English Mediaeval
Architects

THIS EDITION
OF
ENGLISH MEDIAEVAL ARCHITECTS
WAS SPONSORED BY
FRIENDS AND ADMIRERS OF
DR. JOHN HARVEY
AS A TRIBUTE TO HIM
ON
HIS SEVENTIETH BIRTHDAY

English Mediaeval Architects

A BIOGRAPHICAL DICTIONARY DOWN TO 1550

Including Master Masons, Carpenters,
Carvers, Building Contractors
and others responsible for
Design

by

JOHN HARVEY

with contributions by
ARTHUR OSWALD

ALAN SUTTON
1987

OTHER BOOKS BY JOHN HARVEY

HENRY YEVELE
The Life of an English Architect, c. 1320–1400

GOTHIC ENGLAND
A Survey of National Culture, 1300–1550

THE PLANTAGENETS: *1154–1485*

DUBLIN: *A Study in Environment*

THE GOTHIC WORLD
A Survey of Architecture and Art, 1100–1600

A PORTRAIT OF ENGLISH CATHEDRALS
A Selection of Photographs by Herbert Felton

THE CATHEDRALS OF SPAIN

CATHEDRALS OF ENGLAND AND WALES

MEDIAEVAL CRAFTSMEN

YORK

THE BLACK PRINCE AND HIS AGE

THE PERPENDICULAR STYLE: *1330–1485*

MEDIAEVAL GARDENS
(all the above published by B. T. BATSFORD)

ENGLISH CATHEDRALS: *A Reader's Guide*
(NATIONAL BOOK LEAGUE)

AN INTRODUCTION TO TUDOR
ARCHITECTURE
(ART AND TECHNICS)

CONSERVATION OF OLD BUILDINGS:
A Select Bibliography
(ANCIENT MONUMENTS SOCIETY)

CATHERINE SWYNFORD'S CHANTRY
(LINCOLN MINSTER PAMPHLET)

THE MASTER BUILDERS
(THAMES AND HUDSON)

THE MEDIAEVAL ARCHITECT
(WAYLAND PUBLISHERS)

CONSERVATION OF BUILDINGS
(JOHN BAKER)

EARLY GARDENING CATALOGUES
(PHILLIMORE)

EARLY HORTICULTURAL CATALOGUES:
A Checklist to 1850
(UNIVERSITY OF BATH LIBRARY)

MAN THE BUILDER
(PRIORY PRESS)

EARLY NURSERYMEN
(PHILLIMORE)

SOURCES FOR THE HISTORY OF HOUSES
(BRITISH RECORDS ASSOCIATION)

WILLIAM WORCESTRE: ITINERARIES
1478–1480, an edition with translation
(OXFORD: CLARENDON PRESS)

ALAN SUTTON PUBLISHING · BRUNSWICK ROAD · GLOUCESTER

First published 1954
This edition, completely revised, published 1984
Reprinted 1987
First published in paperback 1987
Copyright © 1984 John Harvey

British Library Cataloguing in Publication Data

Harvey, John, 1911–
English mediaeval architects.—2nd rev. ed.
1. Architects—England—Biography
I. Title
720'.92'2   NA996

ISBN 0 86299 034 3 (case)
ISBN 0 86299 452 7 (paper)

Typesetting and origination by
Alan Sutton Publishing Limited. Printed in Great Britain

CONTENTS

Page

JOHN HARVEY. *Photograph by George Hall, 1978*

PREFACE TO THE FIRST EDITION

The study of mediaeval architecture in England has been greatly handicapped by the gratuitous assumption that it was anonymous, and that the master craftsmen who designed our great buildings were not architects, but worked as members of a group inspired by a collective tradition as dominating as the instinct of the hive-bee. Few fallacies at once so ridiculous and so firmly held can have beset the course of serious historical research.

Historians of architecture working in Germany, France, Spain, and other countries have suffered under no such artificial handicap, and it is due largely to the impact of discoveries made abroad that this extraordinary notion has at last been relegated to an occasional appearance in a correspondence column or a popular pamphlet. It can now be seen that the patient work of several generations of English antiquaries had produced an impressive body of evidence which could have stood unsupported by the parallel facts adduced from the continent of Europe. The labours of Dallaway, Britton, Wyatt Papworth, and Lethaby rescued from oblivion the names of most of the great masters of the English Middle Ages and provided a firm foundation for further reseach.

Unhappily the rediscovery of the names of designers has not so far been matched by adequate stylistic criticism and attribution of the surviving works to the masters responsible, except in a few instances where a regional or individual survey has been made. The way was pointed out by Lethaby's two books on Westminster Abbey, where his unrivalled technical knowledge of mediaeval buildings went hand in hand with a warm appreciation of the lives of his predecessors. Further progress in the recognition of stylistic individuality was being made by F. E. Howard, but was lamentably cut short by his early death.

Most of this earlier work was carried out in spite of the inadequate publication of record sources, and this lack has been remedied only within the last generation by the publication of documents relating to building and by the detailed studies of certain aspects of the evidence made by authorities such as Hamilton Thompson and Douglas Knoop. Only now has Mr. Salzman's magistral *Building in England* at last made the documentary background of the mediaeval building trade fully accessible to students. Local research by many hands has meanwhile been embodied in periodicals, guide-books, and even newspapers and parish magazines, providing an embarrassingly rich mass of material.

Without some key to this scattered information, the task of the critic of style is excessively difficult, if not impossible, and it has long been evident that a requisite primary tool was a compilation of the principal known facts regarding those mediaeval architects whose names have so far been recovered. This book was begun as such a compilation, and it was not at first intended to cover sources still in manuscript. Such a limitation proved unworkable in practice, and in its present form the work is extensively based upon material hitherto unpublished. Much of this material has been the generous contribution of others, to whom individual acknowledgments are made.

The form of the book has been dictated by its intended purpose: to make it possible for the architectural student or the general reader to discover what is certainly known of the authorship of buildings erected in England and Wales, or by English craftsmen elsewhere, before the year A.D. 1550. For this reason space has been given to extensive indexes of different kinds, including a topographical gazetteer of dated works and a chronological table serving as a running directory of the masters at work in each period.

Collection of material from printed surces, and intended only for private use, began in 1930; but I should not have attempted to proceed to publication had it not been for the kind encouragement of the late Mr. E. A. Greening Lamborn, and the invaluable collaboration of Messrs. Ralph H. C. Davis and †Arthur Oswald, who have made the architectural histories of Oxford and Cambridge, respectively, the objects of detailed research. Without their most generous expenditure of time and trouble, and unstinting provision of unpublished material, this book could not have been produced. Mr. Oswald has increased my already deep debt to his generosity by contributing some hundred complete biographies.

I must next express my gratitude to the late Douglas Knoop and to Professor G. P. Jones for much valuable information and for copies of their many joint papers on mediaeval masons, as well as for reading a draft of the text; to †Mr. L. F. Salzman, who drew my attention to his *Building in England down to 1540* while it was still in manuscript, and gave me permission to make the fullest use of it, and who further allowed me to comb his exhaustive series of notes from the Exchequer Works Accounts and other records; to †Dr. W. Douglas Simpson who has helped me from his wide knowledge of military architecture and architects; and to †Mr. L. E. Tanner, who read the draft text and has laid open to me the treasures of the Westminster Abbey Muniment Room.

There is a sadly long list of those to whom I can no longer express my thanks, headed by my very dear and revered friend, Herbert Chitty, and that wise counsellor, Thomas Dinham Atkinson, whose scrupulous criticism of the draft text rid it of many obscurities and much verbiage; and including among others who gave me assistance of various kinds, the Rev. J. H. Bloom, Mr. W. P. Blore, Mr. C. J. P. Cave, the Rev. Christopher Chitty, Sir Alfred Clapham, Mrs. K. A. Esdaile, Dr. W. E. St. L. Finny, Sir Henry Hake, Mr. Alec Macdonald, Mr. W. T. Mellows, Mr. J. G. Noppen, Mr. Sydney Pitcher, Mr. Austin Smyth, Professor A. Hamilton Thompson, Professor E. W. Tristram, and Mr. A. K. Wickham.

In addition to individual acknowledgments which appear through the text, I wish here to give my warmest thanks to a number of friends and correspondents whose support and help has been of special value: Mr. Bernard J. Ashwell, Mr. John Charlton, †Mr. George H. Chettle, Mr. H. M. Colvin, Mrs. E. Cottrill, †Dr. F. C. Eeles, †Mr. A. B. Emden, Mr. C. Farthing, Dr. E. A. Gee, †Mr. W. H. Godfrey, †Dr. Rose Graham, †Mr. F. R. Hiorns, †Miss M. B. Honeybourne, †Mr. H. L. Honeyman, †Mr. R. P. Howgrave-Graham, †Mr. H. A. James, Mr. E. Martyn Jope, †Lord Mottistone, †Mr. W. A. Pantin, Dr. Xavier de Salas, †Mr. F. W. Steer, Mr. R. L. Storey, Mr. Arnold J. Taylor, and †Mr. J. Wilson-Haffenden; and further to those who have supplied information and answered repeated queries about certain places, buildings or documents: †Mrs. Dorothy Gardiner and †Mr. William Urry (Canterbury); Mr. C. G. Bulman (Carlisle); †Mr. F. H. Crossley (Chester); †Mr. W. D. Peckham (Chichester); the Ven. S. J. A. Evans (Ely); Mrs. M. E. Clegg and Mr. D. F. Findlay (Exeter); the late Rev. J. Nankivell and †Col. N. H. Waller (Gloucester); Miss K. M. Longley and Mr. H. Cross (Kingston upon Thames); Mr. R. Somerville (Duchy of Lancaster records); †Mr. G. G. Pace and the †Rev. Canon J. E. W. Wallis (Lichfield); †Mr. J. W. F. Hill, Miss K. Major, Mrs. J. Varley, and Miss D. M. Williamson (Lincoln); †Dr. A. H. Thomas and Mr. P. E. Jones (City of London records); Mr. W. Godfrey Allen, the Rev. W. M. Atkins, Mr. G. Henderson, and Miss I. Scouloudi (St. Paul's Cathedral); Dr. W. O. Hassall (Great Milton); †Dr. H. W. Saunders, Mr. A. B. Whittingham, and the †Rev. J. F. Williams (Norwich); †Dr. H. W. Garrod, †Mr. K. B. McFarlane, †Sir John Myres, and Mr. R. L. Rickard (Oxford); Mr. C. E. A. Andrews and Mr. R. N. Bloxam (Pershore); the late Miss M. J. Becker

(Rochester Bridge); †Mr. Joseph Fowler (Sherborne); Mr. L. A. Burgess (Southampton); the Rev. N. Edwards (Tutbury); Mr. R. H. Richardson (Uttoxeter); †Mr. P. B. Chatwin and Mr. E. G. Tibbits (Warwick); †Mr. H. E. Balch and Mr. L. S. Colchester (Wells); †Mr. G. H. Blore, Miss S. Bridges, and †Mr. W. J. Carpenter Turner (Winchester Cathedral); †Sir Ivor Atkins (Worcester Cathedral); †Mr. John Goodchild (Yeovil); and the † Rev. Angelo Raine (York).

For access to books and documents I am indebted to the authorities and staffs of the Public Record Office, the British Museum, the Bodleian Library, Cambridge University Library; the Archives Nationales and Bibliothèque Nationale, Paris; and very many English and Welsh libraries, including the libraries of the Royal Institute of British Architects, the Society of Antiquaries, the Society of Genealogists, and the London Library; the County or Diocesan Record Offices at Chelmsford, Gloucester, Kingston upon Thames, Lincoln, Warwick, Westminster (Middlesex Guildhall), and Winchester; the Corporation Record Offices of Colchester, Guildford, Kingston upon Thames, the City of London, King's Lynn, Norwich, Shrewsbury, Warwick and York; while for permission to inspect ecclesiastical documents I have to thank the Church Commissioners, the Librarian of Lambeth Palace, the Deans and Chapters and Librarians of Canterbury, Gloucester, Lichfield, Lincoln, St. Paul's, Norwich, Peterborough, Westminster, Winchester, Worcester, and York; the Wardens and Fellows of New College, Oxford and of Winchester College and the Master and Fellows and Librarian of Corpus Christi College, Cambridge; and also the Principal Probate Registry at Somerset House and several district registries for facilities to consult early wills and other probate records.

Mr. Oswald wishes to acknowledge his especial indebtedness to the Provost and Fellows of King's College, Cambridge, the Master and Fellows of Trinity College, the Master and Fellows of Gonville and Caius College, and the President and Fellows of Queens' College, Cambridge, the Town Clerk of Cambridge, the Master and Fellows of University College, Oxford, the President and Fellows of Corpus Christi College, Oxford, the Essex Record Office, Chelmsford, and the Bury and West Suffolk Record Office, Bury St. Edmunds, for facilities generously granted in examining documents in their charge. He also expresses his thanks to †Mr. John Saltmarsh, †Mr. Francis W. Steer, †Miss Lilian J. Redstone, and Miss M. A. Farrow for their kind assistance.

My special gratitude is expressed to the Leverhulme Trustees, whose award of a grant enabled me to complete my research, and to the Trustees of the Crompton Bequest, who have made a grant towards the cost of publication. To my publishers I am grateful, not only for much direct help and advice over a number of years, but also for the extended loan of many valuable works of reference; and I would here pay a tribute of affection and esteem to the memory of the late Harry Batsford, whose enthusiasm and encyclopaedic knowledge did so much for architectural research in all its branches. I have throughout had the benefit of help and advice from my father, †William Harvey, and of inspiration and continuous assistance from my wife.

For the form taken by the book and for all its shortcomings I alone am responsible. No such work ever can be complete, but it is hoped that publication will reveal outstanding gaps, and at the same time promote further research. I should be very glad to receive corrections or additions, however slight, with a view to the future preparation of a revised edition; in any case, steps will be taken to ensure the preservation of information thus contributed.

Much still needs to be done in the field of attribution, and this is emphatically a matter for detailed local studies. It is suggested that knowledge of individual styles might be increased if students would make collections of photographs and accurate drawings (including large-scale or full-size moulding profiles) of all the works of a limited period within a given district. Such collections, published or deposited with the National Buildings Record, would form a basis for serious critical studies in the future.

JOHN H. HARVEY

PREFACE TO THE REVISED EDITION

English Mediaeval Architects was published in November 1954, and three interleaved copies were bound up to record corrections and additions. One of these was kept up by Arthur Oswald and one by myself; the third was deposited in the Library of the Royal Institute of British Architects. After five years all our notes were pooled and the results transferred to the R.I.B.A. copy on 11 August 1960. The book remained in print until 1964, ten years after publication, and no opportunity for a revised edition occurred until after 1970. The possibility of a facsimile reprint containing a limited number of corrections and some pages of additions was mooted, but came to nothing. To my great regret it was not until some time after Arthur Oswald's death that a feasible project for complete revision emerged. (See p. xvii for the circumstances in which this has been undertaken).

The incorporation of matter already noted, in both of our interleaved copies, presented a formidable problem in itself. Beyond that it was necessary to consider how far time spent on fresh research could be reconciled with the continuing steep rise in costs. What has been attempted is:
1. the incorporation of all corrections and additions already noted;
2. systematic search of the more important books and papers published in this field since 1954, including particularly the first four volumes of the *History of the King's Works*;
3. the checking from original sources of a substantial amount of material contributed in the form of notes and abstracts, cuttings or copies from newspapers and local periodicals, guides and miscellaneous ephemera;
4. some further search in original records when this could be combined with the process of checking, notably in archives which have reached public repositories in the course of a generation.

Much of the original has been re-written, and the new 'lives' are very numerous (nearly 400 added to the 1300 of the first edition) though mostly short. It is striking that comparatively few major figures have come to light. On the other hand several masters already included now assume a much higher rank in the light of additional information. Attention should be drawn, for example, to: Aelric the Mason, Nicholas de Derneford, Robert Everard, Henry de Eynsham, William Graver, Robert Hulle, Robert Patrington I, Nicholas Portland, Robert Skillyngton, Simon de Tresk, Richard Winchcombe, Thomas of Witney, James Woderofe and Thomas Wolvey. Among the newly added masters, John Montfort, Simon de Pabenham I, John de Weldon, Ivo de Raghton and Robert Vertue junior are outstanding figures.

It has not been easy to draw a precise line around the material included. The first fundamental decision was that there should be no deletion of existing matter simply to make space: apart from mistakes corrected, everything in the first edition remains in the revision. What has been deliberately excluded is a large proportion of the stylistic discussion and attribution of undocumented works which has gone on during the last thirty years. On the other hand, a few important studies have been based upon the central figure of a known master. Notable among these is the work of Dr. Eileen Roberts, who has dealt with the local

Perpendicular style of Hertfordshire as a framework for monographs on the Wolvey family and on Robert Stowell, with detailed consideration of moulding profiles as guides to attribution. Mention must also be made here of the more general study of mouldings by Dr. Richard K. Morris, with his meticulous treatment of some of the as yet un-named masters of the Western School.

I should make it clear that, except for a few stylistic assessments by others, duly acknowledged, all analysis of style is from my personal observation or from that of Arthur Oswald in his signed articles. It has to be emphasized that individuality of output, as well as chronological development, can only be judged by a subjective process which is based upon a study of many objective facts. Among the most important of such facts are the life histories of identified masters, and to that extent this book is deliberately based upon documentary records. Yet it cannot be too strongly emphasized that architectural history depends in the first place on the buildings themselves, to which the documents must be subordinated whenever there is a manifest clash. Certainty is only reached when, within a given period or the product of a particular master, the combined evidence of structure and of documentation fits together without discrepancy.

Considerations of space prevent the recapitulation of acknowledgments to all those new helpers whose initials are appended to material sent from manuscript sources or from obscure printed works (see Abbreviations, I.) Several of those who most notably assisted me in the production of the original edition have laid me under a fresh debt, especially Mr. L. S. Colchester, Miss Kathleen Major and Dr. Arnold J. Taylor. I am also very greatly indebted to Mr. H. M. Colvin who sent me much unpublished information which has now appeared in the volumes of the *History of the King's Works* under his editorship. Many references to the printed version, here given as a matter of convenience for the user, conceal his personal responsibility. Mr. Colvin has also, for the benefit of this edition, sent me extensive series of notes and has answered repeated queries.

Several contributors have approached me spontaneously or in response to appeal, and I am extremely grateful to them for allowing me the use of large bodies of collected material. Notable among these for his great generosity is Mr. Nigel L. Ramsay, who sent me for several months his extensive notes on alabastermen and other carvers. Dr. Simon Cotton and Mr. Paul Cattermole have given me the benefit of their wide and deep researches into Norfolk and Norwich buildings and records, and Dr. Derek Keene has provided me with the skimmed cream from his forthcoming *Survey of Medieval Winchester*, which will contain the references for matter here quoted with the initials (*D.K. Win.*). Mr. G. M. D. Booth kindly sent fully detailed careers of the two important Warwick masters, Simon Grove and John Montfort, and Mr. Michael Begley has given me important material on King's Lynn. I am likewise extremely grateful to Mr. M. G. Snape who has filled many gaps in the history of Durham craftsmen. Others who have given timely help in the final stages of revision are Dr. J. Wyn Evans in connection with St. Davids, Dr. Barbara Clayre in regard to the last years of Hugh Herland, and Mr. and Mrs Brian Gittos who let me know of the initialled tomb-slab of John Barton (died 1483) at South Cave.

To Mr. Philip Oswald and his brother, who now own the copyright in those articles contributed by Arthur Oswald and signed with his initials, I am grateful for permission to reprint and to amend a very few minor errors. In some cases there has been addition of fresh materials left in manuscript by Arthur Oswald; and a few other necessary interpolations have been placed within square brackets. In another place (p. xvii) Dr. Richard K. Morris gives an account of the Fund for republication which has made the present revision possible, followed by a list of donors. I here make formal, but most grateful acknowledgment to the following corporate bodies, who have given substantial assistance: the Ancient Monuments Society; the Ecclesiastical Architects' and Surveyors' Association; the Worshipful Company of Grocers; the Guild of Surveyors; the Provost and Fellows of King's College, Cambridge; the Worshipful Company of Masons; the Mount Trust; Pynford Design Ltd.; the Charles James Robertson Charitable Trust; the Twenty-Seven Foundation; the staff of the Warwick County Record Office; the Dean and Chapter of Westminster; the Warden and Fellows of Winchester College; and the Dean and Chapter of York.

Here I would express my astonished gratitude to the many donors to this fund, and notably to the organizers: Dr. Ivor Bulmer-Thomas, Mr. L. S. Colchester, Professor Ralph H.C. Davis, and Dr. Eric Gee, with the indefatigable Dr. Richard K. Morris whose arduous work as secretary and universal joint has added a heavy burden to his already busy life of scholarship. The actual out-of-pocket expenses of my research for this edition are being covered by a grant from the British Academy, which I most gratefully acknowledge. Finally I must again thank the Marc Fitch Fund for their help in the past, especially towards my book *The Perpendicular Style* (Batsford, 1978), the research for which produced much additional matter for this dictionary. At the same time I wish to voice my gratitude to that Fund for its continuing support to the work of the British Record Society in publishing Indexes and particularly calendars of Wills: a long series of volumes which greatly facilitate much work that would otherwise be virtually impossible of accomplishment. The arduous work of indexers is all too little recognized or praised, and in that context I again thank Mr. L. S. Colchester and Dr. Richard K. Morris for undertaking the revised index and tables to this book.

On behalf of the John Harvey Birthday Fund I also wish to add thanks to the Ancient Monuments Society for opening a special account for the Fund, and especially to Susan Gold for maintaining the list of donors to it. Both from the Fund and from myself especial thanks go to Mr. Philip Oswald who, at an inconvenient time, very kindly undertook the memoir of his uncle to whom this revised edition is in some sense a memorial.

*   *   *   *   *   *   *   *

At this point it is necessary to comment on several aspects of the revised book and to deal with some problems that have arisen in the course of revision.

1. *Illustration.*   Many readers of the first edition have asked for an illustrated supplement of adequate size to portray the styles of the great masters at least. This has up to now been a project which has not commended itself as financially viable to any publisher. As a partial remedy I refer readers to the plates in several of my other books, deliberately chosen with this end in view: *Henry Yevele* as displaying the output of our greatest architect; *Gothic England*, for the outstanding buildings and styles of 1300–1550; *An Introduction to Tudor Architecture* for work of 1485–1547; *The Gothic World* and *The Master Builders* for illustrations of British material within the European framework; *Mediaeval Craftsmen* for relevant details and fittings; *Cathedrals of England and Wales* for our noblest churches from the eleventh to the sixteenth century; and *The Perpendicular Style* for most of our outstanding *dated* works between 1330 and 1485.

2. *The Background.*   Much confusion still exists in the minds of many readers as to the methods by which the remarkable buildings of the Middle Ages were designed and, in particular, as to who were the designers. It has to be repeated that most of the really great architects in the years between A.D. 1050 and 1550 (the Middle Ages for this particular purpose) were men who, *besides any other education they might receive,* underwent a full training as stonemasons or carpenters — sometimes in both crafts. Over and above merely manual skill

they went on to learn by rote geometrical secrets of two kinds: on the one hand these were methods of manipulating a straightedge or square and a pair of compasses so as to produce a right angle; the repeated proportion of the diagonal to the side of a square; the 'Golden Cut' proportion infinitely repeating itself, and the like. Secondly, the secrets concerned structural stability and comprised memorized proportions of depth and bulk of foundations in relation to the width and height of the building proposed, with safety factors allowing for wind-pressure and the thrusts of vaults and roofs against the needed buttresses. So far as the historical evidence exists I attempted to bring it together, primarily for England, in *The Mediaeval Architect*, which contains full texts and translations of a very large number of key documents and particularly the complete text of The Constitutions of Masonry, of c. 1350. The outcome of this review of the evidence is to show that there could not be 'amateur architects' in the period down to 1500 or later, and that the often repeated statements that the monks and the clergy were 'architects' are necessarily false.

3. *Foreign influences.* It has been usual in the past to attribute most of our outstanding art of all kinds to foreign masters or to foreign influences. There is a curious reluctance to admit that Englishmen, unaided, could produce artistic masterpieces in any way comparable with those achieved elsewhere, notably in France and Italy. The substantial proportion of our notable architects now recorded in this book as revised should redress the balance; enough is known of most of them to show that they were Englishmen born and bred apart from a very few cases of doubt. This refers to architectural designers: after about 1470 carvers and other craftsmen of detail certainly began to settle in this country, mostly from the Burgundian realms in the greater Netherlands.

It is not sought to deny that much architectural usage was derived from France in the earlier Gothic period; nor that Norman (Romanesque) building was a continental introduction stemming from the Conquest. On the other hand the evidence of named individuals and of cases of English designers working abroad are sufficient to prove that, even in the earlier phases, the current did not set one way. After the accession of Edward I in 1272, and more especially from the moment of his return from the Crusade in 1274, it was English architecture and English building organization that led the way and were widely copied abroad. Continental Gothic after 1300 owes as great, if not greater, a debt to England than the English Gothic of the reign of Henry III (1216–1272) owed to France.

Astonishingly, the principal foreign source of inspiration for our later Gothic has been consistently underrated: the acceptance of geometrical ideas from the Saracenic world, in part deriving from the Crusades and other direct contacts with Islam, but also largely by way of political alliance with Spain against the central power of France. Edward I's Spanish queen, Eleanor of Castile, had a 'gloriet' within a lake (of Eastern and Moorish antecedents) built at Leeds Castle in Kent in 1278–90, some years earlier than the very famous park with gloriet and Arabic water engines of Count Robert II of Artois at Hesdin (see J. Harvey, *Mediaeval Gardens*, 1981, 106). The unusual centralized plans of the north porch at St. Mary Redcliffe and of the octagon at Ely set out in 1323 by a master from London, reflect the direct contacts between the English and the Mongol Court at Tabriz during Sir Geoffrey Langley's embassy of 1291–93; then the early Perpendicular 'wire-netting' tracery comes straight from the Cairo of the century ending about 1320.

The diplomatic and military intervention of England in the Peninsula in the time of Edward III and under his son the Black Prince led to a second phase of strictly Spanish influence on English architecture. This is well exemplified by William de Helpeston's eastern chapels for Vale Royal Abbey, set out in 1359 on a plan almost exactly copied from the chevet of Toledo

Cathedral of *c.* 1225; and by John Lewyn's remarkable vault over the great kitchen of Durham Priory begun in 1367. Finally, following the exchanges of embassies between Henry VII and the Catholic Sovereigns of Spain, came the remarkable crop of Mudéjar plans in England, starting with Henry VII's Tower in Windsor castle begun by 1499, including the star-polygon windows of the new Chapel at Westminster (1503) and Thornbury Castle (1511), and culminating in the turrets of the great gate of Cardinal College, Oxford (i.e. the substructure of Tom Tower), begun under John Lebons in 1525–29. The parallel to that of the famous clock-tower (*Torre Nueva*) at Saragossa, designed in 1504, is precise.

4. *Evidence.* Professional historians commonly describe as 'evidence' only strict documenta-tion, expressing a clear fact in so many words written down on parchment or paper. When dealing with art, such historians in general fail to pay attention to the factual evidence of the art itself, e.g. the stylistic traits of national or individual identity displayed. This is perfectly natural and intelligible, but has had unfortunate results in the particular case of English architectural history. A very large proportion of the protracted disputes on the individuality of mediaeval art and architecture has been due directly to the fact that few of the disputants possessed any qualifications to diagnose style: hardly any historians are practitioners of any of the graphic arts, least of all architecture. Yet in every case it is the building itself, properly studied in detail, that provides the best evidence of its history and character, even though precise dates and attribution to a named author depend upon written records.

The reader should bear in mind that, so far as the architects of major surviving works are concerned, this book represents an attempt to bring together evidence from the monument itself and from documents related to its designer; even though the individual careers of named designers are the subject of the book, it is the structural evidence which has primacy so far as it exists. It is not a legitimate criticism of statements based upon the style and apparent date of a given work, to state that there is no *written* evidence to prove the case.

Another cause of doubt and energy lost in barren disputes is the failure to discriminate between greater and lesser masters, and the calibre of works produced by each category of artist. Whereas in the earlier part of the period the survival of documentary records is largely a matter of chance, and it may well be impossible to discriminate between the careers of greater and lesser masters, it is usual after 1300, and often even earlier, to form a substantially accurate impression of status from the surviving references and actual works. In such a case as the contemporary fame of two great masters in the royal service, Henry Yeveley and William Wynford, it may be legitimate matter for discussion which of the two was responsible for a given building, or whether both may have had a share in a collaborative project. On the other hand, in the case of a masterwork of the highest level such as the nave of Canterbury Cathedral, the fact that an undermaster Thomas Hoo was in charge on the site (in modern terms, was employed as a site-architect) must not be used to throw doubt on the architectural responsibility of Yeveley for the design as a whole (see the original Introduction, p. xlv).

To those concerned primarily with the interpretation of written records, verbal and literal inconsistencies bulk large, and doubt is often expressed on a basis of merely superficial discrepancy. For example, in the Exeter Cathedral fabric account for 1346–47, two half-yearly payments of the master's fee are recorded (AEC, ii, 274, 276). The first is to 'J. Joye master of the fabric'; the second to 'Master W. Joye'. Now at this period we have no knowledge of any master mason 'J'. Joy, but William Joy was precisely the master who at Wells in 1329 had succeeded to an office presumptively held by the earlier Exeter master Thomas of Witney. Given that the style of William Joy, highly distinctive, appears in the work of the collegiate church at Ottery St. Mary in 1337–45, there can be no doubt as to the identity of the new

Exeter master. Why, then, did he first appear with the initial 'J'.? The answer is mere common form: in very many accounts, the clerk who kept a tally of the names of men paid often did not know their full name at the first payment; and in many cases assigned to such a man the token name 'John', or just the initial 'J'. Later, when the full name was known, it would be duly entered.

Such difficulties occur even more frequently in the case of later copies of original documents. For instance, the contract of the founders of the London Charterhouse in 1371 for the building of the first cell and part of the great cloister is said in a document of *c*. 1500 to have been with Henry 'Revell'; but the mouldings found on fragmentary remains of the first work bear out the natural supposition (given that no 'Revell' is known at all) that the contractor was Henry 'Zevell' or Yeveley. 'Richard Nymes' proves to have been an 18th-century misreading of Robert Nynes, the latter a form of the surname Janyns of the master of the work known from other records. A still more deceptive case is that of the account for works done at Corfe Castle on 'le Gloriet' in 1377–79, kept by the mayor of Corfe. This lists the 17 masons at work in order and states that the master took 6*d*. a day, the others 5*d*. each. In order the names run: 'Joh*anni*s Combe Mag*ist*ri Will*el*mi Wynford Joh*ann*is Harpetre . . .' and so on; and earlier scholars including the late Dr. W. Douglas Simpson had rightly assumed that the famous Wynford was the master; but *The History of the King's Works* with excessive scruple declares in a footnote (I, 623n.[11]) that whereas the master was John Combe, Wynford was working in a subordinate capacity, which 'perhaps throws doubt on his identification as the well-known William of Wynford'. This is to put the cart before the horse; for general knowledge of the background shows that Master William Wynford was precisely the royal architect likely, in that region, to be in charge of such a major work; and that no such master as John Combe is known at all. Careful examination of the roll shows that there is a faint rubbing of the parchment after the title 'Mag*ist*ri', and a pair of very faint strokes of the pen before it. Evidently the mayor's clerk knew the leading mason employed locally, John Combe, and set down his name first, then that of Master William Wynford; thought to correct an ambiguity by putting a stroke between one name and the next but misplaced it after the title; and finally corrected the error. As usually in mediaeval, but not classical, Latin, the title comes before the name and relates to William Wynford.

As the evidence gradually builds up, it becomes more and more clear that there were comparatively few leading designers among the many masters, and that they were sought from afar for their conspicuous architectural ability. Some even travelled hundreds of miles to tender advice or give designs for some new work, on horseback at five miles an hour and some 30 miles a day. Thus William de Ramsey in 1337 rode 118 miles to Lichfield, a journey of four days, and again 118 miles back to London, with his servants, for a fee of £1 (say £600) and travelling expenses to a total of 6*s*. 8*d*. (say £200 now). By that time Ramsey was the king's chief mason and chief surveyor of the royal works south of Trent, more or less Chief Architect or Director of Works under the Crown, but none the less permitted to continue in private practice. It is therefore by no means a cause for surprise that official style should have spread so far and so fast, or that so many works should, on sound stylistic evidence, be attributed to the same master.

5. *Bibliography.* It should be noted that in most cases it has been necessary to limit the references to those concerned with the documentary sources for a given life, or with discussion of that architect's style. There has in recent years grown up a very much larger body of literature relevant to particular styles or periods, to regions or individual buildings, which could not find a place here. No disrespect is intended by the omission of references to a great

deal of this outer circle of study which may have a bearing upon future estimates of style. On the other hand, references have been inserted whenever possible to the volumes (I–IV, 1963–82) of *The History of the King's Works*, to which reference should be made for further details of the careers of many of the greater masters employed under the Crown, and also of many other craftsmen not included here; as well as for the continuing histories of the works at particular buildings. The work of military engineers on fortifications, largely under Edward I and again under Henry VIII, only very lightly touched upon in this book, will there be found in extremely full detail, together with the careers of architectural masters of the later Tudor period. It is, however, necessary to point out that 'HKW' is a history of the administration and organization of the royal works; it is not a history of architecture or of separate buildings.

Attention is drawn to the existence of the revised and enlarged edition of the late L. F. Salzman's masterwork, *Building in England down to 1540*, published in 1967. This virtually eliminates the few minor errors of the first edition and adds an important series of building contracts as Appendix D. Other important revisions are those of D. Knoop and G. P. Jones, *The Mediaeval Mason* (3rd edition, 1967); and of Francis B. Andrews, *The Mediaeval Builder and his Methods* (1974), bringing together with the original book of 1925 the *Further Notes on the Mediaeval Builder* of 1931.

THE JOHN HARVEY BIRTHDAY FUND

The idea of marking John Harvey's seventieth birthday with a new edition of *English Mediaeval Architects* goes back to correspondence in 1979 between a few of his close friends and admirers — Ivor Bulmer-Thomas, L. S. Colchester, Professor Ralph Davis, Dr. Eric Gee and myself. Unknown to John, we formed an *ad hoc* committee to consider ways of celebrating the career to date of one of the outstanding mediaeval architectural historians of this century.

It was Professor Davis who suggested that we should eschew the more usual device of the *Festschrift*, and take instead the unconventional step of arranging for the republication of one of John's greatest works. *English Mediaeval Architects* was an obvious choice. This indispensable reference work on mediaeval craftsmen, written in association with the late Arthur Oswald over twenty-five years ago, had long since been unavailable, and we felt that its re-appearance in a new edition would give lasting pleasure not only to John's many admirers but also to John himself. We knew that he had a special copy interleaved with amendments and additions made since 1954, and also that he had been approached a short time before about a photographic reprint, but had rejected it mainly because this would not allow for a genuine new edition with all the additional material properly integrated with the original text. So the basis of a new edition existed and the idea was in John's mind. Not, of course, that we could go ahead and republish without his consent, but we could raise a subsidy by requesting donations from his friends, acquaintances and admirers to guarantee to a publisher the financial viability of a completely new edition as John envisaged it. Thus, the John Harvey Birthday Fund came into existence, and its success may be measured by the impressive list of donors that follows and by the fact that the new edition is now a reality.

For the engineering of a suitable occasion at which a presentation could be made to John, we have to thank Ivor Bulmer-Thomas. He arranged for John to address the annual general meeting of the Ancient Monuments Society at St. Bartholomew's Hospital in London in June, 1981, just a few weeks after John's seventieth birthday, and afterwards the honour fell to me to present him with the cheque and illuminated scroll, all of which had been kept a secret from him up to that moment. In moving the vote of thanks, I had the privilege to express my feelings about John's work, which were shared by all those present that day, and I am sure that they would wish some of those thoughts to be recorded here.

John had just given us a fascinating account of the architectural history of the church of St. Bartholomew-the-Great, the sort of paper possible only from one who has been deeply committed to the appreciation of the qualities of mediaeval architecture for the whole of his life. This is reflected in the bibliography of his work, published in Volumes 25 (1981) and 26 (1982) of the *Transactions of the Ancient Monuments Society*. Its extent is truly astounding. His published writings on architectural and topographical matters stretch back forty-seven years to 1936: in all but six of those years (three of the six in wartime), something of note has appeared from his pen, and on average two or three works a year. Among over a hundred relevant items in the bibliography, there are a number of books which are indispensable works of outstanding value, including *Henry Yevele, The Gothic World, English Mediaeval Architects, William Worcestre's Itineraries, The Cathedrals of England and Wales*, and *The Perpendicular Style*. In addition, there is a multitude of scholarly articles, so wide-ranging particularly geographically that no student of English Gothic architecture can work for long in the field without being aware of them.

My first meeting with John was in 1967 in York, and what impressed me particularly then was his generosity with material and ideas. Ever since, I have found that he always has well-informed views to offer on anything Gothic, for the issues of the period matter fervently to him, and there can hardly be an aspect or example of later mediaeval architecture to which he has not turned his lively mind at one time or another. He is the worthy successor of the greatest architectural historians of previous generations: of the Reverend Robert Willis, of Francis Bond and of William Richard Lethaby. Moreover, to borrow a phrase which John applied to Henry Yeveley but which applies equally well to himself, he is 'one of the truest sons of England'. We all thank him for the pleasure and enlightenment he has given us over the past half-century, and hopefully for many years to come.

Dr. Richard K. Morris
University of Warwick
January 1984

LIST OF DONORS TO THE JOHN HARVEY
BIRTHDAY FUND

P. V. Addyman
The Ancient Monuments Society
Andrew Anderson
W. C. Andrews
The Marquess of Anglesey
Bernard J. Ashwell
Tony Baggs
Professor Robert Baker
Dr. Caroline M. Barron
F. B. Benger
Keith and Corinne Bennett
Martin Biddle and Birthe Kjølbye-Biddle
Claude and Joan Blair
Dr. John Blair
† J. M. G. Blakiston
Dr. Pamela Z. Blum
Professor Jean Bony
Nancy Briggs
Professor Christopher and Dr. Rosalind
  Brooke
Charles Brown
R. H. Bulmer
Dr. Ivor Bulmer-Thomas
Peter Burman
Dr. Lawrence Butler
F. W. B. Charles
John Charlton
Frederick E. Cleary
Alec Clifton-Taylor
John Coales
L. S. Colchester
Dr. Nicola Coldstream
H. M. Colvin
Norman Cook
Dr. Paul Crossley
Ian Curry
Dr. Roger Custance
Professor R. H. C. Davis
Professor Barrie Dobson
Professor Kerry Downes

The Revd. A. L. Drinkwater
A. R. Dufty
Elizabeth Eames
The Ecclesiastical Architects' and Surveyors'
  Association
Cecil Farthing
P. J. Fergusson
Eric Fernie
T. W. French
Dr. E. A. Gee
John Gerrard
J. H. P. Gibb
Susan Gold
Dr. Antonia Gransden
Irvine Gray
The Worshipful Company of Grocers
Douglas B. Hague
Colonel Cedric Hall
† Ruthven O. Hall
Professor Frank Harrison
Professor P. D. A. Harvey
Cecil A. Hewett
Professor Jacques Heyman
Professor Rosalind Hill
P. B. Hodson
Christopher Hohler
John Hopkins
John Ingamells
Dr. Virginia Jansen
Laurence Keen
The Rt. Revd. E. W. Kemp
Dennis G. King
The Provost and Fellows of King's College,
  Cambridge
Joan C. Lancaster
Philip J. Lankester
R. E. Latham
Dr. Walter C. Leedy Jr.
H. G. M. Leighton
Dr. Leslie J. Macfarlane

xix

DONORS

Michael McGarvie
N. H. MacMichael
Dr. John Maddison
Kathleen Major
Dr. Richard Marks
Professor Andrew Martindale
The Worshipful Company of Masons
Squadron Leader G. W. Massey
Marion Meek
The Very Revd. Patrick Mitchell
Nicholas J. Moore
Dr. Richard K. Morris
Ronald W. B. Morris
Sir Jeremy Morse
The Mount Trust
Julian Munby
Dr. J. N. L. Myres
John Newman
Dr. E. C. Norton
Sir Walter Oakeshott
Philip Oswald in memory of Arthur Oswald
Dr. David Palliser
David Park
John Parker
Pynford Design Ltd.
Dr. C. A. Ralegh Radford
Nigel Ramsay
Dr. Eileen Roberts
The Charles James Robertson Charitable Trust

Alan M. Rome
Anthony Rossi
Georgina Russell
John Salmon
Matthew Saunders
Lord Saye and Sele
Norman Scarfe
Irene Scouloudi
Derek M. M. Shorrocks
H. Gordon Slade
Dr. John Sparrow
Roger Stalley
Professor R. L. Storey
Sir John Summerson
The Guild of Surveyors
Dr. Arnold Taylor
Dr. Michael Thompson
Margaret Tomlinson
Dr. P. Tudor-Craig (Lady Wedgwood)
The Twenty-Seven Foundation
David and Rosemary Verey
Sir Anthony Wagner
The Staff of the Warwick County Record Office
The Dean and Chapter of Westminster
Dr. Christopher Wilson
The Warden and Fellows of Winchester College
† Dr. Raymond B. Wood-Jones
The Dean and Chapter of York

---

† deceased

FOREWORD

Please read this section before consulting the text of the book

THE SUBJECT MATTER of this book is the architectural *function* of the designers of mediaeval buildings, regardless of other functions which may have been fulfilled by them. It is now certain that most mediaeval architects were master craftsmen of the building trades: men who had graduated after practical training as masons, carpenters, or carvers; many if not most of these masters were literate, and they were often artists and geometricians of distinction for their time. A very small number of secular clerics and members of monastic Orders can be shown to have had technical knowledge and to have acted in an architectural capacity, but there is no foundation whatever for the ascription of architectural design in general to monks or to clerks in Orders. The over-familiar names of such clerical 'architects' as Gundulf, Alan of Walsingham, and William of Wykeham, have therefore been deliberately excluded from the scope of the book, and are mentioned only where they serve to draw attention to the architects employed by them. The role of enlightened patronage was indeed vital to the art of the Middle Ages, but as in all other periods it is essential to distinguish between the functions of client and designer. On the other hand, a few traditional architects, such as Walter of Coventry and John Gower, have been included, when no good evidence for their rejection has been found.

The criteria for inclusion are necessarily to some extent subjective, but selection has been based on the following principles:

(1) Craftsmen described as 'Master' (*Magister*) and engaged on the supervision of building operations, are assumed to have acted as architects unless there is evidence to the contrary.
(2) Masters who held office (e.g. as Chief Mason) under the Crown and in certain special jurisdictions are included, even where no evidence exists of their conduct of specific works.
(3) Craftsmen given the title of 'Warden' (*Custos, Gardianus, Apparator, Apparillator*): lieutenant of or resident substitute for the master, are included, since wardenship was normally a step in promotion towards mastery, and there is evidence to suggest that wardens played an important part in the local diffusion of a master's style.
(4) Contractors able to undertake substantial works have been included, even when they are known to have worked to the designs of another master. There is abundant evidence that many contractors also worked in an architectural capacity.
(5) In cases of doubt as to architectural status, inclusion has been the normal rule, but to avoid confusion, those whose architectural status is proven have been distinguished by **BOLD CAPITALS** at the head of each life, and by **bold type** in the topographical index.
(6) Architecture is here considered as the art and craft of designing and supervising the erection of buildings or parts of buildings, and including fittings of stone, brick, or wood. Masters known only as painters, brass-founders or smiths have not been included, but a number of carvers appear since they often undertook the provision of features such as screens, benches, and monumental tombs, all of which are here considered parts of the building. At least in the earlier period the master carver was often himself the architect, or the designer of the building also the chief sculptor of its plastic enrichments.

In the revision (1983) it has been essential to economize space, and a slightly more exclusive policy has been adopted than in the original work. Thus quarry-masters have not been included, and military engineers only when there is reasonably explicit evidence of architectural status. This has applied particularly to the sixteenth century.

Geographically, the architects listed are limited to those who practised in England and Wales, whether native or foreign; and to natives or presumed natives of England and Wales, or of English descent, who worked elsewhere. No attempt has been made to provide full biographies of designers in Renaissance style nor, in particular, of foreigners who worked in England after 1500.

CONVENTIONS

† died.   C.= Carpenter.   E.= Engineer.   M.= Mason.

Master is used in articles only of craftsmen so described in documentary sources.

Italics are used in articles for the first mention of a building or work by the subject of the article.

SMALL CAPITALS are used in the articles for the first mention of the subject of another article.

Namesakes who belonged to the same craft are arranged in chronological order and numbered. *Senior* and *junior* are used only when the men concerned are known or presumed to be related.

Dates expressed thus: 1453–54, indicate that the reference is to a year of account (e.g. from Michaelmas to Michaelmas) which did not coincide with the historical year. The year is indicated thus: 1453/4, in the case of dates falling from 1 January to 24 March inclusive, since these days were by the mediaeval reckoning counted to the old year. No attempt is made to correct the dates, which are in the Old Style throughout.

In the notes, volume numbers are normally in Roman figures in SMALL CAPITALS; reference is normally to pages, but where the work cited is indexed by numbered paragraphs or sections, the reference is to such sections. The volume and page or folio numbers assigned in the case of manuscript authorities are not consistent, as the various original systems of press-marks are followed.

Where the whole or the greater part of an article has been summarized from a secondary source, the abbreviation for this source is printed in bold type, and references to the original sources are not given. Where earlier secondary sources have treated of given individuals, the abbreviations for these sources are placed in parenthesis before the individual references for facts contained in the article.

In every case where a surname appears to be a toponym, efforts have been made to identify the place of origin; it must be understood that in the later part of the period such identification may imply comparatively little. Identifications have only been given where they are certain, or rest upon very strong presumptive evidence.

Changes since 1954.

No notice has been taken of the changes in local government boundaries made in 1965 and 1974; all English and Welsh counties are to be understood in their historical sense. It has not been possible to check the present position of all manuscript holdings, some of which have been moved since the first edition went to press. Some inconsistency will be found in references, which may refer to the same repository under two different names, notably the British Museum (*BM*) which appears in added material as the British Library (*BL*).

Metrication and decimalization are ignored. Very rough calculations suggest that in order to obtain an *approximate* value for mediaeval building costs, amounts should now be multiplied by at least 500 for the period between 1350 and 1550, and by factors between x 600 and x 1000 for the earlier Middle Ages from the Conquest to the Black Death. It must be stressed that the results are such as to give merely a correct mental impression of global costs.

ABBREVIATIONS

I. AUTHORSHIP

Complete articles contributed by Mr. Oswald are signed with his initials in italics: *A.O.* Articles based wholly or mainly on contributed information have the contributors' initials appended in parenthesis, and a similar acknowledgment is given after contributed references to manuscript sources. The abbreviations used are:

(*A.B.E.*)	the late A. B. Emden
(*A.B.W.*)	Mr. A. B. Whittingham, F.S.A., A.R.I.B.A.
(*A.E.B.O.*)	Mr. A. E. B. Owen
(*A.J.T.*)	Mr. Arnold J. Taylor, C.B.E., D. Litt., P.P.S.A.
(*A.M.E.*)	Mrs A. M. Erskine, F.S.A., F. R. Hist. S.
(*A.O.*)	the late Arthur Oswald
(*A.P.B.*)	Mr. Anthony P. Baggs, F.S.A.
(*A.R.*)	the late Rev. Angelo Raine
(*A. Ru.*)	Miss Alwyn Ruddock, Ph.D., F.S.A.
(*A.W.*)	The Rt. Rev. Dom Aelred Watkin, O.S.B., F.S.A.
(*C.B.L.B.*)	Mr. C. B. L. Barr
(*C.E.L.*)	Mr. C. E. Lugard
(*C.R.D.*)	Professor C. R. Dodwell, Ph.D., F.B.A., F.S.A.
(*C.W.*)	the late Very Rev. Christopher Woodforde
(*C.W.D.*)	Mr. C. W. Dowdall
(*D.A.J.*)	Mr. D. A. Johnson, F.S.A.
(*D.F.F.*)	Mr. D. F. Findlay, Ph.D.
(*D.F.R.*)	Mr. D. F. Renn, F.S.A.
(*D.G.*)	the late Mrs. Dorothy Gardiner
(*D.H.T.*)	Mr. D. H. Turner
(*D.J.*)	Mr. David Josephson, Ph.D.
(*D.K.*)	the late Douglas Knoop
(*D.K.Win.*)	Mr. Derek Keene, Ph.D.
(*D.M.W.*)	Miss D. M. Williamson (Mrs. Owen), F.S.A.
(*D.R.R.*)	Mr. D. R. Ransome
(*E.A.G.L.*)	the late E. A. Greening Lamborn
(*E.G.*)	Mr. E. A. Gee, D. Phil., F.S.A.
(*E.M.J.*)	Professor E. Martyn Jope, F.B.A., F.S.A., M.R.I.A.
(*E.W.*)	Lieut. Colonel Eric Ward
(*G.M.D.B.*)	Mr. G. M. D. Booth
(*G.P.C.*)	Professor G. P. Cuttino, D.Phil, F.S.A., F. R. Hist. S.
(*G.P.J.*)	Professor G. P. Jones, Litt. D.
(*G.W.S.B.*)	Professor G. W. S. Barrow, F.B.A., F.S.A.
(*H.B.*)	the late Hugh M. G. Baillie
(*H.C.*)	the late Herbert Chitty
(*H.M.*)	Sir Humphrey Mynors, Bart.

(*H.M.C.*)	Mr. H. M. Colvin, C.B.E., F.B.A., F.S.A.
(*J.F.*)	the late Joseph Fowler
(*J.G.N.*)	the late John G. Noppen
(*J.H.B.*)	the late Rev. J. H. Bloom
(*J.H.H.*)	the author (in articles by Arthur Oswald)
(*J.S.P.*)	the late Rev. Canon J. S. Purvis
(*J.V.*)	Mrs. Joan Varley, F.S.A.
(*J.W-H.*)	the late J. Wilson-Haffenden
(*K.B.M.*)	the late K. B. McFarlane
(*K.H.*)	Professor Kenneth Harrison, F.S.A.
(*K.M.*)	Miss Kathleen Major, F.B.A., F.S.A.
(*L.A.B.*)	Mr. L. A. Burgess
(*L.E.J.B.*)	Mr. Leslie Brooke
(*L.E.T.*)	the late Lawrence E. Tanner
(*L.F.S.*)	the late L. F. Salzman
(*L.S.*)	Professor Lawrence Stone
(*L.S.C.*)	Mr. L. S. Colchester, F.S.A.
(*M.B.*)	Mr. Michael Begley
(*M.E.C.*)	Mrs. M. E. Clegg
(*M.G.S.*)	Mr. M. G. Snape
(*M.J.B.*)	the late Miss M. J. Becker
(*M.McG.*)	Mr. Michael McGarvie, F.S.A.
(*M.R.P.*)	Mr. M. R. Petch
(*N.H.M.*)	Mr. Nicholas H. MacMichael, F.S.A.
(*N.L.R.*)	Mr. Nigel L. Ramsay
(*N.M.H.*)	Mr. N. M. Herbert, Ph. D.
(*P.R.*)	Mr. Paul Rutledge
(*R.A.B.*)	Professor R. Allen Brown, D. Litt., F.S.A.
(*R.D.*)	Professor R. H. C. Davis, F.B.A., F.S.A.
(*R.H.G.*)	The Rev. R. H. Goode
(*R.K.M.*)	Mr. R. K. Morris, Ph.D., F.S.A.
(*R.L.S.*)	Mr. R. L. Storey
(*R.S.*)	Sir Robert Somerville, K.C.V.O., F.S.A., F.R. Hist. S.
(*R.S-M.*)	Mr. Robert Stanley-Morgan, A.R.I.B.A.
(*W.A.K.*)	The Rev. W. A. Kneebone
(*W.C.B.S.*)	Mr. W. C. B. Smith, F.R.I.B.A.
(*W.D.S.*)	the late W. Douglas Simpson
(*W.J.B.*)	Mr. W. J. Blair, F.S.A.
(*W.P.B.*)	The late W. P. Blore

(*W.T.M.*)   the late W. T. Mellows
(*W.U.*)   the late William Urry
(*X.D.S.*)   Sr. Profesor Xavier de Salas

Note: the same initials, without brackets, are used to indicate authorship in the references.

II. SOURCES

Abbreviations in italics refer to sources in manuscript.

A   *Archaeologia*: Society of Antiquaries of London.

AAA   Accounts of the Obedientiars of Abingdon Abbey. (CS, NS, LI, 1892)

AAJ   British Archaeological Association: *Journal*

AAS   Associated Architectural Societies: *Reports*.

ABC   M. D. Anderson: Looking for History in British Churches. (1951)

AC   *Archaeologia Cantiana*: Kent Archaeological Society.

ACA   *Archaeologia Cambrensis*: Cambrian Archaeological Association.

ACC   Accounts of the Chamberlains of the County of Chester. (LCRS, LIX, 1910)

ACW   Probate Court of Archdeacon of Canterbury (in *KAO*)

ACY   G.E. Aylmer & R. Cant edd.: A History of York Minster. (1977)

AEC   A.M. Erskine ed.: The Accounts of the Fabric of Exeter Cathedral, 1279–1353, 2 parts. (DCRS, NS, XXIV, XXVI, 1981, 1983)

AFC   Anglesey Field Club: *Transactions*.

AH   *Architectural History*: Society of Architectural Historians of Great Britain

AHC   F.B. Andrews: The Herlands and other Carpenters; in Birmingham & Midland Institute: *Transactions*, LV, 1931. (1933)

AIN   Archaeological Institute: Norfolk and Norwich 1847. (1851)

AJ   *Archaeological Journal*: Royal Archaeological Institute.

ALF   P.S. & H.M. Allen: The Letters of Richard Fox. (1929)

ALS   *Atti Liguri di Storia Patria* (Genoa)

AMS   Ancient Monuments Society: *Transactions*.

ANJ   *Antiquaries Journal*: Society of Antiquaries of London.

ANT   *Antiquity*.

AO   Alumni Oxonienses, ed. J. Foster (1887–92)

AOG   E. Ashmole: Installation of the Order of the Garter. (1672)

APC   Acts of the Privy Council (Calendars).

APD   Architectural Publication Society: Dictionary. (1849–92)

AQC   *Ars Quatuor Coronatorum*: Lodge Quatuor Coronati, 2076.

ARA   W. O. Ault: Court Rolls of Ramsey Abbey. (1928)

ARC   *Archives*: British Records Association.

ARH   Architectural History (Lists) (NRA)

ASA   J. Amundesham: Annales Monasterii Sancti Albani (RS, 1870).

ATS   Accounts of the Lord High Treasurer of Scotland

BAA   J. Britton: Architectural Antiquities. (1807–26)

BAACT   British Archaeological Association: *Conference Transactions*.

BAE   Lord Braybrooke: History of Audley End and Saffron Walden. (1836)

BAF   C. Bauchal: Nouveau Dictionnaire des Architectes Français. (1887)

BAH   M. S. Briggs: The Architect in History. (1927)

BAJ   *Berks., Bucks. and Oxon. Archaeological Journal*.

BAL   A. B. Beaven: The Aldermen of the City of London. (1913)

BAO   Bristol Archives Office.

BAS   Birmingham Archaeological Society: *Transactions*.

BB   M. J. Becker: Blythburgh. (1935)

BBA   Sir H. Brakspear: Bath Abbey. (1950)

BBB   W.H.B. Bird: The Black Book of Winchester. (1925)

BBC   C. J. Bates: Bamburgh Castle. (3rd ed., 1894)

BBH   C. J. Bates: Border Holds of Northumberland. (1891)

BBW   J. Britton & E. W. Brayley: History of the Palace of Westminster. (1836)

BCA   Beverley Chapter Act Book. (SS, XCVIII, CVIII, 1897–1903)

BCB   A. Boinet: La Cathédrale de Bourges. (Petites Monographies)

BCL   F. J. Baigent: Crondal Records. (HRS, III, 1891)

BCM   Bury St. Edmunds: Corporation Muniments.

BCO   Balliol College, Oxford: Muniments.

BCR   F. B. Bond & B. Camm: English Church Screens and Roodlofts. (1909)

BCS   W. St. C. Baddeley: A Cotteswold Shrine. (1908)

BCW	J. H. Bloom: Original Charters relating to the City of Worcester. (WHS, 1909)	BPL	F. A. Bailey: The Churchwardens' Accounts of Prescot, Lancs., 1523–1607. (LCRS, CIV, 1953)
BDA	F. Barlow ed.: Durham Annals. 1207–86. (SS, CLV, 1945)	BPN	C. N. L. Brooke & M. M. Postan edd.: Carte Nativorum. (NRS, XX, 1961)
BDB	J. C. Blomfield: History of the Deanery of Bicester. (1844)	BPR	The Black Prince's Register (Calendars).
BEC	J. Bentham: Ely Cathedral. (1812; Supplement, 1817)	BRB	M. J. Becker: Rochester Bridge, 1387–1856. (1930)
BED	W. D. Bushell: Elias de Derham (Harrow Octocentenary Tracts, XII, 1906)	BRC	W. G. Benham: The Oath Book or Red Parchment Book of Colchester. (1907)
BFG	G. Bertie: Five Generations of a Loyal House. (1845)	BRL	Birmingham Reference Library.
BFY	J. Browne: Fabric Rolls and Documents of York Minster. (1863)	BRM	E. M. Beloe: The Red Mount, King's Lynn. (1897)
BGL	C. M. Barron: The Medieval Guildhall of London. (1974)	BRS	J. H. Bloom: Gild Register of Stratford on Avon. (1907)
BGT	Bristol & Gloucester Archaeological Society: Transactions.	BRUO	A. B. Emden: A Biographical Register of the University of Oxford to 1500. (3 vols., 1957–59)
BHB	F. J. Baigent & J. F. Millard: History of Basingstoke. (1889)	BSB	H. D. Barnes & W. D. Simpson: 'The Building Accounts of Caister Castle' in NA, XXX, 1951, 178–88.
BHH	J. R. Boyle: History of Hedon. (1895)		
BHJ	University of Birmingham Historical Journal.	BSC	H. D. Barnes & W. D. Simpson: 'Caister Castle' in ANJ, XXXII, 1952, 35–51.
BHN	F. Blomefield: Topographical History of Norfolk. (1805–62)		
BHS	W. Boys: History of Sandwich. (1792)	BW	Registers of Wills proved in the Sacrist's Court at Bury St. Edmunds or in the Court of the Archdeacon of Sudbury (now in Suffolk Record Office, Bury St. Edmunds).
BHT	J. Bayley: History of the Tower of London. (1821)		
BHY	J. Browne: History of the Metropolitan Church of St. Peter, York. (1847–49)		
BIY	Borthwick Institute, York.	BWO	J. Buxton & P. Williams edd.: New College, Oxford, 1379–1979. (1979)
BKJ	Berkshire Archaeological Journal.		
BL	British Library (see also BM).	CAC	Cambridge Antiquarian Society: Communications (later Proceedings).
BLC	E. M. Beloe: Our Churches (King's Lynn). (1899)	CAD	Calendars of Ancient Deeds (PRO).
BLR	F. B. Bickley ed.: Little Red Book of Bristol. (1900)	CAN	C. H. Cooper: Annals of Cambridge. (1842)
BM	British Museum (see also BL).	CAR	G. G. Coulton: Art and the Reformation. (1928)
BMC	J. R. Bloxam: Magdalen College Register. (1892)	CAS	Cambridge Antiquarian Society.
BMF	Bulletin Monumental: Société Française d'Archéologie, Paris.	CAW	Calendar of Ancient Correspondence concerning Wales. (1935)
BMG	Burlington Magazine.	CBC	H. M. Colvin: 'Four 14th-century Building Contracts' in AH, II (1959), 19–25.
BMH	B. Botfield: Manners and Household Expenses of England. (RC, 1841)		
BNP	Bibliothèque Nationale, Paris.	CBD	Cambridge Borough Documents, ed. W. M. Palmer. (1931)
Bodl.	Bodleian Library, Oxford.		
BOF	The Book of Fees (Testa de Nevill). (1921–31)	CCA	J. C. Cox: Churchwardens' Accounts. (1913)
BPA	J. H. Butcher: The Parish of Ashburton. (1870)	CCA	Archives of Canterbury Cathedral
		CCC	Wills proved in the Consistory Court of Canterbury (in KAO).
BPC	The Story of Bodmin Parish Church. (British Publishing Co.)	CCCC	Corpus Christ College, Cambridge.
BPE	H. E. Bishop & E. K. Prideaux: The Building of Exeter Cathedral. (1922)	CCE	Wills proved in the Consistory Court of Ely (now in CUL).
		CCF	Friends of Canterbury Cathedral: Chronicle.

CCH	W. W. Capes: Charters of Hereford Cathedral. (CNS, 1908)
CCL	Records of Commissary Court of London (in *GUL*).
CCM	Muniments of the Corporation of Cambridge.
CCN	Consistory Court of Norwich (now in *NRO*).
CCO	Corpus Christi College, Oxford: Muniments.
CCP	C. R. Peers: 'Carnarvon Castle' in Cymmrodorion Society's *Transactions*, 1915–16.
CCR	Calendars of Close Rolls.
CCS	G. Coolen: La Cathédrale de Saint-Omer. (1958)
CCW	Calendar of Chancery Warrants.
CCY	Canterbury City Archives.
CDB	R. Chambers: The Book of Days. (1879)
CDE	H. Cole: Documents illustrative of English History in the Thirteenth and Fourteenth Centuries. (1844)
CDI	Calendar of Documents relating to Ireland.
CDS	Charters and Documents of Salisbury. (RS, 1891)
CEF	M. E. Clegg: Transcripts of Exeter Cathedral Fabric Rolls, 1279–1353.
CEM	F. H. Crossley: English Church Monuments 1150–1550. (1933)
CFC	J. M. Cowper: Freemen of Canterbury. (1903)
CFL	Calendar of the Freemen of Lynn 1292–1836. (NNA, 1913)
CFR	Calendars of Fine Rolls.
CGB	Cambridge University Grace Books 'A' and 'B': Proctors' Accounts 1454–1544. (CAS, Luard Memorial Series, 1897–1905)
CGF	A. W. Clapham & W. H. Godfrey: Some Famous Buildings and their Story. (*c.* 1913–14)
CGR	Cambridge Gild Records, ed. M. Bateson. (CAS, Publ., XXXIX)
CHC	County History of Carmarthenshire, ed. Sir J. E. Lloyd. 1935–39)
CHD	J. C. Cox & W. H. St. J. Hope: Chronicles of All Saints, Derby. (1887)
CHH	Sir H. Chauncy: The Historical Antiquities of Hertfordshire. (1700; ed. 1826)
CHR	Calendars of Charter Rolls.
CHS	Chetham Society.
CHT	Caernarvonshire Historical Society: *Transactions*.
CIC	J. M. Cowper: Intrantes, a List of Persons admitted to live and trade within the City of Canterbury, 1392–1592.

	(Canterbury, privately printed, 1904)
CIP	Calendar of Inquisitions post Mortem.
CKC	C. J. P. Carter: Notes on King's College Chapel. (1867)
CKH	W. D. Caröe: King's Hostel, Trinity College. (CAS, Quarto Publ., NS, II, 1909)
CKL	H. M. Chew & W. Kellaway: London Assize of Nuisance 1301–1431. (LOR, X, 1973)
CLB	Calendars of Letter-Books of the City of London.
CLE	R. W. Chambers & M. Daunt: A Book of London English 1384–1425. (1931)
CLH	R. Clutterbuck: History of Hertfordshire. (1815–27)
CLR	Calendars of Liberate Rolls.
CLW	R. Chandler: Life of Waynflete. (1811)
CMA	Calendar of Memoranda Rolls 1326–27. (1968)
CMM	G. T. Clark: Mediaeval Military Architecture. (1884)
CMR	C. H. Cooper: Life of Margaret, Countess of Richmond. (1874)
CNS	Cantilupe Society.
CNW	Chester and North Wales Archaeological Association: *Journal*.
COC	G. Cobb: The Old Churches of London. (3rd ed., 1948)
CPL	Calendars of Papal Letters.
CPLO	J. C. Cox: Pulpits, Lecterns and Organs. (1915)
CPM	Calendar of Plea and Memoranda Rolls of London.
CPR	Calendars of Patent Rolls.
CPW	H. Chitty & S. Pitcher: Mediaeval Sculptures at Winchester College. (1932)
CR	The Record of Caernarvon. (Record Commission, 1838)
CRM	Canterbury Royal Museum: Documents.
CS	Camden Society.
CSB	Board of Celtic Studies: *Bulletin*.
CSD	Calendar of Documents relating to Scotland. (1881–88)
CSG	R. Cole & W. H. Stevenson: Rental of the Borough of Gloucester, 1455. (1890)
CSL	G. G. Coulton: Social Life in Britain. (1938)
CSM	Camden Miscellany, VII. (CS, NS, XIV, 1875)
CSP	Calendars of State Papers: Domestic.
CSR	F. R. Chapman: Sacrist Rolls of Ely. (1907)
CSV	Sede Vacante Wills, Canterbury Probate Records (in *CCA*).
CTG	*Collectanea Topographica et Genealogica.*

CTS Chartulary of the Hospital of St. Thomas the Martyr, Southwark. (Privately printed, 1932)

CUH J. E. Cussans: History of Hertfordshire. (1870–81)

CUL Cambridge University Library.

CWA Cumberland & Westmorland Antiquarian and Archaeological Society: *Transactions*.

CWC R. Custance ed.: Winchester College, Sixth Centenary Essays. (1982)

CWE L. S. Colchester ed.: Wells Cathedral, a History. (1982)

CWF L. S. Colchester ed.: Wells Cathedral Fabric Accounts 1390–1600. (1983)

CWM Churchwardens' Accounts of Great St. Mary, Cambridge, ed. J. E. Foster. (CAS, 8vo. S., XXXV, 1905)

CWT Churchwardens' Accounts of Holy Trinity Church, Cambridge, 1504–63. Transcript by Alfred Rogers *penes* CAS.

CWW Churchwardens' Accounts of Saffron Walden Church, Essex, 1438–90. (Deposited in *ERO*)

CWY R. B. Cook: Some Early Civic Wills of York. (AAS, XXXI-XXXV, 1911–20)

CYS Canterbury and York Society.

DAB J. Dallaway: Antiquities of Bristow. (Bristol, 1834)

DAE J. Dallaway: Discourses upon Architecture in England. (1833)

DAR Durham Account Rolls, ed. J. T. Fowler. (SS, XCIX, C, CIII, 1898–1900)

DAR Unpublished Durham Cathedral Muniments.

DAS Dorset Natural History and Archaeological Society: *Proceedings*.

DAT Danish Art Treasures: Catalogue of Exhibition at Victoria and Albert Museum. (1948)

DB Domesday Book. (Record Commission, 1783–1816)

DBB Boldon Book (Survey of Durham). (SS, XXV, 1852)

DBP J. Dunkin: History of Bullington and Ploughley. (1823)

DCB H. Druitt: Manual of Costume as illustrated by Monumental Brasses. (1928)

DCH G. S. Davies: Charterhouse in London. (1921)

DCL R. C. Dudding: The First Churchwardens' Book of Louth. (1941)

DCM Downing College, Cambridge: Manuscripts.

DCN Dean and Chapter of Norwich, Records in *NRO*.

DCRS Devon & Cornwall Record Society.

DCW J. S. Drew: Compton near Winchester. (1939)

DCY Dean and Chapter of York: Probate Records in *YML*.

DEB F. Drake: Eboracum. (1736)

DGB E. M. Dance ed.: Guildford Borough Records, 1514–1546. (SYR, XXIV, 1958)

DHC L. L. Duncan & A. Hussey: Testamenta Cantiana. (1906–07)

DHW W. Dugdale: History of Warwickshire. (1730)

DIE F. Devon: Issues of the Exchequer. (1837)

DKR Reports of the Deputy Keeper of the Public Records.

DM W. Dugdale: Monasticon (ed. Caley, Ellis & Bandinel, 1817–30)

DMM R. H. C. Davis: 'Masons' Marks in Oxfordshire and the Cotswolds' in Oxfordshire Archaeological Society: 84th *Report*, 1938–39.

DNB Dictionary of National Biography.

DRO Devon Record Office.

DRY W. H. Dixon & J. Raine: Lives of the Archbishops of York, I. (1863)

DS Dugdale Society.

DSC W. Dodsworth: Salisbury Cathedral. (1814)

DSM D. Drake: St. Mawes Castle and Pendennis Castle (1937)

DSP Domesday of St. Paul's. (CS, LXIX, 1858)

DST Historiae Dunelmensis Scriptores Tres, ed. J. Raine. (SS, IX, 1839)

DTB F. Devon: Issue Roll of Thomas of Brantingham. (1835)

DUC Documents relating to the University and Colleges of Cambridge. (By direction of the Queen's Commissioners, 1852)

DWC P. Dearmer: Wells Cathedral. (1922)

EAS Essex Archaeological Society: *Transactions*.

EB Encyclopaedia Britannica, 13th Edition. (1926)

EBB D. Willis ed.: Estate Book of Henry de Bray. (CS, 3S, XXVII, 1916)

ECA Eton College Archives.

ECM J. P. Earwaker & R. H. Morris: History of the Church of St. Mary-on-the-Hill, Chester. (1898)

ECP Early Chancery Proceedings (in *PRO*).

ECR Exeter City Records.

EDC Exeter: Muniments of the Dean and Chapter.

EETS Early English Text Society: Publications.

EFN J. L'Estrange: Calendar of Freemen of Norwich. (1888)

EG C. J. O. Evans: Glamorgan, its History and Topography. (1943)

EHI Ensayos Hispano-Ingleses: Homenaje a Walter Starkie. (Barcelona, 1948)

EHR *English Historical Review*.

ELA W. P. Ellis: Liber Albus Civitatis Oxoniensis. (1909)

EOH A. B. Emden: An Oxford Hall in Mediaeval Times. (1927)

EOL H. Ellis: Original Letters. (3 series, 1824–46)

EPNS English Place-Name Society.

ERA East Riding Antiquarian Society: *Transactions*.

ERO Essex Record Office.

ERP F. Ehrle: Historia Bibliothecae Romanorum Pontificum. (Rome, 1890)

EYC Early Yorkshire Charters. (YRS, Extra Series)

FAO H. Focillon: Art d'Occident. (Paris, 1947)

FCC T. Fowler: Corpus Christi College. (1898)

FFE D. F. Findlay: The Fabric Rolls of Exeter Cathedral. (Ph.D. Thesis, Leeds University, May 1939)

FFK Feet of Fines for Kent.

FH *Family History*.

FHB T. Faulkner: History and Antiquities of Brentford, Ealing and Chiswick. (1845)

FHC T. Fowler: History of Corpus Christi College. (OHS, XXV, 1893)

FHS Flintshire Historical Society: Publications.

FNQ *Fenland Notes and Queries*

FOS H. E. Forrest: The Old Houses of Stratford on Avon. (1925)

FPD Feodarium Prioratus Dunelmensis. (SS, LVIII, 1871)

FRH B. Fletcher: Royal Homes near London. (1930)

FRL A. Finn: Records of Lydd. (1911)

FSA H. Fowler: The Boundary Wall of the Monastery of St. Alban. (St. Albans, 1976)

FSG The Friends of St. George's Windsor Castle): *Reports*.

FTG F. F. Fox & J. Taylor: Some Account of the Guild of Weavers in Bristol. (1889)

FWN E. C. Fernie & A. B. Whittingham: The Early Communar and Pitancer Rolls of Norwich Cathedral Priory. (NRC, XLI, 1972)

FYM Friends of York Minster: *Reports*.

GAL W. H. Godfrey: A History of Architecture in London. (1911)

GAT A. Gardner: Alabaster Tombs. (1940)

GBC R. W. Goulding: Records of Blanchminster's Charity. (1898)

GBR R. H. Gretton: Burford Records. (1921)

GBS J. L. Glasscock, jnr.: Records of St. Michael's Parish Church, Bishop's Stortford. (1882)

GCA Gloucester Cathedral: Archives of the Dean and Chapter.

GCC Gervase of Canterbury: Chronicle. (RS, 1879–80)

GCM Gonvile and Caius College, Cambridge: Muniments.

GCW A. W. Goodman: Chartulary of Winchester Cathedral. (1927)

GDC W. Greenwell: Durham Cathedral (1932)

GEC M. Gibbs: Early Charters of St. Paul's Cathedral. (CS, 3S, LVIII 1939)

GHH J. Gage: History of Hengrave. (1822)

GHT J. Gage: History of Thingoe Hundred. (1838)

GLP D. Gardiner: The Story of Lambeth Palace. (1930)

GLR J. Gairdner: Life of Richard III. (1879)

GM *Gentleman's Magazine*.

GMC J. M. Gray: Biographical Notes on the Mayors of Cambridge. (1922)

GMO H. W. Garrod: Ancient Painted Glass in Merton College, Oxford. (1931)

GMS A. Gardner: English Mediaeval Sculpture. (1951)

GOC E. A. Gee: 'Oxford Carpenters, 1370–1530' in *Oxoniensia*, XVII/XVIII (1954), 112–84.

GOM E. A. Gee: 'Oxford Masons, 1370–1530' in AJ, CIX, 1953, 54–131.

GRC A. Gray: The Priory of St. Radegund, Cambridge. (CAS, Octavo Publ., XXXI, 1898).

GRW Joan Greatrex ed.: The Register of the Common Seal of the Priory of St. Swithun, Winchester, 1345–1497. (1978)

GSD T. Garner & A. Stratton: Domestic Architecture of England during the Tudor Period. (1894)

GSM R. Gough: Sepulchral Monuments (1786–99)

GUL Guildhall Library, London.

GUM   *Guildhall Miscellany.*

GVF   T. H. B. Graham: 'Vills of the Forest, part ii' in CWA, NS XXV (1925).

GYM   Great Yarmouth Muniments.

H   *History*: Historical Association.

HAC   J. H. Harvey: Mediaeval Craftsmen. (1975)

HAR   T. F. Hobson: Adderbury Rectoria (ORS, VIII, 1926)

HAW   F. E. Harmer: Anglo-Saxon Writs. (1952)

HBB   The Black Book of Hexham. (SS, XLVI, 1865)

HBC   H. Braun: Castles. (1936)

HBN   W. H. St. J. Hope & W. T. Bensly: 'Recent Discoveries in the Cathedral Church of Norwich' in NA, XIV.

HBP   J. H. Harvey: 'The Black Prince and his Artists' in CCF, no. 70 (1976), 29–34.

HBS   Henry Bradshaw Society.

HBT   A History of Bearsted and Thurnham. (1978)

HCC   A. Hopkins: Selected Rolls of the Chester City Courts. (CHS, 3S, II, 1950)

HCE   J. H. Harvey: Cathedrals of England and Wales. (1974)

HCH   H. J. Hewitt: Mediaeval Cheshire. (CHS, NS, LXXXVIII, 1929)

HCM   B. W. Henderson: Merton College. (1899)

HCT   J. H. Harvey: 'The Church Towers of Somerset' in AMS, XXVI (1982), 157–83

HCW   J. H. Harvey: 'The Building Works and Architects of Cardinal Wolsey' in AAJ, 3S, VIII, 1943

HCY   History of the Metropolitan Churches of Canterbury and York. (1755)

HDC   [R. C. Hussey]: Extracts from Ancient Documents relating to the Cathedral and Precincts of Canterbury. (1881)

HDE   W. G. Hoskins: Devon. (1954)

HDL   H. Harrod: Deeds and Records of King's Lynn. (1874)

HEA   J. H. Harvey: 'The Education of the Mediaeval Architect' in RIBA, June 1945.

HEC   R. H. Hilton: 'Building Accounts of Elmley Castle' in BHJ, X.

HED   H. L. Honeyman: 'Master Elias Dereham and his connection with Durham' in TDN, January 1938, 15–26.

HFH   H. Howard: The Family of Howard. (1836)

HGA   *Hertfordshire Genealogical Antiquary.*

HGE   J. H. Harvey: Gothic England. (2nd ed., 1948)

HGM   J. H. Harvey: 'Great Milton, Oxfordshire; and Thorncroft, Surrey: the Building Accounts for two Manor-Houses of the late Fifteenth Century' in AAJ, 3S, XVIII, 1955, 42–56.

HGW   J. H. Harvey: The Gothic World. (1950)

HHA   Helmingham Hall Archives.

HHC   A. Hay: History of Chichester. (1804)

HHH   W. & J. H. Harvey: 'Master Hugh Herland' in *The Connoisseur*, June 1936.

HHN   J. Hodgson: History of Northumberland. (1827–40)

HHR   Register of Hamo Hethe, Bishop of Rochester 1319–52. (CYS, XLVIII, XLIX, 1914–45)

HHW   T. S. Holmes: History of the Parish and Manor of Wookey. (Bristol, n.d.)

HHY   J. H. Harvey: Henry Yevele. (2nd ed., 1946)

HKC   J. H. Harvey: 'The King's Chief Carpenters' in AAJ, 3S, XI, 1948

HKL   H. J. Hillen: History of King's Lynn. (1907)

HKW   The History of the King's Works, ed. H. M. Colvin, vols. I–IV, 1963–82.

HLC   T. D. Hardy, ed.: Rotuli Litterarum Clausarum. (Record Commission, 1833–44)

HMA   J. H. Harvey: 'The Mediaeval Carpenter as an Architect' in RIBA, 13 June 1938.

HMB   E. Hope: The Church of St. Mary, Beverley. (1937)

HMC   Historical Manuscripts Commission.

HME   J. H. Harvey: The Mediaeval Architect. (1972)

HML   J. W. F. Hill: Mediaeval Lincoln. (1948)

HMO   J. H. Harvey: 'The Mediaeval Office of Works' in AAJ, 3S, VI, 1941.

HMR   J. Hunter, ed.: Magnus Rotulus Scaccarii. (1833)

HMW   Sir R. Colt Hoare: The History of Modern Wiltshire. (1822–43)

HMY   J. H. Harvey: 'Some Details and Mouldings used by Yevele' in ANJ, XXVII, 1947, 51–60.

HP   R. Higden: Polychronicon. (RS, 1865–86)

HPC   J. H. Harvey: 'The Architects of English Parish Churches' in AJ, CV, 1950, 14–26.

HPL   J. H. Harvey: The Plantagenets. (1967 etc.)

HPM	W. J. Hardy & W. Page: Feet of Fines for London and Middlesex. (1892–93)
HPS	J. H. Harvey: The Perpendicular Style. (1978)
HPW	H. Hall, ed.: The Pipe Roll of the Bishopric of Winchester, 1208–09. (1903)
HRB	H. Hall, ed.: The Red Book of the Exchequer. (1897)
HRC	W. H. St. J. Hope: Rochester Cathedral. (1900)
HRG	F. C. Hingeston-Randolph, ed.: Register of John Grandisson, bishop of Exeter 1327–69. (3 vols., 1894–99)
HRL	T. D. Hardy, ed.: Rotuli de Liberate ac de Misis et Prestitis regnante Johanne. (Record Commission, 1844)
HRO	Hereford Record Office.
HRS	Hampshire Record Society.
HSA	[R. C. Hussey]: Excerpta e Compoto Thesaurariae Mon. Sci. Augustini extra Muros Cantuariae A.D. 1432, etc.
HSC	J. H. Harvey: 'St. Stephen's Chapel and the Origin of the Perpendicular Style' in BMG, LXXXVIII, 1946, 192–9.
HSK	J. H. Harvey: 'Side-Lights on Kenilworth Castle' in AJ, CI, 1946
HSLC	Historical Society of Lancashire and Cheshire: *Transactions*.
HSP	Huguenot Society: Publications.
HSS	J. H. Harvey: 'Archbishop Simon Sudbury and the Patronage of Architecture in the Middle Ages' in CCF, no. 76 (1982), 22–32.
HSY	J. Hunter: South Yorkshire. (1831)
HTA	J. H. Harvey: An Introduction to Tudor Architecture. (1949)
HTD	J. H. Harvey: 'Early Tudor Draughtsmen' in The Connoisseur Coronation Book. (1953)
HTM	*The History Teacher's Miscellany*.
HTN	W. Hudson & J. C. Tingey: The Records of the City of Norwich. (1906–10)
HTP	J. H. Harvey: 'The Last Years of Thetford Cluniac Priory' in NA, XXVII, 1939.
HWA	Sir William Hayter: William of Wykeham, Patron of the Arts. (1970)
HWC	W. H. St. J. Hope: Windsor Castle. (1913)
HWG	T. S. Holmes: Wells and Glastonbury (1908)
HWH	A. M. Hind: Wenceslaus Hollar. (1922)
HWI	J. H. Harvey, ed.: William Worcestre, Itineraries. (1969)
HWP	J. H. Harvey: 'Perpendicular at Wells' in BAACT 1981.
HWW	J. H. Harvey: 'William Wynford, Architect' in *Winchester Cathedral Record*, No. 18, 1949, 4–7.
HYM	J. H. Harvey: 'Architectural History [of York Minster] from 1291 to 1558' in ACY, 149–92.
HYR	J. H. Harvey: 'Henry Yevele Reconsidered' in AJ, CVIII, 1952, 100–08.
IAC	C. Igglesden: Ashford Church. (1924)
IDK	Reports of the Deputy Keeper of the Public Records, Ireland.
IPC	Rotulorum Patentium et Clausarum Cancellarii Hiberniae Calendarium ed. E. Tresham. (1828)
IW	Registers of Wills proved in the Court of the Archdeacon of Suffolk (now in Suffolk Record Office, Ipswich).
JAB	E. Jervoise: Ancient Bridges. (4 regional volumes, I-South, 1930; II-North, 1931; III-Mid. & East, 1932; IV-Wales & West, 1936)
JAS	E.F. Jacob: 'The Building of All Souls College' in Essays in Honour of James Tait. (1933)
JBC	G. Jackson: Bolton Castle. (1946)
JCB	I. H. Jeayes: Catalogue of the Charters and Muniments at Berkeley Castle. (1892)
JCC	I. H. Jeayes; Court Rolls of the Borough of Colchester. (1941)
JCM	St. John's College, Cambridge: Muniments.
JDS	*Journal* of the Derbyshire Archaeological and Natural History Society.
JGA	T. G. Jackson: Gothic Architecture. (1915)
JGR	John of Gaunt's Registers, 1372–76 & 1379–83. (CS, 3S, XX, XXI, 1911; LVI, LVII, 1937)
JJC	C. Johnson & H. Jenkinson: English Court Hand 1066-1500. (1915)
JLC	J. H. James: History and Survey of the Cathedral of Llandaff. (1929)
JMO	T. G. Jackson: Church of St. Mary the Virgin, Oxford. (1897)
JNC	H. E. H. Jerningham: Norham Castle. (1883)
JPC	E. B. Jupp & W. W. Pocock: Historical Account of the Worshipful Company of Carpenters. (1887)
JVM	Homenatge a Josep Vives i Miret (Santes Creus, 2 vols., 1970–71)
KAO	Kent Archives Office.
KAR	Kent Archaeological Society: Records Series.
KAW	T. F. Kirby: Annals of Winchester College. (1892)

KBH	N. J. M. Kerling: Cartulary of St. Bartholomew's Hospital. (1973)	LCR	King's Lynn Corporation Records.
KCA	Kingston upon Thames: Corporation Archives.	LCRS	Lancashire and Cheshire Record Society.
KCM	King's College, Cambridge: Muniments.	LCW	R. W. M. Lewis: Walberswick Churchwardens' Accounts, 1450–99. (1949)
KCR	G. W. Kitchin: Compotus Rolls of St. Swithin's Priory, Winchester. (HRS, 1892)	LDC	Lincoln: Muniments of the Dean and Chapter.
KHA	Account Books of King's Hall, Cambridge (among TCM).	LDD	Lincoln Diocese Documents, ed. A. Clark. (EETS, Original S., No. 149, 1914)
KHW	T. Kemp: History of Warwick.	LEC	A. H. Lloyd: The Early History of Christ's College, Cambridge. (1934)
KJC	D. Knoop & G. P. Jones: 'The Rise of the Mason Contractor' in RIBA, 3S, XLIII, 17 October 1936.	LEN	F. Lennel: Histoire de Calais. (1910)
KJE	D. Knoop & G. P. Jones: 'The Building of Eton College' in AQC, XLVI, 1933, 70–114.	LFV	W. C. Leedy: Fan Vaulting. (1980)
		LGC	P. Lavedan: L'architecture gothique en Catalogne. (Paris, 1935)
KJI	D. Knoop & G. P. Jones: An Introduction to Freemasonry. (1937)	LHC	E. Law: History of Hampton Court Palace. (1885–91)
KJL	D. Knoop & G. P. Jones: 'London Bridge and its Builders' in AQC, XLVII, 1934.	LHR	London Husting Rolls: Corporation of London Record Office.
KJM	D. Knoop & G. P. Jones: 'Notes on Three Master Masons' in Miscellanea Latomorum, November 1937.	LHS	Liber Henrici de Soliaco. . . An Inquisition of the Manors of Glastonbury Abbey, 1189, ed. J. E. Jackson. (RC, 1882)
KJS	D. Knoop & G.P. Jones: 'The Sixteenth Century Mason' in AQC, L, 1937.	LI	J. Leland: Itinerary (ed. L. Toulmin-Smith, 1906–10).
		LKC	W. R. Lethaby: Westminster Abbey and the Kings' Craftsmen. (1906)
KJW	D. Knoop & G. P. Jones: 'Master Walter of Hereford' in Miscellanea Latomorum, December 1939.	LMR	H. Littlehales: The Mediaeval Records of a London City Church (St. Mary-at-Hill). (EETS, OS, Nos. 125, 128, 1905)
KJY	D. Knoop & G. P. Jones: 'Henry Yevele and his Associates' in RIBA, 25 May 1935.	LMT	London and Middlesex Archaeological Society: Transactions.
KLR	C. Kerry: A History of the Church of St. Lawrence, Reading. (1883)	LNE	Luc-Benoist: Notre-Dame de l'Épine. (Paris, 1933)
KMM	D. Knoop & G. P. Jones: The Medieval Mason. (1933)	LNQ	Lincolnshire Notes and Queries.
		LOR	London Record Society.
KSM	J. V. Kitto: Churchwardens' Accounts of St. Martin's in the Fields. (1901)	LP	Lambeth Palace Library.
		LPH	Letters and Papers of the Reign of Henry VIII.
KSW	D. Keene: Survey of Medieval Winchester (Winchester Studies, 2; Oxford).	LPP	L. H. Labande: Le Palais des Papes et les Monuments d'Avignon au XIVe siècle. (Marseilles, 1925)
LAA	Lincolnshire Architectural and Archaeological Society: Reports and Papers, New Series.	LRA	Magnum Registrum Album of Lichfield Cathedral. (WSS, 1926)
		LRC	Life Records of Chaucer (Chaucer Society, 1875–1900).
LAG	J. D. LeCouteur: Ancient Glass in Winchester. (1920)	LRS	Lincoln Record Society.
LAO	Lincolnshire Archives Office.	LS	London Survey (London County Council and LS Committee).
LAS	Leicester Archaeological Society: Transactions.	LSF	F. B. Lewis: Surrey Fines. (SYS, 1894)
LAU	Laudate.	LSL	J. J. Lambert: Records of the Skinners of London. (1933)
LBD	A. F. Leach: Beverley Town Documents. (Selden Soc., XIV, 1900).	LTR	London Topographical Record: London Topographical Society.
LBH	London Bridge House Muniments: Corporation of London.	LWA	L. Lyell & F. D. Watney edd.: Acts of Court of the Mercers' Company. (Cambridge, 1936)
LC	J. Leland: Collectanea, ed. T. Hearne. (ed. 1774)	LWR	W. R. Lethaby: Westminster Abbey Re-examined. (1925)
LCA	Lancashire and Cheshire Antiquarian Society.		
LCM	Lichfield Cathedral Muniments.		

LWW   R. Lowth: Life of William of Wykeham. (1759)

MAE   W. D. Macray, ed.: Abbatiae de Evesham Chronicon. (RS, 1863)

MBB   Monumental Brass Society: *Bulletin.*

MBH   N. Moore: History of St. Bartholomew's Hospital. (1918)

MBM   Memorials of Beverley Minster. (SS, XCVIII, CVIII, 1897–1903)

MBS   O. Manning & W. Bray: History and Antiquities of Surrey. (1814)

MCO   Magdalen College, Oxford: Muniments.

MCP   R. H. Morris: Chester in Plantagenet and Tudor Reigns. (1894)

MCR   B. Marsh: Records of the Worshipful Company of Carpenters. (1913–39)

MCS   J. McNulty: Cartulary of Sallay Abbey. (YRS, LXXXVII, XC, 1933, etc.)

MDA   C. T. Martin: 'Sir John Daunce's Accounts. . .' in A, XLVII pt. ii (1883).

MDD   M. Mackeprang: Danmarks middelalderlige Döbefonte. (1941)

MDR   V. Mortet & P. Deschamps: Recueil de Textes relatifs à l'histoire de l'architecture. . .au Moyen Age. (Paris, 1911–29)

MEC   H. C. Maxwell-Lyte: History of Eton College. (1911)

MGA   R. Merrick: A Book of Glamorganshire Antiquities, ed. J. A. Corbett. (1887)

MHC   G. Marshall: Hereford Cathedral. (1951)

MHN   *Middlesex and Hertfordshire Notes and Queries.*

MHO   J. G. Milne & J. H. Harvey: 'The Building of Cardinal College, Oxford' in OXN, VIII/IX, 1945, 137–53.

MLR   J. P. Malcolm: Londinium Redivivum (1803)

MM   Maidstone Museum.

MMM   W. D. Macray: Muniments of Magdalen College. (1882)

MMW   M. E. C. Walcott: Memorials of Westminster. (1851)

MNE   K. B. McFarlane: The Nobility of Later Medieval England. (1973)

MR   *Masonic Record.*

MRC   H. B. McCall: Richmondshire Churches. (1910)

MRT   Merton College, Oxford: Muniments.

MSD   F. Marcham: Catalogue of Surrey Deeds.

MSE   Memorials of St. Edmunds Abbey. (RS, 1890–96)

MSL   B. McClenaghan: The Springs of Lavenham. (1924)

MTM   J. Maclean: The Parochial and Family History of the Deanery of Trigg Minor. (1868)

MVH   Magna Vita S. Hugonis. (RS, 1864)

NA   *Norfolk Archaeology*: Norfolk and Norwich Archaeological Society.

NBR   Nottingham Borough Records.

NCH   Northumberland County History. (1893–1940)

NCM   Norwich Cathedral Muniments (now in *NRO*).

NCO   New College, Oxford: Muniments.

NDR   Norwich Diocesan Registry.

NIM   J. Nichols: Illustrations of Manners. (1797)

NLH   F. M. Nichols: The Hall of Lawford Hall. (1891)

NML   T. North: Churchwardens' Accounts of St. Martin, Leicester. (1884)

NMR   Norwich Museum Muniment Room.

NNA   Norfolk & Norwich Archaeological Society.

N&Q   *Notes and Queries.*

NRA   National Register of Archives.

NRC   Norfolk Record Society.

NRO   Norfolk Record Office.

NRS   Northamptonshire Record Society.

NS   New Series.

NTB   J. F. Nicholls & J. Taylor: Bristol Past and Present. (1881)

NWW   Itinerary of William of Worcester, ed. J. Nasmith. (1778)

NYR   North Yorkshire County Record Office.

OAD   A. Oswald: 'Andrew Doket and his Architect' in CAC, XLII, 1949, 8–26.

OCC   A. Oswald: 'Canterbury Cathedral' in BMG, December 1939.

OCO   Oriel College, Oxford: Muniments.

OCR   *Oriel College Record.*

OEA   Epistolae Academicae Oxonienses, ed. H. Anstey. (OHS, XXXV, XXXVI, 1898)

OED   Oxford English Dictionary.

OHS   Oxford Historical Society.

OMA   Munimenta Academica Oxoniensia. (RS, 1868)

ORS   Oxfordshire Record Society.

OSH   B. H. St. J. O'Neil: 'Stefan von Haschenperg' in A, XCI, 1945, 137–55.

OXN   *Oxoniensia.*

PAS   F. Peck: Antiquarian Annals of Stamford. (1727)

PBA   *Proceedings* of the British Academy.

PCA   W. M. Palmer: Cambridge Castle. (1928)

PCB   E. S. Prior: The Cathedral Builders in England. (1905)

PCC   J. C. Perks: Chepstow Castle (Official Guide-book, 1955).

PCC   Prerogative Court of Canterbury (in *PRO*).

PCH   Matthew Paris: Chronica Majora. (RS, 1872–84)

PCM   Peterborough Cathedral Muniments.

PCO   W. A. Pantin: Canterbury College, Oxford. (OHS, NS, VI-VIII, 1946–50)

PCY   Prerogative Court of York (in *BIY*)

PGL   J. E. Price: The Guildhall of the City of London. (1886)

PHA   Matthew Paris: Historia Anglorum. (RS, 1866–69)

PHM   Peterhouse, Cambridge: Muniments.

PKW   H. R. Plomer: Index of Wills. (Kent Records, VI, 1920)

PMC   Select Pleas in Manorial Courts. (Selden Society, 1888)

PNA   J. Payne-Collier: Norfolk Household Accounts, 1481–84. (RC, 1844)

PPR   Principal Probate Registry, London (all records to 1857 now removed; see *PCC* and consult J. S. W. Gibson: Wills and where to find them).

PR   Calendars of Pipe Rolls: Pipe Roll Society.

PRC   J. S. Purvis: 'The Ripon Carvers' in YAJ, XXIX, 1927–29, 157–201.

PRO   Public Record Office.

PRP   Probate Registry of Peterborough (records now at Northamptonshire Record Office).

PRS   J. S. Purvis: 'The use of Continental Woodcuts and Prints by the Ripon School of Woodcarvers' in A, LXXXV, 1935, 107–28.

PWC   A. N. Palmer: History of the Parish Church of Wrexham. (1886)

PWM   M. R. Petch: 'William de Malton, Master Mason' in YAJ, LIII (1981), 37–44.

QCO   Queen's College, Oxford: Muniments.

R   Report.

RA   *Revue Archéologique.* (Paris)

RAA   H. T. Riley, ed.: Amundesham: Annales. (RS, 1870)

RAC   Chronicle of Ramsey Abbey. (RS, 1866)

RAD   D. R. Ransome: 'Artisan Dynasties in London and Westminster in the sixteenth century' in GUM, II no. 6 (1964), 236–47.

RAM   Registrum Annal. Colleg. Merton. (OHS, LXXVI, 1921)

RAP   J. E. Thorold Rogers: History of Agriculture and Prices. (1866–92)

RAR   *Revista de Archivos.* (Madrid)

RAW   J. A. Robinson: The Abbot's House at Westminster. (1911)

RB   *Records of Buckinghamshire.*

RBA   Rochester Bridge Accounts. (Rochester Bridge Wardens)

RBW   V. B. Redstone: Bury St. Edmunds Wills, 1354–1537. (1907)

RC   Roxburghe Club Publications.

RCAM   Royal Commission on Ancient Monuments (Wales): Inventories.

RCC   J. Raine: Catterick Church. (1834)

RCHM   Royal Commission on Historical Monuments (England): Inventories.

RCW   Wills proved in Rochester Consistory Court (now in *KAO*).

RDC   J. Raine: Brief Account of Durham Cathedral. (1833)

RDL   Reginaldi Dunelmensis Libellus de Admirandis. (SS, I, 1835)

REF   C. Ross: The Estates and Finances of Richard Beauchamp, Earl of Warwick (DS, Occasional Paper no. 12).

RF   T. Rymer: Foedera.

RFP   Records of Finchale Priory. (SS, VI, 1837)

RFY   J. Raine: Fabric Rolls of York Minster. (SS, XXXV, 1858)

RGA   H. T. Riley, ed.; Gesta Abbatum Mon. S. Albani. (RS, 1867–69)

RHD   J. Raine: History of North Durham. (1852)

RIBA   Royal Institute of British Architects: *Journal.*

RJE   M. M. Rowe & A. M. Jackson, edd., Exeter Freemen 1266–1967. (1973)

RKS   J. H. Round: The King's Serjeants. (1911)

RLC   H. T. Riley: Liber Custumarum. (RS, 1860)

RLS   F. L. Ranson: Lavenham, Suffolk. (1947)

RLW   D. Royce: Landboc. . .de Winchelcumba. (1892–1903)

RMC   Cartularium Mon. de Rameseia, ed. W. H. Hart & P. A. Lyons. (RS, 1884–94)

RMF   E. Robo: Mediaeval Farnham. (1935)

RML   H. T. Riley: Memorials of London. (1868)

RMY   A. Raine: Mediaeval York. (1955)

RN   Records of Nottingham.

RND   W. Rye: Calendar of Deeds relating to Norwich: 1285–1306; 1307–41. (1903, 1915)

RNF   W. Rye: Norfolk Feet of Fines. (1885)

RNW   R. B. Rackham: 'The Nave of Westminster Abbey' in PBA, IV, 1909–10.

ROC   R. Richards: Old Cheshire Churches. (1947)

ROD   J. E. T. Rogers: Oxford City Documents. (OHS, XVIII, 1891)

RP   Rotuli Parliamentorum. (Record Commission, 1783–1832)

RPF   W. Rye: Pedes Finium relating to Co. Cambs. (CAS, 1891)

RPL   *Reports and Papers* of the Architectural Society of the Diocese of Lincoln.

RPP   J. H. Round: Peerage and Pedigree. (1910)

RPS   W. B. Rix: The Pride of Swaffham (Swaffham Church). (1950)

RRR	Register of Robert Rede, Bishop of Chichester 1397–1415. (SXR, VIII, 1908)
RRS	Eileen Roberts: 'Robert Stowell' in AAJ, 3S, XXXV (1972), 24–38.
RS	Rolls Series.
RSC	Rotuli Scotiae. (2 vols., 1814–19)
RTW	Eileen Roberts: 'Thomas Wolvey, Mason' in AJ, CXXIX (1973), 119–44.
RUE	H. Reynolds: The Use of. . .Exeter. (1891)
RWC	H. E. Reynolds: Wells Cathedral. (1880)
RYF	W. Rye: Calendar of Freemen of Great Yarmouth. (1910)
SA	Society of Antiquaries of London: Manuscripts.
SAB	J. Summerson: Architecture in Britain 1530–1830. (1953)
SAC	Sussex Archaeological Society: *Collections.*
SAD	Sherborne Almshouse Documents.
SAG	H. Stein: Les architectes des cathédrales gothiques. (Paris)
SAH	St. Albans and Hertfordshire Architectural and Archaeological Society: *Transactions.*
SAK	C. H. Schaefer: Die Ausgaben der Apostolischen Kammer. (Paderborn, 1911–14)
SAP	Somerset Archaeological and Natural History Society: *Proceedings.*
SAW	J. T. Smith: Antiquities of Westminster. (1807)
SBC	R. Stewart-Brown: Cheshire Pipe Rolls 1158–1301. (LCRS, XCII, 1938)
SBD	H. E. Salter, ed.: The Oxford Deeds of Balliol College. (OHS, LXIV, 1913)
SBE	R. Stewart-Brown: Calendar of County Court, City Court and Eyre Rolls of Chester 1259–97. (CHS, NS, LXXXIV, 1925)
SBH	Bishop Hatfield's Survey, ed. W. Greenwell. (SS, XXXII, 1857)
SBL	R. Stewart-Brown: The Tower of Liverpool. (1910)
SBT	Shakespeare Birthplace Trust.
SC	Shrewsbury Corporation Muniments.
SCA	G. G. Scott: Essay on the History of English Church Architecture. (1881)
SCC	W. Somner: Antiquities of Canterbury, ed. N. Battely. (1703)
SCH	H. E. Salter, ed.; Cartulary of the Hospital of St. John the Baptist. (OHS, LXVI, LXVIII, LXIX, 1914–16)
SCM	Select Cases concerning the Law Merchant. (Selden Soc., XXIII)
SCO	*Scottish Historical Review.*
SCP	The Priory of Coldingham. (SS, XII, 1841)
SCR	R. R. Sharpe: Calendar of Coroners' Rolls 1300–78. (1913)
SCT	A. D. Stallard: Churchwardens' Accounts of Tilney All Saints. (1922)
SCW	Swaffham Churchwardens' Accounts.
SD	Sanctuarium Dunelmense. (SS, V, 1837)
SDC	M. G. Snape: 'Documentary Evidence for the Building of Durham Cathedral and its Monastic Buildings' in BAACT 1980, 20–36.
SDD	F. M. Stenton: Documents illustrative of the Social and Economic History of the Danelaw. (British Academy, 1920)
SDN	*Somerset and Dorset Notes and Queries.*
SEC	D. J. Stewart: Architectural History of Ely Cathedral. (1868)
SEJ	R. F. Scott: articles in *The Eagle*, the College magazine of St. John's College, Cambridge.
SEL	Selden Society.
SET	L. F. Salzman: English Trade in the Middle Ages. (1931)
SG	Society of Genealogists: Manuscript Collections.
SGB	Suffolk Green Books. (1894, etc.)
SGC	F. M. Stenton: Transcripts of Gilbertine Charters. (LRS, XVIII, 1922)
SGW	G. G. Scott: Gleanings from Westminster Abbey. (2nd ed., 1863)
SHB	L. F. Salzman: Building in England down to 1540. (1952)
SHC	W. D. Simpson: 'Harlech Castle' in ACA, December 1940.
SHR	Shropshire Archaeological Society: *Transactions.*
SHS	C. F. D. Sperling: A Short History of Sudbury. (1896)
SIA	Suffolk Institute of Archaeology: *Proceedings.*
SJC	St. John's College, Cambridge: Archives.
SJR	L. R. Shelby: John Rogers. (1967)
SJS	W. D. Simpson: 'James de Sancto Georgio' in AFC, 1928.
SLC	H. E. Savage: 'The Architectural History of Lichfield Cathedral' in TNS, XLVIII (1913–14), 113–22.
SMC	R. E. Swartwout: The Monastic Craftsman (1932)
SMO	H. E. Salter: Mediaeval Archives of the University of Oxford. (OHS, LXX, LXXIII, 1917–19)
SMR	Memorials of Ripon. (SS, LXXIV, LXXVIII, LXXXI, CXV, 1882–1908)
SNN	D. J. Stewart: 'Notes on Norwich Cathedral' in AJ, XXXII, 1875.
SNQ	*Sussex Notes and Queries.*
SNR	W. D. Simpson: 'A Further Note on Rothesay Castle' in *Trans.* Glasgow Archaeol. Soc., NS, X, 1941, 78.

SPA	G. de G. Sieveking, ed.: Problems in Economic and Social Archaeology. (1976)	TJS	A. J. Taylor: 'Master James of St. George' in EHR, LXV, 1950, 433–57.
SPE	St. Paul's Ecclesiological Society: *Transactions*.	TNS	*Transactions* of the North Staffordshire Field Club.
SPM	St. Paul's Cathedral, London: Muniments (now in *GUL*).	TPD	H. Turner & J.H. Parker: Domestic Architecture of the Middle Ages. (4 vols., 1851–59)
SQC	W. G. Searle: History of Queens' College, Cambridge, Part I. (CAS, Octavo Publ., IX, 1867)	TRO	W. H. Turner: Records of the City of Oxford. (1880)
SRG	W. H. Stevenson: Calendar of Records of the Corporation of Gloucester. (1893)	TSB	S. Tymms: Sudbury and Bury Wills to 1649. (CS, XLIX, 1850)
SRS	Somerset Record Society.	TSS	J. Topham: An Account of the Collegiate Chapel of St. Stephen at Westminster. (1834)
SS	Surtees Society.		
SSB	L. Stone: Sculpture in Britain: the Middle Ages. (1955, etc.)	TSW	M. Thompson: 'The construction of the Manor at South Wingfield, Derbyshire' in SPA, 417–38.
SSC	T. Serel: Historical Notes on St. Cuthbert's, Wells.		
SSF	H. E Salter; ed.: Snappe's Formulary. (OHS, LXXX, 1924)	TTH	A. J. Taylor: 'Thomas de Houghton' in ANJ, XXX, 1950, 28–33.
SSL	J. Stow: Survey of London.	TVR	A. H. Thompson, ed.: Visitations of Religious Houses in the Diocese of Lincoln. (CYS, XVII, XXIV, XXXIII, 1915–29)
SSS	J. Stow: Survey of London, ed. Seymour. (1734)		
STC	Sir Robert Somerville: Guide to Tutbury Castle. (1964)	TWA	L. E. Tanner: The Story of Westminster Abbey. (1932)
SWD	W. D. Simpson: 'The Warkworth Donjon and its Architect' in *Archaeologia Aeliana*, XIX, 4S, 1941.	TWP	E. W. Tristram: English Mediaeval Wall Painting. (1945–50)
		UCO	University College, Oxford: Records.
SWL	R. R. Sharpe: Calendar of Wills in the London Court of Husting. (1889)	UFT	G. Unwin: Finance and Trade under Edward III. (1918)
SXR	Sussex Record Society.	VA	*Vernacular Architecture*: Vernacular Architecture Group.
SYC	Surrey Archaeological Society: *Collections*.		
SYR	Surrey Record Society.	VCH	Victoria County History.
SYS	Surrey Archaeological Society.	VCL	A. Vallance: Old Crosses and Lychgates. (1933)
TBK	U. Thieme & F. Becker: Allgemeines Lexikon der bildenden Künstler. (Leipzig)	VCS	A. Vallance: English Church Screens. (1936)
		WAM	Westminster Abbey Muniments.
TCB	A. H. Thompson: 'Cathedral Builders of the Middle Ages' in H, July 1925.	WAP	H. Walpole: Anecdotes of Painting in England. (3rd ed., 1782)
TCC	A. H. Thompson: Cathedral Churches of England. (1925)	WBR	J. Wallis: The Bodmin Register. (1830)
TCM	Trinity College, Cambridge: Muniments.	WBW	T. P. Wadley: Notes of Bristol Wills. (1886)
TCR	Register of Thomas of Corbridge. (SS, CXLI, 1928)	WCC	R. Willis & J. W. Clark: Architectural History of the University of Cambridge. (1886)
TDN	Architectural and Archaeological Society of Durham and Northumberland: *Transactions*.	*WCM*	Winchester College Muniments.
		WCO	Worcester Cathedral Obedientiary Rolls: Dean and Chapter's Muniments.
TED	A. H. Thompson: 'Master Elias of Dereham and the King's Works' in AJ, XCVIII–1941, 1942, 1–35.	WCR	Compotus Rolls of Worcester Cathedral Priory. (WHS, 1908–10)
TFC	H. Taylor: Guide to Flint Castle. (1899)	WCV	T. D. Whitaker: The History and Antiquities of the Deanery of Craven. (1805)
TFE	T. F. Tout: 'Firearms in England in the XIVth century' in EHR, 1911, 67, 689–90.	WDA	J. M. Webster: Dunfermline Abbey. (1948)
TGD	T. Gardner: Dunwich. (1754)	WDC	C. E. Woodruff & W. Danks: Memorials of Canterbury Cathedral. (1912)
THS	Thoroton Society.		
THW	L. E. Tanner & R. P. Howgrave-Graham: Unknown Westminster Abbey. (1948)	WDO	G. Webb: 'The Divinity School,

	'Oxford' in *Country Life*, 27 April and 4 May 1929.
WFC	Woolhope Field Club: *Transactions*.
WFL	C. Welch: Register of Freemen of the City of London, 1535–52. (1908)
WFM	J. Weever: Funeral Monuments. (1631)
WGR	Register of Walter Gray. (SS, LVI, 1872)
WHB	R. Warner: History and Antiquities of Bath. (1801)
WHC	J. F. Williams: The Early Church-wardens' Accounts of Hampshire. (1913)
WHP	C. Welch: History of the Pewterers' Company of London. (1902)
WHR	W. J. Williams: 'Henry Redman' in AQC, XXXIX, 1926.
WHS	Worcester Historical Society.
WHT	H. R. Watkin: History of Totnes Priory and Mediaeval Town. (1914–17)
WHW	T. D. Whitaker: The Hundred of Whalley. (1881)
WKA	N. J. Williams: Kingston-upon-Thames Bridgewardens' Accounts 1526–1567. (SYR, XXII, 1955)
WKM	W. J. Williams: 'The King's Master Masons' in AQC, XLIII, 1930.
WLC	Wells Chapter Muniments.
WLE	M. Weinbaum: London unter Eduard I und II. (Stuttgart, 1933)
WMC	H. A. Wilson: Magdalen College. (1899)
WML	W. J. Williams: 'Masons and the City of London' in AQC, XLV, 1932.
WMP	J. C. Wedgwood: History of Parliament — Biographies of the Members of the Commons House, 1439–1509. (1936)
WMW	H. F. Westlake: St. Margaret's Westminster. (1914)
WNC	Winchester Cathedral Muniments.
WNQ	*Wiltshire Notes and Queries*
WOR	Worcester County Record Office.
WPM	R. N. Worth: Calendar of the Plymouth Municipal Records. (1893)

WPR	Register of Worcester Priory. (CS, XCI, 1865)
WPS	W. Papworth: 'Superintendents of Buildings in the Middle Ages' in RIBA *Transactions*, 1887.
WRC	G. Wrottesley: 'Crécy and Calais' in WSS, XVIII, 1897.
WRH	Wykeham's Register, ed. T.F. Kirby. (HRS, 1899)
WRO	Warwick County Record Office.
WRS	T. D. Whitaker: A History of Richmondshire. (1823)
WS	Walpole Society.
WSD	M. White: St. Davids. (1939)
WSG	Muniments of St. George's Chapel, Windsor.
WSH	F. T. Wethered: St. Mary's Hurley in the Middle Ages, Charters and Deeds. (1898)
WSS	William Salt Society.
WTB	C. Welch: History of the Tower Bridge, etc. (1894)
WTM	*Wiltshire Archaeological Magazine*.
WVB	The White Vellum Book of the Scarborough Corporation. (1914)
WWA	H.F. Westlake: Westminster Abbey. (1923)
WWH	Historical Society of West Wales: *Transactions*.
WWL	J. M. Wilson: The Worcester Liber Albus. (1920)
YAJ	*Yorkshire Archaeological Journal*.
YAS	Yorkshire Archaeological Society.
YCF	Register of Freemen of York, ed. F. Collins. (SS, XCVI, 1897, etc.)
YCM	York Corporation Muniments.
YCR	York Civic Records, ed. A. Raine. (YRS, XCVIII, 1939, etc.)
YDC	Muniments of the Dean and Chapter of York (in *YML*).
YDR	York Diocesan Registry.
YHW	G. Young: History of Whitby. (1817)
YMB	York Memorandum Book, ed. M. Sellers. (SS, CXX, CXXV, 1912–15)
YML	York Minster Library.
YRS	Yorkshire Archaeological Society: Record Series.
YTE	Testamenta Eboracensia. (SS, IV, 1836, etc.)

Il reste une oeuvre, un homme et une date. C'en est assez.
Ferdinand Brunetière: *Essais sur la littérature contemporaine,* 1892

. . . there is no formulation of a question which forces us to penetrate so deeply into the essence of the individual work as that concerning the identity of the author . . . every work of man is the product of a personality with qualities existing once and unique. . . . The ultimate, the most fruitful question, even if it cannot be answered, is and remains that which concerns personality.

Max J. Friedländer: *On Art and Connoisseurship,* 1942.

INTRODUCTION

Architectural Attribution in relation to English Mediaeval style

Four centuries have passed since Giorgio Vasari wrote his remarkable book on the lives of Italy's painters, sculptors, and architects: Italy owes much of her pre-eminent reputation as an artistic country to this delightful work. Living in an age of achievement in all artistic fields, Vasari was able to write both of contemporary and past masters, keeping a fair balance between the mediaevals and the moderns, in spite of his predilection for the latter. The keynote of the book is human interest, the personality of each artist being set before us with vividness and fidelity—each is an inspired pen-portrait which seizes on the imagination and endows its subject with a three-dimensional quality rare at that period. France, Germany, Spain, and England, not less endowed with masters of their own, had no Vasari, and we peer into a darkness illumined only by sparse gleams of light.

Had John Leland, while searching for topographical antiquities, collected also the many stories which must have been told of the architects responsible for the buildings he saw; had Cavendish added to the biography of his master, Wolsey, the lives of the artists who were his fellow-servants; had William Worcestre been inspired by his interviews with John Norton the mason of Bristol and Robert Everard of Norwich, to write their lives; these are opportunities that cannot be recalled. That picturesque incidents in the careers of the masters were handed down, we know: for instance where Stow tells us of the replacement of the weathercock on Paul's steeple by Burchwood the King's plumber, after a certain Robert Godwin had been killed by a fall when winding it up.

The public records tell us that 'Burchwood' was John Byrchold, Serjeant Plumber from 1455 to 1494, who took fees of 12*d.* a day; the building accounts of the time would reveal where he executed other work. Such dry details, valuable to the economist or antiquary, fail to give life to the image of John Byrchold; whereas 'Burchwood the King's plumber' stirs the imagination with his gallant task performed 500 feet above the cobbles of St. Paul's Churchyard, so that all London might gaze at the newly gilt cock upon their glorious steeple.

Even the dry documents sometimes yield their tithe of human interest, as in the case related by Lethaby, where William de Ramsey, Mason to Edward III, was involved in a complicated abduction, or fifty years later, when we find his successor, Henry Yeveley, sitting down to table with Bishop William of Wykeham at Winchester House in Southwark. The grand old mason, probably over seventy, may be pictured as telling Wykeham something of his plans for the new nave at Canterbury, which Wykeham was about to emulate at his own cathedral of Winchester; there Yeveley's colleague, William Wynford, was the architect, and on the same intimate terms with his patron.

In what circumstances did Henry III borrow five casks of wine from his mason, John of Gloucester, when at Oxford? At least this debt was honourably repaid. Just how did the design of Westminster Hall roof suggest itself to the brain of Hugh Herland, and were the airy angels, deputising for posts of stout oak, the suggestion of King Richard II himself? We shall never know the answers to scores of similar questions which fill the subject with uncertainty. With few exceptions, our knowledge is limited to the facts recorded in contracts, accounts, and a few other surviving documents.

INTRODUCTION

A craftsman is apprenticed, works for the King, takes a private contract, is asked to advise a prelate on some building problem, travels to seek materials or men and renders a detailed statement, takes a younger man as his partner or warden owing to advancing years, makes a will, perhaps with references to his family, his friends, his colleagues, his work, the tools of his trade; finally he is buried beneath a tomb or brass recording his name and office and begging the passer-by to pray for his soul and that of his wife.

Research and good luck may show that he was the richest man in his village when a Fifteenth was collected, that he was a farmer as well as an artisan, and possibly that he was part-owner of a quarry. There yet remains little but the skeleton of an existence before us—save in rare instances his face and figure are hidden—his temper, his family life, his illnesses, his pastimes; jovial hours spent with his fellows; all have passed away.

Something remains to be said, although it is true that no amount of official records can replace the biography based on personal knowledge. We still have a great deal of the actual work of the masters, in spite of the wastage of wars and time. In these works are the most precious thoughts of great minds embodied in wood and stone, awaiting that detailed study which could throw as much light on their authors' inward existence as the anecdotes of a Vasari on their outward seeming.

This is not to say that no part of such a study has been made; many traces of recognition of individual styles are for example to be found in the work of Wyatt Papworth in the great *Dictionary* (of the Architectural Publication Society), and Lethaby in his two memorable books on Westminster Abbey laid the corner-stone on which a solid structure may be built. It is a matter for the deepest regret that F. E. Howard's untimely death robbed us of further brilliant studies such as that on Richard of Winchcombe. Howard's knowledge of local styles should have resulted in a detailed analysis of individual design, at least for that Perpendicular period so close to his heart.

Up to the present no serious attempt has been made to ascribe to named masters the principal schools of English Gothic architecture, nor to indicate the relationships of these schools on the basis of personal relations between the masters and their pupils. It is only with the discoveries of the last generation that such an attempt has become possible, owing to the enormous increase in publication of local records and of detailed research in connection with individual buildings. In the latter class, St. John Hope's masterly work on Windsor Castle takes pride of place, and is in fact the only modern English work on a major monument undertaken on a satisfactory plan and scale. Similar authoritative works, based on the whole of the documentary evidence as well as on minute survey and inspection of the structural remains, should be prepared with grants from public funds for such buildings as the Tower of London, Hampton Court, Westminster Abbey, the old Palace of Westminster, and some of the greater cathedrals. Meanwhile, sufficient authorities are now accessible for a general view of the main trends of style and the isolation of a number of the great masters.

When Horace Walpole wrote his *Anecdotes of Painting* on the basis of George Vertue's laborious researches, he brought to the task all the qualities of the artistic biographer save one: he lacked, as did every connoisseur of his age, critical appreciation of mediaeval style. The day of Rickman was still ahead, and fumblings in the dark and Strawberry Hill were the outcome. But the vogue of 'Strawberry Hill Gothic' marked a turning-point; for two centuries Gothic had been an unfashionable style, discarded and trodden under until even in the remote country districts the tradition itself died away, though not entirely. One of the most successful 'post-Tudor' works was the rebuilt nave of Lynn St. Margaret's by Matthew Brettingham (1745); and King's Lynn was the centre of the Walpole family's influence.

This sturdy, slightly clumsy building is still genuine Perpendicular—more so than were

Wren's experiments in Gothic style, and far more so than Strawberry Hill. But the comic aspect of the Twickenham style should not blind us to the fact that it led to renewed interest in Gothic, still further aroused by the finely engraved folios of *Ancient Architecture* produced by John Carter at the end of the century. Carter's errors in dating were soon noticed, and Dallaway, Britton, and Rickman put the science of architectural archaeology on a firmer foundation. Finally the Pugins, Parker, Bloxam, and Robert Willis reduced dated attribution to a science, founded on the character of the work itself. Special attention was given to the development, first of window tracery, later of mouldings, which last are probably the surest indication of date, apart from documentary or epigraphic evidence of unquestioned authenticity.

Structural evidence has up to now been used mainly as a guide to chronology; it is clearly of the highest importance in attribution to a named master. Unlike painting, the art of architecture cannot be carried out directly by the master's hand, and the niceties of brush-stroke comparison are not applicable. But mouldings were worked from a full-size template drawn by the master, and it is in mouldings and the smaller tricks of detail that evidence of identity must be sought. Due allowance has to be made for the participation of assistants and for the fact that moulds were frequent bequests to favourite apprentices or junior partners.

Structural indications and documentary evidence are mutually complementary and must be reconciled; both are liable to misinterpretation. Not only the authenticity of a document, but its relevance, must be established beyond question. Far too much reliance has been placed on loosely worded statements, which even if contemporary, are inadequate. Such statements are found in large numbers in chronicles written for the glorification of some religious house and its energetic Abbots or Priors. The usual errors in attribution which may be traced back to these chronicles fall into three main groups: firstly, the statement that a given ecclesiastic built a certain work may mean that he began it, that he ended it, that he carried it through from start to finish, or that he merely executed substantial repairs; secondly, the work in question may not be that which survives, owing to a subsequent rebuilding of which all record has been lost, or else the description is applied to the wrong part of the building, owing to ambiguity; third, and most important for individual ascription, a false impression is generally conveyed that the abbot, prior, sacrist, or other officer who acted as master of the works, was himself the designer or even technical executant of the work.

This last error invalidates many ascriptions set down in the standard works of the nineteenth century and even more recent years. In spite of repeated demonstrations that the most usual (even if not the only) designers were the master craftsmen, discussion still takes place as to the architectural capacity of great ecclesiastics, already renowned as statesmen, philanthropists and promoters of education. The churchman, or the noble or sovereign, who ordered and paid for the work, deserves all the credit due to an enlightened client, who will provide ideas and may even have suggestions of his own in planning. One may go further, and admit that the inspiration of great works of art often stems from the patron. But this is not the same thing as design: the designers of the larger mediaeval buildings were perforce practical geometricians and accomplished draughtsmen, for before a complex and highly articulated building is erected its members must have been set out in advance, either to scale or full size. The final refutation of those who would attempt to controvert this self-evident fact is provided by the massive remains of the Vienna Cathedral 'plan-chest', which in spite of losses still numbers 400 drawings dating from the mediaeval period.*

*See the reproductions in H. Tietze: *Geschichte und Beschreibung des St. Stephansdomes in Wien* (Oesterreichische Kunsttopographie, XXIII, 1931), and especially the biography of the fifteenth-century architect *Hans Puchspaum* by Bruno Grimschitz (Vienna: Wolfrumbücher, 1947).

INTRODUCTION

Let it be admitted that cases can be made out for the artistic capacity of a few exceptional clerics; they remain rare exceptions nevertheless, and it is fruitless to attempt to trace the progress of style outside the ranks of the men who had received an adequate technical training. The architects were those trained craftsmen who had risen above those who worked with hammer and chisel, and were being accused of idleness as early as 1261, when a sermon refers to 'Master Masons with a rod and gloves in their hands' who 'say to others "cut it for me this way" and labour not themselves yet take higher pay', or again when we are told 'in those great buildings there is commonly one chief master who only commands by word of mouth, who seldom or never lays his hand to the job, and yet takes higher pay than the rest'.†

The Middle Ages in England did not conduce to amateur work, nor to the production of 'universal' artists, except possibly in the twelfth and early thirteenth centuries. Of this last-named class Giotto seems to be almost the only important mediaeval representative (if we assign Leonardo to the Renaissance) and his name is constantly brought forward in this connection; deservedly great as is Giotto's reputation, it is still the case that one swallow doesn't make a summer. On the other hand, Villard de Honnecourt and several of the early English 'engineers' undoubtedly had a thorough grounding in several different crafts and branches of art.

In contrast to the over-emphasis on clerical architects, the importance of patronage has been unduly neglected.‡ The supreme value of the artistic taste of King, nobles and prelates must be grasped before mediaeval art and craftsmanship can be seen in their true perspective. It was the demand for beautiful and magnificent buildings which produced the supply, and not the creative impulse of the artist which caused a proportionate demand. Still less was architecture a 'Folk' product arising from anonymous committees of workmen or peasants. In England the greatest single impetus given to art and architecture was due to the interest and taste of King Henry III, no doubt aided by his wife Eleanor, daughter of Raymond Béranger, Count of Provence, one of the most distinguished of a line noted for its cultural achievements, and himself a troubadour of note.

Eleanor's sister, Margaret, married St. Louis of France, and Henry's visits to his brother-in-law fired him to emulate the latter's architectural pursuits. Henry's reputation as a King has suffered from the political and military preoccupation of historians, and his positive achievements have received scant and rather condescending praise. Certainly he was not a great administrator like his son; his character lacked the element of ruthless determination: but when we seek the first flowering of English mediaeval art, it is to Henry's reign that we must look, where his inspired extravagance fostered both art and science. Henry surrounded himself with artists of all types, a court poet, a court painter, sculptors, goldsmiths, and minor craftsmen, while he saw to it that Matthew Paris, monk of St. Albans and painter, should have full opportunities for recording contemporary history, in spite of the fact that Matthew expressed himself with a freedom sometimes rivalling that of a modern journalist. Matthew Paris, as a serious historian, did not abuse the licence allowed him by wilful distortion of the facts, but it is nevertheless a mark of King Henry's benevolence that he encouraged the production of this outspoken record of his reign, a remarkable contrast with the later attitude of the Lancastrian and Tudor sovereigns, who had their shaky titles as excuse for repressive measures.

†G. G. Coulton: *Art and the Reformation*, p. 174, and Mortet & Deschamps: *Recueil de textes &c.*, p. 291.
‡This was written before the appearance of Dr. Joan Evans's works on French and English mediaeval art, which have worthily redressed the balance.

Of all Henry III's activities, it is his pursuit of architecture that gives him the highest claims to the gratitude of posterity, for there can be few who have not felt at least subconsciously the beauty of his new Abbey Church at Westminster. This church marks not only the opening of a new epoch in architectural style, but also of a new method of conducting building operations. The earlier buildings of Henry III, like those of his predecessors, had been erected under the supervision of 'masters of the works' who had had no technical training, though the King's craftsmen had doubtless provided the design and technical oversight of the work.

The old system was the outcome of a kind of centralization by which all the services of the Crown were concentrated for financial purposes into the hands of a small number of officials. The sheriffs of the counties provided the normal channels through which the necessary money was gathered and supplied, and it was convenient to make them responsible for the expenditure, keeping check upon them by constituting for each special purpose a miniature Board of Works which probably included one or more of the royal clerks, and often the chief craftsman. This method can be seen at work (in the Pipe Rolls) from the middle of the twelfth century, though the great engineer Ailnoth during a career of well over thirty years came to occupy a position comparable to that of the Surveyor-General of the Works five hundred years later. Ailnoth was an exceptional man and Henry II an exceptional king, and after their deaths the craftsmen had less share in the organization and administration of the works.

This unsatisfactory state of affairs was the one inherited by Henry III, and it served him during the earlier part of his reign, which was in fact the period of greatest artistic activity. That it proved workable was largely due to the immense energy of the young King, who spared no pains where it was a question of arranging for the proper execution of building works, and himself directed a great deal in person by detailed letters of instruction and by word of mouth. From the wording of the letters which ordered Master John of Gloucester the mason and Master Alexander the carpenter to take over the direction of the works in 1256, it is clear that the King had had trouble caused by leaving craftsmen's work under the supervision of men with purely administrative or clerical training.

From 1256 onwards, it was to be the chief craftsmen who had the direct control of the works, and it is to this fact that we owe our knowledge of many of the greatest mediaeval architects. From the middle of the thirteenth century there is a definite succession of master masons and master carpenters, appointed by patent, and with certain exceptions Crown works executed at a given time may be safely ascribed to the master craftsmen then in office. The Scottish Border, Wales, and the Palatinate of Chester were under separate works establishments, as also was Windsor Castle at most periods when important building operations were in progress; work in the Duchy of Lancaster continued to be managed apart from other Crown works after the union of the Duchy with the Crown in 1399, and special master craftsmen were occasionally appointed to carry out individual works of importance.

The succession of masons and carpenters who held office in Cheshire and North Wales is known from the latter part of the thirteenth century, but those for the Borders and for the Duchy of Lancaster seem not to have been appointed regularly, and it is impossible to ascribe works from these areas with the same accuracy, unless specific records exist.

It is the succession of the King's Craftsmen which is the key to the problem, but while the greatest craftsmen were to be found in the royal service, there were many others of importance as the leaders of local schools, and these men are far more difficult to trace, for we depend almost entirely on the chance survival of individual documents. It is now time to consider the various classes of records which provide the available evidence.

In the first place is the evidence of date upon which the older historians relied, consisting for the most part of monastic and civic chronicles. The whole structure of the architectural chronology which has been built up rests upon these sources, with few major exceptions. It must be mentioned that in spite of the degree of accuracy which has been achieved in relative chronological dating, parallel to the sequence datings of field archaeology, there is still a great amount of error in the correlation of these relative dates to actual years of the calendar. The reason lies not in the misinterpretation of the structural evidence, but in the loose wording, ambiguity, and absence of written records. Upon examining the accepted dating of the various parts of our greater churches, for example, it will be found that the best authorities differ very greatly. In the instances where fabric rolls and comparable documents survive and have been utilized, the contrast is striking: every detail fits into its place, and each part proves the correct solution of its neighbours.

If detailed accounts existed in every case, the matter would only require a certain amount of patience for a full solution to be reached, but this is not so; many classes of documents have to be ransacked, and in the case of the lesser buildings, only too often ransacked to little purpose. The principal classes of evidence may now be taken in order, with the objections which may lie against each.

1. The best evidence is that of *Inscription* upon the fabric itself, setting out the date of erection and the names of those responsible. This method was seldom adopted in its entirety, though there are many instances of the building client's name being recorded, often with the date, and in a few cases the craftsman has signed his work. Where such evidence does occur, it must be subjected to the usual palaeographic tests; secondly, it is necessary to be certain that the inscription has not been removed from its original position. Good examples of craftsmen's inscriptions are 'W. Hal Carpenter mad thys rowfe' in the roof of the north chapel of St. Mary's, Beverley, and 'Robertus me fecit' by a carving of a face on a cap of the south choir aisle of Romsey Abbey, Hants.

These inscriptions are unofficial, but at Winchester College the portraits of the chiefs of the works were included in the great East window of the Chapel, with their names attached. The persons commemorated were 'Sir' Simon Membury the clerk of works, William Wynford, mason, 'the Carpenter', and Thomas the glass-painter. Documentary evidence shows that 'the Carpenter' was Hugh Herland. Other instances must have occurred of portraits included in the glazing, but they have been lost in the immense destruction of painted glass which has taken place in the last three centuries; except that of William Vertue (see Appendix I).

2. Next to inscriptions, literary evidence is the clearest obtainable, but it is seldom free from ambiguity. There have been few periods in which the personality of architects has been a favourite subject with literary men, and this lack of interest in the architect was especially pronounced in the Middle Ages. There are, however, several exceptions to the rule. Of these by far the most significant is the detailed account by Gervase of the rebuilding of Canterbury Cathedral under William of Sens, including the statement that Master William was a most cunning craftsman in wood and stone, and made moulds for shaping the stones, which moulds he delivered to the stone-cutters; this is of crucial importance, for in conjunction with the rest of the story, it establishes a number of fundamental points in connection with mediaeval architecture.

Firstly, the designer (architect) was himself a craftsman; secondly, he was a worker of wood as well as of stone; thirdly, he personally made the moulds or templates from which the stones were to be shaped; lastly, he delivered the moulds to others, for the actual stone-hewing to be done. Except that his education had included training in actual craftsmanship, William of Sens was in all important respects equivalent to a modern architect. The references to the contemporary Richard de Wolveston show that England could produce important architects of her own at the same period.

3. The third class of evidence consists of documents connected with the actual performance of the works themselves, and having the character of archives. Apart from the voluminous official enrolments relating to royal works and the royal craftsmen, there are two special classes of document which often throw light upon the date and authorship of buildings. The first of these consists of the licences to crenellate (printed as an appendix to Turner & Parker's *Domestic Architecture*), and the similar licences granted in the several Palatinate jurisdictions.* These give approximate dates for a large number of domestic buildings, though great care must be taken to check the information with the existing work. It seems also to have been a common practice to begin the work some time before obtaining the licence, but the discrepancy is not likely to amount to more than a few years.

The second class of records relating to non-royal buildings consists of enrolments of writs of aid, licences to impress, and other forms of official assistance. As these often name one or more craftsmen in charge of the building works, they are of particular importance for attribution. Such are the licence granted to Robert Skillyngton, mason, in 1391, to impress men for the works of Kenilworth Castle, the licence to John Hardy, mason of London, in 1444, to use his ship *Le Cristofre* in connection with the works of Syon Convent, and the exemptions from jury-service granted in 1380 and later to Thomas Hoo, mason of Canterbury Cathedral. This last instance must serve as a warning, however, for there is evidence which strongly suggests that Hoo was resident master, but not the designer, of the nave of Canterbury; the consultant position of the great architect Henry Yeveley, together with stylistic evidence, shows that Yeveley rather than Hoo was the architect.

Among the remaining types of documents, two are of supreme importance: accounts and contracts. The accounts in question vary greatly in the amount of information they contain, partly because of differing methods of administration and accountancy, partly by the mere accidents of survival. Detailed accounts must almost always have been drawn up in the first instance, including paysheets with the names of all those employed, and items of expenditure, but it is seldom that these original records survive. Far more common are the summarized accounts prepared for audit purposes, and where these are well kept, they usually indicate quite clearly the status of the master craftsmen. Beside the very large number of official accounts, there are some notable series relating to private works, such as those for Kirby Muxloe Castle and several of the Oxford and Cambridge colleges, as well as the long series of fabric rolls preserved at some of the great churches, notably Westminster Abbey, York Minster, and Durham, Ely, Exeter, and Norwich Cathedrals. In some cases the extant accounts are so much summarized that all names are excluded, but it is generally possible to find a few individual 'rewards' given to the chief craftsmen.

Unusual in that they are not exclusively fabric accounts are the accounts of churchwardens and manorial officers; these often include valuable evidence of building dates, but in many cases only specify the craftsman as 'the mason', 'the carpenter', and so forth. Where they do include names and detail, they sometimes provide examples of the private practices of architects from larger centres, as in the case of Thomas Stanley, one of the Canterbury Cathedral masons, who built the tower of Lydd Church, Kent, between 1442 and 1446.

Where all fabric accounts have perished, it occasionally happens that an account of a different character will supply the required evidence. Kitchen accounts may record the supply

*See alphabetical list of all licences to crenellate 1256–1478, in Henry Godwin: *The English Archaeologist's Handbook* (Parker, 1867), pp. 233–51.

INTRODUCTION

of food to the master craftsmen on the occasion of a visit, or lists of liveries distributed to the
'esquires' or servants of a monastery may include the names of the principal craftsmen. As in
the case of Yeveley and Hoo at Canterbury, care must be exercised in using such evidence, for
the architect was quite often a different man from the permanently resident master attached to
the building.

A most unusual type of evidence is that relating to William of Wykeham's master
craftsmen. Only one of Wykeham's household account rolls is extant, that for the summer of
1393, just at the time when Winchester College was approaching completion. The names of
Membury, the clerk of works, and Wynford the mason, were known from the chapel window
mentioned above, but the carpenter remained unidentified. As no fabric rolls were known to
exist, the late Herbert Chitty was led to examine this household roll in detail, and discovered
that the names of Wynford and Membury frequently occurred in the lists of strangers to whom
meals were served, and that when they were present 'Herland' was generally a third. This
could only be Hugh Herland the great King's Carpenter, who was at that time a colleague of
Wynford's on a commission for the repair of Winchester Castle, and whose style appeared in
the timber 'fan-vault' of the College Chapel. Further, 'Herland' had visited Wykeham by
himself on two occasions earlier in the year, when the Bishop was at Esher, close to Hugh
Herland's home at Kingston upon Thames. Another of Wykeham's visitors in the early part of
the year was 'Yeveley', at a time when the Bishop was living at his palace in Southwark; as
Henry Yeveley the King's Mason lived in Southwark, there can be no doubt as to the identity
of this visitor either. Finally, similar evidence is forthcoming from the Hall Books and Bursars'
Rolls of New College, Oxford, proving visits by Yeveley, Wynford, and Herland to the sister
foundation while structural works were still in progress.

Contracts are second only to accounts in importance, and have the advantage that they
usually specify with greater precision the work to be done, which is often readily identifiable
with existing remains. On the other hand, the existence of a contract is no proof that the work
was carried out, and we know that at Durham, John Middleton failed to carry out the work on
the dormitory which he had contracted for in 1398, a new contract being let to Peter Dryng in
1402.

Some contracts, for example that by which Nicholas Typerton undertook to build the south
aisle and porch of St. Dunstan's in the East, London, in 1381, specify that the work is to be in
accordance with the design of some other craftsman; in the case just mentioned, that of the
great architect, Henry Yeveley. Others mention a 'pattern' or a drawing, as do those entered
into by John Hobbs in 1475, and by Richard Gyles and Thomas Phelypp in 1516, but do not
specify the maker of the drawing or pattern. That this was not necessarily a different person is
shown by William Orchard's contract of 1475, to make the great west window of Magdalen
College Chapel according to his own 'portraiture'.

In other cases the contract supplies a detailed specification of the work to be done, or even
requires the contractor to copy existing buildings; detailed specifications occur in William
Horewode's contract for the nave and tower of Fotheringhay Church and in that of Robert
FitzGiles for a terrace of small houses in York; FitzGiles's contract also refers to certain details
which were to be copied from existing houses, and when Richard Russell and Adam Powle
contracted to build the tower of Walberswick Church, it was stipulated that it was to be like
that of Tunstall, with door and windows like those of Halesworth.

Contracts of these last categories must imply that the contractors were not considered as
architects of high standing, but were employed to copy good work as an economical method of
obtaining a result which appealed to the taste of the client. In addition to the executed
indentures of building contracts, they have sometimes been preserved in the form of registered

copies, as are several in the registers of John of Gaunt, relating to works in the Duchy of Lancaster. Allied to building contracts, are contracts of employment, often granted by capitular authorities to the master craftsmen in their employ, as seems to have been the practice at York Minster, and at Canterbury, Durham, Hereford, and Winchester Cathedrals. Some contracts, such as those of John de Middleton at Durham and of William Wynford at Winchester, include the provision of food, drink, and livery during the execution of specified work or for life.

Probably supplementary to lost contracts of employment were grants of houses, as for example those of Nicholas of Ely at Salisbury and Richard of Abingdon at Oxford. Such grants mentioning that the grantee was at work on a given building at a certain date, are a valuable form of evidence in the period before 1300, when private contracts and accounts are rare or non-existent.

During the later Middle Ages, one of the most important sources for dating buildings is provided by the great numbers of contemporary wills, with their frequent bequests to specific works. In a few cases, wills even mention the architects responsible for work being done at the testator's expense; craftsmen so mentioned are William Wynford, in Wykeham's will of 1403, John Bolron and John Cotom of York, who were to build the church of St. John Hundgate in 1435, and Thomas Nunton, whose contract to vault the tower of Oakham Church, c. 1424, is only known from the will of his client, Roger Flore.

One other form of documentary record deserves special mention, namely the appointments of sworn 'viewers' or 'searchers' of building works in the great municipalities. Usually two masons and two carpenters held office at one time, as for instance Richard de Salynge and Richard at Cherche, masons, and John de Totenham and Richard Shropshire, carpenters, in London in 1363, and John Porter and Robert Couper, masons, and John Foulford and Robert Jackson, carpenters, in York about 1457–58. Their office was equivalent to that of the district surveyors of modern times, for they had power to reject bad workmanship and materials, enforce the building code of their city, and were also arbitrators in case of disputes arising over the code, party walls, ancient lights, and similar matters.

4. The fourth class of evidence comprises documents personal to the architect, such as wills and private deeds, or other private records in which he is mentioned. As a whole, this is not a very fruitful source so far as the attribution of works is concerned, though when John Fustyng of Oxford died in 1508, the inventory of his goods included debts owing to him in respect of the pulpit and Congregation House at St. Mary the Virgin, whose authorship is quite unknown from other sources. The descriptions given of themselves by other craftsmen in their wills are often interesting, as where John Russell junior describes his long career in the royal service, or John Forman tells us of his post at York Minster. Sometimes the witnesses were craftsmen of importance, and when Robert Vertue's two colleagues witnessed his will they added their description as 'the King's Master Masons'. When Stephen Lote made a codicil to his will he was 'in the new lodge of our lord the King of England at Portsmouth' and he must have become ill quite suddenly, for this codicil is in nuncupative form, only used when a notary could not be brought in time to draw up the document in the normal way.

One class of personal deeds has been mentioned above, in the third category of evidence, namely grants of houses and land to craftsmen by the client or patron; purely private deeds also occur, but they seldom do more than confirm the direct evidence of other categories of records; where, however, they take the form of grants by the craftsman to the fabric, they may contain most valuable information, as do the grants of Godwin Gretsyd, and Hugh 'son of the late Master Henry de Reyns, mason', to Westminster Abbey.

5. A fifth form of evidence consists of the sepulchral monuments of the architects, often

containing valuable information as to offices held by the deceased craftsman, in addition to his name and date. The monuments of Richard of Gainsborough, the Wolvey family, Robert Spillesby, and Henry Redman are of this sort, and others exist, or are known to have existed in the past. Except that such evidence is related primarily to the person and not to the building, it partakes of the same character as the inscriptions which formed our first class. In some instances, though the monuments themselves have been lost, the inscriptions have been preserved by antiquaries writing before floors were repaved and old gravestones removed. The inscription on the gravestone of Humphrey Coke has thus been recorded, and notes are extant of the burial-places of some of the master masons of York Minster.

6.   Finally there are many incidental references which may provide valuable information, such as the mention of John Thirsk in the post-mortem inventory of John Bradford, to whom he owed money, and the description of Richard de Farnham, witness to a deed, as 'architect of the new fabric of Durham'. The precise weight of each reference must be judged on its own merits, and as an instance of possible ambiguity, the word translated as 'architect' in the description of Richard de Farnham, is '*architector*' which frequently means not the architect, but the chief roofer, carpenter, or thatcher.

All classes of evidence suffer from possible objections, and it is only where a great many facts are discovered relating to one particular architect that certainty can be reached as to his status. Such reasonable certainty has been reached in a number of instances, of which the most notable are those of Robert of Beverley, James of St. George, Humphrey Coke, John of Gloucester, Walter of Hereford, Hugh Herland, William Hurley, John Lewyn, Thomas Mapilton, James Nedeham, William Orchard, William Ramsey, Henry Redman, Henry de Reyns, John Russell junior, William of Sens, Robert and William Vertue, John Wastell, Richard Wolveston, William Wynford, and Henry Yeveley; a mere score out of the thirteen hundred names included in the following pages.* Even so, our mediaeval architects are better known to us than our musicians of the same period, and at least as well as our painters and sculptors.

Against the remainder, it may be objected that they were building contractors, builder's foremen, stone-hewers and carvers, carpenters or clerics, rather than architects. This may well apply to some of them; but it seems far more probable that many of them may be celebrities as yet unrecognized, whose importance will eventually be disclosed. So far as the craftsmen are concerned, they are mostly 'masters', and there is no doubt that a distinction was drawn between a 'master' and a fully-skilled craftsman who was not a master. It seems, for instance, that only masters could take apprentices, and as master masons at any rate could not normally take more than two apprentices at a time, it is clear that the number of masons who had worked an apprenticeship can have borne only a small proportion to the total number of skilled masons in the country. One of the most puzzling features of the whole problem is our lack of knowledge of the means by which a mason or carpenter graduated as a master. It seems that most of the great mediaeval architects sprang from families of 'masters' who handed on their specialized knowledge to their sons, or else they had been so fortunate as to become the pupils, or at a later period the articled apprentices, of masters of importance. There is perhaps some analogy with the case of Japan, where detailed records of artists and craftsmen extend back for seven or eight centuries, and prove conclusively that the greatest masters of painting, sculpture, carpentry, and metalworking, ran in families, some of which

*To this list should now (1983) be added at least: Michael of Canterbury, Simon Clerk, Nicholas de Derneford, Reginald Ely, John Montfort, Simon Pabenham I, Robert Patrington, Ivo de Raghton, Robert Skillyngton, William Smyth, Simon de Tresk, Robert Vertue junior, Richard Winchcombe, Thomas Witney.

lasted for 500 years, and even more (Edward Dillon: *The Arts of Japan*.) In Europe we have a few recorded instances of the same character, though only carried back to the sixteenth century, notably the musical families of Bach and Couperin, the printers Guasp, and the botanists in the family of de Jussieu. In England we have at least one remarkable instance which does go back to the Middle Ages, that of the Phelps family of Thames watermen, King's bargemasters, and champion scullers. Scotland provides in the architectural field the outstanding family of Mylne, master masons to the Crown of Scotland from 1481 for seven generations, and continuously architects from the fifteenth century to the present day.†

So far we have discussed the different forms of positive evidence for attaching the names of certain architects to their works; such evidence must exist unknown in numerous instances, and still has to be brought to light, but even if all the great collections of accounts and other documents were to be combed for architectural material, there would remain a large residue of buildings, some of them of prime importance, which would even then be anonymous. To assign these to their probable authors, or at least to their schools, a new critical faculty will have to be developed. There has been much use of the word 'schools' in connection with the supposed groups of masons who are said to have wandered over the country in search of jobs. These 'schools of masons' have taken the place of the 'Comacine Masters' of a generation or so back, who were credited with cathedral building on an international scale. It should be emphasized that there is as little practical evidence of nomadic English 'schools' as there is for the more wide-spread 'Comacine Guild'. The study of detailed accounts by the late Douglas Knoop and Professor G. P. Jones has shown that migration of groups of masons did take place under the system of royal impressment, several Canterbury Cathedral men appearing also at Eton College, but no evidence has come to light in favour of the wide-spread activities of building-contractors with large staffs of men permanently in their employ. In a few cases of rather late date, references to a contractor 'and his men' (*et socii sui*) do occur, but these were the employees of a master or firm, not a migratory group. In any case, the employment of the same gang of men would not, any more than at the present day, produce resemblances in design between the works of two different architects.

The critical study of masons' marks is only in its infancy, but some remarkable preliminary results have been reached by my friend and collaborator, Ralph Davis, showing the migrations of a number of individual (though unnamed) masons; but even in the Cotswolds it seems to have been rare for more than one or two masons to go from job to job together. Out of a dozen freemasons who cut the moulded stones of Minster Lovell Church, the mark of only one has been traced elsewhere. Two notable exceptions occur: a group of marks found at Magdalen College, Oxford and also at Southleigh Church, suggests the building of the latter by men in the employ of William Orchard, who was both architect and contractor on a very large scale at Magdalen, and was a quarry-master of considerable importance. The other exception occurs on Wolsey's works, where at least eight different marks (all of them too complicated for chance duplication) connect the great tower at the east end of the Hall at Christ Church, Oxford, with the works at York Place in Westminster. Both the works in question can be dated in or close to 1528, and it may be the stone for both buildings was prepared at a stone-yard remote from the sites. This is rendered the more probable explanation by the existence of contracts for the supply of Kentish hardstone, ready hewn. But the point is architecturally immaterial. In both cases the architectural resemblance is due to a common architect, not to the hewing of the stones by the same craftsmen.

The 'schools' which did in fact exist were schools in the sense in which the word is applied

† It is now (1983) possible to add for England the notable instance of the *RAMSEY* family, q.v.

in painting and music; composed of actual pupils of the master, or of his imitators. In this way we can trace an artistic 'pedigree' for a century between 1360 and 1460 among the 'descendants' of Henry Yeveley.*

One grave difficulty concerns the part played by buildings now destroyed, and of which no illustrations exist. Probably Gloucester Abbey owes much of its stylistic reputation to the complete destruction of its rivals at Evesham, Winchcombe, and Cirencester. Be this as it may, the reconstruction of the styles of these vanished monasteries is not hopeless. All the great religious houses possessed wide-spread manors and churches, and works of importance at these would be carried out by the monastic craftsmen, so that careful investigation should provide a sufficient body of material for critical purposes. By such studies the greater part of our architectural history should ultimately be recovered, and the superstitions of anonymous and 'folk' architecture be finally laid to rest.

EPILOGUE (1983) TO INTRODUCTION

Much that was tentative and exploratory when this book was sent to the printers in 1953 has been confirmed by the research of the last thirty years. In one crucial respect we have now reached certainty: it was actually *impossible* that the clerical order, or any of its members but a few who were completely untypical, should have designed the cathedrals and other great buildings of the Middle Ages. A very few men, it is true, who had first been trained in masonry — in 'the Art of Geometry' — might in later life take holy orders or enter a monastery perhaps as lay brothers; these indeed might be architects in the full sense. Yet the complete and — until late in the fifteenth century — unbroken secrecy of their masonic teaching was able to ensure that the only effective architects of the Middle Ages were those who had served an apprenticeship as craftsmen to masonry or to carpentry. The closely guarded methods of geometrical setting out which provided both for satisfactory aesthetics ensured by right proportion; and also for structurally sound amounts of foundations and buttressing masses, were the living canon of architecture throughout the Gothic age. (See HME, and for the eventual breach in secrecy committed by Mathes Roriczer in 1486, Lon R. Shelby, *Gothic Design Techniques*, Southern Illinois University Press, 1977).

What has just been said is an international truth: it goes for France, for the Germanic lands and Hungary, for the Low Countries and Scandinavia, for Spain and Portugal and, so far as Italy was ever Gothic, also for Italy. Gothic architecture in Western Europe was an art produced exclusively by laymen (i.e. not by ecclesiastics) trained in practical geometry with square and compasses as well as in the handicraft of cutting stone or timber. Since most of the narrative history and literature of the period lay in the hands precisely of clerics and ecclesiastics, it is not surprising that the external evidence has for so long seemed slight and misleading. What had for a long time been adequately demonstrated from archival evidence on the Continent of Europe is now also demonstrable for the insular realms, led in the relevant period by England. More than this, it is now evident that it was from England that the great Germanic system of Building Lodges derived its origin (see HGW, map at p. 23; HME, p. 138). Before 1275, when the German masons adopted it, England already had a free jurisdiction of masons; and this free custom having the force of law is independently evidenced in 1305 as already existing in the free court which Master Walter of Hereford claimed at Carnarvon.

* See HHY, 71–6.

A great deal is still obscure. We do not know precisely what was the carpenter's equivalent to the Constitutions of Masonry (see HME, pp. 191–207), nor whether carpenters held any jurisdiction comparable to that of the free masons. This aspect is obscured by the fact that from time to time it is specified of a given master that he was expert both in wood and in stone. There is considerable ambiguity in the descriptions of some of the leading engineers employed by Henry III and Edward I through the thirteenth century, and it is evident that some of them possessed an overall competence in many respects comparable to that of a modern architect. Even the word 'architect' appears occasionally, as in the description of the conference held at Hereford Cathedral and reported in order to obtain a Papal Bull in aid of works to be done 'upon the ancient foundation which is thought to be firm and solid in the judgment of masons or architects regarded as skilled in their art (*judicio cementariorum seu architectorum qui in arte sua reputabantur periti*)'. Similar conferences are known as far back as the fall of the central tower of Winchester Cathedral in 1107, where the tower as immediately rebuilt was declared by masons (*secundum latomos*) to be the firmest of all towers in the realm of England. Allowing even for substantial exaggeration, it is certain that there was communication between masters over a wide area before the onset of Gothic style. By the middle of the fourteenth century there is the direct evidence of the Constitutions that congregations and assemblies were held both in counties and for larger regions. This is clinched by the marked characteristics of local style, for instance in church towers, which are in some cases distinctive of a single county (e.g. Somerset) but in others show common factors over a large diocese (e.g. Norwich, though there are also minor details more typical of Norfolk or Suffolk respectively).

Purely local style, on a level well below that of the great cathedrals or the royal works directed by the king's craftsmen, may well have lain to some degree in the hands of masters of trade guilds in the towns. It is essential to distinguish these bodies of settled men, 'free' of a given place, from the far more influential body of the 'lodge' masons who held their free courts quite independently of the guilds or companies. This clear distinction has long been well understood in regard to organization on the Continent, but still occasions expressions of surprise at the unimpressive part in municipal affairs played by building craftsmen. (See for example Heather Swanson, *Building Craftsmen in late medieval York*, Borthwick Paper No. 63, 1983, pp. 29–30). The great masters were not tied down to urban life but were extremely mobile, as can be seen from many of the more noteworthy careers outlined in this book. They were in some cases very wealthy men, ranking economically with the merchants, as is indicated by the high assessments to taxation recorded in many instances. Some at least appear to have been descended from the gentry (see *RAMSEY* family, p. 239), and in any case their officially admitted *social* position derived from their skill. The tables of precedence put 'rich artificers' along with 'worshipful merchants' as on the same level, and sitting at the same table, with 'gentlemen well nurtured and of good manners' (see HME, pp. 75–7).

This contrast between the relative poverty of the general run of building workers and even of 'little masters' and the immense prestige and often wealth of the few really outstanding architects, is emphasized by the additions made to the first edition of this book. As has been said above, (Preface, p. x) only a handful of the many new careers are of men of distinction. From about 1300 onwards it can now be assumed that we know the names of a substantial majority of the significant architectural figures, even if the precise part played by each is not yet always explicitly defined. As time goes on it becomes more evident that clients were prepared to send long distances for a master of renown, to pay him high fees, and to treat him with honourable esteem. This is, of course, exactly what has long been accepted as true of the mediaeval architects of the greater European states. It is now possible to discern the individual contributions of most of the great leaders of style; but this is only to restate, for

England, what Wilhelm Vöge laid down as a general principle in his inaugural lecture at Freiburg im Breisgau in 1910: that where significant stylistic trends originate, important masters can be identified (*Zeitschrift für bildende Kunst*, N.F. XXV, 1914). Thus the characteristic and uncommon features of our Perpendicular are due to the express creation of William Ramsey (III), the superb consummation of the English cathedral to Henry Yeveley, the extraordinary innovation of the square-topped tower to his colleague William Wynford.

In view of the far-reaching studies of the whole of the surviving documents for the royal buildings, now published in the first four volumes of *The History of the King's Works*, few major revelations from record sources are likely. What must continue over a very long period is the detailed analysis of the style of each of the greater masters, starting from those works certainly documented, but by no means artificially excluding what has an obvious relationship even if no signed guarantee.

LOOKING BACK FROM 1983

Now that more than half a century has elapsed since the first inception of this book, it may not be out of place to give a short account of how it came into being. My interest in the personalities of mediaeval architects had first been aroused at the age of five, when my father William Harvey was working on the detailed survey and repair of Westminster Hall. On repeated visits to that wonderful building, and taken to examine the timbers of its giant roof at close quarters from the gantry scaffold, I came to regard the name of Hugh Herland almost as that of an adoptive uncle. He, and his colleague Henry Yeveley who designed the new Gothic stonework for King Richard II's rebuilding, were heroic and intimate figures throughout my childhood and youth. The fact that many documents survive, giving the names of those responsible for buildings six and seven centuries old, made a profound impression on me.

Much later, after starting work in an architect's office in Westminster in 1928, I was able to spend my lunch-hours in the Public Reference Library in Great Smith Street, where I devoured Professor Lethaby's books on Westminster Abbey, and on Mondays could explore the Royal Chapels free of charge. The interrelation between the mediaeval Palace — of which Westminster Hall is the chief surviving part — and the immense royal abbey alongside, exercised a powerful fascination and led me to wider reading which went a good deal beyond that needed for my student's work on architectural history at evening school classes. In 1930, after two years at work and at the study of architecture, I began seriously to collect notes of all the mediaeval masters named by Lethaby and the few other relevant authors then available. By this time I was making use of the Library of the Royal Institute of British Architects and discovered the biographies in the *Dictionary of Architecture* of 1849–92, as well as the earlier collections of John Britton and James Dallaway. It soon became obvious that there was a major gap to be filled, if only by the compilation of references to what was already in print. To go beyond this brought up problems of stylistic criticism with which at the time I was not competent to deal.

So matters stood when, in 1931, my father was starting to recover from a long and severe illness and was able to renew his own interest in the details of mediaeval buildings. Out of talks with him at that time arose the project of our collaborating in a new life — of article length — of Hugh Herland. My father had many drawings of the master's details and mouldings and had made a close study of Herland's brilliant structural design; I would attempt to bring together what was known of his life and of his works elsewhere than at Westminster. Thanks to a suggestion from my eldest uncle, Fred Harvey, I extended my researches to the Guildhall Library, open until 5 o'clock on Saturday afternoons. Since I had to work in London on Saturday mornings my season ticket made this an economical access to a campaign of reading spread over the years 1931–33. I cannot adequately express my gratitude for the wonderful help given to an enquiring youth by the staff of the Corporation's splendid library: a treasure-house open freely to all comers. The fact that it was not necessary to obtain a ticket nor to show any qualifications, was — and is — of enormous value to thousands of readers. The knowledge, the courtesy, and the practical help displayed by the staff make the Guildhall Library a remarkable institution of learning, all the more valuable because it is not academic.

Towards the end of this phase I first considered the possibility of turning my private notes into a book. I was much encouraged by a talk with Charles D. St. Leger, the senior under whom I worked at office. It was he who, next after my father, had impressed on me the importance of freehand sketching of architectural detail as a means to the appreciation of the minutiae of style. St. Leger was an enthusiast of the graphic arts and a fine draughtsman in pen-and-ink. He impressed on all of us office juniors how vital it was to study buildings, to visit museums, the Diploma collection of the Royal Academy, and the lesser galleries of London, such as Dulwich. He strongly commended the idea of writing with a view to publication: not as a career but as a means to clear expression. Not long after this my father had been invited to undertake a structural survey of the Church of the Holy Sepulchre at Jerusalem, and took me as his assistant. A second survey, of the Church of the Nativity at Bethlehem, was to follow and it was not until the summer of 1935 that I could again pick up the threads of research in England.

A period out of work, however, gave me a flying start and we were able to get the article on Hugh Herland published in June 1936 (see abbreviation HHH). The later stages of investigation had several important results: I had to get tickets for the British Museum and the Public Record Office, and I renewed the reading of wills in the Literary Search Department at Somerset House, with which a campaign on family history had already made me familiar in 1931. Of even greater value proved the following of a clue to Herland's work at Winchester College, as I thus made the acquaintance of Herbert Chitty, retired Bursar of the College and one of the greatest of antiquaries as well as the best of friends. Through Chitty I came to realise how much information lay in corporate and private muniment rooms rather than in libraries and record offices. Though less true now that so many private archives have been deposited, it has to be remembered that it was not until well after 1945 that there was a more or less complete coverage of the country by record offices officially designated for deposit. Again, it was largely through continuing contacts with Chitty that I began to appreciate the vast amount of archival matter already in print, notably in the official series of calendars.

It was at this time (1936) that, after working through *The Mediaeval Mason* which Douglas Knoop and G. P. Jones had brought out in 1933, I made contact with Professor Knoop. He generously sent me offprint copies of all their long series of detailed studies of masons, and then their new book *An Introduction to Freemasonry* when it appeared early in 1937. The fully documented 'lives' of 20 masons, given as an appendix, were followed in November of that year by three more printed in *Miscellanea Latomorum*. These lives were a model for the documentary side of any comparable treatment, but of course were not concerned with stylistic problems or attribution of undocumented works. Seeing that Knoop and Jones had been able to compile such substantial lives of masons, I decided to concentrate for a time on carpenters, particularly in their architectural function (see HMA). It was this work on carpentry that was to become the trigger, setting in motion all the later stages of progress towards a published biographical dictionary.

LOOKING BACK

Material rapidly accumulated and the process was speeded up by parallel work on three projects (see HMA, HTP and HMO), which considerably added to the scope of the sources covered. Running to earth the Thetford register which formed the basis of HTP brought me into touch with three more great scholars, M. Seymour de Ricci, Mr (now Sir) Anthony Wagner, and Dr. G. Herbert Fowler, and enabled me to carry out a study of cartularies and other ecclesiastical sources in which I could find as many as possible of the masters responsible for the ancient cathedrals and greater monasteries.

The general search for carpenters (HMA, and most of the material published much later as HKC) widened my knowledge of record sources and went hand in hand with consideration of the craftsmen employed in the royal works (HMO), inspired by my joining the Ancient Monuments Branch of H.M. Office of Works in April 1936. In my own time I worked on the sources available for buildings with which I had to deal in the course of my official employment, among them notably the long series of accounts for the Tower of London and for Kenilworth Castle. Another field of special research lay among mediaeval churchwardens' accounts, a large number of which were already in print. Many were discoverable through J. C. Cox's list of 1913 and others were in the Subject Index of the London Library. Some of these accounts are extremely disappointing so far as concerns major building work at parish churches, but in bulk they yielded a great deal which I then drafted into an article, eventually printed (HPC) only in 1950.

The publication of 'The Mediaeval Carpenter as an Architect' in the *R.I.B.A. Journal* of 13 June 1938 marked a turning point and had almost immediate repercussions. Within days of publication it brought me the very generous offer by L. F. Salzman of the use of his unpublished book, eventually to appear in 1952 as *Building in England*. This manuscript and, after the war, his exhaustive notes from Exchequer Works Accounts and other records, jointly provided the largest component of material for the first edition of this dictionary. The debt which I owe to his generosity and scholarly guidance cannot adequately be described. Salzman's original offer in June 1938 was followed at once by notable assistance from E. A. Greening Lamborn and from Ralph H. C. Davis, both based on Oxford and both anxious to remedy the inadequate knowledge of the architecture of the elder University hitherto available, when compared with the masterly account of Cambridge by Willis and Clark. This again led to much help later from Martyn Jope. It was, too, the article on carpenters that after a longer interval brought me into touch with T. D. Atkinson, the importance of whose help was described in the original preface.

By this time I had on loose leaves an alphabet of architects, the first draft of a ready-reference guide but little more. It contained the successive chief masons and carpenters of the royal works, an extensive collection of cathedral masters, and what could be extracted from print on Oxford and Cambridge. In the summer of 1938 a correspondence on architect-craftsmen was carried on in the *Daily Telegraph*, and I submitted a lengthy letter which had the good luck to be printed on 23 June. This announced my project, set out a selection of the outstanding buildings of the period which could already be attributed to named masters, and asked for information. Rather surprisingly, this brought a far slighter response than the publication of the earlier article in a professional journal of limited circulation, but it had one result of crucial importance. About a month later I received the letter from Arthur Oswald which began our long and fruitful collaboration. From the start he most generously put at my disposal his substantial bodies of notes on mediaeval craftsmen, mostly at Cambridge but also at Canterbury and Durham. He also explained that he was himself working on an architectural history of King's College Chapel, in much fuller detail than that by Willis and Clark, and proposed to reserve this biographical material. At a much later date Arthur decided to postpone work on his project and allowed his detailed lives of Reginald Ely, Simon Clerk and John Wastell to appear in the dictionary, with an impressive cast of lesser men. It may be said here that in length, Arthur's contributions amounted to over one-sixth of the main text of the book. The lives written by him almost all concerned East Anglia: out of a total of 87 wholly written by him, 48 at least were mainly concerned with Cambridge, 16 with Bury St. Edmunds, and five each with Saffron Walden and with London. Even this massive group of lives, researched in the closest detail, was very far from being his total contribution. Over a period of fifteen years in all he sent me the results, in this field, of his very wide reading in topographical and antiquarian literature. In that way he provided the raw material for a good many more lives, as well as vital individual facts towards others.

My own work on the project during the last twelve months before the outbreak of war in 1939 was practically confined to the search for wills of masters already known, with some investigation of manuscripts at the British Museum and a study of accounts relating to York Place, Westminster, and to Cardinal Wolsey's works. At the time I envisaged going to press after about another year's work on re-writing the material. Had the war not come, the book would have been a relatively modest compilation mainly depending upon sources already in print, though including a great deal from the official calendars, the printed pipe rolls, cartularies and bishops' registers. Hardly anything could be done during the war years, but as a precaution against total loss I was able to get the existing material typed in triplicate and indexed, and made tentative approaches to the problem of publication later on. After 1945 it was extremely difficult to find time for much work apart from searching methodically to fill gaps such as dates of death. Frequent contact with Arthur was resumed, however, and a fair amount of material was exchanged between us. For several years I was visiting London on business, having gone into free-lance practice, and we were often able to lunch together and discuss the project. It was Arthur who persuaded me that it had now gone too far to be publishable as a mere compilation, and this meant that I had to seek some financial aid to cover living costs and travelling expenses. At the third try I was awarded a research grant by the Leverhulme trustees for the year 1949–50.

It was the award of this grant that made it possible to change the character of the dictionary from what was primarily a compilation of references to printed matter into a work very largely based on a cross-section of original sources hitherto almost entirely untapped, at any rate for this purpose. In the course of a year, by rearrangement of other work, I was able to visit Gloucester, Lincoln, King's Lynn, Norwich, Peterborough, Shrewsbury and Worcester, besides dealing with a substantial amount of material in London at the British Museum, Lambeth Palace, the Public Record Office and the Church Commissioners. Most important, I was able, for all masters of the London area, to check the City Hustings rolls for deeds and wills, and to work through the admirably indexed Westminster Abbey Muniments with the help of Lawrence Tanner, the Librarian and Keeper. I wish here to pay tribute to the unfailing kindness as well as deep learning of Tanner, not only the ideal man in the right place, but a fountain of cheerful interest in the many subjects studied by 'his' readers. For whatever reasons, the surviving muniments of the great abbey incorporate not just the monastic accounts, estates material, title deeds and cartularies, but great quantities of extraneous documents from many sources.

Before obtaining the award I had covered a good deal of the record sources at Canterbury, Lichfield, Warwick and York. At Oxford Sir John Myres threw open the New College archives, and I was able to go through their long series of accounts for estates as well as surviving hall books. Through Chitty I had earlier been able to see some of the muniments in the sister foundation at Winchester, and after I had become consultant architect to the College at the start of 1947 and paid frequent visits to Winchester, was shown a great many by his deputy Austin Smyth. Then in 1949, the year of my grant-aided work, Smyth was injured and unable to return, and Chitty (by then almost totally blind) persuaded the College to appoint me as his deputy on a part-time basis. Six months later, Herbert Chitty died, and I remained the College archivist for the next fifteen years. Although this in fact gave me very little opportunity to use the documents for my own research, the friendly interest of successive Wardens did enable me to incorporate a fair number of references by the time the dictionary went to press. The detailed listing of the College muniments by Miss Sheila Elliott (now Mrs Himsworth), done after publication of this book, has made it possible to use much more for the present revision.

Because of the heavy demands of my professional life, and from 1949 the added duties of an archivist, progress in the last stages was very slow. This did, however, have the major advantage that I was able to inspect a great many more of the buildings concerned and form first-hand estimates of style. Soon after the end of the war I had been able to make measured drawings of much of the output of mouldings by Henry Yeveley and his contemporaries (in part published in 1947 as HMY), and carried on similar works of recording as occasion offered, particularly at Canterbury, Ely, Gloucester, Lichfield, and Norwich, the surviving fragments of Ramsey's work at Old St. Paul's, and at Westminster Abbey. A good deal of this material, already collected well before publication of this book, was published later (1962) in *Studies in Building History*, the memorial volume to Bryan O'Neil edited by Martyn Jope.

In the course of this account I have mentioned the great debt which the book owes to the Guildhall Library of the Corporation of the City of London, as it was the first milestone in my research. The personal contacts enjoyed at the great muniment rooms, notably those of Westminster Abbey, New College at Oxford, and Winchester College, were immensely helpful; and there was also a strongly personal element in the running of the Corporation of London Record Office under both Dr. A. H. Thomas and his successor Mr. P. E. Jones. Though in a naturally more remote way I received much kind help from a number of the Assistant Keepers of the Public Records, and from very many members of the staffs of libraries and record offices all over the country. Certain striking changes in the climate of research, between my work for the original edition and the present revision, are worth a retrospective comment. From 1930 until 1950 or even later, the great bulk of research was necessarily done in libraries, apart from work at the Public Record Office. The reading room of the British Museum was still largely devoted, in its open shelves, to work in the antiquarian field, so that complete sets of *Archaeologia*, of the *Archaeological Journal* and of the *Journal of the British Archaeological Association* could always be consulted. This was an immense boon to workers in this field, sadly now lost. Far more serious in its consequences is the dispersal of probate records from Somerset House. No doubt local workers enjoy convenient access to many of the wills and administrations, as well as inventories, for their own areas; but the concentration of the many courts overlapping in their jurisdictions in the area of Greater London and the Home Counties was of enormous value for any general work such as this. In present conditions of fragmentation it would be impossible for a large and vital part of the research for this book to be done by one man. Incidentally, I must here pay a tribute of warm affection to the memory of the late Miss Helen Thacker who presided for a time, all too short, over the Literary Search Room at Somerset House before its glory departed for ever.

In compensation the whole country has now the benefit of a series of wonderfully efficient county record offices. In several other contexts and during my work on the present revision of this book, I have been accorded extremely helpful treatment, not only on personal visits, but also by correspondence. Much of the checking of individual documents would have been impossible within limited time had it not been for the obliging promptitude with which photocopies were supplied, information given, and private depositors approached on my behalf. I ought in conclusion to stress the fact that many institutions and persons have given me help, perhaps of a merely negative kind, which receives no acknowledgment in this volume. For the apparent neglect I must express my regret, and at the same time give my best thanks to every one of the legion of helpers who have made it possible to produce the book.

ARTHUR OSWALD. *Photograph by Harold Connold, 1940*

ARTHUR STANLEY OSWALD

Arthur Stanley Oswald was born at Muswell Hill in North London on 3 March 1904, the third child of Philip Stanley Oswald LLB, of Lincoln's Inn, and Mabel Gertrude née Harrison. My father, William Harrison Oswald, was the eldest of their seven children. My grandmother was an accomplished watercolourist, whose surviving paintings include detailed studies of the interior of Westminster Abbey and other ecclesiastical buildings, and it was probably from her that Arthur learnt to recognise the principal styles of mediaeval architecture. At any rate, at the age of about seven (by which time his father was a curate in North Finchley) he was photographing the Norman arches of St. Albans Abbey with a newly acquired Brownie camera. Then, during the family holiday at Birchington in Kent in the summer of 1912, he and his mother visited nearby churches such as St. Mary's, Minster-in-Thanet, and St. Nicholas-at-Wade and spent what he described in his diary for 28 March 1931 (recounting his next visit there to 'revive memories') as 'two blissful days seeing the cathedral and the City' of Canterbury. In September 1913 my grandfather became Vicar of All Saints', Sudbury, and Arthur at once made my father bicycle with him to Long Melford for the first of many visits to one of those magnificent East Anglian Perpendicular churches that were to become one of his most absorbing interests.

A few days later he went as a boarder to Tyttenhanger Lodge Preparatory School at Seaford and thence in September 1917 as a scholar to Cheltenham College, his father's school, where he became a day boy for his last two years after the family moved from Sudbury to Cheltenham. At school he won numerous prizes and finally a scholarship to Queens' College, Cambridge, in 1922. There he gained the Bell University Scholarship in 1923, first class honours in Part I of the Classical Tripos in 1924, and the same in Section A (Modern and Mediaeval Literature) of the English Tripos in 1926.

After going down from Cambridge Arthur would have liked to do a course in architecture at the Architectural Association, but, as he felt that he could not expect his parents to spend any more on him and that he 'had no particular aptitude for drawing', he started teaching at Merchant Taylors' School, at that time in Charterhouse Square in the City of London. A year later he moved on to become a Lecturer in English Literature at Bede College, Durham. Even before he went there he had begun to submit articles to *Country Life*, his first attempt, on Regent Street, being read by the manager, Herbert Pratt, 'with very considerable pleasure' but rejected as being 'likely to wound the susceptibilities of a number of advertisers'! He visited The Grange at Rottingdean at the beginning of October 1927, with a letter of introduction written by Edward Hudson, and his illustrated account of the house appeared in the issue of 12 November. In December he was offered a job on the journal's staff, which he at first turned down, but, after changing his mind in April 1928, he took up the post in the following September at an annual salary of £350. From the start, most of his articles were on country houses — a subject that he shared with Christopher Hussey — but as early as 24 November 1928 there appeared the first of a series of scholarly articles (continued till 11 February 1939) on the colleges of Oxford and Cambridge. In another of these, on St. John's

College, Cambridge, published on 18 October 1930, one can see already Arthur's interest in the mediaeval craftsmen who built the colleges, in his mentions of 'Reculver of Grenewich Brikmaker' and 'Swann ye mason' (see the article on William Swayn in this dictionary).

In 1933 Country Life Ltd published Arthur's *Country Houses of Kent*, illustrated by some 200 photographs mostly from the journal's own collection, and in 1935 a companion volume, *Country Houses of Dorset*, of which a second edition appeared in 1959. Between 1931 and 1967 he wrote articles in *Country Life* on nearly twenty houses in the latter county, which he had loved from childhood.

There were also plans to expand the articles on Cambridge colleges into a book to be published by Country Life Ltd, and much of this was drafted before the Second World War. Only the chapter on King's College is extant, in manuscript, but in a note dated 1975 Arthur described this as having 'got out of hand'. His painstaking work on this college's muniments, not completed till about 1950, made it plain to him that what he 'wanted to write was a detailed account of the chapel showing just how much was done under each of the four master masons and considering the share of responsibility of each for the final result'. Thus it was that, when Arthur made contact with John Harvey in July 1938, as described on page (liv) of this dictionary, he at first reserved his detailed findings on Reginald Ely, John Worlich, Simon Clerk and John Wastell. An undated manuscript of a book, provisionally entitled *King's College Chapel and its Architects* and probably mainly written before the Second World War (and certainly all before 1950), still survives but was apparently never fully revised for publication, though part was used for his paper about Reginald Ely (OAD in this dictionary: see later in this account).

In the December 1939 issue of *The Burlington Magazine* Arthur published a paper entitled 'Canterbury Cathedral: the Nave and its Designer' (OCC in this dictionary), in which he presented evidence for the theory that Henry Yeveley, 'the Wren of the fourteenth century', was the architect of the nave at Canterbury. On pages 64–66 of the first edition of *Henry Yevele: The Life of an English Architect* (Batsford, 1944) John Harvey unreservedly accepts the evidence, which confirmed his pre-existing opinion, but systematically dismisses Arthur's criticisms of Yeveley's handling of what is to John Harvey 'the very finest product of English Gothic': Arthur never shared his view of the pre-eminence of Yeveley, and in his working copy of the first edition of this dictionary he crossed out the final paragraph of the article on Yeveley!

On 12 November 1940 Arthur joined the Royal Navy as a volunteer, leaving the second part of his article on 'Bristol — Queen of the West' and three instalments of 'Sudeley Castle, Gloucestershire' to be published in *Country Life* in succeeding weeks. His war service took him as an Ordinary Coder to the North Atlantic, where he was inspected by Winston Churchill on Iceland, and to the Mediterranean, where his destroyer *HMS Southwold* sank after hitting a mine and he was picked up from the sea and landed on Malta, shoeless! He then served as an RNVR Cypher Officer in the Persian Gulf, at Fort Southwick near Fareham and in Northern Germany. He returned to his job at *Country Life* and to his researches into Suffolk and Cambridge wills and other documents in the New Year of 1946. During the last few months of 1944 and early in 1945, while he was at Southwick, he and John Harvey had been corresponding almost weekly about their mediaeval researches and especially about the latter's book on Yeveley, which Arthur reviewed in *Country Life* on 26 January 1945; this correspondence was resumed just before Christmas that year and from September 1951 onwards was mainly concerned with the completion of the dictionary.

In August 1946 Arthur became a member of the Suffolk Institute of Archaeology and early in 1947 of the Cambridge Antiquarian Society, and on 26 April 1948 he gave a lecture to the latter — first mooted in July 1939 — based on his paper 'Andrew Doket and his Architect', later published in the Society's *Proceedings* (OAD). Arthur's identification of Reginald Ely as the first architect of his own college, Queens', as well as his precise analysis of Ely's contribution to the design of King's College Chapel greatly excited John Saltmarsh, with whom also Arthur was corresponding at this period. He also commented in detail on drafts of and made important contributions to Kenneth Harrison's book *The Windows of King's College Chapel Cambridge* (published by the University Press in 1952), and Harrison wrote: 'the chapter on the glaziers, to say nothing of anything else, would have been very thin without your help'. Arthur himself published two papers on early sixteenth-century religious glass in *Journal of the British Society of Master Glass-Painters*, 'Barnard Flower, the King's Glazier' (1951–1952) and 'The Glazing of the Savoy Hospital' (1954–1955). (Flower was responsible for the earliest windows in King's College Chapel.)

While the first edition of the dictionary was in press, Arthur planned a booklet reproducing his articles on the masons concerned with the chapel; but by February 1955 what had originally been intended as a brief introduction to them was 'well on the way to becoming the main part of the book, i.e. the history of the building of the chapel', and he decided that the idea of reprinting the articles would have to be abandoned.

In March 1942 *Country Life* started a series of articles entitled 'Old Towns Revisited', to which Arthur made important contributions. In 1952 eight of these, five of them by Arthur, were published as a book with the same title, edited and with an introduction by him. Arthur retired from *Country Life* in 1969, having been on its staff for 41 years apart from his war service. In 1973 he embarked on a book, at the request of Terence Dalton Ltd of Lavenham, on the careers of Simon Clerk and John Wastell, and it seemed that at last he had found the impetus to revise and update his pre-war work on these early Tudor architects; but sadly, after drafting three of the ten projected chapters, he again gave up. He became increasingly disabled by emphysema and died on 1 March 1979, two days before his 75th birthday.

This brief account of Arthur Oswald's career leaves much about him unsaid. He was a man who experienced things deeply and was not afraid, or ashamed, to show his emotions. He had a strongly developed appreciation of beauty, especially visual beauty, a keen sense of pathos, but also a good sense of humour — shaking at times helplessly with almost silent mirth. He never married, but he had an acute observation of the ways of little children and derived much pleasure from young nephews and nieces and, later, great nephews and nieces. He avoided social events whenever possible, just as he shunned organisational bureaucracy, but he was a delightful companion and conversationalist, especially with just one other person.

Church architecture was his first love, but his range of interests — some amounting for a time to crazes — was impressive. Among them were English literature (especially the Lakeland poets), paintings (especially of John Constable and other English landscape painters of the late eighteenth and early nineteenth centuries), music (at first classical, but later he had a 'Beatles period' and latterly he extended his knowledge of early music and modern composers through BBC Radio 3), ballet, the theatre, photography, the genealogy of the Oswald and Harrison families, ice-skating, hill-walking and, in his retirement, finding British wild orchids (of which he saw twenty species before he died, despite the increasing breathlessness that restricted his mobility). He also composed the weekly *Country Life* crossword for many years — apparently his principal qualification for cypher work in the Navy!

As his obituary in *Country Life* of 15 March 1979 put it, 'Arthur was an intensely shy and retiring man, very gentle and modest.' But, paradoxically, he combined his modesty and diffidence with a tenacious certainty about his own opinions and ways of doing things. Everything he did was done carefully, even meticulously — and a consistently high standard was more important to him than a rapid result. He took enormous trouble in checking and commenting on drafts sent to him by fellow workers and was generous in supplying relevant information from his own researches. It is typical of him that — apart from his articles in *Country Life* — his name appears far more often in other authors' acknowledgements than as an author in his own right. But he was not wholly undervalued: he was made an Honorary Associate of the Royal Institute of British Architects in May 1951 and an Honorary Fellow in October 1971; he was elected to the Council of the Royal Archaeological Institute of Great Britain and Ireland in May 1952; and he was for a few years from 14 March 1968 a Member of the Royal Commission on Historical Monuments for England.

Philip Oswald
November 1983

DIS
MANIBVS

ARTIFICVM PRAETERITORVM

BIOGRAPHIES

Please read the Foreword on page xxi before consulting the text.

Abbendon, Hugh—see ALBEMUNT

Abbot, John—see EVERARD

ABBOTSBURY, William [de Abbotesbury] (*fl.* 1344–1348) Mason (*Abbotsbury, Dorset*)

In 1344 provided stone for *Windsor Castle*;[1] on 12 August 1347 was ordered to take stone for *Westminster Palace*, while the Abbot of Sherborne was to allow him to carry the stone over his manor of Beer, co. Devon. Abbotsbury was paid £1 1s. 0d. for the 21 days 8–28 October spent in obtaining Beer stone 'in the county of Somerset'.[2] In 1347–48 he was *cementarius* and surveyor of works at Westminster Palace, taking 1s. a day.[3]

[1] *PRO*, E.101–492–26 (*G.P.J.*); [2] CPR 1345–8, 367; [3] *PRO*, E.101–470–18 (*G.P.J.*)

ABINGDON, Alexander de [A. *Imaginator*] (*fl.* 1291–1317) Imager (*Abingdon, Berks.*)

Master; described as 'Le Ymagour'; in 1291–94 was engaged on the statues of the Eleanor Crosses at *Charing* and *Waltham*, and with NICHOLAS DYMINGE made the tomb of Queen Eleanor in *Lincoln Cathedral* for £25.[1] In 1305–06 he acknowledged debts to merchants of Gascony[2] and in 1312 he entered into a bond to complete his contract with the parson of *Stanwell Church*, Middx.;[3] perhaps the delicate chancel arcading which still exists.

In 1316–17 Master MICHAEL OF CANTERBURY, with Alexander le Ymagour and others, became sureties that WILLIAM DE HOO and two other masons would rebuild a wall at Eltham Manor.[4]

Mr. Arthur Gardner has drawn attention to the similarity between the Waltham statues of Queen Eleanor and the effigy of a lady at *Aldworth*, Berks., not far from Abingdon, and also to a statue at *Lichfield Cathedral*.[5]

LKC, 177, 245–6; LWR, 197–8
[1] BMH; [2] CLB, 'B', 156, 160, 179;[3] *Ibid.*, 'D', 289; [4] SHB, 27–8, [5] GMS, 167–9

ABINGDON, John [Abyndon] (*fl.* 1396–1398) Mason

Mason contractor who in 1396–98 vaulted two cellars of the great tower of *Portchester Castle*, Hants., for £20. The work was done with masonry of additional thickness (*cum duplic' pendent'*). The master in charge was WALTER WALTON, acting under the instructions of HENRY YEVELEY.

PRO, E.101–479–23

ABINGDON, Nicholas [de Abyndon] (*fl.* 1344–†*c.* 1365) Mason

In 1344 was warden of the masons at *St. Stephen's Chapel, Westminster*, taking 3s. 6d. a week.[1] He was probably the man of this name who by 1366 had died, leaving a tenement in Lime Street in the parish of St. Andrew Cornhill, London.[2]

[1]*PRO*, E.101–470–13; [2] *LHR*, 94(103), 98(146)

ABINGDON, Reginald de (*fl. c.* 1270) Mason

Master mason (*cementarius*), living in St. Thomas's parish near Oseney in Oxford; probably master mason of *Oseney Abbey*; father of WALTER the Mason I.

E. M. Jope in BKJ, LI (1951), 56

ABINGDON, Richard de (*fl.* 1275) Mason

In 1275 was master mason in charge of the work of *St. Mary the Virgin, Oxford* (tower, *c.* 1270–80); and was granted by the rector and parishioners a house called 'St. Mary's Entry' rent free during his work, and thereafter by 12s. yearly rent.

OHS, LXXXV, 77–8, 447 (*E.A.G.L.*)

Ablemond, Hugh—see ALBEMUNT

ACKLAM, Gilbert de (*fl.* 1349–1356) Mason

Master mason of *Calais* from soon after its capture from the French, and in charge of works there from 1349 until JOHN BOX took over in May 1356. In 1351–2 he carried out works on the peel of *Frétun*, 3 miles from Calais, with the carpenter Master STEPHEN OF DUNMOW.

HKW, I, 427n., 451; II, 1054

ACLE, Richard de (*fl. c.* 1276–1285) Mason

Succeeded THOMAS DE WELDON at *Rocking-*

1

ham Castle about 1276 and was still in charge there in 1285.

HKW, II, 817

ADAM the Carver [*Sculptor*] (*fl.* 1314–1324) Carver

Master carver engaged on making images in the choir of *Norwich Cathedral* in 1314–15, when he received a gift of 1*s.* from the prior. In 1323–24 he was paid £2 for making 24 small images for the cathedral clock.

NCM, rolls 23, 230

ADAM the Joiner [Joynour] (*fl.* 1398–1402) Joiner

Rent-collector of *New College, Oxford*, for their London estates; was paid £12 for three cupboards and an altar made by contract for New College, 1398–99; and rode to Oxford to measure the vestry and tower of the college; in 1400–01 again visited Oxford in connection with the canopy over the high altar of the College Chapel, and is again mentioned in 1401–02; work on the canopy was finished in 1406.

NCO, London Acc., 3–6

ADAM the Mason I (*fl. c.* 1225) Mason

In *c.* 1225 described as master, owning land in the parish of St. Margaret, Southwark, next to that of the Abbot of Waverley and of St. Thomas's Hospital.

CTS, 32

ADAM the Mason IA (*fl.* 1227) Mason

In charge of works at *Dover Castle* from March to May 1227, at 3*d.* a day; he was then succeeded by WILLIAM CHANCELLOR.

HKW, II, 636

ADAM the Mason II (*fl.* 1288–89) Mason Master mason; in 1288–89 was paid £2 for making two new windows in the hall of *Carmarthen Castle*, and two others in the tower over the gate. He was probably also the designer of work carried out by contract at the same time by THOMAS HOGUN.

WWH, III, 47

ADAM, Richard (*fl.* 1484–1486) Carver

Held property in Lincoln (part of no. 13 Minster Yard), in 1484–86, rent free; this implies that he was in the service of *Lincoln Cathedral*.

LDC, Bj.5.11 (*K.M.*)

ADDESCOMP, William [Attescompe] (*fl.* 1418–1425) Carpenter (*Addiscombe, Surrey*)

Was master carpenter in *Windsor Castle* in 1418–19,[1] and had probably succeeded WIL-LIAM WYSE in or about 1415. On 24 August 1425 he contracted to make two new houses in Basinghaw, London, for the executors of Richard Whittington by Michaelmas 1426 for £62 13*s.* 4*d.*, the clients finding all materials.[2] JOHN CAUSTON, carpenter, was to make the 'howsyng' for the houses.

[1] HKW, II, 1053; [2] CLE, 228–9 (*N.L.R.*)

AELFRIC the Mason (*fl. c.* 1087) Mason

Appears as the last witness to the charter founding *Hurley Priory*, Berks., of which he was presumably the builder.

WSH, 29 (*C.W.D.*)

AELRIC the Mason (*fl. c.* 1124–1153) Mason

Master mason (*Magister Aelricus cementarius*) who in the 12th century was in possession of the lands of Ledmacduuegil in Fifeshire, Scotland, later known as Masterton. The overlordship of these lands was granted by King Malcolm Canmore to *Dunfermline Abbey*, of whose church (*c.* 1125–50) Aelric is believed to have been the designer. He was probably a Saxon from Northumbria.

WDA, 216 *(G.W.S.B.)*

Aelric—see also AILRIC

Aillyn—see ALLEN

AILNOTH the Engineer [*Ingeniator*] (*fl.* 1157–1190) Engineer

King's Engineer for works at the *Tower of London, Westminster Palace*, and elsewhere. In 1157–58 he was receiving a yearly fee of £10 12*s.* 11*d.*, or 7*d.* a day for 365 days in the year, and was in charge of repairs to the King's houses at Westminster. He continued to draw this fee until 1189, not as a retainer for architectural work, but as keeper of the Old Palace of Westminster, an office which he seems to have held as deputy of the Leveland family.[1] Ailnoth executed repairs to the Solar in Westminster Palace in 1162, and cleaned the King's houses in the following year, when he purchased new rushes for them. In 1165 he made ready the King's Court and houses, and probably designed *Orford Castle*, Suffolk, built in 1165–73.[2]

He viewed the leadwork for the King's houses in *Windsor Castle* in 1167, and was in charge of other works there in that and the following year. In 1169 he was again in charge of building at Westminster, and stone was bought by him for the works at Windsor in 1171; two years later, while still in charge at Windsor, he supervised with Edward Blund and William Magnus the building of the gaol of London, at *The Fleet*. During 1174 a considerable amount of work was done at the Tower under him, and next year he repaired the refectory of *Westminster Abbey* and took with him carpenters and masons to Suffolk to pull down the castle of *Framlingham*; he also hired carpenters to find timber in the wood of Beckenham, Kent, for repairs at the Tower of London. In 1176 the chapel in the Tower was covered with lead under his supervision, and he again visited East Anglia to complete the dismantling of Framlingham Castle, and to serve *Walton Castle* in the same fashion.

In the next year, 1177, timber was provided from the issues of Surrey for works at *Woodstock Palace*, Oxon., to be done under him, and he also repaired the King's chamber at Westminster. In 1178 he did further work to the King's houses, both at Westminster and the Tower, and next year he repaired the glass windows at Westminster; a proof of the early existence of glazing in the windows of the King's houses.

Ailnoth made a wharf at Westminster in 1180, and a cloister between the King's chambers there. Work on the wharf was again in progress three years later, and in 1185 Ailnoth was once more supervising work on the gaol of London. In the following year he mended the houses at Westminster 'for the King's coming', continued the work on the gaol of London, and repaired the King's Hall at 'Radlega' (*Rayleigh*, Ess.). 1187 saw him making a stone arch and the King's seat in the chapel of St. John at Westminster, with various other works there including the wharf, and in the following year he mended the wharf, the wall, and the King's bridge (landing-stairs) there.

He received his usual fee in 1189, but in the next year, the first of Richard Coeur-de-Lion, only had £2 10s. of the King's gift from the issues of Wiltshire; he had probably retired from active work at an advanced age. He was dead by 15 October 1197 when Maud his widow was concerned with land held in Westminster. ROGER ENGANET seems to have been his son.

Ailnoth, who certainly worked at Westminster Abbey, was probably the designer of the Infirmary Chapel of St. Katherine there, built about 1160. The detail is advanced, and

such work would be of the royal school. Ailnoth was versatile, having to do with works of stone, wood, lead, and glass, but there is no doubt that he was a craftsman of technical training, perhaps a carpenter, as were most of the engineers of the 12th and 13th centuries, men accustomed to making the great war-engines which preceded the use of gunpowder. In Ailnoth's time the title covered the functions of an architect.

HKC; *generally* PR
[1]C.T. Clay in EHR, LIX (1944), 1–21; [2] HBC

AILRIC the Carpenter (*fl.* 1165–1168) Carpenter

Rendered accounts in 1165–66 and 1166–67 for 1 mark (6s. 8d.) of the issues of Norfolk and Suffolk, and in 1167–68 for 10s. of the issues of Devonshire. He was probably in the King's service.

PR

Ailric the Mason—See AELRIC

AILYNGTON, Nicholas de [Alyngton] (*fl.* 1342–1347) Mason (? *Elton, Hunts.*)

In September 1342 was warden of the masons working on *St. Stephen's Chapel* in Westminster Palace, taking 3s. a week, continuing until 7 April 1343, when he was succeeded by JOHN DE RAMSEY III.[1]

Was the Black Prince's master mason at the manor of *Kennington*, Surrey, in 1346; on 4 November he was granted £20 for the works there, and a further £10 was allowed on 28 July in the following year.[2] At this time the stone hall was being rebuilt; Ailyngton was succeeded by JOHN DE LEICESTER.
[1]PRO, E.101–470–13; [2] BPR, I, 27, 29, 104

ALAN the Carpenter (*fl.* 1282–1283) Carpenter

Master carpenter to the Bishop of Winchester in 1282–83, when he was paid at *Witney*, Oxon., by order of the Treasurer of Wolvesey, a sum of 11s. 2d. for 9 weeks and 4 days' work.

PRO, Eccl. 2–159305

ALBEMUNT, Hugh de [Abbemund, Abbendon, Ablemond] (*fl.* 1213–1243) Carpenter

Master carpenter in the King's service; was paid 23 marks (£15 6s. 8d.) for work done at *Colchester Castle* in 1213.[1] In 1217 Master Hugh was in charge of work at *Devizes Castle*, with 20 carpenters under him; and in 1222 he was sent to seek timber for the new great hall of *Winchester Castle*.[2] He received fees by in-stalments in 1227 and onwards, his wage-rate being at first 9*d.* a day; from 8 August 1236 it was reduced (as with RALPH BURNELL) to 5*d.* a day while at work, with a retainer of 3*d.* daily when inactive. He was employed on the *Palace of Westminster* in 1233; and was to have timber for repairing the King's chamber and chapel at *Havering-atte-Bower*, Essex, in the following year, together with the carpenters NICHOLAS DE AUNDELEY, SIMON OF NORTH-AMPTON, and WILLIAM RUTIER. Orders were given for the payment of his wages from time to time until Easter 1243. He was perhaps identical with HUGH the Carpenter I.

CLR, *passim*
[1] CMM, I, 421; [2] HKW, II, 627, 858

ALBEMUNT, Robert de [Abbemund] (*fl.* 1214–1228) Carpenter

Was the second King's Carpenter in 1214, taking 6*d.* a day, and worked generally under Master THOMAS. He sometimes was given 20*s.* for a robe, and received a reward of £1 on 23 Jan. 1223/4, as the fourth of Henry III's four master carpenters, with NICHOLAS DE AUNDE-LY, Thomas, and Ralph (? RALPH BURNELL)[1] He continued to draw wages until July 1228.[2]

[1] HLC, I, 178b, 441b, 449b, 477b, 480b, 527b, 582b; [2] CLR 1226–40, 7, 14, 24, 37, 41, 60, 70, 79, 82, 92; HLC, II, 13, 39, 44, 100b, 104, 117b, 141

ALBERIC the Mason (*fl.* 1249–1253) Mason

Master mason in charge of the building of the east cloister at *Westminster Abbey* from 1249 to 1253, and probably from the begin-ning of the work in 1245. He was apparently subordinate to Master HENRY DE REYNS. Alber-ic also undertook the making of windows and tracery by task-work, and in 1253 was paid for 280 feet of voussoirs with fillets, at 3*d.* and 3½*d.* a foot, as well as for 50 'assises' or facing blocks, at 5*d.* each, and for seven steps cut by task, probably those leading up to the Chap-ter House.

One of the entries relating to Alberic men-tions his three companions, which suggests, as Lethaby pointed out, that he was a sub-contractor, and very likely engaged for the whole of the work connected with the Chap-ter House, apparently regarded as separate from the church itself.

SGW; LKC, 154, 159; LWR, 130 ff.; HKW, I, 139

ALBON, Richard [de Sancto Albano] (*fl.* 1345–1373) Carpenter

In 1345–6 Edward III ordered 100 'ribalds' to be made for the Crecy campaign. The woodwork of the carriages was made by Master Richard of St. Albans, master carpen-ter at the *Tower of London*.[1] In 1349 he was carpenter at *Rotherhithe Manor*, when he re-ceived £8 for building houses, with £9 10*s.* 0*d.* in 1350 for repairs. He was warden (*apparila-tor*) of carpenters employed on works at *Rotherhithe* from 7 Feb. 1352/3 to 9 Feb. 1353/4, taking 3*s.* 6*d.* a week.[2] On 12 Jan. 1353/4 a writ of impressment in favour of Richard Albon the King's Yeoman was issued, empowering him to take carpenters for the works at Rotherhithe[3] and on 18 March 1355/6 he was appointed keeper of the houses in the King's manor of *Eltham* with a salary of 6*d.* a day so that he undertook repairs when required.[4] In 1373 Richard Albon and Margery his wife made a grant of a tenement in the parish of All Hallows, Barking, London.[5]

[1] TFE (*A.O.*); [2] PRO, E.101–545–33; [3] CPR 1350–4, 542; [4] *Ibid.* 1354–8, 350; [5] LBH, LR. 29

Albon, Robert—see ST ALBANS

ALBON, William (*fl. c.* 1370–1375) Mason

William Albon and JOHN HAWARDEBY 'rep-aired' the great bridge of *Huntingdon* about 1370–75 at a cost of £200, which they had difficulty in recovering. This work was almost certainly the building of the fine bridge which survives.

PRO, Anc. Petitions, 7937 (*L.F.S.*); JAB, III, 101–2

ALCOCK, William (*fl. c.* 1463–1478) Carpenter

Of Blythburgh, Suffolk; in 1463 cleaned the images in *Walberswick Church*, Suffolk, and mended the font and the Easter Sepulchre there, and in 1472–73 was paid 10 nobles (£3 6*s.* 8*d.*) for making 'Saint Johnnys tabernakyll'.[1] Between 1475 and 1478 he made a beam for a Candle Beam in *Thorington Church*, for £3.[2]

[1] LCW, 15, 33, 35; [2] BB, 45–6

Alderidge, William — see ALDRYCH, Thomas

ALDRYCH, Thomas [Ardrych] (*fl.* 1487–1508) Mason

On 18 Feb. 1487/8 Thomas Aldrych of North Lopham contracted to build within ten years a tower of knapped flint for *Helmingham Church*, Suffolk; it was specified that it should be of the size and form of the tower at Framsden, but following the 'facion' of the tower of Brandeston. Aldrych was to be paid

10s. for each foot of height. A reference to £300 to be paid him by instalments suggests that he was already engaged in extensive works at the church.[1] North Lopham is in Norfolk, about ten miles east of Thetford.

In 1507–08 the great east window of the chancel of *Thetford Cluniac Priory* was built by Thomas Aldrych, mason, who may have been the same man, or possibly a son, and who was in all probability identical with Thomas the Mason who carried out other works at the Priory in 1516-17, and perhaps with 'Master le Mason' who worked on the High Altar for five days in 1523–24.[2]

[1] SHB, 547–9; [2] HTP, 11, 12, 13; *CUL*, Add. MS. 6969, f. 85b.

Robert **ALDWYCK**, mason of Thetford, was in 1432 pardoned for not appearing to answer a debt. His name may well be a version of Aldrych.

CPR 1429–36, 161

William **ALDERIDGE**, a rough-layer, who took up the freedom of Oxford in 1536–37,[1] and who may have been the William Aldryg who worked as a rough-layer at *Nonsuch Palace* in 1538, was probably a relation.[2]

(*G.P.J.*)
[1] TRO, 149; [2] *PRO*, E.101–477–12

Aldwyck, Robert—see ALDRYCH, Thomas

Alee, John—see LEE

Alen—see also ALEYN, ALLEN

ALEN, — (*fl.* 1535) Mason

Alen, a mason of Bersted, Kent, was to finish a tomb in the form of an Easter Sepulchre in the church of *Faversham*, Kent, according to his bargain with Dame Joan Norton, who died in 1535. He was perhaps identical with JOHN ALLEN.

(*A.O.*) Fane Lambarde in AC, XLI, 107–13

ALEXANDER (*fl. c.* 1180) Mason Carver

Signed an inscription on the carved sandstone font of *Tiköb Church*, North Zealand, Denmark. The work is English but the sandstone is from Scania in southern Sweden (in the Middle Ages politically Danish). Alexander was presumably an English mason who worked on the cathedral of *Lund* in Scania.

DAT, 54; MDD, 43, 362 ff., fig. 463–4

ALEXANDER the Carpenter (*fl.* 1234–†*c.* 1269) Carpenter

Worked at *Westminster Palace* as a master carpenter in 1234–40;[1] on 25 November 1237 was allowed £3 9s. 10d. for repair of the Bishop of Durham's houses at *London*; on 4 February 1238/9 the sum of £20 was paid to him for wainscoting the Queen's Chapel at Westminster.[2] He was master carpenter at *Westminster Abbey*, where the work of rebuilding was shortly to begin, and by 1248/9 he was working on the detached belfry at the Abbey, where he continued until 1256, in which year he was paid 20 marks (£13 6s. 8d.). On 29 November in the same year he was appointed keeper of the King's works of carpentry, and advised on the work of the gateway of *Guildford Castle*, with JOHN OF GLOUCESTER, keeper of the masonry works. With Master John he also visited *Portchester Castle* to supervise the works there, and also *Dover Castle* and *Rochester Castle* to take charge of repairs.[3]

On 10 January 1257 Master Alexander was given £2 by the king to buy himself a horse on his appointment, with Master John, to view the defects of the royal castles and buildings south of Trent.[4] On 14 January Alexander was appointed by patent master of all the king's works of carpentry, being the first holder of this new office; he received furred robes twice a year in addition to his fees, which the king had already ordered to be doubled when Alexander was travelling on official business.[5] Alexander's wife Argentine also received robes.[6] Master Alexander was normally associated with John of Gloucester, as on the works of 1257–59 on the queen's apartments in *Windsor Castle*.[7] In 1259, besides his work at the Abbey, he was in charge of building at the Palace, and in 1260 he is mentioned as owning property in Knightsbridge. He continued to be one of the masters in charge both at the Palace and the Abbey until 1267.[8]

On 27 June 1257 Alexander had received a gift of houses in Canterbury and on 27 April 1258 he and his heirs and assigns were granted by royal charter two parts of a messuage opposite to the pillory there.[9] Master Alexander died in or about 1269. Argentine his widow was paid £1 6s. 8d. for land occupied at the Royal Mews, Charing Cross, in 1274–77, and was still alive in 1278.[10] Alexander had been a witness to many charters dated at Westminster between 1246 and 1269,[11] and his son Henry made grants of houses and lands there which he had inherited from his father.[12]

One of Alexander's most important works has survived, the timber roof of Henry III's work at Westminster Abbey; it consists of scissor-braced trussed rafters with upper and lower collars, a type employed in the same period at Ely and Salisbury Cathedrals and the roofs of the eastern arm at Lincoln.[13] The original timbers of the scissors trusses still stand, though much obscured by later strengthening pieces.

HKC; LKC

[1] CCR 1231–4, 413; 1237–42, 208; [2] CLR 1226–40, 298, 364; [3] CLR 1251–60, 304; [4] Ibid., 350; [5] CPR 1247–58, 538; [6] CCR 1256–9, 159, 218; [7] HKW, II, 867; [8] CLR 1260–67, passim; [9] CHR 1226–57, 471; 1257–1300, 9; [10] PRO, E.101–467–7)(3); E.372–123, m. 21 (H.M.C.); [11] WAM, 13753, 15190, 16276, 17086, 17138, 17155 B, 17161, 17337, 17345, 17347–9, 17360, 17367, 17369, 17371, 17379, 17388–9, 17395, 17400, 17410, 17440–1, 17449, 17451, 17455, 17462–3, 17504–5, 17510, 17551; [12] WAM, 17383, 17468, 17544;[13] LWR, 56; cf. A, C (1966), 155 ff.

ALEXANDER the Mason I [Cementarius] (fl. 1262) Mason

Referred to as the heir of JOHN 'Cementarius' (II) in a deed in which he and his sisters Cristina and Alice granted a house in the High Street of Exeter to St. Nicholas Priory.

DRO, ED/SN/48 (A.M.E.)

ALEXANDER the Mason II [Cementarius] (fl. c. 1224–1240) Mason

Mentioned in several undated documents of c. 1215–40 as master mason of the church of St Mary, the cathedral, at Worcester. His work there must have comprised the new choir begun in 1224. Certain stylistic resemblances, and the transfer from Worcester to Lincoln at this time of the polygonal chapter-house plan, make it probable that he was identical with Master ALEXANDER III. The common factors of style had been independently noted by Professor C. M. Girdlestone, who also suspected some connection with contemporary work at the cathedral of Le Mans in France (AJ, CII, 1945–7, 111ff.).

BCW, 3, 5, 7, 119; WPR, 109b; cf. EHR, XLVII (1932), 265; AAS, XXXV (1919), 357

ALEXANDER the Mason III [Cementarius] (fl. c. 1235–1257) Mason

Mason of Lincoln, described as the fellow or colleague of Master GILBERT DE BURGO in a document which they witnessed between 17 June 1235 and 16 June 1239. Called also Alexander, son of Odo of Newport (i.e. Newport, Lincoln) when, probably in 1245–48, he was granted by the dean and chapter of Lincoln a messuage and houses in Pottergate in St. Margaret's parish and other property, by rent of 24s. yearly, he to repair the premises. The lease was to Alexander and his heirs by his wife Thecia.[1] Was master of the work at Lincoln Cathedral about 1240, when he appears as a witness to several deeds conveying lands at Fillingham to the church of Lincoln, for the fabric of the cathedral, and to a grant of land in the parish of St. Peter Eastgate, Lincoln. He is described as 'mason, master of the work', or 'master of the fabric' (cementarius magister operis; magister fabrice). He was still living at Christmas 1257, when he was described as master of the fabric, and was dead by 1270.[2] His daughter Maud was a nun of St. Michael's, Stamford, and living in 1297.[3] Alexander's heiress Thecia, with her husband Laurence of Ingilby, did fealty for the Pottergate property on 24 Oct. 1293, and later sold it to RICHARD DE STOW II on 24 June 1295.[4]

Alexander was presumably in charge of the building of the nave, the chapter house, and the Galilee, together with the upper parts of the west front and the rebuilding of the central tower's lower stage after its collapse in 1237. All of these works are clearly by the same hand, and are of outstanding originality of design. Alexander's innovations in several fields had permanent significance in the development of English Gothic: notably his polygonal chapter house with its many-ribbed vault, his development of the screen-front and of the tower with polygonal buttresses, and above all his insertion of lierne ribs in the vault of the nave. This last, leading as it did to the whole development of patterned vaulting in England and abroad, was one of the fateful achievements in the history of Gothic art. One mark of Master Alexander's style at Lincoln is a trellis pattern on the central tower and also on the upper part of the west front. This occurs also on the lower stages of the towers of Newark and Grantham churches, which he may have designed.

It seems probable that the Lincoln Alexander was identical with ALEXANDER II.

LRS, LXII, (Reg. Ant.), ix, no. 2600; LXVII, passim; LRS, XXXII, 97–8, 101; LDC, D.ij. 80–1–143
[1] LDC, D.ij. 78–2–48 (K.M.); [2] LDC, R. 779, 744; 694, 701–8, 739, 741; D.ij. 78–3–96 (K.M.); [3] LDC, R. 745 (K.M.); [4] LDC, D.ij. 78–2–49; Liber Cantariarum, No. 538 (K.M.)

ALEXANDER the Mason IV [le Machun] (*fl.* 1273–1305) Mason

Leading mason (*cementarius*) employed at *Norwich Cathedral Priory* between 1273 and 1305, but apparently paid only 1*d.* per day, with 2*d.* a week for his boy (*garcio*) in addition. He may have been identical with the Alexander *cementarius* or Le Maczeon for whom the sacrist provided an over-tunic price 6*s.* 8*d.* in 1310–11 and 2 ells of cloth price 2*s.* 6*d.* in 1325–6.

NCM, rolls 5, 10, 11, 211, 218, 223, 226, 231

ALEYN, David (*fl.* 1372–   ) Mason

Is mentioned on 15 December 1372 as mason to John of Gaunt, Duke of Lancaster, at the latter's castle of *Kidwelly*, Carmarthenshire.

JGR 1372–6, 281

Aleyn, John—see ALEYN, Richard

ALEYN, Richard (†1468 or 9) Carver

Of Bury St. Edmunds. The bequests in his will (dated 22 November 1468, proved 20 January following) to 'my Lord the Prior' and 'my master the Sacrist' suggest that he was a salaried craftsman in the Sacrist's office at the Abbey.[1] He left to the 'Monastery of St. Edmund' 40*s.* to be spent according to the disposition of the Prior. In bequeathing 20*s.* to the 'reparation' of the roodloft at *Kentford* he made the qualification: 'provided that the parishioners hold themselves thus contented, otherwise that they settle it as it shall seem best to them and my executors'. The inference seems to be that he was under a contract to make the roodloft and that it was uncompleted. Bequests to the high altars of Barrow, Great Saxham, Hargrave, and Clare may indicate that he had done work in each of those churches. His tools were to be sold by his executors.

John *ALEYN*, also a carver of Bury, who made his will 10 May 1457 (proved 14 June following), was probably a relative, but he mentions no son of the name of Richard.[2] He can be traced in documents from 1439.

A.O.
[1] BW, ia, 118; [2] Ibid., ia, 55

ALEYN, William (*fl.* 1404–1408) Mason

Leading mason employed on the cloisters of *Worcester Cathedral* from 1404 to 1408, taking 3*s.* 2*d.* a week.

WCO, C.78, 79, 80

Aleyn—see also ALEN, ALLEN

ALLEN, John [Aillyn, Aylyn] (*fl.* 1541–1543) Mason

In 1541–43 was a freemason in the King's service at *Dartford*, Kent, at first taking 8*d.* a day, and later warden of the masons there at 9*d.*[1] He was perhaps identical with ALEN, mason of Bearsted, Kent, and with John Alen who with his man was paid 2*s.* 10*d.* for five days 'werking on the florys of the stepull' at *Rainham Church*, Kent, in 1517–19.[2]

(A.O.)
[1] Bodl., Rawl. D. 783, 784 (G.P.J.); [2] AC, XV, 334

Allen—see also ALEN, ALEYN

Allerton, Henry de—see ELLERTON

Almayn, Stephen—see HASCHENPERG

Alnod—see AILNOTH

ALSEBROKE, Henry [Halsebroke] *fl.* 1482–1486) Carpenter

Carpenter of Tattershall, Lincs.; in 1482 was paid £53 2*s.* 2½*d.* in part payment of his carpenter's work on 'le Belle frame' and £1 13*s* 4*d.* out of £9 17*s.* 6*d.* for other work on the bell-tower of *Tattershall Church*, Lincs.'[1] The work was being carried out for Bishop Waynflete of Winchester, executor of Ralph, Lord Cromwell, the refounder of the castle and church of Tattershall. Alsbroke contracted on 25 April 1484 to make a combined ceiling and floor for the chapel and school at *Wainfleet*, Lincolnshire, founded by Bishop Waynflete; it was to be like one in the gatehouse at Esher, Surrey. He was to be paid £25 13*s.* 4*d.* and cloth for a gown or 6*s.* 8*d.* for it.[2] On 14 January 1485/6 he undertook by another contract to build an *Almshouse* for the *College of Tattershall*, Lincs., for £16. The building was to include a hall, chapel, and 13 chambers, with a pillared gallery along the south side.[3] It seems highly probable that Alsbroke was the carpenter at *Esher Palace*, built *c.* 1480, and perhaps for other works of Bishop Waynflete (see COWPER, JOHN).

[1] HMC, De L'Isle, I, 198 ff.; [2] SHB, 542–3; CLW, 369; [3] SHB, 544–5; HMC, De L'Isle, I, 175–6

ALVERTON, John de [Northallerton] (*fl.* 1350–1364) Carpenter (*Northallerton, Yorks.*)

Contracted in 1350 to rebuild the roof of the *Castle Hall* at *Durham* for Bishop Hatfield re-using the old timbers. He also appears as a party to recognizances in 1355, to the Bishop; in 1361 to the Prior; and in 1364 to one Alan de Shotelyngton.

VCH, *Durham*, III, 22, 74; DKR, XXXI (1870), 113

ALWIN the Mason (*fl. c.* 1150) Mason
Witnessed a charter of *c.* 1150 in the chapter house of *Lewes Priory*, of which he was probably the master mason.
SXR, XL, 10 (*L.F.S.*)

Alye, Alygh—see LEE

Ambresbury, Walter de—see HEREFORD

AMBROSE, Richard [Ameros, Amrys] (*fl.* 1504–1557) Carpenter
In 1504 Richard 'Ameros' was apprenticed for 7 years to THOMAS MAUNCY, and took up the freedom of London in 1510 as 'Amrys'. He later served as Warden of the Carpenters' Company[1] and in 1532 undertook a task for timberwork at the *Tower of London*. On 21 June 1535 he was appointed Master Carpenter in the Tower, and drew fees for the office until 25 March 1557.[2]
[1] MCR, II, 154, 244, 262; [2] HKW, III, 267n, 409

Ambrosse, Nicholas—see ANDREWS

AMPILFORDE, Thomas (*fl* –1422) Mason (*Ampleforth, Yorks. N.R.*)
Contracted on 13 Jan. 1421/2, with JOHN GARRETT and ROBERT MAUNSELL, masons, to build the bridge at *Catterick*, Yorks., like the bridge at Barnard Castle. The work was to be finished in 3½ years at a price of 260 marks (£173 6s. 8d.) with a gown to each of the three masons in every year. This very fine bridge still stands, carrying the New North Road across the Swale.
SHB, 497–9; AJ, VII, 56

Andely—see AUNDELY

ANDEWE, Nicholas (*fl.* 1539) Mason
In 1539 Nicholas Andewe (N.B. *not* 'Andrewe') was warden of the masons working on *Camber Castle*, Sussex, under the upper warden or resident master THOMAS POKYLL. Andewe was paid 4s. a week.
HKW, IV, 423

Andrew the Carpenter—see COUPER

ANDREW the Mason [*Cementarius*] (*fl. c.* 1138–1150) Mason
Appears as witness to a document of *c.* 1138–50 at St Paul's Cathedral, London, and may have been the designer of the great Norman nave then in course of erection. Though destroyed in the Great Fire of London, 1666, the nave is known from Hollar's detailed plan and fine engravings of the cathedral.
(LKC, 115); HMC, 9R I, 62a

ANDREWE, John (*fl.* 1487–1496) Mason
Working on St. John's aisle in the church of *St. Andrew, Plymouth*, Devon, in 1487–88.[1] In 1495–96 he made a window of 'morestone' for the Plymouth *Guildhall*.[2]
[1] HMC, IX, 262 (*L.F.S.*); [2] WPM, 93 (*N.L.R.*)

ANDREWE, Nicholas (*fl.* 1539) Carpenter
Master carpenter of the works of *Camber Castle*, Sussex, in 1539, taking 10d. a day.
HKW, IV, 423

ANDREWS, Nicholas [Ambrosse, Andrewes] (*fl.* 1493–1496) Carpenter
Carpenter of Bristol; acted as a viewer of the city in 1493 with JOHN DYMMOK and JOHN WALTER, masons, and RICHARD SOMERE, carpenter; and again in 1496 (Nicholas 'Ambrosse') with RALPH SPORRIER and John Walter, masons, and Richard Somere.
(*A.O.*)   BLR, II, 133–4

Anglicus, Hugo—see WILFRED

Anglicus, Joannes—see ENGLISHMAN, LANGLOIS

ANTELL, John [Auntell] (*fl.* 1459 (?) –1485) Mason
John Auntell in August 1459 was working as a freemason at *King's College Chapel, Cambridge*, under REGINALD ELY.[1] In 1469–70 John Antell, freemason, was admitted a freeman of Norwich.[2] In 1484–85 he received a robe price 6s. 8d. from the Sacrist of *Norwich Cathedral*;[3] in the same year, when the Cellarer of the Priory spent a sum of £24 on the new chancel of *Worstead Church*, Norfolk, John Auntell '*liber lathomus*' and his fellows received £3 14s. 9½d. Antell was also paid 12s. 8d. for making freestone jambs for doors in a new building in the Norwich Cathedral hostry (*hostilaria*).[4]

William Hermer, freemason, admitted a freeman of Norwich in 1509, was described as an apprentice of John Antell.[2]

John ANTIL, who with his servants worked on the Chantry at *Mettingham College*, Suff., for 82 days in 1424–25 for £1 3s. 0d., may have been the father of the freemason.[5]

Robert ANTELL, freemason of Norwich, in 1492 carried out repairs to the steeple windows of *Walberswick Church*, Suffolk.[6] He was presumably the freemason of Norwich concerned with the tower of *Swaffham Church* in 1507,[7] and may have been the Robert Antell who died on 26 April 1538 at Norwich, as recorded in the register of St. Michael-at-Palace.[8] A mason of the same name was working at *King's College Chapel, Cambridge*, in 1508, at the rate of 3*s.* 4*d.* a week.[9]

J.H.H.; A.O.
[1] *KCM*, College Accs., vol. ii; [2] EFN; [3] *NCM*, Sacrist Roll, No. 308; [4] *Ibid.*, Cellarer's Roll, No. 189; Almoner's Roll, No. 577; [5] *BM*, Add. MS. 33985, *f.* 142; [6] LCW, 66; [7] SCW (*S.A.C.*); [8] *NRO*, PD 12/1 (*P.C.*); *KCM*, Building Acc. 1508–9.

Antell, Robert—see ANTELL, John

Aquete—see HUGUET

ARAZ, Baldwin de (*fl.* 1241) Mason
Master; was paid a yearly fee of 10 marks from 22 October 1241 as a mason in the service of Henry III.[1] Presumably from Arras, France.
[1]CLR 1240–5, 81

ARCHE, William (*fl.* 1443–1444) Carpenter
In 1443–44 was paid 4*s.* 8*d.* for making two 'baywyndowes' at *Battle Abbey* in the Almonry and in the Parlour, by contract.
SAC, LXXVIII, 39 n.[2] (*L.F.S.*)

ARCHES, Richard de (*fl.* 1215) Carpenter
Master; was paid 7½*d.* a day for his work on *Oxford Castle* in February 1215.
HLC, I, 168, 188

ARNOLD (*fl. c.* 1113) Mason
Was a lay-brother of *Croyland Abbey*, Lincs., and was apparently the designer of the Norman church begun on 7 March 1113, of which one of the tower arches and several other fragments still remain. He is described as 'a most learned master of the art of masonry' (*caementariae artis scientissimus magister*).
(APD); BAA, IV, 88

ARNOLD, Edmund (*fl.* 1454–1463) Carpenter
Carpenter to the church of *Tilney All Saints*, Norfolk, from 1454; he was paid £1 4*s.* 6*d.* for 41 days' work in 1463, perhaps for part of the fine roof of the nave.
SCT

Artelburgh, John—see ATTLEBOROUGH

ARTHUR the Mason [Masoun] (*fl. c.* 1190) Mason

Arthur 'Masoun', with Wido the Goldsmith and others, was witness to a grant made by the Chapter of *Ripon* to their smith Ralph at a date late in the 12th century, probably *c.* 1190. He was probably the master in charge of work on the church, begun between 1154 and 1181.
SMR, I, 103

Artifex, Radbell—see RADBELL

Artifex, Roger—see LE ENGINNUR

ASKHAM, John [Askam] (*fl.* 1387–†1437) Carpenter (? *Askham Bryan* or *A. Richard, Yorks. W.R.*)
Free of York in 1387; was master carpenter of *York Minster* from 1415 until after 1434[1]. With his wife he joined the Corpus Christi Guild of York in 1429.[2] He made his will on 27 April 1434 and it was proved on 11 January 1436/7.[3] Askham was probably the designer of the wooden high vault of the choir and of the choir stalls. He was apparently succeeded at the Minster by WILLIAM COTTINGHAM.
[1]BHY, I, 211–12, 217–18, 221, 231–2; RFY, 33, 36n., 38, 42n., 45, 50, 52n., [2] SS, LVII. [3] *BIY*, York Wills, 3.479.

ASSER, John, senior (*fl.* 1416–1433) Mason
Was appointed on 22 August 1416, master mason in the counties of Chester and Flint, during pleasure, in succession to THOMAS DE HOLDEN. On Asser's resignation in 1433 the office was granted to his son, JOHN ASSER, junior.
DKR, XXXI (1870), 170

ASSER, John, junior (*fl.* 1433–† 1446) Mason
On the resignation of his father, JOHN ASSER, senior, was appointed for life, on 1 March 1432/3, master mason of the counties of Chester and Flint, with North Wales. On 22 June in the same year he was named supervisor of the building of a chapel to the south of the chancel of *St. Mary-on-the-Hill Church, Chester*. The contractor for this work was THOMAS BATES, mason; it was completed in about two years.[1]
On 10 June 1439 Asser received a grant of the office of surveyor of the walls of the city of *Chester*, and died on 16 June 1446, when he was succeeded by JOHN CAMPTON.
DKR, XXXI, 170
[1] SHB, 503; ECM, 31

ATKINS, John [Atkynnys] (*fl.* 1449–1453) Mason
Seems to have been the master mason in

charge of the tower of *Merton College, Oxford*, for a short period in February and March 1449, in succession to ROBERT JANYNS. He was paid 4*s.* a week, and did not work regularly, which suggests that his position was to some extent consultative or advisory.[1] He also sold stone to the college authorities, and it was probably he, or perhaps a son, to whom WILLIAM ORCHARD conveyed land at Barton in Headington in 1483; the John Atkyns in this transaction was described as 'of Headington', where stone-quarrying was the principal industry.[2]

In 1452–53 4*s.* was paid to John Atkyns and Robert 'Iannyns' (Janyns) for their fee for surveying the new *Divinity Schools* at Oxford and giving information as to the height of the work, and Atkyns also had expenses for declaring to the Taynton quarrymen the sizes of certain stones.[3] He may have been the John Atkyns who was Bailiff of Oxford in 1469–70.[4]

(*R.D.*)

[1] OHS, XVIII, 314–37; [2] HMC, 3R, 318; [3] *UCO*, Smith Transcripts, X (*A.O.*); [4] GOM, 112

Attechirche, Richard—see CHERCHE

Attegrene, John—see GRENE

Attehoke, Simon—see HOOK

Atte Marsh, Mere—see MARSH

Attescombe—see ADDESCOMP

ATTLEBOROUGH, John [Artelburgh] (*fl.* 1376) Mason (? *Attleborough, Warw.*)

In 1376 one of the four masons who represented their craft on the Common Council of London.

W.L. Williams in AQC, XLI, 136; CLB, 'H', 43

ATWOOD, William [Atte Wode, Atwodde] (*fl.* 1490–1507) Mason

Freemason; on 23 October 1490 succeeded WILLIAM SMYTH as master mason of *Wells Cathedral* and the manors belonging to the Chapter, with a fee of £1 6*s.* 8*d.* a year and a house in Wells;[1] in 1498 took up the freedom of Wells, having married the widow of a freeman.[2] Atwood appears in the surviving fabric rolls of 1492–93, 1500–01 and 1505–06 as receiving his fee of 26*s* 8*d.*[3] and was responsible for the rebuilding of the south cloister at Wells, not finished until 1508.[4]

[1] HMC, Wells, II, 120; RWC, 179–80; [2] SRS, XLVI (1931); [3] *WLC*, Fabric rolls (*L.S.C.*) CWF, 25, 31, 39; [4] HMC, Wells, II, 201, 206

AUNCELL, Denys (*fl.* 1459–1460) Carpenter

Carpenter of *Bury St. Edmunds*; in 1459–60 contracted to make a barn, 42 feet long by 20 feet, to be set up at *Bradfield*, Suffolk, for William Pyk, butcher.

ARC, XIV, 19 (*A.E.B.O.*)

AUNDELY, Nicholas de [Andeli, -ly, Áudeley, N. the Carpenter] (*fl.* 1207–†1245) Carpenter (? *Les Andelys, France*)

Master carpenter to King John and to Henry III; he very probably came from Les Andelys in Normandy, where he may have worked on *Château-Gaillard* in 1198. He was in charge of works in the King's houses at *Fifmore* (*Finmere*, Oxon.) and *Gloucester* in 1207,[1] in 1210 was employed at Knaresborough, Yorks., and (at Carlingford and elsewhere) in Ireland,[2] and in 1212 was sent to *Cambridge* to work on the Castle.[3] Soon afterwards he was making engines of war for *Knepp* and *Bramber Castles* in Sussex,[4] in 1214 for *Nottingham*,[5] and in 1215 for *Knaresborough*.[6] At this time he was being paid 9*d.* a day, while three ordinary carpenters received 6*d.* a day each;[7] in November 1215 Master Nicholas also had a grant of land from the King.[8]

Aundely was probably not identical with the Nicholas Rouland (Roeland, Rueland) who in 1217 and 1218 was in charge of repairs to the *Tower of London*, and in 1220 was paid £1 for hiring a cellar to keep the King's wine in London.[9] But it was Aundely who on 23 January 1223/4 received a reward of £1 as did each of Henry III's three other master carpenters, THOMAS, Ralph (? RALPH BURNELL) and ROBERT (DE ALBEMUNT).[10]

From this time forward he seems to have been the senior carpenter in the royal service, but was concerned almost exclusively with the provision of engines of war, though in 1231 he was kept at *Windsor Castle* in charge of the works while the King's other carpenters were sent to Shropshire. At this time he was being paid 1*d.* a day by the Sheriffs of London.[11] In 1235 he build a new timbered hall at *Kempton Manor*, Middlesex, for the King. In 1236 he was put upon the same footing as the other master carpenters, of receiving 5*d.* a day when at work, and 3*d.* on other days.[12] For the rest of his life he seems to have drawn only 3*d.* a day, last paid to him on 1 May 1245.[13] On 8 December order was given to the Bailiffs of Windsor to pay to Huldeburg, late the wife of Master Nicholas the Carpenter, 1*d.* daily for her maintenance.[14]

¹ HLC, I, 80; ² HRL, 161, 195–6, 206, 209, 226; ³ CDE, 232–3; ⁴ Ibid., 241; ⁵ PRO, Pipe Roll 16 John, Rot. 15, m.j. (R.A.B.); ⁶ Ibid., Pipe Roll 17 John, Rot. 1, m.j. (R.A.B.); ⁷ Ibid. (R.A.B.); ⁸ HLC, I, 239; ⁹ Ibid., 345, 357, 415b; ¹⁰ Ibid., 582b; cf. 178b, 473, 527b; II 7, 13, 90, 100b, 117b, 141; ¹¹ CCR 1227–31, 477, 531; ¹² HKW, II, 965; CLR 1226–40, 247, and passim; ¹³ Ibid. 1240–5, 301; ¹⁴ Ibid. 1245–51, 13 (prints 'yearly' for 'daily')

AUSTYN, William (*fl.* 1415–1425)
Carpenter

Of Basingstoke; with JOHN WILLAM, carpenter of the same place, contracted in 1415 to make the flat roof of the church of *Hartley Wintney Priory*, Hants. On 20 February 1424/5 he entered into a bond in £40 with the Warden of *Winchester College*, along with a helier and a smith.

HMC, 15R (10), 174; *WCM* 19996

AYLMER, John [Aylemere, Elmar, -mer, Hilmare, Hylmer] (*c.* 1471–†1548) Mason

Mason of London; contracted on 5 June 1506, as partner of WILLIAM VERTUE, to vault the choir of *St. George's Chapel, Windsor*, before Christmas 1508 for £700. The work was to include the flying buttresses, cresting, and the series of King's beasts to bear vanes.¹ The original contract is lost; the copy from which it is known spells the name as 'Hylmer', but this mason was identical with a well-known London freemason whose name appears in several forms.

In 1512 and until about 1519 Aylmer was master mason at the building of the *Savoy Hospital*, taking 12*d.* a day, and having under him ROBERT BROMEHALL as warden at 10*d.*² (see also HENRY SMYTH). Between 21 July 1515 and 6 March 1517 he was also carrying out work at the *Tower of London*, as appears from an account of money spent for the king by Sir John Daunce: 'To John Hilmare, fremason, for copyng of a breke wall with a harde stone of Kent betwene the gate ayenst the Lion Towre of the Towre of London and the wacche house, and for makyng of an upright steyer of assheler from the Themys as highe as the grounde afore the wacche-house, with other amendementes, and the fynysshyng of the Toure Wharff' £66.³

John Aylemere of Southwark had worked for Wolsey at *York Place* in 1529 and on 28 January 1535/6 gave evidence as to Wolsey's supplies of materials for the work. At the time Aylmer was aged 64; he signed his deposition as 'John Elmar'⁴ This man had been asked to oversee work which WALTER MARTYN, mason, might have in hand at the time of his death in 1513,⁵ was executor of the will of Nicholas Marche, citizen and freemason of the parish of St. Bartholomew the Less, London,⁶ and overseer of the will of HENRY SMYTH, both in 1517.⁷ Marche described him as 'John Elmar son of Josu Elmar', while Smyth's will calls him 'Master Elmer'.

In 1531 HUMPHREY COKE, the King's Carpenter, appointed as one of his executors 'John Aylmere citizen and freemason of London'⁸ and in 1538 'Mr. Elmer' was a member of the Court of Assistants of the Masons' Company.⁹ John Hylmer, citizen and freemason, dwelling in St. Saviour's parish in the borough of Southwark, made his own will on 10 July 1548, and it was proved on 7 August.¹⁰ He desired to be buried 'within the Chapel of the Trinitee before the Alter beneath the steppes there as I have laid a marbull stone all redy for my burial with certain pictures'. He refers to 'my counting house' and 'the wardens of the Craft of the Fremasons of London', and mentions William Hylmer my brother's son dwelling in Essex, William Clerke now apprentice with Henry Hylmer my son, and describes household goods including pictures of a lord and a lady and many other pictures of men and women. These were probably brasses. To his son Henry he left his messuage called the 'Angell upon the Hope' and land at Edmonton.

(APD; BAA)
¹ AOG; ² HKW, III, 202; ³ MDA, 312 (A.O.) ⁴ LPH, X, 194; (S.P. 1–101, f. 206); ⁵ PCC, 23 Fetiplace (A.O.); ⁶ CCL, 43 Bennet; MR, XVI, 171; ⁷ PPR, Peculiar Court of Westminster, 127 Wyks (A.O.); ⁸ PCC, 5 Thower; ⁹ MHN, IV, 19–20; ¹⁰ PCC 10 Populwell; MR, XVI, 205

AYLMER, Thomas (*fl.* 1389–†1407) Mason

On 19 April 1389 contracted to reconstruct a window in the church of *Bradwell-juxta-Coggeshall*, Essex, for the sum of 5 Marks (£3 6*s.* 8*d.*). The window was 14 feet long and 10 feet wide and was to be completed before Michaelmas. The client was Sir John Hende, citizen of London and Lord Mayor in 1391 and 1404, a great benefactor to Coggeshall Abbey.

In 1395 Hende sued Aylmer for failure to perform the contract, Aylmer defending himself on the ground that the work had been well and sufficiently done within the stated time. The case was to go before a jury, but the Sheriff failed to summon a jury for the date set, and the case was adjourned.¹ Thomas Ailmer of London, 'masoun', was a mainpernor for William Shelford, chaplain, in April 1396.[2]

In 1394 and 1402 Aylmer and Joan his wife (daughter of Emma, late wife of William Temple, bladesmith, and kinswoman to Robert Moton, grandfather of said Emma) were concerned with house property in St. Clements Lane, Cannon Street, parish of St. Clement, London.[3]

Thomas Aylmer, mason, of the parish of St. Clement, Eastcheap, made his will on 27 August 1407; it was proved 24 September by his widow Joan, executrix and sole legatee.[4]

[1] EAS, NS, XXII, 354–5; [2] CCR 1396–9, 304; [3] LHR, 123 (115), 131 (11); [4] W.J. Williams in MR, XVI, 80; Archd. Ct. London I, f.179

Aylyn—see ALLEN

AYNHO, Nicholas de [Eynho] (fl. 1294–1295) Mason (Aynho, Northants.)

Master mason in charge of building a stone tower windmill in Dover Castle in 1294, with machinery made by JOHN OF HARTING, to a total cost of £36 6s. 11d. He was paid 3s. per week. In the next year he was working at St. Stephen's Chapel, Westminster.

HKW, II, 638; PRO, E.101–547–18

Aynsham, Henry de—see EYNSHAM

Baard, William—see BAYARD

Bacon, John—see BACON, William

BACON, William [Bakon] (fl. 1466–1468) Carpenter

With WILLIAM HARWARD on 25 June 1466 contracted to make by 1 August 1467 the floors and roof of the Schools at Cambridge for £33 6s. 8d.[1] Like Harward, he was of Halstead, Essex. The roof mentioned still exists, being that of the South Room of the Old Schools (previously the Old University Library). Payments to the carpenters for this work occur in the Proctors' Accounts of 1466–68.[2]

(A.O.)

[1] SHB, 535–6; WCC, III, 13, 93; [2] CGB, 'A' 55–6, 65–6

John BACON, also a Halstead carpenter, was engaged on the 'new work' at Peterhouse, Cambridge, in 1463.

WCC, I, 13

BAGBY, Robert de (fl. 1331–1361) Carpenter (Bagby, Yorks. N.R.)

Carpenter of York; took up the freedom of the city in 1331;[1] in 1361 he was paid £4 for his work on the Hall of the York Merchant Adventurers, building from 1359. He was probably the designer.

[1] York Mercers' account-book 1358–61 (A.R.)

BAGER, William (fl. 1549–1551) Carpenter

Master carpenter from Portsmouth, in charge of works on the fortifications of Alderney, C.I., in 1549–51, under the direction of JOHN ROGERS.

HKW, IV, 454

BAGWORTH, Peter de (fl. 1314–1326) Mason (Bagworth, Leics.)

Master Peter de Bagworth and several other masons of the Earl of Lancaster working at Melbourne, Derbs., came armed to Ravenstone on Sunday 29 September 1314, and assaulted William Gretheved who had killed Robert de Holewell in self-defence. Master mason working for the borough of Leicester in 1326, when 1s. 3½d. was spent on ale given to him and his men on various occasions. The community was also fined 3s. 4d. for having failed to supply Bagworth with his robe until he sued for it.

J.C. Cox in JDS, XXXI (1909), 121 (N.L.R.); SHB, 79

Baiard, William—see BAYARD

BAKER, John (fl. 1503–†1535) Mason

Was appointed master mason of Calais in 1503 in succession to RICHARD COMBES; his appointment was confirmed on 26 December 1509,[1] in succession to THOMAS FERRIER, and in 1528 he was being paid £16 16s. 4d. a year.[2] Between 1510 and 1512 large payments totalling over £300 were made to him for stone bought for the works.[3] From 1520 onwards he held the post jointly with his son WILLIAM BAKER; in 1528 he received £11 3s. 10d. for his fee. John Baker was still master mason at Calais on 10 April 1535 when he was commissioned to take materials for the works.[4] He died soon afterwards.

LPH, II, pt. ii, pp. 1441–1518; HKW, III, 342, 419 [1] LPH, I, 771; [2] Ibid., IV, pt. ii, 5102 (2); [3] Ibid., II, pt. ii, pp. 1441–1518; [4] Ibid., VIII, 632 (16)

BAKER, Richard (fl. 1459) Carpenter

Contracted in 1459 to make the roof of a granary at Felmersham, Beds., for King's Hall, Cambridge (now merged in Trinity College), for 13s. 4d., and also to provide structural timbers and doorposts for 3s. 4d.

SHB 532; (KHA, xii, f. 241)

BAKER, William—see BERKELEY

BAKER, William (fl. 1520–†1545) Mason

Was working under his father JOHN BAKER as joint master mason at *Calais* from 1520. In 1528 he was paid £11 3s. 10d.[1] By 1535 he was master mason at Calais, where work was in progress upon the 'Becham Bulwerke' for which Baker bought many thousands of bricks. In 1540–41 Baker was in charge of works at the castle of *Guisnes*. He died in 1545, when he was succeeded by JOHN WRIGHT.[2]

It seems possible that Baker was identical with the 'William Baker, Jurat of Folkestone', who in August 1539 incurred various expenses in connection with the building of *Sandgate Castle*, Kent, including 2s. for 'ij times Rydyng to the Downes to have certayn communicacon with master controller there concernyng th' use and custome of ffree masons and hard hewars'.[3]

HKW, III, 353, 357, 368n, 419
[1] LPH, IV, pt. ii, 5102 (2); [2] LPH, XXI, pt. i, 302 (3);
[3] KMM, 169

Bakon, William—see BACON

Baldwin Brickmaker—see DUTCHMAN, Baldwin

Bale, John—see LOOSE

BALE, William (*fl.* 1519–) Carver
'Gravor' of *Wymondham*, Norfolk, where with THOMAS STERLYNG he agreed on 7 October 1519 to make the image of a 'riding George' for the parochial church, in the abbey nave.

A, XLIII, 271

BALFRONT, Henry (*fl.* 1432–†1460) Carpenter
Was appointed for life master carpenter of the county of Chester on 26 May 1432, and on 8 May 1438 his grant was renewed to cover Flintshire as well. He died on 24 November 1460 and was succeeded by WILLIAM FRANKELYN.

DKR, XXXI

BALL, Robert, I [Balle] (*fl.* 1336–1337) Mason
Master mason (*cementarius*) in charge of work for the pittancer of *Norwich Cathedral* in 1336–37, on houses 'in the place once of J. Gerard'. Ball was paid 5s. 2d. for 3 weeks' work, and on another occasion 2s. for 6 days' work of himself and his assistant (*garcio*).

NCM, roll 1045

BALL, Robert, II [Balle] (*fl.* 1505–1506) Mason

In 1505–06 was paid for making the 'table' of the south aisle and the vestry window at *Holy Trinity Church, Cambridge*. The south aisle may mean the south transept.

A.O.   CWT, f.79A

BALWE, John (*fl.* 1447–1448) Carpenter
With JOHN HIKKE made seats for *Yatton Church*, Somerset, in 1447–48, for which they were paid £2 18s. 8d., in addition to expenses, and 4d. for drink on completion.

SRS, IV (1890), 85–9

BANBURY, John (*fl.* 1324–1326) Mason
Master mason in charge of works at *Portchester Castle* in 1324–26.

HKW, II, 787

Bank, Robert—see William SPILBERY

BANSTON, William [? Bauston] (*fl.* 1466–1467) Mason
Mason (*lathamus*) employed by the Bishop of Winchester in 1466–67 to provide masonry for works at the manor of *Downton*, Wilts., for £13 6s. 8d. The work was described as consisting of 5 'penons', one buttress, 6 windows, and one window in the chapel.

PRO, Eccl. 2–3–155834

'BANWELL, Master of' (*fl.* 1519–1522) Carver
An unnamed carver undertook to make the roodloft for *Banwell Church*, Somerset, on 6 December 1519, and it was structurally complete by 1522. The design was based on that of the new screen at St. Erth, Cornwall (now destroyed), which was visited by one of the Banwell churchwardens, with Richard Synger and John Morse, who received wages at the rates of 4d. and 3d. a day respectively. The sum of 4d. was paid 'for a paper to draw the draft of ye rode loft'.

C.S. Taylor in SAP, LI (1905–6), pt. ii, 74; BCR, I, 147

BARBOUR, John [Barbur] (*fl.* 1528–1543) Mason
One Barbour was named second to RICHARD LEE as one of the two master masons who on 31 December 1528 were shortly to take to Wolsey 'the whole platte of the college' at *Ipswich*.[1] He was probably the John Barbur of Ipswich, 'Free mason', who on 4 March 1541/2 entered into a bond in £30 to Lyonell Talmache of Helmingham, esquire, to make 'a Battlemente vpon the steple' of *Helmingham Church*, Suffolk, according to a contract, before 24 June 1543. The battle-

ment bears shields with the arms of Tolle-mache and the date 1543.[2]

John BARBOR, mason, was admitted free-man of Great Yarmouth in 1442.[3]

Thomas BARBOR, mason, paid 13s. 4d. rent to the Sacrist of Westminster Abbey in 1506–1509 for a tenement adjacent to Hen-ry VII's Chapel, then in course of building, and close to the house of JOHN CHENEY.[4]

(A.O.)

[1] LPH, IV, 5077; [2] HHA, Study bookcase, Long drawer, 2a/1; [3] RYF; [4] WAM 19762–64

Barcestre, John de—see BURCESTRE

BARNACK, John (fl. c. 1250–1263) Mason

Between 1250 and 1263 the Abbot of Peter-borough granted to John Barnack the abbey's mason, a messuage with the houses on it and the courtyard and meadow attached.

BPN, 188 no. 526 (N.L.R.)

BARNEBY, Stephen de (fl. 1351–1377) Carpenter

Took up the freedom of York in 1351;[1] with ROBERT DE DOUNOM, carpenter, on 14 June 1377, contracted to repair the gaol of York.[2] He was probably related to William Barnby of York, carpenter, whose son John Barnby disposed of lands in York in 1409.[3]

[1] YCF; [2] SHB, 453–4; (PRO, E.101–598–24); [3] CCR 1405–09, 526

BARNET, Thomas [Barnett] (fl. 1350–1386) Mason

A working mason (cementarius) at the Tower of London from September 1350 to May 1351 at 6d. a day;[1] was one of the sworn masons of the City of London in 1368, 1370, and 1371;[2] and in 1376, with RICHARD ATTE CHERCHE and HENRY YEVELEY was concerned in a property transaction in Guildford and the neighbourhood.[3] On 15 February 1376 Bar-net was in possession of two shops in the parish of St. Mary Woolchurch which he held by the courtesy of England in right of his deceased wife Katherine, kinswoman of Michael Tullesan (Tholesan), by whom he had had issue, since dead.[4] In 1377 when he is named as 'latamus', in 1380 with his second wife Alice, and in 1386 he was concerned with the disposal of properties in the parishes of St. Thomas Apostle, St. Mary Wool-church, All Hallows, Barking, and St. Matth-ew, Friday Street, London.[5]

[1] PRO, E.101–471–3; [2] CLB 'G', 223, 228, 257, 279; [3] LSF, 145; [4] CIP, XIV, 283 no. 287 (N.L.R.); [5] LHR, 105 (73), 108 (138), 114 (118)

BAROWE, Thomas (fl. 1478–1485)

Although appointed to the office of Master Mason of Lancashire in August 1478, and maintained in the post by Henry VII in 1485, this was a sinecure, since Barowe was the king's cook.

HKW, II, 1059; III, 178n

BARSHAM, Thomas [de Jernomuta] (fl. 1415–1421) Carver (? Barsham, Suff.)

Carver of Great Yarmouth, Norfolk; in 1415–16 he was paid £3 6s. 8d. for making 12 figures of the Apostles, and 3s. 4d. for a 'woodwyse' (wild man) for the new chapel of Mettingham College, Suffolk. Between 1416 and 1421 he received payments totalling £37 6s 11d. for making and painting two images with their tabernacles, and for painting a 'tabula', all for the high altar of the chapel.

BM, Add. MS. 33985, ff. 91v.–121v.

BARTELOT, John (fl. 1428–1429) Mason

Was paid £5 13s. 4d. for making a stone wall next Southampton Castle in 1428–29, with a reward of 3s. 4d. and 8d. to him and his fellows for drink.

HMC, 11R. III, 140

Bartewe—see BERTY

BARTHOLOMEW the Carpenter (fl. 1355–   ) Carpenter

With his fellows was paid £8 in 1355 for making anew the chapel (corpus communis eccle-sie) at Clarendon Palace, Wilts.

PRO, E.101–459–29; (L.F.S.)

BARTON, John I (fl. 1415–† c. 1451) Mason

A working mason at York Minster by 1415–16, and until 1421, he took up the freedom of the city in 1427. By 1444 he had succeeded JOHN BOWDE as master mason at the Minster, but in 1450 JOHN PORTER was twice sum-moned from Lincoln to give advice, and had become master by 1452.[1] It is possible that Barton had died in 1450, when his house in Lop Lane was described as 'late of John Barton'. This may, however, mean only that he had ceased to occupy a tenement allocated to the master, since his post was not a full time one. In the spring and summer of 1448 Barton was working on the Guildhall of York at 6d. a day, under ROBERT COUPER, the city's chief mason, who took 3s. 4d. a week.[2] It is probable that John was the father of THOMAS BARTON, as this would account for the know-ledge shown by the latter at Durham of the design for the York central tower never completed. John Barton was perhaps identical with JOHN BURTON I or II.

ACY, 191; HPS, 204
[1] *YML*, Fabric Rolls; YCF; BHY, I, 237; RFY, 59, 62n., 65; [2]*YCM*, Chamberlains' Accs., vol. 1A, *ff*. 6ff.

BARTON, John II (†1483) Mason

Mason of Tadcaster, Yorks., whose will was made on 13 January and proved on 7 April 1483. He desired to be buried in the church of South Cave 'in the south corner', left a robe to his apprentice John Osboldson, and mentions a daughter Agnes and his wife Margaret whom he appointed executrix. Barton's grave slab still exists in the church at South Cave: a cross between a shield of arms and a man's bust, with a mason's square and the initials 'I.B.'

PCY, vol. v, 209; Mr. and Mrs. B. Gittos

BARTON, Roger de (*fl.* 1372–1383) Mason

On 2 October 1372 Roger de Barton, mason, contracted to build five gables, windows, and two chimneys etc. at the manor of *Storeton*, Cheshire, a house belonging to the Stanley family. The gables were to be similar to one built earlier by another mason, William Wyntreton.[1] On 6 Sept. 1383 agreed with Henry Percy, Earl of Northumberland, to execute certain works at *Cockermouth Castle*. Barton was to build a wall already begun between the kitchen and the south wall of the castle, with towers above the gateway, together with two side walls for the chapel above the gate, with a staircase, doors, and windows. The chapel walls were to be 3½ feet thick. For the main wall he was to receive 22 marks (£14 13s. 4d.) per square rod, each rod counted at 7 customary ells (*vlnas usitatas*), and for the work of the chapel 12 marks (£8) per rod, without deduction of openings (*absque mensuracione ostiorum fenestrarum sive caminorum in toto dicto opere nisi tanquam pro integro pariete*). Barton had to find all materials and carriage, except that the Earl would provide ironwork, timber for scaffolds (*pro scarfaldis*), 8 loads of firing for burning lime, and free access to a sufficient quarry. The work was to be finished within two years, payment being made at the rate of £20 a quarter until the measured total was reached.

[1] *BL*, Add. Ch. 66294 (*D.H.T.*) [2] *PRO*, E.210–5627 (Ancient Deed D.5627) (*H.M.C.*)

BARTON, Thomas (*fl.* 1447–*c*. 1475) Mason

Was probably closely related to JOHN BARTON I, and took up the freedom of York as a mason in 1447.[1] After a major fire at *Durham*

Cathedral in 1459, Barton was working on repairs there, and was apparently master mason there from 1465 until some ten years later.[2] His design for the lower stage of the central tower, as then rebuilt, owes much to the earlier designs for the lantern of York Minster; the upper storey — intended but never built at York — was added at Durham by JOHN BELL, junior.

HPS, 179, 204; cf. M.G. Snape in TDN, NS III, 1974, 71–4
[1] YCF; [2] DAR

BATAILE, John de la [de Bello] (*fl.* 1278–†1300) Mason

From June 1278 to 1280 was undermaster of the works at *Vale Royal Abbey*, Cheshire, at 3s. a week, under WALTER OF HEREFORD. In 1291–93 he was joint master (with SIMON PABENHAM) of the works of five of the *Eleanor Crosses*, those at Stony Stratford, Woburn, Dunstable, St. Albans, and Northampton. He died in 1300, leaving shops in Newgate Street, London, and houses at St. Albans. Perhaps father of THOMAS DE LA BATAILE and very possibly identical with JOHN DE LEDES.

KJI, 73; SWL, I, 146

BATAILE, Thomas de la (*fl.* 1325–1326) Mason (? *Battle Hall, Leeds, Kent*)

Master Mason (*cementarius*) of Leeds, Kent; in 1323–25 he was paid £66 13s. 4d. for his work on four turrets of the wall next to the White Tower of the *Tower of London* on the east; the work was done by task.[1] In 1326 he was in charge of work at *Caerphilly Castle* for Hugh le Despenser.[2] Perhaps son of JOHN DE BATAILE. Thomas may well have built *Battle Hall* at *Leeds*, a work of this period in highly developed Kentish style.[3]

(LKC)
[1] *PRO*, E.101–469–7 (*L.F.S.*);[2] A.J. Taylor in CSB, XIV, pt. iv (May 1952), 299–300; [3] TPD, II, 46

BATE, Thomas (*fl.* 1380) ? Mason

Of Corby, Lincs.; an inscription gives his name as 'maker' of a column of *Ropsley Church*, Lincs., at Michaelmas 1380.

CAR, 87

BATEMAN, Colmet (*fl.* 1396) Sculptor

In 1396 was embellishing with carvings the south portal of the Abbey of St. Bertin, now the *Cathedral of St. Omer*. His surname strongly suggests English origin or extraction.

CCS, 44 (*A.O.*)

BATES, Robert (Batys) (*fl.* 1515–1535) Carpenter

Was appointed a master carpenter in the

Tower of London in July 1515, with 8*d.* a day, for his services in the wars.[1] In August 1523 he was with the army at Calais, and continued to receive his £12 3*s.* 4*d.* a year until 25 March 1535.[2]

[1] LPH, III, pt. ii, 3288, p. 1371; [2] *Ibid.*, II, pt. i, 2736. pp. 873–7; IV, pt. i, 1939 (q), p. 868

BATES, Thomas [Betes] (*fl.* 1433–1435) Mason

Contracted to build a chapel to the south of the chancel of the church of *St. Mary-on-the-Hill, Chester*, on 22 June 1433. The work was to be under the supervision of JOHN ASSER, junior, chief mason of the County Palatine, and was finished in about two years. Betes was to be paid £20 and a gown for the work.

SHB, 503; ECM, 31; LCRS, CIII, 48

BATH, Robert [Bathe, Robert Carpenter] (*fl.* 1361–1396) Carpenter

Carpenter working in *Oxford* from 1361–62, when he was paid 17*s.* 11*d.* for work on a new room at *Queen's College*, while he appears there again in 1369. At *Merton College* he seems to have been master carpenter at the building of the library, being paid large sums for what must have been contract work: £104 14*s.* 4*d.* in 1371–73, £90 in 1377–78, and £14 13*s.* 4*d.* in 1378–79, besides smaller items. On 21 Sept. 1363 Robert Bathe, carpenter, was living in a house belonging to St. John's Hospital within the East Gate on the south side, and from 1374 to 1376 he was tenant of a house of the hospital in St. Mary Magdalene parish. In 1379 he was paid by Merton for work outside the college, and in the following year he paid 12*d.* to the Lay Subsidy and was living in St. Giles.

Further minor works at Merton from 1383 onwards were followed by his spending 41 weeks at *Ipstone Church*, Bucks., in 1391–92, for which the college paid him at the rate of 2*s.* 6*d.* a week, with 2*s.* a week for his servant. This was probably for work on the chancel roof. As Robert Carpenter, Bath is last heard of in 1395–96 when he was making library windows at Queen's College for 13*s.* 4*d.* His roof for the Merton College library is probably that which survives, though it was altered and ceiled in 1503.

GOC

Battle—see BATAILE

Batys—see BATES

Bauston, William—see BANSTON

BAYARD, William [Baard, Baiard] (*fl.* 1204–1205) Engineer

Was in charge of work at *Nottingham Castle* in 1204–05

(WPS; APD); PR

BAYNES, Robert (*fl.* 1474–1501) Mason

Took up the freedom of the city of York as a tiler in 1474, but was appointed Common Mason of *York* on 2 May 1499. He was dismissed from office in 1501, when he was succeeded by CHRISTOPHER HORNER.

RCHM, *York*, II, 174

BEARE, Nicholas (*fl.* 1341) Carpenter

In November-December 1341 Master Nicholas Beare, carpenter, working with his fellows at *Exeter Cathedral*, was paid 3*s.* 6*d.* weekly for two weeks and 2*s.* 6*d.* for a third week.

EDC, roll 2632 (A.M.E.); AEC, ii, 267, 307

BECKELEY, John [Bockeley] (*fl.* 1430–1455) Mason (*Beckley, Oxon.*)

Of Headington, Oxon.; in 1430–32 was at work on the tenement called *Hans* in *Oxford*, for New College, building a wall, windows, doors, and chimneys there for which he was paid £6 19*s.* 3*d.* in 1430–1 and 18*s.* 10*d.* in 1431–2.[1] He contracted to rebuild the north transept of *Thame Church*, Oxon. in 1442. For his main contract he was paid £4 13*s.* 4*d.* The timberwork was made by JOHN EAST. Many details are given in the churchwardens' accounts, from which it appears that the quarry-master of the same name, dead by 1442, was not the mason.[2] In 1452–53 he provided 986 feet of stone for the *Divinity Schools, Oxford*, at 2*d.* a foot, receiving a total of £8 6*s.* 0*d.*, and 4*d.* for his expenses at the quarry.[3] He was probably identical with John 'Bockeley', stonemason, who purveyed carriage for the works at *Eton College* in June 1441.[4] Beckeley was doing odd jobs for *New College* from 1452 to 1455.[5]

[1] *NCO*, Oxford City Accs., 9–10, 10–11 Hen. VI; [2] BAJ, VII (1901–11); GM, 1865, pt. i, 176–89; [3] *UCO*, Smith transcripts, X, 305–11 (*A.O.*); [4] CPR 1436–41, 573; [5] GOM, 75

BEDEFORD, Robert de [Lenginour] (*fl.* 1286–1304) Carpenter (? *Bedford, Lancs.*)

Was a carpenter in charge of the great engines of war and also concerned with scaffolding for fortifications in the campaigns of Edward I in Wales from 1286, and later in Scotland. He was a master carpenter paid at 12*d.* a day in 1303–04, while with the infantry of Edward I's army in Scotland. Bedeford was in charge of the making of houses in *St. Andrews Castle*, and works at Dunfermline.

BM, Add. MS. 8835, *ff.* 21v., 81, 90 etc.; HKW, I, 412n, 417; II, 1033–35

Beek—see BEKE

BEK, John (*fl.* 1525–1526) Carpenter

Master carpenter, named second after RICHARD GREYHORSE, in charge of repairs at *Tickenhill Manor*, Worcs., in 1525–26. Each took 8*d.* a day.

HKW, IV, 279

BEKE, Richard [Beeke] (*fl.*1409–†1458) Mason

Was working at *London Bridge* at 3*s.* 9*d.* a week in 1409 and later, with special rewards of 13*s.* 4*d.* in 1411 and 1412, and of 10*s.* a year in 1413–16; in September 1417 he succeeded JOHN CLIFFORD as chief bridge mason, taking a yearly fee of £1 in addition to his existing wages. Beke's wife Alice was bequeathed a piece of silverware by Clifford's widow Lettice who died in 1418.[1] Owing to a temporary enforcement of the Statute of Labourers, Beke only received 3*s.* 4*d.* a week from April 1425 to March 1426. In November 1412 the Bridge accounts record a payment to Beke of 12*s.* for 12 tons of ragstone. He was presumably the Richard Beke of Southwark who witnessed deeds connected with some Bridge House properties on 14 February 1428/9.[2]

He continued in his office at the Bridge until 1435, when he was absent for three weeks in February, and left for good at the end of March. On 1 Jan. 1434/5 he had been appointed master of the works at *Canterbury Cathedral* for life, at 4*s.* a week, with a convenient house, or £1 a year in lieu, 8*s.* for fuel, 10*s.* a year for clothes, or a livery, and two pair of hose. If he should become ill and have no power 'to be stere hym selft but for to lye stylle in hys bedde, or be privyd of hys bodyly sygzth and blynde', his wages were to be reduced to 2*s.* a week, with the same allowances as before.[3] From 1432 he had been a consultant at Canterbury, as is shown by his receiving livery of the Prior.[4]

In 1438 the Mayor of London wrote to the Prior of Canterbury asking that Beke should be allowed to inspect London Bridge and advise as to its preservation. Another journey may be indicated in 1446, when the sum of 5*d.* was 'spendit on the mason of Crystchirche for to have ynsyzt yn the Cane stone for the

stepill' of *St. Mary's, Sandwich*. This suggests that either Beke, or less probably his warden, was called into consultation.[5] His name appears regularly as an esquire receiving livery of the Prior of Christ Church, Canterbury, from 1432 to 1457.[4]

Beke died on 16 November 1458, leaving £2 to the work of Canterbury Cathedral, and to the refectory a silver cup with a cover.[6] His obit was kept on 17 November, as he had been admitted to fraternity of Christ Church, Priory on 22 July 1440.[7]

Beke was not one of the great Canterbury designers, but he was in charge of a great deal of work, including the strengthening of the crossing piers and building of the lowest internal stage of the central tower, the addition of tabernacle work to the base of the south-west tower (from 1449), the completion of the north transept and Lady Chapel (*c.* 1448–55), and various works of less importance, including the maintenance of the great complex of surrounding buildings.

KJI, 86; KJL; WDC
[1] *PCC*, 42 Marche (*A.O.*); [2] *LBH*, Deeds E.44, H.71; [3] SHB, 590–1; [4] *Bodl.*, Tanner MS. 165; OCC; [5] BHS, 363; [6] CAS Publ., XXXIV, 76; [7] *BM*, Arundel MS. 68, *ff.* 48v., 63

Bekeley, William—see BERKELEY

BEKHAM, John (*fl.* 1439) ? Mason (*Beckham, Norf.*)

Of Raynham, Norfolk; in 1439 purchased from the Trinity Guild of (King's) Lynn 40 marble stones of two feet in size, and 80 of one foot. Bekham was presumably a carver or monumental mason.

LCR, G.d.61

BEKKE, J[ohn] (*fl.* 1491–1492) Mason

Was probably the mason in charge of the building of the spire of *Yatton Church*, Somerset, in 1491–92.

SRS, IV (1890), 118

BELDHAM, Robert (*fl.* 1471–1473) Carpenter

Carpenter to the Bishop of Winchester at *Farnham Castle*; in 1471–72 made scaffolds for work on the outer wall on the east side of the castle and worked on the carpentry of the new tower. In this and the next year he was paid £7 1*s.* 6*d.* out of a total of £12.

PRO, Eccl. 2–3–155836–7

BELE, Thomas [Bole] (*fl.* 1521–1533) ? Mason

Carried out repairs to the chancel of *Hock-

ham Church, Norfolk, and also to *Hockham Rectory*, between 1521 and 1533, for the Cluniac Priory of Thetford, which had impropriated the rectory. Bele may have been a local mason, or a servant of the monastery responsible for miscellaneous works.

CUL, Add. MS.6969, *ff.* 155v., 199v., 221, 227v., 241

BELL, John, senior (*fl.* 1418–1441) Mason

In 1418 entered into a recognizance to the Bishop of Durham as a surety for THOMAS HYNDELEY, the Bishop's master mason.[1] He was working for *Durham Cathedral Priory* from 1420 when he was engaged upon the Infirmary with his apprentice.[2] He seems to have been in charge, taking 3s. 4d. a week for 45 weeks and also carrying out various parts of the work by agreement. Work on the Infirmary continued for some years, and was not finished until 1429, when the rebuilding of the Prior's Lodging began.

In 1422–23 one John Bell owed 8s. to Finchale Priory, a cell of Durham, apparently as arrears of rent, and this may have been the mason.[3] Bell was the leading mason of the '*Operarii Prioris*' in 1427–28,[4] and probably succeeded Thomas Hyndeley as master in or soon after 1433.

In 1429 the wooden spire of the central steeple of Durham Cathedral had been struck by lightning, and extensive alterations costing £233 6s. 8d. were done on the tower between 1430 and 1437, apparently under Bell's supervision. Meanwhile the Prior's Lodging had been completed in 1432. In 1438–39 Bell and WILLIAM CHAUMERE inserted tracery in four windows of the choir for £2 14s. 8d. and made a doorway into the monks' cemetery for £1 1s. 8d.[5] Two years later he and Chaumere inserted tracery in one of the nave windows at a cost of 12s.[6] The Prior of Finchale owed Bell 6s. 8d. in 1439, possibly for work done there.[7]

[1] DKR, XXXIII; [2] DAR, I, 270; [3] RFP, clxxxiv; [4] DAR, III, 709; [5] *Ibid.*, II, 408, 410; [6] *Ibid.*, 410; [7] RFT, ccxxx

BELL, John, junior (*fl.* 1478–1488) Mason

On 25 October 1478, described as 'mason', and on 13 July 1486 (*latamus*), was a witness to claims to sanctuary at Durham.[1] Possibly son or grandson of JOHN BELL, senior. He was master mason during the building of the upper stage of the central tower of *Durham Cathedral*, from about 1483 to 1490. The accounts for 1483 show that he had a fee of £6 13s. 4d. while his apprentice William Saun-

derson took £4 4s. 7½d. for 55 weeks. The total expenditure on the tower from 1483 to 1488 was £281 10s. 5d.[2]

On 1 April 1488 Bell was appointed 'special mason' to the Prior and Chapter for life as from the Whitsun following. The conditions of his appointment were that he should not depart from his occupation without special licence, that he should have one apprentice of his own, and train another to be appointed by the Prior. His fees amounted to 10 marks (£6 13s. 4d.) a year, payable in eight instalments, as well as a special payment of 10s. each winter at Martinmas (11 November); he was also to have a garment competent to his degree, and the house in which THOMAS BARTON, mason, dwelt while he lived, rent free. If Bell were to be debarred from work by continued infirmity or great age, he was to have a pension of 4 marks (£2 13s. 4d.) a year.[3] The agreement specified that Bell was to serve the chapter for 'all their works of masonry with imagery and other', thus implying that he was a skilled sculptor as well as mason.

He was perhaps identical with the John Bell who took up the freedom of York in 1465, and was a working mason at *York Minster* in 1472.[4]

[1] SD; [2] DAR, II, 415; [3] SHB, 592–4; DST, ccclxxiii; [4] AQC, XLIV, 231, 235

BELL, John, III (*fl.* 1476–1503) Mason

Although he lived and worked for over a quarter of a century in Cambridge, John Bell was probably a new arrival in 1476, when he was engaged as warden of the masons under JOHN WORLICH at *King's College Chapel*, where works were resumed in that year on a restricted scale. His position is described in a document dated 17 August 1476 concerning a dispute in which Worlich and he were chosen as two of the arbitrators.[1] 'Belle lathomus' appears as a guest of the college in hall on Lady Day that year and again on 9 April. In the first week of August there is a note in the kitchen accounts that he began to have commons in the college 'with the fellows'.[2] In the following year up to Michaelmas 1477 he was charged 44s. 7d. for his commons. During these two years he was paid 35s. for 'setting' and made two journeys to Huntingdon to buy stone.[3] Bell did not depart on the appointment of SIMON CLERK as master mason in the summer of 1477, and he seems to have been employed at least intermittently during the

18

next two years. In September 1479 he was paid 3s. 4d. for supplying 'serches' for the well in one of the tenements belonging to the college.[4] In March 1480 he worked for 17 days in the church of *St. John the Baptist* close to the college at 3s. 4d. a week.[5] From 1480 to 1485 the building of the chapel went on at an increased tempo, but it is difficult to judge from the documents how actively or regularly he was employed. He continues to appear occasionally as a guest in hall, but it was with the servants, not the fellows, that he had supper on 7 October 1481.[2] There is a reference to his house in that year;[6] the following year, on 3 October, John Bell of Cambridge, 'ffremason', and Elisabeth, his wife, were granted a lease, for 40 years or for their lives, of a college tenement in St. Edward's parish, probably on the west side of the High Street, at a rent of 13s. 4d. a year.[7] In March 1483 John Bell and Roger Paynter were paid 11s. 2d. for repairing two chimneys in the Provost's Lodge.[8] He was not among those named in the impressment commission of 28 August 1484, so that if he was still on the building staff his status was inferior to that of WILLIAM WRIGHT, who was probably Simon Clerk's deputy. There are occasional small payments to him, as well as appearances of his name in the kitchen accounts, up to 1491. On 18 December 1490 he was a guest in company with JOHN WASTELL, who is named before him.[2] In February and March 1495 he was a guest on three occasions, probably when working on the windows of the hall.

Meanwhile, he had been employed at *King's Hall* during the year 1484–85 to lay a pavement in the chapel.[9] He was working again at King's Hall in 1497–98, when he received 4s. for making a chimney in a new building.[10] The following year he was paid 38s. 6d. by one of the proctors of the university in satisfaction of an old debt in respect of work performed by him at *Great St. Mary's Church*.[11] The rebuilding of the church had been begun in 1478; it then hung fire for ten years, but was continued energetically from 1488 until 1493, when work seems to have been suspended for another ten years owing to lack of funds. In 1503 a long-standing dispute between the university and the town, which had involved them in expensive litigation, was temporarily settled, and to the composition which was drawn up between them there was attached a list of privileged

persons which included 'Belle the Mason of the University'.[12] Taken in conjunction with the entry in the proctors' accounts this might be regarded as evidence that Bell was master mason for the rebuilding of Great St. Mary's, but the nave arcades, clerestory and chancel arch, which probably date from after 1500, are characteristic of the work of John Wastell, and though Bell may have been responsible for the tower, begun in 1491, Wastell is more likely to have provided the design for it. Bell's status was probably that of mason in charge on the spot during the earlier stages of the work. No reference to him later than 1503 has been found.

It is possible that the Cambridge John Bell was identical with the mason of that name who was made a freeman of York in 1465 and was employed at the Minster in 1472 (see BELL, JOHN, junior, above). A contemporary namesake who was five times Mayor of Cambridge between 1494 and 1512 is not known to have been a relation of the mason. He came from Earith in Huntingdonshire, was a fishmonger and also had brewing interests, and on his death in 1523 was buried in St. Nicholas Chapel, King's Lynn, in which town he seems to have settled in his later days.[13]

A.O.

[1] *Bodl.*, Cambs. Charters 34; WAP, I, 171; [2] *KCM*, Kitchen Accs., s.a.; [3] *KCM*, Mundum Book 1476–77; [4] *Ibid.*, 1478–79; [5] *Ibid.*, College Accs., vol. vi; CAC, IV, 353; [6] *KCM*, College Accs., vol. iv; [7] *Ibid.*, Leger Book, *f.* 118; [8] *Ibid.*, College Accs., vol. v; Mundum Book 1482–83; [9] *TCM, KHA*, xvii, 232; [10] *TCM, KHA*, xix, 194; [11] CGB 'B', I, 120; [12] *CCM*, Cross Book, *f.*102; CAN, I, 270; [13] GMC, 20; CBD, 146; Will, *PCC*, 15 Bodfelde

BELL, Roger (*fl.* 1520–1524) Joiner

Of Ashfield, Suffolk; on 30 June 1520 he (named second) contracted with JOHN NUN to make the roodloft of *Great St. Mary's Church, Cambridge*;[1] it was completed about two years later. In 1524 he was taxed at 10s. on lands valued at £10 in the parish of Ashfield; this was the largest sum paid by anyone in the parish.[2]

(A.O.)

[1] CAS Publ. x, 63–7; xxv, 36, 53; [2] SGB, x, 63

BELL, William (*fl.* 1482–1497) Mason

Master mason of *Oxford*; was paid 12d. for laying the first stone of the cloister of *All Souls College* on 26 May 1482, and in the same year was master mason in charge of the building of the chancel of *Wolvercote Church* for Merton College. In 1494–97 he was master for the

BELLAMY, ROBERT

work of *Balliol College* including the south front and old gate-tower now destroyed. This was very like that of St. Bernard's (i.e. *St. John's) College*, in progress from 1483 or soon afterwards.

GOM, 82; R.H.C. Davis in OXN, XI/XII (1946-7), 87–8

BELLAMY, Robert (*fl.* 1500) Carver

One of the sculptors of a dragon, lion, and leopards for the Great Hall of the *Tower of London* in 1500, and may have belonged to the same family as THOMAS BELLAMY II and WILLIAM BELLAMY II.

(LKC, 230; LWR, 171); *BM*, Egerton MS. 2358

BELLAMY, Thomas, I [Belamy] (*fl.* 1473) Carpenter

With JOHN DORAUNT, was working at the Prior's great chamber at *Ely* in 1473, when the two men were paid jointly 8*d.* a day.

CUL, Add. MS. 6387, 47

BELLAMY, Thomas, II [Belamy, Bellame] (*fl.* 1548)? Carver

Probably son of WILLIAM BELLAMY II; bought the carved work of the rood of Lydd Church, Kent, for 10*s.* when it was pulled down in 1548. In view of the circumstances of such demolition at that period, it seems probable that the purchase was on account of family sentiment rather than profit. He was probably the 'belamy' who received minor payments for work at Lydd in 1558.

FRL, 399, 424–5

BELLAMY, William, I (†1513) Carver

Of Bury St. Edmunds. Will dated 9 February 1512/13, proved 11 May 1513. He bequeathed 3*s.* 4*d.* to the church of St. James in Bury and the same sum to the church of Our Lady in Tuddenham. He mentions his brother John, a son Stephen, who was under age, and his wife Christian.[1] Tuddenham St. Mary is a village 2½ miles south-east of Mildenhall. The will of William Bellamy of Tuddenham was proved 31 July 1461[2] and that of Thomas Bellamy of Tuddenham, husbandman, dated 27 June 1495, proved 20 September 1495.[3]

A.O.
[1] *BW*, vii, 23; [2] *Ibid.*, ii, 297; [3] *Ibid.*, v, 74

BELLAMY, William, II [Belamy(e), Belemy] (*fl.* 1519–1535) Carver

Carver of Canterbury, who made a new roodloft and figures for *Lydd Church*, Kent, between 1519 and 1528. In 1535 he made seats for the 'Lady chancel' there.

FRL, 328, 338, 340, 346, 369–70

Benckys, Thomas—see BINKS

Benet le Fremason—see CROSSE, Benedict

BENETT, William (*fl. c.* 1500) Carpenter

Carpenter to *Leeds Priory*, Kent, *c.* 1500, when he was paid fees at the rate of £1 16*s.* 8*d.* a year.

Bodl., MS. Top. Kent d.4 (R); AC, II, 56

Benkes, Thomas—see BINKS

BENSON, — [Bensun](*fl.* 1534) Mason or Bricklayer

In 1534 was working on the central tower of the church of the *Augustinian Priory* at *Little Dunmow*, Essex. Geoffrey Stether, the Prior, paid to 'Bensun' 24*s.* 'for A foote of the stepull' in the middle of May and £11 0*s.* 7*d.* for another 9 feet and a half in early October.[1] No further work appears to have been done up to the Dissolution of the Priory in 1536. Lime for the steeple was being bought by the Prior in 1528, but there is no record of the amount built between that year and 1534.[2]

A.O.
[1] *PRO*, SC6. Hen. VIII, 937; (VCH, *Essex*, II, 153); [2] *BM*, Add. MS. 20021

BEREWIK, John [Berwyke] (*fl.* 1436–1438) Carpenter

Carpenter of Romsey, Hants.; undertook to frame a timbered house and to erect it after its carriage to *Winchester* on a site in St. Pancras Street (Middle Brook Street) there, for the Warden of Winchester College. The house was 'to be y made as the trasyng schewith y drawe in a parchement skyn', between 16 April and 1 August 1436, and for his work Berewik was to receive £7 13*s.* 4*d.*[1] Expenses allowed to college servants in 1437–38 for riding to Romsey on two occasions 'to speak with Henry Berwyke carpenter' may refer to the same man.[2] Berewik entered into a bond with Winchester College in the sum of £10 on 4 December 1438.[3]

[1] SHB, 583–4; *WCM* 1011; [2] *WCM* 22113; [3] *WCM* 20088

'Berham', Helyas de—see DEREHAM

BERKELEY, William [Baker] (*fl.* 1479–1483) Carver

Chief carver at *Windsor Castle* from 1479 to 1483, during work on St. George's Chapel. He was given a yearly reward of £2 13*s.* 4*d.* and 10*s.* for a robe.[1] His name appears on one occasion as 'Baker', and he may perhaps be identical with the William Baker who in the same years painted frescoes on the walls of

Eton College Chapel, across the Thames.[2]
[1] HWC, II, 400–6; *PRO*, E.101–496–19 (*L.F.S.*); [2] WCC, I, 412

BERRY, William (*fl.* 1434) Carpenter
Was paid £3 13s. 4d. for making the carpentry work of a barn at *Ormesby*, Norfolk, in 1434. In addition, £1 2s. 10d. was paid for timber and 8s. 8d. for its carriage from Norwich, while a stonemason (*latome*) received 6s. 3d. for working on the 'fotyng' with his servant for 7½ days. The sum of 1s. 2d. was spent in bread, ale and cheese at 'le Reyseng' of the barn.
HTM, IV, 176

BERTRAM the Engineer [Bertrand] (*fl.* 1248–1250) Engineer
King's Engineer to Henry III between 1248 and 1250; allowed wages of 1s. a day and expenses. He does not seem to have been concerned with building works.
CLR 1245–51, 212, 231, 248, 277, 293

BERTY, Robert (*fl.* –†1502) Mason
Mason of Bearsted, Kent, father of THOMAS BERTY; he died between 4 October 1501 and 17 February 1501/2.[1] He was probably identical with the Robert Berty who farmed the rectory lands of Bearsted for a rent of £4 13s. 4d. paid to Leeds Priory c. 1500.[2]
[1] BFG, 464; [2] Bodl. MS. Top. Kent d.4(R); AC, II, 56

BERTY, Thomas [Bartewe, Barthew, Bartiewe, Bartiue, Bartue, Bartuu, Bartyew, Bert, Bertie, Bertye] (*c.* 1485–†1555) Mason
Elder son of ROBERT BERTY, mason, of Bearsted, Kent, was under 20 when his father made his will (proved 17 February 1501/2) on 4 October 1501. Thomas and his younger brother William were left the reversion to property at Bearsted, after the death of their mother Marion (or Margaret), and also their father's 'working toles such as be for macyns crafte'; their sister Joan, as yet unmarried, was left a house in 'Yerlys Lane', Maidstone.[1] In June 1509 Robert Berty's widow Margaret, late of Godstone but now of Colchester, received a general pardon,[2] and at Christmas 1517 Richard, son of Thomas Bartewe, was born in Hampshire.
Thomas was probably settled in *Winchester* by this time, having married Aline, daughter (according to later pedigrees) of. . . Say of Shropshire. A Thomas 'Bartue' was living in the High Street in 1515–16, and this was almost certainly he.[3] On 23 May 1520 Thomas Berty was granted a void ground at New

Bridge, Winchester, for the term of 40 years, paying to the bailiffs a fine of 40s. and a quit-rent of 1s. 2d. a year.[4] About this time he may have been concerned with work for the Bishop of Winchester at the Priory of *St. Mary Overy, Southwark*, including the design for the top stage of what is now the cathedral tower. In 1532-33 he rendered accounts as deputy of Philip Parrys, treasurer of Wolvesey in Winchester,[5] and was at the same time carrying out the vaulting of the presbytery aisles of *Winchester Cathedral* by contract, receiving a part payment of £5 in this year in addition to an annual retaining fee of 13s. 4d.[6] On 17 February 1533/4 his son Richard was admitted to Corpus Christi College, Oxford, aged just over 16 years.[7] On stylistic evidence it may be suspected that about 1536–40 Berty may have designed the *Holy Ghost Chapel, Basingstoke*, for Lord Sandys; for whom he may also have worked at *The Vyne*. In 1537 he was styled 'yeoman' and was living at Winchester with his wife 'Alice'; from then until 1541 he held office as Bailiff of the Soke, the bishop's liberty. He also held much property in the south and east suburbs.[8]
In the spring of 1538 'Bartyew' was supervising the works at *Titchfield*, where the buildings of the dissolved monastery were being transformed into a spacious residence for Thomas Wriothesley, afterwards Earl of Southampton. In this work Berty seems at first to have been advised by Sir RICHARD LEE, but afterwards to have disregarded Lee's proposals. Surviving letters refer to consultation between Wriothesley's agents and 'Bartyew' concerning windows and chimneys 'in the. . .north yle beneth and other places', and quote his conclusion 'that smoke shall not be avoyded by the chymneys of your chieffe lodgings if the steple stand'.[9]
On 2 August 1538 the Prior of St. Swithun's Cathedral Priory at Winchester granted to Thomas Bartew, bailiff of the Soke, a lease for 81 years of two tenements and a garden on the east side of Kingsgate Street and on the south of the former Whitefriars, with a plot called the 'Alees' (Allies), a rent of 1s. 4d.; and on 15 November of the same year the Prior further granted to him a rent of 40s. for his laudable service in times past, with the supervision of the works of the monastery.[10] The priory was surrendered to Henry VIII exactly a year later. On 13 March 1543/4 'Thomas Bartu of the fortresse

of Hurst Captayne' took a lease from Winchester College of a close of pasture called Dogger's Close (near The Allies), for 20 years at a rent of 13s. 4d., agreeing to hedge and enclose it. The counterpart lease bears the signature 'By me Thomas Bartu'.[11]

During 1539 Berty was given control of the royal building works at *Calshot Castle*, and also at *Cowes* in the Isle of Wight,[12] and between 1541 and 1544 he built *Hurst Castle*, of which he was appointed the first captain.[13] He was also at work on *Southsea Castle* in 1544.[14] The customers of Southampton and Thomas 'Barthew' were ordered in 1543 to report to the Privy Council concerning the arrest of a certain Spanish ship,[15] and in 1546 a letter was directed by the Council to the Chancellor for Augmentations, ordering him to deliver 15 fodder of lead to Thomas 'Bartue' or to one Rigewaye for the fortifications at Haselnorth (*Hasilworth Castle* near Portsmouth),[16] which indicates that Berty was still employed in an architectural capacity in addition to his administrative post as Captain of Hurst. In 1550 he supplied lime for the building of bulwarks at Jersey.[17]

Part of the inherited property at Bearsted was sold by Richard and Thomas 'Bertye' for £60 in 1546,[18] and in 1550 Thomas Bertie of Bearsted, Kent, Captain of Hurst Castle, received a grant of arms.[19] Thomas 'Bartuu' died in 1555, and an inventory of his goods made on 18 May showed that his possessions amounted to £38 8s. 10d. at Hurst, as well as £14 12s. 1½d. at Winchester, where, too, he had a house. Administration was granted to his widow Aline on 6 June.[20]

Berty (or Bertie) is of historical interest as the father of Richard Bertie who later married Katherine, widow of Charles Brandon, Duke of Suffolk, and in her own right Baroness Willoughby de Eresby. But Thomas was himself a man of talent and character, and played a large part in the transformation of the older Perpendicular architecture into the new Tudor-Renaissance style. It seems probable that he was engaged by Fox, Bishop of Winchester, for the design and execution of his remodelling of the presbytery of the cathedral, including the Perpendicular rebuilding of the aisles and their vaults, of the great east window and gable, and the erection of the flying buttresses. The stone screens which stand between the presbytery and aisles bear the date 1525, and carry a parapet with Italian Renaissance enrichments. Fox's chantry chapel has closely similar Gothic detail, but lacks the Italian work, while the later chantry of Bishop Gardiner (1531–1555) containing what are practically replicas of certain Gothic details, is thoroughly classicised in its general design. These works must almost certainly be attributed to Berty, and typify three stages of his artistic development, but the applied Italian detail was doubtless the work of foreign carvers. Closely similar in feeling and detail to these works at Winchester are the Chantry Chapels at *Christ Church Priory* of Prior John Draper II, dated 1529, and of the Countess of Salisbury, of approximately the same date. Both of these are architecturally akin to Fox's screens and chantry at Winchester, and almost identical details are employed: here, too, foreign carvers carried out surface enrichment.

Berty's later domestic and military work at Titchfield and for the Crown belongs to the contemporary official style, which had been initiated by HENRY REDMAN when King's Master Mason. Though unremarkable, the design at Titchfield is impressive and is a most skilful example of the conversion of an existing building (the monks' church) to different uses. Berty may have owed his rapid advancement in some measure to the complaisance with which he adapted his designs to suit the employment of Renaissance decoration, and it is noteworthy that the district in which it worked should so largely coincide with one of the chief areas of early employment of Italian detail. Incapable of the higher imaginative flights of the style which had produced Bath Abbey and Henry VII's Chapel, Berty accepted the fashionable imported detail to please the taste of his exalted patrons — its tentative employment upon the screens at Winchester was safe from Fox's criticism, for the aged Bishop was blind.

J.H.H. in HBT, 26–9

[1] BFG, 464; [2] LPH, I, i, 438(3), p. 252; [3] *D.K. Win*; [4] BBB, 135; [5] BFG, 473; [6] KCR, 216ff.; [7] RPP, I, 35; [8] *D.K. Win*; [9] LPH, XIII, i, 749; [10] *WNC*, Reg. 3 (1533–38), *ff.* 33v, 84v; [11] *WCM* 809A; [12] RPP, I, 38; LPH, XIV, i, 398, p. 151; cf. HKW, IV, 537; [13] RPP, I, 38; [14] HKW, IV, 557; [15] LPH, XVIII, i, 447; [16] *Ibid.*, XXI, i, 154; [17] APC, 413; [18] RPP, I, 35; [19] *Ibid.*, 38; [20] *SG*, Ac. 4088 (F.J. Baigent: Hampshire Wills MS.), p. 130

Berwyke, Henry—see BEREWIK, John

Bery, John—see BURY

Betes, Thomas—see BATES

BEVERLEY, Robert of (*fl.* 1253–†1285)
Mason (? *Beverley, Yorks.*)

Probably of Beverley, Yorks., where he may have been concerned in the building of the choir and transept of the Minster — this work was completed shortly before 1260, when the High Altar was consecrated.

Robert is first heard of in London in 1253 when he was paid £1 12*s.* 0*d.* for working four bosses for the work of *Westminster Abbey;*[1] in 1259 he was working at *Westminster Palace* under JOHN OF GLOUCESTER at the rate of 3*s.* a week, and at the Abbey where he was one of the responsible masters of the works and corresponded concerning the supply of stone with Richard le Wyte of Purbeck.[2] Towards the end of 1260 he succeeded John of Gloucester as King's Master Mason and chief mason of Westminster Abbey on John's death, and on 27 April 1261 was ordered to supply Reigate stones for the Queen's Lodging at *Windsor Castle*: 200 blocks were to be sent in April, and another 300 in August, from the store at Westminster.[3] He was also to allow freestone and lead to be taken for a conduit for the Friars Preachers (*Blackfriars*) of *London.*[4] On numerous occasions Robert of Beverley witnessed deeds at Westminster.[5] In April 1262 the Sheriff of London was to build *Holborn Bridge* of stone and lime by the advice of Master Robert of Beverley the King's Mason. With Master ODO, one of the King's Carpenters, he repaired part of Westminster Palace after a fire in 1263,[6] and for the next four years he was keeper of the works at the Abbey, with ALEXANDER the Carpenter and John of Spalding, a clerk.[7] For these works he received £100 in 1264, and on the following 30 January his own emoluments were augmented by a grant of two robes yearly from the royal wardrobe 'as Master John de Gloucestre used to receive'. Along with Master Alexander, Robert received payments for the works, both at the Palace and the Abbey, from 1263 onwards. At intervals from 1269 to 1272 he 'viewed' the accounts for the Abbey works, and about this time probably provided the designs for the new work of *Hayles Abbey*, Glos., which was in progress from 1270 to 1277.[8]

On 7 November 1271 he was granted a patent as surveyor of the royal works at the *Tower of London*, at the castles of Windsor, *Rochester, Hadleigh*, and manors of *Guildford, Kempton*, and *Havering*. In this document he is called the King's 'principal carpenter' but this must have been a mere scribal error of '*carpentarius*' for '*cementarius*'. At about this time he was purchasing building materials for the works.[9] On 25 February 1272 he was allowed £11 0*s.* 4*d.* for works which he had lately done at the Tower. A year later he was in charge of the making of the tomb of John of Windsor, son of Edward I.[10] His rate of pay was 6*d.* a day, but payable for every day in the year, instead of for six working days in the week.

Later, he prepared the Abbey for the Coronation of Edward I, which took place on 19 August 1274, and from a list of about this period it appears that the Abbot of Westminster by his special grace allotted to Master Robert a provision of wine such as the convent's own officials had.[11] Soon after this he was designing the new works of the outer ward and barbican at the Tower of London, as planed boards for moulds were obtained for him.[12] He was keeper of works at the Tower and Westminster Palace, and rendered accounts for both places from the Coronation in 1274 to May 1277.[13] For the former works he was to have 30 oaks from Windsor Park to burn lime, and another 30 from the Forest of Essex, in June and July 1275;[14] on 21 November he was given a tun of wine by the King, and his fees were increased to 12*d.* a day while working in London, and 16*d.* when journeying outside it.[15]

In January 1276 there is a record that he had received £40 to buy timber for works in the Palace, and 300 pounds of wax for making an image for the King, while Robert himself had £3 6*s.* 8*d.* for making this image.[16] It seems very likely, as Lethaby suggests, that this was a temporary figure of Henry III, whose bronze effigy by William Torel was not cast until 1291. Further works in Westminster Palace were carried out by Master Robert during this year, for which he received over £200 for materials and labour, and with his wife Cecilia he was concerned in a transfer of property at Pirford in Surrey, a manor belonging to Westminster Abbey.[17]

Other works in 1276 were on the Mews at *Charing* (the site is now Trafalgar Square), and he spent 1,000 marks at the Tower,[18] as well as 2,000 marks in 1277, when he was paid 7*s.* a week according to the accounts for the works there.[19]

For the years 1277–79 he was also in

charge of operations at Westminster Palace.[20] In 1278 he had to audit the accounts of the works at the Tower, Westminster, and the Mews,[21] and in January 1277/8 he sat on a commission *ad quod damnum* which decided that the wall of London between Ludgate and the Thames should be pulled down and rebuilt farther west, so as to include the new church and buildings of the *Blackfriars*, for which Robert of Beverley was very probably the architect.[22] Out of a period of 53 weeks in 1278–79 he was working at the Tower for 50,[23] and that the works there were being pressed forward at high speed is shown by the fact that £100 a week was being supplied during the greater part of the year.[24] This work went on through 1279, when the Byward and Middle Towers were completed; in May Master Robert was to have 200 beech trees from the woods of Woodford, Waltham, and Loughton in Essex,[25] and his fees of 12*d*. a day were paid continuously in the Tower accounts until 24 June 1284.[26] Between August 1279 and November 1281, Master Robert also had charge of extensive works at *Kings Langley Manor*, Herts.[27] The upper part of the western Inner Curtain (above the lowest arrow-slits), with the Beauchamp Tower, was only begun in 1281, and finished, even to the timber hoards, by 1284.

In May 1282 and March 1284 Robert of Beverley received orders to audit the accounts, being named as a 'Master of the King's Works'[28]; he died on 11 April 1285[29]. The charge of the works was thenceforward given to the Constable of the Tower. Master Robert's widow Cecily is mentioned in 1293.[30]

Robert of Beverley as a designer is known to us principally from the unaltered parts of the Byward and Middle Towers of the Tower of London, and from the outworks recently uncovered there (1936–39). The ribbed vaults in the chambers of these towers are of great beauty, as are the characteristic fireplaces, and we cannot doubt his artistic inspiration as well as the ingenuity of his planning, though the latter must have owed much to Edward I's military experience in France and Palestine. Master Robert's works at the Tower transformed it into the earliest English example of a true 'concentric' castle, of the type soon to be perfected at Harlech, which was in all probability designed by Robert's successors, JAMES OF ST. GEORGE and RICHARD LENGINOUR.

It is worth noting that at Goodrich castle in Herefordshire there is a barbican almost identical in size and plan with that at the Tower. This latter was completed in 1279, and the Goodrich one may belong to the works in progress in 1280 and 1282, for William de Valence, uncle of Edward I. Either Robert of Beverley designed this also, or it was copied from his work at the Tower.

We have already seen that he probably designed the new work at Hayles Abbey, begun in 1270. This consisted of a five-sided apse with a fully developed chevet of five chapels, similar to the chevet at Westminster, and there can be little doubt that it was at any rate a work of the royal school of craftsmen, for the patron was Richard, King of the Romans, brother of Henry III. It is somewhat remarkable that the neighbouring Abbey of Winchcombe should have engaged for the architect of its own new work, begun about 1278 to rival that of Hayles, WALTER OF HEREFORD, who was to become a royal master craftsman equally famous with Robert of Beverley. Again, while Beverley was concerned with the building of the Blackfriars in London, Hereford was later to bring masons for the building of the Greyfriars.

At Westminster Abbey the 'first work' was finished at the time of John of Gloucester's death, and included the whole of the presbytery and transepts, as well as the Chapter House. The 'second work', consisting of the first four bays of the nave, was carried out by Robert, though he adhered, as had John of Gloucester, to the main principles of design laid down by HENRY OF REYNS in 1245. The close adherence at Westminster to the design of an earlier period has often been remarked on, but it is hardly less characteristic of Beverley Minster, where Robert of Beverley may have been trained. At Westminster, if the wax image made by him in 1276 was indeed that of Henry III, it is probable that Torel's brass figure of 15 years later was copied from it, and may thus preserve the form of Master Robert's work. If so, Robert was a sculptor of the very first class; in support of this theory, it may be pointed out that the face of Henry III's effigy is much more lifelike than that of Eleanor of Castile, made at the same time, while one would expect the reverse to be the case, since Henry had been dead nearly 20 years. If the head were originally the work of Master Robert, this would be explained, since he must have known the old King intimately, and would have had a death-mask to work from.

Robert's work at Windsor was not considerable, and is lost; of Hayles Abbey and the barbican at Goodrich little beyond the plans remain, and the same is true of the London Blackfriars. We have nevertheless enough of his art at the Tower and Westminster Abbey to conclude that he was one of the greatest masters of English architecture, and his official position made him the acknowledged chief of his craft for the quarter century preceding his death, a period of vital development in planning and design.

CLR, *passim*
[1] ANJ, XXVIII, 147; *PRO*, E.101–467–4; [2] *PRO*, E.101–467–3; HMC, 4R, 176; *WAM*, 16000 (g); [3] CCR 1259–61, 373–4, 426; *WAM* 16000 (d); [4] *WAM* 16000 (b, c); [5] *WAM* 17362 of 1 Feb. 1271, and the following undated deeds, 13753; 17336; 17345–8; 17387; 17391; 17400; 17460; 17466; 17504; 17541; 17543; [6] LKC; [7] CPR, 12 Nov. 1265; LWR, 95–6; [8] LKC; [9] *PRO*, C.47–3–7 (52); [10] *PRO*, E.101–471–5, 8; [11] LKC; [12] *PRO*, E.101–467–6 (6); [13] *PRO*, E.101–467–6 (2,5); [14] CCR 1272–9, 192, 200; [15] *Ibid.*, 757–8; [16] CPR 1272—81, 131; [17] LSF; [18] LKC; [19] *PRO*, C.47–3–48 (3); [20] LKC; [21] CCR 1272–9, 444; [22] CPR 1272–81, 258; [23] *PRO*, E.101–467–7 (4, 5, 6); [24] CPR, 26 June 1278; [25] CCR, 1272–9, 528; [26] *PRO*, E.101–467–9, 10; [27] HKW, II, 971; [28] CCR 1279–88, 154, 258; [29] HKW, I, 206; [30] *WAM* 5705

BILTHAM, Ralph (*fl* 1423–1425) Carpenter
Carpenter of Norwich; between 1423 and 1425 made the new roof for the chancel of *St. Saviour* there, rebuilt by JOHN SPYNK and JOHN WESPNADE.

NRO, DCN rolls 531, 533

Bindle, John—see BYNDYLL

BINKS, Thomas, [Benckys, Benkes, Bynkk, Bynks, Bynkys] (*fl.* 1486–1517) Carpenter
In 1486/7, 1487/8, 1489/90, and 1490/1 was one of the wardens of the London Carpenters' Company, and master in 1495/6, 1496/7, 1500/1, 1501/2, 1510/11, and 1514/15.[1] [Between 1498 and 1501 Binks was master carpenter at the rebuilding of *Richmond Palace*, Surrey. He was presumably designer of the roof of the great hall, 100 feet by 40 feet in size. It was described as 'not beamyd ne brassid, but proper knotts craftily corven, joyned and shett to guyders (together) with mortes and pynned hangyng pendaunt from the side roff in the grounde and floure'.[2] This suggests a timber ceiling with carved bosses and wall-posts (pendants). Binks was also the master carpenter employed on the king's new chapel at *Greenwich* in 1499–1504.[3]] In June

1505 he was paid the final-instalment on his indenture 'for the gallery & [in?] the orchard' at *Richmond Palace*.[4] On 30 August 1507 a sum of £66 13s. 4d. was paid to Henry Smyth, 'towards the finishing of [the hall and chapel at Richmond] through Bynks faults', suggesting that his work had been defective.[5] He was living on 31 August 1517, when he made a conveyance of the Bear Inn.[6]

A.O. (HKW, III, 27–9, 195)
[1] JPC, 622; MCR, II, 256; [2] FRH, 164; [3] HKW, IV. 97. 223; [4] *BM*, Add. MS. 7099, f.93; [5] *PRO*, E.36–214, p.186; [6] MCR, II, 256

BIRCH, John (Birche) (*fl.* 1511–1513) Carver
In 1511–12 was paid £6 13s. 4d., and in the following year £1 10s. 0d. for work in the new chapel (Lady Chapel) and Prior's Chapel at *Rochester Cathedral* (*pro complanacione nove capelle et pro factura desse in capella Domini Prioris*).

HRC, 87

BIRD, John I [Byrd(e)] (*fl.* 1510–1532) Carpenter
In 1510 John Byrde, carpenter, contracted with the Mercers' Company of London to build a dwelling house for the school master of St. Paul's Churchyard for £113 6s. 8d.[1] John Byrd of London, 'the younger', carpenter, who may have been the same man, or identical with JOHN BIRD II, contracted to build a three-storeyed tenement before 1526, when he was sued in connection with the work. Litigation continued until 1532. In October 1528 Bird was described as 'late of London, carpenter'.[2]

(*N.L.R.*)
[1] LWA, 377; [2] J.H. Baker in SEL, 93, 94: i, 109, 112, 115; ii (text) 307–10

BIRD, John II (*fl.* 1531–†1554) Carpenter
Was appointed on 26 May 1531 to be chief carpenter of the works of the town and marches of *Calais*, in succession to THOMAS JAY deceased, with the usual fees and the old timber of ships and other perquisites.[1] In 1539 he was a commissioner for the fortification of Guisnes and Calais.[2] He died in 1554.[3]
[1] LPH, v, 278 (40); [2] *Ibid.*, XIV, i, 398, p. 151; [3] HKW, III, 353, 420

BIRD, John [Birde, Byrd] (*fl.* 1512–1522) Mason
Mason of Taunton, Somerset; on 24 December 1512 was granted by the Prior of St. Swithun's Cathedral Priory, Winchester, four loads of wood, and £3 6s. 8d. a year for life in consideration of Bird's good service past and

to come in repairing weirs and doing other works.[1] In 1522 Bird was concerned with the building of a new chancel at *Bishop's Hull Church*, Som., for the Prior of Taunton.[2]

[1] *WNC*, Register 2 (1496–1533), *f.* 76v.; [2] SDN, VII, 264–6

BIRD, Richard [Brid] (*fl.* 1439–1464) Carpenter

In 1439 paid 12*d.* to the London Carpenters' Company; he was warden of the Company in 1440–41;[1] and was sworn as a viewer of his craft in the city in the same year.[2] He may well have been the designer of the original roof of the *London Guildhall* whose stonework under JOHN CROXTON was approaching completion at the time. Our knowledge of the Guildhall's original roof, destroyed in the Great Fire of 1666, is limited to a small sketch reproduced in James Smith's *Specimen of Ancient Carpentry* (1736). Its width of 49 feet was with the single exception of Westminster Hall, the largest open span covered in England in mediaeval times.

On 13 February 1449/50, Richard Bird and JOHN HAYNES, citizens and carpenters of London, contracted to make a pair of desks with panelling and a parclose about the organ loft of the *Beauchamp Chapel* at *St. Mary's, Warwick*. They were to receive £40 for their workmanship, the executors of the Earl of Warwick finding all timber and carriage.[3] The summarised accounts for the work show that the executors spent £35 2*s.* 6*d.* on the costs of 'lez Deske and Organ-house' in 1450/1, and a further £16 0*s.* 4*d.* in the following year. The fine desks with panelled backs are still in the chapel. In 1464 Richard Byrde and others conveyed a tenement in the parish of St. Botolph without Aldgate, which afterwards became a property of the London Bridge House.[4]

[1] MCR, II (1914), 3, 5, 6; cf. 9, 10; [2] CLB, 'K', 257; also CPM 1437–57, 57, 69, 75, 86, 127; [3] DHW; BAA, IV, 11; [4] *LBH*, Deeds, I.42, H.49

BIRD, Thomas [Bryd] (*fl.* 1434–   ) Carpenter

Of Tyryngton (Terrington, Norfolk); contracted on 12 May 1434 to make a landing-place for the Abbot of Bury at *Tilney*, Norfolk, for which he was to receive £13 and a gown of the suit of the abbot's yeomen.

SHB, 504–5; (*BM*, Add. MS. 14848, *f.* 74v.)

BIRLYNGHAM, Simon (*fl.* 1496–†1499) Carpenter (? *Burlingham, Norf.; Birlingham, Worcs.*)

Built the new *Hall of the Pewterers' Company of London* in 1496–98 for £40. Before the design was made members of the Company went 'wt the Carpenter to have a vewe' of several roofs, of the Haberdashers' and Carpenters' Halls, Papey Hospital, and the Dean's roof at Hackney.

An inventory of the goods of 'Symond Byrlyngham', carpenter of London, was taken at Cambridge on 15 December 1499 and shows that he had houses in Wood Street, his chief residence; in Bishopsgate Street, and at Sheen. Debts owed to him amounted to £316 2*s.* 5*d.*, of which £32 15*s.* was for 'diverse stuff boughte' for the King; money was also owed by the Master of Lincoln's Inn, the City churches of All Hallows the Great, St. Alban, St. Margaret Pattens, St. Mary-le-Bow, and St. James; by the Companies of Vintners and Leathersellers, and by Sir John Shaa for gates made at *Old Ford*.

WHP, I, 82–6 (*L.F.S.*); W.M. Palmer in N & Q, 11S, VI, 21 Sep. 1912, 227 (*N.L.R.*)

BISCHOPE, Richard (*fl.* 1487–   ) Carpenter

Searcher of the carpenter's craft of York (with JOHN COUPER) in 1487, when on 24 February (1486/7) they and the keepers of the Fraternity of the Resurrection made an agreement with William Bewyk, Prior of the Austin Friars of York. The convent was to sing two trentals of masses yearly for the souls of the brothers and sisters of the Fraternity, and a trental of masses after the decease of any brother, on payment by the Carpenters and the Fraternity, which was maintained by them, of 10*s.* yearly and 5*s.* for the celebration of the trental for each deceased member who should be notified to the Convent. In lieu of cash payment of 6*s.* 8*d.* of the yearly 10*s.*, the carpenters leased to the Convent two messuages 'upon the corner of the lendyng next Saynt Leonerdes to the watter of Ouse adjoynyng', in length 9 yards and in breadth 8½ yards, for the term of 99 years.

(*A.R.*)   YCM, B/Y, f.201b

BISHOP, William [Busshopp] (*fl.* 1449–†1474) Carpenter

In 1449–50 £7 6*s.* 8*d.*, part of a total sum of £16, was paid to William Bishop for making the roof for the new chancel of *Wighton Church*, Norfolk, begun ten years earlier by JAMES WODEROFE.[1] In 1467–8 William Busshopp, wright, made a roof for the north aisle of *East Dereham* church, Norfolk.[2]

The will of William Bysshop or Busshop, of the city of Norwich, carpenter, was proved in 1474.[3] Bishop wished to be buried in the church of St. Martin 'de Balliam' in Norwich. His house and goods were left to his wife Alice and, after her death, to his younger son John, still a minor. His elder son, Master Robert, was already in priest's orders and was left 10 marks to celebrate for his father's soul for a year. Bishop's own father is referred to as Nicholas Grene, and his brother as John Grene; they were to be joint executors with another son Thomas, who was to have all the tools of Bishop's trade except for 5s. worth to each of his three apprentices: Thomas Welsham, John Gyrlyng and William Awbry. The will was made on 13 April 1474 and twice proved, on 4 January and 9 February 1474/75.

[1] *NCM*, Cellarer's Roll 168 (*S.A.C.; P.C.*); [2] *NRO*, Phillips MSS, Box 5 (*P.C.*); [3] *CNN*, 87, 88 Gelour

BISLEY, Richard de [Birselegh, Bissele, Burseleye] (*fl.* 1351) Carpenter (*Bisley, Surrey*)

Master in charge of works at *Hertford Castle* in 1351.

CPR 1350–4, 60, 80

BLACKSHAW, William (*fl.* 1515) Carver

Of Westminster; in 1515 William Blackshaw 'Kerver dwellyng in Saynt Stephens Ally' was paid 31s. 8d. for stuff and workmanship 'of the Hous of the Sacrament at the High Awlter & for the halpace at the bak of the same' in *St. Margaret's Church, Westminster*

A.O. MMW, Appendix, p. 28

BLAKETOFT, Richard de (*fl.* 1324–1328) Carpenter (*Blacktoft, Yorks, E.R.*)

Carpenter of York, admitted to the freedom of the city in 1324–5.[1] In 1328 he was associated with Master HENRY DE KINGSTON as one of the chief carpenters during the works on the *Archbishop's Palace* to fit it for use by Queen Philippa during the campaign against the Scots. He was paid 6d. a day, Sundays and Feasts included.[2]

[1] *YCF*; [2] *PRO*, E.101–501–8 (*L.F.S.*)

BLASTON, Robert de (*fl.* 1351–) Carpenter (*Blaston, Leics.*)

Agreed in 1351 to serve the Cambridge Corpus Christi Guild for 1d. a week less wages than was customary in the town; the work done was probably on the Old Court of *Corpus Christi College.*

(A.O.) CGR, 37

BLASTON, Roger de (*fl.* 1338–1339) Mason

Freemason at *Carmarthen Castle* in 1338–39, when with his fellow, Roger de Devonschira, he repaired the walls and five towers for 11 weeks for the agreed sum of £3 6s. 8d.

WWH, III, 57

BLEDDYN, Gwilym ap Ieuan (*fl.* 1447–) Carpenter

Was master carpenter of *Kidwelly Castle* in 1447, when he was paid a salary of £24 13s. 4d.

CHC, I, 302

BLITHERE [Blitherus, Blittaere, Blize, Blutere] (*fl.* 1070–1091) ? Mason

Evidently from his name a Saxon Englishman, was master of the works at *St. Augustine's Abbey, Canterbury*; he was described in 1091 as 'the very distinguished master of the craftsmen and director of the beautiful church' (*praestantissimus artificum magister, templique spectabilis dictator*). He was the designer of Abbot Scotland's new church begun about 1070 and completed in 1091.[1] He is probably to be identified with the Blittaere or Blize who at the time of Domesday survey (1086) held Seasalter, Kent, of the monks of Christ Church Cathedral Priory.[2]

[1] SMC, 103 (Historia translationis S. Augustini episcopi, auct. Gocelino p. 17); [2] VCH, *Kent*, III, 217a, 261b

BLOCKLEY, John de [Blockle, Blockcleya, J. de Westminster] (*fl. c.* 1250) Carpenter (? *Blockley, Worcs.*)

Master carpenter of Westminster; in the reign of Henry III he appears in documents of Westminster Abbey and reference is also made to his son Nicholas.

WAM, 'Domesday', ff. 533v., 550, 552v.

BLOIS, Robert de (*fl.* 1186–1210) ? Mason

Master of works of the town of Blois, France, and there built the church of *St. Nicholas*, whose choir he began in 1186; the church was completed in 1210. According to Bauchal he was called to England in 1195 to build *Lincoln Cathedral*, but the evidence for this statement is not clear.

BAF, 57

BLOUND, William le (*fl.* 1292–) Mason

Was in charge of works at the *Palace of Westminster* in 1292, with ROBERT OF WALTHAM, carpenter.

LKC, 180–1

BLOUNHAM, John (*fl.* 1350–1351) Mason (*Blunham, Beds.*)

First working mason (*cementarius*) at the building of a postern at the *Tower of London* from June 1350, and was paid 6*d.* a day; from March 1351 he was put on a weekly rate of 3*s.* and termed *apparilator*, and after 10 May was left in charge of the work which had been under the direction of JOHN LEICESTER.

PRO, E.101–471–3

BLOWE, Hugh [Blouwe] (*fl.* 1237–1238) Mason

Was master mason at *Marlborough Castle* in 1237–38 during works on the great hall; he was paid 2*s.* 6*d.* a week, and had a pair of gloves. He was also paid for making windows at task. His brother, Roger Blowe, also worked at Marlborough, taking 4*d.* a day.

PRO, E.101–476–3 (*G.P.J.*)

Blutere—see BLITHERE

Bochor, John—see BOCHOR, Richard

BOCHOR, Richard (*fl.* 1437–   ) Millwright

Richard Bochor and John Bochor of Pluckley, Kent, millwrights, contracted on 6 November 1437 to build a fulling mill at *Chartham* for the Prior of Christ Church Canterbury. The work was to be finished by 29 September 1438, and the price was to be 22 marks (£14 13*s.* 4*d.*).

SHB, 509–10

Bockeley, John—see BECKELEY

Bocton, William—see BOKTON

BODECOTE, William (*fl.* 1375–1376) Carpenter

Chief carpenter at *Abingdon Abbey* in 1375–76, when he and two other carpenters were paid 6*s.* 6*d.* for three weeks at task for making of windows (? shutters) above (*super*) the Chapter House. He also received 5*s.* by agreement for a tunic with hood. For work on the roof of the south side of the abbey church he and three others were paid £1 2*s.* 4*d.* and board for four weeks.

AAA, 27

BODEKESHAM, William (*fl.* 1351–1371) Carpenter (*Bottisham, Cambs.*)

Bodekesham was the usual mediaeval spelling of the Cambridgeshire village of Bottisham. His name figures among those of seventeen carpenters whose arrest was ordered in March 1351 for withdrawing without licence from the works at *Hertford Castle* for which they had been impressed by the Sheriff of Essex.[1] In 1369–70 he was a salaried carpenter of the sub-Sacrist in the abbey of *St. Edmund at Bury*; he received 12*s.* for a robe, £3 9*s.* 4*d.* in wages by the year and an annual fee of 20*s.*[2] His will is undated, but occurs between wills of December 1369 and October 1372 in the earliest Bury register.[3] He made a bequest of his tools to the Sacrist of the abbey. One of the witnesses was William Mason, no doubt WILLIAM HECHAM, the abbey mason.

A.O.

[1] CPR 1350–4, 80; [2] BCM, Sacrist's Roll, A–6–1–3; [3] BW, i, 35

BOKINGHALE, Robert de [? Roger de] [Bokenhale] (*fl.* 1307–1308) Carpenter (*Bucknall, Lincs.*)

On 8 April 1307 was granted by the Chapter of *Lincoln Cathedral* a yearly pension of 9 marks (£6) as long as he should be the carpenter to the church, and that he should hold the office for life. On 9 April 1308 he took oath to serve the chapter faithfully as master carpenter of the church, and to observe the conditions laid down in his contract of employment.[1]

One Roger Carpenter was employed by the Chapter of Lincoln in 1320–21, and in 1324–25 appears as Roger de Bokenhall, making a new chamber in Micklegate, Lincoln at task for £2 3*s.* 4*d.* He was presumably identical with the 'de Bokenhale', carpenter, who was paid £6 13*s.* 4*d.* in 1336–37 for making a certain new chamber for the poor clerks.[2]

[1] LDC, A.2–22, *ff.* 6v., 11; [2] Ibid., B.j, 2–5

BOKTON, William de [Bocton] (*fl.* 1307–   ) Carpenter

Master carpenter employed at *Knaresborough Castle* in 1307 to direct the work of making a lodge and a tracing house for the masons under HUGH DE TICHEMERS

HKW, II, 689

BOLAZ, Thomas (*fl.* 1309–   ) ? Mason

On 24 November 1309 Thomas Bolaz, assigned to supervise the works of the King's houses at *Dublin* was granted £20 for their repair.

IPC, I, pt. i, 12

Bolde, John—see BOWDE

Bole, Thomas—see BELE

BOLE, Walter le (*fl.* 1341–†1349) Mason

Was in charge of works at *Westminster Abbey* from 1341 until his death in 1349, and was probably designer of the works at the south end of the east cloister walk in 1345. The Abbey accounts for 1341–42 show that in that year he was paid £20 for repairs and for 1 great pillar made by special agreement, as well as £3 for making parapets. He also received dress, boots, gloves, and his food.[1] In 1346 he sold to the Black Prince a ship called *La Marie* for the purpose of carrying stone to the prince's works at Kennington, Surrey.[2] Bole's will, proved in July 1349, shows that he lived in the parish of St. Andrew, Castle Baynard, and that his wife Matilda had died before 1348. He was succeeded at the Abbey by JOHN PALTERTON.[3]

William Asshurst, clerk, son of John Asshurst, woodmonger, and his wife Margery, kinswoman of Walter Bole 'maszon' disposed of tenements in St. Andrew's parish in 1410.[4]

[1] *WAM*, 23452 A and B; [2] *BPR*, I, 29; [3] *SWL*, I, 603–4; [4] *LHR* 137(85)

BOLRON, John (*fl.* 1407–1435) Carpenter
(*Boldron, Yorks. N.R.*)

Took up the freedom of York in 1407,[1] and in 1411 rebuilt *York Castle* bridge.[2] With his wife Matilda was admitted to the Corpus Christi Guild of York in 1429–30[3] and was evidently a carpenter of some standing in the city, for he was chosen by Richard Russell, a prominent York merchant, to be the carpenter for the new works at the church of *St. John the Baptist, Hundgate, York*. The passage from Russell's will (made 1 December, proved 10 December 1435) runs: 'And I will that John Bolron, carpenter, shall make a door, a ladder, and all the woodwork for hanging bells in the tower.'[4] The church of St. John has disappeared.

[1] *YCF*; [2] *PRO*. E.364–45, rot. C; [3] *SS*, LVII, 30; [4] *PCY*; *CWY*, vi; *YTE*, II, 53

BOLRUN, Ralph (*fl.* 1212–1241) Mason
(*Bowerham, Lancs.*)

Mason (*cementarius*) to the castle of *Lancaster* from before 1212 to 1241, when he was holding a carucate of land in 'Bolrun' (Bowerham in Lancaster) worth 2½ marks (£1 13s. 4d.) by this serjeanty. His father Vivian de Bolrun, a benefactor of Cockersand Abbey, had held by serjeanty before Ralph, but probably because Ralph was succeeded by a daughter, Maud, in 1241, the serjeanty was commuted for a yearly payment of 5s.

BOF, I, 370; *HRB*, II, 465; *VCH, Lancs.*, VIII, 37–8

BOLTON, Edward (*fl.* 1488–1503)
Carpenter

Succeeded WILLIAM FRANKELYN as master carpenter of Chester and Flint in 1488, and probably was dead by 1503 when OLIVER BOLTON took over the office.

HKW, III, 418

BOLTON, Hugh (*fl.* 1537–1552) Carpenter

Succeeded OLIVER BOLTON as master carpenter of Chester and Flint on 21 December 1537, and was himself succeeded by WILLIAM BOLTON in 1552.

DKR, XXXI (1870)

BOLTON, John (*fl.* 1412–1413) Mason

Was master mason in 1412–13 at the building of a new parlour in *Stockton Manor*, Durham, for the bishop.

DAR, Stockton account (*M.G.S.*)

BOLTON, Oliver (*fl.* 1503–†1537)
Carpenter

Was appointed master carpenter of the works of *Chester Castle* on 5 March 1503, and on 12 March 1518 was granted the same office during pleasure in the counties of Chester and Flint. He was paid the sum of £9 2s. 6d. in 1526 (? more probably 1524).[1] He was succeeded in 1537 by HUGH BOLTON, probably his son.

DKR, XXXI (1870)
[1] *LPH*, IV, pt. i, p. 872

BOLTON, William (*fl.* 1543–1558)
Carpenter

Sold timber to make the pulpit of *St. Mary, Chester*, in 1543–44,[1] became master carpenter of Chester and Flint on 8 August 1552, and was followed in that office by his son Henry Bolton on 26 March 1558.

DKR, XXXI (1870); *HKW*, III, 170, 418
[1] *LCA*, LIII (1938), 110

Henry BOLTON held the office of master carpenter of Chester and Flint from 26 March 1558 until his resignation in favour of Milo Mather, who took office on 13 January 1592.

DKR, XXXI (1870)

BONEVILE, William (*fl.* 1467–1473)
Marbler

Of Corfe, Dorset; in 1467–68 supplied a marble stone for the tomb of Thomas Goldstone, late Prior of *Christ Church, Canterbury*, for £4 10s. 0d.; in 1472–73 was paid 20s. and £3 7s. 8d. respectively for the 'sarcophagus' of

Prior Petham and for placing a stone upon the tomb of Prior John Oxney there.

CCA, Prior's Rolls, XVII, 11, 12; AC, LVIII, 33–4, 38 (W.P.B.)

BONVERSALL, Michael (*fl.* 1519–1523) Carver

Of Hythe, Kent; in 1519 contracted to make and erect a new roodloft in *Hackington Church*, near Canterbury, to be finished in 1523. Remains of the screen, which has lost its vaulting, still exist.

AC, XLIV, 267–8

BOORE, John (*fl.* 1539–1540) Carpenter

Master carpenter engaged in 1539–40 on the construction of a blockhouse at *Calshot*, Hants.

(A.O.) LPH, XIV, pt. i, 398, p. 151

BORNAT, John (*fl.* 1532–1533) Mason

Was mason at *Winchester Cathedral* in 1532 at 5*d.* a day, in addition to his food; he worked on the vaulting of the north and south chancel aisles for 45 days, and on the hall of the Infirmary. THOMAS BERTY, who took a retaining fee as master mason, was the designer of the work.

KCR, 216 ff.

BOSTON, John (*fl.* 1442) Mason

Described as a certain mason of the City of London (*lathamus quidam Civitatis London*) when he was employed by the *London Charterhouse* in 1442 to instal their water supply, of which he was the designer as well as maker (*artifex fuit et inventor*).

BL, Cotton MS. Nero E.VI, f. 10

Boston, William—see BUXTON

Botiller, John—see BUTLER

BOUDON, Hugh de (*fl. c.* 1310) Mason (? *Bootham, York*)

Described as master of the work of masonry of *York Minster* when he was summoned to *Knaresborough Castle* about 1310 to deputize for Master HUGH DE TICHEMERS. He can only have been the second or deputy master (see SIMON the Mason I).

His name is probably a form of the York suburb of Bootham. He seems to have been responsible for bringing back ballflower enrichment from the royal works to be used, exceptionally, over the west doors of the Minster.

J.H.H. in ACY, 156–7, 159, 190; HKW, II, 689

BOULTON, John de (*fl.* 1301–1302) Mason

Chief mason at *Linlithgow*, Scotland, in 1301–02, when he was paid 5*d.* a day; the working masons received 4*d.* The work was under the supervision of JAMES OF ST. GEORGE.

PRO, E.101–482–20

BOURNE, John de (*fl.* 1340–   ) ? Carpenter (*Bourne, Lincs.*)

Master employed by the Dean and Chapter of Lincoln in 1340 to make a new barn (*orreum*) at *Normanby*, by contract for £2 10*s.* 0*d.*

LDC, B.j, 2–5

BOURYNER, J. (*fl.* 1341) Carpenter

Carpenter to *Canterbury Cathedral* in 1341, when he was paid 5*s.* for making a new 'desk', the Prior's carrell, with 13*s.* 11*d.* for boards, hinges, etc. He also had sums of 14*s.* 4*d.* and 10*s.* for felling timber at Great Chart and Loose for the new Infirmary Hall.

HDC, 12

BOWDE, John [Bodde, Bolde, Boude, Bulde] (*fl.* 1418–†1443) Mason

A working mason at *York Minster* by 1418 and until 1421, when he was receiving special pay as a setter. About 1436 he succeeded THOMAS PAK as master mason; he died in 1443. On 26 May, as John 'Bulde alias Taliour' (carver) he made his will, and it was proved on 31 May. JOHN BARTON was master by 1444.

J.H.H. in ACY, 191; BHY, I, 221, 236; RFY, 56n., 57

BOWDEN, John (*fl.* 1474–1479) Carpenter

Of Burford, Oxon., master carpenter and woodwork contractor at the building of *Magdalen College, Oxford*, between 1474 and 1479. The progress of the works is detailed in connection with the mason, WILLIAM ORCHARD.

(R.D.) HMC, 8R, I

BOWMAN, Ralph [Bolmone] (*fl.* 1501–1511) Mason and Carver

In November 1501 was paid £10 for work on buildings at *St. Paul's Cathedral, London*, required for the marriage of Prince Arthur to Katherine of Aragon, and in the following March received 61*s.* 10*d.* for making images there.[1] Between 1508 and 1511 he received special payments for 'intaylyng' at *King's College Chapel, Cambridge*; he does not appear to have been one of the regular masons employed, but undertook 'taskwork' by agreement.[2] In 1510 he was making imagery for the chapel of *Christ's College, Cambridge*. He received 20s. for an image of Christ over the chapel door, 40s. for a large image of Christ with the sepulchre and the four knights at the north end of the high altar, and 40s. for an image of Our Lady at the south end.[3] These statues were made of stone from Eversden in the south-west of Cambridgeshire. Bowman seems to have had his workshop within the precincts of the Carmelite Friary, for a payment was made for the carriage of the images 'from the white friers' after they were 'fully fynysshed and made'.[4]

A.O.

[1] *BM*, Add. MS. 7099, *ff.* 71, 73; [2] *KCM*, Building Accs. 1508–9 and 1509–15; [3] *JCM*, Account of Henry Hornby 1510–11 printed by R.F. Scott in *The Eagle*, June 1910; [4] *JCM*, Account of John Scott, 1510–11; WCC II, 197

BOX, John (*fl.* 1333–†1375) Mason

A mason working at *Westminster Palace* in 1333–34 at 5½d. a day. May have been a Canterbury man, as he was stated to be in the service of the Prior of *Christ Church, Canterbury*, in 1350, when on 30 May letters close were issued to him, ordering him to appear before the Bishop of Winchester, the treasurer at *Westminster*, to give information concerning certain works at the Palace there, and to carry out other works enjoined upon him by the treasurer. He in fact received £114 in 1350–51 on behalf of works which he was supervising. At the same time an order was sent to the Prior of Christ Church to cause 'Master John Box, *cementarius*' to come 'as the King has learned that John is now staying with the prior in his service'.[1] The treasurer's accounts of Christ Church Priory, Canterbury, show that Box received an annual robe in each of the years 1352/3–1355/6.[2]

In 1353 Box undertook task work at Westminster Palace and was paid £5 7s. 10d. besides his task for taking down and rebuilding the *vice* or spiral stair on the south part of the chapel at the west end;[3] and from 20 June 1351 to 9 October 1357 was taking 12d. a day as master mason in charge of the works at the Palace and at the *Tower of London*; he was also described as working '*super ordinacione operum Regis*'. Meanwhile, from May 1356 until 1358, he was in charge of works at *Calais*.[4]

From 1361 he was chief mason at *Queenborough Castle*, taking 12d. a day; on 24 November 1363 he was appointed with JAMES BROYL and STEPHEN PEYNTOR to impress labour for the works there,[5] and in 1367–8 he was still taking 12d. a day as master mason. At this time he also undertook with MAURICE YONGE and JOHN ROKESACRE to build 55½ perches 1¼ feet of the castle wall called 'Barbican' for £500. The rate was calculated at £9 for each perch of 21 feet in length, 20 feet thick at the foundation, and 21 feet high.[6] On 28 April 1369 Box was again appointed to impress masons for Queenborough Castle with John Rokesacre.[7]

On 20 June 1376 the King, in granting a lease of the manor of La Gare in Kent, allowed that Maurice Yonge, the grantee, should have out of his rent for the first two years a sum of £135 owed to 'the said Maurice, John Box, and John Rokesacre, masons, who lately undertook the task of making the walls of the outer ward called "Le Barbican" of (Quenesburgh) castle. . . for making 15 perches and ½ foot of the said walls, each perch costing £9', Yonge undertaking 'to acquit the King as regards the executors of the said John and John, both of whom (he says) are dead, of whatever of the said sum could be demanded by them'.[8]

Box's work at Canterbury Cathedral may well have included the fine tomb of Archbishop Stratford, made about 1350. He is likely also to have collaborated with HENRY YEVELEY on the Black Prince's Chantry Chapel in the crypt of Canterbury Cathedral, built after 1363, while Yeveley was probably the chief architect of the work at Queenborough.

[1] *PRO*, E.101–469–12; E.372–197; CCR 1349–54, 226; [2] *LP*, MS. 243, *ff.* 84v, 88, 93, 98; [3] LKC; BBW, 169; [4] *PRO*, E.101–471–6, 11; 472–4; 173–7 (*H.M.C.*) [5] *PRO*, E.101–483–20 (*L.F.S.*); CPR 1361–4, 430; [6] *PRO*, E.101–483–25, 502–3 (*D.K.*, *L.F.S.*); [7] CPR 1367–70, 238; [8] CFR 1368–77, 352

Boxton, William—see BUXTON

BOYDELL, William [W. Wright] (*fl.* 1445–   ) Carpenter

Of Little Casterton, Rutland; on 12 September 1445 contracted to make a floor and roof in the Chapter House at *Stamford Nunnery* for £2 6s. 8d. and also a roof for the dormitory there for 7 marks (£4 13s. 4d.).

SHB, 519–20; (*PRO*, E.101–504–19)

BOYDEN, William (*fl. c.* 1308–1326) ? Mason

Is said to have been the architect of the Chapel of the Virgin (the eastern Lady Chapel) in *St. Albans Abbey*, built between 1308 and 1326.

(APD; BAA); RAA, i, 445

BRADLE, Richard (*fl.* 1380) Mason

In 1380 was paid 7*d.* a day as warden of the masons engaged in heightening the main gatehouse of *Carisbrooke Castle*, under the direction of HENRY YEVELEY.

HKW, II, 594

'Bradley', William—see HYNDELEY

BRADSHAW, Lawrence (*fl.* 1542–†1581) Carpenter

In 1542–43 Lawrence Bradshaw took 1*s.* a day as a carpenter working at the king's manor of *Dartford*, and in the next year he was taking 1*s.* 4*d.* a day for drawing plats for work at *Dunstable* and in 1544 rode to view the works there. He was also working at *Ampthill Manor*, Beds., as 'the settar owte of worke and drawing of platte'. The manor at the time was in the king's hands. In September 1544 he was on campaign in France and was a witness to the will of JAMES NEDEHAM.[1]

From 1 May 1547 Bradshaw was appointed by Edward VI surveyor of the King's works, apparently in succession to Sir RICHARD LEE, a post regranted to him by Mary in 1553, and later by Elizabeth, and which he retained until 1561. He was still living as a Queen's Pensioner in 1570, and was concerned with property in the city of London in 1577.[2] He is referred to as 'gentleman' in the grants to him.

The accounts for 1548–49[3] show that during two years he was travelling by land on 318 days, being allowed 4*s.* a day for 'dyettes and Rydinge Charges', in addition to 'goynge by water for the space of 258 days' at 1*s.* 8*d.* a day — these payments seem to have been in addition to his retaining fee; he was also allowed £1 for one year's allowance in respect of 'money bagges, candelles to wryte by, for the makinge of bokes and reconynge by night, and. . . quylles and pyn dost'. His normal fee was 2*s.* a day, with a clerk to assist him, and the traditional appurtenances of the office.

During 1548 he was paid £200 to make new bridges (landing-stairs) at the new *Palace of Westminster* (Whitehall).[4] These bridges may have included the great stairs shown in van den Wyngaerde's sketch of about 1550, whose stone piers were found in 1939. Bradshaw was Master of the London Carpenters' Company seven times, lastly in 1579, and died on 24 May 1581 leaving a widow, Grace.

(APD; JPC, 623); HKW, III, 55–9; IV, 69, 75
[1] *BM*, Add. MS. 10109; D. R. Ransome in GUM, II, 238;

[2] CPR 1547–8, 231; 1554–5, 181; 1557–8, 167; CSP, Add. 1566–79, 315; *LHR*, 262 (48); [3] *PRO*, E.101–474–19; [4] APC, II, 222

BRAMCOTE, William de (*fl.* 1307–1323) Mason (*Bramcote, Notts.*)

Master mason (*cementarius*) in charge of works at *Nottingham Castle* in 1307–08, he received 6*d.* a day. With WILLIAM DE EMBLEBY, carpenter, in 1323 contracted to build houses within the castle for £200.

PRO, E.101–477–19 (*L.F.S.*); HKW, II, 761

BRANCHE, John (*fl.* 1438–1443) Carpenter

Master carpenter at the building of *All Souls College, Oxford*, in 1438–43, when he was paid 3*s.* 4*d.* a week.[1] Branche must have been the designer of the fine hammer-beam roof of the chapel, completed in 1443; the dimensions are 70 feet long by 28 feet span. Certain references in the college accounts suggest that Branche may have been the carpenter of *Abingdon Abbey*.

Branche may have been the John Braunche, carpenter, who in 1407 took up the freedom of Wells, Somerset,[2] and was perhaps identical with the John, carpenter, who in 1413–17 made the chancel roof of *Adderbury Church*, Oxon., by task for £8 13*s.* 4*d.* and received in addition a reward of 13*s.* 4*d.*[3] A John Braunche, whose occupation is not specified, was living at Abingdon in 1448–49,[4] and another Oxford carpenter of the name was given a reward of 1*s.* 8*d.* by *New College* in 1465–66, sold shingles to *Merton College* in 1468, received 40*s.* in part payment for making the new great gates of *University College* in 1475–76, and rebuilt a house on the north-east corner of Carfax for that college in 1476–78.[5]

GOC
[1] JAS, 129; [2] SRS, XLVI (1931); [3] HAR; [4] AAA, 124; cf. E. M. Jope in BKJ, LI (1951), 54; [5] *UCO*, Bursars' Accs. (*A.O.*)

BRANKASTRE, John (*fl.* 1462–1478) Mason (*Brancaster, Norfolk*)

John Brankastr', *lathamus*, worked for the Precentor of Norwich Cathedral Priory on the chapel of *St. Eustachius* at *Great Plumstead*, Norfolk, in 1462–63. Again in 1477–78, when he was described as the mason of the Lord Prior, he was paid 1*s.* 3*d.* for 5 days work on *Plumstead Rectory*.

NCM, Precentor's Rolls, Nos. 930, 938 (*P.C.*)

BRASIER, Hugh [Brasyer] (*fl. c.* 1475–†1487) Mason

Freemason of London, concerned in the

Queen's work at *Havering-atte-Bower c.* 1475–80.[1]

He made his will on 7 May 1487, desiring to be buried in the churchyard of St. Katherine Coleman Street. He left all his residuary estate to his wife Elizabeth and his lands and tenements at Warwick after the death of his mother Joan Brasyer, with remainders to his son Thomas, and daughters Beatrice and Margaret; if they were all to die of minor age, then to his sister Joan. The will was proved on 12 June 1487.[2]

[1] *PRO*, C.1–66–411; [2] *ERO*, Archd. Ct. of Essex, 82 ER 1

BRAY, Henry de (1269–†*c.* 1340) Layman

One of a family of Northamptonshire squires who has some claims to architectural repute; he was born on 31 January 1269, and even before attaining his majority had begun the rebuilding of his manor house at *Harlestone*, Northants. The stone came from a quarry close by, and the timber from his home park. His works included the hall and north chamber, 1289; the south chamber, 1291; a wall and gate in 1292 and 1294; and between 1295 and 1309 several other walls, a pound, herb-garden, pigsty, fowl-house, tower, grange, bakehouse, kitchen, dovehouse, 'fountain', granary, sheepfold, and carthouse, as well as several cottages for his tenants, a water-mill, and a new water-supply system for the manor.

In 1320 the chancel of *Harlestone Church* was built, possibly with his advice; in 1323 he was one of the six jurors who were impanelled to inquire into the state of Northampton Castle and made a return of its defects, with an estimate of the cost of repair. Lastly, in 1325, the remainder of Harlestone Church was rebuilt, the stone and timber being supplied by him, while his son-in-law John Dyve paid for the carpentry work, presumably by hiring carpenters or lending his estate carpenter to the church.

While there is no evidence that Henry de Bray in any way corresponded to an architect of the present day, it seems probable that he had considerable practical knowledge of building work, and would have been in a position to advise the local craftsmen on points of design. His remarkable 'Estate Book' gives evidence of an inquiring and methodical mind.

Carved heads believed to represent de Bray and his wife Mabel are on each side of the church door at Harlestone. He died about 1340.

EBB

BRAY, Reginald *(fl.* 1528–1529) Mason

Citizen and freemason of London; in 1528–29 made 'bases' for the tomb of Lady Margaret Beaufort in *Henry VII's Chapel, Westminster*. His name suggests that he may have been a natural son of Sir Reginald Bray.

(*A.O.*) R.F. Scott in A, LXVI, 365–76

BREDON, John, I (*fl.* 1398–   ) Mason (*Bredon, Worcs.*)

In 1398 Prior John Malverne of Worcester leased to John Bredon, mason, and to Joan his wife a tenement in the corner of Corveser Street, next the tenement of 'Master John Bredon'. It seems doubtful whether the mason could have been identical with the Master John Bredon named (*fl.* 1381–1408), who was five times Bailiff of the city of Worcester.

BCW; cf. J. W. Hobbs in AQC, XL (1928), 147

BREDON, John, II (*fl.* 1466–   ) Mason

Freemason of Belvoir, Leics., to whom lands in and near Belvoir were quitclaimed on 14 October 1466.

HMC, Rutland, IV, 20 (*H.M.C.*)

BREDONE, Thomas de (*fl.* 1356–   ) Mason

Was one of the twelve London masons who in 1356 were to answer touching the articles of the masons' mistery. Bredone was among the six 'Mason-hewers or Freestone-masons'.

(LKC); RML, 280–2; KMM, 249–51

BRERETON, John (*fl.* 1537–1544) Mason (? *Brereton, Chs.*)

Was appointed master mason of the counties of Chester and Flint on 14 May 1537, and held office until the appointment of THOMAS WISSWALL in 1544.

DKR, XXXI (1870)

BRETON, Adam (*fl.* 1335–1336) Mason

Master mason in charge of works at *Carisbrooke Castle*, Isle of Wight, in 1335; he was succeeded in December 1336 by RICHARD LE TAYLLOUR. Breton was paid 2s. a week.

SHB, 60; *PRO*, E.101–490–21 (*L.F.S.*)

BRETON, John (*fl.* 1446–1447) Carpenter

Master carpenter of Hillington, Norfolk. In 1446 the Chamberlains of (*King's*) *Lynn* sent for him to build the *Town Mills* and he was paid for 89½ days' work between Michaelmas and Easter (9 April) 1447, and for a further

$30\frac{1}{2}$ days after Easter, sometimes at the rate of 8*d*. and sometimes at $8\frac{1}{2}d$. a day.

LCR, Ea. 51

BRIAN, John ['Bricine', Bryan] (*fl*. 1470–1496) Carpenter

Was working in *Oxford* from 1470, when he carried out minor works at *New College*, while in 1474–75 he made cresting for the high altar at *Merton College*. In 1474, John Bryan, carpenter, was paid £1 for making the roof of a tower at *Magdalen College*, by task.[1] In 1496 he petitioned the King, Henry VII, for a sum of £9 in view of alterations to the designs for work at *Woodstock Palace*, and implying that he had designed the roof of the great hall there. His petition mentions that 'your Grace had a sight bi picture of the ruffe of your hall of Woodstoke'. The building of Woodstock Palace was in progress between 1494 and 1501, under WILLIAM EAST, mason.[2]

GOC
[1] *MCO*, Accs. (*E.M.J.*); [2] HMC, 3R. 318; OHS, LXXX (1924), 241

'Bricine', John—see BRIAN

Brid, Richard—see BIRD

BRIGGES, Richard [de Ponte] (*fl*. 1312–†1327) Carpenter

Took up the freedom of York as 'Ricardus de Ponte', carpenter, in 1312–13; carpenter to *York Minster*. He died at the beginning of 1327, desiring to be buried in the Minster, and leaving his tools to his son John.

RFY, 207n.

BRIGGS, Thomas, I [Brigges, Brugg] (*fl*. 1469–1485) Mason

Took up the freedom of York in 1469,[1] and was working at *York Minster* at 3*s*. a week in 1472.[2] He was appointed on 15 February 1484/5 to be common mason of the city of York for life, at such daily wages as a mason should take, with a gown yearly, and a house in Walmgate rent free. He succeeded ROBERT DAVYSON.[3]

(*G.P.J.*)
[1] YCF; [2] AQC, XLIV, 231, 235; [3] YCR, I, 112

BRIGGS, Thomas, II (*fl*. 1524–1535) Carpenter

Was appointed carpenter to *Lincoln Cathedral* on 20 September 1524, on the death of ROBERT WYMARKE, at 13*s*. 4*d*. a year, together with a house rent free, in which Briggs was already living. On 18 October 1526 he was admitted to the office of watchman, vacant by the resignation of ROBERT NEWBY, and he was still the cathedral carpenter on 3 September 1535. Robert Wymarke in his will had left Briggs 'one gowne' in 1524; Briggs was presumably his assistant before Wymarke's death.

LRS, XII, 49, 56, 74; XIII, 181

BRIGHT, Richard [Bryght] (*fl*. 1441–1451) Carpenter & Timbermonger

Second sworn carpenter to the City of London (with RICHARD BIRD) in 1441,[1] and appears as a timbermonger in the city in 1444.[2] Bright continues to appear as a sworn carpenter of the City at various dates until 17 December 1451.

[1] CLB, 'K' 257; [2] LHR, 174 (17)

BRIKEMAN, Matthew [Brykemason] (*fl*. 1430–1433) Bricklayer

Was paid £3 6*s*. 8*d*. for his task of building the walls of the chapel at *Rochford Manor*, Essex, in 1430–33. (See also WILLIAM NORFOLK).

BL, Egerton Roll 8347

'BRISTOL, Carpenter of' (*fl*. 1475–1476) Carpenter

In 1475–76 a carpenter of Bristol was paid £2 for making new desks for the chancel of *Cheddar Church*, Somerset, besides 8*s*. spent on timber, 9*d*. for 6 boards (*tabulis*) from Wales, and 1*s*. 8*d*. for nails and ironwork.

PRO, Eccl. 2–135–131916, $\frac{1}{11}$

BROMEHALL, Robert (*fl*. 1512–1515) Mason

Warden of the masons at the building of the *Savoy Hospital* in 1512–15, under JOHN AYLMER.

Bromflet—see BROWNFLEET

Bron, John—see WORLICH, John

BROND, John (*fl*. 1492–†1518) Mason

Of Bury St. Edmunds, can be traced in Bury documents and wills over a period of a quarter of a century. From 1505 to 1511 he was the mason in charge of the building of *Little Saxham Hall*, Suffolk, with THOMAS LOVEDAY, carpenter. The Hall (pulled down in 1773) was built for Thomas Lucas, Solicitor General to Henry VII, and was to be 'according to the patron of an house of Sir John Cutts in his manor of Thaxted' (i.e. Horham Hall, Essex).[1] Loveday paid visits to Horham Hall, and it is possible that both he and Brond had been employed there. Stylistic resemblances in the treatment of windows suggest that the clerestory of the nave of *Thaxted Church*, Essex, which is early 16th century, was the work of the same master mason.

In a list of legacies included in a codicil to the will of John de Vere, 13th Earl of Oxford, is one of 40s. to John Brond. A large number of the Earl's servants received sums of varying amounts 'in reward'; if John Brond was the Bury mason, it is likely that he had been carrying out work for the Earl in Suffolk or Essex. His will was proved 10 May 1513.[2]

John Brond's will is that of a prosperous man (dated 1 October 1517, proved 27 March 1518).[3] He lived in Hatter Street and had several other houses in Bury. He requested 'My ryght Reverende good Lord John Abbott of the Monastery of Bury' to act as the supervisor of his will and also 'to be especiall good lord to Thomas my son'. Evidently John Brond had been employed by the Abbot and he may have succeeded JOHN WASTELL as abbey mason in 1515.

A reference in a will of 1542 shows that *Thomas* BROND was also a freemason.[4]

A.O.

[1] GHT; [2] A, LXVI, 319; [3] BW, viii, 42; [4] PCC, 8 Spert

Bronflet—see BROWNFLEET

BROOK, Geoffrey [Broke] (*fl.* 1477–79) Carpenter

In 1477 undertook to build a new barn at the rectory of *Broad Chalk*, Wilts., for King's College, Cambridge, who owned the advowson. He was paid £21.

(*A.O.*) KCM, Mundum Book 1476–77, 1478–79

BROUN, John (*fl.* 1391) Mason

On 18 February 1390–91 John Broun, mason of Hereford, undertook to build the stonework of a hall at *Lyonshall Castle*, Herefordshire, for its lord Sir John Devereux. The walls were to be 3 feet thick on foundations carried 2 feet below ground level; the internal dimensions being 44 by 25 feet. There were to be buttresses and four doorways of stone, three of them 5 feet wide and the other 4 feet. There were to be three stone windows, one a bay window of ten lights, the others of two lights with a transom. Broun was to be paid 25 marks (£16 13s. 4d.) and a quarter of wheat: a first payment of £4 3s. 8d. at the start of work and the rest quarterly. Broun was also to extend the gate-tower of the castle by 6 feet on each side, but keeping the old width,

to vault the gateway throughout, to perform the masonry work for a new portcullis (*portecolys*) in his new extension. There was to be a little doorway (*petit heuse*) for the porter on one side and a new spiral staircase with a turret above, with two privies and two fireplaces to the two chief rooms with the room above the vault; and a window on each side of each room. Broun was to finish off his new work with machicolations and battlements (*maggecolera et enkernellera*) and to embattle (*enbatillera*) the new work inside. For this second work Broun was to be paid 40 marks (£26 13s. 4d.) and a quarter of wheat. Sir John was to provide all materials, plant and carriage, except masons' tools.

BL, Harl. MS. 7366, *f.* 1v, from original now in *HRO*, A.H. 79 (*R.K.M.*)

BROWN, John, I [Broun] (*fl.* 1391–1409) Mason

Mason employed at *Westminster Abbey*, where the treasurer allowed him a tunic in 1391–92.[1] From 1392 until 1402 he was continuously engaged on the work of the nave, taking 3s. 4d. a week, the highest rate of pay among the working masons.[2]

From 1405 until 1409 a mason of the same name worked on *London Bridge*, where he was paid 3s. 9d. a week.[3] This was presumably the John Brown, mason, of Aldgate Street, who was involved in legal proceedings *c.* 1420.[4]

[1] WAM, 19876; [2] Ibid., 23463–23472; [3] KJL, 12–14; [4] PRO, ECP, 11, 367

BROWN, John, II [Broun] (*fl.?* 1428–1461) Mason

An important mason of this name worked at *King's College Chapel, Cambridge*, under REGINALD ELY up to the cessation of work in 1461. His status is shown by his eating at the Fellows' table when he was entertained as a guest on certain feast days and other occasions.[1] His name can be traced in the Kitchen Accounts from 1448, but he may have been employed from the commencement of building operations. On several occasions he was entertained with Reginald Ely, and like him, he received a pardon from the King on 10 February 1461.[2] His position was probably that of warden of the masons. In the accounts of the Provost, Robert Wodelark, during the years 1459 to 1461, when he was struggling to carry on the works with inadequate funds, there are many payments to John Brown and those working with him 'in regard'.[3] The college made a house available for him, as is shown by a payment under the year 1476–77 for slating the tenement 'where John Brown freemason lately dwelt'.[4]

It is probable that the King's College mason was identical with John Brown of Barrington, who between 1428 and 1431 supplied clunch stone in partnership with Henry Jekke (or Jekkys) to *King's Hall, Cambridge*, for the building of the King Edward gate-tower and an adjoining range.[5] For the lay subsidy of 1451 the lands and tenements of John Brown of Barrington were valued at £3 6s. 8d. and he was assessed at 1s. 8d.[6] There was a John Broun who was sworn a master of the London freemasons in 1441.[7]

A.O.

[1] *KCM*, Kitchen Accs., i; [2] CPR 1452–61, p. 647; [3] *KCM*, College Accs., vol. ii; [4] *KCM*, Mundum Book 1476–77; [5] *TCM*, *KHA*, vii, 246–50; viii, 31; [6] *PRO*, Lay Subsidy 81–103; W.M. Palmer, 'Cambridgeshire Subsidy Rolls, 1250–1695', p. 143; [7] CLB, 'K', 257

BROWN, John [Browne] (*fl.* 1497–1505) Carpenter

Carpenter of *Canterbury*; contracted to build a range of four houses there in 1497. He was to frame the building at the Austin Friars, and was to have £20 for his work, or more if this were considered too little 'by men havyng good insight of carpentary werk'.[1] With EDMOND GODFREY, he was paid £7 7s. 6d. for making the pews and pulpit at *St. Andrew's Church, Canterbury*, in 1505, besides 4s. 10d. for timber. Payment was evidently made as the work proceeded: first two instalments of £2 13s. 4d. each, then 3s. 6d. and 1s. 4d. for timber, an instalment of £1, then one of 16s. 8d. for the pews, while in respect of the pulpit Godfrey was paid 4s. 2d. for 7 days, 'hys ladde' for 7 days, 8d., and John Carver for 6 days, 3s.[2]

[1] SHB, 554–6; (PRO, Anc. Deed B.5740); [2] AC, XXXII, 232

BROWN, John [Broun] (*fl. c.* 1500) Carver

Undertook, with ROBERT FILLE, to make an altar table for the monastery of *Syon*, of ten 'storys' of Our Lady with imagery. The total cost was to be £60, with meat, drink, fuel and other necessaries. The date can be fixed to the years 1493–1500, as the work is described in a petition to a cardinal who was Chancellor, certainly Morton.

PRO, ECP 189.15 (*N.L.R.*)

BROWN, Robert [Broun] (*fl.* 1415–1421) Carver

On 4 February 1414/15 Robert Broun, carver, received £4 13s. 4d. covering the purchase of timber and the making of figures of a swan and an antelope for the King's great ship the 'Holigost', then lately built at Southampton.[1] On 3 October 1418 Broun was paid £2 12s. 0d. for carving swans in the King's chamber at *Shene Palace*.[2] On 31 December 1421 Robert Broun, 'Kerver', living in the Savoy without Temple Bar, London, contracted to carve a tomb of alabaster for Richard Hertcombe, to be set up in the priory church at *Bisham*, Berks. The monument was to comprise a great stone, 11 feet 8 inches long and 5 feet broad, set over 12 niches containing 'mourners', with two alabaster figures, canopies and shafts, and was to be in place by 24 August 1422. The whole work, including the making of a vault beneath the tomb, was to cost £22 13s. 4d.

[1] DIE, 338, 357; [2] G. M. Bark in ANJ, XXIX (1949), 89–91

BROWN, William [Broun] (*fl.* 1380–1415) Mason

Was perhaps identical with the William Le Massone who, with Alice his wife, was assessed 2s. to the Poll Tax of 1380 in the North-east Ward of Oxford;[1] and from then until 1386 engaged on the building of *New College* under WILLIAM WYNFORD. William Broun was fined on four occasions between 30 September 1390 and 11 November 1392 for taking excessive wages, under the Statute of Labourers; his residence in the North-east Ward and later known facts suggest that he was then employed on the building of the New College cloisters (*c.* 1390–95).[2] From 1388 Brown was at New College and on 16 February 1390/1 Brown dined with the Fellows, while Wynford and HUGH HERLAND were at the high table; again on 15 September 1391, when Wynford was at the high table; in 1392–3, 1398, and in 1405–06.[3] He had also dined with the Fellows of *Winchester College* on 12 December 1395.[4] During 1396 and 1397 he had active charge of the building of the tower of New College, and presumably carried this work to completion (1403), as Wynford's warden or undermaster. He was also carrying out extensive work on *Canterbury College* from *c.* 1384 to 1396.[5] From 1398 to 1402 he was building the old hall of *Queen's College, Oxford*, for whose chapel Brown's wife was mending vestments in 1400; in 1409–12 was engaged at the chapel and also at the gatehouse of *Oriel*

College; in 1411–13 worked on *St. Bartholomew's Hospital, Cowley*; and in 1414–15 on the hall of Oriel College.[6] Throughout, Brown was doing small jobs for New College, where he received a livery, but took only the normal mason's pay of 3*s.* a week.

He was possibly identical with William Broun, *cementarius*, who in 1375 built part of the new chapel at the royal manor of *Havering*, Essex, for £46 13*s.* 4*d.*,[7] and with the William Brown, mason, who in 1385 made a great fireplace of two hearths for the Dancing Chamber and the King's wardrobe at *Clarendon Palace* for £25.[8] He may also have been the William Mason who from time to time worked for Queen's College, Oxford, notably on the *Rectory of Sparsholt*, Berks., in 1372–73, and on the chancel there in 1374–75, as well as at the college itself in 1373–74 and 1400–01.[9]

GOM, 63–4; HKW, II, 959, 934
[1] OHS, XVIII, 26; [2] SMO, 5, 21, 43, 97; [3] *NCO*, Hall Books; [4] *WCM*, Hall Book 1395–6; [5] OHS, XVIII, 310, 313–14; HSA, 29, 31; PCO, II, 128, 141–2; [6] E.M. Jope in OCR, April 1946, 8–9; GOM, 63; [7] *PRO*, E.101–464–27 (*L.F.S.*); [8] SHB, 100; E.101–473–2 (*L.F.S.*); [9] GOM, 64

BROWN, William [Broun] (*fl. c.* 1463) Carpenter

About 1463 William and Thomas Broun of *Cockfield*, Suffolk, contracted to make for Lawrence Smyt a new house 43 feet by 18 feet, timbered after the fashion of 'Edmund Ampes hall'.

A.E.B.O. in ARC, XIV, 1979, 19–20

BROWNFLEET, William [Bronflet, Bromflet, Brounflete, W. Carver] (*fl.* 1482–1523) Carpenter (? *Broomfleet, Yorks, E.R.*)

In 1482–3 William Brounflete, carver, took up the freedom of the city of York. The principal master of the 'Ripon School' of carvers, whose work is so uniform that he was probably the responsible designer throughout. The choir-stalls of *Ripon Minster* were made between 1489 and 1494, and those at *Manchester Collegiate Church* (now Cathedral) about 1505–09; some bench-ends now in *Aysgarth Church*, close to Jervaulx Abbey, seem to have been made about 1506, and a screen for *Easby Abbey* (now in Wensley Church) about 1510, at the costs of John, Lord Scrope of Bolton.

Brownfleet was also known as William Carver, and was almost certainly identical with the man of that name who was wakeman or mayor of Ripon in 1511. Before 1518 he

had begun to make the choir-stalls, now destroyed, for *Bridlington Priory*, and probably a screen there, now at Flamborough Church. On 3 April 1518 he contracted to make a loft next to St. Wilfrid's Closet in Ripon Minster as soon as he had finished the Bridlington work, with a 'Georg Apon horsebak' (an equestrian statue of St. George) like one at Kirkstall Abbey; in 1520–21 he had a reward of 6*s.* 8*d.* for supervising the other carpenters at Ripon Minster, and in 1522–23 he was paid 6*d.* a day for work there, including a feretory and carving behind the High Altar; he had several other carvers under his charge. He also travelled to York, Weighton, and Hull on 7–10 July 1522, and bought a large quantity of wainscot and other boards at Hull.[1] About this time he seems to have made the stalls for *Beverley Minster*.

Bench-ends at *Leake*, near Northallerton, made about 1519, and one end at *Over Silton*, three miles north of Leake, are attributed to his workshop, and his influence is seen in others at *Barkstone Church*, Leicestershire, and some now at Durham Castle, originally in the Bishop of Durham's Chapel at *Bishop Auckland*.

(Note: the Paper Book of accounts relating to Brownfleet's work at Ripon is dated in the printed edition as 'Cir. 1520', but on the assumption that Saturday was the normal pay-day, borne out by the dated Ripon accounts, it can be assigned to the period 28 April 1522 to 25 April 1523.)

PRC; PRS; SS, XCVI, 205
[1] SMR, III, 200

BROYL, James [Bruyl] (*fl.* 1363–1366) Mason

On 24 November 1363 was named second (after JOHN BOX) in a commission to impress labour for the works of *Queenborough Castle*, Kent,[1] and in 1365–66 he was the chief mason there (probably ranking as warden), taking 10*d.*. a day.[2]

[1] CPR 1361–4, 430; [2] *PRO*, E.101–483–23; 502–3 (*L.F.S.*)
Brugg, Thomas—see BRIGGS

BRUMLEYE, John de (*fl.* 1336–1337) Mason

Master mason (*Magister cementar'*) at *Scarborough Castle* in 1336–37, when he was paid 2*s.* 4*d.* a week. His main work was the rebuilding of the great bridge in stone.

PRO, E.101–482–4 (*L.F.S.*); HKW, II, 831

Brunell—see BURNELL

BRUSYNGDON, Robert ['Brasington', 'Grasington'] (*fl.* 1395–1396) Carver

Carver of angels bearing shields which carry the hammer-posts of *Westminster Hall* roof. He was paid £1 6*s.* 8*d.* each for four angels; four more were carved by William Canon for £1 each, and six others by PETER DAVYN and Hubert de Villers for 15*s.* each. Finally Brusyngdon himself produced two more at the price of 15*s.* each.[1] These 16 angels (out of a total of 26) are all that are accounted for in the surviving rolls.

Brusyngdon's name has been misread as 'Grasington' and the second item mentioning him has been referred to a 'Richard' Brusyngdon in error.[2]

[1] *BM*, Add. Ch. 27018; [2] LKC, 254; LWR, 150; HGE, 59, Fig. 94; SHB, 218

Bruyl, James—see BROYL

Bryd, Thomas—see BIRD

BUCHAM, Robert (*fl.* 1447–*c.* 1457) Mason

In 1447–48 was working on the cloister of the *Great Hospital, Norwich*, and was paid 6*d.* a day jointly with his servant, taking their board at the hospital table in addition. The roofs were made by the carpenter SIMON TABBARD, whose work continued until 1457.

NRO, Great Hospital, 24a

Buet, del—see LEOMINSTER

BUK, Richard [Buc] (*fl.* 1413–1450) Carpenter

Carpenter employed at the building of the chapel of *Mettingham College*, Suffolk, from 1413 to 1424. His chief work was the making of the stalls; in 1413–14 he rode to Norwich with Master John Warren, a chaplain of the college, for the purpose of viewing stalls. During the next six years he received payments amounting to nearly £40 for the stalls, for a separate pair of stalls and a pulpit, made under another agreement. In 1418–19 he also provided a 'tabula' for the high altar for 13*s.* 4*d.* to be painted by THOMAS BARSHAM and from 1422 to 1424 carried out work on the ceiling of the vestry roof and minor works there, for which he was paid £2 18*s.* 4*d.*[1] In 1450 Richard Buc was paid 8½*d.* for mending the stalls of *Walberswick Church*, Suffolk.[2]

[1] *BM*, Add. MS. 33985, *ff.* 79v.–137v.; [2] LCW, 5

BUK, Robert (*fl. c.* 1411–1454) Carpenter

Is mentioned in accounts as master carpenter at the church of *St. Augustine, Hedon*, Yorks., over a long period in the 15th century, probably *c.* 1411–1454; he was paid 10*d.* a day.

BHH

BUKMER, Gregory [Buckmer] (*fl.* 1509–†1513) Carpenter.

Was appointed master carpenter of *Calais* in succession to ROBERT MAPILSDEN on 26 December 1509, and was killed in a neighbouring skirmish in 1513. He was succeeded in office by BEDE OLIVER on 20 December.

LPH, I, 770, 4611; LEN, ii, 205 (*H.M.C.*)

Bukston, William—see BUXTON

BULFORD, John (*fl.* 1452–1467) Carpenter (*Bulford, Wilts.*)

Of Newbury, Berks., carpenter; on 8 October 1452 entered into a bond in £6 with the Warden of *Winchester College*. In 1466–67 made by contract with the Bishop of Winchester various works at the manor of *Downton*, Wilts., viz. a new roof over the great chamber like the roof of the hall of the rectory there, a new roof to the chapel, with a new roof to the latrine and repairs to the roof of the chamber next the hall, all for £15 6*s.* 8*d.*, with additional payments, 'ex regardo' of £7 5*s.* 0*d.*

WCM 20083; *PRO*, Eccl. 2-3-155834

BULLOCK, Henry (*fl.* 1541–†1561) Mason

In early life servant to JOHN MOLTON, he was in 1541 working at *Westminster Palace* at 3*s.* 4*d.* a week.[1] In 1546 Molton, then King's Master Mason, left to 'John Moore, my prentice, and to John Moore and Henry Bullock, sometime my servants' all his 'portratures' 'plaates', books, tools, and instruments.[2] Bullock was appointed for life master mason of *Windsor Castle* after the death of GUY RAFF on 20 November 1549, with fees of 6*d.* a day.[3] He was in charge of the work on the Lodgings of the Poor Knights in 1557, and of the making of a new fountain in the castle in 1558.[4] Bullock also held the office of King's Master Mason from 1556 to his death.

Bullock made his will on 18 October 1561, and it was proved on 5 November. He desired to be buried in the church of St. Margaret, Westminster, and mentioned his father Thomas Bullock and his mother, his brother Robert Bullock, wife Katharine, and servant Gilbert Carter.[5]

[1] *Bodl.*, Rawl. D. 781; Eng. Hist. b. 192 (*G.P.J.*); [2] W.J. Williams in MR, XVI, 204; [3] CPR 1548–9, 247; WKM, 34; [4] HWC, I, 257, 259; HKW, III, 408; [5] *PPR*, Westminster Court, 164 Bracy

BUNTING, William (*fl.* 1481–1483)
Carpenter

Undertook carpentry work by indenture at *Tendring Hall*, Stoke-by-Nayland, Suffolk, for John, Lord Howard between October 1481 and March 1483.¹ The first indenture was for the chapel. In June 1483 Lord Howard was created Duke of Norfolk.

A William Bunting, carpenter of Bury St. Edmunds, can be traced from 1433; his will was proved 14 July 1456.²

A.O.

¹ PNA, *passim*; ²*BW*, ia, 53

BURCESTRE, John de ['Barcestre'] (*fl.* 1348–   ) Mason (? *Bicester, Oxon.*)

Master mason; on 13 January 1347/8 contracted with Ralph, Lord Stafford to build a castle on the motte at *Stafford*, according to Lord Stafford's '*deuys et ordinaunce*'. The towers were to be 10 feet higher than the walls, which were to be 7 feet thick at the bottom exclusive of the plinths. For every perch of 24 feet of wall, 1 foot in height, Burcestre was to be paid 5 marks (£3 6s. 8d.), and was to have fuel for his lodging and for his men, and hay for his horse.

SHB, 438–9; HMC, 4R. I, 328

BURDON, Richard (*fl.* 1511–1512) Mason

Worked for two weeks at 3s. 8d. a week on the bay-window of the hall of *Little Saxham Hall*, Suffolk, in 1511.¹ In the next year he was rated at £2 in the Cambridge Poll Tax return, and was said to be rated at Ely. He was assessed on movables, and appeared in the category of those with wages between £2 and £10.² He may have been a son or brother of WILLIAM BURDON II.

(A.O.)

¹ GHT; ² CBD, 123

BURDON, William, I (*fl.* 1422–   ) Mason

Of Westminster; with Richard Hert of Blechingley was commissioned early in 1422 to take various conveyances, labourers, etc., for the nave of *Westminster Abbey*.

CPR 1416–22, 420

BURDON, William, II [Burden, Bordon] (*fl.* 1505–1519) Mason

Of Ely; in September 1505 he undertook to make the windows, doors, and other details for *Little Saxham Hall*, Suffolk, where JOHN BROND of Bury St. Edmunds was the general contractor. They were to be of freestone and Burwell stone and he was to receive £19, of which the last payment was made on 21 August 1507. In 1511 he seems to have been consulted over the building of the great bay-window of the hall there on which RICHARD BURDON and Thomas Butler were working, since he was paid 2s. for three days' work and 1s. 8d. for his journey from Cambridge to Saxham and back.¹

At Cambridge he was working on *Great St. Mary's Church* at the time. The accounts of the proctors of the university of 1508–10 show sums of £4 and £4 19s. being paid to Burdon, the first being a payment to WILLIAM SWAYN and Burdon jointly.² The rebuilding of the church was then nearing completion. In 1512 and 1513, when the vestry and south porch were built, he received two payments of 20s. and one of 10s. from the churchwardens.³ It may be inferred that he was the mason in charge of the work during the final stages. In 1519, when some work requiring the employment of two or three masons for several weeks on the new gate-tower of *King's Hall, Cambridge*, was in progress, Burdon received a payment of 10s., probably as master mason.⁴ This gate-tower (now the Great Gate of Trinity College) appears to have been begun as far back as 1490, perhaps from designs by JOHN WASTELL, but though the accounts show that a little work was done on it in 1519, the upper stages were not built and finished until 1528–35.

No documentary evidence has been discovered for work by William Burdon at Ely either on the cathedral church or the monastic buildings.

William BURDON, who worked as a mason at *Westminster Abbey* in 1467–68 at 3s. 4d. a week and for whom vesture was bought,⁵ may perhaps be identified with the William Burdon of Bury St. Edmunds, mason, who died in 1496. In his will, dated 15 May and proved 14 September of that year, his mother and his wife Joan are mentioned as living.⁶ A *William Boredon* occurs in documents at *King's College, Cambridge*, between 1467 and 1473 serving freemasons and 'dawbing' and 'cleying' walls of college buildings and tenements;⁷ in 1480 he was one of the masons employed on the church of *St. John the Baptist*, which adjoined the Old Court of the College.⁸

A.O.

¹ GHT, 139–151; ² CGB, 'B', I, 236, 248; ³ CWM, 14, 20, 21; ⁴ TCM, KHA, xxii, 131; ⁵ WAM, 23533 (J.H.H.); ⁶ BW, vi, 43; ⁷ KCM, Mundum Books; ⁸ KCM, College Accs., vol. vi; J. W. Clark in CAC, IV, 354

BURGESS, William [Burges, Burgeys] (*fl.* 1456–1472) Mason

Mason (*lathamus*) to the Bishop of Winchester at *Farnham Castle*. In 1456–57 he repaired defects in the new tower and built a new stair in it of brick for £1 11s. 8d., while in 1471–72 he repaired the outer wall on the east side.

PRO, Eccl. 2–2–155827, 2–3–155836

BURGO, Gilbert de (*fl. c.* 1230–1235) Mason

Master, apparently of *Lincoln Cathedral*, for a short period between Master MICHAEL and Master ALEXANDER. He held land in the parish of St. Clement in the Bail in or soon after 1232, and between 1235 and 1239 witnessed a deed along with Alexander as his mate (*socio suo*).

LRS, LXII, (*Reg. Ant.*), ix, nos. 2620, 2600 (*K.M.*)

BURNELL, Ralph [Brunell, Burnel the Carpenter, ? Ralph the Carpenter] (*fl.* 1220–†c. 1254) Carpenter

Master carpenter in the service of Henry III; probably identical with Master Ralph who was one of the King's two Master Carpenters in 1212, with NICHOLAS DE AUNDELY, and who received a reward of £1 on 23 January 1223/4, and certainly with the Burnell or Brunell who is named as a carpenter receiving livery and wages of 9d. a day from 1220 to 1223;[1] with Master Hugh his colleague Burnell was engaged in 1226 on the works of *Carmarthen* and *Cardigan Castles*, taking 9d. a day each, and was ordered to stay on the works there on 5 January 1226/7.[2] On 22 July 1227, he was allowed 2 marks (£1 6s. 8d.) in part payment of arrears due to him, and a further mark a week later. His wages of 9d. a day continued to be allowed through 1228 and 1229 by instalments, but were generally considerably in arrears.[3] On 19 July 1229 he was one of the King's Carpenters at work in *Windsor Castle*, and continued to receive pay during the following year. He worked at Windsor Castle in 1233, still paid at 9d. a day, and for 55 days in the following year at the same rate.[4]

On 28 November 1236 he was granted 5d. a day when working and 3d. a day when not working as a retaining fee, as from 8 August 1236, together with Masters Nicholas, Hugh, and William, King's Carpenters (i.e. NICHOLAS DE AUNDELY, HUGH ALBEMUNT, and WILLIAM LE RUTIER). Payments for the carpenters' liveries were authorized from time to time

throughout 1235 and in May 1242 Burnell was being paid 6d. a day as the carpenter at Windsor.[5]

In the meantime he had been working at *Westminster Palace*,[6] and from time to time he appears among the carpenters to whom allowances of 3d. a day were to be paid, until April 1247.[7] He later became master carpenter at Windsor Castle, where he died before 4 December 1254.[8] His son, Thomas Burnell, had been appointed to hold the office in his stead before 22 February 1261/2.

It was afterwards found that Thomas had not been trained as a carpenter and was therefore unable to fill the office. The King, however, in regard for the long service of Ralph granted Thomas the fee of 3d. a day for life of his special grace.[9]

[1] HLC, I, 122, 441b, 449b, 477b, 527b, 582b; [2] WWH, III, 32; [3] CLR 1226–40, 42, 45, 129, 135, 136; [4] HWC; CLR, 1226–40, 138, 141, 147, 156, 169; [5] *Ibid.*, 247; VI, 2222, 2241, 2263, 2291; [6] CCR 1231–4, 200; [7] CLR 1226–40, 470; 1240–5, 7, 150, 167, 181, 184, 194, 225, 247, 277, 301; 1245–51, 21, 47, 87, 115; [8] CLR 1257–60, 187; CPR 1258–66, 202; [9] *Ibid.*, 387

BURREY, Thomas (*fl.* 1527–   ) Mason

Was paid sums of 1s. 3d. and 1s. 10d. in 1527 for work on the church and churchyard wall of *Tilney All Saints*, Norfolk. He and his man were allowed 11d. board in addition to these payments, and it seems not unlikely that Burrey was the 'freemason of Lyne' (King's Lynn) who was paid £5 in 1505, and the 'ffreemason' who made the church battlements and other work in 1523–25, receiving a total of £13 6s. 8d.

SCT

BURTON, John, I (*fl. c.* 1400–1403) Mason

Mason or quarryman employed to break stones for the works of *York Minster*, c. 1400–03. He was paid 1s. 8d. per week and had a robe price 6s. 8d. by agreement. Perhaps identical with JOHN BURTON II.

RFY, 20, 22

BURTON, John, II (*fl.* 1446–   ) Mason

Was master mason (*magister latimus et cementarius*) at *Beverley Minster* in 1445–46. Perhaps identical with JOHN BURTON I, or with JOHN BARTON.

ERA, VI; VII, 64

BURTON, Stephen (*fl.* 1442–†1488) Mason

Of the parish of St. Michael, Cornhill, London. He seems to have specialized in making and supplying stone fireplaces, for his will shows that he had a stock of 'parells' (i.e.

apparels) for chimneys.

In September 1442 Stephen Burton was among the masons working at *Eton College*.[1] On 26 February 1476/7, as one of the four sworn masons and carpenters of the City of London, he made a report on the Abbot of Winchcombe's house in Fleet Street;[2] in 1480, as a churchwarden of St. Michael's Cornhill, received a quitclaim of lands and tenements in Cornhill, granted to that church.[3] On 28 August 1482 John, Lord Howard (created Duke of Norfolk in the following year), paid £1 6s. 8d. to 'Burton of Cornhill at London for the aparayll of a chymeny cont. xj. pesis which was sent to Stoke' (*Tendring Hall*, Stoke-by-Nayland, Suffolk).[4] 'Burton', Mason, and his men' and 'Stevyn Burton' are named as carrying out repairs and inserting chimneys in houses belonging to St. Mary-at-Hill, London, in 1479–81.[5]

In his will,[6] dated 30 October and proved 13 November 1488, he described himself as citizen and freemason of London and desired to be buried in St. Michael's Church, Cornhill, 'vnder the belfrey in the place where the body of Johane my wif lieth buried'. All the tools and instruments pertaining to his craft were to be evenly divided between John Rolle, William Somerby, Thomas Clavell, John Woodale, and Richard Loremere, to each of whom he also bequeathed 'a parell of a Chymney'. John Rolle is described as 'sometyme my servaunt'. His executors were to sell to the best advantage 'all the stonys which I haue vnbequeathed'. Four torches to be used at his burying were afterwards to be distributed between his parish church 'to bren at the lavacion [*sic*] of the blessed sacrament', St. Olave's Jewry ('Saint Tolowse in the old Jurye'), Edmonton parish church and the parish church of Our Lady of Rickmansworth, Herts.; possibly he had carried out work at these churches or some of them. To the Austin Friars of London, where he wished a trental of masses to be said for his soul and his wife's soul, he bequeathed a covered maser with a silver-gilt band. 'To euery pore woman of my Crafte within London' he bequeathed 4d. He named as first executor William Clavell, citizen and freemason.

Richard BURTON and *William* BURTON were freemasons who worked at Eton College, the former from July to September 1448, the latter from September 1448 to June 1449.[7]

J.H.H.; A.O.
[1] KJE; [2] RLW, II, 565; [3] *LHR*, 210(16); [4] PNA, 285; [5] LMR, 104–5, 107–8; [6] *PCC*, 13 Milles; [7] KJE (*G.P.J.*)

BURWELL, John de [Burwelle] (*fl.* 1339–1340) Carver (*Burwell, Cambs.*)

Carved an image on the central wooden boss of the lantern vault at *Ely Cathedral* in 1339–40, being paid 2s. and taking his board at the Prior's table.

CSR, II, 98

BURWELL, Robert (*fl.* 1350–1360) Carver

From 26 April 1350 was engaged on carving the seats (*cedilis*) of the stalls for the chapel at *Windsor Castle*, being paid 2s. a week. In 1351–53 he was carving the stalls of *St. Stephen's Chapel, Westminster*.[1]

In 1359–60 he was paid for 8 weeks work at *Ely Cathedral* at 3s. 4d. a week, for making gargoyles and images for corbels at 'le blakerode'.[2]

[1] *PRO*, E.101–471–5; 492–27; [2] CSR, II, 194

BURY, John [a Bury, Bery] (*fl.* 1472–? 1522) Mason (? *Bury St. Edmunds, Suffolk*)

Of Cambridge; on 22 June and 11 Dec. 1491 contracted to make the masonry, tiling, and ceiling of eight chambers at *Great Chesterford*, Essex, while ALWYN NEWMAN, carpenter of Cambridge, was to perform the timberwork.[1] During the years 1472–74 John Bury was employed on small tiling jobs at *King's College*, including the tiling of the unfinished turrets of the entrance gate-tower of the Old Court for protection from the weather;[2] in 1477 he was paid for tiling the masons' lodge;[3] and in 1504 he received 26s. 8d. for making a chimney in the provost's lodge.[4] At *King's Hall* the accounts show that he was employed in various capacities: in 1486–87 (repairing a chamber), 1489–90, 1498–99 (making or supplying materials for a new wall along the east frontage of the college) and in 1504–05.[5] In 1499–1500 he and his servants were paid 20s. by the treasurers of the borough for the making and workmanship of a wall called 'le Tollebothe Walle'.[6] At *Holy Trinity Church, Cambridge*, he built a wall on the east side of the churchyard in 1506–07 and in the next year was paid for supplying bricks for it.[7]

It is possible that this mediaeval Balbus was identical with a prominent Cambridge townsman, for in the year when he made the

Tollbooth wall, John a Bury also received the freedom of the borough;[6] he was a bailiff in 1502, 1503, and 1506, mayor in 1510 and 1517, M.P. in 1514, and died in 1522.[8] In his will he endowed an obit in St. Sepulchre's Church, where he was buried.[9] The Hagable rentals of 1483, 1491, and 1493 show John a Bury paying a rent on a house in the Ward on the near side of the bridge (*Citra Pontem*); its position is more precisely stated in a rental of 1514–15 in which 2*d.* was paid by John Bury, alderman, on a footbridge behind his tenement leading to the Green Croft, i.e. a few yards east of St. Sepulchre's Church.[10] The entries relating to the mason all refer to comparatively small jobs, but he may have made a profitable business out of bricks and tiles, and the successful local builder then as now could take an active part in municipal affairs. If the mason was the same man as the alderman, his admission to the freedom comparatively late in his career can be explained on the supposition that he was not a native but came from Bury. He had to pay the full fine of 20*s.*

A.O.

[1] SHB, 550–2; JCB, 198, 203; [2] *KCM*, Mundum Books, 1472–3, 1473–4; [3] *KCM*, College Accs., vol. vi; [4] *KCM*, Mundum Book 1503–4; CAC, IV, 295; [5] *TCM, KHA*, xviii, 20, 178; xix, 257; xx, 229; [6] *CCM*, Box 18/71, No. 9; [7] *CWT*, 81a, 18b; [8] CBD, 148 and *CCM*, Cross Book, *ff.* 303 *et seq.*; [9] *PCC*, 5 Bodfelde; [10] CBD, 63, 59, 66, 46

BURY, Richard de (*fl.* 1352–   ) Carpenter
In 1352 was master carpenter at *Trinity Hall, Cambridge*, founded two years previously by William Bateman, Bishop of Norwich. By patent, dated 8 February 1352, protection during pleasure was granted to Master Richard de Bury and other carpenters hired by the Bishop to construct houses for his new college, in carrying the required timber which they had bought in Essex, Norfolk, Suffolk, and Cambridgeshire. The carpenters were, however, to come to the King whenever he required their services.

CPR 1350–4, 225

BUTLER, John [Botiller] (*fl.* 1435–   ) Mason
Of 'Totyngton' (Toddington), Beds.; was commissioned on 14 May 1435 to take stone-cutters, labourers, stone, lime, etc., for the repair of the King's manor of *Clipston* in Sherwood, Notts.

CPR 1429–36, 473

Thomas BOTELER, citizen and mason of London, of the parish of St. Peter Cornhill, made his will on 14 Sept. 1409, constituting his wife Sabina executrix and principal legatee. The will was proved on 21 April 1413.

PPR, Archd. Ct. of London, I, f. 283

BUTLER, Richard [Buttler] (*fl.* 1540) Carpenter
On 16 August 1540 agreed with the mayor and commonalty of *Guildford*, Surrey, to make a market-house, 15 feet out into the street and with an upper storey having three bay windows, the central one 8 feet wide and the others 6 feet. Butler was to have all the necessary timber and boards brought to him and to clean and re-use, or else make new, the bargeboards, doubtless from an older building on the site. The work was to be finished by 8 days after Michaelmas following (7 October 1540) and Butler was to be paid 5 marks (£3 6*s.* 8*d.*)

DGB, 42–3

BUXTON, William [Boston, Boxton, Bukston] (*fl.* 1508–1535) Carpenter
Of Cambridge; from 1508 to 1515 worked at *King's College Chapel, Cambridge*, probably as one of the wardens of the carpenters under the master carpenter, RICHARD RUSSELL. His pay in 1508 was at the rate of 6*d.* a day; he was employed in selecting and supervising the felling of timber in various parks.[1] The Kitchen Accounts of the college show that he and his fellow carpenter, THOMAS WATLINGTON, were frequently entertained in hall in 1512 and 1514.[2] He was also employed by the college on minor jobs, e.g. in 1509–10 repairing the west door of the old chapel; in 1519 working on the gallery over the river and repairing the rails in the churchyard, also repairing the beds of fellows and scholars in diverse chambers.[3] He was much employed at *Holy Trinity Church*. In 1509–10 he made a new stock for the second bell; in 1518–19 he was paid 4*d.* 'for his counseill' when a new frame for the bells was made by John Manhall; between 1524 and 1526 he made new seats for the church and at the conclusion of the work was given 20*s.* 'over and beside his bargain'. In 1525, when he made a new wheel for the great bell, the churchwardens began to pay him a fee of 1*s.* 4*d.* a year for looking after the bells; the item occurs regularly in their accounts until 1530, when there is a hiatus.[4] At *Great St. Mary's Church* he was paid

for making the windows in the vestry in 1514 and for mending the great bell in 1518.[5] Between 1519 and 1533 he was employed four times by the university in setting up and taking down the stage used for the degrees ceremony which when not in use was stored at the Grey Friars.[6] In 1523 he made the gates of the new gate-tower of *King's Hall* (now the Great Gate of Trinity College) which still exist. He contracted to make these gates for £6 13s. 4d. The timber was obtained from Chesterford in Essex, and seems to have been paid for by the college.[7] The upper stages of the gate-tower were not built until 1528 to 1535, when THOMAS LOVEDAY contracted for the woodwork; there is an item, however, in the accounts of 4d. paid to 'Bukston' for setting up the doors.[8] When the stalls in King's College Chapel were erected, Buxton seems to have been one of the carpenters employed in framing them and setting them up. No accounts for the work have been discovered, but the Kitchen Accounts of the college for the year 1534–35 show that joiners, carvers, and carpenters were entertained in hall on several occasions, and their presence is probably to be explained by their employment on the stalls, which from the occurrence of Anne Boleyn's initials can be dated between the years 1532 and 1536. Between October 1534 and August 1535 Buxton was a guest on at least six occasions.[9]

A.O.
[1] *KCM*, Building Accs. 1508–9 and 1509–15; [2] *KCM*, Kitchen Accs., vol. xi; [3] *KCM*, Mundum Books; [4] *CWT*, passim; [5] CWM, 24, 36; [6] CGB, 'B', II, 82, 107, 110, 173, 182; [7] *TCM, KHA*, xxiii, 126, 205; WCC, II, 452, 454; [8] WCC, II, 454; [9] *KCM*, Kitchen Accs., vol. xiv

BYNDYLL, John (*fl.* 1392–1393) Mason
Master mason taking 4d. per day in January 1392/3, when he was in charge of work at the vineyard of *Windsor*.
PRO, E.101–496–1 (*L.F.S.*)

Bynks, Thomas—see BINKS

BYTHAM, John of (*fl.* 1317–   ) Carpenter (*Bytham, Lincs.*)
Charged in the Fair Court of St. Ives in 1317 with having put alder and willow instead of oak timber into a house which he had built for Roger of Moulton. John pleaded that he had used only oak and had not broken any covenant.
SCM, 103

CAKE, Thomas, alias MALLYNG [Kake] (*fl.* 1378–†1413) Mason
Mason of London, and a viewer of the city in 1378–9.[1] He was a Master of the Masons in 1386, and a Common Councillor for Bridge Ward.[2] On 10 February 1409/10 Thomas the son of Robert Kake, alias Thomas Mallyng, was discharged from jury service because of old age.[3] The will of Thomas Cake alias Malling, dated 1 October 1412, was proved on 25 September 1413.[4]
[1] CKL, no. 620; [2] CLB 'H', 273–4, 281; [3] CLB 'I', 83; [4] AQC, XLI, 138, from *PCC* 28 Marche (*N.L.R.*)

CALDHAM, Gabriel [Calldham, Cauldeham, Coldam] (*fl.* 1530–†1570) Mason (? *Coldham, Cambs.*)
Mason working in the London area, and a member of the London Masons' Company. He was working on the repair of *Brent Bridge*, Mddx., in 1530 at 10d. a day, and had two apprentices, of whom the elder, William Holmes, was taking 7d. daily, and the other 5d. Caldham also provided stone for the work. In 1531 he was temporary warden of masons at *Westminster Palace*, at 8d. a day, and made 'parrells' for chimneys there.[1] Next year he provided stone for Greenwich and for Windsor, and in 1533 was warden at the *Tower of London* and was also paid for stone. He provided Reigate stone for *Greenwich Palace* in 1533–34 and worked there at 8d. a day, and also supplied stone for the manor of More. He was again selling stone for the works at Greenwich in 1537 and in 1538 was a member of the Court of Assistants of the London Masons' Company.[2] From 1539 to 1543 he appears as providing stone for Canterbury Manor, Calais and Guisnes, and Dartford; and from 1543 to 1544 had a year's lease of 'St. Helen's Ferme' in 'Estframeling', Kent. His will was proved on 23 August 1570.[3]
KJS
[1] *WAM*, 12257; *PRO*, E.36–251; [2] MHN, IV, 19; [3] AQC, XLVIII, 157

CALNE, Walter de (*fl.* 1354–1359) Carpenter
Master carpenter in charge of repairs at *Clarendon Palace* in 1354–59.
HKW, II, 917

CAMBRIDGE, Matthew of (*fl. c.* 1214–1235) Monk
Benedictine monk; directed the work of the octagonal spire and later of the Lady Chapel

at *St. Alban's Abbey* for Abbot William de Trumpington (1214–1235). Matthew of Cambridge was keeper of the Abbey Seal and Trumpington's private secretary. It is very doubtful whether he can be considered an architect, and he was probably only in administrative and financial control of the works.

(SMC); VCH, *Herts.*, II, 485

CAMBRIDGE, Thomas of [Cantebrugge] (*fl.* 1364–1370) Mason

Thomas de Cantebrugge, citizen of Hereford, in 1364 entered into a bond with the Dean and Chapter of *Hereford* to complete the work of their new chapel of St. John the Evangelist and St. Michael, and the new Chapter House, within seven years from 13 December 1364. In 1367 he received £11 18*s.* 1*d.* for one quarter's payment of a yearly sum of £50 due for this work; the receipt describes him as 'mason and citizen of Hereford'. Thomas may have been a contractor carrying out the designs of JOHN OF EVESHAM, in 1359 appointed master mason to the cathedral.

CCH, 231, 232

CAMPDEN, Nicholas of (*fl.* 1336) Mason (? *Chipping Campden, Glos.*)

In 1336 an enquiry was held into the state of the keep of *Gloucester Castle*. 'Master John the mason', presumably JOHN DE TEYNTON, and 'Master Nicholas the mason of Campden' were called to give expert evidence.

HKW, II, 655

CAMPTON, John (*fl.* 1446–1461) Mason

Was appointed for life master mason of *Chester* and North Wales on 2 July 1446, at the death of JOHN ASSER, junior. He seems to have held the office until 1461, when WILLIAM REDICHE was appointed.

DKR, XXXI (1870)

Cancellar, William—see CHANCELLOR

Canon, Edmund—see ST. ANDREW

CANON, John (*fl.* 1424–1427) Carpenter

Master carpenter, appointed on 8 February 1423/4 to have charge of all the work of carpentry in the castle and lordship of *Hertford*, the castle of *Pleshey*, and all the manors of Queen Katherine in the county of Essex, taking a fee of £2 yearly with 6*d.* for every working day. In the year to Michaelmas 1427 he was paid £22 18*s.* 9½*d.* for repairs of houses in Hertford Castle, as well as his wages for 160 working days.

PRO, D.L. 29–58–1096

CANON, Stephen (*fl.* 1470–1473) Carpenter

Carpenter of *Bristol*; acted as a viewer of the city in 1470 and in 1473 (see RAWLYN WILLIAMS). He was very possibly identical with the Stephen Kerver who about this time made the canopy over the altar of *St. John's, Glastonbury*, and collaborated with George Organmaker on the organ-case there.[1]

(*A.O.; G.M.D.B.*) BLR, II, 132; Sotheby's Catalogue, 13 April 1981, Lot 15
[1] SDN, IV, 282

CANON, Thomas (*fl.* 1385–   ) Marbler

'Marbrer', of Corfe, Dorset; in 1385 was paid £30 6*s.* 8*d.* for making 13 stone images in the likeness of kings to stand in *Westminster Hall*, as well as two larger images at £3 6*s.* 8*d.* each.[1] Some of these are presumably the statues of kings still remaining in the Hall.[2]
[1] SHB, 32; *PRO*, E.101–473–2 (*L.F.S.*); [2] GMS, 229–31

CANTELOU, John [Cantelowe] (*fl.* 1439–*c.* 1449) Mason

Was the chief working mason at *Windsor Castle* in 1439 and 1440, when he was in charge of the making of the great stair leading up to the Donjon. He took 6*d.* a day, working for 126 days in the year from Michaelmas 1439 to Michaelmas 1440. In the account for the next year he appears for 91 days, working on the wall of the Donjon ditch, and upon a new tower in the middle bailey. Meanwhile, on 13 February 1440/1, he had been appointed master mason of the King's works at Windsor Castle, with a lodging in the Castle and 10*d.* a day. He probably held this office until the appointment of JOHN THIRSK in 1449.

HWC, I, 229, 235

CANTERBURY, Alexander of (*fl.* 1313–   ) Mason

Was a sworn surveyor of masons' work to the City of London in August 1313. With Master SIMON DE PABENHAM, mason, and Master ROBERT OF NORTHAMPTON, carpenter, he was to 'make partition of tenements in the city', and to act with the Chamberlain on this survey.

(LKC, 363); CLB, 'B' 15

CANTERBURY, John of (*fl.* 1221–1225) Carpenter

Was one of the King's Carpenters working at *Westminster* in 1221, when on 28 May he was granted 1*d.* in alms by the King.[1] About 1225 'John Carpenter of Canterbury, carpenter of the lord King of England' paid 11s. for the grant of quitrents of 2s. 1½d. in the parish of St. Olave, Southwark.² Canterbury may have been identical with JOHN the Carpenter I. He seems to have lived in Westminster.³

HKC
¹ HLC, I, 451b, 460; ² CTS, 50 (No. 237); ³ WAM, 'Domesday', f. 552v.

CANTERBURY, Michael of [de Cantuaria; M. le Macun] (fl. 1275–1321) Mason

Master mason of Canterbury, where he was renting a tenement in Northgate from Christ Church Priory in 1275 and onwards until 1290.¹ In 1275–76 payments totalling £2 10s. 0d. were made to him by the Treasurer of Christ Church Priory, Canterbury, for work on the *Prior's House* in London, adjoining the church of St. Mary-le-Bow on the west; on 16 August 1277 he was paid 3s. for going to London from Canterbury about the works of the Prior's House and 2s. for another journey thither in the following year, with further sums of 2s. and 4s. later. In 1279–80 he was paid 5s. for the work of the 'new Tower', apparently at *Canterbury*.²

In 1284 Master Michael 'le Macun' was a witness to a grant made by the priory of St. Laurence, Canterbury, of ground in Ruttington Lane next to St. Augustine's Abbey.³ He had probably moved to London by about 1290, for from 1291 until 1294 he was making the *Cheapside Eleanor Cross* at a total cost of £226 13s. 4d.⁴ This Cross was the second in importance of the series: that at Charing cost £650, and those outside London about £134 each. Fragments from the Cheapside Cross are preserved in the Museum of London.⁵

On the morrow of Trinity, 21 Edward I (1 June 1293) a fine was levied at Canterbury whereby Master Michael le Mazun and his wife Mary (by proxy of William Brodeye) acquired a messuage in the suburbs of Canterbury from William le Scriveyn of Oxford and Helewyse his wife, whose property it had been.⁶

On 28 April 1292 work under his charge began at the new chapel of *St. Stephen* in Westminster Palace, and continued for some years until progress was stopped by a fire in the palace which in 1298 made the royal apartments uninhabitable. A lodge for him, and measurements taken by him, are mentioned; he also made purchases of marble.⁷ He was probably the designer of the canopied tombs of Edmund Crouchback and Aveline

of Lancaster in *Westminster Abbey*, both of which must have been made about the time of Earl Edmund's death in 1296.⁸

In March 1306 Master Michael of Canterbury was sent to Winchester to prepare *Wolvesey Castle* for a royal visit.⁹ In 1312 Master Michael was in charge of the works of the *Black Friars* of *London*, then visited by Edward II, who gave a reward to the master and the 24 masons working under him.¹⁰ Canterbury was probably the 'Master Michael le Maceon' who was first named of the commission appointed on 5 March 1315/16 to arrange for the paving of the City of London.¹¹ On 12 May 1315 he was named as designer and supervisor of a wall to be built round *Eltham Manor* by WILLIAM DE HOO and others, and in 1316–17 he became surety for Hoo, who had been ordered to rebuild the wall which had been scamped.¹²

On 29 September 1321 a sum of 20s. was paid for the robe of Master Michael of Canterbury from the account for works in Westminster Palace, including the newly restarted operations of St. Stephen's Chapel.¹³ This important entry shows that Master Michael was still in charge after the long hiatus in the works, but it is likely that he died soon afterwards, since by the next year it was WALTER OF CANTERBURY who was named as master.

The *Michael of* CANTERBURY, marblemason, who on 9 August 1332 was paid 8s. for a boat-load of ragstone for St. Stephen's Chapel,¹⁴ was presumably a younger namesake.

Michael of Canterbury is of outstanding importance as the bearer of the Kentish style to London and the court of Westminster, and as the original architect of the Royal Chapel of St. Stephen. He was probably the designer of the tomb of Archbishop Peckham (†1292) in *Canterbury Cathedral*, which already employs the ogee curve in minor details, as does the monument of Edmund Crouchback and that of Bishop William of Louth (†1298) in *Ely Cathedral*, also to be attributed to him.¹⁵ The chapel of St. Etheldreda at *Ely Place, London*, which seems to have been built for Bishop Louth (1290–98) is significantly a smaller version of the turreted chapel with undercroft introduced by Master Michael at St. Stephen's, Westminster.¹⁶ Elements in the window tracery at Ely Place, and also the alternation of larger and smaller shafts in the doorway, again find their counterparts in the Lady Chapel of *Old St. Paul's, London*, completed *c.* 1307–12.[17] Here, too, the buttress-pinnacles seem to have been an enlargement of the type used by Canterbury on his canopied tombs. Master Michael was certainly the leader of the 'London School' of tomb design,[18] and one of the chief formative influences on English style.

(APD; LKC)

[1] *CCA*, Box D, Rentals (*W.P.B.*); [2] *LP*, MS. 242, *ff.* 27, 33v., 43v., 52; [3] *CCA*, MS. C.20, p. 93–4 (*W.U.*); [4] BMH; [5] VCL, 102; [6] FFK, Edw. I, No. 396 (*N.H.M.*); [7] TSS, 2; BBW, 424–5; *PRO*, E.101–468–6; [8] LKC, 182–4; [9] HKW, I, 207; II, 862–3; [10] HKW, I, 207; [11] CLB 'E', 55–6; [12] SHB, 27–8, 422–4; [13] *PRO*, E.101–469–3; [14] BBW, 155; [15] HSC, 196; [16] RCHM, *West London*, 44–5, 123; GAL, 75–8; [17] HWH, Pl. XLI; [18] Count Paul Biver in AJ, LXVII (1910), 51–65

CANTERBURY, Michael of, junior [de Cantuaria] (*fl.* ? 1292–1334) Mason

May have been the Michael who was warden (*apparitor*) of the masons working on *St. Stephen's Chapel* in Westminster Palace, taking pay at 3*s.* 6*d.* a week from 1292 to 1296, under Master MICHAEL OF CANTERBURY.[1] In 1325 one Michael of Canterbury was first of 25 masons, paid 5½*d.* a day in summer and 4½*d.* in winter; from 1331 to 1334 he was named as *apparilator* and 'lieutenant and keeper' for Master THOMAS OF CANTERBURY, being paid 5½*d.* a day in 1331 and 6*d.* thereafter.[2]

[1] *PRO*, E.101–468–6, 547–18; [2] E.101–469–8, 468–3, 469–11, 12, 469–17, 470–15

CANTERBURY, Peter of (*fl.* 1311–1313) Carpenter

Was chief carpenter at the *Palace of Westminster* from 1311 to 1313, when he was succeeded by JOHN LE ROKE.

LKC, 187

CANTERBURY, Simon of (*fl.* 1299–†1341) Carpenter

Carpenter of London; he lived in the parish of St. Margaret Pattens in Billingsgate Ward, and frequent mentions of his tenement occur in property transactions in that parish. He was also a witness to many of these deeds, from 1299 to 1340.[1] On 11 November 1308 he contracted to build a house in London,[2] and undertook a further contract in 1313, but in this case, owing to the death of his client, he was not able to begin work until 1320.[3]

As 'Simon le Carpenter' of Billingsgate Ward he was assessed to pay 13*s.* 4*d.* in the taxation of 1319, while in that of 1332 he was

to pay 8*s.*;[4] in 1325 he is mentioned as being owed certain payments from a tenement assigned to the New Hospital of St. Mary without Bishopsgate.[5] In 1336 he was the first named of four carpenters on a commission to inquire into the state of the *Tower of London*, the others being JOHN DE TOTENHAM, Robert de Farnham, and Thomas de Gylingham.[6] He was no doubt the most important carpenter in the City at this period, and presumably of considerable age.

On 19 June 1338 he granted a tenement in St. Margaret Pattens to John de Hatfelde, chandler,[7] and his will, made on 11 April 1340, shows that he owned a good deal of property.[8] To his second wife Isabella[9] he left a life interest in his brewery, with remainder to his daughter Alice, who was also to have a house below the brewery called 'la Newewodehous', with an area, solar, and garret, and also another tenement in the parish. A third tenement, also in the parish of St. Margaret Pattens, was to be sold and the proceeds devoted to pious and charitable uses.

In August 1340 Master Simon appeared at the inquest held on his neighbour John Bone, dyer,[10] and he died in the next year, his will being enrolled in November 1341. His daughter Alice is again heard of in 1345, when John Joye of St. Margaret Pattens acknowledged that he owed her the sum of £18.[11]

Simon of Canterbury seems to have graduated as a master about 1316, as he is almost invariably referred to by that title afterwards, but never earlier. He may have been related to PETER OF CANTERBURY.

HEA

[1] *LHR*, 30(59), 32(30), 34(24), 47(74, 114), 53(89), 55(49), 64(99, 131), 65(61); *LBH, passim*; [2] RML, 66; CLB, 'C', *f.*96; SHB, 417–18; [3] CLB, 'E', 21; [4] WLE; UFT, 61 *ff.*; [5] CLB, 'E', 205; [6] BHT, App. to pt. i, 273; [7] *LBH*, D. 12; *LHR* 65(61); [8] SWL, I, 450; [9] Simon's wife in 1301 was Margery de Hadley — *LHR* 30(59); but by 1318 he had married Isabella widow of Richard de Hormede — *LHR* 47(74); [10] SCR, 266; [11] CCR 1343–6, 542; cf. *LHR*, 69(133), 76(43, 44)

CANTERBURY, Thomas of [de Cantuaria] (*fl.* 1323–1335) Mason

In November 1323 was a mason working under WALTER OF CANTERBURY at *Westminster Palace* and the *Tower of London*; in 1325, described as Master Thomas de Cantuaria, he was pledge for Master Walter's completion of work at the Tower; and next year was working at 3*s.* a week on the new chapel in the Palace (St. Stephen's),[1] and on the new passage from the chapel to the Painted Chamber; he also in each year had a grant of £1 for a robe. From September 1325 his pay was raised to 1s. a day.[2] He was continuously in charge until 1335, taking the same salary and £1 for a robe yearly.[3] About this time, 1326, he seems to have begun the new chapel of the *London Guildhall*, where he was paid £7 17s. 0d. in 1332. When work was started upon the upper chapel of St. Stephen's in 1331, Master Thomas of Canterbury was paid 6s. a week from his 'first coming to Westminster' in the week ending 27 May. He also received £1 for a robe. His duties included work 'in tracing the moulds', or 'on the moulds in the tracing house' (*in trasura super moldas operanti*), and 'drawing upon the tracing', or 'on the tracing floor' (*tractanti super trasuram*).[4] He was possibly the Thomas de Cantuar of the Ward of Walbrook in London assessed to pay 17s. 9½d. in 1332.[5] In 1335 he was appointed guardian of the children of John de Wyncestre, the King's plumber.[6] Master Thomas was certainly the designer of the upper chapel of St. Stephen's, which even after mutilation seemed to have been 'the first of all the architectural works of the land'. It was the final flower of the Decorated style in its full perfection, while Master Thomas's immediate successor as King's Master Mason, WILLIAM DE RAMSEY was at the very same time, 1332, at St. Paul's Cathedral, experimenting with novelties which were soon to turn to fully developed Perpendicular.[7]

Master Thomas's detail at St. Stephen's Chapel closely resembled that of the tomb of John of Eltham (†1334) in Westminster Abbey and that of several works at Canterbury, notably the great gatehouse of *St. Augustine's Abbey* (c. 1308), the stone screens surrounding the *Cathedral* choir (1304– c. 1320), the tomb of Archbishop Mepham (†1333), and the great window of St. Anselm's Chapel in the Cathedral, behind Mepham's tomb, built in 1336. It is likely that Master Thomas began his career at Canterbury, and continued to have charge of works there after coming to London.

A mason of the same name who was a working mason at Westminster Palace in 1344 at 4½d. a day,[8] and on 16 August 1355 was ordered to buy 20 loads of Egremont (Totternhoe) stone for the works of the Palace may have been a relative.[9] This man was warden (*apparilator*) of masons' work in 1357, taking 7d. a day.[10]

(LKC; BBW; APD; BAA)

[1] *PRO*. E.101–468–3, 469–7; [2] *PRO*, E.101–468–3; [3] E.101–469–12, 469–17, 470–15; [4] E.101–469–11; [5] UFT, 61ff.; [6] SWL, I, 406; [7] HSC; [8] *PRO*, E.101–469–6; [9] CPR 1354–8, 277; [10] *PRO*, E.101–545–35 (*L.F.S.*); cf. HKW, II, 992

CANTERBURY, Walter of (*fl.* 1319–1327) Mason

Probably identical with the 'Master Walter le Masoun' who in 1319 was assessed to pay 2s. 6d. tax in the ward of Aldersgate, London.[1] In 1324–25, Master Walter de Canterbury, mason, rebuilt the outer curtain wall of the *Tower of London* from the Traitors' Gate to the 'nearer gate towards the hospice', a total of 412½ feet, for which he was paid at the rate of 2s. 6d. a foot.[2] About this time work was continued on the lower chapel or crypt of St. Stephen in Westminster Palace, and Walter was probably the designer of the vaulting and window tracery completed in 1327. He was certainly in charge of work at the Palace in 1322, and was King's Master Mason from 1323, if not earlier.[3]

At Westminster Abbey, Master Walter probably designed the tomb of Aymer de Valence (†1323), which has close affinities to the detail in St. Stephen's crypt.

It seems possible that he was identical with Walter the Marbler (le Marbrer) of London, who in 1281 served on a city jury,[4] in 1287 was surety for Master JOHN DOGET's fulfilment of a contract,[5] in 1293/4 was to pay 6s. 8d. to the subsidy as of Billingsgate Ward, was living near St. Magnus Church in 1327 and died about 1330,[6] leaving a widow Joan, who had been sister of Walter Bacheler.[7]

[1] WLE; [2] *PRO*, E.101–469–7 (*L.F.S.*); [3] *Ibid.*, 469–5; LKC, 188; [4] CLB, 'B', 9; [5] CNW, XXXVII, 295–7; [6] WLE; CLB, 'E', 224, 253–4; [7] SWL, I, 195–6

CAPELL, Walter (*fl.* 1369) Mason

In 1369 made four buttresses to support the wall of the moat at *Eltham Palace*.

HKW, II, 933

CARLTON, Adam [Carleton] (*fl.* 1343– 1359) Carpenter

Chief carpenter of all the King's castles, manors, and other works in *Ireland* between 1343 and 1359. He took at the Dublin Exchequer a yearly fee of £6 1s. 8d. by instalments until 1355, when this was increased to £9 2s. 6d.

IPC, I, pt. i, 44–6, 61–2, 67, 69, 76, 79; *BM*, Egerton MS. 1773, *f.* 22v.

CARLTON, Geoffrey of (*fl.* 1352–1380)
Mason

Was warden of the masons at *Windsor Castle* under JOHN DE SPONLEE, and from 4 June 1352 was in charge of the masons working on the Canons' latrine there.[1] From 27 October 1352 to 24 March 1352/3 he was, however, at work on the south cloister of *Westminster Abbey*, taking 3*s.* a week and a winter tunic price 6*s.* 8*d.*[2] During 1353 he was again in charge of those working on the Windsor cloister, and on the treasury with the vaulted porch beneath it. This work lasted until 1354, and he continued to hold the post of warden (*apparilator*) at 3*s.* 6*d.* a week during the building of the cloisters which lasted until 1356.[3]

He does not appear in the accounts after this but on 1 July 1359 received a grant for life of the office of 'warden of the King's works in masonry in Windsor Castle', at 6*d.* a day and £1 a year for his robe and shoes. This grant was confirmed by Richard II on 17 March 1378, and he took fees to 1380.[4]

The accounts show that he was paid £1 6*s.* 8*d.* for an old house in Windsor Castle in 1365–66.[5]

It is clear that Carlton was never the chief architect at Windsor Castle, as his pay was only half that of the designer (*ordinator*) first John de Sponlee, and afterwards WILLIAM WYNFORD. He was perhaps a son of *William de CARLTON*, who was a mason working at Westminster Palace in 1315, at the rate of 6*d.* a day.[6]

It is possible that this William was identical with the 'Willelmus de Carleton, masoun' who took up the freedom of York in 1294–95, but if so, Geoffrey would probably have been a grandson. *Adam de CARLTON*, mason, took up the freedom of York in 1323–24.[7]

CCR 1354–60, 215, 224
[1] HWC, I, 145; [2] *WAM*, 23455; [3] HWC, I, 150, 157; cf. HKW; [4] CPR 1377–81, 154; cf. HKW, I, 212; [5] *PRO*, E.101–493–22 (*G.P.J.*); [6] LKC; *PRO*, E.101–468–20; [7] YCF

CARLTON, Miles de (*fl.* 1272–1288)
Carpenter

Master carpenter on the works of *Rockingham Castle* in 1272–88.

HKW, II, 817

CAROW, Robert (*fl.* 1491–†1531) Carpenter

Carpenter of Oxford; in 1491–92 he and Thomas Jenkyns were paid 7*s.* by Oriel College for cutting and squaring timber in Stow Wood; in 1493–94, he received 8*d.* for repairs done on St. Mary's (Adam de Brome's) Chapel in *St. Mary the Virgin's Church*, and in the next year 6*s.* for work at *St. Bartholomew's Chapel, Cowley*.[1] In 1494 he also worked on a new vestry for *Queen's College*, and from then onwards was much employed by *Magdalen College*. In 1501–2 he made a new louvre for the hall at *All Souls*. In 1503 he is found acting as a surety for William Patenson, Principal of St. Edmund Hall,[2] and was paid 6*s.* 8*d.* by Magdalen College for timber and for work on the new tower.[3] In 1505–06 timber was bought by Oriel College for *Tackley's Inn*, and in 1507 Carow was working timbers for the building.[4] At the same time he obtained a lease from Magdalen College of a house called the Grammar Hall (now 42 and 43 High Street, Oxford),[5] and rented King's Mill and Holywell Mill from Merton College.[6]

Carow again carried out work at St. Bartholomew's, Cowley in 1510–11, for which he was paid 13*s.* 4*d.*,[7] and from 1511 to 1514 was engaged on the rebuilding of Buckley Hall (part of Tackley's Inn) for Oriel College, by contract. He was paid £5 13*s.* 4*d.* by instalments.[8] In 1516 he was Bailiff of Oxford, being proceeded against in December for impanelling privileged persons upon the Jury for the University Leets,[9] and in 1516–17 was doing minor repairs at *Oriel College*.[10] At this time he was busy upon the carpentry work of the new *Corpus Christi College*, notably that of the library range, 'accordyng to a platt' made by HUMPHREY COKE. This Carow made for £73 13*s.* 4*d.* while he also made 20 beds for the college at 2*s.* each, 'he fyndyng all manner of stoof except nayls'.[11] From 1518 to 1522 he was a Councillor of the city of Oxford and Guardian of Swynstock.[12] In 1518–19 he was paid £1 6*s.* 8*d.* for timber and workmanship at the Provost's Chamber of Queen's College.[13] Next year he was doing minor repairs for Oriel College and was paid a further sum of 6*s.* 8*d.* for work on Buckley Hall, while in 1520–21 he had £2 in part payment for building work on St. Mary's (Adam de Brome's) Chapel in the church of *St. Mary the Virgin*.[14]

At the taxation of 1524 Carow paid 5*s.*, living in the parish of St. Peter-in-the-East, his servants, James Lynche and Richard Sclatter, paying 2*s.* and 4*d.* respectively.[15] In 1524 and 1525 he was paid by Oriel College sums totalling £4 for work at *St. Barth-*

olomew's, *Cowley*, apparently including the timber ceiling which still exists.[16] He was also working at this time for Magdalen and for *New College*. Described as 'Mr Caro' he was warden of the carpenters of *Cardinal College* when work was begun in 1525, and seems to have stood in the same relation to Humphrey Coke, the chief carpenter, as did WILLIAM JOHNSON to JOHN LEBONS and HENRY REDMAN the masons.[17] At the same time he repaired the *South Bridge* for the city, being paid 4s. On 31 May 1529 he signed, as a Councillor of Oxford, the motion to conclude the 'varyances betwene the Towne and th'unyversyte'.[18] He seems to have died intestate early in 1531, as an inventory of his estate is preserved among the records of the Court of the Archdeacon of Oxford for April in that year. The gross value was only £2 7s. 9d., most of which was swallowed up by his funeral expenses and outstanding debts, including wages to Carow's servants, Christian and James. He was buried at St. Peter-in-the-East, the Proctors of the Lady Chapel receiving a fee of 6s. 8d. for his grave. Carow's end must have been a lonely one, for his food was provided by neighbours: among the debts figure 4s. 4d. to Edward Staunton 'for mete and drink and other thinges'; 12d. 'to Herrys wiffe and for brede drynk and vitaile'; 14d 'to Kateryn Ale wiffe for vitayle'; and lastly 10d. 'to a pour woman for keeping him in his sekenes'.[19]

(*E.M.J.*) GOC; HAC, 192, 200–2
[1] *OCO*, Treasurers' Accs., III, 192, 244, 272; [2] *EOH*, 277; [3] *MCO*, Liber Computi; [4] *OCO*, Treasurers' Accs., III, 568, 573, 575; [5] *EOH*, 168–9; [6] RAM, 321; [7] *OCO*, Treasurers' Accs., III, 672; [8] *Ibid.*, III, 722–3, 751; [9] TRO, 14, 15; [10] *OCO*, Treasurers' Accs., IV, 556; [11] *CCO*, Building Accs. 1517–18 (*A.O.*); SHB, 573; [12] TRO, 20–22, 28, 31, 32; [13] QCO, Long Rolls 1518–19 (*E.G.*); [14] *OCO*, Treasurers' Accs., IV, 644, 665; [15] ROD, 69; [16] *OCO*, Treasurers' Accs., IV, 732, 747; [17] MHO, 142, 148–9; [18] TRO, 54, 64; [19] *PPR*, Archd. Ct. of Oxford, S.I., 1, *ff.* 37–8

Carpenter, John—see BRANCHE, GOLDYNG

CARPENTER, Richard (*fl.* 1467–1468) Carpenter
Of Kinver (Kenvare), Staffs.; in 1467–68 was paid £5 6s. 8d. for panelling (*le syelyng*) of the parlour at *Hartlebury Castle*, Worcs., made at task.

PRO, Eccl. 2–128–92487

CARPENTER, Stephen [Carpynter] (*fl.* 1476–1477) Carpenter
Was paid £2 6s. 8d. for making the seats in

St. Ewen's Church, Bristol, in 1476–77.
BGT, xv(1890–1), 270

Carpenter, Thomas—see THOMAS, John; TURRET

CARPENTER, William (*fl.* 1470–1472) Carpenter
Of Bideford, Devon; with JOHN SAM, was responsible for the timberwork of *Bodmin Church*, Corn., in 1470–72. Sam made the roofs of the north and south aisles, while William Carpenter received by instalments £21 3s. 8d. for his task, which evidently included the roof of the body of the church.

CSM, VII, 20, 31

CARTER, John (*fl.* ?1484–1512) Mason
Possibly the John Carter who became free of Exeter in 1484–5.
Freemason (Vre massyn) of Exeter, who between 1506 and 1512 built the north-eastern chapel of St. George at *Croscombe*, Somerset, for £27 11s. 8d., and also vestries at the south-west of the church.[1] One of this name worked as a mason and setter at 3s. and 3s. 4d. a week at *Westminster Palace* in 1531–32.[2]

RJE, 59
[1] SRS, IV (1890), 29–32; [2] *PRO*, T. R. Misc., 251, 252 (*G.P.J.*)

CARTER, William (*fl.* 1434) Carpenter
Of Croydon, Surrey; apparently the chief carpenter employed in 1434 on the building of the Lollards' Tower at *Lambeth Palace*.
GLP, 52–6

CARVER, David (*fl.* 1499–1500) Carver
Carver of Bristol; in 1499–1500 received the final instalment of £21 of his contract of £41 for making seats for *St. John's, Glastonbury*. He was also paid £1 for spending a week with his six servants in connection with transport of the seats from Bristol to Glastonbury.
SDN, IV, 335

Carver, William—see BROWNFLEET

CATELYN, John (*fl.* 1404–1425) Mason
John Catelyn, senior, and John Catelyn, junior were two masons employed on the works of *London Bridge*. The elder first appears in 1404, being paid 3s. 9d. a week, and continued to work at that rate until 1421, when he was joined by his son, John Catelyn, junior, who was paid at the same rate. Both Catelyns were employed until February 1424/5, but after that date only one; which one it is not possible to say for certain, though

49

the younger man is indicated. This man was the leading mason, and after the departure of RICHARD BEKE in April 1435, became chief mason of the Bridge, taking 4s. a week until 19 December 1444.

Nicholas CATELYN, mason, who worked for the *Bridge* in 1405, 1411–12, and 1417, died in 1433. He was a citizen and mason of London, and parishioner of St. Dunstan-in-the-West.[1]

KJL
[1] *PPR*, Com. Ct. of London, 348 More (*A.O.*)

CAUSTON, John (*fl.* 1425) Carpenter
Was to build a 'howsyng' according to a pattern (*patron*) delivered in 1425–26, for two new houses to be erected in Basinghaw, London, by WILLIAM ADDESCOMP for the executors of Sir Richard Whittington.
CLE, 228–9 (*N.L.R.*)

Cauldeham—see CALDHAM

CHAFYN, Thomas [Chaffon(t), Chaffyn, Chawfynt, Schafont] (? *c.* 1520–†1572) Mason
Described in November 1557 as 'of Callaice, Freemason', had on 11 January of that year (as Thomas Chawfynt) taken up the freedom of the Vintners Company of London by patrimony.[1] He was son of Robert 'Chaffon', free as a vintner in 1525 on grounds of his apprenticeship to Stephen Mason or Masson (free in 1516).[2] It seems that Thomas Chafyn must have trained as a mason before becoming a free vintner, since he stated in his will that he had been brought up in 'the science and arte of masonry', and this would presumably have been about 1535–1550.
Stephen Mason made his will on 10 November 1557, leaving residuary estate to Thomas Chafyn ('Chaffon'), including a stone quarry in Boughton Monchelsea, Kent; Thomas's brother John Chaffon is also mentioned, and the fact that their father Robert Chaffon had been Mason's apprentice.[3]
Thomas Chafyn's will, made on 24 April 1567, calls him citizen and vintner of London, but goes on to state that he had been 'appointed by force and aucthorite of our said soveraigne Lady the quenes Majesties commission and in her name comaunded to travaile into the parties and domynyons of Russia beionde the seas there to serve in the workes of the Emperour of Russia (Ivan the Terrible, 1547–1584) in the science and arte

of masonry, wherein I have been traded and brought up. . .'[4]
He left to 'my welbeloved wife' Margaret all his leases, lands at Wavering Street in the parish of Boxley, and a quarry of hard stone at Boughton Monchelsea. His executors were his friend Robert Gybson, citizen and vintner, and his 'cosyn' Robert Eve or Ive, barber; the latter proved the will on 14 April 1572, Gybson having predeceased Chafyn.
[1] *GUL*, MS. 15211/1, *f.* 89/101; [2] *Ibid., ff.* 57v/68v; 55/66; [3] *GUL*, MS. 15364; [4] *PRO*, Prob 11/54, *f.* 78 (PCC 11 Daper)

CHALMER, Thomas (*fl.* 1508–   ) Mason
'Magister latomorum' of *Durham Cathedral* on 23 August 1508 when he witnessed a claim to sanctuary. CHRISTOPHER SCUNE already held this office by October 1515. *Henry 'CHAMER'* in 1510–11 seems to have been the mason in charge of works at *Norham Castle* for the Bishop of Durham.
(*A.O.*) SD; *DAR*, Norham rolls (*M.G.S.*)

CHAMBERLAIN, John [Chamberleyn] (*fl.* 1428–1436) Carpenter
Carpenter of *Southampton*, paid £3 1s. 8d. for timber for the new bridge of Bargate in 1428–29. He presumably carried out extensive works for the town for on 14 December 1436 he (burgess of Southampton) agreed to accept a rent of £4 for 24 years in lieu of £24 owing to him.
HMC, 11R. iii, 83, 135–6

CHAMBERLAIN, Richard (*fl. c.* 1360–†*c.* 1363) Mason
Carried out work by contract of *c.* 1360 at *Rochester Castle*, but had died by about 1363 when his widow is mentioned.
HKW, II, 811n

Chambre, William—see CHAUMERE

CHAMBYR, — [? Chambyn) (*fl.* 1460– Mason
On 27 October 1460 was concerned in the purchase of Taynton stone for the choir of *St. Mary the Virgin, Oxford*; possibly as master mason. The work was in progress from 1459 to 1465.
(*E.M.J.*)*OCO*, Treasury Accs., II, 141; cf. 137, 179, 181, 183, 234, 236

Chamer, Henry—see CHALMER

CHAMPNEYS, William [Champeneys] (*fl.* 1409–1436) Mason
Chief mason of *Rochester Bridge* between 1409 and 1436, usually referred to as *lathomus*.

50

His position was that of a resident sub-master or warden, as at all important works advice or supervision was sought from an outside master, such as STEPHEN LOTE, who was paid 6s. 8d. in 1409–10 for his counsel, or THOMAS MAPILTON who received £4 for supervising the rebuilding of a stone pier and two arches in 1422–26. Champneys and WILLIAM ATTE HELLE were paid £63 6s. 8d. for this work.

Champneys supplied freestone for the works on occasion, and in 1423–25 built the stonework of the new *Crown Inn, Rochester*, which had become the property of the bridge wardens. For this he was paid £9 16s. 8d.

William Champeneys of Strood, mason, was on 18 February 1427/8 ordered to answer William Wade of Faversham touching a debt,[1] and the bridge mason also acted as one of the two wardens who administered the bridge from 1427 to 1431. Champneys undertook journeys in connection with the works, as when in 1409–10 he travelled to Rainham with one of the wardens to interview a mason who was ill, or when in November 1422 he went to London to inform William Sevenoke, an influential citizen, of the state of the bridge fabric.

BRB, x, 75, 84–6, 90; *RBA*, No. 32 (*M.J.B.*)
[1] CPR 1422–9, 437

CHANCELLOR, William [Cancellar] (*fl.* 1227–) Mason

Master of the masons (*cementariorum*) at *Dover Castle* in 1227 taking 3½d. a day, in succession to ADAM the Mason IA.

SHB, 69; *PRO*, E.101–462–10 (*L.F.S.*)

Chapell, Peter—see GARALD, Richard

CHAPMAN, John (*fl.* 1435–1436) Mason

Master of the masons (*magister cementariorum*) engaged on the cloister of *Worcester Cathedral* in 1435–36, when he was allowed board for 13 weeks at 7d. a week, a gown (*toga*) price 6s. 8d. and 2s. 2d. towards the rent of his house. His fees were to be paid by the Almoner whose account is missing. It is clear from the variant detail that it was the west walk of the cloister which was designed by Chapman, and built between 1435 and 1438.

WCO, rolls C.88, 89

CHAPMAN, William (*fl.* 1509–) Mason

Freemason of Chertsey, Surrey; contracted on 26 January 1508/9 to pull down the central tower of the church at *High Wycombe*, Bucks., to rebuild the eastern part of the nave, and to make two doors through the new work 'conveying through all the three rode loftes'. The sureties for his completion of the work were William Billesdon of —, Berkshire, 'fremason', and Nicholas Benet of Clewer, Berkshire. Chapman's price for the work was £33.[1] In the summer of 1508 William Chapman, perhaps the same man, was working as a setter at *King's College Chapel, Cambridge*, being paid at the higher rate of 3s. 8d. a week.[2]

John CHAPMAN, a mason who worked at Westminster Palace and Dartford in 1541 and 1543, may have been a relation.[3]

[1] SHB, 557–9; RB, IX, 13 (*PRO*, Ancient Deed, D.985); [2] *KCM*, Building Acc. 1508–9 (*A.O.*); [3] *Bodl.* Rawl. D.781 (*G.P.J.*)

CHAUMERE, William [Chambre] (*fl.* 1438–1450) Mason

Mason at *Durham Cathedral*, working from 1438 to 1440 under JOHN BELL, senior, and received £1 16s. 8d. in 1439 for work on the paving of the church.[1] In 1450 he did work on the Bishop's new Hall at *Pittington*, Durham, where he and William Knayth were paid £5 for making two windows by contract. They also worked tracery, corbels, ashlar, and other stones for windows and doorways there.[2]

(A.O.)

[1] DAR, II, 408–10; [2] DST, 325

Chawfynt—see CHAFYN

CHENEY, (John) [Chayney] (*fl.* 1521–1522) Mason

Was one of Wolsey's masons at *Hampton Court* in 1521, when he was given special licence to work for *St. Lawrence's Church, Reading*. He built a new arcade between nave and aisle in 1521, and in the next year made a new font for £1 11s. 8d. The churchwardens paid 4s. 4d. for 'a hose cloth to the Surveyor' of Wolsey's works for the licence, and 3s. 4d. riding costs for Cheney.[1] He was perhaps the 'Chany', rough mason, who worked at *Magdalen College, Oxford*, in 1520–21, taking 7d. a day.[2] Cheney was almost certainly identical with the John Cheney, mason, who from 1505 until 1511 was renting from the Sacrist of Westminster Abbey a tenement which had been part of that leased by ROBERT STOWELL and later by ROBERT LEGET. Cheney paid rent of 13s. 4d. yearly, and also 6s. 8d. for a cottage close by, both being adjacent to the site of *Henry VII's Chapel* then being built.[3]

[1] KLR, 14, 24; CCA; [2] GOM, 107; [3] *WAM* 19761–67

CHERCHE, Philip de (*fl.* 1342–) Mason

With RICHARD DE FELSTEDE, carpenter, contracted on 2 December 1342 to build a tavern in *Paternoster Row, London*, in the parish of St. Michael le Querne. Cherche's work was to comprise a stone vaulted cellar and the walls of the ground storey, for which he was to receive £26 and 13s. 4d. for a robe.

SHB, 432–3; (*LBH*, G.16, 17)

CHERCHE, Richard at [Attechirche] (*fl.* 1361–1383) Mason

Was elected one of the sworn masons to the City of London on 21 October 1361, and continued to hold the office up to 1383.[1] In 1362–63 he worked for 110 days at *Windsor Castle* taking 6d. a day,[2] and in 1376 was concerned, with THOMAS BARNET and HENRY YEVELEY, in a property transaction in Guildford and the neighbourhood.[3] Next year he was concerned in the conveyance of a tenement and land to the rector of the church of St. Nicholas Cole Abbey, London, for the purpose of enlarging the church.[4]

Cherche was very likely the 'Master Richard Mason' who in 1385–86 was paid £8 12s. 0d. for various works done by contract at the church of St. Martin-le-Grand, London, including the making of the east window. Henry Yeveley was probably the designer of this work.[5]

[1] CLB, 'G', 129, 158, 223, 257, 279; 'H', 13, 216; [2] PRO, E.101–493–11 (*D.K.*); [3] LSF, 145; [4] *LHR*, 105 (39); 106(110); [5] *WAM*, 13310

CHERYHOLME, Richard (*fl.* 1481–c. 1502) Bricklayer (*Cherryholme near Selby, Yorks.*)

Admitted to the freedom of the City of York as a 'tyler' in 1481–2.[1] On 30 September 1483 licence was granted to Abbot Thomas Boothe of *St. Mary's Abbey, York*, to retain him with his four servants as long as he should please.[2] The work begun for Boothe was the new Abbot's House, now part of the King's Manor, York; it was continued under the next Abbot, William Sever, until 1502. It is entirely of brick above a stone plinth, but the windows are framed in terra-cotta, probably the first use of this substance in English building.

[1] SS, XCVI, 204; [2] *BL*, Harl. MS. 433, *f.* 119v

'CHESTER, Master of the Abbot of' (*fl.* 1463–) Mason

On 9 December 1463 a gratuity of 12d. was given 'to a mason off the Abote of Chester that cam to see my lordys worke at Holt'.

This was *Holt Castle*, Denbighshire, where work was in progress for Sir John Howard, afterwards 1st Duke of Norfolk.

BMH, 56

CHESTER, Nicholas de (*fl.* 1296) Carpenter

Master carpenter; in 1296 built at task the watermill at *Gyffin* by Conway, with Master JOHN DE LONDON.

HKW, I, 350

CHESTERFELD, William [Chestrefeld] (fl. 1416–1432) Mason

In 1416–17 was paid expenses by *Selby Abbey* for going with John Wod to Huddleston quarry.[1] In 1431–32 he received a fee of 6s. 8d. for surveying the stone fabric of the monastery of Selby Abbey and for carving stone there (*pro supervisu fabrice lapid. mon. & sculptura lapid. hoc anno*).[2]

[1] Westminster Dioc. Archives, Se/Ac/9, Minute ...; [2] Hull Univ. Lib., MS DDLO/20/1, Feoda (*N. L. R.*)

CHESTERTON, Handekyn de [Chestreton] (*fl.* 1316–1318) Mason

Undermaster of the works of masonry at *Carnarvon Castle* in 1316–18, under HENRY DE ELLERTON.

PRO, E.101–486–28 (*L.F.S.*)

CHEVYNTON, Richard (*fl.* 1437–1443) Mason

Was master mason of the works of *All Souls College, Oxford*, from 1438 to 1442, taking 3s. 4d. a week with an annual fee of £1 6s. 8d. He was usually at work at the Burford quarries, while ROBERT JANYNS the warden, remained on the site at Oxford.[1]

Chevynton, however, was presumably the general designer of the college, founded in 1437, and structurally completed by 1444; the chapel was consecrated in 1442, and the hall (see BRANCHE, JOHN) finished in 1443.

He was given cloth by *Abingdon Abbey* in 1440–41,[2] probably as a retaining fee as master mason to the abbey. He was dead by 23 August 1443, having left provision for obits for himself and his wife Matilda, who survived him, at St. Nicholas's, Abingdon.[3]

[1] JAS, 128; [2] AAA, 121; [3] E. M. Jope in BKJ, LI (1951), 54

'CHICHESTER, Carpenter of' (*fl. c.* 1228–) Carpenter

Bishop Ralph Neville of *Chichester* wrote to Dean Simon concerning the master carpenter of the cathedral church who, wishing to fulfil his vow as a crusader, had nominated a young man to take his place. The crusade was doubtless that of 1228–29.

SAC, III, 75

CHICHESTER, Ralph of (*fl.* 1287–1294) Marbler

Master; in 1287 undertook with JOHN DOGET to supply marble columns, capitals, bases, and cornice moulding for the works of *Vale Royal Abbey*, Cheshire, worked to a pattern (*exemplar*) sent by Master WALTER OF HEREFORD. Between 1291 and 1294 he supplied cross-shafts and various marble details ready worked for the *Eleanor Crosses* at Charing, Dunstable, St. Albans, Stony Stratford, and Woburn.

A.J.T. in CNW, XXXVII, 296–7

CHILD, John (*fl.* 1307–1308) Carpenter

Master carpenter in charge of work on chambers in *Nottingham Castle*, built in 1307–08.

HKW, II, 761

CHRISTCHURCH, John of (*fl.* 1281–1307) Mason

'*Cementarius*', was granted by the *Abbey of Eynsham* in 1281, for his laudable service in his office, a corrody of a suit with fur as given to the clerks, and 40s. a year which he enjoyed until 1307.

(*E.M.J.*) OHS, XLIX (1906–7), 332

CHRISTIAN the Mason (*fl.* 1183–) Mason

Was mason to Bishop Hugh Pudsey (Puiset) of Durham in 1183, when the Boldon Book records that he held 40 acres in South Sherburn which the Bishop gave him from the moor for 5s. and two bovates which used to belong to Arkill for 14d.; he was, however, to be quit of both rents while he served the Bishop as mason. A gravestone inscribed to 'Christian' and of this period was discovered in Pittington churchyard by Canon Greenwell, and ascribed to him.

DBB, 10; VCH, *Durham*, I, 304, 329

Christian, Richard—see HOLBROOK. Lawrence

CHUDDERE, William (*fl.* 1398–1399) Carver

In 1398–99 was paid £60 for making the pinnacle on the north gable of *Westminster Hall*, and four images of different kings to stand in its four sides.

PRO, E.101-473-11

Clark—see CLERK

CLAVYLL, John [Clauyle, 'Glanyll'] (*fl.* 1390–1391) Mason

Perhaps one of the Claville family of the Isle of Purbeck. Was mason in charge of repairs done for the King at *Gloucester Castle* in 1390–91; he contracted to make nine arches of stone in three corners of the walls, each set of three arches being made to sustain a turret; for the whole of this he was paid £30. He was also paid £15 for work on a ruined round tower between the great tower and the middle gate of the castle.[1]

William CLAVYLLE was on 28 August 1421 ordered to obtain ships for transporting stone from the quarries of Caen for the building of *Westminster Abbey*.[2] William Clavell, citizen and freemason of London, was executor of the will of STEPHEN BURTON in 1488.

[1] *PRO*, E.101–559–33; E.364–27(F); [2] DKR, XLII, 429

CLEMENT, John (*fl.* 1399–) Carpenter

Was granted on 19 November 1399 the office of one of the master carpenters of the Duchy of Lancaster, viz.: master carpenter of the works of the castles of *Kenilworth, Tutbury*, and *Leicester* for life, with the accustomed fees, taking 10 marks (£6 13s. 4d.) yearly. The grant was made in consideration of his 'good and agreeable services' in the past; it is just possible that he had worked on the roof of the great hall of Kenilworth Castle, but this may have been designed by WILLIAM WINTRINGHAM.[1]

In 1402 one John Clement, carpenter, was admitted to the freedom of Wells, Somerset.[2]

[1] *PRO*, D.L.42–15, *f.* 5b.; [2] SRS, XLVI

CLEMENT, William (*fl.* 1532–†1540) Carpenter

An apprentice of JAMES NEDEHAM. On 1 October 1532 was appointed, jointly with JOHN RUSSELL to the office of Chief Carpenter to the King.[1] He is mentioned as the King's Master Carpenter in documents of 20 March 1535 and 16 November 1538, when he appears as due for pay for work done at *Hampton Court*, where he was in charge of the erection of the roof of the Great Hall from 1532 onwards. This roof was at one time considered to be of his own design, but is now known to have been made from drawings by JAMES NEDEHAM.[2] Clement was also master carpenter at *Nonsuch Palace*, and at *Oatlands* from 1537.

On 21 June 1538 Clement, described as

one of the King's Master Carpenters, was granted £25 a year for life,[3] and in 1539 was appointed master carpenter for the construction of three blockhouses in the Downs, at *Deal, Walmer*, and *Sandwich*.[4]

Clement was dead by September 1540, when his will was witnessed by CHRISTOPHER DICKINSON.

HKW, III, 408; IV, 206

[1] JPC, 165; [2] LPH, Addenda, pt. i, 977; pt. ii, 1371; [3] LPH, XIV; i, p. 594; [4] *Ibid.*, No. 398, p.151; [5] *PRO*, E.101–474–19

CLENCHWARTON, Simon [Clenchewardon, -dyn, Clenchwarton, Clensewarton, Gleyngewarton] (*fl.* 1442–1461) Carpenter (? *Clenchwarton, Norfolk*)

Was a working carpenter at *Westminster Palace* in 1442–3. Appointed King's Master Carpenter on 9 July 1451.[1] In 1455–56 he was a warden of the London Carpenters' Company, and appears in their records from 1455 to 1460.[2] He received a general pardon on 28 July 1460, and as King's Master Carpenter was still drawing his fees of 12*d.* a day in the early part of 1461,[3] but was superseded by EDMUND GRAVELEY who received a patent of appointment on 14 October 1461. Graveley's pay was granted him in arrears from 4 March, the date of Edward IV's accession, and it is clear that Clenchwarton's dismissal was due to political causes connected with the deposition of Henry VI. It would seem that the royal craftsmen were considered to be loyal supporters of the House of Lancaster, for almost all of those in high positions lost their offices in 1461.

[1] HKW, I, 222; CPR 1446–52, 456; [2] JPC, 621; MCR, II, 18, 20–1, 27, 31, 260; [3] CPR 1452–61, 589; *PRO*, E.364–100(B)

CLERK, Cornelius [Clerck, Clerke] (*fl.* 1506–1526) Carpenter

Carpenter working in *Oxford*, where he was doing minor works at *Magdalen College* from 1506 to 1508. In 1507 he was living in a tenement of St. John's Hospital within the East Gate, and had moved to another house of the hospital's by 1516.

In March 1517 he undertook to make 16 library desks for *Corpus Christi College* for £16, the design to copy that of the Magdalen College desks, but to have ball finials instead of poppy-heads to the seats. In 1520–21 he was chief carpenter at the building of the Gallery or Election Chamber at Magdalen College, and did other work there. In 1521 he

had moved to a third house belonging to St. John's Hospital, in 1524 paid 4*d.* to the Lay Subsidy, and in 1525–26 was paid for work at Magdalen. His library desks at Corpus, though altered, still exist. He was perhaps related to ROBERT CLERK II.

GOC

CLERK, Henry (*fl.* 1455–1456) Mason

Mason of Coventry; in 1455–56 was admitted, with his wife Agnes, to the Guild of Holy Cross, the Blessed Mary and St. John Baptist of Stratford on Avon.

(*A.O.*) BRS, 123

CLERK, John (*fl.* ?1448–†1459) Mason

Was warden of the masons at *Eton College* in 1453–54. When he made his will in February 1459 he was living in London, in the parish of St. Andrew upon Cornhill (St. Andrew Undershaft). A John Clerk was paid for 15 days' work as an ordinary mason at Eton in October 1448. Owing to gaps in the building accounts of the college it is uncertain when John Clerk became warden of the masons, but he was holding that position in October 1453 under JOHN SMYTH. His apprentice was HENRY JANYNS, who departed with his master at the end of March 1454.[1] In his will Clerk left to Henry Janyns all his tools, 'pictures' and 'portraitures' and 26*s.* 8*d.* in money.[2]

John Clerk was a brother of SIMON CLERK, who at the time when John Clerk made his will was master mason at Eton. He appointed him co-executor with his own wife Amy, left him 20*s.* and forgave him a debt of 20*s.* A daughter, Maude, was a nun at the Cistercian house of Pinley in Warwickshire. A bequest of 16*s.* 4*d.* to 'the felaship of free masons of london' shows that he was a member of the London Masons' Guild. He may have done work at the Priory of *Hounslow*, since he bequeathed 3*s.* 4*d.* to the Prior and Convent of that house to pray for his soul. His will was dated 1 February and proved 16 February 1458/9.

A *John CLERK*, mason, was made a freeman of the city of Wells in 1404.[3] A mason of this name supplied stone for the Guildhall at Norwich in 1410–11.[4] *Richard CLERK* was one of the freemasons working at Canterbury Cathedral between 1429 and 1433.[5] *Robert CLERK*, freemason, was employed at Eton College in February 1445.[1]

A.O.

[1] KJE; [2] *CCL*, Sharpe, *f.* 268; [3] *SRS*, XLVI; [4] *NA*, XV, 164; [5] *Bodl.*, Tanner MS. 165

CLERK, Robert, I (*fl.* 1393—*c.* 1412) Carpenter

Carpenter of Norwich, where he took up the freedom in 1393.[1] In 1410–11 he was making the great doors for the *Norwich Guildhall*,[2] and in the next year was paid £1 13*s.* 4*d.* for the 'kage' or lock-up near the Murage Loft.[3] Probate of the will of a carpenter of this name in the City Court of Norwich is attributed to 1409–10, perhaps in error.[4]

(A.O.)

[1] EFN; [2] NA, XV, 164 ff.; [3] HTN, II, 58; [4] *NMR*, Enrolled Deeds, roll 17 m.25

CLERK, Robert, II [Clarke, Clerck] (*fl.* 1516–1524) Carver

Carver working in *Oxford*, where in 1516–17 he made the presses for *Queen's College* library for £2 5*s.* 3½*d.*, and two chests for the chapel for 7*s.* In 1518–19 he was supplying planks and carving knots and flowers for the new roof of the chancel of *Whaddon Church*, at the expense of New College. During 1520–21 he was carving woodwork for the hall of *Magdalen College*, being paid at 8*d.* a day. He was perhaps related to CORNELIUS CLERK, as his name appears next to that of Cornelius in the Lay Subsidy of 1524, when both were living in the parish of St. Peter-in-the-East, and each paid 4*d.*

GOC

CLERK, Simon [Clerc] (*fl.* 1434–?†1489) Mason

[In 1434 assisted in the making of a niche for a statue on the west side of the Lollards' Tower at *Lambeth Palace* (see JOHN THIRSK).] For some forty-five years, from 1445 or earlier until his death in or shortly before 1489, Simon Clerk was normally resident at *Bury St. Edmunds*, where he was master mason at the *Abbey*. At *Eton College* he was master mason from 1453 to 1461, when the choir of the chapel was nearing completion. From 1477 until 1485 he was master mason in charge of the works at *King's College Chapel, Cambridge*, and when they ceased soon after Henry VII's accession he continued to receive a consultant's fee.

Simon Clerk was a brother of JOHN CLERK, who had been warden of the masons at Eton in 1453–54. In his will, dated 1 February 1458/9, the latter left 'to my brother Symkyn Clerke of Eton', 20*s.* and released him from a debt of 20*s.*; he also left 6*s.*8*d.* 'to Amy wyff of the saide Symond' and 3*s.* 4*d.* to each of their five children; Simon Clerk was appointed co-executor with the testator's wife.[1] 'Symond' and, more often, the diminutive form 'Symkyn' occur in many of the references to Simon Clerk. The identity of the Bury and the Eton mason is confirmed by the will of Thomas Clerk of Bury, who refers to his parents, Simon and Amy. John Clerk mentions another brother, John, a weaver of Stony Stratford. Another relative may have been John Clerk of Monks Risborough (died 1461). The will of the latter, dated 1 February 1461, and a codicil sealed three days later were both witnessed by Simon Clerk and Richard Philpot at Eton, and the testator left the sum of 66*s.* 8*d.* 'to the work of the operations of the King's college of blessed Mary of Eton'.[2] (In March 1454 RICHARD PHILPOT had succeeded John Clerk as warden of the masons at Eton.) In disposing of his property the testator mentions lands and tenements in Monks Risborough, Great and Little Kimble, which he had inherited from his father, so that if Simon Clerk was his brother he is likely to have been born in Buckinghamshire. No details of Simon Clerk's early career have come to light, except that in 1434–5 he was working on Lambeth Palace with John Thirsk, then master mason to Westminster Abbey. He is found in 1445 already holding an important position.

By an indenture dated 12 December 1445 the Abbot and Convent of Bury St. Edmunds granted to Simon Clerk, 'Mason of Bury St. Edmunds', a thirty years' lease of their manor of Hessett, five miles east of Bury, with certain reservations.[3] He was also to receive annually from the Sacrist a robe of the livery of his gentlemen (*generosorum*) on payment of 10*s.* This grant was in lieu of a previous grant, dated 30 November 1445, by which the Abbot and Convent had agreed to pay him an annual fee of £10 for life, the same sum as was stipulated in the seven years' agreement made with JOHN WODE of Colchester on 25 August 1436. The nature of Simon Clerk's appointment is not specified in the agreement, which, if not supplemented by another setting out the terms of his engagement as master mason, must have left him a free hand to undertake work elsewhere, but in the contemporary index of the Register into

55

which the grant was copied it is stated to have been made 'for his faithful labour concerning the new [work?] begun in the monastery'. The uncompleted new work was the rebuilding of the great west tower of the abbey church after the collapse of the years 1430 and 1431. A design for the new tower may have been made by THOMAS MAPILTON, the master mason of the King's works, who had been called in to inspect the old tower a few months before the fall of its south side.[4] In 1436 John Wode was placed in charge of the rebuilding,[5] on which much money is known to have been spent between Michaelmas 1438 and Michaelmas 1441.[6] But the work went on for years, as is shown by numerous bequests in wills, and one made in 1465 'to the more speedy forwarding of the bell-tower of the monastery newly being made'[7] reveals that it was still unfinished the year before the great fire which ravaged the whole church. It is probable that brick was extensively used in the construction of the tower, as in the case of the Bell Harry Tower at Canterbury Cathedral, since the Abbot, William Curteys, made a contract with two German brickmakers on 1 April 1440 to burn bricks at his kiln at Chevington and by December 1441 they had turned out over 230,000.[8]

Whether John Wode died or departed at the end of his seven years' contract is not known, but about 1445 the house belonging to the Sacrist on the north side of the Horsemarket in which he had lived came into the occupation of Thomas Style.[9] Towards the end of the term of office of Thomas Derham, Sacrist 1441–49, Simon Clerk paid a fine of 20s. on acquiring a house on the west side of the Horsemarket, and about 1466, towards the end of the term of John Woolpit, Sacrist 1449–69, he enlarged his premises by acquiring the two adjoining tenements on the south to the corner of Westgate Street.[10] The property probably passed to his son Thomas, who in his will of 1506 bequeathed 40s. to the reparation of the Cross standing in the Horsemarket in Bury and to the mending of the highway from the said Cross to St. Mary's Church.

Simon Clerk's appearance at *Eton* may indicate that work on the western tower at the Abbey of Bury had been temporarily suspended. The Eton building account for [1453–54] shows that he was then master mason,[11] [having succeeded JOHN SMYTH I in 1453]. His brother's will reveals that he was living at Eton in February 1459, and two years later he witnessed the will of John Clerk of Monks Risborough at Eton, so that he is likely to have remained in charge until the cessation of building on Edward IV's accession. The successive enlargements which the chapel had undergone in the mind of the royal founder seem to have resulted in a great deal of wasted building effort and the pulling down of much that had already been erected. The dimensions of the existing chapel accord with those specified for the choir in the King's 'Avyse' which superseded the smaller building as prescribed in the 'Will' of 12 March 1448.[12] JOHN SMYTH was master mason when the existing building was begun in 1449 according to the revised dimensions, but in 1453 he had become master mason at Westminster Abbey; he continued, however, to receive a fee of 40s. a year, probably in a consultant capacity, up to 1460. Between 1458 and 1460 the ironwork for the side windows and the great east window was paid for, so that their tracery was probably inserted at that time. The patterns used for the side windows and for the west window above the antechapel show a close resemblance to that of the tracery in the east window of King's College Chapel, and may therefore have been designed by Simon Clerk. The short window in the west gable must have been inserted after it had been decided to modify the design for the nave, which was to have been of the same height as the choir. There is evidence to show that when Bishop Waynflete resumed the works in 1469 he contemplated building an aisled nave of reduced height before deciding to abandon the idea in favour of a transeptal antechapel on the model of those in Oxford colleges.[13] Simon Clerk may have been employed or consulted by Waynflete for a time in and after 1469, which is the likeliest date for the west window and the great arch below it (subsequently blocked up). The Oxford mason, WILLIAM ORCHARD, supplied the stone for the antechapel, which was built between 1479 and 1483, and he was probably responsible for its design. By that time Simon Clerk will have had his hands full with his work at King's College Chapel and Bury.

There is a reference to Simon Clerk in the long will of John Baret of Bury St. Edmunds, which is dated 10 September 1463 but was not proved until 2 May 1467.[14] He left instructions for the rebuilding of the *Risby Gate* at the north-west entrance to the town, preferably with freestone and brick, but if his executors felt doubtful about the use of brick as 'not sufficient to endure', flint rubble ('calyou and moorter') was to be employed and they were to 'take avys of Symkyn Clerc, mason, of this'. The Risby Gate was pulled down in 1765. John Baret was an official of the Abbey. His tomb with a cadaver is in the easternmost bay of the south aisle of *St. Mary's Church*, where stood the Lady altar; he had had it erected before the date of his will, having commissioned it perhaps from Simon Clerk's workshop, and he had also beautified what was then the Lady Chapel at his own expense. The Jesus Chapel on the north side of the chancel had recently been built, and at the time when he made his will the corresponding chapel on the south side was under consideration. These two chapels were built at the expense of John Smyth, a wealthy merchant and great benefactor of the town, and there would be a strong presumption that they were designed by Simon Clerk had there not been another prominent Bury mason and townsman in the person of JOHN FORSTER. (Note: The tracery of the windows in these chapels is of poor design and quite unlike that found at Long Melford, Hessett and Denston which are more likely to be works of Simon Clerk.) Both Forster and Simon Clerk were among the feoffees named in two feoffments of 10 September 1470 and 20 July 1473 made by John Smyth in connection with the charitable trust which was founded by him for the benefit of the town and annexed to his will.[15]

On 8 January 1475 Simon Clerk was one of the witnesses to the will of Adam Prenteys of Bury, from whom he had acquired the two tenements at the corner of Westgate Street and the Horsemarket,[16] and on 20 October 1479 he witnessed the will of Edward Bush of Bury.[17] The following year he acted as supervisor of the will of THOMAS IDE of Bury, carpenter, dated 20 July 1479 and proved 23 August 1480.[18] Ide was probably one of the Abbey craftsmen. A great many deeds connected with the trusts established by John Smyth and Margaret Odeham are preserved among the Muniments of the Corporation, and Simon Clerk figures in at least eight of these, either as a feoffee or a witness, at

different dates in 1477, 1479, 1484, and 1485.[19] The seal which he used shows a bird with wings displayed holding something in its claws. In some of these deeds his son Clement Clerk was also one of the feoffees. The affairs of the town, to which the Abbot denied any corporate government, were largely in the hands of the Candlemas Guild, to which Simon Clerk probably belonged. At some date before 1484 he seems to have been Alderman of Bury.[20]

Renewal of work on the great west tower of the abbey church must have been abruptly stopped by the fire which on 20 January 1466 broke out in the roof of the nave through the carelessness of plumbers and swept through the church, destroying the roofs of nave, transepts, and presbytery, all of which were unvaulted, and burning the timber spire on the central tower which collapsed, along with the timberwork and bells in the tower itself, on to the floor of the crossing.[21] The central tower, dating from 1362–1388, was damaged but did not fall; the unfinished west tower seems to have been unaffected. It may be assumed that Simon Clerk was in charge of the great work of reconstruction which was put in hand without delay by the Abbot, John Boon, who before his death in 1469 had himself spent 300 marks on the restoration of the nave and left another 200 marks towards vaulting the church.[22] Bequests in wills of 1492 and 1495 to the new vaulting show that this work was still going on after Simon Clerk's death when JOHN WASTELL had in all probability succeeded him as master mason. The great Norman fabric was being given a late Gothic vault, as at Norwich, and at the same time, and it is interesting to speculate whether a lierne or a fan vault was adopted. If it was a fan vault, it will have been an important lost link in the chain of these vaults and must have influenced Wastell in the development of his form of fan design. Bequests to the building of the unfinished west tower begin again in 1475 and continue up to 1504.[23]

Simon Clerk's association with King's College Chapel began in the summer of 1477. Donations and contributions from private sources had made it possible to resume work on the building in the previous year, though only on a restricted scale, with JOHN WORLICH as master mason. The College Mundum Book for 1476–77 records an expenditure of over £77 on the chapel in those two years, and one of the items is a payment of 10s. 'to Simon Master of the masons by way of Reward together with his expenses'. The section covering 'Riding Costs' discloses that one, Thomas Whight, had been sent to Bury 'for the Master of the masons after the Feast of St. John [1477]'. The Bursars' Accounts for the next year are missing, and little seems to have been done in 1478 and 1479, but on Michaelmas Day of the latter year the Vice-Provost gave 'Symkyn the mason' 6s. 8d. in reward 'coming from the Bishop of Lincoln from Woborn'.[24] It was largely through the good offices of Thomas Rotherham, then Bishop of Lincoln and Chancellor of England, that Edward IV was persuaded to give a large sum of money which made it possible to renew building operations on a much increased scale in 1480 under the new Provost, Walter Field, who was appointed supervisor of the works.[25] A day-book of 1480–83, kept by Thomas Clyff, the clerk of the works, shows that Simon Clerk was paid £10 a year as master mason,[26] and from 1481 he received in addition an annual pension of 40s. by a grant dated 20 September of that year.[27] This additional fee, granted to 'Simon Clerke of Bury fremason', described in the margin as 'chief mason of the College', was 'in consideration of his good and sound counsel and service' and was to be paid for 30 years or until his death within that period. It continued to be paid after the works had been suspended in 1485, but by 1489 it had fallen into arrears, for on 22 December of that year 20s. was paid 'to Thomas Clerke of Bury in part of payment of the fee of Simon Clerke his father now dead' and on 10 July 1490 a further 40s. was paid to Clement Clerke 'in part of payment of a larger sum for the fee of his father'.[28]

Living and working less than thirty miles from Cambridge, Simon Clerk must have been familiar with Henry VI's great building project from its inception, and likewise he must have been known to the Provost and Fellows when master mason at Eton, and also as the master mason at the abbey of St. Edmund. In August 1460, when the Provost, Robert Wodelark, went over to Eton for Election Day, he gave a 'regard' of 6s. 8d. 'to the mason of Eton', who very probably was Simon Clerk.[29] In 1477, when Clerk was called in at King's, the ironwork for the great east window and for the easternmost window on the north side was being made and delivered. By the time the works came to a halt after Henry VII's accession five bays of the choir had been roofed;[30] slightly more progress had been made on the south side than on the north. In June 1485 masons were working on the sixth window, but whether on the north or south is uncertain, for the masonry details show that by the time the third phase of building began six windows on the north and seven on the south had been completed.[31] Simon Clerk can have been responsible for little in the design of the chapel as it stands, but the tracery of the east window is probably due to him. He may also have designed the internal stone panel-work above the windows and it is not unreasonable to suppose that he made drawings for the high vault, to which Wastell may have owed something.

Evidence of Simon Clerk making designs occurs in Clyff's accounts. In May 1480, when a 'forel' (*forale*), or thin smooth skin of parchment, was bought for MARTIN PRENTICE, the chief carpenter, on which to draw the roof of the chapel, three more were bought 'for the chief mason'.[26] Again two skins of parchment (*pelles pargameni*) were bought for Simon Clerk on 9 August 1481 and another on 16 December 1482. Clyff's accounts, the College Mundum Books and the kitchen accounts make it possible to follow Simon Clerk's movements between Bury and Cambridge in considerable detail. There are many entries of the expenses of servants 'riding to Bury for Simon Clerk', for instance on 5 July 1481, in May 1482 before Edward IV's visit to the college, on 4 January 1483 and several times in 1484. On 2 June 1483 a servant rode to Newmarket with a letter for Simon Clerk, for whom a horse was hired from Richard Smyth, brewer.[26] Sometimes he was refreshed with wine, and after a visit to London in January 1482 a special refection was served to him on his return. His visits to Cambridge varied from a few days to several weeks. In October 1482 he was a guest for a whole week. From 26 January 1483 he received commons continuously for six weeks or longer, and he was at the college during nearly the whole of April;[32] he also received commons for several weeks between June and October 1484. At other times he was frequently a guest in hall at dinner or supper with the fellows, especially on feast days. On

28 August 1484, when Richard III issued a new commission for impressing masons and other craftsmen and for obtaining materials for the works, Simon Clerk was one of the six named in it.[33]

An entry in Clyff's accounts for the works suggests that Simon Clerk undertook other work on his visits to Cambridge. On 1 April 1481 there is an entry of the receipt from him of 2s. 8d. 'for one stone for the chapel of King's Hall and for another for the doorway (ostio) of the Friars Preachers'.[26] Work on the chapel of King's Hall, which had been suspended for ten years, was resumed in 1480, when an agreement was made with a carpenter, probably for roofing the unfinished structure. The King's Hall Accounts do not reveal the name of the master mason at this time, but if it was Simon Clerk, as the entry suggests, there was the same succession of architects at King's Hall — Ely, Worlich, Clerk, and Wastell — as at King's College. The Dominican Friary, for which Simon Clerk needed a stone for a doorway, occupied the site of Emmanuel College.

Among the many accounts of Thomas Clyff preserved among the King's College muniments there is a day-book covering the period 1484 to 1488 in which he entered not only sums received and expended on behalf of the college but also his personal receipts and expenses. In 1485 on 13 June he paid 2d. 'for wine given to Simon Clerk & Clement Clerk', on 18 June he received 4d. from Simon Clerk, and on the feast of St. John the Baptist (24 June) he received 20d. 'from Simon Clerk John Wastell & ij Chirch Wardens of Walden'.[31] Other entries make it clear that he made a small private income from writing out, and perhaps also drafting, bills, obligations, indentures, and other legal documents for those who required them, and the entry of June 24 doubtless refers to a building contract drawn up between Clerk and Wastell in partnership and the churchwardens of Saffron Walden Church, Essex. The churchwardens' accounts of that church for 1485–86 (Easter to Easter) contain the following items:

It' payd on to Mayster Symkyn ye Mason for hys costis here. And owteward & homward   vijs.

It' payd for paper to make wt owr boke   j d.

It' payd at Cambregge for makyng offe j denter & j oblygacion   viij d.

There are also two items relating to the visit of a quarryman and an agreement for buying stone.[34] All these entries have been crossed out, no doubt because they were transferred to a new book of building accounts, the book for which the paper was bought. The churchwardens' accounts, which are not complete and do not go beyond 1491, throw little light on the nature of the contract, but in 1485 there is a memorandum of £7 paid to the mason for 45 tons of stone, in 1488 there is a reference to the 'Resceyuors for the new werks of the south Ile', and there is an undated account, perhaps of 1490–91, of payments for lead for the church roof, which may have been the roof of the south aisle.[35] As Simon Clerk was dead by December 1489, he can have had little share in the rebuilding of the church, unless he had been previously employed on the north aisle, for bequests in wills show that the building of the nave arcades and clerestory was not begun until 1497 or later, and took some thirty years to complete. It was the usual practice in the rebuilding and enlargement of a parish church to rebuild the aisle walls first, and Simon Clerk may have been responsible for the design of these, although for the windows it seems likely that the patterns had already been set by the work that was carried out in the 1440's and embodied in the great rebuilding scheme begun in 1485. On stylistic grounds as well as from their date the design of the nave arcades and clerestory can be assigned to Wastell.

The entry in Clyff's day-book is important for the evidence it provides of Simon Clerk and John Wastell acting as partners in a contract, the one an old and experienced architect who must have been at least seventy at the time and the other a rising young mason of ability. It establishes the fact that there was continuity in the works at King's College Chapel, in spite of the gap of nearly a quarter of a century between the second and third great phases of building, as there must also have been at the abbey of Bury and at Saffron Walden. At all three buildings Wastell must have been familiar with Simon Clerk's ideas and intentions, and it is possible that a fan vault for King's was already visualised by Simon Clerk when building the choir. [It cannot be supposed that the fan vault of the Red Mount Chapel, King's Lynn, was designed by Clerk, since that can now be dated to 1505–06.[36]]

The loss of the abbey church at Bury makes it difficult to assess the quality of Simon Clerk's work. At the chapels of Eton and King's he was following in the footsteps of others and they afford little indication of his style. But his long career gives him importance among 15th-century architects, and there must be much unrecognised work by him in Suffolk churches and perhaps farther afield as well. It is possible that he designed the noble tower of *Lavenham Church*, Suffolk, to the building of which Thomas Spring made a bequest of 300 marks in 1486. It was built in two stages, *c.* 1486–95 and 1518–25;[37] during the interval the nave was rebuilt, beginning about 1495 and carried on more actively after 1500, and as this is linked stylistically with the naves of Saffron Walden and *Great St. Mary's, Cambridge*, which are manifestly the work of the same master mason, in all probability John Wastell, there may have been the same partnership between Clerk and Wastell at Lavenham as at Walden, with Wastell carrying on after Clerk's death. Simon Clerk may also have had some initial responsibility for the rebuilding of Great St. Mary's, Cambridge, which was begun in 1478 but discontinued for ten years after little more than £20 had been spent.[38] The tower was not begun until 1491, after Clerk's death. It is probable that the aisle walls were undertaken first, and they present an individual feature in the treatment of the internal arches of the north and south doorways, which are of much flattened four-centred form with a pair of cusps on each side placed close to the point where the arch springs. This mannerism also occurs in the internal arches of the west doorway at Lavenham and the south doorway at Saffron Walden and may be regarded as a small piece of evidence pointing to common authorship.

Thomas Clyff's day-book containing the personal entries has a further reference to Simon Clerk dated 14 April 1486, when Clerk paid him 4*d.* 'for writing the release of a tenement in Bury St. Edmunds'.[31] Possibly he parted with one of his houses in the Horse-market at this time, but the business might have been done on behalf of a fellow-townsman. The will of Simon Clerk is likely to have been in the missing Bury register (Herdman), which is known from a few extracts made from it by Sir Symonds d'Ewes:

they are from wills proved between 1483 and 1491.[39] Simon Clerk was probably buried in St. Mary's Church, Bury, perhaps in the Jesus Aisle or Chapel on the north side of the chancel, where his son Thomas directed that his body should be laid and where a chantry priest was to celebrate for two years at the Jesus altar. Thomas Clerk also willed that a 'sangrede' should be kept for six years for the souls of 'Symon & Amye my ffader & moder' and of his two dead wives. As Simon Clerk was already a freemason in 1434 he may have been born about 1410 and he will have been well over 75 when he died.

Both Clement and Thomas Clerk, his sons, lived up to their surname by being clerks in the King's Chancery. Clement figures in Bury deeds and wills from 1477, when he is already described as 'of the Chancery of the lord King'.[40] By a patent of 10 November 1487 he and Gilbert Bacheler received a grant in survivorship of the office of Clerk of the Crown of Chancery.[41] Clement Clerk eventually obtained the appointment, in which he was succeeded by William Porter (12 November 1504).[42] He had three tenements and a garden in Bury, in Maidwater Lane, not far from his father's property,[43] but when he made his will on 16 September 1498, he was living at Great Livermere, north-east of Bury, where he desired to be buried in the parish church at one end of the altar of St. Nicholas. He mentions by name eight sons and three daughters in his testament, which, with his last will concerning his lands and tenements 'in the county of Suffolk and elsewhere', was proved 27 November 1504.[44]

Thomas Clerk describes himself in his will as of Bury, 'Gent'. He held a corrody in the abbey of St. Edmund. No son survived him, and he left all his real estate 'in Bury or anywhere else' to his wife Anastace absolutely. His long will shows that he had ranged widely, and among numerous bequests are sums of money to 'our lady of Mounthaute in London', to the priory of St. Denys 'beside Southampton', and to the master and brethren of St. Thomas of Acres in London, also 'j peyer Chalys' to Hurley Priory in Berkshire, 'to be occupied in the capell of Seynt Leonard'. He died between 10 May and 20 June 1506.[45]

A.O.

[1] *CCL*, Sharpe, *f.* 268; [2] *PCC*, 22 Stokton; [3] *BM*, Add. MS. 7096, *f.* 154v.; [4] *BCM*, A.6–1–6 (Sacrist's Roll

1429–30); HMC, 14R. App.8, 125; [5] *BM*, Add. MS. 14848, *f.* 308v.; [6] *Ibid.*, *f.* 309v.; [7] *BW*, ia, 86; [8] *BM*, Add. MS. 14848, *f.* 318v.; Add. MS. 7096, *f.* 111; [9] *Ibid.*, Harl. MS.58, *ff.* 81v.; 85; [10] *Ibid.*, *ff.* 85v., 91; [11] KJE, 77, 91n.; [12] WCC, I, 366–8; [13] *Ibid.*, 428; [14] *BW*, ia, 95, printed in TSB, 37–8; [15] *BW*, ia, 304; TSB, 68–9; [16] *BW*, ia, 205v.; [17] *Ibid.*, 271v.; [18] *Ibid.*, 281; [19] *BCM*, H.1–2–14, No. 5; H.1–2–2; H.1–5–16; H.1–5–1, No. 3; H.1–1–48, Nos. 1–4; [20] SIA, XXII, 28; [21] *BM*, Cotton MS. Claud. A, xii, *f.* 189v. (CAS, Publications XXVIII, 205); [22] St. John's Coll. Oxford Library, MS. 209; (MSE, III, 298); [23] *BW*, vi, 163; [24] *KCM*, Mundum Book 1478–79; [25] WCC, I, 472; [26] *KCM*, College Accs., vol. iv; [27] *KCM*, Leger Book, 116v.; [28] *KCM*, Mundum Book 1489–90; [29] *KCM*, College Accs., vol. vi; [30] WCC, I, 490–1; [31] *KCM*, College Accs., vol. v; [32] *KCM*, Kitchen Accs., s.a.; [33] CPR 1476–85, 472; [34] *CWW*, *ff.* 136v., 137; [35] *Ibid.*, 140v.; [36] See JOHN WASTELL, ad fin; [37] MSL, 60; [38] CGB, 'A'; [39] *BM*, Harl. MS. 294, *ff.* 156–9; [40] *BCM*, H.1–5–16; [41] CPR 1485–94, 223; [42] CPR 1494–1509, 401; [43] *BM*, Harl. MS. 58, *ff.* 18, 19v., 27; [44] *PCC*, 21 Holgrave; [45] *BW*, vi, 190

CLEUERE, Thomas (*fl.* 1396–1399) Carpenter

Master carpenter in charge of the works at *Portchester Castle*, Hants., in 1396–99, taking 6*d.* a day.

PRO, E.101–497–23, 24

Cleve, John—see CLYVE

CLIFE, John (*fl.* 1416) Mason

First master mason, with JOHN COLCHESTER, in charge of repairs to the walls and towers of *Harfleur*, France, from 1 January 1415/16. He was paid 1*s.* a day.

PRO, T.R. Misc. Bk. 79, *f.* 43 (*L.F.S.*); cf. *PRO*, E.101–69–8 no. 520 (*N.L.R.*)

CLIFFORD, John (*fl.* 1383–†1417) Mason

Probably the John Clifford who worked for a short time at *Windsor Castle* in 1361–62,[1] but his career has not been traced until on 29 September 1383 he acquired, apparently on behalf of HENRY YEVELEY, a toft of ground in Wennington and an acre in Aveley, Essex.[2] In the following February he was associated with Yeveley in acquiring land in Bermondsey,[3] apparently in connection with *London Bridge*, of which Yeveley was a warden. Clifford may already have been chief bridge mason, a post which he certainly held by 1388; from 1384 until shortly before his death he was frequently a party to Bridge House transactions.[4] In August 1386 he was sworn a master of the Masons' Mistery of London,[5] and on 4 November was again concerned with Henry Yeveley in the acquisition of property in the parish of St. Benet Fink, London.[6] Next year he and Yeveley seem to have been owed a total of £360 by nine men, mostly of Maidstone, but this was probably the amount of recognizances entered into by quarrymen for the supply of stone.[7] In 1387–88 Clifford, with Yeveley and others, was a party to two fines concerning property in Southwark,[8] and in 1390 was joint purchaser with Yeveley of tenements in the parish of St. Magnus by London Bridge;[9] these were private ventures and not on behalf of the Bridge Estates. On 1 May 1396 Clifford was one of those who, apparently on Yeveley's behalf, bought 2½ acres of land in Aveley, and on 14 April 1398 was one of the group of feoffees to whom Yeveley granted his Essex lands.[10] In 1400 he was appointed one of Yeveley's executors,[11] and as a feoffee was concerned in 1401 with the transfer of part of the properties to Katherine, Yeveley's widow.[12]

At a date before 1396, Clifford had acted as Yeveley's deputy in an architectural capacity, when he visited *St. Alban's Abbey* to advise Brother WILLIAM STUBBARD on the building of walls from the King's Hall to the Almonry.[13] As master mason of London Bridge, Clifford was paid 3*s.* 9*d.* a week, and an annual retaining fee of £1 until his death.[14] The post implied constant responsibility for maintenance but cannot have afforded much scope for design.

He was dead by 11 September 1417,[15] and was succeeded as bridge mason by RICHARD BEKE, to whose wife Alice a piece of silverware was bequeathed a year later by Clifford's widow.[16] Clifford's will, which had been made on 8 August 1411, and was proved on 17 September 1417,[17] shows that he had held land jointly with Yeveley at Greenwich and Deptford. He seems to have been provided with a house by the city, rent free, for the London Bridge accounts contain the entry on 22 January 1417/18: 'Paid to the parson of St. Mary Magdalene, Bermondeseye, 12*d.* tithe for the croft and garden of the Bridge late (occupied by) John Clifford.'

Clifford's extensive properties were left to his wife Lettice for her life, with remainders to Henry Clopham, son of William Clopham, and to the wardens of London Bridge, on condition that the wardens observed the yearly obit of Clifford and of his wife in the church of St. Olave, Southwark. The properties included: a messuage garden and meadow in the parish of West Greenwich which Clifford and Henry Yeveley had held of the feoffment of Robert atte Melle alias atte Brigge, senior; a plot of ground and a house in the same parish and $4\frac{1}{2}$ acres of land in 'Chirchefelde' which Clifford and his wife had had of the grant of John atte Mille; lands and tenements purchased of Richard atte Vyne in the parish of Lambeth and in the field of Southwark; a messuage and adjoining garden called 'le Crystopher on le hoop' in Deptford, of the grant of Robert atte Wode; lands and tenements purchased of Alice Large in Bermondsey; a messuage with curtilage, gardens, and meadows, and a piece of meadow called 'Horscroft', near Horsleydown, formerly belonging to John Whaplode, in the parish of St. Mary Magdalene Bermondsey; and 40s. rent from three pieces of meadow in East and West Greenwich sold to John Cheseman by Clifford.

(KJI)

[1] *PRO*, E.101–493–10; [2] F.W. Steer in EAS, XXIV, 48; [3] *LBH*, E.23; [4] *LBH*, deeds, *passim*; account roll, 7, m.12; [5] *CLB*, 'H', 273; [6] *LHR*, 115 (61, 93); [7] CCR 1385–9, 431; [8] *LSF*, 154; [9] *LHR*, 119 (61); [10] Steer in EAS, XXIV, 49; [11] SWL, II, 346; [12] Steer in EAS, XXIV, 50; [13] RGA, III, 387; [14] KJL; [15] *LBH*, accounts, vol. ii, *f.* 266 (*L.F.S.*); [16] PCC, 42 Marche (*A.O.*); [17] *PCC*, 38 Marche; *LBH*, L.R.79

CLONYER, John [Clonier] (*fl.* 1399–1427) Carpenter

Probably identical with the Master John, carpenter, in charge of timberwork at the chapel and mill of *Roxwell*, Essex, for New College, Oxford in 1399–1400. From 1405 John Clonyer was carrying out extensive works at the manor of *Writtle*, Essex, being paid £33 6s. 8d. by instalments spread over three years. The warden of New College in 1407 also gave him as reward the price of a quarter of wheat, i.e. 6s. In the following year Clonyer was building a new chamber and carrying out repairs to the houses and barns, while in 1409–10 Clonyer's wife provided oak boards for the door of Roxwell Chapel and in 1412–13 shingles for the chancel roof at Writtle. Clonyer was at work on minor repairs at Writtle in 1426–27, and in the same year 'John Muller clonier' was concerned with the new 'ceiling' of the chancel of Roxwell Chapel.

NCO, Writtle Accs., A.6, 8; B.7–8, 10–11 Hen. IV; C.13 Hen. IV–1 Hen. V; D.5 Hen. VI

CLOPTON, Thomas (*fl.* 1397–†1420) Carpenter

Was appointed master carpenter at *Calais* on 25 August 1397, and held office until his death in 1420, when he was succeeded by THOMAS MATHEW

HKW, II, 1054

CLYDROWE, John (*fl.* 1392–1393) Mason (? *Clitheroe, Lancs.*)

Leading mason on the works of the *Worcester Cathedral* cloisters in 1392–93 at 3s. 2d. a week in winter, rising to 3s. 4d. after Easter.

WCO, C.76

CLYFF, William (*fl.* 1460) Carver

Described as 'Magister' when, in October 1460, Robert Grout bequeathed £26 13s. 4d. to have his gravestone carved by Clyff or another adequately skilled in the said work (*in dicto opere satis experto*), to be placed in *Canterbury Cathedral*.

PCC 21 Stokton (*A.B.E.*)

CLYVE, John [Cleve] (*fl.* 1362–1392) Mason

In 1362–63 received £11 in part payment of 100 marks for building the walls and vault of the salting-house and larder at *Windsor Castle*, and by 1365 had received payment in full.[1] Was master mason of *Worcester Cathedral Priory* in 1376–77 when he was given a robe price 13s. 4d. while in charge of the building of the dormitory. He again received a robe in 1382–83, when a further 20s. was allowed for his board (*coquina*). In 1386 he was paid only for the first quarter of the year, but in 1391–92 he was a creditor of the Cellarer for an outstanding debt of 30s.[2] He was evidently the designer of the early Perpendicular work there, including the tower, north porch, recasing of the chapter house, east cloister (1386–96), and the south arcade and vault of the nave (–1386). The detail of all these works is homogeneous and individual, and shows clearly the influence of the early Court style of Perpendicular. The tower and porch in particular are among the masterpieces of English art, while the nave vault is well adapted to disguise the difference in design of the two arcades.

HPS, 92, 95

[1] HWC, I, 186, 189, 193, 207–8; [2] WCR, 20; *WCO*, C.69, 70, 71, 74

COBB, Robert [Cobbe, 'Cok'] (*fl.* 1508–1537) Mason

Of Cambridge; in 1508 was one of the working masons employed on *King's College Chapel* at the rate of 3s. 4d. a week.[1] He lived in the parish of St. Mary the Great and in the Poll Tax return of 1512–13 for Cambridge was assessed under Market Ward. This shows that he had movables valued between £20 and £40, on which he paid tax of 3s. 4d. His servant, George Wylkynson, was taking wages between £1 and £2; Anne Broughton, another servant, had wages of 10s. and a gown price 5s. Four men, three of whom were freemasons, were 'atte borde with Robert Cobbe'.[2] For the Poll Tax of 1516–17 his goods were valued at £14 and he was assessed at 7s., but this figure seems to have been judged too low, and there is a note inserted 'per Commission' in which the amounts are raised to £18 and 9s. He then had a servant called 'Raaf'.[3]

In 1510 or 1511 he gave a shilling towards the seating of Great St. Mary's Church.[4] From 1516 to 1518 he and John Martyn were wardens of the Sepulchre and Crucifix Lights in the church, and in 1522 he paid 4s. 8d. due by him as 'late warden of the sepulcre light'. In 1518 he bought 'a lytell stone' from the churchwardens for 3d.[5]

About 1523 he built the little chantry chapel on the north side of the chapel of St. John's College. This chantry was founded by Hugh Ashton, Archdeacon of York and former Comptroller of the Household of the Lady Margaret Beaufort, mother of Henry VII, who died on 23 December 1522. His fine tomb, with 'two ymages one lyvely and another dedely', which stood under an arch between the antechapel and the chantry chapel, is now in the antechapel of Sir Gilbert Scott's building. From the terms of Ashton's will, work on the chapel and tomb appears to have been begun before his death.[6] An account of money laid out on the building of the chapel, presumably by his executors, contains several payments to 'Cobb the fremason' both for workmanship and stone. A total sum of £45 16s. 8d. was spent.[7] Cobb was probably also the mason employed on the little court (now destroyed) at the south-west corner of the first court of the college. In the spring of 1529 a payment of 37s. 6d. in part for the new building was made to 'Cok the fremason', as his name is printed by Willis and Clark; no doubt, Cok is a misreading of Cob.[8] The master mason of this small court, built between 1526 and 1529, was WILLIAM ROBYNSON.

In 1535, when the screen and stalls in King's College Chapel were being erected, the choir seems to have been paved. At the Epiphany Feast Robert Cobbe and two paviours were among the guests entertained; he was also a guest on the Feast of the Assumption (August 15).[9] In February 1537 'Master Cobb' was paid 53s. 4d. for making three windows of squared stone complete with ironwork in the gallery of the President's Lodge at Queen's College.[10] [Robert Cobb may have been the freemason 'Cobbe' who in 1533–34 added the battlements to the tower of Swaffham Church, Norfolk.[11]]

Henry COBBE, a quarry owner, in 1459–60 supplied stone for King's College Chapel, Cambridge;[12] and in 1483–4 for Saffron Walden Church.[13]

A.O.
[1] KCM, Building Acc. 1508–9; [2] CCM, Box xvii/23; CBD, 118, 122; [3] CCM, Box x/1; [4] CWM, 40 (wrongly dated 1518 at the head of the page); [5] Ibid., 28, 31, 34, 44; [6] PCC, 4 Bodfelde; WCC, II, 287n.; [7] CMR, 254; [8] WCC, II, 246n.; [9] KCM, Kitchen Accs., vol. xiv; [10] SQC, 196; [11] Churchwardens' accounts (S.A.C.); [12] KCM, College Accounts, vol. ii; [13] Churchwardens' accounts

COBOLD, William [Cobald] (fl. 1401–1430) Carpenter

In 1401–02 was carpenter in the Sacrist's office at the Abbey of St. Edmund at Bury, being paid £5 4s. for the year. In 1417–18 and 1429–30 he was carpenter in the office of the sub-Sacrist and was paid at the same rate of 2s. a week. In these two latter years he received money for robes.[1] He had died before 12 February 1434, when his widow Anabilla made her will.[2] About 1430 he and his wife were granted a corrody of the value of 6d. a week in the Hospital of St. Saviour at Bury for the life of the survivor 'on account of good and laudable service'.[3] He lived in a house on the east side of Reyngate Street. His son William was a monk in the abbey.

A.O.
[1] BCM, Sacrists' Rolls, A.6–1–4, 5, 6; [2] BW, i, 209; [3] BM, Add. MS. 14848, f.21

COBYN, Thomas (fl. c. 1441–1443) Mason

Was paid for the building in freestone (cementrie libere) of the great wall on the west side of the inner court of South Wingfield Manor, Derbyshire, for Ralph, Lord Cromwell. The amounts were £4 in 1441, £8 5s. 10d. in 1442, and £7 8s. 0d. in 1443. The principal mason contractor at the time was RICHARD NORTH.

KAO, U 1475 M 207, by kind permission of Viscount De L'Isle, V.C., K.G.

'Cok the fremason'—see COBB, Robert

Cok, Peter—see KOC

COKE, HUMPHREY

Cokat, John—see COKET

Coke—see also COOK

COKE, Humphrey [Cook] (*fl.* 1496–†1531) Carpenter

On 16 March 1496 was appointed, with GEORGE PORTER, a member of a commission to take craftsmen and labourers for the King's works in the North and on the Marches of Scotland, but was stated to be of London when he was appointed chief carpenter of *Berwick-upon-Tweed* on 23 November 1499. On 7 November 1502 he was again a commissioner for the King's works on the Border.[1] On 22 March 1504 Coke was at work in Westminster, where he received £26 12s. 4d. for building *Henry VII's Almshouses* in the Abbey precinct.

Coke ('Umfrey Cooke') took up the freedom of the London Carpenters' Company in 1504, and was a warden of the Company in 1506/7, 1507/8, 1510/11, and 1519/20. He made periodical payments for 'presenting' his apprentices, and obtained licences in 1512 to employ 'foreigners' (i.e. non-members of the Company) 'at mastyr Gyrforthes yn Bassyng saw' (Bassishaw) and in 1514 for raising a timber frame in Fleet Street.[2]

In 1510/11 he was paid 6s. 8d. for drawing the plan of the cloister at *Eton College*, and he was evidently one of the principal craftsmen there over a considerable period, for he was paid an instalment of £13 6s. 8d. in 1514–15[3] for his work there, and in 1516–17 he designed the woodwork for the west side of the Cloister Court and Lupton's Tower.[4] Meanwhile he was acquiring property at Westminster, where he purchased 'the messuage called the Cristofer, one Close, syx litill tenements and syx gardeyns in the parishe of Seynt Martyns in the Felds' from Robert Chesman of Kentish Town, by indenture dated 4 December 1514.[5] He took a lease of adjacent property from the Abbot of Westminster on 12 December 1516, including a gatehouse which 'was probably the entrance to the alley leading to the river which later became Christopher or Hartshorn Lane'.[6] This was on the south side of the Strand where Northumberland Street was built in later times. Coke's lease was to run for 56 years at 13s. 4d. a year. From 1508 onwards until 1520 or later, Coke was master carpenter of the great hospital of the *Savoy*, which was in process of construction, and was also situated south of the Strand. Coke took 12d. a day and had as his warden JOHN SALLETT who took 8d. (See HENRY SMYTH) After completion of the hospital, Coke was retained as its chief carpenter at a yearly fee of £50.

At the time of the lease in 1516 Coke was living in the parish of St. Martin-in-the-Fields, but was still holding his post at Berwick, and was also able to act as master of the carpentry works at *Corpus Christi College, Oxford*, from 1514 to 1518, where he was paid at the rate of 1s. 8d. a day, when he was at work there, which was sometimes (for instance during 1517) for more than half his time. With WILLIAM VERTUE, Coke provided the plans from which the college was built; and with Vertue and WILLIAM EAST became the victim of assault and threats by members of Brasen-Nose Hall.[7] When ROBERT CAROW, carpenter of Oxford, contracted to make the timberwork of the library range, it was to be 'accordyng to a platt made by Humphray Cooke'[8] and Coke was in charge of the timberwork as a whole. His work doubtless included the design of the hall roof, which is almost identical with a roof from St. Mary's College, now at Brasenose Chapel, but hidden by plastering;[9] this latter roof must also have been of Coke's design.

Bishop Fox, founder of Corpus Christi College, had a high opinion of Coke, whom he entrusted in 1517 with 'the Fundacion under my seall' and other documents and money which he was to carry from Esher to the president-designate of the college at Oxford. On another occasion Fox wrote of Coke that 'he is righte cunnynge and diligente in his werkes. . . if ye take his advise. . . he shall advantage you large monee in the buldinge thereof, as well as in the devisinge as in the werkenge of yt'.[10]

On 22 August 1519 he was appointed the King's Chief Carpenter during pleasure at 12d. a day,[11] an office which he held until his death; he did not surrender his Berwick post until 1524,[12] but no doubt the duties there must have been nominal. In 1520 he was concerned in the preparations for the Field of the Cloth of Gold, with William Vertue the King's Mason.[13]

About this time Coke, with NICHOLAS REVELL, designed and built a house for James Yarford, alderman of London. They were paid £300, but sued Yarford for extras amounting to £64.[14]

In addition to the offices held by Coke as a craftsman he was, at least as early as 1509, keeper of Durham Place and bailiff of 'le Duresme rents' in the Strand, between Durham House and Ivy Lane. While the Crown was in possession of the temporalities of the see, Coke gave evidence on oath concerning Durham Rents in 1522.[15] In 1509 Coke was also master of the Bridge House.

Later he was employed by Cardinal Wolsey as one of the masters of the works at *Cardinal College, Oxford*,[16] now Christ Church, begun in 1525 and continued until 24 November 1529,[17] when Wolsey's downfall put a stop to the works. Fortunately the roof of the great hall had just been finished, and in this we have not only Coke's greatest work, but also the last great work of mediaeval carpentry, uncontaminated by Renaissance influence. Coke must also have designed the wooden vault which was constructed at Sonning in 1528 for the chapel of the college;[18] this chapel was never built, but it is possible that the structure of this vault is that which now covers the chapel at *Hampton Court Palace*. This vault was erected under Henry VIII, after Coke's death, and is plentifully sprinkled with the King's badges, but it is by no means unlikely that the materials were those already prepared for use at Oxford.

Humfrey's son ROGER COKE worked for Wolsey at *York Place*,[19] and we may suppose that Humphrey also was concerned in the design of woodwork there and at Hampton Court. In the absence of accounts, and since no detailed investigation of the Tudor work at Hampton Court has yet been made, it is incapable of proof. There can be little doubt that Coke designed the carved roof of the Savoy Chapel, destroyed by fire in 1864, and it was there that he was buried.

The inscription on his gravestone is recorded as follows:[20] 'Of your Charity pray for the Soul of Humphrey Cook, Citizen and Carpenter of London, and Master Carpenter of all the works to our Sovereign Lord King Henry the Eighth, and Master Carpenter at the building of the Hospital called the Savoy: the which Humphrey deceased the 13 day of March in the year of our Lord God, 1530, and lieth under this Stone.' The year of his death is undoubtedly 1531 (New Style), and the day must therefore have been earlier than 25 March, but the inscription is in error, since Coke made a codicil to his will on 18

March; probably the '13' was a slip for 18. The will itself[21] had been made on 14 March and was proved on 10 July. Coke, who was survived by his second wife Alice, left his property in the Strand to his daughter Christine, who had married JOHN RUSSELL,[22] afterwards King's Carpenter for more than thirty years. Besides Christine and Roger, there were three younger children under 21, Humphrey, Margaret, and Elizabeth.

Coke was one of the busiest of mediaeval craftsmen, and his known work includes the finest carpentry of the earlier and better period of Henry VIII. Coke's noble roof at Christ Church, Oxford, ranks second only to that of HUGH HERLAND at Westminster Hall.

HKC; (HMA; HMO; HCW); HKW, III, 202, 209 [1] CPR 1494–1509, 53, 187, 327; [2] MCR, II, *passim*; [3] WCC, I, 415n.; [4] *Ibid.*, 418n.; [5] *PRO*, C.1–616–17; [6] LS, XVIII, 21; *WAM*, 17188; [7] FCC; FHC, 64; [8] *CCO*, Account 1517–18 (*A.O.; R.D.*); [9] RCHM, *City of Oxford*, 27; [10] ALF, 19–21, 89 (*A.O.*); [11] LPH, III, pt. i, p. 162; [12] *Ibid.*, IV, pt i, 297; [13] *Ibid.*, III, p. 234; [14] SHB, 15; [15] LPH, I, i, p. 216, 438(1); III, 2485; [16] *Ibid.*, IV, 2734; [17] *PRO*, SP.1–55, *ff.* 221–38; [18] *PRO*, E.101–479–9 & *Bodl.* Twyne MS. xxi, 350 (*R.D.*); [19] *PRO*, E.101–474–7; [20] SSS, II, 681 (*A.O.*); [21] *PCC*, 5 Thower; printed in full HGE, 186–9; [22] LS, XVIII, 21

COKE, John (*fl.* 1532–1533) Carpenter
Warden of the carpenters working at *Greenwich Palace* in 1532–33, taking 9*d.* a day.
Bodl., Rawlinson MS. D.775, *f.* 31v.

COKE, Roger (*fl.* 1511–†1545/6) Carpenter
Son of HUMPHREY COKE; took up the freedom of the London Carpenters' Company in 1511, and appears in their records at various later dates, being Junior Warden of the Company in some year between 1515 and 1533.[1] He was the first of the working carpenters at *York Place, Westminster*, when Wolsey's work began there on 5 February 1514/15. He took 7*d.* a day, as compared with the 1*s.* a day usual for a master carpenter, and the 6*d.* a day which was paid to the carpenters under Roger's control.

At the end of the surviving account for 1515 is a separate bill headed: 'Here after foloweth the reparacons and Workemanshypp done in my lord off Yorks place by Roger Coke Carpenter the 11 day off Novembre.' This contains items for the bakehouse, kitchen, and buttery, several 'Pressys for the Wardroppe', bedsteads for the chambers, 'a bedsted for the chylldern off the Chapell', 'a fote off a lectron for the chyldron's chamber where they goo to scole', planks 'for a wrytyng bord', '150 off harte lathe for the ponds for the swannes', and various works in the hall, chapel and subsidiary offices. An additional bill for work done between 11 and 31 March following is for an Easter 'Sepoulker' of wood, with 'a payallme cros & a stafe for palme sonday'.[2]

Roger Coke probably continued to work for Wolsey, but he never attained to his father's reputation, though evidently skilled in all the smaller forms of carpentry. He survived his father nearly 15 years, making his will on 6 September 1545; it was proved on 13 January following.[3]

[1] MCR, II, 203–4, 220, 229, 243, 246; [2] PRO, E.101–474–7; [3] CCL, 75 Thirlby

COKET, John [Cokat, Kokette] (fl. 1430–1444) Mason

In 1430, when the King Edward Gate-tower of King's Hall, Cambridge, was being built, the accounts record several payments to a mason called Koket.[1] As several of the masons who worked at King's Hall about that time were later employed at Saffron Walden Church, Essex, he can be safely identified with the John Cokat or Kokette who worked there between 1438 and 1444. In 1438 and 1441 he was paid at the usual rate of 3s. 4d. a week, but in 1444 he was being paid at 4s. a week, and he seems to have succeeded JOHN GERARD as chief mason for the building then in progress.[2]

A.O.

[1] TCM, KHA, viii, 283–289; [2] CWW, ff. 5v., 21v., 22

COKKER, Richard (fl. 1442–1443) Carpenter

In 1442 was paid £3 6s. 8d., and £6 in the following year, for the timberwork of the kitchen roof at South Wingfield Manor, Derbyshire, as well as £2 to him and William Wright for raising the roof 6 feet at the order of the client Ralph, Lord Cromwell. Cokker was also one of the several carpenters concerned with other woodwork at the Manor (see JOHN MAFELD).

KAO, U 1475 M 207, by kind permission of Viscount De L'Isle, V.C., K.G.

COKSEGGE, Nicholas (fl. c. 1464) Carpenter

Carpenter of Bury St. Edmunds, about 1464 undertook to make for John Brasier of Bury a new house, 34 feet 6 inches long, on the model of 'Mayster John Bukkys house'.

A.E.B.O. in ARC, XIV, 1979, 19–20

COLCHESTER, John [Colchestre] (fl. 1416–1417) Mason

Second master mason, with JOHN CLIFF, in charge of repairs to the walls and towers of Harfleur, France, from 1 January 1415/16. He was paid 1s. a day. On 13 February 1416/17 'Johan Colchestre maceons' was appointed to have charge of the works at 'Hareflieu' for a year with 16 other masons under his control (desouz sa gouuernance), taking 12d. daily for himself and 9d. for each other mason.

PRO, T. R. Misc. Bk. 79, f. 43 (L.F.S.); E.404–32–281 (R.L.S.); cf. E.101–69–8 no. 520; 70–2 no. 610 (N.L.R.)

COLCHESTER, Walter of (c. 1180–†1248) Monk

Sacrist of St. Albans Abbey; described as a painter and carver (pictor et sculptor incomparabilis). With ELIAS OF DEREHAM made the shrine of Thomas Becket at Canterbury Cathedral, c. 1218–20.

TBK, XXXV, 120

COLCHESTER, William (fl. 1385–†1420) Mason

From the beginning of 1385 until Michaelmas 1388 the works of Southampton Castle were under the charge of HUGH KYMPTON and William Colchester as leading masons, each at 8d. a day. On 2 December 1395 William Colchestre, mason, was joined to the Sacrist of Westminster Abbey in a commission empowering them to impress craftsmen and labourers 'for the speedy completion of the nave. . . which the King extremely desires'.[1] At the death of HENRY YEVELEY in the summer of 1400, Colchester became chief mason for the works of the abbey nave taking £5 a year and a furred robe price 13s. 4d. After 1403 work ceased but he continued to receive his robe by way of retainer until 1405 or later.[2] On 14 December 1407 he was appointed by the King as patron to rebuild the fallen belfry at York Minster, being described as 'mason, expert in that art and much commended'.[3] He was unpopular there no doubt because he was a 'foreigner', and a commission was set up on 24 July 1408 to inquire into a conspiracy by certain masons to maim him, which had resulted in severe injuries to him and to his assistant, WILLIAM WADDESWYK[4].

On 6 June 1410 his patent for the York work was revoked,[5] but it is not certain that he ceased to superintend there, as he was still in charge at the Minster from 1415 to 1419 and became a freeman of York in 1417.[6] In

July 1413 Henry V restarted the work at Westminster Abbey, and Colchester's fee for the post of chief mason was increased to £10, so that he presumably had to spend a greater proportion of his time there; his allowance for clothing was increased to 14s. 2½d.[7] On 2 June 1418 the King himself directed a warrant to the Chancellor stating that he was 'fully avysed to make oure maistre mason as maister Steven was — oon that hyght Colchester whiche is maistre mason bothe of the chirche of York, and of Westm.'. This was sent from Bernay in Normandy, and on 6 July Colchester received his patent, granting him the office of King's Master Mason at *Westminster Palace* and the *Tower of London*, in succession to STEPHEN LOTE, at 12d. a day.[8] He died on 5 July 1420, and all his posts were filled by others in the next year; at Westminster Abbey he had been succeeded at Christmas 1420 by JOHN THIRSK who had been his warden.[9] A mason named *William COLCHESTER* was among those working on the Prior's bakehouse at *Worcester Cathedral* in 1420 and 1421, taking 1s. 8d. a week in addition to his meals at the Prior's expense.[10]

Colchester left his mark as a designer at York Minster, in the stone screens at the entry of the choir aisles, buttressing the eastern piers of the tower, which was carried out later, but probably in general accordance with drawings left by him, for a belfry of two stages. He probably also designed the stone altar-screen of the Minster. The buttressing screens, bonded into the aisle walls, have a sliding joint against the shafts of the crossing, an ingenious device to minimize the effects of settlement, while increasing rigidity against wind pressure.

At Westminster Abbey he simply supervised the continuation of work according to the old design, and his short term of office as King's Mason was not marked by much activity.

KJM; (RNW; BHY, I, 211–12, 217, 218); HKW, I, 214; II, 843
[1] CPR 1391–6, 643, 647; [2] WAM, 23470–4; [3] CPR 1405–8, 383; [4] Ibid., 482; RFY, 201; [5] CPR 1408–13, 199; [6] RFY, 34n.; YCF, I, 125; [7] WAM, 23492–4, 23480–8; [8] CPR 1416-22, 170; PRO, C.81/1364 (R.L.S.); [9] WAM, 23489; [10] WCO, rolls C.83, 84

Coldam, Gabriel—see CALDHAM

COLE, John (*fl.* 1470–1473) Bricklayer ['Brekemason']
In 1470 and in 1472–73 was the contractor for bricklaying at the building of the so-called 'Fox's Tower' of *Farnham Castle*, Surrey. The work was begun in 1470 and completed in or soon after 1475.

M. W. Thompson in SYC, LVII, 1960, 88

COLE, John [Coole] (*fl.* 1501–1504) Mason
Master mason at the building of the spire of *Louth Church*, Lincs., from the beginning of the work in 1501 until 1504. He is known to have prepared moulds for the work, and was therefore the architect of one of the finest steeples in existence. From 1505 until the completion of the work in 1515, Cole's place was taken by CHRISTOPHER SCUNE, the architect of the new nave of Ripon Minster. The total cost of the spire at Louth was £305 7s. 5d. Cole was on one occasion paid 2s. 5d. for making moulds for four days, and 3s. 4d. at another time for his expenses in visiting the quarries. In 1503–04, 6d. was paid for 'j wellome skyn for to draw the broch in'.

The date of the tower at Louth is uncertain (*c.* 1450–90) but the arch to the nave is stylistically in the closest agreement with the Perpendicular crossing arches at Ripon Minster. This may be accounted for on the supposition that the Louth arch was pierced at the time of the completion of the spire, perhaps on account of failure in its predecessor, or else that for some reason more than one Ripon mason had worked at Louth.

(APD; BAA; WPS; A, x); DCL, 20–1, 23–6, 35–9, 52–4, 66–7, 73

COLEBROOK, Robert de [Colebrak, -brok] (*fl.* 1278–†*c.* 1300) Carpenter
In 1278 ROBERT OF BEVERLEY, who was in charge of works at the Tower of London, purchased timber 'for the new tower (*turrell*') towards the city' through Robert 'de Colebrak',[1] and further payments were made in 1281–84 'by the hands of Robert de Colebrok', including the costs of carriage of timber from Southwark to the Tower by water. In 1284 he was paid 10s. 4d. for timber and boards for a little boat for the use of the lord Alphonso and for the painting of the same.[2] The lord Alphonso was Edward I's eldest surviving son, born in 1273, but he died later in the year 1284.

In 1288 Robert of Colebrook was the King's principal carpenter engaged on the works at *Westminster Palace*, being paid 3s. a week,[3] and he still held this position until 1297. Between 1292 and 1297 Colebrook was also in charge of works at the *Tower of London*, and received pay at the rate of 9*d*. a day. On 23 October 1292 he was one of the mainpernours at the Exchequer for Master THOMAS DE HOUGHTON who was then sworn in as a serjeant carpenter.[4]

Colebrook paid 20*s*. in the subsidy of 1293–94, when he was living in Broad Street Ward in the City of London, probably in the parish of St. Bartholomew the Less.[5] He and his wife Avice, widow of Robert le Callere, were concerned in property transactions in several London parishes from 1288 until Colebrook's death between 1298 and 1301.[6]

On 8 June 1294 he was ordered to take wood from Pamber Forest, Hants., for the works of St. Stephen's Chapel.[7] When work was in progress at York Place, Westminster, in 1298, after a fire in the Palace had forced the King to borrow the Archbishop's town house, Robert supplied boards for repairing part of the houses there.[8]

HKW, I, *passim*; II, 723
[1] *PRO*, E.101–467–7(6); [2] *Ibid.*, E.101–467–9; [3] *Ibid.*, E.101–467–16; [4] TTH, 29; [5] WLE; [6] LHR, 18 (72, 73, 79), 26 (24), 27 (58), 30 (92), 31 (48); [7] CCR 1288–96, 350; [8] *PRO*, C.47–3–31

COLECHURCH, Peter of *(fl.* 1163–†1205) Priest

A priest, and possibly an instance of a clerical architect; he is said to have built a wooden bridge over the Thames at *London* in 1163, and to have begun the first stone bridge there in 1176, the work going on until 1209. Colechurch died in 1205, and was buried in the bridge chapel, the work being brought to a conclusion under ISAMBERT DE XAINTES.

APD; (BAA; WTB)

COLONIA, John de *(fl.* 1521–1526) Carpenter

Probably a German from Cologne, was working in *Oxford* in 1521, making 22 new stalls for *Magdalen College* chapel. These were removed in 1831. He also made 89 yards of ceiling at 10*d*. a yard, apparently to be fixed within the chapel roof. He also did other minor works, taking 8*d*. a day. From 1523 to 1526 he was living in a house in the parish of St. Peter-in-the-East, formerly inhabited by ROBERT CAROW. He was perhaps identical with JOHN SKOWTE.

GOC

COLWYK, John de [Colewek, Colwik] *(fl.* 1345–1358) Carpenter *(Colwick, Notts.)*

Carpenter of York, where he took up the freedom in 1345–6. In 1357–58 he was paid 3*s*. a week, in charge of work for the Merchant Adventurers, perhaps their *Hall* (see ROBERT DE BAGBY).

SS, CXXIX, 4, 5, 8, 10–13, 16

COLYER, Thomas *(fl.* 1470) Mason.

Mason of *Bristol*; in 1470 acted as a viewer of the city.

(*A.O.*) BLR, II, 132.

COLYN, Piers *(fl.* 1438–   ) Carpenter

Third named of three carpenters, of whom the first was RICHARD WODEMAN, who in 1438 contracted to make the timberwork of the *Guildhall, Canterbury*.

SHB, 510–12; *CRM*, Bundle LVI A(7); (*D.G.*)

COLYN, Thomas *(fl.* 1408) ? Carver

In 1408 an alabaster tomb was made in England at the orders of Queen Joan of Navarre, for her first husband, John, Duke of Brittany (†1399). It was to be conveyed to *Nantes* by John Guychard, merchant, together with three Englishmen who had made the tomb (*qui eandem tumbam operati fuerunt*): Thomas Colyn, Thomas Holewell, and Thomas Poppehowe.[1] The tomb closely resembled that of Ralph Nevill, Earl of Westmorland (†1425) in *Staindrop Church*, Dur.[2]

[1] RF, VIII, 510; CEM, 26–7 (plate); [2] GAT, 11–12

COMBER, William *(fl.* 1440) Carpenter

Of Newport, Isle of Wight, on 9 October 1440 entered into a bond in £10 with the Warden of *Winchester College*.

WCM 20108A

COMBES, Richard *(fl.* 1485–1503) Mason

In 1485 succeeded THOMAS FERRIER as master mason of *Calais*, and held office until the appointment of JOHN BAKER in 1503.

HKW, III, 419

COMPTON, John de *(fl.* 1341–   ) Mason

Master mason of freestones (*cem' libr' lapidum*) in charge of the building of a new chapel at the royal manor of *Ludgershall*, Wilts., in 1341; he seems to have been superseded after the first four months' work by JOHN DE HACCHE.

PRO, E.101–476–1 (*L.F.S.*); HKW, II, 731n.

CONAN the Mason *(fl.* 1129–1130) Mason

Was pardoned sums of 1*s*. and 3*s*. in 1129–30 by writs of Henry I, apparently at London. Two arches ('Arch') of *London Bridge* were made in that year for £25, perhaps stone piers with a timber superstructure (see PETER OF COLECHURCH); work done at the *Tower of*

London cost £17 0s. 6d.
HMR, 148, 150; 144

Cony—see also COYNY

CONY, Robert (*fl.* 1417–†1446) Joiner
Appointed on 3 March 1416/17 King's chief joiner in the *Tower of London* in succession to JOHN WYDMERE, deceased.[1] In 1424 he provided two boards for the new painted signs of the *Crown Inn, Rochester*, for 13s. 4d.[2] He was confirmed in his Crown office on 7 July 1424,[3] and on 12 May 1425 was ordered to impress carpenters and others for the works in the Tower and to purvey materials for the making of lances, chests, platforms (*tabulis*), and pavoises (*pavys*), etc.[4] He received a fresh grant of the office, for life, on 18 October 1439,[5] and was given exemption from serving on juries, etc., on 23 May 1443.[6] Between 1424 and 1443 he had been concerned in several property transactions in London parishes.[7] He was still living on 30 January 1445/6,[8] but seems to have been dead by 5 February, and on 24 March 1446 Margaret his widow and executrix surrendered to the Crown a shop which had been granted to him on 9 November 1432.[9] Cony drew fees of 12d. a day, and received cloth for his annual robe of office.[10]

[1] CPR 1416–22, 66, 85; [2] BRB, 91; *RBA*, No. 32 (*M.J.B.*); [3] CPR 1422–9, 192; [4] *Ibid.*, 304; [5] *Ibid.*, 1436–41, 342; [6] *Ibid.*, 1441–6, 172; [7] *LHR*, 153(4), 164(21), 172(56); [8] CPR 1441–6, 398; [9] *Ibid.*, 402, 425; [10] *PRO*, E.403–695; BM, Add. 17721, *f*.39

Cook—see also COKE, KOC

COOK, Thomas, I [Cok, Koc] (*fl.* 1349–1360) Mason
In 1349 a working mason on the postern of the *Tower of London* at 6d. a day; in 1353, with ROGER STEPHEN, he undertook by task the repair of 5 perches of wall at *Rotherhithe Manor* for £13 6s. 8d. He was probably identical with the Thomas Cook appointed to take carpenters for the works of Eltham and Rotherhithe on 18 November 1353; and on 12 January 1354 was ordered to purvey stone and lime from Kent, Surrey and Sussex for the same places. He was also paid £17 10s. 0d. for a further task of 7 perches of wall at *Rotherhithe*. In 1358–60 he was warden (*apparilator*) of the masons at *Eltham Palace*.
PRO, E.101–471–3; 493–4; 545–33, 34; CPR 1350–4, 522, 542, HKW, II, 990

COOK, Thomas, II [Cookus] (*fl.* 1447–1448) Mason

Mason of Warwick; in 1447–48 was admitted to the Guild of the Holy Cross of Stratford on Avon on his own behalf and for the soul of Joan, formerly his wife.
(*A.O.*) BRS, 109

Coole, John—see COLE

Cooper, Andrew—see COUPER

COOPER, Geoffrey (*fl.* 1370–) Carpenter
In 1370 was paid 20 marks (£13 6s. 8d.) for fitting up rooms 'bien convenablement' in the 'nurserie' built round the great hall of *Cambridge Castle*.
A.O. CAC, XXVI, 87

COORLAND, Walter [Gauterius Coorlandus] (*fl. c.* 1025–1049) ? Mason
Said to have been sent by Emma, Queen of England, to build the monastery of *St. Hilaire-le-Grand, Poitiers*; begun *c.* 1025, and consecrated in 1049. He can hardly have been the 'Gauterius Corloanarius' who witnessed deeds at St. Hilaire *c.* 1077–90.
APD; MDR, I, 141; FAO, 36

COPDOKE, Thomas and John (*fl.* 1464–1466) Carpenters (*Copdock, Suff.*)
From 1464 to 1466 were making additions to *Tendring Hall*, near Stoke-by-Nayland, Suffolk, for Sir John Howard, later Duke of Norfolk. They were brothers and worked under indentures. Up to September 1465 they were paid £30 3s. 4d. From October they and their men were boarded while they were 'framynge and arerynge' the work. In the accounts a distinction is sometimes made between John Copdoke of Halstead, Essex, and John Copdoke of Sudbury, and in October 1465 an agreement was made with 'Young Copdoke' for a year's service. Total payments made on account of the Copdokes' work amounted to rather more than £55.
A.O. BMH

Corant—see also CURRAUNT

CORANT, Henry [Harry Curant, Coraunt, Corra(u)nt, Corraunte, Courant(e), Curraunte, Curraynte (*fl.* 1535–1547) Carver
Carver of Kingston upon Thames; in 1535–36 he was engaged in carving, setting-up, and finishing the sides of the stalls for the chapel at *Hampton Court*. In addition to this work executed in wood, he carved 38 of the King's and Queen's beasts in stone to stand about the ponds in the pondyard there at 26s. each, and also a lion and a greyhound in

69

freestone. Corant was to give advice concerning the bequests of his friend EDMUND MORE in 1536.

Corant rented a house near Kingston Bridge from the Bridge Wardens for 16s. a year from 1536 until 1543; it was apparently that which EDMUND MORE had formerly held. In 1539–40 Corant paid the Bridge Wardens 5s. for old planks and in 1540–41 a sum of 34s. 8d. for 'the rentt of the toll taken at the bridge'. From 1544 until 1547 Corant was himself one of the two Bridge Wardens.

HC, I, 358, 370–1; WKA, xv, 22–4, 27–8, 30, 33, 37, 39

CORBRIDGE, Gilbert de (*fl.* 1226–1248) Carpenter (*Corbridge, N'land*)

Carpenter, son of William the carpenter, and master carpenter to Walter Gray, Archbishop of York, who on 29 December 1226 granted to Gilbert and his heirs 47 acres of waste with common of pasture at 'Wudeburn' for 1 mark of silver yearly. In 1248 Gilbert de Corbrig, carpenter, and his heirs received a grant of 2 bovates and 2 acres of land in Milford and 12½ acres of new assart by rent of 15s. 5½d. This grant was confirmed by the Dean and Chapter of York on the ground that Gilbert had been long in the Archbishop's service and had laboured much and faithfully for *York Minster*. He was no doubt in charge of the carpentry works during the building of the transepts *c.* 1230–60.[1]

It has been suggested that Gilbert was an ancestor of Thomas de Corbridge, Archbishop of York 1300–04.[2]

[1] WGR, 225, 259; [2] TCR, II, xi

CORBY, Robert de (*fl.* 1381–1384) Mason (? *Corby, N'hants.*)

Chief mason at *Rockingham Castle*, Northants., in 1381–84, taking 6d. a day.

PRO, E.101–481–9 (*L.F.S.*)

Corfe, John de—see DOGET

CORFE, John de (*fl.* 1334–1336) Mason

Chief keeper, purveyor, and ordainer of all the King's work in *Ireland* touching the art of masonry (*capitalis custos, provisor et ordinator tocius operacionis Regis in Hibernia que ad officium cementarie pertinet*) in 1334 and during the next two years, when he was paid his fee of 10 marks (£6 13s. 4d.) yearly by instalments at the Dublin Exchequer.

IPC, I, pt. i, 38, 41

CORNWALL, John [Cornwale, Cornwayle] (*fl.* 1377–1409) Mason

Mason (*lathomus*) at *Exeter Cathedral* from 1377, and was warden of the masons in 1389 when part of the masons' house was rented to him. He had evidently succeeded JOHN SWALLOW, and was still in office in 1409.

FFE, quoting EDC, fabric rolls and No. 3550, *f.*51

CORSCOMBE, John de [Coscombe] (*fl.* 1347–1348) Mason (? *Corscombe, Dorset*)

In 1347 the leading mason on the works of *Exeter Cathedral* was one Corscombe, paid 1s. 10d. a week in winter and 2s. 2d. in summer.[1] He was admitted to the freedom of the City of Exeter by gift of the mayor and community on 29 September 1348, at the instance of John de Schareshull the cathedral precentor.[2]

He may have been related to the John de Corscombe, mason, who worked at Exeter Cathedral at 2s. 2d. a week in 1304 and again in 1309–10.[3]

[1] EDC, rolls 2633–34 (AEC, ii, 309–10); [2] RJE, 28; [3] AEC, i, 182, 187, 212

CORVEHILL, William (*fl. c.* 1500–†1546) Monk

Monk of *Wenlock Abbey*, born at Wenlock. At his death in 1546 he was described as having been 'excellently and singularly experte in dyverse of the VII liberal sciences and especially in geometre, not greatly by speculacion, but by experience; and few or non of handye crafte but that he had a very gud insight in them, as the making of organs, of a clocke an chimes, an in kerving, in masonrie, and weving of silke, an in peynting. . . a gud Bell founder and a maker of the frame for bells'.

D.H.S. Cranage in A, LXXII (register of Thomas Butler, vicar of Wenlock)

CORYNGDON, John (*fl.* 1464–1484) Mason

Of Exeter; in 1464 was making a porch before the tower of the church of *Clyst Gabriel*, Devon; and later contracted to hew stone for the Vicars Choral of *Exeter Cathedral*. In 1484 he worked on the *Exeter City Guildhall*.

FFE, quoting EDC, No. 1932; Vicars Choral No. 3349; Exeter City Rec. Roll, 2 Ric. III

'Coteham', John—see TOTTENHAM

COTEREL, Richard (*fl.* 1314) Carpenter

In May 1314 a payment of £2 10s. was recorded for works done by contract by Richard Coterel, carpenter, in *Windsor Castle*.

HKW, II, 870

COTOM, John (*fl.* 1435–1438) Mason

Mason of York; in 1435 he was chosen by Richard Russell, a prominent merchant, to complete the church of *St. John the Baptist, Hundgate*, in *York*.[1] The church has been destroyed. One of the desperate debts owing to the estate of John Bradford, mason of York, at the latter's death on 2 October 1438, was 14*s.* from John Cotom, mason.[2]

(*PCY*; CWY, vi; W. J. Williams in MR, xvi, 129)
[1] YTE, ii, 53; [2] *Ibid.*, iii, 95

COTTINGHAM, William [Cotyngham] (*fl.* 1416–†1457) Carpenter (*Cottingham, Yorks. E.R.*)

Became a freeman of the city of York in 1416–17,[1] and apparently succeeded JOHN ASKHAM as master carpenter of *York Minster* in 1437. Cottingham appears in the extant fabric rolls as the master carpenter, until shortly before his death in 1457.[2] His will made on 2 January 1456/7 refers to him as 'citizen and carpenter of York, dying in the house in which John Hall "sissor" (tailor) now lives, in Petergate'; he desired to be buried in the churchyard of St. Michael-le-Belfry, between the bodies of his deceased sons, William and John.[3]

On 24 January 1436/7 Cottingham had been one of the witnesses to the will of Thomas Best of York, carpenter, proved in 1439.[4] Cottingham's widow Joan died early in 1460, her will being made on 21 July 1459, and proved on 28 March 1460.[5]

William Cottingham was probably the most important York carpenter of his time, and may have designed the roof of the *Guildhall*, whose carvings, however, appear to be by several hands. The principal city carpenter after Cottingham's death was JOHN FOULFORD, and it is perhaps more likely that he was the principal carpenter employed on the Guildhall.

[1] YCF; [2] BHY, i, 236–7, 240–1; RFY, 56n., 57, 59, 62n., 68, 207; [3] *Ibid.*, 207; [4] *PCY*, vol 3, 573; [5] *DCY*, vol. 1, 290

Couper—see also COWPER

COUPER, Andrew [Cowper] (*fl.* 1455–1485) Carpenter

Carpenter of Norwich, taking up the freedom there in 1455–56.[1] In 1484–85 he was paid £3 1*s.* 10½*d.* by the Cellarer of Norwich Cathedral Priory for making the roof of the new chancel of *Worstead Church*, Norfolk and the work went on until 1488 (See JOHN ANTELL). At Norwich he worked on a new building at the hostry of the priory, being paid 13*s.* 4*d.* for taking down the old roof for 8 days; wages of 8*s.* 4*d.* with board costing 5*s.*

2*d.* for 11 days spent on making 'le tresawnce'; and various other works done in 1484–85.[2] He was no doubt identical with the Andrew Carpenter paid 7*s.* 4*d.* in 1481–82 for repairs in the great campanile of *Norwich Cathedral*,[3] and probably father of WILLIAM COWPER.

[1] EFN; [2] *NCM*, Cellarer's Roll, Nos. 189–191, Almoner's Roll, No. 577; [3] *NCM*, Sacrist's Roll, No. 306

COUPER, John (*fl.* 1482–1487) Carpenter

Worked for 20 weeks in 1482 at *York Minster*, taking 3*s.* a week, on the tabernacle of St. Peter in the Choir.[1] He took up the freedom of York in 1483–84,[2] and was second searcher of the York Carpenters' craft in 1487, when with RICHARD BISCHOPE, he entered on behalf of the carpenter's mistery into an agreement with the Austin Friars of York.[3]

[1] BHY, i, 258; RFY, 85; [2] YCF; [3] YCM, B/Y, 201b

John COUPER (†1402), carpenter of York, may have been of the same family. His will made on 29 September and proved on 4 October 1402, mentions his wife Margaret, and a daughter of the same name, Richard 'my brother's son' to whom 'my best bow with 12 arrows' and a sword with 'bukler' were left, and 'Sir' John de Awne, John Taverner, and Robert Cracall, who were to be joint executors with his wife. He desired to be buried in the churchyard of Holy Trinity, Goodramgate.

PCY, vol. 3, 84

COUPER, Robert (*fl.* 1442–†1459) Mason

One Robert Couper, mason, was paid 3*s.* 4*d.* by order of the Abbot of Selby for coming to *Selby Abbey* at the beginning of February 1432 to give advice on the making of the stonework of the north aisle; perhaps identical with one admitted a freeman of the city of York in 1442/3,[1] who soon afterwards was chief mason to the corporation. In 1446–47 he was working on the building of a gate, perhaps that leading to the old Common Hall, taking pay of 3*s.* 4*d.* a week in summer and 3*s.* in winter. He was the mason in charge of the building of *York Guildhall*, where his servant Patrick worked for 20 days during the four weeks ending on 23 February 1447/8. Couper himself first appears in the account for the week ending 20 April, when he was paid 3*s.* 4*d.* for laying stone. He worked there intermittently during the spring, but from August until 2 February 1449, when the account ends, he was continuously at work, taking 3s. 4d. a week, and 3s. the winter rate from 1 December onwards. His servant Patrick was paid 2s. 2d. a week. No other detailed accounts have been preserved, but Couper doubtless continued in charge of the works for several years until c. 1453, when materials were transferred to Walmgate Bar, where Couper supervised repairs.[2] During 1449 Couper was also in charge of the re-building of a house in Feasegate. In 1453 he was also at work on the King's Staith on the east bank of the Ouse below the Bridge, taking 3s. 4d. a week for 5 weeks, and 1s. 3d. for a night's work.

In an undated document of about 1457–58, Couper appears as 'common mason' of the city of York, when, with JOHN PORTER, the Minster mason and two carpenters (JOHN FOULFORD and ROBERT JACKSON) he adjudi-cated on a dispute concerning the discharge of rainwater from a house in 'Northstrete', York, on to an adjoining garden.[3]

In his will, made 13 August 1459, he desired to be buried 'in the Ambulatory before the Crucifix in my parish church of St. Margaret of York'. His bequests included 6s. 8d. to the fabric of the church of Bubwith, of which place he was probably a native; his sons, Nicholas Couper, chaplain, and Robert Couper are mentioned; to the latter, Couper left all his patterns and tools ('exemplar' et instrumenta'). To his wife Marjorie he left his leases of a tenement in 'Walmegate' in York, and other relatives named were John and Joan Walker, children of his deceased sister Agnes; and Thomas Couper of Bubwith, son of his deceased brother William Couper. The will was proved by his wife Marjorie on 20 August 1459.[4]

On stylistic grounds it seems probable that Couper was the designer of the masonry work of St. Anthony's Hall, York, c. 1448–53, but the building has been so altered that few details of the original stonework remain. He may also have rebuilt the church of St. Martin, Coney Street, c. 1443–50.

RMY, 136–7, 165, 223
[1] Hull Univ. Lib., MS DDLO/20/1, Dona (N.L.R.); YCF; [2] YCM, Chamberlains' Accs., vol. 1A, ff. 6–8, etc. (A.R.); [3] YMB; [4] PCY, vol. 2, 415

Coupere, John—see COWPER

Coupere, Robert—see COUPER

COURTLEY, John (fl. 1525–1526) Carpenter

Carpenter, late of Arreton in the Isle of Wight, appointed on 29 Sept. 1525 by an indenture sealed in the chapter house of Quarr Abbey to hold and exercise the office of carpenter to the said abbey for life, either in person or by a sufficient deputy.

Courtley was to receive a yearly rent of 26s. 8d., with a robe of the suit of the abbot's yeomen (unam togam de secta valectorum nostror-um), and a house in Quarr called 'le south-yatehows' and two closes of land called 'Scraggs closes' near the wall of the monas-tery; two loaves of convent bread, two loaves of household bread, three gallons of convent ale, and as many messes of flesh or fish as a monk of the house should have; with allo-wance of enough fuel from the woods of Quarr; as well as two loaves of convent bread, two of household bread, three gallons of ale and a monk's allowance of food with fuel for Joan, Courtley's wife. These per-quisites were to last for their joint lives and the life of the longer liver of them.

PRO, E.326–B.9360, Anc. Deed (L.F.S.)

COVENTRY, Thomas [Coventre] (fl. 1438–†1465) Carpenter

Of Hart Street, London. In 1438 he was one of the three wardens of the London Carpenters' Company, to which he gave three trestles 'for ye medell tabell'. He was warden again in 1445 and 1455.[1] [On 14 February 1447/8 he received a gift from Joan Bertram, widow.[2]] At the time when he made his will, dated 1 November 1464, proved 23 January 1465, he was owed £8 by the church-wardens of St. Olave, Hart Street, but he be-queathed 40s. of this sum 'to the church body' of the church. He was also owed £4 by Robert Gower, the rector of the church, but he forgave this debt on condition that the parson should ceil (syle) or cause to be ceiled as much of the roof of the north aisle of the church as remained unceiled 'according to the werkyng of the seling there nowe begon'. This 'seling' or roof had evidently been begun by Thomas Coventry himself. He desired to be buried in the church of St. Olave beside his wife Lettice. He held a lease of a brew-house called the Cock in Hart Street from the Crutched Friars, to whom he bequeathed all the lead vessels and necessaries in it at the expiration of his term; the 'tenement or cot-age' in which he lived, also held on lease, adjoined the brewhouse on the east. He left a daughter, Thomasin, wife of John Waite of

London, 'yeman'. To three carpenters, John West, John Plane, and Thomas Foxley, who probably were or had been in his employment, he left 6s. 8d. each. To Thomas Fourneys, his apprentice, he bequeathed all his tools and 'hustilments of carpenterie', 40s. in money and all his right 'in a pair of indentures and covenants and sale of timber' made with the prior and convent of Newark beside Guildford in Surrey. His executors after having valued 'the tymbre and borde that is in my hawe' were to allow Thomas Fourneys the option of buying it 'as it is praysed'.[3]

A.O.
[1] JPC, 15, 17, 621; CPM 1437–57, 173;[3] PCC, 7 Godyn

COVENTRY, Walter [? William] of (*fl.* 1187–1199) Mason

Is said to have designed the new work of *Chichester Cathedral* after the fire of 1187; it was sufficiently far advanced for consecration in 1199. On account of the very close resemblance between this work, notably in the retrochoir, with the work which had been completed at Canterbury Cathedral in 1184, it has been suggested that the mason was identical with WILLIAM ENGLISHMAN.

(APD; BAA); HHC, 261

'**COVENTRY**, The Mason of' (*fl.* 1469–) Mason

During the building of the tower of *Ludlow Church*, Salop, in 1469, several specialists were consulted, among them 'ye mason of Coventre', who was paid sums of 6s. 8d. and 5s., with 8d. 'in expenses for the same mason to bring him to Beaudeley' (Bewdley, Worcs.) and 12d. 'in expenses apon the mason of Coventre by Richard Sherman'. (See also MASON, CLEMENT; HOBBS, JOHN.)

SHR, 2S., I (1889), 243

COWPER, John [Coupere] (*fl.* 1453–1484) Mason

Perhaps the son of John Cowper, mason (*lathamus*), who was at work on the buildings of Winchester College in 1456–57, and building a brick wall there in 1458 at 3d. a day;[1] and connected with the Thomas Cowper (*lathamus*) who sold stone to the college in 1465/6, and the latter's son who worked there in that year at 2d. a day. In 1466/7 John Cowper was repairing a chimney in the college, taking 5d. a day while his son took 3d.[2]

The younger John apparently served his apprenticeship as a mason on the works of *Eton College*, where he appears on 1 October 1453, at the rate of 2s. a week. As the immediately preceding accounts are missing, it is quite likely that he had already been working at Eton for a year or more, which would allow of his serving his term of seven years there. He was paid at the same rate throughout the account for October 1453 to September 1454, but was receiving 2s. 6d. a week at the start of the next surviving account in October 1456. He was still being paid at this rate in April 1459 when he left Eton, presumably at the end of his apprenticeship. For two weeks in July 1460 his name appears among the ordinary freemasons, taking the standard wage of 3s. 4d. a week, but he then left, doubtless to take up more remunerative or congenial work elsewhere.[3]

It is also to be remembered that the battle of Northampton was fought at this time, resulting in the downfall of Henry VI and the practical cessation of work at Eton. Bishop Waynflete of Winchester, one of the trustees of the college, may have taken Cowper into his service, as he next appears as a mason of Winchester on 20 April 1477, contracting with the bishop and the latter's foundation of Magdalen College, Oxford, to repair *Bramber Bridge* in Sussex. He was to hew 100 loads of stone, and to be paid £19 for his work. On 9 January in the following year Cowper undertook the completion of this repair in another contract which promised him 20 marks (£13 6s. 8d.) and a gown.[4] Soon afterwards he seems to have gone to *Tattershall*, Lincs., to supervise Bishop Waynflete's work on the collegiate church there, including the belfry stage of the tower.[5] This work did not occupy the whole of his time, as he was able to take on the position of master mason at *Kirby Muxloe Castle*, Leics., which he built for William, Lord Hastings.[6]

Preliminary work on the site began in October 1480, and Cowper was working there at 8d. a day in May and June 1481. He paid frequent visits from Tattershall, worked at Kirby for some 14 weeks in 1481, 19 weeks in the following year, and came twice in the spring of 1483. The resident mason at Kirby was ROBERT STEYNFORTH who, however, sometimes visited Tattershall. In August 1481 oak boards were prepared for the masons' moulds and in the following spring the new towers and gatehouse were begun and rapidly pushed on, the work being almost finished by

October 1482. The gatehouse vault was made in February 1483, and foundations were laid for a new kitchen in March. But before the castle was completed Lord Hastings had been executed, on 14 June 1483, and the works were practically stopped for several months. During the winter, and until September 1484, small works were done, including the laying of floors, but the castle was never finished.

The principal material used at Kirby Muxloe is brick, and it is probable that Cowper also designed the other important brick buildings built for Bishop Waynflete, the new gatehouse tower at *Esher*, Surrey, built *c.* 1475–80, and the school at *Wainfleet*, Lincs., built in 1484.[7] Another work with much resemblance to his style is the tower of the Bishop of Lincoln's Palace at *Buckden*, Hunts., built at the same period.[8] Cowper adapted the somewhat earlier style of Tattershall Castle to the changing needs of a later generation, and his work forms an important link in the development of the brick Tudor which was shortly to become the fashion.

Since Cowper was apprenticed from about 1452 to 1459, he was probably born in 1438, and was therefore 45 when he is last heard of; perhaps he died soon after 1484. On the other hand, it is just possible, though unlikely, that he migrated to Scotland and became one of the chief masons of King James IV; the great donjon or forework of *Rothesay Castle* in Bute was being built in 1512, when two entries occur in the accounts of the Lord High Treasurer of Scotland: on 17 March 'to Johne Cowper to big in Rose (Rothesay) after the Kingis devise, in drinksilvir, iij Franch crounis, xlijs' and on 6 May 'to Huchone (Hugh) Cowpar, maissone in Bute, in drinksilvir, xiiijs'.[9] Hugh Cowper, receiving a smaller sum for his reward, was probably subordinate to John, and very likely his son. If it were the English John Cowper, he would have been 73 or 74 years old, with a grown son capable of supervising the works. It should be noted that the value of the Scots shilling in 1512 would be only about 1*d.* to 1½*d.* English money of the same period, so that John Cowper's reward would have been equivalent to about 5*s.* given to an English mason, and Hugh's perhaps 1*s.* 6*d.*; amounts which would indicate that both masons were of high status.

[1] *WCM*, compotus 1456–7, 1457–8; [2] *WCM*, compotus 1465–6, 1466–7; [3] KJE; [4] SHB, 538–40; (*MCO*, Deeds, Bramber 16, 12); [5] HMC, *De L'Isle & Dudley*, I, 198; [6] A. Hamilton Thompson in LAS, XI, 193 ff.; [7] CLW; [8] RCHM, *Hunts.*; [9] SNR

COWPER, Nicholas (*fl.* 1431–1443) Mason

Built a new tower at the south-east angle of *Liverpool Castle* in 1431–1443. The work was done by contract at £4 for a rod of 21 feet.

HKW, II, 706

Cowper, Robert—see COUPER

COWPER, William (*fl.* 1488–1508) Carpenter

Probably son of ANDREW COUPER; took up the freedom of Norwich in 1488/9.[1] On 8 May 1508 he adjudicated as junior master of the carpenters' craft of the city.[2]

[1] EFN; [2] HTN, II, 29–30

Coyny—see also CONY

COYNY, Robert (*fl.* 1541–1542) Carpenter

Carpenter of London; on 8 March 1541/2 contracted with Thomas Richardes, merchant tailor of London, to frame and set up roofs on a brick house and a dovehouse at *Hacton*, near Hornchurch in Essex. The work was to be according to a signed 'plott', and was to be like the roof in the west part of Lincoln's Inn; it was to be finished by the end of August 1542, but was not completed, owing to Richardes's failure to supply all the timber.

PRO, Early Chan. Proc. 961, 49 (*L.F.S.*)

CRACALL, Richard of (*fl.* 1412–1415) Mason

Possibly son of Robert de Crakall, mason, who took up the freedom of York in 1367–8, and who died in 1395. Was apparently identical with RICHARD OF NEWTON who was living at Patrick Brompton, Yorks., on 28 January 1409/10, when he contracted to rebuild the south aisle of *Hornby Church*.[1] Richard of Cracall (now Crakehall, less than two miles from Newton in Patrick Brompton parish) contracted with Katherine, widow of John Burgh of Burgh, and her son William, to build the chancel, nave, and aisles of the church of *Catterick*, Yorks. The contract is dated 18 April 1412 and stipulates that the work should be finished in three years, the agreed price being 160 marks (£106 13*s.* 4*d.*) with an extra 10 marks (£6 13*s.* 4*d.*) and a gown if the work were completed punctually.

The tower, vestry, western bays of the nave, and the porch were not built until later, the porch being completed in 1491.[2]

(WPS)

[1] SS, XLV, 47n.; SHB, 482–3; MRC, 62; [2] SHB, 487–90; RCC; MRC, 37–40

CRAKALL, John [Crakel, Grakal] (*fl.* 1473–1474) ? Mason

Apparently the mason employed to carry out routine repairs at *Chichester Cathedral* in 1473–74 when he was paid at the rate of 5*d.* a day.

M. E. C. Walcott in GM, 1863, pt. ii, 487–90; SXR, LII (1952), 116–17

Crancewyk, John—see CRANSWICK

CRANEBY, John [Kraneby] (*fl.* 1345–1368) Carpenter

Became a freeman of York in 1345;[1] in 1366–68 he was in charge of the building of houses in *Pavement, York,* for the Guild of the Assumption and also houses in the parish of St. Denis.[2] He also received payments for work and repairs on the Great Hall of the Guild (the *Merchant Adventurers' Hall*) but this may have been designed earlier by ROBERT DE BAGBY.

[1] YCF; [2] SS, CXXIX, 20–25

CRANSWICK, John de [Crancewyk] (*fl.* 1311–   ) Carpenter (*Cranswick, Yorks. E.R.*)

Was sworn carpenter of *Beverley* in 1311, when he undertook repairs to the mansion of St. Andrew's prebend for the Minster authorities.

MBM

CRAVEN, Nicholas (*fl.* 1533–   ) Mason

Contracted, with THOMAS SELLERS, in 1533 to rebuild the aisles of *Burnley Church, Lancs.,* for £60.

(APD); WHW

CRESSING, John [Kersyng] (*fl.* 1315–1326) Carpenter (*Cressing, Essex*)

Master of the king's carpenters under Edward II. In 1315 he worked at *Thundersley,* Essex; in 1322–3 was granted a robe as a valet of the Chamber. In 1325 he was in charge of works on the houses in *Hadleigh Castle* and also built a timber-framed chapel at *Henley Manor* in Surrey. In 1325–6 he was being paid 6*d.* a day at *Dover Castle.*

HKW, I, 174n., 180; II, 638, 662, 960

CRIKYLWODE, Thomas (*fl.* 1461) Mason

Of Southampton; on 29 September 1461 took a lease from Winchester College of a toft with a garden in the suburb without Bargate, Southampton. He was to rebuild the tenement, 30 feet by 13 feet in size, within two years, the College providing 6 loads of timber from Eling or Allington and stones from the shore at Barton, Isle of Wight, Crikylwode providing carriage.

WCM 28860 C, D

CROFTON, William (*fl.* 1440–1444) Carpenter

Appointed chief carpenter of the King's new works at *Calais* on 1 July 1440; on 17 December 1441 JOHN TYRELL was associated with Crofton in the office, and on 12 November 1444 Crofton was succeeded by Tyrell.

DKR, XLVIII, 338, 349, 364

CROKE, Richard [Croc, Croch, Crok] (*fl.* 1309–1334) Mason

Was a leading mason at *Exeter Cathedral* in 1309, when he started the year at the winter rate of 1*s.* 9¾*d.* and later took the summer rate of 2*s.* a week. He worked more or less continuously at the Cathedral until 1334,[1] but on 11 March 1314 had been granted the freedom of the City of Exeter at the instance of Ralph de Monte Ermeli (? Ralph de Monthermer, Earl of Gloucester).[2]

[1] AEC, i, 186–212; ii, 293–303; [2] RJE, 13

Crompe, Thomas—see CRUMP

Crondal—see CRUNDALE

CROSBY, Robert [Crosbe] (*fl.* 1475–1500) Carpenter

Warden of the London Carpenters' Company in 1475/6, 1476/7, 1479/80, 1482/3, and 1485/6; and Master in 1488/9, 1492/3, and 1493/4.[1] In 1484 the Company's accounts record the payment of 8*s.* to 'Stevyn Scalis and Robert Crosbye for to mete the Kyng',[2] and in 1493 Crosby and THOMAS MAUNCY took part in 'settyng the kyng from Eltham'.[3] Crosby presented apprentices on several occasions, and is mentioned up to 1500.[4]

[1] MCR, II, 50, 51, 58, 63, 70, 78, 98, 102; [2] *Ibid.,* 66; [3] *Ibid.,* 99; [4] *Ibid.,* 82, 121, 129, 134

CROSSE, Benedict [Benet le freemason, Crose] (*fl.* 1473–1480) Mason

Mason of Bristol; in December 1473 was living in a house at 'le Pyll yende' belonging to John Shipward the elder, merchant.[1] About 1478–80 William Worcestre, while compiling topographical notes on Bristol noted as a freemason of the city 'Benet Crosse', and on the other side of the same sheet took down the names of the mouldings employed on the south door of *St Stephen's Church*, giving a sketch plan of the door jamb. This he describes as '*de opere manuali Benet le Fremason*', without making it clear whether Cross's 'handiwork' was the drawing or the doorway itself.[2]

[1] WBW, 160; [2] *Corpus Christi College, Cambridge*, MS. 210, p. 129, 130; HWI, 315, 367;

CROSSE, John (*fl.* 1446–1454) Carpenter
Of Cleve in Yatton, Somerset; between 1446 and 1454 Crosse took down the old roodloft and erected another in *Yatton Church*, for the price of £31, with sundry other payments.

SRS, IV (1890), 95–8; VCS, 64

Crouch, Crowche, John—see THIRSK

CROWE, William (*fl.* –1355) Carpenter
Warden (*apparilator*) of the carpenters at *Westminster Palace* from 24 March to 25 August 1355, taking 3*s.* 6*d.* per week.

PRO, E.101–471–11

Crowland, William de—see CROYLAND

CROXTON, John [Crokston, Croxtone] (*fl.* 1411–1447) Mason
Became mason of the *Guildhall, London*, in 1411, when work on the present building was begun, and in 1416 and again in 1419 was sworn as a master of the masons' mistery. By the will of WALTER WALTON, made 16 August 1418, he was bequeathed Walton's 'best compass'. On 7 October 1440 he was granted a shed by the Guildhall, and he continued to work there at least until 1446. On 17 June of that year Croxton presented a petition to the city for £8 2*s.* 0*d.* which he was out of pocket and an additional £2 a year, on the ground that he had worked on all the works of the city and especially the Guildhall 'by XXX yere and more and therin spended hys yonge age', had been 'in attendaunce daily upon your werkes by vj yere and more aboute the fundementez and reisyng of yoᵉ chapell at Guyldhalle and purveyng for the ordenaunce and counseille of the mooldes thereof and upone youre werkes at Padyngtone, Tybourne, Trippeswelle, Charyngcrosse, Crosse in Chepe, and other places'; for this he had only a 'litell house', with £1 a year and clothing. His modest prayer was granted. In 1441 he had been a sworn master of the Carpenters and Freemasons,[1] and from 1444 to 1447 appears regularly as one of the four viewers of the City of London, being named

first on each occasion.[2] Stone was bought from 'Croxton Masoun' in 1446 for works at the college of St. Martin-le-Grand, London.[3]

Croxton was no doubt the designer of the fabric of the Guildhall, which still remains, though greatly obscured by restorations; the crypts and porch are fine specimens of the 'London School' of Perpendicular. The original roof of the Guildhall, destroyed in the Great Fire of 1666, was perhaps designed by RICHARD BIRD, carpenter. The new chapel, now destroyed, was begun in 1429 and roofed in 1446.[4]

In the grant of 1440, mention is made of Croxton's wife 'Anneys', but otherwise nothing is known of his private life.

WML; BGL
[1] CLB, 'I', 172, 207; 'K', 257, 314; [2] CPM 1437–57, 57–8, 68–9, 75, 86, 97; [3] WAM, 13312; [4] PGL, 120

CROYLAND, William de (*fl.* 1392–1427) Mason
Master mason at *Croyland Abbey*, Lincs., from 1392 to 1427 or later, and designed the Perpendicular work there, including the existing north aisle and tower. His other work comprised the west side of the cloisters, the choir aisles and Lady Chapel, and the refectory, all of which have now gone; and probably also the abbot's hall, north and south transepts, and the surviving nave screen. He cannot have been identical with WILLIAM DE WERMINGTON.

(APD; BAA); VCH, *Lincs*, II, 114; SMC, 108

CRUMP, Thomas [Crompe] (*fl.* 1372–1396) Mason
Worked with Ralph Crump who may have been his brother, at *Queenborough Castle* in 1372, at 5*d.* a day, and in 1381 was building the great gateway of *Cowling Castle*, Kent, and supplying worked stone for the castle; he was then described as 'mason of Maidstone'; the designer was HENRY YEVELEY who measured the work for payment.[1] In May 1386 Crump was ordered to impress masons for work at *Leeds Castle*,[2] in 1387 was described as of Otham, near Maidstone,[3] and on 25 June 1389 undertook work on a wharf at the *Tower of London*, with JOHN WESTCOTE, mason of London, and William Jancook, mason of Maidstone; this work also was to be done under Yeveley.[4] In 1395–96 Crump was selling Maidstone ashlar for the use of the works at Westminster Hall.

Ralph CROMPE also appears as a supplier

of stone for the works of Rochester Castle, from 1368 to 1374.[5]

Roger CROMPE of Maidstone was a quarryman concerned with supplies of stone, between 1372 and 1397.[6]

William CROMPE of Otham, 'the younger', mason, acquired rights in a quarry at Boughton Monchelsea in 1486, and another of the same name was involved in a dispute as to quarry rights there in 1536.[7] The will of William Crompe, the elder, of Otham, was proved in 1514, and the will of William Crompe, mason of Otham, in 1537.[8]

KJI

[1] SHB, 461; [2] CPR, 1385–9, 180; [3] CCR 1385–9, 430–1; [4] SHB, 469–70; [5] AC, II, 111 ff; *PRO,* E.101–483–28, 29; [6] *PRO,* E.101–483–27, 28, 495–23; CCR 1385–9, 430–1; *LBH,* L.R.71; accounts, 17 m.2. III (xvi); [7] AC, XXVII, 172, 175; [8] *Canterbury Wills,* A.12, 306; A.21,62

CRUNDALE, Richard [Crondale] (*fl.* 1281–†1293) Mason (*Crundale, Kent*)

Was already a master mason of the City of London when he served on a jury there in 1281,[1] and during the next three years was the principal mason working under ROBERT OF BEVERLEY at the *Tower of London.*[2] In 1284–85 he was working at *Westminster Abbey,* and seems to have succeeded Robert of Beverley as the King's Chief Mason, at least for London works.

He guaranteed account rolls for work at *Westminster Palace* in 1288 and 1290 and was paid £7 in 1288 for working the marble stone of a laver in the Small Hall 'where gilt heads and images are set' (*ubi capita deaurata et ymagines apponuntur*).[3] After Queen Eleanor's death in 1290 he was in charge of the building of *Charing Cross* and of the making of her tomb in the Abbey. He died about 8 September 1293, when he was succeeded by his brother ROGER CRUNDALE at the works of Charing Cross.[4]

(APD); LKC

[1] WKM; [2] *PRO,* E.101–467–9; [3] *PRO,* E.101–467–17 (*L.F.S.*); [4] A, XXIX; BMH, 130

CRUNDALE, Roger [de Crondel] (*fl.* 1290–1298) Mason

Worked at *Westminster Palace* in 1290, and in 1294 completed *Charing Cross,* which had been designed by his brother RICHARD CRUNDALE. He was also paid £1 16s. 8d. for marble for the tomb of Queen Eleanor in Lincoln Cathedral between 1291 and 1294. He also assisted NICHOLAS DYMINGE de Reyns on the

Eleanor Cross at *Waltham.* In 1298 he disposed of a tenement in the parish of St. Mary Magdalen, Old Fish Street.[1]

Other members of this family were:

Thomas CRUNDALE who worked at *Westminster Palace* and St. Stephen's Chapel in 1290 and 1292, and

Walter CRUNDALE who worked at *Westminster Palace* in 1325.

LKC; BMH

[1] *LHR,* 27 (114)

Curant, Henry—see CORANT

Curraunt—see also CORANT

CURRAUNT, Robert (*fl.* 1482–1487)? Mason

Probably a mason-contractor; in 1483–85 built the lower part of the *Red Mount Chapel,* (King's) Lynn.

BRM; HKL, 208–9; *LCR,* KL/C7/4 (*M.B.*); NCM, Lynn Priory Rolls.

Curteys—see RAMSEY, John, senior I

CURTEYS, John (*fl.* 1476–†1490) Carpenter

On 3 November 1476 a case was put to arbitration between John Curteys, carpenter of Canterbury, and Thomas Julle, in regard to Curteys' claim to 40s. due to him for repairs on the belfry of the parish church of *Adisham* ('Addesham'), Kent.[1] In 1485 he made a chest for vestments at *St. Andrew's, Canterbury.*[2] The will of John Curteys, carpenter of Canterbury, was proved in 1490.[3]

[1] CCY — Pleas; [2] AC, XXXII, 213; [3] Archdeacon's Court, Wills 5.245

CURTEYS, Richard [Curtheis] (*fl. c.* 1300–   ) ? Mason

Mentioned in deeds of 1323 as father of JOHN RAMSEY, senior I, mason of Norwich. Probably identical with RICHARD LE MACHUN, mason of Norwich Cathedral 1285–90. The researches of Mr. A. B. Whittingham have shown that the Curteys family had held property under the Abbot of Ramsey at Wyke Fen in Well since the twelfth century.

RND 1307–41, 118, 120; cf. HPS, 47

CUTTING, John [Cuttyng] (*fl.* 1482–1483) Mason

In 1482–83 was employed by John, Lord Howard (soon afterwards created Duke of Norfolk) at *Tendring Hall,* near Stoke-by-Nayland, Suffolk, which seems to have been largely rebuilt at the time. Some of the payments were made to Cutting 'and his fellowship'. A *William CUTTING*, mason, described as his 'cosyn', was employed at the same time.

A.O. PNA (from *SA*)

CUTTING, Richard [Cuttyng] (*fl.* 1485–86) Mason

Circa 1485–86 was partner with JOHN TILLEY in a contract for building the tower of *Little Thornham Church*, Suffolk.

A.O. PRO, ECP, 76–20.

CUTTING, Thomas [Cuttyng] (*fl.* 1499–†1532) Mason

In 1499 was paid 28s. 10d. for making the stair to the roodloft at *Walberswick Church*, Suffolk.[1] In 1523–24 Thomas Cutting of Ipswich, assessed under West Ward, paid £2 10s. for the subsidy of that year; he was one of the wealthier men worth £40 or more who paid the 'Anticipation'.[2] The will of Thomas Cutting, freemason, of the parish of St. Matthew, Ipswich, is dated 28 February 1531/2, proved 27 September 1532.[3] He desired to be buried in his parish church by his wife Emme. A second wife Alice and two sons Gregory and Thomas survived him.

A.O.
[1] LCW, 81; TGD, 156–7; [2] SGB, X, 210, 217, 415–16; [3] IW, XI, 53; CCN 6, 7 Puntyng. Abstract in SIA *Proceedings* VII, 201

CUTTING, William (*fl.* 1482–1483) Mason
Cousin of JOHN CUTTING

DAM, David (*fl.* 1470–1485) Carver

Carver employed at *York Minster* in 1470–71, when 'David carver' was paid 17s. 4d. for carving knots (probably bosses for the roof of the central tower), with 10s. as a reward, and also worked for 18 weeks at the rate of 3s. a week.[1] In 1485 David Dam, carver, was paid at the same rate for 2 weeks' work.[2]

[1] RFY, 74; BFY, 17–18; [2] BFY, 20; BHY, I, 261

DAM, James (*fl.* 1457–1479) Carver (? *Damme, Belgium*)

Took up the freedom of York as a carver in 1457,[1] and was working at *York Minster* on woodwork in 1470. This work seems to have been connected with the roofing of the central tower of the Minster. In 1479 Dam was engaged on stone carving, for he appears in the fabric rolls as a mason, being paid 39s. for 13 weeks' work, and also 14s. 7d. for 'intailyng 175 crokettes'.[2] Dam may well have been a Fleming from Damme, near Bruges.[3] His son John, a goldsmith, was admitted a freeman of York in 1483.

[1] YCF; [2] RFY, 72, 83; BFY, 19; [3] HGE, 119

DAM, Richard [at Dam] (*fl.* 1460–   ) Carver

Of Norwich; in 1460 made a tabernacle for a statue of the Blessed Virgin in *Saffron Walden Church, Essex*.

A.O. CWW, ff. 58–9; BAE

DANYELL, Thomas (*fl.* 1461–1487) Mason

In January 1461 Thomas Danyell was apprentice to THOMAS JURDAN, chief mason of *London Bridge*; the remuneration paid in respect of Danyell's services was 2s. 6d. a week, and that rate was paid until February 1465, after which 3s. a week was paid until he left the Bridge early in July. Danyell was employed elsewhere for three years, but in 1468–69 he was again at work on the Bridge. On 26 July 1465 and again on 20 January 1480, he was a witness to deeds executed in connection with London Bridge, at Greenwich and Deptford.[1] He seems also to have gone into business as a stone merchant, for in 1479 a total of 109 casks of 'Canestone' were bought for the works of *Windsor Castle* from John Shippe and Thomas Danyell for £33 12s. 6d.[2] In 1482 Danyell made a 'parayll for a chymney' for *Tendring Hall*, Stoke-by-Nayland, for which he was paid 20s.[3]

On 27 April 1482 he was appointed King's Master Mason, and in the next month chief mason of London Bridge, with fees of 3s. 4d. a week, in addition to his royal retainer of 1s. a day; both posts were vacant through the death of his old master Thomas Jurdan. Danyell was able to undertake private work, at least for the king's brother-in-law, Anthony, Lord Rivers. A letter from Rivers to 'Daniell, maister mason with the kyng', written on 28 May 1482, concerns mason's work at a large house and concludes: 'I pray you goo to the Mote the soner by cause of this wrightyng', referring to *The Mote* in Maidstone, Kent.[4] Danyell seems to have been temporarily replaced as King's Mason by ROBERT STOWELL but his grant was confirmed by Richard III on 10 October 1484. Danyell may have died in 1487, as he was succeeded in that year at London Bridge by THOMAS WADE, though he is mentioned in 1510 as having 'lately held' the office of King's Master Mason, when it was granted to WILLIAM VERTUE. Danyell's mark ✶ is on record.[5]

KJI; KJL
[1] LBH, Deeds; [2] HWC, II, 379, 400; [3] PNA, 285; [4] GLR, 395; [5] LPH, VIII, pt. i, 546(72); PRO, E.315–468 (H.M.C.)

DARTFORD, Ralph of (*fl. c.* 1220–1245) Mason (*Dartford, Kent*)

Master *cementarius*, living near the Almonry of *Westminster Abbey*; and possibly master mason of the Lady Chapel, begun in 1220 and finished about 1244.

LWR, 73; *WAM*, 17341–2, 17374, 17498

DAUVYLE, John [Dauvyld] (*fl.* 1362–1364) Carpenter

Was paid 6*d.* a day as warden of the carpenters working at *Hadleigh Castle* between 1362 and 1364.

HKW, II, 665

DAVID the Carpenter (*fl.* 1246–1256) Carpenter

One of Henry III's master carpenters; was on 24 December 1246 ordered to have 30 oaks for the work of a house beyond the king's larder at *Clarendon*. At the same period he received pardons for one mark (13*s.* 4*d.*) and for 40*s.* which he had been fined in the forest court of Wiltshire, apparently for illegal ploughing up of waste land.[1] In 1247 he was sent to *Ludgershall Castle*, Wilts., to make a new dais in the hall.[2] On 11 June 1249 the king ordered the sheriff of Wiltshire to pay David the wages he had received from the previous sheriff, and on 20 July 1250 directed that he should be paid £5 to build a house for the use of the king's workmen at *Clarendon*, and to contain their tools.[3]

These works were again mentioned in July 1252 as being under Master David,[4] and in the same year he built the stable in the *Castle of Old Sarum* for £12 5*s.* 8*d.* He was still in charge at Clarendon in 1256.[5]

HKW, II, 730, 827, 916n

[1] CCR 1242–47, 493, 494, 524; [2] CCR 1247–51, 9; [3] CLR 1245–51, 239, 296; [4] CLR 1251–60, 61; [5] CCR 1256–59, 16

Davy, Richard—see FARLEIGH

DAVYN, Peter (*fl.* 1395–1402) Carver

In 1395–96 carved three of the angels for the hammer beams of *Westminster Hall* roof at 15*s.* each. In 1402 he was paid 7*s.* 6*d.* each for 68 keys consisting of angels and arch-angels with scrolls for the ceiling of the King's chamber at *Eltham Palace*.

SHB, 216, 218; *BM*, Add. Ch. 27018

DAVYSON, Robert (*fl.* 1464–†*c.* 1484) Mason

Free of the City of York in 1464; on 3 February 1477/8 was appointed by the *York* city authorities to view and oversee the walls of the city and declare any faults therein to the mayor and chamberlain. He was to receive for himself and his servants working on the walls 'such wages as belongeth to a mason to take by day'; he was also to have a house in 'Walmegate' rent free and a gown yearly. The house had previously been that of ROBERT TONGE, mason, perhaps Davyson's predecessor in office. Davyson probably died in the winter of 1484/5, when he was succeeded by THOMAS BRIGGS.

(*G.P.J.*) YCR, I, 25

DAW, John (*fl.* 1481–1482) Mason

Was building the south aisle of *St. Andrew's Church, Plymouth*, in 1481–82.

HMC, IX, 262 (*L.F.S.*)

DAW, John [Dawe, Dow] (*fl.* 1531–1547) Carver

Of Lawhitton, Cornwall; named first when with JOHN PARES, carver, he contracted on 29 May 1531 to make a roodloft, roodscreen and parcloses for *Stratton Church*, Cornwall. When he entered into a bond on 14 July 1531 his name appears as John 'Dow'. The loft was to be like that of St. Kew, with a crucifix like that at Liskeard. The final payment for the whole of the work was made in 1539.[1]

In *Bere Regis Church*, Dorset, one of the bench-ends is inscribed: 'ION DAV WARDEN OF THYS CHARYS'. They were made in 1547, the date carved on another.[2]

[1] GMS, 18–19; [2] RCHM, *Dorset*, II pt. i, 17, 188

DAW, Richard [Dawe] (*fl.* 1534–1536) Carver

On 10 August 1534 a contract was made at Launceston with Richard 'Dawe', a 'kerver of Lansant' (Lezant) to make a new chancel roof for *Altarnun Church*, Cornwall, by Michaelmas 1536. There were also to be a new gable window of four lights, both roof and window to be 'after the patente' of those of the 'south Ambulatorie' of the church; a new window of two lights on the south side of the chancel; and a celure over the high altar. Daw was also 'to new pynne and rowe caste all the old walls of the seid Chauncell and to whitelyme the Inne walls and side walls of the seide chauncell'. Daw was to take down the old roof, set up the new when framed, and find materials and scaffolds; all for 20 marks (£13 6*s.* 8*d.*)

EDC, no. 606 (*W.A.K.; N.L.R.*)

DAW, Robert [Dave] (*fl. c.* 1540–   ) ? Carpenter

79

DAYFOTE, THOMAS

'Robart Dave maker of this worke' appears on one of a series of carved bench-ends in *Altarnun Church*, Cornwall, made *c.* 1540.

GMS, 18–19

DAYFOTE, Thomas (*fl.* 1451–) Carpenter

In 1451–52 was paid £2 for making a roodloft for the church of *Tintinhull*, Somerset, by agreement.

SRS, IV (1890), 185

Delpeston, Robert—see HELPESTON

DENMAN, John (*fl.* 1522) Mason

Apparently the freemason in charge of the building of a new chancel at *Bishop's Hull Church*, Somerset, in 1522, for the Prior of Taunton. Much confused and conflicting evidence was given in the course of a resulting lawsuit, as recorded in a certificate of 29 August 1522.[1] From this it appears that several different masons were competing for the contract, among them Richard Pytt and John Gyll, while JOHN BIRD obtained the contract at £10 for Denman and John Lawrence. Bird was declared to have no interest in the work himself.

That Denman was the designer of the chancel seems to be inferred from the depositions of Richard Brecher and John Hynde, rough masons, that they 'wrought upon the foundacion at the biddyng of John Denman fremason. And at no nother man ys Request.' The chancel was not consecrated until 1540.[2]

[1] SDN, VII, 264–6; [2] *Ibid.*, XVII, 119

DENYAR, Thomas [Thomas Mason] (*fl. c.* 1406–1416) Mason

Mason and citizen of Hereford; perhaps identical with Thomas Denyas who worked as a mason for 24 days in the winter of 1398–99 at *Portchester Castle*, Hants., at 6*d.* a day.[1] Mason at *Hereford Cathedral*, and about 1412 contracted to build the south walk of the cloister.[2] On 8 July 1414, as 'Thomas Mason' he and his fellows and servants were protected from impressment for the King's works before the completion of the work of the chapel of St. John the Baptist on the south side of Hereford Cathedral.[3]

Denyar was to complete the walling in 2 years and he was to have two robes a year, one each for himself and his partner, or £2 in silver, and 23½ marks (£15 13*s.* 4*d.*) for his labour. For the stone and its carriage he was to be paid 12*d.* per 'sothin' in addition. He was also to vault the cloister at the price of 4 marks (£2 13*s.* 4*d.*) for each bay, completing the whole work within 6 years from the start.

In 1416 'Thomas Mason of Hereford' received a bequest of 10 marks (£6 13*s.* 4*d.*) from John Prophet, Dean of York, in compensation for the loss he sustained in connection with the chapel of St. John the Baptist.[4] Prophet had been Dean of Hereford 1393–1407.

[1] *PRO*, E.101–479–24; [2] SHB, 486; CCH, 232; [3] CPR 1413–16, 226; [4] YTE, III, 53–5

DENYS, Henry (*fl. c.* 1430) Mason

Master of the masons (*Magister lathamorum*) who received a fee of £6 13*s.* 4*d.* in an account for works possibly connected with *Battle Abbey* early in the reign of Henry VI.

PRO, Exch. Misc. B. (*H.M.C.*)

DENYS, John (*fl.* 1407–*c.* 1423) Mason

Acquired the freedom of Canterbury by redemption in 1407.[1] He received esquire's livery as resident master mason of *Canterbury Cathedral* at Christmas 1416, along with STEPHEN LOTE, and may have held the office until the appointment of JOHN MORYS about 1423. Denys' name appears among the esquires in the list of those receiving livery from the Prior in 1416 and 1420, being specified as '*Magister latamorum*'.

[1] CFC; [2] *Bodl.*, Tanner MS. 165

DENYS, Roger [Dynyce] (*fl.* 1418–†1432) Mason

Contracted on 1 November 1418 to rebuild the chancel of *Surfleet Church*, Lincs., to roof it with lead, and to glaze with figures in English glass the five-light east window and three three-light windows on each side. On 11 November 1419 he took on another contract to rebuild the church and tower of *Wyberton*, Lincs., for 190 marks (£126 13*s.* 4*d.*) and in 1420 undertook further work at the latter church. He was later involved in legal proceedings in connection with both these jobs after he had moved from Lincolnshire to London.[1] When he made his will on 14 January 1431/2 he described himself as citizen and mason (*lathamus*) of London, dwelling in the parish of St. Sepulchre outside Newgate. He wished to be buried in the cemetery of St. Paul's called 'Pardowncyrchhawe', and left to his wife Dionysia £20 and a considerable quantity of household goods. The will was proved on 19 January 1431/2.[2]

[1] LNQ, XIV, 231 from *ECP* 7.104; SHB, 495–7; [2] *CCL*, 298 More

80

Depenhale, Robert de—see DIPPENHALL

DEREHAM, Elias of ['Berham', Derham] (*fl.* 1188–†1245) Cleric (*West Dereham, Norf.*)

Secular clerk, and later Canon of Salisbury and Wells. Much is known of his long career as an ecclesiastic and official of the Crown, and only a summary is given below. In 1188 he was a witness to the foundation charter of West Dereham Abbey, Norfolk, founded by Hubert Walter, the Dean of York but in the following year Bishop of Salisbury, and from 1193 Archbishop of Canterbury. Dereham was one of Walter's executors when the archbishop died in 1205, and was concerned with payments to Peter des Roches, Bishop of Winchester. In 1208 he witnessed a charter at Witham Charterhouse, Somerset; during the latter part of the Interdict he was in France with Bishop Jocelyn of Wells and Jocelyn's brother Hugh, Bishop of Lincoln, visiting England in 1212. In 1215 he was present at the sealing of Magna Carta at Runnymede, and was one of the commissioners employed to distribute copies of the charter.

At Canterbury on 7 July 1220 took place the translation of the body of Thomas Becket to the new shrine. Present at the ceremony were the 'incomparable masters WALTER OF COLCHESTER, Sacrist of St. Albans, and Elyas of Derham canon of Salisbury, by whose counsel and invention everything necessary to the making of the shrine, to its setting up and removal were done without cause for blame'. (*Incomparabilibus artificibus magistris Waltero de Colecestria, sacrista de Sancto Albano, et Elya de Derham, canonico Salisburiensi, quorum consiliis et ingeniis omnia quae ad artificium thecae et ipsius elevationis, et translationis necessaria fuerant irreprehensibiliter parabantur.*)[1]

About this time Dereham became a canon of *Salisbury*, where the first stone of the new cathedral was laid on 28 April 1220. The Lady Chapel was completed by 1225 and the eastern arm of the church by 1237. Dereham was in charge of the building works, being described as director of the new fabric (*a prima fundatione rector fuit novae fabricae*) from its foundation for the next 25 years, i.e. until his death in 1245.[2] In Salisbury Close he built for himself the prebendal house known as Leadenhall.

In 1228 he was one of the executors of Stephen Langton, Archbishop of Canterbury, and in 1229 was at Wells as steward to Bishop Jocelyn and witness to a deed disposing of the property of Master ADAM LOCK, the deceased chief mason of *Wells Cathedral*. In 1229 Dereham also went to Durham with Bishop Jocelyn, where both were witnesses to a deed between Bishop Poore, who had been translated from Salisbury in 1228, and the prior and convent of Durham. Within the next year or so he was a witness at Salisbury to a grant by Bishop Bingham to the dean and chapter of a house which was to be occupied by Master NICHOLAS OF ELY the mason, and his heirs.

In 1233, Dereham was in charge of the King's works in *Winchester Castle*, and in the next year at *Clarendon Palace*; in 1236 he was again directing works at Winchester Castle, where the great gatehouse was in progress, and the following year was still in charge at Salisbury Cathedral, acted as executor of Bishop Poore, and was present at Canterbury when Archbishop Edmund Rich chose a site for the building of a college of secular canons. He was also to give his counsel as to the enclosing with a stone wall of the anchoress of *Britford*, Wiltshire.[3] In 1238 he was executor of Bishop Peter des Roches of Winchester, and was at Salisbury making a marble tomb which on 6 March the Sheriff of Wiltshire was ordered to pay for, and to have carried to *Tarrant Keynston* in Dorset for the burial of the King's sister Joan, Queen of Scotland.[4] In 1242 he was given 6 logs for the works of the church of *Harrow*, Middx., of which he was rector.

On 8 March 1244 the King allowed 30 marks (£20) to Master Elias of Dereham to make a cup for the reservation of the Eucharist over the high altar of Salisbury Cathedral.[5] On 10 April 1245 Dereham resigned his prebend of Litton in Wells Cathedral, and died shortly afterwards.

Dereham's precise relationship to the buildings with which he was concerned is nowhere described, and to call him the architect of Salisbury Cathedral and the hall of Winchester Castle is to go far beyond the recorded facts. In the latter case, he only appeared on the scene some years after the start of the works under Master Stephen the Mason. There is even less justification for attributing to him the design of the west front of Wells Cathedral and the chapel of Nine Altars at Durham. Analysis of these works shows differences of treatment and conception quite as striking as the resemblances, and there is no reason for crediting him with the architectural details, which would normally be produced by the chief masons, NICHOLAS OF ELY, STEPHEN, THOMAS NORREYS, and RICHARD OF FARNHAM, respectively.

The evidence for Dereham as an artist, whether as designer or craftsman, or both together, is distinctly stronger, though allowance has to be made for the extremely ambiguous use of the crucial words *artifex*, *facere*, which by no means prove that Dereham worked with his own hands on the shrine of Thomas Becket, the tomb of Queen Joan, or the hanging Pyx for Salisbury. Consideration of probabilities does, however, suggest that in these cases he was more intimately concerned with the production of objects of art than were most administrative chiefs of the Middle Ages or since and that he was at least a distinguished amateur.

Accepting this as a working hypothesis, certain features of the architectural works with which he was associated can be more easily understood. The symmetrical plan of Salisbury Cathedral was made possible by the unencumbered site, but the dimensions of the building as a whole show a more than ordinary preoccupation with systems of proportion, normal as these were in the production of mediaeval buildings. But the application of the proportional rules is carried out with a rigidity extremely rare, and with a resulting discordance of parts. The individual piers, arches, windows, are of exceptional purity of form, yet they are fitted together within an artificial strait-jacket and by means of awkward and freakish expedients. Similar characteristics are to be found, though to a less degree, in the west front of Wells.

In confirmation of this view of Dereham's theoretical position in regard to architecture, it is worth mentioning that he is known to have been interested in theories of cosmography, for one diagram of the world in a series preserved in a St. Albans manuscript is said to be 'according to Master Elyas of Dereham' (*secundum magistrum Elyam de Derham*).[6]

It is reasonable to conclude that Master Elias of Dereham was an amateur artist of some distinction in work of a decorative character, and that acquaintanceship with problems of design so acquired encouraged him to dabble in architecture. He was then a precursor of the dilettante architect of the type of Burlington though it is to be presumed that Dereham's heavy duties as a civil servant and churchman left him comparatively ill-provided with leisure time. It should be noted that Dereham cannot have been identical with ELIAS THE ENGINEER as Horace Walpole suggested on the strength of a misread date: a mistake which, it may be suspected, has contributed greatly to Dereham's supposititious fame as an architect.

TED (BAA; APD; BED; HED)
[1] PHA, II, 242; [2] LI, I, 266; [3] CLR 1226–40, 273; [4] *Ibid.*, 316; [5] *Ibid.* 1240–5, 22; [6] *BM*, Cotton MS. Nero D.I., *ff.* 184–5

DERMAN, John [Dorman] (*fl.* 1450–†1497)
Carpenter

Was probably master carpenter at the *Abbey of St. Edmund*. He was living in Bury St. Edmunds *c.* 1450 and can be traced in Bury wills and other documents up to his death in 1497. William Worcestre, in his first account of the abbey church, has a note recording that 'Dorman de Bury carpenter took from the wood at Cotton Hempnalys 1,200 oak trees for . . .' but the sentence is left tantalizingly unfinished.[1] These oaks may have been required for the new roofs of the church after the fire of 1466. The will of John Derman, dated 9 February, proved 3 March 1496/7, is that of a well-to-do man.[2] In Bury he had houses in Westgate Street and Whiting Street and he also had property in Eriswell. He desired that 'all the boord and tymber beyng in my house that I dwelle in' should be sold after his death and disposed to the Friars of Babwell or to poor folk. One of his executors was John Gy, 'steynor', from whom he had recently bought two tenements in Westgate Street. These he left to his grandson Thomas Prynchet, the younger. The five named witnesses were all craftsmen of Bury.

A.O.
[1] HW1, 160–1; [2] BW, vi, 50

DERNEFORD, Nicholas de (*fl.* 1309–1331)
Mason (? *Darnford, Staffs.*)

Probably entered the royal service to work on the king's castles in Wales about 1309, when JAMES OF ST. GEORGE died. He very likely succeeded St. George as master at *Beaumaris Castle*, although his formal appointment there was not until 12 May 1316.[1] He was then to be paid 7s. a week, but at the time he submitted a petition showing that he had been promised 12d. a day eight years before, but had only been paid at the rate of 8½d.[2]

This clearly implies that he was already a man of distinction by 1309, and his petition refers to the fact that he had even earlier worked at *St. Augustine, Bristol* (now the Cathedral); at *Burton-on-Trent* (presumably the great Benedictine Abbey), and at *Repton* ('Repyndone') *Priory*, which was like Bristol an Augustinian house.

After four years as master at Beaumaris, Derneford was removed from office in 1320 but reinstated the next year.[3] On 10 November 1323 he was appointed master of the works for the North Wales castles of *Beaumaris, Carnarvon, Conway, Criccieth,* and *Harlech,* at 12*d.* a day.[4] This was confirmed in May 1327, and in November the South Wales castles *Aberystwyth, Cardigan,* and *Carmarthen,* were put under his charge, his fee being raised to 2*s.* a day.[5] On 8 May 1331 his appointment was altered to refer to South Wales only, and the fee reduced to 12*d.*[6]

In the context of Derneford's complaint in 1316, it has to be supposed that his earlier work before joining the royal service had been as a chief master of architectural standing, and this in turn suggests that he may have been the designer of the remarkable new choir at Bristol, begun in or soon after 1298, though mostly built between 1311 and 1340. If so, Derneford would rank as an architect of originality and extraordinary genius.

KJM; A. J. Taylor in BGT, XCVIII (1981), 171–3
[1] CPR 1313–17, 457; [2] PRO, E.101–485–24; SC.8–106–5278; [3] CFR 1319–27, 44; CCR 1318–23, 301; [4] CPR 1321–4, 353; HKW, II, 1057; [5] CPR 1327–30, 103, 184; [6] *Ibid.* 1330–4, 50, 115, 343; HKW, I, 470n.[4]

Dervall—see DERWALL

DERWALL, George (*fl.* 1525–1537) Mason
Son of SETH DERWALL with whom he was granted the office of master mason of the counties of Chester and Flint in survivorship, on 1 August 1525.[1] He probably died or retired in 1537, when the office was granted to JOHN BRERETON.

Thomas DARVEWALL, who worked as a rough-layer at *Westminster Palace* in 1531–32,[2] and *Thomas DARRWALL*, a quarryman at Chester Castle about 1580,[3] presumably belonged to the same family.

[1] DKR, XXXI; [2] PRO, E.36–251 (*G.P.J.*); [3] PRO, E.101–489–25 (*G.P.J.*)

DERWALL, Seth [Dervall] (*fl.* 1495–†*c.* 1537) Mason
Was granted the office of master mason in the counties of Chester and Flint, during pleasure, on 24 September 1495, and again on 11 April 1503. At the accession of Henry VIII, Derwall petitioned for continuance in office on 25 May 1509, his petition being endorsed by the King.[1] In 1525 the grant was altered to one for life, jointly in survivorship with GEORGE DERWALL his son; from this it appears that Seth had had a third grant of the office, perhaps to insert a clause of duration for life, on 10 September 1516. He was dead when JOHN BRERETON was appointed on 14 May 1537.[2]

DKR, XXXI
[1] Bradfer-Lawrence MS. 56 (*N.L.R.*); [2] HKW, III, 418

DEWILDE, William (*fl.* 1510–) Carpenter
Of London; on 8 July 1510 contracted to build a house, which was to be framed at Kingston upon Thames for the Prior of *Charterhouse* in *London*, who was to pay Dewilde £10.

SHB, 560; (PRO, Anc. Deeds E.359)

DEYSTER, William (*fl.* 1385) Mason
Of Northampton; in 1385 gave a bond for 19 marks (£12 13*s.* 4*d.*) to *St. Andrew's Priory, Northampton,* presumably for the completion of works there.

BL, Add. Ch. 6045 (*N.L.R.*)

DICKINSON, Christopher [Dyconson] (*fl.* 1528–†1540) Mason
Freemason; was appointed on 27 August 1528 master mason of the buildings in *Windsor Castle,* with fees of 6*d.* a day at the death of HENRY REDMAN.[1] He was still in office in 1538, when he was granted £25 a year for life.[2] In 1531 he was also master bricklayer at *Westminster Palace* (the new palace of Whitehall) taking 12*d.* a day.[3] In 1536 he was apparently in charge of work at *Hampton Court,* for he entered into an agreement with two Kentish masons to supply paving stone for use there.[4] From 1537 he was also in charge at *Oatlands.*[5] In 1539 'Christopher' was appointed master bricklayer, with others, for the construction of the three castles in the Downs (*Deal, Walmer,* and *Sandown*).[6] He witnessed the will of WILLIAM CLEMENT in 1540, but was dead by 23 December, when WILLIAM REYNOLD II was appointed master mason of Windsor Castle in his place.[7]

[1] LPH, IV, pt. ii, 4687, p. 2035; [2] WKM; LPH, XII, pt. i, 1241; XIV, pt. i, p. 594; [3] LPH, V, 952; PRO, E.36–251; [4] SHB, 121–2; [5] HKW, IV, 206; [6] LPH, XIV, pt. i, 398, p.151; LHC, 89; [7] LPH, XVI, 379(48); HKW, III, 31, 304

Henry DYCKENSON, who came from London to advise on the stonework of the chapel of *Trinity College, Cambridge*, in 1559, may well have been a son of Christopher.

WCC, II, 566

DILKYN, William *(fl. 1284–1285)* Mason

Master mason in charge of works at *Rockingham Castle*, Northants., in 1284–85, when new windows were inserted in the chapel.

PRO, E.101-480-28 (*L.F.S.*): cf. HKW, II, 817

DINSDALE, John *(fl. 1398–1404)* Mason

In charge of building the new dormitory in *Durham Cathedral Priory* between 1398 and 1404, in association successively with JOHN MIDDLETON and PETER DRYNG. He too worked by contract, but the document is lost.

SDC, 29

DIPPENHALL, Robert de *(fl . 1335–1344)* Mason (*Dippenhall* in *Farnham, Surrey*)

Possibly son of Walter de Depenhale, a London mason in 1316.[1] Robert was one of four masons who, under WILLIAM RAMSEY III, surveyed the *Tower of London* in 1335. On 13 March 1342 he undertook by contract for £92 to build the stonework of a new chapel and chamber in the Privy Palace at *Westminster*, to be roofed by WILLIAM HURLEY.[2]

On 25 July 1344 an estimate of dilapidations was made concerning the possessions of the Bishop of Hereford in London, after the death of Thomas Charlton. The estimate, totalling £95 7s. 0d., was made by a jury of craftsmen headed by Robert 'de Depenhale', mason, with Richard de Radewelle, mason, the carpenters William de Poterne and William de Ledecombe, a plumber, and a tiler from Winchester.[3]

[1] CLB 'E', 56; [2] HKW, I, 208n., 534; CBC in AH, II, 1959, 20–1; [3] *Bodl.*, MS. Jones 21, *f.* 7

DIXI, Walter *(fl. ? 1277–   )* Mason

'Walter Dixi cementarius de Bernewelle' (Barnwell, Cambs.) made a grant of land to his son Lawrence in 1277 (? or 1312), sealed with his device of a hammer between a half-moon and a star or sun.

APD; A, xxx, 119

DOBSON, John [Dobeson, Tobbeson] *(fl. 1387–1409)* Carpenter

Citizen of London; master carpenter to *St. Paul's Cathedral* in 1387–88, when he was paid fees of £6 13s. 4d., besides receiving pay at 8d. a day for 48 days' work on the *Bishop's Palace*. In 1394–95 he rode to Barnet to choose timber for the works of the Cathedral, and he also sold timber to the fabric, while still in receipt of his annual fee of £6 13s. 4d., which he continued to take in 1396–97.[1]

On 12 April 1402 was appointed for life to be one of the two carpenters of the King's works within the *Tower of London*, the *Palace of Westminster*, and the *Manor of Eltham*, as NICHOLAS WALTON was, receiving 6d. daily so long as he should be occupied on the works in the absence of the other carpenter, HUGH HERLAND.[2]

On 6 September 1405 Dobson contracted to erect buildings on the south side of *Bucklersbury* for the Dean and Chapter of St. Paul's Cathedral,[3] for £46 13s. 4d.

On 21 July 1409 the sheriffs of London were ordered to release JOHN MASSINGHAM who had been imprisoned for quitting the service of John Dobson, carpenter, before the expiry of his term of apprenticeship.[4] Dobson probably died about this time, as his post at St. Paul's was held by WILLIAM GOLDYNG at Michaelmas 1409.[5]

[1] PRO, E.101-473-1, 4, 9; *SPM*, B.95.6; [2] CPR 1401-5, 83; [3] SHB, 478-482; (*SPM*, MS. 1717); [4] CCR 1405-9, 455; [5] *SPM*, B.95.7

DODINGTON, John (?) [Dodyngton] *(fl. 1412–?1427)* Mason

Was master mason during the erection of certain new buildings at *King's Hall, Cambridge*. In connection with a new bakehouse he is described in the accounts of 1411–12 as master of the work; he was paid 13s. 4d. and was entertained to dinner with his wife and servant and given wine.[1] The bakehouse stood between the kitchen and the hall on the east side of the mediaeval quadrangle. In 1417 a new library on the north side of the quadrangle and a range of chambers running southward at its west end were begun and completed by 1422. In the account of 1416–17 Dodington received a payment of 6s. 8d., probably as master mason. The range of chambers still exists, forming part of the King's Hostel at Trinity College, projecting northward behind the Great Court.[2] In 1427 work was begun on a new gate-tower, the structure of which was finished by 1432. The accounts record many payments to the principal mason, but his name is not given. There is a payment, however, 'to Dodyngton's servant' in the account of 1426–27, the year in which the work started,[3] so that it is likely that Dodington was still being employed by the college as their master mason. The gate-tower formed the south entrance to the college from the north end of Milne Street. It was taken down in 1600 and re-erected about thirty yards northward on the north side of the Great Court west of the chapel. This gate-tower, known as King Edward's Gate, is the prototype of the Cambridge college gate-tower with four corner turrets. The identification of its architect is, therefore, a matter of some interest. In W. D. Caröe's paper on King's Hostel, Dodington's Christian name is given as John, but without reference to any entry in the accounts.[4] There are Doddingtons in Lincolnshire, Northamptonshire, and the north of Cambridgeshire.

A.O.
[1] *TCM, KHA*, v, 319; WCC, II, 440n.; [2] WCC, II, 442; CKH; [3] *KHA*, vii, 153; WCC, II, 444; [4] CKH, 4, 22

DOGET, John [J. de Corfe] (*fl.* 1287–1294) Marbler

Master; in 1287 Masters John Doget and RALPH OF CHICHESTER undertook to supply marble columns, capitals, bases, and cornice moulding worked to a pattern (*exemplar*) sent by WALTER OF HEREFORD, master of the works of *Vale Royal Abbey*, Cheshire. The finished work was to be sent by sea (probably from Purbeck) to Frodsham in Cheshire. In 1291–94, John de Corfe, almost certainly the same man, was supplying marble for *Charing Cross*.

A. J. Taylor in CNW, XXXVII, 295–7

DORAUNT, John (*fl.* 1426–1473) Carpenter

Carpenter of Norwich; in 1426–27 he supplied timber for the repairs of the common inn of the city, *The Peacock* in Market Square.[1] In 1439–40 he was working for the *Cathedral Priory* on the great gates of the 'Prechyngyerd' next the Carnary.[2] A carpenter of this name worked on the great chamber of the Prior of *Ely* in 1473, being named second to THOMAS BELLAMY.[3] See also DURRANT.

[1] HTN, II, 65; [2] *NCM*, roll 287; [3] *CUL*, Add. MS. 6387, p.47

Dorman, John—see DERMAN

DOUNE, Geoffrey atte [Downe] (*fl.* 1385–1397) Mason

Supplied stone for the domestic buildings of *Rochester Cathedral Priory* in 1385–6, 'crest' for the chapel of the dormitory and in 1396–7 stone for a new latrine.[1] In 1386, with THOMAS CRUMP (Crompe) and William Okeangre, Doune was commissioned to press masons

and workmen for the repair of *Leeds Castle*, Kent.[2] On 4 August 1387 Geoffrey de Doune of 'Hartlepe' (Hartlip near Chatham) was one of nine men of Maidstone and the surrounding district bound in a recognizance of £360 to John, Lord Cobham, HENRY YEVELEY, JOHN CLIFFORD and others, for the supply of stone for Lord Cobham's works.[3] He was described as of Maidstone on 6 March 1397, when he and four others were licensed to press masons for the repair of the walls and gates of *Rochester*.[4]

(*A.O.*)
[1] HRC, 191; [2] CPR 1385–9, 180; [3] CCR 1385–9, 430–1; [4] CPR 1396–9, 137

Doune, John—see DOUVE

DOUNOM, Robert de [Downam] (*fl.* 1364–*c*. 1404) Carpenter

Took up the freedom of York in 1364. Robert de Dounom and STEPHEN DE BARNEBY, carpenters, contracted on 14 June 1377 to repair the *Gaol* of York;[1] in the accounts for *York Minster* from 1399 to 1404 he appears as Robert Downam or Downham, the master carpenter.[2]

[1] SHB, 453–4; (*PRO*, E.101–598–24); [2] BHY, I, 194, 197, 201; RFY, 14n., 20, 21, 25n.

DOUSE, John [Douce, Dous, Dowce, Dowsce] (*fl.* 1427–1445) Carpenter

Was chief carpenter at *King's Hall, Cambridge* during the years when the gate-tower (the King Edward Gate of Trinity College) was being erected. A range of chambers was also built, stretching northward from the gate-tower towards the mediaeval court. When the gate-tower was begun in 1427, Douse made the masons' lodge; he also took down some old chambers to clear the site. The accounts of 1428–29 record payments to him for making the centering for the great gate. In the next year he received the final instalment of a sum of £40 for work on 'the new building', probably the timber floors and roof of the gate-tower and/or the range of chambers.[1] He was given a gown in 1429–30 and 1430–31.[2] In 1432–33 he supplied timber ready fashioned for the Warden's Chamber. In 1436–37 he was paid 13*s*. 4*d*. for 'studies' (*studiis*) and in 1439–40 was working on a stair turret built in the angle between the gate-tower and the range of chambers.[3] His name appears again in the account of 1444–45, when he was paid 8*s*. 7*d*. for seventeen days' work.[4] He seems to have come from

Haverhill in Suffolk, for certain payments were made to 'John Dowce minor de Haueryll', probably his son.[5]

A.O.
[1] *TCM, KHA*, vii, 174, 211, 249, 283–9; *WCC*, II, 444–5; [2] *KHA*, vii, 270; viii, 11; [3] *Ibid.*, viii, 111; ix, 39, 40, 227; *WCC*, II, 446n; [4] *KHA*, x, 182; [5] *Ibid.*, vii, 295

DOUVE, John [Dowve] (*fl.* 1385–   ) Carpenter

Appointed master carpenter to *Lichfield Cathedral* on 16 June 1385, at £1 yearly and 2s. 6d. per week.

LCM, Acta Capitularia 1384–1438, *f.* 5v. (*A.B.E.*); (*D.A.J.*)

DOVER, John (*fl.* 1431–1437) Mason

Mason concerned with the works of *Winchester College*. In May 1431 he dined with the Fellows of the College, in company with six other masons (*lathami*) none of whom are named. In 1436–37 he was paid £1 for making a stone doorway from the new stairs leading directly from the kitchen to the hall. This doorway is now within the First Hatch.

WCM 22824, Hall Book 1430–31; Compotus 1436–37

Dow, John—see DAW

DOWELL, William (*fl.* 1508–   ) Carpenter

Master Carpenter of *York Minster* in 1508.
BHY, I, 268

DOWLAND, Thomas (*fl.* 1496–   ) Mason

Contractor for the nave, north porch, and west tower of the *Holy Cross Guild Chapel* at *Stratford on Avon*, begun at about the time of the death of Hugh Clopton, the donor, in 1496. Stylistic resemblances suggest that Dowland may also have built the chancel of *Stratford Parish Church* (*c.* 1465–90) and the nave clerestory (*c.* 1495).

Dowland worked in a regional style which appears in a number of churches, and notably in towers and steeples, on the border of Warwickshire and Worcestershire. Some at least of these were begun before his time, but that nearest in date to the Stratford chancel is the steeple of *Sheldon*, Warks., begun in 1461, apparently by Henry Ulm, according to two inscriptions in the church. The first states that in 1461 'ye stepel was begon ye mason had thr[ee] and forti pond vi.[s] viii.[d] for makyng of the st'pel'. The other graffito is in part unintelligible, but has been read as: 'Henry Ulm [y[e] he?] of [? Horsod] M[o] CCCC lxi y[t] to begon'. There is no certainty that Henry Ulm, even supposing that the name has been correctly read and is complete, was either the mason who received £43 6s. 8d. for building the tower, or the designer.

VCH, *Warwickshire*, III, 276; IV, 203

Downe, Geoffrey atte—see DOUNE

DOWNER, John (*fl.* 1435) Carpenter

A carpenter of Weald in the parish of Harrow, Middlesex, who with others entered into a bond in 100 marks on 1st August 1435 with the Warden of *Winchester College*. This may have been in connection with the building of a new barn at *Harmondsworth* (see WILLIAM KYPPYNG).

WCM 20151

DOWNES, Edward (*fl.* 1486–   ) Carpenter

Of Worksop, Notts.; in March 1485/6 contracted to build a new bridge at *Newark*, Notts., of twelve timber spans over the Trent, for the sum of £40. The previous bridge had been destroyed in a great flood. The work was to be done at the costs of the Bishop of Lincoln, lord of the town, who provided £66 13s. 4d. for the making of the bridge, and its approaches of stonework, the money being intrusted to John Philipot, alderman, and three others.

SHB, 546–7; LDD, 256

Downham, Robert de—see DONNOM

DOYLE, John (*fl.* 1482–   ) Carpenter

Master carpenter of *Kirby Muxloe Castle*, Leics., during its erection in 1482, taking 8d. a day.

LAS, XI, 193 ff.

DRAWSWERD, John [Drawesworde] (*fl.* 1486–1489) Carver

Was paying 6s. 8d. rent for a tenement (3 Greestone Place) in Lincoln in 1486 and was there for the next two years, but had left by 1489.

LDC, Bj. 5.11 no. 2 (*K.M.*)

DRAWSWERD, Thomas [Drawswerde] (*fl.* 1495–†1529) Carver

Of York; was one of a family of image-makers and carvers. In 1495–96 he took up the freedom of the city,[1] and in 1498 is mentioned in the fabric rolls of York Minster as 'mending the dove for the paschal candle';[2] he was Chamberlain of York in 1501, and Sheriff in 1505–06, when he submitted an estimate for image-work in *Henry VII's Chapel* at *Westminster*. On 10 November 1508 he was elected alderman. At this time we learn of his great work, finished ten years before, for *Newark Church*, Notts. On 21 December 1508 the churchwardens of Newark gave Drawswerd a release from all actions in respect of the great reredos of their church (*pro factura de le Reredose ecclesie predicte*). The work done by him was not the roodscreen (as mistakenly suggested by Dimock on the supposition that a 'carver' worked only in wood). What was done, on the reredos behind the high altar, was apparently completed in 1498, and the release ten years later doubtless freed Drawswerd from responsibility after the period in which he was liable for replacement of defective work.[3] He was elected Member of Parliament for York on 2 January 1511/12, and was Lord Mayor of York in 1515 and 1523. Drawswerd was one of the aldermen commissioners for the Lay subsidy of 1524, which assessed him for £18 worth of lands and mentions that he had spent £22 on bearing civic offices since the first levy.[4] Holtby Hall in Davygate, York, was granted to Drawswerd, who regranted it to the commonalty of York when he was Mayor in 1524.[5]

By his will made on 28 January 1528/9, and proved on 30 July 1529, he desired to be buried in the churchyard of 'Sancte Martyn's in Conyngstrete, before the roode', and bequeathed his house at 'Jubergate now in the holding of Roberte Lowther, mylner, after my wif deith, to Sancte Martyn's kirke warke'. To 'George Drawswerde my sone' he left his house in Bootham called the Bell, and he also disposed of many other tenements in York. 'Mawde my wif' was appointed executrix, and 'Maude my doughtour' and 'Cristabell my sone wif' are also mentioned.[6] Drawswerd's merchant's mark was ☖ .[7]

LKC; PRS

[1] YCF; [2] RFY, 92; [3] Newark Corporation Records no. 263 printed by Dimock in RPL, vol. IIIA (1856), 1–13 (*A.O.*); [4] YAJ, IV (1877), 173, 201; [5] RMY, 127, mistakenly printing 'William' Drawswerd; [6] YTE, v, 267; [7] YCM (*A.R.*)

DRAWSWERD, William (*fl.* 1525–1526) Carver

Paid 21*s*. 8*d*. for carving on the feretory at *York Minster* in 1525–26.

RFY, 101

DREWRY, Roger [Drury] (*fl.* 1398–1432) Carpenter

Appointed master carpenter of the castle of *Chester* and in the counties of Chester and Flint for life, on 1 February 1411/12. He died on 7 April 1432 and on 26 May was succeeded in the office by HENRY BALFRONT.

Before his appointment Drewry had been granted livery of the Crown with 6*d*. a day for life, in 1398.

DKR XXXI

Ralph **DRURY**, carpenter, was in 1400 granted wood for the repair of the mill of *Northwich*, Cheshire, on the representation of WILLIAM DE NEWHALL, master carpenter of Chester.

DKR, XXXI

DRIFFELD, William (*fl.* 1382–1385) Mason

Mason working on the choir of *Lichfield Cathedral* in 1382–85, in a subordinate position though described as 'Magister'.

Bodl., MS. Ashmole 794, *f*. 194 (*D.A.J.*)

DRUE, John (*fl.* 1489–)? Carpenter

In 1489 John Drue gave a receipt for £5 paid to him 'for making the chancel' or screen? (*pro factur' cancell'*) of *Puriton Church*, Somerset, on behalf of the Dean and Canons of Windsor. The payment was made at Bridgwater.

WSG, xv, 60, 65 (*H.M.C.*)

Drury—see DREWRY

DRYFFELD, Robert (*fl.* 1393–1395) Carpenter

From 1393 to 1395–96 was paid £20 for making new choir-stalls for the church of *Bicester Priory*, by task, besides 23*s*. 4*d*. for making 30 finials for the stalls.

(*E.M.J.*) DBP, II, 229

DRYNG, Peter (*fl.* 1364–†1404) Mason

Mason of Durham; he was associated with JOHN LEWYN in the reconstruction of *Finchale Priory*, co. Durham, from 1364 onwards,[1] and in 1368–69 was one of the masons working on the new kitchen of *Durham Cathedral Priory*.[2] About 1388 he obtained a lease of the tenement of Dryburn in the city of Durham,[3] in 1389–90 entered into a recognizance to John de Sutton, chaplain, at Durham,[4] while in 1392 a Peter Dryng who may have been the same man is mentioned as having sold wine and ale. In 1400 and 1401 Dryng was paid a retainer of £1 6*s*. 8*d*. each year by instalments at Whitsun and Martinmas.[5]

On 2 February 1401/2, Dryng contracted to continue the walls of the new dormitory in the monastery of Durham, begun by JOHN MIDDLETON, to be completed by the feast of

All Saints 1404. From 20 March 1402 to 1 November 1404 he was to have each day one white loaf and one flagon of ale, and a mess from the kitchen such as the Prior's squires received. In addition, he was to be paid 10 marks of silver (£6 13s. 4d.) for every rod of work, each rod consisting of 6½ yards of 1 yard square, the money to be paid by instalments, £40 at the beginning of the work, and £40 at the completion of each 6 rods.[6]

In 1402/3, with Walter Lewyn, son of John Lewyn, he entered into a recognizance to the Bishop of Durham to deliver John de Kellowe, late farmer of the vill of Durham, to the gaol there,[7] and was also a party to several other recognizances in the same year. At this time, work was in progress upon the Chantry Chapel and tomb of Bishop Walter Skirlaw, and it seems that Dryng was the master mason in charge.[8] Dryng died in 1404, leaving no male issue.[9]

[1] RFP; [2] DST, 132n; [3] VCH, *Durham*, III, 165; [4] DKR, XXXIII; [5] DAR, II, 337; SDC, 28, 35; [6] SHB, 476–7; DST, 186; [7] DKR, XXXIII; [8] DAR, II, pp. lix–lxi; [9] VCH, *Durham*, III, 165

Ducheman, Baldwin—see DUTCHMAN

DUDDASON, Leofsi [Leofsi de Lundonia] (*fl. c.* 1050–1066) ? Mason

Saxon Englishman in charge of the building of the new *Westminster Abbey* for Edward the Confessor, *c.* 1050–1066 (*qui preerat illius ecclesie cementariis*). He gave 2½ hides of land at Wormley, Herts., to the Abbey. It seems probable that Leofsi was not the architect (see GODWIN GRETSYD) but an administrative chief. It is, in any case, of outstanding interest that the two men who between them must have been responsible, should both have been English, in spite of the predominantly Norman character of the work.

F. E. Harmer in EHR, LI (1936), 98; HAW, 292, 355, 566

DUNMOW, a Mason of (*fl.* 1500) Mason

Was paid 9s. 4d. for making the battlement on the north side of *Bishops Stortford Church.* He was described as 'one of Dunmow and his 3 servants'.

GBS, 24 (*A.O.*)

DUNMOW, Stephen of (*fl.* 1351–1357) Carpenter

Master carpenter at *Calais*, with WILLIAM OF TILNEY, in 1351–57; he also had charge of works on the peel of *Frétun*, 3 miles from Calais, in 1351–2, with Master GILBERT ACK-LAM the mason.

HKW, I, 428n., 451; II, 1054

DURAND the Carpenter [Durandus] (*fl.* 1086–) Carpenter

Was one of the officials of William the Conqueror in 1086, when Domesday Book shows that he held the small manor of 'Alfrunetone' (now Afflington), Dorset, worth 6s. He is described as 'carpenter', the entry occuring among the 'lands of the King's thanes'. He also held the manor of Moulham, near Swanage, where later his descendants held by serjeanty of finding a carpenter to work on the Great Tower of Corfe. This suggests that Durand had been responsible for the Conqueror's original wooden tower at *Corfe.*[1]

DB; VCH, *Dorset*, II, 335n.
[1] W. D. Simpson in DAS, LXXIII, 74

DURAND the Mason [Durandus *cementarius*] (*fl.* 1224–*c.* 1233) Mason

French mason, visited England to take charge of work at *Beaulieu Abbey*, Hants., in 1224.[1] He was very probably identical with the carver of the bosses of the nave of *Rouen Cathedral*, one of which bears the inscription: *Durandus me fecit.* This dates from about 1233, but it has been suggested that Durandus was master mason of the nave from 1214 to 1251.[2]

[1] HLC, I, 625b; AJ, LXIII, 136; [2] WPS; cf. APD; RA, 5S., XI (1920), 319

DURRANT, John (*fl.* 1441) Carpenter

Carpenter of Norwich, but not recorded as free of the city. Made a new roof for the chancel of the church of *Thurlton*, Norfolk, in 1441 for £5 13s. 4d.; JOHN MARWE was the mason employed. The sum of 4d. was paid for a horse to enable Durrant to take the measure of the roof, with 12d. for his journey from Tivetshall with expenses. See also DORAUNT.

NRO, Great Hospital, 24.51 (*S.A.C.*)

DUTCHMAN, Baldwin [Ducheman] (*fl.* 1433–1455) Brickmaker

Probably from the Low Countries, or from the Baltic lands, where brick fortifications were usual. Baldwin undoubtedly supervised the making of the bricks or 'wall-tiles' when *Tattershall Castle*, Lincs., was being built between 1433 and 1455, and it has been suggested that he was an expert in fortification of the type of Tattershall, most unusual in England, but normal in the countries ruled by the Teutonic Knights.

(*W.D.S.*) AAJ, 2S., XL, 177–92; HMC, *De L'Isle &*

Dudley, I, 198, 210, 215

Dyconson—see DICKINSON

DYLKESTON, Richard (*fl.* 1365–1369) Mason (? *Ilkeston, Derbs.*)

Master mason (*cementarius*) in charge of works at *Nottingham Castle* in 1368–69, when he was paid 3s. 4d. a week, and also received £4 for his task of building a wall of 'la Damisele Chambre' 46 feet long, 8 feet high, and 3 feet thick. He was almost certainly the master who had been in charge at the same rate of pay since 1365, when the windows of the Castle chapel were renewed.

PRO, E.101–478–7, 8 (*L.F.S.*)

DYMINGE, Nicholas [Dymenge, de Legeri] (*fl.* 1292–   ) Mason

Called 'de Reyns', and perhaps from Rheims in France, though 'Reyns' and 'Leger' are known forms of Rayne and Layer in Essex; he was mason of the *Eleanor Cross* at Waltham, and of the tomb of Queen Eleanor in *Lincoln Cathedral*, made in 1292. He may perhaps have been related to Master HENRY DE REYNS.

(LKC); **BMH**

DYMMOK, John (*fl.* 1493–   ) Mason (*Dymock, Glos.*)

Mason of *Bristol*; in 1493 acted as a viewer of the city with JOHN WALTER, mason, and NICHOLAS ANDREWES and RICHARD SOMERE, carpenters.

(*A.O.*) BLR, II, 133

DYMOKE, Hugh de (*fl.* 1303–1304) Carpenter

Master carpenter of the works of *Beeston Castle*, Cheshire, in 1303–4, during repairs to the three towers of the inner ward; he also made two machines called 'springalds' for the castles of Flint and Rhuddlan, by agreement with Master RICHARD LENGINOUR.

ACC, 42; FHS, III, 47

DYNCOK, John (*fl.* 1426–1440) Mason

Admitted to the freedom of *Norwich* in 1426,[1] and Junior Warden of the Masons' Guild there in 1440.[2]

[1] EFN; [2] AQC, XV (1902), 202

Dynyce, Roger—see DENYS

DYTTON, Walter (–†1413) Marbler (*Long Ditton, Surrey*)

Was born in the parish of (Long) Ditton, Surrey. On 5 October 1413 made his will as a citizen and marbler of London, residing in the parish of St. Dunstan in the West, Fleet Street, where he wished to be buried. To the Fraternity of St. Dunstan he left 6s. 8d. for his name to be kept in special memory; and he bequeathed a like sum to the parish church of (Long) Ditton. The will mentions his parents John and Alice Dytton, his wife Alice and John his brother. The will was proved within two days.

GUL, Archdeaconry Court of London, vol. I, *f.* 298.

EAST, John, I [Est] (*fl.* 1356–1369) Mason

During the absence of JOHN PALTERTON on pilgrimage, the position of master on the works of the south cloister of *Westminster Abbey* was taken by John Est from 25 January 1355/6 to 6 March 1356/7. He received wages of 2s. a week with a year's fee of £2; his arrival was a week before Palterton's departure and he left a month after Palterton's return.[1]

From 1363–69 he was master mason in charge of works on *Morende Castle* in Yardley Gobion, Northants., taking 4s. a week.[2]

A John Est, mason, worked in *Westminster Palace* at 6d. a day in the autumn of 1319.[3]

[1] *WAM*, 23455; [2] *PRO*, E.101–544–31; 476–11 (*L.F.S.*) (*G.P.J.*); HKW, II, 743; [3] BBW, 121

EAST, John [Este] (*fl.* 1442–   ) Carpenter

Of 'Fynchamstede' (Finchampstead, near Wokingham, Berks.); in 1442 made and set up the roof of the new north transept at *Thame Church*, Oxon., for £4 6s. 8d. (see BECKELEY, JOHN).

(*R.D.*) BAJ, VII; GM 1865, pt. i, 176–89

EAST, William [Easte, Eist, Est, Este] (*fl.* 1494–1526) Mason

Possibly identical with the William Est (*latamus*) who worked at *Westminster Abbey* for 40 weeks in 1482–83, taking an apprentice's rate of 2s. a week.[1]

From 1494 was rebuilding the palace of *Woodstock*, Oxon.; for the period up to 1501 he was paid £800 for the works.[2] From 1503 onwards East had a contract to maintain the manor of *Langley* near Leafield, Oxon., along with Woodstock, for £5 a year, later raised to £6, and this continued to be paid until 1520. On 1 July 1505, with two others, he entered into a contract of quite a different nature — to make a clock for *Magdalen College, Oxford*. The clock was to be of new iron, both house, hammer, and wheels, with bars and hand to the dial, and was to go truly for a year and a day, all repairs within the year to be at the expense of the makers; the price was to be

£10.[3] East was described as 'of Abingdon, mason'; possibly he may have been a master mason to *Abingdon Abbey*.

From 1511 to 1520 he was paid an annual fee for keeping the palace of Woodstock in repair; for the first four years the fee was £5, and afterwards £6. He had charge of the manor of *Langley*, Oxon., as well as Woodstock; in December 1519 he was still living at Abingdon.[4] Between 1512 and 1518 he was building *Corpus Christi College, Oxford*, under the direction of WILLIAM VERTUE.[5] In the summer of 1512 East was gravely wounded by, or at the instigation of members of Brasen-Nose Hall, and threats were employed against his colleagues Vertue and HUMPHREY COKE. By August 1514 East had recovered and the affair was patched up.

In 1513 he was paid £1 by Oriel College for work on the Lady Chapel of *St. Mary the Virgin, Oxford*. In 1520 East made a sundial in the churchyard there, designed by Nicholas Kratzer.[6]

He built the antechapel of *Queen's College, Oxford* (begun 1516) by contract, and in 1519 was paid £3 for his completion of the large bay-window of the Provost's house there.[7]

East was one of the masters of the fraternity of the Holy Cross at Abingdon when on 23 January 1519/20 they obtained licence to hold a fair.[8] Either East moved soon after this, or had a quarry at Burford, Oxon., in addition to his home at Abingdon, for on 3 April 1522 'Master William Eist mason of Burfurth' contracted to make windows for the chapel of *Balliol College, Oxford*;[9] it is hardly likely that two different men are in question. William Est was taxed 4s. on £8 of goods in the township of Burford in each of the lay subsidies of 1524, 1525, and 1526, and his tenement in the High Street of Burford, next but one to the south of the way leading to the church, is referred to on 2 August 1526.[10]

The windows which East agreed to make were 'iii great wynd(ows) both the soolls & hedds of the south syde of the new capell with a litill wyndow to ye vestre with corbell table & iiii corbylls' with certain other masonry in the vestry. For this he was to have £8, having for the purpose such stone already in the college as would serve. He was to find all other stone, carriage, scaffolding, lime, and workmanship.

East seems to have been a contractor on a large scale, but it is difficult to assess his position as an architect; his work at Woodstock was probably built to the design of ROBERT VERTUE, the King's Chief Mason, just as William Vertue was the designer of Corpus Christi College.

GOM, 88–9; HKW, IV, 160, 351
[1] *WAM*, 23557; [2] *BM*, Add. MS. 7099, *ff.* 19, 22, 50, 52, 54, 59, 63, 69 (*A.O.*); [3] HMC, 8R, App. i, 266; [4] LPH, II, pt. ii, pp. 1441 ff.; III, pt. ii, pp. 1533 ff; *PRO*, E.36–214, pp. 61, 156, 199, 262 (*A.O.*); [5] FCC; FHC, 64; [6] E. M. Jope in *Oriel Record* (April 1946), 8; (*OCO*, Treasury Accs. III, 749); JMO 187n.2; [7] *QCO* Long Rolls (*E.G.*); [8] LPH, III, pt. i, p.206; [9] *BCO*, Register (*R.D.*); SHB, 573–4; [10] GBR, 599, 601, 603, 672

EASTAWE, John [Estow] (*fl.* 1525–1538) Mason

In 1525 contracted to execute the masonry and brickwork of *Hengrave Hall*, Suffolk. The work was completed in 1538. Eastawe was to do all the work 'according to a frame which the said Ihon has seen at Comby'. He and 'all his company yt he setts a worcke for ye said house' were to be boarded at the house of Thomas Shethe for 16d. a week; Eastawe was to make all the necessary mortar and the chimneys were to have sides of 'roubed bryck'. The price to be paid was £200, a first instalment of £10 when he began the foundation, and further sums of £20 as the work should proceed, by estimation.

The client, Sir Thomas Kitson, was to make (i.e. have made) a bay-window in the hall on the south side, of freestone, and also the freestone work 'of the gate coming in at the bridge'. These works were performed by JOHN SPARK, mason, and the woodwork by THOMAS NEKER, carpenter. It seems from this exclusion of the specially difficult works from Eastawe's contract, that he was simply a building contractor, and the 'frame' which he was shown was evidently a design prepared by someone else, perhaps John Spark the freemason.

GHH, 41; SHB, 574–5

Eastington—see ESTINTON

ECCLESTON, Nicholas de (*fl.* 1346–1361) Carpenter (? *Eccleston*, Ches.)

Was granted the office of chief carpenter of the counties of Chester and Flint on 14 September 1346, with fees of 2½d. a day and 10s. for a robe, altered on 15 October to 3d. a day, with the same provision for a robe; from 2 February 1350 his fee was raised to 4d. During 1351 he was in charge of repairs to the roof of the great hall of *Chester Castle*, repaired the mill-pond at *Northwich*, and carried out repairs to the hall of *Flint Castle* by contract. On 12 February 1352/3 Eccleston was ordered to go to *Carnarvon* to raise the new weir there begun, and on 14 September he received a new grant as master carpenter in Chester, Flint, and North Wales, at 6*d.* a day, with a robe yearly worth 10*s.*

In 1357–58 he repaired the mill at Northwich and carried out work on the manor of *Frodsham*; from 1358 to 1360 he was one of the farmers of the Dee mills and fishery at Chester. He was dead by 21 October 1361, when his successor RICHARD ERCALO was appointed.

BPR, III, 88, 119, 489; HCH, 94–6; FHS, RS. No. 2, pp. 21–2, 25, 54–5, 59, 75, 77, 80–1, 98, 99, 103; ACC, 122–3, 148, 160, 166–7, 182, 222, 245, 258, 269

Ednoth—see WORCESTER, Ednoth of

EDRICH, William (*fl.* 1369–1370) Carpenter
Was master carpenter at the *Abbey of St. Edmund, Bury*, in 1369–70. In the Sacrist's Roll for this year 10*s.* for his robe is entered.[1] Work on the rebuilding of the central tower under the Sacrist, John Lavenham, was in progress at this time.

A.O.
[1] *BCM*, Sacrist's Roll, A.6–1–3

Edward—see ODO, Edward fitz

EDWARD the Carpenter (*fl.* 1321–1323) Carpenter
Master Edward the carpenter was in charge of repairs to the great hall and other buildings of *Bristol Castle* between April 1321 and December 1323.

HKW, II, 580

EDWARD (? *fl. c.* 1020–1046)? Mason
Mentioned after THURUERD as one of the builders of the abbey church of *St. Benet Holme*, Norfolk; probably of the work founded by Canute and built *c.* 1020–46.

DM, III, 62, 88; NRC, II, 33

EDWIN (*fl. c.* 1100–1140) Carpenter
Was one of the King's Carpenters in the 12th century, when he held the manor of Cadishead in Barton, in the parish of Eccles, Lancs., by serjeanty of carpentry in the royal castle of *West Derby*, under 'King Henry', probably Henry I.

VCH, *Lancashire*, IV, 371; HKW, I, 27n.[10]

Eist—see EAST.

ELAND, William de (*fl.* 1382) Mason (*Ponteland, N'land*)
In 1382, when Sir John Heron was Gov-

ernor of *Norham Castle*, William de Eland was paid £3 6*s.* 8*d.* for masonry work.

JNC, 175 (*A.O.*)

ELESER, John (*fl.* ? *c.* 1540) Mason
Was recommended to the chapter of *Exeter Cathedral* about 1540 for the office of 'Maystre Mason'.

RUE, 63 (*N.L.R.*)

ELIAS the Carver [Helias sculptor] (*fl. c.* 1200) Carver
Witnessed a charter at *Lewes Priory, c.* 1200, in company with Master ROGER the Mason, Philip the Carpenter and John the Glazier, presumably the building staff of the Priory at the time.

SXR, XXXVIII, 180 (*L.F.S.*)

ELIAS the Engineer [E. the Mason, Elyas, Helie, Elias of Oxford] (*fl.* 1186–1203) Engineer
Referred to indifferently as carpenter, mason, and engineer (*carpentarius, cementarius, ingeniator*).[1] From 1186 he was in charge of the King's houses in *Oxford*, and received fees of 1*d.* a day as keeper of Beaumont Palace until 1200. He was also paid £5 yearly for his sustenance until in 1201 he took payment for a half-year only. In 1191 he was at *Winchester*, in the next year at *Portchester*, in 1194 took siege engines to Nottingham, in 1195 had charge of works at *Rochester, Hastings, Pevensey, Westminster Palace*, and both Beaumont Palace and the castle at Oxford, while in 1197 he was at the royal manor of *Freemantle*, Hants., and at *Marlborough*, Wilts. In 1198 he was supervising repairs at Westminster Palace and from 1199 to 1203 he was engaged on works at the *Tower of London*. He was also active at Portchester and the royal lodges in the New Forest in 1200.

Elias the Engineer certainly belonged to an earlier generation than Master ELIAS OF DEREHAM, with whom he was mistakenly identified by Horace Walpole.

PR
[1] The identity of Elyas the mason with Elyas the carpenter and engineer has been established by Mr R. Allen Brown. (Unpubd. D. Phil. Thesis, Oxford)

Elias the Mason—see ELIAS the Engineer

ELIAS the Mason I [Helyas] (*fl. c.* 1175–1200) Mason
Mason (*cementarius*); witnessed a grant to *Bullington Priory*, Lincs., in the late 12th century, together with RALPH W(U)DEMAN, carpenter, Osbert the plumber of Sempringham,

and Martin the smith. These men may have formed the works staff of the Gilbertine Order at the time.

(*H.M.C.*) SGC, 94

ELIAS the Mason II (*fl.* 1313–1314) Mason

Was master mason in charge of the building of *Dunstanburgh Castle*, which began in 1313. Quarrying was started on 7 May, and by Michaelmas 1314, 16 perches of a moat 80 feet broad and 18 feet deep had been dug on the west side of the site, a hostelry 80 feet by 20 feet in size had been built for the workmen, at a cost of £1 16*s*. 1*d*., and the main building was in progress.

Master Elias had contracted to build the 'bows' of the gatehouse to a height of 80 feet, with a tower above either side of the gateway; for this he was to have £224, of which he had been paid £65 10*s*. for work already completed in the autumn of 1314. The licence to crenellate was not granted until 21 August 1316, and the work must have been structurally complete soon after.

BBH, 169–70

Elis—see also ELLIS, ELYS

ELIS, Robert (*fl.* 1477–1478) Carver

Was paid £40 in 1477–78, with JOHN FILLES for making six tabernacles for the choir of *St. George's Chapel, Windsor*.

PRO, E.101–496–17 (*L.F.S.*)

ELKIN, Thomas [Elkyn, Elkyns] (*fl.* 1440–†1449) Mason

Mason (*lathomus*); of Gloucestershire origin, holding land at 'Berynton' (Berrington).[1] He contracted on 16 January 1439/40 to complete the work of the *Divinity Schools, Oxford*,[2] begun by RICHARD WINCHCOMBE. Elkin was already at work before undertaking the contract, which instructs him to continue as he had already begun, to restrain the undue enrichment of the work (*supervacuam talem curiositatem dicti operis*), which had been reproved by magnates of the realm and others. He was to have a yearly fee of 1 mark (13*s*. 4*d*.), with weekly pay of 4*s*. in summer and 3*s*. 4*d*. in winter.

Elkin witnessed a deed at Balliol College on 20 June 1445,[3] and died between 29 September and 6 October 1449, having apparently lived in Oxford since 1440. In his will he desired to be buried in the Austin Friars of Oxford, left 1*s*. 8*d*. to the repairs of St. Mary Magdalene without the North Gate,

and his tenement in Catte Street to Katherine his wife and John Elkyns his son; his apprentice William was to have his tools and various other items.[4]

The distinction between the original details of Winchcombe and the simpler work by Elkin is clearly visible in the Divinity Schools.[5]

[1] AJ, LXXI (1914), 221n.; [2] SHB, 513–14; OEA, I, 192; [3] GOM, 74; [4] OMA, II, 595; OHS, XCIII, 191; cf. 128, 169, 180–1, 195; XCIV, 341; [5] F. E. Howard in HAR, 34

ELLERTON, Henry de [Allerton, Elreton] (*fl.* 1304–1322) Mason

Worked at *Carnarvon Castle*[1] as undermaster to WALTER OF HEREFORD, taking 4*s*. per week; in 1304 he petitioned Parliament for arrears of £30 15*s*. 5*d*. for his work at Carnarvon, while Walter of Hereford petitioned for over £130. Warrants were made out for their satisfaction, charging the amounts to the Chamberlain of Carnarvon.[2]

In 1307 Ellerton obtained licence to build a chantry chapel on his burgage in Carnarvon, and in 1309 he became master of the works on the death of Walter of Hereford,[3] and was responsible for the building of the King's Gate and northern walls of the castle. He also contracted to repair part of the town quay in 1316, and was still in office in 1322, but he probably died in the following year, as NICHOLAS DE DERNEFORD became master of works for all the North Wales castles in November 1323. While undermaster, Ellerton's wage was 4*s*. a week, raised to 14*s*. after he became master on the death of Walter of Hereford. His post was formally enlarged in March 1318 to that of master and surveyor of the King's works in the castles of North Wales.[4]

Ellerton's work at Carnarvon Castle follows closely on the style of Hereford's earlier sections of the building, but the King's Gate in particular is a very notable design for which Ellerton must take some of the credit.

KJI; (APD;BAA)
[1] CCP, 7; cf. PRO, E.101–486–1; A. J. Taylor in ANT, XXVI, 25–34; [2] BAA, IV, 169; RP, I, 167b.; [3] A. J. Taylor in CHT (1948), 17–18; HKW, I, 468

ELLIS, John (*fl.* 1520–1542) Mason

Probably identical with the John Ellis who worked as a mason at *Westminster Abbey* for two weeks in 1520–21 at 3*s*. 4*d*. a week, and for 7½ days in 1523–24 at 8*d*. a day.[1] He was working as a setter at 3*s*. 8*d*. a week at *Westminster Palace* in 1531, when he became second warden of the masons under JOHN

MOLTON, after which he received 8*d*. a day. He was also paid his expenses for impressing masons.² In 1534 John 'Ells' of Westminster, freemason, cut two 'bullyns' of freestone for the vault of the bay-window in the new hall at *Hampton Court* for 10*s*. each.³ In 1542 he worked at Westminster Hall at 9*d*. a day⁴ and later took 10*d*. a day at *Rochester* for work as a freemason.⁵ He may have been the father of NICHOLAS ELLIS.

He or Nicholas Ellis may have been the 'Mastr. Ellys the King's Mason' who in 1544 arranged for the removal of material from the dissolved Abbey of Abingdon to the works of *Christ Church, Oxford*.⁶

(*G.P.J.*)
¹ *WAM*, 23608, 23610; ² *PRO*, E. 36–251, 252; ³ LHC, I, 350; ⁴ *BM*, Add. 10109; Plut. clxxii-D.; ⁵ *Bodl*., Rawl. D.781; ⁶ E. M. Jope in BKJ, LI (1951), 57–8

ELLIS, Nicholas [Ellice, Ellys] (*fl*. 1529–†1556) Mason

May have been a son of JOHN ELLIS. In 1529–30 Nicholas Ellys (*lathomus*) worked for 50 days at *Westminster Abbey*, taking 8*d*. a day.¹ He was warden of the masons at *Whitehall Palace* in 1541, taking 4*s*. a week,² and on 19 April 1547 was appointed Master Mason of the King's Works,³ and was being paid his fees of 12*d*. a day in 1548 and 1549.⁴ His patent granted him his wages as from 23 January 1547, as he had occupied the office since that date, when JOHN MOLTON died. In 1549 his riding charges appear in the accounts⁵ and on 28 August 1551 Ellis was ordered by the Privy Council to provide for the making of a conduit in *Windsor Castle* 'as many tonne of stone of the provision that was made for buylding of the front of the Quyre in the College as shall be sufficyent'.⁶ He or John Ellis may have been the 'Mastr. Ellys the King's Mason' who in 1544 arranged for the removal of material from the dissolved Abbey of Abingdon to the works of *Christ Church, Oxford*.⁷

In June 1545 Ellis was a warden of the London Masons' Company⁸ and between 1546 and 1552 was concerned with the purchase and lease of various premises in Westminster, being referred to as 'Esquire; mason of Westminster; officer of the King's Buildings, and chief Mason to Edward VI'.⁹ He died in November 1556.¹⁰

(*G.P.J.*)
¹ *WAM*, 23619; ² *Bodl*., Rawl. D.781; Eng. Hist. b.192; ³ CPR 1547–8, 100, 117; ⁴ *PRO*, E.101–474–19; ⁵ *Ibid*.; ⁶ HWC, I, 256; WKM, 34; ⁷ E. M. Jope in BKJ, LI, 57–8;

⁸ WFL, 80; ⁹ *WAM*, 18051, 28336, 35843, 36388; ¹⁰ HKW, III, 408

ELNINGTON, Simon de (*fl*. 1329–   ) Mason

In 1329 appears as '*cementarius*' in a list of the servants of *Croyland Abbey*, Lincs.

(SMC, 170); DM, II, 121

Elreton, Henry—see ELLERTON

ELTHAM, Richard de (*fl*. 1240–1259) Mason (*Eltham, Kent*)

Master mason (*cementarius*) of Westminster, where he appears as holding land in Tothill Street, and in connection with *Westminster Abbey*, together with his brother *John de ELTHAM*, mason (*fl*. 1242–1271)´ (See also WILLIAM DE WAUZ.) Orders were given for robes to be issued to Master Richard de Eltham as one of the king's craftsmen at Westminster from 1255 until 1258;¹ and for Master John de Eltham in 1265.²

WAM, 'Domesday' ff. 560, 384, 344v., 445v., etc.
¹ CCR 1254–6, 91, 239–40, 312; 1256–9, 13, 54, 159, 218; ² CCR 1264–8, 14

ELWARD, Richard (*fl*. 1489–1490) Mason

In 1489–90 Richard Elward, 'fremason', was paid £1 3*s*. 4*d*. for making a new east window for the chancel of the church at *Stoke Holy Cross*, Norfolk, together with repairs to other windows. He apparently cut the stones at Norwich, for transport to Stoke. It is possible that he was identical with RICHARD ELWARE.

NRO, DCN, Chamberlain, No. 450 (*P.C.*)

ELWARE, Richard [Elwar] (–†1521) Mason

The will of Richard Elwar of 'Becclis', freemason, made on 20 May 1521, left 6*s*. 8*d*. 'and more if it may be borne' to the making of the church tower at *Beccles*.¸ It was built between 1515 and 1547. Elware had been twice married, first to Alice, and was survived by his second wife Ellen, who died in 1526.² Elware's house in the parish of St. Martin at Oak in Norwich was to be sold for pious uses. He was perhaps identical with RICHARD ELWARD.

John ELWARE, mason, possibly the father of Richard, was admitted a freeman of Lynn by purchase in 1458-9.³ *Thomas ELWARE*, perhaps a son or grandson of Richard, freemason, was admitted a freeman of Norwich in 1531–2.⁴

¹ *NRO*, CCN 115 Alblaster; ² CCN 127 Groundesburgh; ³ *CFL*, 56 (*P.C.*); ⁴ EFN

ELY, Nicholas of (*fl.* 1230–) Mason (*Ely, Cambs.*)

Mason (*cementarius*) to the cathedral church of *Salisbury*; was granted a messuage on the east of the cloister, 169 feet in length by 119½ feet in breadth, for a rent of two wax candles of 2 lb. weight yearly on the vigil of the Feast of the Assumption. The original grant was by Bishop Richard Poore (1217–1229) and it was confirmed by Dean William de Wanda (1220-1238); this makes it extremely probable that Ely was the designer of the cathedral, standing in the same relation to Master ELIAS DE DEREHAM as WILLIAM WYNFORD did to Bishop William of Wykeham a century and more later. It is interesting that Derham is one of the witnesses to the confirmation above mentioned, while 'Hugh, carpenter' is another.

The first work at Salisbury was the Lady Chapel, built 1220–25, followed immediately by the eastern arm and eastern transepts, finished before 1237; the great transepts and nave followed, all but the west front being complete by 1258. The design of all this is probably that of Ely.

HMC, *Var. Coll*, I, 382

ELY, Reginald or Reynold (*fl.* 1438–†1471) Mason

As the first of the four master masons responsible for the building of *King's College Chapel, Cambridge*, Reginald Ely can be claimed as one of the outstanding architects of the 15th century. During the thirty-three years of his working career for which there is documentary evidence he lived at Cambridge, but he seems to have been of Norfolk origin. In his will he made a bequest of 40s. to the building of the tower of the church at Coltishall ('Cowdesdale') in Norfolk 'to pray for the souls of me and my parents'; he also left 20s. to the building or repair of the bridge at Coltishall, 26s. 8d. to the building or repair of the bridge at Wroxham, and 6s. 8d. to the Guild of the Holy Trinity at Sloley. All three places are in the same district between seven and ten miles north-east of Norwich. It may be inferred that his parents were buried at Coltishall and that either he had been born there or had spent some of his early years in that part of Norfolk. Residence at Bungay in the north of Suffolk is suggested by a bequest of 6s. 8d. to the high altar of the parish church of St. Mary and St. Thomas in that town 'for

tithes forgotten'; he also left 15s. to the use of that church 'to pray for the souls of me and my wife', implying probably that she had died there, perhaps when he was working on the church. It is possible that he acquired a topographical surname only after he had settled at Cambridge, in which case there will have been a period of work and residence at Ely.

At Cambridge he first appears in 1438–39 working at *Peterhouse*, where he built the newel stair of the library on the west side of the mediaeval court.[1] A contract for the building of the range had been made in 1431, with a quarryman mason, JOHN WASSYNGLE. The stone stair still exists, but the building is disguised by later refacing. On 16 June 1444 a commission was issued to Reginald Ely and two others to impress masons and craftsmen for the works at King's College and to obtain all necessary materials and the carriage and freightage for them.[2] In this patent Reginald Ely is described as 'chief mason of our royal college of the blessed Mary and Saint Nicholas of Cambridge'. He retained this position until building stopped in 1461.

A fragment of a building account covering the four weeks 6 July to 3 August and referable to the year 1443 contained the name of Reginald Ely,[3] and it is probable that he had been master mason of the college since the first foundation of 1441. On 15 February of that year Henry VI had made a grant to the college of the stone of the hall of Cambridge Castle for their buildings[4] which, as at first projected, would have been confined to the area west of the Schools. By the summer of 1443 considerable progress must have been made on the building of what came to be known as the Old Court of the college, but on 10 July of that year the King granted his second charter for the vastly increased foundation which necessitated the purchase of a large area of property south of the Schools and which would have rendered obsolete the buildings under construction. The Old Court was finished off in makeshift fashion on the assumption that it would provide only temporary accommodation. It continued in use, however, until 1829 and the lower part of the unfinished gate-tower, the foundation-stone of which was laid by the King on 2 April 1441, still stands, now incorporated in university buildings. Drawings and engravings show that the Old Court in the quality of its

94

design was superior to any college building hitherto erected in Cambridge and the gate-tower was intended to be a splendid feature.[5] Its architectural detail discloses idiosyncrasies that recur in parts of the chapel built in Reginald Ely's time and also in other buildings that he is likely to have designed, and there is every reason for believing that he was the architect responsible for it.

Before work on the magnificent chapel for the new foundation could be begun the site had to be acquired and cleared. These operations took more than three years, and it was only on 25 July 1446 (St. James's Day) that the King was able to lay the foundation-stone. Even then the design cannot have been settled, for the King's 'Will and Intent' concerning his two colleges, which contains detailed specifications and measurements for their buildings, is dated 12 March 1448.[6] Doubtless, the plans as laid down were the result of joint consultations between the King, his administrative officials, and the master masons, and it is probable that the advice of ROBERT WESTERLEY, chief mason of the King's works, was obtained for the Cambridge college as well as for Eton. There is no evidence, however, that he had any direct responsibility for the buildings at King's, where Reginald Ely was undoubtedly the master mason on the spot and in all probability the architect who designed the elevations and details of the portions of the building completed in his time. There were considerable divergences from the original specification during the later stages of construction, and one departure — the decision to build side chapels between the buttresses of the choir as well as those of the antechapel — seems to have been taken while Ely was still master mason. As Willis and Clark have pointed out, the portion of the building erected during Henry VI's reign can be determined by the presence of the white magnesian limestone from Yorkshire which was not used during the later phases of construction.[7] An agreement for obtaining stone from a quarry at King's Cliffe in Northamptonshire had, however, been made in June 1460 before the works came to a halt.[8] On the evidence of the Yorkshire stone the whole of the chapel had been laid out in Ely's time, but at the west end the walls and turrets were only six to eight feet above ground while the eastern turrets had risen to a height a little above the

springing of the arch of the east window. More progress had been made with the buttresses and walls of the first two bays on the north side of the choir than on the south. The side doorways in the choir and the easternmost pair of chapels on the north (which were originally intended as a vestry) together with their lierne vault were probably designed and completed by Ely. Stylistically they show close analogies with the gate-tower of the Old Court. If the high vault had been erected in Ely's lifetime it would almost certainly have been of lierne instead of fan design.[9] Neither the great east window nor the side windows were far enough advanced for their ironwork or tracery to be inserted; it was only in 1476 that the ironwork for the large windows began to be obtained, and it is therefore doubtful whether Ely designed the tracery of any of them; the tracery of the great east window was in all probability designed by SIMON CLERK. On the other hand, the tracery of the east window of the eastern-most chapel on the north side can be assigned to Ely with confidence. It is remarkable for its curvilinear design making use of a four-lobed pattern that derives from 14th-century prototypes at Ely and in the cloister at Norwich. On a smaller scale it was used for the tracery of nearly all the side chapels but in company with a quite different pattern of Perpendicular character. Curvilinear tracery makes belated appearances in many Norfolk churches and Ely's use of it may be taken as another pointer to a Norfolk origin.

There are no building accounts for the first phase of construction of the chapel, but Reginald Ely's name occurs in other college documents. In the earliest surviving kitchen account beginning at Michaelmas 1447 'Raynold' appears as a guest in hall on several occasions and on 1 September 1448 he is specified as 'Raynold lathamus'. He was a guest several times in 1450–51 and 1455–56, and was present at the St. Nicholas Feast (December 6) and on New Year's Day in both those years.[10] On 3 February 1449 the Provost went to *Huntingdon* to inspect the reconstruction of an inn called *The Hart* belonging to the college. He took with him William Roskyn, the clerk of the works, Reginald Ely, and THOMAS STURGEON, the master carpenter, but the inn, on which over £85 was spent, seems to have been a timber-framed building.[11] William Roskyn died early in

1452, and Reginald Ely was a witness to his will, dated 20 May 1449 with a codicil of 1 September 1451.[12] By a deed dated 3 February 1456 John Teynton alias Robyns of Fairford, Glos., freemason, as heir to his uncle, John Teynton alias Robyns, clerk, released to the Provost and Scholars of the college all his right and title in the manors of Grantchester.[13] On the same day Reginald Ely and John Bartilmew, a college servant, were appointed attorneys to take seisin of the manors on behalf of the college from the Fairford freemason.[14] This meeting of two masons, one from Cambridge, the other from the West Country, albeit over a legal matter, is not without interest.

During the 1450's work on the chapel slackened owing to the uncertain supply of funds caused by the Wars of the Roses, but in 1459 a fresh effort to stimulate building operations was made by the Provost, Robert Wodelark, and on 26 February of that year a new commission was issued for impressing masons and craftsmen and obtaining all necessary materials and carriage.[15] Reynold Ely was one of those appointed to act. Between 23 April 1459 and 13 April 1461 he was entertained by the Provost on over thirty occasions, and on 17 May 1459 was present when WHETELEY, the Eton carpenter, was a guest while on a visit to the college, no doubt in some consultative capacity.[8] Wodelark's day-books of this period have survived. He was in difficulties over paying the masons and other workmen,[8] and on 4 November 1459 he borrowed £10 from Reginald Ely but was able to repay him a month later. Ely's own salary was badly in arrears. Henry VI's 'Will' had specified that the master mason at King's should receive £16 13s. 4d. a year, compared with £13 6s. 8d. for the master mason at Eton,[16] but by 1459 this figure may have been reduced. On 9 April 1460 Ely was paid £7 8s. 8d. in part payment of £27 8s. 8d. owing to him for the two previous years and he received another £8 10s. on 5 June.[8] A payment of 20s., made to his executor as late as July 1474, shows that the arrears due to him were not settled in his lifetime,[17] and it is therefore not surprising that among the numerous bequests in his will there is none to King's. On 15 April 1460 a payment of 33s. 4d. was made to him for his expenses 'riding to the quarry',[8] perhaps to arrange about the supply of stone from a quarry at King's

Cliffe, Northants., over which an agreement was made two months later.

On 10 February 1461 Reginald Ely received a general pardon, as did JOHN BROWN, who was probably warden of the masons.[18] Although the pardons were granted by Henry VI, he was at the time virtually the prisoner of the Duke of York and his party, and the two men probably thought it politic to safeguard themselves under the new government. Between 1461 and Ely's death ten years later only two further references to him have been found among the college muniments. In September 1463 he supplied a thousand 'Rede' for Grantchester, presumably for thatching there,[17] and in 1468, when the precinct wall of the college was being built along the south side adjoining St. Austin's Hostel, four 'crestes', probably coping stones, were bought from him.[19]

The building of the chapel entailed the destruction of the parish church of *St. John the Baptist*. It was rebuilt on a smaller scale close to the hall on the north side of the Old Court of the college, and it is likely that Reginald Ely was required to design the new church, which was in existence by 1453.[20] Both Clare Hall and Trinity Hall made use of the old church of St. John, and as accommodation for them could not be provided in the new church, negotiations were started for obtaining from Barnwell Priory the advowson of *St. Edward's Church* on the west side of Peas Hill. In 1446 it was transferred to Trinity Hall, and the church was greatly enlarged by the building of broad aisles on each side of the chancel, the north aisle being appropriated to Trinity Hall and the south aisle to Clare Hall.[21] The east windows of both chapels are 19th-century inventions, but the side windows, though restored, reproduce the original patterns of the tracery, which is curvilinear in character with four-lobed forms recalling the windows in the side chapels at King's but smaller in scale. The attribution of these two chapels to Reginald Ely is strengthened by the fact that he had at one time been a parishioner of St. Edward's, as he states in his will. The cost of building these aisles would not have fallen on the parish, but at some date Ely had been employed to do work by the parishioners, who at the time of his death owed him 40s., 'as appears in my compotus for the church of Saint Edward', half of which he remitted.

When he made his will in 1463, Ely was living in St. Botolph's parish, probably in a house on the north side of what is now called Silver Street some twenty or thirty yards east of Queens' Lane. A tenement in that position belonging to him is mentioned in the first charter of foundation of St. Bernard's College (3 December 1446)[22] which within eighteen months was to become *Queens' College*. Adjoining Ely's house was one belonging to Andrew Doket, the first President and virtual founder of Queens'. Ely bequeathed a house to the college, and he also left money for a chaplain fellow of Queens' to celebrate mass in the college chapel daily for a year after his decease. Doket died thirteen years after Ely, but he makes very particular mention of him in his will, in which he left instructions for the celebration of an annual obit in St. Botolph's Church on the anniversary day of Reginald Ely.[23] The inference that the two men had been closely associated during the building of the college and that Ely had been Doket's architect as master mason of the original court is borne out by stylistic resemblances between the design of the gate-tower and that of the Old Court of King's College. The Queens' court, a brick-faced building with stone dressings, was built with a strict regard for economy, but its gate-tower may be considered as a simplified version of the other translated into brick with stone dressings and less elaborate ornaments.[24] At both colleges Thomas Sturgeon was the master carpenter, and as Reginald Ely was living within a few yards of the site of the projected college and was a parishioner of the church of which Doket was rector, it would have been the natural course for Doket to engage him as master mason. The brick range facing the river on the west side of the Cloister Court was probably built during Ely's lifetime and may also have been designed by him. The first court of Queens', compact and conveniently arranged within the quadrangular frame, marks a considerable advance on any of its predecessors and it exerted a long-lasting influence on Cambridge college buildings.

In 1449 Reginald Ely was employed at *King's Hall*, the college subsequently absorbed by Trinity College, over the construction of a stone watercourse to the buttery and kitchen with a drain to the river.[25] The supply of water was probably obtained from the water pipe belonging to the Grey Friars, a section of which followed the course of King's Hall Lane. The college had been granted the right of taking water by a lead-pipe from this a few years previously. The account for 1448–49 records the purchase of a capon for 'Ruskyn' (the clerk of the works at King's College) and 'Reginald' and the expense of 22*d*. on a meal at which they and others were present.[26] In the account for the following year, in which there are payments for a new building that entailed the purchase of a considerable amount of worked stone from Barrington, Reginald Ely was entertained to dinner with Roskyn and John Brokeshaw (who was to be his executor).[27] In the section of the accounts giving figures of 'repasts' or sizings, the name 'Reginald' is entered in the three years 1448–49, 1449–50, and 1451–52. The totals of these meals, which were paid for by the college, were 6*s*. 10½*d*., 14*s*. 8½*d*., and 8*s*. 2½*d*, showing that he gave detailed supervision of whatever works were in progress.[28] Other college buildings on which Ely may have worked or been consulted were the kitchen building of Peterhouse (1449–50) at the west end of the hall, and the library built over the hall at *Pembroke College* in 1452. The windows of both buildings were of the kind used in the first court of Queens' and the Old Court of King's College. The mediaeval hall and library at Pembroke were destroyed in 1875.

The fact that Reginald Ely's will was proved before the Vice-Chancellor in the University Court shows that he was a privileged person by virtue of being an official or servant of the University, and he may therefore be presumed to have been mason of the University as JOHN BELL is known to have been in 1503. The building of the *Schools Quadrangle* was proceeding by slow stages in his time, as the Proctors' Accounts show, but as a rule they record only the lump sums handed out to those entrusted with the supervision of the works. Occasionally detailed payments made by the Proctors themselves are given, and in 1463 there are two entries probably referring to Ely — a payment of 4*d*. 'to one working with Master Raynald' and another of 5*s*. to 'Raynald'.[29] These items occur at a time when security measures were being taken after one of the University chests had been robbed and a new door was made to the vestibule leading to the chapel in the north range. But payments were also being made over the building of the south range containing a new school of civil law and a library over it. This building was begun in 1459, and as Robert Wodelark, the Provost of King's College, was appointed supervisor of it,[30] and the range actually adjoined the Old Court of the college, it is highly probable that Ely was the master mason. The contract for the structural woodwork was not signed until June 1466 (see WILLIAM HARWARD and WILLIAM BACON) and the range was finished about three years later. Only the north wall facing the court retains its mediaeval character and that has lost its window tracery so that little can be gained from stylistic comparisons. The east range seems to have been begun in 1470 or 1471,[31] but it was not completed until four or five years after Reginald Ely's death. There was a richly treated entrance doorway with schools on either side of it and a library occupying the whole of the first floor. The library was built at the sole expense of Thomas Rotherham, then Chancellor of the University and Bishop of Lincoln, but Loggan's engraving shows that the whole range between the staircase tower at its south end and the divinity school to the north was a single balanced design. When the range was pulled down in 1754, the stones of the entrance doorway were purchased by Sir John Cotton[32] and it was re-erected at Madingley Hall to the west of Cambridge, where it still remains. Comparison with Loggan's engraving shows that the archway has been widened by the insertion of an ogee at the apex of the four-centred arch. In its design and detail this gateway shows a marked resemblance to the outer arch of the gate-tower of the Old Court of King's. If it was designed by Ely, it must have been almost his last work, but it could with almost equal reason be attributed to JOHN WORLICH, who after having worked under Ely since 1443, if not earlier, would have been very familiar with his style. The Proctors' Accounts throw no light on this point.

Reginald Ely's will is dated at the beginning 14 October 1463, dated a second time at the end and witnessed 16 July 1471, and was proved before Edmund Coningsborough, the Vice-Chancellor, two days afterwards.[33] Doubtless some alterations and additions were made at or shortly before the later date. He described himself as 'of Cambridge, Mason', and desired to be buried in St. Botolph's Church on the north part 'before the image of Saint Christopher'. No children are mentioned, and his wife, who is referred to but unnamed, seems to have died many years before. He can hardly have been less than sixty years of age and may have been older. His executors were John Brokeshaw and John Melford. The former had for many years been on the administrative staff of King's College as a bailiff, collector of rents, and clerk. John Melford is mentioned as Ely's apprentice earlier in the will, evidently in the part composed in 1463. He was probably a son of Robert Melford, of St. Edward's parish, a wax-chandler, who died in 1468 and appointed Reginald Ely a supervisor of his will,[34] in which a son John is named.

Ely's will is a long one, containing many pecuniary legacies and charitable bequests, and several debts owing to him were remitted either wholly or in part. He left 40s. to the use of his parish church, St. Botolph's, to be disposed by the churchwardens. The bequests to St. Edward's Church, Cambridge, and to the church of St. Mary and St. Thomas at Bungay have already been mentioned. St. Mary's, Bungay, formed the nave of the priory church of Benedictine nuns dedicated to the Holy Cross; it was in great part rebuilt and much enlarged during the first half of the 15th century. Its fine tower, of the octagonal corner buttress type, standing at the south-west angle, is shown by bequests in wills to have been in course of erection between 1441 and 1474, but it cannot be said to disclose characteristics definitely recognisable as in Ely's style so far as it can be assessed. On the other hand, the north porch of Thaxted Church, Essex, shows marked resemblances of detail to the gate-tower of the Old Court of King's, and the fact that Ely bequeathed to the use of the parish church of 'Thakstede' in Essex his best belt of green silk bossed with silver makes it a reasonable assumption that he had worked at the church and designed this porch and perhaps also the north transept. Ely was a member of the Guild of Our Lady of Boston, to which he made a bequest of 6s. 8d. Apart from the additional evidence this gives of the wide range of his activities it suggests the possibility that he had worked on the famous 'Stump'. Even farther from Cambridge than Boston was the house of Trinitarian Friars at Thelsford in Warwickshire, on the banks of the Avon, to which Ely left 'a piece of silver without a cover called a "flatpece"'.

The will makes no mention of the church at *Burwell*, north of Cambridge, but on stylistic grounds it can be attributed to Reginald Ely with a fair degree of confidence. It can be accurately dated both by bequests in wills and by an inscription on the wall above the chancel arch which states that the wall itself and the carpentry of the nave were erected at the expense of John Benet in 1464. The whole church, apart from the tower, was rebuilt to a single homogeneous design. John Heigham, rector, who died in 1467, left directions in his will that the chancel 'newly begun' should be 'entirely built and completed' from his goods and at his proper costs.[35] A bequest of 1454 shows that the north aisle was then beginning and another of 1460 was for glazing of windows in the south aisle.[36] The window tracery of the church is remarkable for its curvilinear forms, which make use of the four-lobed pattern previously noted in the side chapels of King's College Chapel and the chapels of St. Edward's Church, Cambridge; and in the panelled work above the chancel arch there is a band of decoration displaying motives that occur also on the gate-tower of the Old Court of King's and on the north porch of Thaxted Church. There is a tradition in the village, which may well be right, that the church was built by the architect of King's College Chapel. There is also a hint that points to the same conclusion in the will of John Mason, of Sudbury and Melford, Suffolk, who died in 1509 and may have been identical with the John Melford who was one of Ely's executors. John Mason refers in his will to 'my maister, Reynold Ely', and after bequests to the churches of Melford and Lavenham there is one of 6s. 8d. to 'the church of Borwell', comparatively far away but on which perhaps he had worked under his master in earlier days.[37] In *Long Melford Church*, in the Martyn Chapel on the south side of the chancel, there are two windows with tracery quite different from that of the other windows in the church, and displaying the four-lobed pattern in their heads. The Martyn Chapel was built in 1484, but it looks as though two windows some twenty or thirty years earlier were taken down and reset, perhaps for the sake of the glass they contained. Windows with two of the patterns of tracery found at Burwell occur

in the south aisle of *Cavendish Church*, Suffolk, which was in course of erection in 1471.[38]

Besides the house in which he lived Reginald Ely had another tenement in Cambridge; he left this to Queens' College. He had lands in Barton and Comberton, to the west of Cambridge, and part of the rent of these was to be applied to the support of the three almsmen in the almshouse which he founded under his will. His executors were directed to build the almshouse in St. Clement's parish or anywhere else where a plot of land could be acquired. They obtained a site in St. Michael's parish, on the north side of Michael Lane (now Trinity Lane), at a spot a little to the east of the south-east corner of the Great Court of Trinity, where the almshouse was built between 1473 and 1476. It remained there until 1864, when it was rebuilt near St. Paul's Church.[39] In founding this almshouse Reginald Ely was probably influenced by the example of his friend, Andrew Doket, the President of Queens', who founded an almshouse for three poor women close to his college.

A.O. **OAD**

[1] WCC, I, 12, 16; [2] CPR 1441–6, 269; WCC, I, 594; [3] CKC, 11; [4] CPR 1436–41, 507; [5] WCC, I, 326, Figs. 7, 10, 11 and 12; [6] *Ibid.*, I, 368–70; [7] *Ibid.*, 486; [8] *KCM*, College Accs., vol. ii; [9] SCA, 181, Plates 36 and 37 give drawings suggesting the form a lierne vault might have taken; [10] *KCM*, Kitchen Accs., vols. i and ii; [11] *KCM*, Mundum Book, 1448–49; [12] *KCM*, Leger Book, *f.* 1; [13] DUC, I, 54; [14] *KCM*, Leger Book, *f.* 11v.; [15] CPR 1452–61, 478; [16] WCC, I, 378; [17] *KCM*, College Accs., vol. vi; [18] CPR 1452–61, 647; [19] *KCM*, Mundum Book 1467–68; [20] WCC, I, 550; [21] *Ibid.*, 80, 220, 549; III, 495–7; [22] SQC, 9; [23] *Ibid.*, 57; [24] CAS, Proceedings, XLII, 9, 10, 23, 24; [25] WCC, II, 449; [26] *TCM*, King's Hall Accs., xi, 77, 115; [27] *KHA*, xi, 131; [28] *Ibid.*, 100, 151, 205; [29] CGB, 'A', 37, 38; [30] *Ibid.*, 14; [31] WCC, III, 14 and CGB, 'A', s.a.; [32] WCC, III, 18; [33] *GCM*, Box xxi, No. 18; [34] *PCC*, 23 Godyn; [35] *Ibid.*, 20 Godyn; [36] *BW*, ii, *ff.* 231, 256v.; [37] *PCC*, 22 Bennett; [38] *BW*, ii, f.494v.; [39] WCC, II, 419

Elyas—see ELIAS

ELYE, Robert (*fl.* 1333–1334) Carpenter

Carpenter to the treasurer of *Christ Church Priory, Canterbury*, in 1333–34, when he was paid a fee of 13s. 4d., and 1s. 9d. per week.

LP, MS. 243, *ff.* 49v., 55

ELYNGHAM, Robert (*fl.* 1365–1394) Mason (*Ellingham, Norf.*)

Took up the freedom of Norwich 1365–66,[1] in which year John ELYNGHAM, mason, was also made free; in 1375 was one of several Norwich masons attached to the carpenters' guild,[2] in 1383 made the churchyard wall of

St. Peter's, and in 1387–88 supplied 62 lb. of plaster of Paris to the Norwich City treasurers for 2s. 4d.[3] In 1392–93 he was paid £2 10s. 0d. for repairs of the chancel of *Costessey Church*, Norfolk, and also 7s. for freestone. In the following year he made a cross for the gable of the chancel for £1, and was paid 13s. 10d. for the stone for the cross and gable.[4]

[1] EFN; [2] AQC, X (1897), 17; [3] HTN, II, 47, 49; [4] NRO Great Hospital, 24.c (*P.C.*)

Elys—see also ELIS, ELLIS

ELYS, William (*fl.* 1474–1475) Mason

Mason of New Sarum; in 1474–75 was working on the window of the great chapel in the outer court of *Clarendon Palace*.

PRO, E.101–460–13 (*L.F.S.*)

EMERY, Thomas (*fl.* 1446–1470) Carpenter

Carpenter to the Bishop of Winchester. In 1454 he was paid £5 6s. 8d. for making a house at task in the Soke of *Winchester*. In 1456–57 he made a new chamber for 'le Ewery' at *Highclere*, Hants., at the north end of the hall of the bishop's manor house for £4 1s. 8d., and in the same year built a new kitchen in a house in the Soke by Winchester called 'Newbrigge' for £1 6s. 8d. In 1466–67 he was working on a new house in *Wolvesey Palace, Winchester*, and was engaged on minor works there in 1469–70. Thomas Emery was living in Colebrook Street between 1446 and 1464, and worked regularly on repairing house property for *St. John's Hospital*. The accounts sometimes call him *architector*. Tax records show him as a little above the average for the city.

PRO, Eccl.2–159444, 2–2–155827, 2–3–155834, 155835; (*D.K. Win*)

EMLER, Lawrence [Ymber] (*fl.* 1492–1506) Carver

In 1492 Lawrence Emler was paid £2 for making a new statue of St. Thomas, to stand on the west side of *London Bridge*.[1] Described as a native of Swabia in 'Almain', he was granted a patent of denization on 8 January 1505/6,[2] and at this time produced an estimate for images for Henry VII's tomb at *Westminster*, to be cast in bronze from his wooden patterns.[3] Emler must have been the Master Lawrence who in 1503 carved the beautiful head of the funeral effigy of Queen Elizabeth of York, being paid 13s. 4d. jointly with 'Fredrik' his mate;[4] it has also been suggested that the existing bronze screen surrounding the tomb of Henry VII is to his design.[5]

[1] WTB, 67; [2] CPR 1494–1509, 473, 487; [3] LPH, I, pt. i, No. 307, p.141; [4] W. H. St. J. Hope in A, LX, 550–1; [5] LKC, 235

ENEMETHE, Thomas ['Euemeche'] (*fl.* 1357–   ) mason (*Emneth, Norfolk*)

Mason at *Ely Cathedral* who in 1357–58 was paid 3s. per week and also undertook task work; perhaps identical with Master THOMAS the Mason VIII.

CSR, II, 180

ENGANET, Roger [Engane] (*fl.* 1177–1216) Engineer

Probably son of AILNOTH and perhaps identical with ROGER LE ENGINNUR. He appears frequently as witness to deeds dated at Westminster between *c.* 1177 and the early years of Henry III,[1] and in 1197–98 was Praepositus of Westminster, where he had a stone house.[2] In 1193 was paid £2 for repairing the King's house at *Westminster*, in 1194 received sums totalling £9 2s. 8d. for the same purpose, and in 1199 supervised work at the *Tower of London*. In 1197 and 1201 he was concerned with lands in Westminster, with property in Battersea in 1200, and in Middlesex in 1214.

C. T. Clay in EHR, LIX (1944), 7
[1] WAM, 'Domesday', ff. 508v., 557, 568, 625, etc.; [2] Ibid., f.473; WAM, 17438

Engineer—see ENGANET; LE ENGINNUR; LENGINOUR

Enginnur, Roger le—see LE ENGINNUR

Englishman, John—see LANGLOIS

ENGLISHMAN, John the [Anglicus, Englicus] (*fl.* 1336–1341) Mason

Master mason; working at *Avignon* between 1336 and 1341 on the walls of the Papal Palace on the north side, near the cathedral of Notre-Dame-des-Doms. He was probably the Englishman who about this time was responsible, at least in part, for the tomb of Pope John XXII, who died on 4 December 1334. The detail of the tomb is distinctively of the 'Canterbury School'. Lasteyrie and others have mistakenly ascribed this tomb to Jean Lavenier of Paris quite without authority.

LPP, I, 60; II, 139; ERP, I, 614; SAK, II, 51, 252, 681

ENGLISHMAN, William [William the E.] (*fl.* 1174–†*c.* 1214) Mason

Worked under WILLIAM OF SENS on the

rebuilding of *Canterbury Cathedral* from 1174, and after Sens was injured in 1177 continued the work, which was completed in 1184.[1] It has been suggested that he was identical with the William or WALTER OF COVENTRY who was in charge of the new work at *Chichester Cathedral* from 1187 to 1199. He is described by the chronicler Gervase as 'small in body, but in workmanship of many kinds acute and honest', and it is to him rather than to William of Sens that the credit for the principal stylistic innovations at Canterbury is due,[2] for the Trinity Chapel and Corona, which were built after Sens had returned to France, are far more advanced than the choir.

It is possible that the mason of Canterbury was identical with the 'William the Englishman' who built a church at *St. Jean d'Acre* in Palestine about 1192,[3] after the recapture of the city by Richard Coeur-de-Lion in 1191. But this William is described as a chaplain of Ralph de Diceto, dean of St. Paul's.

In 1214 Canterbury Cathedral Priory received a bequest of 40*s*. under the will of William 'Anglicus' by the hands of the Abbot of *St. Radigunds*, near Dover.[4] This abbey had been founded in 1191, and may have been built by Master William. It is also not unlikely that he was identical with the William Anglicus or Le Engleis who was taking 9*d*. a day in the King's service in 1214, apparently as a carpenter or engineer. On 28 November 1214, 25*s*. for the Michaelmas quarter of William's annual pension of £5 was paid to his wife, probably an indication of his illness or death. By 1218 this pension had been granted to THOMAS the Carpenter.[5]

(APD;BAA; WDC)

[1] GCC; SHB, 373; [2] A, XLIII, 73 ff.; [3] APD; PCH, II, 360–1; [4] HDC, 20; [5] HLC, I, 178–9

'Enterpas', John—see EUTERPACH

ERCALO, Richard [Erkaloo] (*fl.* 1361–1377) Carpenter (? *High* or *Childs Ercall, Salop*)

Was granted the office of chief carpenter of Chester and Flint in succession to NICHOLAS DE ECCLESTON on 21 October 1361, and held the post until 1374, when he was succeeded by WILLIAM DE NEWHALL. Ercalo is referred to on one occasion as William, but this seems to have been a scribal error.

HCH, 94–6

Erkaloo—see ERCALO

ERNALD the Mason († *c*. 1180) Mason

Mason of Lincoln, apparently master at *Lincoln Cathedral*. His tenement in the Bail was sold by his widow, 'Lady Lecia', to Richard of Kyme, one of the canons, between *c*. 1180 and 1186. His son Andrew later appears as a witness.

LRS, LXII, Reg. Ant. ix, nos. 2605, 2648 (*K.M.*)

ESSEX, John [Herd] (*fl.* 1447–1454) Marbler

Marbler of London in 1447 concerned in the acquisition of a tenement in the parish of All Hallows London Wall;[1] was living in St. Paul's Churchyard, London, in 1454, when he was sent for to attend King Henry VI at *Westminster*, where the King proposed to have his tomb prepared. The position of the intended tomb had been marked out in the abbey by JOHN THIRSK the abbey mason (who had died in 1452), and Essex, with Thomas Stephens, coppersmith of Gutter Lane, went to Westminster, where they 'bargained with the king for his tomb and received 40*s*. on account', according to a later deposition by Thomas Fifelde, who had been Essex's apprentice at the time, and had been given a groat from the earnest money on the following day, when the two craftsmen were discussing the matter in Essex's house. The tomb was not actually made, on account of the civil confusion which so soon followed.

Essex and Stephens in 1454 contracted to make a part of the tomb of Richard Beauchamp, Earl of Warwick, with William Austen, founder. Essex had probably supplied the design for the marble tomb itself, which was made by John Borde, marbler of Corfe Castle in Dorset, between 1449 and 1457. The tomb definitely belongs to the 'London School' of design, and the *Beauchamp Chapel* in *St. Mary's, Warwick*, is itself in a style as much related to that of London as to the local work in Warwickshire. Essex may even have had a hand in the design of decorative parts of the chapel, though the master mason was probably THOMAS KERVER of Warwick. In the little chantry chapel on the north side of the Beauchamp Chapel itself, is a fan-vault of exquisite design, with pendant conoids: this vault appears to be the prototype of that of Henry VII's Chapel at Westminster.

The documents relating to Essex's contract with Henry VI give his name as 'John Essex alias Herd'.

(LKC, 209); DHW; BAS, LIII
[1] *LHR*, 176(24)

ESSHYNG, Thomas (*fl.* 1363–1368) Mason

Of Betchworth, Surrey (Bechesworthe); in 1363 contracted with Sir William de Echyngham to make 5 windows each of 3 lights for the church of *Etchingham*, Sussex. Esshyng sued Sir William in a plea of contract in 1368, but the actual windows in the church are of 2 lights.

PRO, De Banco Roll, Hil. 42 E.III, 174 d. (*L.F.S.*)

Este—see EAST

ESTINTON, Stephen de (*fl.* 1223–1224) Carpenter (? *Eastington, Dorset*)

Master carpenter engaged on repairs to the hall of *Sherborne Castle*, Dorset, in 1223–4.

HLC, I, 528b, 532b

Estow—see EASTAWE

EUDO the Carpenter (*fl. c.* 1280) Carpenter

Master carpenter; witness to a deed at Westminster.

WAM, 17510

'Euemeche'—see ENEMETHE

EUTERPACH, John [Euterpas] (*fl. c.* 1440) ? Mason (? *Waterbeach, Cambs.*)

The building of the hall of *South Wingfield Manor*, Derbyshire, for Ralph, Lord Cromwell, was begun about 1440 under a contract made with one John Euterpach or Euterpas, but the actual work was done by RICHARD NORTH, and finished by about 1443–44. The position of Euterpach in relation to the work has been described as 'architect',[1] but is not defined in the surviving account.[2]

[1] MNE, 94; [2] KAO, U 1475 M 207, by kind permission of Viscount De L'Isle, V.C., K.G.

EVERARD, John [alias Abbot, Everhard] (*fl.* 1429–1475) Mason

John Everard, alias Abbote, mason, was admitted to the freedom of Norwich in 1429–30;[1] in 1440 he was a warden of the Norwich Masons' Guild, with JOHN DYNCOK.[2] He was paid £4 in 1440 for whitewashing in the cathedral church and 13s. 4d. for making the jambs of a gateway to the Preaching Yard, apparently to the design of JAMES WODEROFE;[3] on 13 March 1441 he was arrested in the church of St. Martin and bound over to keep the peace towards Elizabeth Botry.[4] He completed the whitewashing of the cathedral in 1442 for £3 6s. 8d.[5]

From 1437 to 1444 and again from 1452 until 1475, Everard was constantly engaged on minor repairs and works in the church, and on the monastic buildings and properties.[6] Hardly any of his work seems to have been of much significance, with the possible exception of the repair of two panels in the vaults next to the Bishop's Oratory in 1465–66,[7] and mending the walls of the presbytery and Lady Chapel in 1468–69.[8] It seems probable that he always worked under the direction of another, JAMES WODEROFE until 1451 and ROBERT EVERARD after that date. In 1438–39 and 1447–48 John Everard also worked for the Great Hospital of Norwich.[9] His apprentices Robert Brygge and James Broun became free of Norwich in 1453–54.[10]

Everard appears in the Norwich muster of *c.* 1457 as living 'over the water' (*ultra aquam*)[11] and in 1461–62 John Everard, mason and citizen of Norwich, and Margaret his wife conveyed to Robert Everard, freemason, and others, properties in All Saints de Fibriggate in Cowgate, Norwich.[12] In 1471–72 he is described as John Everard the elder when engaged on repairing and white-washing the north aisle of the cathedral nave, for which he was paid £1 1s. 8d.[13] He last appears in 1475, working at Bawburgh for the Sacrist.[14]

[1] EFN, 49; [2] AQC, xv (1902), 202; [3] HBN, 110n.; SNN, 187; [4] HTN, I, 327; [5] HBN, 110n.; [6] NCM, Sacrist's rolls 285–304; Communar's rolls 1082–95, Camera rolls 84–92; [7] SNN, 43; NCM, roll 299; [8] NCM, roll 300; [9] NMR, G.24.a., Great Hospital account rolls; [10] EFN; [11] HTN, I, 410; [12] NMR, Deeds roll 19A, m.4 (*A.O.*); [13] HBN, 110n.; NCM, roll 302; [14] NCM, roll 304

EVERARD, Robert [alias Abbot, Everhard] (*fl.* 1440–1485) Mason

Robert Everard, alias Abbot, mason, took up the freedom of Norwich in 1440–41.[1] In the same year he worked for the Almoner of *Norwich Cathedral Priory*, being paid £7 11s. 11½d. for the work he and his servants did on three tenements in the parish of St. Peter Hungate, Norwich.[2] In 1449–50, with Margery his wife, he conveyed property in Great Hautbois to Nicholas, prior of Horsham St. Faith and others.[2] He appears working for *Norwich Cathedral* in 1452–53, when he was paid £4 for freestone and the making of a new doorway to the Exchequer of the Great Cellar.[3] In the previous year JAMES WODEROFE had made his last appearance as master mason to the cathedral, and it seems probable that Robert Everard took his place. By the Infirmarer Everard was paid 12s. 8d. for repairing a window on the south side of the chancel of *St. Gregory's Church, Norwich*, in 1453–54.[5] In the next year he was employed by the Great Hospital to make a new east window for the chancel at *Repps*, for which he was paid £2, as well as £1 12s. 4d. for building buttresses there, and 7s. for roughcasting and limewashing the chancel walls.[6]

With John Everard, Robert was paid £1 2s. 0d. for repairs to the presbytery in 1457–58,[4] and was carrying out minor works in 1459–60.[5] In 1461–62 Robert was paid 17s. 4d. for works about the cathedral church.[6]

Robert Everard, like his predecessors, worked not only on the cathedral, but at other churches belonging to the priory. In 1456–57 he was paid £13 6s. 8d., part of a total of 100 marks (£66 13s. 4d.) for rebuilding the chancel at *Martham Church*, Norfolk; the work was not finished until 1469, and was regrettably demolished to give place to a new chancel of 1855–61.[10] He was again employed by the Great Hospital in 1458–59 when he was paid 12s. for choosing freestone for the chancel at *Hardley*, Norfolk, rebuilt in 1458–62. The stone was worked in Norwich, which rather suggests that Everard was responsible for design. The work survives.[11]

In 1466 Robert Everard was paid 10s. for the carriage of timber needed for the cathedral works,[7] in 1468–69 he made a new west window of the northern 'vault' (? nave aisle triforium) for 6s. 8d.[8] and next year was mending 'Lady Harcourt's window'.[9] In 1463 the central tower had been struck by lightning, and much damage done to the nave by fire. The nave was provided with a stone vault, *c.* 1463–72, and a stone spire was built. The bells were recast *c.* 1469. No record of these works appear in the cathedral accounts, and they were evidently paid for from the Bishop's purse or outside funds, but an indication of work in connection with them is given by the payment recorded in the Sacrist's roll for 1471–72 of £3 13s. 4d. to Robert Everard for finishing off two columns of the bell-tower by task (*pro consummacione ij columnarum campanilis in grosso*).[10] In 1474–75 Everard received 18s. 4d. for work on the altar of the Lady Chapel and elsewhere.[11]

That Robert Everard was the architect of the stone spire seems to be confirmed by a memorandum in William Worcestre's notebook (the so-called Itinerary), in connection with Worcestre's discussion of architectural problems and nomenclature with the Bristol freemasons, JOHN NORTON and BENEDICT CROSSE: 'to inquire of Robert Everard of Norwich

"How many inches doth the spere of Trinite chyrch of Norwich bater yn. vj. feete."[12] This note was made during Worcestre's survey of Bristol in 1478–80.

In 1481–82 Robert Abbot, alias Robert Everard of Norwich, mason, Margery his wife, and Robert Brampton conveyed a tenement in the parish of St. Martin, before the Palace Gates, Norwich, to a number of persons including William King, rector of Badingham. In the next year Everard was defendant in a Chancery suit brought by William son of Walter Fornefeld, concerning a messuage in Norwich,[13] and he is last mentioned in the cathedral rolls when in 1484–85 he received a robe of the Sacrist's household livery, price 6s. 8d.,[14] together with JOHN ANTELL, who was probably his assistant and perhaps his successor as cathedral mason. At this time Everard and Antell were both cutting windows and doorways for the new building at the Cathedral hostry.[20] In 1465–66 Everard had taken a lease from the cathedral priory of a parcel of meadow and paid 6s. 8d. yearly rent until 1483–84 (the Gardener's roll of 1484–85 being missing).[21]

The design of the Perpendicular vaults is an extremely fine one: indeed, the Norwich examples must be regarded as the supreme triumph of the lierne School. The pattern is satisfying, and demonstrates its essential structure, unlike some of the later vaults. The transition from Norman walls and piers to the later roof is well managed, and the rising cross-ridges greatly add to the apparent height. The spire, though of lesser inspiration, is well detailed, and has a delicate entasis; its buttressed bottom stage groups well with the pinnacles added to the Norman tower. In proportion, the spire seems too small for the tower, but this was doubtless a structural necessity, especially in view of the fires and storms from which the steeple had already suffered.

[1] EFN; [2] *NRO*, DCN, Almoner No. 544 (*P.C.*); [3] RNF, pt. ii, 28 Hen. VI, No. 238; [4] *NCM*, roll 88; [5] *NRO*, DCN, roll 982 (*P.C.*); [6] *NRO*, Great Hospital 24f, 24g; (*P.C.*); [7] *NCM*, roll 295; [8] *Ibid.*, roll 296; [9] *Ibid.*, roll 297; [10] *NRO*, DCN, Cellarer 172–77 (*S.A.C.*; *P.C.*); [11] *Ibid.*, Great Hospital 24e (*P.C.*); [12] SNN, 43; [13] *NCM*, 300; SNN, 43; [14] *NCM*, roll 301; [15] *Ibid.*, roll 302; [16] Ibid., roll 304; [17] *Corpus Christi College Cambridge*, MS. 210, p. 130; cf. WWI, 367; [18] *NMR*, Deeds, roll 19K, m.3; *PRO*, *ECP*, Bundle 62, No. 91 (*A.O.*); [19] *NCM*, roll 308; [20] *Ibid.*, Almoner No. 577 (*P.C.*); [21] *NRO*, DCN, rolls 1017–1019

103

EVERSOLT, Gilbert de [Eversold] *(fl. c. 1200–)* Monk

Benedictine monk; was in charge of the works of St. Albans Abbey *c.* 1200, after the unsuccessful start on the west front made by HUGH DE GOLDCLIFF. No serious progress was made under Eversolt, and it may be doubted whether he had any technical knowledge.

(BAA); RGA, I, 219

EVESHAM, Henry of *(fl. c. 1300–†1319)* Mason

Also called Henry Lathom (*Lathomus*); was the master mason of *Evesham Abbey* from about 1300 until his death in 1319. He built the Chapter House, which was a ten-sided building over 50 feet across; only the entrance archway of the vestibule now survives. He also built the dormitory, refectory, abbot's hall, and kitchen, all now completely gone.

(APD; BAA); LC, I, 249

EVESHAM, John of *(fl. 1359–)* Mason

Mason of Worcestershire; was appointed master mason of *Hereford Cathedral* on 9 April 1359; he was to work upon the fabric of the cathedral and the chancels of churches belonging to the Chapter (*refeccionem sive emendacionem concernentibus ecclesie antedicte sive cancellorum pertinencium ad ecclesiam antedictam*) during the rest of his active life, instructing the labourers under him in the arts of masonry and carpentry. He was to live in Hereford, and not to work elsewhere without the leave of the Dean and Chapter. His remuneration would be 3s. a week for his life and a white loaf daily, and a house was to be let to him at 10s. a year; should he be absent from work through illness, he was to receive full pay for not more than two weeks, and thereafter only 1s. a week. Evesham was perhaps designer of the works done by THOMAS OF CAMBRIDGE.

SHB, 587–8; CCH, 230–1

EYE, Robert de *(fl. 1300–1301)* Carpenter

Master Robert de Eye, carpenter, was in 1300–01 paid 25 marks (£16 13s. 4d.) for finding timber and making the chapel of St. Louis in the church of the *Greyfriars, London*.

EHR, LVI (1941), 447–550

Eynho—see AYNHO

EYNSHAM, Henry de [Aynsham, Aynesham, Einisham, Eynesham] *(fl. 1301–1343)* Mason (*Eynsham, Oxon.*)

Henry de Aynsham, 'maceoun' petitioned Parliament in 1303 for £19 5s. 0¼d. owing to him from the time when he was employed on the King's works in *Carnarvon Castle*.[1] This implies a substantial period going back before February 1301, and probably a fairly high rate of pay. The claim was at once allowed. It is extremely likely that Eynsham was the Master Henry le Mason put in charge of important repairs at *Clarendon Palace* in 1316–17 (see HENRY the Mason II). What seems certain is that he was the Master Henry de Eynesham, 'machon', who in 1322 granted an extensive estate to the Prior and Convent of Monk Bretton, Yorks., for his soul and those of his ancestors and benefactors.[2] The property comprised four messuages, a watermill, a large area of land and nearly £6 in yearly rents near the priory and in Bolton upon Dearne, Billingley and Worsborough.

It is possibly significant that Monk Bretton Priory was subordinate to that of Pontefract, and lay in the Honor of Pontefract, for Master Henry de Eynesham next appears as in charge of building a great tower at *Pontefract Castle*, from 6 February 1323 until 1326 or later. The cost of works amounted to nearly £500, and Master Henry received fees of £10 a year as well as £2 10s. 0d. for his robes.[3] By 1328 Master Henry de Einisham, 'machun' or *cementarius*, was at Spalding, Lincolnshire, and in the next three years was acquiring properties there and at Pinchbeck which he granted to *Spalding Priory*, presumably in exchange for a corrody in the house by way of pension.[4] He was no doubt in charge of works at the priory, and seems to have stayed there for the rest of his life, as in 1343 Henry de Eynsham, *cementarius*, was licensed by the Bishop of Lincoln to hear divine service in any place within his chamber in Spalding Priory (*infra cameram suam in prioratu de Spaldyng*).[5] By this time he was no doubt aged and infirm.

The career of Master Henry is of considerable interest as that of a 'freelance' architect obtaining work within the civil service and outside it, and concerned with military, probably civil, and ecclesiastical buildings. He may well have trained on the works of the Benedictine abbey at Eynsham, Oxfordshire, and as a young man already of some distinction have been pressed into the king's service for Edward I's campaign of works at Carnarvon begun in 1295–6. The evidence of the Spalding cartulary in particular is important in showing that the same man might commonly be referred to in legal documents by his surname and occupation, yet on other occasions by his Christian name and occupation only.

[1] RP, I, 164b; [2] YRS, CVII, 121; CPR 1321–4, 206–7; BL, Stowe Ch. 434; [3] CMA 1326–7, 2167 (a xxxvi); HKW, II, 782; [4] BL, Add. MS. 35296, ff. 159–65 (N.L.R.); CPR 1327–30, 369; 1330–4, 100; [5] LAO, Episcopal Register 7, f. 165v (D.M.W.)

EYTON, Nicholas de [Eton] (fl. c. 1270–1275) Mason

'Cementarius', appears as the sixth of eleven witnesses to a grant by THOMAS LE WALEYS to Lichfield Cathedral. He was probably related to WILLIAM DE EYTON.

LRA, 265

EYTON, William de [Eiton, Eton] (fl. 1322–1336) Mason

Master mason (cementarius) of Lichfield Cathedral; on 13 February 1321/2, with his seven masons, took an oath to aid the Chapter of Lichfield in the defence of the Close.[1] In 1327 he was assessed at 1s. 6d. to the lay subsidy, and in 1332 at 3s. 4d.;[2] on 25 October 1336 an agreement was made by the Chaplain of St. Mary's altar in the cathedral whereby Master William was to receive a yearly rent of 18d. which had been assigned to the fabric by THOMAS LE WALEYS.[3] He was probably dead before 23 May 1337, when WILLIAM DE RAMSEY III was appointed master.

Eyton's work consisted of the Lady Chapel (probably designed c. 1310) with its vault and the eastern bays of the aisle walls of the presbytery.

[1] Bodl., MS. Ashmole 794, f. 2v; [2] WSS, VII, 236; X, 83; [3] Bodl., MS. Ashmole 794, f. 56

FAGAN, Robert (fl. 1391–c. 1414) Mason

On 25 October 1391 contracted to build the bell-tower of St. Asaph Cathedral, Flintshire, to be finished by All Saints, 1392 for 100 marks (£66 13s. 4d.); Fagan's work was to contain 5 yards or rods (virgae), as well as 1½ virgae of battlement; the upper part of this tower was blown down in 1714 and rebuilt.[1]

On 18 June 1396 Fagan was granted the office of master mason of the county of Chester and North Wales, in succession to WILLIAM HELPESTON. He received a commission on 11 April 1398 to take workmen for the repair of North Wales castles, and his sphere of activity was said to include Chester, Flint, and North Wales, the last including the modern counties of Anglesey, Carnarvon, and Merioneth. A further writ of aid was issued on his behalf on 18 April 1399.[2]

As Fagan's grant was for life, it is probable that his death took place in 1414, when he was succeeded by THOMAS DE HOLDEN.[3]

[1] SHB, 470; RCAM, Flints., 86; [2] DKR, XXXI; CPR 1396–9, 552; [3] DKR, XXXI

FAGION, Antonio (fl. 1538)

Antonio Fagion, Sicilian, received a reward of £10 'for making of certain devices of bulwarke and blockhouses and other devices' and 'for his long waiting and offering of his said service', recorded in the King's Book of Payments in March 1538.

LPH, XIII pt. ii, 1280, f. 7 (A.O.)

Fairchild, Fayerchild—see NICHOLAS the Mason III

Fakenham, Robert—see FEKENHAM

FAMBELER, Giles (fl. 1532–   ) Carver

Was employed at Queens' College, Cambridge, in 1532 to carve panelling for the hall.[1] The carved heads, coats of arms, and early Renaissance detail were the work of DYRIK HARRISON, Giles Fambeler and Lambert, all of whom were probably Flemings. Much of this panelling, removed from the hall in the 18th century, is now in the study in the President's Lodge. [Possibly identical with Giles Van Beller or Vanbellaer, tried at York for heresy in 1534.[2]]

A.O.
[1] WCC, II, 45, 61–66; [2] BIY Archbishop Lee's Register (J.S.P.)

Fant—see also FAUNTE

FANT, Thomas [Flant, Frant] (fl. 1366–†1383) Carpenter

In 1366 supplied 1,000 heart-laths from Croydon for the works of Westminster Palace.[1] Second sworn carpenter of London, with RICHARD SHROPSHIRE, on 13 January 1369/70, when the two men, with the sworn masons of the city, RICHARD ATTE CHERCHE and THOMAS ATTE BARNET reported as to the dimensions of a tenement near Holborn Bridge. On 17 February 1370/1 these four masters successfully petitioned to be excused from paying taxes and subsidies, as their predecessors in office for one hundred years had been. Thomas Fant was again sworn as carpenter on 26 October 1375, and was dead by 9 October 1383, when William Dudecote, carpenter, was sworn in his place.[2] He was, no doubt, the Thomas Fant of London, carpenter, who with Simon Mannynge of

Cudham, Kent, bought all the trees in a wood at Farley, Surrey, from Merton College, Oxford, on 27 January 1376/7.[3]

[1] BBW, 190; [2] CLB, 'G', 257, 279; 'H', 13, 216; [3] MRT, Surrey Deeds, 625

FARELE, William (*fl.* 1392–) Mason

Of Dunstable; with PHILIP LESSY undertook, on 1 November 1392, to build the tower of *Houghton Conquest Church* within three years. They were to receive 10*s.* a foot for the foundations, 13*s.* 4*d.* a foot from the ground up, and 6 quarters of corn.

Deed in Sale Catalogue of H. T. Wake, Derby, 1882 (*R.H.G.*)

FARLEIGH, Richard of [Farlegh, ? of Reading] (*fl.* 1332–1365) Mason (? *Monkton Farleigh, Wilts.*)

Possibly identical with the Master Richard of Reading who in 1332 was paid £3 6*s.* 8*d.* for carving images for the gable of *St. Stephen's Chapel, Westminster.*[1] Master Richard of Farleigh was in charge of work at *Reading*, and also at *Bath*, before July 1334, when he was appointed by the Dean and Chapter of *Salisbury* to be master mason of the *Cathedral* taking 6*d.* a day, with the reversion to the pension of the Keeper of the Fabric of 10 marks (£6 13*s.* 4*d.*) a year if he should survive 'Robert the Builder' (see ROBERT THE MASON, VII). The contract of employment stipulated that he should not neglect or delay the works notwithstanding his prior obligations at Bath and Reading.[2] On 30 April 1335 he was granted the reversion of a corrody by Bath Cathedral Priory.[3] At Salisbury his work must have been the great tower and spire; he is thought, on stylistic grounds, to have designed the tower of *Pershore Abbey*, Worcs., which closely resembles that of Salisbury.[4] He is also referred to as Richard Davy of Farleigh, and it is probable that he came from Monkton Farleigh, close to the Somerset border; Farleigh is near to Bath Abbey, on whose works he may have been trained.

Preparations for the construction of the upper part of the tower at Salisbury had begun about 1320, and Farleigh's appointment probably marks the start of actual work. The spire was not completed until well into the second half of the 14th century, but the design of tower and spire forms a perfect unity, and must have been the conception of one man, probably ROBERT the Mason VII.

In 1352–53 'Master Richard Farleigh' was master of work at *Exeter Cathedral*, taking 3*s.* a week while at Exeter, and receiving a reward of 20*s.* from the Chapter.[5] He had apparently succeeded WILLIAM JOY. Farleigh may also have provided a design for St. Anne's Gate and Chapel on the east side of the Close at Salisbury, built by the Chapter *c.* 1350–54.[6]

In 1360, and again in 1363, fines are recorded whereby Richard de Farleygh, mason, and Margaret his wife acknowledged the right of John de Mershton to 6 messuages, 16 acres of land, and 3 acres of meadow in Keynsham, Somerset, on payment to them by John of 20 marks of silver.[7] In 1364–65 there was an action in the Court of Common Pleas by Henry de Forde against Richard de Farlegh and Margaret his wife for recovery of a toft in Bath.[8]

(APD)

[1] SAW, 201; [2] DSC, 151n.; VCH, *Berkshire*, II, 66; [3] SRS, VII, 171; [4] F. B. Andrews in BAS, LVII, 9–10; [5] *CEF (M.E.C.)*; AEC, ii, 290; [6] CPL 1342–62, 538; [7] SRS, XVII (1902), 46; [8] SRS LXXII, 302/6

FARNHAM, Richard de [Farinham] (*fl.* 1242–1247) ? Mason

Perhaps master mason of the chapel of the Nine Altars (eastern transept) at *Durham Cathedral*, begun at Michaelmas 1242 and not finished until after 1254; the design has also been attributed to ELIAS DE DEREHAM. In a contemporary deed in which Farnham's name appears as a witness he is described as 'architect of the new fabric of Durham' (*Magister Ricardus de Farinham tunc architector nove fabrice Dunelm*).[1] He was also a witness to a deed of 1247 between the bishop and the prior concerning the advowson of Waldenwton Church (Newton-le-Wold, Lincs.).[2] The interpretation of 'architector' is doubtful: 'carpenter' is a possible meaning, but the word was probably used as equivalent to '*ingeniator*' and implied general responsibility for the works.[3] Master Richard was perhaps related to Nicholas de Farnham, bishop of Durham at the time.

[1] GDC, 48; cf. VCH, *Durham*, III, 95; [2] DST, lxxvii; [3] cf. MDR, II, 237

FAUDY, John (*fl.* 1398–1400) Carpenter

Of Salle, Norfolk; on 10 May 1398 entered into a contract with Sir Edmund de Thorpe to make the roofs for the nave and north chapel of *Ashwellthorpe Church*, Norfolk, within two years for 17½ marks (£11 13*s.* 4*d.*)

BHN, 149; *NRO*, Frere MSS., Hundred of Depwade (*S.A.C.; P.C.*)

FAUNTE, Thomas [Fant(e), Fantt, Forard,

Forente] (*fl.* 1524–†1550) Mason

Was a working mason at *Westminster Abbey* for 25 weeks in 1524 and thereafter continuously until midsummer 1529, taking 3*s.* 4*d.* a week as well as additional 'setting money' on occasion. In the four years from Michaelmas 1525 he was also given a robe worth 10*s.*[1] In 1531–32 was first warden of the masons on the works of the *New Palace* at *Westminster*, being paid 8*d.* a day.[2] He may have been the Thomas 'Forard' who in 1538 rode to Glos., Wilts., and Herefs. for 30 days to impress masons for *Nonsuch Palace*,[3] and who was working at Nonsuch at 3*s.* 4*d.* a week.[4] His will, dated 3 September and proved 15 September 1550, asked for burial in the churchyard of St. Margaret, Westminster.[5]

[1] *J.H.H.* in AJ, CXIII, 1957, 97; [2] *PRO*, E.36–251; [3] WKM; [4] *PRO*, E.101–477–12 (*G.P.J.*); [5] W. J. Williams in MR, XVI, 205

FAWLEY, — (*fl. c.* 1380–) Mason

Master mason for the chapel of *St. Mary's College* at *St. Davids*, Pembrokeshire; the chapel stands over a vaulted basement, and is a fine piece of early Perpendicular work. The college was founded in 1377 by John of Gaunt, Duke of Lancaster, and Bishop Adam Houghton.

(*R.D.*) WSD, 50

Fayerchild, Nicholas—see NICHOLAS the Mason III

FAYREBOWE, John (*fl.* 1444–) Carpenter

Carpenter of Busshopestrowe (Bishopstrow, Wilts.); contracted on 16 December 1444 to make a frame building at the '*Blue Boar*' in *Salisbury*, within eight months at a cost of £20.

SHB, 516–17; WTM, XV, 330

FAYTH, Richard (*fl.* 1375–1376) Carpenter

Master; in 1375–76 was paid by the dean and chapter of Lincoln for going to *Harrington* ('Haryngton'), Lincs., to survey defects of the chapel there.

LAO, LDC, Bj.5.2, *f.* 19

FEKENHAM, John (*fl.* 1419–1423) Mason

In 1419 undertook repairs at *Roxburgh Castle* after the siege of 1417. In 1423 he was a commissioner for repairs at *Berwick*.

HKW, II, 821

FEKENHAM, Robert [Fakenham] (*fl.* 1422) Mason

In 1422 Thomas Langley, Bishop of Durham, gave instructions to Sir Robert de Ogle, Governor of *Norham Castle*, to build a new tower there. Robert Fekenham, mason, was paid £22, and Robert Skirwent, 'quawrreour', and his associates received £20 16*s.* 0*d.* for winning stone in the quarry for the works.

JNC, 178 (*A.O.*)

FELS, William (*fl.* 1535–) Mason

Was chief mason of *Lincoln Cathedral* in September 1535, but then resigned, and was succeeded later in the month by WILLIAM KITCHIN. His fee was 13*s.* 4*d.* a year.

LRS, XIII, 181

FELSTEDE, Richard de (*fl.* 1322–1347) Carpenter (*Felsted, Essex*)

Carpenter of London, sent to the king at York in 1322; he worked at *Hanley Castle*, Worcs., from 1322 to 1326, by which time he had succeeded ROBERT DE GLASHAM as master of the king's works there. On 8 December 1337 took a 20 years' lease from the city of the gate of Aldersgate, with a parcel of land in the west and a garden on the east, by rent of £1 6*s.* 8*d.* a year.[1] With PHILIP DE CHERCHE, mason, contracted on 29 December 1342 to build a tavern in *Paternoster Row, London*.[2] Felstede's work comprised a timber-framed house of two storeys, each jettied, and attics, with two gables towards the street, built above the stone cellar and ground storey to be supplied by Cherche. The timber was to be supplied by the owner, Felstede receiving £24 for workmanship and 20*s.* for a gown. On 16 October 1347 an agreement was made between the chief officers of Henry, Earl of Lancaster and Master Richard de Felstede, citizen and carpenter of London, to make roofs for the hall, pantry, buttery, and kitchen of *Kenilworth Castle*, as soon as the masonry should be ready, for 250 marks (£166 13*s.* 4*d.*).[3] He was also to have a robe of the earl's gentlemen (*gentils hommes*).

[1] HKW, I, 180; II, 668–9; CLB, 'F', 18; [2] SHB, 433–4; (*LBH*, G.16, 17); [3] SHB, 436–7; (*PRO*, D.L. 42–11); cf. VCH, *Warwicks.*, VI, 135

FELSTEDE, William de (*fl.* 1252) Carpenter

Master carpenter of the works at *Havering*, Essex, in 1252, along with RICHARD DE WAUD.

CLR 1251–60, 44

FERRIER, Thomas [Ferrar, Ferrour] (*fl.* 1459–1485) Mason

Appointed master mason of the works at

Calais on 30 August 1460 but had held office since 1 September 1459;[1] he was succeeded by RICHARD COMBES in 1486.[2] A Thomas Feroure, who had been a scholar at Oxford, became a yeoman mason by 1439.[3]

[1] DKR, XLVIII, 443; [2] HKW, III, 419; [3] BRUO, II, 680

FETHURSTONE, William [Fedderston, Fedurstone, Fetherston] (*fl. c.* 1447–1471) Carpenter

Carpenter of the new *Divinity School, Oxford*; ordered to be paid £3 2s. 1d. in 1452 for his bill for work done *c.* 1447–49.[1] Fethurstone worked for *All Souls College* in 1450–51 and about that time was a warden of St. Peter's-in-the-East. With his wife Emmota he was concerned in various court cases, and was later connected with *Queen's College* from 1468 to 1471.

GOC
[1] OMA, II, 735

FIFEDE, John de (*fl.* 1320–1321) Mason (*Fyfield, Essex*)

Mason (*cimentarius*) of Maldon, Essex, summoned in 1320 to *Hadleigh Castle* to assist in the survey made by the engineer ROBERT DE GLASHAM. He may have been 'the mason of Maldon' who built a chamber above the castle gate in 1311–12.

HKW, II, 661

FILL, Robert [Fills, Fylle] (*fl.* 1479–1503) Carver

On 3 November 1479 Robert Fill of London, 'Kervor', witnessed the will of another London carver, John Elys.[1] With JOHN BROWN, carver, contracted to make an altar table for the monastery of *Syon* at a date probably between 1493 and 1500. He was paid sums of 100s., 100s. and £8 by Henry VII in 1502–3 for making two tabernacles for *Richmond* parish church. In the first two entries the name is given as 'Sill' and 'Sills' by Craven Ord in transcribing, no doubt incorrectly. His reading for the third entry is Fylle.[2]

[1] GUL, CCL, Wilde 279; [2] BL., Add. MS. 7099, ff. 75, 81 (*A.O.*)

FILLES, John (*fl.* 1477–1478) Carver

Named second to ROBERT ELIS in 1477–78, when the two men were paid £40 for making six tabernacles for the choir of *St. George's Chapel, Windsor*.

PRO, E.101–496–17 (*L.F.S.*)

FILYON, Thomas (*fl.* 1513) Mason

Thomas Filyon was appointed master mason of *Pontefract Castle* under the Duchy of Lancaster on 9 March 1513.

HKW, III, 178n.[6]

FISHER, John [Fysher] (*fl.* 1486–1504) Joiner and Carver

Citizen and joiner of London; on 11 August 1486 contracted to make a roodloft for *Merton College, Oxford*, modelled on those of Magdalen College Chapel and of the church of St. Mildred, Poultry, London. He was also to make statues for it, each 11 feet high, of characters to be decided by the Warden. This roodloft has been destroyed; the college was to pay Fisher £27 and find meat and drink for him and two or three servants while he was there. Fisher carried out minor works at Merton in 1489–90, 1494–5, and in 1503 altered the roof of the library there for 5 marks (£3 6s. 8d.); in 1504 he was again working there with his son. He also worked for *Magdalen College*, where in 1490–92 he made an oratory for the President over the south walk of the cloister, and in 1502–03 made new cupboards for the hall and worked at *Horsepath*.

GOC; (HCM, 210; AJ, II, 181; Reg. Coll. Merton, 520)

FISHER, William [Fyssher] (*fl.* 1447) Carpenter

Of Downton, Wilts., on 26 May 1447 entered into a bond in 10 marks with the Warden of Winchester College.

WCM 20009A

FitzDalber—see MOYSES, Thomas

FITZGAMEL, Alan (*fl.* 1260–1261) Mason

Master mason (*cementarius*) in charge of works done for the town of *Shrewsbury* in 1260–61, on the wall at Gatepol, and the tower beneath the castle. JOHN GYMEL carried out much of the work by contract.

HMC, 15R, x, 25–6; SC, Bailiffs' Acc., No. 308

FITZGILES, Robert (*fl.* 1327–1335) Carpenter

Was admitted to the freedom of York in 1327, and on 22 June 1335 contracted with the parishioners of St. Martin, Coney Street in *York* to build a timber-framed range of houses on the north side of the church, and fronting to Coney Street and to St. Martin's Lane.

The houses were to be 100 feet in length, and 18 feet in breadth towards Coney Street, narrowing to 15 feet at the west end, and were to comprise seven tenements. The house to the street was to have a projecting gallery in front, and the remaining six houses were to be under one roof. The sizes of timber to be used are specified, but the details were to follow the design of certain houses which are named. The work was to be completed by Michaelmas, under pain of excommunication, and Robert was to be paid 62 marks (£41 6s. 8d.) for the whole, in instalments, and a robe in addition. Fitzgiles also contracted in 1335 to build five houses under one roof in Aldwark, York, between the corner of St. Andrewgate and the house of the Prior and Convent of Guisborough.

SHB, 430–2; *YDC*, Registrum Antiquum (*A.R.*); RMY, 5

FITZROGER, William (*fl.* 1200–) Carpenter

William son of Roger, carpenter, was in 1200 paid £4 10s. 0d. for carrying timber from Cheshunt to the Tower of London.

PR

FITZTHOMAS, William [William the Mason] (*fl. c.* 1250–†*c.* 1270) Mason

Master *cementarius of Lichfield Cathedral*, son of Master THOMAS the Mason I, whose properties in Lichfield he inherited. He was living after 1254, but was dead by 1275, when his daughters Alice and Juliana disposed of his houses outside the gate of the precinct, towards the north.

LRA, Nos. 33, 213, 235, 499, 507, 508

FITZWICHING, Richard (*fl.* 1169–1188) Carpenter

Richard son of Wiching, carpenter, was allowed £1 for his robes in 1169–70, and in 1173–74 the sum of £2 15s. 3d. was paid for the hire of two horses with their gear when he was sent by the King to Huntingdon. In 1187–88 Richard the carpenter, Geoffrey the carpenter, and Ralph the smith were allowed £36 0s. 11d. for the King's works.

PR

FLANDERS, John of [de Flandria, de Sancto Albano, de St. Omer] (*fl.* 1249–1258) Carver

Master carver to Henry III from 1249, when he was in charge of the painting of the King's wardrobe in *Westminster Palace*. He was then ordered to make a great lectern for the Chapter House of *Westminster Abbey*, like that in the Chapter House at St. Albans, where he was working in 1251; on 30 August he was granted a robe of the King's gift.[1] He was perhaps identical with the ditcher (*fossiator, le Fossur*) of this name, who in 1241 had been granted livery of 12d. a day for his works at the *Tower of London*.[2] The sculptor was certainly identical with John of St. Albans, sculptor of the King's images, who received a winter robe on 22 December 1257,[3] and who on 2 May 1258 was said to have worked long upon the King's 'candelabrum'.[4] He may also have been the John of St. Albans, lay-brother, for whom, with his wife and two sons, the convent of Lire (Eure, France) was asked to provide for the term of six years by Henry III in 1254.[5] A carver named John of St. Omer was paid 7s. 6d. at Christmas 1292 for cutting three capitals of Caen stone for the lower chapel of *St. Stephen* in *Westminster Palace*.[6]

[1] CCR 1247–51, 203, 495; TWP, *13th century*, I, 459; [2] CLR 1240–5, 23; CCR 1237–42, 251, 256; [3] *Ibid.* 1256–91, 79; [4] *Ibid.*, 217; [5] CPR, 1247–58, 386; [6] *PRO*, E.101–468–6, rot. 35

Flant, Thomas—see FANT

Flexman, John—see GYE

FONOYLL, Raynard [Fonoll, Fonolly] (*fl.* 1331–1362) Mason

English master mason and sculptor; from 1331 to about 1341 was in charge of building the south cloister of the Catalan monastery of *Santes Creus*. Some years later he was probably working on the royal palace attached to the monastery but, possibly to escape the Black Death, moved to *Montblanch*, where he began building the church of *Santa Maria* in 1352. He was still master of the work of Montblanch in 1362 when, on 17 January, his two sons John and Thomas by a spinster Elisenda were legitimized, as Raynard had no issue of his marriage.

The few available documents show only that Fonoyll was at Santes Creus in 1331, 1332, and on 25 June 1340, when he took as apprentice for four years Guillem, son of Berenguer de Valoria; and of Montblanch in 1352 (?), 1359 and 1362. The stylistic evidence derived from his most unusual, and specifically English, sculptures of babewynes, portrait busts and other details, suggests a considerably wider sphere of work and influence at the cathedrals of *Tarragona* and *Lérida*, the royal monasteries of *Pedralbes* at Barcelona and *Poblet*, and the town church of *Morella*. The evidence, with full illustration, was collected by the late Josep Vives i Miret and published posthumously.[1]

Fonoyll is of outstanding importance in the history of Spanish art in that his work is by far the earliest flamboyant (curvilinear) known in the Peninsula. The style of his grotesque carvings, moreover, is notably precocious for 1330, when he must at the latest have left England; and suggests an origin in the South Midlands.[2] In view of the stylistic certainty that Fonoyll's art was English, confirming the explicit statement of the first record of his appearance in Spain on 3 February 1331 that he was '*Anglicus*', his names deserve consideration. The Christian name, appearing in the documents as Raynardus, Raymardus, Renaudus, Raynaldus, is almost unknown in Catalonia in the thirteenth and fourteenth centuries but is equivalent to the English Reginald or Reynold. On the other hand, Fonoll is a well known Catalan surname, identical with the plant fennel, and occurring as a minor place-name. It is possible that the forms in the records represent simply a translation of the English surname Fennell; but the occurrence on more than one occasion of the preposition *dez* or *deç* rather suggests localization in Catalonia after Raynard's arrival.

(*X.D.S.*) LGC, 33; EHI, 313–14; cf. *J.H.H.* in JVM, I, 225–35
[1] *Reinard des Fonoll* (Barcelona: Blume, 1969); [2] Professor Lawrence Stone, *in litt.*, 1961.

Forard—see FAUNTE

Forcinus—see FORTIN

FORD, William (*fl.* 1442) ? Mason

In 1442 gave an acquittance for 22 marks (£14 13s. 4d.) paid him for work done in the church of the *Bodmin Greyfriars* 'about the tomb of the late Thomas Peverell esquire according to an example portrayed on a certain parchment, with French (? free) stone in a goodly chapel'.

MTM, I, 188

Forente—see FAUNTE

FORMAN, John (*fl.* 1515–†1558) Mason

In 1515 John Forman was warden of the masons under JOHN LEBONS at the building of Wolsey's *Hampton Court*, and in May held a royal commission to impress masons for the works. It was presumably to the influence of Wolsey as Archbishop of York (1514–1530) that Forman owed his next promotion, for he was appointed master mason at *York Minster* in succession to CHRISTOPHER HORNER prob-

ably during 1523. In 1525 he was in charge of the works of the church of *St. Michael-le-Belfry, York*, just by the Minster. This church was practically complete by 1536.[1] In 1530 Forman was owed £58 for 'stuff' for Wolsey's works at Southwell, Scrooby, or Cawood, or possibly at all of these.[2] He continued to hold his office of Minster mason until his death in the summer of 1558; his last work was the Catholic redecoration of the Minster in 1557. In January 1538 Forman had been one of a commission to survey *Pontefract Castle*, Yorks., along with JOHN TOMSON, carpenter. He was also deputy to GEORGE LAWSON at *Berwick-on-Tweed*, where he was appointed Master Mason on 7 February 1543.[3]

In his will, made on 20 March 1557/8, he described himself as 'the maister of the maysons in the Cathedrall churche of Yorke' and appointed his wife Agnes as executrix; he desired to be buried in the Minster. The will was proved on 13 June 1558.[4]

A mason of the same name worked in 1473–74 at the quarries where stone was prepared for the works of the central tower of Durham Cathedral,[5] and another John Forman, of Selby, was paid 22s. 6d. for 9 loads of plaster for the York Minster works in 1478–79.[6]

(APD; WPS)
[1] BHY, I, 271; RFY, 99n., 102, 103n., 104, 106–8, 110–12; [2] LPH, IV, pt. iii, p. 3048; [3] HKW III, 288, 416; IV, 127; [4] PCY, 15, pt. 2, 286; [5] DAR, II, 413; [6] RFY

FORSTER, John [Foster] (*fl.* 1456–1473) Carpenter

In 1457 became master carpenter of *York Minster* on the retirement of WILLIAM COTTINGHAM, and continued there until 1473.[1] He took up the freedom of York in 1457–58.[2]
[1] BHY, I, 240–1, 249–50; RFY, 74; [2] YCF

FORSTER, John [Foster] (*fl.* 1433–†1494) Mason

Although no work of this mason is known, his career can be followed over a period of sixty years and presents several points of interest. He began by being apprenticed to a London brazier, Thomas Boston, who when at Bury St. Edmunds on 10 August 1433 released him of 'alle maner acciouns' but bound him by an obligation of 20s. if Boston should get him the freedom of London.[1] The bond was to be met at Christmas 1436 and was put in the keeping of WILLIAM LAYER, to whom John Forster was probably apprentice at the time. A declaration rehearsing the above was made by the alderman and bailiff of Bury and seven other leading townsmen, including William Layer, on 18 October 1438. In it John Forster is described as 'masoun'. [On 18 August 1460 Forster let what was probably a sub-contract to THOMAS NUNNE, carpenter, to make a parlour to be set 'where the olde halle is late Richard Parmenter', in Bury.[2]]

John Forster figures in Bury wills and deeds from 1444 up to his death. In 1473 as alderman of Bury he held the highest municipal office for which a townsman was eligible under the rule of the Abbot.[3] He acted as a feoffee for the two great benefactors of the town, John Smyth (died 1481) and Margaret Odeham (died 1492), over numerous properties which formed the endowments of the charitable trusts established by them.[4] Margaret Odeham was the widow of John Odeham, draper of Bury, and John Forster seems to have been closely associated with both of them from 1454 onwards. The seal which he used was probably that of John Odeham; impressions attached to deeds show a merchant's mark with the letters 'i', 'o', and 'd'.

In his will John Forster desired to be buried in the churchyard of St. James 'under a stone by me laid be fore the brasen doore', i.e. the great west door of the abbey church.[5] Although it was not proved until 12 August 1495, he died between 10 September 1493 and 4 June 1494, when his widow Margaret made her will, in which she refers to 'John fforster late my husbonde now dede'.[6] He appears to have been owed considerable sums of money at his death.

John Forster was clearly a prominent man in his craft as well as in the life of the town. There must be many Suffolk churches containing unrecognised work by him. Several of those for whom he acted as executor were masons or servants of the abbey, and it is probable that at least during part of his career he was employed there. In view of his early training as apprentice to a brazier he may have specialized in making designs for brasses, as other masons (for example WILLIAM HYNDELEY and HENRY YEVELEY, as evidenced by their wills) are known to have done.

A.O.
[1] *BM*, Add. MS. 14848, *f*. 303v.; [2] *A.E.B.O.* in ARC, XIV, 1979, 19–20; [3] *BCM*, H.1–5–6; [4] *Ibid.*, H.1 *passim*; [5] *BW*, vi, 35; [6] *Ibid.*, vi, 60v.

FORTIN [Forcinus] (*fl.* 1204–) Engineer

Was engineer in charge of works at *Colchester Castle*, Essex, in 1204. No remains of this period can now be seen.

(APD; WPS); **PR** LVI, 46

Foster, John—see FORSTER

FOULFORD, John [? J. Wright] (*fl.* 1444–?1466) Carpenter

Of York; probably identical with John Wright, carpenter, who took up the freedom of the city in 1444–45.[1] During 1448–49 Foulford was working for the city authorities on the gate of 'Fishergate' for 12 days, taking 5*d*. a day.[2] It is possible that he was the carpenter of the roof of the new *Guildhall* of York, of which the masonry work was in progress in 1448 and 1449.

In about 1457–58 Foulford was one of a commission of two masons and two carpenters (he was named before the other carpenter ROBERT JACKSON) to adjudicate on a dispute connected with the York building code (see JOHN PORTER and ROBERT COUPER).[3]

In 1465 William Foulford, cordwainer, took up the freedom of York as son of John Foulford, wright,[4] but there is no trace of the latter's entry into the freedom, unless he is identical with the John Wright who entered in 1444–45 and made his will on 10 November 1466. This will describes him as 'John Wryght, carpenter'; he wished to be buried in the church of St. Michael-le-Belfry, and left to John Wilson his servant one 'dolobrium' (hewing axe) and one 'blokker'.[5]

The timber roof of *All Saints Church, North Street*, in *York*, built *c*. 1450, is probably by the same designer as that of the Guildhall, containing similar figure carvings of angels with musical instruments, grotesques, and the like.

[1] *YCF*; [2] *YCM*, Chamberlains' Accs., MS., vol. 1A, *f*. 48; [3] YMB, 219; [4] *YCF*; [5] RFY, 207–8

FOUNDYNG, William [Foundy, Funden, -yng, Houndling] (*fl.* 1446–1487) Mason

Apparently the mason in charge of work at *Exeter Cathedral* from 1459 to 1487, and perhaps at earlier and later dates; he presumably succeeded JOHN HARRY about 1456, and it may be significant that a William Foundyng took up the freedom of Exeter in September 1455. He is first mentioned in 1446–47, when he was paid 6*d*. a day for intermittent work, and from 1459 onwards was in receipt of a regular pension or fee of £1 6s. 8d. yearly.[1] He rode to the stone quarries at Beer in 1459–60, and in 1476–77 was proceeded against for not fulfilling his contract to build a house for Henry Hull esquire.[2] He was probably the William Fundy who, with William Gervays, made two windows for the chancel of *St. Mary's, Dawlish*, in the late 15th century.[3] Between 1467 and 1472, William Fundyng 'late of the cete of Exeter. . .Fremacyn' and Robert Russell of the same, 'Belmaker', were involved in legal actions before the Mayor and Bailiffs of the city, and were defendants in a Chancery suit.[4]

(*D.F.F.*)

[1] RJE, 52; *EDC*, Fabric rolls; [2] *ECR*, 16–17 Edw. IV, m.26; [3] *EDC*, No. 961; [4] *PRO*, C.1–46–69

FRANKELYN, John [alias Temple] (*fl. c.* 1440) Carpenter

Was master carpenter at *Caen* in Normandy towards the end of the English occupation. He was presumably the father of WILLIAM FRANKELYN (1461–1504).

HKW, I, 463

FRANKELYN, Roger [Fraunkelyn] (*fl.* 1369–) Carpenter

On 7 April 1369, John Frankelyn and JOHN PAGE of London, carpenters, contracted to build 20 shops and a gateway for the Dean and Chapter of St. Paul's, between the north door of the capitular bakehouse and the south corner of the same, and thence to the houses of the abbey of Peterborough on the west. There were to be 20 houses fronting as shops to the high road, with gables to east and west; the work was to be finished in 2½ years, and Frankelyn and Page were to receive £303 by instalments.

SHB, 441–3; (*SPM*, MS. 1796); HMC, 9R. App. i, 50

William FRANKELYN, carpenter, built a long chamber in *Windsor Castle* for which he was paid 200 marks (£133 6s. 8d.) in 1361–65. He was very likely the carpenter of that name who on 29 Sept. 1383, with his wife Juliana, leased a tenement above Candiche in Holywell, Oxford, from St. John's Hospital, and who was fined there under the Statute of Labourers in 1391.

GOC

FRANKELYN, William [Frankeleyne, alias Temple] (*fl.* 1461–†1504) Carpenter

Probably the son of JOHN FRANKELYN alias Temple; held office as Master Carpenter of the counties of Chester and Flint from 29 August 1461. He was appointed for life master carpenter of the *Castle of Chester* on 30 December 1461, a new grant of 12 April 1463 later extending the scope of his office to the counties of Chester and Flint. The office was confirmed in 1467, 1484, and on 1 November 1485, and Frankelyn held it until the appointment of EDWARD BOLTON in 1488.[2] As William Temple, he was then appointed Master Carpenter of *Calais* in succession to WILLIAM WOODWARD, and held office until his death on 30 June 1504. He was succeeded by ROBERT MAPILSDEN.[3]

Frankelyn may well have been the designer of the stalls for *St. Asaph Cathedral*, made during the episcopate of Bishop Redman (1471–1495).

[1] DKR, XXXI; [2] HKW, III, 418. [3] *Ibid.*, II, 1056; III, 419

Frant, Thomas—see FANT

FRAUNCEYS, Robert (*fl.* 1385–†1388) Carpenter

Master carpenter in *Windsor Castle*, appointed on 3 February 1384/5; he died on 29 May 1388.

HKW, II, 1053

FRAUNCEYS, Thomas (*fl.c.*1388–†*c.* 1403) Carpenter

Master carpenter in *Windsor Castle*, taking fees of 6d. a day and a yearly livery, presumably in succession to ROBERT FRAUNCEYS. He was succeeded by WILLIAM WYSE on 15 April 1403.

CPR 1401–5, 218

FREEMASON, William (*fl.* 1462–1463) Mason

Of Bodmin, Cornwall; in 1462–63 made three new windows for the hermitage chapel belonging to *Restormel Castle*.

HKW, II, 805n

FREMAN, John (*fl.* 1482–1483) Carpenter

Carpenter engaged to make centres for the nave vault of *Westminster Abbey*, being paid 8d. a day in 1482–83.

WAM, 23557

FRENGEY, John (*fl.* 1391–1392) Carpenter

Was paid £8 for making the woodwork of two rooms within two stone towers at 'le Waterloks' of *Canterbury* in 1391–92, by contract.

PRO, E.364–27(D)

FRETON, John (*fl.* 1388–1389) Carpenter

Master carpenter at *Dover Castle* in 1388–9,

when NICHOLAS PEYNTOUR was the mason in charge.

HKW, II, 639, 1052

FROGBROOK, Roger (*fl.* 1536–1538) Carpenter

Made the timberwork of the new steeple at *Bolney Church*, Sussex, from 1536 to 1538. On one occasion he was paid 4*s.* 6*d.* for travelling to the Isle of Wight, but for what purpose is not stated. The masonry work was built by THOMAS POKYLL.

SAC, VI, 244–52

FROST, Hugh (*fl.* 1390–1391) Carpenter

Carpenter to the Trinity Guild of (King's) Lynn in 1390–91, when he received 7*s.* 5*d.* for his livery.

LCR, G.d.53

FRYTHEBY, Robert de (*fl.* 1356–   ) Mason

Master mason (*magister cementar'*) in charge of works at *Berwick-upon-Tweed* in 1356, being paid 12*d.* a day.

PRO, E.101–482–16

FULBOURNE, William of (*fl.* 1341–1342) Carpenter (*Fulbourn, Cambs.*)

In January 1341 the great tracing-house of the Master Mason in *Westminster Palace* was repaired by William of Fulburne at task for 13*s.* 4*d.*.[1] In the next year he undertook by contract to build two stables at Westminster, mainly of timber but including the stone foundation walls, ironwork, plaster and tiling.[2]

[1] *PRO*, E.101–470–10; [2] HKW, I, 186; CBC in AH, II, 25

FULLER, John [Fullour] (*fl.* 1423–1448) Carpenter

Appointed master carpenter of the King's works at *Calais* on 2 September 1423 and was still in office as late as 1448, although in 1440 WILLIAM CROFTON had been appointed master carpenter of the New Works there. After the destruction of *Newenham Bridge* on the bounds of Calais in 1436 by the Burgundian forces, Fuller carried out a speedy restoration.

DKR, XLVIII, 227; HKW, I, 437; II, 1054

Funden, William—see FOUNDYNG

FUSTYNG, John (*fl.* 1506–†1508) Carver

Of Oxford, where he lived in 1507 in a house in St. Mary's parish belonging to St. John's Hospital; died in 1508, the inventory of his goods showing that he was a carver in both wood and stone, and also a tombmaker.

He left £30 worth of timber, wrought and unwrought belonging to work he had undertaken for *Godstow Abbey*, £7 6*s.* 8*d.* worth of stone, a debt of £11 still outstanding of £20 he was to have had for the pulpit at the church of *St. Mary the Virgin, Oxford*, another debt of £6 owing to him for work at the 'Sembly House' (*Congregation House*) at St. Mary's, and a third debt of £1 2*s.* 4*d.* for a tomb for 'Master Croston', doubtless the Edmund Croston, parson of Biggleswade (†1507) whose brass still remains in the tower of St. Mary's Church. Fustyng had carved stones for the *Magdalen College* bell-tower during the two years previous to his death.

(*R.D.*) **JMO**, 215; GOM, 90; GOC

Fynt, William—see VYNT

GABRIELL, Denis (*fl.* 1433–1434) Mason

In 1433–34 made the stone screens of the chapels of St. Paul and St. John Baptist in *Exeter Cathedral*. On stylistic grounds it seems likely that Gabriell also designed the chantry chapel of Bishop Nicholas Bubwith (†1424) in *Wells Cathedral*, and the North Chapel (*c.* 1446) at *North Bradley Church*, Wilts.

BPE, 19, 133

GAINSBOROUGH, Richard of [Gaynsburgh] (*fl. c.* 1300–*c.* 1350) Mason (*Gainsborough, Lincs.*)

Mason of *Lincoln Cathedral* in the first half of the 14th century. His tomb slab is in the cloisters, and appears to date from *c.* 1325–50. It shows him clothed in a belted tunic and with a square beside him.[1] The day of his death is given as 21 May, but the year is partly obliterated, only the letters 'MCCC . . .' remaining; the description (*olym cementarivs istivs eclesie*) suggests that he was the master in charge, and he may have been identical with RICHARD OF STOW II. On the other hand, the only Lincoln citizen of this name discoverable in documentary sources is Richard de Gaynsburgh, 'poyntour', whose will was proved in the Burwarmote Court on 14 March 1350/1, in so far as concerned a free messuage in the parish of St. Margaret Wigford; this refers to Richard's widow Sarra as one of his executors.[2] It is possible that 'poyntour' is a variant of painter, and that the word was used in its occasional mediaeval sense of sculptor or imager. Gainsborough may have been the Richard Mason who was left 2 chisels and a 'hakhamer' under the will of Martin le Payntour, made 30 November, and proved 6 December 1332.[3] (See Appendix I.)

(APD; BAA)
[1] BAH, 120–1; [2] *LDC*, MS. 169, *f*.213v (*J.V.*); [3] *LAO*, Amc. 5/Misc./1 (*D.M.W.*)

GALAMPTON, John (*fl.* 1486–1487) Mason

At *Exeter Cathedral* in 1486–87 to oversee the masons (*ad supervidend. lathomos*) when he was paid 5*d*. a day on two separate occasions, and also received £1 6*s*. 8*d*. for his yearly pension or fee.

EDC, Fabric roll 1486–87 (*D.F.F.*)

Galfron'—see GEOFFREY the Mason

GALMETON, Robert de (*fl.* 1312–1326) Carpenter

Presumably from one of the two places in Devon called Galmpton; was the leading carpenter at *Exeter Cathedral* from 1313 to 1322, and again in 1326, being paid at the rate of 2*s*. 2*d*. a week in summer and 1*s*. 10*d*. in winter, compared with the 3*s*. paid to the visiting master THOMAS OF WINTON. Galmeton was in addition paid £4 in 1317 for making the bishop's throne by contract. The throne is one of the best examples of mediaeval woodwork, and is the earliest and certainly the finest of the few bishops' thrones in existence. Responsibility for the design must be attributed to Master THOMAS OF WITNEY though there are few points of resemblance to the Winchester Cathedral stallwork of 1308–10, carried out by WILLIAM LYNGWODE.

BPE, 12, 16, 18, 53; *CEF*, from Fabric rolls Nos. 2611, 2613

GAMELYN, ? Robert [Gammelyn, Gamlyn] (*fl.* 1481–1483) Carpenter

From March 1481 to the end of March 1483 was working under contract at *Tendring Hall*, near Stoke-by-Nayland, Suffolk, for John, Lord Howard, later Duke of Norfolk. There are references in the accounts to his 'bargen of the houssyng that he must make' and to 'the new byldyng'. He received £77 in all. He and his men were boarded while the work was going on. His Christian name is not given, but he may be identical with one Robert Gamelyn mentioned elsewhere in the accounts.

A.O. PŇA (from *SA*)

GAMSTON, Philip (*fl.* 1400–*c*. 1415) Mason

Master mason of *Pontefract Castle* under the Duchy of Lancaster, confirmed in office on 28 June 1400. He had been succeeded by ROBERT GAMSTON by 1415.

HKW, II, 1060

GAMSTON, Robert (*fl.* 1415–†*c*. 1428) Mason

Was probably the son of PHILIP GAMSTON, whom he had succeeded as master mason of *Pontefract Castle* by 1415. He held office until his death about 1428.

HKW, II, 1060

GARALD, Richard [Gerald] (*fl.* 1441–†1458) Mason

Mason in charge of the building of the tower of *Fulham Church*, Middx., in 1441, when on 5 May a patent was issued prohibiting interference with him or his colleague, Peter Chapell, while engaged on the work, or the stoppage of stone for it coming from the quarry at Maidstone.[1] Garald made his will on 22 March 1456/7, describing himself as Richard Gerald, mason, of the parish of St. Sepulchre, London, and leaving bequests to his son William and wife Matilda, who proved the will on 23 January 1457/8.[2]

(*A.O.*)
[1] CPR 1436–41, 530; [2] *CCL*, 237 Sharp; W.J. Williams in MR, XVI, 160

Garard, Walter—see GERARD

GARRETT, John, (*fl.* 1421–1422) Mason

The second of three masons (with THOMAS AMPILFORDE and ROBERT MAUNSELL) who contracted to build *Catterick Bridge*, Yorks. on 13 January 1421/2. Garett had apparently undertaken the whole of the work by an earlier contract which he had been unable to fulfil.

SHB, 497–9; AJ, VII, 56

GASE, — (*fl.* 1274–   ) ? Mason

Servant of *Norwich Cathedral Priory* who in 1274 was sent to Caen with a colleague (*socio suo*) to buy stone for the works.

NCM, roll 3

GELIS, John (*fl.* 1496–   ) Mason

Supplied alabaster for the works of *Stirling Palace*, Scotland, in 1496, when he was described as 'Inglisman'.

ATS, II, lxxx

GEOFFREY the Carpenter I (*fl. c.* 1308–1326) Carpenter

'Master Geoffrey' was the craftsman in charge of the making of the choir-stalls of *St. Albans Abbey* in 1314; it is not improbable that he was also the designer of the splendid timber vault of the presbytery, of approximately the same period.

It is stated that Master Geoffrey and his servant (*garcio*) were paid a joint fee of 4*s.* weekly, and that Geoffrey received a yearly robe of the suit of the Abbot's esquires, as well as other profits and fees.

RGA, II, 124

GEOFFREY the Carpenter II (*fl.* 1370) Carpenter

Of Chesterton, Cambs.; in 1370 made a porch and external staircase at *Cambridge Castle*, and repaired the constable's chamber there for £13 6*s.* 8*d.*

HKW, II, 587

GEOFFREY the Engineer [de Leveland, Ingeniator] (*fl.* 1129–1130) Engineer

Apparently the keeper of the *Old Palace of Westminster* in 1129–30, when he received a fee of 7*d.* a day; he was also pardoned a sum of 2*s.* in the issues for Kent, showing that he was connected with that county. It has been suggested that he was a member of the family of de Leveland, who held Leaveland near Faversham from the time of the Conquest, and who were also hereditary keepers of the Old Palace of Westminster.

C. T. Clay in EHR, LIX (1944), 1–21

GEOFFREY the Mason I (*fl. c.* 1270) Mason

The name 'GEFRAI LE MACHVN' is carved upon the chancel arch of *Berden*, Essex, a work of *c.* 1270.

RCHM, *Essex*, I, 23

GEOFFREY the Mason II [Galfron'] (*fl.* 1359–) Mason

Probably chief mason of *Lincoln Cathedral* in 1359, as the will of Richard de Whitwell, canon of Lincoln, then left 'to Master Galfron the mason (*sementarius*) for two white stones, 20*s.*'.

LRS, v, Wills i, p. 9

GEOMETER, William the [Villam le (G)eometer] (*fl.* late 13th century) ? Mason

A tomb slab with inscription to 'Villam le (G)eometer' asking for prayers for his soul, was found in the vestibule of the Chapter House of *Bristol Cathedral*, and is now in the north choir aisle. It is apparently of late 13th century date, and may perhaps commemorate the master of the east end of the Elder Lady Chapel, altered *c.* 1280, or the designer of the new choir of hall-church type, whose plan goes back to *c.* 1298. The stone has been damaged, destroying the initial letter, and the name has also been read as 'Someter'.

(Personal observation); BGT, LXXIV (1955), 177–9

GEORGE the Mason [*Latimus*] (*fl.* 1459–) Mason

Mason who in 1459 undertook to make the walls of a new granary at *Felmersham*, Beds., for King's Hall, Cambridge. He was to be paid £2 6*s.* 8*d.* and a gown or 6*s.* 8*d.* for it.

SHB, 532; (*TCM, KHA*, xii, *f.* 241)

Gerald, Richard—see GARALD

GERARD [Girard] (*fl.* 1240–1256) Carpenter and Engineer

King's Carpenter and Engineer to Henry III; he was engaged on the works of *Corfe Castle*, Dorset, on 13 February 1239/40,[1] and on 26 January 1240/1 orders were given to pay him 1 mark (13*s.* 4*d.*) of the King's gift for a robe and his livery of 7½*d.* a day from All Saints to the Feast of Purification.[2] Further warrants for his livery were issued from time to time,[3] and on 12 November 1242 he seems to have been employed at *Bordeaux*, during the King's expedition to Gascony.[4]

In 1244 he was engaged on works of fortification at *Bywell*, Northumberland; *Newcastle-upon-Tyne*; *Bamburgh Castle*; and *Nottingham*, and drew timber for making war-engines from the forest of Carlisle.[5] Stones for the engines were to be cut from a form and mould supplied by him.[6]

On 10 January 1245, Gerard was made keeper of the King's houses in *Winchester Castle* at a fee of £2 yearly and was granted houses in Winchester for his own dwelling.[7] From time to time orders were made for the delivery to him of materials for the repair of the castle and of his own houses, and for payment of his fees.[8] He also received generous gifts from Henry III: 4 marks (£2 13*s.* 4*d.*) to buy a horse in 1244,[9] in 1246 £6 10*s.* 0*d.* to Gerard's wife Denise and £2 10*s.* 0*d.* for their two sons, and a further £2 for Denise in 1247.[10]

Gerard was at *Chester* making catapults in September 1247,[11] and during the following summer was again in charge of repairs at Corfe Castle.[12] During 1249 this work continued, and in Winchester Castle Gerard repaired the 'Jews' Tower', built a new chamber, and was to have shingles for re-roofing the King's houses in the castle.[13] Repairs at Winchester continued under Gerard's charge at least until 1252, when he was to have oaks to joist the Salsary Tower.[14] But in 1250 he had been sent to North Wales to ordain the King's engines and view the works at the castles of *Deganwy* and *Diserth* ('Gannoc' and 'Dissard')[15] and in 1251 he was carrying out repairs at the King's lodge of *Fremantle* in Hampshire and made a new bridge at Corfe Castle.[16] At this time his salary was said to amount to 12*d.* a day, and he was paid heavy arrears due to him.[17]

Master Gerard once more accompanied the King on his expedition to Gascony in 1253;[18] in 1255 he was named as one of the intendents of the custody of *Dover Castle*, and was sent to Carlisle to make engines of war.[19] He was still at Carlisle on 18 January 1255/6.[20]

Master Gerard's fees continued to be heavily in arrears and repeated orders were sent by the King to secure payment between 1252 and 1255. At this time he was in charge of the buildings of Winchester Castle, and had again been concerned with Corfe Castle in 1253, when he built a bridge. Later he was to make a leaden counterpoise for the King's engines of war in Gascony, to be shipped from Southampton. In 1254 he was allowed expenses for work at Chester; in 1255 was once more at Corfe, and worked on two catapults at *Carlisle Castle* until 1256. In May he was paid £1 7*s.* 10*d.* for timber commandeered from him, an indication that Master Gerard was not exclusively employed on official works.[21]

The high rates of pay and distinguished treatment accorded to Master Gerard show that he was one of the principal technical officers in Henry III's service. Building works were certainly placed under his charge, but he seems to have excelled in the construction of engines of war and ammunition.

(HKC, 18)
[1] CCR 1237–42, 174; [2] CLR 1240–5, 26; [3] *Ibid.*, 56, 119; [4] CCR 1242–7, 3; [5] CLR 1240–5, 230, 245, 250, 258; CCR 1242–7, 200; SBC, 79; [6] CLR 1240–5, 255; [7] CCR 1242–7, 282, 287; [8] CLR 1240–5, 289, 290; 1245–51, *passim*; [9] CLR 1240–5, 258; [10] *Ibid.* 1245–51, 91, 93, 132; [11]*Ibid.*, 141; [12] CCR 1247–51, 61, 73; CLR 1245–51, 207–8; [13] *Ibid.*, 222, 226, 237, 245, 260–1; CCR 1247–51, 146, 167, 251; [14] CCR 1247–51, 264, 304; *Ibid.* 1251–3, 92; [15] *Ibid.* 1247–51, 324; SBC, 102, 104; [16] CCR 1247–51, 394–5, 406, 431; [17] CLR 1245–51, 362, 373, 376; [18] CPR 1247–58, 348; [19] CCR 1254–6, 137, 181, 235; [20] CPR 1247–58, 509; [21] CLR 1251–60, *passim*

GERARD, John (*fl.* 1410–1418) Carpenter
On 20 August 1410, John Gerard, carpenter, and John More, timbermonger, contracted to build three houses in *Friday Street*, London, according to a detailed 'patron'

drawn on parchment, and according to the directions of WALTER WALTON, mason, who in his will pardoned him a debt of 6*s.* 8*d.*, and left 6*s.* 3*d.* to his wife Joan, in 1418.

SHB, 483–5; (*SPM*, MS. 1462); PCC, 22 Marche (*A.O.*).

GERARD, John (*fl.* 1439–1441) Mason
In 1439 was working at *King's Hall, Cambridge*, when a turret staircase was built in the angle between the gate-tower and the adjoining range of chambers.[1] In 1440 and 1441 he was at *Saffron Walden Church*, Essex, where he seems to have succeeded JOHN WOLMAN as master mason in the spring of 1441. Like his predecessor, he was paid at the rate of 3*s.* 8*d.* a week. In 1440 he was paid 8*d.* for 'un estrich bord' to make moulds for the great window. This window was probably one described as 'the west window of the new work', for the ironwork of which a payment was made in June 1441. The new work was the north aisle rebuilt at this time. Among the contributions collected for the work was one of a shilling from John Gerard. Payments were made to his servant, Nicholas Porter or Nicholas Sconys, apparently the same man, whose weekly rate was 3*s.* 2*d.* By the spring of 1444 he had been succeeded as master mason by JOHN COKET.

A.O.
[1] TCM, KHA, ix, 179, 227; [2] CWW, *ff.* 12–24

GERARD, Walter [Garard] (*fl.* 1368–1373) Mason
Mason working at *Rochester Castle* for 252 days in 1368–69, taking 6*d.* a day.[1] On 3 June 1369, described as of Sutton Valence, Kent, he was commissioned to take masons and others for the works of *Leeds Castle* and *Langley Park*.[2] He was master mason at Leeds from 1369 to 1373, probably under the direction of HENRY YEVELEY; his pay was 6*d.* a day, the same as that of the leading working masons[3]. Gerard also carried out contract work to the value of £102 6*s.* 3*d.* on the repairs at Leeds.[4]
[1] AC, II, 123; [2] CPR 1367–70, 255; [3] PRO, E.101–466–19 (*L.F.S.*); HKW, II, 701

Gerves, John—see JERVEYS

GIBBON, John
Mistakenly said to have been 'marbler' to Edward III, and to have designed *Queenborough Castle*, built 1361–67, under William of Wykeham as clerk of works. In fact, on 1 June 1339, John Gybboun of Sandwich the King's mariner, was granted for life the

profits of the passage between Sandwich and Stonore.

(APD); CPR 1338–40, 266

GIBBON, John [Gybbon] (*fl.* 1532–1550) Mason

In 1532 John Gibbon was a setter at *Westminster Hall* at 3s. 8d. per week.[1] He was living in St. Saviour's parish, Southwark, in 1541, with a foreign servant named Hayes.[2] In 1545 he was paid 20s. for drawing the 'platt' for *Redgrave Hall*, Suffolk, and during the first six years of work there received £8 10s. 0d. as master mason.[3]

[1] *PRO*, E.36, vol. CCCII; [2] HSP, X, 1, 37; [3] SIA, XXIX, 5–6, 11, 23, 32 (*A.O.*)

GILBERT the Carpenter I (*fl. c.* 1154–1189) Carpenter

Witness to a charter at Westminster of the reign of Henry II.

WAM, 17079

GILBERT the Carpenter II (*fl.* 1256–1273) Carpenter

Was one of the royal carpenters in charge of works at *Windsor Castle* on 22 January 1256, when he was to have timber for the repair of the hall and chambers in the upper castle, 'where the King's children have been nursed'. His appointment may have dated back to the death of RALPH BURNELL in c. 1254. Orders were given for the issue of robes to him in 1257–58. In 1258–59 he was allowed 5 marks for wages, and livery of £7 17s. 6d., and was one of the surveyors of the works. At this time the chief carpenter of Windsor Castle was nominally THOMAS BURNELL, who succeeded his father Ralph in 1254; but Thomas was not a trained craftsman. In 1262 Master Gilbert was to wainscot the queen's chamber at Windsor. On 26 January 1265, robes were ordered to be issued to Gilbert the carpenter, GILBERT THE MASON, and Thomas Burnell the viewer of the works, and orders were given on 7 July 1270 to pay arrears. Gilbert was granted 6d. a day as King's Carpenter in Windsor Castle on 10 October 1273.[1]

HWC, I, 66, 68, 71, 81; CCR, CLR *passim*
[1] CCR 1272–9, 34

GILBERT the Mason I (*fl.* 1265–1266) Mason

On 26 January 1264/5 and 8 October 1265 orders were given for robes to be issued to GILBERT THE CARPENTER, Gilbert 'le Macun', and Thomas Burnell (see RALPH BURNELL), viewer of the works at *Windsor Castle*, and on

28 December 1266 Gilbert the mason of Windsor Castle was again to have a robe. He was presumably the chief technical officer in charge.

CCR 1264–8, 15, 75, 279

GILBERT the Mason II (*fl.* 1385–   ) Mason

On 3 March 1384/5 was master of the masons and masonry work of *Lichfield Cathedral*, when the Chapter decided that two working masons should be provided to work under his direction. He was to have £2 a year and 3s. 4d. a week when at work.

WSS, VI, pt. ii, 86; *LCM*, Acta Capitularia 1384–1438, ff. 2v., 9v. (*A.B.E.*); (*D.A.J.*)

GILDENE, John (*fl.* 1338–?1356) Mason

'Cementarius' working for *Canterbury Cathedral Priory* from 1338 to 1341. In 1338 he was engaged in building the Prior's new chamber at the manor house of *Eastry*, Kent.[1] One J. Geldene who was receiving an annual robe without fur from the Prior between 1351 and 1356 may have been the same man.[2]

(*W.P.B.*)
[1] AC, LVIII, 30–1; [2] LP, MS. 243, ff. 79, 84v., 93, 98

Giles—see GELIS, GYLES

Giles, Robert—see FITZGILES

GLANFORTH, William (*fl.* 1466–1468) Mason

In partnership with JOHN POLLARD contracted in 1466 to build a new porch at *Saffron Walden Church*, Essex.[1] This was the south porch; the fan vault must have been inserted later, early in the 16th century. In 1467 and 1468 he was at work on the south range of the *Schools* at *Cambridge*.[2]

A.O.
[1] *CWW, ff.* 73–5; BAE, 219 *et seq.*; [2] CGB, 'A', 56, 57, 65

'Glanyll', John—see CLAVYLL

'Glapham', Adam de—see GLASHAM

GLASHAM, Adam de ['Glapham'] (*fl.* 1300–1314) Carpenter (? *Glasson, Cumb.*)

Was working in 1300 at 6d. a day upon making engines at the siege of *Caerlaverock Castle* (which has been misinterpreted as Carnarvon). Master Adam de Glasham, carpenter of Cumberland, was also to work on the fortifications of *Dumfries Castle*, Scotland,[1] and on 12 February 1301/2 was one of the master carpenters in charge of works at *Linlithgow Peel*, with THOMAS DE HOUGHTON.[2] In 1304 he was one of the carpenters at the siege of

Stirling Castle.[3] At *Northallerton* Master Adam was engaged in building a peel tower in 1314.[4]

(APD; DAE); HKW, I, 217
[1] *PRO*; E.101–482–17 (*L.F.S.*); [2] TTH, 30; [3] *Ibid.*, 31; [4] HKW, I, 235

GLASHAM, Robert de (*fl.* 1305–*c.* 1325) Engineer

Master carpenter in charge of works at *Beeston Castle*, Cheshire, in 1305, when he was paid 6*d.* a day.[1] As 'the king's engineer' he was making engines at Windsor in 1307–8 and in the same year worked on a new gate at *Chester*. In 1310–11 master carpenter in receipt of 7½*d.* a day with summer and winter robes worth £2 yearly,[2] and in 1312 was employed at *Scarborough Castle*. Apparently succeeded RICHARD LENGINOUR as master engineer of the county of Chester on 24 January 1314/15 and like his predecessor farmed the mills, fishery, and bridge of Chester for £200 a year. He was still receiving the fees of his office, 12*d.* a day, up to 30 September 1320.[3] He surveyed *Hadleigh Castle*, Essex, in 1320–21, and from 1323 to 1325 was master of the works at *Hanley Castle*, Worcs.[4]

[1] *PRO*, E.101–458–16 (*L.F.S.*); [2] *BM*, Cotton Nero C. VIII, *f.* 18v.; [3] ACC, 86, 89, 92; [4] HKW, II, 661, 668

GLASIER, Thomas [Glasyare] (*fl.* 1437–*c.* 1465) Mason

Was a freemason at *Eton College* at 3*s.* a week from October 1444 to June 1446 and in the latter year had a reward of 20*s.*, being described as a carver (*keruer*).[1] In 1451 'Thomas Glasyare, mason' took up the freedom of Canterbury on his marriage to Alice, daughter of Nicholas Munden;[2] in 1458 he succeeded RICHARD BEKE as master mason of *Canterbury Cathedral*. He received robes there as an esquire of the Prior in 1458 and 1459, but had been succeeded by another (possibly THOMAS REDMAN) by 1466; this Glasier was an apprentice at Canterbury Cathedral in 1437, and appears as a mason from 1439 to 1442, and in 1454.[3] Identity with the Eton man is probable, for several other masons from the Canterbury works were impressed for the building of Eton College at about the same period. Glasier was admitted to fraternity of Christ Church, Canterbury, at an unknown date, and his obit was kept there (*Thomas Glasier magister lathomorum frater noster*) on 8 October. His name was added to the calendar at a date *c.* 1465–85.[4]

[1] KJE; [2] CFC, 123; [3] *Bodl.*, Tanner MS. 165 (*A.O.*); [4] *BM*, Arundel MS. 68, *f.* 44v. (*A.B.E.*)

GLASTON, John de (*fl.* 1. Carpenter

Master carpenter employed *Cathedral* for 14 weeks in 1310 to stalls from the Norman church int choir; he was paid 2*s.* 3*d.* a week have been the master carpenter of C *Abbey* where the choir furnishings h made between 1291 and 1303.

BPE, 15, 52; *CEF*, from Fabric roll No. 2609

Glenchwarton; Gleyngewarton, Simon—see CLENCHWARTON

GLOSSE, — (*fl.* 1524–1525) Carver

Carver employed at work in the church of *Stogursey*, Som., in 1524–25, when he was paid £8 in addition to 13*s.* 4*d.* when he went to Bristol, 2*s.* 4*d.* 'for his charges into Wales', and 3*s.* 4*d.* on another occasion.

HMC, 6R, 348–50

'Gloucester Mason, the'—see HOBBS, John

GLOUCESTER, John of (*fl. c.* 1245–†1260) Mason

A deed of *c.* 1245 conveys from Richard le Symphanur of Gloucester to Master John the Mason (*cementarius*) and his heirs a shop in the drapery of Gloucester, at a yearly rental to the abbot of 2*s.*, Master John paying Richard 40*s.* for the grant.[1] In 1249–50 order was given to the Sheriff of Gloucester to distrain on 'John le Macun' and others for wine bought of the King,[2] and about the same time 'Master John the King's Mason' appears as holding property in Puck Lane near the Northgate of Gloucester and as a witness to Gloucester deeds from 1250 to 1253.[3] In 1252 he was to view the king's works at *Woodstock* and was to be paid 1*s.* a day by the bailiffs there from 21 February 1253. He continued to have charge of these works for the rest of his career. On 11 June 1253 John of Gloucester was granted a robe as the King's Mason of Westminster; the robe was in respect of the previous Christmas term. In 1255 he was promised 10 librates of land for his services at *Gloucester, Woodstock, Westminster*, and elsewhere, and was to have two robes yearly, with furs of good squirrels, 'such as the Knights of the Household receive'. From 1255 onwards he was in charge of works at the *Tower of London* and also at *Windsor Castle*, where the Queen's Lodging was rebuilt to his design. A sum of £20 was allowed towards this work on 10 January 1256, the Queen's old chamber in the upper bailey was to be repaired, and a new garderobe made 'by counsel and oversight' of Master John, in April 1257. In June new lodgings of two stories were being made under his supervision, and in January 1258 he was ordered to provide for a turret with an oriel to be made beside the Queen's new chamber. In March 1256 Master John was to give his counsel on the repair of the great fireplace in the King's chamber at Windsor and also in regard to the repairs of *Oxford Castle*; in April was to view the works at *Havering* and the cleaning of the ditch of Gloucester Castle.

Between 1254 and 1256 Master John was in charge of repairs to the hall and other parts of the royal palace at Guildford, next to the Castle, damaged by fire, according to the king's personal instructions by word of mouth. In September 1255 he was directing work on the chapel at Havering, then in 1256 was to decide the site for rebuilding the kitchen in Gloucester Castle, and to have a fireplace built in the steward's chamber at Woodstock. In October of 1256 he was to direct work by the sheriffs of London on the stone quay below the Tower and to supervise the roofing with lead of the great wardrobe there.

Meanwhile, he was also in charge of the works at *Westminster Abbey*, and in 1255–56 he lent, at the King's order, to the Dean of *St. Martin's-le-Grand, London*, freestone for the works there from the stores at Westminster, and also gave to St. Martin's the roof timbers of the Lady Chapel of the abbey, which was being re-roofed with stone. The rebuilding of St. Martin's-le-Grand continued for several years; marble columns for a pulpit there were to be given in March 1258, and on 12 May 1259 Master John was ordered to supply the keepers of the works there with five figures of kings cut in freestone and other hewn stone. He was also instructed to give materials to the Friars Preachers (Dominicans or *Blackfriars*) for their London works (1259–61).[4]

In 1256 Master John was in charge of repairs at the *Tower of London*. The King returned to him five casks of wine, in lieu of ones taken at Oxford. He was granted an estate at 'Blechesdon' (Bletchingdon, Oxon.) and about the same time was concerned in the transfer of some Southwark property. He was also, at an unspecified date, the grantee

of land in Middlesex and Surrey.[5] On 3 November 1256 the king by charter granted him two properties in Northampton, for his good service. On 29 November 1256 he was ordered to take charge of the whole of the royal works, with Master ALEXANDER the Carpenter 'because the King had suffered much damage through causing his works to be carried on by Sheriffs and other officers'. Among the first duties carried out by the two craftsmen was the viewing of marble from Purbeck which was being purchased for the works of Westminster Abbey. The new arrangement was confirmed on 14 January 1257, when John of Gloucester was granted a patent as master mason of the King's works. Both he and his wife Agnes were provided with furred robes twice a year, at Christmas and Whitsun from 1254 onwards. At this time he was giving his 'view and counsel' on the erection of the new gateway of *Guildford Castle*, part of which still stands in Quarry Street, Guildford. In this he was accompanied by ALEXANDER the Carpenter, with whom he also visited *Portchester Castle* to supervise the works there. He was in charge of work at Everswell by Woodstock and at Havering in Essex.

In 1257 Gloucester was ordered to repair the king's chambers in *Merton Priory*, Surrey, and on 21 May he was to have the oversight of £200 worth of works on the *Castle* of Salisbury (*Old Sarum*). In 1258 he was granted for his good services a house at Bridport, Dorset, and two in Oxford, as well as exemption from certain taxes and jury service. In the same year he and Master Alexander directed the rebuilding of the tower over the prison in *Winchester Castle*, the work being done by the local master HENRY the Mason IA. Next February (1258/9) he was ordered to send marble columns from Westminster for the Queen's chamber in Windsor Castle, of which, as we have already seen, he had been in charge since 1255. He received later in the year £410 to pay arrears of wages to the workmen at Windsor, and in June advised on the paving of the King's new chapel at Woodstock. During 1259 he was supervising various small works at the *Palace of Westminster* as well as the rebuilding of the Abbey: among these works were the repair of a chimney which threatened to fall, and of the conduit of water which supplied the King's lavatory, and the making of a drain through which the refuse of the kitchens could flow into the Thames, 'which conduit the King ordered to be made on account of the stink of the dirty water which was carried through his halls, which was wont to affect the health of the people frequenting them'.

John of Gloucester's range of activity was very wide, and during the last five years of his life he was in charge of works at the royal castles of Gloucester, Oxford, Portchester and Salisbury as well as at the king's manors of Feckenham, Guildford, Havering, Hensington and Woodstock, apart from his heavy commitments in London, Windsor and Westminster. Among the various tasks which fell under the supervision of the mason was, for example, the preparation of the King's iron lectern for Master William to paint, and in 1260 a further order to Master John directed him to have the lectern put together in the new Chapter House. He seems to have had the general supervision of the Abbey works, for it was to 'his friend Master John le Mazun' that the Sheriff of Lincoln wrote informing him that lead had been dispatched from Boston to London according to the King's order.[6] At this time orders were given that his wages should be doubled when he was travelling on business for Westminster Abbey, but in spite of this he seems to have been in financial difficulties. He died between 30 June and 20 October 1260, being at the time bound to the King in the sum of 80 marks (£53 6s. 8d., probably equivalent to some £25,000 in the values of 1982) by reason of arrears in the King's works, and though it was agreed that the debt might be compounded for a yearly payment on 5 marks, it was found by inquisition taken on 3 January 1265/6 that the income from his possessions was less than 2 marks a year. This seems surprising, since in addition to his considerable property in the provinces he owned a house and curtilage in Westminster, but it is probable that difficulties had arisen out of the new method of administration of the royal works, which threw so much responsibility upon the chief mason.

John of Gloucester left a widow Agnes and a son Edmund. (See Appendix 1)

(APD; HWC; LKC; LWR, 94; TPD, I, 248–52); **KJI**; CLR 1251–60; CHR 1226–57, 452
[1] *GCA*, Charters, IX, 2; [2] CCR 1247–51, 317, 361; [3] SRG, Nos. 439, 446, 487; cf. St. Clair Baddeley in BGT, XL (1917), 147–66; [4] *WAM*, 15999; [5] *PRO*, Anc. Deed. B.8278 (*H.M.C.*); [6] *WAM*, 16000 (f)

GLOUCESTER, Robert of (*fl.* 1359–1361) Mason

Was working as warden of the masons at *Windsor Castle* in the summer of 1359, and on 6 January 1360 received a commission to take masons for the King's works in Windsor Castle. In this commission he is named as 'the King's mason', but the accounts show that he held the rank of warden (*apparellator*) only, and that he was succeeded by WILLIAM WYNFORD in that office at some date before 12 April 1361.

HWC, I, 218–19

GLOUCESTER, Thomas of (*fl.* 1354–1358) Mason

Worked under JOHN BOX as warden (*apparilator*) of the masons at *Westminster Palace* in 1354 and 1355, taking 3s. 6d. a week.[1] In 1356 he was the principal mason working at *St. Stephen's Chapel, Westminster*[2] and also appears as the fifth of the six 'hewers' who represented the Freestone Masons upon the commission for regulating the masons' craft in the city of London in that year.[3] He was still working at Westminster Palace as warden in charge of the masons in 1357–58.[4] It is hardly likely that this mason can be identical with the Thomas de Gloucestr', a working mason at *Exeter Cathedral* from Michaelmas 1310 to February 1311, when he was paid at the top rates of 2s. 3d. per week in summer and 1s. 10½d. in winter.[5] He might, however, have been the THOMAS the Mason VII who was in charge at Winchester Cathedral, in view of the marked influence of Gloucester style upon Bishop Edington's work there.

(LKC)
[1] *PRO*, E.101–471–9, 11; 502–17 (*L.F.S.*); [2] *Ibid.*, E.101–471–15, 16; [3] RML, 280–2; KMM, 249–51; [4] *PRO*, E.101–472–4; [5] AEC, I, 187–8

GLYDON, William (*fl.* 1478–   ) Mason

On 26 April 1478 contracted to build a stone malt-house at *Exeter*, Devon, outside the south gate and opposite to 'Wynardis almyshous'. He was to be paid £8.

SHB, 540–1; *PRO*, Anc. Deed A.11545

Goche, Thomas—see GOOCH

GODARD the Carpenter (*fl. c.* 1219) Carpenter

Master Godardus, the carpenter of the cathedral church of Salisbury, and Cecilia his wife, about 1219 were holders of land belonging to the 'carpentaria' of the church.

HMC, *Var. Coll.* I, 369 (*L.F.S.*)

GODARD, John (*fl.* 1466–   ) ? Carpenter

Of Bucklebury, Berks., 'hosbondman', when on 11 June 1466 he contracted to make 37 desks with forms for the *Divinity School, Oxford*, for £22.

AJ, LXXI (1914), 244

GODERICH, John (*fl.* 1384–1396) Mason

Master mason of *Calais* in 1384–96.

HKW, II, 1054

GODFREY, Edmond (*fl.* 1505–   ) Carpenter

With JOHN BROWNE was paid £7 7s. 6d. for making the pews and pulpit at *St. Andrew's Church, Canterbury*, in 1505, besides 4s. 10d. for timber.

AC, XXXII, 232

GODWIN the Mason I (*fl.* 1167–1172) Mason

In each of the years 1167–68, 1169–70, and 1171–72 the sum of 1 mark (13s. 4d.) was allowed for the robes of Godwin the mason of *Windsor Castle*, who was no doubt in charge of the masonry works there, under the general direction of AILNOTH the Engineer. Perhaps identical with GODWIN the Mason II.

PR; (HWC, I, 19)

GODWIN the Mason II [Godwyn] (*fl. c.* 1170–1190) Mason

Master mason (*cementarius*) appearing as a witness to a grant to Byland Abbey, Yorks., of a spring in 'Dale' called 'Woodkelde', *c.* 1170–90. He was presumably the designer of *Byland Abbey*, begun *c.* 1175, and completed soon after 1200. Perhaps identical with GODWIN the Mason I.

EYC, III, 449, No. 1839

GOLDCLIFF, Hugh de (*fl. c.* 1195–1214) Mason (*Goldcliff*, Mon.)

No doubt from the Benedictine Priory of Goldcliff near Newport, Monmouthshire; was master mason of the work at the west front of *St. Albans Abbey* (*c.* 1195–1214) but was dismissed without pay owing to the collapse of the work through his carelessness or jerry-building; he was described as a 'clever but deceitful craftsman' (*vir quidem fallax et falsidicus, sed artifex praeelectus*). In spite of his lack of success as a builder he must be given credit for the very beautiful design of the western porches, which were slowly carried up over a long period.

(BAH; APD; BAA); RGA, I, 218–19

GOLDYNG, John (*fl.* 1426–†1451) Carpenter

Possibly identical with the John Goldyng who in 1405 sold timber to the wardens of London Bridge, and with one of that name concerned in the purchase of houses in Aldgate Street in 1418.[1]

In 1425–26 John Goldyng, carpenter, was paid 7s. 4d. for drawing the design of the kitchen (*pour portratur' del patron de cuzine*) and for his work for the *Merchant Taylors of London* at their Hall. In 1436 he was assessed as having lands and rents in London worth £5 yearly. He was appointed King's Carpenter during good behaviour on 25 July 1426 at a yearly fee of £20 and a robe, as WILLIAM YERDEHURST had had, and obtained a new grant on 10 April 1438.[2] He may have designed the roof of *Eton College Chapel*, though the work was carried out by ROBERT WHETELY, the warden of the carpenters there, who had been granted the reversion of Goldyng's office. Goldyng may have been the 'John Carpenter of London' who made doors for Fromond's Chantry in *Winchester College* in 1438–39 (the glazing of the windows was carried out by John Prudde, the King's Glazier, five years later).[3] 'John Carpenter of London' in 1435–36 was also paid £20 in part of a contract of £66 13s. 4d. for making a new house of eight tenements for the Bishop of Worcester in London.[4] In 1435–6 an inquisition was held to establish that John Golding of London, carpenter, was not identical with another John Golding.[5] Goldyng had a regrant of his office on 19 May 1444, and was succeeded by SIMON CLENCHWARTON on 9 July 1451. Goldyng made his will on 14 September 1450, describing himself as citizen and carpenter of London, dwelling in the Close of St. Bartholomew's Priory, Smithfield; the will was proved on 26 January 1450/1 by Alice, his widow and executrix.[6]

The John Goldyng, carpenter, who in 1450–51 received 6s. 8d. in recompense of his heavy losses on a contract to make 'le Waturwerk and lez flodezates' of the mill of *Sudbury*, Suffolk, for the Duke of York must have been another man.[7]

(HKC; APD)

[1] *LBH*, Accs., 17 m.3 (xxi); *LHR*, 146(18); [2] 1st book of accounts, f. 166v; S.L. Thrupp, *Merchant Class of Mediaeval London*, Chicago 1948, 381 (*N.L.R.*); CPR 1422–9, 395; 1436–41, 164; cf. *BM*, Add. MS. 17721; [3] *WCM*, Compotus 1438–9; [4] *PRO*, Eccl. 2–128–92475; [5] *PRO*, E.143–24 (*H.M.C*); [6] *CCL*, 39 Sharp; [7] *WAM*, 12167

GOLDYNG, William (*fl.* 1409–1410) Carpenter

Master carpenter to *St. Paul's Cathedral, London*, at fees of £6 13s. 4d. a year, in the year Michaelmas 1409–10. He had probably succeeded JOHN DOBSON in the office, about 1409.

SPM, B.95.7

GONELD, John [Gonell, Gonyld] (*fl.* 1432–†1445) Carpenter

Of Bury St. Edmunds, where he was one of the administrators of the goods of William Saverey, mason, grant 14 August 1432,[1] and witness to a deed, 24 February 1432/3.[2] In 1437 he received livery of the Prior of *Christ Church, Canterbury*, as a carpenter employed (*hoc anno*) in the office of the treasurer,[3] by whom he was engaged to make the timber-work of 'le Sunne' in the summer of that year; the masonry had been provided by RICHARD SMYTH and the sign was made by JOHN MASSINGHAM III.[4] In 1445 John Gonell, doubtless the same man, was master carpenter of the repairs of *Rochester Bridge*. The Archbishop had given a commission to the bridge wardens to collect labourers and materials after the fall of an arch of the bridge at Easter of that year.[5]

The will of John Goneld of Bury, occupation not stated, but in all probability the carpenter, was dated 'at Wulwyche in the county of Kent' 2 July 1442 and proved in the Court of the Sacrist of Bury 20 November 1445.[6] In the grant of probate it is stated that John Goneld 'while he lived of the diocese of Norwich. . . at the time of his death was known to have had movable goods in diverse dioceses of the province of Canterbury'. He referred to his lands and tenements in the town of Bury and named as supervisor John Bury and executors Thomas Goneld, Edmund Galyon, and his wife Margaret.

A.O.; J.H.H.
[1] *BW*, i, 201v.; [2] *BCM*, H.1–2–17; [3] *Bodl.*, Tanner MS. 165; [4] *Ibid.*, MS. Top. Kent, c.3, *ff.* 147v.–149; [5] BRB, 88; [6] *BW*, ia, 17

GOOCH, Thomas [Goche] (*fl.* 1478–83) Carver

Of Sudbury, Suffolk; in 1478 was engaged on a contract for making the roodloft in *Clare Church*. John Horold, clothman of Clare, in his will dated and proved that year, refers to 'the new rood loft' in the church 'being made according to the form of a certain indenture made between the wardens of the same

church and Thomas Goche of Sudbury keruer'.[1]

In 1482 (15 March) Thomas Goche, carver, was a witness to the will of Thomas Wurtham of Sudbury.[2] The will of Thomas Goche of Sudbury, dated 17 March 1482/3, was proved 17 December following.[3] He was survived by his wife Isabel, two sons, both named Thomas, and four daughters. The elder son, one of his executors, was a chaplain in the college of St. Gregory at Sudbury; his will was proved in 1510.[4] He used his father's occupational designation ('Kerver') as his surname.

A.O.
[1] *PCC*, 35 Wattys; [2] *BW*, iii, 250; [3] *Ibid.*, 298; [4] *CNN*, 266 Spyltymber

Gore, John—see GOWER

GOSEDEN, Robert (*fl.* 1340–1382) Mason

Was master mason to the Bishop of Winchester for works at *Farnham Castle* in the middle of the 14th century. With ROBERT LE HORE he contracted to rebuild the outer walls, the work being done in 1340–42 at a cost of £97 15s. 4¾d.

In 1342 he also added a chamber to a small building 'on the left facing the keep', and in the next year with a man and a boy he rebuilt two fireplaces in the kitchen. In 1347 he began the work of the Great Chapel, probably to the east of the hall, but after 1348 work was suspended owing to the Black Death. It was resumed in 1353, and must have been speedily completed, as the walls were plastered in that year.

The last mention of Goseden shows that he sold stone to the bishop from his quarry at Bentley in 1382.

(*A.O.*) **RMF**, 126–7, 136, 139, 140, 142

GOUSHILL, Richard de (*fl.* 1335–1337) Mason

Master mason of the works carried out for Edward III after his capture of *Roxburgh Castle*, in 1335–37. He may have been the 'Master Richard' who was in charge of further works there in 1357–61.

HKW, II, 819

GOUSHILL, Robert de (*fl.* 1359–   ) Carpenter

Carpenter in charge of repairs to the timberwork of the chancel of 'Bondeby', *Bonby Church*, Lincs., in 1359. He may have been associated with Goxhill Priory.

PRO, E.101–458–28 (*L.F.S.*)

GOWER, John [Gowere] (*fl. c.* 1450–1460) Mason

According to a traditional rhyme — 'John Gowere, who built Campden Church and Glo'ster towre' was the mason who built the great tower of *Gloucester Cathedral*, about 1454–57, and the nave and tower of *Chipping Campden Church*, built *c.* 1450–60.

It is just possible that this John Gowere was one of the two masons named John Gore who worked as setters at *Eton College* for four weeks in May and June 1445; John Gore, senior, was paid at the rate of 6*d.* a day, while John Gore, junior, presumably his son, took only 4*d.*[1]

The 'Mason Bracket' in Gloucester Cathedral is said to represent the master mason of the tower and his apprentice, who was killed by a fall; there seems to be no authority for naming the mason 'John Tully',[2] (but see TULLEY, ROBERT) while the bracket certainly dates from the work of *c.* 1337.

(APD)

[1] KJE; [2] BAH, 91

GOWSELLE, John (*fl.* 1440–   ) Austin Canon

At a visitation of the Augustinian Priory of Torksey, Lincs., held on 6 April 1440, the Prior gave evidence that Brother John Gowselle, though learned in the art of stone masonry, would not take heed to the works of the church and priory, but was disobedient. Torksey was a small and poor house, and the canons were perhaps attempting to carry out repairs for themselves.

TVR, II, 383n.

Graham, Thomas—see GRANTHAM

Grakal, John—see CRAKALL

GRANTHAM, Hugh (*fl.* 1390–†1410) Mason (*Grantham, Lincs.*)

Mason working on the choir of *St. Andrew's, York*, in 1390 and 1392. Grantham made his will on 8 March 1409/10 and it was proved on 16 March. He left £40 to his wife Agnes and £40 13*s.* 4*d.* to his son, dom. Thomas Grantham. An inventory of his goods shows that his estate amounted to £207 15*s.* 3*d.*, not less than £100,000 in values of 1982. He owed, among many other debts, 6*s.* 8*d.* for stone for a window in *All Saints, North Street, York*, and various amounts for other stone and owed to masons.

RFY, 129; YTE (SS, XLV, 1865), iii, 47–53

GRANTHAM, John (*fl.* 1372–   ) Carpenter

Carpenter to John of Gaunt at *Leicester Castle*, and was granted £2 a year for his good services on 4 August 1372.

JGR 1372–6, 439

GRANTHAM, Thomas [Graham] (*fl.* 1277–1295) Mason (*Grantham, Lincs.*)

Master mason in charge of the building of *Flint Castle*, begun in 1277, when he was paid 1*s.* a day; the design was probably by RICHARD LENGINOUR and JAMES OF ST. GEORGE. Grantham, who had brought 200 masons from Lincolnshire to Chester on 17 July 1277, was sent on later from Flint to *Ruthin Castle*. He was probably the Master Thomas the Mason recorded as a burgess of Ruthin in 1295.

HKW, I, 309, 327–8

SHB, 70; *PRO*, E.101–485–19 (*L.F.S.*)

GRAVELEY, Edmund (*fl.* 1444–1484) Carpenter

Free of the London Carpenters' Company in 1444;[1] was appointed to the office of King's Chief Carpenter on 14 October 1461, at the customary fee of 12*d.* per day,[2] superseding SIMON CLENCHWARTON who may have been under suspicion as a Lancastrian sympathiser. In 1462–63 Graveley was a warden of the Carpenters' Company, and in 1467 was concerned in certain transactions in the city.[3] He must be regarded as the designer of the roof of the *Eltham Great Hall*, the principal work of carpentry carried out in Edward IV's reign. The building of the new hall at Eltham took place between 1475 and 1480,[4] when Edward IV's early policy of economy had been reversed.

Graveley received a regrant of his office from Richard III in 1483, and in 1484 was granted the office for life at 12*d.* a day and a yearly robe, with arrears of pay from 7 July 1483.[5] He was probably the 'Edmund Graveley, esquire' who was a witness at Lewisham, Kent, in 1483.[6]

There are two villages called Graveley, one in Hertfordshire, near Hitchin, the other in Cambridgeshire some five miles south of Huntingdon. Probably from the latter place was Robert Graveley of Cambridge, who in his will of 1465 mentions his brother Edmund, apparently of London. It appears from the will[7] that Robert and Edmund were bound to John Mydelton, citizen of London, in the sum of £20, by reason of a debt of £14 owed by Edmund, and that Edmund owed Robert 10 marks. It is quite likely that this Edmund was the carpenter, and that he had undertaken work for John Mydelton, with his brother Robert providing some of the capital.

HKC

[1] MCR, II, 10; [2] CPR 1461–7, 50; cf. HKW, I, 222n.[5]; [3] MCR, IV, 36–7, 260; CLB, 'L' 75; [4] PRO, E.101–496–21; [5] CPR 1476–85, 443; [6] LBH, I, 43; [7] PCC, 10 Godyn (A.O.)

GRAVELEY, John (*fl.* 1451–1452) Carpenter

In 1451–52 the chamberlains of (King's) Lynn paid John Graveley for felling timber and making the arms and other parts of the mill called 'Scalesmylle' at *Lynn*.

LCR, Ea. 52

GRAVER, William (*fl.* 1462–1493) Mason

Mason of Winchester, dwelling in St. Maurice's parish towards the east end of the High Street on the south side; he also had property in Colebrook Street at the same period, 1462–*c.* 1472. From 1463 to 1468 he also owned tenements near St. John's Hospital.[1] In 1465–66 he was engaged on paving the kitchen of *St. Mary's College*.[2] In 1466–67 he was the leading *cementarius* at *Wolvesey Palace*, in charge of building a new house over 'le surveynge place' between the great hall and the kitchen. He was paid 7*d.* a day with 2*d.* a day for his apprentice.[3]

He was presumably identical with the William '*lathamus*' who in 1469–70 received £2 13*s.* 4*d.* for his work on the new reredos of *Winchester College Chapel*, since in the following year it was William Graver, *lathamus*, who was paid 10*s.* for setting iron bars in the reredos and doing other work in connection with it.[4]

Graver twice dined with the Fellows of the College in July 1476,[5] and in 1481–82 worked for 8½ days on 'le condyte' at the College, taking 6*d.* a day for himself and 4*d.* a day for his servant.[6] On 20 April 1493 Graver was granted by *Winchester Cathedral* Priory, for his past and continuing good services, as chief mason of the cathedral ranking as a *generosus*, a life corrody of food and drink in hall, with £3 6*s.* 8*d.* yearly and a gown of the livery of the *generosi* of the prior's chapel, and a second gown of the livery of the *Custos Operum*.[7]

[1] (D.K.Win.); [2] WCM, Compotus 1465–6; [3] PRO, Eccl. 2–3–155834; [4] WCM, Compoti 1469–70, 1470–1; [5] Ibid., Hall Book 1475–6; [6] Ibid., Compotus 1481–2; [7] GRW, no. 507

GRAVOUR, William [Granere, Gravere] (*fl.* 1433–1436) ? Mason

Master of the works of Sir John Fastolf's castle at *Caister*, Norfolk, from 1433 to 1436.[1] It is nowhere stated that he was a mason, and he may have been purely an administrative clerk of works, though a clerk John Elys was associated with him. Gravour received pay at 6*d.* a day and also a yearly fee of £3 6*s.* 8*d.* In any case he is probably to be identified with the William Gravour of Norfolk who on 1 May 1434 was to take oath not to maintain peace-breakers.[2] The works of the castle began in 1432 and were completed by 1446.[3]

[1] BSB; [2] CPR 1429–36, 407; [3] BSC, 36

GRAY, William (*fl.* 1487–   ) Mason

Was paid £3 3*s.* 9*d.* in 1487 for work on the *Church House* in North Street, *Ashburton*, Devon

BPA

GRENE, John atte (*fl.* 1334–†1350) Mason

Possibly identical with the John atte Grene of Tasburgh, Norfolk, who took up the freedom of Norwich in 1322–23,[1] or with the John atte Grene (son of John, son of John atte Grene of Bury) who, with his wife Isabella, disposed of tenements in the parish of St. Mary-le-Bow, London, in 1339.[2] The Norfolk man, though his craft is not mentioned in the entry of his freedom, was presumably the mason who was warden of the work of the *Norwich Cathedral* cloisters in 1335–37,[3] under JOHN DE RAMSEY I. In 1334 a mason of this name received a fee of £1 and 13*s.* 4*d.* for a robe at *Ely Cathedral*. Letters were sent to him in 1337, when he had a reward of 5*s.* and 14*s.* 10*d.* for a robe, but not being named as master until 1339, he was probably not identical with Master JOHN the Mason VII in charge of the works of the Octagon there from 1322 to 1328. John atte Grene was still master mason at Ely in 1345–46 when he had a house there, and his son John worked under him.[4]

He was already 'master of the masonry and works of the King' south of Trent by 30 June 1349 but was probably dead of the plague before 30 May 1350 when JOHN BOX was called from Canterbury.[5]

[1] EFN; [2] LHR, 66(109); [3] NCM, roll 1044; [4] CSR, II, 68, 82, 84, 97, 99, 110, 116, 122, 128, 137; [5] CPR 1348–50, 387

GRENE, Robert (*fl.* 1533–1538) Mason

Mason of Norwich, admitted to the freedom in 1533–34.[1] In 1538 he and his three servants were paid for helping to lay a gravestone in *Norwich Cathedral*, apparently under the directions of WILLIAM THACKER, freemason and marbler.[2]

[1] EFN; [2] *NRO*, DCN, Liber Misc., Liber 3.

GRENE, Thomas (*fl.* 1456–1457) Carpenter

Was paid 3s. 4d. in 1456–57 for making an oriel in the mansion house at *Macclesfield*, Cheshire.

(A.O.) A, XXIII, 106

GRETSYD, Godwin (*fl. c.* 1050–1067) Mason

Was the master mason in charge of the building of *Westminster Abbey* by Edward the Confessor between 1050 and 1065, perhaps working under the control of LEOFSI DUDDASON. Godwin appears also, with his wife Wendelburh, in a list of persons to be prayed for in Hyde Abbey at Winchester, to which he was a benefactor.

In 1067 Godwin seems to have given certain land and houses in Southampton to Westminster Abbey, reserving the use of them to his son Ælfwin for life. Though the existing source is a spurious charter of a later date, it seems probable that these facts are historical.

(LKC, 102; LWR, 4, 19); F. E. Harmer in EHR, LI (1936), 98

GREYHORSE, Richard (*fl.* 1525–1526) Carpenter

Master carpenter employed, along with JOHN BEK, on repairs at *Tickenhill Manor*, Worcs., in 1525–26, taking 8d. a day each.

HKW, IV, 279

GROSMONT, Ralph of (*fl.* 1177–1191) ? Engineer (*Grosmont*, Mon.)

Was in charge of works at *Hereford Castle* in 1177–79; then in 1182–3 was visiting Grosmont and Skenfrith and a horse was bought for him. Work costing £14 was done on *Grosmont Castle* in 1183–4, and in 1185–88 some £130 on *White Castle*, 'by view of Ralph of Grosmont', who received a personal reward of £2. In 1187–91 he was keeper of the works of *Skenfrith Castle*, on which £64 2s. 8d. was spent.

HKW, I, 59; II, 657, 837, 853

GROVE, Simon [le Grove] (*fl.* 1408–†c. 1450) Carpenter

Carpenter to Richard Beauchamp, Earl of Warwick, from c. 1418 onwards, and prob-ably worked on many of the buildings attri-buted to Earl Richard by William Worcestre.[1]

He first occurs in 1408–9 when he under-took to build a new porch onto the *Guildhall* at *Stratford-upon-Avon*, and to rebuild part of the kitchen there. For this he had £2 0s. 4d., and also seems to have been allowed an entry fine of £2 13s. 4d. to the Guild.[2] The timber came from Packwood, where Simon Grove was living in 1414,[3] and held property as late as 1443.[4] In 1410 he was paid 21s. by the Master of the Stratford Guild for building a house in the town.[5] He first appears in the service of the Earl of Warwick in 1418–19, in which year he supervised the felling of timber at the Earl's manor of Tanworth-in-Arden for the construction of the new stable at the gate of *Warwick Castle* mentioned by Worcestre, for the building of which he was presumably responsible.[6] From then on he remained in the Earl's service, being frequently described as 'the lord's carpenter'.[7] By the Earl's letters patent of 20 May 1421 he received an annuity of 2d. a day for life from the issues of the manor of Tanworth.[8]

His recorded works for the Earl, apart from the new stable at Warwick, include repairs to the manor of *Kirtling*, Cambs., in June 1421,[9] the making of mangers in the stables of the Earl's old hospice in *London* in 1422–23,[10] the repair of a house in *Warwick* subsequently leased to him for life on 15 April 1423,[11] and the building of a new lodge at *Claverdon* in 1430–31.[12] He also supervised the making of laths at Tanworth for use at Warwick Castle in 1421–22 and 1422–23,[13] and was presum-ably in charge of the carpentry works in progress.[14]

No references to his work are found after 1431, except for £20 due to him in 1442–3 for building a house in *Stratford* for the Guild,[15] but he is mentioned up to 28 January 1449.[16] By this time he was resident at Aspley in the parish of Tanworth. He was dead by Michaelmas 1451 as his annuity does not appear in 1451–2.[17]

(G.M.D.B.)

[1] HWI, 218–21; [2] *SBT*, BRT 1/3 XII no. 20; BRS 12; [3] *BRL*, deed in Keen Collection; [4] *Ibid.*; [5] BRS, 14; [6] *SBT*, DR37/box 108; [7] *SBT*, DR37/box 83; [8] *SBT*, DR37/box 108; [9] REF, 9, quoting Receiver General's account of 1421–2; [10] *WRO*, CR1886/373; [11] *Ibid.*, CR1886/485; [12] *SBT*, DR37/box 108; [13] *Ibid.*; [14] A 'new tower' and a 'new building next the high tower' were under construc-tion in 1422–3: *WRO*, CR1886/485; [15] *SBT*, BRT 1/3; [16] *SBT*, DR37/954; [17] *Ibid.*, DR37/box 108

GROVE, WILLIAM

GROVE, William (*fl.* 1473–†1479)
Carpenter

Was granted the office of master carpenter in *Windsor Castle* for life on 25 February 1472/3.[1] He may have been the Grofe, carpenter, who in 1448–52 had worked at *Merton College, Oxford*.[2] He was dead when JOHN SQUYER succeeded to his office on 20 September 1479.[3]

[1] CPR 1467–77, 373; [2] GOC; [3] CPR 1476–85, 163

GROWDON, Roger (*fl.* 1449–1452) Mason

At the beginning of 1449 was appointed by the corporation of *Totnes*, Devon, master mason for the building of the new belfry of the church. Overseers were appointed and in 1450 it was decided that they should view the steeples of Callington (Cornwall), Buckland (? Monachorum), Tavistock, and Ashburton, and that Totnes steeple should be built with the best of them as a pattern. The work was in progress in 1452 and later.

The Totnes tower is in fact closely similar to that at Ashburton, but is more ornate than its model.

(*A.O.*) WHT, I, 396, 407; II, 956–7

Gruff' le Wright—see WRIGHT

GRYME, John (*fl. c.* 1428) Mason

In *c.* 1428 was paid £4 for new making the church porch of *St. John's, Glastonbury*, and covering it with freestone and 'walston' by piecework.

SDN, IV, 143

Henry GRYME, mason, was admitted to the freedom of Wells in 1427.

SRS, XLVI, 141

Henry GRYME, freemason, was recruited in July 1448 to the works of *Eton College* and worked at 3s. a week until 1453.

KJE, 87, 103 (*A.O.*)

GUELDERS, Henry of (*fl.* 1371–1375)
Carpenter

Was master carpenter at *Calais* in 1371 and until 1375, when he was succeeded by RICHARD HEMMYNG.

HKW, II, 1054

GUNDULF (*fl. c.* 1022–†1108) Monk

A Norman monk of Bec, who became Bishop of Rochester in 1077. He is said to have designed his castle at *Malling*, Kent, built about 1070; *Rochester Cathedral*, begun about 1080, of which a tower, parts of the crypt, and other remains are incorporated in the existing building; parts of *Rochester Castle* now destroyed (not the keep, often attributed to him but dating from *c.* 1130; there are slight remains of Gundulf's rubble walling); and the White Tower or keep of the *Tower of London*, about 1081. It has also been suggested that he designed the tower of *Malling Abbey* and the early parts of *Dartford Church*, both in Kent. He died on 8 March 1108.

It is not likely that Gundulf actually designed the buildings attributed to him, but he was probably an enlightened patron and able administrator, with special knowledge of building (*in opere cementarii plurimum sciens et efficax*).

APD; (BAA; CMM)

GUNTON, John de (*fl.* 1319–†1349)
Carpenter

Carpenter and burgess of Great Yarmouth, Norfolk, one of the sons of WILLIAM DE GUNTON and Margaret his wife. On 4 October 1319 was joined with ROGER DE GUNTON and his mother Margaret in undertaking to make a roof for the nave of the church of *Norton next Haddiscoe (Subcourse)*. With his brother ROBERT DE GUNTON on 16 April 1330 he took on the making of a roof for the church of Holy Trinity, (*East*) *Caister* of 29 couples of heart of oak, each couple 25 feet long and in size according to a pattern (*eskauncellyn*), framed with tiebeams, collars and ashlars cross-braced (*chescon couple serra lye des soebemes wyndbemes de asshelers croyses parmy le Wyndbemes*) by 8 September 1330, for the timber of the old roof and £7 3s. 4d.

John de Gunton, probably smitten by the plague, made his will on 9 May 1349, and it was proved two days later, showing that his wife Beatrix had predeceased him and that he left only a daughter Isabella.

GYM, C.4/53, m. 18v. (*A.P.B.* and *P. R.*); HAC, 198–200

GUNTON, Robert de (*fl.* 1330–1337)
Carpenter

Carpenter of Great Yarmouth, son of WILLIAM and brother of JOHN DE GUNTON. On 16 April 1330 with his brother John undertook to make a new roof for the church of (*East*) *Caister*, Norfolk. From a plea of 11 January 1336/7 it appears that he was son of William de Gunton and Margaret his wife.

(*P.R.*); HAC, 200

GUNTON, Roger de (*fl.* 1319–1320)
Carpenter

126

Carpenter of Great Yarmouth; with WILLIAM DE GUNTON on 1 May 1319 undertook to make the chancel roof for the church of *Norton (Subcourse)*, Norfolk; and after William's death was a party to a further contract of 4 October 1319, with William's widow Margaret and son JOHN DE GUNTON to a separate contract with the parishioners to make a roof for the nave, of 32 rafters at 12*s.* 6*d.* each according to the size of the timbers in the chancel. The work was to be finished by 29 September, 1320, a year after the chancel roof which had been acknowledged as complete by 4 October 1319.

GYM, C.4/43, m. 1 (*A.P.B.* and *P. R.*); HAC, 198–9

GUNTON, William de *(fl. 1303–†1319)* Carpenter

Carpenter of Great Yarmouth, party to a deed in 1303. On 1 May 1319, with ROGER DE GUNTON, undertook to make a roof for the chancel of *Norton next Haddiscoe (Subcourse)*, Norfolk, of 25 couples of oak according to the size of patterns (*eschankelyons*), the work to be finished by 29 September. William died in the interim, but Roger appeared on 4 October 1319 to prove that the work was done. William was the father, by his wife Margaret, of JOHN and ROBERT DE GUNTON.

GYM, C.4/42, m.4 (*A.P.B.* and *P.R.*); HAC, 198–200

GUYNES, John *(fl. 1499–†1510)* Joiner

Carpenter of Windsor, usually called 'the joiner'. For *Windsor Castle* he made 22 doors for which he was paid £2 4*s.* on 31 October 1499, with a further payment of £2 on 24 April 1500. In August he received £3 6*s.* 8*d.* 'opon his indentur', which seems to have been a contract for roofs, as he soon afterwards had £3 12*s.* 4*d.* in full payment for 'the two middell roffes'.[1] Guynes made his will on 24 September 1509 and it was proved on 16 February 1510; he desired to be buried in the church of St. John the Baptist by his late wife Margaret, and mentions his mother Isabella as still living. He left bequests to her and to his sister Isabell, as well as many tools to several craftsmen: Axes, augers, chisels and gouges are followed by 40 'enbowyng planes', that is planes with shaped blades for shooting mouldings, showing the highly sophisticated character of the joinery of the time.[2]

[1] HKW, III, 307; [2] *PCC*, 26 Bennett (*A.O.*)

Gwilym ap Ieuan—see BLEDDYN

GYE, John [Gye alias Flexman] *(fl. c. 1525)* Carpenter

At an uncertain date between 1518 and 1529, when Cardinal Wolsey was Chancellor and also Legate *a latere*, a petition was submitted by John Gye alias Flexman of Whittlesford Bridge, Cambridgeshire, carpenter, alleging that he had not been paid an agreed sum for the work of taking down the old *Great Bridge* at *Cambridge* and setting up another in its place. It is known that a special tax was raised, from 1499 until 1546, for new building the Great Bridge; Thomas Hutton, gent., who had been one of the commissioners for the tax, sent for Gye, 'for takyng vpp of the kyngs brygge in Cambryg beyng then so dekeyd and sonkken that nowther horsse ne man covld passe over', and asked for an estimate. Gye had declared that he would 'not gladly' do the work for £40, but took on the job and was given an advance of 20 marks (£13 6*s.* 8*d.*) to begin work. After demolition Gye got the foundation laid 'within the water', but was unable to obtain any further advance. He borrowed £10, hired a yard in 'Bukkyngham' College (i.e. Magdalene, beside the Bridge) 'to lye in hys Tymbre and bords', but was unable to pay the rent so that the materials were sold by the college.

PRO, C 1–510–54; cf. JAB, III, 106

GYLES, — *(fl. 1507–1509)* Mason

Freemason in charge of the building of the steeple of *Swaffham Church*, Norfolk, from 1507 to 1509; Gyles visited the work from elsewhere bringing with him on various occasions his son or two apprentices.

RPS, 29–30

GYLES, Richard [Gelys] *(fl. 1516–1518)* Mason

Freemason of Winchester; with THOMAS PHELYPP of Oxford, mason, contracted to build a farmhouse according to a plan, at Holywell in Oxford, on 11 May 1516; this still exists, being known as *Holywell Manor*; Gyles and Phelypp were to be paid £29.[1] In 1517–18 Richard Gelys was master mason in charge of works at *Warblington*, Hants., being paid 3*s.* 8*d.* a week.[2] He was perhaps identical with the 'Gills' who was partner to THOMAS POKYLL in a contract to build the tower of *Bolney Church*, Sussex, in 1536.[3]

[1] SHB, 570–1; RAM, 461; [2] *PRO*, E.101–490–12 (*L.F.S.*); [3] SAC, VI, 244–52

GYLES, William *(fl. 1463–1464)* ? Mason

William Gyles was paid 12*d.* in 1463–64 for repairs to a window in the steeple of *East*

Dereham Church, Norfolk.

NRO, Phillips MSS. box 5, 40973 (*P.C.*)

Gylkes, Gylkys—see JYLKES

GYLYS, Richard (*fl.* 1492–   ) Carpenter
Carpenter; on 10 March 1491/2 was paid
13*s*. 4*d*. for making the new building at *Dean*,
Oxon., for Oriel College.

(*E.M.J.*) *OCO*, Treasurers' Accs., Bk. iii, 198

GYMBOLL, Robert [Grymboll, Gymbold]
(*fl.* 1511–1517) Carver
Of Aldermanbury, London, when (as
'Goodman Gymbold') he was in 1511 paid £2
for carving new tabernacles for the altars of
the Holy Name of Jesus and of St. Clement in
the church of *Allhallows Staining, London*.[1] In
1517 he carved ten king's beasts of wood for
the lantern of the *Savoy Hospital*.[2]

[1] MLR, II, 19; [2] HKW, III, 204

GYMEL, John [*Cementarius*, le Mazun] (*fl.*
1259–1261) Mason
Mason (*cementarius*) engaged to work upon
the town walls of *Shrewsbury* in 1259–1261. He
was sometimes paid by contract (*convencio*) for
specified tasks, such as 4½ marks in 1260 for
the wall from the gate next the house of John
de Thonge to the castle; on other occasions he
received 2*s*. per week in summer or 1*s*. 8*d*. in
winter. Besides the walls he was building at
the Dominican Friary in 1259, St. Rumold's
Gate and St. George's Bridge in 1261. The
designer may have been ALAN FITZGAMEL.

HMC, R.15, pt. X, 25; *SC*, Bailiff's Accs., Nos. 305,
307, 308

GYST, Walter (*fl.* 1377–1406) Carpenter
Master carpenter of *Exeter Cathedral* in 1377
and subsequently until 1406, when he was
granted a yearly fee of 14*s*. and 4*d*. a day for
his good services.

BPE, 91–2; *FFE*

HACCHE, John de (*fl.* 1341–   ) Mason
Master mason (*cementarius*); in 1341 succeeded JOHN DE COMPTON in the charge of the
works of the new chapel at the royal manor of
Ludgershall, Wilts. He was paid 2*s*. 2*d*. a week,
the rate received by the working masons
being 1*s*. 10*d*.

PRO, E.101–476–1 (*L.F.S.*); HKW, II, 731n.

'Hacket'—see HUGUET

HALES, James [Halys] (*fl.* 1507–   )
Carver
Was paid £5 in or shortly before 1507 for
carving the patron or wooden model for a
copper image made for the Earl of Derby,
and formerly in *Burscough Priory* in the parish
of Ormskirk, Lancs. The fact was mentioned
as a memorandum appended to the estimates
made in 1506–07 for the tomb of Henry VII
at Westminster.

LPH, I, 775

HALES, William (*fl.* 1382–   ) ? Mason
Appointed surveyor of the works of *Kenilworth Castle* on 4 February 1381/2, as HENRY
SPENCER, mason, had been, with the same
fees.

JGR 1379–83, 1110; (DL.42–14, *f*. 120)

HALL, Geoffrey (*fl.* 1448–1460) Carpenter
Between Michaelmas 1448 and Michaelmas 1451 more than £85 was spent by King's
College, Cambridge, on the building of an
inn at *Huntingdon* called the *Hart in the Hoop*.
Considerable payments were made to Geoffrey Hall, the carpenter in charge of the work.
The Provost made three visits of inspection,
and on the first, on 3 February 1449, he was
accompanied by William Roskyn, REGINALD
ELY, and THOMAS STURGEON, respectively clerk
of the works, master mason, and master
carpenter at King's College.[1] In 1450–51
timber worth 16*d*. was bought from Geoffrey
Hall for the reconstruction of a tenement in
Barnwell belonging to the nuns of St. Radegund's Priory at Cambridge.[2] Two sums of
10*s*. and 2*s*. were paid to Geoffrey Hall by the
Provost of *King's College* in 1460 in satisfaction of creditors of the college.[3]

A.O.

[1] *KCM*, Mundum Books; [2] *GRC*, 169; [3] *KCM*, College
Accs., vol. ii

HALL, Thomas (*fl.* 1532–   ) Carpenter
In or about 1532 JOHN KYNGE and Thomas
Hall, carpenters of London, were to build
three new houses next the King's lodging in
the *Tower of London*.

LPH, V, 1781, 1086, 1307

HALL, W(illiam?) [Hal] (*fl. c.* 1520–   )
Carpenter
Made the wooden roof of the north chapel
of *St. Mary's Church, Beverley*, Yorks., as is
shown by the inscription 'W. Hal Carpenter
mad thys rowfe', accompanied by a square,
carpenter's axe, and compasses.
He may also have made the timber ceiling
of the nave, completed in 1524; the two roofs
are apparently of nearly the same date.

HMB

HALLEY, Bartholomew (*fl.* 1446–1461)

Was not a craftsman but apparently a lawyer and M.P. He held office as King's Joiner in the Tower of London from 1446 after the death of ROBERT CONY, until 1461, but must have appointed a deputy.

HKW, I, 225n.; II, 1051

Halsebroke, Henry—see ALSEBROKE

Halywode, Nicholas—see WAREYN, Richard

Hamelhampsted, William de—see HEMEL-HEMPSTEAD

HAMME, John (*fl.* 1480–   ) Carpenter

In 1480 was paid £10 for taking down the old steeple frame of *Hythe Church*, Kent, and putting up a new one. He and his two assistants were allowed 6*s.* for board for 2 weeks while pulling down the old work.

HMC, 4R, 432–3

HAMOND, John (*fl. c.* 1463–   ) Carver

Made an image of Our Lady for *Saffron Walden Church*; the date is given in print as 1464, but seems to have been 1462–63.

(*A.O.*) BAE, 219 ff.; *CWW*

HAMOND, William (*fl.* 1476–1479) Mason

With two other masons, Ralph Hamond and Miles Alenson, on 4 November 1476 undertook to take down and rebuild the church of *Oldham*, Lancs. It was to be 20 feet wide with four arches on each side, 12 feet wide between the pillars and 18 feet high. There was to be an 'yling' on each side 10 feet wide, with a wall 12 feet high, five windows on the south and four on the north. The masons were to be paid in six instalments of £28 6*s.* 8*d.*, and the work was to be finished by Easter Day (11 April) 1479. The church was again rebuilt in 1843.

W.H. Rylands in HSLC, L (1900), 141–3 (*N.L.R.*)

HAMPTON, John (*fl.* 1455–1474) Mason

Mason of Bath; in 1455 owned a tenement in Redcliff Street, Bristol, and in 1474 was bequeathed 3*s.* 4*d.* by the will of William Canynges on condition of attending his funeral at Redcliff Church.[1] He may have been the mason of this name working at *Eton College* in 1442 who in the week 2–7 July was paid for 4 days only 'for late cuming and gooth from his werke out of tyme'.[2]

(*A.O.*)
[1] WBW, 135, 151; [2] KJE, 93

HANCOCK, William [Hancok] (*fl.* 1384–†1389) Mason

In 1384 acquired a tenement in the parish of St. Mary at Hill, London;[1] made his will on 12 February 1388/9 as a parishioner of St. Faith-by-St. Paul's, leaving 12*d.* to the fraternity of masons of London founded at St. Thomas of Acre, and his residuary estate to his wife Joan, who proved the will on 29 March 1389.[2]

Henry HANCOCKE in 1434 assisted in making a niche on the west side of the Lollards' Tower at *Lambeth Palace*.

GLP, 52–6
[1] *LHR*, 113(22); [2] *CCL*, 177 Courtney; (AQC, XLI, 130–1)

HARDTHONG, Thomas (fl. 1375–1384) Mason

Master mason of *Calais* in 1375–84.

HKW, II, 1054

HARDY, John (*fl.* 1441–1451) Mason

In 1441 was senior warden of the London Masons' Mistery,[1] and on 18 March 1443/4 took a 50 years' lease of a tenement and shop on the east side of Gracechurch Street, London on condition of building a new house of timber within five years.[2] He was apparently in charge of the works of the monastery of *St. Saviour, Syon* (Brentford), Middlesex, in 1444, as on 3 November of that year he was granted a licence for seven years to use his ship 'Le Cristofre' for those works without hindrance of the King's purveyors or ministers.[3]

In 1451 Hardy was paid £10 in two instalments by the keeper of the new work of *Westminster Abbey* for 'Northirnstone' bought from him for the great south rose.[4] On 17 December of the same year Hardy appears as one of the four sworn masons and carpenters acting as viewers of the City of London.[5]

[1] CLB, 'K', 256; [2] *LHR*, 172(52); [3] CPR 1441–6, 312; [4] *WAM*, 23517–18; [5] CPM 1437–57, 127

HARDYNG, John, I (*fl.* 1326–1327) Carpenter

Admitted to the freedom of York in 1326–27,[1] and at some time later in the reign of Edward III was master carpenter in charge of works at *York Castle*.[2]

[1] YCF; [2] *PRO*, E.101–501–12 (*L.F.S.*)

HARDYNG, John, II (*fl.* 1443–1446) Carpenter

Carpenter of *Southampton*; in 1443–45 repaired a tenement outside Bargate belonging to Winchester College. He was the first named of two carpenters (see RICHARD HOLNERST) who on 4 March 1444/5 contracted to build the *Angel Inn, Andover*, Hants., for the college according to a 'portature' or drawing. They were to be paid £90 and to complete the work within two years. Hardyng gave the Warden of the College a bond in 10 marks (£6 13s. 4d.) on 25 April 1444, payable at Michaelmas; and he and Holnerst four further bonds (for £90, £10, £10 and 10 marks) at intervals until 2 July 1446. In the same year Hardyng was paid 3s. 4d. for drawing the '*portratura*' or design, but was later told not to begin work until further instructions from the Warden were given. The carpenter of Eton College, who visited Winchester College on 2 April 1445, was paid 3s. 4d. for giving his counsel on the design and execution of the work and a further 6s. 8d. for making a 'portratura' of the inn drawn on a skin of parchment, as well as 1s. 8d. given to his servant. This carpenter may have been ROBERT WHETELY. In July 1445 Hardyng visited Froxfield, Hants., to obtain timber for the work. The actual building at Andover seems to have been done by Holnerst.

SHB, 517–19 (*WCM* 2522); cf. Compotus *WCM* 22119–20; bonds WCM 20115, 22833; 20090–93

Harley, John—see HERLEYE

HAROLD the Mason [Eraldo] (*fl.* 1129–1130) Mason
In 1129–30 was pardoned 13s. 4d. by the king's writ at Colchester. He was probably in charge of works at *Colchester Castle*.

HMR, 138

HARPOUR, Ellis (*fl.* 1375–1421) Carpenter
Carpenter employed by *Durham Cathedral Priory* from 1375 and through the rest of his life until 1421. Henry Bowet, Archbishop of York, wrote on his behalf to the prior, asking a place for him and his wife in the Almshouse of St. Mary Magdalen, Durham, on the grounds that he had spent most of his life in the priory's service, and that his wife had been a servant to Bowet's mother.

DAR, Loc. XXV.51 (*M.G.S.*)

HARPUR, Henry (*fl.* 1508) Carver
In 1508 Henry Harpur and WILLIAM MOORECOCK of Burton, Staffs., undertook to make a tomb for Henry Foljambe, deceased, in St.. Mary's choir in the church of *Allhallows, Chesterfield*, by 26 Oct. 1510. It was to be as good as the tomb of Sir Nicholas Montgomery at 'Colley' (Great Cubley), and was to have an image of Henry Foljambe of copper and gilt upon a table of marble (alabaster) with two shields of arms at the head

and two at the feet, with 18 images (weepers) with arms below the table. Harpur and Moorecock were to be paid £5 in hand and £5 on completion. The tomb, which still exists, has finely cut weepers; the 'image' is a brass set in the slab. The Cubley tomb used as a model is of exactly the same type and was doubtless also made by the same firm, to whom Mr. Arthur Gardner also assigns tombs at Ashover and Norton, both of *c.* 1510–20.

CTG, I, 354; GAT, 9–10

Harrenden—see HERUNDEN

HARRESONE, John (*fl. c.* 1540–?†1551) Carpenter
A carpenter of 'Wallton' (? Waltham Holy Cross), Essex, who contracted *c.* 1540 to build a farmhouse at *Wormley*, Herts., for William Woodlyffe, mercer of London. The house, for the tenant farmer William Curle, was to be of two storeys, 24 feet long by 15 feet wide; later, Woodlyffe wished it to be enlarged, agreeing to pay the extra cost. After Harresone had laid out over £10 against an advance from Woodlyffe of £2, a dispute arose with the tenant Curle over costs of carrying timber, and Curle sued Harresone before the City Sheriffs. Harresone petitioned the Lord Chancellor, Sir Thomas Audley (1538–44).
He may have been the John Harryson, yeoman of Waltham Holy Cross, Essex, who made his will on 4 January 1550, leaving his house and lands to his wife Agnes and mentioning a son William and three daughters. The will was proved on 28 April 1551.

PRO, C.1–1010–18; ERO, Archdeaconry Court of Essex 76 ER 7

HARRISON, Dyrik (*fl.* 1510–1532) Joiner
Of London; perhaps a Fleming. In 1510 he worked on the stalls of *Christ's College, Cambridge*; these were replaced in 1702–03. Harrison and Henry Plowman, another joiner, were paid 3s. 4d. 'for ther costes and cariege of ther tolys from London to Cambrege with rewardes for lettyng of certen daies werke or ther toles came'.
Between 18 November 1531 and 21 July 1532, Harrison carved panelling for the Hall of *Queens' College, Cambridge*, and at the conclusion was given a reward of 8d. in addition to his fees 'by order of the President'. The panelling was removed in the 18th century,

but much of it remains in the study of the President's Lodge.

(*A.O.*) WCC, I, 197–8; II, 45, 61–6

HARRY, John (*fl.* 1407–1447) Mason

Mason of Exeter; was at work on *Exeter Cathedral* in 1407 at the rate of 2*s.* 1*d.* a week, his pay rising to 2*s.* 6*d.* and to 2*s.* 8*d.* by 1408; he left the works in 1409, but returned as a 'fremason' in 1420, when he received 3*s.* a week and a fee of 6*s.* 8*d.* a quarter. On 21 July, 1427 he took up the freedom of the city of Exeter, and visited the Beer quarries on behalf of the cathedral. He had also repaired the bishop's manor houses at *Chudleigh* and at *Faringdon*, Hants., in 1424–25 and 1425–26, his visit to Faringdon being combined with a journey to London. He was paid nothing by the Chapter in 1430–31 and 1431–32, as he was absent on pilgrimage, but thereafter appears as master mason of the cathedral at 3*s.* a week. In 1447 he visited Salcombe on behalf of the Chapter, and in the same year was paid by the city for transcribing a roll of chronicles. He was dead by 1456, when mention is made of the tenement lately his in the parish of St. Mary, Exeter. He was succeeded as master at the Cathedral by WILLIAM FOUND-YNG. Harry's principal work as master seems to have been the new vestry added to the south side of the Lady Chapel; only its doorway survives.

(APD) *FFE*, from Fabric rolls; *ECR*, Receiver's roll 25–26 Hen. VI; *MCR*, 5–6 Hen. VI

HART, — (*fl. c.* 1490–1525) Mason

According to Rice Merrick's *Book of Glamorganshire Antiquities* written in 1578, the tower of *St. John's Church, Cardiff* 'was made by — Hart, a Mason, who made the tower of Wrexham and of St. Stephen's in Bristow'.[1]

Wrexham Church tower was certainly in course of erection between 1505 and 1525;[2] at *St. Stephen's, Bristol*, the lower part of the tower was begun *c.* 1453, and works were in progress in 1480 (south porch) and 1493;[3] while the Cardiff tower closely resembles the original north-west tower of *Llandaff Cathedral*, built in 1486–95.[4] 'Hart' was probably identical with WILLIAM HORT.

[1] MGA, 124–5; [2] PWC; [3] NTB; *Corpus Christi Coll., Cambridge*, MS. 210, p. 129; WBW, 170; [4] JLC, 25–6

HARTING, John of (*fl.* 1250–1294) Carpenter (*Harting, Sussex*)

Resident master carpenter at *Dover Castle* from *c.* 1250 until 1294 or later, paid at 4*d.* a day. His work was mainly concerned with the continuous repairs of the royal apartments in the castle. When travelling, as he did in 1256, 1261, 1266, 1269 and 1272 to obtain timber for the works from the Forest of Essex, he was paid at the double rate of 8*d.* In 1294 he provided the machinery for a windmill built by NICHOLAS AYNHO.

HKW, II, 638; CLR 1251–60, 291, 372; 1260–7, 32, 46, 220; 1267–72, nos. 671, 2117

HARTSHORNE, Thomas (*fl.* 1531–1532) Carpenter

In 1531–32 was in charge of repairs to the staircase at *Sunninghill*, Berks.

HKW, IV, 272

Harunden, Thomas—see HERUNDEN

HARWARD, William [Hereward, Herward] (*fl.* 1449–1468) Carpenter

Of Halstead, Essex. In 1450 he was paid £2 3*s.* 4*d.* for his bargain at *Peterhouse, Cambridge*, where he made the solar over the buttery and a partition dividing the buttery and pantry.[1] On 25 June 1466, in partnership with WILLIAM BACON, he entered into a contract to make the floor, roof, doors, windows, and staircase roof for the south range of the *Schools Quadrangle* at Cambridge. This work was to be finished by 1 August 1467; the two carpenters were to receive £10 in hand and a further £23 6*s.* 8*d.* during the progress of the work.[2] Payments to the carpenters in respect of this contract occur in the Proctors' Accounts of the university between 1466 and 1468.[3]

In 1449, when King's College were carrying out repairs at *Merton Hall, Cambridge*, they bought 900 laths for 4*s.* 6*d.* from William Herward at Barnwell Fair.[4] The reference might be to the Midsummer Fair or the more famous Stourbridge Fair, but in either case it is interesting in showing how Suffolk and Essex carpenters attending the Cambridge fairs might be able to obtain building work at or for the colleges.

In 1450 Andrew HERWARD, probably a relative, was one of the carpenters working under GEOFFREY HALL on the *Hart Inn* at *Huntingdon*.[4]

A.O.

[1] WCC, I, 12n.; [2] *Ibid.*, III, 13, 93; SHB, 535–6; [3] CGB 'A', 54, 57, 65, 66; [4] *KCM*, Mundum Book 1448–9

HASCHENPERG, Stephen von [S. the Almayn, Hassenpergk, Hassynberk] (*fl.* 1539–1543) Engineer

'Gentleman of Moravia'; German military

engineer and designer of fortifications. He was employed by Henry VIII to design a part of the new scheme of coastal defences, begun about 1539. He seems to have received the fee of 4s. a day, and was certainly the designer of *Sandgate Castle*, built in 1539–40,[1] and also of *Deal*, *Sandown*, and *Walmer* castles at the same time. At Sandgate he is named in the accounts 'devisor' and 'engineer', and signed the ledger books as 'Ic(onomus)' or 'overseer' of the works. On 20 October 1539 Haschenperg was granted an annuity of £60 which was increased to £75 on 25 July 1540. In 1539–40 Haschenperg ('Master Stevyn the devysour') was in charge of the new work at *Camber Castle*, and added to the earlier tower of 1512–14.

After his work at Sandgate, Haschenperg was sent to Calais to produce a survey map of the English territory, completed at the end of 1540.

From the spring of 1540 the works of St. Mawes Castle in Cornwall were in progress; Stephen 'the Almaine' is said to have designed this castle and Pendennis, though the latter was not built until 1542–46.[2] From 1541 von Haschenperg was principally engaged on the fortifications of *Carlisle*, until he was suspended in May 1543.[3] Haschenperg went to the continent and after a fruitless effort to regain the favour of Henry VIII apparently returned to his native country and became steward (*Hofmeister*) to Marcus Kuen, Bishop of Olmütz 1553–65.

The typically English decorative details of the coastal forts such as windows, doors, and moulding profiles, were doubtless designed by the King's Master Mason, JOHN MOLTON.

OSH
[1] AC, xx, 246, 247; [2] DSM; [3] LPH; HKW, IV, 422, 667

HASILL, John (*fl.* 1427–1428) Carpenter
Master carpenter at the building of the *Grammar School, Stratford on Avon*, in 1427–28, when he was paid at the rate of 6d. a day.
FOS, 30

HASSOCK, John [Hassok] (*fl.* 1443–1450) Carpenter
In 1443–44 made 'stoling' for *Rochester Bridge Chapel*.[1] Of St. Margaret next Rochester, he was granted a pardon on 7 July 1450 for having taken part in Jack Cade's insurrection.[2]
(*A.O.*)
[1] BRB, 20; [2] AC, VII, 263

HATHERLEY, John de (*fl.* 1323–1324) Carpenter (*Hatherley, Glos.*)
Master carpenter at *Gloucester Castle* in 1323–24, when he was paid 2s. 2d. a week for work on the hall of the long stable, and repairs to the drawbridges towards the town and towards the meadow beyond Severn, with the 'Garites' over each bridge. The carpenters working under Hatherley were paid 1s. 6d. or 1s. 8d. a week.
PRO, S.C.6–854–7

Hause, John, Haus, Richard—see HOWES

HAWARDEBY, John (*fl. c.* 1370–1375) Mason (*Hawerby, Lincs.*)
Partner of WILLIAM ALBON in repairing the great bridge of *Huntingdon*, c. 1370–75.
PRO, Anc. Petitions 7937 (*L.F.S.*); JAB, III, 101–2

HAWES, — [Hawe] (*fl. c.* 1430) Mason
Mason of Occold, Suffolk, near Eye; was called in c. 1430 to design and estimate for alterations to the chancel of *Wingfield Church*, Suffolk. The chancel and south (Lady) chapel were to be lengthened by 14 feet, with a new arch between them and a new window in the south aisle wall. The old east window of the chapel was to be rebuilt in the new gable, and another new window on the north of the chancel, as well as a new east window to the chancel, which was to be heightened with a clerestory. Hawes put the total cost at £75 7s. 4d., of which mason's work would account for £33 6s. 8d., stone from Lincolnshire and Burwell £23 17s. 4d., and brick £4 3s. 4d. The work seems to have been carried out about 1430 and in part was to the earlier design of c. 1415.
Bodl., MS. Bodley d.d. Ewelme a.6, A.37

Hawes, John—see HOWES

Hawkin of LIÈGE—see LIÈGE.

HAWKINS, John [Hawkyns] (*fl.* 1525–1534) Carpenter
Carpenter of London; in 1530 undertook by contract to build two houses in *Shoreditch* for Katherine Adams, but was sued by her for having failed to do so. Hawkins defended himself on the ground that he and all his servants had been pressed to work for the King at *York Place*. In 1534 he appealed to Thomas Cromwell to obtain payment of a debt of £4 10s. owed to him for nine years by *St. John's Priory, Clerkenwell*.
SHB, 38, 98; LPH, VII, no. 1640 (*N.L.R.*)

HAYGHT, Edward (*fl. c.* 1516–1529)
Carpenter
At the building of *Chevet Hall* near Wakefield, Yorks., in *c.* 1516–29, £3 6*s.* 8*d.* was paid to Edward Hayght 'for tymbur wark of the sayd hall wt iij gavyll ends and the hawtt playsse over the deesse'. The masonry of the hall had been built by JOHN PRESTON.

YAJ, XXXII (1936), 326–30

HAYNES, John (*fl.* 1450–   ) Carpenter
Citizen and carpenter of London; with RICHARD BIRD undertook on 13 February 1449/50 to make desks for the *Beauchamp Chapel, Warwick.*

DHW; BAA, IV, 11

HAYS, Richard (*fl.* 1498–1526) Mason
Rough mason and later freemason of *Oxford.* He carried out a large number of minor works at *Magdalen College* from 1498 until 1526, and from time to time was employed by other colleges, as by *New College* in 1500–01, when he built a chimney in the hall, and by *Lincoln College*, for which he repaired properties in 1505–07. At this period his normal wage was 6*d.* a day.

From 1507 onwards he was doing more important work at Magdalen College, building the range of chambers eastward of the great tower, supplying the moulds (*exemplaribus vulgar. dict. le mowlde*) for which he was paid 8*d.* While most of his employment continued to be at Magdalen, Hays in 1511 also worked at *Oriel College*, and in 1516 for Lincoln College.

From 1520 he was in charge of the building of the gallery or *Election Chamber* at Magdalen, an extension to the President's Lodge. He was paid 3*s.* 4*d.* a week at times, and also received sums for squaring ashlar and cutting quoins and stringcourses. He is last mentioned in 1526.

GOM, 86–7

Hayward, John—see HEYWARD

HECHAM, William (*fl.* 1369–   ) Mason
Was a salaried mason at the abbey of *St. Edmund* at *Bury* in 1369–70. The Sacrist's Roll for that year shows him receiving 12*s.* for a robe. He is described as *cementarius* and no other mason is named. The wages of the *cementarius*, unnamed but presumably William Hecham, are entered as £4 6*s.* 8*d.* for the whole year.[1] At this time the central tower

was being rebuilt under the Sacrist, John Lavenham. William Mason, who was one of the executors of WILLIAM DE BODEKESHAM, carpenter, *c.* 1370, may have been William Hecham.[2] A gift of 3*s.* 4*d.* made '*apud Sanctum Edmund*' to a mason working on the bell-tower occurs in the Treasurer's Roll at Ely for 1370–71.[3]

A.O.
[1] *BCM*, A.6–1–3; [2] *BW*, i, 35; [3] *CUL*, Add. MS. 6388, p. 57 (*J.H.H.*)

HEDON, Hugh de (*fl.* 1394–†1408) Mason
(*Hedon, Yorks. E.R.*)
Took up the freedom of York in 1394 and was paid as master mason of *York Minster* in 1399,[1] and also visited the stone-quarries at Thevesdale and Stapleton in that year and in 1404; he seems to have held the office until WILLIAM COLCHESTER was sent from London to take charge of the works at the end of 1407. This was in consequence of the collapse of the old central tower while being underpinned with new crossing arches and under stress from a great tempest. Hedon died soon after, as his will was proved by his wife Agnes on 1 September 1408.[2] He had been one of the executors of the will of John Hyndeley of York, mason, who died in August or September 1407[3] (see HYNDELEY, WILLIAM).

William HEDON, mason, in 1429 left his sword, two bows and twelve arrows, to the Light of St. Mary in St. Maurice's Church outside Monk Bar, York.[4]

BHY, I, 197, 201; ACY, 167–9, 190
[1] YCF, i, 94; RFY, 14n.; [2] PCY, ii, 584; [3] *Ibid.*, iii, 271; [4] RMY, 277

HELEY, John (*fl.* 1446–†1475) Mason
Was appointed by the Duchy of Lancaster master mason in Lancashire from 30 April 1446 and held office until his death in December 1475. He was in charge of building a new gatehouse at *Halton Castle*, Cheshire, in 1450–57, for the Duchy.

HKW, II, 667, 1059

Helie—see ELIAS

HELLE, William atte (*fl.* 1422–1426) Mason
In November 1422 called into consultation by WILLIAM CHAMPNEYS concerning a defective pier of *Rochester Bridge*. The pier had to be rebuilt with its two arches, Helle and Champneys being paid £63 6*s.* 8*d.* for the work on its completion in 1426. He was probably identical with WILLIAM HILLE.

BRB, 85–7

HELMESFIELD, Adam de (*fl.* 1368–1369) Carpenter

Master carpenter in charge of works at *Nottingham Castle* in 1368–69, when he was paid 3*s.* 4*d.* a week.

PRO, E.101–478–8 (*L.F.S.*)

HELPESTON, John de [Helpstone] (*fl.* 1296–1326) Mason (*Helpston, N'hants.*)

John de Helpeston was a burgess of Ruthin in 1296 and was evidently concerned with the works of Edward I's castles in North Wales. Undertook to build the round water-tower on the walls of *Chester* by contract in 1322–23; it was to be 24 royal ells (90 feet) high, and Helpeston was to be paid £100.[1] In 1324 he did a large amount of work at *Flint Castle,* a sum of £22 still outstanding being paid to him in 1326.[2]

(APD; BAA); SHB, 428–9; HKW, I, 329
[1] MCP, 244; [2] FHS, III, 83

HELPESTON, Robert de [Delpeston] (*fl.* 1319–1344) Mason

Robert de Helpeston was a working mason at *Carnarvon Castle* in 1319–20, and in 1323–4 made the stone piers for a bridge at *Harlech Castle*.[1] In 1325 was paid by the Chamberlain of Chester £11 6*s.* 8*d.* for works carried out in *Chester Castle*, and £8 for work at *Shotwick Manor*.[1] Was appointed master mason of the castles of North Wales (*Beaumaris, Carnarvon, Conway, Criccieth,* and *Harlech*) on 20 January 1330/1, at 1*s.* a day in succession to NICHOLAS DE DERNEFORD. His grant was confirmed on 10 October 1332.[2] He was probably dead when HENRY DE SNELLESTON was appointed his successor in 1343–4.

[1] HKW, I, 388n.; [2] ACC, 96; [3] CPR 1330–4, 50, 343

HELPESTON, William de [Hulpeston] (*fl.* 1319–1375) Mason

A mason called William de Helpeston was working at *Carnarvon Castle* in 1319–20, but he may well have been an elder relative of the later master. Master mason to the Black Prince for Cheshire and North Wales, taking 6*d.* a day and on 20 August 1359 contracted to build 12 chapels at the east end of *Vale Royal Abbey*, Delamere, Cheshire. These were to equal in height a chapel already built by him adjoining the choir of the church. The Prince was to pay him 200 marks, yearly (£133 6*s.* 8*d.*) up to a total of £860, and Helpeston was to have a life-pension from the abbey on completion. Helpeston was to change and ordain the moulds at will (*chaun-*

ger et ordiner ses moldes a sa volentee).[1] On 6 July 1360 he was commissioned with four others, to impress masons and other workmen for this work.[2] He may have died in 1375, and in any case before 1396, when his office was granted to ROBERT FAGAN.[3] Helpeston's warrant of appointment as master mason in Chester, Flint, and North Wales was dated 4 December 1361,[4] in 1365 was given a special reward of £2 for his trouble and expense in the prince's service, and he was still in charge of works at Vale Royal in 1368, when he was commissioned to take workmen for the abbey on 3 March. The last surviving record of payment of his official fee is in 1374, and it is uncertain whether he survived into the reign of Richard II.

In 1375 a mason called Helpeston was assaulted by a gang who mistakenly believed him to be the man of the same name employed by the Abbot of Vale Royal.[5] Helpeston, like his predecessor JOHN DE TICHMARSH, combined his official post in the County Palatine with that of supervisor of murage of the city of *Chester*, for which he was paid 4*d.* a day.[6]

Helpeston's unusual plan for the church chapels at Vale Royal is derived from that of Toledo Cathedral. This must indicate a connection with the recent (1357–58) diplomatic activity leading to a treaty between England and Castile.[7]

HKW, I, 388n., 469; II, 1056–7 (*H.M.C.*); HME, 161; HPS, 95
[1] BPR, III, 344–5, 361–3, 445; SHB, 439–41; AQC, XLIV, 225; [2] CPR 1358–61, 441; [3] DKR, XXXI; [4] BPR, III, 428; [5] HCH, 153–4; [6] BPR, III, 425–6; [7] HME, 161, 216–18

HEMELHEMPSTEAD, William [Hamelhampsted] (*fl.* 1353–   ) Mason (*Hemel Hempstead, Herts.*)

Warden (*apparilator*) of the works of masonry at *Rotherhithe* Manor, from 1 April to 20 May 1353, taking 3*s.* 4*d.* a week.

PRO, E.101–545–33; cf. HKW, II, 990n.

HEMMYNG, Richard (*fl.* 1363–1384) Carpenter

Warden (*apparilator*) of the carpenters employed at the *Tower of London* from 25 September 1363 to 1 October 1364, taking 3*s.* 6*d.* a week.[1] In 1375–1384 he was master carpenter at *Calais*, apparently in succession to HENRY OF GUELDERS.[2]

[1] *PRO*, E.101–472–12; [2] HKW, II, 1054

HENDY, Robert (*fl.* 1316–1317) Carpenter

Master carpenter in charge of works at

Clarendon Palace in 1316–17 taking 3*s.* 4*d.* a week.

PRO, E.101–459–27 (*L.F.S.*); HKW, II, 917

HENRY the Carpenter IA (*fl.* 1248) Carpenter

Master carpenter to the Bishop of Winchester in 1248, when he was paid for 10 weeks' work upon a mill at *Southwark*, and for 42 weeks' supervising the felling of timber at Wargrave, Berks. He was paid at the rate of 3*s.* 10*d.* a week, and was given a summer robe price 10*s.* in addition.

PRO, Eccl. 2–159457

HENRY the Carpenter I (*fl.* 1280–1286) Carpenter

Described as 'frater Henricus', appears as chief carpenter of the works of *Corfe Castle* in 1280–86. He was probably a lay-brother of the Cistercian Abbey of Bindon.

SHB, 4; PRO, E.101–460–27; 462–16 (*L.F.S.*)

HENRY the Carpenter II (*fl.* 1358–1360) Carpenter

In 1359–60 was paid £6 by the treasurer of *Westminster Abbey* for making the new roof of the cloister by contract, together with 6*s.* 8*d.* for felling timber in the previous year, 6*s.* 8*d.* for a tunic, and sums totalling 16*s.* 8*d.* for minor works and materials.

WAM, 19854

HENRY the Mason IA (*fl. c.* 1240–1265) Mason

'Magister Henricus Cementarius de Hyda' appears as a witness to deeds executed at *Hyde Abbey, Winchester*, in the time of Abbot Walter (1222–47).[1] He also witnessed deeds enrolled in the Hyde Abbey cartulary and executed *c.* 1253, *c.* 1262 and at dates in the abbacies of Roger de St. Valery (1248–63) and William of Worcester (1263–81).[2]

This was doubtless the Master Henry who in 1258 undertook to rebuild the tower over the prison in *Winchester Castle* under the direction of JOHN OF GLOUCESTER and ALEXANDER the Carpenter.[3]

[1] WCM 12099, 12100, 12112, 12125; 1317; [2] BL, Cotton MS. Dom. A.XIV, *ff.* 25, 34, 36v, 37, 37v, 38v; cf. WCM 12106, 12116; [3] HKW, II, 860

HENRY the Mason I (?   –†*c.*1300) Mason

Henry *cementarius* of Ecclesall, appears in the obituary roll of *Beauchief Abbey*, Derbs., in a hand of the second half of the 13th century. His commemoration was on 9 August.

BM, Cotton MS. Caligula A. viii, *f.* 18v. (*H.M.C.*)

HENRY the Mason II [le Mason] (*fl.* 1316–1317) Mason

Master mason in charge of works at *Clarendon Palace* in 1316–17, taking 3*s.* 4*d.* a week. He may well have been HENRY DE EYNSHAM.

PRO, E.101–459–27 (*L.F.S.*); HKW, II, 917

HENRY the Mason III [*latamus*] (*fl.* 1400–) Mason

Mason in charge of building the hall porch of *King's Hall, Cambridge*, in 1400, when allowance of 1*s.* 10*d.* a week was made for his dinners (the usual amount was only 2*d.* a day).

KHA, Bk. v, *f.* 73 (*L.F.S.*)

HENWICK, Robert [Henwyk] (*fl.* 1376–) Mason

Mason of London; in 1376 was elected as one of the four masons who were to represent the trade on the Common Council of the city.

(*A.O.*) CLB, 'H', 43; Williams in AQC, XLI, 136

HEOSE, William (*fl.* 1313–) Mason

Of 'Roventon' (Rowington, Warwickshire); with John de Pesham contracted to build a gatehouse of stone at *Lapworth*, Warwicks., for Sir John de Byssopesdon, on 12 November 1313. John de Pesham was apparently the lessee of a quarry, from which the necessary stone was to be provided. The gatehouse was to be completed before the Feast of All Saints following (1 Nov. 1314), and a total payment of 25 marks (£16 13*s.* 4*d.*) was to be made by two equal instalments on the Feast of the Purification (2 February 1313/14) and upon the completion of the work.

The gatehouse was to be 40 feet long and 18 feet wide within the walls, and was to contain a chamber on each side of the gateway and a large upper chamber taking up the full size of the building. One of the base chambers was to have a chimney and a garderobe projecting outside the room, and the upper chamber was to have two chimneys and two garderobes. The external walls were to be 3½ feet thick, and the other walls 2½ feet; the ground storey was to be 11 feet in height, and the upper storey 9 feet, while a battlementing 2½ feet high was to crown the walls, and provision for a drawbridge was to be made.

APD; TPD, II, 5; SHB, 421–2

Herd, John—see ESSEX

HEREFORD, Henry of (*fl.* 1277–1298) Mason

Mason sent from Chester to Carmarthen on 18 July 1277, to take charge of work on *Aberystwyth Castle*. He was presumably the master of this name who in 1298 held a burgage tenement at Carnarvon, and was very likely related to WALTER OF HEREFORD.

HKW, I, 300

HEREFORD, Walter of [de Ambresbury, Herford] (*fl.* 1277–†1309) Mason

Probably of Harford, Glos., in the parish of Naunton.

On 22 January 1278 'Master Walter of Herford, mason' (*cementarius*) contracted with John Yanworth, Abbot of *Winchcombe*, that he should serve the abbot and his successors faithfully and finish their 'new work'. This was probably the Lady Chapel in the cemetery, begun under Abbot Yanworth. The contract continues: 'Other work, except the works of our Lord the King, he shall not begin without leave of the Abbot and Convent. We grant the same Master Walter, while with us, such victuals as the chief servants of the Lord Abbot receive; but if it should happen that the said Master Walter, through sickness or other reasonable cause, choose to remain in his chamber, he shall have two monastic loaves daily, two jugs of convent ale and two dishes from the Abbot's kitchen; and for his two servants such allowance as the Abbot's servants receive. He shall have also for two horses a measure of oats each night while he is attending to the various works. If, however, the said Master Walter, on account of infirmity or old age, should abide continuously with us, he shall have two monastic loaves, two jugs of ale and two dishes, but allowance only for one servant and one horse. He shall have, moreover, a robe every year such as the seneschal of our house receives, and for two servants such robes as the Abbot's servants receive. The said Abbot and Convent have also granted him leave to build, at his own expense, a chamber next to the granary, the Abbot finding stone and timber; which chamber he shall have while he lives. And he shall have from the Abbot's chamber every night two candles of wax, and from the sub-cellarer four of tallow, from Michaelmas to Easter, and every week, a load of firewood.'[1] The reference to the works of the King doubtless refers particularly to Master Walter's existing involvement in the design of Vale Royal Abbey, whose first stone had been laid on 13 August 1277.

From 28 March 1278 until 1290 he was master of the works at *Vale Royal Abbey*, Delamere, Cheshire, for the King, being paid 2s. a day for 365 days a year from 1278 to 1280, as well as £2 6s. 8d. for his robes.[2] In 1287 he sent a pattern (*exemplar*) of columns, capitals, bases, and cornice moulding needed for the work at Vale Royal to London to be made by the marblers, Masters JOHN DOGET and RALPH OF CHICHESTER. In the meantime, Master Walter may have been sent to begin the new monastery of *Aberconway* in 1284. In 1304–05 he was master mason at *Carnarvon Castle*: he had certainly been in charge since 1295; on 16 June 100 masons and 30 or 40 smiths were to be sent to him as keeper of the works there.[3] He was described as Master 'Watier de Ambresbury'; this suggests that he had been at Amesbury, Wilts., in connection with the tomb of Queen Eleanor of Provence. In 1304 he petitioned for arrears of pay at Carnarvon amounting to £131 6s. 0d., a warrant for which was ordered to be made out. Again in 1305 Master Walter petitioned the Crown in connection with the works at Carnarvon, and especially that he might continue to keep his free court of the castle workmen as he had been wont to do; this was allowed him, with the fines consequent on breaking of contracts and undertakings made by the workmen.[4]

In 1300 he was employed on the Scottish campaign and an advance of £1 8s. 6d. on his fees was paid at Carlisle to his wife Alice.[5] He continued to be stationed at Carnarvon until his death in 1309, at wages of 7s. a week, but this was not his only employment, for in March 1304 he was at Edinburgh Castle and was sent to Perth and Stirling in connection with military operations, having a writ of 7 March in that year to take masons and bring them into Scotland for the royal works there, sheriffs, bailiffs and other ministers being ordered to be assistant to him.[6] He took masons to London in 1306 for 'the Queen's work', the building of the *Grey Friars' Church* at *Newgate*, endowed by Queen Margaret. In 1308 he paid the costs of appropriating the church of Enstone, Oxon., to Winchcombe Abbey.

Master Walter was still alive on 30 November of that year, when he was ordered to attend at the Exchequer to render account for the works at Carnarvon, but was dead by 13 February 1308/9, when HENRY DE ELLERTON was put in charge.[7]

Master Walter was, apart from JAMES OF ST. GEORGE, the principal mason-architect employed by the Crown between 1285 and 1309, and his connection with the Queen's work at the Grey Friars of London suggests that his was the principal influence which formed the new type of 'preaching church' destined to have so vital an effect on the church design of the later Middle Ages. At the royal towns of Winchelsea and Hull we may also see Master Walter's influence in the two splendid churches of *St. Thomas, Winchelsea* and *Holy Trinity, Hull*, both of which must have been designed within a few years of the turn of the century, and probably within the five years 1295–1300. The plan of the church at Hull is almost the same as that of the Grey Friars in London, and is only slightly smaller, but Hull still retains a projecting transept, which was, however, reduced to a mere vestige of its previous significance.

As a military architect, Hereford had complete charge of the works at Carnarvon Castle, though there is reason to think that the plan had been settled beforehand by James of St. George and RICHARD LENGINOUR, the military experts. Walter may well have been the designer of the 'second work' at *Denbigh Castle*, including the great gatehouse, begun about 1300. There can be little doubt that most or all of the other castles built during the Edwardian settlement of Wales were designed by a great military engineer, and there is evidence to show that this was Master James of St. George, aided by Richard Lenginour. Only thorough re-examination of the buildings and manuscript sources could show the precise shares of these three great designers in the Edwardian castles, but that they were jointly responsible for the whole series seems certain.[8]

A *Walter de HEREFORD*, mason, with Hugh de Peck, was paid £4 for work done in *Beeston Castle*, Cheshire, in 1325.[9]

(APD); **KJI; KJW**; G. H. Jack in WFC 1933–35 pt. ii; HKW, I, 205, 248–52, 339
[1] RLW, I, 136–8; [2] CNW, XXXVII, 295–7; [3] CCW 1244–1326, 63; CAW, 150; [4] RP, I, 167b; CR, 220; [5] A. J. Taylor in CHT (1948), 16–19; [6] BM, Add. MS. 35293, ff. 36, 38v. (*A.J.T.*); Taylor in SCO, XXXIV no. 117, 44–6;

[7] Taylor in CHT (1948), 17; [8] cf. A. J. Taylor in ANT, XXVI (1952), 25–34; [9] ACC, 96

Herford, Walter—see HEREFORD

HERLAND, Hugh [Harland, -londe, Herlonde] (*c.* 1330–† *c.* 1411) Carpenter

Carpenter of London, probably son of WILLIAM HERLAND and perhaps grandson of JOHN HERLAND. He was probably born about 1330, as he was described as 'verging on old age' in 1383. Though possibly identical with Hugh 'Kervour', who in June 1350 was working among the carpenters engaged on making the stalls for the chapel at *Windsor Castle*, taking 6*d*. a day,[1] he is first mentioned by name in 1360, when William and Hugh Herland were commissioned to impress carpenters for work at *Westminster Palace* and the *Tower of London*, on 16 August.[2] On 3 March 1364 Hugh was granted, during pleasure, wages of 8*d*. a day by the hands of the clerk of the King's works in the Palace of Westminster and the Tower of London, and for some time after this he was working at the Palace, where the fittings of *St. Stephen's Chapel* were being completed.[3]

Hugh Herland had perhaps spent the whole of his early career on the royal works, for on 10 October 1366 he was granted 10 marks (£6 13*s*. 4*d*.) yearly for life, for his long service, and about the same time a small house by the Palace in the outer ward was delivered to him for keeping his tools and moulds.[4] On 26 July 1368 he was granted the office of the Pesage of Wools at Queenborough, Kent,[5] where a remarkable castle was just being finished. This office was again granted to him on 29 September 1370,[6] and it is possible that he had work at this time at Queenborough, Rochester, or elsewhere in the neighbourhood, for at a later date he is found living at Upchurch, six miles from Queenborough, and quite possibly he had purchased land there at this time.

The tester over the tomb of Queen Philippa in Westminster Abbey may be Hugh's work, or that of William Herland; the pierced spandrils are extremely like Hugh's known work, and the date of the tester is uncertain, though the tomb was supplied in 1367 by HAWKIN OF LIÈGE, of Paris, two years before the Queen's death. Another work with exactly the same type of pierced spandril is the roof of the Abbot's Hall at Westminster Abbey, built about 1375, and this, too, must have been designed by one of the Herlands, probably Hugh.[7] It was in this year that William Herland died, and on 10 June Hugh was granted the same position of 'disposer of the King's works touching the art or mistery of carpentry', with 12*d.* a day from the clerk of the works at the Palace of Westminster and Tower of London during the continuance of the works, and afterwards at the Exchequer, and a winter robe yearly 'of the suit of the Esquires of the Household'. The allocation of his wages suggests that he had been working at Westminster for some time before the date of the grant, which was 'during pleasure'.[8] In 1376 Herland had the oversight of work done at *Havering Manor* under WILLIAM LOVE as his warden.

Edward III died on 21 June 1377, and on 20 September Herland was again granted the Pesage of Wools at Queenborough, and on 31 January following, the Pesage of Wools at Sandwich, Kent.[9] On 6 March 1378 his pension of 10 marks was confirmed, and in April he was appointed carpenter and controller of works at *Rochester Castle*, where he was paid his wages of 12*d.* daily from 19 April, in accordance with a royal letter issued to William Basynge, master of the hospital of Strood and clerk of the works; this letter, given under the Privy Seal on 12 October 1378, ordered that 'to our well beloved master Hugh Herland carpenter, Controller of our said works, you shall cause to be paid twelve pence the day for his wages for the time since the Feast of Easter last past'.[10]

During this period Hugh must have designed the tester over Edward III's tomb, which marks the very highest point in the design of decorative woodwork, and foreshadows his design for the chapel vault at *Winchester College*, some ten years later. The delicate cusping and fine proportions of the tester, together with the avoidance of superfluous ornament, put this little work quite beyond criticism as one of the finest compositions of Gothic art.

Hugh's work at Rochester Castle continued, and he was reappointed on 17 March 1379 until the Feast of All Saints following, while on 24 March he received a new appointment as one of the King's Master Carpenters, with fees of 1*s.* a day and a robe yearly. On 2 August 1380 the scope of his Rochester appointment was altered to include work at *Leeds Castle*, Kent, and he continued to act as controller of the works at Rochester Castle until 1386–87. He had other duties in addition, for on 14 March 1380/1 RICHARD SWIFT and Hugh Herland, carpenters, were commissioned to impress 50 carpenters for service in Brittany with the Earl of Buckingham.[11] On 6 June the Kentish rebels captured and plundered Rochester Castle, but the repairs continued in the succeeding years as before, Herland being again mentioned as controller when a new clerk of works was appointed on 7 May 1384. Herland was concerned with other royal works, as when in 1385 he directed subordinate carpenters on the works of *Portchester Castle*.[12]

In 1383 Master Hugh surrendered his position as one of the King's Master Carpenters because he was 'verging on old age', but on 7 December he was granted a pension of 1*s.* a day and a robe yearly, which left him as well off as before, though without such heavy responsibilities. A few years later, as will be seen, he must have resumed his duties. In 1384, along with HENRY YEVELEY and WILLIAM WYNFORD, he let a contract for the repair of the timberwork of the battlements of *Carisbrooke Castle* to ADAM OLIVER.[13]

Herland's first association with William of Wykeham is uncertain, though they may have met in 1360 or 1361 when Wykeham was clerk of the works at Windsor Castle, or later at Queenborough. Herland certainly worked for Wykeham from 1387 onwards, and he designed the timberwork for Wykeham's *New College, Oxford*, probably about 1384, as the masonry work of the college was started in 1380, and the buildings were occupied on 14 April 1386. When Wykeham's manor house at *Highclere*, Hants., was being largely rebuilt in 1387, Master Hugh Herland was paid 6*d.* a day for 4 days spent there and 10*d.* was allowed for 6 lb. of oats for the horse of 'Master Hugh Harlond coming for divers turns'.[14] In 1388–89 Herland, with WILLIAM WYNFORD, visited New College on various occasions. On 25 March 1389 they dined at the high table together in company with HENRY YEVELEY. Wynford and Herland again dined at New College on 16 February 1390/1.[15]

Herland's next official work took him to *Winchester*, where the *Castle* required repair; on 3 March 1389/90 a commission was issued for the works to be done under Master Henry Yeveley and Master William Wynford, and Hugh Herland, carpenter, and the accounts of the constable speak of repairs done 'according to the ordinance and advice' of the three masters.[16] Wynford was at this time building Winchester College for Wykeham, and Herland must have been the designer of the timberwork, including the existing timber vault of the chapel; the roof of the hall, though not original, seems to have retained his typical design of pierced spandril pieces beneath horizontal tie-beams.

On 8 May 1390 an order was made for repairs to be done on the keep of *Canterbury Castle* under the supervision of the King's Master Mason and Master Carpenter, presumably Henry Yeveley and Hugh Herland; on 28 April following, Herland's pension of 10 marks a year was made payable out of the fee-farm of the city of Winchester, which suggests that he was spending a great part of his time there on the works of the castle.[17] Probably on account of this shift to the west of his principal works, he acquired a considerable property at Kingston upon Thames, Surrey, from Philippa, daughter of William Voirdyre; on 20 July Philippa gave to 'Hugh Herlonde of Upchirche of Kent and Joan his wife' and to their heirs, quitclaim with warranty of 'all the lands with houses, buildings, tofts, commons, rights, etc.' in Kingston 'sometime of her said father'. Hugh Herland was assessed at $11\frac{1}{2}d.$ for property in 'Souterrowe' Kingston, in a rental of about this time. On 18 October 1392 he obtained a lease for 60 years from Wykeham of the 'Bishop's Hall' in Kingston, a large mansion belonging to the see. The lease, confirmed by St. Swithun's Cathedral Priory of Winchester on 3 September 1393, names Hugh Harland, Joan his wife, and Thomas, William, Hugh, and John their sons, as lessees by rent of 4s. a year.[18]

About this time died WILLIAM WINTRING-HAM, chief carpenter to John of Gaunt, who was then rebuilding a large part of *Kenilworth Castle*, where the new hall was given the great span of 45 feet, the widest span yet attempted, apart from the nave of York Minster, which was vaulted in wood by PHILIP OF LINCOLN between 1350 and 1375. It is quite probable that Herland was called in to advise on the construction of the Kenilworth roof, which was destroyed during the Commonwealth period. Unfortunately no drawing of it seems to have been preserved. About the same time he may have been consulted by

John Holland, Duke of Exeter, the King's half-brother, who was building *Dartington Hall* near Totnes in Devon, between 1390 and 1399. The great hall has a span of 38 feet and though the original roof is lost, its form is known, and has been reproduced in the modern roof. It is a hammer-beam roof of proportions closely similar to those of Westminster Hall, but lacking the great arch-rib, Westminster's special feature for overcoming the difficulties of an immense span.

Herland visited William of Wykeham in 1393, dining at the bishop's table at Esher on 28 May and 11 June, and at Wolvesey Palace, Winchester, or at Marwell 5 miles away, on 26, 27, and 31 July, 21, 22, and 24 August, and 14 September. William Wynford was also at table when Herland visited the bishop at Winchester, and on most occasions so also was Simon Membury, Wykeham's clerk of the works at Winchester College.[19] The King and Queen twice visited Wykeham at Winchester during the summer, on 25 July and on 16–17 September, and it may have been the sight of the fine work being done for Wykeham by the royal craftsmen that caused Richard II to decide upon the rebuilding of *Westminster Hall*, though extensive repairs were already in contemplation.

It was on 21 January 1393/4 that the works at Westminster were put under the charge of John Godmeston as clerk of works, with Hugh Herland as carpenter and controller, and the work proceeded steadily until shortly after 1400, at a cost of nearly £2,000 a year for the six years; the total cost of the new hall would be equivalent to about six million pounds in 1982.[20]

By 1 June 1395 matters were so far advanced that order was given for 30 strong wains to convey the timber wrought at a place called 'the Frame' by Farnham, Surrey, to 'Hamme' upon Thames, thence to be brought to Westminster by water.[21]

Herland was constantly at work on the hall through these years, and he probably had little spare time for other work, as his control-ment of the accounts must have imposed on him heavy duties in addition to the design and supervision of the timberwork and the anxiety inseparable from the construction of a work on such a vast scale, 240 feet long by 70 feet in span. On 11 November 1395 an order was made to the Keeper of the Great Wardrobe to deliver Master Hugh's annual robe, and grants of 28 April and 20 June in the following year secured to him for life the possession of the 'little house lying in the outer little ward of the Palace of Westminster, near the house of the clerk of works, for keeping his tools and for making his models and moulds for his carpentry work', which had been delivered to him by the order of Edward III 30 years before.[22]

On 28 February 1396/7 the commission to Yeveley, Wynford, and Herland for the repair of Winchester Castle was renewed for another seven years, and on 26 May he was granted for life, for his long and good service as chief carpenter, controller, and surveyor of the works within the Palace of Westminster, the Tower of London, and elsewhere, a pension of £18 5s. 0d. a year at the Exchequer. Besides this, he had on 17 October 'all the croppings and coppices. . . which lie cut and remaining over in a wood near Kyngeston-upon-Thames' from the trees provided for the Hall and other works.[23] His connection with Kingston is also evidenced by the fact that he witnessed a deed there on 23 May 1398.[24]

A new harbour at *Great Yarmouth* was being constructed in 1398, and on 10 August Master Hugh Herland and others were appointed to impress labour for the works there. This is the last evidence of his connection with building works other than those of Westminster, apart from a possible connection with the repairs of Kingston Bridge in 1400. Next year the dynastic revolution took place, but Henry IV continued the works at the Hall, and confirmed the royal craftsmen in their offices; on 10 November 1399 Hugh Herland was confirmed in his appointment as controller to John Godmeston at Westminster Hall, and on 19 November had confirmation of his three grants of 10 marks yearly, of 1s. a day, and of £18 5s. a year.[25]

During 1400 he continued to work as carpenter and controller at the Hall, but the work there was almost finished, and he probably spent a great deal of his time at Kingston, for on 18 November a commission was issued 'to William Loveney, Richard Kays, serjeant-at-arms, and Hugh Herland, to enquire into the report that certain men of the town of Kingston upon Thames, lately appointed by Richard II to take divers customs for the repair of the bridge of the town from merchandise passing by the bridge, have thus received divers sums of money and

retained the same to their own use, and to collect these sums and expend them on the repair of the bridge'. It is not clear whether Master Hugh was to take part in the police investigation, or only to advise upon the repair of the bridge, which was of timber.[26]

His pension of 10 marks a year from the fee-farm of Winchester was evidently difficult to collect, for an order had to be made to the bailiffs of Winchester on 22 June 1403, to cause them to pay to ˙Hugh Herland the arrears from 19 November 1399, when the patent was confirmed, and to continue to pay the pension during Herland's life.[27] Master Hugh must now have been quite an old man, as he had been verging on old age 20 years before. 'Mr. Hugo Harlend' had supper in the Warden's Chamber at Winchester College on Thursday 17 August, 1402, along with Nicholas Porter, constable of the Soke, and John Harleston.[28] He retained his office until the end of 1404, when upon surrender it was regranted to WILLIAM TOUTMOND on 12 January 1405 as 'the office of chief carpenter, disposer and surveyor of the King's works . . .' with fees of 1s. a day and a winter robe yearly. Herland's other pensions would of course continue until his death. Orders and receipts for half-yearly payments of 5 marks, or of arrears of his pension from Winchester continue until 18 October 1411 and imply his death by April 1412 at latest.[29]

Nothing further is known of Hugh's wife Joan who was living in 1391–92 when he acquired his Kingston properties, but their sons Thomas and William referred to in the lease of 1392 can be identified. William Herland of Kingston upon Thames was one of the seventy original scholars of Winchester in 1394 and stayed there until 1397 when he proceeded to New College, Oxford, but died in August 1398. Thomas Herland succeeded to his father's lease of Bishop's Hall and in 1413–14 entertained King Henry V there; he continued to appear as a Kingston resident until 1433, while in 1434 Juliana Herland, presumably his widow, was occupying the property. A rental of the spring of 1417 shows Thomas Herland as assessed at 1s. 4½d. on his land and tenement in 'Souterysrowe', 3d. for three half-acres of land, 4d. for 'Tabardys', and 3d. for his garden. In 1433 he was presented as a 'common brewer', being fined 8d., and Juliana was similarly presented in the following year.[30]

In addition to Hugh Herland's known works, and those mentioned above of which he may have been the author, there is the roof of the guardroom in Lambeth Palace, which dates from *c.* 1390, and is closely linked to his style. Though its span is only 28 feet, the roof is of particular interest because it so closely resembles the lower part of the roof of Westminster Hall, below the hammer-beams. It may be that this arched roof was one of the links in the chain of development which led to the design of Westminster Hall roof, which is not only the earliest known hammer-beam roof of any considerable size, but also incorporates the principle of the arch-braced roof on an enormous scale. Another probable work by Herland is the wooden vault of the collegiate church at *Arundel* (the Fitzalan Chapel), built *c.* 1380–1400.

The importance of Westminster Hall roof to the history of art and building construction is so great that it tends to overshadow Herland's life; the exquisite proportions of all its parts, and the harmonious play of light and shade between its trusses make it incomparably the most beautiful work of its kind. Roofs of greater span have since been constructed of timber, though quite without architectural pretensions: such were Peter the Great's Riding School at Moscow, and the original timber barrel-vaults of King's Cross Station in London, each 100 feet in span; there is one mediaeval roof of greater span than that of Westminster Hall, that of the Palazzo della Ragione at Padua, with a span of 84 feet; but its design has no aesthetic quality, while its construction depends entirely on an elaborate network of iron tie-rods. It is said to have been designed about 1306 by frate Giovanni, an Austin friar, who brought back from the East the drawing of a great palace roof in India, which he proceeded to copy for the Paduans.

The carved tester over the tomb of Edward III has already been mentioned. On the underside is a series of vaulting ribs of wood, suggesting the fan-vault design, and Herland developed this principle much further in the vault of Winchester College Chapel, where he so disposed his bunches of ribs that they produced fans bounded by somewhat tilted ribs forming pointed arches on plan. Herland's timber vault fails geometrically to be a true fan vault in that its ribs do not all follow the same curvature, but from its appearance it must be classed as one of the parents of the fan vault in England. The origin of the fan vault in masonry has been traced to Tewkesbury and to Gloucester, where it was being used structurally for the cloisters at some time after 1357 and before 1412, but no fan vault of large span is known earlier than that of the choir of Sherborne Abbey, Dorset, designed before, and built soon after, the fire of 1436.

Not much of Herland's minor work is known, though in his long career he must have designed a great deal, but it is possible that there is work of his still extant which has not been recognised. The portrait in the stained glass of the east window of Winchester College Chapel, named 'Carpentarius' must be of Herland, for no other carpenter is found at that time (1393) closely associated with Wynford and Membury, whose figures in the glass are beside that of the carpenter. Unfortunately the existing glass is only a copy of the original, but certain original panels are in existence which show that the drawing, though not the colour, of the present glass is close to that of the original. (See Appendix I.)

(HHH; HMA; LKC)

[1] *PRO*, E.101–492–27; [2] *CPR* 1358–61, 449; [3] *Ibid*, 1361–4, 474; *PRO*, E.101–472–14, 16; [4] *CPR* 1364–7, 312, cf. 1391–6, 707, 725; [5] *Ibid*. 1367–70, 147; [6] *Ibid*., 464; [7] *LWR*, 144; [8] *CPR* 1374–7, 189; [9] *Ibid*. 1377–81, 13, 135; [10] *Ibid*., 138, 213; *PRO*, E.101–480–5; [11] *CPR* 1377–81, 334, 338, 540, 607; [12] *Ibid*. 1381–5, 398; *PRO*, E.101–480–5, 8, 10, 12; HKW, II, 790; [13] *CPR* 1381–5, 341; HKW, II, 595; [14] *PRO*, Eccl. 2–159395 (*J.H.B.*); [15] *NCO*, Hall Books, Bursar's Acc. 1388–89; [16] *CPR* 1388–92, 237; *PRO*, E.101–491–21; *PRO*, Foreign Roll 13 Ric. II (A) (*L.F.S.*); [17] *CPR* 1388–92, 249, 261; *CCR* 1389–92, 252; [18] *CCR* 1389–92, 477, 485; *KCA*, D.III.e(1); MBS, I, 345; [19] *WCM*, Wykeham's Household Acc. 1393 (*H.C.*); [20] *CPR* 1391–6, 349; *PRO*, E.101–470–17, 473–11, 12, 13, and Pipe Rolls; *BM*, Add. Ch. 27018, cf. HKW, I, 533; [21] *CCR* 1392–6, 352; SHB, 218; [22] *CCR* 1392–6, 436; *CPR* 1391–6, 707, 725; [23] *CPR* 1396–9, 116; [24] *CCR* 1396–9, 318; [25] *CPR* 1396–9, 407; 1399–1401, 70, 254; [26] *Ibid*., 413; [27] *CCR* 1402–5, 88; [28] *WCM* 22815; [29] *CPR* 1401–5, 479; *PRO*, SC6–1283–9 (box 2), a reference owed to Dr. Beatrice Clayre; [30] *WCM*, Register (*H.C.*); *NCO*, Register and Hall Books; *CCR* 1413–19; *PRO*, E.101–406–21; *KCA*, D.III.e(2), (3); G.198, 208, 212, 214; C.I.1,2

Michael HERLAND was a London carpenter who died before 1397; his widow Constance remarried to Richard Greystoke, who paid over 10 marks bequeathed to Michael's daughter Alice, on 13 February 1397; Alice married John Ryngsone, tailor, before 15 January 1398.

CLB, 'H', 435

HERLAND, JOHN

HERLAND, John [Hurelonde] (*fl.* 1329–) Carpenter

Probably from one of the places called 'Hurlande' in Surrey, notably that in Dunsfold which gave its name to a family occurring there in the 14th century.[1] Master carpenter of the works of *Westminster Palace*, at 6*d.* a day, in 1329, when he was in charge of the building of a timber bridge (water stairs) and constructed a pile-driver, and on one occasion was sent by the clerk of works to Kingston upon Thames to select timber.[2] It is possible that he was the designer of the original timber vault of *St. Stephen's Chapel*, which was prepared in or before 1328, though not erected until 1348. His unusual surname suggests that he was related to WILLIAM and HUGH HERLAND. Perhaps identical with the John Herland who in 1332–33 was paid a sum of £2 18*s.* 6*d.* by the treasurer of *Christ Church Priory, Canterbury*, which had been owing from 1328,[3] and possibly with the John de 'Hylaunde' who in 1332 was assessed to pay 5*s.* 4*d.* to the taxation, in Queenhithe Ward, London.[4]

[1] EPNS, VI, 20, 159; XI, 211, 236, 388; MSD, Dunsfold No. 483; [2] PRO, E.101–467–6, (1); HMA, 739; [3] CCA, Treasurer's Accs., bk. ii; [4] UFT, 61 ff.

HERLAND, William [Herlonde] (*fl.* 1332– †1375) Carpenter

Carpenter of London; in August 1332 William de Herlond was sawing moulds for the work of *St. Stephen's Chapel* at 5*d.* a day, and he probably continued in royal employment. He was already warden (*apparilator*) of the King's carpentry works in 1347–48;[1] with WILLIAM HURLEY the King's Chief Carpenter, he was commissioned to engage carpenters for the work at *Eltham* and *Windsor Castle* on 30 June 1350,[2] and was paid 8*d.* a day as '*apparilator* of all the works of carpentry there' from 26 April 1350 to 7 August 1351.[3] At the same time he was working at *St. Stephen's Chapel* in *Westminster Palace*, being paid 3*s.* 6*d.* a week;[4] he was working at St. Stephen's in August, September, and November 1351, and in February, March, and June 1352, on the making of the stalls, and was paid 8*d.* a day as *apparilator* until 20 June 1352, from which date he received 1*s.* a day, the same rate as William Hurley, the master.[5] In September 1351 he had been working under William Hurley on the Seneschal's Chamber at Westminster, and among other payments to him was one of 10*d.* for two pounds of glue which

he furnished for the work of the stalls in the chapel on 13 May 1351; on 2 January 1351/2 he was paid £3 for wainscot.

He apparently succeeded William Hurley as King's Chief Carpenter upon Hurley's death in 1354, though he does not seem to have been granted a patent of office. From Michaelmas 1354, however, he was being paid at the rate of 1*s.* a day, and his services were described as 'the ordaining of divers works of the King'.[6] During the following year he supervised work at Westminster Palace and the *Tower of London*, and was in charge of the preparatory works for the making of the great hall roof at Windsor Castle.[7] In 1356 he was paid £6 for making good the ceiling of the cloister beside the King's Chapel at Windsor, but a further £12 was withheld from the full payment for this work as he had not completed the 'task' he had undertaken by 31 October 1356;[8] he was still working at Windsor in 1357.

Early in 1358 he was at Westminster Palace, and on 6 June was appointed to have the 'view and disposition of the repairs' of *Hadleigh Castle* in Essex,[9] where he worked during the next year. On 14 July 1360, Herland was discharged of a sum of £23 3*s.* 3¾*d.* for which he was responsible, on account of his 'industry about the making of stalls in the King's Chapel of Westminster, the sale of the wood of Reyndon, and of the lop and crop of divers oaks bought for the King's use and by him sold',[10] and on 16 August he was commissioned, with HUGH HERLAND to take labour for work at Westminster and the Tower. Herland also had responsibility for works at *Rotherhithe Manor*, where a carpenter William Bercholt built a new bridge to the river wharf in 1361 by contract made with Master William.[11]

His work at Westminster Palace continued until 1366,[12] and he seems to have spent part of the year there even when engaged on other work, as he was from 1 November 1363, when he was associated with Stephen Scarlet as a 'controller and surveyor of the works' at the King's manor of 'Retherhethe' (*Rotherhithe*). This work lasted until 1370,[13] and on 7 June 1367 he and Scarlet were granted a patent of appointment as controllers there.[14] In 1368 he was also concerned in work at *Rochester Castle*, where four little brass wheels for the hoisting engine were purchased from him at 3*s.* 4*d.* each.[15]

142

On 26 March 1370, Herland was commissioned to press 80 carpenters and bring them to London so that they should be there immediately after Easter,[16] and in the same year he was paid for 'cords of Spanish thread for the engines' which he provided for the works of the Tower of London.[17]

Herland must have been approaching old age, for on 27 March 1371 he was granted 'for his long service' a tenement 'in the parish of St. Mary Bothawe in the ward of Dowgate, London, sometime of John son of John Adam, spicer, called Hachesham, held of the King in burgage. . . of the clear yearly value of 40s.'.[18] From this time we hear no more of William Herland until his death in the summer of 1375. From the grant to Hugh Herland of William's office of 'disposer of the King's works . . . of carpentry' it appears that he was dead by 10 June,[19] though his will is dated 6 July; this may be the date of granting probate; the will was not enrolled in the Court of Husting until 16 July.

The will provides that he should be buried in the church of St. Peter the Less near 'Pauleswharf' before the image of St. Katherine in St. Mary's Chapel. He left bequests to the church and its ministers, and to the 'old work' of St. Paul's Cathedral, namely the chapel of St. John the Baptist near 'le northdore'. No children are mentioned, but the Husting enrolment is probably incomplete; the will was proved in the Archdeaconry Court of London, and registered on folio xvj for 1375, but the register for this period is lost.[20] To Agnes his wife he left his tenement in the parish of St. Peter aforesaid, and a tenement near 'la Dragoun' at Dowgate in the parish of St. Michael 'Paternostercherche' in the 'Riole' for her life, she to sell the reversion, if possible, immediately after his decease, and to devote the proceeds to pious uses.[21] It seems clear that the two tenements at Dowgate are one and the same, for on 15 July 1383 an order was given for livery of a tenement in the parish of St. Mary Bothaw in Dowgate to John Frost and Agnes, widow of William Herland, who had willed it to her by his will enrolled in the Court of Husting on Monday before the Feast of St. Margaret 49 Edward III (16 July 1375).[22] Probably the house lay on the boundary of the adjoining parish of St. Michael Paternoster Royal.

Herland's other house, evidently his own home, can be identified as having stood on the south side of Thames Street immediately opposite St. Peter's, Paulswharf; from his will we know that it stood in the parish of St. Peter, and an enrolment of 1388 mentions that the tenement 'late of Master William Herlonde carpenter' formed the eastern boundary of a tenement in the parish of St. Benet 'atte Wodewharf' and in Baynard's Castle Ward; the Herland house was therefore the westernmost in the parish of St. Peter.[23]

(LKC; HKC)

[1] PRO, E.101–469–11; 470–18 (L.F.S.); [2] CPR 1348–50, 588; [3] HWC, I, 151; PRO, E.101–492–27; [4] LKC, 196; E.101–470–19; [5] PRO, E.101–471–5, 6; [6] Ibid., E.101–471–11; [7] HWC, I, 155; [8] Ibid., 158; [9] CPR 1358–61, 53; [10] CCR 1360–4, 44; [11] CPR 1358–61, 449; HKW, II, 991n.; [12] LKC; E.101–472–14; [13] PRO, E.101–493–20; 494–2, 12; [14] CPR 1364–7, 414, 417, 427; [15] AC, II; [16] CPR 1367–70, 384; [17] PRO, E.101–472–18; [18] CPR 1370–4, 59; [19] Ibid. 1374–7, 189; [20] PPR, Archd. Ct. of London, I, prefaced index; [21] SWL, II, 175; [22] CCR 1381–5, 318; [23] Ibid., 1385–9, 480; cf. LHR, 108(25), 110(3), 112(33)

HERLEYE, John [Harley, Herling] (*fl.* 1381–1382)? Clerk

Surveyor of the works of *Kenilworth Castle* for John of Gaunt, appointed on 4 December 1380 with a fee of 10 marks (£6 13s. 4d.). He was apparently an administrative officer as his term of office overlaps the appointment of WILLIAM HALES as surveyor and chief mason.

JGR 1379–83, 486, 607, 668, 786, 880, 885, 1083

Herlonde—see HERLAND

HERMAN, Nicholas (*fl.* 1492–1493) Mason

In the summer seasons of 1492 and 1493 Nicholas Herman, freemason, worked for some four months each year on the 'stepyll' of *East Dereham Church*, Norfolk. This was the upper part, now removed, of the central tower. Herman was paid at rates approximating to 3s. 4d. a week, together with his servant, William Makrell at 4d. a day, Herman's uncle at 3s., and their two 'laddes' or 'chyldyr' paid 1s. a week each.

Church accounts (S.A.C.;P.C.)

HERMANZONE, Arnold [Termassone] (*fl.* 1536–) Carver

Tomb-maker, born in Amsterdam and working at Aire in Artois; on 1 March 1535/6 undertook to make tombs for Sir William and Margaret Sandes to be delivered at Antwerp within seven months, for setting up in *Basingstoke Holy Ghost Chapel*, Hants. The tombs were to be of black Antoing stone and each was to bear a copper or brass cross.

BHB, 158–9, 692–3; VCH, *Hants.*, IV, 137–8

HERMER, John (fl.   –†1509) Mason

From a passage in his will, which was made at Cambridge, dated 6 February 1507/8, proved 9 May 1509, it is evident that he had been engaged on work at the Premonstratensian abbey of *West Dereham*, Norfolk.[1] He bequeathed to the abbot and convent 10 marks 'to be taken and rebated of the some of money that he oweth me'. He also made provision for one of the canons to sing masses for his soul for two years. He desired to be buried in the church of the Grey Friars at Cambridge 'before our lady in the south yle there'. Bequests to 'the Abbey of Bury Seynt Edmund' and to the church of St. Mary the Great at Cambridge may indicate that he had worked on both those buildings. He mentions his wife Alice, three daughters, and his mother Katherine who was living at Saxham, near Bury St. Edmunds. As he left 20s. to the high altar of Saxham Church for tithes forgotten, he had evidently lived in that parish and may have been born there. The will of a John Hermer of Great Saxham who died in 1441 is in the earliest register of Archdeaconry of Sudbury wills.[2]

John Hermer left to his apprentice William Reed all his tools and instruments belonging to his occupation 'wheresoever they may be found'.

A.O.
[1] *PCC*, 14 Bennett; [2] RBW

HERMER, Nicholas and Thomas [Harmer] (fl. 1520) Masons

An entry in one of the Hall Books of the corporation of King's Lynn under 29 October 1520 records the sealing of an indenture made between the Mayor and Burgesses and Nicholas Harmer of East Dereham in Norfolk and Thomas Harmer of 'Borewell in Norfolk', freemasons, for making the *South Gate* in *South Lynn*.[1] The South Gate of Lynn, which still stands, had been rebuilt just a century earlier by a London mason, ROBERT HERTANGER, who failed to fulfil his contract. 'Borewell' was a common mediaeval spelling of Burwell, which though in Cambridgeshire was in the diocese of Norwich.

These two masons, who may have been brothers or father and son, were probably relations of JOHN HERMER and of *William HERMER*, freemason, apprentice of JOHN ANTELL, who was admitted to the freedom of Norwich 1508–09[2] and is likely to have been the William Hermer who was a member of the Guild of St. George in Norwich between 1512 and 1530.[3] William Hermer was paid £1 for two 'bussellis doleis' of freestone for the chancel of *St. Peter Parmentergate, Norwich*, in 1511–12.[4]

A.O.
[1] HKL, 760–1; [2] EFN; [3] NRC, IX, 108, 131; [4] *NRO*, DCN, Infirmarer no. 993 (*P.C.*)

Heronden—see HERUNDEN

HERTANGER, Robert (fl. 1409–1416) Mason (? *Hartanger, Barfreston, Kent*)

In or shortly after 1416 Robert Hertanger, a London mason, contracted to rebuild the *South Gate* at *King's Lynn*, which was found to be in a dangerous condition. Before half the work was completed he had spent all the money voted but was excused 'because of his poverty'. Another mason finished the building of the gateway, which, however, needed to be rebuilt again a century later, when NICHOLAS and THOMAS HERMER were the contractors.[1]

During the late summer and autumn of 1409 Robert Hertanger was one of the masons employed at *London Bridge*.[2] *Richard HERTANGRE*, mason, [who] worked at *Merton College, Oxford*, in 1448,[3] [may have been identical with the mason Richard 'Hertangr' imprisoned for debt in London in 1435 at the suit of JOHN BURTON, mason.]

A.O.
[1] HKL, 760–1; [2] KJL; [3] GOM, 113; CCR 1435–41, 234

HERTE, John (fl. 1449) Mason

Mason of Bristol. On 8 December 1449 an agreement was made between the proctors of the parish of 'Holywylle' (*Holywell, Oxford*) and John Herte, to go to arbitration, presumably in regard to payment for work done on the church. In case the arbitrators should not be unanimous, John Beke, rector of All Saints, Oxford, was to be assessor.[1] The north arcade of the nave and north aisle were rebuilt, 'about the middle of the 15th century'.[2]

[1] OHS, XCIII (1932), 194; [2] RCHM, *City of Oxford*, 129

HERUNDEN, John, I [Harrenden] (fl. –†1509) Mason

Mason; died in 1509, when he left his tools to be sold for the benefit of the repairs of Twyford Bridge and Yalding Church.

(*A.O.*) DHC, *West Kent*, 84; *RCW*, vi, 249

An earlier *John HERYNDEN* of 'Boughton Monchelsey' died in 1488.

CCC, C.3, 189 (*A.O.*)

HERUNDEN, John, II (*fl.* 1524–†1532) Mason

Mason of Boughton Monchelsea, Kent, in 1524. He died in 1532.

(*A.O.*) AC, XXVII, 173; *CCC*, A.19, 275

HERUNDEN, Thomas (*fl.* 1529–†1534) Mason

On 4 February 1529 was granted the office of King's Master Mason in survivorship with JOHN MOLTON.[1] Molton seems to have been generally referred to as the King's mason, perhaps because Herunden was the owner of quarries at Boughton Monchelsea in Kent, where he lived. In 1531–32 he was paid for hardstone for Westminster Palace, being described as of 'Bolton Monshelley, Kent, mason', and at the same time a *Thomas HARUNDEN* possibly a son, was working there as a hardhewer, taking 3*s.* 4*d.* a week.[2] He died in 1534, his will being proved by his widow Elizabeth on 30 September. He left three sons, John, Edward, and William, the last still an apprentice. Edward was to have the dwelling-house, lands, and quarries at Boughton.[3] Other bequests were to the parish churches of Boughton, Loose, East Farleigh, and St. Margaret's, Westminster. The will was evidently made in Westminster, for 'Sir' Henry Mott, curate of St. Margaret's, was a witness. John Clyffe of East Farleigh, mason, was to be overseer, to assist Herunden's wife in the sale of the stone from his quarry.

WKM
[1] LPH, IV, pt. iii, 5336; [2] *PRO*, E.36–251, 252 (*G.P.J.*); *WAM*, 12257; [3] *PCC*, 18 Hogen

Herward, William—see HARWARD

HEYDON, John (*fl.* 1471–1475) Mason

In 1471–72 John Heydon was paid £5 as part of his contract to build a new chancel at *Hempstead-by-Holt Church*, Norfolk, and in 1474–75 the final instalment of £7. The work was done for Norwich Cathedral Priory. A John Heydon died in 1480 as lord of Losehall Manor in Hempstead.

NRO, DCN, Cellarer, nos, 180, 181 (*S.A.C.; P.C.*)

Heyndele, John—see HYNDELEY

HEYWARD, John [Hayward] (*fl.* 1354–1359) Carpenter

Carpenter working at *Rotherhithe Manor* for the king in 1354–56, and for the Black Prince at *Kennington* in 1358–59.

HKW, II, 993, 968

HEYWOD, John (*fl.* 1438–†1448) Carpenter

Of Ditton Valence (now Wood Ditton), Cambs. By an indenture made with John Edward, Mercer of Bury, 2 November 1438, John Heywod contracted to roof the chapel of *St. John at Hill* in the abbey cemetery at *Bury St. Edmunds* and to do some minor work for £10 6*s.* 8*d.*[1] The roof was to have six 'pryncepal couplys Arche bounden' and the principals, purlins, and 'iopez' were to be 'enbowyd' (i.e. moulded). The will of John Heywode 'de Saxton hamelett' in the parish of Ditton Valence, dated 4 April 1448, proved 14 July 1448, is probably that of the same man, although there is no indication in it that he was a carpenter.[2] His wife was dead and no child is mentioned.

A.O.
[1] *BM*, Add. MS. 14848, *f.* 304; SHB, 512–13; AAJ, XXI, 118; [2] *BW*, ii, 120v.

HIKKE, John (*fl.* 1447–1448) Carpenter

With JOHN BALWE made seats for *Yatton Church*, Somerset, in 1447–48.

SRS, IV (1890), 85–9

HILDER, Christopher (*fl.* 1480–1481) Mason

In 1480–81 was paid £3 13*s.* 4*d.* for making a buttress on the north side of the chancel of *Northallerton Church*, Yorks., N.R., by agreement. The chancel was pulled down and rebuilt in 1779.

(*A.O.*) DAR, III, 647

HILDOLVESTON, W[illiam] de (*fl.* 1292–1293) Carpenter (*Hindolveston, Norf.*)

Master carpenter employed by *Norwich Cathedral Priory* on the construction of a new bakehouse in 1292–93; he was paid £3 6*s.* 8*d.*

NCM, roll 11

Hill—see also HYLL(E)

HILL, John (*fl.* 1448–1483) Mason, Carver

John Hill, freemason, was admitted to the freedom of Wells, Som. in 1448.[1] In 1476–77 one 'John Hille, kerver' was paid 1*s.* 9*d.* for 1 day's work by himself and 2 days' work by his men in the church of *St. Ewen, Bristol*.[2] In 1480–81 'John Hylle the kerver' was paid 3*s.* 4*d.* 'for selynge of the wall yn the Northe Ile . . . by the Image of Jesus' in *All Saints Church, Bristol*, and £2 3*s.* 4*d.* was paid in the same year 'to the kerver for makyng of a Newe Fronte otherwyse callyd a Reredose wt. iij. howsys for Seynt Thomas awter'.[3] 'John Hylle, kerver' bought 'stuff yt was lafte' after the building of an 'aller' (? passage) by the Bristol Tuckers in 1482–83; he may also have been the unnamed 'kerver' paid for work at this time, for example 16*d*. for 2½ days.[4]

(A.O.)

[1] SRS, XLVI (1931), 147; [2] BGT, XV (1890–91), 270; [3] BAO, Churchwardens' accounts; [4] FTG, 76 *(E.W.)*

HILL, Nicholas *(fl. 1491–1499)* Imager

Carver of Nottingham who in 1491 brought action to recover from a salesman the value of 58 carved heads of St. John Baptist. In 1494–95 he was himself sued by a carrier who had taken carved heads to London, and was again involved in a suit concerning a St. John's head in 1499.

W.H. St. John Hope in AJ, LXI (1904), 234; RN, III, 18, 28, 499

HILL, Walter *(fl. c. 1495)* Alabasterman

Concerned in indentures for the making of a tomb for the body of King Richard III, with Sir Reynold Bray and Sir Thomas Lovell. See also JAMES KEYLEY.

PRO, C.1–206–69 *(A. Ru.)*

HILL, William [Hylle] *(fl. 1466)* ? Carpenter

Of Ipswich; in March 1466 undertook to make a new quay and a new house at *Harwich* for Sir John Howard, later Duke of Norfolk, for £6. An agreement with a mason was made in the same month to build a tower at Harwich.

A.O. BMH

HILLE, William *(fl. 1425–)* Mason

Paid £13 6*s*. 8*d*. for building two perches of the wall between *Maidstone College* and the River Medway in 1424–25. He was probably identical with WILLIAM HELLE.

MM, Steward's Acc. 1424–28 *(J.W-H.)*

HILLES, Ralph *(fl. 1552–1554)* Mason

Succeeded ROBERT SYLVESTER as master mason of the Court of Augmentations on 29 September 1552 and held office until the Court was dissolved on 23 January 1554. In 1553 Hilles, with the master carpenter JOHN REVELL and the chief joiner Richard Pye, was in charge of fitting up *Somerset Place* for the Princess Elizabeth.

HKW, III, 420; IV, 253

Hilmer, John—see AYLMER

HIPPIS, John [Hypps] *(fl. 1515)* Marbler

Of Lincoln; on 6 April 1515 contracted to make a tomb for John Willoughby, son of Sir Henry Willoughby, in *Wollaton Church*, Notts., for £5 6*s*. 8*d*. It was apparently to be of alabaster, bearing brasses.

THS, Rec. Ser. XXI (1962), 1–2 *(N.L.R.)*

HIRDE, John *(fl. 1396–1397)* Mason

Mason of Pembroke; in 1396–97 was paid £20 for laying and rebuilding a wall at *Carmarthen Castle* 145 feet in length.

WWH, III, 72

HIRTON, Roger de [Irton] *(fl. 1344–1348)* Mason

A mason employed at *York Minster* in 1344 when he was said to have been paid for working although absent. Mistakenly claimed as master mason of the Minster. He took up the freedom of York in 1348. One Roger de Irton was a tenant owing suit to the Portmote Court of Tutbury, Staffs., on 10 July 1342 when he was essoined of common essoin (i.e. as being absent through illness) by John 'Sutor'.

APD; KMM, 32; *PRO*, DL 30–109–1618, m.4

HOBBS, John [Hobbes] *(fl. 1455–1475)* Mason

Of Gloucester, where he held property in the parish of St. John's in 1455 as tenant of the Abbot;[1] in 1475 ('of Gloucester') he contracted with Sir John Beauchamp, Baron of Powick, to build a new chapel for the latter on the north side of the choir of the *Black Friars' Church at Worcester*, together with a tomb in the chapel. The chapel and tomb were to be built 'according to the patroun of the portretor' specified in an indenture which is not known to survive. An alabaster image was to be placed on the tomb.[2] Hobbs was perhaps the 'Gloucestre mason' consulted at the building of the tower of *Ludlow Church*, Salop, in 1469; this mason received a reward of £1 6*s*. 8*d*., and 6*d*. was spent on him 'and his man at a dyner'.[3] It seems not unlikely that he designed the Lady Chapel of *Gloucester Cathedral*, built between 1457 and 1483.

John Hobbs may have been a son of *William HOBBYS*, mason, who in 1441–42 was paid 6*d*. a day for 8 days for riding to the quarries at Upton and Frome 'to choose and examine good stones called Cropstone' for the repairs of *Gloucester Castle*.[4]

[1] CSG, 64, 76; [2] VCH, *Worcs.*, II, 167; [3] SHR, 2 Ser., I (1889), 242; [4] *PRO*, E.101–473–18

'Hobyns', John—see LEBONS

HOCKERING, William [Hokeryng] *(fl. 1423–1426)* Mason *(Hockering, Norfolk)*

Appointed master mason of the King's works at *Calais* on 18 December 1423, in succession to JOHN PYNKHILL. He was succeeded by WILLIAM WARLOWE in 1426.

DKR, XLVIII, 228; HKW, II, 1054

Hocton, Thomas de—see HOUGHTON

HOGUN, Thomas [Hugun] (*fl.* 1288–1289) Mason

Mason contractor who in 1288–89 was paid £5 15*s.* 0*d.* for making a new wall below *Carmarthen Castle*, on both sides of the postern towards the Bridge of Towey. In the same year he received £2 for whitening and repairing the whole of the castle walls, and with two fellows a further £3 for building the walls of a stable. It is probable that these works were under the direction of Master ADAM the Mason II.

WWH, III, 47

Hoke, Simon—see HOOK

Hokynton, Thomas—see HOUGHTON

HOLBECH, Hugh (*fl.* 1398–1412) Carpenter (*Holbeach, Lincs.*)

Of (King's) Lynn; in 1398–99 he and his associates were paid £6 12*s.* 7½*d.* for 10 weeks' work on making a house at the *South Gates* of *Lynn* for the town chamberlains. In 1411–12 the chamberlains paid him 12*s.* for three long beams bought from him for the bridge at the South Gate.

LCR, Ea, 40, 45

HOLBROOK, Laurence [Holbrok] (*fl.* 1450–1461) Carpenter and Joiner

On 7 July 1450 a pardon was granted to 'Laurence Holbroke of Rochester joynour' for having taken part in Jack Cade's insurrection.[1] In 1460–61 Holbrook and Richard Christian, carpenters, made a new parlour for the *Crown Inn, Rochester*.[2]

(A.O.)
[1] AC, VII, 263; [2] BRB, 92

HOLDEN, Thomas de (*fl.* 1414–†1429) Mason

Was granted the office of master mason in the counties of Chester and Flint, during pleasure, on 6 October 1414; he seems only to have held the post two years, as JOHN ASSER, senior, was appointed on 22 August 1416. As master mason for North Wales he held office as surveyor of the works there until his death on 19 February 1429.

DKR, XXXI; HKW, I, 467 n.; II, 1057

Holewell, Thomas—see COLYN, Thomas

HOLM, Henry (*fl.* 1423–1424) Carpenter

Was paid £9 11*s.* 0*d.* in 1423–24 for making various chambers in the new *Crown Inn,* *Rochester* by contract.

BRB, 90; *RBA,* No. 32 (*M.J.B.*)

HOLMCULTRAM, Robert de [de Ulmo] (*fl.* 1298–1309) Engineer (*Holme Cultram, Cumb.*)

Cistercian lay-brother and carpenter and engineer employed by Edward I. In 1298 he was associated with THOMAS DE HOUGHTON in sending engines of war by sea from Carlisle to Ayr, and on 3 May 1309 was appointed to succeed Houghton as master carpenter and engineer of the works of *Carlisle Castle*.

TTH, 32

HOLME, Henry (*fl.* 1381–1383) Mason

On 20 July 1383 contracted to build the new gatehouse of *Dunstanburgh Castle* for John of Gaunt, Duke of Lancaster.[1] He had been doing work at the castle since 1 December 1381, as JOHN LEWYN seems to have left certain works unfinished, perhaps on account of the pressure of his (Lewyn's) other work. In the autumn of 1382 Holme was paid his arrears and in 1383 a sum of £20 for making six 'houses' with vaults, chimneys, and windows, in addition to his work on the gatehouse, which was to be paid for at the rate of 10 marks (£6 13*s.* 4*d.*) for each rod completed; this payment was to include the costs of quarrying lime, sand, carriage and all other things necessary to the work, but Holme was to be allowed to take the old gatehouse to help the works of the new one.[2]

(BBH)
[1] SHB, 463; [2] JGR 1379–83, 624, 723, 903, 923

Holmesfield—see HELMESFIELD

HOLNERST, Richard [Holhurst, Holnehurst] (*fl.* 1445–1450) Carpenter

Carpenter of Romsey, Hants. Second named of two carpenters, with JOHN HARDYNG II who undertook to build an inn at *Andover* for Winchester College on 4 March 1444/5. The design was in the first place made by Hardyng, a Southampton carpenter, but this was apparently superseded by a fresh drawing prepared by the carpenter of Eton College (probably ROBERT WHETELY). Holnerst evidently carried out the actual building work on the site and was being paid instalments for the work in 1447–48. In 1449–50 one JOHN LEWYS, carpenter, rode from Winchester to Andover to value the work done by Holnerst as extras beyond the contract.

SHB, 517–19; *WCM,* Compoti 1444–5, 1447–8, 1449–50

Homurvill, William—see HUMBERVILLE

HOO, Thomas (*fl.* 1380–1398) Mason

Was probably resident master mason of *Canterbury Cathedral* during the rebuilding of the nave under HENRY YEVELEY; on 10 July 1380 he was granted two years' exemption from serving on juries while engaged on this work, and again on 7 February 1389/90 for three years.[1] In 1398 his name appears as an esquire of the prior of Christ Church Priory, receiving a livery at Christmas;[2] this suggests that he held a position of importance on the staff. In February-April 1351/2, Thomas Hoo, mason (*cementarius*), was paid 5½*d.* per day for work at *Westminster Palace*, while from Michaelmas to Whitsun 1354–55 he was paid 2*s.* a week for 31 weeks' work.[3]

Thomas HOO, perhaps the son of the Canterbury mason, worked as a mason on the nave of *Westminster Abbey* for 43 weeks in 1395–96, taking the apprentice's rate of 2*s.* a week.[4]

[1] CPR 1377–81, 530; 1388–92, 196; [2] *Bodl.*, Tanner MS. 165 (*A.O.*); [3] SAW, 202; *PRO*, E.101–471–6, 11; [4] *WAM*, 23464–5

HOO, William de [Hove] (*fl.* 1292–1317) Mason

A mason working under MICHAEL OF CANTERBURY, at *St. Stephen's Chapel* in *Westminster Palace* in 1292,[1] and made the casket (*cista*) for the heart of Queen Eleanor of Castile buried in the *Blackfriars' Church, London*.[2] On 5 March 1315/16 he was a member of a commission of masons to arrange for the paving of the city of London.[3] Named as master, on 12 May 1315, he with three other masons, John de Offynton, John de Hardynggesham, and John de St. Omer, contracted to make a wall round the manor of *Eltham* by Michaelmas 1316 to the design and under the supervision of Master Michael of Canterbury. Owing to their fraudulent workmanship and use of inferior materials, the masons were imprisoned and heavy damages assessed against them, but they were released on undertaking to rebuild the work properly, with Michael of Canterbury, Alexander Le Ymagour (DE ABINGDON), and other citizens going surety for them.[4]

[1] TSS, 2; [2] BMH; [3] CLB, 'E', 55–6; [4] SHB, 27–8, 422–4

HOOK, Simon at [Hoke, Hooke] (*fl.* 1354–1396) Mason

Worked as a mason (*cementarius*) at *Westminster Palace* for 150 days in 1354–55, taking 5½*d.* a day, the standard rate;[1] was overseer of the masons' work during the repairs of *Rochester Castle* from 1368 to 1377 taking 8*d.* a day,[2] and in 1383 was partner of WALTER WALTON in undertaking the repair of the church of the *Hospital of St. Thomas of Acon* in *London*.[3] In August 1386 he was sworn as one of the masters of the mistery of masons in London.[4] Between 1392 and 1396 Hook was concerned in several property transactions in the City of London.[5]

(APD; KJI, 84, 125)
[1] *PRO*, E.101–544–25; E.101–545–8 (*L.F.S.*); [2] AC, II, 122; [3] CPR 1381–5, 310; [4] CLB, 'H', 273; [5] *LHR*, 120(150), 122(87–90), 124(10), 125(24)

HOORE, Stephen (*fl.* 1386–1395) Carpenter

Of Wickhambrook, Suffolk; in 1386, in partnership with JOHN PAYN of Depden, Stephen Hoore contracted to build a kitchen at *King's Hall, Cambridge*, of the same excellent timber in quantity and workmanship as that of the kitchen of the Friars Preachers at Cambridge. It was to have a solar annexed on the west side, with a covered staircase leading to it, and a larder on the east. These buildings were to be finished by 24 June 1387 and to cost 30 marks (£20).[1] Each of the contractors was to receive in addition a tunic and a hood. The kitchen stood at the northeast corner of the mediaeval court adjoining the ground of St. John's Hospital. In 1394–95, when a chimney was built in this kitchen, payments were made to Stephen, carpenter, among others.[2]

A.O.
[1] WCC, II, 438; [2] *TCM*, *KHA*, iv, 105

HOPKINS, Stephen (*fl.* 1470–   ) Mason

Mason of *Bristol*; in 1470 acted as a viewer of the city.

(*A.O.*) BLR, II, 132

HORE, John (*fl.* 1434–   ) Carpenter

Of Diss, Norfolk; contracted on 20 June 1434 to build a new windmill at *Tivetshall*, Suffolk, for the Abbot of Bury. Hore was to have the material of the old mill, with 9½ marks (£6 6*s.* 8*d.*) and a robe.

SHB, 505; (*BM*, Add. MS. 14848, *f.* 74v.)

HORE, Robert le (*fl.* 1340–1344) Mason

With ROBERT GOSEDEN contracted to rebuild the outer walls of *Farnham Castle*, Surrey, in 1340; the work went on until 1342.[1] He was the owner of a quarry at Bentley, Hants., whence he sold 233 feet of stone for 10*s.* 6*d.*, for the works of *Windsor Castle* in 1344.[2]

[1] RMF, 126; [2] HWC, I, 117, 125

HORE, Thomas (*fl.* 1414–1415) Mason

On 15 February 1414 he was one of a large number of men of the town of Cirencester who received a pardon for all treasons, insurrections and the like. Thomas Hore of Cirencester, mason, was on 26 November 1415 pardoned for not appearing before the justices of the bench to answer Thomas Mulle touching a debt of £40.

CPR 1413–16, 168, 316 (*A.O.*)

HOREWODE, William [Horwod] (*fl.* 1434–) Mason

Freemason, 'dwelling in Fodringhey'; contracted to build the nave, aisles, and tower of *Fotheringhay Church*, Northants., on 24 September 1434; Horewode was to be paid £300 for the work.[1] It is not unlikely that he was identical with the William Horwode, citizen of London, to whom Roger Mapulton, mason of Watford, Herts., owed 40s. in 1459.[2] (See MAPILTON, THOMAS*.)

The new work at Fotheringhay was to be modelled upon the quire which had been built some years before, and there is some reason to suppose that the original design may have been by Thomas Mapilton and STEPHEN LOTE who had collaborated in making the tomb of the Duke of York there. This Duke was killed at Agincourt in 1415, and the new quire of Fotheringhay was in progress at the same time as his tomb. Horewode's work at Fotheringhay was probably nearing completion in 1441, when an unnamed mason from thence went to work on All Souls College, Oxford.[3]

(APD; BAA)
[1] SHB, 505–9; KMM, 245–8; DM, VI, 1414; [2] CPR 1452–61, 454; [3] GOM, 60

HORNE, John (*fl.* 1417–1428) Mason Carver

Mason; took up the freedom of Norwich in 1417–18.[1] In 1427–28, as a carver (*le gravour*) he was working with WILLIAM REPPYS on bosses of the vault of *Norwich Cathedral* cloister.[2]
[1] EFN; [2] SNN, 174; *NCM*, roll 1077

HORNER, Christopher (*fl.* 1478–†1523) Mason

Was an apprentice at *York Minster* at 2s. 6d. a week in 1478–79 and 1481–82, and in 1489 was admitted a freeman of York. In 1490 he was committed to prison with WILLIAM HYNDELEY while an inquiry was made to discover whether they had murdered John Partrik, a tyler, during the dispute between the masons and the tylers.[1] By 1495 he was taking 3s. a week for work at the Minster, and in 1505 was appointed master mason there, in succession to William Hyndeley.[2] On 20 November 1499 a licence was issued to the curate of St. Michael-le-Belfrey, York, to marry Christopher Horner and Agnes Wilkinson.[3] On 17 September 1501 Horner was appointed Common Mason of York in succession to ROBERT BAYNES, and held the office until 1506 when he was succeeded by ALEXANDER WILSON. Horner was again in trouble in 1504 when he was committed to prison in connection with disturbances at the election of the mayor on 15 January. He was released on 10 June and later again gaoled for misbehaviour.[4] Horner made his will on 12 February 1522/3, leaving all his tools within the lodge to the work of the fabric, and died before 9 April 1523, when the will was proved.[5] He was succeeded in office by JOHN FORMAN.

KJI; RCHM, *York*, II, 174
[1] YCR, II, 60, 61; [2] BHY, I, 266, 268–9; RFY, 94, 95, 96n., 97; [3] YTE, III, 361; [4] YCR, II, 191–4; III, 1–7; [5] YTE, V, 165; *DCY*, II, 135

HORS', Stephen de (*fl.* 1294–) ? Mason

At the court held for Ramsey Abbey in the manor of *King's Ripton*, Hunts., on 20 January 1293/4, the whole township was ordered to pay 3s. 4d. unjustly withheld from Stephen de Hors' from his pay (*stipendio*) for making a certain stone cross.

ARA, 216

HORSSALE, Richard (*fl.* 1511–) Mason

Freemason of Tetbury, Glos.; on 25 March 1511 he contracted with the feoffees of the church of *Sherston*, Wilts., to build a *Church House*, 60 feet by 19 feet, and 16 feet high, with doors and windows as specified in the contract for £10, the whole to be completed on St. Luke's Day, 18 October. The building still exists, though partly rebuilt, in Sherston High Street.

SHB, 561–2; WNQ, VI, 448–50

HORT, William (*fl.* 1509–1526) Mason

'Fremason'; in 1509–10 was paid £2 10s. 0d. for work on the spire of *Yatton Church*, Som. In 1524 he received £1 for repairs to the chancel there and also supplied stone for the work. In that and the following two years he was paid over £9 for the new *Cross* in the churchyard. He is probably identical with 'HART'.

SRS, IV (1890), 130, 140

Horwood—see HOREWODE

Hoton, Thomas de—see HOUGHTON

HOTON, William, senior (*fl. c.* 1348–†1351) Mason

Was master mason at *York Minster* perhaps in succession to THOMAS PACENHAM until his death in 1351, when he was succeeded by his son WILLIAM HOTON, junior. Hoton supervised the building of the Zouche Chapel, begun by 1350; the chapel may, however, have been designed by another master for the Archbishop.

RFY, 166

HOTON, William, junior (*fl.* 1351–†*c.* 1368) Mason

Became master mason of *York Minster* on 1 October 1351, in succession to his father WILLIAM HOTON, senior. He lived in a house in the close previously inhabited by THOMAS PACENHAM. He was to have £10 a year, payable at Whitsun and Martinmas, and a house in the cathedral close for life. If he became unable to direct the work through blindness or disease, he was to pay half the wage of the undermaster from his own fee of £10.[1] Hoton's full-size setting-out for the tracery of the aisle windows of the choir, begun in 1361, still survives on the plaster floor of the tracing-house above the vestibule of the chapter-house.

He died before January 1368/9, when he was succeeded by ROBERT PATRINGTON, senior. The Hoton family seems to have been engaged in the same craft for several generations.

> William *HOTON* of York, mason, died before 4 July 1392, when probate of his will was granted to his brother James of Hoton.[2]

KJI; *J.H.H.* in FYM 1968 (1969), 11; HYM, 163
[1] *SHB*, 586–7; RFY, 1, 166; [2] *PCY*, i, 48

HOUGHTON, Thomas de [Hocghton, Hoctone, Hoghton, Hokynton, Hoton, Hotton, Houtton, Octon] (*fl.* 1288–1318) Carpenter

Master carpenter and engineer in the royal service. In 1288 he was one of the viewers of works at the little hall of the *Palace of Westminster*, being paid 6*d.* a day,[1] but on 25 July 1290 he was given a regular appointment with only 4½*d.* a day while at work, with a clothing allowance of £1 yearly. He was paid from 31 July to 19 November having charge of works in Westminster Palace, and procuring timber at Kingston upon Thames. In 1292 he built a stable at the royal mews and altered the palace kitchen by contract, receiving £6 3*s.* 4*d.*, and made the carved wooden screen and canopy for the tomb of Queen Eleanor in *Westminster Abbey* for which he was paid over £20. On 23 October he gave pledges at the Exchequer and took oath to serve as a serjeant carpenter, one of his sureties being Master ROBERT DE COLEBROOK.

The rest of his career was associated with military work; in Wales from the spring of 1293: at *Beaumaris Castle* in 1295 he was paid 9*d.* a day as one of two *ingeniatores* ranking as esquires-of-arms; was at Wingham, Kent in October and there received prest money to proceed to Cumberland to build engines of war. In September 1298 he sent engines from Carlisle to Ayr by sea, for use in the Scottish campaign, and in February 1300 he was with the army at *Edinburgh Castle*. In 1302 he was one of two master carpenters (with ADAM DE GLASHAM) in charge of works at the building of *Linlithgow Peel*, and was taking 1*s.* a day. From November 1303 to February 1303/4 he was with the Court at Dunfermline, and from April to August 1303 he was the senior of seven master carpenters directing works at the siege of Stirling. He was at Westminster in March 1305, but on 3 September 1306 was sent from Newbrough-in-Tyndale to the siege of Kildrummy in Mar which shortly capitulated. In November 1307 he was selecting timber for the works of *Dover Castle*, and then took charge at *Carlisle Castle*, where he was succeeded as chief engineer on 3 May 1309 by Brother ROBERT OF HOLMCULTRAM. In February 1312 he was directing the construction of engines for the defence of the *Tower of London*, and he was making engines in the castle of *Berwick-on-Tweed* shortly before it was captured by the Scots in 1318.

TTH; HKW, I, 216–17
[1] *PRO*, E. 101–467–16

Houke, Simon—see HOOK

'Houndling', William—see FOUNDYNG

HOWEL the Mason (*fl.* 1468–†*c.* 1470) Mason

Of Penllyn, North Wales; about 1468 he began the bridge of *Pont-y-Pair* over the Conway at *Bettws-y-Coed* but died before its completion.

JAB, IV, 42

HOWELL, Geoffrey ap (*fl.* 1447) Carpenter

Succeeded JOHN ROUS as master carpenter of the royal castles in South Wales at some date after 1435, but had ceased to hold office by April 1447.

HKW, II, 1057

HOWELL, John (*fl.* 1538–1539) Mason

Described as master; warden of the masons at the pulling down of *Chertsey Abbey* in 1538 and *Abingdon Abbey* in 1539, taking 5*s.* a week.

PRO, E.101–458–1; 459–22 (*L.F.S.*) (*G.P.J.*)

HOWES, John [Hause, Haves, Hawes] (*fl.* 1466–1523) Mason

Mason of Norwich, took up the freedom of the city in 1466/7;[1] on 8 May 1508 he was adjoined to the masters of the masons' and carpenters' crafts of the city at the mayor's command, to adjudicate in a dispute.[2] John Howes, son of John Howes, mason, took up the freedom as a tailor in 1522/3.[3] A younger *John HOWES* took up the freedom of Norwich as a mason in 1518 as apprentice of JOHN HOWES and died in 1552, leaving his wife Elizabeth his sole executrix. He wished to be buried in the churchyard of St. Mary of the Marsh in the Cathedral precinct.

NRO, Dean & Chapter Wills, Reg. 1461–1559, f. 115
[1] *EFN*; [2] *HTN*, II, 29–30; [3] EFN

HOWES, Richard [Haus] (*fl.* 1493–? †1528) Mason

In 1493–94 Richard Haus, mason, took up the freedom of Norwich after serving apprentice to John Spylman.[1] In 1508, at the command of the mayor, he was adjoined to the masters of the masons' and carpenters' crafts of Norwich to settle a building dispute.[2] He was paid £2 13*s.* 4*d.* in 1511–12 for work on rebuilding the chancel of the church of *St. Peter Parmentergate, Norwich*.[3] He may have been the Richard Haus(se) who died at the abbey of St. Benet Hulme in 1528, leaving a widow Letice.[4]

[1] *EFN*; [2] *HTN*, II, 29–30; [3] *NRO*, DCN, roll 993 (*P.C.*); [4] *CCN* 169 Haywarde (proved 1528)

HOWLETT, William [Howlot] (*fl.* 1462–1466) Carpenter

Admitted to the freedom of Norwich in 1462–63;[1] in 1465–66 he was working in the choir of *Norwich Cathedral*, and also made new doors for the chancel of *Scratby Church*. He seems to have been paid at the rate of 6*d.* a day, plus his board.[2]

(SNN)
[1] *EFN*; [2] *NCM*, roll 299

HUBAL the Mason (? 12th century) Carver

Carver of the Norman tympanum formerly at *Pennington Church*, Lancs., mentioned in a Runic inscription.

VCH, *Lancashire*, VIII, 340–1

HUDDE, John (*fl.* 1500–1515) Carver

One of the carvers, with ROBERT BELLAMY and others, of the dragon, lion, and leopards for the royal cipher in the Great Hall of the *Tower of London* in 1500; and also carved two lions and a great rose with an imperial crown above it, over the north door in *Westminster Hall*, in 1500–02. He may have been employed in the next few years on the statues or enrichment of *Henry VII's Chapel* at Westminster.[1]

Between 1510 and 1515 'Jehan Hudde' was one of the carvers employed at *Bourges Cathedral*, France, on tabernacles and details of the north porch and tower.[2]

(LKC, 230; LWR, 171)
[1] *BM*, Egerton MS. 2358; [2] BCB, 18

Huet—see HUGUET

Hugh the Carpenter—see ALBEMUNT

HUGH the Carpenter I (*fl. c.* 1230–) Carpenter

Probably carpenter at the building of *Salisbury Cathedral*, as he appears as a witness to the confirmation of a messuage to NICHOLAS OF ELY the cathedral mason, *c.* 1230. He may have been identical with HUGH ALBEMUNT.

HMC, *Var. Coll.*, I, 382

HUGH the Carpenter II (*fl.* 1359–1396) Carpenter

Was master carpenter of *Worcester Cathedral* from 1359 to 1396, taking 1*s.* a week plus 6*d.* 'companagium' or 3*d.* a day. This small wage suggests that he was a resident jobbing carpenter, and this is borne out by references to the minor works he did. In 1382–83 the sum of 8*d.* a week was paid to Richard his apprentice.

(WCR); *WCO*, rolls C.65–7, 69–71, 74–7

HUGH the Carver (*fl. c.* 1150–) Carver

Master; perhaps identical with Master Hugh the Sacrist of Bury who died *c.* 1200. About 1150 the doors at the front of the abbey church of *Bury St. Edmunds* were carved by the hands of Master Hugh 'who, as he excelled all men in his other works, in this marvellous piece of work excelled himself'.

SHB, 253; MSE, II, 289

HUGH the Mason I (*fl.* 1086–) Mason

At the compilation of the Domesday survey of Hampshire, *c.* 1086, Hugh the mason (*cementarius*) held land for two ploughs which had belonged to one Giraud in Chilcomb near Winchester, a manor in the hands of Bishop Walchelin. There can be little doubt that Hugh was the master in charge of the building of the Norman *Winchester Cathedral* (1079–93).

VCH, *Hants.*, I, 463–4

HUGH the Mason II (*fl. c.* 1160–   ) Mason

Mason (*cementarius*) of Lincoln; appears with Gervase and Walter de Archeseia, *cementarii*, among witnesses to a grant of land at Honington, Lincs., to Stixwould Priory early in the reign of Henry II.

(*H.M.C.*) SDD, 281

HUGH the Mason III (*fl.* 1291–   ) Mason

Was master mason at *Hereford Cathedral* in 1291, while the work of the outer walls and windows of the nave aisles, presbytery, and north-east transept was in progress. His fee was £5 a year. He may have been Hugh, son of HENRY DE REYNS.

CCH; MHC

HUGUET [Aquete, 'Hacket', Huet] (*fl.* 1402–†1438) Mason

Probably French or Flemish master mason of the friary church of *Batalha*, Portugal, from 1402 until his death in 1438. The claim that he was of Anglo-Irish origin rests upon nothing more than an impossible identification with David Hacket, bishop of Ossory 1460–78, under whom the crossing vault of *Kilkenny Cathedral* was built. The very strong English influences on the design of Batalha had already been present under Huguet's Portuguese predecessor, Affonso Domingues, (See STEPHEN STEPHENSON.)

TBK, XVIII, 96–7; HGW, 106

Hugun, Thomas—see HOGUN

HULLE, Robert [Hylle] (*fl.* 1400–†1442) Mason

Mason of Winchester; possibly identical with the Robert Hulle invited to visit Winchester College on 10 December 1400, when 'Guy, cook at St. Cross' was given a reward of 12*d.*[1] This may perhaps indicate that Hulle was at the time engaged on some work at *St. Cross Hospital.*

On 7 March 1411/12 Hulle was already master mason (*Magister Latomorum*) of *Winchester Cathedral*, presumably in succession to WILLIAM WYNFORD; he was then granted by the Prior and Convent a lease of their tenement in the constabulary of the city of Winchester, at a rent of 6*s.* 8*d.* a year, a yearly robe furred with lamb of the suit of the Prior's esquires, a 'standing' in the monastery at the Prior's costs, with 3*s.* 4*d.* a week when engaged on the work of the church, with his dinner in the Prior's Hall, while his servant (*garcio*) was to take his meal at the servants' table.[2] The house was at the south end of Great Minster Street on the west side; he was still living there in 1430 but had probably moved away by 1436. Hulle also had another property close by his house. Before 1426 he had saved the life of John Schaldene, butler and attorney of the cathedral priory, who gave him property in the city, the gift being recorded in 1426 while Hulle was at Salisbury.[3]

In 1412–13 Hulle supplied 6 tons of Beer stone for the works of *Winchester College.*[4] In 1417 he was assessed at 6*d.* to the Tarrage of the city in respect of the tenement he held of the Priory, next but one to the Minster Gate;[5] while in 1418–19 he was paid 6*s.* 8*d.* by Winchester College for riding to *Alresford* to superintend their works in progress on the *Angel Inn* (see THOMAS WOLFHOW), and for his advice on matters touching his trade.[6] In 1439–40 Robert Hulle was paid £6 in part of his contract of £12 for 'la Kervyngworke Rodeloft' at *St. John's, Glastonbury.*[7] Hulle was in charge of the building of *St. John's Hospital, Sherborne,* Dorset, being paid £19 by instalments from the summer of 1440 until about April 1442.[8]

Hulle must have been dead by 1 June 1442, when a fresh grant was made of his tenement by Winchester Cathedral Priory.[9]

[1] *WCM*, Compotus 1400–1; [2] *WNC*, Reg. 1, *f.* 29v.; [3] (*D.K.Win.*); [4] *WCM*, Compotus 1412–13; [5] *WCM*, City of Winchester 2; [6] *WCM*, Compotus 1418–19; [7] *SDN*, IV, 192; [8] *SAD*, Building Accs. (*J.F.*); [9] *WNC*, Reg. 1, *f.* 61

HULLE, William (*fl.* 1534) Carver

In 1534 was paid 8*s.* 8*d.* for making 'the gorge and the dragonne' for *Wigtoft Church*, Lincs.

NIM, 225 (*N.L.R.*)

Hulpestone—see HELPESTON

HUMBERCROFT, Simon (? *fl. c.* 1305) Mason

Mason who was possibly in charge of work *c.* 1305 at *St. Mary's Church, Beverley*, Yorks.

John Bilson quoting Beverley Chapter Acts (*M.R.P.; W.C.B.S.*)

HUMBERVILLE, William [Humbervyle, Homurvill, Umbyrvil, Umbyrvyle, Vmbreuill, Wymberuill] (*fl.* 1351–1379) Mason

In June 1351 William Umbrevill was one of the working masons employed at *Windsor Castle* at 5½*d.* a day, and was still there in 1353–54 working on the aerary;[1] and leading mason on the works of *Wallingford Castle*, Berks., in 1375, taking 6*d.* a day.[2] He was master mason in charge of the building of the library of *Merton College, Oxford*, in 1369–79. In connection with the work he journeyed with Bloxham, warden of the college and surveyor of the works, to Sherborne, Salisbury, Winchester, and London; they went to London 'with the purpose of viewing the library of the Preaching Friars'. He was paid 4*s.* a week in summer and 3*s.* 4*d.* in winter, spending part of his time at the quarry at Taynton. He was also paid for supplying Taynton stone for the works in 1378.[3]

(*R.D.*) (GMO, 48n; GOM, 61)
[1] *PRO*, E.101–492–27; HWC, I, 150; [2] *PRO*, E.101–490–3 (*L.F.S.*); [3] *Bodl.*, MS. top. gen. c.20, pp. 127–37

HUMFREY the Mason [Vnfr'] (*fl.* 1129–1130) Mason

Was paid £7 12*s.* 1*d.* for the year 1129–30 for his work for the Crown, out of the issues of Oxfordshire, amounting to 5*d.* daily for every day in the year. He was probably in charge of building at *Woodstock*, or perhaps at *Oxford Castle*.

HMR, 1

HUNGERFORD, John of (*fl.* 1333–1334) Carpenter

In October and November 1333 was working on the new scaffold for *St. Stephen's Chapel*, Westminster, and continued there in the following spring. Was in charge of works on the 'great bridge' of the *Tower of London* in 1334, when he was paid at the rate of 5*d.* a day.

PRO, E.101–469–17, 18; 470–15

HUNT, William, I (*fl.* 1440–†1486) Carver

Carver of London; in 1440 was paid for making 2 whole 'knottes' (i.e. carved bosses), 6 half knots, and 4 corner knots for the wooden ceiling of a new tower in the *King's Mews* at *Charing Cross*.[1]

In 1467/8 William Hunt, 'kerverr de London' was paid 3*s.* 4*d.* for coming to *Winchester College* to design and draw out the new rood-loft for the chapel (*pro novo Rodi soler imaginando et excogitando*).[2]

When William Worcestre, the antiquary, was at Shene in Surrey in 1480, he noted down items from the calendar of a breviary of Bayonne or Bordeaux, belonging to one Hunt, a carver there (*pertinenti—Hunt, kerver de Kyngston Shene*).[3] This was very likely the same man; probably he was identical also with the WILLIAM HUNT II who carved gates for the Schools at Cambridge in 1479.

William Hunt of 'Schene', by his will proved on 19 September 1486, left many small bequests to lights in the church of St. Mary Magdalen, and the residue of his estate to his wife Joan and son Edmund.[4]

[1] SHB, 216n.; [2] *WCM*, Compotus 1467–8; [3] Corpus Christi College, Cambridge, MS. 210, p.221; NWW, 297–8; [4] *PPR*, Archd. Ct. of Surrey, 44 Spage

HUNT, William, II (*fl.* 1479–) Carpenter & Carver

Contracted to make the new gates of the *Schools* at *Cambridge* in 1479, when he was paid £2 in part of a larger sum. These were the gates of the recently completed east range of the quadrangle. Loggan's engraving of the Schools (*c.* 1690) shows that these gates were finely carved. He was probably identical with WILLIAM HUNT I.

A.O.. CGB, 'A', 131

HUNTE, Robert (*fl.* 1468) Mason

Mason of Folkestone; in 1468 contracted to build stone walls and gates round the town of *Sandwich*, Kent.

KAO, Sa/AC1, f. 184v (*N. L. R.*)

HUNTER, Thomas (*fl. c.* 1498–) Mason

Was apparently the mason in charge of building the tower of *Witton (Northwich) Church*, Cheshire, begun *c.* 1498. The tower of *Great Budworth Church* is also attributed to him on account of its very close resemblance.

ROC, 11, 362

HUNTINGDON, Hugh of (*fl.* 1349–†1356) Mason

Was the Black Prince's mason in the counties of Chester and Flint and North Wales from 4 November 1349, taking 6*d.* a day for 329 days. In 1349–50 he spent 67 days at *Carnarvon*, and in the next year 192 days in North Wales.[1] He was in charge of repairs to *Chester Castle* in 1350–51; received a formal grant of appointment as the Prince's mason on 14 July 1351, and in 1354–55 was comptroller of the works at Chester Castle, when the stone wall of the inner bailey was repaired. He died about 1356, when JOHN DE TICHMARSH became mason. Hugh's widow Matilda is mentioned in documents of 1356 to 1359.

HCH, 94–6; ACC, 129, 167, 170, 230
[1] FHS, RS No. 2 (1929), 27, 54

'HUNTINGDON, Mason of' (*fl.* 1405–1406) Mason

A certain mason (*cimentarius*) of the county of Huntingdon was paid 6s. 8d. in 1405–06 for surveying the defects of the western tower of *Ely Cathedral*, and 1s. was paid to a groom (*garcio*) seeking the said mason in the said county.

CUL, Add. MS. 2956

Hurelonde—see HERLAND

HURLEY, John (*fl.* 1273–   ) Carpenter

A master carpenter working at *Westminster Palace* in 1273, apparently engaged in renewing the ceiling of the Painted Chamber burnt in 1262. He may well have been an ancestor of WILLIAM HURLEY.

LKC, 172

HURLEY, Simon [Hurle] (*fl.* 1350–1355) Carpenter

From April 1350 was one of 13 carpenters working on the stalls of the chapel at *Windsor Castle*, and also on the 'trasour' there, at 6d. a day.[1] In 1351–52 he was warden (*apparilator*) of the carpenters, taking 3s. 6d. a week, while work was in progress on the royal pew and on the new clock in the great tower of the castle. On 9 May 1352 Hurley was ordered to impress carpenters and sawyers for Windsor from Berks., Bucks. and Wilts.,[2] and in that year was one of three contractors who built 23 timbered lodgings for the canons to the north of the Dean's Cloister, for a total sum by taskwork of £107 6s. 8d.[3] In 1354–55 Simon Hurle was one of the carpenters employed at *Westminster Palace*.[4]

[1] PRO, E.101–492–27; [2] CPR 1350–54, 261; [3] HWC, I, 132, 138, 146–7, 152; [4] PRO, E.101–471–11

HURLEY, William [Horlee, Hurle, Hurlee, Hurlegh] (*fl.* 1319–†1354) Carpenter (?*Horley, Surrey; Hurley, Berks.*)

Presumably identical with the William de Hurlee who in 1319 was assessed to pay 1s. 8d. to the subsidy in the ward of Farringdon Within, London.[1] He probably came from Horley in Surrey, or possibly from Hurley, Berks. Hurley may have been the Londoner who visited *Ely Cathedral* in 1323–24 to ordain the new work of the Octagon and was paid 3s. 4d. by the Sacrist (*cuidam de Londonia ad ordinand. novum opus*), but his earliest certain work is in 1323–24 when Master William de Hurley was in charge of works at the *Tower of London* at 6d., and at *Tonbridge*, Kent, at 12d. a day felling timber for Westminster.[2] At this time Sir Stephen de Asshewy, knight, of Kent, entered into a recognizance in £40 to William de Hurleye, citizen and carpenter of London.[3] In 1326 Hurley was working at *St. Stephen's Chapel*. In the same year, Hurley was to take carpenters to *Caerphilly* to carry out works on the castle for Hugh le Despenser in conjunction with THOMAS DE LA BATAILE, master mason. Despenser ordered his bankers, the Peruzzi, to pay Hurley 40s., for which Hurley gave his receipt on 4 March 1325/6; his seal is attached bearing three shields point to point between fleurs-de-lis, one of the shields charged with a stag's head.[4] In 1332 Hurley was paid £2 17s. 2d. and £1 for a robe for work at the chapel of the *London Guildhall* and probably continued to have charge of the work at the Guildhall until its completion about 1337.[5] In 1332 a carpenter named Walter de Hurley is named as 'keeper of carpentry for the King's works' but this Walter is not otherwise heard of, and this is a printer's error for William.[6]

In 1334 William Hurley was advising Ely Cathedral on the construction of the timber vault and lantern above the Octagon; he received a fee of £8 a year from the Ely fabric fund for several years and thereafter £1 yearly until his death in 1354.[7] In addition to the remarkable work of the Lantern, he must have designed the choir-stalls, which are in advanced London style.

On 1 June 1336 he was granted a patent as chief carpenter and surveyor of all the King's works of carpentry at the Tower and elsewhere south of Trent and Humber, with fees of £18 5s. 0d. a year and an annual robe.[8] During the next year he and his wife Idonea disposed of tenements in the parish of St. Mary Aldermanbury[9] and a house was built for him at the Tower of London; he also certified certain measurements there, with WILLIAM OF RAMSEY, the King's Master Mason.[10] In 1338 Hurley took a large engine to Scotland for the siege of Dunbar: the journey began on 15 February and lasted 11 weeks. From then onwards he seems to have spent much of his time at St. Stephen's Chapel, and most of the carpentry there was erected under his supervision, the timber vault being set in position in 1347–48, though it had probably been designed by 1320–25. (See HERLAND, JOHN.) In 1342 he had to bring an engine of war from Sandwich to London, perhaps a sign that the old combination of the offices of 'engineer' and 'carpenter' was not yet quite obsolete.[11] He was also, for £50, to roof a new chamber in the Privy Palace at *Westminster*, built by ROBERT DE DIPPENHALL.

On 16 February 1343/4 he and William of Ramsey were commissioned to take men for work at *Windsor Castle*,[12] and he personally worked there from February to April, and again from late July until the works ceased on 27 November. On 20 April 1346 he was to take carpenters for the works of *Westminster Palace*, and on 30 June 1350 for felling timber for *Eltham Palace* and Windsor Castle.[13] He was again in charge of work at Windsor in 1350 when nails and laths were bought for the repair of 'Master William Hurley's chamber', and two daubers were employed on its walls a few weeks later. Four months after this 500 'spikynges' (spike nails) were bought for 'mending the house in which Master William Hurley turns the chapiters for the stalls', and 16 pins of iron were procured 'for a certain wheel to turn the chapiters for the same stalls'.[14]

At the same time Hurley was master carpenter at St. Stephen's Chapel, and in 1352 he was being paid at 1*s*. a day while working on the stalls there; he was described as master of all the works belonging to carpentry at the Palace, Tower of London, and Windsor Castle.[15] He died in 1354,[16] and was succeeded in his office of King's Carpenter by WILLIAM HERLAND.

As designer of the Ely Lantern, Hurley ranks as one of the outstanding structural inventors, and he was evidently a specialist in the design of stalls also; unfortunately those at Windsor and St. Stephen's Chapel have been destroyed, but the series at Ely, though probably less magnificent than those produced under his direct supervision for the King, are among the finest which survive.

He may have provided the design for the great hall roof at *Penshurst*, built between 1341 and 1349 for Sir John Pulteney, four times Mayor of London. The span, 39 feet, is considerable, and only one of the foremost carpenters of the period would have been prepared to design so large a roof.

(LKC; HKC)

[1] WLE; [2] CSR, II, 45; SHB, 301; PRO, E.101–469–7; 485–14 (*L.F.S.*); [3] CMA, 1532; [4] A.J. Taylor in CSB, XIV, pt. iv (May 1952), 299–300; [5] CLB, 'E', 273; [6] LKC, 189; [7] CSR, I, 44 ff.; [8] CPR 1334–8, 305; [9] *LHR*, 64(166); [10] PRO, E.101–470–1; [11] CPR 1340–3, 566; [12] *Ibid*. 1343–5, 279; [13] *Ibid*., 1345–8, 112; 1348–50, 588; [14] HWC, I, 131–3; [15] LKC; PRO, E.101–471–6; [16] CSR, II, 168

At the Tower of London in 1336 Master *Humfrey de HURLEY* was working on the smoke louvre of the great hall, taking 6*d*. a day, and *Walter de HURLEY*, at 5*d*., assisted him.

John HURLEY and SIMON HURLEY were carpenters employed at *Westminster Palace* in 1354–55.

PRO, E.101–471–11

HUY, Thomas (*fl.* 1391–1397) Carpenter

Carpenter; made the new roof for the chancel of *Costessey*, Norfolk, in 1391–97, when this was repaired by ROBERT ELYNGHAM, mason.

NRO, Great Hospital rolls, 24c (*P.C.*)

HYDES, Pers (*fl.* 1479–   ) Carpenter

Carpenter of Lenton, Notts.; with Roger Hydes, perhaps his son or brother of the same place, contracted on 13 July 1479 to build a house in *Nottingham* for £6.

SHB, 541; RN, II, 389

Hykenam—see ICKENHAM

HYLL, William (*fl.* 1458–1459) Mason

Mason paid £3 for paving the church of *Yatton*, Som., in 1458 and working on the battlements and west end in 1459, when he was paid £1 16*s*. 0*d*.

SRS, IV (1890), 100–2

Hylle—see also HILL

Hylle, Robert—see HULLE

HYLLE, Thomas (*fl.* 1477–†1483) Mason

In 1434 a mason named Thomas atte Hill built the wall of the Lollards' Tower at *Lambeth Palace* to a height of 50 feet. He may have been the Thomas Hille who, with Thomas Bridde, John Carter, John Hook, and John Tyllie, quarrymen of Kent, undertook on 4 April 1442 to supply stone for the building of *Eton College*, worked to patterns sent to them by the clerk of the works.[1] Hille may have been identical with the Thomas Hylle who was sworn master with STEPHEN BURTON of the masons in London when on 26

February 1476/7 a report was made on the Abbot of Winchcombe's house in Fleet Street.[2] In 1482 he acquired a cottage in the parish of St. Stephen, Coleman Street,[3] and on 27 February 1482/3 made his will, proved 21 March 1482/3. In this he describes himself as citizen and freemason of London, of Ware, Hackney, and the parish of St. Stephen, Coleman Street.[4]

[1] GLP, 52–6; SHB, 515–16; WCC, I, 385; [2] RLW, II, 565; [3] LHR, 212(11); [4] CCL, 371 Wilde

Hylmer, John—see AYLMER

HYNDELEY, Thomas (*fl.* 1401–1433) Mason

Worked as a mason at *Durham Cathedral Priory* from 1401, when he made two windows in the church and placed certain images in position.[1] In 1402–03 he worked under PETER DRYNG on the tomb of Bishop Walter Skirlaw. For his work in the church he was paid a total of 7 marks (£4 13s. 4d.), spread over two years.[2] He probably worked on the cloisters for some years, at first under THOMAS MAPILTON, but in 1416 Hyndeley became chief mason and on 29 September he and four sureties were bound in the sum of £200 that he should complete the work of one fourth part of the cloisters of Durham Cathedral by Michaelmas 1418.[3] In 1418 he entered into a further recognizance to the bishop 'for the performance of covenants in certain indentures between the Lord Bishop and Thomas Hyndeley mason, John Ole, Roger Esyngwold, and John Glover of Framwelgate'.[4] On this occasion one of Hyndeley's sureties was JOHN BELL, senior.

In 1425–26 'Hyndley meistre mason' was paid 8s. 'for rydyng fro Duresme to Scardeburgh for to devyse & ordeine the moste siker grounde of the Constable Toure' of *Scarborough Castle*. In 1426–27 Thomas Hyndeley, mason, was paid for working at the castle 58 days at 6d. a day, and in 1428–29 for 16 days 'wirkyng there ad devysyng the foresaide werk'.[5]

As master mason at Durham, Hyndeley's yearly retaining fee amounted to £5 6s. 8d. and a robe;[6] his wages are not certainly known, but 3s. 4d. a week seems to have been the normal pay of a master mason at Durham when not engaged on contract or task-work. Hyndeley completed the cloisters, and in 1433 was paid 40s. 'by agreement' as well as payments for Egliston marble for the work of

the new octagonal lavatory in the centre of the cloister.[7]

(APD)

[1] DAR, II, 393–4; [2] *Ibid.*, III; [3] DST, 204; [4] DKR, XXXIII; [5] *PRO*, E.101–482–8 (*L.F.S.*); [6] RDC; [7] DST, 443

HYNDELEY, William ['Bradley', Hendeley, Hyndlay, Hyndle] (*fl.* 1466–†1505) Mason

Left Norwich, where he had taken up the freedom in 1466,[1] to become (*c.* 1471) first warden of the masons' lodge at *York Minster* and then, on the death of ROBERT SPILLESBY, in 1473, the master mason. He held office until his death in 1505 when he was succeeded by CHRISTOPHER HORNER. In 1473 he took up the freedom of York. He may perhaps have been related to THOMAS HYNDELEY. William Hyndeley was warden of the York Minster masons' lodge for 24 weeks in 1472, while the office of master was vacant, and for his service at this time he was paid at the rate of 3s. 4d. a week with a special gratuity of 13s. 4d.[2] He was generously treated by the York authorities, who gave him £5 for his expenses in bringing his wife and children from Norwich in 1476, and for his defence in a suit maliciously brought against him in London. In 1475 Hyndeley had charge of the battlementing of the south side of the Minster.

In 1490 he was committed to prison with Christopher Horner while an inquiry was made to discover whether they had murdered John Partrik, a tyler, during the dispute between the masons and the tylers.[3]

His will of 24 June 1505, proved on 21 November, states that he wished to be buried under the new 'campanile' of the Minster near the tomb of his first wife; Margaret his wife and Henry Plomer his son [*sic*] were residuary legatees. He left his mason's tools to the Minster, and his tools pertaining to 'les gravyng in plaite' to William Gilmyn his parish clerk.[4] Hyndeley had died on 1 November, as was recorded on his gravestone now destroyed, but noted by Dodsworth before the Civil War. His name was misread by Drake, who also introduced other minor errors. The inscription seems to have run: (In the south Ile under the Great bells:) '*Sepultura Willm̄i. Hyndley armigeri et latomi quondam magistri Cementariorum fabrice huius ecclīe metropolitani Ebor. qui obijt in Festo omniū Sanctorū anno dn̄i millīmo quingentessimo quinto cuius aīāe ppicietur Deus Amen*'.[5]

(APD); BHY, I, 252, 254, 257–8, 261–6; **RFY**, 77, 80,

83, 88, 90n., 92
[1] EFN; [2] BHY, I, 252; BFY, 18; [3] YCR, II, 60, 61, 77; [4] DCY, ii, 49; YTE, IV, 240; [5] Bodl., MS. Dodsworth 157, f. 26; cf. DEB, 498

John HYNDELAY (*fl.* 1385–†1407) mason of York made his will on 16 August 1407; it was proved on 10 September. In it he desired to be buried in the church of the Friars Preachers in York, and mentioned his wife Agnes and three executors, Brother John Parys of the Order of Preachers in York, 'Sir' William Barton, vicar of Acle, and HUGH OF HEDON, mason, to whom he left £1. He was no doubt the John Heyndele, mason, who in 1385 was named second to ROBERT PATRYNGTON in Richard II's order to build a memorial cross to Sir Ralph Stafford.

PCY, iii, 271; CPR 1385–9, 13

ICKENHAM, John, senior & junior [Hykenam] (*fl.* 1395–1419) Carpenters

It has not so far proved possible to distinguish with certainty between the father and son of the same name. On 1 November 1395 John Hykenham, senior and John Hykenham, junior both dined with the Fellows of *Winchester College*, and in January 1396/7 John Ykenam did so. In 1417–18 one of the name, probably the son, supplied boards for a new chest in the college treasury, and in the following year was making chests for the muniments.

WCM, Hall Books, Compotus Rolls

ICKENHAM, William, senior & junior [Hykennam, Ikenham] (*fl.* 1388–†1424) Carpenters

It has so far been impossible to distinguish with certainty between the careers of father and son of the same name. In 1388–89, 1390–91, 1392–93, and 1399–1400 William Hykennam, carpenter, was a guest at *New College, Oxford*, where he had probably been engaged on the works.[1] On one occasion his son and an apprentice are mentioned, and in 1391 he was paid 32*s.* 4*d.* for a partition in the upper chamber of the Warden's Lodging and panelling in the oratory. In 1394, William Ikenham, senior and William Ikenham, junior, carpenters, both worked for seven weeks on the chapel and other parts of William of Wykeham's episcopal manor of *Highclere*, Hampshire.[2] In 1396–97 William Ikenham and his son were carrying out various works at *Winchester College*, and in the next year a William Ikenham made gates to

the garden there, with panelling for rooms, and provided timber for the Exchequer Tower at the west end of the hall. At this time he also made the roof of a dove-house at *Hamble*, Hampshire, as well as a new chamber there, and presumably also the new church roof, finished in 1402 at a cost of £17 7*s.* 1*d.*[3]

From 1399 to 1402 William Ikenham was much employed at Winchester College, making doors on stairs, and desks in 1399–1400, work on the stable and new chamber in 1401, while in the next year he carved wooden bases for images in the chapel.

Again from 1409 until 1413 one of the two men, probably the son, was kept busy at Winchester making the gates of the so-called 'Non Licet' gateway in 1409–10, bedsteads in 1410–11, altering a staircase in the college brewery in 1411–12, and making cupboards for the Exchequer in 1412–13. The remains of a fine oak cupboard in the Old Bursary (Exchequer Room) may be part of this last work. In 1413, jointly with John Schaldene, the butler and attorney of the cathedral priory, he bought a tenement in Colebrook Street from Simon Membury, treasurer of Wolvesey, but disposed of it in 1420.

In 1418–19 William Ickenham was one of a party from the college which went to measure their Inn at *Alresford*, Hampshire (later the George), which was to be rebuilt.[4]

The son made his will on 16 October 1423, desiring to be buried in the nave aisle of Winchester Cathedral. Bequests included 1*s.* to the parish church of 'Kyngate' (i.e. St. Swithun the Less, Winchester), to Nicholas his servant all his carpenter's tools and £3 'which I owe him of my father's bequest', £3 to John West, and 6*s.* 8*d.* to Henry Hatypays, both of them carpenters of Winchester. The only living relative named is his sister Isabel Turnour, who was left £20 and made residuary legatee of all his effects at Uxbridge, Middlesex. Ickenham bequeathed £5 6*s.* 8*d.* to a chaplain to celebrate masses in the church of Ickenham, Middlesex, for the souls of his parents and grandparents; £30 to be distributed to the poor in Hampshire and in other places 'where I have acquired my goods' (*ubi bona mea adquisivi*) and another £30 to the poor of Middlesex. The total value of the bequests in money amounted to over £107, a great sum for the period. The will was proved on 8 November 1424.[5]

GOC; (AJ, VIII, 81, 86; KAW, 41, 49, 60, 159) (*D.K.*

157

IDE, THOMAS

Win)
[1] *NCO*, Hall Books; [2] *PRO*, Eccl. 2–159403 (*J.H.B.*); [3] *WCM*, Roll of Extraordinary Expenses; [4] *WCM*, Compotus, *sub annis*; [5] *PCC*, 3 Luffenam (*H.C.*)

IDE, Thomas (*fl.* 1463–1480) Carpenter

Of Bury St. Edmunds. John Baret of *Bury* in his will, dated 10 September 1463 and proved 2 May 1467, directed his executors to have a timber cross made before the gate of his house 'be the avys of Thomas Ide'; it was to be 'such a work of timber with four posts and a cross as is at Eye' (in the north of Suffolk).[1] The will of Thomas Ide, made at Bury 20 July 1479, was proved 23 August 1480.[2] He left a wife, Margaret, and two sons, both named John, the elder of whom was 'brother of the house of Sudbury', by which is probably meant the Dominican Friary there. He made a bequest of 6*s*. 8*d*. to 'the new fabric of the bell-tower' of the Abbey at Bury.

A.O.

[1] TSB, 20, 43; (*BW*, ia, 95); [2] *BW*, ia, 151

IRELAND, William of [de Hibernia] (*fl.* 1291–1294) Mason Carver

Described both as mason and imager (*cementarius, imaginator*); carved the statues which still survive on the *Hardingstone Eleanor Cross*, Northants., between 1291 and 1294. He was paid £3 6*s*. 8*d*. for each and for making statues for other of the Eleanor Crosses now destroyed. He also made the central shaft for the Lincoln Cross, otherwise the work of RICHARD DE STOW.

BMH

IRLAM, John [Kerver alias Irlam] (*fl.* 1510–1535) Carpenter

In 1510–11 John Kerver alias Irlam was appointed Master of the King's Works in North Wales at 6*d*. a day. Much maintenance work was carried out under him at *Carnarvon, Conway* and *Harlech Castles* until 1528, and at *Beaumaris Castle* as late as 1534–35.

HKW, III, 171–2

Irton, Roger de—see HIRTON

IVES the Engineer [Yvo] (*fl.* 1172–1174) Engineer

Was probably working at *Berkhampstead Castle*, Herts., in 1172–73 and in the following year hired carpenters to make 'machines' when the King came to Huntingdon.

PR

JACKSON, Robert [Jakson] (*fl.* 1428–1458) Carpenter

Carpenter of York, where he entered the freedom in 1428–29;[1] in *c*. 1457–58 he was one of a commission of four craftsmen who were to adjudicate on a dispute which came under the York building code, being named after JOHN FOULFORD. (See also PORTER, JOHN and COUPER, ROBERT, masons.)[2] The four craftsmen in question were the 'searchers' of their craft in York, corresponding to the sworn craftsmen of London.

[1] YCF; [2] YMB, II, 219

JACKSON, William [Jacson] (*fl.* 1529–) Mason

A freemason of Bratoft, Lincs., who on 10 July 1529 contracted to supply the battlements of the church of *Orby*, Lincs.; their design was to be similar to that of those at 'Weston Admeals' and 'Est erkele' (East Keal, Lincs.). Jackson was impressed for the King's works, and nothing was done.

SHB, 575; (PRO, ECP, 613–10)

JACOB the Joiner [Junctor, Junur] (*fl.* 1253–) Joiner

Was paid £3 4*s*. 2*d*. for panels for the chambers of the King and Queen in *Westminster Palace* in 1253, and £3 6*s*. 6*d*. for work on the King's bed and at the Exchequer, together with the cost of fir boards.[1] He may have been the designer of the stalls of *Westminster Abbey* begun at this time, but of which only fragments survive.[2]

[1] SGW, 239, 242; [2] LKC, 23, 160

Jagell, Jakyll—see JEKYLL

JAGRYN, John (*fl.* 1480–1481) Joiner

Made panelling and parclose screens for *Yatton Church*, Som., in 1480–81 for £1 18*s*. 8*d*.

SRS, IV (1890), 112

JAKELYN, Thomas (*fl.* 1533) Carpenter

In 1533 was warden of the carpenters engaged on the repairs of *Woking Palace*.

HKW, IV, 345

JAKES, John [Jeckys] (*fl.* 1444–1449) Mason

In 1444–45 John 'Jeckys' worked with JAMES WODEROFE on making the lavatory in the cloister of *Norwich Cathedral Priory*, when they were paid £2 2*s*. 0*d*. Jakes was separately paid 3*s*. 8*d*. for images of St. John Evangelist and St. Barbara brought from Trowse and set in the chapter-house. In 1446–47 he received a cape as livery, and in 1449 accompanied Woderofe to Eton College.

NRO, DCN, Communar, no. 1083 (*P.C.*)

Jakson—see JACKSON

JAMES, John (*fl.* 1431–†1455) Mason

Presumably English; master mason in charge of the works of the cathedral of *Notre Dame* in *Paris*, from 1431 to 1447, and also master of the works of the city of *Paris* from 1431 to his death in 1455.

BAF; SAG, 103 ff.

Jannings—see JANYNS

JANYN, John (*fl.* 1416–1422) Carpenter

Second master carpenter, with THOMAS MATHEWE, in charge of repairs to the walls and towers of *Harfleur*, France, from 1 January 1415/16. He was paid 1*s*. a day. (See JENYN, JOHN.) In 1418–19 Janyn played an important part in the siege of Rouen by building a timber bridge over the Seine, and he still had charge of the works of carpentry at Harfleur in 1421–22.

HKW, I, 458–9, 462
PRO, T.R. Misc. Bk. 79, *f.* 46 (*L.F.S.*)

JANYNS, Henry [Jenyns] (*fl.* 1453–1483) Mason

Was probably the son of ROBERT JANYNS, senior, who was warden of the masons at Eton College from February 1448/9. By 1453 JOHN CLERK was warden of the masons at Eton, and had as his apprentice Henry Janyns, who worked under him until Clerk left Eton on 30 March 1454.[1] Janyns presumably accompanied Clerk to other work, and there completed his training. Clerk in his will made in February 1459, left to Henry Janyns all his tools, 'pictures', and 'portraitures'.[2] He was very likely the son of Robert Janyns concerned in the carving for the gateway of *Merton College, Oxford*, in 1463–64.

The construction of the new chapel of St. George in *Windsor Castle* seems to have been decided upon in 1474, and the site was being cleared in June 1475. It was probably about this time that Henry Janyns was appointed chief mason of the works, with a fee of £12 yearly and a gown. His name appears in the accounts from 1478, when he bought 9,755 feet of Taynton stone for the works of the chapel at 2*d*. a foot, and drew his fee of £12.[3] In addition to his fee, he was given a 'reward' of £3 6*s*. 8*d*. in 1481, and 4*s*. was paid him for the rent of a house at Burford, leased and occupied for the King's work by his masons working there. He had a reward of £2 16*s*. 8*d*. in 1482, and one of £3 6*s*. 8*d*. in 1483. In each year he drew his fee of £12 and a sum of 10*s*. for a robe.[4] On stylistic grounds a probable attribution to Henry Janyns is the monument to Cardinal Bourchier († 1486) on the north side of the high altar in *Canterbury Cathedral*. A formal grant of the place of burial had been made on 16 April 1480. The detail has the same delicacy and small-scale ornament to be seen on the front of Edward IV's monument in the choir of St. George's Chapel; the four-lobed motive in the spandrels of the four-centred arch may be compared with the tracery of the west window in St. George's.[5]

Henry Janyns was probably the father of ROBERT JANYNS, junior, who was later in charge of works in Windsor Castle.

(APD)
[1] KJE; [2] *CCL*, 268 Sharp (*A.O.*); [3] PRO, E.101–496–17 (*L.F.S.*); [4] HWC, II, 378, 403–6; [5] SCC, App., 4 (*A.O.*)

JANYNS, Robert, senior [Jannings] (*fl.* 1438–1464) Mason

Was warden of the masons at the building of *All Souls College, Oxford*, under RICHARD CHEVYNTON, who was usually engaged at the quarries at Burford, while Janyns had charge of the building work in Oxford. He was paid at the rate of 3*s*. a week and also had a yearly fee of 13*s*. 4*d*. The work began in February 1438 and ended with the completion of the hall in 1443.[1]

Janyns is next heard of in 1448, when he had obtained the position of master mason in charge of the building of the new bell-tower of *Merton College, Oxford*, begun in July, where he was paid 8*d*. a day. During his work at Merton, his expenses were paid for travelling to 'Sydeley' (Sudeley, Glos.) on business connected with the hiring of a mason, and his wife Elizabeth was paid 1*s*. for four days spent in bringing straw for thatching the masons' lodge (*casam latomorum*).[2]

During the first week of February 1448/9 he worked at Merton College, but from 10 February he is found at *Eton College*, where he was warden of the masons (*gardianus lathomorum*) at a fee of £10 a year. Later he was paid £6 13*s*. 4*d*. for providing Taynton stone for the works.[3] In spite of his work at Eton, Janyns still appears as 'Master of the Works' at Merton in 1451. In 1452–53 one Robert 'Iannyns', doubtless Janyns, was associated with JOHN ATKINS in measuring the work done at the new *Divinity Schools, Oxford*.[4]

Janyns was also sent on journeys to Burford and to Abingdon, and received small fees from Merton College for occasional visits. He continued also to do jobs for All Souls, and in

1449–50 3s. was paid for two pullets for a meal given to Robert Janyns by the Warden in his own room. In 1452 he was paid 8d. by Merton College for repairing the chancel arch of *St. Peter's-in-the-East*, and he made and fixed the carving above the gateway of Merton College, with his son, in 1463–64.[5] The career of Robert Janyns is somewhat unusual in that although apparently a man of considerable capacity, he did not reach the top of his craft, and after having worked as master at Merton College, being paid for irregular supervisory and consultative work, he had to accept a regular post at Eton, at an assured wage it is true, but of a subordinate character, and with by no means high pay. On the other hand, though his wife was prepared to undertake carter's work, the payment to her of 3d. a day must be considered an adequate wage for the period. The probability is that the Janyns family found it difficult to make 'both ends meet' and that the result was to force Robert into the Civil Service. Such results, proceeding from inadequate financial support while building up a private practice, are not unknown in more recent times. It is at least satisfactory to know that two masons, who we may feel assured were Robert Janyns's son and grandson, rose to eminence in the King's works. (See JANYNS, HENRY and JANYNS, ROBERT, junior.)

(*R.D.*) GOM, 72–3

[1] JAS; [2] RAP, III, 720 ff.; [3] KJE; *ECA*. Accs. (*G.P.J.*); [4] *UCO*, Smith Transcripts, X (*A.O.*); cf. OXN, XXI, 48–60; [5] GOM, 73

A *John JENYN* and *Thomas JENYN* were working at *Windsor Castle* in 1426 and 1427 as masons; they were sometimes ranked among the *sementarii*, sometimes as setters (*positores*) and their wages raised from 5d. to 6d. a day each.[1] The former may have been the John Jenyns who carried out repairs for *All Souls College* in 1469–71.[2] In a Windsor account of 1418–19, Thomas 'Janyne' is mentioned as the son of 'Genyne Westynangere', presumably of Westenhanger, Kent.[3]

[1] *PRO*, S.C.6–1302–4 (*A.O.*); [2] GOM, 97 (*H.M.C.*); [3] *PRO*, S.C.6–755–9

JANYNS, Robert, junior [Jenins, Jenyns, 'Nymes'] (*fl.* 1499–1506) Mason

Probably the son of HENRY JANYNS; he was chief mason of Henry VII's Tower in *Windsor Castle* by January 1499, and continued in that office until 1505. The principal work done was the building of *Henry VII's Tower*, of star-polygon form, undoubtedly derived from the contemporary Mozarabic designs at Saragossa by way of the embassies exchanged with Ferdinand and Isabella. In 1506 he was one of the three masons described as 'the King's Master Masons' who submitted to Henry VII an estimate of the cost of works at Henry VII's new chapel at Westminster, the others being ROBERT VERTUE and JOHN LEBONS. Janyns and Lebons also described themselves as 'the King's Master Masons' when they acted as witnesses to Robert Vertue's will on 10 May 1506.[1] He may have been the Robert Janyns of Burford, Oxon., who made his will there in 1501, leaving a house and lands to his wife Agnes. The will was proved on 9 October 1506.[2] Janyns bequeathed to the Lady Chapel in *Burford Church* 'a stondynge cuppe covered and gilte for to make a chalys'. The chapel had been recently reconstructed and was referred to in 1500 as the 'new chapel of Blessed Mary of Burford'. Janyns may well have been the master for the reconstruction in the 1490s: the flattened four-centred windows with a minimum of tracery, a type very rare in parish churches, may be compared to those in the aisles of St. George's Chapel, Windsor, Eltham Palace and other royal works.[3]

It has been suggested that Janyns was the mason in charge of the building of the new Palace of *Richmond*, after the destruction of the old Shene Palace by fire in 1497, and also that he designed *Thornbury Castle* begun about 1511 for the Duke of Buckingham, and left unfinished at the Duke's execution in 1522.

(APD; LKC; WKM)

[1] HWC, I, 247; [2] *PPC*, 11 Adeane; cf. GBR, 675–7; [3] GBR, 114 (*A.O.*)

JAY, Thomas (*fl.* 1523–†*c.* 1531) Carpenter

Was appointed master carpenter of *Calais* in 1523, at a salary of £16 16s. 4d. a year, in succession to BEDE OLIVER, with 21 carpenters under him. He died before 26 May 1531, when he was succeeded by JOHN BIRD.

LPH, IV, pt. ii, p. 2227; HKW, III, 419

JEKYLL, Hamund [Hamidius, Hammudus; Jagell, Jakyll, Jekel] (*fl.* 1415–1442) Carpenter

Carpenter of *Exeter*; in 1415–16 was paid for viewing the cathedral vestry (that on the south side of the choir) with the canons; in 1441/2, as master carpenter of the cathedral, he was being paid 3s. per week.

BPE, 98–9; *FFE*

JEKYLL, Walter [Jacol, Jagell] (*fl.* 1405–1431) Carpenter

A working carpenter at *Exeter Cathedral* in 1405–06, and master carpenter there in 1430–31, when he was renting a house from the Chapter. He also leased a garden in 1425–26. Jekyll took up the freedom of Exeter on 22 April 1409.

(*D.F.F.*);   *EDC*, Fabric rolls; RJE, 40

JENKYNS, Thomas (*fl.* 1498–1505) Mason

Mason of *Oxford*, who in 1498–99 was paid for building a buttress at *Magdalen College*; he took 6d. a day. He did other small jobs for the college in 1500–01 and 1504–05.

Although not apparently a master, he must have had an independent business, for in 1505 he sold three chimneypieces to *Lincoln College* for 6s.

GOM, 85

JENYN, John (*fl.* 1440–1442) Carpenter

Carpenter at the building of *St. John's Hospital, Sherborne*, Dorset. He was paid fees by instalments amounting to £3 in 1440–41 and £11 in 1441–42, as well as expenses for riding in search of timber to North Perrott, Somerset, and elsewhere. (See JANYN, JOHN.)

SAD, Building Accs. (*J.F.*)

Jenyns—see JANYNS

Jernomuta, Thomas—see BARSHAM

JERVEYS, John [Gerves, Jerves] (*fl.* 1482–†*c.* 1510) Joiner

On 21 October 1482 succeeded WILLIAM LEE as the King's Chief Joiner at the *Tower of London*, with 12d. a day; he was regranted the office on 20 August 1484 with arrears from 7 July 1483.[1] Although Henry VII discontinued the practice of appointing master craftsmen by patent, Jerveys seems to have retained his post, being ordered to impress carpenters and others to serve with the King's Army in France on 26 November 1491 and 9 May 1492,[2] and on 13 December 1496 he was ordered to repair the carriages for the ordnance to be sent towards Scotland.[3] He was probably identical with John Gerves, taking 8d. a day for 223 days' work at the Tower of London as chief carpenter *c.* 1500,[4] and was dead by 23 May 1510.[5]

[1] CPR 1476–85, 314, 514; [2] *Ibid.* 1485–94, 393, 397; [3] *Ibid.* 1494–1509, 92; [4] *BM*, Egerton MS. 2358; [5] LPH, I, 1058.

(In the calendars, 'junctor' has been misread as 'janitor' and translated as 'porter'.)

JESTELYN, John (*fl.* 1509–1511) Mason

Worked at *Eton College* in 1509–10, being sent to Taynton to procure stone for the cloister. In the next year he was paid 10s. for certain work on the cloister for which he had contracted.

WCC, I, 415

JOHN the Carpenter I (*fl. c.* 1229–1241) Carpenter

At some time between 1229 and 1241 was granted by the Dean and Chapter of St. Paul's Cathedral, London, certain stone-built houses which lay without their churchyard on the north, at a rent of 15s. a year.[1] Master John, carpenter of St. Paul's, was a witness to charters in and about 1236.[2] He may have been identical with the John the Carpenter who was in the royal service in 1231 and 1233; in the former year he was on two occasions ordered to take timber for making windows at the Palace of *Clarendon*, and in 1233 a letter close was issued concerning the fee of 1d. a day which 'he was wont to take'[3] (see also CANTERBURY, JOHN). This Master John held land in King Street, Westminster, and witnessed charters there.[4] He was perhaps the John the Carpenter who in March 1221 had been ordered to build a barn 150 feet long and 34 feet wide at *Bamburgh Castle*; its cost was £46 18s.0d.[5]

[1] HMC, 8R, I. 10; [2] GEC, 117, 254; Nos. 151, 317; [3] CCR 1231–4, 4, 14, 190; [4] *WAM*, 17082, 17145, 17370, 17384; [5] BBC, 13; HHN, III, iii, 129

John the Carpenter (*fl.* 1250–1294)—see HARTING

JOHN the Carpenter II (*fl.* 1256–   ) Carpenter

Carpenter of the Bishop of *Norwich*; bequeathed 3 marks (£2) by the will of Bishop Walter de Suffield in June 1256. Possibly identical with JOHN the Carpenter IV.

BHN, IV, 491

JOHN the Carpenter III (*fl.* 1260–   ) Carpenter

Employed by the town of *Shrewsbury* in September 1260 to make the roof of the new tower below the castle by contract (*convencio*).

SC, Bailiff's Accs. No. 308

JOHN the Carpenter IV (*fl.* 1272–1305) Carpenter

Master Carpenter of *Norwich Cathedral*

Priory; possibly identical with JOHN the Carpenter II. He was paid a regular retaining fee of 6*s.* 8*d.* a year until 1283; after this he is not mentioned until 1298–99 when he was paid 13*s.* 4*d.* for half a year and thereafter until 1304–05 received £1 6*s.* 8*d.* yearly. In 1273–74 he was allowed £14 to cover the cost of timber bought at Hamburg and his expenses thither.

NCM, rolls 2–6, 13, 15–17

JOHN the Carpenter V (*fl.* 1287–1295) Carpenter

Was master carpenter at *Cambridge Castle* when it was rebuilt between 1283 and 1299. In December 1287 Master John the Carpenter was being paid at the rate of 2*s.* a week as compared with 2*s.* 6*d.* paid to the master mason. There are no detailed accounts before November 1286, by which time the new hall had been built, but in 1288 Master John spent a week in making the garderobe opening off it. In June of that year he was working on the prison in the postern tower and in August at the postern gate. [He was still in charge in November 1295.]

A.O.
CAC, XXVI, 72–81; *PRO*, E.101–459–15, 16 (*L.F.S.*)

JOHN the Carpenter VI (*fl.* 1381–   ) Carpenter

On 26 September 1381 John of Gaunt, Duke of Lancaster ordered his receiver in Yorkshire to pay the expenses for the erection of new rooms between the gate and the kitchen in the manor of *Cowick* (near Goole, Yorks.) 'as the duke has "devised" to master John his chief carpenter there', and on the same date the forester of the honour of Pontefract was ordered to provide timber for these works.

JGR 1379–85, Nos. 598, 599

JOHN the Carpenter VII (*fl.* 1384–1385) Carpenter

Master carpenter in charge of works at *St. David's Cathedral* in 1384–85, when he was paid 4*s.* a week.

WWH, IX, 82, 96, 102

John the Carpenter (*fl.* 1399–1427)—see CLONYER

John the Carpenter (*fl.* 1413–1417)—see BRANCHE

JOHN the Carver (*fl. c.* 1500–   ) Carver

One 'John' signed the roodscreen of *Chulmleigh Church*, Devon, made *c.* 1500.

AAJ, 2S, XXXIII (1928), 162

JOHN the Mason I (*fl. c.* 1180–1185) ? Mason

Brother John the Mason (*Frater Johannes Cementarius*), a Knight Templar, was a witness to a charter dated at the Temple, London, *c.* 1180–85. He was possibly the designer of the circular nave of the *Temple Church*, consecrated in 1185.

WAM, 13752

JOHN the Mason IA (*fl. c.* 1200–   ) Mason

A charter of *c.* 1200–11 grants land and stone houses in Bury St. Edmunds near the west gate of St. Edmund's cemetery, which had belonged to John the mason (*cementarius*). It seems not unlikely that John had been master mason to *Bury Abbey*.

(*R.D.*) CS, 3S, LXXXIV, 80

JOHN the Mason II [*Cementarius*] (*fl. c.* 1250) Mason

Referred to as dead in a deed of 1262–63 relating to *Exeter*. His heir, ALEXANDER the Mason I, is also mentioned.

DRO, ED/SN/48

JOHN the Mason III (*fl.* 1212–1213) Mason

Master mason (*cementarius*) of *Canterbury Cathedral* in 1212–13, when he was paid 21*s.* by the treasurer; in the next year was succeeded by Master RALPH the Mason III.

(*W.P.B.*) CCA, Treasurer's Accs. 1198–1227

JOHN the Mason IV (*fl.* 1256–   ) Mason

Mason of the Bishop of *Norwich*; was bequeathed 3 marks (£2) by the will of Bishop Walter de Suffield in June 1256. Master John *Cementarius* was in *c.* 1250 witness to a charter conveying Norwich property to Ely Cathedral Priory.

BHN, IV, 491; Ely 'Liber M', transcript p.152 (*S.J.A.E.*)

JOHN the Mason V [le Masun] (*fl.* 1281–   ) Mason

Mason in charge of works for the Prior of *St. Swithun's Cathedral Priory, Winchester*, in 1281.[1] Building at the Prior's House (now the Deanery) was in progress and this may have been the open porch which still exists.

[1] EHR, LXI, No. 239 (1946), 97, 101

JOHN the Mason VI [le Mazun] (*fl.* 1309–   ) Mason

Master mason appointed to take charge of the works of *Carlisle Castle* on 3 May 1309.

TTH, 32

JOHN the Mason VII [*Cementarius*] (*fl.* 1322–1326) *Mason*

Master mason at *Ely Cathedral* during the building of the Octagon. His name appears in the surviving Sacrist's rolls from 1322 to 1326; he received a fee of £2 a year in addition to wages (which are not stated) and a robe with furs.[1] The price of the robe with furs was at first 16*s.* 9*d.*, but in 1325–26 was only 15*s.* 3*d.* On the other hand, in this year a payment of 11*s.* 9*d.* occurs for a room hired for him.[2] In the absence of detailed wage-lists it is impossible to show whether he was permanently employed at Ely, but it seems more probable that his appointment was on a consultative basis.

It is clear that Master John was not identical, as has been suggested, with his successor JOHN ATTE GRENE, nor can he have been the unnamed visitor from London who was paid 3*s.* 4*d.* in 1323–24 for ordaining the new work (*cuidam de Londonia ad ordinand. novum opus*).[3] It is, however, quite possible that the latter was WILLIAM HURLEY the carpenter, who was to take charge of the timber vaulting and Lantern. A close relation between the masonry of the Octagon (1322–28) and Lady Chapel (1321–49) with contemporary work at both Norwich and London is evident and it would be reasonable to identify Master John with one of the members of the RAMSEY family: the elder John rather than the younger, suggested by Chapman.[4] (See Appendix I.) (TCC)

[1] CSR, II, 34, 48, 61; [2] *Ibid.*, 27, 40, 42, 61; [3] *Ibid.*, 45; [4] *Ibid.*, I, 22n.

JOHN the Mason VII.A (*fl.* 1406–1424) *Mason*

John le Mason 'le Yrishman', who had previously built the tower of Sir John Stanley, kt., at *Liverpool* (in 1406–), with a second John le Mason 'Northerenman', who had made the inner chamber for Sir Henry Norreis, kt., together made a tomb in *Hale Church*, Lancs., for John Leyot, rector of Malpas (†1428) in 1424.

HSLC, L (1900), 139; SBL, 13–14

JOHN the Mason VIII (?–†*c.* 1500) *Mason*

John le mason of Chesterfield, with Cecily his wife and his children appear in the obituary roll of *Beauchief Abbey*, Derbs., in a hand of *c.* 1500; a full commemoration service was celebrated on 14 August.

BM, Cotton MS. Caligula A. viii, *f.* 18v. (*H.M.C.*)

John the Mason—see WASSYNGLE

JOHNSON, Thomas (*fl.* 1530–1536) *Carver*

Carver of London; in 1530–36 made 29 of the King's Beasts on the battlements, and the lantern of the great hall at *Hampton Court*. Johnson may well have been the Thomas Johnson who in 1505–6 paid 20*s.* rent to the Sacrist of Westminster Abbey for three-quarters of a year, for a tenement close to the site of Henry VII's Chapel, then in course of erection. In 1511–12 Thomas 'Johnston' paid 10*s.* rent for a shop close by.

LHC, I, 347; PRO, E.36–237, *f.*145 (*L.F.S.*); WAM 19761, 19768

JOHNSON, William [Jonson] (*fl.* 1501–1538) *Mason*

In 1501–02 one William Johnson 'prentis' served under THOMAS WADE for 21 days on the works of *London Bridge*.[1] In 1518–19 one 'Jonson lathamus' and another were at work on the wall at the end of the chapel of *Queen's College, Oxford*;[2] and in 1525 William Johnson was warden or resident master (under JOHN LEBONS and HENRY REDMAN) and taking part in the design and setting out of *Cardinal College* (now Christ Church), *Oxford*.[3] As Lebons's partner he contracted on 20 February 1527/8 to make traceried windows for the chapel of *Balliol College*, for £14 3*s.* 4*d.*[4] He was presumably the Mr. Johnson, mason, who in 1528 was paid 3*s.* 4*d.* for work at Merton College.[5]

Between 1530 and 1536 William Johnson, freemason of Barrington in Cotswold, was supplying worked stone for the great hall of *Hampton Court Palace*,[6] and in 1538 William Jonson was named first among the liverymen of the Company of Freemasons of London.[7] The 'Wyllm Jonson' employed as a bricklayer at *Whitehall Palace* about 1540 was perhaps a different man.[8]

[1] KJL, 28; [2] QCO, long rolls (*E.G.*); [3] OXN, VIII–IX, 139; [4] *Ibid.*, 146; SHB, 574; [5] GOM, 94; [6] SHB, 111; PRO, E.36–237, 238; LHC, I, 347, 355; [7] MHN, IV (1898), 19–20; [8] *Bodl.*, MS. Engl. hist. b. 192, *f.* 21

JORDAN the Carpenter (*fl.* 1224–1230) *Carpenter and Engineer*

On 22 October 1224 order was given to pay 5 marks to Master Jordan the Carpenter who made the King's trebuchet at Dover, and further payments were made to him for a trebuchet which he was constructing at *Windsor Castle* in 1225; on 19 November he was ordered to take two beams of timber in the forest of Odiham for this purpose, and on 8 June 1226 he had 3 marks in part payment of his livery while engaged on the works of Windsor Castle.

That he was engaged in an architectural capacity, as well as a military engineer, is shown by other payments, as for example on 26 February 1225/6, when 10 marks were to be given to him to be taken to Windsor for repairing the ditch in the great bailey between the hall and the tower. Further payments of 2 marks and 5½ marks were made to him on 10 December 1226 and 31 July 1227, and on 22 July in the latter year he also had 7 marks as part of his arrears of wages as one of the King's Carpenters.

On 10 May 1229 he was granted 12d. a day as the King's Catapult-maker, and from 1227 to 1230 the works of Windsor Castle were 'viewed' by the master trebuchetor, who was clearly Master Jordan.

CLR, *passim*; HWC

Jordan, Thomas—see JURDAN

JOY, Richard [Joye] (*fl.* 1356) Mason

Named first of six masons, layers and setters to draw up regulations, with six hewers, for the London masons in 1356.

CLB 'G', *f.* 41; KMM, 249

JOY, William [Joye] (*fl.* 1329–1347) Mason

After working for some time in a subordinate position, was appointed master mason at *Wells Cathedral* on 28 July 1329, within two months of the election of Bishop Ralph of Shrewsbury. Joy was granted for his good service the office of master of the fabric, with a fee of £1 10s. 6d. yearly for life, payable half-yearly by the keeper of the fabric, in addition to his stipend when at work. Later* the yearly fee was increased to 40s., with '6d.. each day he shall abide in the city of Wells.

* Note: the grant of 30s. 6d. per year was for good service in the past and to come, in addition to his existing wages, unspecified. This is on *f.* 181 of the *Liber Albus*, two folios after the other grant, whose date was on Thursday after St. Matthew (21 September) of 13. ., the last part of the year being illegible. This (*f.* 179) was for 40s., with 6d. a day on conditions. It is to be noted that on *f.* 181v is a grant, otherwise irrelevant, made in chapter on Thursday after St. Matthew 1329; and that both grants to Joy were made by Dean John de Godeley, dead before 9 February 1333. The second grant must, therefore, be of 1332 at the latest, and was almost certainly of 1329. In that case it must be taken as an amendment probably due to negotiation following appointment. The grant on *f.* 179 is added in a different hand and ink, in a space at the bottom of a leaf.

and be engaged upon the fabric and works'. He was bound to 'oversee repairs in the said church and give his counsel, care and aid thereupon'.[1] These terms are the same as those granted in 1365 to WILLIAM WYNFORD, and it is clear that like Wynford, Joy had a practice independent of his work at Wells.

On 21 March 1335/6 Edward III issued letters recommending one William Joye to a dwelling and corrody at Bath Priory; this was resisted by the house, and after an inquiry had been held, the King ordered Joye not to trouble the Prior further.[2] If this Joye was the mason, the grant would imply that he had been in the royal service. The mason appears outside Wells in 1346–47, when Master W. Joye was paid £2 for his yearly fee as master of the work of *Exeter Cathedral*, where he had probably succeeded THOMAS WITNEY about 1342. He was presumably dead by 1352, when RICHARD FARLEIGH was in charge at Exeter.[3]

The history of the building at Wells in the early 14th century is complicated, and involved not less than eight separate works of considerable importance. Of these the Chapter House (*c.* 1295–1310), the Lady Chapel (built by *c.* 1319), and the raising of the central tower (1315–22) had certainly been carried out before Joy took charge; for one THOMAS le Masun had been at Wells in 1323, and there is reason to think that this was Thomas Witney. But about 1325 a grand design for the enlargement of the eastern arm of the church was put in hand; its general plan must have been settled considerably earlier, as the building of the new Lady Chapel implies the eastward extension of the 12th-century choir. The precise stages by which operations were completed are obscure, but it is certain that demolition of the old east end had taken place by 1332, and that much still remained to be done in 1338. In 1338 the fabric was said to be badly broken and deformed (*enormiter confracta et deformata*) and this probably refers to the serious settlement of the new tower, which led to the insertion of the great strainer-arches at the crossing, and the works of consolidation of the upper part of the tower.

On stylistic grounds these works on the central tower, the pulpitum and stalls (the latter known to have been begun in 1325), the cloaking of the Early English choir, the building of the presbytery with the new vault over

164

presbytery and choir together, and the re-trochoir, must all have been done between 1325 and 1350, and Joy is to be regarded as the architect responsible. His work is markedly in the Bristol manner, and it is in that region that his training must have taken place, very possibly on the works of the new choir of St. Augustine's Abbey (now *Bristol Cathedral*). The tracery of the great east window of the Wells presbytery, with its mullions of Perpendicular character, can hardly have been designed before *c.* 1335, and betrays contact with masters from London, or at least information as to the work in progress at St. Paul's Cathedral and at Gloucester. The royal visit of Edward III to Wells in the winter of 1332–33 may well have provided an opportunity for the transmission of information by members of the household. Besides the work at the cathedral, Joy may have been concerned with the gatehouses and walls of the *Close* and *Bishop's Palace* at Wells, built under a licence to crenellate issued in 1340. Joy's style seems to be closely related to the works done at *Ottery St. Mary* collegiate church in 1337–45.[4]

At least the lower part of the screen added to the west front at Exeter must have been in progress while Joy was in charge there, but its design probably goes back to Thomas Witney, and it was not completed until *c.* 1375.

[1] HMC, *Wells*, I, 220, 222; [2] SRS, VII, 137–8; [3] *CEF* (*M.E.C.*); AEC, ii, 274, 276; [4] *J.H.H.*. in FSG. 1961. 55n.[3]

JOYNER, Lambert (*fl.* 1531–1538) Joiner

In 1531–32 was one of the joiners working in the hall of *Queens' College, Cambridge*; in January 1533 he received £2 as a final pay-ment for panelling and panelled the Com-bination Room there for £2, and in 1536–37 worked on the windows of the President's Gallery, when he was paid 6s. for 6 'wooden fabrics' (*ligneis fabricis*).

In 1538 he was paid for making panelling in the hall of *St. John's College*; this still exists, though moved in 1862. At Christmas 1538 the payments made for this panelling were: 'To Lambert jun' (*junctor*) for selyng ye hall 24 yardes — 14 yardes £3 10s. and 10 yardes 20s. — £4 10s. 0d..' (i.e. in all).

(*A.O.*) WCC, II, 34n., 49n., 61–66, 309n.

Joynour, Adam—see ADAM

JURDAN, Thomas [Jordan] (*fl.* 1444–†1482) Mason

A hardhewer of this name took 6*d.* a day on the works of *Eton College* from 1444 to 1446.[1] In the middle of January 1460/1 he became chief mason of *London Bridge*, at 4s. a week, this sum being reduced to 3s. 4d. in the following December, probably owing to his becoming the King's Mason. He took wages as 'Serjeant of the King's Masonry' from 27 July 1461, at 12*d.* a day,[2] and was master mason of the King's works, as well as chief bridge mason, at his death on or shortly after 20 April 1482. His successor, THOMAS DANYELL was appointed King's Mason on 27 April.

Jurdan must have designed the great hall of *Eltham Palace*, built between 1475 and 1480 and for which he bought paving stone, and was presumably the principal architect em-ployed for Edward IV's works, apart from those carried out by ROBERT LEGET and HENRY JANYNS at Windsor Castle.

KJL; HKW, I, 215; II, 937, 1050
[1] KJE; [2] *PRO*, E.364–100(B)

JYLKES, John [Gylcous, Gylkes, -ys] (*fl.* 1397–1433) Carpenter

Carpenter employed by *New College, Ox-ford*, to carry out work at their rectory of *Swalcliffe*, Oxon., including the hall and stables in 1397–98, farm buildings in 1408–09 and 1412–13, and chambers and chapel in 1432–33. He worked too at *Adderbury, Drayton*, and *Heyford*, as well as at the college itself. Jylkes also, with JOHN WILTSHIRE, repaired *Patys Inn* in Oxford for the college in1427–29.

GOC; *NCO*, Swalcliffe Accs. A, B, C, D; Oxford City, 6–7 Hen. VI

Kake—see CAKE

KALE, John [Cale, Calle, Calley, Kayll, Keale, Keell, Keill, Kele, Kell, Keyl, Keylle] (*fl.* 1484–1535) Carver and Joiner

Of Cambridge; perhaps son of Henry Kale or Kele, who was a bailiff of the town in 1491 and 1492, and Mayor in 1500 and 1505.[1] For the year 1484–85 John Kale began to pay rent to the treasurers of the borough on a house in the Market Place which had recently been in the occupation of JOHN SAY.[2] For the Poll Tax of 1512–13 John Kale, 'cerver', was assessed under Market Ward and paid 1s. on movables between the value of £2 and £10; his son John Kale who was 'takyng no wage', paid 4d.[3] He was assessed for the same amount of tax in 1517, when his movables were valued at £2, but there is no mention of his son.[4]

In April 1508 he made a window by agreement in the Provost's Lodge at *King's College*, for which he was paid 2s. 6d., and also worked for three and a half days on other small jobs there at the rate of 6d. a day.[5] In 1508–09 he made two bell wheels for *Holy Trinity Church, Cambridge*, for 6s. 8d., finding the stuff himself. In 1509–10 he was paid a shilling for looking after the bells there for three-quarters of the year; in 1517–18 he made the wheel for the third bell, and in 1524–25 a new staff for a processional canopy which had cost the parish over £11.[6] At *Great St. Mary's Church* in 1513–14 he received three payments amounting to 33s. 4d. for making 'the Chirche dore', probably the south door. In 1510 or 1511 as a parishioner he had contributed to the seating of the nave of the church. Small payments to him were made in 1523, 1526, and 1527, in the two latter years over repairs to the organs.[7]

His name frequently appears in the accounts of the Proctors of the University between 1516 and 1531, effecting small repairs and cleaning in the Schools.[8] In 1523–24 he was paid 6d. 'for a table to hang on the copy of ye mayers submyssyon in ye scolys' and in 1528–29 he made a box, price 1s. 2d., for keeping the charters. Like WILLIAM BUXTON, he was employed several years to set up and take down the 'frame' or staging erected in Great St. Mary's Church for Commencement. From 1519 or earlier he was the University Crier and bell-ringer. To Kale, *stentor*, fell the task each September of proclaiming the rights and privileges of the University at the opening of Stourbridge Fair.

'Kele', along with Buxton and others, was among those present at dinner in hall at King's College on New Year's Day 1535 and may have been one of the joiners employed on the screen and stalls in the chapel.[9]

A.O.
[1] CCM, Cross Book, ff. 303 et seq.; [2] CCM, Box xviii, No. 71; [3] CCM, Box xvii, No. 23; CBD, 120; [4] CCM, Box x, No. 1; [5] KCM, Mundum Book 1507–08; [6] CWT, ff. 85b, 26b, 53a, 75b; [7] CWM, 19, 40, 53, 59, 64; [8] CGB, 'B', II, *passim*; [9] KCM, Kitchen Accs., vol. xiv

KAMESHAM, Richard de (fl. c. 1250) Mason (*Keynsham, Somerset*)

In the time of Abbot John de Felda (1243–63), the Abbey of Gloucester granted land in Castle Street, Gloucester, to Richard de Kamesham, mason.

GCA, Charters III.1

Karver—see also KERVER

KARVER, Thomas (fl. 1459–) Carpenter

Of Lichfield; on 9 April 1459 agreed to make 40 choir-stalls for the nuns' church at *Nuneaton Priory*, Warwickshire; they were to be 'after the forme of a pyktur' kept by the prioress and 'with a syllur [celure, canopy] a cordyng wt ye same pyktur', and were to cost £1 1s. 8d. each.

VCH, *Warwicks.*, II, 67; BM, Add. Ch. 48698

Keale, John—see KALE

Kenbury—see KENTBURY

KENDAL, William (fl. 1333–) Carpenter (*Kendal, Westd.*)

Master carpenter in charge of demolishing the old timber-framed chapel of *Haywra*, Yorks. W. R., in 1333, and rebuilding it, with 16 carpenters working under him.

HKW, II, 672

KENE, Richard (fl. 1353–) Carpenter

Master carpenter to the Bishop of Winchester at *Farnham Castle* where he made a timber frame and roof for a small hall in the keep in 1352–53. During 1353 he also made a timber belfry for the great chapel. This belfry was blown down in the great storm of 1361 and rebuilt. Kene's normal wage was 5d. a day.

(A.O.) RMF, 140, 151

KENT, John de I (fl. 1310–) Carpenter

Master carpenter; from 1310 onwards was building a new kitchen, wardrobe, knights' chamber and stable at *Byfleet Manor*, Surrey, for Edward II.

HKW, II, 906

KENT, John II (fl. 1537–) Carpenter

Was carpenter to the sub-Sacrist in the abbey of *St. Edmund* at *Bury* in 1537–38. He was in receipt of a fee of £5 4s. and a robe.[1] On 6 April 1538 the abbot and convent granted him a 60-year lease of a tenement on the south side of Eastgate Street, Bury, near the river.[2]

A.O.
[1] BCM, A.6–1–7; [2] BM, Harl. MS. 308, f. 138v.

KENT, William de (fl. c. 1202–1207) Carver

Carver (*sculptor*) to whom a grant was made by Humbert, Prior of *Lewes*, Sussex (1202–c. 1207), of a messuage next the great gate of the Priory towards the Hospital.

SAC, xxxv, 116; *PRO*, Exch. T. R. Anc. Deed. A. 15657 (*H.M.C.*)

KENTBURY, Robert [Kenbury, Kentebury] (*fl.* 1369–1397) Mason

Mason of Westminster; on 27 August 1369 was to assist WILLIAM WYNFORD to impress 30 masons from the home counties for foreign service.[1] From 1373 he appears as a landowner in Westminster;[2] in 1381–83 was working at the *Royal Mews* at *Charing*;[3] on 12 January 1386 was appointed to purvey building materials for the works of *Westminster Palace* and about this time carried out works on the drain of the great palace kitchen at task.[4] From 1387 to 1391 was warden under HENRY YEVELEY at *Westminster Abbey*, receiving 13*s.* 4*d.* yearly for a furred robe.[5] Mentions of his wife Agnes occur in 1390–91.[6] In 1392 he was paid £1 6*s.* 8*d.* for making two windows at *Windsor Castle*, and did another small task there in the following year.[7] In 1395–96 he worked at Westminster hall and elsewhere in the Palace and carried out a task of £23 for making the walls of the belfry next to the hall.[8] On 28 June 1397 order was given to arrest Robert Kentbury and distrain upon him for treading down and wasting the crops of the Abbot of Westminster at Westminster.[9]

[1] CPR 1367–70, 287; [2] *WAM*, 5906, 16245, 17688, 17698, 17701, 17703, 17710, 17713; [3] *PRO*, E.101–495–14 (*L.F.S.*); [4] CPR 1385–9, 71; *PRO*, E.101–473–2; [5] *WAM*, 23460–62; [6] *WAM*, 17711–12, 17714; [7] HWC, I, 222, 225n.; [8] LKC, 217; *BM*, Add. Ch. 27018; [9] *WAM*, 12768

Simon KENTBURY was paid 6*d.* a day at *Westminster Hall* in 1397–99 as purveyor of stonemasons.

PRO, E.101–470–17, 473–11

Thomas KENTBURY, mason of Westminster, perhaps Robert's son, is mentioned on 9 April 1404 and 28 July 1406.

CCR 1402–5, 360; 1405–9, 145

Kersyng—see CRESSING

Kerver—see also KARVER

KERVER, Geoffrey (*fl.* 1463–1464) Carpenter

Of Worcester; in 1463–64 was paid £13 6*s.* 8*d.* for the carpentry work and carving of the library and desks built at *All Saints Church, Bristol*.

PRO, Eccl. 2–128–92484

Kerver, John—see IRLAM

KERVER, Laurence (*fl.* 1473–1475) Carpenter

In 1473–75 carried out the timberwork of a new building at *Tickenhill Manor*, Worcs., for £24 6*s.* 8*d.* (see also JOHN ROGERS I).

HKW, IV, 279

KERVER, Robert, I (*fl.* 1409–1410) Carver

Is mentioned in 1409–10 as living in a house in the churchyard of *Worcester Cathedral* belonging to the monastic almoner; at this time the building of the cloisters was in progress and Robert may have been engaged upon the carving of the vault bosses.

WCO, roll C.189

KERVER, Robert, II (*fl.* 1469–   ) Mason

Was called in to advise upon the building of the tower of *Ludlow Church*, Shropshire, in 1469, when he was paid 4*d.* for his expenses.

SHR, 2S., I (1889), 242

KERVER, Thomas (*fl.* 1441–   ) ? Mason

With John Mayell and John Skynner, all three of Warwick, had a writ of aid in 1441 for engaging workmen to build the *Beauchamp Chapel* at *St. Mary's Church, Warwick*. On account of his name it has been suggested by Mr. P. B. Chatwin that Kerver was the master mason of the chapel, which was under construction from 1442 to 1448, while the glazing, carved work, and furniture were in progress for several years more, the completion coming about 1457. The tomb of the Earl of Warwick in the chapel was probably designed by JOHN ESSEX, marbler of London, and the stalls and woodwork were made by RICHARD BIRD, a London carpenter.

BAS, LIII

KERVER, William (*fl.* 1422–1423) Carver

Of Castle Acre, Norfolk; in 1422–23 was paid 40*s.* by the Trinity Guild of (*King's*) *Lynn* for work in connection with the rebuilding of the *Guildhall*.

LCR, G. d.58

Kervour, Hugh—see HERLAND (p. 137)

KETEN, Robert de (*fl.* 1329–   ) Carpenter (*Ketton, Rutland*)

Appears as carpenter of *Croyland Abbey*, Lincs., in a list of the abbey servants in 1329.

(SMC, 103, 170); DM, II, 121

KEYES, Roger (*fl.* 1441–1452) Clerk

A clergyman; in September 1441, shortly after work had begun, he was appointed supervisor of the works of *All Souls College, Oxford*, of which he became warden a few months later. In 1448 he became master of the works of *Eton College*, and may have had something to do with the design of the chapel, as he travelled to Winchester and Salisbury to measure the choirs and naves of the cathedrals there, and later travelled to London to show the King, Henry VI, a drawing (*portratura*) of the college, though it is not stated that he made this drawing himself. He was presented to the living of High Ongar in April 1449, and in 1452 was granted two stags yearly from Dartmoor Forest for his good services to the Crown at Eton. In connection with Keyes's claim to recognition as an architect, it must be pointed out that there is little relationship between the work of All Souls and that of Eton; the probable architects were the master masons, RICHARD CHEVYNTON and ROBERT WESTERLEY, respectively.

(APD; BAA); KJE; WCC, I, 396–8

Keyle—see KALE

KEYLESTEDS, William de (*fl.* 1321–   ) Mason

Mason (*cementarius*); on 2 May 1321 contracted to pull down and rebuild *Darley Hall*, Derbyshire. He was to receive 8 marks (£5 6s. 8d.) and a servant's robe. The house built by Keylesteds survived until 1771, when it was demolished.

(APD; WPS); SHB, 427–8; *BM*. Add. MS. 6670, *f.* 122

KEYLEY, James (*fl.* 1495–   ) ? Carver

Was paid £10 1s. 0d. for making the tomb of Richard III in the church of the *Grey Friars, Leicester*, in September 1495. See also WALTER HILL, alabasterman.

(APD); *BM*, Add. MS. 7099, *f.* 129

KILBOURN, John de (*fl.* 1335–1338) Mason

A working mason at *Haywra*, a fortalice in Knaresborough Forest, in 1335;[1] was appointed in March 1337 master mason of the king's works in Scotland.[2] He was concerned with extensive repairs at *Stirling Castle* in 1336–37, and his main work consisted of the rehabilitation of *Edinburgh Castle* in 1337–38.[3] He was paid 7s. a week.

[1] *PRO*, E.101–482–25 (*L.F.S.*); [2] RSC, I, 486; [3] HKW, I, 421–2

KILHAM, John (*fl.* 1473–1488) Mason

Master mason of *Peterborough Abbey* when on 17 November 1473 he was granted a yearly rent of 40s. and a gown of the suit of the Abbot's gentlemen, for his faithful counsel and supervision in his art, recent and to come.[1] On 30 January 1487/8 he appears as an alderman of the Guilds of St. Mary, St. John the Baptist, and SS. James and George in the parish church of Peterborough.[2]

On 8 March 1492/3 an annuity of 8 marks (£5 6s. 8d.) was granted to Thomas Kilham, son of the above John, probably as master of the Bede House known as the chapel of St. Thomas Becket.[1]

[1] PCM, 'The Book of Roger Bird' (*W.T.M.*); [2] NRS, IX (1939), 195

King—see KYNG

KINGSTON, Henry de [Kynggeston] (*fl.* 1320–1328) Carpenter

In 1320–21 had charge of works at *Knaresborough*, Yorks., as a carpenter of the King's Household.[1] In 1328 he was master in charge of the carpentry works at the *Archbishop's Palace* in York, when it was fitted up as a royal residence for Queen Philippa during the campaign against the Scots. He was paid 6d. a day, Sundays and feasts included.[2]

[1] HKW, II, 690; [2] *PRO*, E.101–501–8 (*L.F.S.*)

'KIRKBY MALHAM, Master of' (*fl. c.* 1450) Mason

In the middle of the 15th century a single mason (as proved by his mark) worked on a series of churches of similar style on the borders of Yorkshire, North Lancashire, and Westmorland. The conclusion has been drawn by the Rev. H. Poole that the owner of this mark was a working master who both designed and erected the buildings in question. They comprise the whole church of *Kirkby Malham*, and the chancel aisles and arcades at *Dent*, both Yorks. W.R.; the south aisle and arcade of *Arkholme*, the whole of the very small church of *Over Kellet*, and the aisles, arcades, and porch at *Warton*, all in Lancashire; and the chancel aisles and arcades of *Beetham*, Westmorland.

H. Poole in **AQC**, XLIV, 236–8

KITCHIN, William [Kechyn, Kychin] (*fl.* 1527–1559) Mason

William Kechyn 'inteylar' was paid £3 16s. 8d. for 33 weeks' work at *York Minster* in 1527–28.[1] It was probably the same man who was granted the office of mason to *Lincoln Cathedral* by the Dean and Chapter on 11 September 1535. He is stated to have done good service there already, for which he was to have the office for life at a fee of £1 a year as well as his stipend when employed on the works of the cathedral, with all wages, fees, etc., belonging to the office which he was to have from Michaelmas 1535. It was decided shortly afterwards that 13s. 4d. of his fee was to be paid by the clerk of the works, and 6s. 8d. by the dean, precentor, chancellor, and sub-dean 'in consideration of the great need and ruinous state of the fabric' (*nimiam fabrice inopiam et ruinositatem*).

On 11 April 1543 he was granted the office of one of the four vergers of the cathedral, vacant through the death of John Gallaye, and on 18 June 1558 he was regranted the office of mason or stone-worker (*latomii seu fabri lapidarii*) at the increased fee of £3 a year. He was probably quite old, as in the next year the reversion of his post as one of the vergers was granted to John Hill. Kitchin probably built the chantry of Bishop Longland who died in 1547.

(*A.O.*) LRS, XII, 194, 195; XIII, 74; XV, 152, 165
[1] BHY, I, 271; RFY, 102

KNIGHT, Reginald (*fl.* 1433–†1469) Mason

Working as a mason (*lathamus*) at *Canterbury Cathedral* from 1433 to 1442, when he was first of the working masons.[1] On 20 February 1444/5 he first appears as bridge mason of *London Bridge* at 4s. a week, and was chief bridge mason until superseded by THOMAS JURDAN in January 1460/1.[2] He had acquired the freedom of Canterbury by redemption in 1452,[3] and again received livery of the Prior of Christ Church in 1454 as a mason and in 1455 and 1456 of special grace as one of the 'valetti', while in 1457 he was ranked among the 'Generosi'.[1] He died at Canterbury in 1469.[4]

(*A.O.*)
[1] *Bodl.*, MS. Tanner 165; [2] KJL; [3] CFC; [4] Canterbury Wills, A.2.358

KOC, Peter [Cok] (*fl.* 1272–1308) Carpenter

Carpenter employed by the Sacrist of *Norwich Cathedral* from 1272 to 1308. Though never described as master, he held a responsible position, and usually received a retaining fee of 13s. 4d. a year. In the years from 1291–92 to 1297–98, during which he was engaged in the building of a timber spire on the central tower of the cathedral, he was also given a yearly tunic valued at 5s. When this work began he visited Ely and Bury St. Edmunds, but there is nothing to show whether this was for the purchase of materials or to obtain ideas in design and construction.

NCM, rolls 210–20, 222–5

Kokette, John—see COKET

Kraneby—see CRANEBY

Kychin, William—see KITCHIN

KYMPTON, Hugh [Kymton] (*fl.* 1343–1388) Mason

May well have been a son of the *Thomas KYMPTON* who was overseer of the masons at *Windsor Castle* in 1345. Hugh was commissioned to take cartage for stone in Beds. and Herts., for Windsor Castle on 24 February 1343/4; in 1361 he was warden (*apparator*) of the masons there at 3s. 4d. a week, and he held the same office for parts of 1362, 1363, and for 13 weeks in 1365–66, for three of which he was paid at the rate of 4s. a week. He also worked 'crest' and 'table' stone from the quarries of Careby and Holywell, Lincs., at 4d. a foot in 1364, and in 1365–66 he built a wall at task, with JOHN MARTYN and JOHN WELOT for which they were paid £102 13s. 4d.

It is not certain, though it seems probable, that Kympton actually went to Lincolnshire in 1364 to work at the quarries. His payments as warden (first working mason) at Windsor are not continuous, and his other absences may perhaps be accounted for by his being sent away to supervise the provision of stone from various quarries.

In 1384–85 Kympton was paid 8d. a day as master of the masons working and ordaining the masons' work (*magistro lathomorum operant' et ordinant' opus cementar'*) at *Portchester Castle*, Hants., under the instructions of HENRY YEVELEY (*per ordinacionem Magistri Henrici Yeveley*).[1] From 1386 to 1388 Kympton held a similar position at Southampton Castle.[2]

KJI; HWC, I, 113, 185, 189, 197–8, 208–10
[1] *PRO*, E.101–479–22 (*L.F.S.*); [2] HKW, I, 212

KYNGE, John [Kyng] (*fl.* 1527–1532) Carpenter

John Kyng, carpenter to the Mercers' Company of London was in 1527 paid an annuity of 20s. above his wages.[1] About 1532 John Kynge and THOMAS HALL, carpenters of London, were to build three houses next the King's lodging in the *Tower of London*.[2]

[1] LWA, 764; [2] LPH, V, 1781, 1086, 1307

'Kyng', Richard—see NORTH

Kynggeston, Henry de—see KINGSTON

KYPPYNG, William [Kyppyns] (*fl.* 1423–1425) Carpenter

KYRTON, John

Carpenter employed by *Winchester College*. In 1423–24 he rode to *Downton*, Wilts., in connection with making a new roof for the chancel there, and he was probably the William Carpenter who was paid 6*s*. 8*d*. in the same year for work at *Andover*, Hants.

In the following year William Carpenter was making seats in the entry of the College Chapel, being paid 1*s*. 4*d*. a week for himself and 1*s*. 3*d*. and 8*d*. respectively for his two servants. William Kyppyng was paid £6 for his work at Downton on the chancel roof, and also journeyed to Surrey and Middlesex to view the timber with one John atte Oke 'next Kyngston' (upon Thames) for a new barn at *Harmondsworth*, Middlesex. This barn was building in August 1427, but it is to be noted that in 1434–35 a carpenter of Uxbridge visited Winchester College to make a contract for building a new barn at Harmondsworth. (see JOHN DOWNER). It is therefore uncertain whether Kyppyng was the author of the magnificent rectorial barn which still exists there.

A Commoner surnamed Kyppyng appears in the hall-books of Winchester College for 1447.

WCM, Compotus rolls, *sub anno*

KYRTON, John (*fl.* 1415–   ) Mason

Mason of Winchcombe, Glos.; with Joan his wife owed 40*s*. for entry to the Guild of *Stratford on Avon* in 1415–16, but the fine and 'light silver' were pardoned by the Master and Aldermen in consideration of Kyrton's work on *St. Mary's Guild Chapel* (now Clopton Chapel) in the parish church.

BRS, 23

L. (*fl. c.* 1218–1220) Carver

Servant of the Dean of Wells *c.* 1218–20, for whose loan Abbot David of Bristol asked, to carve detail of the (Elder) Lady Chapel at *St. Augustine's, Bristol* (now the Cathedral). On stylistic evidence it seems likely that 'L.' was Master ADAM LOCK.

Rosalind Hill in BGT, LXV, 152; cf. CWE, 62, 105

LAKENHAM, Henry (*fl.* 1372–†1387) Marbler

Probably son of RICHARD LAKENHAM, and mentioned in 1372. On 2 May 1376 undertook to make a tomb for Sir Nicholas de Loveyne in the *Abbey of St. Mary Graces* (Eastminster), *London*. It was to have a freestone effigy of a knight (*chivalrot*) with a helm beneath the head and a lion at the feet, on a chest of marble with laton shields and inscription, 7 feet long by 3 feet wide and 2½ feet high.[1]

Lakenham's will, made on 16 June 1387, was proved in the Commissary Court of London on 8 August. It shows that he was a citizen and marbler, of the parish of St. Faith. He wished to be buried in St. Paul's churchyard and left his property to his wife Agnes and daughter Helen. The executors were his wife, John Ashwyth and Henry Cook, and the bequests show that he was worth over £60. His apprentice, WILLIAM WEST, was to be released from four years of his term.[2]

[1] PRO, E.210–6436 (*W.J.B.*); [2] *W.J.B.* in ANJ, LX (1980), 66–74

LAKENHAM, Richard (*fl.* 1355–1380) Marbler (*Lakenham, Norfolk*)

Of London; in 1355–56 supplied figures of St. Mary and St. George for *St. Stephen's Chapel, Westminster*. In 1363 he contributed to a present to the king, and witnessed a London deed in 1368. He was evidently well off, as he bought a house and land at Mitcham, Surrey, in 1367, which he and his wife Christine sold in 1371. In the following year he bought land in Buckinghamshire. In 1379 he was a feoffee of a tenement in St. Sepulchre's parish, and was apparently the Richard 'Marborer' acting for *St. Bartholomew's Hospital* in 1380.

W.J.B. in ANJ, LX (1980), 66–74

'LALYS' (*fl.* 1111–1147) Mason

Is said to have been a Saracen mason taken prisoner on Crusade, who built widely in South Wales. He is credited with *Laleston Church*, mistakenly said to owe its name to him, *Neath Abbey* (founded 1111), and *Margam Abbey* (founded 1147); and is said to have become architect to Henry I.

APD; EG, 268; AJ, III, 277

Lambert Joiner—see JOYNER

LAMBERT the Marbler [*Marmorarius*] (*fl.* 1183–   ) Marbler

Held 30 acres in Stanhope, Durham, in 1183, to be held by rent of 4*s*. a year while he was in the service of the Bishop of Durham. He presumably worked the marble columns for the Galilee of *Durham Cathedral*.

(APD); DBB, 10; FPD, 133n.

LANDRIC (*fl.* 1086–   ) ? Carpenter

Possibly the master carpenter of *York Castle* in 1086, when Domesday Book shows that he held Chetel's Manor in Acaster Selby.

EYC, I, 356, No. 462n.

LANGEFORD, John (*fl.* 1428–1429)
Carpenter

Carpenter at the manor of *Wethersfield*, Essex, in 1428–29, when he made new doors for the hall for 10s. Timber had been cut in the park at a cost of 1s. 7d., brought from the park to the manor house for 1s. 2d., and thence to 'le Framyngplace' for a further 10d.

PRO, D.L.29–42–822

LANGLEY, Reginald (*fl.* 1463–1464) Mason

Mason of London, in 1463–64 was employed to carve the royal arms of Edward IV to be set on the new gatehouse of *Hertford Castle*.

HKW, II, 680

LANGLOIS, Jean (*fl.* 1263–1267) Cleric

Perhaps 'John the Englishman'; treasurer in charge of the works of *St. Urbain, Troyes*, France, built 1263–66. Langlois in 1267 left Troyes on pilgrimage to Jerusalem.

BMF, 1922, 480

LANGTON, J(ohn) [Langeton] (*fl.* 1363–1365) Carpenter

Master carpenter during works on *Morende Castle* in Yardley Gobion, Northants., from 1363 to 1365, taking 4s. a week. (See JOHN EAST I)

PRO, E.101–544–31 (*L.F.S.*)

LARDYNER, Robert [Lardener] (*fl.* 1390–†1414) Carpenter

Appears as a party to several conveyances of property in the City of London between 1390 and 1396,[1] and was the second sworn carpenter of London in 1412, when with WALTER MYLTONE and the sworn masons of the city (see WALTON, WALTER) he viewed a plot of land by the church of St. John Walbrook, which the parishioners wished to exchange.[2] Robert Lardener, carpenter and citizen of London, made his will on 12 March 1413/14. He was apparently a parishioner of St. Michael's, Cornhill, and left to his servant Joan Hygyn his best brass pot, largest maser, second-best bed, and 6 silver spoons, while constituting his wife Clemency chief executrix and residuary legatee. The will was proved 19 April 1414 by Clemency and John Wyng, chaplain, her co-executor.[3]

[1] *LHR*, 119(18, 168), 120(122), 122(119), 123(22), 125(83); [2] CLB, 'I', 102; [3] *PPR*, Archd. Ct. of London, I, f. 312

Lathom, Henry—see EVESHAM

LATTHEBURY, Richard (*fl.* 1393–1404) Mason

Tiler and mason (*tegulator et latamus*) of the Isle of Wight; on 6 March 1392/3 undertook to repair all the buildings of *Barton Oratory*, Isle of Wight, at such times as William Love, the Archpriest, should consider necessary. All expenses of repair were to be paid by the Archpriest, who was also to provide a labourer and to give Latthebury his food with a yearly gown and a fee of 10s., and feed for a horse. Latthebury was to be free to take on other work when not occupied at Barton. He evidently held the post on 23 January 1403/4 when the agreement was sealed.

A, LII (1890), 307–9; (WCM, Barton 70)

LAWSON, Sir George (*fl.* 1514–†1543) (not a craftsman).

On 10 March 1514 was to purvey munitions to Berwick-upon-Tweed for its defence against the Scots,[1] was appointed master mason of the works at *Berwick-upon-Tweed* on 12 May 1515,[2] and on 24 April 1524 received the office of master carpenter at the same place, with wages of 12d. daily, on the surrender of the office by HUMPHREY COKE. In addition to the wage the office carried with it the appointment of a soldier in the town with £6 a year for his wages and 20s. a year for a yeoman under him.[3]

Lawson is mentioned very frequently as the holder of administrative offices at Berwick, where he was appointed treasurer on 22 May 1517; and also one of the Receivers-General for an extensive area in the north on 23 July of the same year.[4]

In 1530 Lawson was still 'Treasurer of Berwick' when granted the oversight of various storehouses and buildings in Berwick and on Holy Island,[5] and in August of the same year he was paid £126 2s. 3d. for repairs carried out at Berwick.[6] In view of his diverse appointments it is unlikely that Lawson was an architect, and his offices were sinecures so far as actual craftsmanship is concerned. He died in 1543.

[1] LPH, I, 4868; [2] *Ibid.*, II, i, 973 (pp. 261 *ff.*); [3] *Ibid.*, IV, i, 297 (p.126); [4] *Ibid.*, II, 3273, 3505; [5] *Ibid.*, IV, iii, 6418; [6] *Ibid.*, V, pp. 303–6; HKW, III, 416; IV, 622

Lawyn—see also LEWYN

LAWYN, Simon (*fl.* 1397–   ) Mason

On 15 March 1397 STEPHEN LOTE and Simon Lawyn, masons, were commissioned to impress masons to build a 'place' outside

LAYER, WILLIAM

Temple Bar, London, for the Earl of Rutland.
(*A.O.*) CPR 1396–9, 92

LAYER, William [Leyr] (*fl.* 1419–†1444) Mason

An important and well-to-do mason working in *Bury St. Edmunds* during the first half of the 15th century. In his will he refers to his property in 'the town of Leyr', one of the three Layer villages in Essex, from which he took his surname. By 1419 he was married to Margery Clerk, for in an enfeoffment of a messuage and land in Rougham (east of Bury) made by her in 1453 it is stated that she and her husband William Leyre, 'Masoun', were enfeoffed in the property by a deed dated 16 June 1419.[1]

The Sacrist's Roll of 1429–30 records a payment of 33*s.* 7*d.* to William Mason, probably William Layer, for making a chimney in the house of Richard Barbour in the Cook Row and carrying out repairs there.[2] From 1430 until his death William Layer figures in a number of Bury wills and deeds. Between 1433 and 1438 he seems to have had as his apprentice JOHN FORSTER. In 1439 he was one of 29 men of Bury who were summoned to appear before the Justices at Westminster for contravening the recently enacted Statute of Cambridge by throwing garbage into the streets and lanes of the town and near the Abbey, doubtless to the great dislike of the energetic, reforming Abbot, William Curteys.[3] At his death in 1444 he left a son George, a mason, and three daughters. The executors of his will, dated 20 January and proved 20 April of that year, were his wife Margery, his son George, and Stephen Gardener of Bury.[4] His property included a capital tenement and a house adjoining it in the Cornmarket at Bury, two adjoining houses in Risbygate Street, a grange and two gardens in the west suburb of the town, land in the fields of Bury and Westley and at Fornham All Saints, and lands and tenements at Rougham and at Layer in Essex.

William Layer made a bequest of 4 marks to the fabric of the new bell-tower of the monastery of St. Edmund. Although JOHN WODE of Colchester was the mason in charge of the rebuilding of the tower, having been appointed in 1436, it is probable that William Layer worked with him as a partner or assistant, for in 1439–40 John Wode and William '*socius suus*' went over to *Ely* to supervise repairs to the chapter house of the cathedral.[5] If the nave of *St. Mary's Church, Bury,* rebuilt between 1424 and 1444, was designed by a local mason, William Layer is the likeliest candidate. He may also have designed the tower of *Rougham Church,* to the building of which he made a contingent bequest of 20 marks. The money was to be raised out of the sale of his property at Rougham in the event of his son George predeceasing his mother. George Layer died in 1452, eight years before his mother, and the deed of enfeoffment of 1453 mentioned above was probably in execution of the clause in William Layer's will.

George *LAYER*, by his will, dated 3 September, proved 4 October 1452, also made a bequest to the building of the new bell-tower of the Abbey.[6] His widow Margaret had become the wife of Henry Banyard of Bury before 1460. He left two sons, Thomas and William, and the latter became a man of substance and importance in Bury, describing himself as 'gentleman' and in 1497 holding the office of Alderman of the Candlemas Guild.

A.O.

[1] *BCM,* H.1–2–10; [2] *BCM,* A.6–1–6; [3] *BM,* Add. MS. 14848, *f.* 303v.; [4] *BW,* ia, 6; [5] *CUL,* MS. Add. 2956, *f.* 158 (extract from Sacrist's Roll 1439–40) (*J.H.H.*); [6] *BW,* ia, 38

Lea—see LEE

LEBONS, John ['Hobyns', Lobbens, Lovyns, Lubyns] (*fl.* 1506–1529) Mason

In 1506 was one of the three masons described as 'the King's Master Masons' who submitted to Henry VII an estimate of the cost of works at the King's new chapel in *Westminster Abbey,* the other two being ROBERT VERTUE and ROBERT JANYNS, junior. When Vertue made his will on 10 May in that year, Lebons and Janyns were witnesses and put 'the King's Master Masons' after their names.[1] A John 'Hobyns', freemason of London, mentioned in 1510, was probably identical with Lebons.[2] He may have been the John Lubyns who built a chimney at the *Christopher Inn, Oxford,* for Lincoln College in 1509–10.[3]

Lebons at a later date passed into the service of Cardinal Wolsey, who employed him as master mason at the building of *Hampton Court* from January 1515, at a yearly fee of £6 13*s.* 4*d.* He presumably continued in charge as long as Wolsey's works lasted (certainly until 1527), but by 1525 he had become the resident master mason in charge of the new works of *Cardinal's College* (now Christ Church) at *Oxford*. Licence to found the college was granted on 13 July 1525, and in that year 'Mr. Lubbyns' was already in receipt of a yearly 'pension' of £10 chargeable on the assets of the monasteries suppressed by Wolsey.[4] According to the accounts, the works had already begun on 16 January 1524/5, in anticipation of the licence, so Lebons was clearly in charge from the beginning. In addition to the annual fee of £10, he had 12*d.* a day for his wages throughout the period of the works, which went on until 24 October 1529.[5] HENRY REDMAN shared the post of master mason with Lebons, but Redman had also to look after the offices of King's Mason, mason in Windsor Castle and mason to Westminster Abbey, so that he cannot have spent much time at Oxford.

A letter of 29 December 1526 speaks of the great progress which had been made, owing to the exertions of 'Mr. Lovyns, Mr. Redman, and Mr. Coke' (HUMPHREY COKE the carpenter).[6] In spite of Lebons's high rate of pay, he was not precluded from undertaking other work, as is shown by a contract which he undertook for the Master and Fellows of *Balliol College*, on 20 February 1527/8. This specified that 'mr. John Lobbens (mr. off my lorde Wa(*rkes*)) & William Jonsons fremason to werke or cawse to be wroghte iii heides off wyndos off iiii lyghtes & one off iiii lyghtes off ye northe syde & the heid off ye eiste windoe off v lyghtes euery wyndow to be wrowghte with wovsers & chawmerantes & ye said mr. Lobbens to see all maner off stones to be conveid & caryed into our college off Ballial sayff & sownde withowt brekyng or bressing or if so by yt any stone be broke in caryage then the said mr. Lobbens to cawse to be mendyd or to be reparyd. And the said maister and fellows to p(*ay*) for the caryage off ye stones. And ye said maister & fellows to pay or cawse to be payd to ye said mr. Lobbens (& William Jonson) for ye performyng of ye premisses xxi markes iiis. iiiid.' (£14 3*s.* 4*d.*).[7]

In 1515 'paper Riall for platts' was bought for his use.[8] This item shows that Lebons was concerned in the preparation of drawings, and thus no doubt in the design of works in the modern sense. The size of 'Royal' sheets of paper is 25 inches by 20.

John 'LYBYN' born in Somerset, who was admitted scholar of Corpus Christi College, Oxford on 29 March 1541 at the age of 18, proceeded to a fellowship in 1547 and vacated it in 1551, may have been a son of the master mason.[9]

(APD; WKM); GOM, 93–4; HKW, IV, 127
[1] LPH, I, 307; [2] *Ibid.*, 2nd ed., I, i, 438(4); [3] GOM, 93; [4] LPH, IV, pt. i, 1138; [5] *PRO*, E.101–479–11; [6] LPH, IV, pt. ii, 2734; [7] SHB, 574; *BCO*, MS. Register (*R.D.*); [8] VCH, *Middlesex*, II, 372; [9] AO

LEDES, John de (*fl.* 1288–1292) Mason

Master mason, doubtless from Leeds, Kent. In 1288 he was in charge of work for the little hall of the *Palace of Westminster*,[1] and on 23 October 1292 was one of the mainpernours for THOMAS DE HOUGHTON at the Exchequer.[2] It is very possible that Ledes was identical with JOHN DE LA BATAILE.[3]

[1] *PRO*, E.101–467–16, 17; [2] TTH, 29n.4; [3] LKC, 179

LEE, John [a Lee, Alee, Alye, Alygh] (*fl.* 1487–†1522) Mason

During the final phase of building at *King's College Chapel, Cambridge*, John Alee was joint master mason with JOHN WASTELL. Little about his career has so far come to light, but he must have been one of the more important architects in Henry VII's reign and the early years of his successor, and there is reason for thinking that he was the grandfather of SIR RICHARD LEE, the architect and engineer.

In 1487–88 a mason named John Alygh was working on the nave of *Westminster Abbey* the whole year at 3*s.* 4*d.* a week.[1] In the previous year a Thomas Alye was paid at the same rate for 21 weeks; this may have been the same man with his Christian name entered incorrectly. In 1497–98 John a Lee undertook a contract for mason's work at the royal manor of *Langley* near Leafield, Oxon., for which he received £120.[2] [In 1500–04 John a Lee was partner with ROBERT VERTUE in a contract for works costing £900 at Greenwich.]

Preparations for resuming work on King's College Chapel began in 1506 as a result of the King's visit when he spent St. George's Day at Cambridge. On 1 May 1507, when HENRY SMYTH and WILLIAM VERTUE, the King's Master Mason, visited the college, probably for a conference, Lee was with them and all three were entertained with wine.[3] On 8 July John Lee, described as chief mason (*capitalis lathamus*), was paid 8*d.* for two 'tables' (*pro ij tabulis*) in the hall.[4] Early in the following year

John Lee, freemason, received 56s. 8d. for work which his men did at *Biggin* (? in Barkway), Hertfordshire, one of the college estates, on the repair of the chapel there.[5]

When building operations at King's College Chapel began in earnest in the spring of 1508, there is no mention of Lee in the book of building accounts going up to 1 April 1509. But from May of that year until the completion of the fabric in July 1515, John Alee was joint master mason with John Wastell and he was paid at the same rate, £13 6s. 8d. a year.[6] It seems likely that he was appointed to take the place of WILLIAM SWAYN, who during the first year is described as comptroller. Alee took no part in any of Wastell's contracts and probably had no share in the designing of the building. His name is always second to Wastell's. The kitchen accounts for the period that survive show Lee being entertained on three occasions against twelve for Wastell. John Alee was frequently paid for 'Purveyor's Costs' up to March 1512, and this fact suggests that he was chiefly employed in obtaining men and materials for the work. His salary was paid up to 29 July 1515.

John Alee of St. Albans, freemason, made his will 20 November 1521; it was proved 6 February 1521/2.[7] It is very brief. He desired to be buried in the churchyard of St. Peter's and named as his executrix his wife Margaret, to whom he left all his goods to dispose as she thought best. It cannot be proved that all the above facts relate to one man, but they are consistent with a single career. No document has been found to show that John Alee was master mason at *St. Albans Abbey*, as he may well have been, and there is no definite proof that he was grandfather of Sir Richard Lee, the architect and engineer, but there are certain suggestive facts. In Sir Richard Lee's pedigree his father is given as Richard Lee 'of Hertfordshire' and his grandfather as John Lee, who married Elizabeth, daughter of Ralph Shirley, servant to the Earl of Arundel.[8] John Alee, the freemason, mentions his wife Margaret, but she may have had a predecessor; and the omission of any reference to a son may be explained by the fact that the very brief will was made when he was 'syke in body'. Sir Richard Lee between 1538 and 1540 obtained the site of Sopwell Priory and the manor of Sopwell, just outside the town, and there is evidence of his interest in St. Albans some years previously. More-

over, he was buried in the chancel of St. Peter's Church.[9] According to the pedigree, John Lee's father, also John, came from Sussex, apparently from Fittleworth, where there is a Lee Farm. If John Alee was master at St. Albans Abbey he is likely to have been the designer of the Ramryge Chantry on the north side of the high altar, with a little fan vault (for Abbot Thomas Ramryge, 1492–1521).

A.O.; HKW, IV, 97

[1] *WAM*, Novum Opus Rolls (*J.H.H.*); [2] *BM*, Add. MS. 7099, *ff.* 42, 44, 46, 51; HKW, IV, 160; [3] *KCM*, Mundum Book 1506–7; [4] *Ibid.*; [5] *Ibid.*, 1507–8; [6] *KCM*, Building Accs. 1509–15; [7] *PPR*, Archdeaconry of St. Albans, 181b Walingford; [8] *CLH*, I, 105; [9] *Ibid.*, I, 120

LEE, Richard [a Lee] (*fl.* 1525–1535) Mason

Between 1525 and 1533 'Master Lee', freemason of Ely, designed and made a tomb for John Fisher, Bishop of Rochester, which was intended to stand in his chantry chapel on the north side of the sanctuary of the chapel of *St. John's College, Cambridge*. In 1524–25 a payment of 3s. 4d. was made 'to the Master mason of Ely for drawing a drawght' for the tomb 'and for his avyse of the chapell'; in 1532–33 'M' Lee the fremason' received £6 13s. 4d. 'for makyng and settyng uppe the tumbe' and this was followed by a final payment of £3.[1] Fisher was never buried in the chapel, and after his execution the tomb was removed, but its sides and two ends, carved in clunch, were discovered intact in 1773, when they were seen by William Cole and sketched by James Essex before they were turned out into the open where they soon perished.[2] The fact that the tomb was in full Renaissance style, having pilasters at the angles carved with arabesques and with pairs of *putti* placed on each side of a panel intended for an inscription, shows that Lee was abreast of the new fashions and suggests that he may also have been responsible for Bishop West's Chapel at *Ely Cathedral* in which Renaissance motives occur. Three late Gothic arches of four-centred form were pierced in the wall between Fisher's Chapel and the main chapel, and these still survive, having been taken down and inserted in the south wall of the antechapel of the new chapel built in 1864–69.[3] Lee's Christian name is disclosed in a letter to Thomas Cromwell from William Cavendish, written from Ely in 1533, in which he refers to a secret commission which he had entrusted to 'an honest man, one

Richard a Lee, a freemason, whom ye right well know'.[4]

Richard Lee is mentioned as master mason, with (? John) BARBOUR, at Wolsey's College at *Ipswich* in 1528 and in a letter from William Capon to Wolsey dated 12 April 1529.[5] This may well have been the same man and probably the Richard 'a Le' appointed overseer of the will of EDMUND MORE on 31 August 1535; More seems to have been at Ely when he made his will.

In the summer and autumn of 1535 Richard Lee is mentioned several times in letters to Thomas Cromwell reporting on the progress of building works at his houses at Hackney, 'Friars Austins' and Ewhurst, e.g. (3 September) 'Ric. a Lee is busy about your buildings'.[6] It is difficult, however, to decide whether this was the Ely mason or SIR RICHARD LEE, the engineer and military architect. The Ely mason may indeed have been the father of Sir Richard Lee and son of JOHN LEE, the St. Albans master mason.

A.O.

[1] WCC, II, 282–3; [2] *Ibid.*, 285–6, where Essex's sketch is reproduced; [3] *Ibid.*, 243; [4] LPH, V, No. 1494; [5] LPH, IV, pt. iii, 5077, 5458; [6] LPH, VIII, No. 1142; IX, Nos. 66, 259, 339, 340, 413, 414

LEE, Sir Richard (? 1513–†1575) Architect & Engineer.

The first English architect to be knighted, Sir Richard Lee was primarily an expert in fortification. He has found a place in the *Dictionary of National Biography*, to which reference should be made for the latter part of his career, which, falling outside the scope of this work, is only briefly summarised here.

In the Visitation of Hertfordshire, 1572, his parents are set down as Richard Lee 'of Hertfordshire' (son of John Lee) and Elizabeth, daughter of Robert Hall, of More.[1] According to the *D.N.B.* he was born about 1513, in 1528 was page of the King's cups, being granted an annuity of £6 by the King on 20 August of that year, and in 1533 was serving with the army at Calais. He seems to have been in the service of Thomas Cromwell, and he may have been the Richard Lee mentioned in letters to Cromwell as being concerned with building works at his houses at *Hackney*, 'Friars Austins', and *Ewhurst* between July and September 1535.[2] In a letter dated 28 September 1535 John ap Rice, writing to Ralph Sadler, whose son, Edward, afterwards married Sir Richard Lee's daughter Anne, mentioned that he and Richard Lee were going to St. Albans, where Sadler should write if he wished to give them instructions about his farm there.[3] A few weeks later, John ap Rice was at Bury St. Edmunds reporting to Cromwell on the character of the abbot and the state of the monastery, and in his letter dated 5 November he wrote: 'Of Ely I have written to you by my fellow Ric. a Lee.'[4] These references to St. Albans and Ely are suggestive, for if the individual mentioned was the future Sir Richard Lee, they lend support to the possibility that his father was identical with RICHARD LEE the Ely mason and his grandfather with JOHN LEE, the mason of St. Albans.

On 12 August 1536, at Cromwell's request, the King granted to Richard Lee the office of surveyor and paymaster of the fortifications of *Calais* with £20 a year, a further annuity of £10, and a messuage and mansion in the parish of St. Nicholas near the Boleyn Gate which his predecessor, William Lelegrave, had had.[5] On 26 September he reported to Cromwell on the state of the works at Calais, using the language of one experienced in masonry.[6] For several weeks in the winter of 1536–37 he was in England, and Lord Lisle, the Deputy of Calais, made use of him as an intermediary to secure for him through Cromwell the priory of Frithelstock in north Devon.[7] In April 1537 William, Lord Sandys, Captain of the Castle of Guisnes, wrote to Cromwell asking for money to be employed in the fortifications by the surveyor, whom he regarded as 'a discreet man'.[8] Lee continued to be surveyor of Calais until December 1542. He played an important part in the operations against the French in the summer of 1540, when he made a map of Calais and its environs which is now in the British Museum. As a military engineer he was of great service in the attack on the castle of Fiennes three years later.

In March 1538 Lee is found acting in a different capacity, if the Richard Lee who wrote to Thomas Wriothesley on the 28th of that month was the surveyor of Calais. Wriothesley had received a grant of *Titchfield Abbey* in Hampshire and was engaged in building a house, now itself a ruin, where the nave of the abbey church had been. His master mason was THOMAS BERTY or Bartew, but the letter from Richard Lee shows that he had been consulted by Wriothesley and had recently visited Titchfield. He wrote from Lewes, reporting that the work was proceeding well but that they intended to make the roof of the hall 'shorter than I purposed hit by reson they will have the Screne covered which verely shalbe a disvigueryng of it'. Lee refers to his ship, which had recently been to Titchfield laden with 'stuff' for Wriothesley.[9]

As one of Cromwell's henchmen, Lee himself was not slow to profit by the opportunities presented of securing church property. In February 1540 he obtained a grant of the manor of Sopwell, just outside the town of St. Albans.[10] This included the site and buildings of the Priory, where he built a mansion which he called *Lee Hall*. In 1550 he was granted the monastic buildings of St. Albans Abbey which had been promised him by Henry VIII,[11] but the abbey church was excluded from the grant and in 1553 was sold by the Crown to the townspeople for £400. Lee also obtained some of the abbey's estates, including the manor of Langleybury, which he subsequently sold to Queen Elizabeth.

On 13 March 1544 Lee received a patent granting him the office of General Receiver of the Court of Wards and Liveries, with a fee of £66 13s. 4d. and the usual profits. [He seems also to have succeeded to the post of surveyor of the works after the death of JAMES NEDEHAM and to have held it until the appointment of LAWRENCE BRADSHAW in 1547.][12] In the spring he was present at the attack on Leith and Edinburgh, and on his return displayed to the King a plan of the city and its port to enable him 'to perceyve the scituacions of the same'. As a result he was knighted (11 May 1544). From this expedition he brought back the brazen font belonging to Holyrood Abbey and presented it to St. Albans Abbey, having added to it a vain-glorious inscription describing his exploit.[13] It disappeared during the Civil War, but the eagle lectern which he also brought from Holyrood is still at St. Albans, in St. Stephen's Church.[14] Later that year he accompanied the army to Calais and was in charge of the defence of Boulogne when the French unsuccessfully besieged the town. On 4 October he received a patent granting him a coat of arms.

Early in 1545 he was sent to survey the defences of *Tynemouth Castle*, taking with him two Italian experts in fortification, Antonio da Bergamo and Giovanni Tomaso Scala.[15] One of the plans then made has been preserved.[16] In May he examined defences in the Isle of Thanet. Later he gave advice about the defence of *Yarmouth*, and in August about works round *Kelso*. The same year the Duke of Suffolk asked for his assistance at *Portsmouth* [, but he remained captain of the town and paymaster for only six weeks. He may, however, have designed *Sandown Castle*, I.o.W.] In May 1546 he was again at Calais making plans to show the boundaries proposed by the French commissioners for a treaty of peace. In February 1547 he was at *Boulogne*, and in the spring and summer of that year accompanied the Protector Somerset on his expedition into Scotland in the capacity of military engineer. [In July 1550 Lee inspected *Norham Castle*.]

During the next ten years he seems to have lived a retired life and to have busied himself with his buildings at Sopwell, but a new period of activity began in 1557, when he went to the Netherlands as trenchmaster with the English force operating with the Spaniards under the Earl of Pembroke and was present at the siege and capture of St. Quentin. In January 1558 he was sent to *Berwick* as surveyor of fortifications and until 1565 he spent much of his time in the North, principally at Berwick, though there were intervals when his services were required on other affairs. In November 1559 he was sent on a secret commission to Antwerp, in 1560 he prepared the designs for the building of *Upnor Castle* on the Medway, and in October 1562 he went with an English force to Dieppe and Le Havre. As late as 1573 the Earl of Essex requested that Lee might be sent to Ireland to construct a fort near Belfast.

He died on 25 April 1575[17] and was buried in the church of St. Peter at St. Albans, where there was a slab with a Latin inscription in the chancel commemorating him and his two daughters.[18] He married Margaret, daughter of Sir Richard Greenfield, who had served with him at Calais. A portrait of Sir Richard Lee, about a foot high, painted on board and showing him with his sword by his side, belonged to Nicholas Stone, the sculptor. It afterwards went to his great-nephew, Charles Stoakes, by whom it was given to Benjamin Jackson, King's Master Mason, who died in 1719.[19]

A.O. (APD; DNB); HKW, IV, 507, 554, 680
[1] *BM*, MS. Harl. 1504; CLH, I, 105; [2] LPH, VIII, No. 1142; IX, Nos. 66, 259, 339, 340, 413, 414; [3] LPH, IX, No.

466; ⁴ *Ibid.*, IX, No. 772; ⁵ *Ibid.*, XI, Nos. 277, 385(13); ⁶ *Ibid.*, No. 498; ⁷ *Ibid.*, Nos. 1358, 1369; XII, Nos. 353, 451; ⁸ LPH, XII, No. 961; ⁹ *PRO* L & P Dom. Hen. VIII, vol. 130, *f.* 129; AJ, LXIII, pp. 231 ff.; ¹⁰ LPH, XV, No. 282(123); ¹¹ CPR 1550–3, 5; ¹² LPH, XIX, pt. i, No. 278(34); HKW, III, 13; ¹³ WFM, 569; ¹⁴ CPLO, 167; ¹⁵ LPH, XX, 99; NCH, VIII, 157; ¹⁶ *BM*, Cotton. MS. Aug. I, ii, 7; reproduced in Arch. Ael. (*2d.* ser.), xix, 68; ¹⁷ CUH, 289; ¹⁸ CLH, I, 120; ¹⁹ WS, Vertue Notebooks, i, 130, 148; ii, 25

Where references are not given the information is taken from the article in DNB.

LEE, William (*fl.* 1461–†1482) Joiner

Brother of Sir Richard Lee, citizen and grocer of London and Lord Mayor in 1461–62 and 1470–71, who released William of a debt of £20 by a codicil made on 26 September 1471.¹ William Lee, 'joynour', had been ordered on 7 January 1460/1 to purvey lances and other things for the King's use,² and on 9 March 1460/1 as 'citizen and joynour of London' was granted the office of 'porter' in the *Tower of London* at 12*d.* a day (a confusion in the printed calendars between 'junctor' and 'janitor'). On 31 March he was to find carriage for three great bumbards for the siege of 'Thorpwaterfeld' Castle (Thorpe Waterville, Northants.).³ On 30 October 1462 he was to impress carpenters and find timber for making lances, chests, tables, 'pavys', and other things for the works of his office, which was clearly that of King's Joiner.⁴ His will made on 16 October 1482 was proved on 10 June 1483.⁵ In it he desired to be buried in the chapel of St. Peter in the Tower, referred to his daughters, and left bequests to the 'feleschipp of Joynours of London', to EDMUND GRAVELEY, the King's Carpenter, and to John Crochard and William Neve, King's Smith and Glazier respectively. Lee was dead by 21 October 1482, when his office was granted to JOHN JERVEYS.⁶

¹ PCC, 37 Wattys (*A.O.*); ² CPR 1452–61, 655; ³ *Ibid.*, 1461–7, 9, 28; ⁴ *Ibid.*, 207; ⁵ CCL, 347 Wilde; ⁶ CPR 1476–85, 314, 514

Legeri, Dyminge de—see DYMINGE

LE ENGINNUR, Roger [Artifex] (*fl. c.* 1152–1173) Engineer

Engineer to Roger de Clare, 2nd Earl of Hertford (1152–73) who granted to him land at Foscote, Bucks., 'for the artificer's work which he shall show in the earl's business, and wherever he shall be in his service he and his assistant and his horse shall be at the earl's expense'.¹ Le Enginnur, who may have been identical with ROGER ENGANET, was suc-

ceeded in his properties at Foscote and in the neighbourhood by his son John le Enginnur, whose son Roger le Enginnur granted certain property at Silverstone, Northants., to Luffield Priory (see also ROGER 'Artifex').²

(*L.E.T.*)
¹ *WAM*, 2602; ² *Ibid.*, 2590

LEGET, Robert [Legate] (*fl.* 1462–1484) Mason

On 21 February 1461/2 was granted for life the office of chief mason at *Windsor Castle*, superseding ROBERT STOWELL. Leget received a confirmation of this grant on the same date in 1484, and his name is mentioned in the grant of the office to HENRY REDMAN in 1520 as Redman's predecessor, though it is hardly likely that he was in charge there for so long as 59 years; some years may have elapsed without an appointment. In 1479 Leget was paid £26 13*s.* 4*d.* for making the great 'baywyndowe' of the Queen's chamber,¹ and in 1481 for making 21 'mantell jamys and Bordurs' of Reigate stone.²

Leget was very probably identical with the Robert Leget or Legat who from 1503/4 to 1505 was paying rent of 13*s.* 4*d.* to the Sacrist of Westminster Abbey for a tenement which had been part of that leased by ROBERT STOWELL from 1476 to 1497, and in which Leget was succeeded by JOHN CHENEY. It would seem that Leget was concerned with the building of *Henry VII's Chapel*, whose site was adjacent.³

A curious feature of Leget's term of office is that other masons were put in charge of the principal works in progress; thus HENRY JANYNS was chief mason of St. George's Chapel from *c.* 1475 to 1483, and ROBERT JANYNS, junior, was in charge of the building of Henry VII's Tower from 1498 to 1505.

WKM; (HWC; CPR; LPH)
¹ HWC, I, 239; ² *PRO*, E.101–496–24 (*L.F.S.*); ³ *WAM* 19759–61

Thomas LEGET, mason, worked at *Eton College* from 1456 to 1460; he was perhaps the father of Robert Leget.¹ He was possibly the Thomas Legett who had supplied an image of St. Margaret for Canterbury Cathedral *c.* 1446–49.²

(*A.O.*)
¹ KJM; ² AC, LIII, 15

William LEGATT, mason, was in charge of the building of a wall by *St. Ewen's Church, Bristol*, in 1464–65.

BGT, XV, 177

LEGH, Richard de (*fl.* 1325–1335) Carpenter

Master in charge of carpentry works at *Chester* and *Beeston Castles* in 1325, and on 12 June of the following year was appointed to do the King's repairs in carpentry in the county of Chester, etc., at wages of 4*d.* a day.[1] In 1326 he was also paid £9 for work done by him at *Flint Castle*, and the accounts show that he continued to draw his pay of 4*d.* a day until 1335 or later.[2] In 1328 he was paid £1 12*s.* 6*d.* for work at Flint Castle and in 1331 repaired the Bridge of *Rhuddlan*, Flintshire.[3] He probably died before September 1346, when NICHOLAS OF ECCLESTON was appointed master carpenter for Cheshire.

[1] HCH, 94–6; ACC, 96, 97, 103; CCR 1330–3, 186; [2] FHS, III, 83, 89, 92; ACC, 103, 110; [3] FHS, RS. No. 2, p. 4; JAB

LEICESTER, Edward [Leycester] (*fl.* 1526–) Mason

Was master mason of *Bath Abbey* in 1526/7, when the reversion of the office was granted to JOHN MOLTON.

BM, Harl. MS. 3970; WHB, App. LVIII, p. 55

LEICESTER, John [Leycestre] (*fl.* 1349–1351) Mason

Mason (*cementarius*) in charge of the building of a postern at the *Tower of London* from April 1349 until 9 May 1351. He was at first paid 3*s.* 6*d.* a week, the working masons receiving 6*d.* a day; from August 1349 his pay was increased to 5*s.* a week and he is described as '*ordinator omnium operum Regis ibidem* [sc. the Tower] *pertinentium ad sementariam*'; ordainer of all the King's works there touching masonry. In 1350 or 1351 Leicester contracted to complete works at *Kennington*, Surrey, for the Black Prince, begun by NICHOLAS DE AILYNGTON.

PRO, E.101–471–2; HKW, II, 967

Leicester ?, John—see LEYCETT

LEICESTER, Richard [Leycestre] (*fl.* 1352–1353) Mason

Mason working for the Black Prince in 1352–53, when he took stone prepared for the works of Westminster Abbey for the Prince's manor of *Kennington*, paying £2 3*s.* 0*d.* for it.

WAM, 23455

LEMYNG, Lawrence (*fl.* 1511–1520) Mason (? *Leeming, Yorks. N.R.*)

Mason engaged on the building of the spire of *Louth Church*, at first as apprentice to CHRISTOPHER SCUNE in the spring of 1511 when 'Lawrence' was being paid 3*s.* a week.

In August 1512 his pay rose to 3*s.* 4*d.*, the highest journeyman's rate on the job, and he seems to have acted thenceforward as a resident warden during the long absences of his master, Scune. At the completion of the spire in 1515, although Master JOHN TEMPAS had been called in from Boston to take charge he drew only 3*s.* 4*d.* a week while Lawrence received 4*s.* and a reward of 20*s.* against that of 6*s.* 8*d.* given to Tempas.

Lemyng evidently settled in Louth for some time after the spire had been finished, for he was mending a window in the choir of *St. Thomas Church* in 1516–17, was at work on the church walls in 1517, and in 1520 had an apprentice working under him. His career is of unusual interest in that, if he was out of his apprenticeship in 1512 at the age of 20, he was earning a master's pay 3 years later, and when 28 had an apprentice of his own.

HEA; (DCL)

LENGYNNOUR, Andrew (*fl.* 1357–1360) Carpenter

Master carpenter; was ordered on 16 February 1356/7 and 10 March 1359/60 to take men and materials for the repair of *Dover Castle*.

CPR 1354–8, 512; 1358–61, 340

LENGINOUR, Richard [Richard the Engineer] (*fl.* 1272–†*c.* 1315) Engineer

Described as Master Richard the King's Engineer in the winter of 1272–73, when he was allowed 20 marks (£13 6*s.* 8*d.*) reduction off the rent which he owed for the Dee Mills at Chester.[1] Richard accompanied Edward I as an engineer during the King's advance into North Wales, and with Master JAMES OF ST. GEORGE was in charge of the works at the building of *Flint* and *Rhuddlan Castles*, begun in 1277 and in the main completed by 1282.[2] In 1281–82 he was supervising the building of *Rhuddlan Bridge*,[3] directed the repair of *Hope Castle* in 1282 after the Welsh rising, and also took carpenters to Anglesey for the building of a temporary bridge over the straits, and from 1283 was probably one of the principal architects of the fortifications of *Conway Castle* and town.[4] On 20 October 1284, 'Master Richard Ingeniator' the King's Serjeant, was granted 12*d.* a day for life, and on 4 June in the following year was granted letters of simple protection for one year.[5] Payment of Richard's fees can be traced in the Pipe Rolls and Chamberlain's Rolls for

178

the county of Chester up to the end of his life; his daily fee of 1s. was allowed for 364 days in each year.[6]

In 1285–86 Master Richard and HENRY OF OXFORD, carpenter, contracted to build the hall and chambers of Conway Castle for £100.[7] Richard's home was in Chester, and on 26 September 1284 he had been granted the custody of the King's mills and fishery there for 12 years at a rent of £200. He was to keep the mills, causeway, and fishery in good repair, and might take timber for the purpose from Delamere Forest, but he was not to be held responsible for destruction by fire during war, or flood.[8] From time to time he was allowed rebates from his farm in compensation for damage caused while he was absent from Chester on the King's service: at Carnarvon in 1283–84, in Wales from 1284 to 1287, and at 'Drosselan' (Treflan, Carnarvonshire).[9] On Richard's return about 1288–89 he claimed in respect of losses sustained through damage to the fishery in his absence, amounting to £40 and £54. An inquisition was held in 1289 which found that the fishcrates had been swept away during three successive years while Richard was engaged in the King's service at Rhuddlan and Carnarvon, and that the loss amounted to £60.[10]

In the following year Richard was indicted for seizing and carrying off to Chester Castle a cart-load of bread belonging to William Fox, which the complainant had bought at Warwick and brought to Chester for sale. Master Richard successfully defended himself on the plea that such importation of bread was prejudicial to the interests of the Dee Mills, and that he was acting according to precedent.[11] Other suits in the Chester Courts refer by name to a considerable number of servants of Master Richard, and it is evident that he controlled a numerous staff.[12]

During this period and until 1312 a great deal of work was carried out at *Chester Castle* under Master Richard's supervision,[13] and when further works were required at Flint or Rhuddlan Castles, it was his duty to make the necessary arrangements. For example, Master HENRY DE RYHULL, carpenter, was paid £28 5s. 0d. in 1301–02 for making 'one great wood work upon the great tower of Flint Castle together with one noble and beautiful box. . .with windows and steps, by a certain agreement in gross made with him. . .by the Justice and Master Richard the Engineer — except the carriage of the timber to be made at the expense of the Lord by the same agreement', and Robert de Melbourn, mason, had £7 3s. 4d. for 'stonework fitted into the said tower for receiving and sustaining the said woodwork, by an agreement in gross'. The same mason was paid £4 by another agreement 'for making one stone turret in Rothelan (Rhuddlan) Castle. . .in place of the gate of the same castle which was against the Friars Preachers of Rothelan, except the battlements of the same turret, so that the wall of the same contain in thickness ten feet'. For other works at Rhuddlan Castle Master HENRY OF OXFORD, carpenter, was paid £8 6s. 8d.[14]

In the following year £14 was paid to Geoffrey de Boneville, mason, 'making one great stone wall by order of the Justice, between the great tower of Flynt Castle and the inner bail. . . by a certain agreement made with him' and a further £14 was spent on the carriage of mortar and stones, while at Rhuddlan Castle Henry of Oxford and others were making two machines called 'mangonels' for which they were paid £26 17s. 7d.[15] In January 1302/3 Master Richard travelled to Windsor to advise the King concerning the making of pontoons at *Lynn* for the transport of troops to Scotland. The actual making of these pontoons was supervised by Henry de Ryhull, Lenginour's undermaster of carpenters, who took twenty from Chester to Lynn for the work.[16] In 1303–04 two machines called 'Springalds' were made by Master HUGH DE DYMOKE, engineer, one for Flint Castle and one for Rhuddlan, by an agreement made with Master Richard the engineer; Master Hugh received £4 for these engines.[17] In 1303–4 Master Richard had general direction of work at *Beeston Castle*, Cheshire, supervised by Master WARIN the Mason and HUGH DE DYMOKE.

In 1305–06 Master Richard Lenginour was Mayor of Chester[18] and seems to have worked for the Abbey of St. Werburgh's there about this time, presumably as architect of the choir of their church (now *Chester Cathedral*). In 1310 the Abbot gave a recognizance for £40 to Richard 'Ingeniator' and another for £20 13s. 0d. in 1312–13 to Master 'Lenginour'. In the last-named year Giles Lenginour gave a recognizance for £12 to 'Master Richard Ingeniator citizen of Chester'.[19] Works in *Chester*

Castle done in 1312–13 by RICHARD DE PARIS, mason, and WILLIAM DE WAKEFIELD, carpenter, were carried out under an indenture between the Chamberlain and Aymer, son of Richard Lengynour. About this time further small works were in progress at Flint Castle, where £4 6s. 8d. was paid to Robert de Stokelegh and Hugh de Dersbur, carpenters, 'for the woodwork made on the upper stage of the tower above the prison. . .according to a certain agreement', and at Rhuddlan, Henry de Moddreshale, carpenter, and his fellows, were paid £5 17s. 4d.[20]

Richard Lenginour's fees were paid for 1313, but by 1315 he was dead. In that year his son Giles Lenginour paid a fine for a lease of land in Eccleston bequeathed by his father, and ROBERT DE GLASHAM had succeeded to Richard's office on 24 January 1314/15.[21] Master Richard held the Manor of Belgrave and is said to have been an ancestor of the family of Grosvenor, Dukes of Westminster.[22] He also owned land in Watergate Street, Chester, and lived in Bridge Street.[23]

The career of Master Richard Lenginour is a long and remarkable one, and it is obvious that he held a very special position in connection with the military architecture of Edward I. In the first few years of the reign, fortification was almost confined to the works at the Tower of London, which were carried out under Master ROBERT OF BEVERLEY who had been appointed surveyor of the King's works in 1271 by Henry III, and had his wages increased to 12d. a day by Edward I in 1275. Robert of Beverley last appears on 24 June 1284, and it seems significant that within the next four months Master Richard Lenginour received a grant for life of 12d. a day, while on the same day Master James of St. George was granted the much higher allowance for life of 3s. a day.

Master Richard was clearly a craftsman of great importance, notwithstanding the higher fees accorded to James of St. George, and if the latter was the expert designer of the extraordinary series of fortifications built in North Wales, it was Richard who was for many years in charge of the routine supervision and upkeep of these works.

[1] SBC, 108–9; [2] MCP; WPS; TFC; A, XVI; [3] JAB, IV, 36–7; [4] A, LXXXVI; [5] CPR 1281–92, 137, 170; [6] SBC, 154, 163, 176, 182, 208; ACC, 5, 24, 40, 78; [7] A, LXXXVI; [8] CPR 1281–92, 135; [9] SBC, 156; [10] MCP, 104; [11] *Ibid.*, 101; [12] SBE; HCC; [13] HCH; MCP, 95; [14] FHS, III, 15, 16; [15] *Ibid.*, 34; [16] CSD, II, 352–3; [17] FHS, III, 47; [18] MCP,

577; CCR 1302–7, 417; [19] DKR, XXXI; [20] ACC, 79; FHS, III, 66, 67; [21] ACC, 78, 83; [22] HCH; WPS; [23] HCC, lxvii; cf. *BM*, Add. Ch. 72246, 72251, 72253, 72257

Lenginour, Robert—see BEDEFORD

LENGYNOUR, Robert, I (*fl.* 1308–1327) Mason

Was master mason of *Glastonbury Abbey* for a period of at least 19 years; he was enfeoffed for life of the office for surveying and directing the works of the church by Abbot Geoffrey and the Convent on Thursday before St. Dunstan 2 Edward II (1308) and received yearly 12 marks (£8) and a robe of the suit of the esquires worth 20s.; every day he was to have for himself in bread, ale, and cooked food (*coquina*) 5¼d. and for his horse yearly four wainloads (*plaustrata*) of hay worth 10s. He was still a member of the abbey household in 1324, and in 1327 was taxed at 3s. to the lay subsidy.

SRS,. XXXIX, 19, 22–3; *PRO*, Memoranda L.T.R. Roll 94, 17 Edw. II, m.54 (*L.F.S.*); SRS, III, 204

LENGYNOUR, Robert II [Ingeniator] (*fl.* 1324–1341) Engineer

Took fees of £18 5s. 0d. a year at the Dublin Exchequer on 28 October 1324, and was in charge of military works on Irish castles until 1341 or later.[1] In 1339 reference is made to his having repaired the castle of *Arklow* in 1333, and to his having done other work at *Leixlip Castle*. He was also in arrears with his payments as farmer of the King's mill near Dublin Castle and the King's mill at Leixlip.[2]

[1] IPC, I, pt. i, 30, 38, 41; *BM*, Egerton MS. 1773, *f.* 22; [2] IDK, 47R, App., 33, 58

Leofsi de Londonia—see DUDDASON

LEOMINSTER, Henry de [del Buet] (*fl.* 1277–1280) Mason

Master mason employed as a military engineer at *Builth Castle* in 1277, being given a reward of £2 at Chester in November. He was paid 4s. 4½d. a week during the seasons of 1278–80.

HKW, I, 295–6

LESSY, Philip (*fl.* 1368–1392) Mason

Of Totternhoe, Beds. In 1368 was working on the King's Manor of *Chiltern Langley*, taking 5½d. a day.[1] On 1 November 1392, WILLIAM FARELE and Philip Lessy contracted to build the tower of *Houghton Conquest Church*.[2]

[1] *PRO*, E.101–466–4 (*L.F.S.*); [2] Deed in sale catalogue of H. T. Wake, Derby, 1882 (*R.H.G.*)

LESYNGHAM, Robert (*fl.* 1376–1394) Mason

Was master mason of *Exeter Cathedral* during the building of the new cloisters (now destroyed) and the upper part of the screen of the west front, as well as of the great east window. He visited the work there from about 1376 to 1394, taking an apprentice in 1382 and, after the completion of his term, another in 1389.

Lesyngham apparently came from Gloucestershire, since JOHN SWALLOW, who is known to have come from that county, was sent (*versus partes proprias*) to bring Lesyngham from his own home. It is evident that Lesyngham had other important work in hand and the style of the Exeter east window suggests that this work consisted of the cloisters of *Gloucester Abbey* where Lesyngham was probably master. Lesyngham was given very high pay at Exeter: a fee of £5 yearly and 1*s.* a day when he was surveying and ordaining the work there, with a house rent free in the Close. Skins of parchment were brought for Lesyngham to 'show the form of the work of the new cloister' in 1377–78 and to paint the design of the new east window in 1389–90. In 1387 he was engaged on the repair of houses in the Exeter Close.

FFE, quoting Fabric rolls and Chapter Archives no. 3773

LETCOMBE, William de [Ledecombe, Letecombe] (*fl.* 1351–1354) Carpenter (? *Letcombe Regis, Berks.*)

Carpenter in charge of the Queen's works at her manor of *Banstead*, Surrey, commissioned to hire craftsmen in August 1351 and June 1354.

CPR 1350–4, 161; 1354–8, 73

Leveland, Geoffrey de—see GEOFFREY the Engineer

LEWES, John (*fl.* 1436–†1449) Mason

Was one of three masons commissioned on 8 February 1435/6 to take workmen for the repair of *Woodstock.*[1] On 23 July 1443 he received a life grant of the office of chief stonemason at the castles of *Carmarthen, Cardigan,* and *Aberystwyth,* South Wales, in succession to JOHN UNDERWOOD, deceased.[2] Lewes was dead by 12 July 1449, when the office was granted to William Brian and Richard Pole in survivorship.[3] Brian and Pole seem to have had a sinecure, for Brian belonged to the King's cellar for the mouth, and Pole was groom of the chamber.

Simon LEWYS, mason, was on 6 June 1415 ordered, along with John Benet, to take 100 men of their trade for Henry V's campaign in Normandy. See also THOMAS MATHEWE.

HKW, I, 457 (WKM)
[1] CPR 1429–36, 527; [2] *Ibid.* 1441–46, 188; [3] *Ibid.* 1446–52, 246

LEWISHAM, John [Leuesham] (*fl.* 1441–1445) Mason (*Lewisham, Kent*)

Mason employed on the works of *London Bridge* from November 1441; he succeeded JOHN CATELYN as bridge mason in January 1444/5, but was superseded a month later by REGINALD KNIGHT.

KJL

Lewyn—see also LAWYN

LEWYN, John (*fl.* 1364–†c. 1398) Mason

Perhaps identical with John Loewyne (*cementarius*) who worked on repairs at *Westminster Palace* for one week in June 1351, taking $5\frac{1}{2}d.$ a day.

Was the principal mason to *Durham Cathedral* and the Palatinate in the latter part of the 14th century. In 1364 he was sent from Durham to *Coldingham Priory,*[1] a Scottish dependency of Durham, and in 1367 he was in charge of the building of the great kitchen of Durham Priory, on which work continued until 1374.[2] Lewyn took as his fee £3 6*s.* 8*d.* each quarter, and had a robe worth 13*s.* 4*d.* every year. In 1368–69 he was granted exemption from jury service as 'the Bishop's Mason', and also had from Bishop Hatfield 4 acres of land in 'Framwelgate' and other parcels of land formerly in the tenure of John de Reine.[3] Although a servant of the Bishop of Durham, Lewyn was appointed by the Crown to take workmen for the repair of *Bamburgh Castle* on 21 May 1368, and some of the work seems to have been done by the summer of 1372, but on 9 March 1375 a commission was appointed to inquire into an information that John Lewyn, who had received at Bamburgh divers sums of the King's money by the hands of the executors of Ralph, Lord of Nevill for the repair of the said castle, retained the moneys without having done the repairs.[4]

In 1370–71 Lewyn had from Bishop Hatfield a grant of the wardship and marriage of Robert, son and heir of Thomas Coxside of Durham,[5] and he was still holding lands in the parish of Lanchester as executor of Thomas Coxside after 1382.[6] In 1371–72 he was a party to recognizances with Ralph de Eure and others,[7] and in June 1378 bought certain rents and services in the vill of Broomley in the parish of Bywell St. Peter, Northumberland, giving power of attorney to his son Walter Lewyn to take possession.[8]

At this time there was a sudden spate of castle-building in the north, probably due to the fear that the accession of the boy Richard II in England would provoke Scottish raids. Bishop Hatfield had rebuilt the keep of *Durham Castle*, and it is highly probable that the architect was John Lewyn; this would have given him considerable prestige in the north, and probably accounted for the fact that his services were in request at several widely separated places within a short time.

On 10 July 1378 he received a Crown commission to take masons for works at *Carlisle* and *Roxburgh Castles*,[9] and he contracted with the Crown to execute these works. At Carlisle, by indenture of 13 April 1378, a tower with a gate and barbican was to be built, for which Lewyn would receive 500 marks (£333 6s. 8d.);[10] while at Roxburgh the new works were described in the contract of 1 August 1378 as to consist of a wall with three towers. Roxburgh, a castle several miles beyond the Scottish border, was continuously in English hands from 1346 to 1460, but a special clause in Lewyn's contract freed him from blame in the event of interference by the Scots. The new wall was to run across the castle from north to south, 30 feet high with three towers, each 50 feet high, the central tower being provided with a gate and barbican. The work seems to have been finished by 1387.[11]

Only two months after the start of these very considerable works, Lewyn contracted with Sir Richard le Scrope to build two towers, a gateway, and other buildings at *Bolton Castle*, Yorks., on 14 September.[12] This was apparently in completion of work which had been begun there a short time before, but the whole castle is of uniform design, and Lewyn had evidently had charge of the work from the start. The new contract provided for works which can be identified with the eastern range of the castle, together with the eastern rooms of the south range. Sir Richard was to find wood for burning lime and for centres and scaffolds, and to pay for the carriage of materials; Lewyn was to execute the work and to provide stone and lime, being paid at the rate of £5 for each perch of masonry, consisting of 20 superficial feet, 1 yard thick, together with a fee of 50 marks (£33 6s. 8d.). Sums due from a previous account are mentioned and confirm Lewyn's earlier work on the castle.

During 1378 John, Lord Neville obtained from Bishop Hatfield licence to crenellate his mansion of *Raby*, and a considerable part of the existing castle dates from this period, including the kitchen, which has many points of resemblance to that of Durham Priory. John Lewyn may well have designed these works, and also the great castle of *Sheriff Hutton*, for which Lord Neville had a licence on 26 April 1382. As we shall see, Lewyn certainly worked for Ralph, Lord Neville, son and successor of John, and the resemblance between the castles of Bolton and Sheriff Hutton is very marked. Lewyn was perhaps also responsible for the castles of *Lumley*, Durham, and *Wressle*, Yorks. E.R., whose plans closely resemble those of Bolton and Sheriff Hutton.

Meanwhile, Lewyn was undoubtedly a busy man, for he was engaged on the important works at Carlisle and Roxburgh for several years. His work at the former castle was evidently completed by 1383, for on 8 October a commission was issued for the survey of a gate and tower which John Lewyn had contracted to build there, but other works at Carlisle, and those at Roxburgh, lasted until 1387; on 24 November in that year orders were given for the survey of Lewyn's works at both castles.[13] He had, however, been tempted to undertake work at another important castle, for John of Gaunt. This was *Dunstanburgh*, built in the early part of the century by ELIAS the Mason II; the lapse of only two generations was considered to have rendered its enormous gate-tower obsolete, and a complete transformation was projected. Lewyn contracted on 25 October 1380 to make a new 'mantelet' of freestone by the great tower (the original gatehouse) of Dunstanburgh, finding materials, carriage, and workmanship. This mantelet was undoubtedly undertaken first as a precaution against surprise during the building of the intended new gatehouse, and we can hardly doubt that Lewyn provided the general design for the new works, though the contract specifies that the mantelet was to be 'in a certain place pointed out to him by the said John, King of Castile and Duke of Lancaster, and his council' (*en certein lieu a lui divise*, etc.).[14] The work was to be finished by Michaelmas 1381; Lewyn seems to have built the mantelet and to have begun other works, but he left them in an unfinished state, with the result that John of Gaunt called in another mason, HENRY HOLME, who took over on 1 December 1381. No doubt Lewyn's commitments exceeded his powers at this time, and the campaign on the borders in 1379–81 must have resulted in increased difficulties and at the same time official pressure to complete his works for the Crown.

The register of John of Gaunt shows that Lewyn was to be paid all arrears in connection with the mantelet in July 1381, in addition to payments 'for another work made by our device there'; this work is later mentioned as 'the new work joining the new made mantelet', so that there can be little doubt that Holme simply continued what had been designed and begun by John Lewyn.[15] About 1382 Lewyn is entered as a free tenant in Newton Cap, Darlington Ward,[16] and he also held land at Lanchester in addition to his trusteeship of the Coxside Estate there.[17] Notwithstanding his work at such distant points as Carlisle, Roxburgh, and Bolton, in 1384–85 Lewyn was appointed a commissioner of array for the city of Durham by Bishop Fordham, and in the same year John Lewyn, Walter Cokyn, Roger Aspour, and Henry Shyrbourne were granted the borough of Durham to farm, with all the rents and services appurtenant, for the term of 6 years at a yearly rental of £86 13s. 4d. In the following two years Lewyn was a party to recognizances connected with this 'farming' of the borough.[18] Lewyn also did work for the Crown at Berwick-on-Tweed in 1385–86.

It has been suggested by Dr. W. Douglas Simpson that at about this time Lewyn was engaged on the design of the great donjon of *Warkworth Castle* for the Earl of Northumberland. Heraldic evidence strongly suggests that this was built soon after 1380 at the latest, and at that time no mason of the first rank other than Lewyn is known to have been in practice in the north.[19]

On 3 July 1388 the King committed to Sir William de Fulthorp certain lands forfeited by his father Roger Fulthorp by mainprise of

John Lewyn and others,[20] and on 4 November order was given to the collectors of customs at Newcastle upon Tyne to secure to Lewyn the payments due to him for his works at Roxburgh Castle.[21] The method by which Lewyn was to secure payment seems curiously complicated, but it would appear that he must have been in business as a shipper of wool and woolfells. A subsidy of 20s. the sack had been granted by the King to the Duke of Gloucester and others, and the full export duty was at a rate in excess of this; Lewyn was to have allowance of this excess upon such wool as he should ship oversea, up to a total of £398 13s. 9d., the amount owing to him. This seems a most inequitable method of payment, as even at best Lewyn would not receive a penny, except from the increased profits of his export trade. Not only this, but in 1391 Lewyn forfeited 18 sacks and 13 cloves of wool, 68 woolfells, and 8 dickers of hides, because he shipped them from Newcastle for the staple of Calais and they were taken to 'Middelburgh in Seland' contrary to the King's prohibition.[22] Lewyn can hardly have been encouraged by these results of his hard work, but a year later he entered into a further contract for additional works at Roxburgh Castle;[23] his private practice was perhaps more remunerative, for he entered into an agreement with Ralph, Lord Neville that he and his son Walter Lewyn would sufficiently renew all defective roads at *Brancepeth* within two years of being asked to do so, for the sum of 200 marks (£133 6s. 8d.). Lord Neville agreed to release the Lewyns from a recognizance to him, which was cancelled, and it is quite possible that this was the outcome of building operations at Brancepeth Castle for Lord Neville on which John Lewyn had been engaged.[24]

John Lewyn was a party to several recognizances at Durham between 1390 and 1397,[25] and in 1395 and 1398 he was paid sums due to him for his work at *Finchale Priory* for the Durham conventual authorities, to whose rule Finchale was subordinate.[26] The association with Lewyn of his son Walter in 1391 suggests that he was then getting old, and he is last heard of in 1398, when the bishop granted to one William Warde a piece of waste ground 'under the walls of the castle of Durham on the East, viz. in length from the King's Gate to the quarry where John Lewyn digs stones, and in width from the wall of the

LEWYS, JOHN

aforesaid castle to the water of Wear to hold and enclose in severalty'.[27]

Lewyn is not mentioned in connection with the rebuilding of the dormitory at Durham Cathedral Priory, which JOHN DE MIDDLETON, mason, contracted to carry out, on 21 September 1398. It seems probable that by that time Lewyn had died, or else was too infirm even to give counsel.

At the Priory of Durham Lewyn was certainly the designer of the kitchen and the cloisters, of which the earlier part was carried out in his time. He was probably responsible for the throne above Bishop Hatfield's tomb, and may have had something to do with the Neville screen, but the latter was made in London and sent to Durham in pieces by sea in 1376. Stylistic evidence suggests that the screen, which had been put in hand by 1372, was designed by HENRY YEVELEY.

Lewyn was the most important provincial architect of mediaeval England of whose career we have adequate details. His strength lay in his grasp of construction, and the splendour of massive structural work, properly carried out. He was in fact what would now be called a functionalist, but though there is little purely decorative detail in his known works, it cannot be doubted that he had beauty as well as utility in mind when he invented for the kitchen at Durham the vault of intersecting ribs which forms a perfect support for the lantern and at the same time delights the eye with its interwoven star. The resemblance of this vault to examples in Persia and in Spain affords an unusual problem in the diffusion of style.

Lewyn's work is an outstanding example of the adaptability of the mediaeval mason; already holding an important position as an ecclesiastical architect, he undertook work for the Crown, for the Duke of Lancaster, and for private clients; he held a prominent place in the affairs of the city of Durham, was the owner of several country properties, and was apparently an exporter of wool on a very large scale.

SWD; (APD); HKW, II, 569
[1] SCP; [2] DAR, II, 571–4; [3] DKR, XXXII, 287 *ff.*; [4] CPR 1374–7, 143; NCH, I, 40; [5] DKR, XXXII; [6] HBB, 59, 60; VCH, *Durham*, III, 140, 206; [7] DKR, XXXII; [8] NCH, VI, 146–50; [9] CPR 1377–81, 257; [10] SHB, 456–7; *PRO*, E.101–483–31; [11] SHB, 457–9; *PRO*, E.101–483–32; [12] SHB, 455–6; AQC, X, 70; VCH, *Yorks. N.R.*, I, 272; JBC, 10–11; [13] CPR 1385–9, 367; [14] JGR 1379–83, 922; SHB, 460–1; [15] JGR 1379–83, 410, 566, 624, 723, 923; [16] SBH, 47; [17] HBB, 59–60; [18] DKR, XXXII; [19] SWD;

[20] CFR 1383–91, 241; [21] CCR 1385–9, 544; [22] CPR 1388–92, 355; [23] *PRO*, E.101–483–4; [24] DKR, XXXIII, 43 ff.; [25] *Ibid.*; [26] RFP, cxii, cxv, cxx; [27] VCH, *Durham*, III, 22

LEWYS, John [Lewes] (*fl.* 1435–1460) Carpenter

Carpenter of Winchester, evidenced there from 1435 to 1460, and living in Colebrook Street in 1446. He also had property in the suburb to the south. In 1441 he made the roof for the Great Hall of *Wolvesey Palace* and worked for *St. John's Hospital* in 1459–60. He had an extensive business as a timber merchant. In 1449–50 Lewys rode to Andover to value work there done by RICHARD HOLNERST.

(*D.K. Win*); WCM 22124

LEYCETT, John [Leicester ? or Lycett] (*fl.* 1458–1460) Carpenter or Carver

An indenture of 25 December 1460 shows that the four churchwardens of *Newark*, Notts., had paid to 'Johanni Leycett Karuffar' various sums over the two (?) previous years totalling £36 13s. 4d.; also to Robert 'caruffar' a total of £34 13s. 4d. This may have been for work on the roofs of the nave and aisles.

(*A.O.*) Newark Corporation Records no. 218 printed by Dimock in RPL, vol. IIIA (1856), 7

Leyr, William—see LAYER

LIEGE, Hawkin of [Hennequin] (*fl.* 1361–†1382) Carver

Of France; was paid 200 marks (£133 6s. 8d.) on 20 January 1366/7 for making the marble tomb for Philippa, Queen of Edward III, in *Westminster Abbey* during the Queen's lifetime. The effigy is evidently a portrait.[1] As 'Hennequin de Liège' he is known to have worked for the Count of Flanders and for the French Court.[2]

[1] DIE, 189; [2] TBK, XVIII, 461–2 (Jean de Liège)

LIES, William (*fl. c.* 1420–) Carpenter

Was warden of the King's works of carpentry in the time of Henry V taking fees of 10d. a day.

PRO, E.101–473–18

LILYE, Simon (*fl.* 1344–1347) Mason

Leading mason or warden at the building of the west walk of *Norwich Cathedral* cloisters, from 1344 to 1347. He was paid 2s. 4d. weekly and received a robe priced at 14s. 2d.; he also went to Yarmouth in connection with purchases of marble. In 1346–47 he was paid 6s. 8d. for '*doctrina Toft*' presumably a book acquired by the monastery.

NCM, rolls 1050–52

LIMOGES, John of (*fl.* 1282–   ) Tomb-maker

John, citizen of Limoges (*Johannes Burgensis Limovicensis*), in 1282 made the tomb of Walter de Merton, Bishop of Rochester, and came to England to supervise its erection in *Rochester Cathedral*. He was paid £40 5s. 6d. for his work, probably a wooden effigy covered with enamelled plates. In addition £2 6s. 8d. was spent on one of the bishop's executors travelling to Limoges to order and provide for the making of the tomb (*ad ordinandam et providendam constructionem dictae tumbae*), 10s. 8d. on the expense of a groom (*garcio*) going to Limoges to bring it and Master John to England, and £22 on masonry work about the tomb.

HRC, 126

LINCOLN, Philip of (*fl.* 1346–1375) Carpenter

Was appointed master carpenter at *York Minster* on 1 August 1346, during good conduct, at 1s. 8d. a week and the other accustomed profits of the office, and in addition the office of janitor of the Close at 10s. a year.[1] In 1350 his offices were regranted to him for life and the weekly fee increased to 2s.; at this time and for some years subsequently he was engaged on the construction of the great timber vault of the nave, 45 feet in span.

In 1371 his fees were raised to 3s. a week, and on 29 January 1374/5 he received a grant of houses beside the gable of 'Berefride's choir' (i.e. the church of St. Michael le Belfry beside the Minster). Master Philip did not take up the freedom of York, so he had probably been brought from Lincoln, as were other York craftsmen.

[1] SHB, 586; BHY, I, 168, 190; RFY, 165, 1, 5, 185

Philip may have been related to *Robert of LINCOLN*, carpenter, who took up the freedom of York in 1323–24,[1] and was taxed 2s. 3d. in the parish of St. Michael le Belfry, York, in 1327;[2] and to *Henry de LINCOLN* who took up the freedom there in 1326–27.[3]

[1] YCF; [2] YRS, LXXIV, 1929; [3] YCF

Lindsey—see LYNDESEY

Lobbens, John—see LEBONS

LOCK, Adam [Loeck] (*fl. c.* 1215–†c. 1229) Mason

Master mason at *Wells Cathedral* for some years previous to his death in or about 1229, when he was apparently succeeded by THO-MAS NORREYS, mason, a witness in September 1229 to a charter connected with Lock's property, and still living in 1249.

Adam left a widow Agnes and a son Thomas; he must have been a man of considerable standing, as the sub-dean of Wells and another canon were executors of his will, and he owned several houses and some land in Wells worth 10 marks of silver. Master ELIAS OF DEREHAM was one of the witnesses to Agnes Lock's confirmation in 1229 of a grant of land made by her son Thomas.[1]

On the assumption that the west front of Wells was begun c. 1220, Adam Lock has been credited with the design, but this chronology is very improbable. It was shown by Armitage Robinson and Bilson[2] that the building of the front is not likely to have begun until c. 1230, and further that there is no documentary evidence for the often repeated statement that the church was entirely finished by 1242. So early a date is indeed refuted by much of the statuary on the front, which would have been placed in position while the great scaffold was up; the later statues and some of the decorative details cannot be earlier than c. 1250–60, an approximate date which receives some confirmation from the career of Master SIMON DE WELLS, sculptor.

It must therefore be accepted that Lock was the master under whom the second work of the nave, west of the north porch, was carried out, from c. 1215. He was probably identical with 'L.', sent from Wells to carve the detail of the (Elder) Lady Chapel at *St. Augustine's Abbey, Bristol*, about 1218–20. There is no stylistic reason why he should not also have been responsible for the earlier work of the cathedral, whose plan and detail, exclusive of the west front, form a single unity. Either Lock adhered to the design of a predecessor in an exceptionally conservative spirit, or he was himself the original MASTER OF WELLS. (See Appendix I.)

CWE

[1] HMC, *Wells*, I, 35; II, 550–1; [2] AJ, LXXXV (1930), 11n., 65–7

LOCO, Peter de (*fl. c.* 1340–c. 1357) Joiner

King's Joiner to Edward III; mentioned as the predecessor in office of JOHN WYDMERE.

CPR 1391–6, 363; HKW, I, 224

LOMHERST, Stephen (*fl.* 1373–   ) Mason

Described as 'de Souttune'; on 1 August

185

LONDON, JOHN

1373 contracted to build a new cloister at *Boxley Abbey*, Kent, together with windows and doors leading to the church, dorter, and refectory. One walk was to be built in a year, and the four walks together with four windows in the south wall of the church, above the cloister, were to be finished within five years. Lomherst was to use stone from a quarry of the Abbot and Convent at 'Chyngele' of which he had a lease, and was to adhere to the details and drawings (*formas et mensuras moldas et portreturas*). For the whole work he was to be paid £120 by instalments. 'Souttune' is probably to be identified with Sutton Valence, then an important stone quarrying centre some 7 miles to the south of Boxley.

SHB, 448–50; (*PRO*, E.101–622–46)

LONDON, John de (*fl.* 1295–1296) Carpenter

Master carpenter; in 1295 carried out work on the hall in *Carnarvon Castle*, and in the next year was partner to Master NICHOLAS DE CHESTER in building the watermill near *Conway*.

HKW, I, 350n., 381n.

London, Leofsi of—see DUDDASON

LONDONEYS, William [Londynays] (*fl.* 1381–1392) Mason

On 11 May 1381 a protection for one year was issued in respect of William Londoneys, mason, working with the Archbishop of Canterbury on the new *City Wall* of *Canterbury*,[1] and on 1 February 1386–7 he and Richard Cook and James Gilet of Canterbury were granted a commission to impress masons and others to work on the walls of Canterbury at the wages of the commonalty.[2]

In 1391–92 one of the same name of the parish of St. Margaret, Canterbury, with William Pylland of Boxley, John Waleys of Boxley, and John Smyth, mason, of East Malling, Kent, bound themselves in £120 to John Baddyng of Rye, Sussex, apparently in connection with some building work.[3] An account for the period Easter 1391–Michaelmas 1392, for works at *Bermondsey Abbey*, shows that Londoneys received £20 13s. 4d. for building the south aisle of the church, and 16s. 8d. for carting rubbish away.[4] Simon the Carpenter, who received £10 for his share of the work, may have been the Simon Carpentere who in 1398 had a livery of the Prior of Christ Church, Canterbury,[5] and who in

1411, as Simon Carpenter of London, was paid £13 19s. 9d. by the Prior of Christ Church.[6]

[1] CPR 1381–5, 8; [2] *Ibid.*, 1385–9, 271; [3] HMC, 5 R, 512; [4] Dr. Rose Graham in AAJ, 3 S, II (1937), 148–9; [5] Bodl., MS. Tanner 165 (*A.O.*); [6] CCA, Prior's account roll xvii.1 (*W.P.B.*).

Londres, Nicholas de—see RAMSEY

Londynays, William—see LONDONEYS

LONG, John (*fl.* 1394–†*c*.1425) Mason

Worked as a mason at the building of the nave of *Westminster Abbey* continuously from 29 September 1394 to 25 November 1399, and for 28 weeks in 1400–01, taking 3s. 4d. a week.[1] In 1421 he was in York, when he took up the freedom of the city,[2] and in 1421 was appointed master mason of *York Minster* in succession to William Colchester. He took fees of £10 a year and was still in office at the end of 1423. In January 1426 he was succeeded by WILLIAM WADDESWYK.

(APD; BHY, I, 221, 225)
[1] *WAM*, 23464–70; [2] YCF; [3] RFY, 42n., 46, 50

LONGE, Laurence (*fl.* 1368–1369) Mason

Warden (*apparillator*) of the masons at work on *Leeds Castle*, Kent, in 1368–69, at the rate of 6d. a day.

HKW, II, 700

LOOSE, John [alias Bale] (*fl. c.* 1455–1478) Mason

Of Burston in Norfolk, near Diss, and later of Cambridge. He built a new stone wall at the *Friars Preachers* there about 1456, and he was working at *Peterhouse* in 1456–57.[1]

On 4 September 1457 he contracted with *Corpus Christi College* to build a wall 81 feet in length next to St. Botolph's churchyard. He was to receive either 40s. with food and lodging for himself and his four men, or to be paid at the rate he had been taking at Peterhouse.[2]

On 4 December 1459 he made a further contract with the same college to build a bakehouse. The work was to begin on 12 March and be finished by 1 August 1460. For it he was to receive £7 13s. 4d. and 'a gown of yeoman's livery, or else a noble' (6s. 8d.), and also provision was made that 'the sayd John schal haue withinne the sayd College a chambre, j bedsteed, and a bedde, and his mete to be dyght in the kechyn at [the college's] costis, as longe as he is werking in the said werk'.[3] He is described as a 'leyer', so that he is presumably to be considered as a building

186

contractor rather than an architect. Payments to Loose in respect of this and other work at the college are entered in the White Book kept by John Botwright who was master of the college from 1443 to 1474.[4] In 1477–78 Loose was paid two sums of 3s. and 3s. 4d. for whitening the walls of the School of Canon Law in the *Schools* at *Cambridge*.[5]

[1] *PHM*, Bursars' Rolls (*L.F.S.*); [2] SHB, 531–2; WCC, I, 261, 310; [3] SHB, 532–4; WCC, I, 259, 308; [4] CAS Proceedings, XXII, 76–90; [5] CGB, 'A', 123

Loot—see LOTE

LORD, Adam (*fl.* 1490–) Mason
Mason (*latamus*); on 29 June 1490 was granted by the Bishop of Ely, John Alcock, a fee of £2 yearly for life so long as he should remain in the city of Ely, and 8d. a day when employed. This grant was confirmed by the Prior and Convent on 5 July. Lord may have been identical with ADAM VERTUE. He was probably the designer of *Bishop Alcock's Chantry* in *Ely Cathedral*, built at this time.
CUL, Add. MS. 6392, *f.* 417

LORYMERE, Henry (*fl.* 1488–1489) Marbler
Of London; in 1488–89 was paid £9 6s. 8d. in part payment for the making of the tomb of the 13th Earl of Oxford at *Earl's Colne*, Essex.
ERO, D/DA 139 (*L.S.*)

LOTE, Stephen [Loot, Loth, Lotte] (*fl.* 1381–†1417/18) Mason
Probably came from Newington-next-Hythe, Kent. Was warden under HENRY YEVELEY of the new lodge of *St. Paul's Cathedral* in 1381–82, taking pay of 4s. 6d. a week.[1] Between 1390 and 1394 he carried out works for the Queen, Anne of Bohemia at her *Wardrobe* in London, payment for which was still outstanding after her death on 7 June 1394,[2] and at some time in 1393–94 he was working at 6d. a day upon the watergate of the *Savoy Palace* in London, for John of Gaunt, Duke of Lancaster.[3]
On 1 April 1395 Lote was partner to Yeveley in a contract for making a tomb for the King and Queen in *Westminster Abbey*, to be completed within two and a half years.[4] On 26 November 1394 Yeveley and Lote were paid £20 as an instalment for work done upon the tomb of Archbishop Langham in Westminster Abbey.[5]
In 1397 Lote and SIMON LAWYN were commissioned to take masons for the building of a place by the Earl of Rutland outside *Temple Bar*,[6] and on 29 July 1398 Lote, with Henry Yeveley and others, was witness at Wennington in Essex to a deed concerning property there.[7] On 6 October 1400 he became the King's Master Mason at *Westminster* and the *Tower of London*[8] in succession to Yeveley of whose will Lote was an executor. He seems to have acted as Yeveley's assistant in connection with the new works of the nave of *Canterbury Cathedral* for he, like Yeveley, received a robe of the suit of the esquires of the Prior of Christ Church in 1398. In 1400–01 Lote sold stone for the making of a chimney in the King's oratory in the Tower of London,[9] and in 1405 was paid £33 6s. 8d. for making the battlements on the east side of Westminster Hall.[10]

Lote had similar grants of robes at Canterbury in 1412 and 1416, the only years for which lists survive at this period, so that he was presumably consultant architect to the cathedral during the completion of the nave, the building of the new cloisters, and the continuation of the work on the transepts, which were not finished until after Lote's death.[11] He was almost certainly the designer of the pulpitum (*c.* 1410) and of the tomb of Henry IV (†1413) in the cathedral. Lote may also have continued Yeveley's work on *Maidstone Church*. In 1409 he was called in to give advice on the repair of *Rochester Bridge*, where he received 6s. 8d. for the hire of his counsel.[12] No doubt Lote was frequently passing Rochester Bridge on his journeys to Canterbury, and the bridge authorities were thus able to save the travelling expenses which they would otherwise have had to pay.

On 5 December 1414 Lote was granted protection for life from serving on juries and the like. It was in this year that he was put in charge of the great rebuilding of the royal manor of *Sheen*, Surrey, for Henry V.[13] Lote may soon after have been the designer of the new collegiate church of *Fotheringhay*, Northants., founded by the Duke of York; the Duke was killed at Agincourt in 1415, and Lote was engaged upon his tomb at the time of his (Lote's) death; as the work of the choir of the new church and the erection of the tomb were going on at Fotheringhay at the same time, it seems highly probable that the same mason would be the designer of both. The choir of Fotheringhay was destroyed in the 16th century, but the nave of the church was built after the model of the choir, according to a contract made with WILLIAM HOREWODE, mason, in 1434. In 1421 Peter Mabawe had left £4 to the building of the college and making of a window, showing that work was in progress.[14]

Lote acquired property in Essex with Henry Yeveley in 1394, and possessed lands at Wennington until his death.[15] In one case Lote is described as 'latoner' which may indicate that he produced monumental brasses.

On several occasions between 1391 and 1417 he was concerned with JOHN CLIFFORD and other masons in the transfer of properties connected with the London Bridge House in Bermondsey and Deptford.[16] Towards the end of his life he was put in charge of the King's works at *Portsmouth*, and this, no doubt, was connected with Henry V's invasion of France. Lote died in the winter of 1417/18, and his will, proved on 10 February 1417/18, contains many interesting particulars.[17] The will was made on 31 October 1417; Lote described himself as citizen and mason of London, and desired to be buried in St. Paul's churchyard next the great cross 'where the body of Alice my late wife lies buried'. A codicil of 7 December mentions that his sons and daughters were also buried there. Among his bequests were £10 to his parish church of St. Faith-within-St. Paul's and £1 to the church of 'Newton' (Newington-next-Hythe), Kent, 'to pray for my soul and the souls of my father and mother', who were presumably buried at Newington. He also left a wax torch to the church of 'Wynyngton' (Wennington) in Essex, where he held land.

To THOMAS MAPILTON, citizen and mason of London, he left 13s. 4d. a year for four years 'from my shops situate in the great cemetery of the church of St. Paul, London, in which John Parker and Walter Lucy dwell so that he be friendly and well disposed (*amicus et benevolens*) in the making of the tomb of the Duke of York'. (It may be noted that in 1422–23 the rent paid for these shops by Parker and Lucy to the Dean and Chapter was £1 13s. 4d.)[18] John Capell, his apprentice, was left 'my part of the shop also situated in the said cemetery and which I now occupy' with storehouses for stone and vacant land adjoining, subject to Capell's good behaviour, and the expending of half its value for the good of Lote's soul.

Robert Bery, citizen and fishmonger of London, and the said John Capell, were to have the house (*mansum*) 'which I inhabit', with the chapel, etc., and to make certain payments therefrom. Two other apprentices, Richard and John Stotheley, were to have £1 each, and Thomas Mapulton was left 'my whole bed in my chamber at Schen (Shene Palace) and all patterns that be there'.

WALTER WALTON, mason, was to have 13s. 4d. a year for four years from the rents of Lote's shops, and Robert Bery and Walter Walton were executors and residuary legatees. Various small bequests went to his servant, John Here; to Philip Vegerous, citizen of London; William Wilmoot; Peter Pountefrette; Katherine Wyseman; Master Thomas Wulvesley (perhaps THOMAS WOLVEY the mason); Stephen Wood, son of John at Wood, carpenter, dwelling in Mark Lane; Anne, daughter of Master John Nuburgh; Isabell, daughter of John Twyford, marbler; and Margaret, daughter of William Symonds, junior of 'Schene'.

The codicil is in the form of a memorandum or nuncupative testament 'that on the 7th day of December 1417 in the new lodge (*le nove logge*) of our Lord the King of England at Portsmouth . . . Master Stephen Loot principal master and keeper of the masons of our lord the King as well at Schene as at Portesmoth being in good health of mind but sick in body made this codicil'. Thomas Mapulton, mason, Robert de Bury, fishmonger of London, and Walter Walton, mason, were each left a piece of silver with a cover, while 'his cover that is by itself at London' was to go to the parish church of Hythe in Kent to be made into a chalice. Thomas Mapilton was present at the making of the codicil and was added as co-executor; he was to have a bed of 'tapisserwerk' with a coverlet cut for the same, and 'all and singular necessary belongings that are in his (Lote's) kitchen and room in London'.

Mapilton was also to have the terms still to come to Lote from John Studeley his apprentice. Ten marks were left to the church of St. Thomas at Portsmouth for its repairs, and other bequests were 'To Alice Chaumberleyn of "Braynford" (Brentford) a nut with a cover of silver which Dan John her son, monk of Christ Church, Canterbury, while he lived gave to him', and to Katherine the woman looking after him in his infirmity until death.

He left his one grey 'Ambeler' to Robert Bedyngton, knight of the Lord King, and 'he willed that our Lord the King if it pleased him should have his mule, otherwise he left the said mule to the reverend father in Christ and lord Thomas Langley Bishop of Durham and now Chancellor'. Henry V, in appointing WILLIAM COLCHESTER to succeed Lote, stated in the warrant that he was to be 'maistre mason as maister Steven was'.[19]

Lote was not one of the greatest of mediaeval architects, but he was evidently a competent and trustworthy craftsman, well fitted to carry on the work of Henry Yeveley and to form a link with the younger generation, of which Mapilton was the leader. All the close associates of Yeveley, John Clifford, Walter Walton, and Lote, died within twelve months, September 1417 to September 1418. William Colchester, who succeeded Lote as King's Mason, only survived him for two years, so that by 1420 Mapilton was left almost without a rival.

KJI; KJY; (APD; BAA); HKW, I, 213–14
[1] *PRO*, E.101–473–1; [2] *Ibid.*, E.101–502–19; [3] A, XXIV, 299 ff.; [4] RF, III, iv, 105; *PRO*, E.101–473–10; [5] HMC, 4R, 179; *WAM*, 6318; [6] CPR 1396–9, 92; [7] CCR 1405–9, 88; [8] CPR 1399–1401, 361; [9] *PRO*, E.101–502–23 (*L.F.S.*); [10] *Ibid.*, E.101–502–26 (*L.F.S.*); [11] OCC; [12] BRB, 84; [13] CPR 1413–16, 270; HKW, II, 998; [14] *PCC* 55 Marche in AJ, LXX, 279 (*S.A.C.*); [15] F. W. Steer in EAS, XXIV, 48–50; *LHR*, 123(34); [16] LBH, H.25, 26, 28; I, 1; L.R. 71, 72; [17] *PCC*, 40 Marche (*A.O.*); [18] *PRO*, Eccl. 2–137–171463(2); [19] *Ibid.*, C.81/1364 (*R.L.S.*)

Loudham, Thomas de—see LUDHAM

LOUNE, William (*fl.* 1434) Mason
In 1434 constructed a niche on the west side of the Lollards' Tower at *Lambeth Palace*.
GLP, 52–6

LOVE, William (*fl.* 1376–   ) Carpenter
Warden (*apparator*) ordaining the work of the carpenters under Master HUGH HERLAND at the royal manor of *Havering*, Essex, in 1376, when he was paid 3s. 6d. a week for 17 weeks during alterations to the chapel.
SHB, 53; *PRO*, E.101–464–30 (*L.F.S.*)

LOVEDAY, Richard (*fl.* 1501) Carver
Of Middleton, Suffolk; about 1501 contracted to make a screen between the nave and chancel of *Carlton St. Peter Church* next Kelsale, Suffolk, near Saxmundham. The work was to be done for the churchwardens, who were to pay 11s. 8d. on completion, in addition to 10s. already paid by Robert Bumpsted, priest, 'to Mr. Richard Loueday grauour and Robert Willatt of Middilton seruant of the said Richard'.
CCN, 85 Popy

LOVEDAY, Thomas (*fl.* 1503–†1536) Carpenter
Of Sudbury, Suffolk; later of Gestingthorpe and Castle Hedingham, Essex. The first known reference to him is in a deed dated 22 May 1503, when he was associated with John Wyner of Sudbury, draper, over the sale of two messuages with gardens in Sudbury to Robert Fynch of Bulmer, Essex, clerk, and Joan Dawson of the same, widow.[1] Between 1505 and 1510 he was the chief carpenter employed by Thomas Lucas, Solicitor-General, in the building of *Little Saxham Hall*, Suffolk, where the chief mason was JOHN BROND of Bury St. Edmunds.[2] He entered into several contracts with his employer, covering different parts of the building, and supervised the selection and felling of timber. In the autumn of 1505 he went to London to see the house of Angel Donne ('Aungil Donn ys hows') in Tower Street near St. Margaret Pattens Church. Angel Donne was a wealthy merchant and his house was notable for a belvedere tower of brick (added by Sir John Champneis *c.* 1530–40), which is singled out for mention by Stow in his *Survey of London* as 'the first that ever I heard of in any private mans house'.[3] He also made several visits to *Hornham Hall*, near Thaxted, Essex, which Thomas Lucas prescribed as the model of his house and on which Loveday may also have worked. In 1515 Thomas Loveday was one of the twenty-four burgesses of Sudbury who with the mayor and five former mayors subscribed their names to a set of regulations for the government of the town.[4]

On 1 November 1516 Loveday, still 'of Sudbury', contracted for much of the woodwork at *St. John's College, Cambridge*, for which he was to receive just over £100.[5] He undertook to make the stalls and roodloft of the chapel, three pairs of gates, ten doors, a 'Lantorn' over the stair turret of the gate tower, the floors of chambers, and desks for the library. The stalls were to be as those in Jesus College, the seats, roodloft, and library desks as those in Pembroke Hall. The stalls are now in the new chapel built in 1864–69; part of the rood screen is in Whissendine Church, Rutland. No detailed building accounts for the college are known to exist, but it is probable that Loveday had been the chief carpenter from the beginning of building operations in 1511 and that he was responsible also for the hammer-beam roof of the hall and the roof of the chapel destroyed in 1869. In 1528–29, doubtless through his connection with St. John's, he was employed at *King's Hall*, where the entrance gate-tower (now the Great Gate of Trinity College), which had for many years stood half built, was at last completed.[6] He was paid £8 for making the upper floor and roof, but the last instalment was not received until 1535. He also made the floors in the four turrets.

The Lay Subsidy rolls of 1523–24 show Thomas Loveday assessed under Gestingthorpe, a village in Essex about 5 miles from Sudbury.[7] In *Gestingthorpe Church* his name and that of his wife Alice are carved on the double hammer-beam roof of the nave, probably as two of the donors, but there can be very little doubt that it had been designed and constructed by Loveday.[8] It shows affinities both with the hall roof at St. John's College, Cambridge, and with the double hammer-beam roof over the nave of the church at *Castle Hedingham*, where Loveday was living when he made his will. On stylistic grounds both the roof at Castle Hedingham and the little hammer-beam roof at *Sturmer Church*, near Haverhill, may be attributed to him, and there are several other late roofs among the churches of north Essex for which he is likely to have been responsible, e.g. the south aisle roof at *Steeple Bumpstead*, the roofs of the north aisle, the chancel, and the Macwilliam Chapel at *Stambourne* and the north aisle roof at *Wimbish* (dated 1534). Loveday's work shows little refinement; it tends to be rather heavy and cumbrous and is marked by a multiplicity of roll mouldings. Shortly before his death Loveday had been roofing part of the church of *Little Coggeshall Abbey*, as appeared in evidence given by one of the monks who stated (23 January 1536) that Loveday should have been paid 100 marks but that he had only received £30.[9]

Loveday's will, dated 27 December 1535,[10] describes him as of Castle Hedingham, where he wished to be buried in the churchyard of St. Nicholas. He refers to his wife Alice, two sons and a daughter, and to John Sibley, who was perhaps his wife's brother or nephew. He left his house to his wife for life with remainder to John Sibley. He mentions the 'instruments and tolys' that belonged to his

'occupacion of carpynters craft'. He probably died early in 1536 since the will is endorsed 1535 (Old Style) but without particulars of probate. From the will of John Sibley,[11] who died in 1570, it appears that the names of Loveday's children, whom he describes as his 'kinsfolke', were Richard, John, and Joan. The name of *John LOVEDAY* appears in the Lay Subsidy rolls of 1523–24 assessed under Castle Hedingham.[7]

A.O.; J.H.H.

[1] Bodl., Suffolk Charters, Nos. 371, 373; [2] *BM*, Add. MS. 7097, *ff.* 175 *et seq.* Extracts in GHT, 139–51; [3] SSL, 1633 ed., p. 137; [4] SHS, 24–33; [5] SHB, 571–2; WCC, II, 243–4; [6] WCC, II, 452–4; [7] *PRO*, E.179-108-163; [8] RCHM, *Essex*, I, pp. xxvii–xxviii, 99, 100; [9] LPH, IX, p. 60; [10] *PPR*, Archdeaconry of Essex, unregistered will; [11] *PPR*, Commissary of Essex & Herts., 138 Meade

LOVELL, Thomas (*fl. c.* 1480–1501) Mason

Freemason, engaged by Robert Long of Steeple Ashton, Wilts., to rebuild the north aisle of *Steeple Ashton Church* for £80.[1] At Long's death in 1501[2] only £31 had been paid and Lovell, who had finished the work, sued Long's executors for the balance. Lovell must have carried out the complete rebuilding of the nave with its porches and the chancel chapels. The aisles are vaulted and the central nave was intended to have, but did not receive, a stone vault.

AJ, LXXVII, 351

[1] *PRO*, Early Chancery proc. 367–38; [2] *PCC*, 4 Blamyr

Lovyns, John—see LEBONS

LOWE, Stephen (*fl.* 1546–1552) Mason

Mason employed by the town of *Shrewsbury* to rebuild the stone bridge in 1546–48, and probably to design the old buildings of the *Free School* (now the Public Library) in 1551–52.

HMC, 15R, x, 35–6

Lubyns—see LEBONS

LUDHAM, Thomas [Loudham] (*fl.* 1344–1348) Cleric

Mistakenly described as master mason of York Minster from 1347. In 1345 he was described as 'dominus' and as keeping the keys of the fabric to the exclusion of the master mason. He was still in charge of the fabric in 1348. (See PACENHAM, THOMAS DE.)

APD

LUKE, Henry (*fl.* 1412–1417) Carpenter

Received livery among the craftsmen (*artifices*) as leading carpenter of *Canterbury Cathedral* in the surviving lists of Christmas livery for 1412, 1416 and 1417.

Bodl., MS. Tanner 165

LUVE, William (*fl.* 1310–1313) Mason

Was master mason (*cementarius*) of *Exeter Cathedral* in succession to ROGER from 1310 to 1313, when the choir was nearing completion. He received fees of £6 13*s*. 4*d*. yearly, and £1 12*s*. 0*d*. in rent was paid for his house.

CEF; (BPE); AEC, i, 66, 68, 70

LYLE, John (*fl.* 1481–   ) Mason

Superseded ROBERT STEYNFORTH as warden of the masons at *Kirby Muxloe Castle*, Leics., in October 1481, under JOHN COWPER. Lyle had not previously worked at Kirby Muxloe and his origin is unknown.

LAS, xi

LYNCHE, Henry (*fl.* 1399–1400) Mason

Mason of London, who on 1 December 1399 received a silver censer worth £5 in part payment for works he had done on the hospice of John Holand, Earl of Huntingdon, in Thames Street, *London*.

PRO, E.159–176 (East., Recorda, rot. 44)

LYNDESEY, John (*fl.* 1353–1366) Carver

In 1353–54 was making images for the stalls in the chapel of *Windsor Castle*, being paid 3*s*. 4*d*. a week.[1] On 10 December 1365 he was paid £20 in part of £50 for a retable with carved figures for St. George's Chapel, Windsor; and on 23 October 1366 a further instalment of £6 13*s*. 4*d*. for what is evidently the same wooden retable was paid to 'William de Lyndeseye', carver of wooden images in London.[2]

[1] *PRO*, E.101–492–30 (*L.F.S.*); [2] DIE, 187–8

LYNDON, Peter (*fl.* 1458–   ) Bricklayer

German (Docheman); at *Tattershall College*, Lincs., in 1458 built for £3 5*s*. 10*d*. a brick turret at the north-east corner of the buildings from the depth of 24 feet to a height of 15 feet.

De L'Isle & Dudley MS. 219 (*L.F.S.*)

LYNES, John (*fl.* 1433–1434) Mason

In 1433–34 John Lynes, stonemason, was paid £3 6*s*. 8*d*. for repairs to the gable of the chancel of *Worstead Church*, Norfolk.

NRO, DCN, Cellarer no. 159 (*S.A.C.*; *P.C.*)

LYNG, Hervey de (*fl.* 1385–1415) Mason

Senior mason at work on the cloisters of *Norwich Cathedral* from 1385 to 1415. At first he was certainly subordinate to ROBERT WODE-HIRST and is never described as master in the surviving rolls. In 1385–86 he worked for 48 weeks at 2*s*. 2*d*. weekly; in the following year he was paid for 14 weeks 4 days' work, but also received a robe price 9*s*. 10½*d*.; in 1388–89 he was paid for 33 weeks, with a robe price 13*s*., and his expenses going to Burwell and Santon on various occasions. His name again appears in 1411–12, when he and his son were paid for 11 weeks' work at 6*s*. 8*d*. jointly, with 10*d*. a week for his son's board in addition. Lyng received a robe price 13*s*. 4*d*. in 1413–14, and he and his son were paid £5 5*s*. 0*d*. for their work; in 1415–16 they did 9 weeks' work for £3. Hervey Lyng was no doubt the warden or resident master who continued to supervise routine work whose design had already been settled. As 'Henry' Lyng he was in charge of works carried out for the Almoner of Norwich Cathedral Priory at *Wicklewood Church*, Norfolk, in 1412.[2]

[1] *NCM*, rolls 1058–60, 1068–70; [2] roll 520 (*P.C.*)

LYNGWODE, William (*fl.* 1308–1310) Carpenter (*Lingwood, Norf.*)

Carpenter of Blofield, Norfolk; began to make the choir-stalls of *Winchester Cathedral* in 1308, when Bishop Henry Woodlock (1305–16) wrote to John Salmon, Bishop of Norwich (1299–1325) to request that Lyngwode should be excused from doing suit at the manor court of Blofield until Michaelmas 1309. Apparently the work was not then finished, and a second letter was sent to ask for a similar concession until its completion.

The Winchester stalls are among the greatest masterpieces of mediaeval woodwork, and the unusual circumstances of Lyngwode's employment strongly suggest that he had already become famous, but the stall-work at Norwich Cathedral is of the 15th century, and nothing of his period seems to exist there now.

AJ, LXXXIV, 125

LYNNE, Richard (*fl.* 1333–†1341) Mason

Worked as a setter at St. Stephen's Chapel in *Westminster Palace* in 1333;[1] his will, proved in 1341, shows that he lived in the parish of St. Andrew, Castle Baynard, London. He left to his daughter 1 acre of arable land and half his sheep at Enfield, as well as 40 quarters of malt and 6 quarters of grout-malt; to his son he bequeathed all his 35 sheep at Brixton.[2] If Lynne were an architect at all, it would have been in a small way, but he was evidently a man of some substance who was able to combine farming with the practice of his craft.

[1] LKC; [2] SWL, I, 452

LYNNE, Thomas (*fl.* 1501–   ) Mason

Was appointed resident mason at *Bath Abbey* during the rebuilding, begun in 1501, on the recommendation of ROBERT VERTUE.

SAP, LX, pt. ii, 1–4

LYNSTED, Robert (*fl.* 1522–†1542) Mason (*Lynsted, Kent*)

Admitted freemason of Canterbury in 1522 by his marriage with Dorothy, daughter of Robert Sare, grocer;[1] he was working as a hardhewer at 3s. 4d. a week in 1531–32 at *Westminster Palace*,[2] and in 1539–40 was the warden of the masons at the building of *Sandgate Castle*, Kent, being paid at the rate of 10d. a day.[3] Lynsted worked under STEPHEN VON HASCHENPERG, the German engineer and 'devisor' but the design of detail was probably the work of JOHN MOLTON. Lynsted certified the accounts, signing his name and adding his mason's mark. Lynsted is at first described as warden, signing with the mark ✷; from June until September 1539 he is described as 'Upper Warden', having Nicholas Rychard as underwarden, but does not sign; while from 14 September onwards he is described as 'Mr. Mason', signs as 'mason', and with the mark ⅋, which he perhaps acquired on attaining mastership. In spite of his fairly high standing in the administration of the works, he is found in the late summer of 1541 working on a comparatively unimportant job at *Dartford*, at the reduced wage of 9d. a day.[4] He was also, however, paid 7d. a day extra in respect of the services of his son Francis. Robert Lynsted died in 1542.[5] *Francis LYNSTED* was working at Dartford on his own account at 8d. a day in 1543,[6] was admitted a freeman of Canterbury by patrimony in 1544,[7] and died two years later.[8]

[1] CFC; [2] PRO, E.36–251 (*G.P.J.*); [3] AC, XX; *BM*, Harl. MS. 1647, 1651; [4] KJS; [5] Canterbury wills, A.22, 244; [6] *Bodl.*, Rawl. D.783; [7] CFC; [8] Canterbury wills, A.24, 100

MACHON, Richard (*fl.* 1347–1348) Mason

Master mason in charge of works on *Emlyn Castle*, Carmarthenshire, in 1347–48. He took 1s. 2d. a week for marking the stones for the working masons.

HKW, II, 647

MACHUN, Richard le (*fl.* 1285–1290) Mason

Master mason of the works of *Norwich Cathedral* in 1285–86 when he received £2 4s. 0d. pay, in 1288–89 when he was paid £3 6s. 8d., and in 1289–90 when his fee was 15s. and timber was bought for his house. He was probably identical with RICHARD CURTEYS.

NCM, rolls 214–16, 1030

MAFELD, John ['Masele'] (*fl.* 1440–1443) Carpenter

John Mafeld and William Mafeld, carpenters, undertook by a contract for £26 13s. 4d. to make the timberwork of a range of new chambers on the west side of the inner court at *South Wingfield Manor*, Derbyshire, for Ralph, Lord Cromwell. They received £4 in 1440, £6 13s. 4d. in 1441, £1 0s. 4d. in 1442 and £12 2s. 11d. in 1443, when a further sum due of £3 6s. 9d. was still unpaid. For the erection of the framework John Mafeld was assisted by William Wright and his servant, hired at 11d. a day between them for 11 days. Mafeld was also one of the carpenters engaged on making centering, scaffolds and other things for the work of the hall (see RICHARD NORTH).[1] Mafeld's name has been mistakenly transcribed as 'Masele'.[2]

[1] KAO, U 1475 M 207, by kind permission of Viscount De L'Isle, V.C., K.G.; [2] TSW, 432–3

MAGHULL, John de [Moghale] (*fl.* 1283–1291) Carpenter (*Maghull, Lancs.*)

Was master carpenter of the works of *Aberystwyth Castle* in 1283, and was probably the John the Carpenter at *Harlech Castle* in 1289, making joists and roofing the south tower towards the town. In 1291 he was bailiff of Conway.

HKW, I, 305, 363

MAGSDEN, Robert (*fl.* 1517–1523) Mason

In 1517 HENRY SMYTH left to Robert Magsden 'all my Bokis of purtiturys', that is portraitures in the sense of designs. Magsden was paid 12d. in 1523 for the workmanship of six shields of freestone with the arms of the Goldsmiths' Company, to be set on the ovens in the *Bridge House*, Southwark, for which Sir John Thurston, citizen and goldsmith, had left a legacy of £200.

WTB, 97

MAIDSTONE, John (*fl.* 1387–1390) Carpenter

Was chief carpenter at *King's Hall*, Cambridge, *c.* 1387–90 when a new hall was built. An account beginning 15 August 1387 contains a schedule of sums paid to 'John

Maydeston Carpenter' amounting to £33 6s. 8d. in all.[1] In 1390 he received fifteen payments amounting to £24 9s. 8d.; the first was made on the morrow of St. Gregory (13 March).[2] It was assumed by Willis and Clark that John Maidstone was the master mason,[3] but he is definitely described as carpenter. The master mason may have been JOHN SHARP.

A.O.

[1] *TCM, KHA*, iv, 24; [2] *Ibid*., iii, 46; [3] WCC, II, 439

MAIDSTONE, John (*fl*. 1352–?1397) Mason

A John Maydeston, paid as a common mason at 5½d. a day, worked on *St. Stephen's Chapel, Westminster*, in 1352.[1] In 1391–92 and again in 1396–97, John Maydestone senior, mason, carried out taskwork on properties belonging to the London Bridge House.[2]

[1] BBW, 167; *PRO*, E.101–471–6; [2] *LBH*, accounts, 11, m.9 (xxviii); 15, m.7 (xxxii)

MAJANO, Giovanni da (*fl*. 1521–1536) Sculptor

Italian sculptor; was already working for Cardinal Wolsey by 1521 when he asked payment for eight painted and gilt terra-cotta medallions of Roman Emperors for *Hampton Court*, and three reliefs of the works of Hercules. He must also have produced the relief of Wolsey's arms, dated 1525. In 1527 he was at work in connection with a banqueting hall being made at *Greenwich*, and in the next year was receiving an annuity of £20 from Henry VIII. After Wolsey's fall, Majano worked at *Windsor Castle* with BENEDETTO ROVEZZANO to complete the tomb intended for Wolsey but which was being finished for the King. For Henry VIII he doubtless also made terra-cotta medallions, fragments of which were found on the site of *Whitehall Palace* in 1939, and which are seen in views of the 'Holbein Gate', Whitehall.

TBK, XIV, 124–5

Mallyng, Thomas—see CAKE

MALTON, William de (*fl*. 1335–1338) Mason

Of Huggate; was appointed master mason of *Beverley Minster* on 25 October 1335, in succession to WILLIAM DE LA MARE. Malton supervised the completion of the nave of Beverley, but the design followed closely that of the earlier work farther east. He has a better claim to architectural distinction as the probable designer of the tomb of Lady Eleanor Percy, erected about 1340, the highest development of its type before the Black Death.

There is no reason to doubt that the architect was the William de Malton to whom Nicholas de Hugate, Provost of Beverley, left a horse and a piece of plate with a cover in 1338. Hitherto no other documentary evidence for his career has come to light, but a serious case has been made out by Mr. M. R. Petch for reconstructing Malton's working life as a mason at York Minster from *c*. 1315–20, then at *Bainton Church* and from the early 1330s on the north aisle wall arcade of the nave at Beverley Minster, on a basis of his mark (an X formed of pairs of lines) and the graffito 'Maltun'. As a master, stylistic evidence links the north nave aisle with the reredos, with the Percy tomb, and with the priest's tomb in *Welwick Church*.

MBM; PWM

MALVERNE, Alduin de (*fl. c*. 1120–   ) ? Mason

Was surveyor of the works of the *Wye Bridge* at *Hereford*, originally built about 1120. It is rather unlikely that he was the designer of the bridge. It is not clear whether the surveyor of the Hereford bridge was identical with his namesake who was the founder of Great Malvern Priory, *c*. 1086.

(APD; BAA); LI, VIII, 58; cf. VCH, *Worcs*., II, 136–7; PCH, ii, 174

MAN, Robert (*fl*. 1425–1444) Benedictine Monk

Benedictine monk of Peterborough, and from 1425 to *c*. 1444 Prior of the Benedictine House at Daventry. At a visitation in 1442 he was said to be 'of no account in matters temporal . . . albeit he has some degree of experience in the craft of stonemason and carpenter'.

TVR, I, 61; VCH, *Northants*., II, 113

MANNING, John [Mannyng] (*fl*. 1545–†1551) Joiner

Apprentice of JOHN RIPLEY; was granted the office of Chief Joiner of the King's works in England in succession to THOMAS WARE on 22 October 1545, at the suit of Sir Anthony Denny.[1] He was also to have the office of chief joiner in the Tower of London, with a house there when the house and the office were vacated by JOHN RIPLEY; Ripley was, however, still in office when Manning died on 10 July 1551, to be succeeded as chief joiner of the

MAPILSDEN, ROBERT

works by Richard Pye.[2]

[1] LPH, xx, ii, 706(50), 707(41); [2] CPR 1550–3, 162–3

MAPILSDEN, Robert (*fl.* 1504–1509) Carpenter

Was master carpenter at *Calais* in 1504, in succession to WILLIAM TEMPLE. He presumably held office until the appointment of GREGORY BUKMER in 1509.

HKW, III, 419

MAPILTON, John [Mapulton, Mapylton] (*fl.* 1390–†1407) Marbler (*Mappleton, Derbs.*)

On 10 June 1390 pardon of outlawry was granted to John Mapilton, mason, for not appearing before the Justices of the Common Bench to answer John Edward, citizen of London, for retaining in his service Edmund Brecham, late the servant of the said John Edward who had left without his leave, and for refusing to restore him when required to do so, he having surrendered to the Fleet prison.[1]

In 1395–97 Mapilton, described as 'marbeler', acquired premises in Fleet Street, which were disposed of by Agnes his widow in 1407, after her remarriage to Robert Fann, skinner.[2]

John Mapilton, marbler of London, occurs in 1400,[3] and on 2 August 1407 the will was proved of John Mapylton, citizen and marbler, of St. Dunstan's, Fleet Street.[4] In the will, made 9 February 1406/7, Mapilton desired to be buried in the church of the Carmelites, Fleet Street, before the image of St. Christopher painted on the wall, next to the grave of William Abyndon deceased. In addition to a bequest of 20*s.* to the house of Carmelites and one of 3*s.* 4*d.* to the high altar of St. Dunstan's, a further 20*s.* was left for the making of 'le Rodeloft' there, 13*s.* 4*d.* to the Fraternity of St. John Baptist of the Tailors of London, 3*s.* 4*d.* to the Fraternity of St. Dunstan, and £4 3*s.* 4*d.* between the four orders of friars. To the church of 'Eleleston' (? Elvaston), Derbyshire, where he was born (*ubi sum oriundus*), Mapilton left a vestment and a silver chalice, and 6*s.* 8*d.* to Swarkeston ('Swareston') Bridge in the same county. Various bequests were made to his mother Agnes, sister Isabel, brothers Philip, Thomas (my best furred robe), Peter, and Roger; 40*s.* to William Pychard when out of his apprenticeship, and 20*s.* to Walter Showe his apprentice. Mapilton's tenement in the parish of St. Dunstan's, and all his marble stones

(*petras meas marmoreas*) were to be sold by his executors; in lieu of dower in this tenement, his wife Agnes was to have £40, the residue of household goods unbequeathed, and the term still to come in the apprentice Walter. Agnes, with Thomas Mallyng and William Mirton, were executors. It seems all but certain that John's brother Thomas was identical with THOMAS MAPILTON, the mason.

[1] CPR 1388–92, 258; [2] *LHR*, 124(111), 126(95), 135(19, 23, 43); [3] CCR 1399–1402, 284; [4] SWL, II, 375; *PPR*, Archd. Ct. of London, I, f.179

MAPILTON, Thomas [Mapulton, Mapyltone, 'Stapylton'] (*fl.* 1408–†1438) Mason

Mason of London, and probably brother of JOHN MAPILTON, mason and marbler. His first post of importance was, however, that of master mason at *Durham Cathedral*, where he was in charge of the building of the cloisters from 1408 to 1416. He was given a yearly fee of £5 6*s.* 8*d.* and a robe of the value of 13*s.* 4*d.*[1]

At Durham he seems to have rented a house in the Bailey or Elvet from the Prior of Finchale, to whom in 1411 he owed one quarter's rent of 6*s.* in arrear.[2]

In 1416 he returned to London and at any rate until 1418 was warden of the masons at *Westminster Palace* and the *Tower of London*. He was described as 'citizen and mason of London' in the will of STEPHEN LOTE made in 1417, and was evidently one of Lote's friends, and arrangements were made that he should continue Lote's work on the tomb of the Duke of York, receiving a rent-charge of 13*s.* 4*d.* a year for four years after Lote's death. Mapilton also had bequests of a piece of silver with a cover, Lote's bed and 'patterns' in his room at Shene Palace, and the terms still to come from Lote's apprentice John Stothley. Mapilton had evidently entered the royal service at this time, and was present in the 'new lodge' at *Portsmouth* when the codicil to Lote's will was made on 7 December 1417. Between 1417 and 1422 Mapilton was involved in legal difficulties over goods which had belonged to John Chamberleyn, clerk of the King's works at Portsmouth, and which had been given to him by Alice, Chamberleyn's widow.[3]

Portsmouth was being used as the base for Henry V's second campaign in France, and on 6 March 1417/18 Mapilton and Robert Rodyngton received a commission to take eight discreet and sufficient stone-cutters and bring them beyond the seas to the King's

194

presence with all possible speed.[4] Mapilton was probably in France with the King's retinue until peace was made in the spring of 1420.

A passage in Vasari's Lives opens up the possibility that as soon as the peace made travelling feasible, Mapilton went on to *Florence* to give his counsel on the vaulting of the central space of the Duomo. Vasari states that Filippo Brunelleschi, architect to the church of S. Maria del Fiore, suggested to the wardens that they should obtain the advice of foreign and Italian architects of repute in consultation; the wardens agreed to this in 1417, but 'a great deal of time was lost before the architects assembled. They were summoned from afar by means of directions given to the Florentine merchants living in France, Germany, England and Spain, who were commissioned to spend any amount of money to obtain the principal, most experienced and gifted men of those regions. At length, in 1420, all these foreign masters and those of Tuscany were assembled at Florence with all the principal Florentine artists, and Filippo returned from Rome. They all met together in the Opera of S. Maria del Fiore, in the presence of the consuls and wardens, and a chosen number of the ablest citizens, so that, after the opinion of everyone had been taken, the method of vaulting the tribune might be determined.'

At the time that the Florentine merchants were trying to obtain the advice of the principal masters, practically the whole of the older generation of English masons was dead; JOHN CLIFFORD, STEPHEN LOTE, and WALTER WALTON all died in the year 1417–18, and WILLIAM COLCHESTER was apparently fully occupied as mason to York Minster and Westminster Abbey, as well as filling the office of the King's Master Mason, until his death which took place on 5 July 1420. Of course it was Brunelleschi's own project of an immense dome which was the outcome of the consultation, but the mere fact of such a visit to Italy would no doubt greatly increase the prestige of any English mason. Whether or no Mapilton was one of those who visited Florence, he was promoted to the office of King's Master Mason on 6 June 1421, with the title of 'Disposer of mason's work at Westminster',[5] and about this time he became consultant mason to *Canterbury Cathedral*, where he designed the south-west tower,

on which work was in progress from 1423 to 1434.[6] This work was encouraged by Archbishop Chichele, a keen patron of architecture. Owing to his official position, Mapilton was only able to visit Canterbury from time to time, the actual work being carried on under JOHN MORYS, the warden of the lodge masons.

Probably on one of his journeys to Canterbury, Mapilton gave advice to the wardens of *Rochester Bridge* in 1422, for which he was paid £4.[7] Stephen Lote had given advice there under precisely similar circumstances. Mapilton's name, as 'master mason' appears in the lists of esquires of the Prior of Christ Church, Canterbury, who received robes in 1423 and 1429, and it is probable that he continued to hold the position of consultant architect there until 1432, when his place was taken by RICHARD BEKE, chief mason of London Bridge.[8] Mapilton may have found himself too busy to continue regular visits to Canterbury, for in 1429 he undertook the building of *St. Stephen's Church, Walbrook*, in London, and on 11 May he was one of eight important persons who laid memorial stones on the foundations of the new church; 'Maistir Thomas Mapilton, the kyngis mason than beyng Maistir mason of the seyd chirche werke'. The chief promoter of this work was Sir Robert Chichele, grocer, a brother of the archbishop. The church was not completed until 1439, shortly after Mapilton's death.[9]

In 1429–30 Mapilton was called in by the *Abbey of Bury St. Edmunds* to survey the great western tower which was in a dangerous condition. A payment of 26s. 8d. was made to 'Master Thomas Mapyltone, mason of the lord King, coming from London to survey the great bell-tower and giving his counsel upon repairing the same', while 6s. 8d. was given to 'another mason' who accompanied him, and 3s. 4d. to their servants.[10] The tower was evidently too far gone to be saved, for the south side fell on 18 December 1430, and the east side a year later. The remainder was pulled down in 1432, and in 1436 a contract was entered into with JOHN WODE, mason of Colchester, for the rebuilding.[11] It is quite likely that Mapilton may have supplied designs for the work.

Mapilton was in charge of works at Portsmouth in 1420–22 and in 1430 and his pay of 12d. per day was being charged to the account for works at Portsmouth 'Tower' in

1437–38.[12] In 1434/5 he received his yearly robe, together with a second one in arrear for 1433/4. In 1434 Mapilton was also concerned with extensive repairs to the *Prince's Wardrobe* in London.[13]

In 1435–36 Mapilton was admitted to membership of the London Skinners' Fraternity of Our Lady of the Assumption, which had an altar in the church.of St. John the Baptist, Walbrook,[14] and he must have died towards the end of 1438, for he is mentioned as being dead in the patent of appointment of ROBERT WESTERLEY, his successor as King's Mason, granted on 6 January 1438/9.

There are no surviving royal works of importance dating from the period of Mapilton's office, but he probably designed the Lollards Tower of *Lambeth Palace* for Archbishop Chichele; the tower was begun in 1434. On the other hand it must be noted that it was JOHN THIRSK (Triske) who provided a statue of St. Thomas of Canterbury for the river front of the tower, being called 'Magister de les Fremasons'. Mapilton's design for the western towers of Canterbury is a sturdy and typically English work, and had considerable influence on the towers of parish churches built in Kent during the succeeding half-century; notable examples of this school are the towers of Lydd (1442–46) and Tenterden (*c.* 1449–61) designed by THOMAS STANLEY, who was the principal lodge mason at Canterbury under Mapilton and John Morys. Mapilton was probably concerned with Chichele's foundations at *Higham Ferrers*, the *College* and *Bedehouse*, both begun about 1423, and showing points of style in common with the Canterbury tower. For the Archbishop's later colleges, *St. Bernard's* (now St. John's) and *All Souls*, at Oxford (1437), Mapilton may have produced the first plans which he did not live to carry out.

Thomas Mapilton may have had a son of the same name, for while he was consultant mason to Canterbury Cathedral in 1429, another *Thomas MAPILTON* received a livery from the prior as one of the lodge masons, but nothing further is known of his career.[15]

Roger MAPILTON [Mapulton] mason, appears in 1450 as of Tottenham, Middlesex, and in 1459 as of Watford, Herts., when he was pardoned for not appearing to answer William Horwode, citizen of London, touching a debt of 40*s.*[16] This WILLIAM HORWODE may have been the mason of Fotheringhay Church.

(APD; WKM)

[1] RDC; [2] RFP; [3] HKW, I, 214; *PRO, ECP*, 48, 232; [4] CPR 1416–22, 148; [5] *Ibid.*, 374; [6] WDC; AC, XLV, 37–47; [7] BRB, 84; [8] OCC; [9] LMT, V (1879), 330–1; [10] HMC, 14R, VIII, 125; [11] A, XXIII; [12] *PRO*, E.101–479–7, 25 (*L.F.S.*); [13] *BM*, Add. 17721, *f.* 39; HKW, II, 982; [14] Skinners' Co., MS. (*A.O.*); LSL, 79; [15] *Bodl.*, Tanner MS. 165; [16] CPR 1446–52, 345, 370; 1452–61, 454

MAPLETON, Goldyng (*fl.* 1425–) Carpenter

Carpenter of London; was paid 7*s.* 4*d.* in 1425 by the Merchant Taylors' Company for the design for their new kitchen (*pur portratur del patron de cuzine*).

SHB, 20

Mapulton, Mapyltone—see MAPILTON

MARAYS, William le (*fl.* 1296) Mason

Mason (*cementar'*) hired in 1296 to rebuild a fallen wall on the north side of the great east tower of *Mere Castle*, Wilts., with two new buttresses and an arch built above the entrance gate, for a total sum of £2. This had included purchase and carriage of freestone. A further 8*s.* 8*d.* was spent on digging and transport of rubble stone (*velutis petris*).

HMW, *Hundred of Mere*, 210 (*M. McG.*)

MARCHANT, Thomas [Marchaunt, Merchaunte] (*fl.* 1485–†1526) Mason

Mason of Norwich; admitted to the freedom in 1485–86.[1] In 1508 he was the first sworn master of the Norwich masons,[2] and died in 1526.[3]

(*A.O.*)
[1] EFN; [2] HTN, II, 29; [3] CCN, 92, 93 Hay3warde

MARE, William de la (*fl. c.* 1325–†1335) Mason

Was master mason of *Beverley Minster* until his death in 1335, when he was succeeded by WILLIAM DE MALTON. He cannot have held the office for many years, as in 1322 the mason was RALPH OF WHITBY. At this time the works of the nave were in progress, but the design followed that of the earlier work.

MBM

MARLOW, William [de Merlawe] (*fl.* 1284–1293) Mason

As Master William the mason, was in charge of building a chapel and new royal apartments in *Chester Castle* in 1284. In 1292–93 he was master of the works there when the new Outer Gatehouse was built.

HKW, II, 610–11

MARRY, Nicholas (*fl.* 1544–   ) Carver

'Graver' of Norwich; in 1544 carved the city arms on the beam over the gateway of Monastery Yard, Elm Hill, *Norwich*, being paid 15*d.* for two days' work. The beam was removed in 1914 and is now in the Norwich Museum.

(*A.O.*)   Norwich Museum

MARSH, Ralph atte [atte Mere] (*fl.* 1335–1339) Carpenter

Master carpenter at *Carisbrooke Castle* in 1335–39, during the period for which ADAM BRETON and then RICHARD LE TAYLLOUR, masons, were responsible. Marsh took 2*s.* per week.

HKW, II, 592–3

MARTYN, John (*fl.* 1351–1368) Mason

Was a layer at *Windsor Castle* and also a minor contractor there. He was being paid 5½*d.* a day from 1351 to 1356, and at 6*d.* in 1361–63. In 1362/3 he was in addition paid £40 and £16 13*s.* 4*d.* for making a vault at task, in 1364 £295 6*s.* 8*d.* (jointly with JOHN WELOT) for building a wall at task; in 1365–66 £102 13*s.* 4*d.* (jointly with Welot and HUGH KYMPTON) for building a wall at task; in 1367–68 £150 11*s.* 1*d.* , £5 6*s.* 8*d.*, and £2 6*s.* 8*d.* for building a wall at task, and in 1368 £90, £22, and £2 for building a wall, making a gate at task, and building a chimney. He may just possibly have been the mason of this name who was living in Oxford in 1380 and later, and worked on the barn of *New College* there in 1402–03.[1]

KJI; HKW, II, 877–80
[1] GOM, 116

MARTYN, Walter (*fl.* 1500–†1513) Mason

Worked at *Greenwich Palace*, *Westminster Palace*, and the *Tower of London*, from 1500 to 1502, but his position seems to have been little more than that of a working mason of good standing.[1]

He made his will on 24 April 1513 and it was proved on 7 June. In it he desired to be buried at St. Bartholomew's Priory, Smithfield, in the 'parish chapel' by his first wife, and left £2 to the reparations of the priory. After reference to his daughter Joan Martyn and his wife Margaret, he arranged for any mason's work he might have undertaken to be completed by his servant and two apprentices under the oversight of JOHN AYLMER.[2]

[1] *BM*, Egerton MS. 2358; [2] *PCC*, 23 Fetiplace

MARWE, John (*fl.* 1400–1442) Mason

Was admitted a freemason of Norwich in 1400/1,[1] and probably began the building of the *Norwich Guildhall* in 1407; he was in charge there in 1411 at 6*d.* a day, with 5*d.* a day for his brother Thomas Marwe. John Marwe worked there for 68 days during the year, and his brother Thomas for 59 days.[2] In 1428–29 Marwe was a feoffee of property in Trowse, along with JOHN WODEROFE, freemason.[3]

On 10 July 1432 John undertook to rebuild *Conisford Quay* for £53 6*s.* 8*d.* and cloth for a gown at Christmas, the Norwich authorities finding a house for him and his workmen.[4] He was a member of the Guild of St. George at Norwich, and a Common Councillor of the city.[5] In 1441 Marwe made a new window of freestone for the south side of the chancel of the church of *Thurlton*, Norfolk. He was paid 16*s.* 4*d.* for the window, which was to his own design. At the same time a new roof was built by JOHN DURRANT. The rectors were the Great Hospital, Norwich.[6] He is last mentioned in 1442 as a Brother and Alderman of the Guild of St. George.[7]

(KJI)
[1] EFN; [2] NA, XV, 164 ff.; [3] *NMR*, Court Roll 18, m.16; [4] SHB, 501–3; [5] HTN, II, 389, 399; [6] *NRO*, Great Hospital, 24.51 (*S.A.C.*); [7] NRC, IX, 31, 38, 39

MARYS, John [Maryce] (*fl.* 1442–   ) Mason

Mason of Stogursey, Som.; on 29 September 1442 contracted with the parishioners of Dunster to build the central tower of *Dunster Church* to the design of RICHARD POPE within three years. He was to be paid 13*s.* 4*d.* for every foot built, with £1 for the pinnacles.

SHB, 514–15; AJ, XXXVIII, 217

'Masele', John—see MAFELD

MASON, Andrew (*fl.* 1449–1450) Mason

With Robert Taillour, mason, rebuilt the chapel of *St. Mary Magdalene's Hospital, Durham* in 1449–50. They were paid £6 for making walls, windows, and doors, with two buttresses; this included a 'reward' in addition to the agreed price. The ruins of this chapel still exist.

(*A.O.*)   DAR, I, 238

MASON, Clement (*fl.* 1469–1471) Mason

Was apparently master mason at the building of *Ludlow Church* tower, Salop. The work began in 1453 but there is no evidence that he was employed from the beginning. In

1469 one John Peion was paid 3s. 4d. 'to fetche home Clement mason' from elsewhere; Clement was paid only 3s. 8d. for two weeks' work but he may not have been working full time, or else the low wage may be explained by the fact that a number of specialists were also called into consultation, only named as the 'Gloucestre mason' and 'the mason of COVENTRY' who were paid £1 6s. 8d. and 12s. 8d. respectively, and ROBERT KERVER II, who had 4d. for 'seeing the werk of the stepill'. The Gloucester mason may have been JOHN HOBBS.

SHR, 2S., I (1889) 235–43

Mason, Gilbert—see GILBERT the Mason II

MASON, John, I (*b.c.* 1348, *fl.* 1403) Mason
Was the master mason of the work of the fabric of *Chichester Cathedral* in 1403, while work was in progress on the Vicars' Close and also at the high altar. In giving evidence of malversation of building materials on 26 May 1403, Mason described himself as 55 years old.

(PCB); RRR, 116–21

MASON, John, II (*fl.* 1409–1414) Mason
Mason employed to build the new chapel of *Mettingham College*, Suffolk, from 1409 to 1414. In 1410–11 he was paid 5s. for his expenses on going to Lincolnshire for free-stone, and he spent most of the first two years at Mettingham with his men. In the three succeeding years he spent only an occasional week or fortnight on the site, being paid 2s. a week when present. The total paid to him for work done by his men amounted to more than £30.[1]

He was probably identical with the John Masun of Bungay who in 1422–23 was paid 12s. for making two 'lavatoria' of freestone for the cloisters of the college.[2]

APD; (AJ, VI (1849), 62–8)
[1] BM, Add. MS. 33985, ff. 55v.–79v.; [2] Ibid., f. 132v.

MASON, John, III (*fl.* 1479–   ) Mason
John Mason of 'Seghtford' (Seighford, Staffs.), mason, and Nicholas Mason of Stafford, mason, were sued for damages of 20 marks (£13 6s. 8d.) by John Harecourt in 1479, on the ground that they had contracted to build a tower at *Swynnerton* for a certain sum paid to them but had built it so negligently that it had collapsed.

(A.O.) WSS, NS, VI (1903), pt. i, 112

Mason, Nicholas—see MASON, John, III

MASON, Philip (*fl.* 1415) Mason
Undertook a contract to make the chapel of St. Anne in *Bridgwater Church*, Som., in 1415–16, when he was also paid 13s. 4d. for completing work on the Trinity Chapel.

SRS, LVIII (1943–5), No. 576

MASON, Richard (*fl.* 1398–1401) Mason
Mason working at *Winchester College* in 1398–99, when he fixed windows in the vestry and carried out other minor works. He was possibly the Richard Rede, mason, who made windows in a new room at the end of the hall in 1398–99. In 1399–1400 windows in the room over the Bursary (probably Cheese Room) were made by Richard Mason, who in 1401 was in charge of further works including the stables; the sum of 10s. was given in reward to him, and to the clerk writing the particulars of account. He was perhaps identical with RICHARD the Mason V.

WCM, Compotus rolls; Custus operum roll 1401

MASON, Robert le [Massoun] (*fl.* 1332–1337) Mason.
Master of the works of *London Bridge* in 1337 when he granted to Ralph de Haynton, chaplain, a quitrent from a tenement in the parish of St. Peter, Broad Street.[1] At the same time a 'Robert le Masoun' was living in the parish of St. Benet, Paul's Wharf, evidently he who in 1332 had been assessed to pay 1s. 4d. to the taxation in Castle Baynard Ward.[2] He may perhaps have been identical with ROBERT the Mason VI.
[1] LHR, 64 (101); [2] SCR, 224–5; UFT, 61 ff.

MASON, Robert (*fl.* 1472) Mason
At a Visitation held in 1472 it was stated that an agreement had not been performed by Robert Mason, to make a bell-tower for the parishioners of *Ampleforth*, Yorks. Order was given that it should be built by Easter 1474 under a penalty of 40s..

RFY, 255 (A.O.)

MASON, Thomas, I (*fl.* 1394–1395) Mason
Mason to *Whitby Abbey*, Yorks., in 1394–95 when he was paid £1 11s. 0d. for 93 days' work on the building of the Fee-house.

YHW, II, 927

MASON, Thomas, II (*fl.* 1498–   ) Mason
Mason, probably of Boston, Lincs. The accounts of the churchwardens of Leverton, about 5 miles north-east of Boston, contain a number of items connected with work on the steeple of *Leverton* in 1498. The stone quarry

seems to have been at or near Swineshead, about 7 miles west of Boston. A sum of £1 19s. 8d. was paid 'for ston at ye qwarryll' and 5d. for 'Expencys at ye qwarryll & at Boston as wye com howmward'. (Expenses doubtless covered drinks.) 'Thomas Macyn for goyng wyt us to ye quarryll' had another 4d. Further 'expencys at ye sam time' accounted for 1s. 2d. in addition.

Later 5d. was paid 'for a wendds (windlass, winch) & a man a day' and another trip to the quarry cost 6d. 'in expencys qwan wye went for Swynsyd fayr to the quarryll'; Swineshead Fair was kept on 2 October. Lastly, 'Thomas Masyn' received £1 6s. 4d. 'for wyrkyng of ye stepyll'.

A, XLI, 333 ff.

Mason, Thomas—see DENYAR

Mason, William—see BROWN; MAYSON; ORCHARD, William

MASON, William [Masen, Masson] (*fl.* 1482–1504) Mason

Of *Bishop's Stortford*, Herts., and for many years in charge of various works and repairs at the church there. In 1482 he was paid 8s. 2d. for making windows on the north side of the church, and in 1491 £1 for making battlements, while in 1504 he mended the cross, doubtless in the churchyard, and part of the floor, for 10d. He may have been responsible for the workmanship of the fine north porch, built c. 1490–1500, but the design was probably supplied by the master mason of St. Paul's Cathedral, since Stortford belonged to the bishop, and his mason would be likely to visit the church from time to time. In 1503 the sum of 6d. was 'payde for the fremasenys dynare', perhaps indicating such a visit.

GBS

MASOUN, Gilbert (*fl.* 1324) Mason

Received a reward in 1324, apparently in connection with the works of *Hanley Castle*, Worcs., which RICHARD DE FELSTEDE had in charge.

HKW, II, 668n.

MASSINGHAM, Bartholomew de (*fl.* 1264–1265) Mason (*Massingham, Norf.*)

Mason (*cementarius*) and master of the work of the Prior at *Norwich Cathedral* in 1264–65, when he was paid among the masons working from Michaelmas to St. Nicholas, and again from Easter to St. Mary Magdalene's day, and received a robe price 10s.

NCM, roll 1

MASSINGHAM, John de, I (*fl.* 1337–1338) Carpenter

Paid 5s. 8d. in 1337–38 by the Town Chamberlains of (*King's*) *Lynn* for boards bought from him for the south gates, made by JOHN DE QWYNBERGWE.

LCR, Ea. 7

MASSINGHAM, John, II [Massyngham] (*fl.* 1354–1378) Carpenter

One of the working carpenters at *Westminster Palace* in 1354–55,[1] and warden (*apparilator*) of carpentry there from 27 September 1361, when he was being paid 3s. 6d. a week.[2] On 1 February 1364/5 he received a grant of 10 marks (£6 13s. 4d.) a year for life.[3] On 27 January 1369, HUGH HERLAND and John de Massyngham were described as carpenters among the craftsmen serjeants of the royal household (*valletz de mestere de nostre houstel*), and on 1 September of the same year they were issued with mourning cloth to attend the funeral of Queen Philippa.[4] On 23 August 1369 Massingham was to impress carpenters for foreign service, and on 26 March 1370 for the royal works.[5] On 11 July 1376 Massingham was described as one of the King's Carpenters, when he was paid an instalment of £3 6s. 8d. of his pension of 10 marks[6] and this was confirmed to him by Richard II on 5 March 1377/8.[7]

Thomas MASSYNGHAM, citizen and carver (*keruere*) of London, made his will 26 January 1389/90. A parishioner of St. Benet Fink, he made various bequests to that church and its chaplains, and left his wife Alice executrix and residuary legatee. It was proved 3 February 1389/90.[8]

[1] *PRO,* E.101–471–11; [2] *Ibid.,* 472–9, 10; [3] CPR 1364–7, 123; [4] LRC, III, 174; [5] CPR 1367–70, 287, 384; [6] *PRO,* E.403–460; [7] CPR 1377–81, 137; [8] *CCL,* Courtney 195v.

MASSINGHAM, John, III, senior [Massyngham] (*fl.* 1409–1450) Carver

Possibly identical with the John Massingham, carpenter of London, who on 21 July 1409 was ordered to be set free after imprisonment for leaving the service of JOHN DOBSON, carpenter.[1] In the will of Richard Sponewey of London, carpenter, made 26 August 1426, John Massyngham was pardoned 6s. 8d. of the moneys which he owed to Sponewey.[2] From 1429 to 1431 the carver was living in *Canterbury*, where he paid

4d. yearly among the 'Intrantes' (licenced foreigners not free of the city) of 'Newyngate and Redyngate',[3] while in 1432 he purchased his freedom.[4] In August 1438 a total of 13s. 4d. was paid him in two instalments by the hands of his wife for making an image for the sign of the 'Sun' (pro ymagine pro le syne at Sonne) at Canterbury,[5] and about this time he may have carved the four later statues of Kings (Richard II, Henry IV, V, and VI) for the cathedral pulpitum.[6]

Between 1438 and 1442 he was master carver at All Souls College, Oxford, where he received the high pay of 4s. 8d. a week besides his board and lodging, assisted by his son JOHN MASSINGHAM IV, junior, who was paid 2s. a week. Massingham was also paid for travelling between Oxford and London, and visiting the Founder at Croydon. His own work probably included the statues of Henry VI and Archbishop Chichele on the main gate (now in the cloister), and imagery on the great reredos of the chapel.[7] He may also have designed or produced figures for the interior of the new Divinity Schools at Oxford, in progress between 1430 and 1455.[8]

In 1448–49 he made in London an image of the Virgin for Eton parish church, and for this he was paid £10.[9] He was meanwhile, from 1447 onwards, doing work for the enrichment of the Beauchamp Chapel, Warwick, for which he was paid £3 6s. 8d. in prest by 1449.[10] In 1450, when he is named as a citizen of London, he was to make the wooden pattern for the effigy of Richard Beauchamp, Earl of Warwick, to be cast in bronze by William Austen of London. At the same time Roger Webb, warden of the Company of Barber Surgeons, was engaged presumably to give expert advice on anatomy which is portrayed with unusual fidelity in the effigy.[11]

Massingham was the first sculptor to introduce into England the new canons of realism initiated on the continent by Claus Sluter in the second half of the 14th century. Massingham's realism was, however, tempered by adherence to the architectural use of sculpture traditional in England. In addition to his documented works, his influence can be seen in the figures of Henry V's Chantry in Westminster Abbey, with their animated attitudes and (for the first time in England) use of landscape backgrounds to the groups. These carvings were made c. 1440–50.[12]

[1] CCR 1405–9, 455; [2] CCL, More, f. 172; [3] CIC; [4] CFC; [5] Bodl., MS. Top. Kent c.3, f. 149; [6] GMS, 232; CCF, Apr. 1935, No. 20; [7] JAS, 130–1; GOM, 71; [8] AJ, LXXI (1914), 217–60; GMS, 235; [9] WCC, I, 402; [10] BM, Add. MS. 28564, f. 257; [11] Ibid., f. 267; A, LXXVII (1928); [12] A, LXV (1914), 129 ff.

MASSINGHAM, John, IV, junior (fl. 1438–1478) Carver

Son of JOHN MASSINGHAM III, senior with whom he was at work at All Souls College, Oxford, between 1438 and 1447.[1] He was presumably identical with a distinguished carver and polychromist who worked at Winchester on many occasions between 1452 and 1478.

The accounts of Winchester College for 1452–53 show that 7d. was spent 'on the house of Messyngham making the sign for the inn at Andover'.[2] The Angel at Andover, Hants., was an important property of the college and Massingham was probably given accommodation in a nearby tenement belonging to the college while he made the sign. John 'Messyngham' appears as a witness to a will made on 16 May 1454, and to a grant of 27 August 1472, both concerning a house in the parish of St. Peter Colebrook, Winchester, acquired by William Fulford, mason, and his wife Cristina.

In 1465–66, 'Messyngham' was at Winchester, painting the stone statue of the Virgin and Child over the outer gate of the college,[3] in 1469–70 he was paid £26 13s. 4d. and a reward of £2 for his work on the images of the chapel reredos and 16s. was allowed for his commons for 16 weeks, with £2 6s. 8d. for the commons of his servants.[4] In 1473–74 'Masingame' was entertained in hall with his wife and servant;[5] he was given refreshments on 19 and 20 August 1475,[6] and was again entertained in 1475–76, when he was paid £1 for a crucifix for the new roodloft in the chapel.[7] In 1477–78 he received a further sum of £1 6s. 8d. for sculpture and painting of the companion images of St. John and St. Mary.[8]

Massingham's career brings into special prominence the link between sculpture and painting and shows that a sculptor of distinction would paint not only his own new works, but also existing figures.

[1] JAS, 130–1; [2] WCM, Compotus 1452–3; [3] Ibid., 1207, 1208; Compotus 1465–6; [4] Ibid., 1469–70; [5] Ibid., Hall Book 1473–4; [6] Ibid., Compotus 1474–5; [7] Ibid., Hall Book and Compotus 1475–6; [8] Ibid., Compotus 1477–8

Massone, William le—see BROWN

MATHEU, John (fl. 1304–   ) ? Mason

In 1304 John Matheu, surveyor (*supervisor*) of the works of the houses of the castle and Exchequer of *Dublin* was granted £30 to effect repairs.

CDI, 1302–7, 108

MATHEWE, Thomas [Matthew] (*fl.* 1415–1423) *Carpenter*

With William Gille, was empowered to impress carpenters and other workmen for Henry V's campaign in Normandy in 1415, and with WILLIAM TEMPLE was one of the master carpenters in charge of the body raised, taking 12*d.* a day. He was first master carpenter, with JOHN JANYN, in charge of repairs to the walls and towers of *Harfleur* from 1 January 1415/16. In 1417 he had 119 carpenters under him there, and on 24 March 1419/20 was appointed master carpenter at *Calais*. He held office until 1423 when he was succeeded by JOHN FULLER.

PRO, T.R. Misc. Bk. 79, *f.* 46 (*L.F.S.*); cf. E.101–69–8 no. 518 (*N.L.R.*); HKW, I, 458–9, 461; II, 1054

MATHIE, Adam (*fl.* 1374–1377) *Mason*

Named first, with JOHN MEPPUSHAL, mason, when they contracted on 31 October 1374 to rebuild parts of *Merton Hall, Cambridge*. This building, known as the School of Pythagoras, still exists, showing both the original Norman work, and the parts rebuilt by Mathie and Meppushal, including the west wall and the south wall for a distance of 18 feet. They also added four buttresses and repaired the stone steps. They were to be paid £32 13*s.* 4*d.* by instalments.[1]

Between 1375 and 1377 Mathie seems to have been employed at *King's Hall, Cambridge*. In an account containing items for the roofing of chambers Master Adam Mason was paid 20*s.* for making a gutter (*aqueductile*) and walls of stone by agreement.[2] As a plumber was paid 'for making the gutter round a new chamber', presumably the mason had built this chamber and made a gutter of stone, which the plumber lined with lead.

[1] SHB, 451–2; CAS, 4to Publ. NS, IV, 29, 31, 52; (*MRT*, Deeds No. 1639); [2] *PRO*, E.101–348–14 (*A.O.*)

MATHU, John (*fl.* 1519–1523) *Carver*

Described as 'Graver'; was paid for making an altar table of the Blessed Virgin Mary for the parish church of *Little Walsingham*, Norfolk; he was paid £3 in 1519 and £1 more in each of the years 1520 and 1523.

AIN, 149 (*N.L.R.*)

MATTHEW the Mason I (*fl.* 1287–1288) *Mason*

Master in charge of building the chapel in *Leeds Castle*, Kent, for Queen Eleanor of Castile in 1287–88, for £50, perhaps only in part payment.

HKW, II, 695

MATTHEW the Mason II (*fl.* 1450–   ) *Mason*

Mason of *Alnwick Abbey*, Northumberland, in 1450, when he was paid £1 10*s.* 0*d.* for carving the stone lion over the gateway of the *Bondgate* of Alnwick, which had been begun about 1443.

Licence to enclose the town with embattled and machicolated walls had been granted to the 2nd Earl of Northumberland and the burgesses of the town in 1434, but the Bondgate tower was not finished until 1450, when a total of £17 17*s.* 2*d.* was spent on it, inclusive of the 30*s.* to Matthew who may well have been the designer of the works.

BBH, 21

Matthew, Thomas—see MATHEWE

MAUNCY, Thomas [Maunsel, Maunsey, Maunsye, Mawsell, Mawsill] (*fl.* 1479–†*c.*1504) *Carpenter*

Took up the freedom of the London Carpenters' Company in 1479, and was a warden of the company in 1492–93, 1493–94, and again in 1500; in 1493 he accompanied the master, ROBERT CROSBY, in 'settyng the kyng from Eltham'. On several occasions between 1488 and 1504 he paid fees for 'presenting' his apprentices and journeymen, and was evidently in a large way of business.[1] By 1496 he was employed as King's Chief Carpenter, and in 1496–98 built new chambers at *Westminster Palace*, and superintended the rebuilding of *Baynard's Castle* from 1496 to 1501, when he was described as the King's Carpenter.[2]

Mauncy was also chief carpenter of *London Bridge* from 1487, being paid 4*s.* a week until 1492, when he lost his job for causing the arrest of Bridge workmen for the royal works. In 1495 he was re-engaged as joint chief carpenter with WALTER REVE, taking only 3*s.* 4*d.* a week. In 1499 he was found to be absent from work and 'noe good dothe there in eny wyse yit by the sufferaunce of the mayre and his brethren the same Thomas taketh wekely for his wages this yere iii.*s.* iiij.*d.*' He was not employed in 1500 but appears again from 1501 to Christmas 1503 as master carpenter, taking £8 13*s.* 4*d.* yearly and having Robert

Maunsy as his warden. During Mauncy's periods of office he engaged many others of his family to work on the Bridge, viz. James, Robert, Richard, Roger, John, John junior and Thomas junior; of these only James remained in the regular service of the Bridge.[4]

HKC
[1] MCR, II, *passim*; [2] LKC, 226; *BM*, Add. MS. 7099, *ff.* 36, 38, 44, 47 (*A.O.*); cf. HKW, IV, 50; [3] FRH, 164; [4] P.E. Jones in AAJ, 3 S, XVI (1953), 62

MAUNSELL, Robert (*fl.*   –1422) Mason
The third of three masons (with THOMAS AMPILFORDE and JOHN GARRETT) who contracted to build *Catterick Bridge*, Yorks., on 13 January 1421/2.

SHB, 497–9; AJ, VII, 56

MAURICE (*fl.* 1174–1187) Engineer
Is described as mason (*cementarius*) at the building of the keep of *Newcastle upon Tyne* in 1174–75; the work lasted from 1171 to 1177 and there is good reason to suppose that Maurice was the designer, for the Newcastle keep has many points of resemblance to that at *Dover*, where Maurice, under the designation of engineer (*ingeniator*) was in charge from 1181 to 1187.

He was paid at the rate, unusually high for the period, of 1*s*. a day while at Dover; Maurice was undoubtedly a specialist in castle building, and was treated accordingly. In 1181 he was allowed £3 0*s*. 2*d*. for cloths (*pannis*) in addition to his high pay. The works done under him included the keep and at least a part of the curtain-wall, and there is no doubt that Maurice was the greatest, as he was the last, of the exponents of the square donjon. Dover and Newcastle both have elaborate forebuildings, and the entrance in both was on the second floor; both are of great height, and have walls of immense thickness pierced by chambers and galleries. At Newcastle one of the corner towers is polygonal, thus foreshadowing the next great development in fortification.

Maurice was probably employed at least in an advisory capacity on other works, though his name is not recorded elsewhere; it has been suggested that he was the designer of the stone domestic buildings of *Farnham Castle* which were erected about 1180.[1] It is to be noted, however that one URRICUS seems to have been the engineer employed on works in London and Surrey at about this period.

(APD;WPS); **PR**
[1] HBC, 52

MAYNE, John (*fl.* 1513–*c*. 1526) Carpenter
Devon carpenter; between 1513 and 1516 was paid £11 in instalments for making the seating for *Ashburton Church*, as well as £2 19*s*. 3*d*. for other timberwork there. He was probably also the designer of the roodloft, and screens separating the chancel from the chapels of St. Thomas and St. Mary on the north, which were put up between 1521 and 1526 at a total cost of £30 13*s*. 9¼*d*., in addition to £3 16*s*. 0*d*. for extra seats made in 1522.

BPA

MAYSON, William (*fl.* 1487–1488) Mason
Rebuilt the chancel of *Ellingham Church*, Northumberland, in 1487–88. He was paid £18 16*s*. 4*d*. for various works including dressing stone, making three windows, and battlementing the roof. The church was rebuilt in 1805 and again in 1862, so that all trace of his work is now lost.

DAR, III, 651

MAZZONI, Guido [Paganino, Pageny] (*fl.* 1473–†1518) Sculptor
Of Modena, Italy; visited England and in 1506 made designs for the tomb of Henry VII, not carried out.

(APD); TBK, XXIV, 315

Meepshall, John—see MEPPUSHAL

MELBOURNE, Robert de (*fl.* 1301–1304) Mason
Between 1301 and 1304 built a new turret on the site of the Friary Gate at *Rhuddlan Castle*. His contract was to build the masonry for £4.

HKW, I, 326; cf. HAC, 134

MEMBIRI, William de (*fl.* 1313–1317) Carpenter (*Membury, Devon*)
Chief working carpenter at *Exeter Cathedral* from 1313 to 1317, taking 2*s*. 3*d*. a week, as Master WALTER the Carpenter (II) had done.

AEC, i, 71, 74, 76, 79, 84, 193–5

Mentam, Richard—see MYNTHAM

MENYVER, J[ohn] (*fl.* 1403–1404) Carpenter
Master carpenter of works at *Hereford Castle* in 1403–04, when he was paid 6*d*. a day.

PRO, E.101–544–14 (*L.F.S.*)

MEPPUSHAL, John [Mepsale, Meepshal (1), Mepeshale, Mepissal] (*fl.* 1374–1418) Mason
Mason; perhaps of Meppershall, Beds.; on

31 October 1374 he was named second to ADAM MATHIE, mason, in a contract to rebuild part of *Merton Hall, Cambridge*, now known as the School of Pythagoras.[1] This building still exists, and clearly shows the original Norman work and the repairs done under the contract of 1374. This included four buttresses, the repair of the stone steps, and the rebuilding of the west wall, and the south wall for a distance of 18 feet. They also rebuilt the vault, but this was removed in the 18th century.

Meppushal was working at *Ely Cathedral* in 1389–90 repairing the Lantern (Octagon) and the vault below the dormitory; his pay was 4d. a week in addition to his diet. In 1395 he was engaged on repairing the vault of the Almonry Chapel; in 1396–97 he was in charge of the work on the great new gate-house or 'Ely Porta', then begun, and in 1399 repaired the vault below the Almonry Hall. From 1405 to 1407 he was strengthening the north side of the great west tower with a new arch, apparently by contract. Meppushal was still living in 1418, when he was the owner of a house in Ely which was long afterwards known as 'Mepsale's Corner'.[2]

Meppushal's great gatehouse is a work of the highest importance and restrained nobility of treatment but the design may be due rather to ROBERT WODEHIRST.

[1] SHB, 451–2; (*MRT*, Deeds No. 1639); CAS, 4to Publ. NS, IV, 29, 31, 52; [2] BEC, 50, and Suppl.; SEC; *CUL*, MS. Add. 2956, *ff.* 158 ff.; 2957, *ff.* 1 ff.

Mepsale, John—see MEPPUSHAL

Merchaunte, Thomas—see MARCHANT

MERE, John de [More] (*fl.* 1316–1347) Carpenter

In 1316 contracted for £14 3s. 4d. to take down the old hall of Prince Llewelyn at Conway, ship it to *Carnarvon Castle*, and re-erect it there.[1] He was probably identical with the John de More who was granted the office of master carpenter in North Wales on 20 July 1347.[2]

[1] CCP, 17; [2] BPR, I, 95

Merlawe, William de—see MARLOW

MERYMAN, Richard (*fl.* 1418–) Mason

Mason (*lathamus*) was paid 20s. towards the cost of building a lodge at *Dunster Castle*, Somerset, on 16 January 1417/18. He was quite possibly identical with the mason who had previously come from Bridgwater 'to

view the lord's hall in the Castle, about to be rebuilt' and who had been paid 3s. 8d. for his expenses.

AJ, XXXVIII (1881), 77

MICHAEL the Carpenter I (*fl.* 1280–1281) Carpenter

Master carpenter of *Exeter Cathedral* in 1280–81.

AEC, i, 4, 5

MICHAEL the Carpenter II (*fl.* 1382–1385) Carpenter

Master Michael, carpenter, presumably chief carpenter to *Norwich Cathedral* in 1382–85, made a new roof for the chancel of the church at *North Elmham*, Norfolk.

NRO, DCN, Master of the Cellar, nos. 60–62 (*P.C.*)

MICHAEL (*fl. c.* 1210–†c. 1234) Mason

Master of the work (*Magister operis*) of *Lincoln Cathedral* when, c. 1230, he was holding land of Newhouse Abbey in the parish of St. Michael on the Mount, Lincoln. He had already been in possession before the Barons' War. In or soon after 1235 his land near the East Gate was sold by Peter, son and heir of Master Michael the mason (*cementarii*).[1]

HML, 113
[1] BL, Harl. Ch. 44.1.49 (*K.M.*)

Michael 'le Macun'—see CANTERBURY

MICHELL, Richard (*fl.* 1510–†1515) Mason

Was appointed master mason of *Berwick on Tweed* at 8d. a day on 10 August 1510, and surrendered the office in 1515, when it was granted on 12 May to GEORGE LAWSON.[1] Michell died shortly afterwards.

The *Richard MICHELL* who worked at *Westminster Palace* in 1531–32 as a rough-layer, taking only 7d. a day[2] can hardly have been the same man, but he and *Thomas MICHILL*, roughlayer at *Nonsuch* in 1538[3] may have belonged to the same family. *John MICHELL*, leading mason at the rebuilding of the Constable Tower in *Scarborough Castle* under THOMAS HYNDELEY in 1426–28 at 6d. a day, was very probably a common ancestor.[4]

[1] LPH, I, 1206; II, i, 973 (p. 261); [2] *PRO*, E.36–251 (*G.P.J.*); [3] *Ibid.*, E.101–477–12 (*G.P.J.*); [4] *Ibid.*, E.101–482–8

MIDDLETON, Geoffrey de (*fl.* 1336–1350) Carpenter

Geoffrey was the resident carpenter in charge of work at *Ely Cathedral* from 1336, receiving a furred robe worth 14s. 10d. and a reward of 4s. In 1341 his name is given as Geoffrey de Middylton, when he was being paid 2s. 9d. a week; in the following year he was called 'Master' and was provided with a house rented at 6s., paid by the Sacrist. He is last mentioned in 1350. His brother John worked with him, and may be the John Carpenter who was paid from 1352 to 1360.

CSR, II, 84, 97, 110, 113, 116, 119, 122–3, 137, 142

MIDDLETON, John de (*fl.* 1398–1401) Mason

Contracted to rebuild the dormitory in *Durham Cathedral Priory* on 21 September 1398; the work was to be completed by Christmas 1401, but Middleton failed to bring the work to a conclusion, and it was finished under another contract by PETER DRYNG. Payment was to consist of a suit of esquire's livery, food and drink for the mason and his boy while working, and 10 marks (£6 13s. 4d.) for every rod of work, the rod consisting of 6⅔ superficial ells (*ulnae*). The existing vault was to be retained intact, and the walls were to be of equal strength to those of a tower in the castle of Brancepeth called 'Constabiltour', which tower was to be the pattern of the work. There were to be 9 windows, of which 5 of carved work like the middle window of the Communar's house, and the west wall was to be 60 feet high, with battlements, and 2 yards thick at the foundation, with 4 offsets in its height, or more, according to a pattern to be provided. So much detail is given that it is to be presumed that Middleton was a simple contractor rather than an architect.[1]

Middleton may have been the man referred to in a letter from Thomas Langley, Bishop of Durham, to Henry V, written about 1416–17, concerning the King's treasure deposited in the church of Durham. The money was 'under the warde of two monkes of the Churche, and the last Prior that ded is, and of a man that is clepet Mydeltone'.[2]

(APD; WPS)
[1] SHB, 473–5; DST; [2] EOL, 2S, I, 51

MIDDLETON, Thomas de (*fl.* 1290–1292) Mason (? *Milton, Dorset*)

Master mason supervising the works carried out at *Corfe Castle* by PHILIP SEROYL in 1290–92.

HKW, II, 622

MILDENHALL, John de [Mildenhale] (*fl.* 1374–   ) Carpenter

Of Cambridge; on 17 September 1374 contracted for the timberwork 'of all the chambers to be newly built' at *Trinity Hall, Cambridge,* and also for the range to be built 'from the north end of the hall northwards to Heneylane'. By elimination the first part of the contract can be referred to the north range of the mediaeval court, which together with the continuation of the hall range still exists, though with a Georgian facing towards the court. The new chambers were to be modelled on those of the east range already built; the other building was to conform to the hall. The hall and east range doubtless formed part of the buildings for the timberwork of which RICHARD DE BURY had been responsible in 1352. John de Mildenhale was to receive £100 to be paid by instalments: £50 at Michaelmas, sums of £10 at Christmas, Easter, and Midsummer, and £20 within 15 days of completion. The north range was stripped and reconstructed in 1928–29, and an illustrated account of the discoveries then made was privately printed for the Master and Fellows. Floor beams and partition walls of 1374 were disclosed, but the roof appears to have been of later date.

A.O. SHB, 450–1; WCC, I, 217, 238

MILEHAM, John (*fl.* 1505–1517) Mason (*Mileham, Norf.*)

Mason of Norwich, apprenticed to John Bedford and free of the city in 1505–06.[1] On 8 May 1508 he was second master of the masons' craft of Norwich, with THOMAS MARCHANT,[2] and in 1510–11 his own apprentice John Dowe was admitted to the freedom.[3] On 3 April 1517 Mileham was admitted to the Guild of St. George.[4]

(A.O.)
[1] EFN; [2] HTN, II, 29–30; [3] EFN; [4] NRC, IX, 113

MILTON, William (*fl.* 1375) Mason

In 1375 William Milton, mason, built by contract four buttresses to support the hall of *Beckley Manor,* Oxon., a royal hunting-lodge, for £1 each.

HKW, II, 899

MODY, William (*fl.* 1439–1459) Mason

On 3 March 1438/9 William Mody was first named of the four sworn masons and carpenters of the City of London. He was appointed on 1 July 1440 chief mason of the new works at *Calais* and soon afterwards succeeded WILLIAM WARLOWE as master mason. Mody was instructed to visit quarries in Yorkshire and Lancashire, and on 24 February 1440/1 he was ordered, with John Noreys of Gainsborough, to take stone and workmen from Doncaster for the works of Calais, and on 16 August 1441 was given a commission, with Simon Baron, to arrest workmen to carry on the Calais work. He had a fresh grant of office on 4 February 1447/8, and probably died shortly before the appointment of THOMAS FERRIER in 1459.

DKR, XLVIII, 338, 343, 348, 376, 443

Moises, Thomas—see MOYSES

MOLTON, John [Moulton, Multon] (*fl.* 1524–†1547) Mason

Mason (*lathomus, cementarius*) engaged in carving by piecework (*entayling in gross'*) at *Westminster Abbey* from 1524 until 1528.[1] He was one of the witnesses to the will of WILLIAM VERTUE on 11 March 1526/7, and in that year he was granted the office of master of the works of *Bath Abbey*,[2] which he held until the dissolution of the abbey on 27 January 1539/40. HENRY REDMAN, master mason to the King and to Westminster Abbey died on 10 July 1528, and Molton succeeded to both these offices. Molton was master mason to the dean of *St. Stephen's Chapel* at Westminster by 1528, and was to succeed Henry Redman on Wolsey's works at *Cardinal College, Oxford*. At *Westminster Abbey* he was appointed jointly with WILLIAM TAYLOR and with him held office until 1534 when the threat of Dissolution put a stop to the work.[3] Molton's work at the Abbey probably included the chantry of Abbot Islip (†1533).

It was not until 4 February 1528/9 that he and THOMAS HERUNDEN received a patent granting to them in survivorship the office of 'Head master of the works in the Tower of London and in the Kingdom of England and elsewhere.'[4] Herunden died in the summer of 1534, and Molton alone held the office for the remainder of his life; Herunden was in any case a quarry owner of Boughton Monchelsea, Kent, and probably took little part in the design of buildings.

Molton's first work of importance was the extension of Wolsey's York Place and its transformation into the King's new *Palace of Westminster*, or Whitehall as it soon became known. A detailed book of accounts which runs from 7 May 1531 to 20 April 1532 shows that Molton was in charge of the work at York Place, having associated with him CHRISTOPHER DICKINSON master of the bricklayers, and JOHN SMYTH II, who was paid 10*d.* a day for his assistance in 'devysing and drawing'. The wardens of the working masons were THOMAS FAUNTE and JOHN ELLIS.[5] The accounts show that Molton was being paid 12*d.* a day as well as payments made to him for lifting tackle and stone for chimneys.[6] At this time another aspect of Molton's work is illustrated by a commission ordering him to approve the quality of 200 tons of Luke stone and 300 tons of Caen stone, sold by Nicholas Tyrrye, purveyor, to Thomas Cromwell, to be delivered at the Tower of London wharf.[7]

In 1532 Henry VIII also began the new works at *Hampton Court*, including the great hall, and for these works Molton was responsible; much of his time was spent there, as for example between 24 December 1532 and 1 February 1532/3 when he received 1*s.* a day, and 19 December 1534 and 16 January 1534/5 when he was paid £1 for 20 days spent at Hampton Court; he was still at work there in 1536.[8]

On 28 October 1537 Molton and JOHN RUSSELL were to have the allowance of beer and bread which Westminster Abbey had paid to the Priory of Kilburn; on 1 November 1538 one 'John Mowlton, yeoman of Westminster' who may have been the mason, was granted an 80 years' lease of land at Speen, Berks., by Westminster Abbey; and in 1545–46 John Multon, officer of the King's Buildings, petitioned for licence to acquire tenements in Westminster.[9]

In 1539 Molton and John Russell were supervising work on the forts at *East* and *West Cowes*, Isle of Wight, which had probably been designed by THOMAS BERTY. He continued to hold the office of chief mason until his death on 23 January 1546/7, when he was succeeded by NICHOLAS ELLIS.

Molton made his will on 30 November 1546; he described himself as 'master masonne unto the King's majestie' and desired to be buried in St. Margaret's on the right hand of his wife Cicely, lately deceased. He left lands in Westminster and Middlesex to his only daughter Agnes, wife of John Moore, and to John Moore his prentice and John Moore and HENRY BULLOCK sometime his servants, all his 'portratures, plaates, books . . . tooles and instruments'. John Russell, Master Carpenter to the King's Majesty, was to be overseer of the will.[10]

Molton died only five days before Henry VIII, and there can be little doubt that he was the designer of all the important building works carried out for the King after the downfall of Wolsey. These included, besides the new Palace of Westminster and the extension of Hampton Court, the *Palaces of St. James, Bridewell,* and *Nonsuch,* though a great part of the detail at this last was apparently supplied by Italian artists, Antonio Toto dell' Nunziata of Florence and JOHN OF PADUA.[11] 'Mr. Molton' had been specially appointed master mason for *Camber Castle* in 1539, and he was probably also in charge of the forts built at *Deal, Walmer,* and *Sandown.*[12] Indeed Molton as official devisor of the King's works doubtless supplied the architectural details of all the coastal forts though their planning was probably due to (Sir) RICHARD LEE, STEPHEN VON HASCHENPERG, and other military engineers.

The importation of foreign artists must have been a bitter blow to the native craftsmen such as Molton who had been trained in the old traditions, and the result was ultimately to kill Gothic as a stylistic unity. Though old planning and to a less extent the old detail lasted through the remainder of the century, John Molton must be regarded as the last great English architect of the old school. Unfortunately he does not seem to have had the inventive genius of Henry Redman, who might, had he lived, have avoided the complete subjugation of English art by fantastic and often foolish imitations of antiquity.

(APD; WPS; WKM); HKW, IV, 537

[1] *WAM,* 23612–17; [2] BBA, 15; *BM,* Harl. MS. 3970; [3] *PRO,* SP Hen. VIII, 235, *f.* 290 *(D.J.);* RNW; [4] LPH, IV, pt. iii, 5336; [5] *Ibid.,* v, 952; [6] *PRO,* E.36–251, 252 *(G.P.J.);* [7] LPH, v, 261; [8] *PRO,* E.36–237 *(L.F.S.);* LHC, I, 127; [9] *WAM,* 7241, 18051; [10] *PPR,* Consistory Court of London, 101 Thirlby; W. J. Williams in MR, XVI, 204; LPH, XIII, i, p. 583; [11] CGF, 6; [12] LPH, XIV, i, 398 (p. 151)

MONTACUTE, William *(fl.* 1303–1313) Carver (? *Montacute, Som.)*

Chief carver at *Exeter Cathedral;* produced bosses, capitals, and carved heads for the work of the choir between 1303 and 1313.

(BPE); *CEF*

MONTFORT, John [Mo(u)n(t)fort, Mo(u)n(t)ford, Momford] *(fl.* 1376–†*c.* 1405) Mason

Probably related to, or conceivably identical with, the John Mountford or Mountfort,

mason, paid for minor works at the Earl of Warwick's castle at *Elmley,* Worcs., in 1345/6 and 1346/7, and also related to the Thomas Mountfort who hired masons to build a new larder at Elmley Castle in the same period.[1]

John Montfort, mason, surrendered a cottage and land at Elmley, held of the Earl, on 26 January 1376.[2] He was excused attendance at manorial courts held there in 1381 and 1382 'because he was on the lord's service'.[3] In 1377–78 the bailiff of Tanworth-in-Arden, another Warwick manor, delivered 6,500 laths to John Monford, mason.[4] In 1391–96 he was engaged on various works at Elmley Castle, including a contract to build part of the outer walls for £40.[5] After the fall of Thomas Beauchamp, Earl of Warwick, in 1397, Montfort had two suits brought against him in the Elmley manorial court,[6] and he was made to pay rent for a quarry on Bredon Hill,[7] which after the Earl's restoration in 1399 (and presumably before 1397) he held freely 'to the lord's use'.[8] He died about 1405: his quarry was leased to Thomas Abbot of Pershore on 24 April 1405,[9] and his Elmley lands granted to others in 1407.[10]

The mason was presumably identical with the John Montfort who lived in Warwick between 1379 and 1405.[11] The records show both in the Earl's service from *c.* 1377 to *c.* 1399;[12] when in a petition to Earl Thomas the Warwick man states that he had served the earl over 22 years '*et en toutz voz trouailles deyns le dit temps ad este oue vous*',[13] probably referring to building works. The Warwick Montfort was a prominent townsman and a valued servant of the earl.[14] He was thus likely to be the 'mason of the Earl of Warwick' paid 3s. 4d. by the Prior of Worcester in 1392–93.[15] At that time he would almost certainly have been at work on Guy's Tower in *Warwick Castle,* under construction in that same year.[16] He may also have worked on Caesar's Tower and other parts of the east front of the castle, though their dates are less certain. In spite of the sparsity of explicit records, Montfort must rank among the leading military architects of the late fourteenth century.

(G.M.D.B.)

[1] HEC, 81–7; [2] BL, Add. Roll 25961; [3] *WOR,* 899:95, rolls 5 & 6; [4] *SBT,* DR37/box 107; [5] *WOR,* 899:95, rolls 70–74; [6] *WOR,* 899:95, rolls 10 & 11; [7] *Ibid.,* roll 10; [8] *PRO,* SC 6–1304–42; [9] *Ibid.;* [10] *WOR,* 899:95, roll 78; [11] John Montfort of the Smithstreet, Warwick, occurs in many deeds dated there between 1381 and 1392 (e.g. *WRO,* DR115/ 15, 16 and 75, CR26/1 (1) X, HR11/4. The earliest

reference is in a writ of 7 March 1379 (CCR 1377-81). He was a founder of the Guild of the Holy Trinity and St. Mary in 1383 (*PRO*, C.66–315, m. 11); the latest reference to him as alive is in a rental of 28 August 1405 (*WRO*, CR26/3, *f.* 47.); [12] For Montfort's service see the petition of 1399 below; [13] Petition, *WRO*, CR1886/481; [14] Arrested as a supporter of Earl Thomas, Montfort had to sue for pardon in 1398: *PRO*, C.67–30, m. 30; [15] See p. 315, 'WARWICK, Master of the Earl of'; [16] *SBT*, DR473/293, *f.* 12

Moore, Edmund, Richard—see MORE

MOORECOCK, William (*fl.* 1508–1510) Carver

In 1508 HENRY HARPUR and William Moorecock of Burton, Staffs., undertook to make a tomb for Henry Foljambe at *Chesterfield*, by 26 October 1510.

CTG, I, 354

MORE, Edmund [Moore] (*fl.* 1523–†1536) Carver

Freemason and carver of Kingston upon Thames; between 1523 and 1533 carved statues for Bishop West's chantry chapel in *Ely Cathedral*; he was paid £9 'upon a reckoning for the images'. In 1530–32 he was engaged on carving three 'tables' of the King's Arms for *Hampton Court* by contract for the sum of £34 4s. 10d. In 1535–36 he was carving in wood on the stalls of the chapel, taking 12d. a day, as did his colleague Peter Cleyff, who was probably from Cleves in the Rhineland. More was also paid, over and above his wages, 12d. a day for four days, riding to Amersham, Chenies, Henley, Thatcham, and Kingsclere to impress carvers.[1]

More's will, proved at London on 10 September 1536, was made on 31 August 1535. He describes himself as of Kingston, Surrey, but was apparently not there at the time of making the will, and it is to be presumed that he was at Ely ('the town of Ele'), where he had a house, as well as one in Kingston; both houses and the whole of his goods were left to his mother Margaret More, widow, with remainders to various relatives including children of his sisters Ellyn and Mary, and his brother William More. Three boats on the Thames were bequeathed, one of them being in the custody of '[John] Lovell of Richemount the King's gardyner'; recompence was to be given to those 'that have taken payne wt. me in my seekenes' on the advice of his friends Harry Curant (CORANT) and Thomas Bucknall, while Richard 'a Le' (RICHARD LEE) was named overseer.[2] More was evidently still at work upon Bishop West's Chapel.

His house at Kingston was rented by him from the Bridge Wardens at 16s. a year from 1529; in 1530–31 there is a reference to 'the brygge howse pale, where More dwelles', and after his death the house seems to have been taken by Harry Corant from 1536 to 1543, when it passed to William Bayard, tenant in 1547 of 'a tenement lying toard the grett bryg'.[3]

[1] VCH, *Cambs.*, IV, 73; LHC, I, 125, 158, 358; [2] *PCC*, 40 Hogen; [3] WKA, 8, 9, 11, 13, 15, 17, 19

More, John de—see MERE

MORE, John (*fl.* 1386–) Mason

On 1 March 1385/6, John More, mason, and Nicholas Mason were ordered to take masons to repair the great bridge of *Dublin*.[1] More was presumably identical with the John More, 'clerk of the works' (*clericus operacionum*), who had been allowed £20 on 30 April 1372 for works on *Dublin Castle* and elsewhere in Leinster, and on 18 September 1381 £20 to be spent on *Carlow Castle*.[2]

[1] IPC, I, pt. i, 128; [2] *Ibid.*, 82; *BM*, Egerton MS. 1773, *f.* 22

MORE, Mathy (*fl.* 1491–1495) Carpenter

Carpenter and joiner; on 7 December 1491 contracted to provide new fittings for *Bodmin Church*, Cornwall, including seating with carved bench-ends, and a pulpit and screen, for £92. The work was to be completed by Michaelmas 1495. Some of this woodwork still remains in the church. The work in general was to follow the pattern of that in St. Mary, Plympton, while the pulpit was to be like that at Moretonhampstead.

(BPC); WBR, No. 3, 33

MORE, Richard [Moore] (*fl.* 1446–1450) Carpenter

Appears as one of the carpenters of the Prior of Durham in 1446, when the priory owed him £18 2s. 8d. In 1450 he took down the old hall at *Pittington* and made a new roof to the hall by contract for £5, and his wages at 6d. a day for 21 days.

(*A.O.*) DST, 325

MORE, W[illiam] (*fl.* 1403–1407) Mason

Master mason in charge of work at *Hereford Castle* in 1403–04, when battlements were added to the gatehouse and walls repaired. On 14 June 1407 licence was given to the parson of the church of St. Ouen, Hereford, with others including William More, mason, to set up a chantry in Hereford at the altar of the Holy Trinity in that church, endowed with five messuages in the city.

PRO, E.101–544–14 (*L.F.S.*); CPR 1405–8, 337, cf. 259; CCR 1405–9, 254

MOREL, Peter (*fl.* 1285–   ) Mason
Master mason engaged on the works of *Harlech Castle* in 1285; the design of the castle was by JAMES OF ST GEORGE.

PRO, E.101–485–26 (*L.F.S.*)

MORELL, John (*fl.* 1482–   ) Carpenter
Carpenter to James Goldwell, Bishop of Norwich, in 1482 when he was paid £13 by instalments for work at the bishop's manor of *Gaywood* near Lynn, and also for repairs to the lord's barn at *Langham*, Norfolk.

NDR, Bishop's Rolls, Bundle 1, roll of arrears of ministers

MORGAN, Stephen (*fl.* 1472) Carpenter
On 17 November 1472 Stephen Morgan, carpenter, agreed with Alice Chester widow of Harry Chester, draper of Bristol, 'to make wele werkmanly and surely of good tymbre and bordys a newe hous in the high strete of Brystowe (*Bristol*) with flores wyndowes dorrys and partesons and all other thyngis of tymbre werk belongyng to the same hows, excepte latthes and latyces, . . . and the seide Stephen shall make in the seide hows a shop a hall above the same with an oryell, a chambre above the hall with an oryell and a nother chambre above that'.

The house was to be completed within four months and Morgan was to receive £6 13*s.* 4*d.* in three instalments, £3 at Christmas, 33*s.* 4*d.* 'atte Floryng of the seide hows' and 40*s.* on completion by 'the feste of Annunciacion'.

SHB (2nd ed. 1967), 598

MORWENT, Roger (*fl.* 1517–   )
Carpenter
Carpenter; undertook in 1517 to make panelling, floors, and other woodwork for *Corpus Christi College, Oxford*, for £5. HUMPHREY COKE was evidently the designer and let the contract.

SHB, 572

MORYS, John (*fl.* 1423–1429) Mason
Mason working at *Canterbury Cathedral* in 1423, when he received livery as an esquire (*armiger*);[1] in 1426–27 he went to Merstham, Surrey, to order stone, being named as warden of the masons;[2] he still held this position at Christmas 1429.[1]

[1] *Bodl.*, Tanner MS. 165 (*A.O.; W.P.B.*); [2] AC, XLV, 45

MOTT, John [Mote, Motte] (*fl.* 1480–1491)
Carpenter
Perhaps son of Thomas Mott, carpenter, who between January and April 1480 worked at the church of *St. John the Baptist, Cambridge*, under MARTIN PRENTICE and in August and September of the same year was one of the carpenters employed on buildings in the Old Court of *King's College*. Thomas Mott was paid at the rate of 6*d.* a day; John Mott, who worked for 37 days on the church and for 15½ days in the Old Court, received only 4*d.* a day and so may still have been an apprentice.[1] In 1491, when over £37 was spent on repair and alterations of the Tolbooth or *Guildhall* at *Cambridge* and the adjoining gaol, John Mott undertook work by agreement in the Old Gaol 'called le Peloureschambre' which seems to have occupied part of the space beneath the Tolbooth.[2] The Tolbooth was replaced by the Guildhall built by James Essex in 1782, but small portions of the old walls were left standing at the west end.

A.O.

[1] *KCM*, College Accs. vol. vi; CAC, IV, 353–6;[2] *CCM*, Treasurers' Acc., 1490–91, Box 18/71, No. 6

Moulton, John—see MOLTON

MOUNTSORREL, Thomas (*fl.* 1276–1307)
Mason
Succeeded Master WILLIAM DE MOUNTSORREL, probably his father, as viewer of the works of *Bristol Castle* in 1276. He was sent for to give advice on the works of *Aberystwyth Castle* in 1280. In 1280–82 the bridge leading towards St. Philip's church from Bristol Castle, on the south-east side, was rebuilt and in the following twelve months the chapel of St. Martin and some adjacent chambers, Master Thomas certifying the cost of £267. He remained in charge of the works, which included rebuilding sections of the curtain walls in 1288–89 and in 1294–95, until 1307 or later, but had died by 1327. His latest known work was the building of the new great gate towards the town in 1305–07 at a cost of £31 13*s.* 4*d.*

HKW, I, 303; II, 580; CPR 1272–81, 186

MOUNTSORREL, William (*fl.* 1253–†1276) Mason
Had presumably been working at *Bristol Castle* before 24 January 1253, when the bailiffs of Bristol were ordered to pay him 12*d.* a day during the king's pleasure instead of his previous daily wages of 6*d.* This may

mark his promotion to the position of viewer of the works at the castle, which he held until 1276. In the meantime, in 1253–55, he was sent to take charge of works at the king's manor of *Gillingham*, Dorset. At Bristol Castle he was succeeded by THOMAS MOUNTSORREL, presumably his son.

CLR 1251–60, 101; CPR 1272–81, 186; HKW, II, 580, 945

MOYSES, Thomas [T. M. FitzDalber] (*fl. c.* 1240–1242) ? Mason

An inscription records that Thomas Moyses laid one of the stones of a buttress of the chapel of Nine Altars at *Durham Cathedral c.* 1242; he was presumably identical with the man of this name who *c.* 1240 granted a burgage in Elvet.

VCH, *Durham*, III, 101

MULSHAM, John (*fl.* 1381–1382) Carpenter (*Moulsham, Essex*)

Carpenter; in 1381–82 contracted to make the timberwork of a new hall at the manor of *Moulsham by Chelmsford*, Essex, with a chamber annexed. He was to be paid £2 16s. 8d., apparently in addition to the materials of an old hall on the site. The sum of 1s. 11d. was paid for felling 34 oaks and oak saplings for the work. The walls were plastered by John Wavel at task for 16s. 9d. and pointed by him for 8s. 9d. Further sums were spent upon nails, 1600 laths, lime and tiling.

ERO, D/DM M87

Multon, John—see MOLTON

MUMER, Harry (*fl.* 1533) Carpenter

On 5 October 1533 Harry Mumer was paid £10 for making, framing and setting up a new 'garnell and malte house' in the *Castle of Guisnes*, by a bargain made with William Lambert, surveyor, and the King's Master Carpenter.

LPH, VI, 1477 (*A.O.*)

MUNFORD, Robert [Monteforde] (*fl.* 1454–1480) Carver

As Robert Monteforde, graver, in 1454–55 took up the freedom of Norwich.[1] He was paid £9 2s. 4d. for a new font-cover for *East Dereham Church*, Norfolk, in 1478–80, with another £2 16s. 10d. for accessories and expenses; 2s. 4d. also had to be spent on repairing the glass of the west window, broken during the installation.[2]

[1] EFN; [2] Church accounts (*S.A.C.;P.C.*)

MYLTONE, Walter (*fl.* 1412–1428) Carpenter

Was one of the sworn carpenters of London (with ROBERT LARDYNER) in 1412, when on 18 April a petition was granted to the parishioners of St. John Walbrook regarding the exchange of a plot of land (see WALTON, WALTER). Myltone and Lardyner had been present at the survey in their official capacity.[1] Walter Mylton and Edmund WARLOWE, masons and citizens of London, received a grant of tenements in Mincing Lane in 1427–28.[2]

[1] CLB, 'I', 102; [2] PRO, Ancient Deed C.10225 (*H.M.C.*)

MYNTHAM, Richard [Mentam] (*fl.* 1477–1480) Carpenter

Rebuilt the watermill of *Tingewick*, Bucks., for New College, Oxford, by contract in 1477–80, for £6.

NCO, Tingewick Accs., 97–9

N. . ., R. . . de (*fl. c.* 1240–1270) Carpenter

Master carpenter of *Durham Cathedral*, had spent his working life there and, when aged, was granted by Prior Hugh (1258–1278) a weekly allowance from the Cellarer of 7 loaves and 7 gallons of ale, 3 messes of meat and 4 of fish, with 3 ells of russet or bluet cloth yearly from the Prior's chamber.

BDA, 183

NARBURGH, John (*fl.* 1466–1467) Mason

Mason working at *East Dereham Church*, Norfolk, in 1466–67. He was paid 10d. for two days work in connection with the lead roof of the south aisle, and his man had 5d. for the same two days. They also worked together repairing the church doorway, taking 12d. for the two, with board and lodging. Narburgh was also paid by the churchwardens for materials sold by him: 4d. worth of lime, and on another occasion 12d. for lime and tile, again 6d. for one comb of lime. He was also employed to fix the hooks for the hinges of new shutters made to the treasury by William Pylche, carpenter.

NRO, Phillips MSS., Box 5 40973 (*P.C.*)

NASSINGTON, John of (*fl. c.* 1260–c. 1280) Mason

Of Lincoln; between 1263 and 1272 entered into an agreement with the dean and chapter as to buildings next the churchyard of St. Andrew-in-the-Bail; his daughter and heiress Margery in 1285–86 released all her rights in these buildings to the chapter. This may indicate that her father had died, but he appeared as a witness on a number of occasions between 1263 and 1279.

LRS, LXII, Reg. Ant. ix, nos. 2514; 2515; 2511–12, 2524, 2527–8; cf. 2516 of A.D. 1305 (*K.M.*)

Nedham—see NEDEHAM

NEDEHAM, Christopher (*fl.* 1514–)
Carpenter

A member of the London Carpenters' Company in 1514; father of JAMES NEDEHAM.

MCR, II, 230

NEDEHAM, James [Nedam] (*fl.* 1514– †1544) Carpenter

Of Wymondley Priory, Hertfordshire; son of CHRISTOPHER NEDAM, citizen and carpenter of London; he became free of the London Carpenters' Company in 1514, and was warden of the Company between 1515 and 1533. In May 1521 James Nedeham, carpenter, showed to the Court of Assistants of the Mercers' Company of London his 'platt' of a louvre for the *Mercers Hall*, and agreed to make it for £16 by Easter 1522.[1] On 26 September 1522 he was granted a protection because going overseas in the retinue of Lord Berners, deputy of Calais. In the following year he was a master carpenter taking 1*s.* a day in Skevyngton's retinue beyond seas,[2] and he probably remained abroad until 1525, when the war between England and France came to an end. During the three years of the war the English Armies covered a great deal of ground in northern France, and on one occasion advanced to a point within sight of Paris, so that Nedeham probably had some opportunity of seeing the early Renaissance work which was then more advanced in France than at home.

After his return a post as gunner in the Tower of London, probably a sinecure by way of pension, was found for Nedeham; the grant was issued on 1 September 1525, and appointed him to the post held by Robert Fyssher deceased, at the rate of 6*d.* a day. He held this for rather more than a year, when a senior gunner, Robert Best by name, died, leaving a vacancy at 8*d.* a day, which was granted to Nedeham on 1 December 1526, in lieu of his existing office then surrendered.[3]

At this time Wolsey's immense architectural schemes at York Place, Hampton Court, Ipswich, and Oxford were in progress, and Nedeham was soon in a high position in the technical administration of the building operations at *York Place*. Nedeham's precise position is not clear, but after Wolsey's fall he

petitioned the Crown for payment of the balance of money which he had spent on the works of York Place, and which had never been paid him. The King examined him as to whether he had spent the whole £1,000, and finding that it was so, ordered that he should be paid the remainder of the debt on 17 May 1530.[4] The King also retained his services for the continuation of the works at York Place, and between October 1530 and February 1531 Nedeham was paid a total of 50 marks (£33 6*s.* 8*d.*) by instalments for making a private 'bridge' or landing-stairs at York Place.[5]

At the same time he was able to undertake work for private clients, for on 15 February 1529/30 he contracted to make wooden galleries round three sides of the walled garden at the mansion of the Marquess of Exeter in the parish of St. Lawrence Pultney, London, for £110.[6] In the contract he is called 'one of the King's master carpenters'. HUMPHREY COKE was then the chief carpenter, but Coke died towards the end of March 1531, and Nedeham succeeded him at once, the grant being issued on 14 April.[7] His salary was 1*s.* a day, and the accounts for 1532 show that he received it regularly, being entitled 'the King's carpenter'.

In the summer of 1532 Nedeham was in charge of works at the *Tower of London* and on 11 June contracted to re-edify St. Thomas's Tower (the Traitors' Gate) for £120.[8] These works were the result of a survey of the Tower undertaken earlier in the year, which showed that extensive repairs were required. Nedeham's work included the timber-framed north wall of the Traitors' Gate, with its three windows above the great arch.

The autumn of 1532 was the crisis of his career; it seems evident that the King was dissatisfied with the existing administration of building operations, and called for the resignation of Thomas Flower, clerk and surveyor of the works. The latter surrendered his office, and it was immediately granted to Nedeham, on 4 October 1532, with pay of 2*s.* a day. Nedeham had already given up his post of chief carpenter, which was granted on 1 October to JOHN RUSSELL and WILLIAM CLEMENT in survivorship, and he also surrendered his post of gunner in the Tower.[9] The appointment of Nedeham as 'clerk and overseer' of the works was revolutionary, for the post had in the past been held by clerics, not by men trained in the building crafts.

Nedeham undoubtedly owed his sudden promotion to the rise of Thomas Cromwell, who had supervised Wolsey's building operations and thus must have come into close contact with the principal craftsmen. Almost immediately after his appointment, on 17 October, Nedeham was engaged on Cromwell's work,[10] evidently that 'large and spacious' house in Throgmorton Street of whose building Stow tells an unsavoury story. 'This house being finished (by Thomas Cromwell), and having some reasonable plot of ground left for a garden, he caused the pales of the gardens adjoining to the north part thereof on a sudden to be taken down; twenty-two feet to be measured forth right into the north of every man's ground; a line there to be drawn, a trench to be cast, a foundation laid, and a high brick wall to be built. My father had a garden there, and a house standing close to his south pale; this house they loosed from the ground, and bare upon rollers into my father's garden twenty-two feet, ere my father heard thereof; no warning was given him, nor other answer, when he spake to the surveyors of that work, but that their master Sir Thomas commanded them so to do; no man durst go to argue the matter, but each man lost his land, and my father paid his whole rent, which was 6s. 6d. the year, for that half which was left. Thus much of mine own knowledge have I thought good to note, that the sudden rising of some men causeth them to forget themselves.'[11]

Nedeham was presumably the principal surveyor engaged on this scandalous business, but one cannot help admiring the resource and skill shown in moving a house 22 feet on rollers before its owner was aware of the matter. Cromwell's house was afterwards Drapers' Hall, and the present Drapers' Hall stands upon the same site.

The works of *Hampton Court Palace* were now being pushed forward for the King, and the great hall was added to Wolsey's existing buildings; in his accounts for his first year as surveyor, Nedeham includes an item 'for riding to Hampton Court and being there in drawing of platts and making of moulds for the new hall by the space of 22 days within the time of this accompte, at 4s. the day £4 8s. 0d.'.[12] This clearly shows that Nedeham made the drawings and templates for the timberwork of the hall, and its similarity to the roof

of Christ Church hall at Oxford shows his debt to Humphrey Coke, under whom he must have learned much.

As surveyor, Nedeham was officially responsible for the very extensive building works of the last 15 years of Henry VIII's reign. He was not of course the designer of the masonry and brickwork, which came within the scope of JOHN MOLTON the master mason, but it is now impossible to say how much of the credit for the carpentry works should go to him, and how much to John Russell, the King's Carpenter, who was Humphrey Coke's son-in-law.

Nedeham's sudden promotion had made him bitter enemies among the old-established clerics of the civil service and Cromwell received (about 1534) an unsigned letter from the comptroller accusing. Nedeham of malpractices on a large scale. The correspondent (who may have been either George Lovekyn, appointed comptroller in 1529, or David Martin, who was granted the reversion of the office in 1534) stated that when he was appointed, the office had not been exercised for a long time; he pointed out that Nedeham had opportunities to take an illicit commission on materials which he ordered, and suggested that some men were receiving double pay, including Nedeham himself, 'for he makes his own book and pays without comptrolment'. Meanwhile Nedeham was having difficulty in getting money at all, for on 26 July 1534 he wrote to Cromwell asking for money to pay wages for the work done at the Tower of London.[13]

On 17 December he was ordered by Cromwell to make a survey of the parsonage at *Bishops Hatfield*, Herts., where repairs to the amount of £90 3s. 4d. were found to be required.[14] Nedeham is said to have settled in Hertfordshire in 1536, and he obtained a lease of the dissolved priory of Little Wymondley for 21 years from Michaelmas 1537; he later acquired the freehold which descended in his line to the latter part of the seventeenth century.

A large proportion of Nedeham's accounts as surveyor has survived;[15] they show that work was in progress at Hampton Court, Greenwich Palace, Whitehall Palace, and the Tower of London, besides the lesser royal manors of Eltham, More, Grafton, Canterbury (the fitting up of the surrendered St. Augustine's Abbey as a royal residence in

1539), and Dartford. Other work of importance was at Windsor Castle, Bridewell Palace, Nonsuch, the coastal forts built in and after 1539, and demolition work at several of the abbeys, as for example Chertsey in 1538, Merton in 1539, and Barking in 1541 and 1542. The destruction of these monastic buildings provided material for the new works, as Merton did for Nonsuch, and Barking for Greenwich Palace.

About 1540 work was in progress at Petworth, Sussex, and at Knole in Kent, manors which had fallen into the King's hands.[16] Petworth is only five miles from Cowdray, where the famous Buck Hall was built for the Earl of Southampton in or about 1540; this roof, destroyed by fire in 1793, is only known from a drawing[17] but it was exceedingly like that of Hampton Court on a smaller scale, and was designed by Nedeham or by one of the royal carpenters.

In 1534, 1535, and 1542 Nedeham was Master of the London Carpenters' Company.[18] In 1536, perhaps as a result of the anonymous communications, Cromwell made a memorandum that the accounts of the clerk of the King's works should be surveyed, but nothing discreditable to Nedeham seems to have come to light.[19] From 1539 onwards Nedeham had charge of work on the forts at *Tilbury*, *Sheerness* and elsewhere in the Thames estuary. On 4 July 1541 Nedeham was appointed one of the commission sent to *Rochester Cathedral* to appoint stalls in the choir, places in the chapter house, and dwellings for the Dean, and in the following year he was in charge of works at *King's College, Rochester*.[20]

At the same time work was proceeding at Whitehall, including the building of the Privy Gallery between 1542 and 1544, and the office of works was housed in 'the New office for the King's Survays in the fysshe yard'. The accounts give Nedeham the titles of 'accountant, Surveyor General, and Clerk of the King's Works', and show that he was paid 2s. a day for himself, with 6d. for a clerk, 4s. a day riding costs when travelling by road, and 1s. 8d. a day for boat hire when going by water.[21]

In 1543 James Nedeham 'Esquire' with Alice his wife and Edmund their son acquired properties in Gracechurch Street, London, in the parish of All Hallows, Lombard Street.[22]

There was another financial investigation in 1543–44, as a result of which a warrant was issued on 29 April 1544 'to the general surveyors and to the auditors of accounts of paymasters, clerks and surveyors of building to allow all the accounts of James Nedeham since the 4th of October 24 Henry VIII (when he was appointed clerk and surveyor of the King's works in England, as largely as Henry Smythe and Thomas Flower held the said offices) and his wages of 2s. a day for himself, 6d. a day for his clerk, 4s. a day for riding costs, 20d. a day for going by water from London to Westminster or Greenwich, and all other necessary charges'.[23]

On 27 June 1544 Nedeham was appointed General Receiver of forfeited lands in Yorkshire, but died during Henry VIII's campaign in France on 22 September, and was buried 'in our Ladies Church in Boloigne', as we are informed by a memorial brass in Little Wymondley Church, Herts. Nedeham's will, made on his death-bed, was proved on 5 February 1544/5 by his wife Alice and John Nedam his son.[24]

Nedeham left 40s. each to the parish churches of Little Wymondley and Chislehurst, Kent, and bequeathed his manor house of Wymondley and the rectory there to his wife, under condition of permitting his son John 'and his wif wyth one man servaunte and one mayde servaunt to have meate and drinke wyth house rome and lodging wythin my sayd manour' or else Alice was to pay John £13 6s. 8d. a year. John was to occupy lands at Hitchin, Ilford, 'Polletts' (Ippollitts), Graveley, Hertford, Letchworth, 'Moche Wymondley', and Abingdon. Alice was also to have a house and land at Chislehurst and the rectory there, the remainder being left to 'my son Edmond' and his heirs; Alice was to have silver plate to the value of £33 6s. 8d. and £66 13s. 4d. in cash, her jewels, clothing, and two chests. William, Henry, and Andrew Nedeham are mentioned as younger sons, and Margaret and Anne, daughters. Plate to the value of £400 was to be realised to provide £6 13s. 4d. a year each to the four younger sons 'to fynde them to scole', and they were to have the principal when 23 years of age.

Nedeham's signature (*Jamys Nedam*) occurs several times in the Court Book of the Carpenters' Company.[25] His office of surveyor seems to have passed to Sir RICHARD LEE, who held it before 20 September 1547 when it was granted to LAWRENCE BRADSHAW who had been one of the royal carpenters, and had recently had charge of works at the manor of Ampthill. He had been left £6 13s. 4d. in Nedeham's will and was evidently a close friend.

Nedeham was accounted a gentleman, his father Christopher being the son of 'Black John' Needham of (High) Needham, Derbyshire. The family bore arms of *Argent on a bend engrailed azure two buck's heads cabossed sable*, which James differenced with an *escallop gold*. There is a Hertfordshire tradition that Nedeham repaired *Hunsdon House* for Henry VIII, which could only have been in the period of known works in 1525–28, well before Nedeham's succession to the post of the king's carpenter.[26]

The extent to which Nedeham may be regarded as an architect is by no means certain, as there are other possible claimants in the case of practically all the works with which he was concerned. At York Place he may have designed the roof of Wolsey's great hall, which was in course of erection in 1528, but Humphrey Coke is perhaps more likely, though it is by no means improbable that Nedeham collaborated with the older master. At Hampton Court it is at least certain that Nedeham made the drawings and the moulds or templates for the roof of the hall, but much of the Renaissance detail was almost certainly designed and executed by foreign craftsmen, and the shares of John Russell and William Clement in the work cannot be overlooked.

The events of Nedeham's life and his somewhat spectacular career leave an impression that he was a pushing and able administrator, well able to pick the brains of the most creative artists around him, and if so he was neither the first nor the last man in such a position to win a reputation by these means.

(APD); HKC; HMA; HKW, IV, 602

[1] MCR, III, 211; LWA, 531; [2] LPH, III, pt. ii, 2587, 3288; [3] *Ibid.*, IV, 1676(1), 2761(1), 2839(12); [4] *Ibid.*, IV, 6390; [5] *Ibid.*, V, pp. 752–3; [6] SHB, 575–7; (*PRO*, Anc. Deed D.10097); [7] LPH, V, g.220(20); [8] SHB, 579–80; LPH, V, 952, 1086, 1307, ii; [9] *Ibid.*, VI, p. 191; JPC, 165; LPH, V, 1370(5); [10] *Ibid.*, V, 1442; [11] SSL; [12] Bodl., Rawlinson MS. D.775; [13] LPH, VII, 1012, 1011; [14] *Ibid.*, VII, 1551; [15] Bodl., Rawlinson MS.D.775–85; *BM*, Add. MS. 10109; Harl. MS. 1647, 1651; *PRO* E.101–459–22, 477–12, 483–14, 489–12; [16] *BM*, Arundel MS. 97; [17] GSD, I; [18] JPC; [19] LPH, X, 254; [20] *Ibid.*, Addenda, pt. ii, 1502; Bodl., Rawlinson MS. D.785; [21] *BM*, Add. MS. 7100, No. 81; Add. MS. 10109; [22] LHR, 243(116, 125); [23] LPH, XIX, i, 444(17); [24] PCC, 21 Pynnyng; [25] MCR, III, 21, 22, 211 [26] CHH, II, 109–11

NEKER, Thomas [Nekyr, Nykyr] (*fl.* 1530–1538) Carpenter

Carpenter and joiner of Great Fransham, Norfolk; in 1530 made the new door of the church at the *Cluniac Priory of Thetford*, being paid £2, and also £1 13s. 8d. for his time and that of his 'boy' for 50 days' work, as well as 4s. for making a new door for the buttery there.[1]

On 20 January 1537/8 he contracted with Sir Thomas Kitson to make the panelling and other woodwork for *Hengrave Hall*, Suffolk, which had been built by JOHN EASTAWE, mason. Sir Thomas was to provide all the timber, hewn and sawn into scantlings of the proper sizes, and should find and set up 'al maner of stayings as shall be necessary', while Neker was to have £116 for the work, which comprised the panelling of the hall, 7 chambers, 2 parlours, 2 great chambers, 16 lodgings on the first floor, and other small rooms, together with the entrance gates and benches and cupboards. The work was to be finished by Easter 1539, and Neker was to be paid £116 by instalments.[2]

[1] HTP; *CUL*, MS. Add. 6969, f. 227b; [2] SHB, 582–3; GHH, 42

NETILTON, William [Netylton] (*fl.* 1500–†1506) Mason (*Nettleton, Lincs.*)

Mason employed at *Louth Church*, Lincs., during work on the western porch and at the building of the spire, and apparently the resident warden from 1500 until his death in the summer of 1506. He was at first paid 6d. a day, and later 7d. On occasion he rode to the quarry to choose stone, and it was he who in 1501 spent four days riding 'to get a master masson for to take charge of the said brooch', obtaining the services of JOHN COLE. Netilton himself was paid for tracing (drawing) and making moulds for the spire in the spring of 1501. His wife Margaret seems to have died before 1500.

DCL, 6–7, 9–12, 17, 20, 23–5, 35–7, 56, 67, 73, 87–8

Neuhall, Richard de—see NEWHALL

NEWBY, Robert (*fl.* 1524–1526) Mason & Bricklayer

Was appointed master bricklayer of *Lincoln Cathedral* in 1524 at 13s. 4d. a year; he also held a post as a watchman there, which he resigned in 1526. His office was identical with that of chief mason, as he is more than once referred to in later documents as having held the office of stone-cutter or stonemason (*latho-*

mo seu fabro lapidario). He no longer held the post in 1535, as WILLIAM FELS was the mason named in a schedule to the Valor Ecclesiasticus taken in that year.

(*A.O.*) LRS, XII, 56, 74, 194; XV, 152; XIII, 181

Newenham, Adam—see NEWNHAM

NEWHALL, Richard de (*fl.* 1289–)
Carpenter (*Newhall, Ches.*)

At the County Court for Chester held on 20 September 1289, Richard de Swetenham entered into a recognizance to pay the whole cost of the carpenter's work for the chancel of 'Thorpelegh' (*Tarporley*), Ches., to be finished by Christmas by Richard de Neuhall, 'carpentator'.

SBE, 151

NEWHALL, William de [Newehall] (*fl.* 1374–†1412) Carpenter

Was appointed master carpenter in the counties of Chester and Flint during pleasure on 2 May 1374 and 20 April 1377, and the office was regranted to him for life in 1387. In 1390 he was ordered to deliver one oak out of the wood of Ewloe for the repair of the coal-mines of Ewloe, and on 15 March 1391/2 order was given for timber to be delivered from the forest of 'Mara' for the repair of *Northwich Bridge*, by view of William de Newehall the King's Carpenter. During the ensuing year Newhall supervised the repairs of this bridge.[1]

On 28 March 1397 William de Meysham, lessee of the manor, town, lordship, and coalmines of Ewloe, Flintshire, was ordered to have three oaks delivered to him by William de Newehall the master carpenter in recompense of the costs of certain repairs made by de Meysham on the said property. Next year, on 8 April 1398, a petition was submitted to the King by ROBERT SCOT, carpenter, praying the office of master carpenter in the county of Chester then held by William de Newhall who was too old and feeble to fulfil the duties of the office; Scot did not succeed in displacing Newhall, but he was granted the reversion of the office after Newhall's death.

After the accession of Henry IV, Newhall obtained a new grant of the office for life on 20 October 1399, but on 13 February following Robert Scot was appointed by Henry, Prince of Wales in the room of William de Newhall. Newhall, however, was still able to maintain his position and on 2 June obtained

a warrant from John, Bishop of St. Asaph and Chamberlain of Chester to Roger Brescy, for a grant to him in the name of Henry, Prince of Wales, of the office of master carpenter of Chester and Flint for life. On 24 July Henry, Prince of Wales issued a warrant to John Doune, master forester of Delamere, to deliver wood for the repair of *Northwich Mill* to Ralph Drury, carpenter, on the representation of William de Newhall, master carpenter of Chester.

On 9 January 1401/2, John Williamson, apprentice of Newhall, swore faithfully to fulfil his duties for the remainder of his term of 6 years, viz. 2 years 3 weeks. Probably Newhall was not so feeble as Scot would have liked to make out, as he was still competent to have an apprentice. Newhall was still in office more than six years after, for on 3 October 1408 a bond was inrolled whereby GRUFF' LE WRIGHT undertook to make, repair and mend the bridge of Northwich according to the advice of William de Newehall, master carpenter in the county of Chester; he died on 12 January 1411/12 and on 1 February his office was granted to ROGER DREWRY.[2]

No official timberwork from the period of Newhall remains, but there is at least a possibility that he designed the beautiful choir-stalls of St. Werburgh's Abbey (now *Chester Cathedral*) which were made about 1380–85, and the roof of *Tabley Old Hall*, which dates from the same period. Tabley is only four miles from Northwich, where Newhall was engaged on official work. These works follow closely the designs of the King's Craftsmen in London, and HUGH HERLAND may be ultimately responsible.

DKR, XXXI
[1] JAB, IV, 8; [2] *PRO*, SC6–775–14 (*H.M.C.*)

NEWMAN, Alwyn (*fl.* 1490–1495)
Carpenter

Of Cambridge; in 1490 Alwyn was one of the carpenters employed by King's College on repairs to *St. Augustine's Hostel*.[1] On 7 July 1491 Alwyn Newman contracted for £43 6s. 8d. to make the timberwork of eight chambers at *Great Chesterford*, Essex, where JOHN BURY, mason, was responsible for the rest of the contract.[2] In 1495 Alwyn Carpenter, no doubt the same man, contracted to make a timber building, 22 feet long and 18 feet wide, at the east end of the bakehouse at *King's Hall, Cambridge*. He was to receive 33s. 4d., the college paying for laths and splints.[3]

A.O.
[1] *KCM*, Mundum Book 1489–90; [2] SHB, 550–1; JCB, 199; (Berkeley Castle MSS. S.C. 656, 657); [3] *TCM, KHA*, xix, 1

NEWMAN, John [Neuman, Neweman] (*fl.* 1362–1381) Mason

Was granted pontage for ten years on 24 February 1361/2 and for three years in 1381, so that he should carry out the necessary repairs of the bridge at *Redbridge*, Hants.

CPR 1361–4, 172; JAB, I, 67–8

NEWMAN, Robert [Neweman] (*fl. c.* 1450–1456) Mason

Mason; contracted with Abbot William de Newnton (1413–57) to vault the nave (bouvke)* of *Pershore Abbey* for a certain sum of money, and 20s. and a gown yearly for life. Newnton's successor, Edmund Hert (1457–79), refused to pay these annuities. The nave has been destroyed, but the vault of the south transept, also made in Newnton's time, may have been by Newman.

* The word bouk(e) means belly, trunk or body (OED), clearly referring to the nave of a church, and is used in the same sense by William Worcestre of 'the boke of the chyrch' of Great Yarmouth in 1479 (HWI, 184–5). It cannot mean the surviving transept as suggested by F. B. Andrews (LAU, x, 1932, 82).

PRO, C.1–73–10

NEWNHAM, Adam de [Newenham] (*fl.* 1351–) Carpenter

A Cambridge carpenter, who with ROBERT DE BLASTON agreed to serve the Cambridge Corpus Christi Guild for 1d. a week less wages than usual; probably on the buildings of the Old Court, *Corpus Christi College*.

(*A.O.*) CGR, 37

NEWTON, Elias de [Neweton, Niwaton, Nyweton] (*fl.* 1316–1331) Mason

Was one of the leading masons at *Exeter Cathedral*, working on the high altar and elsewhere from 1316–17 until 1330–31. He took wages of 1s. 10½d. a week in winter and 2s. 3d. in summer.[1] On 3 May 1322 he took up the freedom of the city of Exeter, paying a fine of £1 6s. 8d.[2]

[1] AEC, i, 196–211; ii, 296–300; [2] RJE, 17

NEWTON, John (*fl.* 1418–) Marbler

Was proceeded against in the Consistory Court of York in 1418 by the executrix of John Brompton of York, mason, for breach of contract in connection with work at *St. Leonard's Hospital, York*.

(*A.R.*) YDR, Consistory Court cases Cur. Ebor. Cap.F.80

NEWTON, Richard of (*fl.* 1410–) Mason

Of Newton in Patrick Brompton, Yorks.; contracted on 28 January 1409/10 to rebuild the south aisle of *Hornby Church*, Yorks., for 51½ marks (£34 6s. 8d.). He was almost certainly identical with RICHARD OF CRACALL.

SHB, 482–3; MRC, 46, 62; VCH, *Yorks. N.R.*, I, 317

NICHOLAS the Carpenter (*fl. c.* 1180–1190) Carpenter

Was witness to a deed at *Wells Cathedral* in the time of Bishop Reginald (1174–91), and was presumably the master in charge of building the original roof of the choir.

HMC, *Wells*, I, 491

Nicholas the Carpenter—see AUNDELY; OBEDONE

NICHOLAS the Mason I (*fl.* 1218–) Mason

Master mason (*cementarius*) apparently in charge of the building of *Leiston Abbey*, Suffolk, in 1218, when he witnessed a document dated at Leiston with two canons of the house and Denis and Robert de Snape, two other masons. He may perhaps have been identical with the Master Nicholas *cementarius* of *Ely Cathedral*, who was a witness to Bishop Eustace's charter of *c.* 1215.

(*S.J.A.E.*)
(*H.M.C.*) BM, Cotton MS. Vesp. E. xiv, *f.* 59v.

NICHOLAS the Mason II [Mazon] (*fl.* 1221–) Mason

Nicholas Mazon was paid 5 marks (£3 6s. 8d.) in December 1221 for making a well in the *Tower of London*.

HLC, I, 483

NICHOLAS the Mason III [Machun] (*fl.* 1278–†c. 1290) Mason

Master mason of *Norwich Cathedral* by 1278, when Master Nicholas and his boy (*garcio*) received 2s. 10d. from the Master of the Cellar.[1] In 1282 he was in receipt of a yearly robe, and was in charge of work on the east window of *Trowse (Newton) Church* for the prior; he and his men were paid a total of £2 15s. 6¼d. for this in 1282–83, and the glazing of the window cost £3 3s. 0¼d.[2] During the next year he and his 'mate' were paid £2 5s. 6½d. for work done for the Prior,[3] and the sum of £1 was paid for robes for Nicholas Fayerchild and his son, perhaps the same.[4] In 1288–89 the robe for Nicholas 'le machun' cost 14s. 6d.,[5] but he had disappeared by the next year when RICHARD LE MACHUN (? CUR-TEYS) was given a robe.

FWN, 48, 53

[1] *NRO*, DCN, Master of the Cellar roll 4; [2] *Ibid.*, Communar 1029A; Master of the Cellar roll 6 (*P.C.*); [3] *Ibid.*, roll 6; [4] *Ibid.*, roll 7; [5] *Ibid.*, Communar 1030

NICHOLL, Walter (*fl.* 1475–1477) Carver

Carver of Southwark; on 15 August 1475 contracted with Bishop Waynflete to make the roodloft and stalls for *Eton College Chapel* for 100 marks (£66 13s. 4d.). The west side of the roodloft was to be like that in Winchester College Chapel (designed in 1468 by WILLIAM HUNT I), and the east side like that in the College (Hospital) of St. Thomas of Acre in London. The work was to be finished by the Feast of the Assumption (15 August) 1477, and the payment was to be £66 13s. 4d. and two gowns, while a workshop and lodging were to be provided.

On two occasions in 1476 'Walter the carver' accompanied the Eton College authorities on visits to the Bishop of Winchester (Waynflete), once with the chief mason and carpenter, and the second time by himself. Nicholl is probably to be identified with the 'Watkyn kerver' living in 'le spytell' (St. Thomas's Hospital) in Southwark in 1478, near to Robert Wyse the fuller, mentioned by William Worcestre. This rather suggests that Nicholl was a foreigner.

WCC, I, 409, 596; HWI, 42–3

NICOLL, John (*fl.* 1489–   ) Carpenter

Made seats for *St. Martin's Church, Leicester*, in 1489, when he received £2 3s. 4d., with other payments for materials, etc.

NML

NIKEL, John (*fl.* 1372–   ) Carpenter

On 15 December 1372 John Nikel is mentioned as carpenter to John of Gaunt, Duke of Lancaster, at *Kidwelly Castle*, Carmarthenshire.

JGR 1372–6, 281

NOIERS, Geoffrey de [du Noyer] (*fl.* 1189–1200) ? Mason

Probably came of a Norman family which had settled in Lincolnshire; he has been claimed as a French architect brought to England by St. Hugh, though Viollet-le-Duc was unable to accept the design or detail of the Lincoln work as French. He is described as 'builder of the noble fabric' (*nobilis fabricae constructor*) of St. Hugh's choir in *Lincoln Cathedral* built between 1192 and 1200, and it is clear that this work formed part of a single plan for the cathedral conceived at this time. But Geoffrey's precise function is uncertain, and it seems more probable that his contemporary RICHARD the Mason I was architect of the cathedral.

(APD; BAF, 449); MVH, 336

NORFFOLK, William (*fl.* 1430–1433) Carpenter

Fulfilled a contract of £12 in 1430–33 to make and erect all the timberwork of the chapel of *Rochford Manor*, Essex, over and above what had been done under another contract by John Rampton, carpenter. See also MATTHEW BRIKEMAN.

BL, Egerton Roll 8347

None, John—see NUN

Norhampton—see NORTHAMPTON

NORMANBY, Robert de (*fl.* 1368–1369) Mason

Mason employed by the Dean and Chapter of Lincoln in 1368–69 to carry out repairs to the chancel of the church of (*Castle*) *Bytham*, Lincs. He was paid by instalments a total of £8.

LDC, B.j, 2–6

NORREYS, Richard (*fl. c.* 1250–1270) ? Mason

Employed, apparently as a craftsman, by *Wells Cathedral* in the middle of the 13th century. He was probably related to THOMAS NORREYS, and may have succeeded him as master mason of the cathedral.

HMC, *Wells*, I, 139, 202, 331, 450, 476; II, 562–3, 572–3

NORREYS, Thomas [Norais, Noreis] (*fl.* 1229–1249) Mason

Mason (*cementarius*), appears as a witness to documents in connection with the bequests of Master ADAM LOCK to *Wells Cathedral* in 1229. He probably succeeded Lock as master mason of the cathedral, and is named as 'Master' in a deed of *c.* 1245, during the building of the west front.[1] On 13 December 1249, Thomas '*cementarius*' was witness to a deed at Glastonbury,[2] and may have been identical with Norreys (see THOMAS the Mason IA).

As discussed in connection with Lock, it is probable that the work of the west front was not begun until *c.* 1230, and Norreys was presumably its designer. The style is related to that of Salisbury Cathedral, and ELIAS OF

DEREHAM was concerned with both buildings, but it should be noted that there are great differences of detail and that the Wells design is relatively more advanced in style.

[1] HMC, *Wells*, I, 36, 527; II, 552, 556; [2] C.M. Church in A, LI (1888), 346; *Wells Almshouse Charters*, No. 3 (*L.S.C.*)

NORTH, Richard ['Kyng'] (*fl.* 1440–1447) Mason

Mason (*cementarius*) paid for building the stone walls of the undercroft of the hall and other parts of *South Wingfield Manor*, Derbyshire, for Ralph, Lord Cromwell. In 1443 he received £20 for the foundations of the hall and the vault of its undercroft and work was proceeding at the same time on the great west curtain-wall. Mention is made of three sums totalling £68 10*s*. 11*d*. which had been paid to North in preceding years under his contract. For other work North was paid by task, or at the rate of 3*s*. 4*d*. per week. North was also due to receive another £6 13*s*. 4*d*. over and above the amount of a contract made with Lord Cromwell by JOHN EUTERPACH, but the relation between Euterpach and North is not made clear.[1] North was probably the Collector for Wingfield manor named in 1447.[2]

[1] *KAO*, U 1475 M 207, by kind permission of Viscount De L'Isle, V.C., K.G.; [2] TSW, 427

Northallerton, John—see ALVERTON

NORTHAMPTON, Adam de (*fl.* 1253) Mason

Master Adam de Northampton, mason (*cementario*) was on 9 June 1253 appointed under contract the Master of the Fabric at *Glastonbury Abbey*, with responsibility also for the abbey's other works as well as having charge of the abbey church. He was granted a corrody for life as if one of the monks, with pay of 1*s*. 8½*d*. weekly, 13*s*. 8*d*. at Michaelmas for clothing, and a house in the churchyard of St. John's Church at a yearly rent of 12*d*. payable to the Sacrist, to whom the house would revert after Adam's death. Even if stricken with serious illness or permanent disability, the whole corrody would still be paid. This exceptionally liberal arrangement reflects Master Adam's high reputation.

Longleat MS. 10590, *f*. 59 (*A.W.*)

NORTHAMPTON, John (*fl.* 1417–1423) Mason

In 1417, with Joan his wife, acquired a tenement outside 'le Forgate', Worcester.[1] He was working as a mason at *Worcester Cathedral Priory* in 1423, when with Walter his mate he

received a joint wage of 5*s*. a week.[2]

[1] BCW, 55; [2] WCR

NORTHAMPTON, Ralph of (*fl.* 1227) Canon

Augustinian canon of St. James, Northampton, sent for by Henry III on 22 April 1227 to repair the fishpond at *Woodstock*.

CLR 1226–40, 28

NORTHAMPTON, Robert of [Norhampton, Northamptone] (*fl.* 1293–1319) Carpenter

Master carpenter of London; was concerned in several property transactions in the city between 1293 and 1313, when his wife Marjorie is mentioned.[1] In 1313 he was sworn carpenter to the City of London.[2] On 15 June 1315 John, son of Nicholas le Barber of London, granted to Master Robert 'de Northamptone', carpenter, his tenement in the parish of St. Bartholomew the Less, between the land of John de Middeltone on the west, the tenements formerly of John de Gildeforde on the east, and in length between the moor of Walbrook on the north and the King's highway on the south, at a rent of 6*s*. 8*d*. to 'Le Menchene' of Clerkenwell, and 40*d*. at 'Kinggesrente'.[3]

In 1319 he paid 2*s*. 6*d*. to the subsidy, being assessed in the ward of Cripplegate Within,[4] and may have died in the following year, when ADAM DE ROTHYNG was sworn carpenter to the city. Northampton's son James and the latter's wife Joan, disposed of some of the family property between 1331 and 1344.[5]

[1] LHR, 23(17), 26(29), 42(18); CLB, 'B', 189; [2] CLB, 'B', 15; [3] LBH, C.58; [4] WLE; [5] LHR, 59(144), 70(91, 92), 72(6, 12)

NORTHAMPTON, Simon of [Simon the Carpenter] (*fl.* 1226–1252) Carpenter (? *Northington, Hants.*)

On 10 December 1226, Master Simon de Northampton was one of the five King's Carpenters, and payments on account of his fees are recorded for many years.[1]

On 31 July 1234 Simon de Northampton was named as one of the four 'King's Carpenters' who were to take timber for the repair of the chamber and chapel at the King's manor of *Havering-atte-Bower*.[2] There seems to be little doubt that he was identical with the Simon who was working as a carpenter at *Windsor Castle* two years later, and who had charge of works there for nearly 15 years. In

1236 he was called 'Symon the King's Carpenter' when orders were given to the keeper of Windsor Forest to let him have two twisted posts for mending a kitchen at Windsor, with timber for making a gutter in another of the King's kitchens there and props to push back the King's wardrobe which had gone over on one side.

A very much greater quantity of timber was provided in August 1240, amounting to 190 oaks and a beech tree for making tables for the King's kitchen, besides firewood for a kiln. In the following January the King ordered that Master Simon should have timber 'for lengthening the chamber of Edward our son and making an alley from the kitchen to the hall'. During March the King's chamber was being built and more timber was procured, and by November it was probably ready for roofing, for the Constable and Keepers of the Tower of London had orders to send 10 fothers of lead to Master Simon, on the 15th of the month.

Through 1242 very extensive works were going on, and some £350 was paid to Master Simon for them in several instalments; the chapel is on one occasion specified as in course of erection. Further large sums were allotted to Master Simon in 1243, and he is named as one of the keepers of the works, the others being Hugh Giffard and William le Brun, who were not craftsmen. On 15 June the bailiffs of Wargrave were instructed to let Master Simon have 6 good oaks for making shingles for the works, and on 12 January 1243/4 the keepers, including Simon, were allowed £200 for the cost of obtaining material for the buildings. By December the King's lodgings were ready for wainscoting, for which Simon was to have 10 marks.

Master Simon was evidently the King's Chief Carpenter for all works, and not merely for those at Windsor, for in 1245 he was associated with Master HENRY DE REYNS, the King's Master Mason, when the latter was sent to view the defences of *York Castle*, and to confer there 'with other masters expert in the science', as to how it should be fortified.[3] From 1244 to 1249 Simon's name appears as one of the keepers of the works at Windsor Castle; in October 1249 he was supervising the completion of the barbican with Master THOMAS the Mason II, of Windsor, and an account for the five years ending in 1252 includes a payment to him of £5 for paving

the King's lodging. He probably died in or soon after 1252, as he is not again mentioned.
HKC; **HWC**
[1] CLR, *passim*; [2] CCR 1231–4, 488; [3] *Ibid.* 1242–7, 293

NORTHWICH, Thomas de (*fl.* –†1207) Benedictine Monk

Monk of *Evesham* and physician; is said to have built the tower of the abbey church. This tower collapsed soon after his death in 1207.
SHB, 10–11 qu. MAE, 108, 224

NORTON, John (*fl.* 1480–) Mason

Freemason of Bristol and master of the work of the church of *St. Mary Redcliffe* in 1480, when William Worcestre took down from him particulars of its dimensions.[1]

He may have been identical with the John Norton, mason, who was working at *Southampton* on the water-house in 1428–29, taking 3s. or 3s. 4d. a week;[2] with the John Norton who in 1434 assisted in the making of a niche on the west side of the Lollards' Tower at *Lambeth Palace*;[3] and with the John Norton (*lathamus*), who worked at *Eton College* from 16 September 1448 until September 1449 or later, at 6d. a day.[3]

(APD)
[1] *Corpus Christi Coll., Camb.*, MS. 210, pp. 130, 158; HWI, 366–7; DAB, 133, 202, 207; cf. A, XXXV (1853), 279–97; [2] HMC, 11R, III, 134 ff.; [3] GLP, 52–6; [4] KJE, 36; (AQC, XLVI, 103) and *ECA*, Accs. (*G.P.J.*)

NOTTINGHAM, John [Notyngham] (*fl. c.* 1457–1467) Mason

Between 1457 and 1467 was paid 23s. 4d. for making buttresses by agreement at *Corpus Christi College, Cambridge*. These are probably the buttresses in the Old Court of the college. He also contracted to make two windows for 48s. 8d. The payments to him occur in an account book kept by the master of the college, John Botwright, covering the years 1457–67.[1] Between 1460 and 1462 John Notyngham was working on the south range of the *Schools* at Cambridge.[2]

A.O.
[1] CAC, XXII, 76–90; [2] CGB, 'A', 28, 34

Nottingham, Peter of—see PETER

NOTTINGHAM, Ralph de (*fl.* 1278–1282) Mason (*Nottingham*)

A working mason under WALTER OF HEREFORD at Vale Royal Abbey in 1278, had become master in charge of the works of *Hope Castle*, Flints., by 1282, taking 3s. per week.

He was subordinate to Master JAMES OF ST. GEORGE.

HKW, I, 331

NOTTINGHAM, William de [Notingham] (*fl.* 1276) ? Carpenter

Master (? carpenter); in charge of works at *Westminster Palace* and the *Royal Mews* from August to October 1276, taking apparently 7s. a week.

PRO, E.101–467–7(2)

Noyer, Geoffrey du—see NOIERS

NUN, John [None, Nunne] (*fl.* 1518–?†1536) Joiner

Joiner and carver of Drinkstone, Suffolk; on 30 June 1520 contracted in partnership with ROGER BELL to erect the roodloft at *Great St. Mary's Church, Cambridge*, by Whitsun 1522, for £92 6s. 8d. The Christ was to be as at Triplow, Cambs., while the 'Backside' was to be modelled on that at Gazeley, Suffolk.[1] Nun and Bell were already receiving payments in 1518, and the final payment was made in 1523.[2] This roodloft, 'magnificently constructed and partly gilded', was taken down by order of Archbishop Parker in 1562.[3]

In 1524 Nun's lands at Drinkstone were valued at £2, the tax being assessed at 2s.[4] In 1527–28 John Nunne, carpenter, received a robe from the cellarer of the Abbey of Bury. He and his fellows were paid 52s. 8d. for felling trees and planing them for reparations within the monastery.[5] He may have been the 'John Nunne of Woolpett' (Woolpit) whose will was proved at Bury St. Edmunds on 17 March 1535/6.[6]

(*A.O.*)

[1] CAS, Publ., x, 63–7; [2] CWM, 36, 53; [3] *Ibid.*, 150–1; CAS, Publ., x, 81; CGB, 'B', II, 86; [4] SGB, x, 332; [5] *BM*, Add. Ch. 53140; [6] RBW, 209

NUNNE, Thomas (*fl.* 1460) Carpenter

Carpenter of Rougham, Suffolk; on 18 August 1460 entered into a contract with JOHN FORSTER, mason of *Bury St. Edmunds* to make a parlour to be set 'where the olde halle is late Richard Parmenter'. Nunne was to receive £1 in advance, and to complete the work by midsummer 1461.

A.E.B.O. in ARC, xiv (1979), 19–20

NUNTON, Thomas (*fl.* 1424–) Mason (*Nunton, N'hants.*)

Contracted with Roger Flore esquire of London and Oakham, to vault the tower of *Oakham Church* for 5 marks, of which he had received a noble in earnest at some time before 15 April 1424, when Roger Flore made his will. The will refers to this agreement in the following terms:

'If ye voute of Okeham stepill be not made in my lif, ye which I haf made covenaunt of with Thomas Nunton, mason, to gif him v mark for ye werkmansshipe (of ye which I have paied him a noble on ernest) I wol ye same covenaunt be fulfillid of my good after my decesse as sone as myn neebours wul ordeyn for ye stuffe yat shall go yerto of ye which stuffe Richarde Oxenden haith paied to Fairchilde quarriour . . . xiijs. and iiijd. for freestone.' The will was proved (*PCC* 69 Luffenam) on 20 June 1428, but it is not clear whether the work was ever carried out.

EETS, LXXVIII, 65–74

Nunziata—see TOTO

Nykyr, Thomas—see NEKER

'NYMES, Richard' A misreading of Robert Nynes—see ROBERT JANYNS junior

OBEDONE, Nicholas de [Nicholas the Carpenter] (*fl.* 1351–1360) Carpenter

Carpenter employed by *Worcester Cathedral Priory* from 1351 to 1360 and perhaps earlier and later, with a yearly fee of 20s. in addition to payments for work done.

WCO, Cellarer's rolls

OCLEYE, John de (*fl.* 1283) Mason

Master mason in charge of the works of repair at *Aberystwyth Castle* in 1283, when he was paid 7s. a week.

HKW, I, 305

Octon, Thomas de—see HOUGHTON

ODO the Carpenter (*fl.* 1246–1263) Carpenter

Master; of Westminster in 1246[1] and subsequently, when he was the owner of land there and witnessed various charters;[2] was working at *Westminster Abbey* in 1248–49, under Master ALEXANDER and was in charge of repairs at the Palace in 1263, after it had been partly destroyed by fire in the preceding year. He must have made the wooden ceiling of the Painted Chamber which was then put up. The keeper of the Tower of London was ordered at this time to deliver to Master Odo the King's Carpenter the engine called 'Truye' (i.e. Sow) to raise timber. Though subordinate to Master Alexander, Odo was of high standing, as he was provided with a furred robe each year from 1255 or earlier.

(LKC, 154, 162, 172)
[1] *WAM*, 17155B; [2] *WAM*, 17085, 17148A, 17148B, 17161, 17349, 17353, 17369, 17379, 17389, 17511; [2] CCR 1254–6, 91, 239–40, 312; 1256–9, 13, 54, 159, 218

ODO the Goldsmith (*fl.* 1218–†*c.* 1242) Goldsmith

Keeper of the Palace of Westminster; there are frequent records of money being paid to him for repairs of the King's houses there, from 1218 onwards until about 1242. He was not an architect, but a financial administrator. His son EDWARD FITZ ODO succeeded him.

APD

ODO, Edward fitz (*fl.* 1239–†*c.* 1264) Clerk

Son of ODO the Goldsmith; was associated with his father in 1239, and was later Keeper of the works of the Palace, and one of the keepers of the works of Westminster Abbey, from 1243 to the end of 1263. He was not an architect, but was smelter to the Exchequer, Treasurer, and later King's Clerk.

(APD; CLR; LKC); J. G. Noppen in ANJ, XXVIII, 138 ff.; XXIX, 13 ff.; HKW, I, 101–4

OFFORD, John (*fl.* 1380–   ) Mason

On 7 March 1379/80 John of Gaunt, Duke of Lancaster granted 'of special grace to our well loved John Offord "maceon" a cottage with appurtenances in our town of Saham (Saham Toney), Norfolk, once of Katherine de Dereslee, containing 1 acre'; the grant was to John Offord and the heirs of his body, by rent of 8*d.* a year and suit of court. (See UFFORD, THOMAS.)

JGR 1379–83, 962

Offord, Thomas—see UFFORD

OKEY, William [Okay] (*fl.* 1525–1531) Carpenter and Carver

In 1525 a certain W. Okay, carpenter, was warden carver at Wolsey's works of *Cardinal College*, Oxford.[1] He was almost certainly identical with the William Okey of 'Gippeswiche' (Ipswich), carpenter, who was paid for 12 days' work at Ipswich in 1531 at 7*d.* a day, for looking after the King's storeyard there in connection with the works of *Whitehall Palace*.[2] The storeyard at Ipswich contained the materials from Wolsey's intended college there, which were transported by sea to Westminster for use in the King's work.

[1] HCW, 54n.; [2] PRO, E.36–251

OLIVER, Adam (*fl.* 1384–1385) Carpenter

In 1384–85 repaired all the timberwork, such as shutters, on the battlements of *Carisbrooke Castle*. The work was done by contract for £43, made with HUGH HERLAND the King's carpenter and the two King's masons HENRY YEVELEY and WILLIAM WYNFORD.

HKW, II, 595

OLIVER, Bede [Olyver] (*fl.* 1513–*c.* 1523) Carpenter

'Master Carpenter of the Vanguard', was appointed master carpenter of *Calais* on 20 December 1513 and his name occurs in the expenses of war in 1514. He was succeeded in 1523 by THOMAS JAY.

LPH. I, 4611; 5724; HKW, III, 419

OLIVER, (William ?) (*fl.* 1507–1508) Mason

Between October 1507 and March 1508 a mason called Oliver was employed at *Little Saxham Hall*, Suffolk, to carry out masonry work. He was paid 21*s.* 8*d.* for three two-light windows in the chapel, a two-light window in the gable-end and a single light in the stair, and for making a doorway; also 4*s.* 8*d.* for a light in the gable-end of the parlour and 3*s.* 4*d.* for another window.[1] More important masonry work was undertaken by WILLIAM BURDON. The building contractor was JOHN BROND. Oliver was probably the William Oliver who in the summer and autumn of 1508 was working at *King's College Chapel* at 3*s.* 4*d.* a week and on 1 October received a reward of 16*d.* for four weeks' 'intayling'.[2]

A.O.
[1] GHT, 145–6; [2] *KCM*, Building Acc. 1508–09

ORCHARD, John (*fl.* 1376–1395) Brassworker

Brassworker (*latoner*) of London, was paid £5 on 31 May 1376 for providing angels for the tomb of Queen Philippa of Hainault in *Westminster Abbey*.[1] He was not a mason (*latomus*) though he has sometimes been so described in error. In 1377 he acquired a house and garden in Tothill Street, Westminster, and may have been engaged on the making of the bronze effigy of Edward III.[2] In 1395 he disposed of houses in the parish of St. Olave Old Jewry, London.[3]

(APD; LKC)
[1] *PRO*, E.403–460; [2] LKC, 289; [3] *LHR* 124(108)

ORCHARD, William [Orcheyerd, W. Mason] (*fl.* 1468–†1504) Mason

Freemason and citizen of Oxford; was probably employed by *Balliol College*, which in 1472 granted him a lease of the Pike Inn on favourable terms; at this time mention is made of his wife Agnes and son John.[1] He had been from 1468 master of the work of Bishop

Waynflete's *Magdalen College* and also undertook considerable sections of the work by contract. The walls surrounding the site were put up between 1467 and 1473, and in the latter year the buildings were set out, probably by Orchard as responsible designer. The foundation-stone was laid on 5 May 1474, and work proceeded rapidly, so that the buildings were occupied by 1480. On 2 October 1475 William 'Orcheyerd' and his wife Agnes had been granted the rent of a tenement in Oxford for William's 'good and praiseworthy service and counsel' (*bona et laudabilia servicium et consilium*), and the rent of an adjoining house was conveyed to them on 26 March 1477; the rent of a third house, next to the previous two, in St. Aldates, was added in 1483, bringing Orchard's total fee up to £4 yearly.[2]

Orchard's first contract was made on 16 September 1475, when he agreed to make for 20 marks (£13 6s. 8d.) the great west window of the chapel in 7 lights, according to his own 'portraiture', to make 22 cloister windows, and buttresses, at 48s. 4d. for each window and buttress, and to cut freestone for 12 doors and 102 other windows at 6s. 8d. each. The cloister windows were to be 'as good as those of All Souls College or better'. He was also to make two-light windows for the library at 13s. 4d. each.

The building accounts show that Orchard was actively directing the operations, and incidentally that he had other work of his own. His expenses were paid for riding with Robert Baron to London and then on to Waltham to speak with Waynflete, and he was paid a reward of £1 for his diligence in attending to superintend the work on various occasions 'to the hindering of his own work'. In addition he had 10s. for his livery, and on some occasions acted as paymaster to the subordinate masons; he also had 10s. which he paid to the Abbot of Rewley for 'a great instrument called a crane to lift stones and mortar high up over the wall'.[3]

In 1478 Magdalen College leased to Orchard land at Barton in the parish of Headington for 59 years, and he may have farmed this land in addition to stone-quarrying at Headington. On 5 October 1478 he acquired a tenement in Oxford in the parish of St. Michael at the South Gate, between 'Waterhall' on the south and a toft of St. Frideswide's on the north.[4] In January 1479 he undertook by a further contract with Magdalen College to make buttresses and battlements for the chapel and to do work on the hall, library, and towers.[5] At the same time he contracted to supply stone for Waynflete's works at *Eton College* from the quarry at Headington which he leased from the King, where he would set to work 'quarryours, masones and laborares';[6] he was evidently in charge of Waynflete's work at Eton, including the antechapel.

In April 1479 he undertook a third contract, whereby he was to make the 'vyse' or staircase of the Founder's Tower at Magdalen, and a spire 16 feet in height, with pinnacles 11½ feet high, the pinnacles to cost 11s. 1d. each and the spire 9 marks (£6). Between 1480 and 1483 the vault of the *Divinity School* (begun by RICHARD WINCHCOMBE in 1430) was made, and the occurrence upon it of the initials W.O. has suggested that he was the responsible mason and this is confirmed both by the evidence of style and by the fact that he took an oath to serve the university in the year 1478–79, rode to visit the Bishop of London on behalf of the university in 1482–83, and was paid for supplying stone for the university's use in the same year.[7]

This evidence is confirmed by a request made in 1479 by the University of Oxford, that the masons who had just finished Magdalen College should not be impressed by the Crown for Windsor, but should be left in the university's employment.[8] In 1482 Orchard sold stone for the School of Canon Law at Oxford,[9] and in the following year he conveyed land at Barton to John Atkyns of Headington, being described in the deed as 'of Oxford, esquire'.[10]

His own lease of land at Barton from Magdalen College was altered in 1486 to a term of 20 years or for his lifetime, at the nominal rent of a red rose payable on the Feast of St. John the Baptist. The college reserved to themselves the working of the quarries on this land, but Orchard's title to two acres which he had acquired was conceded.[11] He was then referred to as 'William Orchard commonly called Master William Mason'.

On 20 August 1490 Orchard made a will which was later revoked. In it he described himself as 'of the towne of Oxford, esquier' and desired to be buried in St. Frideswide's

Church; to the priory he left 6s. 8d. yearly for prayers for his soul and that of his wife Agnes, this rent charge to be paid out of his house in Grampound without the South Gate of Oxford. He had bought this house from Robert Fisher in 1478. His 'ferme place of Edyngton (Headington) named sumtyme Jenyns Place' was to be charged with a like sum of 6s. 8d. to Magdalen College. His rights in Jenyns Place, and 2½ acres of quarry at Headington, were to go to Orchard's son 'John the younger', while his daughters Elisabeth and Anne were to have Fisher's house, and a house in Headington called 'Hils house' respectively. The references to St. Frideswide's (now Oxford Cathedral) suggest that Orchard was responsible for the new works there including the pendant vault of the choir (c. 1478–1503) and the cloisters (c. 1489–99).[12]

In 1490 he leased some of his Headington land, being again styled 'esquire'.[13] Throughout this period he must have been in charge of the new works at Magdalen College, where the President's lodging was built from 1485 to 1488, the Muniment Tower in 1487–88, while the south cloister was finished in 1490. The great Bell Tower was begun in this year, though it was not completed until 1509, five years after Orchard's death.[14]

About 1500 work was proceeding on the aisle and arcade of Waterstock Church, Oxon., for Thomas Danvers, lord of the manor. Danvers was Waynflete's agent for the purchase of lands for Magdalen College, and the work at Waterstock Church is in Orchard's style, so that it seems probable that he carried out the work or provided designs.[15] This work was still in progress in 1501, when Orchard again leased a portion of his land at Headington.

On 25 May 1502 he contracted with the Abbot of Fountains, Yorks., to provide stone for the Cistercian College of St. Bernard (now St. John's College) in Oxford. The abbot was to be responsible for removing the soil from the quarry, so that stone should be laid bare not only for the building of the college but also for other buildings which Orchard might be supplying.[16] By another contract of 13 February 1502/3, for completion of the work at the end of 1504, it is clear that he was engaged on the building of this college, which was still in progress when he died in 1504.

Orchard's final will was made on 21 January 1503/4; in this he refers to his second wife, Katherine, to whom he left a close of land at 'Heddyngton townys end' and a garden in Oxford by Jury Lane.[17]

Orchard lived in Oxford, in a house which he rented from Balliol College.[18] His elder son, John, evidently the 'John son of William Mason' who was a chorister at Magdalen in 1484/5, took the degree of B.C.L., and was a brewer in 1505. He was living in 1513, when he sold some of the Headington property. A document in the archives of Magdalen College gives a picturesque account of the negotiations for sale on 7 March 1512/13, when John Orchard and his brother-in-law Harry Oldame and others went to Headington Quarry 'and called all the said men working in divers mens quarries together, and they all sat down upon a green bank and did drink a pennyworth of ale' as a preliminary to the surrender by John Orchard of his right in the property by the transfer of a symbolic straw.[19]

William's daughter Isabella (alias Elizabeth) had married Edward Mawdisley, tailor of Oxford, about 1490, married secondly Harry Oldame of Oxford, and died before September 1513. Orchard asked in his will to be buried in St. Frideswide's Priory Church and bequeathed to the Priory the house in Crampolle (Grandpool or Grandpont) after the decease of his wife Katherine.

William Orchard was undoubtedly one of the greatest architects of his time, and he is of particular interest in that he remained, so far as is known, outside the orbit of the royal works. His position as a quarry-owner was evidently of considerable importance, and his social standing was high; in all probability he was the designer of a great deal of work in and near Oxford during the last thirty years of his life, though there must have been other architects working there. In spite of considerable differences in detail between the two great pendant vaults of the Divinity Schools and St. Frideswide's, circumstantial evidence favours Orchard as the builder of both. That of the Divinity Schools was certainly intended at a much earlier date, and it may be that it to some extent follows a design laid down by Winchcombe or by THOMAS ELKIN. The vault of St. Frideswide's probably dates from between 1485 and 1500.

In his earlier career Orchard may perhaps have designed several works for Sir Robert Harcourt, high steward of the university from

1446 to 1471; the Harcourt aisle of *Stanton Harcourt Church* (*c.* 1470) and 'Pope's Tower' there, and the church of *Southleigh*, a chapelry of Stanton; perhaps also the tower of *Kempsford Church*, Glos., which had close stylistic similarities. The piers of the Harcourt aisle are identical in section with those of the antechapel of Magdalen.[20]

KJI; GOM, 75–9; (DNB; APD; BAA; WDO)
[1] SBD, 126; [2] SCH, II, 161–2; III, 282; [3] BMC, II, 227 ff.; [4] ELA, No. 264; [5] WMC, 21–4; [6] WCC, I, 410; [7] SMO, II, 324, 338–9; [8] SMO, II, 291; OEA, 448; [9] SMO, II, 339; [10] HMC, 3R, 318; [11] Magdalen Coll. Ledger 'A', *f.* 50v.; [12] SSF, 216; [13] HMC, 3R, 318; [14] RCHM, *City of Oxford*, 69a; [15] Will of T. Danvers, made 1 Nov. 1501 (*E.A.G.L.*); [16] OHS, NS, I, 28–9, 83–4; [17] SSF, 217; [18] SBD; [19] MMM, 20–1; [20] DMM

ORGAR, John [Orger, Orgoure] (*fl.* 1508–†1546) Mason

In 1508, and probably earlier, was warden of the masons on the staff of *London Bridge*, taking 4s. a week for 43 weeks in the account for 1508–09. In 1513 he was promoted to the office of chief bridge mason in succession to THOMAS WADE, at a yearly salary of £10. He was also paid for the services of his apprentices, Robert Holte, whose rate varied from 6d. to 7d. a day, from 1514 to 1518, and Thomas Felde from 1519 to 1525, in respect of whom Orgar was paid 4d. a day for the first two years, 6d. a day for the next three, and 7d. a day for the last two years.[1]

Orgar was presumably identical with the John Orgar who supplied '150 foote of hardston of Kent at 8d. the foote redy hewyn' in February 1514/15, for the works of York Place, and in the following August supplied 50 feet of 'passe stone' ready hewn, also at 8d. a foot, for the same works.[2] In 1531–32, John Orgar of Boulton (Boughton Monchelsea) Quarry in Kent supplied 'hard stone of Kent called ashlar' for Henry VIII's extension of York Place (i.e. the *New Palace of Westminster*, or Whitehall).[3] He was working as a mason there at 12d. a day being described as 'John Orgoure of Boulton Mounchelsea' and on 28 January 1536 he signed by mark (|𝒷) a deposition as to the sale of stone to York Place.[4]

In 1538 'John Orger' was the fifth named in the list of the Court of Assistants of the London Masons' Company, and in 1546 the will was proved of John Orgar of London and Boughton Monchelsea, Kent.[5]

This Orgar may perhaps have been a son of *John ORGAR* who was a hardhewer on

the works of *London Bridge* in 1475–76.[6]
[1] KJL, 15, 28, 32; [2] PRO, E.101–474–7; [3] LPH, v, 952; [4] PRO, E.36–251 (*G.P.J.*); *WAM*, 12257; LPH, x, 194, iv; (S.P.1–101, *f.* 208); [5] MHN, IV, 19–20; *PCC*, 24 Alen; [6] KJL, 15

ORTON, David (*fl.* 1464–1472) Carpenter

Carpenter, employed by the Bishop of Winchester at his manor of *Witney*, Oxon., from 1464 to 1472. In 1464–65 Orton made a new roof for the chapel of the manor for £3 0s. 1d., and worked on the grange and on the new roof over the chapel altar for £1 2s. 0d. In the following year he roofed the chamber next the chapel, in 1466–67 worked on the grange, and in 1471–72 was paid £2 1s. 0d. for work on the great kitchen.

PRO, Eccl. 2–2–155832, 2–3–155833, 155834, 155836

OSBERT the Mason (*fl.* 1129–1130) Mason

The Pipe Roll for 1130 records a payment of £1 15s. 0d. to Osbert the Mason of Baenburg (*Bamburgh*, Northumberland), as well as the sum of 7d. spent on repairing the gate of the castle there. The existing stone keep was not built until 1164–70.

(BBH, 234); HMR, 35

OSEKYN, John [Osekin] (*fl.* 1274–   ) Carpenter

Was paid 8d. a day in 1274 when in charge of works at the *Tower of London*; perhaps father of ROBERT OSEKYN.

PRO, E.101–467–6(4)

OSEKYN, Robert (*fl.* 1300–†1311) Carpenter

Was a sworn carpenter of the City of London in 1300, and master carpenter at the *Palace of Westminster* in 1307, taking 1s. a day. In 1310 he was paid 12 marks (£8) for making two 'loggeas' next the great hall for the masons to work, and to store the stones cut for St. Stephen's Chapel. He died in October 1311, leaving considerable property in the parishes of St. Bartholomew and St. Benet to his wife Joan (a daughter of William le Callere) with reversion to his sons John and Simon.

SWL, I, 223; *PRO*, E.101–468–21, *f.* 116v; cf. *LHR*, 35(76), 40(28), 44(98, 100), 53(31), 54(69), 56(61–4, 67, 70–2), 58(3), 92(2, 3)

OSMUND the Mason (*fl. c.* 1175–1200) Mason

Mason (*cementarius*), apparently concerned with the King's works at *Clipston*, Notts., in the late 12th century, when with ROGER 'Artifex' he witnessed a charter granting land at Morton, Notts., to Rufford Abbey.

(*H.M.C.*)   SDD, 275, No. 370

OSWESTRE, David (*fl.* 1416–   ) Carpenter (*Oswestry, Salop*)

Carpenter of Coventry; in 1416–17 was granted by the Holy Trinity Guild a lease for 24 years of cottages in Bishop's Street, Coventry, by yearly rent of 6*s.*, on condition that he rebuilt the cottages within two years.

HMC, 15R, x (1899), 144

OTES, John [Otys] (*fl.* 1508–1527) Mason

A mason-setter at *King's College Chapel, Cambridge*, in the summer of 1508, receiving the higher rate of pay of 3*s.* 8*d.* a week;[1] was in charge of the building of the tower of *All Saints Church, Derby* (now the cathedral) in 1527, and probably throughout from about 1510 until its completion in or after 1532. His normal rate of pay was 3*s.* 4*d.* a week, but during the 27 weeks from Passion Sunday to All Saints, 1527, he lost pay for holidays in five weeks, taking only 1*s.* 8*d.* in the week after Palm Sunday, Pentecost, and the week of St. James, and 2*s.* 10*d.* in the weeks after Low Sunday and Corpus Christi.[2]

[1] *KCM*, Building Acc. 1508–09 (*A.O.*); [2] CHD

Ouguet—see HUGUET

Oxford, Elyas of—see ELIAS the Engineer

OXFORD, Henry of (*fl.* 1281–1302) Carpenter

Carpenter engaged on carting timber for the works of *Flint Castle* in 1281–82; as carpenter of *Rhuddlan Castle* in 1282 he took 8*d.* a day,[1] and was also working at *Hope Castle* and on the bridge near Bangor. He was master carpenter of the works of *Carnarvon Castle* in 1283–84,[2] and later master carpenter at the building of *Conway Castle*; in 1285 he undertook, with Master RICHARD LENGINOUR to build the hall and chambers there for £100.[3] In 1301 he was paid £8 6*s.* 8*d.* for work at Rhuddlan Castle, and in the following year he and others were paid £26 17*s.* 7*d.* for making two mangonels there.[4]

WPS; HKW, I, 331, 333, 356–7

[1] A, XVI, 32; [2] H, NS, XXXV, 260; [3] A, LXXXVI; [4] FHS, III, 16, 34

PABENHAM, John de (*fl.* 1292–1293) Mason

In 1292 was working at *St. Stephen's Chapel* in Westminster Palace. A later John de Pabenham was working at Westminster Palace in 1319 as a mason's assistant at 3½*d.* a

day.[1] The Pabenham family of masons was a large one, and besides Masters SIMON PABENHAM I and II comprised:

Adam de PABENHAM who in 1278–80 was employed at the quarry of the works of *Vale Royal Abbey*.[2]

Henry de PABENHAM and *William de PABENHAM*, who worked as stone-layers at *Westminster Palace* in 1307.

Hugh PABENHAM, mason, who worked on repairs at *Westminster Palace* in 1351, and at *Rotherhithe Manor* in 1353,[3] and

Walter PABENHAM, mason, who was paid 5*d.* a day as one of the masons working on the little hall at *Westminster Palace* in 1287–88.[4]

LKC

[1] BBW, 123; [2] PRO, E.101–485–22; CNW, XXXVII, 296; [3] PRO, E.101–471–6; 545–33; [4] *Ibid.*, E.101–467–17

PABENHAM, Simon de I [Papenham, Papinham, Pappenham] (*fl. c.* 1262–†*c.* 1280) Mason (*Pavenham, Beds.*)

Simon de Papinham, '*apparilarius*' (warden of craftsmen), was a witness to a grant of land belonging to the fabric of *Lincoln Minster* at a date between 1262 and 1273;[1] and at Michaelmas 1272 Simon de Pappenham, mason, was granted a tenancy of 4 years in a house in the parish of St. Margaret-on-the-Hill in Lincoln Close. SIMON DE TRESK, the master mason of the Minster, was the first witness.[2] This would seem to imply the expectation that Pabenham was to continue to be Tresk's warden at Lincoln until late in 1276.

On the other hand, there is conclusive evidence that one Master Simon de Papinham, mason (*cementarius*), was the master in charge at the new building of the church of *St. Mary's Abbey, York*, begun in 1270 though not finished until 1294. He was probably but not certainly the *Magister Simon cementarius* who was witness to a deed concerning rent payable to the Vicars Choral of York Minster from property in Goodramgate, York; though undated, the deed appears to be of *c.* 1269–70, considerably too early for any likelihood of identity with Master SIMON the Mason I (†1322).[3]

The list of obits maintained by St. Mary's Abbey included one for '*Symon Cementarius*' on 13 May;[4] which, apart from general probability, could not be in respect of the Simon who died in 1322. The cartulary of the obedientiaries of St. Mary's Abbey contains not only title to property at Rudston, Yorks. E.R., left for the maintenance of the obit of Master Simon de Papinham, *Cementarius*, but also the copy of a Final Concord in reference to the transaction, dated June 1280. It is therefore probable that Simon had died on 13 May 1280 or possibly in the previous year on 13 May 1279.[5]

It is quite conceivable that the Lincoln Simon, a warden but not a master *c*.1262–72, was a son of the architect of St. Mary's Abbey, York, and furthermore that he was identical with Simon the Mason I (q.v.). This would go far towards explaining the stylistic relationships between the Minster chapter-house of *c*. 1260–90 and St. Mary's Abbey, and the different but more remotely related style of the Minster nave, designed by 1290. Likewise the certainty of a connection with Pavenham in Bedfordshire, and thus with a family or group of important masons engaged on the king's works, explains the transfer of elements of the Court style to York.

J.H.H. in ACY, 149–56

[1] *LDC*, Reg. Ant. 2722 (*K.M.*); [2] *LAO*, VC 2/1 no 224 (*K.M.*); [3] *YML*, Vicars Choral deeds (*C.B.L.B.*); [4] HBS, LXXXIV (1949–50), iii (1951), 370; cf. SS, CXLVIII, 112; *A.B.W.* in AJ, CXXVIII, 123; [5] *YML*, MS. XVI.A.2, *ff*. 86, 85v

PABENHAM, Simon II [Pabingham] (*fl.* 1282–†1334) Mason

The most important of a large family of London masons who probably came from Pavenham, a few miles north-west of Bedford. At the *Tower of London* in 1282, the sum of £3 1*s.* 2½*d.* was paid to Simon de Pabenham and his fellows for vaulting the tower towards St. Katherine's at task.[1] In 1287 he was a surety on behalf of Master RALPH OF CHICHESTER, marbler, that the latter would carry out his contract to supply marble columns and details for the works of *Vale Royal Abbey*, Cheshire.[2] Pabenham purchased houses in St. Sepulchre's parish, London, in 1292,[3] and in 1293 he built the *Eleanor Crosses* at Northampton and St. Albans with JOHN DE BATAILE.[4] In 1298 he quarrelled with RICHARD DE WYTHAM and both were taken before the mayor and aldermen at the Guildhall, where they were reconciled, agreeing that the one guilty of first renewing the quarrel should give £5 to the fabric of London Bridge. Pabenham went back to the royal service as master mason at the Tower of London from 1307 to 1311.

Master Simon was sworn as a viewer of the masons' craft in the City of London in 1313, when he was to survey party-walls and other matters connected with the building code together with the chamberlain of the city, and ALEXANDER OF CANTERBURY, mason; for the works of carpentry they had associated with them Master ROBERT OF NORTHAMPTON, carpenter.[5]

Two years later Simon Pabenham was one of a commission of London masons who met to chose six paviours for the repair of the pavements of the city. Pabenham died in 1334; his will, proclaimed in the Court of Husting on 16 January 1334/5, shows that he lived near St. Sepulchre's Church, Newgate, to which church he made bequests. His tenements and shops in the parish were to be sold to pay his legacies, while the rest of his property including other tenements was to remain for his wife Amicia and his daughters Alice and Roesia.[6] Many references occur to Pabenham (or Papenham) as owner of properties in West Smithfield, London, ranging in date from 1295 to 1328.[7]

(APD; LKC); HKW, I, 174n.

[1] *PRO*, E.101–467–10; [2] *CNW*, XXXVII, 297; [3] *LHR*, 21(71); cf. 63(67); [4] A.J. Taylor in CNW, XXXVII, 297; [5] CLB, 'B', 15; [6] SWL, I, 400; [7] KBH, nos. 130, 217, 224–5, 240, 254, 259

Pacche—see also PAGE

PACCHE, John (*fl.* 1445–1485) Carpenter

In 1445/6 John Pacche, carpenter, worked at *Westminster Abbey* for 4 days at 8*d.* a day.[1] On 10 March 1454/5 he was appointed the King's Master Carpenter at *Calais* in succession to JOHN TYRELL,[2] and was still in office there in 1472, when the reversion was granted to RICHARD WELLYS,[3] and until 1485, when he was succeeded by WILLIAM WOODWARD.[4]

[1] *WAM*, 23511; [2] DKR, XLVIII, 404; [3] CPR 1467–76, 313; [4] HKW, II, 1054

PACCHE, Richard (*fl.* 1468–) Carpenter

Master carpenter at *Westminster Abbey* in 1468 when he was at work on the roof of the nave.

RNW, 62

Pace—see PAYS

PACENHAM, Thomas de ['Pakenham', 'Patenham'] (*fl. c.* 1339–1348) Mason (? *Passenham, Northants.*)

Was master mason of *York Minster* in the second quarter of the 14th century, probably on the death of Master IVO DE RAGHTON and being succeeded there by WILLIAM HOTON, senior. He had an official residence in the Close, in which later masons were accommodated.[1] (See HOTON, WILLIAM, junior.) Thomas Sampson, Canon of York, in his will made on 15 June 1348 left £20 to the work of the new choir of the cathedral on condition that it should be effectually begun within one year, 'as I have often said to Sir Thomas de Loudham and Thomas de Pacenham'. Loudham was the clerical master of the fabric.[2] (See LUDHAM.)

(APD)

[1] RFY, 166; [2] YTE, I, 54

PADUA, John of (fl. 1543–1556) Architect

On 30 June 1544 was granted a fee of 2s. a day for his services to the King in architecture and to others in music, as from 25 March 1543.[1] This was regranted to him on 25 June 1549 by Edward VI.[2] A later reference of 1555–56 has recently been discovered by Miss E. Auerbach.[3] His life and work remain obscure, though many early Renaissance buildings have been attributed to him, probably without foundation. The question is fully discussed in the Architectural Publication Society's Dictionary, and in the Dictionary of National Biography.

It seems hardly likely that this John can be identical with the John de Padue who was paid for unspecified services at the rate of £1 a month in 1506–07.[4]

SAB, 11; (DNB; APD; BAA)

[1] LPH, XIX, pt. i, p. 505; [2] CPR 1548–9, 338; [3] SAB; (PRO, E.405–122); [4] PRO, E.36–214, pp.113, 126 (A.O.)

Page—see also PACCHE

PAGE, John (fl. 1369–1375) Carpenter

Named second to ROGER FRANKELYN in a contract of 7 April 1369 to build shops in the City of London for the Dean and Chapter of St. Paul's.[1] On 7 February 1374/5 Page took a lease from the Chapter of a shop with a solar above it, outside the wall of the belfry in the eastern part of St. Paul's churchyard.[2]

[1] SHB, 441–3; [2] HMC, 9R, I, 51; (SPM, A.71.1807)

PAGE, Thomas (fl. 1317–1326) Carpenter

Carpenter of Newport, Essex; on 1 April 1317 he contracted to make, for Robert Taper, 28 stalls in the choir of the monastery of Hatfield Regis (Hatfield Broad Oak), Essex, with a proper entrance at the west end and all things appertaining to them, to be as 6 stalls lately put up.

He was to prepare the woodwork at his own house, cutting, sawing, and framing the stalls, and to bring them to the church for carving and polishing. When working at the church he was to receive from the monastery 2 loaves of white bread daily and a gallon of the best ale, with a dish of cooked meat from the kitchen, flesh on flesh days, fish on fish days, or 4 herrings or 6 eggs.

Taper was to pay him £30 as it was required for carrying on the work, which was to be finished by Easter 1319. At the same time Robert Taper paid for the building of the chapels of the Holy Cross and of the Blessed Virgin, the masonry work of the new dormitory, repairs to the old presbytery, and glazing of the new presbytery, and the great south and west windows of the parish church; he also gave a great bell. Only the parochial nave of the church now remains.[1]

As 'Master Thomas the Carpenter', Page worked for Ely Cathedral during the building of the Octagon; in 1322–23, soon after work began, a letter was sent to him at Newport, and he was paid 2s. for his expenses in travelling from Newport to Ely and back with 6s. 8d. for setting up a hoisting machine (le Ferne). In the following year another letter was sent to him, and he was paid 5s. and his board at the Prior's table for 4 weeks while setting up posts; in 1325–26 he received a furred robe costing 15s. 3d.[2]

[1] EAS, NS, II, 134, 136; (ERO, D/DBa T1/36); [2] CSR, I, 21–2, 29, 70; II, 29, 33, 45, 47, 61

Pageny—see MAZZONI, Guido

PAK, Thomas (fl. 1418–†c. 1435) Mason

Was a working mason at York Minster by 1418 (not in 1416) and until 1421 (50 weeks only), when he took up the freedom of York. His wages were 3s. a week. In 1432 he became master mason of York Minster at a yearly fee of £10 in succession to WILLIAM WADDESWYK. In 1435–36 Pak was named as late tenant of Monk Bar, York, probably implying his death, as he was succeeded at the Minster by JOHN BOWDE c. 1436.[1] The south-west tower was begun in 1432 under Pak, but perhaps to Waddeswyk's design; it was not completed until 1456, and the north-west tower, to the same design, not until 1470–74.

(APD; BHY, I, 231–2); RFY, 50, 52; J.H.H. in ACY, 191

[1] YCM, C.82/5

'Pakenham', Thomas de—see PACENHAM

PALDEN, James (*fl.* 1444–1460) Mason

Licence was granted on 3 November 1444 for James Palden, mason, of Laughton, Yorks., to use his ship called *'la Marie'* for seven years for the works of the monastery of *St. Saviour, Syon*, without hindrance of the King's purveyors (cf. JOHN HARDY).[1] In 1459–60 Palden was paid £1 19s. 7d. at 10d. per doliate for conveying 47½ doliates of Huddleston stone from the quarry to Cawood for the building of *Eton College*.[2]

(*A.O.*)

[1] CPR 1441–6, 312; [2] KJE, 14

PALDEN, William [Paulden] (*fl. c.* 1475–1485) Mason

Perhaps a son of JAMES PALDEN; about 1475–85 brought a Chancery suit against Thomas Shaxton for delivering freestone sold on Palden's behalf to the churchwardens of *North Repps*, Norfolk, at the rate of 16 feet to the ton instead of 12 feet.

ECP, bundle 66 no. 268 (*A.O.*)

PALMER, John (*fl.* 1536–1540) Carpenter

In 1536–37 John Palmer of East Farleigh, Kent, took a lease of Tynton Manor.[1] He may have been identical with the master carpenter of this name who was in charge of work at *Sandgate Castle* in 1539–40.[2]

(*A.O.*)

[1] LPH, XIII, pt. i, p. 569 (1519.68.3), p. 582 (1520); [2] AC, XX, 228 ff.

PALMER, Thomas (*fl.* 1505–1506) Mason

Mason (*latamus*) working on repairs of *Ely Cathedral* priory in 1505–06. He and his servant were paid 18d. for 3 days' work on the repairs.[1]

He was probably related to John Palmer, a mason, who had worked for Ely Cathedral in 1440,[2] and Henry Palmer, who had assisted THOMAS PEYNTOUR in 1473.[3]

Thomas Palmer may have been in charge of the rebuilding of the east walk of the cloisters at Ely, a work which cost £124 6s. 9d. in 1509–10.[4]

[1] CUL, Add. MS.2956, ff. 158 ff.; [2] Ibid. [3] CUL, Add. MS. 6387, p.53; [4] CUL, Add. MS. 2956, ff. 158 ff.

PALTERTON, John [Palderton, Paltirtone] (*fl.* 1344–†*c.* 1379) Mason (*Palterton, Derb.*)

A working mason at *Westminster Palace* in 1344, when he was paid 4½d. a day.[1] Probably the unnamed mason in charge of the work of the south cloister of *Westminster Abbey* from 1349, receiving pay of 2s. a week throughout the year, with livery of bread and ale worth 1s. weekly, a yearly fee of £1 6s. 8d. and a robe valued at 13s. 4d.[2] The same fees were paid from 1352 to John Palterton, who continued to have charge of the building of the south and west walks of the cloister until its completion on 20 July 1365.[3]

In 1352–53 Palterton refused his robe because it was not delivered punctually; and on 3 February 1355/6 he set out on pilgrimage, from which he did not return until 6 February 1356/7. During his absence his place was taken by JOHN EAST I. In 1358 he paid into the fabric account a sum of £4 on behalf of the spiritual welfare of his dead colleague, Thomas Duffield, who had died in mid-February; Palterton was probably acting as Duffield's executor. The two men were presumably both of Derbyshire origin. Duffield had worked alongside Palterton at Westminster Palace in 1344.

Palterton continued to be the mason in charge of the works of the Abbey, but payments to him were made through various monastic officials, and it is clear that the whole of the works organisation was transferred departmentally more than once during the spate of building which took place in the late 14th century. The 'Novum Opus' came temporarily to an end with the completion of the cloister, and Palterton and his subordinates were at once transferred to the Infirmarer, from whom Palterton received his pay for 10 weeks before Michaelmas 1365, and for the accounting years 1365–67.[4] The support of the works staff fell to the treasurer from 1367 onwards, and Palterton's yearly fee was at the same time raised from £2 to £2 10s. 0d. This appears in all the surviving treasurer's accounts up to 1378–79 inclusive. From 1375 onwards firewood was purchased for Palterton's use.[5] At the same time he was paid a weekly rate when actually at work, but this was not charged on the treasurer's general account, but on that of the Obedientiar concerned. Thus in 1373–74 Palterton was paid a salary of £5 4s. 0d. (2s. a week for the whole year) by the Sacrist,[6] and he was presumably the John Mason paid for 24 weeks' work on the New Gate at 3s. 8d. by the Cellarer in 1374–75, and for 10 weeks' work on the Abbot's house in the next year at the same rate.[7] Palterton's name does not occur in the treasurer's roll for 1380–81, and by that time he was presumably dead.

Palterton was not described as master until 1361, and the extent of his responsibility for the design of the buildings on which he worked remains doubtful. It was pointed out by Lethaby that the character of the doorway from the little cloister to St. Katherine's Chapel, put up in 1371–72, seems earlier than that of the great cloister done between 1349 and 1365; and he suggested that HENRY YEVELEY may have been responsible for the advanced character of the latter work.[8]

(RNW; LWR, 135–8)

[1] *PRO*, E.101–469–6; [2] *WAM*, 23454; [3] *Ibid.*, 23455–23459; [4] *Ibid.*, 19344–5; [5] *Ibid.*, 19863–9; [6] *Ibid.*, 19634; [7] *Ibid.*, 18857–9; [8] LWR, 136–7

PANTON, William (*fl.* 1515–1532) Mason

In 1515 was warden of the masons at *York Place* at 3s. 4d. a week,[1] and in 1531–32 was working at *Whitehall Palace* at the same rate.[2]

[1] *PRO*, E.101–474–7 (*G.P.J.;L.F.S.*); [2] *PRO*, E.36–251 (*G.P.J.*)

PARES, John [Parrys] (*fl.* 1531–1539) Carver

Of North Lew, Devon; named second when with JOHN DAW he contracted in 1531 to make a roodloft, roodscreen, and parcloses for *Stratton Church*, Cornwall. The final payment for the work was made in 1539. Pares also worked on the rood-screen at *Atherington*, Devon, of *c.* 1530.[2]

[1] GBC, 91–4; [2] *ECP*, 1116–49, in HDE, 272

PARIS, Richard de [Parisius, Parys] (*fl.* 1301–1313) Mason

Master mason sent from Chester to Flint in connection with the building of the great tower of *Flint Castle* in 1301, being paid for three days at the rate of 4d. a day. In 1302–03 he was paid £8 for building a stone wall with three buttresses and two windows for the kitchen of *Chester Castle*, by contract for Master RICHARD LENGINOUR. In 1312–13 he carried out various works on the chambers of Chester Castle, and built a new kitchen by the great hall.

ACC, 6, 25, 79, 80

PARKER, John (*fl.* 1542–1552) Carpenter

Was appointed master carpenter of the Court of Augmentations on 29 September 1542, along with ROBERT SYLVESTER the mason. He held office until 29 September 1552, but from 25 March 1550 discharged the office by deputy, JOHN REVELL, who succeeded him. In 1547 he visited the manor of *Havering*.

HKW, III, 420; IV, 151

PARKER, Richard (*fl. c.* 1530–1544) Carver

Presumably the 'Parker, alabaster man of Burton' who, with JOHN SMYTH, freemason of Derby, was to make a tomb for William, 4th Lord Mountjoy, in the church of *Barton (Blount)*, Derbyshire. The tomb had been devised before 1534. As an 'alablaster man', Richard Parker was in 1543–44 paid £20 for making a tomb of alabaster at *Bottesford*, Leics., for Thomas, Earl of Rutland († 20 September 1543) and his countess.

NLH, 341, 347 (*N.L.R.*); HMC, Rutland, IV (1905), 340–1

PARTRYCHE, William (*fl.* 1458–   ) Carpenter

Was appointed warden of the carpenters at *Sheen* in 1458 in succession to RICHARD WHELER.

HKW, II, 1001n.

PASMYCHE, John [Pasmych] (*fl.* 1523–1525) Carpenter

In November and December 1523 was paid for 25½ days work on making the bell-frame for *Prescot Church*, Lancs., at 4d. a day with 2d. daily for his board. In 1524 he and ROBERT RACHEDALE, mason, received 10d. for their labour and costs coming to Prescot 'to see the steple and bellefraye' in the presence of Mr. Bolde and other gentlemen of the parish.

BPL, 1, 3–5, 7

'Patenham', Thomas de—see PACENHAM

'PATRICE'

Imaginary English master, stated by an historical confusion to have designed the church of Notre-Dame-de-l'Epine, near Chalons-sur-Marne, France. It has been demonstrated that this statement rests on a misunderstanding of documents showing that a French master, Etienne Poutrise, was in charge of the continuation of the works in 1453.[1]

(APD)

[1] LNE, 19

PATRICK the Mason (*fl.* 1344–1352) Mason

Master Patrick the mason, with Master ROBERT OF ST. ALBANS, the carpenter, a plumber and a smith, made a survey of the castle of *Berwick-upon-Tweed* in 1344. In 1347–52 he rebuilt one of the bridges between the castle and the Douglas Tower.

HKW, II, 567

PATRINGTON, Robert, I (*fl.* 1352–1385) Mason

Took up the freedom of York in 1352, and on 5 January 1368/9 was appointed master mason of *York Minster* after the death of WILLIAM HOTON, junior. His contract of employment provided that he was to have a fee of £10 a year, but this was to be reduced to £6 13s. 4d. if he became blind or incapacitated so that he was unable to direct the work. If, through his occupation elsewhere, he were to neglect the Minster fabric and, after being warned three times, fail to return, his salary was to cease until he did so. He was to have the house in the Close in which Hoton had dwelt; 1s. 6d. was spent on two 'lovers' (louvres) for it in 1371.

Besides having charge of the work of the Minster, Patrington made marble tombs for six archbishops between 1368 and 1373, for which he was paid by Archbishop Thoresby.

Patrington completed the presbytery (Lady Chapel) of the Minster, which had been begun by his predecessor, and it is possible that he was the designer of the later parts of *Patrington Church*, endowed by his namesake Robert de Patrington, treasurer of York Minster at this time (1368–71).

On 7 July 1369 Archbishop Thoresby allowed 14 marks (£9 6s. 8d.) to Master Robert de Patrington, master mason, for repairing the windows of the chapel in the manor of *Cawood*.[1] Patrington at the head of twelve other masons on 31 October 1370 swore to abide by the regulations made by the Dean and Chapter. Master Robert de Patrington, *cementarius*, on 7 December 1381 undertook to make by 1 August 1382 a marble stone 8 feet by 4 feet, for an image of laton in likeness of a chaplain decently ornamented, carved etc. This was to be placed on the tomb of dom Thomas de Thweng formerly rector of 'Lython', and a laton etc. with the name of the deceased, to be set up by Patrington.[2]

In 1385 Robert Patryngton, mason, and John Heyndele (see under WILLIAM HYNDELEY), mason, were to build a Cross at the spot where Sir Ralph Stafford had been killed by Sir John Holland, Richard II's half-brother. The Cross, made at the King's orders, was on the Bishopthorpe Road a mile or more south of York.[3]

(APD); BHY, I, 163–4, 166, 168, 171; RFY, 5n., 10, 12, 180, 181n.; *J.H.H.* in ACY, 163–7, 190

[1] DRY, I, 464; [2] YML, L 1 2, p. 56 col. 4; [3] CPR 1385–9,13

PATRINGTON, Robert, II (*fl.* 1410–†1430) Mason

Took up the freedom of York in 1410; on 1 May 1424, Robert Patrington of York, mason, granted all his goods to Thomas Brasebrygge, mayor of York, and others,[1] but by his will, made on the Monday after the first Translation of St. Thomas 1426, and proved on 10 May 1430, he left a number of bequests, including 2s. to St. Paul's Cathedral in London, 3s. 4d. to St. Mary at Lincoln, 3s. to St. John of Beverley, and 6s. 8d. to York Minster. He also left 20d. to the church of St. Michael at the Bridge, in York, where he wished to be buried. He described himself as mason and citizen of York and left his wife Agnes to be executrix.[2]

Ralph de PATRYNGTON, mason of York, died in 1391, his will made on 15 June being proved on 20 June in the Court of the Dean and Chapter.[3] He may well have been the Rauff de Patrington who in 1363 was one of twenty-nine masons pressed in Yorkshire for the works of *Windsor Castle*.[4]

[1] YMB; [2] PCY, ii, 669; [3] DCY, i, 101; [4] PRO, E.101–598–7; AQC, XLIV, 227

PATRINGTON, William, I [Padryngton] (*fl.* 1351–1372) Mason

Master; engaged on carving various images and angels at *St. Stephen's Chapel, Westminster*, from 1351 to 1358, partly by task-work, sometimes at 8d. and sometimes 1s. a day;[1] on 24 May 1372 had licence to go to Scotland to make the tomb of King David II at *Holyrood*.[2]

John PATRINGTON, mason, worked on the cloister of the Queen's Pew at *Westminster Palace* in 1357–58, taking 6½d. and 6d. a day.[3] He was pardoned of the death of two chaplains, of which he had been indicted, on 20 August 1372.[4]

SAW; BBW, 164, 166–7, 176
[1] PRO, E.101–471–6; 472–4; [2] RF (Rec. Comm.), III, 942; [3] PRO, E.101–472–4; [4] CPR 1370–4, 199

PATRINGTON, William, II [Padryngton, Patrynton] (*fl.* 1382–1397) Mason

Mason working for the Sacrist of *Westminster Abbey* between 1382 and 1393 at 3s. 8d. a week until 1389 and later at 3s. 4d., and a yearly tunic worth 6s. 8d., and thereafter for the new work of the Abbey until 1397, taking

PAYN, JOHN

normal wages of 3s. 4d. a week.

WAM, 19640–51; 23463–66

PAYN, John (*fl.* 1386–) Carpenter

Of Depden, Suffolk; in 1386 contracted with STEPHEN HOORE to make a new kitchen with larder and solar, at King's Hall, Cambridge (now *Trinity College*). For this they were to receive 30 marks (£20) and each was to have a tunic and hood in addition. The timber and workmanship were to be as in the kitchen of the Friars Preachers in Cambridge.

WCC, II, 438

Paynter—see PEYNTOUR

Paynter, Stephen—see PEYNTOUR

PAYS, Henry [Payse] (*fl.* 1473–1496) Mason

Mason in charge of work at *Walberswick Church*, Suffolk, from 1473 to 1496. In 1473 four 'scheppy skynnys for paternys' were bought, and Pays was paid sums of 12s. and 10s. for his expenses on two visits to Boston, as well as 6s. 8d. for a third journey thither in 1474. He received various sums spread over a number of years, including 10s. for a gown in 1482, and work seems to have proceeded intermittently until 1496, when he was paid £4 4s. 0d. for 16 yards of battlement on the aisle, and £6 16s. 0d. for other battlements and for windows.

LCW, 34–5, 38, 49, 50, 56, 62, 75, 77

PEKKER, John (*fl.* 1423) Carpenter

Carpenter of Cambridge, engaged by the Brewers' Company of London on 8 June 1423 to amend the woodwork of their *Hall* and to make a bay window on the south side 'as be the bay windowes yn the newe corner rente of the Chartre hous yn Cornhill of London with vj. bayes with a vawte . . . vnderneth the same', and two other plain windows of two bays (? lights) each on the south side. A variation provided that another bay should be made to 'vndersette the seide halle affter the sample of the Bay windowe that is yn the In of the Erll of Warwikk'. The total cost was £16 18s. 1½d., plus a gown of livery for Pekker costing above 16s., of 4 yards of ray and 3 yards of coloured cloth. The carpenter's brother was his namesake John Pekker, vintner.

CLE, 162–7

PENINGTON, John (*fl.* 1548–1569) Mason

Was appointed Master mason of *Ripon Minster* by the Duchy of Lancaster on 18 February 1547/8, and was still in receipt of his yearly fee of 6s. 8d. in 1568–69.

HKW, III, 182n

PEPERTON, R. . . (*fl.* 1442) Mason

Freemason; about 1442 built the north aisle of the church of *East Bergholt*, Suffolk, with a bequest of £100. A lawsuit ensued on account of the poor quality of the freestone employed: 'certeyn fremasons beyng expert & connyng in the seid crafte' declared that the stone was bad and that because it would certainly decay, it ought to be taken down.

PRO, C.1–789–43 (*L.F.S.*); cf. HAC, 121

PEPPER, John [Pepyr] (*fl.* 1456–1461) Carpenter

John Pepyr, carpenter, undertook to make a new roof for the chancel of *Hardley Church*, Norfolk, for £5 6s. 8d., and received £2 10s. 0d. in part payment in 1456–7. In 1460–61 he was paid £1 as part of £1 13s. 4d. for new desks for the chancel. The desks were carted from Harleston, presumably the site of Pepper's shop.

NRO, Great Hospital, 24.e (*P.C.*)

PEPPER, Roger [Peper] (*fl.* 1380–) ? Mason

In 1380–81 was paid £5 3s. 4d., part of a total of 20 marks (£13 6s. 8d.) for making the parclose screen 'ad Tria Altaria' on the north side of the feretory of *Ely Cathedral*. It appears that this screen was a stone construction.

CUL, Add. MS. 2956, *ff.* 158 ff.

PEPPER, William (*fl.* 1501–†1517) Mason

Freemason; one of three men enfeoffed by ROBERT BERTY with estates in Bearsted and Maidstone in 1501.[1] Pepper acquired the freedom of Canterbury by marriage in 1508,[2] and died in 1517.[3]

(*A.O.*)

[1] BFG; [2] CFC; [3] Canterbury Wills

PERKYNS, Thomas (*fl.* 1518–) Carpenter

Master carpenter in charge of works at *Warblington Castle*, Hants., from February to November 1518, being paid at first 8d. a day for visits, and later at the rate of 3s. 4d. a week.

PRO, E.101–490–12

PETER the Mason [le Maceon] (*fl.* 1367–1372) Carver

One Peter the Mason lived in St. Mary's Gate, Nottingham, from 1362 to 1370, and may have been identical with PETER DE STEPPINGLEY. In 1361–62 there is a reference to John, son of Peter the Mason.[1] Carver of

Nottingham; was paid £200 between 1367 and 1372 for making an alabaster reredos for *St. George's Chapel, Windsor*.

W.H. St. J. Hope in AJ, LXI (1904), 244–5
[1] *NBR*, Court Rolls

PETER, Henry (*fl.* 1514–1515) Joiner

In 1514–15 was paid £4 for making a tester (*tectura*) above the high table in the hall of *King's Hall, Cambridge*; he also received 4 marks, apparently for carving around the high table.[1] A payment to Peter 'sculptor' occurs in the King's Hall accounts of 1516–17 when wainscot was bought for the hall.[2]

A.O.
[1] *TCM, KHA*, xxi, 18; [2] *KHA*, xxvi, 364

PETER, Matthew (*fl.* 1521–1523) Carver

A Spanish carver employed by the Wardens of *London Bridge* to execute a number of commissions, including carving of four new statues in freestone of Saints Peter, Paul, Michael and George set up on the great gate of the Bridge, and also a statue of St. Katherine made 'in the honour of the Quene's Grace of Englonde' (Catherine of Aragon).

WTB, 66, 67, 97

PETIT, John (*fl.* 1541–　) Mason

Of Wellingborough, Northants.; with THOMAS PHILLIPS of Bristol he contracted in 1541/2 to rebuild the *Cross* at *Coventry* for £187 6s. 8d. It is not stated that Petit was a craftsman, and he may have been Phillips's sleeping partner.

(APD); *BM.*, Harl. MS. 6466, *ff*. 35–36v.

PETTE, Robert atte (*fl.* 1383) Mason

On 25 January 1383 Robert atte Pette, mason of Luddesdown (two miles south of Cobham, Kent), gave an acquittance to John, Lord Cobham, for payment for all the work he had done in the *College* and *Schoolhouse* at Cobham, of which £2 2s. 6d. was in respect of all former debts owing to him.
(A.O.) *BL*, Harl Chart, 48 E.46, printed in AQC, XLV, 53

Thomas atte PETTE supplied 12 cartloads of ragstone in 1368–69 for works at *Rochester Castle*.

AC, II, 115

Stephen PETTE was a freemason who worked at *Canterbury Cathedral* in 1431, and at *Eton College* in 1445–54.

Bodl, MS. Tanner 165, *f*. 136; KJE (A.O.)

PETTYT, Thomas (*fl.* 1543–1545) Mason

Was master mason during Henry VIII's repairs to *Wark Castle*, Northumberland, between 12 February and 10 November 1543.

He certified the expenses for wages and materials with Thomas Gower, surveyor of the works, and had 1s. a day for his wages for a total of 302 days.[1] Pettyt was a surveyor and draughtsman of great skill, as can be seen from the beautiful 'platt of the Lowe Countrye att Calleys, drawne in October, the 37th Hen. VIII (1545) by Thomas Pettyt'.[2]

[1] BBH, 349; [2] *BM*, Cott. MS. Aug. I, ii, 70

PEYNTOR, Henry (*fl.* 1345–1355) Mason

Was master mason (*Magister cementar'*) of the works of *Dover Castle* and town from 1345 to 1355, being paid 2s. 2d. a week. He also undertook work at task in 1354 repairing the vault under the tower ('*turell*') called 'Bodouresin' for £6 13s. 4d.

PRO, E.101–462–16, 18 (G.P.J.; L.F.S.)

PEYNTOUR, Nicholas (*fl.* 1382–1389) Mason

Master mason in charge of work at *Dover Castle* in 1382–89.

HKW, II, 639–40, 1052

Peyntour, Simon le—see WELLS

PEYNTOUR, Stephen [Payntor] (*fl.* 1363–1375) Mason

JOHN BOX, JAMES BROYL, and Stephen Peyntour were appointed to impress labour for the works of *Queenborough Castle* on 24 November 1363;[1] master mason (*Magister cement'*) in charge of work at *Dover Castle* in 1372–75, taking 8d. a day.[2]

[1] CPR 1361–4, 430; [2] *PRO*, E.101–462–23 (L.F.S.)

PEYNTOUR, Thomas [Peyntor, T. Mason] (*fl.* 1471–1495) Mason

On 1 October 1471 was granted a patent for life as master mason to the *Cathedral Priory of Ely*.[1] He was to have 11 marks yearly, a suit of clothes as provided for the gentlemen of the Prior's household, and a fortnight's holiday. In case of old age or infirmity his fee would be reduced to a pension of 6 marks and his livery. During his tenure of office he was to train three apprentices, one after another, for the works of the priory. In 1473 he was in charge of the making of a new wall by 'le Newewerk' and in 1476 of the strengthening of the great western tower.[2] In 1478 he was also serving as farmer and rent-collector to the warden of the Lady Chapel,[3] in 1483–84 was making a window opposite the tomb of St. Alban; in 1487–88 was employed on the southern battlements of the church. He was still drawing his fees in 1494–95.[4]

In March 1483 a *Roger PAYNTER*, freemason, possibly a son of the Ely mason, assisted JOHN BELL in the repair of two chimneys in the Provost's Lodge at *King's College, Cambridge*.[5]

(APD)
[1] *CUL*, Add. MS. 6392, f. 396; [2] *Ibid.*, Add. MS. 6387, pp. 41, 53, 67, 73; [3] *Ibid.*, Add. MS. 6383, p.69; [4] *Ibid.*, Add. MS. 2956, *ff.* 158 ff.; [5] *KCM*, Mundum Book 1482–83 (*A.O.*)

PHELYPP, Thomas (*fl.* 1516–   ) Mason
Freemason of Oxford; with RICHARD GYLES of Winchester, mason, contracted to build a farmhouse at Holywell, Oxford, on 11 May 1516, for Merton College. This is still in existence, being known as *Holywell Manor*.

SHB, 570–1; RAM, 461

PHILIP the Carver [Philippus sculptor] (*fl.* 1534–1535) Carver
A craftsman with this Christian name, probably a foreigner, is likely to have been one of the principal carvers who worked on the screen and stalls of *King's College Chapel, Cambridge*, which from the presence of Anne Boleyn's initials can be dated between the years 1532 and 1536. The college kitchen accounts for the year Michaelmas 1534–35 show that carpenters, joiners, and paviours were among the guests on several occasions in hall. On New Year's Day 1535 'Philip with another stranger' was among those at dinner, when WILLIAM BUXTON, Gere, and Kele (JOHN KALE), all of them carpenters, were also present; on 5 January 'Philippus sculptor' dined in hall 'with five other strangers'. At the Epiphany Feast he may have been one of two unnamed joiners who were among the twenty-seven guests present.

A.O. KCM, Kitchen Accs. 1534–35

PHILLIPS, Thomas (*fl.* 1541–?†1552*) Mason
Of Bristol; with JOHN PETIT of Wellingborough he contracted in 1541/2 to rebuild the *Cross* at *Coventry* for £187 6s. 8d.[1] Phillips and Petit undertook to build the new cross by Michaelmas 1543, with freestone from the quarries of 'Attilborrow and Rounton' (Attleborough and Rowington), and steps of harder stone to be had from the dissolved cathedral priory of Coventry. It was to be set up in the market-place called Cross-cheapinge, and was to resemble the cross 'redie made and set up' in Abingdon, Berks. (of *c.* 1442), except that while the Abingdon Cross 'is begone in 8 panes and chaunged in the second storie into 6 panes, to the deformitie of the same crosse', the Coventry Cross should be six-sided

throughout, and that it should stand on four steps, instead of eight as at Abingdon. Detailed provisions as to the stages of the work and the corresponding instalments of payment are laid down, it being expected that the cross would stand 20 feet above the top step by midsummer 1542, 25 feet high by Michaelmas, 40 feet high by midsummer 1543, and 45 feet 'or higher (yf the said crosse in Abington be higher)' and 'finished in all poynts as well in ymagerie work pictures and fynialls as otherwise accordynge to the due forme and proportion of the said crosse in Abington'. The image of 'a beast or a foule holding up a fane' was to be set on each main pinnacle of the lowest storey, and on each main pinnacle of the second storey 'a naked boy with a target and holding a faine'. The cross was being made under a bequest of £200 left by Sir William Hollies, knight, in his will of 25 December 1541. It is said to have stood 57 feet high, and was taken down in 1771.[2]

(APD)
[1] *BM*, Harl MS. 6466, *ff.* 35–36v.; [2] BAA, I, Q.15–18
* Possibly the Thomas Phillips freemason, buried at St. Edmunds, Dudley, Worcs., 25 March 1552; when work on *Dudley Castle* was in progress.

PHILPOT, Richard (*fl.* 1445–1461) Mason
Worked as a freemason at *Eton College* for many years, and became warden of the masons there in March 1454 in succession to JOHN CLERK. He was still at Eton in 1461.

KJE 40; AQC, XLVI (1933), 107

PICKERELL, John (*fl.* 1384–1397) Carpenter
Was given a life grant as master carpenter of the works at *Calais* in 1391, but had held office since 1384. He was succeeded by THOMAS CLOPTON in 1397.

HKW, II, 1054

Pinkhill, John—see PYNKHILL

PLANTAGENET, Richard (*c.* 1469–†1550) Bricklayer
Illegitimate son of Richard III; after his father's death became a bricklayer's apprentice and towards the end of his life was master of the building of Sir Thomas Moyle's mansion at *Eastwell*, Kent. He was aged over 80 when buried at Eastwell in 1550.

CDB, II, 728

PLAT, Richard (*fl.* 1533–   ) Mason
Master mason at the building of the tower of *Mobberley Church*, Cheshire, in 1533, as is shown by an inscription, naming 'Richard

Plat Master Mason' after the patrons Sir John Talbot and his wife Margaret.

ROC, 11, 238

PLAYSER, Robert (fl. 1427–1437) Mason

Was master mason in charge of the building of the tower of *St. Augustine's Church, Hedon*, Yorks., from 1427 to 1437. In addition to his wages he had a yearly retaining fee of £1 7s. for his vesture, and lived rent free in a dwelling over the Grammar School. His stipend, including certain sums which he was to disburse to other masons, amounted to £5 8s. 4d., but the accounts do not mention the daily rate taken by him.

This tower is one of the finest in England in its composition and restrained but fine detail; it is also interesting as a late example of a central tower added to a parish church. Playser's style has not been identified in other existing buildings of the neighbourhood.

BHH, 119 ff.

PLOUGHWRIGHT, Richard [Plow-wryghte] (fl. 1367–1368) Carpenter

Of Trumpington, near Cambridge; in 1367–68 bound himself in the sum of £20 to erect for John Pilate and complete before the Feast of St. Peter ad Vincula (1 August) next following, eight annexes (*annexas*) in a void place in the parish of All Saints, *Cambridge*, at the end of Nunneslane abutting on the highway. He was to receive for timber and work £5 2s. 6d. in three instalments; the 'sparre' used was to be of value not less than 2d.

A.O. GRC. 94

PLUMPSTED, Thomas de (fl. 1310–1336) Carpenter (*Plumstead, Norf.*)

The principal carpenter employed by the Prior of *Norwich Cathedral* from 1310 to 1336; he was usually paid a retainer of £1 6s. 8d. a year, but sometimes had extra payments or furs in addition.

NCM, rolls 21–29, 31, 33

PODDING, John (fl. 1359–1381) Mason

In a proof of age taken at Ross-on-Wye on 8 March 1381, John Podding, Richard of the Purye and Thomas Schepherd, all aged 50 and over, stated that on Saturday 15 June 1359 they had begun to build the belfry of the church at *Little Dewchurch*, Herefordshire.

IPM, xv (1970), no. 447 (*H.M.*)

PODE, Richard (fl. 1363–1366) Carpenter

Between 1363 and 1366 was a carpenter much employed at *Eltham Palace* and also made the 'Queen's Cross' outside it, by the town of Eltham.

HKW, II, 934

POKYLL, Thomas [Puckyll] (fl. 1536–1540) Mason

Contracted to build the steeple of *Bolney Church*, Sussex, in 1536, at 18s. the foot; the work was completed during the next two years, Pokyll receiving a total of £9, while two setters, William Holmes and John Corker, were paid £21 14s. 6d. apparently for 24 feet of work. It is not clear whether this implies a height of 34 feet altogether, or if Pokyll was in fact paid for the design and general supervision of the work carried out by Holmes and Corker.

Two of Pokyll's 'servants' are mentioned as receiving 18s. for altering the church wall to the steeple, doubtless bonding them together, and board for two masons was allowed at the rate of 5s. 4d. a month each. The timberwork of the steeple was made by ROGER FROGBROOK. Pokyll's contract is not preserved, but it was evidently executed on St. Mary Magdalen's Day, 22 July 1536, when the churchwardens' accounts record the payment of £1 as 'ernest' to Pokyll and his partner Gills.[1] (See GYLES, RICHARD). Pokyll ('Puckyll') was resident master mason at the works of *Camber Castle*, Sussex, in 1539–40. He was termed 'upper warden', being subordinate to the King's Master Mason JOHN MOLTON, and was paid 5s. per week. John Corker also appears at Camber, as a setter at 3s. 8d. a week.[2]

Pokyll may have been related to *Robert PUCKELL*, who was warden of the masons at *Berwick-upon-Tweed* in 1557, at 1s. 4d. a day.[3]

William Holmes may have been the apprentice of GABRIEL CALDHAM of that name, taking 7d. a day at *Brent Bridge*, Middlesex, in 1530, and who in the following year was a mason at *Whitehall Palace* at 3s. 4d. a week.[4]

[1] SAC, vi, 244–52; [2] HKW, iv, 423; [3] PRO, E.101–483–16 (*G.P.J.*); [4] PRO, E.36–251

POLEYN, John (fl. 1434) Carpenter

Of Allington, Hants.; on 13 August 1434 entered into a bond in £10 with the Warden of *Winchester College*, presumably for the performance of building work.

WCM 19960

POLLARD, John (fl. 1466–   ) Mason

In partnership with WILLIAM GLANFORTH, contracted in 1466 to build the south porch at *Saffron Walden Church*, Essex.

A.O. CWW, ff. 73–75; BAE, 219 *et seq.*

PONDOUR, William (*fl.* 1512–   ) Carver

Described as 'joyner, carver or carpinder'; contracted on 22 August 1512 to make an enclosed chapel of wood above the chancel of *Tempsford Church*, Beds., together with a reredos and a carved window for which he was to find all materials, stone, iron, and timber. The work was to cost £3 8s. 4d.

SHB, 563–4; HMC, 8R, 262

PONTEFRACT, Robert de (*fl. c.* 1312–1328) ? Mason

Perhaps a mason; was employed by Prior Henry de Aberford (1312–28) to build a new choir at *Nostell Priory*, Yorks. He ran the convent into such heavy expense that the work had to be stopped.

HSY, II, 207

POPE, Richard (*fl.* 1442–   ) Mason

Freemason; in 1442 provided the design for the tower of *Dunster Church*, Somerset, which was built by the mason-contractor JOHN MARYS of Stogursey; the contract speaks of 'a patron made by the avyce' of Pope, i.e. a drawing. This sturdy central tower is still in existence. It has single windows and diagonal buttresses, and a simple battlemented parapet with angle pinnacles.[1]

It is possible that Pope the freemason was identical with the Richard Pope who was paid 6s. 8d. in 1440–41 for 'his friendship towards the work' of building St. John's Hospital, Sherborne, Dorset. If so, he may have been the contemporary master mason of *Sherborne Abbey*, and designer of the noble choir then in course of erection. Pope was sought by a man on horseback, and therefore must have resided away from Sherborne.[2] He was perhaps of Exeter, where Thomas Pope (*cementarius*) worked at the cathedral in 1395–1414, and Walter Pope, who took up the freedom in 1421, also worked as a mason on the cathedral in 1450.[3]

[1] SHB, 514–15; AJ, XXXVIII, 217; [2] SAD, Building Accs. (*J.F.*); [3] FFE

Poppehowe, Thomas—see COLYN, Thomas

PORTER, George (*fl.* 1482–1499) Carpenter

Probably identical with the 'Richard' Porter who was appointed master carpenter of *Berwick-upon-Tweed* in 1482. He was formally granted on 4 October 1485 the office of chief carpenter of the town and castle of *Berwick-upon-Tweed* at 12d. a day, and a fishery. He was also allowed 6d. a day for a yeoman under him, and a reward of £9 because he had exercised the office from the previous Easter. The fishery was that called 'le Prise Fysshe' in the town of 'Newbrigging' (Newbiggin-by-the-Sea), Northumberland.[1]

On 16 March 1496 Porter and HUMPHREY COKE were commissioned to impress carpenters, masons, smiths, and other workmen and labourers for the King's works in the northern parts and the marches towards Scotland. Porter had died before 3 November 1499, when Coke was appointed to his office.[2]

[1] CPR 1485–94, 16; [2] Ibid. 1494–1509, 52

PORTER, John (*fl.* 1423–†1465) Mason

Was master mason of *York Minster* by c. 1452; in 1466 he was succeeded in the office by ROBERT SPILLESBY. He had worked at Lincoln before taking up his York appointment, and in 1450 was twice called to York to advise on work at the Minster.[1] He became a freeman of York in 1454,[2] and died in the winter of 1465–66, having made his will on 20 December. It was proved on 7 January 1465/6.[3] In 1457 he was one of four craftsmen called in to adjudicate on a dispute concerning the discharge of rainwater from a house in 'Northstrete', York, over the adjoining garden.[4]

His will includes bequests for masses to be said in the church of St. Michael le Belfry, where he was to be buried, and leaves 20s. to the fabric of the Minster. Porter also left legacies to Mount Grace Priory, Lincoln Cathedral, the church of St. Peter 'Estgate', Lincoln, and to the Guilds of St. Mary of Louth and Corpus Christi of York. Relatives mentioned are Agnes his wife, to whom he left his lease of a messuage in the parish of St. Peter 'Estgate' at Lincoln, belonging to the Prior and Convent of 'Tixhill', his daughters Agnes and Elena, and John Porter, son of his deceased son John.

It seems probable that Porter was master mason of Lincoln Cathedral when he was called to advise at York, and he was very probably the original designer of the steeple at *Louth*, completed by JOHN COLE and CHRISTOPHER SCUNE. The Louth tower must have been begun soon after the chancel for whose roof oak trees were granted by the Lincoln Chapter on 26 May 1431.[5] He was probably the John Porter, already married, who was living in the parish of St. Mary Magdalene, Lincoln (i.e. the cathedral precincts), in 1423.⁶

(APD)
¹ BHY, I, 240–1; RFY, 65, 66n., 70n., 72n.; ² YCF; ³ *PCY*, iv, 109; ⁴ YMB; ⁵ *LDC*, Chapter Acts, A.2/32, *f.*57v.; ⁶ *Ibid.*, *ff.* 26v., 27v.

PORTLAND, Nicholas (*fl.* 1394–†*c.* 1406) Mason

Became master mason of *Salisbury Cathedral* in 1394. He probably carried out measures of consolidation to buttress the tower, which had been in danger of falling in 1387. In 1396 Philip Dunstaple, a Winchester mason and innkeeper, sold a house there in Middle Brook Street to Nicholas Portland and his wife. From then until 1405 Portland was engaged on the rebuilding of *St. John's Hospital*, and was paid at least £70 from city funds. The main block of the hospital (other than the chapels) was entirely rebuilt at the time. By 1407 Portland was dead, as his widow then disposed of the house.

(*D.K. Win*)
(APD); DSC, 158

POTTE, John (*fl.* 1353–   ) Carpenter

Contracted in 1353 to rebuild the great bridge to the outer gate of *Farnham Castle*, Surrey, for £12. The Bishop of Winchester, his client, was to supply the timber and other necessaries, such as the 'bayardes' or hand-barrows for the masons.

RMF, 128, 145

POWLE, Adam (*fl.* 1425–1426) Mason

Of Blythburgh, Suffolk; the second of two masons (with RICHARD RUSSELL of Dunwich) who contracted to build the tower of *Walberswick Church*, Suffolk. The tower was to be like that of Tunstall and the door and windows like those of Halesworth.

(APD); SHB, 499–500; (*BM.*, Add. Ch. 17634)

PRATT, John (*fl.* 1375–   ) Imager

'*Ymaginator*', carving figures for the west front of *Exeter Cathedral* in 1374–75, when he was paid 9*d.* and 10*d.* a day. He probably made the upper range of figures on the screen of the front.

BPE, 90; *FFE*

PRENTICE, Martin (*fl.* 1459–1487) Carpenter

Was employed at *King's College, Cambridge*, between 1459 and 1462, and became master carpenter in 1480, when the works on the chapel were resumed on a large scale. The efforts of the Provost, Robert Wodelark, to carry on the building of the chapel when the flow of funds had been interrupted by the Wars of the Roses resulted in the issue of a new commission for obtaining the necessary men and materials dated 26 February 1459.¹ Although THOMAS STURGEON was still master carpenter, the Kitchen Accounts of the Provost show that 'Martyn carpentarius' was frequently a guest along with other craftsmen from April to August 1459 and on several occasions between December 1460 and February 1461.² In August 1460 he was paid 13*s.* 4*d.* for services unstated; in December of that year he was sent to London with others to supervise the transport of the new bells back to Cambridge and received a reward of 6*s.* 8*d.* for his share in the work of hanging them in the timber belfry.³ In June 1462 Sturgeon and he were paid a small sum for supervising the repair of this bell-cage. He does not seem to have been a native of Cambridge but rented a house whilst working for the college. In September 1461 a sum of 22*s.* representing part of the money owing to him was handed to two (no doubt, clamorous) women 'for payment of his rent for the house in which he stays'.⁴ In the accounts of this period his surname never occurs, but his identification with the master carpenter of 1480 hardly admits of doubt, seeing that Martin Prentice was frequently described as 'Martin carpenter' in the later accounts.

In October 1479 a new provost, Walter Field, was appointed to succeed Wodelark, and through his activity and the influence of Thomas Rotherham, the chancellor, Edward IV advanced a large sum of money for the building of the chapel, which had made very little progress since 1461. On 22 December 1479 'Martyn Carpentarius' was a guest at supper in hall and he was entertained twice in June 1480, on the 18th with SIMON CLERK, the master mason, when his surname is given in the entry.⁵ Letters patent were issued on 10 July appointing Martin Prentice and John Sturgeon to take carriage for timber for the works of the college and for other wood which the King had bought from the Abbot of Walden for the building.⁶ Meanwhile, between February and April Martin Prentice had been paid 4*s.* a week for eight weeks in charge of work in the little church of *St. John the Baptist* adjoining the college, which included the making of a roodloft and a 'crest' for the high altar.⁷ Carpentry work went on between May and October in the unfinished court of the college to the west of the Schools, but this seems to have been chiefly entrusted to JOHN STURGEON, though Martin Prentice in November was paid 16s. by the Provost 'for 32 days about the stable and other places of the college'. No doubt, preparations for work on the chapel and the provision of the timber required had kept him fully occupied during the summer. A memorandum of a payment made to him on 26 April definitely describes him as chief carpenter (*principalis carpentarius*).[8]

This item occurs in a day-book kept by Thomas Clyff, the clerk of the works, and covering the period April 1480 to April 1483. On 27 April 1480 nails for cleats for the scaffold were purchased and poplar boards for 'centours', and shortly afterwards a penny was paid for a 'forel' or skin of parchment (*pro vno forali*) for Martin Prentice 'on which he proposed to draw the roof of the Church' (*in quo proposuit tractare tectum Ecclesie*). The roof above the fan vault is a remarkable piece of timber construction. The five eastern bays of the chapel were roofed between 1480 and 1483; the remainder of the roof is thirty years later, but Prentice's design was followed by RICHARD RUSSELL, the master carpenter during the final phase of building. In May, June, and July Prentice was busy superintending the felling of timber in Stansted Park, Essex, and in the woods of the abbot of Walden. He was at Walden again in October with John Sturgeon. In 1481 there were a number of payments to Martin Prentice 'and his fellows', including one of 40s. made on 27 August when they were at Huntingdon. In January 1482 he went to London with Clyff,[9] the clerk of the works, on some business, perhaps concerned with the King's gift of timber from the royal forest of Weybridge, near Huntingdon. From March to the end of May or later he was engaged in supervising his men working on the oak trees felled in the forest of Weybridge; in July they were working at Sapley, north of Huntingdon, another royal forest from which the college obtained underwood for fuel by a grant of Henry VI and now, perhaps, were allowed to take some oaks.[10] At Whitsun this year (not 1481, as stated by Willis and Clark)[11] Edward IV paid a visit to the college. A special 'closet' in the Provost's Lodge was prepared for the King, and Martin Prentice and other carpenters were paid 33s. for their work in making it.[12] In

October Prentice was paid 8s. for a fortnight's work in making a door in the Provost's Lodge.[13] Information about the carpenters' activities in 1483 is scanty, but on 26 March Clyff received £8 from the Provost 'for Martin Prentice and his men'.

The Kitchen Accounts for 1482, 1483, and 1484 show Martin Prentice being entertained in hall on many occasions, but his visits became especially frequent from August 1484 up to the end of the year.[14] After having slackened for a time the works received a new impetus as a result of Richard III's gift of money. On 28 August 1484 a fresh commission, drafted in wide terms, for impressing workmen and obtaining materials, was issued to six of those concerned with the building, of whom Martin Prentice was one.[15] Since March there had been preparations going on for the glazing of the great east window entailing the erection of a new scaffold.[16] A pair of gloves was given to the carpenter on 6 August, when this scaffold was completed.[17] William Neve, the King's Glazier, and John Byrchold, the King's Serjeant Plumber, came to give advice. They were entertained in hall on the Feast of the Assumption (15 August) and the following day; Martin Prentice was present as a guest on both occasions, and, no doubt, they conferred with him.[18] There is a gap in the Kitchen Accounts from April 1485 to Michaelmas 1486, but Martin Prentice appears as a guest on All Saints Day 1486.[19] This is the latest occurrence of his name in the college muniments that has been noted. In the year Michaelmas to Michaelmas 1486–87 Martin 'Carpenter' was employed by King's Hall to repair barns and other buildings at *Chesterton*, near Cambridge, and to make and fix 'mantiltrees' in the college kitchen.[20]

Martin Prentice's 'fellowship', no doubt, included *William* and *Thomas* PRENTICE, both of whom worked at the church of St. John the Baptist in February and March 1480 and in the Old Court of King's College in August and September of that year, each receiving 6d. a day.[7] They were probably sons of Martin. William's name occurs occasionally in the accounts for the chapel: for instance, 24 March 1481 removing 'le fferne' and 1 August 1482 repairing 'le Crane'.[8] In June 1485 he and two others were paid 17d. 'for taking down le fferne broken by the wind', 2s. 11½d. for making a scaffold for the sixth window (on the south side of the chapel) for the masons, and 2s. 1½d. for making beds at the college manor of *Grantchester* 'towards the arrival of the lord Archbishop of York'.[17]

A.O.

[1] CPR 1452–61, 478; [2] *KCM*, College Accs., vol. ii; [3] *Ibid.* and CAC, IV, 230; [4] *KCM*, College Accs., vol. vi; [5] *Ibid.*, Kitchen Accs.; [6] CPR 1476–85, 203, repeated 213; [7] *KCM*, College Accs., vol. vi; CAC, IV, 353–6; [8] *KCM*, College Accs., vol. iv; [9] *Ibid.*, vol. vi; [10] *Ibid.*, vol. iv; [11] WCC, I, 472n.; [12] *KCM*, College Accs., vols. iv and vi; [13] *Ibid.*, Mundum Book 1482–3 and College Accs., vol. vi; [14] *Ibid.*, Kitchen Accs., vol. vii; [15] CPR 1476–85, 472; [16] *CUL*, Clark MSS., Add. 5062, p. 58; [17] *KCM*, College Accs., vol. v; [18] *Ibid.*, Kitchen Accs., vol. vii; [19] *Ibid.*, vol. ix; [20] *TCM, KHA*, xviii, 16, 22

PRENTYS, Thomas (*fl.* 1414–1419) Carver

Carver of Chellaston, Derbyshire; in 1414 sold alabaster to Alexandre de Berneval, the principal master mason of Rouen, who visited England by way of a long sea passage to Newcastle-upon-Tyne.[1] On 14 February 1418/19 Prentys and ROBERT SUTTON, another carver of Chellaston, undertook to make an alabaster tomb with two images and an arch of alabaster over it, to be set up in *Lowick Church*, Northants., by Easter 1420. The tomb, of Ralph Greene and his wife Katharine who was to pay £40 for the work, still stands in Lowick Church.[2] St. John Hope assigned to Prentys the great tomb of Thomas, Earl of Arundel (†1416) at *Arundel*, and that of Henry IV and Joan of Navarre in *Canterbury Cathedral*.[3]

[1] AJ, LXIV, 32–7; LXIX, 484; [2] CEM, 29, 30, 34; [3] AJ, LXI (1904)

PRESTON, John [Pryston] (*fl. c.* 1516–1529) Mason

Mason who supplied stonework at the rebuilding of 'Cheyet' (*Chevet Hall*), near Wakefield, Yorks., begun in 1516 and finished by 1529. Preston was paid £10 for 'Ston wark of the hall wt. the chymnay and the batellynge', £6 13s. 4d. for the stonework of the kitchen, and £12 for stonework of 'the grett Chambur in the neythur end of the Hall'.

YAJ, XXXII (1936), 326–30

PRESTON, William de (*fl.* 1323–   ) Mason

Master mason (*cementarius*) was on 2 November 1323 paid 23s. 4d. for 35 days, expenses at 8d. a day, being sent by the King from Halton Castle to *Carlisle Castle* to survey defects there.

PRO, E.101–379–19

PREWET, Walter (*fl. c.* 1450) Mason

Appears as warden of the masons at *Shene*, Surrey, for 49 days in an unnamed year of Henry VI, in succession to ROBERT WESTERLEY. He was paid 8d. a day.

PRO, E.101–503–15 (*L.F.S.*)

Priors, William de—see WILLIAM SPILBERY

PRITELWELL, Andrew de (*fl.* 1253–1259) Mason

Master mason in charge of the king's works at *Guildford* in 1253, when he was paid £17. On 13 January 1259 the sheriff of Surrey was ordered to let Pritelwell have arrears of £4 10s. 0d.

CLR 1251–60, 125, 447

PRITTLEWELL, Roger of (*fl.* 1293–   ) Mason

Master mason of Prittlewell, Essex; on 6 September 1293 contracted with Sir Richard de Southchurch to build a chapel 50 feet long and 20 feet wide in the churchyard of *Southchurch*, Essex.

(*A.O.*)   EAS, XXI, 268

PROWCE, Thomas (*fl. c.* 1470)? Carpenter

At an uncertain date after the middle of the fifteenth century Thomas Prowce petitioned for payment of 100 marks (£66 13s. 4d.) which he stated was due to him for building a house and chapel for John Lambard, mercer of London.[1] Lambard is evidenced from 1446, was an Alderman in 1460–70, Sheriff of London 1460–61, and died in 1487.[2]

[1] A, LIX, 2 (*ECP*, 66–370); [2] CLB 'K', 318; CPM 1437–57, 103; BAL, I, 146, 416; II, 12

PRUIST, William (*fl.* 1366–1374) Carpenter

Warden of the carpenters at *King's Langley*, where he worked both on the royal manor-house and on the Priory between 1366 and 1374.

HKW, I, 262–3; II, 974–5

PRYMEROSE, Hugh (*fl.* 1411) Mason

In April 1411 was repairing the walls of the vestry of *St. Mary's Church, Grimsby*, Lincs.

LAA, VI pt. i, 30 (*C.W.*)

Pryston, John—see PRESTON

Puckell—see POKYLL

PULEBERG', John (*fl.* 1279) Mason

In April 1279 one of the witnesses to a grant of a quarry for the works of the Cistercian Abbey of *Newenham*, Devon, was Master John Puleberg', mason. He was presumably in charge of the building of the abbey, begun in 1254.

Bodl., MS. Top. Devon d.5, *f.* 25

PYCHE, W. (*fl.* 1468) Mason

Mason employed in 1468 by the church-wardens of *East Dereham*, Norfolk, to make the Seven Sacraments font for the church at a cost of £12 18s. 9d.

A.C. Fryer in AJ, xc (1933), 102 (*K.H.*)

PYNKHILL, John (*fl.* 1401–†1423) Mason

Appointed master mason of the King's works at *Calais* on 11 July 1401 in succession to JOHN STUCLEY, and held office until his death in 1423.[1] He was the author of a surviving letter concerning technical problems of the work on the chapel within the castle at Calais in 1421. This was addressed personally to Henry V by royal command, and contains interesting comments on stone decay and the use of linseed oil to prevent erosion by damp.[2]

[1] HKW, II, 1054; [2] CS, LXXXVI (1863), 19–21; HPL, 176

QUADRATARIUS, Peter (*fl.* 1322–1326) Mason

Probably a mason quarryman at *Ely Cathedral* in 1322, when he received a robe worth 13s. 4d.; he was presumably identical with the 'Peter' who in 1325–26 had a furred robe price 15s. 3d. along with Master JOHN the Mason VII and THOMAS (PAGE) the carpenter.

CSR, II, 33, 61

QWYNBERGWE, John (*fl.* 1337–1338) Carpenter

Carpenter in charge of the making of new gates for the East Gate and South Gate of (*King's*) *Lynn* in 1337–38.

LCR, Ea. 7

RACHEDALE, Robert (*fl.* 1524–1525) Mason (*Rochdale, Lancs.*)

In 1524 was paid, along with JOHN PASMYCHE, carpenter, 10d. for visiting *Prescot Church*, Lancs., to view the steeple and belfry; and later 8d. and 4d. board for his work for two days on fitting the bell-frame.

BPL, 7

RADBELL the Artificer [Rabellus] (*fl. c.* 1086–   ) ? Engineer

Radbell 'Artifex' held land on Mousehold Heath, near Norwich and at Filby in East Flegg Hundred, at the time of Domesday Survey (1086). He was perhaps in charge of William the Conqueror's work at *Norwich Castle*.

VCH, *Norfolk*, II, 39, 191

Radulphus the mason—see RALPH

RADWELL, John de [Radewell] (*fl.* 1311–1320) Mason

Mason employed at the *Palace of Westminster* between 1311 and 1320, taking at first 3d. and then 6d. a day.

BBW, 120–1; LKC, 186; *PRO*, E.101–468–20, 469–1

RAFF, Guy (*fl.* 1545–†1549) Mason

Was appointed master mason of *Windsor Castle* on 27 November 1545, after the death of WILLIAM REYNOLD II.[1] He was buried at St. Margaret's, Westminster, on 17 August 1549 and was succeeded by HENRY BULLOCK in November.[2] His mason's mark was ✕.[3]

He may have been related to *Thomas RAUFFE* who was working as a mason at Westminster Palace in 1531–32,[4] and at the Tower of London in 1535.[5]

[1] LPH, xx, pt. ii, 910 (68); [2] HKW, III, 304–5; CPR 1548–9, 247; [3] (*H.M.C.*); [4] *PRO*, E.36–251 (*G.P.J.*); [5] *Bodl.*, Rawl. D. 778 (*G.P.J.*)

RAGHTON, Ivo de (*fl.* 1317–†c. 1339) Mason

Took up the freedom of the City of York as a mason in 1317,[1] and in 1327 was living in the parish of Holy Trinity, Goodramgate, where he was assessed to the lay subsidy at £3 15s. 5d., the third richest man in the parish.[2] He was by far the wealthiest mason in the whole of York at the time, and evidently of pre-eminent standing. His very rare Christian name makes it virtually certain that he was the 'Master Ivo the mason' who was paid £3 6s. 8d. by Archbishop Melton on 24 June 1331 for 'our work at York'.[3]

Archbishop Melton promoted the works of York Minster from 1321 onwards, and himself paid sums of £20 for the shrine of St. William and £466 13s. 4d. towards the completion of the western part of the nave and west front. The works done for Melton, which included the great west window of 1338–39, were in Curvilinear style, contrasting with the Geometrical style of the earlier work of the nave built under Master SIMON (the Mason I) from 1291 to 1322.

There was only one family named 'de Raghton', from Raughton in Cumberland in the parish of Dalston; the family from the middle of the twelfth century onwards held land of the Crown by the Grand Serjeanty of keeping the King's hawks in the Forest of

Carlisle. The family bore arms: *Sable a chevron argent between three quatrefoils pierced argent*, and in their recorded pedigree the name Ivo descends for at least three generations, the last Ivo de Raughton being dead by 1328.[4] He may well have been the father of the mason.

On stylistic grounds the west front of *York Minster* must in any case be closely related to the east front of *Carlisle Cathedral* (designed between 1318 and 1322), the reredos behind the high altar at *Beverley Minster* (in progress 1324–1334), and the great east window of *Selby Abbey*, begun about 1330. The shrine of St. William at York, of which substantial fragments survive, the pulpitum at *Southwell Minster*, and the south rose window of the great transept of *Lincoln Cathedral* all belong to the same twenty years and all show the impact of a highly individual style, revolutionary at the time. Furthermore, almost all of these works were in one way or another under the patronage of Archbishop Melton.

At the apex of the great west window of York Minster there is a change of style in certain minor details, probably indicating the death of Master Ivo shortly before its completion, in 1339.[5] As the new details suggest the onset of Perpendicular style from the South, this would agree with the assumption that the next master, THOMAS DE PACENHAM, took his name from Passenham in the south of Northamptonshire.

HME, 79–80, 282
[1] YCF, 17; [2] YRS, LXXIV (1929), 166; [3] DRY, I, 432; [4] GVF, 303–10; [5] *J.H.H.* in ACY, 157–8

Rainald, John—see REYNOLD

Ralph the Mason—see DARTFORD

RALPH the Mason I (*fl. c.* 1150) Mason

Master mason (*magister latomus*) who witnessed a lease by the Chapter of St. Paul's Cathedral of their manor of Chingford, Essex, *c.* 1150. The use of *latomus* rather than *cementarius* to designate a mason is of great rarity at this period in England.

DSP, 135

RALPH the Mason II [Radulphus] (*fl.* 1170–1182) Mason

Was King's Mason at *Dover Castle* in 1170–71, and at *Chilham Castle* in the following year. He continued to be mason at Dover Castle until 1182, though probably not constantly there. He was subordinate to MAURICE the Engineer. His normal pay is not recorded, but in 1170–71 he was granted £2 as a gift for his service to the King, and a further sum of £2 in the following year 'for his service for two years by the King's brief'. In 1181–82 he had 1 mark (13*s.* 4*d.*) as a gift for his work at Dover where £815 was spent on the works of the tower, keep, and castle. He may have been working at *Winchester Castle* in 1174–75, when he had a gift of 13*s.* 4*d.* from the issues of Hampshire, for work in the King's chapel there was in progress at the time.

He was perhaps identical with 'Master Robert Cementarius' who in 1168–69 was paid £1 for the works of Dover.

(LKC); PR

RALPH the Mason III (*fl.* 1213–1215) Mason

Master *cementarius* of *Canterbury Cathedral Priory*, and was paid £1 in 1213–14 and 1 mark (13*s.* 4*d.*) in 1214–15. He apparently succeeded Master JOHN the Mason III.

(*W.P.B.*) CCA, Treasurers' Accs. 1198–1227

RALPH the Mason IV (*fl.* 1278–†1293/4) Mason

In charge of work for Roger Bigod III, Earl of Norfolk, on *Chepstow Castle* from about 1278 until his death in 1293–94. The buildings comprised the hall, kitchen, and subsidiary apartments on the north side of the Lower Bailey, completed by 1285, and the Marten's Tower at the south-east angle of the castle, finished by 1293. In 1291 Master Ralph travelled to Framlingham to see the earl and this journey was followed by the building of the eastern part of the upper storey of the Great Tower at Chepstow. He was almost certainly identical with RALPH TOTEWYF.

PCC, 8–9

RAMSEY family: general introduction

The phenomenon of particular arts and crafts running in families is well known (see Introduction, p. xlix), and this is sometimes — perhaps often — linked to the emergence in the arts of individuals from families of social distinction. Society in the Middle Ages was largely based upon primogeniture, and a necessary corollary of the descent of property to the eldest son was the need of younger sons to find their own way in the world. Hence it is not surprising that members of 'the gentry' should be found among the ranks of the more outstanding masters of such crafts as masonry. This is, after all, what the masons themselves (in their 'Constitutions') were claiming by the fourteenth century if not earlier: that their craft took its rise from the need to find a livelihood for 'great lords' children freely begotten'. Setting aside tradition and social snobbery, it is a fact that trainees for the mason's art had to be of free status and legitimate birth.[1]

There is also the contrary phenomenon, that of the man who succeeds in reaching an eminent position by the exercise of his talents, and who is then accepted as being of gentle standing and even, for example, granted a coat of arms as THOMAS BERTY was in 1550 at the end of our period. Without benefit of a formal grant, WILLIAM RAMSEY III (below) was using a magnificent armorial seal before his death in 1349, clearly made to his specification and perhaps to his own design. There are several cases of master masons habitually described in documents as 'gentleman', 'armiger' or 'esquire', and there is more than a mere suspicion in some cases that this indicates relationship to a family of coat armour: SIMON CLERK, IVO DE RAGHTON and ROBERT STOWELL provide instances and, though the evidence is less explicit, WILLIAM WYNFORD may well have derived from a family of manorial lords.

Without insisting upon strictly gentle birth, it must be recognized that considerable numbers of masters were born into yeoman families of standing and, in some cases, of ancient lineage, as with the REDMAN family of masons who were proud of their descent from the Abbot of Ramsey's serjeants who held hereditary office as riding-bailiff (*Ridemannus*) from as far back as the mid-twelfth century. It is a remarkable coincidence that the distinguished family of masons surnamed Ramsey should likewise be documented as tenants of the same abbey for at least two centuries. From Norwich deeds long ago printed by Walter Rye, it was known that the father of JOHN RAMSEY I was RICHARD CURTEYS: such changes of surname are by no means uncommon in the thirteenth and early fourteenth centuries. More recent research by Mr. A. B. Whittingham has shown that the family of Curteys or Curteis can be traced back, as holders of property under the Abbot of Ramsey at Wyke Fen in Well, to one Alfelin who flourished in the middle of the twelfth century and from his personal behaviour acquired the cognomen of '*Facetus*', the courteous. Alfelin, probably of Saxon descent, was the father of

Walter Curteys who went on pilgrimage to Jerusalem, presumably before its capture by Saladin in 1187; and Walter Curteys was father of William Curteys, holding the lands at Wyke Fen in 1202. The estate descended to Simon Curteis who flourished in the reign of Henry III, and from him to a Richard Curteis who was probably father of the master mason of the name.[2]

The members of the Ramsey family who were notable master masons were certainly all closely related, but it is not yet possible to draw up a clear pedigree to include both the Norwich and the London members, although some of them were identical and moved from one city to the other. Wills and other records show conclusively that there were two generations of London masters, the elder consisting of the three brothers JOHN II († 1349), NICHOLAS, and WILLIAM I; the younger of two brothers, JOHN III (†1371) and WILLIAM III, the great King's Mason and creator of the Perpendicular style. It is probable but not absolutely certain that the second generation were children of the elder William de Ramsey.

[1] HME, 76, 148, 200; [2] *A.B.W.* in AJ, CXXVII, 285–9; cf. HPS, 47–8

RAMSEY, John de, I [Rames', Rameseye, -heye, Ramyseye, -sseye] (*fl.* 1304–1339) Mason (? *Ramsey, Hunts.*)

Mason of Norwich, son of RICHARD CURTEYS. He was already named as master at *Norwich Cathedral* in 1304–05, when he was in charge of work on the detached belfry, and received a 'courtesy' of 6s. 8d. from the sacrist.[1] In 1305–06 he was paid £10 13s. 5d. for 8 circular windows for the belfry, being described as 'John de Rames' *lathomus*'.[2] In 1306 he and his wife Agnes Picot disposed of properties in the parishes of St. James and St. Martin-de-le-Hill.[3] For the two accountant's years 1306–08 he was paid fees in arrears of 13s. 4d. by the cathedral Sacrist,[4] and in 1309–10 he received £5 18s. 3d. for the making of the Infirmarer's new chamber by himself and his fellows.[5]

After 1310, and mainly in the years 1316–25, Ramsey was probably in charge of the building of the Norwich *Carnary Chapel*; and about the same time he seems, on stylistic grounds, to have designed *Cley Church*, Norfolk; both works employ circular windows.

John and WILLIAM RAMSEY II were perhaps identical with the William and John, sculptors, who were given robes worth 18s. each in 1319–20; John 'sculptor' may have been concerned with work on the chancel of *Bawburgh Church*, Norfolk.[6] In 1314–15 John de Ramsey the mason bought property in the parish of St. Paul, Norwich,[7] and in 1321 with his wife Agnes he was selling houses in the parish of St. Martin-before-the-Gates.[8] In 1323–24 he was buying property in the parish of St. Mary-the-Less, close to the cathedral;[9] this he sold in 1331–32, when his wife is named as Elena.[10]

When work began on the south walk of the Cathedral cloisters (1324–30), parchment was bought for moulds, and robes were given to Master John for which 17s. and 15s. were paid at Christmas and Whitsun 1324–25. Again in 1325–26 he was presented with a robe worth 17s. 6d.;[11] in 1333–34 he had a gift of 9d.; finally in 1338–39 he received a fee of 21s. in connection with work on the cloisters and Infirmary, and a robe price 16s. 8d.[12]

Master John was probably only intermittently resident in Norwich, and seems to have ceased to have his home there by 1332. He was very probably identical with Master JOHN the Mason VII, who had charge of work at Ely from 1322 until 1326 or later, and also with JOHN DE RAMSEY II of London.

[1] *NCM*, roll 223; [2] *Ibid.*, roll 224; [3] RND 1285–1306, 116, 117; [4] *NCM*, roll 225; [5] *Ibid.*, roll 19; [6] *Ibid*, roll 226; [7] RND 1307–41, 53; [8] *Ibid.*, 100; [9] *Ibid.*, 118, 120; [10] *Ibid.*, 160; [11] *NCM*, rolls 1040, 1041; [12] *Ibid.*, rolls 38, 1046

RAMSEY, John, II, senior [Rammeseye] (*fl.* 1336–†1349) Mason

Mason of London, where he acquired a house in the parish of St. Michael-le-Querne[1] in 1336, and with his wife Juliana disposed of properties in St. Mary-at-Hill, St. Margaret Pattens, and St. Andrew Hubbard in 1344,[2] and bought a tenement in Golding Lane in the parish of St. Giles Cripplegate in 1348.[3]

Described in documents as 'the Woodward' and the 'Mason', he made his will on 15 March 1348/9, and it was proved in November 1349.[4] He left to his wife Juliana his houses in St. Michael-le-Querne and St. Giles Cripplegate for her life, with remainder to his children for their lives. His brother NICHOLAS RAMSEY was to have certain houses in Golding Lane until he should have repaid himself out of the rents a sum of money owed to him. Master William de Rameseye, another brother, is also mentioned; this must have been WILLIAM RAMSEY I, senior. John's

daughter Margery married Richard de Kent, fishmonger, who was dead by 1390.[5] John was possibly identical with JOHN RAMSEY I of Norwich, and with JOHN Mason VII of Ely.

[1] *LBH*, G.43; [2] *LHR*, 71(99); [3] *Ibid.*, 75(171); [4] SWL, I, 625; *LBH*, D.41; [5] *LBH*, I.17

RAMSEY, John, III, junior [Rammesye] (*fl.* 1343–†1371) Mason & Marbler

Mason and marbler of London. He is probably to be identified with the John de Rammeseye who was warden (*apparitor*) of the masons at *St. Stephen's Chapel, Westminster*, from May 1343 to 1348, being paid 3s. 6d. a week. In November 1343 he undertook by contract for £50 to build a chamber of two stories in the Privy Palace.[1] In 1363–65 he was supplying marble for paving the cloister in the upper ward of *Windsor Castle*,[2] and he died in 1370/1. His will, made on 26 August 1370 and proved 24 February 1370/1, expresses his desire to be buried in the church of St. Botolph (Aldersgate) and leaves bequests for the maintenance there of chantries for his soul and the souls of Master WILLIAM DE RAMSEY III his brother, Christiana, wife of William, and others; he also left to the church a missal, a portifory, and two graduals. His houses in the parish were left to his wife Felicia, with reversion to his son Ralph, and 100 marks (£66 13s. 4d.) were to be divided equally between his three daughters, Alice, Margery, and Mariota.[3] His widow Felicia was still living in 1397, when her son Ralph de Ramsey, fishmonger, disposed of the reversion to certain properties.[4]

[1] *PRO*, E.101–469–6, 470–13, 18 (*G.P.J.*; *L.F.S.*); HKW, I, 535; CBC, 24; [2] HWC, 187, 207; *PRO*, E.101–493–16, 17 (*A.O.*); [3] SWL, II, 138; CLB, 'G', 279; 'H', 26, 44; [4] *LHR*, 126(82, 108)

RAMSEY, Nicholas de (*fl.* 1331–1349) ? Mason

Brother of WILLIAM RAMSEY I, senior, and of JOHN RAMSEY II of London. He was a member of the party which on 20 November 1331 was concerned in the abduction of Robert Huberd and his marriage to William Ramsey III's daughter Agnes;[1] and is mentioned in the will of John Ramsey II, made on 15 March 1348/9.[2] In 1348 he supplied plaster for the works of *Westminster Palace*.[3] He may perhaps have been identical with Nicholas de Londres who was master of the works of the city of Paris in August 1333.[4]

[1] CLB, 'E', 266; [2] SWL, I, 625; [3] LKC, 194; [4] BAF

RAMSEY, William de, I, senior [Rameseye]

RAMSEY, WILLIAM

(*fl.* ?1294–1349) Mason

Mason of London, brother of JOHN RAMSEY II and of NICHOLAS RAMSEY, and perhaps father of WILLIAM RAMSEY III and of JOHN RAMSEY III. He may have been the William de Ramisseye who from 10 August 1294 was one of the working masons at *St. Stephen's Chapel, Westminster*, taking 2*s.* 6*d.* a week,[1] and he is possibly to be identified with WILLIAM RAMSEY II of Norwich.

On 20 November 1331 he was a member of the party concerned in the abduction of Robert Huberd and his marriage to Agnes, daughter of William Ramsey III, junior, but was one of those who could not be found when a case was brought on.[2] He is referred to as Master William de Ramseye, mason, on 23 July 1336,[3] and also on 15 March 1348/9, when his brother John made his will.[4]

[1] TSS, 35; *PRO* E.101–468–6; [2] CLB,. 'E', 266; [3] *LBH*, G.43; [4] SWL, I, 625; *LBH*, D.41

RAMSEY, William de, II [Ramysseye] (*fl.* 1326–1331) Mason

Mason of Norwich, perhaps identical with the William 'sculptor' who, with John Sculptor, was given a robe worth 18*s.* by the Sacrist of *Norwich Cathedral* in 1319–20.[1]

The south walk of the Cathedral cloisters was begun in 1324 under JOHN DE RAMSEY I, who continued in charge for two years, but in 1326–27 it was to Master William Ramsey that a robe price 16*s.* 8*d.* was given.[2] In an account for the two years 1329–31 an item of 15*s.* 10*d.* for a robe for Master William de Ramysseye appears,[3] while work was in progress on the cloisters and on a chapel, perhaps St. Ethelbert's Chapel over the Great Gate of the Precincts, certainly under construction about this time.

An undated account, which can, however, be fixed to between 1324 and 1330 on internal evidence, refers to payments of 16*s.* 8*d.* each for two robes for Master William and his brother, with 3*s.* 4*d.* each for their furs, as well as 16*s.* 8*d.* paid for their expenses on journeys from Norwich to London and London to Norwich, and for the keep of their horses while at Norwich. Brother John de Wurthstede also spent 7*s.* 8*d.* on travelling to and from London to obtain moulds for the work of the cloister.[4] This evidence strongly suggests identity between Master William and one of the two masons named WILLIAM RAMSEY I, senior, and III, junior, of London. One of the Norwich masters must presum-

ably have been the William de Ramseye who repaired windows at *Ely Cathedral* in 1336–37. He was paid 8*s.* 8*d.* by the Sacrist, taking fees of 2*d.* a week as well as his board, for his work '*in officio*', and a yearly robe.[5] It is likely that he was in charge of the rebuilding of the choir in succession to JOHN the Mason VII (? JOHN RAMSEY I).

[1] *NCM*, roll 226; [2] SNN, 473; *NCM*, roll 1042; [3] *NCM*, roll 1043; [4] *Ibid.*, roll 1136; [5] CSR, II, 81

RAMSEY, William de, III [Ramesey(e), Rameseyei, Ramessey(e)] (*fl.* 1323–†1349) Mason

One of the masons working at *St. Stephen's Chapel, Westminster*, in 1323, and in 1325, on the making of the cloister or passage (*alura*) between the chapel and the Painted Chamber; at this time he was paid the ordinary rate of 6*d.* a day.[1] From 1326 to 1331 a 'Master William de Ramesseye' was the visiting master mason of *Norwich Cathedral*, and this man (see RAMSEY, WILLIAM, II) may be the same. On 20 November 1331, the London mason and his wife Christina went with others (including Master WILLIAM DE RAMSEY I, senior, and NICHOLAS DE RAMSEY, apparently brother of the elder Master William) to the house of John Spray, without Aldersgate, and forcibly removed his ward, Robert Huberd aged 14, who was the heir to considerable property, and married him to Agnes daughter of William de Ramsey, junior. William and his wife Christina and Thomas de Chacombe were arrested and charged, but since the marriage was an accomplished fact, it was adjudged that Robert Huberd should choose whether or no he would remain with the Ramseys. He preferred to do so, and William de Ramsey produced sureties for the performance of his duties as Robert's guardian, John Spray being discharged from the guardianship.[2] Agnes must have been at least 10 years old, and was probably more, so that it is likely that William de Ramsey was in his early thirties at the time.

Ramsey was engaged by *St. Paul's Cathedral* as master of the new work of the chapter house and cloister there, and on 13 July 1332 was, on account of his giving 'especially and assiduously his whole attention to the business of the same church', granted exemption from jury service.[3] The deeds by which the Dean, the Chapter, and the Bishop granted the site, and an indulgence to those assisting the work, dated 14, 15, and 17 June, state that chapter house and cloister were to be begun at once, and pressed on to completion.[4] In this year he was assessed to pay 13*s.* 4*d.* to the subsidy in Aldersgate Ward; this was a large sum and shows that he was already a man of substance.[5]

In the autumn of 1335 a survey of the condition of the *Tower of London* was ordered, and William de Ramsey was one of four masons who were members of the commission (see also ROBERT DE DIPPENHALL, Peter de Tytemersshe under JOHN DE TICHMARSH, REGINALD WYTHAM), which returned its findings on 14 December.[6] Probably the state of affairs revealed by this survey was an important factor in the decision to reorganize the royal works. This was done on 1 June 1336, by issuing a patent to William de Ramsey as chief mason in the Tower of London and chief surveyor of the King's works in the Tower and other castles south of Trent; the appointment was for life, with a fee of 12*d.* a day and a robe every year; Master WILLIAM DE HURLEY was given a similar patent as chief carpenter and surveyor of carpenters' work, and Walter le Fevre as chief smith, at 8*d.* a day.[7]

During the next two years Ramsey was in charge of repairs at the Tower of London, including work on the great hall there, and his duties as surveyor are well illustrated by an extract from the accounts: 'for recrenellation and cresting of the wall which runs from the gate of the Watergate and the common latrine next the postern opposite the gate of the Mint, which wall contains in length by measure measured in the presence of Master William de Rameseye mason and Master William de Hurle master carpenter, 2 royal perches each of which contains 16½ feet. . . .'[8]

Ramsey's private practice continued, for not only was he still in charge of the new work of St. Paul's, but on 23 May 1337 he entered into an agreement to advise upon the works of *Lichfield Cathedral*, where the presbytery was in course of erection; for each visit he was to receive £1, with 6*s.* 8*d.* for the travelling expenses of himself and his servants coming from London, which was then a journey of 4 days in each direction.[9] He was to give sound counsel regarding the repair of defects and to provide ordinance and instruction to the other masons touching the erection of the new work (*sanum consilium suum circa emendacionem defectuum et ordinacionem suam et informacionem aliis cementariis circa instruccionem novi operis*).

From 1337 Ramsey was also in charge of work at St. Stephen's Chapel, Westminster,[10] and his official work must have been considerable. As a prominent London citizen he was assessed to pay £10 in 1340 towards the city's loan of £5,000 to the King. This implies that he was a man of very considerable wealth; he contributed later on to the gift and loan which the city made in 1346.[11]

On 16 February 1343/4 Ramsey was ordered to impress masons for the works of *Windsor Castle*, where the 'Round Table' building was to be made for the King's projected order of chivalry; Ramsey was further commissioned on 24 February to buy stone for the works, and he was working at Windsor as 'first cutting mason' from 16 February until 27 November, when the work was stopped. A great deal of work was done during this period, but it was abandoned and later destroyed.[12]

Ramsey evidently had business or interests in east Kent, for on 12 April 1345 a commission of oyer and terminer was appointed to hear his plaint that the Abbot of St. Augustine's, Canterbury, and his retinue had carried away his (Ramsey's) goods at Reculver and assaulted his servants, whereby Ramsey lost their services for a great time.[13]

He was commissioned to impress masons for the works of Westminster Palace on 20 April 1346, where work on St. Stephen's Chapel was still in progress, having been ordered on 11 April, with WILLIAM OF WINCHELSEA, to take 24 masons and 39 carpenters with their tools for Edward III's French expedition.[14] In 1347 he was Common Councillor for the Ward of Aldersgate, London, while still in active charge of work at St. Stephen's Chapel. It was at this time that the wooden vault of the chapel was erected, and tracery was made for the windows of the clerestory.[15] During the following year he purchased property at Enfield,[16] which he was not to enjoy for long, for he died on or about 3 June 1349, probably of the Black Death. By 30 June 1349 JOHN ATTE GRENE was the King's Chief Mason. After Ramsey's death his daughter Agnes, as his executrix, submitted accounts relating to his office of chief mason from 1336 to 1349. These accounts show that Ramsey, during the 13 years he had held the office of chief mason and surveyor of masons' work (*Capitalis Cementarius et supervisor*), had received only £136 10s. 0d. out of £254 13s. 8d. due to him for his fees and robes.[17] On 1 August 1376 Agnes received a final payment of £65 9s. 1d. of the arrears; to obtain this payment Agnes agreed to forgo a sum of £32 14s. 7d. still outstanding.[18]

Ramsey had owned a number of properties outside Aldersgate,[19] one of which he conveyed to his daughter Agnes, 'wife of Robert Huberd citizen and mason of London' on 29 May 1349, a few days before his death. This he sealed with his own exquisitely cut seal bearing on a shield the canting arms which he had assumed: a pair of compasses between two rams' heads erased in chief and a gateway in base.[20] The workmanship of this seal and the unchallenged assumption of armorial bearings which it implies speak eloquently of the position and wealth to which Ramsey had attained. A William de Rameseye who is in several cases certainly identical with the King's Mason appears as a witness to transactions in the parish of St. Botolph, Aldersgate at dates from 7 February 1328/9 to 14 October 1348,[21] while Agnes, daughter of Master William de Ramesey, late mason, was engaged in transfers of property at various dates until 1399.[22] Agnes would seem to have carried on her father's shop, as she was paid for making the tomb of Queen Isabella of France, widow of Edward II, in 1358–59, to a total of £106 18s. 11d. according to an agreement made with her by the queen during her lifetime. The tomb was set up in the *London Greyfriars*, and is said to have been made of alabaster. The iron grill placed about the tomb was made by Andrew 'Faber' or Le Fevre, the King's smith in the Tower of London, for £110, and £10 was paid to a London mason, Robert Burton, for masonry work about the tomb.[23]

In addition to his known works it seems not improbable that Ramsey gave advice or a general design for the hall and other buildings at *Penshurst*, Kent, which was built by Sir John Pulteney between 1341 and 1348. Pulteney was a grocer and four times Mayor of London, in 1330, 1331, 1333, and 1336. He was a keen patron of architecture, and according to Stow 'In 1337 built a fair chapel in St. Paul's church, wherein he was buried. He founded a college in the parish church of St. Lawrence, called Poultney; he built the

parish church called Little Alhallowes in Thames Street; the Carmelite friars church in Coventry'; he died in 1348. Such an extensive programme of building would probably imply at any rate the consultant services of a prominent mason; the chapel at St. Paul's Cathedral indicates that Ramsey would be the obvious man to approach, while the work at Coventry suggests a possible reason for Ramsey's intervention at Lichfield.

Ramsey is a master of supreme importance for his influence in the formation of the Perpendicular style. Unfortunately his known works have been destroyed or greatly damaged but we have a detailed view of the St. Paul's chapter house and cloister by Hollar, which shows that the design was of Perpendicular character throughout. This is confirmed by abundant remains of the detail *in situ* or recovered in fragments and now in the south triforium of new St. Paul's. The design for these buildings must have been ready by the time work began in the summer of 1332; it already included the 'key' Perpendicular detail of mullions cutting the curve of the arch, the extensive employment of the bowtell, the fully developed use of the double-ogee and casement mouldings, the quatrefoil-in-square, and the characteristic base with circular roll, bell, and cushion above an octagonal sub-base of bell form. It also displayed the four-centred arch with flattened upper arcs, and the square-framed arch with cusped blind spandrels. While some of these elements were derived from antecedent work at Westminster and others suggest a direct knowledge of recent work in France (notably the south doorway of Clermont-Ferrand Cathedral, carried out by Pierre Deschamps between 1287 and 1325), the conjoint effect is something wholly new and constituting a radically different conception of Gothic art. The connections of Ramsey's family, if not of himself, with Norwich and probably with Ely are of particular interest, for the Norwich south cloister built by JOHN RAMSEY I and WILLIAM RAMSEY II between 1324 and 1330 provides the immediate source of the traceried wall-arcading in the Ely Lady Chapel, carried out slowly between 1321 and 1349. One variant of this tracery, in two interpenetrating planes, seems to have provided the suggestion for the type-pattern of Perpendicular tracery, first seen in the work at St. Paul's begun in 1332, and in the great south window only of the Gloucester south transept. The date of the Gloucester transept as a whole lies between 1331 and 1337, but the abrupt change from the curvilinear traceries of the side windows to the south window with its Kentish and first Perpendicular forms shows that the introduction of these features is an afterthought, undoubtedly due to the impact of the new invention in London.

Comparison of the St. Paul's fragments with the details of Gloucester and of Lichfield is revealing. At Lichfield the markedly individual features of Ramsey's style are present in the bays of the presbytery and retrochoir arcades, though only in the two westernmost bays of the aisle walls, the eastern parts of which are of one build and like detail with the Lady Chapel of WILLIAM DE EYTON. Bases and arch-mouldings were evidently cut directly from Ramsey's moulds. At Gloucester the case is different: the great south window (c. 1335?) shows the influence of Ramsey's work upon another mind; but the whole design of the new choir, apart from its complicated lierne vaulting of western (Tewkesbury, Malmesbury) character, is intimately penetrated by Ramsey's conceptions, though still detailed by another hand.

As the King's Chief Mason for all works south of Trent, Ramsey was officially responsible for Gloucester Castle, and the new work at the Abbey was the direct outcome of the royal tomb of Edward II and the abundant offerings at this new martyr's shrine. Ramsey's advice as consultant must have been obtained before the work of recasing the choir was begun, and he presumably provided the small-scale drawings on which the general ordinance of its parts was based, and possibly advised from time to time.

The identity of the master responsible for the actual detail at Gloucester remains mysterious, for though his mannerisms (notably the use of hexagonal sub-bases and capitals, and the occasional employment of skeleton vault-ribs) have points of contact with Bristol, the detail and mouldings differ very greatly from any Bristol work of the period. Nor is there the slightest likeness to the previous work at Gloucester itself: the south nave aisle of c. 1318–29. The closest analogy seems to be with JOHN DE SPONLEE'S work at Windsor, begun in 1350, and there is reason to suppose that Sponlee may have

been connected with the works of Winchcombe Abbey. Winchcombe had in the previous generation (see WALTER OF HEREFORD) been of far greater architectural importance than Gloucester, and it would seem probable that it was Winchcombe rather than Gloucester that was the true centre of Cotswold masoncraft. It is even possible that it was Sponlee himself who was Ramsey's collaborator at Gloucester.

Be this as it may the work done at Windsor Castle from 1350 onwards, including the vestry, treasury, and cloisters, is very close to Ramsey's style, and designs for some of the work may well have been prepared by him before his death, as the work was projected in consequence of the foundation of the Order of the Garter in 1348. The chapel was made collegiate on 6 August 1348, but no actual work was carried out until April 1350, when Sponlee was already master mason.

(LKC; APD; WKM)

¹ *PRO*, E.101–469–8, 468–3; ² CLB, 'E', 266; ³ *Ibid.*, 263; RML, 185; ⁴ *SPM*, A.24.865; A.73.1902; A.ii.1077; ⁵ UFT, 61 ff.; ⁶ BHT, I, App. 273; ⁷ CPR 1334–8, 305; ⁸ *PRO*, E.101–470–1; ⁹ SLC, *Bodl.*, MS. Ashmole 794, f.57v.; ¹⁰ *PRO*, E.101–470–2; ¹¹ CLB, 'F', 48, 146, 149; ¹² HWC, I, 114; ¹³ CPR 1343–5, 502; ¹⁴ *Ibid.* 1345–8, 112; French Roll 20 Edw. III, quoted in WRC (*A.O.*) ¹⁵ RML; *PRO*, E.101–470–18 (*G.P.J.; L.F.S.*); ¹⁶ HPM, I, 124; ¹⁷ *PRO*, E.101–501–28; ¹⁸ *Ibid.*, E.403–460; ¹⁹ *LHR*, 60 (36), 62 (51), 65 (37), 67 (56); *SPM*, A.6.7; ²⁰ *SPM*, A.6.1; ²¹ Guildhall Deeds Nos. 62–64; *SPM*, A.6.6; MBH, I, 567; ²² *SPM*, A.6.5; *LHR*, 77 (212), 78 (34), 95 (2,6), 114 (108), 115 (39), 124 (17, 18), 128 (45); ²³ F.D. Blackley in International Society for the Study of Church Monuments, *Bulletin* 8 (1983), 161–4 (*N. L. R.*)

RASYN, John (*fl.* 1409–1414) Carpenter

Was master carpenter in charge during the building of *Durham Cathedral Cloister* from 1409 to 1414, when he was succeeded by JOHN WADLEY.

DAR (*M.G.S.*)

RAYE, William (*fl.* 1477–   ) Carpenter

Junior sworn master of the carpenters' craft of London in 1476/7, when on 26 February a report was made on the Abbot of Winchcombe's house in Fleet Street.

RLW, II, 565

RAYNER the Carpenter (*fl.* 1086–   ) Carpenter

One of the carpenters of William the Conqueror, who held of the King the manor of 'Merstune' (now Marston, Herefordshire), worth 4s., when Domesday Book was compiled in 1086.

DB; VCH, *Herefs.*, I, 344

Rayner, William—see REYNER

Raynold, William—see REYNOLD

READING, John [Reding, Redyng] (*fl.* 1442–†c. 1471) Mason (? *Reading, Berks.*)

Was working as a freemason on the works of *Eton College* in 1442, at the standard rate of 3*s.* a week; in the week 19–24 November he was fined 'ffor going without lycens', being paid for 4½ days only.[1] This suggests that he may have had other work which he was undertaking privately.

He next appears in 1460, when he succeeded JOHN SMYTH as master mason of *Westminster Abbey*;[2] in that year 'John Redyng mason' paid 13*d.* for a pew for his wife in St. Margaret's Westminster, as is shown by the churchwardens' accounts.[3] Reading probably died in 1471, when he was succeeded as Abbey mason by ROBERT STOWELL. His fees, like those of his predecessor John Smyth, amounted to £5 a year, with wages of 3*s.* 4*d.* a week when at work, £2 for the rent of his house, and a robe worth 13*s.* 4*d.* He ceased active work in February 1470/1, but his fees were paid up to Michaelmas.

[1] KJE, 26, 37; [2] RNW; WAM, 23525–36; [3] WMW, 138

Reading, Richard of—see FARLEIGH

REDE, William (*fl.* 1516–1521) Carver

Carver of Blythburgh, Suffolk; on 10 May 1516 agreed with the churchwardens of *Redenhall* ('Rednale'), Norfolk, to ceil the roof of the chancel there with timber called 'waynscote' within eight weeks for the sum of 5 marks (£3 6*s.* 8*d.*). The churchwardens later sued Rede in the Court of Common Pleas on the ground that he had fraudulently substituted wood of poplar and ash ('popyll & Asshe') for oak wainscot and claimed damages of £10, later reduced to 10 marks. The attorneys for the parties were set a day to imparle in 15 days after Easter (31 March) 1521, but there is no record of the outcome.

PRO, CP 40–1031, m. 328 (*N.L.R.*)

REDE, William le [Redee] (*fl.* 1367–1374) Mason

Warden of the masons at *King's Langley* from 1367, taking 6*d.* a day. He also carried out taskwork on the cloister of the Priory there until 1374.

HKW, I, 260, 263; II, 975

REDE, William (*fl.* 1482–1515) Mason

Freemason working on the vaults of the nave of *Westminster Abbey* in 1482–84.[1] In 1515 was perhaps warden of the London Guild of Masons. The will of John Bayly, of Bury St. Edmunds, who appears to have been identical with a freemason of that name was made at London, 20 October 1515, and witnessed by 'Master Nevell and William Rede Wardens of the Craft'.[2]

Another *William REDE* was apprentice of JOHN HERMER, freemason, who in his will made at Cambridge, 6 February 1507/8 left to him his tools and remitted his two years' service still to come.[3]

A.O.
[1] WAM, 23558–59; [2] BW, viii, 39; [3] PCC, 14 Bennett

Redee, William—see REDE

REDICHE, William (*fl.* 1461–†c. 1495) Mason

Was appointed for life to be master mason of the castle of *Chester* on 20 December 1461; he may have held the position until the grant on 24 September 1495 to SETH DERWALL.

DKR, XXXI

Reding, John—see READING

REDMAN, Henry [Redmayne] (*fl.* 1495–†1528) Mason

Descended from the ancient family of Reedman or Rideman, who held land of the Abbot of Ramsey by serjeanty of acting as his riding-bailiff (*Ridemannus*) at least as early as the mid-12th century.[1] He was a son of THOMAS REDMAN I of Westminster. In 1495–96 and 1496–97 he was a working mason at *Westminster Abbey*, taking wages of 3*s.* 4*d.* a week, and after March 1496, 6*d.* per working day by the 'new statute'.[2] In June 1496 he was working with his father on the setting of the great windows in the new work.[3]

After 1501 he was working at *Richmond* on the buildings of the *Friars Observant*, who received special patronage from the King. With Robert Nevill, a brickmaker and bricklayer, and THOMAS BINKS, he undertook the whole of the work by a contract now lost, but upon which they were paid £1180 by May 1504. Another £30 in final payment was received by Redman and Nevill at Easter 1506. On 10 July following they were paid 75*s.* 5*d.* in addition 'upon their bill'.[4]

In 1509 Redman was given a 'reward' for visiting *King's College Chapel, Cambridge*, with WILLIAM VERTUE.[5] Two years later he stood surety for Vertue's performance of a contract at St. George's Chapel, Windsor.[6] His father died early in January 1515/16, and he succeeded to the post of chief mason to Westminster Abbey; the work of the nave was reaching completion, but in addition the chancel of *St. Margaret's Church* was rebuilt by Abbot Islip between 1516 and 1523, and for this Redman was the master mason, being paid 3*s*. 4*d*. a week, which he returned to the fabric fund, doubtless because he was already in receipt of fees and wages from official and other sources. He was also the designer of the tower and porch of St. Margaret's, built between 1516 and 1522, when the bells were being hung.[7]

As master mason to the Abbey, Redman received the usual fee of £5 a year, with 13*s*. 4*d*. for clothing.[8]

During 1516 he assisted William Vertue to produce the 'platte' or design for the new work at *Eton College*, consisting of the west side of the court and Lupton's Tower.[9] In the autumn he gave warranty of premises in 'Westbraynford' (Brentford, Middlesex) against the Abbot of Westminster, which probably implies that Redman was a tenant of the Abbey there.[10] Meanwhile he had become the architect of Wolsey's vast building projects: in the accounts for the new work at *York Place*, which begin on 5 February 1514/15, Henry Redman is named as the master mason, but no salary is entered against his name, probably because he was paid in the account for *Hampton Court*, now lost. Among the earliest purchases at York Place were 'two waynscotts to make moolds of for masons', each costing 1*s*., 'whereof one remayneth here and one other is send to Hampton Courte'. Other necessaries included 'glewe and sprigg nale for Mr. Redmayn to make his tools'.[11]

The work at Hampton Court went on for 10 years, until Wolsey presented it to the King in 1525, while at York Place operations were continued until Wolsey's fall in 1529, after Redman's death. Redman must have been a busy man, for he was also in the royal service: from 1516 until February 1519 he was working at *Greenwich* and was paid £33 6*s*. 8*d*. for the making of two new tiltyard towers there.[12] On 12 September 1519 he received a grant of the office of King's Master Mason jointly with William Vertue,[13] who had surrendered his patent, perhaps on account of age. Next year, on 19 July 1520, Redman had a grant of the office of chief

mason in *Windsor Castle* at 6*d*. a day, perhaps a sinecure.[14]

Redman's post as mason to Westminster Abbey included work at the Abbey's widespread properties, and in 1520 he went to *Chelmsford* to advise on the repair of the bridge between Chelmsford and Moulsham, where he was paid 1*s*. for his 'labor to se the bridge and to have his counsell, and his brekfast'.[15]

In 1525 Wolsey began his third great architectural work, the Cardinal's College at *Oxford*, now *Christ Church*. The licence to found the college was granted on 13 July and the masons and others were immediately ordered to 'set forth the ground', i.e. to lay out the plan, and the foundation stone was laid on the 15th.[16] The accounts show that Redman and JOHN LEBONS were the masons: 'to John Lubbyns and Henry Redemayne master masons of the foresaid werks for theire wags euery of them 12*d*. by the day'.[17] They were paid for every day, including Sundays, in the accounts for the first three years of the work; the later accounts do not give their names, but doubtless the same arrangement continued.

A letter of 29 December 1526 mentions the great progress made in the Oxford works, due to the exertions of 'Mr. Lovyns, Mr. Redman, and Mr. Coke' (HUMPHREY COKE).[18] One of Redman's last official works was the completion of the charming cloister and cloister-chapel of St. Stephen's College in *Westminster Palace*; it was begun about 1526, and was presumably the joint design of Redman and William Vertue: Vertue died in March 1527, after which Redman held the office of King's Mason independently.

Redman died, probably at his home at Brentford, on 10 July 1528; on the following day Thomas Heneage wrote to Wolsey that the King 'has shown Mr. Herytage such buildings as he desires at Tittenhanger and is sorry for the death of Mr. Redman, his mason'.[19] The King might well be sorry to have lost such a servant, who, had he lived, might have shown the superiority of the native style to the strange misreadings of antiquity which were so soon to overwhelm English architecture.

Redman made his will on 1 July 1528, describing himself as 'Henry Redman of West Brentford fremason'. He desired to be buried on the north side of the choir of St.

Laurence at Brentford, 'there where the vestre would be made'. He made a number of bequests to Brentford Church, and 10 marks a year for a priest 'to synge and rede for my soule and good helthe of my wyfe, and the soules of my father and mother and for my wyfes father and mother and all that I am bound to praie for and for all christiane soules'. He left to the convent of Syon 13s. 4d., and to the parishioners of Brentford premises there which would suffice to pay £3 6s. 8d. yearly to the parish priest.

These premises were to remain to his wife Joan during her life, and comprised 'the George', a cottage with garden grounds of William Chapman next to the George on the west side, and a cottage next to 'the Maydenhead', and 4 acres of ground late of Agnes Tuttill, 2½ acres of it lying at Burding Bushes, 1 acre 'butting upon a close of Robert Angers' and ½ acre 'in long shoote butting to the Kyngs higheway'. The trustees were to be Master John Spylman and his son John, and Elizabeth Spelman, daughter of Sir Henry Frowick, with others.

Finally comes a clause which throws some light on the Redman family: 'Also. . . to Willm Reedman, the sonne of Thomas Reedman of Westminster, the howse that I dwell in and the lands not bequest ne given after the decease of my wife Jone, if the said Willm Reedman dye without heyres before my wife Joanne all that lands and howses to give and to sell at her discretion yff the said Willm Reedman lyve after my wyfe, then I will that my dwellyng howse with the lands not bequest remayne to the next heyre male of my blood beyring the name of Reedmans in Huntingdonshire, besyde our Lady of Reedbone, also I give and bequethe to my wife Joanne which Joanne I ordeyne and make my sole executrics and Richard Parker nt her and he to have for his labor as my wife thinketh convenient, and Thomas Reedman my overseer, and he to have for his labor 10s.'[20] The chapel of Our Lady of Reedbone was at Hepmangrove in the parish of Bury, near Ramsey.

Thomas Reedman of Westminster was almost certainly the Thomas Redman who was 'kinsman' to THOMAS REDMAN I, father of Henry, and probably identical with the Thomas Redman of New Brentford 'fremason' who on 9 September 1536 enfeoffed Richard Parker and others of a cottage in New Brent-

ford between the tenement of his brother John Redeman and a tenement in the tenure of 'Myghele Andrew'. 'John Redeman fremason' was to deliver seisin, being named as Attorney for that purpose.[21]

Henry Redman was buried in Brentford Church, where his brass and those of his wife and two daughters still remain. His brass has now lost its head, but Lysons made a drawing of it when perfect, of which the late Professor Lethaby published a copy. The inscription begins: 'Py̅ for the Soule of Henry Redman su̅tyme chefe M. Mason of ye Kyngs works and Joha̅ his wyf sp'all benefactors of this churche' and after enumerating their bequests, ends 'deceased July 10 1528. O' whos' soulle Jhu have M'cy'.[22]

Henry Redman succeeded in adapting the traditional English architecture to new requirements and to the new material, brick. Although he could design vaulting and masonry detail in the elaborate style of William Vertue, he was far more a master of composition on broad lines than Vertue had been. This is seen at its best at Hampton Court, where the effect of the exterior is obtained entirely by the general form, and by the breaking of the horizontal line by means of the sharp vertical stress of the turrets. The positions of windows are governed by convenience and structural necessity, and the purely formalistic symmetry which was later to produce such monstrosities as sham windows painted black or even fully glazed, had no place. The horizontal stringcourses kept order, and in consequence the eye is never struck by the quite irregular fenestration. Had Redman lived only a few years longer, he might have been able to establish 'Tudor' as a lasting style; what he did achieve was sufficient to ensure that the minor brick buildings of England for some three centuries should be well fitted for their purpose, suited to their surroundings, and a pleasure to the eye. Happily these smaller works were prevented by expense from copying the grand Renaissance styles, and were able to follow some of the quiet graces of the style of Henry Redman. (See Appendix I.)

APD; HCW; WKM; WHR; GOM, 93; HKW, III
[1] RMC, III, 68, 92, 271; ARA, 6, 27, 46, 66, 114, 116, 118, 129, 135, 142, 202, 204; PMC, 53n3, 69, 72–3, 75–6, 80–1; [2] WAM, 23572–4; [3] Ibid., 33291, ff. 5v., 6; [4] HKW, III, 195; PRO, E.36–214, pp. 55, 77 (A.O.); [5] KCM, Building Acc. 1509–15 (A.O.); [6] HWC; [7] WMW; [8] WAM, 23601–17; [9] WCC, I, 418; [10] HPM; [11] PRO, E.101–474–7;

¹² LPH, III, pt. ii, pp. 1533 ff; HKW, IV, 101; ¹³ LPH., pt. i, 458; ¹⁴ Ibid., pt. ii, 933; ¹⁵ JAB, III, 134–5; ¹⁶ LPH, IV, 1499; ¹⁷ PRO, E.101–479–11; ¹⁸ LPH, IV, 2734; ¹⁹ Ibid., pt. ii, 4497; ²⁰ FHB, 61; ²¹ PRO, Anc. Deed, A.13095; ²² AQC, XL, 170; cf. LMT, XI, 51–4

REDMAN, John [Redmanne] *(fl.* 1490–1505) Mason

Mason of *Westminster*, where he worked on the Abbey from 1490 to 1500, and again from 1501 to 1505 taking 3*s*. 4*d*. a week.[1] He may have been the John Redmanne, 'karver' who in 1496–97 worked in the church of St. Mary-at-Hill, London, in connection with the removal and re-erection of the roodloft.[2]

¹ *WAM*, 23563–85; ² *LMR*, 224

REDMAN, Thomas, I, senior *(fl.* 1490–†1516) Mason

Appears at *Westminster Abbey* as a working mason at Michaelmas 1490 and had probably been entered for the previous 31 weeks as 'WILLIAM' REDMAN; for the next 15 years he was paid 3*s*. 4*d*. a week and had a yearly robe worth 10*s*. like the other working masons; when engaged on setting he received extra pay of 4*d*. a week. In 1499/1500 he was absent for 12 weeks and for 6 weeks in the following year, but he was otherwise continuously employed, being the leading mason from 1500 onwards. In the autumn of 1505 he succeeded ROBERT STOWELL as master mason of Westminster Abbey and held office until his death in January 1516, when the post was given to his son HENRY REDMAN.[1] His will, made on 3 and proved on 9 January 1515/16, describes him as 'of the Town of Westminster mason'; he wished to be buried in St. Margaret's Church. He left to his son Henry Redman a silver salt, and to Thomas Redman his kinsman 'all my tooles that long to Masonry'. His wife Alice was executrix.[2]

A mason of the same name in 1466 had livery as an esquire of the Prior of Canterbury; he may have been master mason of the cathedral.[3] This was more probably the 'Thomas Rodman' whose obit was kept at Canterbury on 11 November.[4]

(WKM)
¹ RNW; ² PPR, Westminster Peculiar, 108 Wyks; ³ Bodl., Tanner MS. 165 (A.O.); ⁴ BM, Arundel MS. 68, f. 48

REDMAN, Thomas, II, junior [Reddman] *(fl.* 1499–†1536) Mason

Mason working at *Westminster Abbey* from 1499, when he received a robe as an unpaid apprentice. He was paid 1*s*. 8*d*. a week from 1500 to 1503, then for 9 weeks at 2*s*. and thenceforward until he left the works in February 1505/6 at 2*s*. 4*d*. After an absence of 3 years he returned to the works as a freemason at the full rate of 3*s*. 4*d*. a week, and continued in full employment until 1532, in most years receiving a robe priced at 10*s*.[1]

He was related to HENRY REDMAN, father of William Redman, and brother of JOHN REDMAN.

His will made on 10 September and proved 22 September 1536, refers to his lands at Ealing, Isleworth, and New Brentford.[2]
¹ *WAM*, 23576–86, 23591–623; ² W.J. Williams in MR, XVI, 204; (CCL, 276 Tunstall)

REDMAN, William [Redeman] *(fl.* 1490–) Mason

A mason of this name appears as working at *Westminster Abbey* for 31 weeks in 1490, but his name is probably a scribal error for THOMAS REDMAN I.

WAM, 23563

Redyng, John—see READING

REED, John *(fl.* 1391) Carpenter

In 1391 was working at the *Abbey of St. Mary Graces* (Eastminster) on Tower Hill, making two new doors for the church, etc., for 12*s*.

A.W. Clapham in A, LXVI, 354, 394

Reginald the Carpenter—see SWAFFHAM

REGINALD the Mason *(fl. c.* 1224–) Mason

Master mason of the Prior and Convent of *Coventry* before 1224–25, when reference is made to his houses outside the wall of the cemetery.

(A.O.) MRA, 179

REMUS, James *(fl.* 1494–) Marbler

Marbler of St. Paul's churchyard, London; according to the will of Sir Brian Rowcliffe, made in 1494, he was to be paid 10*s*. for making Rowcliffe's monument (*epitaphium*) in the *Temple*, according to an indenture which had been drawn up.

YTE, IV, 104

Renell, Nicholas—see REVELL

RENGWYNE, John *(fl.* 1321–) Mason

Of 'Wogham' (Offham, Sussex), mason; contracted with Sir Geoffrey de Say on 6 March 1320/1 to construct a hall at 'Hammes' (*Hamsey*), Sussex, 60 feet in length by 36 feet in breadth. He was to dig and hew the stone and provide sand and lime, while Sir

Geoffrey was to arrange for carriage. The payment was to be made from month to month, and the building was to be finished within 18 months. The total payment was fixed at 35 marks (£23 6s. 8d.) and one quarter of wheat.

SHB, 426–7; AJ, XXIV, 6; (*WAM*, 4063); SNQ, III, 133–6

REPPYS, William (*fl.* 1428–　) Mason Carver (*Repps, Norf.*)

'Gravour' of Norwich; in 1428 was paid £2 for carving 6 bosses for the north cloister vault of *Norwich Cathedral*.

SNN, 173–4; *NCM*, roll 1077

REPYNGDON, William (*fl.* 1348) Carpenter (*Repton, Derb.*)

Master carpenter in charge of works at *Nottingham Castle* in 1348, when a new roof of seven couples was made for the chapel. He was paid 3s. 4d. a week, the working carpenters receiving 2s.

PRO, E.101–544–35

REREY, Richard (*fl.* 1505) Carpenter

Carpenter of Maldon, Essex, who in 1505 framed four new tenements for the London Bridge House, for their property in Rood Lane, St. Margaret Pattens, *London*, for £45 13s. 4d.

P.E. Jones in AAJ, 3 S, XVI (1953), 63

REVE, Walter (*fl.* 1480–1499) Carpenter

Warden of the carpentry of *London Bridge* in 1480, and appointed in 1495 joint chief carpenter with THOMAS MAUNCY, with whom he was in office until 1499.

P.E. Jones in AAJ, 3 S, XVI (1953), 62

REVELL, John (*fl.* 1550–1554) Carpenter

Was appointed deputy on 25 March 1550 to JOHN PARKER, master carpenter to the Court of Augmentations. On 29 September 1552 he succeeded Parker, and held office until the Court was abolished on 23 January 1554. In 1553, with the master mason RALPH HILLES, was in charge of fitting up *Somerset Place* for the Princess Elizabeth.

HKW, III, 420; IV, 253

REVELL, Nicholas (*fl.* 1508–1522) Carpenter

Nicholas Revell became a freeman of the London Carpenters' Company in 1508.[1] In partnership with HUMFREY COKE designed and built a house for James Yarford, Alderman of London, about 1520. They were paid £300 for the work but in 1522 sued Yarford for extras

amounting to £64.[2]

[1] HKW, III, 61; [2] SHB, 15 (*ECP*, 489–6)

Rewlan, James—see ROYALTON

REYNER, William [Rayner] (*fl.* 1413–　) Carpenter

Of Worlington, Suffolk; contracted on 8 June 1413 with ROBERT STRUT of Hartest to make the woodwork of a new bakehouse at *King's Hall, Cambridge* (now Trinity College). The contract itself is lost, but Reyner undertook to convey the timber for the work from Brandon Ferry or 'Totrynghethe' to Cambridge. The accounts for 1413–14 contain entries: 'Watton and his horse for 2 days to inquire after Reyner our carpenter and his bondsman' (evidently Strut), and 'Richard Wrythe riding to Myldenale (Mildenhall) for the carpenter', and writs of *Capias* and *Exigent* were taken out against him, from which it would seem that Reyner was a somewhat elusive personality.

WCC, II, 440, 441; SHB, 46

REYNOLD, John (*fl.* 1391–　) Carpenter

In 1391 made a new house and chamber on the west side of the *Abbey of St Mary* (Eastminster), Tower Hill, London, on the east side of the Abbot's small garden, with three new tenements next the King's highway towards the west, for £52.

The abbey, founded by Edward III in 1350, was at this time practically complete, the church was being paved with stone and tile, and the infirmary was being built.

A, LXVI, 353–64

REYNOLD, John [Rainald, Raynold] (*fl.* 1350–1360) Mason

On 10 June 1350 John Raynold, stonemason, was appointed to impress masons from Essex, Herts., Norfolk and Suffolk for works in the new chapel (? St. Stephen's) in the Palace of Westminster.[1] He was warden (*apparilator*) of the masons employed on the works of the *Tower of London* in 1358–59, taking 3s. 6d. a week.[2] In 1360 Reynold was commissioned to take workmen for the repair of *Hadleigh Castle*.[3]

[1] CPR 1348–50, 584; [2] *PRO*, E.101–472–5, 6; [3] CPR 1358–61, 330

REYNOLD, William, I (*fl.* 1468–1505) Mason

Worked as a mason-setter at *Magdalen College, Oxford* from 1468, taking 3s. 4d. a week; later he was working there mainly on piecework and between 1494 and 1505 was paid some £70 for work on the bell-tower. This was probably designed by WILLIAM ORCHARD as its first stone was laid in 1492.

(*E.M.J.*) BMC, II, 231; *MCO*, Liber Computi (*G.P.J.*); GOM, 79–80

REYNOLD, William, II [Raynold, Reynalde, Reynold(e)s] (*fl.* 1531–†1545) Mason

In 1531 succeeded RICHARD WATCHETT as warden of the masons at *Hampton Court*, where Henry VIII was building great additions to Wolsey's Palace. Reynold was paid 4*s.* a week until 1536,[1] when the work at Hampton Court was nearing completion.[2] He was evidently a skilled carver, for the accounts include payment to 'William Raynoldes, freemason for entayling of two crounys in freston standyng over the Kinges armes at the Chappell dore at 5*s.* the pece, by convencyon'. These arms at the chapel door bear the cyphers of Henry VIII and Jane Seymour and were made in 1536.

Reynold was appointed master mason in *Windsor Castle* on 23 December 1540, on the death of CHRISTOPHER DICKINSON,[3] was in charge of the fortifications of *Hull* in 1542 (see JOHN ROGERS),[4] and died in the summer of 1545, when he was succeeded in that office by GUY RAFF.[5] He made his will on 22 July 1545, the first witness being 'Marster John Rogers' the King's Mason of Calais; the will was proved on 26 September.[6]

The *William REYNOLD* who was working as a mason at 3*s.* 4*d.* a week at *Westminster Palace* in 1531–32 was presumably a different man,[7] while the *Thomas REYNOLD* who worked there for the same wages as a hardhewer, and in 1539 to 1542 as a freemason at 8*d.* a day at *Canterbury Manor, Dartford*, and *King's College, Rochester*,[8] may have been another member of the same family.

(HCW; WKM; HKW, III)
[1] LHC, I, 127; *PRO*, E.36–237 (*L.F.S.*); [2] LHC, I, 358; [3] LPH, XVI, 379 (48); [4] HKW, IV, 474–5; [5] *Ibid.*, XX, pt. ii, 910 (68); [6] *PCC*, 35 Pynnynge; [7] *PRO*, E.36–251 (*G.P.J.*); [8] Bodl., Rawl. D. 779, 783, 784, 785 (*G.P.J.*)

REYNS, Henry de (*fl.* 1243–†*c.* 1253) Mason

Possibly of Rheims in France, but more probably deriving his name from sojourn there than as a native. The problem of his origin will be discussed later, as it is of special importance in connection with his career.

He is first mentioned by name on 10 December 1243, when the King, then at Windsor, ordered that 'Henry master of the King's masons' (*magistro cementariorum regis*) should have a robe consisting of tunic and overtunic; the same order includes a robe for Master William le Brun, one of the keepers of the works at *Windsor Castle*,[1] and the inference is that Henry was already master mason there.

On 13 March 1244/5 Henry was ordered to view the defences of *York Castle* with SIMON DE NORTHAMPTON the King's Carpenter; they were to confer with 'other masters expert in the science' as to how it should be fortified.[2] Next year the rebuilding of the great church of *Westminster Abbey* was begun, and Henry was associated with EDWARD son of ODO the Goldsmith as a keeper of the works. The demolition of the east end of the old church of Edward the Confessor began on 6 July 1245.

Master Henry was put in possession of two houses at Westminster,[3] and on 2 May and 4 June 1246 the King ordered payment of 60 marks (£40) for houses for the work of Master Henry the mason.[4]

The new work seems to have begun with the building of the crypt for the new Chapter House, probably in 1246, the walls of the superstructure following in the next year. The first detailed account relates to 1248/9, and shows that Henry was master of the works, while task-work was being done on the three bays of the cloister which led to the Chapter House; the transept and eastern arm must also have been begun. The next year included the continuation of work on the cloister, Chapter House, and transept, and Master Henry paid out £26 13*s.* 4*d.* for task-work.[5]

During 1250 the structure of the church must have risen rapidly, and in 1251 the piers were ready for the marble shafts, for on 30 October 1251 Master Henry was ordered to hasten the work by getting all the marble work raised during the winter so far as was possible without danger.[6] In 1251–52 he was again paid £26 13*s.* 4*d.* for task-work, and the work on the church must have been practically complete by 1252, when timber was procured for the roof and stalls.

Meanwhile Master Henry had not been engaged solely on Westminster Abbey, for on 12 October 1250 the King had ordered the issue of £30 to the Constable of the *Tower of*

London to make a turret between the King's Chapel and the Thames, by view of several persons, including 'Master Henry keeper of the King's works'.[7] Probably Henry is also included in other cases where the phrase 'by view of the keepers of the King's works' is used.

The virtual completion of the first section of the church and of the Chapter House came in 1253 when work included the provision of marble columns, the filling of the vault with chalk, paving of floors, and the making of iron bars for the windows; in the Chapter House the windows were evidently finished but unglazed as canvas was provided to close them.[8] After this time Master Henry disappears from the scene, and he was presumably dead by the time a robe was issued to JOHN OF GLOUCESTER as 'the King's mason of Westminster' on 11 June 1253.[9]

On 20 March 1260/1 Hugh 'son of the late Master Henry de Reyns, mason' (*filius quondam magistri Henrici de Reyns cementarii*) assigned to the Abbey a rent of 5*s*. from a messuage in Westminster given him by his father and in the tenancy of WALTER the Imager, for the support of a lamp in the Lady Chapel.[10]

The problems of Master Henry's origin and of his work as a designer are closely connected. The discovery of his surname, together with the well-known resemblance of the Abbey to Rheims Cathedral, gave rise to the suggestion that Master Henry was brought from Rheims for the purpose of designing the new church at Westminster. There are very serious objections to this theory. All experts are agreed that the detail of Westminster is English, although the general conception is closely based on French models. The weight of Lethaby's lifelong knowledge cannot lightly be set aside; he wrote in 1925 of 'my conviction, the result of all I know about mediaeval architecture — that Westminster Abbey Church is English work'.[11] It was further shown by Lethaby that on stylistic grounds the King's Chapel in Windsor Castle, of which the masonry work was built between 1239 and 1243, must have been designed by the architect of the new church of Westminster. The moulding sections in particular are almost identical, and the provision of 'moulds' or templates was always the duty of the master mason in charge of the work, however much individual

latitude may have been allowed to the carvers of foliage and enrichments. This of course strongly supports the documentary evidence suggesting that Henry was master of the masons at Windsor in and before 1243, but the structural evidence by itself is overwhelming, and if Master Henry did come from France it would have been before 1239. In any case, he is hardly likely to have come direct from Rheims in 1242–43, at the time of Henry III's unsuccessful war against St. Louis on the borders of Gascony. It is far more likely that Master Henry was an English mason who had at an earlier date been employed at Rheims, perhaps during his wander-years, and who thus had first-hand knowledge of the great French designs of the period.

Master Henry may have supplied designs for the abbey of *Hayles* in Gloucestershire, founded in 1246 by Richard, King of the Romans, Henry III's brother; the resemblances to Westminster are probably too close to be the result of mere imitation. Whatever may be the truth concerning Master Henry, the great church he designed is his best memorial, and while its French features had little or no effect upon the development of English architecture, it has remained a constant source of inspiration to English architects and to all beholders. (See Appendix I.)

(WKM; LKC; LWR, 81 ff.)

[1] CCR 1242–7, 141; [2] *Ibid.*, 293; [3] HPM; [4] CLR 1245–51, 47; CCR 1242–7, 428; [5] *PRO*, E.101–466–29; [6] CCR 1251–3, 174; [7] CLR 1245–51, 306; [8] *PRO*, E.101–467–1; [9] CCR 1251–3, 365; [10] WWA; *WAM*, 17358; [11]LWR, 89

REYNS, Hugh de [Reins] (*fl.* 1261) Mason

Son of Master HENRY DE REYNS, and using a seal inscribed '*S HVGON' D' REINS SIMENTARI*', showing that he was himself a mason. He assigned to Westminster Abbey a rent of 5*s*. from a messuage in Westminster given to him by his father and in the tenancy of WALTER the Imager, on 20 March 1260/1.

Nothing further is known of him unless he was the Master HUGH the Mason III who received a retaining fee of £5 a year at *Hereford Cathedral* in 1290–91. If Hugh de Reyns were the Hereford master it would explain the very close similarities between the details of the north transept there and those at Westminster. The difficulty of the gap of 30 years is more apparent than real: Henry de Reyns seems to have died in middle life, when his son may still have been a minor. The assignment of 1261 may indeed indicate that Hugh had only recently come of age and was therefore born *c.* 1240. On the other hand, the retainer of £5 was, for a provincial cathedral of the time, a very handsome one, suggesting that Hugh was an eminent master.

WAM 17358

Reyns, Nicholas—see DYMINGE

RICARDO of Burgos (*fl. c.* 1180–1226) Mason

Mason in charge of the building of the monastery of *Las Huelgas*, near *Burgos*, Spain begun *c.* 1180 and almost complete in 1223. On 9 July of that year, King Alfonso VIII of Castile granted an estate at Solarzal to Master Ricardo, his wife Alda, and their sons and daughters, in consideration of Ricardo's praiseworthy service in the building of the convent. At this period the name 'Ricardo' when found in Spain invariably indicated an English or Angevin origin, and Ricardo had presumably come to Castile in the train of Alfonso's Queen, Eleanor, daughter of Henry II.

Ricardo probably designed the monastery of *Santa Maria* at *Aguilar de Campóo*, completed in 1222, and to which he disposed of his property at Solarzal in 1226. His influence is also seen in the style of other contemporary works.

(*X.D.S.*) Julio González in RAR, LII (1947)

RICHARD the Carver I (*fl. c.* 1150–   ) Carver

Carved the Romanesque font at *Bridekirk*, Cumberland, which is inscribed: 'Rikarth he me iwrokte and to this merthe gernr me brokte.' A little figure of a man working with hammer and chisel is carved in a loop of the scrolling vine.

(*A.O.*) ABC, 105; GMS, fig. 18

RICHARD the Carver II (*fl.* 1427) Carver

Was paid £1 10s. 0d. for work at *St. Mary's Church, Stamford*, Lincs., in 1427.

PAS, Bk. XIV, ch. iv

Richard the Carpenter—see WALLINGFORD

RICHARD the Carpenter (*fl. c.* 1245–1275) Carpenter

Between 1222 and 1246 land on Tothill, Westminster, was acquired from Richard the Carpenter; he appears later in the reign of Henry III, and as Master Richard, carpen-

ter, early in the reign of Edward I.

WAM, 17344, 17404, 17509

Richard the Engineer—see LENGINOUR; WOLVESTON

RICHARD the Mason I (*fl. c.* 1195–   ) Mason

Mason of *Lincoln*; named as '*Magister*' when holding land near the Close of Lincoln at the end of the 12th century. He was probably St. Hugh's master mason and responsible for the original design of the Gothic Cathedral. (See Appendix I.)

HML, 113 quoting *LDC*, D.ii, 79–2–16

RICHARD the Mason II (*fl. c.* 1195) Mason

Mason (*cementarius*), son of Hereward the Plumber; perhaps master mason to *Rochester Cathedral* when he granted to the Hospital of Strood a rent of 11s. 3d. and 6 hens yearly, by an undated deed of soon after 1193.

(*H.M.C.*) HHR, 6

RICHARD the Mason III [*cementarius*] (*fl.* 1208–1209) Mason

Apparently mason to Peter des Roches, Bishop of Winchester, in 1208–09, when he was given 4 marks (£2 13s. 4d.) for the work of Winchester (*ad opus de Wintonia*), perhaps the new retrochoir of *Winchester Cathedral* (1202–*c.* 1235). Richard in the same year paid a fine for land in Farnham, Surrey, of half a mark (6s. 8d.). Richard may also have worked on the eastern arm of *St. Mary Overy, Southwark* (Cathedral), where building was in progress from *c.* 1213 to 1235.

HPW, 38

RICHARD the Mason IV (*fl.* 1267–   ) Mason

Master (*cementarius*) of *Salisbury Cathedral* in 1267, when he was bequeathed 1 mark (13s. 4d.) by Robert de Careville the treasurer.

CDS, 345

RICHARD the Mason V (*fl.* 1398–1399) Mason

Mason hired by New College, Oxford, in 1398–99 to make a new doorway in the chancel of *Roxwell Chapel*, Essex, for which he was paid £1 6s. 8d. He was perhaps identical with RICHARD MASON.

NCO, Writtle Accs., A.5

Richard the Mason—see GOUSHILL, MACHUN

RICHOWE, Richard (*fl.* 1469–1472) Mason

Was the principal contractor at the building of *Bodmin Church*, Cornwall, between 1469 and 1472. He was paid £22 for the pillars of the nave, £6 for those between the chancel and St. John's aisle, and £17 8s. 0d. for the north and south walls, all by taskwork. He received in addition sums totalling £17 9s. 10d. for cutting stone for windows and porch, and carriage of stone from the moor, and he was occasionally paid a daily rate of 6d. for his services, apart from the task-work. On one occasion a payment of 3s. 4d. to William Mason his brother is recorded.

CSM, VII, 12–15, 27

RICKLING, Thomas [Rikelyng] (*fl.* 1348–) Mason (? *Rickling, Essex*)

Mason (*cementarius*) of 'Berkweye' (Barkway, Herts.); contracted with the Dean and Chapter of St. Paul's on 11 July 1348 to rebuild the chancel of *Sandon Church*, Herts., for 20 marks (£13 6s. 8d.). The work, which still exists, is in the Decorated style.

AJ, LXXXVII, 21–23; SHB, 437–8; (*SPM*, No. 1264)

Ridge, Richard—see RYDGE

Rihul, Henry—see RYHULL

RIPLEY, John [Rypeley] (*fl.* 1525–†c. 1570) Joiner

Appointed King's Joiner in the *Tower of London* on 3 September 1525 in succession to THOMAS STOCKTON.[1] In 1529–30 Ripley was paid 18s. each for carving 'king's beasts' for the Privy Orchard at *Hampton Court*, and in 1532 supplied doors, panelling, cornices and pendants for the great gallery of *York Place*.[2] On 23 March 1532 there is a reference to carriage of wainscot boards from St. Katherine's Pool to the house of John Ripley, joiner, in the parish of St. Giles without Aldersgate, there to be wrought for the King.[3] In 1535 Ripley was producing carvings for the royal barge, and he also made the stalls for the Chapel at *Whitehall Palace*.[4] Between 1536 and 1538 a John Ripley, probably the joiner, made a contribution of 1s. 8d. to St. Martin-in-the-Fields, Westminster.[5] In 1544 and 1550 Ripley acquired houses in the parishes of St. Katherine Coleman, and St. Martin Outwich, London.[6] Ripley continued to hold office as King's Joiner until 1569, taking fees of 12d. a day and a Christmas robe.[7]

HKW, III, IV
[1] LPH, IV, i, 1676(12); ii, 2540(12); [2] SHB, 253, 258; [3] LPH, V, 92; [4] HKW, III, 33; [5] KSM, 56 (*A.O.*); [6] LHR, 244 (30); CPR 1549–51, 358; 1547–53 App., 112; [7] CPR 1554–5, 283; HKW, III, 409

Ripon, William of—see WRIGHT

RISSEBURGH, John de [Riseburgh] (*fl.* 1337–1339) Mason (*Risborough, Bucks.*)

Carried out repairs to the chancel of the church of 'Stokhalling' (? *Stoke Mandeville,* Bucks.) for the Dean and Chapter of Lincoln in 1339; described as master mason (*cementarius*).[1] He was probably the John de Riseburgh, who was working at the *Tower of London* in 1324, at 5d. a day,[2] and who, with John Glorye, carpenter, carried out a survey of *Berkhampstead Castle* on 14 February 1337.

CUH, III, xiii–xiv, 52 (*N.L.R.*)
[1] LDC, B.j, 2–5; [2] PRO, E.101–469–7

RIVER, William de la [Ryvere] (*fl.* 1452–1453) Carpenter

Master carpenter engaged by the town of *Shrewsbury* to build the new mill by the stone gate on the Severn in 1452. In the year 1452–53 he was paid £21 2s. 1d. in part of his contract price of £26 13s. 4d.

SC, Bailiffs' Accs., Box XVIII, No. 879

Robert the Carpenter—see FITZGILES

ROBERT the Carpenter (*fl.* 1446–) Carpenter

In 1446 was paid £4 for taking down and rebuilding the spire of *St. Mary's Church, Sandwich*, Kent.

BHS, 363

ROBERT the Carver (*fl.* 1460) Carver

In 1460, as Robert 'caruffar', was paid £34 13s. 4d. for work done in *Newark Church*, Notts., with JOHN LEYCETT.

(*A.O.*) Newark Corporation Records printed by Dimock in RPL, vol. IIIA (1856), 7

ROBERT the Mason I [Rodbertus, ? St. Albans, Robert of] (*fl. c.* 1077–1119) Mason

In charge of the original work at *St. Albans Abbey Church*, consisting of the transepts, the eastern part of the nave, and the great tower; this work went on from 1077 until towards 1100. Robert was described as excelling all the masons of his time, and was given a house in St. Albans and lands for his good service to the abbey.[1] He yearly gave 10s. to the abbey, and on his deathbed restored to the monks the greater part of the lands granted to him.[2]

A mason named *Robert of ST. ALBANS* appears as witness to a deed endowing *Ramsey Abbey* with 10 acres of land in 1122; at this time the rebuilding of the abbey was in progress. He appears as witness to several further deeds until *c.* 1135.[3]

(APD; BAF, 506)
[1] RGA, I, 63–4, 72; [2] CLH, I, 34; [3] RAC, 239, 246, 262, 272

ROBERT the Mason IA (*fl.* 1129–1130) Mason

Was allowed 12*s.* 6*d.* for his winter livery in Hampshire in 1129–30. The second membrane for the county is missing from the Pipe Roll, but it may well be that Robert was retained for the year and was in charge of works at *Winchester Castle*.

HMR, 40

ROBERT the Mason II (*fl.* 1169–1170) Mason

In 1169–70 the sum of £1 was allowed to Master Robert the Mason (*cementarius*) for the works of *Dover*. He was perhaps identical with RALPH the Mason II, his name being incorrectly entered.

PR

ROBERT the Mason III (*fl. c.* 1185–1198) Mason

Mason of London, witness *c.* 1185–98 to a deed of land outside Newgate granted to the Bishop of Coventry.

(*A.O.*) MRA, 28

ROBERT the Mason IV [*Cementarius*] (*fl.* 1278–1279) Mason

Mason to the treasurer of *Christ Church Priory, Canterbury*, in 1278–79, when he was paid £7 13*s.* 4*d.* for making the walls of new shops in Burgate.

LP, MS. 242, *f.* 48

ROBERT the Mason V (*fl.* 1304–   ) Mason

In 1304 did work on *Bramber Bridge*, Sussex, for the Priory of Sele, which was responsible for its upkeep. He was also receiver of offerings at the chapel of the bridge.

JAB, I, 52

ROBERT the Mason VI (*fl.* 1305–1309) Mason

Master mason at *Westminster Abbey* in 1305–06 when he was paid 9*d.* a day and had charge of extensive alterations to the refectory.[1] At Michaelmas 1309 Master Robert 'de Westmon' granted a 7-year lease of a garden in Longditch at Westminster.[2] He was perhaps identical with ROBERT LE MASON.

[1] R. B. Rackham in AJ, LXVII (1910); LWR, 133;
[2] *WAM*, 17560

ROBERT the Mason VII (*fl. c.* 1310–†*c.* 1335) Mason

Mason (*cementarius*) of *Salisbury*; is said to have controlled the work of the *Cathedral* for 25 years and is evidently identical with the Robert who was still living in July 1334 when RICHARD FARLEIGH was appointed master. His obit was kept up on 17 August.

Since Robert was living in 1334, his period as master of the work need not have begun as early as 1310, and the occurrence of Master WILLIAM DE SCHOVERWILLE as a Salisbury master giving professional advice at Exeter in 1311 strongly suggests that Robert did not take over until 1312 or later. Robert may have designed the great tower at a date around 1320, taking account of its stylistic dependence upon the Hereford tower then only approaching completion. On grounds of detail, notably the profusion of ballflower ornament, the project is to be dated in the 1320s rather than later, and so is unlikely to be the work of Farleigh.

(APD); DSC, 133; HCE, 167, 215–16

ROBERT the Mason VIII (*fl.* 1377–1379) Mason

Apparently the master in charge of the building of the old chapel of *Queen's College, Oxford* (1373–80). He was paid at rates varying between 2*s.* 6*d.* and 3*s.* a week, and was employed for the whole of the year of the surviving account for 1377–78. He lived elsewhere, for a payment of 10*d.* was made to someone to bring him to the college, and in addition to his pay he received a livery priced at 8*s.*

The chapel, pulled down about 1712, had an east window of late Decorated character, much resembling those of the western Lantern of Ely Cathedral, probably designed by ROBERT WODEHIRST, with whom Robert may perhaps have been identical.

GOM, 62

ROBERT (*fl. c.* 1120–1150) ? Carver

'Robertus me fecit' is inscribed on a carved capital of the south choir aisle of *Romsey Abbey*, Hants. (*c.* 1120–50).

A, XIV, 136; XV, 304

ROBERT 'Sculptor' (*fl.* 1292–   ) ? Carver

A member of the English embassy under Sir Geoffrey de Langley which in 1292 was sent by Edward I to Kaikhatu, Ilkhan of Persia. It is not certain that he accompanied the expedition from England, as the extant accounts cover only the journey from Italy to Persia and back, by way of Brindisi, Constantinople, and Trebizond.

ALS, XIII (1877–84), 537–698

ROBSON, John (*fl.* 1475–1490) Carpenter

Master carpenter working on the buildings of the bishopric of Durham. In 1475 he was paid his expenses coming from London and in 1490 he was the master in charge of making a timber frame to support the bishop's chamber at *Bishop Auckland*. He also worked on various mills.

DAR, clerk of works accounts (*M.G.S.*)

Robyns, John alias Teynton—see REGINALD ELY, p. 96

ROBYNSON, John (*fl.* 1526–1529) Mason

Warden of the masons at the building of the second court, now destroyed, of *St. John's College, Cambridge*, from 1526 to 1529. He received 3*s.* 4*d.* a week.

SJC, Bk. II (*L.F.S.*)

ROBYNSON, Robert (*fl.* 1508–1523) Mason

In 1508 was one of the masons working on *King's College Chapel, Cambridge*, at the rate of 3*s.* 4*d.* a week;[1] in 1512 Robert Robinson of Barnwell, 'laborer', was assessed under Preacher's Ward for movables valued between £2 and £10, and then had three masons 'atte borde' with him (unless they were boarded with Robert Robynson, 'burgeyse and brewer', also assessed in the same ward);[2] in 1510–11 Robert Robynson, mason, gave 1*s.* towards the seating of Great St. Mary's Church, and he was one of the electors of church officers in that church in 1523.[3]

A.O.

[1] KCM, Building Acc. 1508–09; [2] CBD, 127, 128; [3] CWM, 40, 52

ROBYNSON, William (*fl.* 1526–1529) Mason

Of Grantham, Lincs.; master mason at the building of the second court, now destroyed, of *St. John's College, Cambridge*, from 1526 to 13 January 1528/9. He was paid 4*s.* a week.

SJC, Bk. II (*L.F.S.*)

ROCHE, John (*fl.* 1460–1464) Mason

Mason (*lathomus*) to the Bishop of Worcester, by whose order he was paid £1 6*s.* 8*d.* by way of a reward in 1460–61, besides £2 of arrears due to him. In 1463–64 he received £4 for his contract on making the stonework of the bishop's new *Library* at *Bristol* (above the north aisle of the church of All Saints), besides rewards totalling 14*s.* 4*d.* The Library was that of the Bristol Guild of Kalendars,

newly endowed by Bishop John Carpenter, who at the same time (1447–74) was building a college at *Westbury-on-Trym*. It seems likely that Roche would have been in charge of this work also.

PRO, Eccl. 2–128–92483, 92484

ROCHE, Roger (*fl.* 1333–1350) Mason

Working at *Exeter Cathedral* in 1333/4 and 1340/41,[1] at first at 1*s.* 1*d.* a week, later at 1*s.* 4*d.* until November 1334; in the next surviving roll at 1*s.* 5*d.*, rising in 1341 to 1*s.* 8*d.* These amounts show that he was still of junior standing. He became free of the City of Exeter on 7 September 1349, by gift of the mayor and commonalty; this was no doubt in consideration of important work on the bridge already done by him.[2] In 1350 he was master of the masons (*mestre des masouns*) at work on *Exebridge* at Exeter, receiving a fee of £2 and also 1*s.* a day when at work.[3]

(*M.E.C.*)

[1] EDC, Fabric rolls 2630–1; AEC, ii, 302–6; [2] RJE, 29; [3] ECR, Acc. of wardens of Exebridge 24 Ed. III

Rodbertus—see ROBERT the Mason I

RODES, William (*fl.* 1486–) Carpenter

Was paid 7*s.* for his labour and that of three men in building a timber span of *Nottingham Bridge* in 1486.

JAB, III, 11

Rodman, Thomas—see REDMAN, Thomas, I

ROGER, 'Artifex' (*fl. c.* 1175–1200) ? Engineer

Roger the King's '*artifex*' at *Clipston*, Notts., was a witness to a charter granting land at Morton, Notts., to Rufford Abbey in the late 12th century. He may have been identical with ROGER ENGANET.

(*H.M.C.*) SDD, 275, No. 370

ROGER the Mason I (*fl. c.* 1160–) Mason

Mason (*cementarius*) who witnessed a charter granting land in the parish of Harbrough, Lincs., to Newhouse Abbey, early in the reign of Henry II.

(*H.M.C.*) SDD, 196

ROGER the Mason IA (*fl. c.* 1200) Mason

Master *cementarius*; witnessed a charter at *Lewes Priory*, Sussex, about 1200, in company with ELIAS the Carver, Philip the carpenter and John the glazier, presumably the masters of the building staff of the priory at the time.

SXR, XXXVIII, 180 (*L.F.S.*)

ROGER the Mason II (*fl.* 1296–†1310) Mason

The Dean and Chapter of *Exeter Cathedral* were already paying a rent of 16*s.* for a house 'in which Master Roger the mason now dwells' by 26 March 1297,[1] and this rent is recorded in the Steward's account for 1296–97.[2] There is nothing to suggest that Roger had only recently taken office, and it is quite likely that he was the 'Master R.' who was being paid 2*s.* 1¼*d.* a week from July 1280 until the following Easter.[3] Roger was certainly the master mason (*cementarius*) and one of the keepers of the new work of *Exeter Cathedral* which was probably designed, and certainly executed by him, including the presbytery, of which the masonry was completed in 1299, and the choir finished about 1310; the works of the crossing and nave were completed by his successors WILLIAM LUVE and THOMAS WITNEY. Roger died in July 1310 when the burial of Roger *latomus* was recorded.[4] Master Roger lived in a house in the Close, for which the rent was paid by the Dean and Chapter, and throughout the surviving rolls was paid fees of £6 yearly. (See Appendix I.)

(BPE; TCC); *CEF (M.E.C.)*; AEC, *passim*
[1] *EDC*, 350, 2123 (*A.M.E.*); [2] *Ibid.*, 2777 (*A.M.E.*); [3] AEC, 3–5; [4] Obit Book 3673, *f.* 97v (*A.M.E.*)

ROGER the Mason III [*Lathomus*] (*fl.* 1315–) Mason

Master in charge of work for *Merton College, Oxford*, in 1315, perhaps the building of the kitchen. He was paid 2*s.* a week, no more than other masons employed on the job, and less than one, who received 2*s.* 2*d.* for setting freestone.

(*E.M.J.*) MRT, Rec. 3642

ROGER the Mason IV (*fl.* 1337–) Mason

Was master mason (*cementarius*) of *Durham Cathedral* in 1337 when he, with his two servants (*garciones*), was paid £5 8*s.* 2*d.* for building a new buttress at the corner of the chapel over the abbey gate. He probably designed the great west window, begun about 1341.

DAR, II, 535

ROGER, Luke (*fl.* 1376–1377) Carpenter

Carpenter to the treasurer of *Christ Church Priory, Canterbury*, in 1376–77, when 4*s.* was paid for his house.

LP, MS.243, *f.* 171

ROGERS, John I (*fl.* 1473–1475) Mason

Was in charge of new building at *Tickenhill Manor*, Worcs., in 1473–75, being paid £6 6*s.* 0*d.* (See also LAURENCE KERVER).

HKW, IV, 279

ROGERS, John II [Rogiers] (*fl.* 1533–†1558) Mason

Freemason; possibly identical with the John Rogers to whom, as a member of the household of Edward Stafford, Duke of Buckingham, 3 yards of cloth for livery were issued in 1514–15. If so, he may have been the designer of *Thornbury Castle*, building from 1511 until 1522.[1] In 1523 John Roger, freemason, was among the inhabitants of Lavenham, Suffolk, in the Muster Roll for Babergh Hundred, and was assessed at 10*s.* At this time the building of the upper part of the tower of *Lavenham Church* was in progress.[2] In 1533–35 he worked as a setter at *Hampton Court* at 3*s.* 4*d.* a week, and also carved label-stops for the doors and chimney-piece of the King's Great Watching Chamber with the King's badges and the Queen's letters.[3] In 1541 he was King's Master Mason at *Calais* and *Guisnes*,[4] and in the following year appears as surveyor of the fortifications of *Hull* and *Berwick*.[5] In June 1542 he was sent from Hull to inspect *Wark Castle*. While at Hull, Rogers produced plans of the Royal manor house and of the bulwarks, and a beautiful bird's-eye view of the former is almost certainly from his hand.[6] On 22 July 1545 he witnessed the will of WILLIAM REYNOLD the King's Mason of Windsor Castle.[7]

Rogers became master mason of Guisnes, about 1540, and he was greatly trusted as a responsible craftsman in charge of the important fortifications around Calais. In June 1541 he was said to have lately advertised the King concerning the works at Guisnes; in July he was about to cross to England to report upon the works; on 9 July 'Rogers the King's mason was sent to mark the works at Arde (Ardres) and Mountory' and esteemed them nothing in comparison with those of Guisnes. On 22 August the Privy Council ordered the surveyor at Calais 'to set labourers to work in such manner as Rogiers master mason at Guisnes should declare', and at Berwick in 1542 he was to report to the King by word of mouth concerning deviations from the 'platts'.

(WKM); **SJR**; HKW, IV

ROKE, JOHN

[1] *PRO*, E.101–631–20; [2] Grimsthorpe MSS. per Miss L. J. Redstone (*A.O.*); [3] *LHC*, I, 127; *PRO*, E.36–240 (*L.F.S.*); [4] *LPH*, XVI, 917, 944, 986, 1036, 1108; [5] *Ibid.*, XVII; [6] *BM*, Cotton MS. Aug. I. i. 84, I. Supp. 4; HTA 91; HTD, 100; [7] *PCC*, 35 Pynnynge

Roke—see also ROOK

ROKE, John le [Rooke] (*fl.* 1313–1320) Carpenter

Was the principal carpenter working at *Westminster Palace* from 1313 to 1320. On 3 December 1313 a writ of aid was issued on behalf of 'John de Roke the King's Carpenter'[1] and his name appears in the surviving accounts for several years.[2] His wages were 6*d*. a day. In 1320 he constructed a penthouse to cover the stones which had been worked for St. Stephen's Chapel.[3]

He seems to have succeeded PETER OF CANTERBURY who was carpenter at Westminster Palace until 1313, but it is uncertain when his term of office came to an end. The next known carpenter at the palace is JOHN DE HERLAND in 1329.

Possibly identical with the John Roke who was paid 1*s*. 6*d*. in 1339–40 for carving one of the wooden bosses of the Lantern vault at *Ely Cathedral*.[4]

[1] CPR 1313–17, 48; [2] LKC, 187; [3] BBW, 121; [4] CSR, II, 98

ROKESACRE, John (*fl.* 1364–†*c.* 1375) Mason

From 1364 onwards did much contract and taskwork, and later with JOHN BOX was appointed to impress masons for the works of *Queenborough Castle* on 28 April 1369;[1] he had been responsible for building a part of the walls of the outer ward called 'Le Barbican', but was dead by 20 June 1376.[2]

Laurence de *ROKISACRE* was a mason employed in 1361–62 on *Leeds Castle*, Kent.[3] A receipt by *Thomas* (?) *ROKESACRE* to the clerk of the works at Queenborough Castle was sealed in 1367.[4]

[1] CPR 1367–70, 238; [2] CFR 1368–77, 352; [3] HKW, II, 700; [4] PRO, Anc. Deeds R.S. 216 (L.F.S.); HKW, II, 796–802

ROLL, William (*fl.* 1410–1417) Carpenter

Master carpenter employed by *Oriel College, Oxford*, to make new stalls for the chapel between 1410 and 1413. He was paid in all £25 11*s*. 5*d*. In 1417 he was renting a house from Exeter College.

GOC

ROLLES, William (*fl.* 1436–1437) Mason

Was the principal mason working at *St. Paul's Cathedral, London*, in 1436–37, when 1*s*. 11*d*. was paid for a breakfast (*jantaculo*) for him, John Blomefeld a carpenter, and Bartholomew 'Plumer' (probably the King's plumber Bartholomew Lathe, 1433–42), for their labour for half a day searching the defects of the bell-tower. Rolles also took pay when at work at the rate of 8½*d*. a day.

PRO, SC 6–917–18; cf. HMO, 76

ROLLESBY, John and Stephen (*fl.* 1450–1451) Carpenters (*Rollesby, Norf.*)

John Rollesby was given a reward of 3*s*. 4*d*. for his work in connection with the Duke of York's mill at *Sudbury*, Suffolk, in 1451. In the same year, Stephen Rollesby was paid sums totalling 17*s*. 8*d*. for works on the duke's castle at *Clare*.

WAM, 12167

ROLLESBY, Nicholas and Peter (*fl.* 1421–1451) Carpenters

In 1421–22 Nicholas Rollesby of Bacton, Suffolk, was paid £33 5*s*. 0*d*. for timber and the building of the *Guildhall* of (*King's*) *Lynn*, then the hall of the Trinity Guild. In the following year Peter de Rollesby, carpenter, and his associates, were paid £9 2*s*. 10½*d*. for work beyond their contract.[1] Peter Rollesby was paid £2 6*s*. 8*d*. for works at *Clare Castle*, Suffolk, for the Duke of York in 1450–51.[2]

[1] LCR, G. d. 57, 58; HMC, 11R, III, 227, 230; [2] WAM, 12167

ROLLESTON, William (*fl.* 1407–1410) Mason

Mason of Beverley, Yorks., living in Walkergate in 1407;[1] in 1409–10 with the other eleven members of the town council was in charge of the building of *Beverley North Bar*,[2] a brick structure which still stands, and in that year was seized in right of Joan his wife of premises in Beverley held by knight service.[3] There seems to have been a second William Rolleston, a merchant, living in Beverley at the same period. The mason may have been designer of the west front of Beverley Minster.[4]

(*G.P.J.*)
[1] LBD, 25; [2] KMM, 40; [3] CPR 1422–9, 417; [4] HGE, 79–80

ROOK, John (*fl.* 1367–1378) Mason

Working mason at *Rochester Castle* in 1367; in 1377–78 he was chief mason there taking 7*d*. a day.

PRO, E.101–479–28; 480–5, 6 (*L.F.S.; G.P.J.*)

Rooke, John—see ROKE

ROTHERHAM, William [Roderam, Rod-rome] (*fl.* 1508–1545?) Mason (*Rotherham, Yorks. W.R.*)

In August 1508 was working as a setter at *King's College Chapel, Cambridge*, receiving the higher rate of 3*s*. 8*d*. a week.[1] In the Cambridge Poll Tax return of 1512–13 William Roderam, freemason, was assessed under Market Ward on movables valued between £10 and £20 and paid 1*s*. 8*d*. tax.[2] In 1514 'Rodrome', mason, was paid a shilling for two days' work about the vestry in *Great St. Mary's Church, Cambridge*; in 1534 Rotheram, freemason, was paid sums of 4*s*. and 2*s*. for mending and pargetting the church walls, 16*d*. for mending and paving the chapel (the Lady Chapel) and for setting up a holy water stoup, and 12*d*. for six bushels of lime; in 1545 a payment of 4*d*. was made 'to father Rotheram when he vewed the steple'.[3] The tower of the church was only half finished, but its completion does not seem to have been contemplated at that time; Father Rotherham's advice may have been sought in connection with the work carried out the following year, when a more substantial covering of timber and slates was put up.

A.O.

[1] *KCM*, Building Acc. 1508–09; [2] *CBD*, 118; [3] *CWM*, 24, 76, 77, 107

ROTHING, John [Rothyng] (*fl.* 1398–1399) Carpenter

Master Carpenter in charge of roofing the cloister of *Selby Abbey* in 1398–99 at its rebuilding under WILLIAM DE SUTHWELL, mason. John Brennand, carpenter, was working under Rothing on carving of bosses for the ceiling (*nodes pro invulturis* (?) *celature*).

Westminster Dioc. Archives, Se/Ac/5 (*N. L. R.*)

ROTHINGE, Richard (*fl.* 1310–†*c*. 1330) Carpenter (*Roding, Essex*)

Carpenter of London, contracted on 13 April 1310 to build a range of three shops of timber in London.[1] On 25 January 1312/13 he was a surety for Adam le Marbrer in the latter's contract to pave four bays of the new Lady Chapel of St. Paul's Cathedral.[2] In 1313 and 1315, with Isabella his wife, he was concerned in conveyances of houses in the parish of St. Botolph Aldersgate; after his death the property was quitclaimed to their daughters Avice and Elena by his widow in 1333.[3] He may be identical with the Richard 'de Rothingg' who paid 3*s*. 4*d*. at the subsidy of 1319 in Bridge Ward.[4] From January to June 1327 Master Richard de Rothing was in charge of repairs to the detached belfry of *St. Paul's Cathedral*, taking 3*s*. a week.[5]

Adam de ROTHINGE (*fl.* 1310–†*c*. 1325) was surety for Richard de Rothinge on 13 April 1310; sworn carpenter of the City of London in 1320, and lived with his wife Katherine in the parish of St. Martin-in-the-Vintry.[6] Between 1317 and 1319 they were acquiring a house in the parish of St. Andrew Cornhill, disposed of by their son Andrew in 1332 after Adam's death.[7] He is hardly likely to be identical with the Adam de Rothyng who was living in Lime Street Ward in 1319, when he paid 1*s*. 1½*d*. to the subsidy.[8] The carpenter was dead when JOHN DE TOTENHAM, senior, was sworn carpenter in his stead in June 1325.

John de ROTHYNG was a carpenter working at the *Tower of London*, taking 4*d*. a day, in 1323.[9] In 1332 he was assessed at 8*d*. to the lay subsidy in the ward of Broad Street.[10]

[1] *SHB*, 418–19; (*SPM*, MS. 1497); [2] *SHB*, 420; [3] *LHR*, 42 (71), 44 (40), 61 (74); [4] *WLE*; [5] *SPM*, A.52.10; [6] *LKC*, 363; [7] *LHR*, 46 (50), 47 (19), 48 (56), 60 (141); [8] *WLE*; [9] *PRO*, E.101–469–7; [10] *UFT*, 80

ROUCESTRE, Simon de (*fl.* 1352–1359) Mason (*Rocester, Staffs.*)

Mason employed at *Westminster Palace* in the summer of 1352 at 5½*d*. a day;[1] he was working on the south cloister of *Westminster Abbey* from 29 September 1357 to 29 June 1359, at the special rate of 3*s*. a week, higher than that paid to the chief mason, JOHN PALTERTON.[2]

[1] *PRO*, E.101–471–6; [2] *WAM*, 23455

ROUGE, Thomas (*fl.* 1449–   ) Marbler

Marbler of London; in 1449 was paid £10 6*s*. 8*d*. for a gravestone for Prior John Elham of *Canterbury Cathedral Priory*.

C. E. Woodruff in AC, LIII, 7

Rouland, Nicholas—see AUNDELY

ROUNE, J(ohn) [Rovne] (*fl.* 1454) Carpenter

Was paid £1 6*s*. 8*d*. in 1454 by the Bishop of Winchester for making at task the seats and desks for the choir in the chancel (*pro sedil' et les dextes in choro cancell'*) of *Hambledon Church*, Hants.

PRO, Eccl. 2–159444

ROUS, John (*fl.* 1407–1435) Carpenter

Was appointed master carpenter of the

royal castles in South Wales by Henry, Prince of Wales on 11 November 1407, and had a new grant from Henry VI on 23 February 1423, continuing in office until after 1435, at fees of 6d. a day. He was succeeded by GEOFFREY AP HOWELL.

CPR 1422-9, 87

ROUS, Philip (*fl.* 1378–1393) Carpenter

Drew fees as master carpenter of the King's castles in South Wales from 10 February 1377/8, and was in office after 18 August 1393.

HKW, II, 1057.

ROUSBY, Robert de (*fl.* 1367–1375) Mason

Chief mason at *Berwick-upon-Tweed* in 1367–1375.

PRO, E.101-483-2 (*L.F.S.*); 482-30 (*H.M.C.*)

ROVEZZANO, Benedetto da (1474–†*c.* 1552) Sculptor

Of Pistoia, Italy. Worked in England for Cardinal Wolsey from *c.* 1524 on the making of the Cardinal's tomb, left unfinished at Wolsey's fall in 1529. In 1526 he was paid for setting up the Lady Altar in *Westminster Abbey*.[1] Work was resumed at *Windsor* under Rovezzano and GIOVANNI MAJANO, in 1531, and continued for five years or more, with the intention of converting it into a monument for Henry VIII. Rovezzano was in Florence by 1543.

TBK, III, 314–16 (Benedetto)
[1] *WAM* 30626

ROYALTON, James [Rewlan] (*fl.* 1472–1473) Carpenter

In 1472–73 was brought from Southampton to Waltham, Hants., and to Winchester for the bishop's works. At *Waltham* he was paid £1 19s. 0d. as well as his board for 78 days' work on making the new 'Galerie' in all works of carpentry, as well as 4d. for a journey to survey the site beforehand. At *Wolvesey Palace* he viewed the old postern bridge and contracted to replace it, being given a reward and journey money amounting to 2s. 4d. in all. On completion of the new bridge at task, he was paid £2.

PRO, Eccl. 2-3-155837

Ruge—see RYDGE

RUSSELL, John, senior (*fl.* 1474–1518) Carpenter

John Russell was employed on the works of *Westminster Abbey* at times from 1474, and in 1478–80 at *St. Margaret's Church, Westminster*,

making the 'halpasse' in the Trinity Chapel, a new door and two 'haches' in the choir, for which including timber and stuff he was paid £4 6s. 8d. He was also paid 33s. for making 11 pews 'in the said halpasse' with material for the same.[1] This work was carried out before the rebuilding of the church. In 1490 John Russell paid 12d. to the London Carpenters' Company 'for presentyng of Jhon Parys is couenantman'.[2] In 1497–98 John Russell was one of the carpenters working at Westminster Abbey in the nave at 6d. a day (15 days). In 1513–14 and 1515–16 he worked for 47 and 38 days respectively, when his daily wage was 8d. In 1517 and 1518 John Russell 'senior', was employed for 165 days at 8d. on the chancel of St. Margaret's Church, Westminster.[3] He was probably a close relative, either brother or cousin, of RICHARD RUSSELL, and he appears to have worked under him at *King's College Chapel, Cambridge*. The book of building accounts for 1509–1515 gives few details, but in the fortnight ending 10 April 1513 John Russell received a payment for purveying.[4]

Between 1498 and 1518 *Robert RUSSELL* and *Thomas RUSSELL*, also carpenters and doubtless members of the same family, were employed at *Westminster Abbey* with Richard Russell. Robert's rate of pay rose from 6d. a day in 1499 to 7d. in 1500 and 8d. in 1514; Thomas was paid 6d. a day in 1499 and 7d. from 1500 to 1518. Both men also worked on the chancel of *St. Margaret's Church* in 1517–18, Thomas for 171 days at 7d., Robert for 136 days at 6d. and for 30 days at 4d.; possibly a Robert junior is to be understood by the latter payment. In the same account a payment of 20s. to Thomas Russell 'Joyner' for making the 'selyng' above the high altar occurs.[3] In 1517 Thomas Roossell of Westminster was paid for carving 98 knots and 43 half-knots (i.e. bosses) for the roof of the chapel of *Corpus Christi College, Oxford*, at 16d. each knot.[5] He was working at *Hampton Court* in 1525.[6]

A.O.; *J.H.H.*
[1] WMW, 147; [2] MCR, II, 82; [3] *WAM*, 23575, 23597, 23600, 23602; [4] *KCM*, Building Accs. 1509–1515; [3] SHB, 217; [6] GOC

RUSSELL, John, junior (*fl.* 1515–†1566) Carpenter

Carpenter of Westminster; was the younger

son of RICHARD RUSSELL, carpenter, who was master carpenter of Wolsey's works at *York Place* when they began in 1515. 'John Russell, apprentice', began to work there on 25 June 1515, at the rate of 4*d*. a day;[1] if, as is quite probable, John Russell was then starting his apprenticeship, he would have been born about 1500. John Russell, 'junior', worked at *Westminster Abbey* in 1517–18 at 8*d*. a day.[2]

After his father's death in 1517, the tenement called the 'Bell' in King Street, close by York Place, went to John's elder brother William, a wax-chandler, who took a new lease of it from the Abbot of Westminster in 1521; in 1524 this was changed into a lease of the principal tenement to William Russell, while the three smaller tenements were let separately, one of them being taken by John Russell, who no doubt lived there until 1531, when the King bought the premises for the extension of his new palace to the west side of King Street. The house was handed over to the King on 18 May 1531, John Russell being paid £20 in compensation for his rights.[3]

John Russell had just become the possessor, in right of his wife, of property in the Strand. This came to the Russells in March 1531, on the death of HUMPHREY COKE, whose daughter Christine had married John Russell. Owing to the death of Coke's younger children a few years later, Christine later succeeded to Coke's large freehold estate in the Strand, consisting of an inn called the 'Christopher', with a close, six tenements and six gardens, on the south side of the Strand where Northumberland Street now stands. The freehold of a tenement with a gatehouse adjoining to this property passed to the King in 1546, when Russell purchased it.[4]

In 1531 Russell was working on the King's extension of York Place as warden of the carpenters at 5*s*. a week,[5] and he had probably been there, under Wolsey and the King, since working out his apprenticeship. He also provided carved antelopes and two 'antyke heddes' for the King's Gate.[6] His marriage to the daughter of the King's Carpenter probably hastened his promotion, and after the brief period when JAMES NEDEHAM held the office, John Russell and WILLIAM CLEMENT jointly had a grant of the office of chief carpenter to the King on 1 October 1532.[7]

On 28 October 1537 JOHN MOLTON and Russell were granted the allowance of beer and bread which Westminster Abbey had paid to Kilburn Priory,[8] and in 1538–39 Russell was paid £1 13*s*. 4*d*. for work done to the chancel of *Aldenham Church*, Herts., for Westminster Abbey.[9] From 1555 or possibly earlier, until his death, he was surveyor to the fabric of the Abbey, apparently the first holder of this new office.[10]

On 27 January 1540/1 Russell took over one of William Clement's apprentices, William Bedell; and in August was paid £152 for the buildings at *Otford*, Kent. The Court Book of the London Carpenters' Company records on 7 July 1545 that 'Master Russell made a bankett for hys surfewerschype' (surveyorship). In 1546 he was concerned with work on the ceiling of the Presence Chamber at *Hatfield*.[11]

Russell, 'Master Carpenter to the King's Majesty' was appointed overseer to the will of John Molton on 30 November 1546.[12]

Russell was a churchwarden of St. Martin-in-the-Fields in 1534–36, and appears in the churchwardens' accounts as a donor to the church in 1536–38, 1542–43, and 1555. He set his mark to the accounts for 1550–52, and in 1561 took down the roodloft and made other alterations in the church, putting in an account which he signed as 'John Russell Carpent'.[13] In 1550 he was master of the London Carpenters' Company, and in 1556 accounts show that 'John Russell Mr. Carpenter' was paid £10 for repairing 'the house where the tomb of copper standeth at Westminster, that the same may be more safely kept'.[14] On 15 October 1552 Russell was granted the arms: *Or on a fess embattled azure an estoile between 2 crescents argent inter 3 leopards' faces gules*; crest: *on a falcon's head erased sable 3 guttys de leau, and in beak a pair of compasses or*.[15]

In 1557 Russell was in charge of the carpentry work for the Poor Knights' Lodgings in *Windsor Castle*, and in the following year was concerned in the making of the new fountain there.[16] He is almost certainly the 'Mr. Russell' who was paid £2 13*s*. 4*d*. by *Trinity College, Cambridge*, in 1559–60 'for his paynes in commynge from London to devise the chappell worke'.[17] This would imply that he designed the roof of the college chapel, which was then in progress.

Russell must have been feeling the effects of his age in 1564, for he made his will on 19 December[18] and on the 8th of the following February a new grant of his office adjoined with him William Colbrand, carpenter.[19] He died in 1566 and was buried at St. Martin-in-the-Fields on 4 July, the fees paid amounting to 3s. 8d.[20] In his will, proved on 13 July, he described himself as 'Citizen and Carpenter of London dwelling in the parish of St. Martin in the feilds, Maister Carpenter as well to the quenes ma^{tie} as also hath ben to her moste deare father and brother the famous Kinge Henrie the eighte and King Edward the sixte and also to the late King Philippe and quene Marie.' He must have been a wealthy man, for in addition to his considerable properties, he left to his 'well-beloved wief' his 'best Antique cuppe with a cover all gilte, sixe gilte spounes, sixe Apostles spones', and a deal of household goods.

Russell was probably a 'ghost', hidden during the lifetime of James Nedeham, but he was clearly a carpenter of great importance just at the period of transition from mediaeval to Renaissance design; Nedeham's roof at Hampton Court combined the form which had been brought by Coke to such perfection at Christ Church, Oxford, with classic ornamentation, but the design and mouldings are still those of the Middle Ages.

Russell's career as a designer belongs properly to the period of the early Renaissance in England, but his youth was passed in a country still imbued with the mediaeval spirit, and he was the King's Carpenter for over five years before the dissolution of the monasteries. His life and official career is in this respect a link almost unique between two worlds which were artistically poles apart, but had a common basis in the traditional construction of which Russell was a master.

(HKC); HKW, IV, 149, 218

[1] *PRO*, E.101–474–7; [2] *WAM*, 23602; [3] *LS*, XIV, 4; [4] *Ibid.*, XVIII, 21; [5] *LPH*, V, 952; [6] *WAM*, 12257; [7] *JPC*, 165; [8] *LPH*, XIII, i, p. 583; [9] *WAM*, 32107; [10] *WAM*, 37557, 37923, 38005–8, 38103–4, 38243–9, 38255–7; [11] MCR, III 14, 27; [12] W. J. Williams in MR, XVI, 204; [13] KSM; [14] JPC; [15] FH, IV no. 20, May 1966, 61 (*N.L.R.*) [16] HWC, I, 257, 259; [17] WCC, II, 566; [18] *PCC*, 21 Crymes; [19] *PRO*, MS. CPR; [20] KSM

RUSSELL, Richard (*fl.* 1420–†*c.* 1441)
Mason

Of Dunwich, Suffolk, and M.P. in 1420 and 1427; contracted in 1425–26 (probably on 26 February) to build the steeple of *Walberswick Church*, Suffolk, with ADAM POWLE of Blythburgh. The tower was to be like that of Tunstall, with doors and windows similar to those at Halesworth. They were to be paid £2

for each yard in height, together with a cade of herrings each year, and a gown of livery each.[1] The work was proceeding in 1432.[2] Russell was a Bailiff of Dunwich in 1430–31 and 1440–41, and was rented 13d. yearly on his property there from 1427 to 1437. He probably died *c.* 1441. On stylistic grounds it is probable that Russell designed the tower of *Kessingland Church*, and had built the lowest 30 feet at the time of his death.[3]

[1] SHB, 499–500; (*BM.*, Add. Ch. 17634); [2] *NCC*, Surflete 89 (*S.A.C.*); [3] C. Chitty in SIA, XXV, 164 *ff*

RUSSELL, Richard (*fl.* 1490–†1517)
Carpenter

Of Westminster; from 1490 to 1516 Richard Russell was the chief carpenter employed at *Westminster Abbey*. The *Novum Opus* rolls show that he was not a salaried craftsman but was engaged for varying periods when his services were required, being paid 8d. a day when employed. In 1505 he worked for as many as 99 days, in 1510 and 1511 for only three days in each year. During this period work on the west front and on the vaulting of the nave and its aisles was proceeding. In 1490–91, when £60 was spent on carpentry, Richard Russell was paid for making the great scaffold high up in the nave and moving centres to the next bays, for working at 'le Frith' making a new scaffold for the side aisles, also for raising it and for making a new lodge in the timber hawe. In the next year he was employed to make and remove the scaffold in the great west window, and in the year following he made a pentice over the west window, covered the jambs, and raised and took down the centres and scaffold there, also repaired the great bell-wheel. In 1501–02, when the vaulting of the westernmost bay was completed, Richard Russell and other carpenters were paid £17 for working on 'the last frame' in the new work. The next year he was employed for 73 days on work which included making scaffolding for taking down the chapel of St. Erasmus adjoining the old Lady Chapel, the removal of which was a necessary preliminary to the commencement of Henry VII's Chapel.[1] As the building accounts for the latter have not survived, it is not known who was the master carpenter employed to make the scaffolds and centres for it, and to erect the timber roof above the fan vault, but Richard Russell is likely to have been entrusted with this important but unspectacular work.

As a parishioner of *St. Margaret's, Westminster*, Richard Russell took part in the rebuilding of that church. The work began about 1488 with the rebuilding of the south aisle; the nave and aisles were completed by 1504. A new vestry was also built. The churchwardens' accounts show that Richard Russell was paid £2 in 1494–95 'for closyng in of the quere from the syde dores to the hy Auter & for ij basys for synt margaret & synt Katrine' and £1 'in yernest of a bargayne for selyng and planckyng with ij deskys a presse and wyndowes a grate wt other standards in the Vestry'. In the following year he received £3 6s. 8d. for this work 'and all other thyngs fynesshyng in the vestri accordyng to hys bargayne'.² There can be little doubt that he was also responsible for the roofs of the nave and aisles. In 1517 and 1518 the east end of the chancel was rebuilt at the expense of the abbot and convent. Richard Russell and at least four other members of his family, including his son John, were employed on the work, but Richard Russell died soon after it was begun, and he was paid only for five days in making the roof of the chancel and four days on scaffolding work, whereas JOHN RUSSELL, senior, and Richard's son JOHN, junior, were paid respectively for 165 and 149 days' work. All three men received 8d. a day. Two other Russells, Thomas (171 days at 7d.) and Robert (136 days at 6d. and 30 days at 4d.), were also employed. Thomas Russell 'Joyner' was paid 20s. for makyng the 'selyng' over the high altar.³

From 1509 to 1515 Richard Russell was master carpenter at *King's College Chapel, Cambridge*, during the final phase of building. He was paid an annual salary of £18 5s. (i.e. at the rate of a shilling a day), and the summarised book of building accounts shows that he received four 'rewards' between 1510 and 1512.⁴ He will have been responsible for the scaffolds needed for the construction of the antechapel and also for the scaffolds and centering for the high vault. The five eastern bays were already covered by a timber roof, designed by MARTIN PRENTICE in 1480 and erected in the course of the next four years. Russell will have roofed the seven remaining bays, keeping to the design of Prentice's work. The timber roof was finished before the end of 1512, in which year the plumbers were at work on the lead covering between the beginning of April and the end of December. During the last fortnight in March of that year Russell was at Cambridge and was three times entertained in hall. On 23 March he was a guest with Wastell and Lee, the two master masons, on 26 March with the chief plumber (John Burwell).⁵ The staging and centres for the fan vault and the laying of the lead roof must have been under discussion. Wastell's contract for the fan vault was made a few weeks later. Before his departure Russell received a reward.⁴ His salary, like those of the other master craftsmen, was paid up to 29 July 1515.

Russell's experience with scaffolding and centres for high vaults at Westminster Abbey and perhaps also in Henry VII's Chapel must have marked him out as the best man for the work at King's. Henry VII seems to have discontinued the practice of appointing by letters patent a master mason or master carpenter of the King's works; otherwise Russell would probably have succeeded THOMAS MAUNCY as King's Master Carpenter, for the posts which he filled show that he was regarded as the foremost carpenter during the early years of the 16th century. Wolsey, who was able to obtain the services of the royal craftsmen, employed him as his master carpenter at *York Place, Westminster*, and at *Hampton Court*, when he began his works in February 1515. An account for York Place covering the year 1515 records payments to Richard Russell in April for work on the masons' lodge. At Christmas he was paid £3 6s. 8d. as master carpenter 'for the ouersight & ordring of the Carpentre Work aswell in this place as at Hampton Court from the begynnyng of the works to Cristemasse'. In June his son JOHN, later to be King's Master Carpenter, began working at York Place as an apprentice for 4d. a day.⁶ For the first six months in Wolsey's employment Richard Russell was still drawing his salary for his post at Cambridge. He is likely to have been still in Wolsey's service at his death, which occurred on 14 May 1517.

Richard Russell's will, dated 14 February 1513/14, was proved on the day of his death.⁷ He appointed his wife Custance as his executrix and John Otwell of Westminster, 'gentilman', as overseer. He refers to his children, who were evidently under age, but the only one mentioned by name is William, to whom he bequeathed his lease of an inn called the

'Bell' in King Street, Westminster, subject to the life interest of his wife. Richard Russell had taken a lease of this inn from the Abbot of Westminster on 14 July 1512; it was re-granted to his son William Russell, who was a wax-chandler, in 1521, and in 1524 it was divided into four tenements, of which William retained the chief messuage while his younger brother John the carpenter had another.[8] That John Russell, junior, the King's Master Carpenter, was a son of Richard Russell is disclosed by the will of William Russell (died 1543), who made his brother John overseer.[9] The relationship of JOHN RUSSELL, senior, to Richard is uncertain, but he seems to have been of the same generation and is more likely to have been brother or cousin than father.

A.O.
[1] WAM, 23566–9, 23575–6, 23579–81, 23584–6, 23589–600 (J.H.H.); RNW, 74–8; [2] WMW, 157–8; [3] WAM, Novum Opus Roll, 23602 (J.H.H.); [4] KCM, Building Accs. 1509–15; [5] KCM, Kitchen Accs., vol. xi; [6] PRO, E.101-474–7 and E.36–236; [7] PPR, Commissary Court of Westminster, 124 Wyks; [8] LS, XIV, 3, 4; [9] PPR, Consistory Court of London (Bishop of Westminster), 31 Thirlby

RUSSELL, Richard (fl. 1434) Carver
In 1434 was described as 'kerver' and paid for 19 days work in making angels and fixing them to the ceiling of the Post Room (the vestibule of the Chapel) at Lambeth Palace.

GLP, 52–6

RUTIER, William le [Rutar, -er] (fl. 1225–†1266) Carpenter
Appears as a carpenter at Windsor Castle on 15 May 1225, when he was granted 20s.,[1] and was one of the King's Carpenters ordered to work at Westminster Palace on 14 March 1233. On 31 July 1234 he was one of four carpenters commissioned to take timber for the repair of the chamber and chapel of the King's palace at Havering-atte-Bower, Essex.[2] On 28 November 1236 he was granted fees of 5d. a day when working for the King, and 3d. a day when not working, and orders for the fee of 3d. a day to be paid to him were made until 25 April 1256.[3] On 7 January 1266/7 a pardon was granted to Richard le Harpur for the death of William le Ruter who may have been the carpenter.[4]

[1] HLC, II, 39; [2] CCR 1231–4, 200, 488; [3] CLR 1226–40, 247, 470; 1240–5, 7, 150, 167, 225, 247, 277, 301; 1245–51, 21, 115, 147, 194, 205, 232, 259, 285, 310, 353, 384; 1251–60, 42, 78, 124, 163, 179, 210, 248, 282; [4] CPR 1266–72, 23

RYDGE, Richard, I [Ruge] (fl. c. 1490–1499) Carver

Was probably the Richard Ruge who erected the roodloft of the Chapel of St. Mary in the market place at Lichfield for £16 13s. 4d. The work was done for Thomas Heywood while Dean of Lichfield, 1457–1492, perhaps shortly before his death.[1] Of Staffordshire, 'kerver'; with his son ROGER RYDGE contracted on 26 February 1498/9 to make a roodloft for the church of St. James, Bristol, to be like that in St. Stephen's, which had been made about 1487. They were to be paid £105, and another £5 if the work was liked. He was perhaps the Richard Ryge who in 1494–95 worked at Magdalen College, Oxford, and may have been identical with RICHARD RYDGE II.

AAJ, XXXII, 350
[1] J.C. Cox in A, LII (1890), 621

RYDGE, Richard, II (fl. 1532–1535) Carver
Carver of London; between 1532 and 1535 provided a large quantity of carved work for Hampton Court. It included 2 greyhounds and a leopard on the spiral staircases about the new hall at 18s. 4d. each; 32 lintels with the King's and Queen's badges for the hall screens at 2s. 2d. each; and a large number of pendants for the roof of the hall. These comprised 16 beneath the hammer beams at £3 3s. 4d. each, 28 'in the cross-mowntyn above the hammer beame' at 25s. each, 20 standing in the 'upper purloyns' also costing 25s. each, 4 hanging upon the 'femerell' or lantern at 40s. each, and a crowned rose for the crown of the vault of the lantern at 13s. 4d. He also carved 28 heads at 12d. each for the hall, and cut and carved 25 turned pendants for the King's Great Watching Chamber at 2s. each.[1] At The More near Rickmansworth in 1536 Rydge worked on the roof of the new chamber,[2] and in 1537 he was paid £20, as a joiner of London, for work on the roof of the king's privy chamber at Greenwich.[3]

Rydge worked in the 'antique' or Renaissance style, but was possibly, though not very probably, identical with RICHARD RYDGE I. Carved panelling at Weston Manor, Oxon., brought from Notley Abbey, and (on stylistic grounds) other woodwork in the Abbot's House at Thame, have been attributed to Rydge upon insufficient evidence, for the name 'Richard Ridge' carved to a large scale on the work at Weston is clearly that of the last abbot of Notley (1532–39).[4]

[1] SHB, 165, 218–19; LHC, I, 348, 352, 354, 356, 365; [2] HKW, IV, 167; [3] Ibid., IV, 104; [4] W. H. Godfrey in AJ, LXXXVI, 59–68

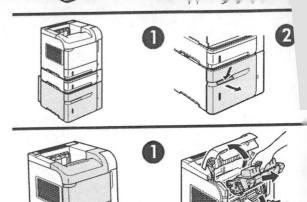

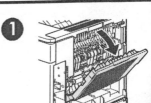

RYDGE, Roger (*fl.* 1499–1508) Carver

Of Kinver ('Kynware'), Staffs. Son of RICHARD RYDGE I and with him in 1499 undertook to make the roodloft for the church of *St. James, Bristol.*[1]

On 1 August 1505 contracted to make two parclose screens for the chancel there, with an (Easter) sepulchre on one side and three 'howsyngs' (sedilia) on the other, as well as a ceiling for the nave with 'Richmonds' and other knots. All the work was to be finished by Michaelmas 1508, for £43.[2]

[1] *AAJ*, XXXII, 350; [2] F. W. P. Hicks, 'The Mediaeval History of St. James, Bristol' — Bristol M.A. Thesis 1932 (*N.L.R.*)

RYHULL, Henry de [Rihul] (*fl.* 1301–1303) Carpenter

Master carpenter at *Flint Castle* in 1301, but subordinate in rank to Master RICHARD LENGINOUR, with whom in 1303 he made pontoons at *Lynn*, Norfolk, and went north with them to Berwick.

A.J. Taylor in *EHR* (Oct. 1950), 449n.[1]

Rypeley, John—see RIPLEY

St. Albans, John of—see FLANDERS

St. Albans, Richard—see ALBON

ST. ALBANS, Robert of [Albion, de Sancto Albano] (*fl.* 1325–1349) Carpenter and Engineer (*St. Albans, Herts.*)

Leading carpenter of the household (as Robert Albon) to Edward II when, in 1325, he was at the head of a group of eleven working on *St. Stephen's Chapel, Westminster.*[1] In 1333 he was master in charge of the working carpenters and also of the siege engines at *Berwick-upon-Tweed* after its capture by Edward III. He also directed work by carpenters at *Roxburgh Castle* in 1335–37, and was one of those making a survey of *Berwick Castle* in 1344. He remained in charge there until 1349.[2]

[1] *HKW*, I, 180; [2] *Ibid.*, II, 566–7, 819

St. Albans, Robert—see ROBERT the Mason I

ST. ANDREW, Edmund of [Edmund Canon] (*fl.* 1355–1360) Carver and Carpenter

Canon of the Augustinian Priory of Newstead, Notts.; his home was probably Andreskirk, near Breedon-on-the-Hill, Leics. In 1355 an order was sent to cause his tools and those of other carpenters about to work under him to be sent from Newstead to Westmins-

ter; in 1357–58 he was employed on the stalls of *St. Stephen's Chapel, Westminster,* as master carver (*Magister talliator*) at 1*s.* 6*d.* a day, and on 17 November 1360 he was given a commission to impress carpenters in which he is called 'Master of the work of the stalls'.

A. H. Thompson in *THS*, XXIII, 96; *PRO*, E.101–472–4

ST. GEORGE, James of [*Ingeniator*, le Mazun, 'St. Gregory'] (*fl.* 1261–†*c.* 1309) Mason (*St.-Georges-d'Espéranche, France*)

Master mason in charge of the building of Edward I's great chain of fortresses in North Wales.

The great period of castle building is clearly divided into three sections, each being the result of a separate conflict between the English forces and the Welsh. The first stage was due to the war of 1276–77, which ended at the Treaty of Aberconway on 9 November 1277. During the campaign Edward I had three castles built, for the purposes of securing his own lines of supply and of keeping the Welsh bottled up in the mountainous area of north-west Wales. These three castles, begun in the summer of 1277 and completed within the next five years, were Flint and Rhuddlan in the north, and Aberystwyth in the west. With Master RICHARD LENGINOUR, James of St. George was in charge of the works at *Flint* and *Rhuddlan*, with his headquarters at the latter place, and he doubtless supplied the designs from which *Aberystwyth* and *Builth Castles* were built at the same time, as on 9 April 1278 he is referred to as travelling to Wales to ordain the works of the castles there (*ad ordinandum opera castrorum ibidem*).

Master James is mentioned as one of the keepers of the works at Rhuddlan on 27 July 1279, and on 7 January following he was ordered to deliver the King's woods near Rhuddlan to be rooted up, probably so that they might not be used as cover for an attacking Welsh force. On 9 December 1280 he was granted a simple protection for seven years.

By 1282 the three castles were practically finished, but a new war broke out and the Welsh succeeded in capturing the castle of Aberystwyth. It was not until 1283 that Edward I was able to starve out the Welsh, and annex the principality to the English crown. The annexation led to the immediate founding of four great castles with English boroughs attached to them, to provide rallying points within the conquered land.

The town walls of *Conway, Carnarvon*, and *Denbigh* were all begun in 1282–83; at Conway the castle was started at the same time, while at Carnarvon the town walls were connected to an early Norman castle which commanded the harbour. At Denbigh the work was under the Earl of Lincoln, but the walls and towers follow the designs used by the royal craftsmen at the other new boroughs. Finally in 1284 the great castle of *Harlech* was begun, on a concentric plan similar to that of Caerphilly Castle in Glamorgan.

The architectural genius behind these great works must have been that of James of St. George, and we find him ordered on 11 September 1283, to leave Rhuddlan and go in person to take seisin of the town of 'Maynan' (Maenan) on the Conway. In 1284 he was keeper of the works at Conway, being responsible for an expenditure of almost £6,000 in the course of the year, and on 20 October he was named the King's Serjeant, and granted an allowance of 3s. a day for life, with a pension of 1s. 6d. a day to his wife Ambrosia if she should survive him. On the same day Richard Lenginour had the more modest, but still generous, grant of 1s. a day for life.

Conway was the headquarters of Master James for several years, and he appears in the works accounts as 'the mason'.¹ The two-storey building in the inner bailey of the Castle is said to have been built by task-work in 1285 for the sum of £320 by 'Master James of St. Gregory, mason', but the name Gregory is simply a misreading for George.

The plan of Carnarvon Castle is so like that of Conway that the setting-out must be attributed to Master James, but the actual building, started about 1285, was put under the charge of Master WALTER OF HEREFORD, who had been engaged on the Abbey of Vale Royal in Cheshire. The more highly finished work of Carnarvon reflects the outlook of this civilian mason, who was nevertheless able to render Carnarvon one of the strongest and most impressive of castles.

In the meantime James of St. George obtained higher promotion, being appointed Constable of Harlech Castle, then nearing completion, on 3 July 1290. His fees, inclusive of his existing stipend, amounted to 100 marks (£66 13s. 4d.) a year. He held this office for more than three years, until 28

December 1293, when he was ordered to deliver up the castle to Robert de Staundon, Justiciar of North Wales. In the next eighteen months he was probably in charge of routine work in and near Chester, for during the last Welsh revolt in 1294–95, on 4 March, he was ordered to take 'all the boats he can find in Wirhale (Wirral) and elsewhere on the coast to carry the pontoons to the King at Aberconeway', and the order was sent by a chancery clerk to Master James 'in Wirhale or elsewhere where he makes the King's pontoons'.

Probably as a reward for his services at this time he was granted on 21 August the manor of Moston in the cantred of Englefield, to hold during his life at a rent of 3s. yearly at the Exchequer at 'Kaernarvan'. The manor was stated to be worth £25 16s. 7d. a year, so that altogether Master James was in receipt of over £80 a year in official emoluments, equivalent to some £40,000 in modern values (1983), a very high remuneration indeed for a mediaeval architect.

This Welsh revolt, which succeeded in taking Carnarvon and was only put down with difficulty, was the cause of the last of the three periods of castle building before mentioned. An entirely new castle was begun at *Beaumaris* in Anglesey, new works were put in hand at Carnarvon, and soon afterwards the great gatehouse and 'second work', probably designed by Walter of Hereford, were built at Denbigh.

James of St. George was put in charge at Beaumaris as one of the two keepers of the works, the other being a clerk, Walter of Winchester. William de Felton, constable of the castle, and James of St. George were on 16 January 1297 ordered 'to cause the goods and chattels of certain clerics from Ireland, shipwrecked near Anglesey, to be appraised by the oath of lawful men and sold' and on 2 April 1299 St. George is again mentioned as keeper of the works in connection with a payment to him and Walter of Winchester of the sum of £44 11s. 5½d. The castle was completed about this time, with the exception of the outer curtain, added in and after 1316 under NICHOLAS DE DERNEFORD; the plan of this outer ward must have formed part of St. George's original design.

Soon after this Sir William de Felton, constable of Beaumaris, is found as governor of Linlithgow in Scotland, and on 29 April

1302 Master James of St. George was to take charge of the works there. While Beaumaris Castle was under construction much had happened on England's northern border: Edward I had conquered Scotland in 1296, only to find it in revolt under Wallace in the following year. Edward had decisively beaten Wallace at Falkirk, a few miles west of Linlithgow, in 1298, but found it necessary to consolidate his position by building fortifications in several places during the next six years, for it was not until 1304 that Scotland was pacified.

James of St. George was probably in charge of the most important of these works. On 30 June 1302 the Sheriff of Northumberland was ordered to send '30 of the best carpenters he can find without delay' to assist Master James of Saint George in the construction of *Linlithgow Peel*. An account of the same year mentions that 'Mestre James de Seint George le Machoun' had been ordered to build certain gates and towers of stone, but that the King had changed his mind and would have the gate and towers of timber and the peel itself to be built of untrimmed logs.[2]

In 1303 St George was probably engaged on the great gatehouse of *Kildrummy Castle*, closely akin to that of Harlech both in plan and scale, as has been pointed out by Dr. W. D. Simpson; no direct documentary evidence survives. That English craftsmen were still working in Scotland is known from the fact of Walter of Hereford's presence in Edinburgh Castle in 1304.

Master James was present at the siege of Stirling in 1304, and received an imprest in respect of wages on 4 September 1306; he must have died shortly before 20 May 1309, when the manor of Moston in Englefield, which had been held for life by 'Master James de Sancto Georgio, deceased', was granted to Adam de Stanay, the King's yeoman.

As a military designer of the late 13th century James of St. George stands without a rival, except for the unknown architect of Caerphilly Castle, which so closely resembles Harlech. No detailed documentation of Caerphilly has survived, but the fact that works were in progress there in 1267 and 1271 has generally been taken to mean that the whole of its concentric design had then been decided. This is not very probable, and modern authorities regard Caerphilly as having developed over a considerable period of years before its essential features were all in being.[3] The great similarity between Caerphilly and Harlech is such as to suggest a common designer, and if so, Caerphilly can only have been the work of James of St. George; for the present this may serve as a tentative hypothesis on which to base further research.

Among the castles of North Wales, the distinct origin of Carnarvon and Denbigh (the second work) from the remainder is obvious, and the presence of Walter of Hereford at the former castle amply explains this. The original layout of both Carnarvon and Denbigh, however, seems to have been settled by that section of the royal office of works of which St. George and Richard Lenginour were in charge. Master Richard is known to have worked at Carnarvon between 1283 and 1287, and he may well have been supervising the erection of the town walls there. That there was some division of responsibility between the administration of the works at Carnarvon Castle and those elsewhere is shown by the complaints which in 1295 arose out of the concentration of attention on Beaumaris, to the detriment of Carnarvon.[4]

The Edwardian castle-plan, with its emphasis on truly concentric lines of defence, which could be employed simultaneously against the besiegers, has always aroused special interest, and while its very ancient origin in the Near East is beyond question, the precise date of its introduction into England has been extremely doubtful. If it could be proved that the concentric defences of Caerphilly were actually designed in the reign of Henry III, the English concentric plan would have been introduced before the date of Edward I's crusade, but as stated above, this is unproven and even improbable. The earliest concentric works with a certain date are those added to the Tower of London by Edward after his return to England in 1274; this makes the old tradition of the introduction of concentric works by Edward directly from Palestine highly probable, and the tradition seems only to have been given up because of the (disputed) dates of Caerphilly, and the attribution of the outer ward of the Tower to Henry III, an attribution quite unsupported by documentary or structural evidence, except in so far as the Traitors' Gate and quay can be said to form a part of the outer ward's design.

The building of the outer land walls at the Tower, with the Byward and Middle Towers and Barbican (Lion Tower), was in progress between 1274 and 1284, the gate-towers were complete by 1279, but the building of the upper part of the *inner* curtain (from the lowest arrow-slits up) was not begun until 1281, and was not complete until 1284. These works were under the control of Master ROBERT OF BEVERLEY.

Several concurrent lines of evidence suggest that St. George was a foreigner, and various origins have been suggested. It has recently been established by Mr. A. J. Taylor that he was identical with a certain Master James the Mason (*lathomus*) who worked for the counts of Savoy from 1261 until 1275, at first with his father, Master John the Mason (*cementarius*). He was engaged on the construction of the new castle and tower of Yverdon, founded about 1260, and the remains of the castle show a close relationship to St. George's works in Wales. Further, his name can be derived from St.-Georges-d'Espéranche, a favourite residence of the counts of Savoy, and the place where Philip of Savoy did homage to Edward I on his return from crusade in June 1273. Master James of St. George was therefore among the last, but by no means the least, of the Savoyard servants of the Kings of England.

SJS; TJS
[1] *PRO*, E.101–485–28 (*L.F.S.*); [2] *Ibid.*, E.101–482–21 (*L.F.S.*); [3] SHC, 155; [4] CCP

'St. Gregory', James—see ST. GEORGE

Saintes, Isambert—see XAINTES

St. Omer, John of—see FLANDERS

SAKKAR, John (*fl.* 1511–   ) Carver
In 1511 was paid £1 for making a carved tabernacle for the high altar of *Allhallows Staining, London*.
MLR, II, 19

Salisbury, Robert of—see ROBERT the Mason VII

SALLETT, John (*fl.* 1512–1515) Carpenter
Was warden of the carpenters at the building of the *Savoy Hospital* in 1512–15, under HUMPHREY COKE.
HKW, III, 202

SALLYNGE, Richard, I [Salyng] (*fl.* 1350–1366) Mason (*Saling, Essex*)
Was working as a mason at *Windsor Castle* in 1350–51, taking wages of 5½d. a day,[1] and in 1356 appeared as one of the six freestone masons of London who were chosen to agree upon the articles of the trade. One of the others was *Walter de SALLYNGE*, probably a relative.[2] From 1353 to 1356 Richard de Salyng was acquiring property in London.[3] In 1357–59 Richard was fined 2s. for a breach of the Statute of Labourers, and was a surety for John de Lesnes, mason.[4] In 1363 he was sworn as a surveyor of the masons' craft in London with RICHARD AT CHERCHE,[5] and from 1362 to 1366 was working at *Hadleigh Castle*, Essex, as warden of the masons (*apparillor*),[6] being paid 1s. a day, Sundays included.

Walter de SALYNGE, mason of London, made his will on 11 December 1339; it was enrolled in the Court of Husting on 17 January 1339/40.[7] He desired to be buried at East Bedfont, Middx., and left rents to the Master and Brethren of St. Thomas of Acon, his wife Cristina and kinsman Roger de Salyngg being executors. Walter and Cristina had claimed a tenement in the City of London in 1319.[8]

(D.K.) (APD)
[1] *PRO*, E.101–492–27; [2] RML; [3] *LHR*, 81 (101), 87 (77–8), 94 (10, 61); [4] CLB, 'G', 116, 118; [5] *Ibid.*, 158; [6] *PRO*, E.101–464–6, 8; CPR 1361–4, 312; [7] SWL, I, 436; [8] *Ibid.*, 283

SALLYNGE, Richard, II [Salyng] (*fl.* 1392–1401) Mason
Mason of London; with Laura his wife, was engaged in the conveyance of property at Budge Row in the parish of St. John Walbrook, and elsewhere in the City of London, between 1392 and 1401.
LHR, 121(20), 122(7), 129(103)

Salopia, Richard de—see SHROPSHIRE

SALTER, John (*fl. c.* 1491–1502) Carpenter
Between 1491 and 1502 was employed as chief carpenter on new buildings at *King's Hall, Cambridge*. These probably included ranges of chambers on either side of the entrance gate-tower (now the Great Gate of Trinity College), which seems to have been begun at the same time, and perhaps also a range of chambers running east and west on the south side of the King's Hall property. There are no details in the accounts throwing light on the men employed during the first two years' work (1491–92), when much was done, and John Salter's name does not appear until the account of 1496–97, when he

was paid 10*s.* and also 8*s.* for timber 'beyond his first agreement'. Two years previously there is a memorandum of an agreement whereby a carpenter was due to receive £27 for roofing a new building, and there can be no reasonable doubt that the carpenter was Salter. Other payments to Salter occur in connection with the new buildings in the accounts for 1497–98 (when he made a door in the new wall fronting what is now Trinity Street), 1500–01, and 1501–02.[1]

In 1491 John Salter was occupying a house in the Market Ward as the tenant of WILLIAM SWAYN, probably the mason, who also worked at King's Hall at this time.[2]

A.O.
[1] *TCM, KHA,* XIX, 54, 147, 194, 386; XX, 42; [2] CBD, 61

SAM, John (*fl.* 1470–1471) Carpenter

Perhaps from Bideford, Devon; in 1470–71 worked at *Bodmin Church,* Cornwall, where he made the roofs of the north and south aisles; he was paid altogether £30 14*s.* 8*d.* The screenwork and fittings were not made until twenty years later, by MATHY MORE. The main roofs seem to have been constructed by WILLIAM CARPENTER.

CSM, VII, 17, 27, 29

SAMMESBURY, David (*fl.* 1483–) Carpenter

On 20 June 1483 David Sammesbury, carpenter, contracted to build a house by the Black Friars Gate in *Gloucester,* for £14.

SHB, 542; HMC, 12R, IX, 415–16

SAMPSON the Mason (*fl. c.* 1250–†*c.* 1274) Mason

Master mason (*cementarius*) of *Ely Cathedral Priory* in the 1250s, when he seems already to have been an old man, and until *c.* 1274, when he died.

Ely, 'Liber M' transcript, 284, 287, 304, 395, 405 (*S.J.A.E.*)

SAMPSON, John (*fl.* 1388–1396) Mason

Sampson twice appeared before the justices in Oxford in 1390 and 1391 for receiving wages above the rates fixed by the Statute of Labourers, but the cases were dismissed on the ground that he was 'a master mason in freestone and capable and skilled in that art and in carving, and because on account of the high discretion and knowledge of that art, the wages of such a mason cannot be assessed in the same way as the wages of masons of another grade and status'. Since Sampson was living in the North-east ward, and was

given commons at *New College* between 1388 and 1396, it seems clear that he was working there, but in what capacity is unknown, though it has been suggested that he was the chief carver of the figure sculptures there, and perhaps also at *Winchester College.*[1]

(R.D.) SMO, II, 3, 22; GOM, 65
[1] BWO, 163–4; CWC, 85, 116

SAY, John (*fl.* 1469–1485) Carver

Of Norwich; in 1469–70 John Saye, 'graver', was admitted to the freedom of Norwich.[1] At some date between 1475 and 1485 Richard Panyes of Norwich filed a Chancery petition against the Sheriff of Norwich concerning an action of debt brought by John Say of Norwich, 'graver', upon a forged obligation.[2]

Between 1482 and 1484 he contracted to make the stalls in the chapel of *King's Hall, Cambridge.* In the account of 1482–83 there is a payment of 13*s.* 4*d.* to John 'Carwer' in part of his stipend; there is also a note that 'John Carwer had his commons at dinner (*in prandio*) at his coming for one week'; in the following year John Say, described both as 'gravor' and 'carwer', undertook to complete all that remained to be done in the chapel for 40*s.* beyond all former sums received by him.[3] While the work was going on he rented a house in the market-place 'above the corner of the new building'. He seems to have carried out some work for the town, for the treasurers noted in their accounts that the tenement had been 'granted to him by the whole commonalty until he shall have received £3 13*s.* 4*d.*'. The treasurers' account for 1484–85 shows that JOHN KALE was occupying the house 'late in the tenure of John Say'.[4]

A.O.
[1] EFN, 9 Edw. IV; [2] *PRO, ECP,* 64–721; [3] *TCM, KHA,* xvi, 132, 245, 271; WCC, II, 451; [4] *CCM,* Box xviii–71, Nos. 1 and 2

SCARDEBOURG, Walter de (*fl.* 1305–1306) Mason (*Scarborough, Yorks.*)

Master mason in charge of works at *Lanercost,* Cumb. for Edward I in 1305–06, taking 8*d.* a day.

PRO, E.101–501–22 (*L.F.S.*)

Schafont—see CHAFYN

Schalston, William—see SHALDESTON

Scharp, John—see SHARP

Schokerwych—see SHOCKERWICK

SCHOVERWILLE, William de (*fl.* 1311–) Mason (?*Shorwell, Isle of Wight*)

Was a master mason of Salisbury, when in 1311 he visited the work in progress at *Exeter Cathedral*.

AEC, i, 57

Scoign, Christopher—see SCUNE

SCOT, Robert (*fl.* 1398–*c.* 1412) Carpenter

On 8 April 1398 petitioned the King, praying a grant of the office of master carpenter in the county of Chester, then held by WILLIAM DE NEWHALL, who he alleged was too old and feeble to fulfil the duties of the office. Scot, however, was granted only the reversion of the office, but on 13 February 1399/1400 was appointed by Henry, Prince of Wales to supersede Newhall, only to be relegated a few months later to his reversionary status. Newhall died on 12 January 1412, and Scot too was in all probability dead by 1 February 1411/12, when ROGER DREWRY had a grant of the office. Perhaps son of WILLIAM SCOT.

DKR, XXXI

SCOT, William (*fl.* 1353–1354) Carpenter

In 1353–54 the mill of *Northwich*, Cheshire, was repaired by William Scot, carpenter, taking 1*s.* 8*d.* a week for 4 weeks, and his son, who worked 3 weeks 2 days at 1*s.* 4*d.* a week. The son may have been ROBERT SCOT.

HCH, 37n., 7

Scremerstone, Walter de—see WILLIAM SPILBERY

Scroyl—see SEROYL

SCUNE, Christopher [Scoign, Scoyne] (*fl.* 1505–1521) Mason

Succeeded JOHN COLE as master mason at the building of *Louth* steeple, Lincs., in 1505, and continued to have charge of the work until it was nearing completion. He first appears at the end of 1505, when he was 'makyng molds to the broche' for 2 days. Between 19 May and 29 November he spent most of his time at Louth, but was absent on 6 occasions for a week or more. While at work he received 4*s.* a week, as well as expenses for travel and riding to the stone quarry. He was also paid a fee of 10*s.* for a half-year, and had a reward of 10*s.* in addition. Scune afterwards only visited Louth at rare intervals: in July 1506; August 1507; April 1508; April 1509 and again for a week in June; April 1510; February 1511 and for a month in August and September; for a fortnight in August 1512. Four or five letters were sent to him in 1514, on one occasion to Ripon. Finally in the spring of 1515 comes the entry: 'Paid Lourence Mason for ridying to his master in north countre for to spure him whether he would make ende of the broch and he said he wolde dell no more with itt, bot he shewed his councell, 6*s.* 8*d.*'; JOHN TEMPAS was then called from Boston to take charge.[1]

At some date after 1508 Scune succeeded THOMAS CHALMER as master of the masons at *Durham Cathedral* and is mentioned there on 3 October 1515 and 3 August 1519.[2]

We have seen that Scune was at Ripon in 1514, and in 1520–21 'Christopher Scoign' had a reward of 10*s.* 'for his good diligence in supervising the masons working on the fabric' of *Ripon Minster*.[3] There can be little doubt that he was the responsible master for the whole of the new work of the nave, begun in 1503 and structurally complete soon after 1520. It is almost certain that the same architect was responsible for the tower and tower arch at *Fountains Abbey*, built for Abbot Huby between 1494 and 1526.

It is at least possible that 'Scoign' was identical with Christopher Gascoigne of Cawton in Gilling, Yorks. N.R., who made his will on 4 February 1538. It was proved on 2 October by his widow Agnes the executrix, one of the witnesses being William 'Maison'. There is mention of a son George, who was to have the farm, and a daughter Alice. A bushel of wheat was left to Byland Abbey.[4]

(APD; HEA)

[1] A, x; DCL, 79–81, 89, 90, 100, 106, 110, 113, 119, 127–9, 137, 146, 161, 166, 169, 179; [2] SD; [3] SMR, III, 181; [4] *BIY, PCY*, vol. 11, *f.* 326

SEBYSTE, Henry (*fl.* 1466–1484) Joiner

Joiner working at *St. Margaret's, Westminster*, in 1466, when he mended the pulpit. In 1478–80 he made doors for the church, and between 1482 and 1484 provided desks for the vestry.

(*A.O.*) WMW, 140, 145, 150

SELLER, Robert (*fl.* 1381–) Mason

Mason (*latomus*) to *Sallay Abbey*, Yorks., in 1381.

(*L.F.S.*) WCV, 66

SELLERS, Thomas (*fl.* 1533–) Mason

With NICHOLAS CRAVEN contracted in 1533 to rebuild the north and south aisles of *Burnley Church*, Lancs., for £60; the work was to be completed within 4 years.

(APD); WHW

SELOT, William (*fl.* 1366–1378) Carpenter

Carpenter of Twickenham, Middlesex; was the principal carpenter at the royal manor of *Sheen*, Surrey, in 1366 and later, and in 1370 was granted 6*d.* a day for life to keep in repair the royal manors of Sheen, *Banstead* and *Isleworth*. The grant was confirmed by Richard II in 1378.

HKW, II, 964, 996

SEMARK, Henry [Semerk, –e] (*fl.* 1482–†1534) Mason

The surname Semark occurs at Barnack and Weldon during the 15th and 16th centuries, suggesting that Henry Semark came from that stone region of Northamptonshire, perhaps from a quarryman's family. There are occasional references to him between 1482 and 1487 among the accounts of Thomas Clyff, clerk of the works at *King's College Chapel, Cambridge*, and the earliest is an item dated 14 August 1482, when on the 'half day' of the Vigil of the Assumption a penny was paid 'for beer to the hands of H. Semark over the carriage of Weldon stone', large quantities of which were being brought to the college at the time for the works.[1] In December 1484 there is an obscure payment of 12*d.* 'to the hands of John Collys in money given to H. Semark and the wife of the same'.[2] As John Collys was a mason of Bury St. Edmunds, where in 1498 he possessed a house in School-hall Street 'in right of his wife', Semark may already have been living in Bury. Other references to Henry Semark occur in 1486, and on 18 April 1487 he was given a reward, but the amount is not stated. Although large-scale operations on the chapel ceased in 1485, there may have been some attempt to carry on with limited resources during the next two or three years, and these items read in such a context may indicate that Semark occasionally came over from Bury as SIMON CLERK'S deputy. In 1500 'Herry Semerke' was one of the executors of William Barker of Bury (will dated 23 September, proved 26 September 1500);[3] on 16 November 1506 he was one of nine feoffees concerned in a grant of a piece of land with a dovecote in Churchgovel Street, Bury, to Margaret Carew of Bury, widow, and four others by a deed executed at Bury to which JOHN WASTELL was one of the witnesses;[4] the

following year he acted as co-executor with Thomas Herrys of the will of John Hermer of Bury, weaver, of St. James's parish (dated 13 November 1506, proved 12 January 1506/7).[5]

From 1508 to 1515 Henry Semark was one of the wardens of the masons at King's College Chapel during the final phase of building when John Wastell was the master mason and ROBERT WORLICH the second warden, both of them his fellow townsmen. Semark's arrival seems to be indicated by the entry in the building account for the fortnight ending 25 June 1508: 'Herry Mason for coming 40 miles 12*d.*' Travelling expenses to Cambridge were paid at the rate of 6*d.* for every twenty miles. Semark and Worlich as wardens were paid 3*s.* 8*d.* a week;[6] in addition, they seem to have received 40*s.* a year paid in quarterly instalments by way of 'reward'.[7] In 1512 Semark was Wastell's partner in the contract for the high vault of the chapel, for which they were to receive £1,200. A subsidiary agreement dated 7 June 1512 sets out their respective duties and responsibilities. The whole profit was to go to Wastell, who undertook to bear 'almaner charges' during his life, paying Semark 20 marks (£13 6*s.* 8*d.*) for his continual attendance on the work; in the event of Wastell's death Semark was to share the profits and charges with Wastell's son Thomas.[8] Weldon stone was used for the vault and if, as has been suggested above, Semark came from Weldon or its vicinity, he would have been specially fitted to ensure that sound stone was supplied by the quarrymen. In Wastell's subsequent contracts Semark is not named and had no share.

The fact that Semark had been associated with King's College Chapel under Simon Clerk, his subsequent appearance at Bury and his position as senior warden of the masons under Wastell during the final stage of building at King's, taken together suggest that he was Wastell's most trusted assistant, and doubtless he worked under him on other buildings, at the abbey at Bury, for instance, and on the eastern chapels at Peterborough. He would also have been the most likely mason to be employed on buildings left unfinished at the time of Wastell's death, and even if JOHN BROND became master mason at the abbey of Bury, Semark may have carried to completion the works at *St. James's Church, Bury*, and at *Saffron Walden*. No doubt also he was responsible for unrecognised work in other churches on his own account, e.g. the fan-vault dated 1529 beneath the tower in *Fotheringhay Church*, Northants.

At some period Henry Semark was living in a house in Northgate Street, Bury, on the west side.[9] He was probably still there in 1524, when he was assessed for the subsidy under 'North Ward' and paid 40s. on goods valued at £8.[10] Thomas Bereve, a wealthy Bury clothmaker, who had much to do with the rebuilding of St. James's Church and was a generous benefactor to it, was living at the time when he made his will (17 July 1525) in a house in Burmans Lane, Bury, which together with its garden he had 'purchased of Herry Semark ffremason'.[11] Henry Semark must have been at least 75 years of age when he died in 1534. By a deed of gift dated 13 March 1533 he made over and confirmed to Christopher Bowyer of Bury, tanner, absolutely, all his goods and chattels, movable and immovable, in Bury or elsewhere, and on 2 June 1534, after Semark's death, this document was produced by Bowyer before the Sacrist in the presence of the four men who had witnessed it. The Sacrist sealed and confirmed it after Bowyer had declared that Semark had made the gift 'freely and spontaneously. . . moved by sure love and especially on account of some services and good deserts rendered to the aforesaid Henry by the said Christopher in times past'.[12]

Edward SEMARK, freemason, no doubt a relation and probably a son, was living in Bury in 1540, when he was renting a house in the High Street (an alternative name for Northgate Street). In the first minister's account of the possessions of the dissolved abbey it is noted that he owed 2s. rent on the above tenement for the year ending Michaelmas 1539.[13]

A.O.

[1] KCM, College Accs., vol. iv; [2] *Ibid*., vol. v, Day-book, 1484–88; [3] *BW*, vi, 97v.; [4] *BCM*, H.1–5–16; [5] *BW*, vi, 186; [6] *KCM*, Building Acc., 1508–09; [7] *Ibid*., Building Accs., 1509–15; [8] WCC, I, 479, 608–9; [9] *BM*, Harl. MS. 58, *f*. 7v.; [10] SGB, x, 355; [11] *BW*, viii, 137; [12] *Ibid*., xiv, 21; [13] SIA, XIII, 311

SENDELE, John (*fl*. 1489–1490) Carpenter

In 1489–90 John Sendele, carpenter, was paid £2 4s. 8d. for making the new roof for the chancel at *Stoke Holy Cross*, Norfolk.

NRO, DCN, Chamberlain no. 450 (*P.C.*)

SENS, William of (*fl*. 1174–†1180) Mason

Was called from Sens, France, to supervise the new work of *Canterbury Cathedral* in 1174, having won a 'competition' between various masters; he entirely remodelled the choir in three years, but in 1177 was crippled by a fall from a scaffold, after which the work was continued by WILLIAM ENGLISHMAN.[1] Sens returned to France and died there on 11 August 1180.[2]

The work of William of Sens at Canterbury marks an epoch in the development of English Gothic architecture, but the great stylistic innovations there were largely due to his successor, William Englishman. William of Sens was described as a most cunning craftsman in wood and stone (*in ligno et lapide artifex subtilissimus*) and made moulds which he delivered to the masons for cutting the stones.

In 1937 *The Zeal of thy House*, a play based on the facts of Sens' life, by Miss Dorothy Sayers, was produced in London.

(APD; BAA; BAF; WDC)
[1] GCC; [2] BAF

SERLE, William (*fl*. 1427–1452) Carpenter

In 1427 contracted to make a roodloft and a clerk's chamber for the church of *St. Mary-at-Hill, London*, and was further paid £12 for the stalls and £8 for a new porch. William Serle and his fellow carpenters and masons of the City of London made an award on 13 April 1440, and on 23 March 1452 William Serle, carpenter, and Alice his wife granted to John Dedham the unexpired portion of a 99 years lease of a plot outside Aldgate.

NIM, 96; LMR, 64, 69, 71; CPM 1437–57, 23, 120

SEROYL, Philip (*fl*. 1290–1292) Mason

Mason of Corfe, Dorset; in 1290–92 he was paid £7 3s. 4d. for lengthening the west chamber next the Queen's chamber in *Corfe Castle* by 8 feet, and for making a new gable and window for the same room, by contract. The work was under the direction of Master THOMAS DE MIDDLETON.

PRO, E.101–460–28 (*L.F.S.*)

SEWY, John [Shewey] (*fl*. 1474–1478) Mason

Mason of Reading; in 1474–78 built the hall and outbuildings at *Great Milton Manor*, Oxon. His contract to build the stonework was dated 11 December 1474. He was to receive 15 marks (£10) and a gown; to hew the stone at the quarry, but carriage to be at the lord's cost.

WAM, 9217, *ff*. 9v.–16, 24v. (*Dr. W. O. Hassall*.); SHB (2nd ed. 1967), 599

SHALDESTON, William [Schalston] (*fl.* 1363–1375) Carpenter (*Shalstone, Bucks.*)

Master carpenter at *Wallingford Castle,* Berks., from 1363 to 1375, taking 3*s.* per week.

PRO, E.101–490–2, 3 (*L.F.S.*)

SHARNHALE, William (*fl.* 1368–1384) Mason

In 1368 was first setter during works at *Rochester Castle,* taking 6*d.* a day; he was also paid £5 6*s.* 8*d.* for setting a vault by taskwork, within the inner gate of the castle. He and his mates were paid £110 for making a new tower, finishing another, and laying 6 perches of wall by task.[1] From 1381 to 1384 he was building *Cowling Castle,* Kent, by contract, for the sum of £456 which he was to be paid by Lord Cobham; it seems probable that the design was by HENRY YEVELEY. Sharnhale is last heard of in September 1384 when he received £3 18*s.* 0*d.* for lime, jointly with THOMAS CRUMP. Sharnhale was probably a small farmer in his early days, as in 1368 he sold three trusses of hay to the keepers of the works at Rochester Castle, for plastering a wall there.

A William Sharnale of East Malling, Kent, was on 11 May 1408 party to a recognizance to abide the award of the Archbishop of Canterbury on all actions or disputes between the Abbess of Malling and certain persons, of whom Sharnhale was one.[2] Very probably Sharnale had been doing work at *Malling Abbey,* over which dispute had arisen. He was quite possibly the same man as the contractor of 25 years before, or perhaps his son.

KJI; AC, II, 99, 123
[1] *PRO,* E.101–545–8 (*L.F.S.*); [2] CCR 1405–9, 393

SHARP, John [Scharp] (*fl. c.* 1387–1395) Mason

Was probably the master mason in charge of the hall built at *King's Hall, Cambridge,* on the south side of the mediaeval court between 1387 and 1390. In the account of 1389–90 there are schedules of payments made to JOHN MAIDSTONE (who was the chief carpenter), to the plumber, and to John Scharp, who was, presumably, the master mason. Sharp received payments totalling £7. By that time most of the masonry work is likely to have been finished. Further payments to Sharp were made in 1395 in connection with a chimney for the kitchen.[1]

In 1439 a portion of the wall of *Cambridge Castle* was repaired by Robert *SHARP,* mason, for £3 3*s.* 4*d.*[2]

A.O.
[1] *TCM, KHA,* iii, 46; iv, 105; [2] *PRO,* Sheriff's Acc. 12–21; PCA, 20

SHERBORNE, Robert (*fl.* 1473–1493) ? Mason

In 1473 undertook to do works in the chancel of *High Wycombe Church,* Bucks., but twenty years later had not done them, so that the chancel was ready to collapse.

(*R.D.*) VCH, *Bucks.,* III, 129n. 24

SHEREFF, John (*fl.* 1528–1535) Mason

Was master mason when the great gate-tower of *King's Hall, Cambridge,* now the Great Gate of Trinity College, was completed between 1528 and 1535. The gate-tower seems to have been begun as far back as 1490 under JOHN WASTELL and WILLIAM SWAYN. Although a little work on it was done in 1519 and the gates for it were made in 1524, it lacked the two upper stages, which were built by John Shereff. In 1528 he was paid an earnest of 10*s.* and a first instalment of £10 at the sealing of the indentures for the work; during the next seven years he received further sums probably totalling about £30; the amount of his second payment is missing owing to the page in the account being torn. He probably came from London, where one of the instalments is stated to have been paid.

A.O. WCC, II, 453, 454

SHERES, Thomas (*fl.* 1532–1545) Carpenter

Undertook to build offices by the kitchen of the royal lodges in the *Tower of London* in 1532. In 1545 he was Master of the Carpenters' Company.

HKW, III, 267n.

SHERRINGHAM, J[ohn] (*fl.* 1481–   ) Carpenter (*Sheringham, Norf.*)

In 1481 undertook to take down the old roof of *St. Margaret's Church, Lynn,* Norfolk, and to cover the church during alterations for 8 marks (£5 6*s.* 8*d.*) and the old spars.

BLC, 92 (*L.F.S.*)

Shewey, John — see SEWY

SHOCKERWICK, William of [Schokerwych] (*fl.* 1316–   ) Mason

Possibly of Shockerwick, Somerset, in the Bath stone-quarrying district; Master *cementarius* of *Worcester Cathedral* in 1316, when in exchange for £60 in silver he was granted a corrody for life. This was to consist of a monk's loaf and a white loaf 'of the old weight' every day for life, with two gallons of the best ale, a mess of meat every flesh day and two dishes of pottage such as the monks in the infirmary receive; supper equal to that of two monks; and on fish days what is served to a monk in the refectory. He was also to have a chamber in the tailor's shop, a stable for his horse, and whatever is needed for his servants.[1] Shockerwick probably designed the north arcade of the nave (1317–24).

W. de Shokerwyk was a mason working on the King's manor of *Clarendon* in 1316–17[2].

(TCC)
[1] WWL, 153; [2] *PRO*, E.101-459-27 (*L.F.S.*)

Showt, John—see SKOWTE

SHROPSHIRE, Richard [de Salopia] (*fl.* 1359–1370) Carpenter
Carpenter of London; on 25 October 1359 the Black Prince ordered that he should be paid £52 for works done by covenant at the Prince's manor of *Kennington*, and was carrying out other works there for several years, for which he was to receive payment in 1362.[1] Master Richard was one of the sworn carpenters of London in 1363, 1367, 1369, and 1370, and in the last year, with RICHARD AT CHERCHE and THOMAS BARNET, sworn masons, and THOMAS FANT, carpenter, petitioned that they should be made free from taxes, as their predecessors in office had been for a century. The petition was granted, for so long as they should remain in office.[2]
[1] BPR, IV, 327, 476; [2] CLB, 'G', 158, 223, 257, 279

'Sill', Robert—see FILL

SIMNEL, Thomas (*fl.* 1475–1479) Joiner
Joiner of *Oxford*, living in 1475 in a house belonging to Oseney Abbey in St. Thomas's parish. He was perhaps partner to William Wootton, who in 1488–89 made the organ for *Merton College*, for he is elsewhere described as organ-builder, and in 1479 lived next door but one to Wootton. In 1478–79 Simnel was working for *Lincoln College* on a new oratory for the rector. His son Lambert (*fl.* 1477–1534) was the notorious pretender to the throne, crowned as King Edward VI in Dublin in 1487.
GOC; (RAM, xxxiii)

Simon the Carpenter—see NORTHAMPTON

Simon de Well'—see WELLS

SIMON the Mason I [Symon] (*fl.* 1301–†1322) Mason
It seems possible that the Simon de Papinham who was warden of the masons at *Lincoln Minster* under Master SIMON DE TRESK between 1262 and 1276 was a son of SIMON DE PABENHAM I and identical with the subject of this article. Paid 2 marks (£1 6s. 8d.) to the Lay Subsidy of 1301 in the city of York; this large amount compares with 16d. and 11d. paid by two other masons.[1] He was evidently master mason of *York Minster* and was referred to as 'Magister Symon' when he took up the freedom of York in 1315.[2] Master Simon died in 1322, when by his will made on 24 June he desired to be buried in the nave of the Minster, left to his wife Alice one acre of land in 'Boutham', 'at the rent of a rose in the season of roses', and arranged for the sale of his marble stones for tombs.[3] The fact that this will was proved in the court of the Dean and Chapter shows that he lived in the Minster Precincts. He was probably the responsible master for the building of the nave from the start in 1291.
(APD)
[1] YRS, XXI (1897), 119; [2] YCF; [3] RFY, 207n

SIMON the Mason II (*fl.* 1386–87) Mason
In a Hostilar's Roll of *St. Saviour's Hospital, Bury St. Edmunds* of 1386–87 there is an item among payments for ornaments for the chapel of St. Thomas of 5s. paid to Simon, the abbey mason, for a base bought from him for the image of St. Thomas to stand 'ad dextrum cornu altaris'.[1] The chapel of St. Thomas stood near the hospital outside the North Gate.
A.O.
[1] HMC, *Var. Coll.*, 14R. VIII, 129

SIMPSON, Richard [Symson] (*fl.* 1500) Mason
A London mason in 1500, when he supplied a chimneypiece ('a parell of a chymney of frestone') for the new parlour in the *Hall* of the *Carpenters' Company*.
JPC, 221

SIMPSON, Thomas [Sympson] (*fl.* 1526–1527) Mason
Was master mason at *Ramsey Abbey*, Hunts., in 1526–27 when he received 20s. in two payments 'for his stipend' from the steward in the absence of the abbot, John Wardeboys.
A.O. PRO, Treasury of Receipt Misc. Bk. E.36-107

SIMSON, George [Symson] (*fl.* 1538–†1556) Mason

A member of the Court of Assistants of the London Company of Freemasons in 1538,[1] was working at *Whitehall Palace* at 3s. 4d. a week in 1541,[2] and died in 1556, when he was said to be of the parish of St. Peter West-cheap, London, and Westerham, Kent.[3]

[1] MHN, IV, 19–20; [2] *Bodl.*, MS. Eng. hist. b. 192; [3] *PCC*, 16 Ketchyn

SKIDMORE, Thomas (*fl.* 1470–1473) Carpenter

Carpenter of *Bristol*; acted as a viewer of the city in 1470 and in 1473.

(*A.O.*; *G.M.D.B.*) BLR, II, 132; Sotheby's Catalogue, 13/4/1981, Lot 15.

SKILLYNGTON, Robert [Skelyngton] (*fl.* 1391–1400) Mason

Was granted a writ of aid on 8 July 1391, to impress within the county of Warwick, masons, carpenters, and labourers to the number of twenty in all, for the new works at *Kenilworth Castle*, for John of Gaunt, Duke of Lancaster.[1] Skillyngton was evidently the mason who had contracted for these works, as in 1392 he was paid £43, in part payment of his 'covenant in gross', £300 having already been paid in 1391; a further £202 1s. 7½d. was paid in 1393.[2]

These works consisted of a great hall, 90 feet by 45 feet, with a tower at each end, and a series of state apartments. The kitchens were also rebuilt and other alterations made.

The details and mouldings of Skillyngton's work at Kenilworth closely resemble those of the choir of *St. Mary's, Warwick* (1381–96), and of the tower of *St. Michael's, Coventry* (1373–94).

In 1397 and in 1400 Skillyngton was master mason of the *College of St. Mary in the Newark* at *Leicester*;[3] and in the latter year he was also master mason at *Tutbury Castle* when a new tower was built and part of the curtain wall rebuilt. A commission for taking masons and workmen for the works was issued in January 1400 to the constable, the receiver, and Robert of Skillington.[4]

(APD; HSK)
[1] CPR 1388–92, 449; [2] *PRO*, D.L.29–728–11979; 43–15–7 (*R.S.*); [3] CPR 1399–1401, 230, 247; HKW, I, 267n.; [4] HKW, II, 847

SKOWTE, John [Showt] (*fl.* 1525–1530) Carver

Carver working in *Oxford*, where he was doing minor works for *Magdalen College* from

1525, taking 8d. per day. In 1527 he made new stalls for St. John's Chapel at a cost of £7 10s. 8d., and also worked on a new organ and other things. He was presumably the John Showt who in 1529–30 made a new organ for Magdalen, and who was from London and possibly a German. It seems not unlikely that he was identical with JOHN DE COLONIA.

GOC

SKYNNER, John (*fl.* 1455) Mason

Mason of Gloucester who occupied a house near the North Gate there, rented from the Abbot, in 1455.

CSG, 104a, 185a

SLEGH, Robert (*fl.* 1334–) Mason

Master in charge of works at *Somerton Castle*, Lincs., in 1334 when he was paid 2s. 6d. a week; the working masons received 2s.

PRO, E.101–484–11 (*L.F.S.*)

SMALDANE, William (*fl.* 1423–1427) Carpenter

Carpenter in charge of the works during the building of the south-west tower of *Canterbury Cathedral*, under the general direction of THOMAS MAPILTON.[1] He and his fellows appear among the *artifices* in the livery list of the Prior in 1423.[2]

[1] C. E. Woodruff in AC, XLV, 46; [2] *Bodl.* Tanner MS. 165 (*A.O.*)

SMYTH, Henry (*fl.* 1506–†1517) Mason

Is shown by his will to have been working at the *Hospital of the Savoy* at the time of his death in November 1517. He was leading setter, taking 3s. 8d. a week. He has to be distinguished from his namesake and contemporary, an administrative official, who in 1500 became comptroller of the King's works at Windsor Castle, in 1509 was granted the office of clerk and surveyor of the King's works throughout England and died in 1528 or 1529.

On 1 May 1506 Henry VII, at the end of his St. George's-tide visit to Cambridge, gave £100 towards the building of *King's College Chapel*. This gift marked the beginning of his awakened interest in his uncle's great project and led to the resumption of works on a large scale in the spring of 1508 and the completion of the whole fabric in the summer of 1515. The entry in the King's Book of Payments records the delivery to the Provost of King's of £100 'vpon an Indenture betwext Henry Smyth & the said Province [*sic*] towards the bildings of the Church of the said College'.[1]

275

Exactly a year later what seems to have been an architects' conference took place at the college, for the Mundum Book for 1506–07 contains an item of 16d. laid out in wine on 1 May 'upon Henry Smith, Vertue and Lee',[2] the two last-named doubtless being WILLIAM VERTUE and JOHN LEE.* On 4 June following a fee of 10s. was paid to Henry Smyth 'by order of the Provost'. His name has not been found again in the years that follow among the bursars' accounts or the building accounts of 1508 to 1515, but the reference to the indenture may indicate that Henry Smyth undertook a limited amount of building between May 1506 and May 1507. Early in 1508 the building of the Savoy Hospital was begun,[3] and perhaps one should connect Smyth's departure from Cambridge with his work at the Savoy. In the upshot JOHN WASTELL became master mason at King's College Chapel with John Lee as second master mason with him, and it is noteworthy that the latter is named chief mason in a small payment made to him by the college on 8 July 1507,[2] just after the last payment to Smyth.

In his will, dated 5 November and proved 19 November 1517, Smyth desired to be buried in the church or churchyard of St. Margaret, Westminster.[4] He mentions his mother and two brothers, John and William, all living; his wife had predeceased him. He left to Robert Cutler 6s. 8d., his hammer and 'my Compasse in the Savey'. To William Wurth he left his new former, his best axe, four of his best square irons, and four of his best round irons; to Robert Magsden 'all my Bokis of purtiturys'. He directed that all his other tools both in his house and in the Savoy should be divided 'among the masons ther' and that 'the trowell in the Savay be delyuered to the master of the werks for it doyth Long to that place'. He named as his executors Thomas Manser (or Mauser) and his wife Alice and Master Elmer (see AYLMER, JOHN), freemason of the City of London, to the last of whom he bequeathed half a dozen silver spoons which he had in his keeping. The residue of his goods was to be divided equally between Manser (or Mauser) and his wife's daughter, Joan Carter.

According to Dallaway, Henry Smyth was master mason at *Richmond Palace* in 1505.[5] His authority was probably the King's Book of Payments,[6] which during the years 1505 to 1509 shows large sums being paid out to Henry Smyth 'upon his boke signed' in respect of works at Richmond Palace and at the church of the *Friars Observant at Richmond*. It seems more likely that this Henry Smyth was the comptroller of Windsor Castle and the same may be surmised of two payments to him of £60 and £100 in November 1503 and January 1504 towards the 'garnishing' of the manor of *Greenwich*.[7]

A.O. (DAE)
[1] *PRO*, E.36–214, p. 57; [2] *KCM*, Mundum Book, 1506–07; [3] *PRO*, E.36–214, p. 250; [4] Westminster Commissary Court, Wyks *f*. 127; [5] Dallaway, *On Gothic Architecture*, p. 423; [6] *BM*, Add. MS. 7099 and *PRO*, E.36–214; [7] *BM*, Add. MS. 7099, *ff*. 84, 86

Henry SMYTH (*fl.* 1500–1528), clerk and surveyor of the King's works, on 13 April 1500 was granted the office of comptroller and clerk of the works in Windsor Castle during pleasure with 6d. a day from 1 November 1499;[1] on 3 July 1502 was granted for life the office of keeper of the leads at Windsor Castle with 2d. a day from the revenues of the castle;[2] on 11 June 1509 was granted the office of clerk and surveyor of the King's works in England by a patent which he surrendered on 14 May 1528, when this office was regranted to him and Thomas Flower in survivorship.[3] He had died before 13 August 1529, when a pardon was granted to Jacobina Smyth, as his administratrix.[4]

A.O.
[1] CPR, 1494–1509, 200; [2] *Ibid.*, 281, 285; [3] LPH, IV, pt. ii, No. 4313 (p. 1897); [4] LPH, IV, pt. iii, No. 5906 (p. 2640)
* [Note: It now seems certain that it was Henry Smyth the clerk and surveyor, not the mason, who went to King's College with Vertue and Lee. (HKW, III, 188)]

SMYTH, John [Symyth] (*fl.* 1423–1425) Carpenter
Jehan Smyth or Symyth appears in the accounts of the Receiver-General of Normandy for 1423–25 as in receipt of 1,200 sols tournois yearly as carpenter of the Regent of France (John, Duke of Bedford). As the sol tournois then stood at 160 to the £ sterling, this was equivalent to £7 10s. 0d. a year in contemporary English money.
BNP, MS. fr. 4485, p. 165; 4491, *f*. 8

SMYTH, John OI (*fl.* 1391–1392) Mason
Of 'Est Malling, mason', was bound with WILLIAM LONDONEYS in 1391–92 in connection with work at Rye.
HMC, 5 R, 512

SMYTH, John, I (*fl.* 1429–†c. 1460) Mason
Was one of the lodge masons at *Christ*

Church Cathedral Priory, Canterbury, in 1429, and by 1433 had risen to the position of first mason, which he still occupied in 1439. He was made warden of the masons at *Eton College* when the works began early in 1441, taking £10 a year; he was subordinate to ROBERT WESTERLEY, the King's Master Mason.[1]

In February 1448 Smyth was named as the master mason at Eton in the estimate for the enlarged design of the chapel.[2] In 1445–46 John Smyth '*capitalis lathamus*' was receiving a salary of £13 6s. 8d. a year, also vesture of cloth costing 3s. a yard; expenses of the chief mason being at London to have the advice of the Marquess of Suffolk about the hall were also paid.[3]

In 1448–50 John Smyth (*magister lathomorum; principalis lathomus*), received salary of £13 6s. 8d. and livery 'de mustard vylours' costing 3s. 4d. a yard. He was living in a house in Eton belonging to Richard Spragott for which the college paid 5s. a quarter.[4] On 14 December 1458, John Smyth received for his wages for two terms 20s.[5]

In 1453 Smyth became master mason of *Westminster Abbey* at the death of JOHN THIRSK, and retained this post until 1460, when he was succeeded by JOHN READING.[6] He had the same yearly fee of £5 as Thirsk but his robe in the first year cost only 9s. 3d. In addition he was paid 3s. 4d. a week when at work at the Abbey for 39 weeks in 1455–56, for 26 weeks in the following year, and for full time thereafter. A rent of £2 a year was paid to the Sacrist for his house in Westminster, which he evidently occupied rent free.[7]

Smyth gave up his position at Eton on accepting that at Westminster Abbey. The account of the clerk of the works at Eton for 1452–53 includes a payment of £20 to Smyth as 'late master mason', while the post was held by SIMON CLERK in 1453–54.

Thomas SMYTH (*fl.* 1448–1460) may have been John's son. He appears in the Eton accounts first as an apprentice and later as a mason earning the full wage.[8]

(APD)
[1] KJE, 91; [2] WCC, I, 399; [3] ECA, Vady's Acc. 1445–46 (*G.P.J.*); [4] ECA, Keys' Compotus 1448–50 (*G.P.J.*); [5] ECA, Medehill's Compotus 1458–60 (*G.P.J.*); [6] RNW; [7] WAM, 23519–24; [8] KJE, 22, 23

SMYTH, John II (*fl. c.* 1530) Mason
Freemason of Derby, who before 1534 agreed with (RICHARD) PARKER to make a tomb for William, 4th Lord Mountjoy, in the church of *Barton (Blount)*, Derbyshire.
NLH, 341, 347 (*N.L.R.*)

SMYTH, John, III (*fl.* 1531–1541) Mason
John Smyth, mason, perhaps brother of HENRY SMYTH, was at *Whitehall Palace* in 1531 'adjoined with the master mason (JOHN MOLTON) in devysing and drawing'.[1] He was still working at the Palace in 1541, taking 3s. 4d. a week.[2]
[1] PRO, E.36–252, f. 335; [2] Bodl., MS. Eng. hist. b. 192

SMYTH, Richard (*fl.* 1437–   ) Mason
Mason (*latamus*) employed by the treasurer of *Christ Church Priory, Canterbury*, to carry out the stonework for 'le Sunne' in the summer of 1437; the timberwork was made by JOHN GONELD, and the sign carved by JOHN MASSINGHAM III.
Bodl., MS. Top. Kent, c.3, ff. 147v.–149

SMYTH, William (*fl. c.* 1465–†1490) Mason
At *St. John's Church, Glastonbury*, window arches and other works were done by William Smyth, T. Ryel and others for £16 10s. 8d. in an uncertain year probably *c.* 1465.[1] Smyth was master mason to *Wells Cathedral* before 1480, and it is likely that he was the man of that name who took up the freedom of Wells in 1475, whose trade is not specified.[2] At the cathedral in 1480–81 he received an annual fee of £1 6s. 8d. and a house as master mason (*lathamus*).[3] Smyth had died before 23 October 1490, when he was succeeded by WILLIAM ATWOOD.[4]

The remains of the Cloister Lady Chapel at Wells, built for Bishop Stillington in 1477–88, show a markedly individual style which appears also in the crossing vault inserted beneath the lantern of the cathedral's central tower. In both cases fan vaults are employed, as is the case also, on a miniature scale, in Sugar's chantry chapel in the nave, built very shortly after the death of Dr. Hugh Sugar in the spring of 1489. These works are sufficient to establish the characteristics of a personal style which can be recognized in several other buildings of the region. Thus the fan vaults closely resemble those of the nave of *Sherborne Abbey*, built *c.* 1486–93, and that of the crossing of *Milton Abbey*, Dorset, designed soon after 1481. The remains of blind tracery of the west wall of the Cloister Lady Chapel are very closely akin to the design of the Sherborne nave clerestory windows.

At the *Deanery* at Wells extensive work was

carried out by Dean Gunthorpe from *c.* 1473 and probably completed before the first visit of King Henry VII to Wells in 1491. The great oriel in Gunthorpe's new hall has a fan-vault with many points of resemblance to that over the crossing of the cathedral, and this again is clear evidence that Smyth was the architect. Further afield, the nave and west front of *Crewkerne Church*, Som., built *c.* 1475–90, form an outstanding work bearing all the marks of Smyth's style, in tracery, panelling and details.

HWP, 40; HPS, 202–4; *J.H.H.* in CWE, 94–6; LFV
[1] SDN, IV, 284; [2] SRS, XLVI, 156; [3] *WLC*, Fabric roll 1480–81 (*L.S.C.*); CWF, 19; [4] HMC, Wells, II, 120

SNAPE, Robert (*fl.* 1386–1399) Mason

Mason of Norwich, admitted to the freedom in 1386–87.[1] In 1398–99 he was paid 9*s.* for 12 shotholes at 9*d.* each, made for the dungeon, i.e. the *Cow Tower* of brick in the city wall of *Norwich* which was rebuilt at this time and still exists.[2]

(A.O.)
[1] EFN; [2] HTN, II, 52

SNELLESTON, Henry de (*fl.* 1343–1347) Mason (? *Snelson, Ches.*)

Was at work for the Black Prince as early as 1343, apparently in succession to ROBERT DE HELPESTON, and was formally appointed master mason to the Black Prince in Chester and North Wales on 29 September 1346, taking 1*s.* a day. In 1347 he designed the *Dee Bridge*, at *Chester*, much of which still survives, and in the same year was to give his 'view and advice' on the repairs of the Prince's Hall and other parts of *Conway Castle*. He had a new grant of his office on 20 July 1347, but was probably dead by 1349, when HUGH HUNTINGDON is mentioned as the prince's chief mason.

Snelleston's work from the stylistic evidence of date included the traceried windows inserted in the buildings within the inner ward of Conway Castle.

BPR, I, 46, 83, 95

SNITTERFIELD, Simon of (*fl.* 1371–1373) Mason (*Snitterfield, Warks.*)

Was master mason of *Calais* in 1371–73, and perhaps somewhat earlier and later.

HKW, II, 1054

SOMERE, Richard (*fl.* 1493–1496) Carpenter

Carpenter of *Bristol*; in 1493 and 1496 acted as a viewer of the city.

(A.O.) BLR, II, 133–4

SOMMER, John (*fl.* 1543–) Mason

Mason (*latomus*) of Portsmouth; on 10 August 1543 he visited *Chichester Cathedral* at the dean's request to survey the tower and steeple (*ad supervidendum Turrim et ly Stiple*). He was paid 3*s.* 4*d.* for his expenses and trouble, with the pay of his servant, for two days.

M.E.C. Walcott in GM (1864), pt. i, 233–6

'SPALDING, Master of' (*fl. c.* 1438–1439) Mason

At a visitation of the Benedictine Priory of *Spalding*, Lincs., held on 1 October 1439, it was reported that a new master of works, Brother John Bostone the elder, had driven away the masons employed, while the master mason (*magister lathomus*) would not stay unless he were guaranteed a life pension from the monastery, although he was offered a fee of 12 marks (£8) yearly.

TVR, II, 336

SPARK, John (*fl.* 1525–†1531) Mason

Built the bay-windows and probably the gatehouse of *Hengrave Hall*, Suffolk, for Sir Thomas Kytson.[1] These works in freestone, carried out between 1525 and 1538, had been expressly excluded from the general masonry and brickwork contract, which had been let to JOHN EASTAWE. According to Gage, the historian of Hengrave, Spark was an artisan from London, but there was a freemason of this name living at Bury St. Edmunds at the time, and from Bury came the glazier and some of the other craftsmen mentioned in the accounts.

John Sparke of Bury, 'ffremason ye Elder', made his will in 1530 (day and month omitted); it was proved 4 April 1531.[2] To Agnes, widow of William Wright alias Cowper, 'whom I intend by ye grace of god to take to my wyff', he left 40*s.* Two daughters by his deceased wife are mentioned. Two namesakes, father and son, who were weavers, were living in Bury at the same time, and the elder witnessed the freemason's will. It is, therefore, difficult to decide which of the two John Sparks entered in the Subsidy Returns of 1523–24 under Bury St. Edmunds was the mason. One in Risbygate Ward was assessed at £26 13*s.* 4*d.* and paid £1 6*s.* 8*d.*, another in West Ward was assessed at £60 and paid £3.[3] For 'the Anticipation' levied on every man worth £40 the assessment of the latter was £80, but this was reduced to 100 marks. In this return the John Spark of West Ward is described as 'yoman'. The freemason refers in his will to his tenement in Westgate Street, but there is nothing to suggest such affluence as the returns for the subsidy imply.

A.O.   (APD)

[1] GHH, 47, 54; [2] *BW*, XIV, 5; [3] SGB, X, 354, 357, 424

SPENCER, Henry [Spenser] (*fl.* 1372–†*c.* 1381) Mason

Was master mason and surveyor of the works at *Kenilworth Castle* for John of Gaunt, Duke of Lancaster, in 1372, when 400 marks were spent on new building. He was apparently dead by 4 February 1381/2, when WILLIAM HALES was appointed surveyor in his stead.

JGR 1372–6, 1156; 1379–83, 1110

SPENCER, William (*fl.* 1520–   ) Mason

Freemason of Lincoln; on 23 April 1520 he and his fellows contracted to rebuild the *Lincoln Guildhall*.

(*A.O.*) HMC, *Var. Coll.*, 14 R. VIII, 27; AQC, XLVIII pt. i, 154

SPENDLOVE, Thomas [Spendloff] (*fl.* 1508–1521) Carpenter

Carpenter and 'graver' of Norwich, adjudicated as senior master of the carpenters' craft of the city on 8 May 1508.[1] In 1520/1 Richard, son of Thomas Spendloff, graver, was admitted to the freedom of the city.[2]

[1] HTN, II, 2930; [2] EFN

Spenser—see SPENCER

Spielsby, Robert—see SPILLESBY

SPILBERY, William (*fl.* 1408) Mason

In 1408 when the west gate of *Norham Castle* was rebuilt from the ground in 298 days, the masons were William de Priors, William Spilbery, Robert Bank and Walter de Scremerstone, who received 3*s.* 4*d.* a week.

JNC, 177, 97 (*A.O.*)

SPILLESBURY, John (*fl.* 1370–1397) Mason

Perhaps of Spelsbury, Oxon.; mason employed at the episcopal manor of *Highclere*, Hants., where Bishop William of Wykeham was carrying out considerable works of repair and rebuilding, for which the architect was probably WILLIAM WYNFORD. Spillesbury, however, was evidently a man of good standing, as in 1370 he was paid 6*d.* a day for 142 days spent in cutting freestone for the two windows of the lord's chamber in the manor, and 'coynes' for the angles of the wall. He had a reward or retaining fee of £1 in several

years, including 1376, 1382, 1385, and 1386, when he was working on the 'new building', and also in the next year, when in addition to his fee he was paid £5 14*s.* 0*d.*, representing some eight months' work. In 1388 he worked on the construction of a new wall, and received payments for various works and new buildings in 1392, 1394, and 1397.[1]

He was perhaps identical with the John Spellesbur', mason, who was working in 1395–96 on the cloisters of *Worcester Cathedral Priory.*[2]

(*J.H.B.*)

[1] *PRO*, Eccl. 2–159380, '84, '89, '92–95, '98, 159403, '04; [2] *WCO*, C.77

SPILLESBY, Robert [Spielsby, Spyllesby] (*fl.* 1445–†1473) Mason (*Spilsby, Lincs.*)

A working mason at *Eton College* from July 1445 to February 1446; on 20 December 1466 was appointed master mason of *York Minster* in succession to JOHN PORTER, taking up the freedom of York in the same year.[1] Spillesby died in the early spring of 1473, being buried in the nave, near the west door. His grave slab, now removed, bore the inscription:

'Hic jacet Magister Robertus Spielsby, quondam Magister Cementariorum hujus Ecclesiae qui obiit Anno Dom. 1472 Cujus Animae, etc.'[2] (Here lies Master Robert Spielsby once master of the masons of this church, who died A.D. 1472 [/73], on whose soul, etc.)

Spillesby was paid £7 15*s.* 10*d.* for 46 weeks' work in 1470, approximately 3*s.* 4*d.* a week, and he also received £1 17*s.* 4*d.* for riding with his servant for 'les merblers' (marblers) for 28 days, while in June he spent 4*s.* in riding for masons to different places. The marblers were brought to York to carve the new base for the shrine of St. William, now in fragments in the Yorkshire Museum. He also had a yearly fee of £1 6*s.* 8*d.* This was for the building of the north-west tower of the Minster, begun in 1470. He was succeeded at the Minster by WILLIAM HYNDELEY.

(APD); BHY, I, 248–9, 250, 252; RFY, 72n., 73, 74, 77; *J.H.H.* in ACY, 175, 181, 191

[1] D. Knoop and G. P. Jones in AQC, XLIV, 228; [2] HCY, 89

Spink, John—see SPYNK

SPONBEDDE, Martin of (*fl.* 1319–1320) Mason (*Spoonbed in Painswick parish, Glos.*)

In the year 13 Edward II (1319–20) the Priory of Lanthony by Gloucester leased to Martin of Sponbedde, mason, and his wife

279

Dionysia two 'selds' (stalls or shops) in Gloucester, for as long as they pay the rent of 8s. yearly. The priory owned stone quarries on an estate in Painswick in which Spoonbed was a tithing, and very likely the birthplace of Martin. The rent was a substantial one and implies that Martin was of quite high status; on the other hand it is hardly likely that he was retained by Lanthony Priory, as in that case he would be termed 'Master' even if not fully described.

It is an interesting possibility that Spon-bedde may have been the master employed by *Gloucester Abbey* (now the Cathedral) for rebuilding the south aisle of the nave, a work begun by 1319 and finished by 1329.

PRO, C 115–K1–6681, *f.* 136 (*N.M.H.*)

SPONLEE, John de [Sponle] (*fl.* 1350–†*c.* 1386) Mason

Probably of Spoonley by Sudeley Castle, near Winchcombe, Glos.;[1] was master of the masons working on the new chapel at *Windsor Castle* when, on 8 April 1350, he was empowered to appoint deputies to take masons and other workmen. The existing accounts show that from 26 April he was taking 1s. a day as 'the chief of the King's masons being there about the ordinance of the works'. On 4 May 1354 he was granted 1s. a day for life at the Exchequer for his wages, on account of his good service, and the Windsor accounts show that he was working there full time as chief mason or 'ordinator' of the works until April 1361. From 12 April 1361 WILLIAM WYNFORD is also named as 'ordinator' and both masons were paid 1s. a day. Sponlee continued to work at Windsor until 1368, but on 27 October 1364 he had been given a corrody at Reading Abbey at the King's request;[2] this form of pension was generally reserved for those who were incapacitated by illness or age, and the facts rather suggest that Wynford was promoted to a position where he could take some of the responsibility from Sponlee. Sponlee's high rank in the royal service is shown by the fact that, with WILLIAM HERLAND, he ranked as an esquire of great estate when he was given a robe to attend Queen Philippa's funeral in 1369; he also had a robe for the funeral of Edward III in 1377.

Sponlee had a confirmation of his life-grant of 1s. a day from Richard II on 8 March 1377/8,[3] and in the same month Master HENRY YEVELEY and Master John Sponle were sent to advise on 'the foundation of a certain tower about to be built for the defence of Southampton'.[4] Sponlee's pension was last paid on 23 September 1382 and by December he was stated to be dead when his corrody was granted to John Rose, yeoman of the King's chamber. Another grant, however, of 28 June 1386, states that John de Sponley was then to give up his corrody and to receive one jointly with Henry Chandeler, a yeoman of the King's chamber.[5] The *John SPONELE* who in 1368 was paid 13s. 4d. for making a chimney in Windsor Castle, was clearly not the great mason, as he is not entitled 'Master', and the item refers to his 'cutting' the chimney thus making it clear that he was a working mason. He was probably our Sponlee's son.

Sponlee's work at Windsor is known in detail, thanks to the research of the late Sir W. St. John Hope, who has shown that work began on the vestry and Chapter House in May and June 1350. The former was completed by the following February, and the Chapter House with the warden's lodging above it in January 1352. The canons' lodgings followed, being finished in July 1353, and the treasury with the vaulted porch beneath it was built between June 1353 and December 1354, while the cloisters, begun about the same time, were not finished until 1356. In 1357–58 the Spicery Gate was rebuilt, and in 1359–60 the New Gate in the inner bailey and the belfry tower were built. From 1358 to 1365 the royal lodgings were being remodelled, and the inner gatehouse and the space beneath the King's chamber were vaulted in 1362–63.

General plans for the works connected with the chapel may have been prepared in 1348–49 by WILLIAM DE RAMSEY, but to Sponlee belongs the credit of building the first works ever constructed in the developed Perpendicular style; no sooner had the Black Death passed away than these buildings began, as they were to proceed, in the new fashion. Sponlee may also have planned the refashioning of the royal lodgings in the upper ward, so long attributed to William of Wykeham, who had charge of the works administration at Windsor, as clerk of the works, from 30 October 1356 to 31 October 1361. The rising man at the time was William Wynford, however, and Wynford's later work at Winchester College and New College, Oxford, strikingly resembles that of these royal apartments. Wynford suddenly appears in 1360, at the highest rate of pay for a master, and it would not be surprising if he had already been taking an important part in the work without recognition. It is obvious that Sponlee was getting old by 1364, and this suggests that he must have already had a long career before his appearance at Windsor in 1350, but his early story is still unknown. If he did come from Spoonley in Gloucestershire, he may well have been master mason to *Winchcombe Abbey*. The possibility that Sponlee may also have worked at Gloucester Abbey deserves consideration.

(WKM); **HWC**

[1] RLW, II, 392–3; BCS, 86; [2] CCR 1364–8, 76–7; [3] CPR 1377–81, 140; [4] HKW, II, 842; [5] CCR 1381–5, 239; *Ibid.*, 1385–9, 256; cf. HKW, I, 212n.

SPORRIER, Ralph [Sporryowre] (fl. 1473–1496) Mason

Mason of *Bristol*; in 1473 and 1496 acted as a viewer of the city.

(*A.O.*; *G.M.D.B.*) BLR, II, 134; Sotheby's Catalogue 13/4/1981, lot 15

SPROICH (*fl. c.* 1190–   ) ? Carpenter

Built a timber bridge over the North Tyne at *Bellingham* for the cathedral priory of Durham in the late 12th century.

JAB, II, 15

Spyllesby, Robert—see SPILLESBY

SPYNK, John (*fl.* 1423–†1430) Mason

In 1423–24 John Spynk, 'sementar', was paid £12 for materials and building of the walls of the chancel of *St. Saviour, Norwich*. The stonework of the windows was provided by JOHN WESPNADE.[1] Spynk's will was made on 16 November 1430 and proved on 4 December. He wished to be buried in the cemetery of the Hospital of St. Giles, and left his wife Agnes and Edward Snetesham joint executors.[2]

[1] NRO, DCN, Almoner no. 531 (*P.C.*); [2] NRO, Acta & Comperta roll 8 (*P.C.*)

SQUYER, John [Squier] (*fl.* 1479–1507) Carpenter

On 20 September 1479 received a grant for life of the office of chief carpenter at *Windsor Castle*, on the death of WILLIAM GROVE.[1] He had a reward of £2 13s. 4d. and 10s. for a robe each year from 1480/1 to 1483/4; he was the principal carpenter engaged on the work of *St. George's Chapel*, and must have made the stalls set up during 1482 and 1483.[2] He was

also concerned with routine repairs to the Castle in 1489–90, and in 1499–1500 was employed on the new tower in the Upper Ward. In 1506–07 he constructed the new gallery at *Richmond Palace* by contract for which he was paid £80 and £6 13s. 4d. in reward.[3]

[1] CPR 1476–85, 163, 183; [2] HWC, II, 382, 402–6; HKW, II, 886n; III, 306, 313n.; [3] PRO, 3.36–214, pp. 94, 107, 118, 130

SQUYER, Robert (*fl.* 1520–21) Mason

Mason (*lathamus*) at *Ripon Minister* in 1520–21, when he was given 6s. 8d. for his good diligence about the works of the church. CHRISTOPHER SCUNE was the visiting master, and Squyer was presumably warden of the works.

SMR, III, 181

Stabbard (John)—see STUBBARD

STACY, John (†1409) Carver

Made his will on 3 September 1409 as a 'kirver' of the parish of St. Peter Broad Street, London. He refers to his three brothers Nicholas, William and Thomas, and made his mother Joan, and Richard Ase, carpenter, his executors. The will was proved on 9 September.

GUL, Archdeaconry Court of London, vol. I, *f*. 216

Stafford, Henry—see STAUNFORD

STAFFORD, John (*fl.* 1354–   ) Carpenter

John Stafford, carpenter, and Petronilla his wife were on 29 September 1354 granted a 40–year lease of a shop within the Abbey of Westminster, viz. the last shop at the north end of seven new shops at the West Gate, by rent of 10s. a year. Stafford was to serve the Sacrist in the work of carpenter whenever required, before all other clients except the King, being paid at the official rate (*stipendium regale*) of 3s. for a whole week.

WAM, 17656

STAFFORD, Thomas (*fl.* 1512–   ) Carpenter

By an indenture sealed in the chapter house of *Arbury Priory*, Warwick, on 3 May 1512, Thomas Stafford, carpenter, was retained to serve the convent 'in the mistery and crafte of carpentry duryng the lyfe naturell of the seid Thomas'. Stafford was to work 'to the best avayle and profyte of the seid Priour and Couent as in chosyng, fellyng, squaryng of tymbre, framyng, reasyng, makyng and fynysshyng of houses and other such werks' as he should be ordered to do 'that longeth or perteyneth a carpenter to do and make after his powre and cunnyng'.

He was to be paid £1 6s. 8d. a year 'aslong as he is myghty in body and abile to worche as a carpenter ought to doo', having the house 'that he nowe indwelleth. . . which he hath taken of the seid priour and Couent be copye of Court Roll which house lieth in Lutmansyend'. The rent of this house, 13s. 4d. a year, was to count as part of his stipend, the other 13s. 4d. being paid in ready money quarterly. Stafford was also to take 'mete and drynke dayly duryng the seid terme suche and in like forme as the hed yomen in the seid priory shall dayly haue and be serued and also barbour and launder wekely as the couent wekely ther haue', and yearly 'iij brode yerds of wollen clothe for his gowne' as the said head yeomen wear.

When Stafford was no longer able to work, he should have the house for the rest of his life, with 'mete and drynk barbour and launder' but no cash. Should he later wish to surrender the house, he should have in exchange 'a chambre with a chymney within the seid priory' with his meat, drink, and other perquisites, as well as 'fuell for his fire sufficient for a man of his age'. The Prior and Convent also undertook to provide 'grasse and pasturyng for a horse or a cowe. . . and hey in wynter for the same,' while Thomas was to 'enforme, instruct and teche a yongman such as the seid priour shall assigne and put vnto the seid Thomas to worche vnder hym as aprentice in the mystery and crafte of carpentry the best wyse he can or may, the seid priour fyndyng the seid yongman all maner tole such as he shall worch with'.

PRO, Anc. Deed. B.9826; (E.36–9826); (*L.F.S.*)

STAINEFIELD, Oliver de (*fl.* 1305–   ) Mason (? *Stainfield, Lincs.*)

Was master mason of *Beverley Minster* in 1305, and probably designed the nave, built from 1308 onwards.[1] At the request of Henry Lacy, Earl of Lincoln, he had been given leave of absence by the Chapter but was summoned to return in February 1305; in June it was resolved that his further absence should be permitted but that he should pay 1 mark a year to the fabric fund of Beverley while non-resident.[2] The Earl of Lincoln was the builder of *Denbigh Castle*, and it is possible that Stainefield may have worked for him there, though the style of the work at Denbigh suggests that the designer was WALTER OF HEREFORD, the great architect of Carnarvon Castle. It is, however, to be noted that Hereford probably visited Hull between 1296 and 1299 in connection with Edward I's buildings there, and that Beverley is the nearest place where skilled masons would be found.

[1] MBM; [2] BCA

Standlee, Thomas—see STANLEY

STANLEY, Thomas [Standlee, Stanlee, Stonley] (*fl.* 1429–†1462) Mason

Built the church tower of *Lydd*, Kent, between 1442 and 1446, apparently by contract, the total price being £280. A gallon of wine, and bread, at a cost of 8d. were provided for him when he left the work. In 1446–47 he also received £2 'in curtesy for his reward about the belfry'.[1] He was one of the senior masons at *Canterbury Cathedral*, having been named first among the lodge masons (*lathami de la loygge*) there in 1429, coming after THOMAS MAPILTON, the master, and JOHN MORYS, the warden, who were among the 'esquires'. He was still the senior working mason in 1431, and in 1432 was promoted, appearing as an esquire. Next year, however, he had been relegated to the *lathami* where he was second to JOHN SMYTH. His name does not appear in the next full list, that for 1437.[2] In 1445 he obtained the freedom of Canterbury by purchase.[3] His will was proved in 1462 in the Court of the Archdeaconry of Kent.[4]

From its stylistic resemblance to that of Lydd, the tower of *Tenterden Church* must have been designed by Stanley; it is known to have been in process of erection from 1449 to 1461. The towers at Lydd and Tenterden are based on the south-west tower of Canterbury Cathedral, designed by THOMAS MAPILTON and built in 1423–34. The tower at Ashford (*c.* 1460–90) is also clearly influenced by those of Lydd and Tenterden.[5]

John STANLEY, possibly son of Thomas, was first of the *lathami* at Canterbury Cathedral in 1445.

[1] FRL, 82–4, 89, 90, 94, 96, 115; [2] *Bodl.*, Tanner MS. 165 (*A.O.*); [3] CFC; [4] Reg. i, 278; [5] IAC (1924), 10, 12

STANLOWE, Robert (*fl.* 1398) Carpenter

'Wryght'; sued in Easter term 1398 by Sir John Bagot for 40 marks damages for having failed to build properly a certain house at 'Blythefeld' (*Blithfield*), Staffs. Stanlowe had constructed the house so negligently and unskilfully (*tam negligenter et inartificialiter construxit*) that it had fallen into ruin.

WSS, xv, 86 (*A.O.*)

'Stapylton', Thomas—see MAPILTON

STAUNFORD, Henry de [Stafford] (*fl.* 1372–) Carpenter

Was master carpenter of the Duchy of Lancaster for works at *Bolingbroke Castle* and bridge, Lincs., in May 1372. On 30 August of the same year he was appointed master carpenter of the work of the Duchy in the counties of Lincoln and Huntingdon at £10 a year.

JGR 1372–6, 569, 965

STAUNTON, Thomas de (*fl.* 1345–) Mason

On 26 January 1345 contracted with the Mayor and Commonalty of *York* to build 20 perches of the city wall from Fishergate Bar to the Foss. The contract makes no mention of an earlier wall between these points. For each completed perch, Staunton was to be paid £7.

RCHM, *York*, II, 13–15

Stephen the Almayn—see HASCHENPERG

STEPHEN the Carpenter (*fl. c.* 1190–1200) Carpenter

Master carpenter; witnessed a grant of *c.* 1190–1200 conveying land in Carles and Snainton, Yorks., to the nuns of Little Mareis at Yedingham.

EYC, I, 487, No. 618

Stephen Carpenter—see CARPENTER

Stephen the Carpenter—see ESTINTON

STEPHEN the Mason [le Macun, Mazun] (*fl.* 1213–1228) Mason

Possibly identical with the Stephen *cementarius* who with his mates was paid £22 in 1180–81 for making the wall of the King's forge (*fabrica*) at *Winchester*.[1] Master *cementarius* in charge of the King's works at *Corfe Castle*, Dorset, in 1213, when he was paid 50 marks (£33 6s. 8d.) in respect of their cost.[2] In 1222 he was paid £8 for work done on the hall and other parts of *Winchester Castle*,[3] and between 1226 and 1228 he had 20s. of the King's gift, and sums of money: 40s. on 8 November 1227, and again 40s. on 10 December 1228, on account of his pay.[4]

Master Stephen was the original designer of the great hall at Winchester, and may also have worked for Bishop Peter des Roches in the retrochoir of *Winchester Cathedral* (1202–*c.*

1235), and the choir and retrochoir of St. Mary Overie (*Southwark Cathedral*), built between 1208 and 1235.

[1] PR; [2] CDE, 257; [3] PRO, E.101-491-13 (*L.F.S.*); [4] CLR 1226–40, 9, 59, 113

STEPHEN, Roger (*fl.* 1353) Mason

Warden (*apparilator*) of the masons at *Rotherhithe Manor* from 20 May to 9 September 1353, taking 3s. 4d. a week. With THOMAS COOK he also undertook the repair of a wall at task for £13 6s. 8d.

PRO, E.101-545-33

STEPHENSON, Stephen (? *fl. c.* 1387–1400) ? Mason

James Murphy in his *Travels in Portugal*, states with reference to the building of the *Abbey of Batalha*: 'According to the account of those who are supposed to have had their information from the records preserved in the Royal Archives of Lisbon, the name of the architect of the church was Stephen Stephenson, a native of England.'

It is known that the chief master of the works at Batalha was the Portuguese Affonso Domingues (*fl.* 1387–†1402), but English influence upon the design of the church is very strong,[1] and it is very probable that at least one English master may have been sent out in the train of Philippa, daughter of John of Gaunt, at the time of her marriage to King John of Portugal, which coincided with the founding of Batalha.

J. Murphy: *op. cit.* (1795),44
[1] HGW, 106

STEPPINGLEY, Peter de (*fl.* 1366) Mason

Of Nottingham; with his wife Alice in 1366 acquired four messuages in St. Mary's Gate there. These they demised later in the same year to William de Askham, chaplain, for life. Steppingley may have been identical with PETER the Mason.

NBR, Court Rolls

STEPUL, John de (*fl.* 1390–) ? Mason

Agreed in 1390 with the Abbot of Darley to build a new bridge over the Derwent near *Derby* at 'Wattestonwell' ford in return for spiritual benefits. There is nothing to indicate that Stepul was himself a mason or building contractor.

(APD); HMC, *Rutland*, IV, 38

STERLYNG, Thomas (*fl.* 1519–) Carver

'Gravor' of *Wymondham*, Norfolk, contracted on 7 October 1519 to make an image of St. George for the church there, in partnership with WILLIAM BALE.

Sterlyng and Bale were to provide the timber and workmanship of the image 'callyd a rydyng George wt ye horse to ye same ymage of xv hande hye and a dragon wt a beme vowted to sett ye seyd ymage horse and dragon upon'. The 'patron' for the work was to be the riding George of 'Leystofft' (Lowestoft) 'except the lyeng of the Dragon schall vary from their seyd patron for thys Dragon schall lye rampyng on the seyd beme'.

The image was to be set up in the body of the parish church (i.e. the nave of Wymondham Abbey) by the Nativity of St. John the Baptist (24 June 1520) and Sterlyng and Bale were to have altogether £13, of which £7 was paid on the day the contract was made.

A, XLIII, 271

STEVENS, Henry [Stevyns] (*fl.* 1479–   ) Mason

Mason of *Salisbury Cathedral* in 1479, when he rode over to Haslebury Quarry to select stone for work on the new vault.

(*L.F.S.*) Salisbury Cath. Fabric Rolls

STEVENS, William (*fl.* 1364–1384) Mason

A working mason at *Wallingford Castle* under ROBERT YEVELEY in 1364–65 when he was paid 3s. 4d. a week.[1] Resident mason at *Abingdon Abbey*, Berks., under WILLIAM WYNFORD in 1375–76, when he received a robe price 12s. 10d. In 1383–84, he was paid at the rate of 3s. a week for 45 weeks in the year, and was given a robe worth 13s. 4d. In both years he was also allowed expenses for visiting the quarries at Taynton, Oxon.[2]

[1] *PRO*, E.101–490–2 (*L.F.S.*); [2] AAA, 28, 47–9; cf. E. M. Jope in BKJ, LI (1951), 54

STEYNFORTH, Robert (*fl.* 1481–   ) Mason

Was warden of the masons at *Kirby Muxloe Castle*, Leics., under JOHN COWPER until October 1481, when he was superseded by JOHN LYLE and reduced in wages from 3s. 4d. a week to 6d. a day.[1] He may have been related to

William STAYNFORD, one of the masonsetters employed on the foundations of the *York Guildhall* in 1448, when he was paid 3s. a week.[2]

[1] LAS, XI; [2] *YCM*, Chamberlains' Accs., MS. vol. 1A, *ff.* 6–8

STIWARD, John (*fl.* 1363–1370) Mason

Principal mason working at the King's manor of *Sheen*, Surrey, in 1363–70. His work, on doorways, walls and foundations, was mostly done by contract.

HKW, II, 996–7

STOCKTON, Thomas [Stokton] (*fl.* 1509–†1525) Carver & Joiner

Like EDMUND MORE of Kingston and some other carvers in the late Middle Ages, Stockton seems to have worked in stone as well as wood. From 1509 to 1515 he was master carver at *King's College Chapel, Cambridge*, receiving an annual salary of £18 5s. (i.e. at the rate of a shilling a day). The building accounts show that 'rewards' were paid to him in July 1510, September 1512, and January, April, and May 1513. As no carved woodwork was made for the chapel during the years when Stockton was master carver, he must have been responsible for the heraldic carving of the antechapel, where the achievements of the royal arms with their supporters and the crowned badges suggest the technique of the carver in wood and might indeed have been carried out in that material. The classified fortnightly summaries of wages in the building accounts show that carvers were employed from October 1512 until August 1513 and that not more than five were working at any one time.[1] Thomas Stockton himself may only have made drawings or models of the carvings. His official duties as King's Joiner would have precluded constant attendance and work on the spot.

On 17 May 1510 Thomas Stockton had been appointed chief joiner in the *Tower of London* in place of JOHN JERVEYS with 12d. a day, a house in the Tower, and a robe yearly as worn by Esquires of the Household. (In Brewer's *Letters and Papers of Henry VIII* the post is given wrongly as that of King's porter; presumably 'junctor' was read as 'janitor'.)[2] On 28 January 1511 a warrant was issued to the Chancellor, the Archbishop of Canterbury, for a commission to Thomas Stockton, the King's Joiner, to employ joiners, carvers, and 'intailers' in the King's works at the Tower of London, Westminster, or elsewhere, and to provide timber and other things necessary for the same works.[3] In June 1513 George Lord, 'purveyor of the King's timber', was delivering timber for works at the Tower to Thomas Stockton by command of Master Almoner;[4] wainscot was taken from Greenwich to the Tower by Richard Baker and John Doffe,[5] and Stockton himself requisitioned elm timber belonging to the works at London Bridge for delivery on Tower Wharf.[6] About this time Sir Thomas Lovell presented a petition on behalf of Lord, who asserted that by the order of the council he had provided five loads of timber for work at the Tower and that Stockton had refused to pay for it.[7] On 10 October in that year Stockton acknowledged receipt of 4,406 staves from Nicholas Robartes in five several parcels at 2*d*. for 4 staves;[8] there were further deliveries of timber from Robartes in November.[9]

In 1515 Thomas Stockton was master joiner at *York Place, Westminster*, where Wolsey began extensive alterations in February, a few months after he had been made Archbishop of York. In the surviving account covering the year 1515 Stockton's name and post are given without any entry against them; probably work had not progressed far enough for the joiners to begin their operations.[10] The master carpenter, RICHARD RUSSELL, held the same position at Hampton Court, and Stockton may also have been master joiner there. In 1520, during the feverish preparations for the Field of the Cloth of Gold, Stockton was one of the many craftsmen to whom 'prests' were delivered.[11] He continued to hold the office of King's Joiner in the Tower until his death, which occurred in 1525 at some date before September 3, when he was succeeded by JOHN RIPLEY.[12] That he had died and had not just retired or been dismissed is proved by a grant, dated 5 October 1525, to William Cowper, yeoman of the pantry, of two tenements in the parish of St. Giles Cripplegate 'late belonging to Tho. Stokton deceased'.[13] A twenty years' lease of a tenement with garden on the west side of Grub Street in the parish of St. Giles Cripplegate, 150 feet in length and 20 feet in breadth, had been granted to Thomas Stockton on 28 July 1514.[14] Evidently he had improved the property by dividing the house or building a second one. But he seems to have owned another property in the same street which was acquired in 1565 by Robert Bestney, gent., from Marion, 'heiress of Thomas Stockton late joiner', as daughter of his sister Agnes, and from her second husband Gerard Hone, glazier, of South-

wark, and her son (by her first husband) Thomas Rolfe.[15]

A.O. (HKW, III, 32-3, 192, 204)
[1] *KCM*, Building Accs. 1509-15; [2] LPH, I, pt. i, 485 (57); [3] LPH, I, pt. i, 682 (37); [4] *Ibid.*, pt. ii, 1954; [5] *Ibid.*, 3613 (460-1); [6] *Ibid.*, 3613 (458); [7] *Ibid.*, 3614 (vi, 24); [8] *Ibid.*, pt. ii, 3614 (vi, 215); [9] *Ibid.*, pt. ii, 3613 (465); [10] *PRO*, E.36-236; [11] LPH, III, pt. i, 826; [12] *Ibid.*, IV, pt. i, 1676 (p. 749); [13] *Ibid.*, 1736 (p. 772); [14] *Ibid.*, I, pt. ii, 3107 (52); [15] *LHR*, 254 (33) (*J.H.H.*)

STOCKTON, William (*fl.* 1506–1513) Carver

Was doubtless a close relative of Thomas Stockton, the King's Joiner. In 1506 he was paid £6 8*s*. 'upon a bargain' for making a carving of St. George for *Holy Trinity Church, Cambridge*, where there was a flourishing Guild of St. George at the time.[1] Henry VII, who spent St. George's Day in Cambridge that year, contributed 20*s*. towards the cost.[2] The carving was probably a 'riding George', like that erected at Wymondham, Norfolk, in 1519, the carvers of which were THOMAS STERLYNG and WILLIAM BALE, but costing only half as much, the Cambridge example will not have been so large.

Between 1511 and 1513 William Stockton was employed at *King's College Chapel, Cambridge*, where Thomas Stockton was the master carver.[3] The building accounts show that he received a reward of 9*s*. in February 1511 and that he was reimbursed for purveyors' costs in December 1512, January and May 1513 during the period when the carvers were at work on the antechapel. He may have acted as Thomas Stockton's deputy, superintending the carving and providing the men and materials.

A.O.
[1] *CWT*, f. 84a; [2] *Ibid.* and *PRO*, E.36-214: [3] *KCM*, Building Accs. 1509–1515

STONARD, John [Stonhard] (*fl.* 1428–1429) Mason

Was chief mason working on the aqueduct and conduit of the town of *Southampton* in 1428–29. He was paid 6*d*. a day, later increased to 8*d*. JOHN NORTON was one of the masons working with him.

HMC, 11 R iii, 134ff.

STONE, John (*fl. c.* 1365–1395) Mason

Leading mason (*cementarius*) at *Wells Cathedral* during the latter part of the 14th century; he was presumably warden or undermaster to WILLIAM WYNFORD. He was living in a house in New Street, Wells, *c.* 1365–72,[1] and in the Fabric roll of 1390–91 was being paid at the rate of 3s. 8½d. a week. He also bought timber from the works.[2] In 1394–95 he was supervising repairs to the bells.[3]

[1] HMC, *Wells*, II, 18, 627; [2] *WLC*, Fabric roll 1390–91 (*L.S.C.*); CWF, 5, 7, 8; [3] *WLC*, communar's account 1394–95

STONE, Peter of [? 'Sutton'] (*fl.* 1263) Carpenter

Described as the king's carpenter, was on 4 March 1263 ordered to supply oaks for the buildings at *Westminster*.

CLR 1260–7, 120

STONEHOUSE, William [Stonhowse] (*fl.* 1446–   ) Mason

Mason working on the upper stage of the tower of *Yatton Church*, Somerset, in 1446.

SRS, IV (1890), 83–4

STORY,—— (*fl.* 1498) Carpenter

Was paid 40s. for making a gallery at *Greenwich* in 1498.

BL, Add. MS. 7099, *f.* 45 (*A.O.*)

STORY, William (*fl.* 1455–   ) Mason

Was appointed on 7 January 1454/5 to report on the state of the fabric of Salisbury Cathedral.

Salisbury Cath., Act Book 'Burgh' (*L.F.S.*)

STOW, Richard, I (*fl. c.* 1198–   ) ? Mason

Contracted about 1198 to build a house for the Prior of Southwark, in the Prior's manor of *Stow*, Cambs., as part of the services by which he held his land. The house was to be such as to afford honourable entertainment to the Prior, and was to be completed before the second Easter after the election of Master Philip (of Poitou) as Bishop of Durham; i.e. by 18 April 1199.

(APD); *BM*, Cotton MS. Nero C.III, *f.* 201

STOW, Richard de, II [Stowa] (*fl. c.* 1270–1307) Mason

Probably identical with the Richard de Stow who about 1275 was one of the jurors of the second class at the Hundred Rolls inquiry in Lincoln.[1] He appears as a witness to deeds concerning the cathedral, *c.* 1275–1300,[2] being subordinate to Master SIMON DE TRESK until 1291, and in 1291–93 was master mason at the erection of the *Eleanor Cross* at *Lincoln*.[3] On 24 June 1295, as master of the fabric of *Lincoln Cathedral*, he acquired property in Pottergate which had belonged to ALEXANDER the Mason III.[4] In 1306 he contracted to build the upper stage of the cathedral's cen-

tral tower.[5] The work was begun under an order of the Chapter dated 14 March 1306/7,[6] and was completed about 1311. Stow's work on the cross is lost, but his belfry stage of the tower is one of the glories of the greatest age of Gothic art.

It is rather improbable that Stow was identical with RICHARD GAINSBOROUGH.

(APD); AJ, XL, 404

[1] HML, 114, 399; [2] *LDC*, D. ii, 77–3–10, 57; R. 742; Reg. Antiq. nos. 2527, 2535, 2585, 2642–3 (*K.M.*); [3] BMH, pt. ii; [4] *LDC*, Liber Cantariarum, No. 538 (*K.M.*); [5] A, IX, 125; [6] *LDC*, Chapter Act Book, A. 2–22, *f.* 5

Stowe, Robert—see STOWELL

STOWELL, John (*fl.* 1457–1470) Mason

Freemason; took up the freedom of Wells, Somerset, in 1458;[1] in 1457–8 he was in receipt of a regular fee at the rate of £2 a year as the consultant master mason of *Wells Cathedral*, apparently starting from Christmas 1457.[2] In 1461–62 he was making a lavatory under the cupboard in the hall of the bishop's *Manor* at *Wookey*, Somerset.[3] In 1470 he contracted with the master of the city of Wells to make a 'fronte innynge to ye altar of our Ladye' in the south aisle of *St. Cuthbert's Church*. Part of this reredos still exists, though greatly mutilated; the subject was the Tree of Jesse.[4] Stowell's apprentice, John Wyne, was admitted to the freedom of Wells in 1485.[5] Stowell is likely to have been the master mainly employed by Bishop Bekynton. He probably belonged to the Somerset family Stowell of Stowell (see ROBERT STOWELL).

[1] SRS, XLVI (1931); [2] HMC, *Wells*, II, 88 (10 R, App. III), 290; [3] HHW, 49; [4] SSC, 20; [5] SRS, XLVI

STOWELL, Robert [Stowe] (*fl.* 1452–†1505) Mason

Was appointed master of the stonemasons at *Windsor Castle* on 12 November 1452, at the death of JOHN THIRSK. His appointment was for his good services, but on 21 February 1462 the office was granted to ROBERT LEGET.[1] There seems little doubt that this was for political reasons, due to the accession of Edward IV in the previous year.

Stowell worked as a mason at *Westminster Abbey* from June 1468 taking 3s. 4d. a week. He was absent from Michaelmas 1469 to February 1470/1; at Michaelmas 1471 he was appointed master mason in succession to JOHN READING. Until Michaelmas 1475 Stowell was paid wages for working as a mason in addition to his fees, and was allowed a house from the Abbey authorities, first in Tothill Street and later in the Sanctuary. In 1489–90 he gave £3 6s. 8d. to the new work on condition that he and his wife should be admitted to the fraternity of the convent, i.e. that they should share in the spiritual benefits of the masses and prayers of the Abbey.[2]

From the Abbey leases, combined with entries in the churchwardens' accounts of St. Margaret's, Westminster, it is possible to reconstruct a little of Stowell's personal life. He was apparently the son of William Stowell and his wife Joan, who leased the tenement called 'St. Albans' from 1473–74; William died in 1476, after which the lease was transferred to Robert, jointly with his mother, his own first wife having died in 1474–75. In 1477–78 the Tothill Street houses which Robert had occupied since 1471 were transferred to Edmond Adam, mason; in 1488 Robert's mother died and, as Robert Stowell, Gentleman, he took a 44 years lease of tenements in the Sanctuary on the west side of the entrance 'de le Brodegates', for 40s. a year. By this time he had remarried and in 1490 paid 1d. for his wife's pew in St. Margaret's; Joan by name, she died in 1500–01. The parish accounts of 1490, 1492 and 1504 were audited by 'Mr. Robert Stowell Esquyer'. In 1505 they record the payment of 6d. for ringing his knell, and 6s. 8d. for his grave in the church.

Stowell probably stopped working as a mason at the Abbey because he now had a private practice, for on 25 June 1476 he contracted to lengthen towards the east the south aisle of *Broxbourne Church*, Herts., and to make a table-tomb there for Sir John Say.[3]

At *St. Margaret's Church, Westminster*, beside the Abbey, the churchwardens' accounts for 1482–84 show that he was paid 4s. for 2 masons who worked 4 days on the Lady Chapel;[4] probably these were masons on the Abbey staff who were 'lent' when the Abbey work was slack. Stowell was probably consulted as to these works, and the more extensive ones begun about 1488. The south aisle of St. Margaret's was rebuilt between 1488 and 1491, and the nave was completed by 1504, and Stowell was probably designer of the whole body of the church. The chancel and tower were rebuilt between 1515 and 1523, under HENRY REDMAN.

The office of King's Master Mason was granted to 'Robert Stowell esquire' on 13 December 1483, though THOMAS DANYELL was already in occupation of the office, and when Danyell was given a new patent in 1484, he was said to have occupied the office from 7 July 1483, at the King's command.[5] Stowell's patent cannot have been effective, perhaps for the same reasons that had lost him his post at Windsor in 1462. He may have had pronounced Lancastrian sympathies, but if so he reaped no reward after the battle of Bosworth, when he might have expected to be reinstated. He still retained his office as master mason to Westminster Abbey, where in addition he undertook work by contract in 1488–89; he was to make the vault of three bays and the arch at the top of the nave for £120, of which he had £74 in 1489 and the balance in the following year.[6]

In 1494 one, William Depyng, merchant, was pardoned for not appearing to answer 'Robert Stowe, alias Stowell, of the town of Westminster . . . "gentilman", alias esquire, touching a debt of 40s.', and in 1491 and 1502 Stowell was a warden of the Guild of St. Mary in Westminster.[7] He died in November 1505, when he was succeeded at the Abbey by THOMAS REDMAN.[8]

Stowell had made a will on 13 November 1505, naming as his executors his son-in-law Thomas Burges and his son William Stowell; he desired to be buried in St. Margaret's, Westminster, and left money for obits at Brentford and Ealing, Middlesex. The executors appeared on 18 November and renounced probate, after which Stowell's goods were administered by the Court.[9]

Stowell's career was a long one, and is also somewhat unusual in other respects. He was peculiarly unfortunate in losing two Crown appointments, for reasons which probably had no connection with his capacity, as he had already done good service in 1452, when he can hardly have been over 30. Secondly he is regularly referred to as 'gentleman' and 'esquire' and this would seem to denote a higher rank by birth than was usual among masons, who took rank as esquires after reaching the top of their craft, but were seldom referred to as such in documents. It seems likely that Robert Stowell, and also JOHN STOWELL, belonged to the Somerset family of Stowell of Stowell, near Wincanton, who bore arms: *Gules a cross lozengy argent*.[10]

(KJM; WKM) **RRS**

[1] CPR 1452–61, 41; [2] RNW; *WAM* 19720–1, 19734,

23533–585; Reg. Bk. I, *ff.* 27, 95; St. Margaret's churchwardens' accounts (*L.E.T.*); ³ SHB, 537–8; (*PRO*, Anc. Deed, D.2638); ⁴ *WMW*, 150; ⁵ CPR 1476–85, 409, 484; ⁶ RNW; *WAM*, 23563–4; ⁷ *WAM*, 17898; cf. 31811; CPR 1494–1509, 280; ⁸ RNW; *WAM*, 23585–6; ⁹ *PPR*, Peculiar Court of Westminster, 21 Wyks; ¹⁰ HME, 80

STRETFORD, Robert de [Stratford] (*fl.* 1351–1354) Mason

Master mason, granted commissions on 28 October 1351 and 4 July 1354 to impress workmen for the building of the *Hospital of St. Mary* by the castle of *Leicester*, of which he must have been in charge, for Henry, Duke of Lancaster.

(*A.O.*) CPR 1350–4, 170; 1354–8, 84

STRUT, Robert (*fl.* 1413–   )

Of Hartest, Suffolk; with WILLIAM REYNER contracted in 1413 to make the woodwork of a new bakehouse at *King's Hall, Cambridge.* Strut is mentioned as 'bondsman' for Reyner, so that he may well have had no connection with the work except a financial one. Since the contract itself is lost, it is impossible to be certain of his precise status.¹ Thomas Strut of Hartest, whose will was proved 26 November 1449, was doubtless a relative.²

(*A.O.*)
¹ WCC, II, 440, 441; ² RBW, 60

STUBBARD, John [Stobart] (*fl.* 1349–1360) Mason

Mason at *Ely Cathedral* in 1349–50, when he was paid £4 13*s.* 4*d.* for 44 weeks' work; in 1352–53 he was paid 2*s.* a week and had certain allowances of food, while from 1357–60 he received £5 4*s.* 0*d.* a year and a robe, but ate at his own table. Though not the master, he was certainly of senior standing and had a servant, John Lenne, working under him.

CSR, II, 194

STUBBARD, William (*fl.* 1357–c. 1390) Carver

Lay brother of *St. Albans Abbey;* he was celebrated as a stone-carver in the time of Abbot de la Mare (1349–96); his tomb is in the north transept of the abbey church.¹ He was advised by HENRY YEVELEY.²

¹ W. Page: *St. Albans Cath. Guide* (1898), p. 29; SHB, 4; ² RGA, III, 387; ASA, 440; cf. *BL*, Cotton MS. Nero D.vii, *f.* 83

STUCLEY, John (*fl.* 1396–1401) Mason

Appointed master mason of *Calais* on 8 September 1396, and in office there until 1401.

HKW, II, 1054

STURGEON, John (*fl.* 1480–1490) Carpenter

Worked at *King's College, Cambridge*, between 1480 and 1484. Though subordinate to MARTIN PRENTICE he was named in the commission of 10 July 1480 for taking carriage for timber for the works of the college¹ and also in the wider commission of 28 August 1484 for impressing workmen and obtaining materials.² In March and April 1480 he supplied timber for the roodloft in the little church of *St. John the Baptist* adjoining the college.³ Between May and October of that year, when certain works were carried out in the Old Court of the college to the west of the Schools that included the building of a pantry and the addition of a timber porch to the hall, Sturgeon provided timber for the pantry and was responsible for the building of the porch, for which he received a final payment of 40*s.* on 3 November.⁴ During the same period he was much occupied in supervising the felling of oaks and the cartage of timber from the Abbot of Walden's wood at Ashdon Hales and from the parks of Thaxted and Bardfield ('Barvile') in Essex. In addition to payments for this work he received 8*s.* in July for scaffold timber bought from him; on 9 October Martin Prentice and he were paid 15*d.* for their expenses at Walden.⁵ A detailed account of the timber brought from Ashdon Hales, near Saffron Walden, in 1480 shows that it was used for the scaffold in the chapel, for the pantry and other buildings in the Old Court, for the new carpenters' lodge, the masons' lodge, and the college stable,⁶ but the great oaks bought from the abbot will have been required for the roof of the eastern bays of the chapel erected at this time. In 1484 messengers were sent to John Sturgeon on four occasions,⁷ and the kitchen accounts show that he was three times a guest in hall that year, on each occasion in company with Martin Prentice.⁸ In April 1486, after the works on the chapel had stopped, he was paid 14*s.* for making a new gate at the back of the college 'towards the field'.⁹ In the same year the churchwardens' accounts of *Saffron Walden Church* record a payment of 2*s.* to 'Sturgyn and hys man' for work in repairing the steeple and the expenditure of another 2*s.* for their board. The repairs effected, which cost 33*s.* 10½*d.*, concerned the lead covering either of the roof of the tower or of a spirelet.¹⁰ Sturgeon was probably the carpenter responsible for the roof of the south aisle. Among payments for the lead covering of the roof *c.* 1490–91 is one: 'It. payd to Scharlet (?) for ye hows yt Sturgyn had of hem ix.*d.*', implying that Sturgeon had been staying in Walden while the roofing was in progress. 'Sturgyn' appears in 1488–89 making a new kitchen and other rooms at *Birchanger*, Essex, for New College, Oxford.[11]

John Sturgeon was doubtless a close relative of THOMAS STURGEON, the master carpenter at King's in Henry VI's reign. It is possible that he was the father of John Sturgeon of Hitchin, an important official in the reign of Edward IV, who was Master of the King's Ordnance from 1477 to 1482, a Commissioner of the Peace in Bedfordshire and Hertfordshire and several times a Commissioner of Array. In his will, dated 20 June 1492, proved 30 June following, John Sturgeon of Hitchin, 'esquier', named John and Agnes Sturgeon, his father and mother, among those for whose souls he endowed a chantry in Hitchin Church.[12] The fact that the college servant sent to fetch 'Sturgyn' to Cambridge in October 1484 was paid for riding to Hitchin suggests some relationship between the two men.

A.O.

[1] CPR 1476–85, 203, repeated 213; [2] *Ibid.*, 472; [3] *KCM*, College Accs., vol. vi; CAC, VI, 353–6; [4] *KCM*, College Accs., vol. vi; [5] *Ibid.*, vol. iv; [6] *Ibid.*, vol. vi; [7] *Ibid.*, vol. v; [8] *KCM*, Kitchen Accs., vol. vii; [9] *Ibid.*, College Accs., vol. v; [10] *CWW, f.* 141v; [11] GOC; [12] *PCC*, 18 Doggett

STURGEON, Thomas [Storgeon, Storion, Sturgyn, Sturion] (*fl.* 1443–1462) Carpenter

Of Elsenham, Essex; on 17 December 1443 as chief carpenter of the works at *King's College, Cambridge*, Thomas Sturgeon was given a commission to impress carpenters and other workmen and to obtain timber and carriage for the works of the college.[1] At this time a beginning was being made with the acquisition of property and clearance of the site for the greatly enlarged college, projected by Henry VI's second charter of foundation of 10 July 1443, and it was not until 1446 that the present chapel was begun. Work, however, must have been proceeding with the buildings in the original court on the west side of the Schools (begun in 1441) in order to provide what was meant under the enlarged scheme to be only temporary accommodation. REGINALD ELY and Thomas Sturgeon had probably been respectively master mason and master carpenter from the outset, and

both men continued to hold those posts until work on the chapel stopped in 1461. For some years previously the works had been languishing owing to the irregular supply of funds, but in 1459 the Provost, Robert Wodelark, had attempted a resumption on a larger scale, and Thomas Sturgeon was among those named in the commission dated 26 February of that year for obtaining the men and materials needed.[2] Documentary evidence for the first phase of construction of the chapel is very scanty, but the kitchen accounts show that Sturgeon was occasionally a guest in hall, as for instance on 18 April 1448, when he dined at the fellows' table,[3] and between March 1459 and April 1461 he was a guest of the Provost on at least fourteen occasions, once accompanied by his father. Some accounts of the Provost's day-to-day receipts and expenditure of that period contain a few payments to Sturgeon for boards and timber for the works.[4]

Sturgeon's part in the building of the chapel will have been confined to making scaffolding and such centering as was needed. The timber roof was not begun in his time. But the bursar's accounts show that he was much employed in other ways, repairing buildings on estates belonging to the college and providing timber. In 1448 and 1449 he was paid sums of 66*s.* 8*d.* and 52*s.* 11*d.* for work at *Grantchester Mill* and *Merton Hall, Cambridge*.[5] Between 1448 and 1451 the college spent over £85 on rebuilding the *Hart Inn* at *Huntingdon*. The carpenter in charge of the work was GEOFFREY HALL, but Sturgeon was paid £6 for sawing of timber at Blackley for the inn, and on two or three occasions he accompanied the Provost on journeys from Cambridge to inspect the progress of the work.[6] In 1450–51 he was paid £4 for repairing the barn on the college estate at *Felstead* in Essex.[7] In 1453 the college received a grant of the underwood in the Forest of Sapley, near Huntingdon, and in 1457 Sturgeon was employed in 'measuring certain acres' there. During the year 1458–59 he supplied two loads of timber for the repair of the college barge.[8] In 1460 the college sent their bells to London to be recast, and great care was taken about the carriage of the new bells back to Cambridge. In November Sturgeon was in London on this business and early in December MARTIN PRENTICE and another also went to London, whence the bells were transported to

Cambridge in time for Christmas. They were housed in a temporary timber belfry, the marks of which can still be seen on the lawn to the west of the chapel. Sturgeon was paid £6 7s. 4d. for bell-wheels and other necessary expenses and on Christmas Eve he was given a reward of 6s. 8d. for the hanging of the bells.[4] The timber belfry had doubtless been made by Sturgeon at an earlier date. On 9 June 1462 he and Martin Prentice were paid 8d. for supervising its repair.[4]

Between 1448 and 1450 Sturgeon was undertaking the carpentry work in the building of the first court of *Queens' College, Cambridge*. In partnership with John Weyse or Veyse, draper, also of Elsenham, Essex, who no doubt provided the financial backing, he entered into two contracts. The first, dated 14 April 1448, was for all the woodwork of the north and east ranges, and about two-thirds of the south range, measuring altogether 240 feet in length, for which the contractors were to receive £100 in three instalments. The second contract, dated 6 March 1449, was for the roof and benches of the hall, the roofs and other woodwork of the buttery, pantry, and kitchen, lying south of the hall, and also of the return of chambers completing the south range. The work was to be carried out as rapidly as the building of the walls would allow, and the contractors were to receive £80 in six instalments.[9] Sturgeon's work remains substantially intact, including the fine open timber roof of the hall, for which there is a detailed specification in the contract.

Thomas Sturgeon's name appears in the churchwardens' accounts of *Saffron Walden Church*, Essex, under the year 1451–52, when he was paid 6s. for 9 oak boards ('ix waynscotis of ynglyng ok').[10] It is possible that by 1460 he had moved from Elsenham to the market town of Newport, five miles to the north, for on 17 November of that year John Grene obtained a ten years' lease of the manor of Newport and the hamlet of Birchanger, which were committed to him by mainprise of Richard Wednesbury of London, gentleman, and Thomas Sturgeon of Newport, 'yoman'.[11]

A.O.

[1] CPR 1441–6, p. 247; [2] *Ibid.* 1452–61, p. 478; [3] *KCM*, Kitchen Accs., vol. i; [4] *KCM*, College Accs., vol. ii; [5] *KCM*, Mundum Books 1448 and 1448–49; [6] *Ibid.* 1448–51; [7] *Ibid.* 1450–51; [8] *Ibid.* 1458–59; [9] SQC, 15 and WCC, II, 8–11; SHB, 528–30; [10] *CWW, f.* 42; [11] CFR 1452–61, p. 288

SUTHWELL, William de (*fl.* 1398–1399)
Mason

Master mason to *Selby Abbey* in 1398–99, when he was paid £2 for his yearly fee. The leading mason under him was John del Wod, probably the John Wod who still held the same position in 1431 (see WILLIAM CHESTERFIELD). The main work in progress was the rebuilding of the cloister.

Westminster Dioc. Archives, Se/Ac/5 (*N. L. R.*)

SUTTON, John (*fl.* 1396–   ) Mason
Carver

In 1396 was working on the choir of *St. Mary's Church, Warwick*, and according to Dugdale 'did cut the arms of the Ancient Earls of Warwick upon it'.

KHW, 103

'Sutton', Peter of—see STONE

SUTTON, Robert (*fl.* 1419–   ) Carver

Carver of Chellaston, Derbyshire; in 1419 undertook to make an alabaster tomb to stand in *Lowick Church*, Northants., being named second to THOMAS PRENTYS in the contract.

CEM, 29, 30

SWAFFHAM, Reginald of (*fl.* 1306–†1314)
Carpenter

Probably the 'master Reginald the carpenter' who was in charge of the wainscoting and fitting up of a new hall, chapel, and great chamber at the Archbishop of York's house in Westminster (later *Whitehall Palace*) in 1306, when it was being used by Queen Margaret and her young children on account of the destruction by fire of a large part of the Palace of Westminster. He was also sent to Winchester, with Master MICHAEL OF CANTERBURY the mason, to prepare *Wolvesey Castle* for a royal visit. Master Reginald was paid for 8 days in the middle of April 1306, at the rate of 1s. a day, but was then removed from his office.[1] The reason for his dismissal is not given.

In 1309 Master Reginald de Swafham was sworn as surveyor of tenements in the City of London, as far as pertained to the trade of a carpenter,[2] and died in 1314. His will, proclaimed in the Court of Husting on 4 November 1314, left his house to Alice his wife for her life, with remainder to his children, unnamed.[3]

[1] *PRO*, E.101–369–11; cf. HKW, II, 862; E.101–468–11; [2] CLB, 'D', 14; [3] SWL, I, 250

SWALLOW, John [Swalwe, Swolwe] (*fl.* 1376–1400) Mason

Mason of Gloucestershire, being so identified in 1397 when he was one of the sureties for Thomas Wolvey's completion of work at Henley Church. He was working at *Exeter Cathedral* in 1376, taking pay of 3s. a week in summer and 2s. 6d. in winter; in the next year he was sent to his own home (*versus partes proprias*) to fetch the master, ROBERT LESYNGHAM. From 1381–82 he was warden of the masons, taking 3s. 4d. a week, and continued in this position until the end of 1388, when he left Exeter.[1] He was succeeded as warden by JOHN CORNWALL. On 18 March 1394/5 he undertook, with RICHARD WASHBOURNE, to make the new cornice and corbels for *Westminster Hall*, to a design to be supplied by HENRY YEVELEY.[2] Two years later he was a surety for the completion of Henley Church by THOMAS WOLVEY, and in 1398–1400 with William Yford was again working at Westminster Hall, on the 12 windows in the side wall, for which they received £96.[3] Though we have direct evidence in one instance that the design of the work he carried out was not his own, his Gloucestershire origin is of interest, and further evidence may show that he was one of the contacts between the schools of Gloucester and London.

(APD; LKC)

[1] *FFE*; [2] SHB, 472–3; [3] *PRO*, E.101–470–17; 473–11; CCR 1396–9, 239

SWAN, John (*fl.* 1454–1455) Carpenter

In 1454–55 was paid for the new roof of *Lydd Church*, Kent.

HMC, 5 R App., 521 (*N.L.R.*)

SWAYN, William [Swane, Swann, Swanne, Swayne] (*fl.* 1483–†1525) Mason

Was a prominent mason in *Cambridge* during the reign of Henry VII. Between 1492 and 1505 he was employed on new buildings at *King's Hall*, where he seems to have been the chief mason in charge of the works carried on intermittently during those years. A new building begun in 1490 is probably to be identified as the east range of an outer court, now forming part of the east range of the Great Court of Trinity College and including the lower part of the Great Gate Tower. Payments made to JOHN WASTELL point to him as the designer, but, not living in Cambridge and having other work on hand, he cannot have given continuous supervision. The account for 1491–92 records sums of 41s. and 13s. 4d. paid to William Swanne 'for certain windows and doorways (*ostiis*) and other things'.[1] In 1495–96 'Swayne *lathamus*' was given commons on three occasions;[2] in the following year William Swayn was paid 10s. and in 1497–98 3s. for 5 days.[3] In 1502–03 Swayne received 6s. 8d. 'for two weeks'.[4] In 1505, at Whitsun, William Swayne was paid 33s. for six tons of stone and during the following weeks there are entries of wages paid to him at the rate of 4s. a week.[5] The King's Hall accounts frequently record only lump sums expended on new building, and masons and carpenters are more often than not unnamed, but the items quoted show that Swayn was employed fairly regularly when building was in progress.

When the final phase of building at *King's College Chapel* was begun in the spring of 1508, William Swayn was comptroller during the first year, and his annual salary of £13 6s. 8d. was the same as that of John Wastell, the master mason.[6] His duties seem to have been those of a purveyor. At the end of September he bought timber and nails at Stourbridge Fair; two months later he was paid 3s. for his riding costs 'ridyng to take up Carts and to see the tymber carted to the worke from Barnesfeld [perhaps Bardfield, Essex] and Cartlyng [Kirtling] parkys'; and on 16 December he received £4 'for prest' for Yorkshire stone. In May 1509 JOHN LEE appears in the accounts as second master mason, and he seems to have taken the place of Swayn, whose name does not occur again.[7] Possibly other work prevented him from giving the time required for his duties. The proctors' accounts for 1508–09 record the delivery of a sum of £4 'to William Swayn and Burdon freemasons' for *Great St. Mary's Church*,[8] showing that he was working on that building in some capacity at the time, and he was carrying out work by contract at *Christ's College*. On 24 August 1510 £10 was paid to him for various works at that college which included the making of a threshold at the chapel door, a holy water stock, enlarging the vestry door, making a window in the master's study, embattling the clock tower, making 18 capitals ('chaptrelles'), and in reward for lengthening the chapel by half a foot and heightening it by 2 feet 'over and beside his old covenants'.[9] From this reference to previous contracts it may be inferred that Swayn had already undertaken other work entailed by

291

the alteration and heightening of the old chapel of Godshouse in adapting it for Lady Margaret Beaufort's newly-founded college.[10] He may also have been responsible for the building of the lodge on the south side of the chapel and for the alteration of the gate-tower, though the carved work applied to the outer elevation is more likely to have been the work of a mason carver, perhaps RALPH BOW-MAN, who made an Easter sepulchre and imagery for the chapel.

In 1510 Lady Margaret Beaufort's second Cambridge college, St. John's, was founded, and the building of the first court was begun. It is not known who was the master mason, but Swayn seems to have been in charge of the work in the early stages. In a letter dated 12 February and, from internal evidence, of the year 1511 the master, Robert Shorton, wrote to John Fisher, Bishop of Rochester, one of the Lady Margaret's executors: 'We haue sent Swann the mason ffor slatt & frestone & takyn to hym x li. to make barganys for it.'[11] The carved work on the outer face of the gate-tower has an obvious resemblance to that on the gate-tower at Christ's, and the fact that Swayn was employed at Christ's might suggest that he was responsible for the design of both colleges. The work at Christ's, however, entailed only the adaptation of the existing buildings of Godshouse[10] and the completion of the court-yard, whereas at St. John's a new court was planned and built, though the chapel on the north side incorporated the walls of the 13th-century chapel of St. John's Hospital. It is difficult to estimate Swayn's precise status as a mason, but as he seems to have worked under Wastell at King's Hall, and probably also at Great St. Mary's Church, and was certainly not employed in an architectural capacity at King's College Chapel, it is possible that the plan and design of St. John's College were also provided by Wastell and that Swayn was the mason in charge. The lack of detailed building accounts leaves the situation obscure, but the gate-tower has a fan vault of the Wastell type and the design of the court as a whole is not inconsistent with an attribution to him.

As early as 1483 William Swayn was paying hagable rent on a house in Cambridge, in Market Ward. In 1491 he had as tenant of it JOHN SALTER, no doubt the carpenter who appears in the King's Hall accounts.[12] Since 1440 King's Hall had been in possession of the advowson of Chesterton, and the college accounts between 1483 and 1500 contain entries of payments made to Thomas Swayn of Chesterton, thatcher, for work done on their buildings there and also on the college buildings. The thatcher may have been the father of William Swayn the mason, who seems to have been identical with a parishioner of Chesterton who was living there between 1500 and 1525. The accounts of 1499–1500 record a payment of 12d. 'to W. Swanne pro le ferey apud Chesterton'.[13] This ferry belonged to an inn by the river called the Tabard, and both are mentioned in the will of William Swayn of Chesterton in 1525 as belonging to him.[14] The riverside situation of Chesterton would have had special advantages for a mason contractor supplying stone which reached Cambridge by water.

William Swayn was one of the executors of Thomas Philippe of Chesterton (†1504)[15] and also executor of the will of William Sade of Chesterton (†1515),[16] possibly identical with William Sadde, whose name appears in the pay-roll of masons working at King's College Chapel in 1508.[6] In 1522 William Swayne of Chesterton was granted exemption from serving on juries,[17] probably on account of his age. The will of William Swayn of Chesterton (dated 4 May and proved 4 June 1525) is that of a well-to-do man. His Chesterton property included 'the Cheker' and five cottages, besides the Tabard, where he lived, and the ferry belonging to it; and in Cambridge he owned a tenement 'that I late purchased of John Bell of Cambridge', and another 'whiche was late Disshers And afterward of the Kyngis College'. He left 20s. to the high altar and 20s. to the reparation of Chesterton Church, also a fother of lead 'when the parisshoners shalhaue nede therof', four new torches and 3s. 4d. to the reparation of the bells, and he made provisions for a chantry in the church. There were also bequests to the four houses of Friars in Cambridge and to the Prior and Canons of Barnwell, and £8 was to be distributed to poor people in Chesterton. He appointed his wife Isabel sole executrix. Two sons, Godfrey and Richard, are named. All his children were under age, so that if the will is that of the mason he must have married late or have taken a second wife much younger than himself.

A.O.
[1] *TCM, KHA*, xviii, 296; [2] *KHA*, xix, 86; [3] *Ibid.*, 147, 194; [4] *Ibid.*, xx, 103; [5] *Ibid.*, 229; [6] *KCM*, Building Acc., 1508–09; [7] *KCM*, Building Accs., 1509–1515; [8] CGB, 'B', pt. i, 236; [9] WCC, II, 200; [10] LEC, 314–36; [11] SEJ, vol. XVI, No. 93 (Dec. 1890); [12] CBD, 61, 64; [13] *KHA*, xix, 299; [14] *PRP, CCE*, 'J', 102v.; [15] PCC, 20 Holgrave; [16] *Ibid.*, 8 Holder; [17] LPH, III, pt. ii, p. 892

SWIFT, Richard [Swyft] (*fl.* 1375–1406) Carpenter

On 18 May 1375 a commission was issued to William Potenham, Richard Swift, carpenter, and Thomas de Trafford, to take craftsmen and materials for the repair of the castle of Edward, Prince of Wales at *Berkhampstead*, Herts. In 1377 two 'petites canons' presumably toy guns, were delivered to the young King Richard II by the hands of Richard Swyft the King's Carpenter.[1] Soon after the accession of Richard II, HUGH HERLAND, the chief carpenter, was appointed controller at the works of Rochester Castle, and apparently in anticipation of this, Swift was on 1 January 1377/8 appointed to be the King's Master Carpenter during pleasure, with 12*d.* a day and a winter robe yearly. His salary was paid at long intervals for it was not until 1382 that he received £55 13*s.* 0*d.* for his pay from 14 April 1378 to 2 May 1381.[2] He received an additional grant of £5 0*s.* 8*d.* yearly on 12 March, a pension which he retained for nearly thirty years.

On 27 January 1379 John Polymond of Southampton and Richard Swift were ordered to sell the bark and branches of 60 oaks which the keeper of Melchet Forest had been commanded to deliver to Swift, and thus to pay for the carriage of the timber to *Southampton* for the works in erection of a tower and four turrets and for making a bridge and three gates and three portcullises there. Swift and Hugh Herland were commissioned on 14 March 1381 to impress carpenters for service in Brittany, and Swift continued to hold his office until April 1394, when he surrendered it to NICHOLAS WALTON; his 'small house with two low chambers annexed, together with the small garden . . . within the palace of Westminster' was granted shortly afterwards to John Stepenhull, one of the yeomen of the kitchen. His fees of 1*s.* a day were allowed in Geoffrey Chaucer's account as clerk of the works for the period 12 July 1389–17 June 1391.[3]

Swift is last heard of on 22 July 1406, when he surrendered his pension of £5 0*s.* 8*d.* in favour of William de Lynne.

CPR, passim
[1] T. F. Tout in EHR (1911), 666–702; (*PRO*, E.101–396–15, 397–19, 398–1); [2] *PRO*, E.364–15 (J); [3] LRC, IV, 293, 304; *PRO*, Foreign roll, 14 Ric. II (C) (*L.F.S.*); cf. HKW, II, 843

SWIFT, Richard II (*fl.* 1428–1429) Carpenter

Of 'Ippesley' (Ipsley), Worcs. At *Grafton Manor*, Worcs., on 25 June 1428 he undertook to build a barn for Humfrey Stafford by 3 May 1429, for £20 with meat and drink. There were to be ten bays each of 10 feet, and 22 feet wide; the walls were to be 12 feet high.

BL, Add. Ch. 73588 (*N.L.R.*)

SWYNNOW, Andrew [Swynhoe] (*fl.* 1481–) ? Mason

Named in an inscription as having begun the south jamb of the tower arch of *Coton Church*, Cambs., on St. Wulstan's Day (7 June) 1481.[1] There is an identical tower arch with the same mouldings at *Caldecote*, nearby.[2]

[1] CAR, 87; [2] (*E.G.*)

SYEKES, John [Sykys] (*fl.* 1531–†1546) Carpenter

Made timberwork for the new church of *St. Michael-le-Belfry, York*, in 1531–32 by contract, under which he was paid £8 3*s.* 4*d.* On 7 February 1543 he was appointed Master Carpenter at *Berwick-upon-Tweed* and held office until his death, being succeeded by John Sykys junior on 2 July 1546.[1]

RFY, 107
[1] HKW, III, 417; IV, 618

SYKES, Robert (*fl.* 1476–1495) Carpenter

Appointed Master Carpenter of *Pontefract Castle* on 3 May 1476 in succession to Thurstan Euxton. Sykes continued to hold the position under Henry VII until 1495 or later, but had no successor.

HKW, II, 1060; III, 178n.

SYLVESTER, Robert (*fl.* 1542–1552) Mason

Was appointed master mason to the Court of Augmentations on 29 September 1542, along with JOHN PARKER, master carpenter. In 1545 he was given £1 for his expenses in riding to St. Albans, Ampthill and Dunstable. He was succeeded by RALPH HILLES on 29 September 1552.

HKW, III, 420; IV, 75

SYMON, Walter (*c.* 1484–*fl.* 1534) Mason

Accounted for £40 out of a total of over £100 spent on building and repairs at *St. John's Hospital, Bath*. Giving evidence in 1534 as to this expenditure of the Prior of Bath, Symon put his age at about 50. His colleague William Grace, mason, was about the same age, and William Hunt, mason, about 60. These works had been done in the time of Prior William Holoway alias Gibbes, since 1525.

SRS, XXVII (1911), 156 (*N.L.R.*)

Sympson—see SIMPSON

Symyth, John—see SMYTH

TABBARD, Simon (*fl.* 1440–1469)
Carpenter

Carpenter of *Norwich Cathedral Priory* from 1440 to 1469. At first employed by the Sacrist on piece-work of various kinds, and in 1441–42 on the repair of the great gates he worked also for the Communar and Pitancer on the new Dorter in 1450–51, and in the following year was paid £5 6s. 8d. by the Sacrist for making a certain work behind the high altar (*pone magnum altare*). In 1454–55 he was repairing the nave roof and hanging the church doors, and in 1465–66 working above the vaults of the cloister.[1] Tabbard seems never to have been paid a retaining fee, and undertook work for other employers; he was, for example, engaged on the roofs of the cloister of the *Great Hospital, Norwich*, in 1450–51 and 1456–57.[2]

[1] *NCM*, rolls 92, 288–90, 293–6, 299, 300, 1088, 1092;
[2] *NMR*, G. 24.a

Taillour, Richard—see TAYLLOUR

TAILLOUR, Robert (*fl.* 1449–1450) Mason
With ANDREW MASON, rebuilt the chapel of *St. Mary Magdalene's Hospital, Durham*, in 1449–50. Fragments remain.

DAR, I, 238

TANNER, John (*fl.* 1412–1424) Carpenter
In 1412–13 was master carpenter in charge of making a new floor for the principal chamber in *Stockton Manor*, Durham, for the bishop. Carpenter of Thomas Langley, Bishop of Durham; in 1423–24 he supervised the rebuilding of the *Crown Inn, Rochester*.

BRB, 90
DAR, Stockton account (*M.G.S.*)

TARELL, John (*fl.* 1399–   ) Carpenter
In 1399 was master carpenter at the building of the *Sessions House* at *Ipswich*. He was paid £1 14s. 7d. for 83 days' work, i.e. at 5d. a day. *Thomas TARELL* was paid at the rate of 3d. a day for the same period.

(*A.O.*) *PRO*, E.101–575–28

TAVERNER, John (*fl.* 1413–   )
Carpenter
Of *Halstead*, Essex; on 18 November 1413 contracted with the Dean and Chapter of St. Paul's, London, to make the new roof of the choir in the parish church of *Halstead*. It was to be a 'chare' roof like the chancel roof of Romford Church; apparently a wagon roof, boarded throughout. He was to be paid 19 marks (£12 13s. 4d.), and for having the walls repaired and raised 3 feet, an additional £1 6s. 8d. and new cloth for a gown worth 6s. 8d. This roof still exists, but is covered by a plaster ceiling.

SHB, 490–1; (*SPM*, MS. 329)

TAYLLOUR, Richard le [Taillour] (*fl.* 1336–1338) Mason
Master mason at *Carisbrooke Castle*, Isle of Wight, succeeding ADAM BRETON in February 1336. A new tower over the gate was being built at the time, with works continuing until 1338.

SHB, 60; *PRO*, E.101–490–21 (*L.F.S.*); HKW, II, 593

TAYLOR, William [Taylour] (*fl.* 1519– †1543) Mason
Possibly identical with the William Masson working at *Westminster Abbey* in 1518–19; from 1519–20 Taylor was employed as a full-time *cementarius* on the works of the nave until he became joint master mason there with JOHN MOLTON after the death of HENRY REDMAN on 10 July 1528. Taylor's name appears in the account rolls until 1533–34, when he worked for 28 weeks.[1] In 1532 he had charge of arrangements for Abbot Islip's burial.[2] On 10 February 1542/3 administration of the goods of William Taylor of Middlesex, deceased, was granted to his widow Elisabeth.[3]

(RNW)
[1] *WAM*, 23604–26; [2] *WAM*, 6325; [3] *PPR*, Consistory of London (Bishop of Westminster), 216 Thirlby

TEGGE, Richard (*fl.* 1515–1519) Carpenter
Master carpenter in charge of the timber works of *Thornbury Castle* for the Duke of Buckingham between 1514/15 and 1518/19. His name is recorded incidentally in a memorandum of disallowed items in the accounts.

WAM, 22909

TEINFRITH (*fl. c.* 1057–1066) Carpenter
'Churchwright' to Edward the Confessor at the time of the building of *Westminster Abbey* in 1050–65. This probably implies that he

was a carpenter experienced in framing the roofs and timber fittings of churches. He received a grant of land at Shepperton, Middlesex, at a date *c.* 1057–66.

(LWR, 19); HAW, 292, 353–4, 573; F.E. Harmer in EHR, LI (1936), 98

TEMPAS, John (*fl.* 1515–   ) Mason

Master mason from Boston, Lincs., brought to *Louth* in 1515 to finish the spire, after the refusal of CHRISTOPHER SCUNE to do so. Tempas and his apprentice worked at Louth from 25 June until the completion of the work on 15 September 1515, though Tempas was absent for two whole weeks at the beginning and end of August. He was paid 3*s.* 4*d.* a week for himself and 2*s.* 8*d.* for his apprentice, as well as travelling expenses, and rewards of 2*s.* at his first coming and 6*s.* 8*d.* when the work was finished. It seems probable that Tempas was the master of the lantern of the famous *Boston* 'Stump'.

DCL, 176–9

Temple, William—see FRANKELYN

TERELL, Robert (*fl. c.* 1540–   ) Mason

Mason of Fremington, Devon; built a guild chapel (the north aisle) to the church of *Heanton Punchardon*, Devon. He was to be paid £46 13*s.* 4*d.* for the work, intended to be 80 feet long by 14 broad, but the length was curtailed by 6 feet owing to the existence of an old vestry, and a dispute arose as to payment at some time in the years 1539–44. The work is of a rough character, and the windows have uncusped elliptical heads to the lights.

PRO, ECP, 1074, 18

Termassone, Arnold—see HERMANZONE

TEYNHAM, Thomas [Tenham] (*fl.* 1429–†1488) Mason (*Teynham, Kent*)

Was an apprentice mason at *Canterbury Cathedral* in 1429, and appears in lists of *lathami* there in 1433 and 1437.[1] From April to June 1442 he was a freemason employed on the works of *Eton College*, and he was warden of the masons there by 1445–6 and until the end of 1448.[2] In 1454 he was again one of the lodge masons at Canterbury Cathedral.[3] In 1468–69 he was paid 13*s.* 4*d.* for two livery cloaks due to him from St. Augustine's Abbey, Canterbury, a probable indication that he held the office of master mason to the Abbey.[4] Thomas Tenham of the parish of St. George, Canterbury, made his will on 11 February 1487/8 and it was proved on 11 August 1488.[5] He desired to be buried in the cemetery of St. Augustine's Abbey, to whose 'New work' he left 3 quarters of corn; his wife Elen and son William Tenham are mentioned.

William TEYNHAM, mason, was admitted to the freedom of Canterbury by redemption in 1483; he may have died in 1500–01.[6] (*A.O.*)

[1] *Bodl.,* Tanner MS. 165; [2] AQC, XLVI; [3] Tanner MS. 165; [4] C. Cotton in AC, LI, 100; [5] CCC, Arch. Reg. 8, *f.* 71; [6] Cant. Wills, C.vi. 11

TEYNTON, John de (*fl.* 1324–1336) Mason (? *Taynton, Oxon.*)

Master mason (*cymentarius*) in charge of work on the walls and battlements of *Gloucester Castle*, begun on 30 September 1324. The work included operations on the 'gate towards the meadow'. Teynton was paid 2*s.* a week, while each of three masons working under him received 1*s.* 8*d.*[1] Teynton may have been the unnamed mason in receipt of 2*s.* weekly who appears in the accounts of 1322–24 as repairing the gate towards Edward's Chamber.[2] Teynton was presumably the 'Master John the mason' who gave expert evidence at a survey of the castle in 1336, along with NICHOLAS OF CAMPDEN.[3]

[1] *PRO,* S.C.6–854–8; [2] *Ibid.,* 854–7; [3] HKW, II, 655

Teynton, John alias Robyns—see REGINALD ELY

THACKER, William [Thakker] (*fl.* 1526–1538) Marbler

Admitted to the freedom of the City of Norwich in 1526 as a freemason, son of John Thakker, butcher, who had been made free in 1455.[1] In 1538 was paid for laying a gravestone in *Norwich Cathedral* with a brass on it, and for his 'bourdage', 3*s.* 8*d.* in all.[2]

[1] EFN; [2] J.R. Greenwood in MBB 27 (1981), 5

THEOBALD the Mason (*fl.* 1170–1171) Mason

Theobald *Cementarius* was paid 5 marks (£3 6*s.* 8*d.*) for his work on the walls of *Winchester Castle* in 1170–71, besides another 5 marks (received as 'Thedbald') for unspecified services.

PR, XVI, 34, 35

THIRSK, John [Thresk, Thrisk, Triske, Crowche] (*fl.* 1420–†1452) Mason

Came from Yorkshire, presumably from the town of Thirsk; his original name seems to have been Crowche. At Michaelmas 1420 he was warden of the masons working at *Westminster Abbey* and received a robe of the suit of the esquires but without fur, price 12*s*.; at this time he took over active control of the works from WILLIAM COLCHESTER. For the year running from Christmas 1420 Thirsk received the fee of £10 as chief mason 'in the place of Master William Colchester for the disposing and ordering of the whole work', while in 1421–22 he was given a furred robe of the suit of esquires, price 13*s*. 4*d*. He continued to hold the office until his death. His fees varied from time to time, as from 1424 until 1430 he was paid for actual work at 6*s*. 8*d*. a week with a yearly robe price 13*s*. or 13*s*. 4*d*. From 1430/1 to 1450/1 he received a fee of £5 a year, with robes price 13*s*. until 1431/2; 14*s*. until 1442/3; 13*s*. 4*d*. until 1449/50, in which year £1 was also contributed to his rent. In the year 1450/1 he received no robe, but £2 of his rent was paid by the Abbey.[1] Apart from the continuation of the work of the nave, Thirsk was responsible for the beautiful chantry of Henry V, inserted in the eastern ambulatory. The work of this chantry lasted for many years. In 1422–23 Thirsk was paid for making the great east window of *St. Margaret's Church, Westminster*.[2] Thirsk's work in the Abbey also included the great altar-screen finished in 1440–41.[3]

John 'Triske, Magister de les Fremasons' was in 1434–35 paid £1 13*s*. 3*d*. for a statue of St. Thomas of Canterbury for the river front of the Lollards' Tower at *Lambeth Palace*, built for Archbishop Chichele. In 1435–36 Thirsk was admitted to the Skinners' Fraternity of the Assumption of Our Lady, in company with THOMAS MAPILTON and in 1438 an inventory of the goods of John Bradford of York, mason, showed that Thirsk owed his estate the sum of £1, which ranked as a desperate debt. Thirsk is described as 'John Thryske master of the masons at Westminster'.[4]

Henry VI, about 1448–49, decided to have a tomb for himself built in Westminster Abbey, and going there to select the position 'commanded a mason to be called to mark out that ground. Whereupon by th'advyse of th'Abbot aforesaide oone callyd Thurske that time being Master mason in the making of the Chapelle of King Henry Vth. which mason incontinently came out and then and there he by the commandment of the said King Henry the VIth and in his presence

with an instrument of iron whiche he browght with hym marked out the lengthe and brede of the said sepulture there to be made in the place aforesaid.'[5] Henry VI was of course not buried in the Abbey, but eventually at Windsor. (See also ESSEX, JOHN.)

Possibly as a result of his interview with the King, Thirsk was granted for life the office of master mason in *Windsor Castle*, on 28 June 1449.[6] He did not live long to enjoy his new office, as he died towards the end of 1452. He was succeeded at Westminster Abbey by JOHN SMYTH I and at Windsor Castle by ROBERT STOWELL, appointed on 12 November 1452.

(WKM)

[1] RNW; *WAM*, 23489, 23494–23518; [2] *WAM*, 19663–64; [3] TWA; [4] *LP*, Court Roll no. 562 (*C.R.D.*); cf. GLP, 52–6; YTE, iii, 195; [5] A, LXV; [6] CPR 1446–52, 256

Thirsk, Simon—see TRESK

THOMAS, John (*fl.* 1456–1466) Carpenter

Carpenter to the Bishop of Winchester. In 1456–57 John Thomas was working at *Wolvesey Palace, Winchester*, on the making of the Janitor's new house, taking 6*d*. a day, while John Thomas, junior, who worked with him, received 5½*d*. John Thomas, senior, also received 3 yards of russet cloth as his winter livery as one of the bishop's servants, under the terms of his contract of employment. He was perhaps identical with the Thomas Carpenter who in the same year made doors and other woodwork, and the roof of the new tower for *Farnham Castle*, and made a partition in the great chamber of *Winchester House, Southwark*.

In 1459–60 John Thomas (perhaps the younger man) was paid 5½*d*. a day for 62 days' work on the east side of the granary and south side of the grange at Wolvesey, but it was probably John Thomas the elder who in 1462–63 made a desk for the bishop's oratory, a great bed for the chamber before the door of the wine-cellar, set boards in the window-seats of the lord's high chamber, and executed repairs at the rate of 6*d*. a day.

In 1464–65 John Thomas was doing repairs at Wolvesey at the rate of 5*d*. a day, but was paid 6*d*. in the next year when the palace was repaired before a visit from the Duke of Clarence.

PRO, Eccl. 2-2-155827, 155828, 155831, 155832, 2-3-155833

THOMAS, William (*fl.* 1415–1420) Carpenter

Carpenter employed from 1415 on preparing timber for the roodscreen of *Bridgwater Church*, Som. He was connected with the work until its completion about 1420.

SRS, LVIII, Nos. 576, 601

THOMAS the Carpenter (*fl.* 1214–1229)
Carpenter

On 21 November 1214 orders were given by King John to pay his carpenters, Master Nicholas de Audeley (AUNDELY) and William Angl' (WILLIAM ENGLISHMAN) at 9*d.* a day, Robert de Albemont (ALBEMUNT) and Thomas at 6*d.* a day, and Hugh de Barentin, Laurence de St. Anguino, and Baudewin at 3*d.* a day.[1] Soon after this, William Anglicus seems to have died, and by 17 August 1218 Master Thomas, then the King's Carpenter in *Nottingham Castle*, had been granted the pension of £5 a year which William had had, in addition to his daily wages.[2] Orders were made from time to time for the payment to Thomas of this pension, of his wages at 9*d.* a day, and for the issue to him of livery or a sum of 20*s.* in lieu of it.[3] On 2 November 1221 Master Thomas was sent with his fellows Burnell (RALPH BURNELL) and Robert (de Albemunt) to repair the King's houses at *Geddington*, Northants., a work which lasted for the next year.[4]

On 30 January 1222/3, 3 marks (£2) were issued to Thomas the Carpenter of *Windsor Castle* and his two mates in part payment of their liveries, and Master Thomas was also given 20 marks to begin the King's Hall at Windsor, in part payment of 70 marks owed to him for that work. A further payment of 20 marks was ordered on 3 May, and another 15 marks on 15 September. On 23 January 1223/4 he received a reward of £1.[5]

By the summer of 1224 work on this hall must have been well advanced, for on 26 May the Sheriffs of London were ordered to supply 100 of fir wood for doors and windows of the hall at Windsor, to Master Thomas the Carpenter; on 24 June he was ordered to go with his fellows to Bedford to take part in the siege, but by 13 November he was back at Windsor, another 10 marks in part payment of the works being then issued to Master Thomas the Carpenter and Nicholas his mate.[6]

On 7 July 1225 Henry fitz Aucher was ordered to cause Master Thomas the King's Carpenter to bring 20 oaks from the park of Havering, Essex, for the work of a small tower made at the *Tower of London*.[7] On 15 December Matilda, wife of Master Thomas the Carpenter, received 15*s.* for a robe.[8] Thomas continued as one of Henry III's chief carpenters, receiving regular fees, until 1229.[9] In July 1227 he and Master Nicholas were in charge of the transport of mangonels from Rochester Castle to Sandwich and thence to Portsmouth, and a month later they were obtaining timber from Herefordshire to make three mangonels and two petraries,[10] but Thomas seems usually to have been engaged on architectural work.

(HWC)

[1] HLC, I, 178b; [2] *Ibid.*, 368; [3] *Ibid.*, 370b, 419b, 441b, 449b, 473; [4] *Ibid.*, 477b, 480b, 527b; [5] *Ibid.*, 531b, 543b, 557, 564; [6] *Ibid.*, 601b, 606b; II, 7; [7] *Ibid.*, II, 49; [8] *Ibid.*, 90; [9] *Ibid.*, 13, 39, 44, 100b, 104, 117b, 128, 141; CLR 1226–40, 7, 14, 24, 37, 41, 60, 70, 79, 82, 92, 110, 118, 121; [10] CLR, 1226–40, 41, 47

Thomas the Carpenter—see PAGE; TURRET

Thomas the Mason—see DENYAR; WALEYS

THOMAS the Mason I (*fl.* 1230–†*c.* 1250)
Mason

Master mason (*cementarius*) of *Lichfield Cathedral* during the period *c.* 1230–50, when he is mentioned in several deeds. He died before 1254, leaving to his son WILLIAM FITZTHOMAS properties in Lichfield which he held by rent of 18*d.* and 14*d.* yearly.

LRA, Nos. 33, 34, 36, 100, 213

THOMAS the Mason IA (*fl. c.* 1230–*c.* 1253)
Mason

Thomas the Mason (*cementarius, Machun, le Masun*) appears at Glastonbury, Somerset, from *c.* 1230 until *c.* 1250, holding land of the abbey in Glastonbury and at 'Domerham' (South Damerham, Hants), and also acting as a witness to deeds. From *c.* 1230 onwards he is described as master (*Magister T. Cementarius*), and he was presumably master mason to *Glastonbury Abbey*. He had probably died before the appointment of ADAM DE NORTHAMPTON on 9 June 1253. It is possible that he was identical with THOMAS NORREYS.

(*L.S.C.*) SRS, V, 111, 169; LXIII, 252, 258, 262, 269, 298, 303, 305

THOMAS the Mason II (*fl.* 1243–1252)
Mason

Robes against Christmas were granted to 'Master Thomas the King's Mason' at *Windsor Castle* on 22 December 1243,[1] and he was mentioned as master mason there in 1248. In October of the following year the keepers of the works at Windsor were given £40 for the completion of the works and for making of the barbican, which the King had provided to be made by the counsel of Master Thomas the Mason and Master Simon the King's Carpenter.[2] (See NORTHAMPTON, SIMON.) On 7 April 1252 the Royal Wardrobe was ordered to provide a robe for Thomas the Mason of Windsor, and another for his wife, of the King's gift.[3]

HWC

[1] CCR 1242–7, 148; [2] CLR 1245–51, 256; [3] CCR 1251–3, 73

THOMAS the Mason III (*fl. c.* 1175–1190) Mason

Perhaps master mason of *Bath Abbey, c.* (1174–91), when he was witness to a charter there. He may have been 'The Master of WELLS'.

HMC, *Wells,* I, 470

THOMAS the Mason IV (*fl.* 1286–1299) Mason

Was master mason at the rebuilding of *Cambridge Castle* between 1286 and 1299, being paid 2s. 6d. a week and taking a robe worth £1 at Christmas. The work included a hall, curtain-wall, great gate, a 'new tower towards the East' built between 1286 and 1288, and another new tower near the hall, built in 1295–99.[1] The design was probably by one of Edward I's principal craftsmen, such as Master JAMES OF ST. GEORGE. In 1287 Master Thomas accompanied Geoffrey Andrew, one of the viewers of the work, on a journey to Peterborough, perhaps to arrange for supplies of stone, which came from Barnack.[2]

[1] CAC, XXVI, 66 ff.; *PRO,* E.101–459–15, 16 (*L.F.S.*); [2] PCA, 9

THOMAS the Mason V [le Masun] (*fl.* 1323–1327) Mason

Witness to a document at *Wells Cathedral* in 1323 in company with members of the Chapter. He was presumably the master in charge of the works, and probably identical with THOMAS WITNEY. The lay subsidy of 1327 names 64 citizens of Wells, among whom three were assessed at 20s. each, then three at 10s., one of whom was Thomas 'Mascon'. This was very probably the cathedral master (cf. IVO DE RAGHTON, SIMON the Mason I, for comparable status).

HMC, *Wells,* I, 225; SRS, III, 272

THOMAS the Mason VI [*Lathomus*]

(*fl.* 1330–1332) Mason

Master mason in charge of work at *Merton College, Oxford,* in 1330–32, receiving 2s. 5d. per week, 2d. more than the other masons. The work in progress consisted of the crossing of the chapel. He was probably identical with THOMAS WITNEY.

(*E.M.J.*) *MRT,* Recs. 3661, 3665

THOMAS the Mason VII [Le Masson] (*fl.* 1355–1356) Mason

Mason to *Winchester Cathedral Priory* in 1355–56, when he was paid an annual fee of 20s. At this time Bishop Edington's work on the new west front was in progress. He may be the same Thomas 'Cementarius' who was given clothing in 1333–35 by the receiver of the Prior's treasury, though this was more probably THOMAS OF WITNEY.

WNC, Receiver's Accs. 1355–56; KCR, 124, 235

THOMAS the Mason VIII [Masoun] (*fl.* 1356–1360) Mason

Master mason of *Ely Cathedral* in 1356–60 where he received a fee of 13s. 4d. by contract, with a robe price £1 yearly, and was paid small sums for making moulds and other work; perhaps identical with THOMAS ENEMETHE or with THOMAS UFFORD.

CSR, II, 194; *CUL,* Add. MS. 6383, p. 11

THOMAS the Mason IX (*fl.* 1365–1366) Mason

Mason to *Halesowen Abbey,* Worcs., in 1365–66, when he was paid 10s. for his yearly fee, and payments were made for steeling and sharpening his tools.

(*H.M.C.*) *SA,* MS. 535

THOMPSON, Nicholas (*fl.* 1549–1558) Mason

Master mason at *Calais* in succession to JOHN WRIGHT, from 1549 until the surrender to the French in 1558.

HKW, III, 419

THORN, John (*fl.* 1439–1442) Carpenter

Between 1439 and 1442 was chief carpenter for works then in progress at *Saffron Walden Church,* Essex. In 1439 he supervised the felling of timber and was paid £7 in part for his bargain 'de le Roofe', the roof of the north aisle, completed in 1445.

A.O. CWW, ff. 13–21

THORNE, William (*fl.* 1519) Mason

The Mercers' Company of London was on 1 July 1519 granted by letters patent the right to retain in their service William Thorne, freemason, then working for them with 20 others, masons, bricklayers, carvers, joiners etc.

AQC, XLI, 136 (*N.L.R.*)

THORNGATE, Thomas (*fl.* 1522–†1534) Carver and Joiner

Of Goudhurst, Kent; made a bargain to carve a tabernacle for the image of St. Peter in the chancel of *Yalding Church* in 1522, at the costs of William Astyn.[1] The will of Thomas Thorngate, 'joyner' of Goudhurst, was proved in 1534.[2]

[1] SPE, VI (1906–10), 297; [2] PKW, Archdeaconry Register 20, *f.* 67 (*N.L.R.*)

THORNTON, Richard (*fl.* 1491–1492) Carpenter

In 1491 carpenter to the Mercers' Company ('our carpenter') when he was paid 4 marks (£2 13*s.* 4*d.*) a year for life. He was still the Company's carpenter in 1492.

LWA, 220, 232

THORNTON, William de (*fl.* 1359–   ) Mason

Mason in charge of repairs to the chancel of *Bonby* ('Bondeby') *Church*, Lincs., in 1359. He may have come from Thornton Abbey.

(*L.F.S.*)   PRO, E.101-458-28

Thresk, Simon de—see TRESK

Thrisk, John—see THIRSK

THURUERD (*fl. c.* 1020–1046) ? Mason

A bede-roll of the *Abbey of St. Benet Holme*, Norfolk, compiled *c.* 1200, contains the names of Thuruerd and EDWARD, builders of the church (*edificatores huius ecclesie*); presumably this refers to the church founded by Canute and built *c.* 1020–46.

DM, III, 62, 88; NRC, II, 33

THWAITES, Richard de (*fl.* 1313–1322) Mason

Mason in charge of the building of a new chapel at *Kenilworth Castle* from 1313–14, when over £140 were spent on the works, for some ten years. The chapel was probably that known as 'John of Gaunt's' in the lower ward of the castle. On 2 August 1322 orders were given to release to Thwaites provisions and other goods seized into the King's hands at the castle by reason of the forfeiture of Thomas, Earl of Lancaster.

VCH, *Warwicks.*, VI, 135

THWAYT, Richard de (*fl.* 1361–   ) Mason

Mason commissioned on 21 June 1361 to impress stonecutters to work at Stapleton and Roche, Yorks., to provide stone for *Hadleigh* and *Queenborough Castles*.

CPR 1361–4, 30

TICHEMERS, Hugh de (*fl.* 1307–1317) Mason

Master mason sent from London to Carlisle in August 1307, but then ordered to go to *Knaresborough Castle*, Yorks., where he had charge of works from 15 September but was repeatedly called away (see HUGH DE BOUDON). In 1315–16, as one of the principal masons of the City of London, he served on a commission instructed to elect six paviours of experience to repair the pavements of the city. In 1317 he was a surety for the rebuilding of works at Eltham Palace by defaulting masons (see MICHAEL OF CANTERBURY).

LKC, 187; HKW, II, 689, 931

TICHMARSH, John de [Tychemerssh] (*fl. c.* 1356–†*c.* 1361) Mason (*Titchmarsh, N'hants.*)

Was the Black Prince's mason for Chester, Flint, and North Wales in succession to HUGH OF HUNTINGDON, from 3 December 1356 until 1361. Tichmarsh drew official fees of 6*d.* a day from 29 September 1356, and in addition 4*d.* a day as supervisor of murage in the city of *Chester*. He was dead by 21 October 1361, and was succeeded in office by WILLIAM DE HELPESTON.

(HCH; ACC, 235); BPR, III, 236, 311, 424

Henry de TISCHEMERSH was a mason at *Westminster Palace* and the *Tower of London* in 1311–15, taking 5*d.* a day.

LKC, 186

Peter de TYTEMERSSHE was the first named of four masons who were members of a commission to inquire into the state of the *Tower of London* in 1335, and was a juror of Broad Street Ward, London, at coroner's inquests held on 30 November 1339 and 22 July 1340.

BHT, App. to pt. I, 273; SCR, 242, 261

TIDEMANN (*fl.* 1306–   ) Carver

Carver from Germany, working in London in 1306, when he had supplied a carved crucifix to the rector of *St. Mildred, Poultry*. This crucifix was confiscated by the order of Ralph Baldock, Bishop of London, on the ground that its arms were not of the true form of the Cross. Tidemann had to make an oath that he would henceforth neither make, nor suffer to be exposed for sale within the City or diocese of London, any such crucifix, and the offending object itself was to be handed back to Tidemann at some place outside the diocese (presumably Southwark). It was to be borne forth from the Priory of Holy Trinity, Aldgate, whither it had been taken at the bishop's order 'at early dawn or late in the evening, when it can be done most secretly and with least scandal', Tidemann surrendering the rector's bond for the purchase price of £23 sterling.

CSL, 473–4

TIGHELERE, Thomas le (*fl.* 1289–1317) Carpenter

Carpenter, miller, and contractor of Farnham, Surrey; in 1289 he rented High Mill and 'La Medmulle', with Bourne Mill, at £5 13s. 6d. a year. In 1307–08 he was paid £20 for building four new houses of timber, lath, and plaster, within the keep of *Farnham Castle*, the Bishop of Winchester his client supplying the timber. He also undertook to keep the roofs of the castle in repair for £1 a year.

In 1309 he was paid £21 12s. 0d. for making new dykes and a sluice for the pond of Bourne Mill, and in the next year he supervised similar work at the bishop's mill at Southwark, for which he was paid £10. In this year, too, he represented Farnham in Parliament as one of its two first M.P.s; obviously he must have been a man of considerable substance acquired by industrialism of a type rather unusual in the Middle Ages. He last appears in 1317, when £30 was paid to Thomas 'Tegulator' of Farnham, for repairs to the head of Frensham Pond.[1]

RMF, 54, 58, 146, 181
[1] *PRO*, Eccl. 2–159332

TILLEY, John (*fl. c.* 1485–1486) Mason

Circa 1485–86 was partner with RICHARD CUTTING in a contract for the building of the tower of *Little Thornham Church*, Suffolk, 'after the patron' (with certain alterations) of the tower at 'Easthorp', probably Thorpe Abbotts, Norfolk. An action was brought against the two masons for defective work.

A.O. PRO, ECP, 76–20

TILNEY, William of (*fl.* 1351–1377) Carpenter

Master carpenter of the king's works at *Calais*, with STEPHEN OF DUNMOW, in 1351–58. He was maimed and granted a pension of £10 a year which he was still receiving in 1377.

HKW, I, 428n.; II, 1054

Tirell, John—see TYRELL

Tiryngton, John—see TYRYNGTON

Tobbeson—see DOBSON

TODDE, John (*fl.* 1415) ? Mason

With Robert Todde and Nicholas Hayforth in 1415 agreed with Thomas de Langton and Thomas Rose to erect a cross chamber and a new entrance etc. for *Wynyard Hall*, Co. Durham.

ARH, II (1970), 2357 (*Londonderry* 11528)

TOFTS, Nicholas [Toftys] (*fl.* 1452–   ) Carpenter

Of Reach, Cambs.; on 6 June 1452 contracted to build the new roof of the nave of *St. Benet's Church, Cambridge*. This was destroyed in 1872, but drawings of it have been preserved.

SHB, 530–1; WCC, I, 282

TOMSON, John (*fl* 1538) Carpenter

With JOHN FORMAN, mason, was one of a commission to survey *Pontefract Castle*, Yorks., in January 1538.

HKW, III, 288

TONGE, Robert (–†c. 1477) Mason

Mason of York; possibly predecessor in office to ROBERT DAVYSON as sworn mason of the city.

(*G.P.J.*) YCR, I, 25

Tornour, Richard—see TURNER

TORRIGIANO, Pietro [Torrysany] (1472–†1528) Sculptor

Of Florence, Italy. About 1510 Torrigiano was in England, working on the tomb of Margaret, Countess of Richmond, mother of Henry VII, and on 26 October 1512 undertook by contract the tomb of Henry VII and Elizabeth of York, which he completed in 1518. While in England he also produced the monument of Dr. John Young (1516), formerly in the Rolls Chapel, now in the Public Record Office, and several works of portrait sculpture. He returned to Florence in 1519, but was again in England c. 1520–22.

TBK, XXXIII, 306–7

Totemound—see TOUTMOND

TOTENHAM, JOHN de, I, senior [Cotenham] (*fl.* 1325–1347) Carpenter

Was appointed sworn carpenter to the City of London in June 1325,[1] in 1332 was assessed to pay 1s. 4d. to the taxation, and was thereafter living in the parish of St. Martin Outwich.[2] In 1335–36 he was the second of the carpenters upon the commission to inquire into the state of the *Tower of London*.[3] In 1339 and 1340 he appeared at certain inquests concerning the parish of St. Martin Outwich,[4] and on 1 July 1342 Edmund son of Walter Cropyn acknowledged that he owed £100 to John de Totenham of London, carpenter.[5]

Finally, on 22 July 1347 'Master John de Totenham' was witness to an indenture concerning a great messuage in the parishes of St. Peter Cornhill, St. Benet Fink, and St. Martin Outwich.[6] This John was almost certainly the father of JOHN DE TOTENHAM II.

Between 1327 and 1347 Totenham was acquiring property in the parish of St. Martin Outwich and elsewhere in the City of London; his wife Alice is mentioned from 1344 onwards.[7] Some of his property was disposed of in 1373 by Walter de Tudenham who had married Totenham's daughter Joan.[8]

(LKC)
[1] CLB, 'E', 201; [2] UFT, 61ff.; CLB, 'E', 269; [3] BHT, App. to pt. i, 273; [4] SCR, 242, 258, 260; [5] CCR 1341–3, 552; [6] *Ibid.* 1346–9, 365; [7] LHR, 56 (19), 58 (16), 60 (110), 71 (24, 76–7), 72 (121), 74 (44); [8] LHR, 102 (25)

TOTENHAM, John de, II, junior [Tudenham] (*fl.* 1358–1368) Carpenter

In 1358 was the holder of a tenement belonging to London Bridge, in the parish of St. Martin Outwich, London. The tenement was on the west side of Bishopsgate Street, immediately to the south of the church of St. Martin, and had four shops annexed to it on the north and five on the south; the rent was 3s. yearly.[1] In 1363 John de Totenham became a sworn carpenter of the city, and was reappointed to the office on 13 March, 1367/8.[2] He may have died soon after.

In 1367 John de Totenham and Cristina his wife conveyed to Stephen atte Mersshe, the King's Chief Smith, and his wife Margery, a messuage in the parish of St. Mary Matfelon without Aldgate.[3] The tenement of Master John de Totenham in the parish of St. Martin Outwich is mentioned in 1375.[4] John and Christian were probably the parents of Margaret, first wife of HENRY YEVELEY, and her sister Isabella, wife of William Palmer, citizen and horse-dealer of London. Yeveley was in 1383 possessed of Totenham's tenement and shops

in the parish of St. Martin Outwich, apparently as Margaret's dower.[5]

(LKC)
[1] LBH, Deeds, S. R. 76d.; [2] CLB, 'G', 158, 223; [3] HPM, p. 144; [4] LHR, 103 (299, 300); [5] LMT, II, 262; BM, Harl. Ch. 58D.30

Totewyf—see also TUTTEWYF

TOTEWYF, Ralph ['Totewys'] (*fl.* 1279–†1294) Mason

Master mason employed at *Corfe Castle* in 1279–80, during the completion of the great entrance gatehouse. He was almost certainly identical with Master RALPH the Mason IV.

AJ, XXII (1865), 218

TOUTMOND, William [Totemound, Tudmund] (*fl. c.* 1400–1414) Carpenter

In *c.* 1400 was working on the King's house at *Sutton*, Middlesex. On the surrender of the office of King's Chief Carpenter by HUGH HERLAND at the beginning of 1405, the post was granted on 12 January to William Toutmond,[1] who like Herland was living at Kingston upon Thames. He received his yearly robe for 1408–09 by warrant of 24 November 1408.[2] Toutmond died in or before 1415. On 20 October 1415, Joan, widow of William Totemound, granted to John Lorchon a garden in Hethenstret, Kingston, bounded by the grange and garden of John Lorchon on the east and west, the garden formerly of Thomas Carpenter on the north, and the way leading to Feldereys-style on the south; a later deed, of 10 June 1427, mentions a piece of waste-land 73 feet long from east to west, and 2 feet wide, next to the corner tenement of Thomas Cryps in Thamestrete, Kingston, bounded by a tenement late of William Tudmund on the south, the highway from Thamesstrete to Bysshopeshalle and to the Thames on the north, Thamesstrete on the east, and the garden late of William Tudmund on the west.[3]

Toutmond's official work may be represented by the fine carved tester over Henry IV's tomb in *Canterbury Cathedral*, certainly the work of the royal craftsmen.

(HHH; HKC)
[1] PRO, E.101–502–15 (*H.M.C.*); CPR 1401–5, 479; [2] PRO, E.101–405–22; [3] KCA, Misc. Deeds, G.187, 218

TOWNSHEND, John (*fl.* 1473–1496) Carpenter

Was Master Carpenter at *Tutbury* under the Duchy of Lancaster by 1473–74 and continued to hold office under Henry VII until 1496.

HKW, II, 1060; III; 178n.

TRESK, Simon de [de Tresco] (*fl. c.* 1255–†*c.* 1291) Mason

Presumably from Thirsk, Yorks.; he was living in Lincoln from a date between 1251 and 1263, and may have been warden of the masons at *Lincoln Cathedral* under ALEXANDER the Mason III until the latter's death in 1258 or later. In documents of 1263 and later he is described as master and in 1274–75 specifically as Master of the work of the cathedral (*tunc magister operis matricis ecclesie*); he was certainly in office until early in 1291, when he seems to have been succeeded by RICHARD DE STOW II who had probably been his warden from *c.* 1276 in succession to SIMON DE PABENHAM I. He was the first witness to a grant by Simon de 'Pappenham', mason, in 1272.

Simon de Tresk held houses belonging to Barlings Abbey in the Bail at Lincoln, and also a property near the Eastgate belonging to Spalding Priory, which he held by a rent of £1 6s. 8d. a year and the duty of providing lodging for the prior with his servants when he came to Lincoln.[1] It is to be noted that he cannot have been identical with Simon de Beverley, *cementarius*, who acquired lands and buildings in the parish of St. Peter Eastgate, Lincoln, from soon after the middle of the 13th century, as they were both concerned in a deed of between 1257 and 1262.[2]

It is clear that Master Simon de Tresk was in charge of the building of the Angel Choir throughout, from its inception soon after 1256 until its completion in 1280 or a little later. He thus takes his place as one of the most significant designers of his time. It was his style, moreover, that his warden Simon de Pabenham took to York for the new church of St. Mary's Abbey, described by Brieger (1957) as 'the most grandiose representative of the style of the Angel Choir in the north'. The work of Lincoln Cathedral was certainly one of the vital nerve-centres of architecture in the later years of Henry III.

HML, 114; (*LDC*, D.ii–78–1–130, 80–1–141, 183); *BM*, Cotton MS. Faustina B.i, *f.* 57d; *LDC*, R.742; LRS, LXII, Reg. Antiq. ix, nos. 2483, 2511, 2535, 2555, 2560, 2618; LXVII, x, 2722, 2820–1, 2875 (*K.M.*)
[1] Spalding Cartulary, f. 283 (*K.M.*); [2] LDC, Reg. Antiq. no. 2724 (*K.M.*)

TRIELL, John (*fl.* 1406) Mason

On 9 May 1406 contracted with the Warden of Winchester College to make a new floodgate of freestone at the new Mill of *St. Cross* by Newport, Isle of Wight, at the rate of 4d. per square foot of stone.

WCM 17233

TUDDENHAM, Henry [Codenham, Tudenham] (*fl.* 1415–1427) Carpenter

Carpenter of Norwich; admitted to the freedom of the city in 1415–16.[1] In 1426–27 he carried out repairs to the *common inn* of the city (*The Peacock* in the Market Place), including a new bay-window. For this work he was paid £4 6s. 8d.[2]

(*A.O.*)
[1] EFN; [2] HTN, II, 65

Tudenham—see TOTENHAM

TUGNEY, Richard (*fl.* 1518–1519) Mason

Mason (*cimentarius*) of *Peterborough*, employed by the Sacrist to make a freestone chimney in 1518–19, for which he was paid 10s.

PCM, Sacrist's Acc. 1518–19, *f.* 247

TULLEY, Robert (–†*c.* 1481) Monk

Benedictine monk of Gloucester, and later Bishop of St. David's. He is often stated to have been the architect of the tower of *Gloucester Abbey* (now cathedral) built *c.* 1450–57, but he was in reality in financial control as 'master of the works'. There is a tradition that the builder was JOHN GOWER.

APD

TURNEPE, Nicholas (*fl.* 1337–1338) Mason

Mason in charge of building a sluice at (*King's*) *Lynn* in 1337–38, when he was paid by the town chamberlains at the rate of 3s. a week.

LCR, Ea. 7

TURNER, Richard [Tornour] (*fl.* 1481–1483) Carpenter

In March 1481 was working at *Colchester* 'upon the new tenanterys' of John, Lord Howard (later Duke of Norfolk), for which he received £8 3s. 4d. In October 1481 he undertook to take down Lord Howard's 'new house' at Colchester and lay the timber in a barn ready for it to be taken to Stoke-by-Nayland at Candlemas. There he was to set it up, making the 'gryse' and windows, all for £2 6s. 8d. In May 1482 he undertook to make a new wall at Colchester with a foot-and-a-half between the studs.

A.O. PNA (from *SA*)

Turner—see also TURNOUR

TURNOUR, John (*fl.* 1421–1422) Mason

Possibly master mason at the building of the new *Guildhall* of (*King's*) *Lynn* after the destruction of the old hall of the Trinity Guild by fire on 23 January 1420/1.[1] The guild accounts for 1421–22 show a payment of £21 to the workmen of John Turnour (*in Vadijs Johannis Turnour operancium ibidem*) engaged on the building. The timber roof was made by NICHOLAS and PETER ROLLESBY.

LCR, G. d. 57; HMC, 11R, III, 227
[1] HDL, 28

TURNOUR, William [Turner] (*fl.* 1484–1492) Mason

Was a mason at *Westminster Abbey* in 1484, under ROBERT STOWELL then the Abbey master mason. Turnour was never himself the master in charge. He was, however, on 3 November 1484, described as 'the king's maister mason', apparently in charge of Richard III's works at *Nottingham Castle*. On 11 February 1488 William Turnour of Nottingham, freemason, was disposing of a messuage in Castlegate; and on 2 May 1492 a grant of all lands in Welburn by Turnour and his wife Alice was enrolled.

(APD, Westminster); *WAM, Novum opus* rolls; SRN, III, 428, 431

TUROLD the Carpenter (*fl. c.* 1150–1200) Carpenter

Carpenter who was granted by the abbey of Burton-on-Trent a mill for a rent of £1 yearly, and in lieu of his fees for doing all the works of the church (probably *Burton Abbey* itself) belonging to his office, both of wood and lead.

WSS, 1916, 239

TURPYN, John (*fl.* 1457–1478) Mason

In 1457–58 executed the paving of the 13 bays of the east walk, plus one bay of the south walk, of the cloister at *Wells Cathedral*, for £6 11s. 3d. or ¾d. per square foot, with a reward of 10s. in addition. He was also paid 3s. 4d. for making three stone door frames for the doors of the plumbery.[1]

In 1478 John Turpyn, presumably the same man, was engaged in impressing masons for the work of *St. George's Chapel* in *Windsor Castle*.[2]

[1] HMC, 10 R. App. iii (1885), 289; *WLC*, Fabric roll 1457–58 (*L.S.C.*); CWF, 13; [2] HWC, II, 378, 399

TURRET, Thomas [Thomas the Carpenter, Thomas Wright] (*fl.* 1391–1397) Carpenter

Carpenter of *Ripon Minster* between 1391 and 1397. His pay varied from 5d. to 6d. a day, according to the time of year. During the winter of 1391–92 he made divers necessaries for hanging the sacrament above the altar, taking 1s. for two days' work; in January and February he repaired the timberwork of the south and central towers, and mended the stocks of the bells; he worked for 3 weeks at 2s. 6d., then at 2s. 9d. for the next two weeks. He worked almost constantly for the Minster authorities for the next three months, generally at 3s. a week; the work done included making a 'Glasehows', probably the glazier's workshop, repairs to the 'Ledehows', doubtless the plumber's shop, and work on a number of houses and on the belfry tower. At the end of May he was taking down boards from the old ceiling of the choir in the church, with an assistant, for a whole week.

In the autumn of 1392 he worked on a new chamber next the Chapter House, and had £3 10s. 0d. in part payment of £4 3s. 4d. which he was to have for making a new house next the churchyard. Other works during the winter included repairs to the windows of the north side of the church and those of the great tower, and making a wooden wheel for the bells. In October 1393 he made a windlass and began three weeks' work upon the great tower (*clocher*) and during the winter carried out a number of small tasks. During the last week of January 1394 he and John Mede his mate spent 5 days repairing defects in the great tower 'after the great winds at that time'. In May, Thomas made stakes for fixing the 'Tent of St. Wilfrid' in the fields at Rogationtide, and he had 13s. 4d. to make up the balance due to him for the construction of the new house south of the church in the previous year.

During the winter of 1396–97 Thomas was frequently called in to repair the great tower and to make and mend windows in the south tower, where he was to have £1 for his work by agreement. Turret was evidently not a contracting carpenter on the same large scale as his contemporary WILLIAM WRIGHT, but he seems to have been a competent routine craftsman, and he undertook the building of a complete timber-framed house.

SMR

Tuttewyf—see also TOTEWYF

TUTTEWYF, John (*fl.* 1438–   )

TWYFORTH, THOMAS

Carpenter

Second named of three carpenters, after RICHARD WODEMAN, who in 1438 undertook to make the timberwork of the *Guildhall, Canterbury.*

SHB, 510–12; *CRM,* Bdle. LVI A. (7)(*D.G.*)

TWYFORTH, Thomas (*fl.* 1364–1384)

Mason

Master mason of *Ely Cathedral Priory* in 1364–65 and 1383–84 when he is mentioned in the accounts of the keeper of the Lady Chapel, having a house and a furred robe.

Ely accounts (*S.J.A.E.*)

TYLLOK, Richard (*fl.* 1439–1441) Carver

Chief carver at *All Souls College, Oxford,* in 1439–41. He made desks and other fittings for the library, while in 1440 he received £2 16*s.* for making the angels in the chapel roof. When employed by time-work his rate seems to have been 4*s.* a week.

GOC

TYNEHAM, Alexander [Tynham] (*fl.* 1387–1392) Mason (*Tyneham, Dorset*)

Master Alexander Tyneham was Provost of Yeovil, Somerset, in September 1387,[1] at which time *Yeovil Church* was in process of erection, perhaps to the design of WILLIAM WYNFORD. The burgesses of Yeovil, in that or subsequent years, petitioned the chancellor to make Alexander Tynham, mason, to give up the Town Seal and other insignia of the office, from which they had discharged him.[2] It is not known for what reason Tyneham was discharged from the office. He was presumably identical with the 'Saundre' Tynam who was Bailiff of the Hundred of Stone, Somerset, in 1392.[3]

[1] Yeovil; Woburn's Almshouse Muniments, *ex. inf.,* John Goodchild esq. of Yeovil; [2] *PRO,* C.1–69–213; [3] *Ibid.,* C.1–69–70

TYNLEGH, John (*fl.* 1412–1413) Mason

Was probably a visiting master mason of *Exeter Cathedral* in 1412–13 when he viewed the ruin of the Chapter House with the Canons, and was paid 12*d.* for his trouble.

(BPE, 96); *FFE,* quoting *EDC,* 2668

TYPERTON, Nicholas (*fl.* 1381–)

Mason

On 24 December 1381 contracted to build the south aisle and porch of the church of *St. Dunstan-in-the-East, London,* to designs (*devyse*) of HENRY YEVELEY; he was to be paid 25 marks (£16 13*s.* 4*d.*) by instalments.

SHB, 462–3; AQC, XLII, 111

TYRELL, John [Tirell] (*fl.* 1441–*c.* 1455)

Carpenter

On 17 December 1441 John Tirell was appointed as the associate of WILLIAM CROFTON in the office of chief carpenter of the King's works at *Calais.* On 20 February 1443/4 Tyrell was granted the houses and shops at Calais attached to the office and on 12 November 1444 he was appointed to hold the whole office in place of Crofton. In August 1453 he was granted protection as master carpenter at Calais in the retinue of the Duke of Somerset, and was probably dead when JOHN PACCHE was appointed in his stead on 10 March 1454/5.

DKR, XLVIII, 349, 361, 364, 397, 404

TYRYNGTON, John [Tiryngton] (*fl.* 1325–1361) Mason

Perhaps from Terrington, Norfolk; was a working mason at *St. Stephen's Chapel, Westminster,* taking 4½*d.* a day in November 1325, along with Hugh de Tiryngton. He was concerned with work on the postern of the *Tower of London* in 1349;[1] in August 1351 he contracted with John Pouke, mason, to carry out mason's work at *Kennington Palace* for the Black Prince. In 1356 Tyryngton was one of the six freestone masons of London who met to agree upon the articles of the trade in the City of London. On 8 June 1353 and again on 14 March 1360/1 he was ordered to impress workmen for the new abbey of *St. Mary Graces-by-the-Tower, London.*[2]

(APD); KJY 468–3;
[1] *PRO,* E.101–468–3; 471–3; [2] *CPR* 1350–4, 465, 471; 1358–61, 567

Tytemerssh—see TICHMARSH

Ufford, John—see OFFORD

UFFORD, Thomas (*fl.* 1374–1376) Mason

Master Thomas de Ufford, mason (*cementarius*), is mentioned in the Sacrist's roll of *Ely Cathedral* for 1374 as receiving no fee because he had done no work that year. In 1376 a mason of this name of Saham (Soham, Cambs.) was party to a fine concerning property in Newmarket, Suffolk. (See OFFORD, JOHN; THOMAS the Mason VIII.)

[1] *CUL,* Add. 6389, p. 165; [2] *RPF,* 128

UFFORD, William (*fl.* 1394–1396) Mason

Between 1394 and 1396 made seven new fireplaces in chambers at the royal manor of *Old Windsor.*

HKW, II, 1008

Ulm, Henry—see THOMAS DOWLAND

Ulmo, Robert de—see HOLMCULTRAM

Umbyrvil, William—see HUMBERVILLE

UNDERDONE, William de [Underdown] (*fl.* 1325–1331) Carpenter

In 1325 was warden (*apparillator*) of the carpenters at *St. Stephen's Chapel, Westminster*, under Master WILLIAM HURLEY, taking 6*d.* a day. In 1331 he was paid by Richard Oxenden, Prior of *Christ Church, Canterbury*, for the timberwork of the monastic dormitory. Underdone had made this by contract for £7 6*s.* 8*d.*, while he was paid an extra of 16*s.* 11*d.* for works not mentioned in the contract.

[1] *PRO*, E.101–469–8; [2] *AC*, LVIII, 30

UNDERWOOD, John (*fl.*   —†*c.* 1443) Mason

Held the office of King's Mason for the castles of South Wales; he died before 23 July 1443 when the office was granted to JOHN LEWES.

CPR 1441–6, 188

UPPEHALLE, Richard (*fl.* 1297–   )

Recorded in an inscription as the founder of the work of the east walk of the cloister at *Norwich Cathedral*, begun in 1297. A stone on the north side of the Chapter House door bore the words: *Ricardus Uppehalle hujus operis inceptor me posuit*, of which the name alone is now visible.

(APD); HWI, 397; D. J. Stewart in AJ, XXXII (1875), 165

URRICUS the Engineer (*fl.* 1184–†*c.* 1216) Engineer

Was one of Henry II's engineers in 1184–85, when the King gave him a reward of £1, and the Sheriff of Surrey provided a further sum of £1 for his sustenance. In 1187–88 he was allowed £1 0*s.* 8*d.* for his cloths (*pannis*). In 1193–94 Urricus was in charge of the making of engines at *Nottingham*, and in the next year was mentioned as 'arbelaster' and 'balistarius'.[1]

Urricus may have built the stone domestic buildings of *Farnham Castle*, Surrey, which were in course of erection about this period[2] (see also MAURICE), and he may have been identical with WULFRIC.

In 1201 Urricus accompanied King John to Normandy to make engines;[3] and in 1210 accompanied the King to Ireland to the siege of Carrickfergus.[4]

On 13 November 1216 Master Urricus was stated to be dead, when Henry III made grants of the lands he had held at Canewdon and Wodeford, Essex, and Sutton, Surrey.[3]

[1] PR; [2] HBC, 52; [3] HRL, 14 (*D.F.R.*); [4] RKS, 15–16

VALE, Richard (*fl.* 1362–1377) Carpenter

Master carpenter of the works at *Dover Castle* from 1362 until 1377.

HKW, II, 639, 1052

Vallibus, Theobald—see WAUS

VANCASTELL, Giles (*fl.* 1477–1478) Carver

The second of two, presumably Flemish, carvers employed at *Windsor Castle* in 1477–78 to make an image of St. George and the Dragon, with St. Edward and a crucifix, for which they were paid £11 10*s.* 0*d.* (See VANGROVE, DIRIK.)

(*L.F.S.*)   *PRO*, E.101–496–17

VAN DALE, Walter (*fl.* 1524) Carver

In February 1524 the General Court of the Mercers' Company of London considered the making of a new retable for the altar in their chapel. 'In consideracion wherof was shewed a platt devised and drawen by oon Walter Vandale of Andewerp karver, whiche parson was brought hyther. . . for thentent aforsaid. Wheruppon a Platt therof was shewed vnto the said assemble with the which they were well content, and uppon that the said Walter was called yn before the said Courte . . . & he said he could do it for £90 Flemish'; the estimate was accepted.

LWA, 673–4

VANGROVE, Dirik (*fl.* 1477–1478) Carver

The first named of two, presumably Flemish, carvers employed at *Windsor Castle* in 1477–78 to make an image of St· George and the Dragon, with St. Edward and a crucifix, for which they were paid £11 10*s.* 0*d.* (See VANCASTELL, GILES.)

(*L.F.S.*)   *PRO*, E.101–496–17

VERTUE, Adam [Vertu] (*fl.* 1475–1485) Mason

Worked as a mason (*cementarius*) at *Westminster Abbey* from January to December 1475, taking 3*s.* 4*d.* a week, the standard rate. In May his son ROBERT VERTUE began work at 1*s.* 8*d.* a week. Between 1477 and 1485 Adam Vertu was paid £6 for 11 stone fireplaces for the lodgings over the new cellar at *Eltham Palace*. Adam may have been identical with ADAM LORD.

WAM, 23543–46; HKW, IV, 78

VERTUE, Robert [Vartu] (*fl.* 1475–†1506) Mason

Son of ADAM VERTUE; first appears as a junior mason at *Westminster Abbey* in May 1475, being paid 1s. 8d. a week; after a year this pay was increased to 2s. and he worked continuously until July 1478, in the years 1476–77 and 1477–78 being given a robe worth 8s. in addition to his pay. After two months' absence he worked again until February 1479–80, at the rate of 2s. 4d. a week, and taking each year a robe worth 9s.

After an absence of three years (probably his 'wander years'), he reappeared at the Abbey as a fully-trained mason in March 1482/3, and continued at work until 24 April 1490, taking 3s. 4d. in normal weeks, but being paid an extra 4d. a week for setting on occasion, and in 1484 for staying at the Reigate quarry for 4 weeks.[1]

He probably became the King's Master Mason after the death of THOMAS DANYELL about 1487 but he was not given a patent of appointment, as the practice seems to have been suspended by Henry VII. From October 1499 until July 1504 he was certainly in charge of work for the King at *Greenwich*.[2]

With his brother WILLIAM VERTUE he designed the new *Bath Abbey Church*, begun in 1501, and they were working there in 1503; Robert recommended THOMAS LYNNE for the position of resident mason.[3] Robert Vertue and his brother declared to Bishop Oliver King 'of the vawte devised for the chancelle. . there shall be noone so goodely neither in England nor in France. And therof they make theym fast and sure.'

In 1501 and 1502 Robert Vertue was paid £100 for building a new tower at the *Tower of London*[4] and in November 1502 £10 was advanced to him in part payment for 'the new platt' at Greenwich, by which a drawing for new works at the royal manor is to be inferred.[5] About this time 'Maister Vartu', probably Robert Vertue, or possibly his brother William, was paid £1 for work in connection with the church of *St. Mary-at-Hill, London*. This seems to have included windows in the tower and the building of a new south aisle, all carried out by Robert Mawnde or Mayndy, mason of Maidstone. A copy of Mawnde's contract 'was delyuerd to Maister Vartu' in 1502 and cost 4d.[6]

At this time he or his brother was also working for *St. Anthony's Hospital*, Thread-needle Street, London, whose Master's account for 1501–02 shows that £3 was paid 'To Vᵣtu the mason for stuff and making a new window'. The Hospital belonged to St. George's Chapel, Windsor.[7]

He must also have been occupied with the design of *Henry VII's Chapel* at Westminster whose foundation-stone was laid on 24 January 1502/3.[8] When estimates were submitted for various works in connection with the King's tomb in 1506, Robert Vertue, ROBERT JANYNS, and JOHN LEBONS were 'the King's three master masons' who estimated the cost of the stonework of the tomb.[9] Robert Janyns and John Lebons were witnesses to Robert Vertue's will on 10 May in that year, describing themselves as 'the King's Master Masons'.

Vertue died before the year was out, for the will was proved on 12 December by the executors, his wife Eleanor and his brother William Vertue.[10] In the will he refers to himself as 'citizen and freemason of London', desiring to be buried in the abbey of St. Augustine at Canterbury. He owned lands at Greenwich and at Canterbury, which he left to his wife for the benefit of his son William, who was still in his apprenticeship. Other bequests were to the parish church of St. Paul without Canterbury, and to his brother William, who was left 'my best gowne, my best doublett and my best Jackett, and my best ryng wt. a dyamond'.

Vertue's connection with Canterbury may explain the close relationship between his style and that of JOHN WASTELL. The direction that he should be buried in the abbey church of *St. Augustine, Canterbury*, suggests that he had been master mason there. Bequests in wills show that a new bell-tower was being built between 1461 and 1516;[11] and although the work must have been begun under another architect, Vertue may have been the master mason in charge from about 1490 onwards, during the years when at Christ Church, Canterbury, JOHN WASTELL was building the Bell Harry Tower. The interesting possibility thus arises that the two pre-eminent architects of Henry VII's reign were building contemporaneously and in healthy competition two rival towers in the city and this may explain both the differences and the basic likeness between the styles of the two men. It is hardly possible to draw any distinction between the styles of Robert and

William Vertue, and as the latter completed or continued his brother's works, they will be considered in connection with William's career.

(APD; WKM)
[1] *WAM*, 23543–53, 23557–64; [2] *BM*, Add. MS. 21480, *f.* 179 (*A.O.*); HKW, IV, 97; [3] SAP, LX, pt. ii, 1–4; [4] *BM*, Add. MS. 7099, *ff.* 70–1, 73, 78; [5] *Ibid.*, *f.*78; [6] LMR, 244–5, 254, 257; [7] *WSG*, XV.37.25 (*H.B.*); [8] LKC; LWR, 161ff.; [9] LPH, I, p. 142; [10] PCC, 8, 9, 10, 13 Adeane; printed in full HGE, 183–5; [11] AC, XXXI, 46–8 (*A.O.*)

VERTUE, Robert junior (*fl.* 1506–1555) Mason

Younger son of ROBERT VERTUE senior, mentioned in his father's will of 10 May 1506 and then apparently a boy (since his elder brother William was not yet out of his apprenticeship). He was presumably the Robert Vertue, master of the works of *Evesham Abbey* who received a pension of £6 13*s.* 4*d.* at the dissolution in 1539. He will have been the architect of the notable buildings of Abbot Clement Lichfield (1514–1539); the surviving *Bell Tower* and the Lichfield Chapels, both with fan-vaults of Westminster style, in the two parish churches of *All Saints* and *St. Lawrence, Evesham.*[1]

Vertue was probably living on 31 May 1555, when Richard Grace, former monk of Evesham, made his will.[2]

(*A.J.T.*)
[1] LPH, XV, 38; cf. *PRO*, E.315–254; [2] C.W. Clarke in *Vale of Evesham Historical Society's Research Papers*, II (1969), 27–37; cf. D. Knowles in EHR, LXXIX (1964), 776

VERTUE, William (*fl.* 1501–†1527) Mason

Is first heard of as master mason of the works of *Bath Abbey*, jointly with his brother ROBERT VERTUE, when the work began about 1501.[1]

About 1502–03 the vaults of the nave, aisles, and transepts of *St. George's Chapel* in *Windsor Castle* were in course of erection and it is probable that the Vertues, with ROBERT JANYNS (junior) were responsible for this work. At any rate, William Vertue and JOHN AYLMER, a London mason, contracted on 5 June 1506 to vault the choir of the chapel according to the roof of the body (nave), in seven severies or bays, together with the flying buttresses, parapets, pinnacles, and the carved figures of the King's beasts, finding all stone and timber with carriage and other necessaries; the work was to be completed by Christmas 1508, and Vertue and Aylmer were to be paid £700. Of this sum £100 was defrayed by Henry VII and Henry VIII, as is shown by two entries in the King's Books of Payments dated 7 July 1507 and 4 August 1509.[2] The first payment of £50 was made on behalf of 'the kings grace & my lord prince'. Another £200 was advanced for the work to the Dean of Windsor on 11 September 1511.[3]

Entries in documents at *King's College, Cambridge*, show that Vertue paid at least three visits to the college in connection with the completion of the chapel. On 1 May 1507 HENRY SMYTH, Vertue, and Lee were given wine,[4] doubtless at a conference at which plans for resumption of work on the unfinished building were discussed. Henry Smyth may have been the mason who was soon to be employed at the Savoy Hospital, work on which was begun in the following year, but he had a namesake who was comptroller of the works at Windsor, an administrative official whom Henry VIII in 1509 raised to the office of clerk and surveyor of the King's works throughout England. Lee was probably JOHN LEE, who was appointed joint master mason with JOHN WASTELL. In December 1509, when building was in full swing, William Vertue paid another visit to the college in company with HENRY REDMAN, perhaps to give advice about the fan vault. They were paid 37*s.* 4*d.* in reward, a fee which probably covered their travelling expenses.[5] A third visit is recorded by an entry in the kitchen accounts of the college. On 30 July 1512 Master Vertue dined in hall having Wastell as a companion.[6] Wastell's contract for the high vault had recently been signed, so that reading between the lines one may suppose that as the pre-eminent master of the fan vault Vertue had been summoned to give his advice just as the great undertaking was beginning.

Vertue was granted the office of King's Master Mason at the *Tower of London* and elsewhere, on 28 July 1510, with the usual fees of 1*s.* a day and a robe at Christmas. The office was said to have been lately held by THOMAS DANYELL, but it is probable that the practice of issuing patents for such offices had been in abeyance during Henry VII's reign.[7] From this time onwards Vertue was exceedingly busy, for the work of *Henry VII's Chapel* at *Westminster* continued for several years, and he must have had charge of this since his brother Robert's death in 1506.

At Windsor Castle he undertook a second contract on 20 December 1511, to vault the roof of the Lady Chapel and to finish the outside of the building with parapets and buttresses, as well as finishing the gallery between the chapel and the church (St. George's Chapel); he was to have £326 13s. 4d. for these works, which were to be finished by Michaelmas 1514. Henry Redman stood as surety for his completion of the work.[8]

Soon after this he began to design and supervise the buildings of *Corpus Christi College, Oxford*, built between 1512 and 1518 by WILLIAM EAST, a mason-contractor. Vertue and HUMPHREY COKE the carpenter provided, 'a double platt made for the over and the nether lodginge', i.e. ground- and first-floor plans; but these are not known to survive. Vertue visited the job from time to time, being paid at the rate of 1s. 8d. a day when he was there, as he was for example for 8 days at the end of June 1517, when the work was nearing completion. He also rode to the Taynton quarries.[9] While the work was in progress, certain members of Brasen-Nose Hall assaulted East so that his life was in danger and used threatening language towards Vertue and Coke; incidents began in the summer of 1512 and ended on 20 August 1514 when Formby, the late Principal of Brasen-Nose, was bound over to keep the peace towards the three masters of the works at Corpus Christi; and Coke and East undertook not to prosecute Formby outside the university.[10] About 1511 the Duke of Buckingham began building *Thornbury Castle*, Gloucestershire, and many details of this are so like work at Windsor and Westminster that it seems certain that one of the royal masons supplied the design. This is the more probable in that the Duke, as Lord High Constable, was closely connected with all Court affairs, and he had in 1508 contributed £20 towards the work of St. George's Chapel.[11]

A fire at the Tower of London in 1512 destroyed the old chapel of *St. Peter ad Vincula*, and the charming little Perpendicular church which took its place must be of Vertue's design, since he was *ex officio* mason of the Tower. It was finished by September 1520.[12] In September 1515 he supervised alterations at *Woking Palace*,[13] and in 1516 he and Henry Redman were each paid a fee of 13s. 4d. for devising the 'platte' of the west side of the court of *Eton College*, which includes Lupton's Tower. Humphrey Coke had a fee of 6s. 8d. at

the same time, and it is clear that these three men were the architects of the new work at Eton.[14] Vertue had probably designed Lupton's Chantry in the chapel, completed by 1515; the style appears to be his, and furthermore closely resembles that of an early drawing in ink, tinted, of the monument intended for Henry VI in *Westminster Abbey*.[15] This accomplished drawing, probably from Vertue's own hand, shows a turreted chantry chapel surmounting a flat-topped table-tomb with panelled sides.

This again shows marked resemblances to the tomb of Sir John Spencer (†1522) at *Great Brington*, N'hants. Another early drawing which may be from Vertue's hand is a design for a parapet of alternating pinnacles and panelled merlons, to a scale of 3 feet to 1 inch, apparently intended for Henry VII's Chapel.[16]

This great quantity of work was evidently more than he could undertake, for in 1519 he surrendered his grant as King's Master Mason, and on 12 September a new grant was made of the office to him and Henry Redman jointly. In the spring of 1520 Vertue took a prominent part in the preparations for the meeting between Henry VIII and Francis I of France which took place near Calais in June, at 'The Field of the Cloth of Gold'.[17] He also prepared apartments for the King of France in the Exchequer at Calais according to a 'platt', a drawing which is still in existence.[18] Vertue also found time to continue his supervision of the new work at Eton College, for he had a reward of 10s. there in 1520; the works were finished in the following year.[19] Among the works of Vertue's last years was the delightful cloister and cloister chapel of St. Stephen's in *Westminster Palace*, which must be attributed to him on the strongest stylistic grounds. The accounts show that he was paid his fees of £18 5s. 0d. for the year 1526.[20]

Vertue made his will on 11 March 1526/7, describing himself as 'William Vertewe Squier marster mason unto the Kinges grace'. He left property at Kingston upon Thames, including an inn called the Three Cranes, which was to go to his son-in-law John Agmondesham, and he also made a bequest to his daughter Margery, the wife of Thomas George. Vertue wished to be buried in Kingston Church, where his wife already lay; one of the witnesses to the will was JOHN

MOLTON, no doubt the mason of that name.[21]

Vertue's style was the culmination of the main tendencies of English architecture up to his time: these tendencies included the deliberate increase of surface ornamentation, and the introduction of quaintness, such as the multi-angular windows of Henry VII's Tower at Windsor, and the chapel at Westminster. Though such profusion of decorative work was carried to an extreme where it obscured the structural sense of the building, as at Henry VII's Chapel, Vertue's detail was applied with a masterly touch. His fondness for the fan vault enriched English art with some of the finest roofs the world can show, and the structural skill and masoncraft of Henry VII's Chapel are quite unparalleled. Even those who are ready to condemn as excessive the degree of ornamentation, can hardly fail to respond to the appeal made by the corona over the apsidal east end of the chapel, where six fans, and the rudiments of two more growing from the panelled arch, are made to support a pendant surrounded with the royal badges.

Another splendid design is that of the fan vault over the crossing at St. George's Chapel in Windsor Castle; it was not built until 1528, after Vertue's death, but the whole conception seems to be his. The broader treatment, with much less intermediate tracery, is in keeping with the high vaults of nave and choir. The side intersections of the rows of diamond-shaped panels containing shields is less fortunate than the rest of the design, and this may be an indication of the great artist's failing powers, though few architects have had a more profound and sustained influence in their own lifetime than William Vertue.

A particular interest attaches to Bath Abbey, as it is an example of the great church of the period, designed as a whole, and executed according to that design, without the changes of style found in our other cathedral and minster churches. An important afterthought at Bath was the decision to vault the main spans, instead of depending on a flat timber roof. When the change was made, the east window was already complete, but the west window, which was to have had a four-centred arch, like that of St. George's Chapel, had only reached the springing level, and was redesigned to suit the intended vault. The roofs seem to have been in progress by 1503, when the chancel vault had already been designed. The change of scheme must therefore have taken place during Robert Vertue's life, though it may have been William who devised the improved west window. The vaults of the choir and aisles were completed by 1518.

The west front is a satisfactory and straightforward piece of work, emphasising the structural forms of the building behind it, and adapted for the display of the ladders with angels going up and down, commemorating Bishop King's dream which led to the building of the new church. The rather weak tracery of the great window was probably added by John Molton, Vertue's successor. But perhaps the finest conception of all at Bath is the tower, which not only overcomes the difficulties of its oblong plan, but makes of them its greatest asset, and in its lack of symmetry proves itself one of the most successful central towers we have. William Vertue's 'filigree' style, though sternly repressed in the building itself, had its opportunity in Prior Bird's Chantry, begun in 1515, a miniature masterpiece.

As a whole, it must be admitted that Vertue's architecture looked back, not forward; its inspiration was the desire to sum up all that had gone before in a work richer, more daring, and more skilfully put together than its predecessors, but it found no way out from the impasse which had been reached by Gothic architecture. Vertue's friend and partner, Henry Redman, found that means of escape, as Hampton Court and Christ Church, Oxford, remain to tell, and had it not been for his death so soon after Vertue's, English art might have shown itself strong enough to overcome the catastrophe of the Renaissance. Lovely as is the work of Vertue and Wastell, its lack of structural vitality (in spite of its immense structural ingenuity, quite a different thing) is its own condemnation. At Henry VII's Chapel we see the apotheosis of an age which had lasted for 500 years, and produced the essential greatness of England; but though Vertue was not destined to know it, by the time he had seen the last stone set in its place, that age itself was dead. (See Appendix I.)

(APD; BAA; WKM; LKC); GOM, 89–90
[1] SAP, LX, pt. ii, 1–4; [2] *PRO*, E.36–214, p. 172; *BM*, Add. MS. 21481, *f*.69v. (*A.O.*); [3] HWC; SHB, 556–7; [4] *KCM*, Mundum Book 1506–07 (*A.O.*); [5] *Ibid.*, Building Acc. 1509–15 (*A.O.*); [6] *Ibid.*, Kitchen Accs., vol. xi (*A.O.*); [7] LPH, I (2nd ed.), 546 (72); II, pt. i, 2736; [8] HWC; SHB,

562–3 collated with *WSG*, XVII.37.3; [9] FCC, 61; SHB, 14; [10] FHC, 64; [11] LPH, III pt. i, 1285, p. 497; cf. Bryan Little in SAP, XCVI (1952), 186–7; [12] LPH, III pt. ii, pp. 1533–45; [13] *Ibid.*, II pt. ii, p. 1468; *BM*, Add. MS. 21481, *f.* 199 (*A.O.*); [14] WCC, I, 417, 418; [15] HTD, 100–1; [16] Hatfield Maps; *BM*, MSS. Facs. 372, vol. ii. 13 (*A.O.*); [17] LPH, III, pt. i, pp. 162, 234; [18] *BM*, Cott. MS. Aug. I, Supp. 7; HTD, 979; [19] WCC, I, 418; [20] LPH, IV, p. 869; [21] *PCC*, 17 Porch; printed in full, HGE, 185–6

VESEY, William [Veysy, Wesey, Weysey] (*fl.* 1437–1462) Brickmaker

Brickmaker and King's Serjeant who was appointed on 10 October 1437 to search for earth suitable for making *tegulae* called 'brike' and to make such tiles for the work of the King's manors at *Shene* and elsewhere.[1] On 29 January 1441 Richard Lownde and Vesey were granted the office of searchers of beer-brewing, for good services to the King, and this was confirmed on 5 April 1443.[2] Meanwhile, on 4 July 1442 Vesey had been ordered to impress masons and bricklayers for the works of *Eton College*.[3] In this year he appears as an elector in Middlesex, and on 12 January 1445 he was granted wages of 6*d.* a day and a fee of £10 yearly, in addition to his joint patent with Lownde as searcher of beer-brewing, and with a fresh appointment for life to seek brick earth and to make bricks and tiles. In February 1448 Vesey founded a chantry in St. Stephen's, Coleman Street, London; was M.P. for Lyme in 1449 and for Wareham in 1449–50; and was Bailiff of the Water of Thames in 1453 and 1454. He continues to be mentioned until 1462, when the survey of beer-brewers was granted to others.[4]

It is possible, as suggested by Dr. W. Douglas Simpson, that Vesey may have been concerned with the design of brick buildings at Eton, and with the similar courtyard plan of *Herstmonceux Castle*, Sussex (1441–).

WMP

[1] CPR 1436–41, 145; [2] CLB, 'K', 270; CPR 1436–41, 495; 1441–6, 184–5; [3] CPR 1441–6, 93; [4] In AJ, XCIX (1943), 119

VILE, Thomas [Vyal, Vyell] (†1472) Carpenter

Of Ixworth, Suffolk; by his will, dated 11 October 1472, proved 9 December 1472, Thomas Vyell the elder of Ixworth bequeathed to the steeple of his parish church 6 marks.[1] His gift is recorded on a tile on the west face of the tower. He is likely to have been employed both at the parish church and at the Augustinian Priory, to the Prior and Canons of which he made bequests. He left two sons, Thomas and John, and bequeathed to the former his tools, which are identifiable as those of a carpenter. His executors were his wife Christian and his brother John. The will of another Thomas Vyell of Ixworth, probably his son, is dated 10 October 1479.[2]

A *Thomas VYELL*, 'graver', was admitted a freeman of Norwich in 1461–62.[3] He seems to have been a different individual from the Ixworth man, since a Thomas Veyle was a prominent member of the Guild of St. George at Norwich between 1470 and 1472.[4]

A.O.

[1] *BW*, ii, 375; SIA, I, 99; [2] *BW*, ii, 587; [3] EFN; [4] NRC, IX, 65–71

VYNT, William [Fynt] (*fl.* 1374–1388) Carpenter

Carpenter of Colchester, who took up the freedom in 1374.[1] On 27 January 1387/8 the first named of three carpenters (with Alexander Tilfyk of Colchester and John Artour of 'Kirkeby' (probably Kirby-le-Soken) who contracted to build two new watermills in the parish of St. Olave, *Southwark*, for HENRY YEVELEY and JOHN CLIFFORD, masons and citizens of London, for £45.[2] He was dead by 1418 when a mention of his widow Dionysia occurs.

[1] BRC, 70, 99; JCC, III, 63; cf. 72–3, 79, 81; [2] SHB, 467–9; *MCO*, Deeds, *Southwark* 33

W., T. de—see THOMAS OF WITNEY

WADDESWYK, William [Wadiswyk] (*fl.* 1398–†1431) Mason (*Wadswick, Wilts.*)

Was a working mason (*cementarius*) in 1398–99 when he was paid 3*s.* 4*d.* a week for 28 weeks on the nave of *Westminster Abbey*, under HENRY YEVELEY.[1] In 1402 he was engaged on the works of *York Minster* for 12 weeks, and returned there with WILLIAM COLCHESTER as assistant in 1408. Both Colchester and Waddeswyk were seriously injured as a result of a conspiracy by some of the local masons, so that Waddeswyk was described as '*mutilato latomo*', but he was granted wages for life by the chapter. By 1415 he was warden of the masons under Colchester and continued under his successor JOHN LONG. In 1422–23 he was paid 3*s.* a week for 48 weeks' work.[2] After Long's death he was appointed master mason of the Minster on 28 January 1425/6, at £10 a year for life; in 1427 he took up the freedom of York.[3]

Waddeswyk made his will on 12 July 1429,

and it was proved on 2 November 1431.[4] He must be regarded as the probable designer of the western towers of York Minster, which are in a somewhat banal version of the Westminster style brought to the North by Colchester and based on the official work of Henry Yeveley before 1400.

[1] *WAM* 23467; [2] BHY, 1, 221, 225; RFY, 46, 199; *YML*, E 3/11; [3] *YML*, M 2(5), f. 222; YCF; [4] *BIY*, Wills 2.655

WADE, Thomas (*fl.* 1487–1513) Mason

Became chief mason of *London Bridge* in succession to THOMAS DANYELL in 1487. In the following year he sold a small quantity of stone to the church of St. Mary-at-Hill, close to the north end of the bridge,[1] so he was presumably in business on his own account in addition to his post at the bridge, which brought him in a fee of only 10 marks (£6 13s. 4d.) a year.

Wade had a succession of apprentices at the bridge, beginning with Robert Oliver in 1489–91, in respect of whose services he was paid 6d. a day for the first year and 3s. 4d. a week afterwards. From 1496 to 1500 Wade's apprentice was John Browne, at 3s. per week, and from 1506 to 1513 one Thomson, at 6d. a day for the first few weeks, and afterwards at 7d.

In 1488–89 Wade was paid for bridge ashlar 'by him purveyed and bought' at 42s. 2d. per 100 feet, and in later years he was frequently paid for stone bought at Maidstone at 35s. the 100 feet. Wade was succeeded as bridge mason by JOHN ORGAR in 1513.

KJL
[1] LMR, 136

Wadherst, Robert—see WODEHIRST

WADLEY, John (*fl.* 1414–1437) Carpenter

Succeeded JOHN RASYN as master carpenter at the building of *Durham Cathedral Cloister* in 1414, and until completion of the roofs in 1419. He also worked on the priory's mills, and continued in regular employment until 1437. His son *Thomas WADLEY* was also in the priory's employ.

DAR (M.G.S.)

Wadlyngton, Thomas—see WATLINGTON

WAKEFIELD, John [Wackefeld] (*fl. c.* 1330–   ) Mason (*Wakefield, Yorks. W.R.*)

Master mason in charge of work at *York Castle* early in the reign of Edward III.

(L.F.S.)   PRO, E.101–501–12

WAKEFIELD, William de (*fl.* 1312–1313) Carpenter

Was associated with RICHARD DE PARIS, mason, in carrying out works at *Chester Castle* in 1312–13, and was named as carpenter of the castle, taking pay of 1s. 9d. a week for 12 weeks.

ACC, 79, 80

WALDIN, — (*fl.* 1086–   ) Engineer

Is mentioned in Domesday as the engineer of *Lincoln Castle* in 1086. Parts of the existing curtain-wall are probably his work, and the plan is his, apart from the addition of the larger mound with its shell-keep of the late 12th century.

He held considerable land in Lindsey in the wapentakes of Aslacoe, Bradley, and Wraghoe; these no longer belonged to him in 1114–16, when he was presumably dead.

DB; (APD; WPS)

'Waldon, Watkin'—see WALTON, Walter

WALEDEN, Robert de (*fl.* 1251–   ) Mason

Master *cementarius*; on 25 August 1251 undertook to complete the masonry work of two chambers with private apartments and other details, at the royal manor of *Havering*, Essex, by task for £95. Timberwork was to be supplied by Master RICHARD DE WAUD', carpenter.

CCR 1247–51, 556; CLR 1251–60, 44

WALEYS, Nicholas (*fl.* 1366–†1403) Mason

A mason of standing at Bristol, called in to build the church spire of *Bridgwater*, Somerset, in 1366. One William Crese was paid 18d. for fetching him from Bristol, and he was paid £61 by indenture in addition to further payments totalling £29 7s. 4d. In 1374–75 'Nicholas the mason', probably the same man, was engaged to repair the tower, and William Waleys, mason, was granted £2, 'by a precept of the stewards of the Gild and other chief and elder men in the Gildhall'.[1]

Nicholas Waleys died in 1403. In his will, made on 22 March 1402 and proved on 9 June 1403, Waleys desired to be buried in the abbey church of St. Augustine, by the side of his wife Margery. He left bequests to the vicar of St. Augustine the Less, to the fabric of the church of St. Michael of Bristol, and to each order of friars. Two shops in 'Horstrete' with a hall, were left to his daughter Isabel, and four other shops in Horstrete are mentioned; his servant Margery, Peter Webbe, and John Bridport were to be his executors.[2] Waleys' wife Margery had predeceased him in 1390.[3]

Waleys may have been master mason of *St. Augustine's Abbey* and have designed the central tower of the church, known to have been in course of building in 1394 though not completed until *c.* 1470.[4]

[1] SRS, XLVIII, 159, 220; [2] WBW, 65; [3] *Ibid.*, 38; [4] WBW, 39

WALEYS, Thomas le [Thomas the Mason] (*fl. c.* 1270–*c.* 1275) Mason

Master Mason of *Lichfield Cathedral* in or shortly before 1270, apparently in succession to WILLIAM FITZTHOMAS. He was still living in 1275 and perhaps later.

LRA, Nos. 114, 124, 237, 404, 405, 556, 564; cf. Bodl., MS. Ashmole 794, *f.* 56

WALFRAY, John [alias Walford] (*fl.* 1450–1453) Carpenter

In Trinity Term 1450 the churchwardens of Capel, Surrey, sued John Walfray of London, carpenter, for a sum of £2. Walfray did not appear and judgement was entered against him; at the Surrey County Court held on 29 September 1451 he was outlawed, but eventually surrendered to the Fleet Prison. On 31 January 1453 a pardon of outlawry was issued to him in the name of John Walfray alias Walford. Probably Walfray had defaulted in respect of a contract, perhaps for the framing of the bell-turret and spire of *Capel Church*.

PRO, C.47–80–4 no. 106; CPR 1452–61, 7

WALLINGFORD, Richard of [Walyngford, Richard the Carpenter] (*fl.* 1347–1353) Carpenter

On 3 March 1346/7 the Black Prince ordered that 'Richard le Carpenter' who was in charge of works at the manor of *Byfleet*, should have 5*d.* a day, and on 12 March 1350/1 Master Richard de Walyngford the Prince's yeoman and carpenter was to carry out works at Byfleet and elsewhere. Next year he was at *Wallingford Castle*, but there was a stoppage of work there, so that it was necessary to order on 30 April that his wages of 5*d.* a day should continue as before. On 8 March 1352/3 he was appointed to be in charge of works in timber at Wallingford Castle.

BPR, I, 49; IV, 6, 48, 62, 83

WALRED, Nicholas (*fl. c.* 1170–) ? Carpenter

Built the original *Severn Bridge* at *Gloucester*, probably a timber structure, about 1170, and also a house for the workmen. It was afterwards enlarged and became the Hospital of St. Bartholomew, which remained responsible for the upkeep of the bridge. The old bridge and the hospital were destroyed in 1809.

APD

Walshe, Richard—see WELCH

WALSINGHAM, Alan of (*fl.* 1314–†1364) Monk

Monk of Ely by 1314 and noted for his skill in goldsmith's work, and later Sacrist from 1321, and Prior from 1341 to his death. As Sacrist he had charge of the works at *Ely Cathedral* from 1321 onwards. These comprised the Lady Chapel, 1321–49; the Octagon, 1322–28; the Lantern, 1328–42; Prior Crauden's Chapel and repairs to the guest hall, 1330; the choir, 1338–50.

The credit for the design of these works must probably be given to the master craftsmen, JOHN the Mason VII, JOHN ATTE GRENE, mason, and WILLIAM HURLEY, carpenter.

(APD; BAA); CSR, I, 10 ff.

WALTER, John (*fl.* 1493–1496) Mason

Mason of Bristol; in 1493 acted as a viewer of the city with JOHN DYMMOK, mason, and NICHOLAS ANDREWES and RICHARD SOMERE, carpenters; and again in 1496 with RALPH SPORRYOWRE, mason, and Nicholas 'Ambrosse' and Richard Somer, carpenters.[1] He may have been the John Walter of Bristol whose will was proved in 1502.[2]

(A.O.)

[1] BLR, 133, 134; [2] CSV, F.262b

Walter of Coventry—see COVENTRY

WALTER the Carpenter I (*fl.* 1229–) Carpenter

In 1229 payments were made in Dublin to Walter the Carpenter for the building of towers of *Dublin Castle* and other works there.

IDK, 35R, App., 30

WALTER the Carpenter II (*fl.* 1300–1313) Carpenter

Master carpenter at *Exeter Cathedral* in 1300, when he was paid 2*s.* 3*d.* weekly in summer, and 1*s.* 10½*d.* in winter. He continued to take 2*s.* 3*d.* weekly for irregular periods of work until late in 1313, when he was replaced by WILLIAM DE MEMBIRI.

CEF, from Fabric rolls, Nos. 2602, 2609; AEC, i, 176–93

WALTER the Imager (*fl.* 1261–   ) Carver

Carver of Westminster; tenant of a house which Hugh de Reyns, son of Master HENRY DE REYNS, had inherited from his father; it was situated between a house of the Abbot of Westminster on the north, and one of Walter the Clerk on the south.

WAM, 17358

Walter the Marbler—see CANTERBURY

WALTER the Mason I [*Cementarius*, Le Masun] (*fl.* 1277–1278) Mason

Son of Master REGINALD DE ABINGDON; perhaps identical with WALTER the Mason III; possibly master mason of *Oseney Abbey*.

E. M. Jope in BKJ, LI (1951), 56

WALTER the Mason II (*fl. c.* 1300–   ) Mason

Master mason (*cementarius*), who *c.* 1300 held a toft and 1/5 virgate of land at Bescaby, Leics., by rent of 6*s.* payable to *Croxton Abbey*. Since Bescaby is adjacent to Croxton, Walter was presumably in charge of the abbey buildings.

(*H.M.C.*) Belvoir Castle, Add. MS. 70, *f.* 55v.

WALTER the Mason III (*fl.* 1301–   ) Mason

The so-called 'Burcester Rolls', the account rolls of *Bicester Priory*, Oxon., record the payment of a sum of 2*s.* in 1301 as the last part of the stipend of Walter the Mason for his work on the Prior's Chamber there; perhaps identical with WALTER the Mason I.

BDB, pt. ii, 143

WALTER the Mason IV [le Machon] (*fl.* 1301) Mason

On 22 February 1301 witnessed a deed of the Prior of *St. Bartholomew's* in *Gloucester*.

SRG, No. 758

WALTHAM, John (*fl.* 1391–1403) Carpenter

Carpenter retained by *Westminster Abbey*. In 1391–92 he was given a robe price 9*s.* 8*d.*,[1] and in 1393–94 was working for four weeks with another carpenter, the two men receiving 5*s.* 4*d.* a week between them.[2] In 1397–98 he again had a robe and mended panelling in the refectory, being paid 6*d.* for one day's work.[3] In 1402–03 he submitted an account for work done on a house belonging to the Abbey.[4]

[1] *WAM*, 19876; [2] *Ibid.*, 19879; [3] *Ibid.*, 19882; [4] *Ibid.*, 23740 A

WALTHAM, Nicholas (*fl.* 1408) Carpenter

In 1408 Master Nicholas Waltham, carpenter, contracted with the Chamberlain of St. Paul's Cathedral to erect seven shops in Knightrider Street, *London*, on the north side of the garden of the great hospice, for £55. This was to include all carpentry work except tilepins. The underground latrines, walls, chimneys and foundations were to be built for £20 by John Teffe, mason; and tilers and others were also employed, and materials bought.

HAC, 35; *PRO*, E.101–473–15

WALTHAM, Robert de (*fl.* 1283–1309) Carpenter

Was principal carpenter at the *Tower of London* in 1283, when he carried out work on the roof of the Great Hall and moved the plumber's workshop.[1] About 1292, with WILLIAM LE BLOUND, mason, he was in charge of works at the *Palace of Westminster*.[2]

At the taxation of 1293/4 'Robert de Waltham charpenter' was assessed to pay 2*s.* in the Ward of Cripplegate;[3] in 1309 he disposed of a house in the parish of St. Michael, Hoggen Lane.[4]

[1] *PRO*, E.101–467–9; [2] LKC, 181; [3] WLE; [4] *LHR*, 38(3)

Walton, John—see WATTON

WALTON, Nicholas ['Wilton'] (*fl.* 1394–†*c.* 1402) Carpenter

On 30 April 1394 received a grant, during good behaviour, of the office of King's Master Carpenter and disposer of the works of carpentry, surrendered by RICHARD SWIFT. His fees were to be 12*d.* a day, from the clerk of the works as long as the works should continue, and from the Exchequer when they ceased, with a robe every winter at the Great Wardrobe.[1]

This office was a 'double' of that held by HUGH HERLAND, for on 12 April 1402 JOHN DOBSON was appointed for life to be 'one of the two carpenters of the King's works' as Nicholas Walton had been.[2]

(APD; BAA)
[1] CPR 1391–6, 427; [2] *Ibid.* 1401–5, 83

Walton, Richard—see WILTON

WALTON, Walter ['Watkin Waldon'] (*fl.* 1383–†1418) Mason (? *Walton in Deerhurst, Glos.*)

Mason of London; in 1383 was hired to

repair the church of the *Hospital of St. Thomas of Acon* in *London*, with SIMON AT HOOK.[1] In 1385 he made the tabernacles for six statues of Kings to be placed in *Westminster Hall* for £4 13s. 4d. and was concerned with the making of these and other images by THOMAS CANON.[2] At the rebuilding of Westminster Hall in 1394–95 he was warden or deputy to HENRY YEVELEY, then the King's Master Mason, who was an old man; the contract for making the new cornice and corbels of the hall, on 18 March 1395, stipulated that the contracting masons, RICHARD WASHBOURN and JOHN SWALLOW, were to make them 'according to the purport of a pattern and mould made by the advice of Master Henry Yeveley and delivered to the said masons by Watkin Walton his warden'.[3]

On 29 April 1396 Walton was commissioned to impress masons for the works of *Portchester Castle*, Hants. He was paid 6d. a day for his work and while travelling, spending 33 days on three visits in 1396, 34 days in 1397, and 80 days in 1398 and the first six months of 1399. Constant superintendence of the works, which included a new hall, kitchen, pantry and buttery, and repairs, was exercised by WALTER WESTON the subwarden, also paid at 6d. a day.[4] Very close stylistic resemblance to Walton's work at Portchester indicates that he was the designer of the pulpitum (miscalled 'Arundel Screen') and of the Cloisters at *Chichester Cathedral*, possibly also of the detached belfry there, all works to be assigned to c. 1400–1410. On 26 November 1397 Walton was appointed by bill of the treasurer to be 'chief surveyor of all stonecutters and masons for the King's works in England', a special appointment doubtless due to Henry Yeveley's advancing years.[5] In the same year Walton and John Swallow stood as sureties that THOMAS WOLVEY would complete the mason's work of *Henley Church*, Oxon., where substantial rebuilding was in progress.[6]

Walton's position as a royal surveyor gave him an assured livelihood, and he seems to have worked regularly at the palace of *Shene* with STEPHEN LOTE. He was employed by the Council of the Duchy of Lancaster to travel to *Little Hallingbury*, Essex, in 1404 to survey the great chamber there; works were also done on the lodge. He evidently maintained a private practice in London as well, for in 1410 he was to direct the building of three houses by JOHN

GERARD, carpenter, and in the spring of 1412 he was one of the sworn masons of the City of London who surveyed a plot of waste ground 21 feet long and 7 feet 3 inches wide on the north side of St. John's Church in Walbrook.[7] The rector and parishioners were granted their petition that this ground might be given them for building an extension to the church, in exchange for 5½ feet of land to the east of the choir which was wanted for street widening.

In 1412–13 Walton ('of London, mason') and his wife Joan made a conveyance of the manor of 'Seymores' in Blo Norton and Garboldisham, Norfolk; the manor belonged to the revenues of the abbey of Bury St. Edmunds, which Walton may have served.[8]

On 20 March 1417 Walton was commissioned to take stonecutters and others for the works at *Shene Charterhouse*,[9] and soon after this became an executor of the will of Stephen Lote who died early in 1418, leaving Walton a number of bequests. Walton did not long survive him, dying before 6 October, when his will was proved.[10] In the will, made on 16 August, he described himself as a citizen and mason of London, and desired to be buried in the church of St. Andrew Baynard's Castle. He left a hewing axe and 6 irons for masonry to his apprentice John Oldland, at the end of his time; to Ralph Oldland, mason, he left his compass at Shene; to JOHN CROXTON, mason, 'my best compass', to Thomas Poynts, mason, 'my livery cloak of my old free mistery', and 'to the fraternity of my art' the sum of 6s. 8d. His wife Joan and brother John Walton survived him. A bequest of 16s. 8d. to the rebuilding and maintenance of 'a certain Chapel called Lee, Gloucestershire' may suggest Walton's place of origin: Leigh is 4 miles south of Tewkesbury and adjacent to Walton in Deerhurst, a manor belonging to Westminster Abbey.

Walton, Lote, and JOHN CLIFFORD were the successors of Henry Yeveley and William Wynford; though not among the greatest masters themselves, they kept alive the best traditions of the royal school of masoncraft in London and Westminster, and handed on those traditions to the younger generation.

(APD); WKM; KJI
[1] CPR 1381–5, 310; [2] DIE, 227–8; *PRO*, E.101–473–2; [3] RF, III, iv, 105; *BM*, Add. Ch. 27018; [4] CPR 1391–6, 702; *PRO*, E.101–479–23, 24; [5] CPR 1396–9, 261; [6] CCR 1396–9, 239; [7] *PRO*, DL 28–4–4; CLB, 'I', 102; [8] RNF, II, 401; BHN, I, 244; [9] CPR 1416–22, 87; [10] *PCC*, 42 Marche — W. J. Williams in AQC, XLI (1929), 137–8

Walynford, Richard—see WALLINGFORD

'Wand', Richard—see WAUD

WARDEN, William (*fl.* 1370–1377)
Carpenter
Between 1370 and the end of Edward III's reign built a new lodge at the royal manor of *Isleworth.* (See also WILLIAM SELOT).
HKW, II, 964

WARE, Thomas (*fl.* 1544–†1545) Joiner
Described as the King's servant when on 30 May 1544 he was appointed chief joiner of the King's works in England, with fees of 12*d.* a day and was granted the reversion of the office of joiner in the Tower of London after JOHN RIPLEY.[1] Ware died on 28 June 1545,[2] and was succeeded by JOHN MANNING.
[1] LPH, XIX, i, 610 (110); [2] *Ibid.*, XX, ii, 707(41)

WAREYN, Richard (*fl.* 1493–   )
Carpenter
On 2 March 1492/3 Richard Wareyn and Nicholas Halywode, carpenters of *Westminster,* undertook to build a brewhouse at the Rose by Charing Cross, for £8 13*s.* 4*d.*
SHB, 552–3; (*WAM,* 17178)

WARIN (*fl. c.* 1223–   ) ? Monk
Was keeper of the works of *Sallay Abbey,* Yorks., about 1223. It is rather improbable that he was the architect of the work.
MCS, 111

WARIN the Mason (*fl.* 1303–1304) Mason
Master mason at *Beeston Castle,* Cheshire, in 1303–04; in charge of making the great gate and drawbridge of the 'Dungon', and crenellating the three towers of the inner ward.
ACC, 43

WARLOWE, Edmund (*fl.* 1413–†1433)
Mason
In 1413–14 undertook to build masonry walls to carry the timber framing for a building called 'Byfleet' at the royal manor of *Sheen,* Surrey.[1] A brother of WILLIAM WARLOWE, he died in January 1433, leaving to William his cup called 'le Note' (i.e. a coconut cup), a baselard harnessed with silver and a gown of violet and 'sangwaiyn' with fur. To his former apprentice Richard Mady he left £1 and all tools belonging to his craft at the Black Friars of London; and all residue to his wife Joan.[2]

[1] HKW, II, 999; [2] *GUL,* Commissary Court of London, Reg. More, *f.* 323v.

WARLOWE, William (*fl.* 1426–*c.* 1440)
Mason
Was appointed Master Mason at *Calais* in 1426, in succession to WILLIAM HOCKERING, and remained in office until *c.* 1440. His successor was WILLIAM MODY, already mason of the 'new works' at Calais.
HKW, II, 1054

WARNER, John (*fl.* 1500–†1518) Mason
Citizen and freemason of London; in 1500 made over his goods to the Recorder and an alderman of the city.[1] In 1513–14 he was paid £24 for making the battlements of the middle aisle (i.e. nave) of the church of *St. Mary-at-Hill, London,* and £3 for those of the south aisle.[2] The latter had probably been designed by ROBERT VERTUE about 1501. In 1515 Warner built the foundation walls for timber-framed storehouses at the *London Bridge House,* using 68,800 bricks.[3]
Warner was of the parish of St. Alban, Wood Street, when he made his will on 7 February 1518; it refers to property in Goldynglane and to his house at Enfield, Middlesex; it was proved on 15 February.[4]
[1] JJC, I, 247; [2] LMR, 287–8; [3] P. E. Jones in AAJ, 3 S XVI (1953), 63; [4] *GUL,* Commissary Court of London, Reg. Bennet, *f.* 112 (*N.L.R.*)

'WARWICK, Master of the Earl of' (*fl.* 1392–   ) Mason
The mason (*cementarius*) of the Earl of Warwick at Warwick; was there given 3*s.* 4*d.* in 1392–93 by the Prior of Worcester.[1] At this time the upper storey of the great gate (Edgar Tower) of the Priory at *Worcester* was being built, and the stylistic resemblances to the great gatehouse of *Warwick Castle* indicate a common authorship. The lower storey of the Edgar Tower had been built in 1346–47 at a cost of £42 18*s.* 2*d.*[2] JOHN MONTFORT was master mason to Thomas Beauchamp, Earl of Warwick, from about 1376 to 1405.
[1] *WCO,* C.76; [2] *Ibid.,* C.61

WARYN, William (*fl.* 1351–1355) Carpenter
Of Kingston, Surrey; in 1351–52 was paid £24 for the carpentry of a new roof for *St. George's Chapel* in *Windsor Castle.* The work was undertaken by contract and was no doubt designed by WILLIAM HURLEY.[1] On 8 March 1353 Waryn was appointed with John Sakers to buy materials and retain craftsmen at the King's wages to rebuild the barns and

315

other buildings accidentally burned in the manor of the Prior of St. John of Jerusalem at *Hampton (Court)*, Middlesex, when the royal household was in residence.[2]

On 16 February 1355 Waryn was one of those commissioned to take craftsmen for the repair of buildings in the Queen's manor of Isleworth.[3]

[1] HWC, I, 139; [2] CPR 1350-4, 417; [3] CPR 1354-8, 178

WASHBOURNE, Richard [Wascheborne] (*fl.* 1387–1396) Mason

Probably from Washbourne, Glos.; in 1387–88 he worked at *Westminster Abbey* for five weeks under HENRY YEVELEY, at 3*s.* 8*d.* a week, the highest rate paid to the working masons.[1] On 18 March 1394/5 he contracted, with JOHN SWALLOW, to make the new cornice and corbels for *Westminster Hall*, to a design supplied by Yeveley.[2]

The two masons were to raise the old walls with a level cornice, 'according to the purport of a pattern and mould made by the advice of Master Henry Yeveley and delivered to the said masons by Watkin Walton his warden'. They were to receive 1*s.* a foot for this cornice, and for each of the 26 corbels, made of Marr stone, and set in position with sawn Reigate stone filling above them, £1. The King was to find all materials and necessaries, including stone, lime, sand, scaffolds, and engines, but not labour or masons' tools. Lodging was also to be found for the masons and their companions for the whole time they were engaged on the works. Half of the work was to be completed by 24 June, and the remainder by 2 February following, i.e. in 1395/6. Extant accounts include the payments made.[3]

(APD; LKC)
[1] *WAM*, 23460; [2] SHB, 472-3; RF, III, iv, 105; (*PRO*, E.101-473-21); [3] *BM*, Add. Ch. 27018

Wassel—see WASTELL

WASSYNGLE, John (*fl.* 1431–) Mason (*Washingley, Hunts.*)

Of Hinton, Cambs.; contracted to build the library of *Peterhouse, Cambridge*, on 12 February 1430/1. This was the west range of the old court; though refaced, the shell remains intact. Wassyngle's name appears frequently in the college accounts of the period. He was to be paid at specified rates for working the stones for doors and windows, and to take 3*s.* 4*d.* a week for building; if the work gave satisfaction, the college would also provide him with a gown of their livery.[1] He was probably identical with the John '*lathamus*' who in 1424–25 had been paid 7*s.* 4*d.* a week for himself and his apprentice, while the north range was being built.[2]

[1] SHB, 500-1; WCC, I, 10, 73; [2] *PHM*, Bursars' Rolls (L.F.S.)

WASTELL, John [Wassel, Westyll] (*fl.* 1485– ?†1515) Mason

Outside the ranks of the royal master masons John Wastell is perhaps the most significant figure in the last age of Gothic architecture in England. During the greater part of his career he was working in the eastern counties with Bury St. Edmunds as his place of residence, but he was also employed at *Canterbury* on the great central tower of the metropolitan cathedral. The only royal work on which he is known to have been engaged is *King's College Chapel*, but the fan vault and the other finishing features, which he designed, show that while he was acquainted with and influenced by the school of the Vertue brothers, he developed a distinct and easily recognisable style of his own.

In the earliest reference to him so far discovered he was partner with SIMON CLERK in a building contract of 1485 made with the two churchwardens of Saffron Walden Church, Essex.[1] As Wastell succeeded Clerk as master mason at King's College Chapel and probably also at the abbey of Bury, this evidence of partnership with the older man, then near the end of his long career, may indicate that Wastell had begun as Clerk's apprentice and worked under him during the second phase of building at King's (1476–85). No wage-lists of masons who worked on the chapel during that period exist, and apart from one isolated reference, in a day-book of Thomas Clyff among the King's College muniments, of beer given to John Wastell on 13 March 1486,[1] it is not until 1490 that his name occurs in the college accounts. On 18 December of that year he was entertained at the Fellows' table at dinner in hall and also at supper when JOHN BELL was likewise present; he was a guest again at supper with the Fellows on 9 January 1491.[2] As the Saffron Walden contract was drawn up at Cambridge by Thomas Clyff (see Simon Clerk), Wastell's connection with Cambridge, and probably with King's, went back at least to 1485.

It is possible, however, that the abbey

church at *Bury*, and not King's College Chapel, was the first building on which he worked if he started as an apprentice under Simon Clerk. Between 1486 and 1490, towards the end of the term of office of John Swaffham as Sacrist (1472–90), relief of 4*s.* 8*d.* was paid by 'John Wastell ffremason' on entering half a tenement on the west side of Churchgovel Street, Bury St. Edmunds, now Crown Street, which leads from Westgate Street to the west end of St. Mary's Church.[3] There is no definite proof that Wastell was master mason at the abbey, but as Simon Clerk died in or shortly before 1489, this record of Wastell acquiring a house in Bury may well indicate that he had recently been appointed to succeed Clerk, and there is plenty of evidence to show that Bury was normally his place of residence until his death. He acted as executor for a neighbour, Richard Sterre, thatcher, whose will was dated 6 August 1492 and proved 24 September 1493.[4] In 1500 he was one of the executors of John Worlych of Bury (will dated 10 June 1498, proved 22 October 1500).[5] Worlych was probably a mason, and John Wastell, who is described as 'ffremason', had as his co-executors the testator's widow, Elianore, and another freemason, John Baly; one of the witnesses was Robert Wastell, 'wever', who is likely to have been his father. Robert Pulham of College Street, Bury, freemason, appointed John Wastell, 'ffremason', supervisor of his will, dated 2 October 1500 and proved 31 December 1501, and made him a bequest of 6*s.* 8*d.*[6] Pulham left 20*s.* to 'the building of the new work in the monastery', where doubtless he had been employed. On 18 August 1502 John Wastell was one of a number of new feoffees appointed by a deed of that date to administer trust property bequeathed to the town by Margaret Odeham in 1492.[7] The feoffees seem all to have been members of the influential Candlemas Guild round which the civic life of Bury revolved. On 16 November 1506 he witnessed a deed in which Thomas Chirche, the well-known Bury bellfounder, and eight other feoffees were concerned,[8] one of the eight being HENRY SEMARK, who was to be Wastell's warden of the masons at King's College Chapel a few years later. Finally, there is the will of 'John Wastell of Bury Seynt Edmonds', dated and proved in May 1515,which is probably that of the mason although he is not so described in it.[9]

The nature of the work in progress at the abbey from 1490 onwards is known only from bequests in wills, but it is clear that the programme of restoration and reconstruction necessitated by the disastrous fire of 1466 had not been completed by the time of Simon Clerk's death. It included the vaulting of the whole church. The possibility that a fan vault was used has been discussed in the article on Simon Clerk, where it is suggested that some of the distinctive features of Wastell's fan vaults may have been derived from him. Bequests to the new vaulting occur in wills of 1492 and 1495,[10] and less specific bequests to 'the new work' continue up to 1500. In the account of the fire of 1466 the timber spire on the central tower of 1362–88 is stated to have been burnt, but it telescoped on to the floor of the crossing, and the tower itself survived and did not have to be rebuilt. The west tower, the rebuilding of which had been begun as far back as 1436, was unfinished at the time of the fire, and its completion was deferred in favour of more urgent work, but several bequests towards it occur in wills between 1492 and 1504, in one of which it is definitely specified as 'the newe stepyll at the west dore of the Monastery'.[11] It is possible that a complete upper stage was built by Wastell, or he may have carried to completion work of Simon Clerk or even the original design of *c.* 1435. Dr. Henry Rudde, priest, in his will of 1506 left £10 'towarde the making of ij blynd windowes. . .biside Seint Christopher'.[12] This is almost the last bequest to the fabric of the abbey church, but from stylistic evidence it is virtually certain that Wastell designed the church of *St. James* at *Bury* (now the cathedral), the rebuilding of which was begun in 1503.

Experience in tower-building gained by Wastell at Bury may have been one of the considerations which led Cardinal Morton to engage him to build the great central tower of *Canterbury Cathedral*, now usually known as the Bell Harry Tower but formerly as the Angel Steeple. As Bishop of Ely from 1478 to 1486 Morton is likely to have become aware of Wastell as a rising young architect and he may even have employed him on some of the buildings which he erected, at Wisbech and Hatfield, during his tenure of the see. The Angel Tower was built between Easter 1494 and Michaelmas 1497 largely at the expense of Morton, whose rebus and badges are carved on it. An account of 1493–94 records a 'regard' of 20s. 'given to a certain master mason sent by the lord Cardinal',[13] and his identity is disclosed in an undated letter from the Prior to Morton about the design to be adopted for the pinnacles at the four corners. The bearer of the letter was 'John Wastell your mason' with whom the Prior had communed 'to perceyve of hym what forme and shappe he will kepe in reysyng up of the pynaclys of your new towre here: He drew unto us ij patrons of hem', which are then described.[14] Morton must have chosen the design which harmonised with the finials of the south-west tower, but Wastell's drawing for his alternative suggestion of 'croketts and single fineall' has been preserved among the archives of the Dean and Chapter. Work on the central tower had been begun in 1433, when RICHARD BEKE was master mason, but it had remained unfinished at the level of the ridges of the roofs, and all above that line is the work of Wastell. The beauty and grace of this tower both in its proportions and detail give it a place among the masterpieces of Perpendicular architecture, although the duality implicit in the design of the elevations is, perhaps, too insistent for the unity of the whole composition.

The two straining arches strengthening the tower piers and the four others subordinate to them were introduced by Wastell, who used a graceful pattern of quatrefoils—one of his favourite motives—for their pierced stone grilles. The internal fan vault of the lantern cannot have been built before 1503, since it has the arms of the see impaling Warham, who became Archbishop in that year, but in its design it corresponds exactly to Wastell's fan vaults at King's College Chapel, and it can therefore be safely attributed to him.

It is interesting to compare with the arches at Canterbury the two strainer arches across the naves of *Rushden* and *Finedon* churches, Northants., inserted to counteract the inward pressure of arches between transepts and aisles. Both arches were clearly designed by the same mason. Their details show quite close analogies with those of the strainer arches at Canterbury and the pierced arches connecting the new work to the Norman apse at Peterborough.

That Wastell was not merely the Archbishop's architect, paying occasional visits, but became master mason at Canter-bury is shown by an entry in a register of Christ Church, Canterbury, which records receptions into fraternity of the Prior and Chapter and dates of obits. He was received into fraternity as master of the masons on 7 April 1496 (*Johannes Wastell magister latomorum*).[15] He could not, however, have been continuously resident, for while the tower was being built, he had work on hand at Cambridge, and presumably also at Bury. Morton may have employed him on other works of his, which included his gate-tower at *Lambeth Palace*, his manor house at *Ford*, near Reculver, and reconstructions and additions at the palaces at Canterbury, *Charing*, and *Maidstone*. At Cambridge Wastell appears among the guests entertained at King's College on 9 March and 29 May 1495.[16] As the chapel was then at a standstill, no particular significance can be attached to these visits, but he had work at *King's Hall*, where in the three years 1490–92 nearly £150 was spent on a new building, which was not complete in 1495.[17] Professor Willis identified this building with a range of chambers known to have existed on the south side of the court, but a careful study of the accounts suggests that it was the east range at right angles to the chapel, now forming part of the east range of the Great Court of Trinity College and including the lower part of the Great Gate Tower. A payment in 1492 'for the covering for the porter's lodge with the walls and towers with a lock for the same',[18] which Professor Willis took to refer to a building shown in Hammond's view projecting from the east side of the King Edward Gate,[19] is more reasonably interpreted as the covering from winter frosts of the porter's lodge and turrets of the Great Gate Tower forming part of the new building. The ranges of chambers on either side of it were finished first — an agreement for roofing was made with a carpenter in 1495 — but shortage of funds delayed the completion of the gate-tower for over forty years, and the two upper stages were not built until 1528–35. Under 'expenses concerning the new building' there is a payment of 10s. to 'Wastell freemason' in 1491–92, and in 1496–97 there are two more of 4s. and 6s. 8d., the latter sum having been paid 'to Master Wastell the freemason at two terms (*ad duos terminos*)'.[20] There are also payments to WILLIAM SWAYN, who was probably the resident master mason in charge of the work, but the payments to Wastell show that he was at least consulted, and he may have been responsible for the plan and the elevations of the lower portion of the gate-tower, though not the whole as executed. The ornament above the smaller side entrance is characteristic and may be compared with his treatment of the spaces above the lower tiers of windows in the Angel Tower at Canterbury.

Another work which may have required Wastell's presence in Cambridge from time to time was *Great St. Mary's Church*, slowly being rebuilt by the university with the aid of donations from outside as well as from local resources. A start was made in 1478; then little seems to have been done for nearly a decade, when work was actively resumed until 1493; after another lull fresh activity began about 1502 and the fabric was completed, except for the upper stages of the tower, in 1514. The tower is known to have been begun in 1491,[21] and it was originally designed to stand clear of the aisles, which by an afterthought were extended westward to the line of its west face. A passage for a processional pathway with north and south doorways runs through the ground storey and has a panelled barrel vault of segmental form ornamented with cusped and floriated ogee motives and quatrefoils. A duplicate of this feature with doorways and panelled vault almost identical in their details is found in the ground storey of the tower at *Dedham Church*, Essex, which was begun a year or two later: it is first mentioned in bequests in wills of 1494 and 1495. At both churches this piercing of the tower by a pathway was done because the towers were built out to the extreme western limit of the churchyard. They are clearly the work of the same master mason in spite of the difference in the materials used, brick faced with knapped flintwork and stone dressings at Dedham, Northamptonshire freestone at Great St. Mary's, Cambridge. In connection with the latter church John Bell received a deferred payment in 1498–99 and he is described as mason of the university in 1502, but though he was, no doubt, the mason in charge of the work, it is possible that Wastell was the actual designer of the tower and, if so, by inference, of the tower at Dedham. The entry in the kitchen accounts of King's College under 18 December 1490, when Wastell and Bell were both guests together in hall,

only a few months before the first stone of the tower of Great St. Mary's was laid at an official ceremony,[21] gains interest and possible significance read in this context. It should be added that the lower stages of the fine tower at *Soham Church*, Cambs., must also have been designed by the master of the towers of Dedham and Great St. Mary's.

The stylistic evidence of these towers is inconclusive, although remarkably similar panelled vaulting of segmental form occurs in conjunction with a fan vault foreshadowing the Wastell type in the *Red Mount Chapel* at (*King's*) *Lynn*, built about 1485 by ROBERT CURRAUNT. This little building has such an ingenious plan that in considering the possible claims of Simon Clerk and Wastell to its design one is more inclined to see in it the work of a young and fresh mind than of an old and experienced architect. It was in 1485 that Simon Clerk and Wastell acted as partners in a building contract for *Saffron Walden Church*, Essex, the reconstruction of which as a great town church of almost cathedral-like proportions began then with the rebuilding of the south aisle. Stylistic considerations had pointed to Wastell as the designer of the nave arcades and chancel arch of this church before any documentary evidence came to light, and he may be presumed to have continued as sole master mason after Clerk's death until his own death, when the work was still unfinished. Bequests in wills show that the building of the arcades and clerestory began about 1497. The detail of these arcades and of the chancel arch with its ornamented spandrels is highly characteristic of Wastell, and other features recalling his work are the fan vault of the south porch and the crocketed ogee-shaped tops to the rood-loft turrets, miniature versions of those surmounting the turrets of King's College Chapel. The treatment of the nave arcades and of the chancel arch at Great St. Mary's, Cambridge, bears such a close resemblance to the work at Saffron Walden that they may be safely attributed to the same designer, so that if there is uncertainty about Wastell's responsibility for the tower of Great St. Mary's, there can be little or no doubt that the arcades, clerestory, and chancel arch (probably not begun before 1500) were due to him. Although payments to William Swayn (in 1509) and to WILLIAM BURDON (between 1509 and 1513) occur in the proctors' and the churchwardens' accounts, these are at a late stage in the work, and the fact that Wastell's name nowhere appears can be explained by the lack of detailed building accounts for the important years. The King's College muniments, however, show that he was still paying visits to Cambridge from time to time. For instance, in May 1499 he and his servant were entertained in hall two days running, and the following day Master Asplond, steward of the college estates at Grantchester and Kersey, forgathered with him at the Bull (*apud signum nigri tauri*), where 4s. (? 4d.) was spent.[22] And in December of that year the Provost sent a messenger to John Wastell who duly appeared to see him in Cambridge on 6 January.[23]

The naves of Saffron Walden and Great St. Mary's, Cambridge, have stylistic affinities with the nave of *Lavenham Church*, Suffolk, built between 1495 and 1515. The parallels are not so close, but allowance has to be made for the difference in effect produced by the Northamptonshire freestone used in the interior of Lavenham, in comparison with the clunch employed in the other two churches, and also for the fact that Lavenham is a more richly treated church on which money was lavished without stint. Several of Wastell's individual traits can be found in it. The aisle windows with their four-centred heads and minimum of tracery are of a Tudor type used at St. George's Chapel, Windsor; though not characteristic of Wastell, they occur in the west windows of the aisles at Great St. Mary's, Cambridge. If, as it is reasonable to suppose, Bury masons were employed at Lavenham, Wastell may again have followed Simon Clerk, to whom the design of the tower, begun about 1486, may be due.

St. James's Church, Bury, can be attributed to Wastell with confidence. Not only was he living in Bury when the rebuilding began in 1503, but his style can be clearly discerned. The side windows may be compared with those in the eastern chapels at Peterborough; the west window of the nave is a smaller version of the great west window at King's College Chapel with tracery of a similar kind; the buttresses of the west front are decorated with vertical panels of ornament much like those on the Angel Tower at Canterbury, and the same pear-shaped quatrefoils occur in each; flanking the west doorway there are niches with tabernacles closely resembling those which Wastell used at King's College Chapel. Rebuilding of the church began by extending the nave westward to the line of the street, as is shown by bequests in wills to 'the new work that is begun in Saint James Church end'.[24] From 1521 onwards bequests for the glazing and ornaments are more numerous than for the fabric, most of which appears by then to have been completed. By comparison with Lavenham this was a cheap church, and the parishioners were evidently more concerned about rivalling the nave of St. Mary's in length and by the height of their arcades than about richness of effect. The arcades are almost devoid of ornament, but the capitals of the shafts of the piers have Wastell's characteristic flower motives in the necking; regarded closely these arcades are seen to be simplified versions of those at Saffron Walden and Great St. Mary's and disclose the same general ordinance of the parts. They are beautifully proportioned and a very fine effect is achieved with a remarkable economy of means. This nave is an altogether more satisfactory design than that of St. Mary's if the splendid roof of the latter church is left out of account.

No building documents for the eastern chapels of *Peterborough Cathedral* are known to exist, but their design shows an exact correspondence with Wastell's authenticated works. These chapels, still often called 'the New Building', were commissioned by Robert Kirton, Abbot, 1496–1528, whose name and rebus occur several times on the bosses and ornaments. A misreading of the letters A.R.K'TON (*Abbas Robertus Kirton*) seems to have given rise to the unfounded statement that the work was begun by Abbot Ashton (1438–71). From the presence of the Prince of Wales's feathers among the ornaments the date can be narrowed down to Henry VII's reign and the years 1496–1509. Wastell will therefore have been engaged on this building before beginning the great work of completing King's College Chapel. The fan vault is recognisably from the same hand as those of King's, and among other close parallels are the pierced parapet and the internal wall panelling below the windows with its elaborate double cusping. The capitals of the vaulting shafts are similar to those used in the nave arcades at Saffron Walden and Great St. Mary's, Cambridge, and the pierced arches linking the new work to the

Norman apse recall in their treatment the strainer arches in Canterbury Cathedral. The beauty of this eastern ambulatory, the skill shown in setting out and accommodating a square termination to the Norman apse and the technical mastery of fan vault design make this one of the most notable examples of late Perpendicular architecture.

Entries in the King's College muniments already quoted show that the Provost and Fellows had been in touch with Wastell since Simon Clerk's death. The awakening of Henry VII's interest in the unfinished chapel dated from his visit to Cambridge in April 1506, when he kept St. George's Day in the temporary chapel of the college.[25] The funds which he made available enabled the college to resume building operations in the spring of 1508 and the structure was finished by the summer of 1515. John Wastell as master mason received an annual salary of £13 6s. 8d. The building account for the first year shows that William Swayn, who had worked with Wastell at King's Hall, received the same salary as comptroller, but from May 1509 until the works came to an end Swayn's place was taken by JOHN LEE (or Alee), who acted as joint master mason and was paid at the same rate but whose chief function seems to have been that of a purveyor, though he may have been more regularly resident than Wastell, who as the actual architect only visited the work when required. In the summarised book of building accounts from May 1509 to July 1515 there are several notes of payments made to Wastell under the heading 'Purveyors' Costs'. The two kitchen accounts for the period that survive, 1511–12 and 1513–14, show that he was entertained as a guest on twelve occasions. On one of these occasions, 30 July 1512, just after Wastell had entered into his contract for the high vaults, 'Master Vertue' was another of the guests present in hall.[26] This is the third recorded visit of WILLIAM VERTUE, the royal master mason, who had been summoned to a conference at the college along with HENRY SMYTH and Lee in May 1507[27] before the works started and had paid another visit accompanied by HENRY REDMAN in December 1509.[28] These consultations are interesting in showing that Wastell was in touch with the royal school of masons and may have made use of suggestions and advice given by Vertue and Redman.

Wastell was responsible for building the whole of the antechapel from a few feet above ground level and for completing the choir, five bays of which had been roofed in Simon Clerk's time. Externally Wastell's work can be recognised by the presence of the Tudor badges added to the buttresses for which he was responsible. The internal elevations of the antechapel with their heraldic adornments are due to him and so is the design of the nine-light west window, the tracery of which is markedly different from that of the east window but shows the same motives as appear in the west window of St. James's Church, Bury. After the shell had been finished Wastell undertook the vaulting of the building and most of the finishing features by a series of contracts.[29]

Between 22 April and 7 June 1512, in partnership with Henry Semark, one of the wardens of the masons and a fellow townsman of Bury, he undertook to make the high vaults of the whole chapel 'accordyng to a platt therof' signed by the King's executors. The contractors were to receive £100 for each of the twelve bays and the work was to be completed in three years. The college agreed to supply the necessary tackle and to allow the contractors the materials of two bays of the great scaffold after it had been dismantled. By a supplementary agreement made between Wastell and Semark and dated 7 June the latter disclaimed any share in the profits and was freed from any liability but undertook to give diligent attendance on the work for the sum of 20 marks a year and not to be absent without Wastell's leave; if Wastell died before the work was completed, it was agreed that profits and liabilities should be equally shared between Semark and Wastell's son Thomas.

In the three subsequent contracts that have been preserved Semark had no share actual or potential. On 4 January 1513 Wastell undertook to make 21 pinnacles of the buttresses, using as a model, though with slight modifications, a pinnacle already in position, and also to complete one of the four corner towers, receiving for the 22 pinnacles £140 and for the tower £100; the college was to provide ironwork worth 5s. for each pinnacle. A further contract of 4 March following provided for the erection by Wastell of the three remaining corner towers by 24 June at the price of £300 in all. Finally, on 4 August of the same year, 1513, he agreed to make the vaults of the two porches for £25 each, the vaults of seven chapels in the nave for £20 each, the vaults of nine chapels behind the choir 'of a more course worke' for £12 each, together with the battlements of all the porches and chapels, comprising twenty bays in all, for £5 per bay or £100 for the twenty. The nine vaults of a more coarse work are tierceron vaults, while the others are fan vaults; lying behind the choir, the chapels with these tierceron vaults are less conspicuous, but it is probable that they were given vaults of this form because the springers for them were already in position. Whereas the sixth chapel from the east on the north side has a fan vault, the corresponding one on the south side has tiercerons, and it is clear that when work ceased soon after Henry VII's accession, more progress had been made on the south side than on the north. It is possible that the openwork parapet above the main walls was the subject of another contract that has been lost. All these different works were to be carried out according to 'plattes' or drawings, and though it is not stated by whom they were made, there can be no doubt that the designs were those of Wastell himself. In the British Museum there is an early ink-and-wash drawing of the whole chapel viewed from the north which may be the approved design of the building, as it was to appear when completed, from Wastell's own hand.[30]

In giving the chapel a Tudor magnificence that entirely disregards the founder's behest about the avoidance of curious carving and busy moulding Wastell was, no doubt, acting in accordance with the instructions he received. The exterior of the new work at Peterborough and the interior of St. James's Church, Bury, show that he knew the value of plain wall surfaces and could dispense with ornament when necessary. His heightening and elaborate finishing of the four corner turrets may be criticised for giving them an undue emphasis and altering, not for the better, the proportions of the exterior as a whole; and the openwork parapet, graceful though it is and well related to the tall pinnacles, gives a frilly finish, teasing to the eye on a building of such length. The fan vault, which is the glory of the interior, depends largely for its effect on the succession of strongly emphasised transverse arches,

breaking up the compartments and providing just the right contrast to the spider's web of the vault itself. The springers of these arches may already have been in position in the choir and decided the form of the design. It is this emphasis on the structure that makes the vault of King's College Chapel a more satisfying work of architecture than the Vertues' vaults at Bath Abbey and Henry VII's Chapel. In evolving his type of fan vault Wastell seems to have adopted a pattern that he felt best expressed the structural form. The ribs radiate geometrically and in subdividing he carefully avoided the ogee forms illogically introduced by the Vertues in their fan vaults; the circular ribs of the conoids are clearly defined and are decorated with brattishing, sufficient to enliven the pattern without distracting the eye unduly. With such modifications as each interior required this was Wastell's almost standardised form of fan vault, admirable for the pure logic of its geometry.

In addition to the examples already mentioned, there are vaults of Wastell's type in the gate-tower of St. John's College, Cambridge, and in the tower of Fotheringhay Church, Northants. St. John's College was founded in 1510, and advantage may have been taken of the presence of Wastell in Cambridge to obtain from him plans and designs for the entrance court and gate-tower, though William Swayn appears to have been the mason in charge.

The will of John Wastell of Bury St. Edmunds is dated 3 May 1515 and was proved before the Sacrist of Bury on 25 May following.[9] It gives the impression of having been drawn up rather hastily by the testator himself without the aid of a clerk or notary. He bequeathed to the high altar of St. Mary's Church, Bury, 10s. for tithes forgotten and another 10s. to be distributed among the priests of the church for a trental of masses. He also directed that 5s. should be spent on painting an image of St. Dorothy, lately given to the church by his father. This shows that his father, if not still living, had only recently died. (Robert Wastell, the weaver, who witnessed the will of John Worlych in 1498, when John Wastell was one of the executors, was still alive in December 1519, when he was a witness to the will of John Hynseley, a carpenter of Bury.)[31] The testator left 6s. 8d. to each of his sisters, who are not named, and appointed as joint executrices his wife Jane and his mother Margaret, bequeathing to his wife 5 marks and all his 'apparell' and to his mother 10s. There are several references to Cambridge: to Nicholas Colyn, 'Frensheman in Cambrygge', 10s. was to be paid to defray a debt; there are bequests of a shilling each to three of the Houses of Friars in Cambridge and one of 10s. 'to the helpyng of some ornament in the Kyngis Colage'; all the testator's books at Cambridge were to be sold to the performing of his will. There is also an interesting mention of 'Richard Pynson of London prentor and Frensheman', who was to be paid 33s. 4d. 'in recompense for re-kenynge betwyn hym and me'.

The references to Cambridge and the bequest to King's College make it highly probable that this was the will of the master mason. But if it was, it is strange that there is no mention of his son Thomas who was to share the profits and liabilities of the contract for the high vault with Henry Semark by the agreement of 7 June 1512 if his father died before the work was finished. As there was a three-year time limit for the construction of the vault, which had not expired by May 1515, Thomas Wastell may have reaped some advantage from it. Alternatively, the absence of any reference to him might be explained by his being still under age: the building account of 1508–09 shows him being paid an apprentice's rate of a shilling a week. He was certainly living in July 1514, when John Wastell and Thomas Wastell together received 8s. 6d. under 'Purveyors' Costs'. The will does not suggest any great affluence, rather the reverse; but Wastell may not have come well out of his contracts. His salary continued to be paid up to 29 July 1515, and there is no mention of his death in the book of building accounts for the chapel in which this final payment is recorded. There is a remote possibility that the will of 1515 is that of a son of the master mason. On 9 May 1506 Henry VII, when returning from Walsingham, a little more than a week after his visit to Cambridge, broke his journey at Bury, and a few days later there is an entry in The King's Book of Payments recording the delivery of 33s. 4d. 'to M' Secretary for one John Wastell a scoler of Cambrige for his exebucion for one half yere begynnyng ye ixth Day of May'.[32] No John Wastell has been traced among the scholars of King's College or King's Hall

about that time. The death of the mason had certainly occurred before 20 May 1518, when new feoffees were appointed to administer the Margaret Odeham trust property in Bury to take the place of those deceased, one of whom is stated in the deeds to have been John Wastell.[33]

A further doubt arises from a reference to Wastell in the will of Thomas Howard, 2nd Duke of Norfolk, which was dated 31 May 1520 but not proved until 16 July 1524.[34] His body was to be buried in the priory church at *Thetford* before the high altar beneath a tomb, preparations for which had been made some years before. Reference is made in the will to an indenture, dated 31 August 1516, whereby his executors were empowered to raise from the issues of certain of his manors and lands the sum of £133 6s. 8d. for the making of his tomb, which was 'to be made and sett in the said Church of the priory of Thetford directly before the high awter where it was deuised by vs maister Clerk maister of the kings workis at Cambrige and Wastell fremason of Bury in the Countie of Norffolk [*sic*]. And the pictours of vs and of Agnes our wife to be sett togider theryppon as well as it may be with the said summe of cxxxiij li. vjs. viijd. In the same writing Indented specified by the aduyse of our kynnesmen Executours and frends'. 'Maister Clerk' is evidently the copyist's misreading of the surname of Thomas Lark, surveyor of the works at King's College. If Wastell died in May 1515, this conference at which he was present with the Duke and Thomas Lark must have taken place well over a year before the date of the indenture. It is clear from the wording of the will that the tomb had not been made at the date of signature (31 May 1520), so that Wastell cannot have been responsible for it, though he may have provided the design which was carried out by someone else. Excavations in the priory church at Thetford made in 1935 brought to light many fragments of a late Gothic tomb which, from its position, must have been the tomb of the 2nd Duke of Norfolk. The very small pieces remaining show a style consistent with Wastell's known work.[35] The tomb must have been destroyed within twenty years of its erection, soon after the Priory was dissolved. The Duke's body was reinterred in Lambeth Church, where there was formerly a brass commemorating him, perhaps removed from the tomb at

Thetford if the 'pictours' mentioned in the will were brasses and not sculptured effigies.[36]

It is possible, but very unlikely in view of his youth, that the freemason consulted was Thomas Wastell. No one with the surname of Wastell appears under Bury St. Edmunds in the return for the subsidy of 1523–24, whereas the names of Wastell's two wardens of the masons at King's College Chapel, Henry Semark and ROBERT WORLICH, are both entered.[37] Thomas Wastell and his mother may have left Bury and gone to live at Canterbury, where in the lists of 'Intrantes' — persons admitted to live and trade within the city on payment of an annual fine — the 'widow of John Wastell' appears under Westgate between the years 1518–19 and 1525–26 paying a fine of 4d.[38] Possibly, John Wastell married a Canterbury girl whom he met when he was at work on the Angel Steeple, and after his death she may have decided to return to her native city. There was a Thomas Wastell living at Canterbury in Northgate parish in 1546,[39] whose will, dated 16 December 1548, is entered in the Archdeaconry register among wills proved in September 1552.[40] He left to his wife Joan a life interest in his property in Canterbury and also a house and garden at Leeds (near Maidstone) with remainder to William and Robert, sons of his 'son in law', Nicholas Mallard. 'Son in law' probably has the common mediaeval meaning of stepson, for the house in Northgate had previously belonged to Thomas Mallard,[39] who was, presumably, his wife's previous husband. A brother, Piers Wastell, is mentioned, but there is no indication in the will that the testator was a mason.

If it can be assumed that the John Wastell of the will of 1515 was the freemason, he can hardly have been more than 55 years old at the time of his death seeing that his mother was still living and his father perhaps as well. When he joined Simon Clerk in the Saffron Walden contract of 1485, he is likely to have been at least 25 years of age, so that a date about 1460 is suggested for his birth. The surname of Wastell has not been found in Bury records before the arrival of the mason in the town, though it occurs in some Suffolk parishes from early in the 14th century. There was, however, a family of this name settled at Melbourn, south of Cambridge, in the early years of the 16th century to which the mason might have belonged. At Aston Abbots, near Aylesbury, there were Wastells living during the second half of the 15th century, and a namesake of the mason was Prior of Dunstable from 1495 to 1525. The surname also occurs between 1450 and 1550 in London, Middlesex, Norfolk, and in several parishes in Kent. *Martin WASTELL*, of Boughton Monchelsea, near Maidstone, was a mason with interests in a quarry. On 4 February 1534 he witnessed a deed concerning land in Boughton Monchelsea;[41] in 1536, in partnership with Thomas Young of Boughton, he supplied hard stone of Kent for Hampton Court;[42] and in his will, dated 1 March 1547 and proved 20 September 1548, he left to his son Oliver all his quarry tools and to his brother John, whom he named overseer, the sum of 6s. 8d.[43] His father was probably Roger Westell or Wastell, of Staplehurst, who died in February 1527, leaving three sons, Martin, John, and Thomas.[44] Though no relationship with this quarryman can be traced, a Kentish origin for John Wastell, the eminent mason, cannot be ruled out, in view of the migratory tendencies of masons in their early years, and indeed is as likely as any other.

A.O.
[1] *KCM*, College Accs., vol. v; [2] *Ibid.*, Kitchen Accs., vol. ix; [3] *BM*, Harl. MS. 58, *f.* 97; [4] *BW*, vi, 21; [5] *Ibid.*, 69, 99; [6] *Ibid.*, 117; [7] *BCM*, H.1–1–49, Nos. 3 and 4; [8] *Ibid.*, H.1–5–16; [9] *BW*, vii, 15v.; printed in TSB, 113; [10] *BW*, vi, 6 and 44; [11] *Ibid.*, 6; [12] *PCC*, 12 Adeane; [13] HDC; [14] CS, NS, XIX, 61; WDC, 208; [15] *BM*, Arundel MS. 68, *f.* 8 (*J.H.H.*); [16] *KCM*, Kitchen Accs., vol. x; [17] *TCM, KHA*, vols. xviii and xix; [18] *KHA*, xviii, 296; WCC, II, 452; [19] WCC, II, 460; [20] *KHA*, xviii, 296; xix, 147; [21] *CAS*, Publications, vol. x, 11; [22] *KCM*, Kitchen Accs., vol. x; Mundum Book 1498–99; [23] *KCM*, Mundum Book 1499–1500; [24] *BW*, vi, 128, 137v., 151v., etc.; [25] AOG, 487; WCC, I, 536n.; [26] *KCM*, Kitchen Accs., vol. xi; [27] *Ibid.*, Mundum Book 1506–07; [28] *Ibid.*, Building Accs. 1509–1515; [29] WCC, I, 608–14; SHB, 564–70; [30] *BM*, Cotton MS. Augustus I, i, 2; HTA, 72–3; [31] *BW*, viii, 69; [32] *PRO*, E.36–214, p. 60; [33] *BCM*, H.1–1–50, Nos. 2, 4, and 5; [34] *PCC*, 23 Bodfelde; [35] Information from *J.H.H.*; [36] HFH; [37] SGB, x, 348–58; [38] CIC; [39] KAR, XII, 4; [40] *ACW*, xxvii, 243; [41] AC, XXVII, 174; [42] SHB, 121; [43] *ACW*, xxvi, 249v.; [44] *Ibid.*, xvii, 173v.

[The following notes on buildings and monuments showing affinity to Wastell's work were entered by Arthur Oswald in his copy of the book:] (p. 318) The two western towers of *Lincoln Cathedral* show a similarity of treatment to the lower part of the Bell Harry Tower. They are usually dated late 14th century, but there appears to be no documentary evidence, and they could perhaps with better reason be claimed as late 15th century. Wastell might then have designed them.

(p. 319) Other work in East Anglia attributable to Wastell.

The south porch of *Rattlesden Church*. The front of this is built entirely of freestone. The design of the doorway and the treatment of its spandrels are characteristic of Wastell. So is the design of the plinth (cf. W. front of St. James's, Bury). The battlements show two motives, both typical: the ogee-headed panel with two cusped circles (cf. vaulted passageways under the towers of Dedham and Gt. St. Mary's, Cambridge) and the cusped lozenge used on Bell Harry Tower, at King's College Chapel, Lavenham and elsewhere. The porch is not vaulted. The parapet, similarly ornamented, is continued the full length of the aisle and across its east and west walls. The tracery of the aisle windows is of a kind used in the second quarter of the 15th century, and the parapet was evidently added when the porch was built. So too, probably, were the octagonal buttresses at the S.E. and S.W. corners of the aisles. They have crocketed finials.

The porch has been thought to be 16th century (J. R. Olorenshaw, "Notes on the Church of Rattlesden", p. 86, where the porch is illustrated). A date between 1485 and 1500 is more likely. The porch may have been a gift of Thomas Rattlesden, abbot of Bury 1479–97. He is believed to have been a native of the parish. The manor of Clopton Hall in Rattlesden belonged to the abbey of Bury.

(p. 320)

(Re Lavenham): He may also have been responsible for the rebuilding and heightening of the nave of *Isleham Church*, Cambs., at the expense of the Peyton family in or a little before 1495. There is an inscription on the roof dated 1495 and made at the expense of Christopher Peyton. The 14th-century pillars were kept but new arches with ornamented spandrels and a tall clerestory were built. The design of the spandrels is similar to those of Lavenham.

(Re tabernacles at King's College Chapel): cf. also those flanking the west doorway in the tower of *Aldington Church*, Kent, said to have been built by Archbishop Warham and possibly designed by Wastell. Other Wastellian detail appears among the decorative work

below the west window of this tower.

The fan vault at Fotheringhay is dated in Arabic numerals on the N.W. springer: "A^o D^o 1529to". It could not, therefore, have been designed by Wastell, but might have been the work of Henry Semark, who came from that region. (V.C.H. *Northants.*, ii, 575)

Monuments attributable to John Wastell; those of: Cardinal Morton, Archbishop of Canterbury 1486–1500, in crypt of Canterbury Cathedral.
William Warham, Archbishop 1503–32. In N. transept of ditto. No doubt erected in his lifetime, presumably before 1515.
Richard Redman, Bishop of Ely 1501–05. In Ely Cathedral, N. side of presbytery.

A.O.

[(p. 321) It can now be added to the account of the eastern chapels at Peterborough that the detailed record of the works of Abbot Robert Kirton (*Bodl.*, MS. Top. Northants. C.5, p. 174) shows that the abbot spent £2000 on the complete new building at the east end '*ultra et retro magnum siue summum altarem*'. It seems very probable that the great mason was John, son of John Wastell of Thetford. The elder John made his will on 25 January 1480/81, and it was proved on 5 April. In it he desired to be buried in the churchyard of the Holy Trinity at Thetford, to whose bell-tower he left 1*s*. His house was left to his wife Agnes and after her death to his son John unless she should have been forced to sell it. A daughter Agnes was to have £2 after her mother's death. The son John was made joint executor with his mother Agnes, showing that he was presumably an adult by the beginning of 1481. (*NRO*, Norwich Archdeaconry Court, Reg. 1469–1503, *f.* xix).

In my view it is unlikely that the will of John Wastell of Bury is that of the great master mason. *J.H.H.*]
[Note on the *Red Mount Chapel* at *Lynn*. (p. 319) Detailed investigation of the building and of the documents by Mr. Michael Begley shows clearly that only the lower part of the Chapel could have been built in 1483–85 by Robert Curraunt. The upper part of the Chapel, with the vaulting, was built in 1505–06 at a cost of £21 18*s*. 4*d*. (*NRO*, DCN, roll 1199). There can be no doubt that the vault was designed by Wastell (not by Simon Clerk).]

WATCHETT, Richard (*fl.* 1531) Mason

Warden of the masons at *Hampton Court* until 1531, when he was succeeded by WILLIAM REYNOLDS.

HKW, III, 304n.

WATERDEN, Geoffrey de (*fl.* 1264–1265) Carpenter (*Waterden, Norf.*)

Master Carpenter of *Norwich Cathedral Priory* in 1264–65.

NCM, roll 1

WATKINSON, Robert (*fl.* 1524–1525) Carver

Carver of Lilleshall, Salop; on 31 January 1524/5 contracted to make for the Palmers' Guild of Ludlow 'three substantial stories' at the east end of the chapel of St. John the Evangelist in the parish church of *St. Laurence, Ludlow*. The 'stories', i.e. figure-carvings, were to be 'according to his paper and better', and he was to be paid £10, with a further reward of £3 6s. 8d. if the work were satisfactory. The carvings were to be set up before Christmas 1525.

SHR, 3S, III (1903), i (after p. 138)

WATLINGTON, Richard [Watlyngton] (*fl.* 1539–) Carpenter

Warden of the carpenters at the pulling down of *Abingdon Abbey* in 1539.

(*L.F.S.*)   PRO, E.101–458–1

WATLINGTON, Thomas [Wadlyngton] (*fl.* 1511–†1535) Carpenter

From 1511 to 1514 worked at *King's College Chapel, Cambridge*, probably as one of the wardens of the carpenters under RICHARD RUSSELL. He received payments for purveying, but his name seems to have been sometimes confused with that of another carpenter, Richard Wadlingford (perhaps Wallingford). The other warden of the carpenters seems to have been WILLIAM BUXTON. The kitchen accounts of the college show that Watlington and Buxton were on several occasions entertained at dinner in hall, Watlington more often than Buxton.[1]

In 1529 Thomas Watlington was warden of the carpenters at *Cardinal College, Oxford*. He was paid for making a bridge over the water in Cowley Mead between St. Edmund's Well and the east side of the college, and two gates, one near the well, the other near a spot called Our Lady in the Wall.[2]

The will of Thomas Watlington, carpenter, of Warfield, Berks., was proved 24 January 1535.[3]

A.O.
[1] *KCM*, Building Acc. 1509–1515; Kitchen Accs., vol. xi; [2] *Bodl.*, MS. Top. Oxon. b. 16; Gutch, 'Collectanea Curiosa' (1781), I, 206; [3] *PPR*, Archd. of Berks. Reg. A. 302

WATSON, Thomas (*fl.* 1525–) Carpenter

In 1525 was paid £1 for making the 'selyng' or celure over the rood in *Bramley Church*, Hants.

WHC, 17

WATTON, John de (*fl.* 1327–) Mason

Master mason (*cementarius*); chief mason in charge of works done at the *Archbishop's Palace, York*, in 1327, taking 6d. a day, Sundays and feasts included. The palace was being fitted up as a royal residence for Queen Philippa during the campaign against the Scots.

SHB, 70; PRO, E.101–501–8 (*L.F.S.*)

WAUD, Richard de [Waude, 'Wand'] (*fl.* 1251–1252) Carpenter

Master carpenter; on 25 August 1251 undertook to provide the timberwork of two chambers in the royal manor of *Havering*, Essex, by task for 50 marks (£33 6s. 8d.). The masonry was to be built by Master ROBERT DE WALEDEN. Waud was to be paid £10 by order given on 1 May 1252.

CCR 1247–51, 556; CLR 1251–60, 44

WAUS, Theobald de [de Vallibus] (*fl.* 1277–1280) Carpenter

Was King's Carpenter *c.* 1277–80; in the former year he received a writ of aid on 16 June,[1] and before 1280 he was at work on the repairs of *Burghfield Bridge*, Berks., as in that year a commission was appointed to decide the responsibility for payment.[2] He may have been the Master Theobald the carpenter who worked at *Chillon* (Vaud, Switzerland) in 1266 and at *St.-Georges-d'Espéranche* (Isère, France) in 1274–75, being apparently the 'Master Theobald of St. George, carpenter' in charge of works in Savoy in 1281–90.[3]

[1] CPR 1272–81, 214; [2] JAB, I, 20; [3] A. J. Taylor in HKW, II, 1036

WAUZ, William de [Waus] (*fl.* 1255–1261) Mason

Master mason; from 1255 to 1258 orders were regularly given for livery of robes to him;[1] and in 1259 he was one of two masters with RICHARD OF ELTHAM in charge of repairs at *Westminster Palace*, under JOHN OF GLOUCESTER. In 1261 he was concerned with property transactions at Plumstead, Kent.[2]

[1] CCR 1254–6, 91, 239–40, 312; 1256–9, 13, 54, 159, 218; [2] ANJ, XXVIII, 139

WAVERLEY, John of (*fl.* 1226–1251) Mason (*Waverley, Surrey*)

Cistercian lay-brother and mason (*cementarius*) who, in spite of the regulations of his Order to the contrary, took charge of building works for lay patrons and notably for King Henry III. He probably took part in the rebuilding of the church of *Waverley Abbey*, whose sanctuary and transepts were completed in 1231.[1] On 22 March 1237 he was ordered to make the Queen's Chamber in *Westminster Palace*[2] and was engaged on the work until February 1239;[3] between 1246 and 1251 he was building the Cistercian Abbey of *Hayles*, Glos.[4] On 5 May 1251 he was sent by Henry III to *Darnhall*, Cheshire, to build a new retaining wall for the King's fishpond.[5]

(APD; LKC)
[1] CLR 1226–40, 8; CCR 1227–31, 491; [2] CPR 1232–47, 177; [3] CCR 1234–7, 425, 500; 1237–42, 12; CLR 1226–40, 258, 271, 276, 285, 298, 300–1, 364; [4] BCS, 27; [5] CCR 1247–51, 439; CLR 1245–51, 350

WAYTE, Robert (*fl.* 1415–   ) Mason

Contracted to do repairs to *Salisbury Cathedral* in 1415, when the tower and spire had sunk and were causing anxiety, in spite of the repairs which had been done towards the end of the 14th century (see PORTLAND, NICHOLAS). The renewed danger probably led to the insertion of the pair of strainer arches beneath the tower, which seem to belong to this period.

(APD; WPS); DSC, 151, 160

WEBBENHAM, Peter de (*fl.* 1370–   ) Mason

Peter de Webbenham, mason of London, contracted with the Dean and Chapter of St. Paul's to build a range of 18 shops in London, on 24 February 1369/70. He was to be paid 50 marks (£33 6s. 8d.) for the stone-work, with a coat and hood.

SHB, 443–4; (*SPM*, MS. 1074)

WELCH, Richard [Walshe, Welsch, -e] (*fl.* 1474–1478) Carpenter

Carpenter of Abingdon; in 1474–78 made the timberwork of the hall, chambers and other buildings of *Great Milton Manor*, Oxon., including an oriel over the gate.

Welch's contract for the carpentry work provides that he should be paid 14 marks (£9 6s. 8d.) and a gown, he to fell and hew the timber, but carriage to be at the lord's charge. He was also to make a gallery from the new chamber for 10s.

WAM, 9217, *ff.* 9v.–16, 42; SHB (2nd ed. 1967), 599–600; HGM

WELDON, John de (*fl.* 1308–   ) Mason

Master mason (*cementarius*) appointed on 4 December 1308 by Ralph Baldock, Bishop of London, to have permanent charge of the works and repairs of *St. Paul's Cathedral, London*. He was to be responsible for the upkeep of the whole of the old work, both of wood and of stone (*tam operis lignei quam lapidei*), and of the tower or belfry as well as the church (*tam in turri sive campanili quam corpore ipsius ecclesie*), reporting defects to the Keeper of the Fabric, and if the latter should neglect them, directly to the Bishop, or in his absence to the Chapter. In pursuance of his duty to watch for defects he was to put aside all other work except the New Work of the cathedral, on which he was also engaged. His fees were to be 2 marks (£1 6s. 8d.) yearly (apparently in respect of the New Work), plus £2 yearly payable at the octave of St. Paul and at Easter; with 8d. a day when working on the tower, 6d. a day when employed on the church, and 6d. likewise if he should be absent on the business of the works and leave a suitable substitute in charge. He was also to have two shops in the churchyard which Master Adam le Marbrer had held, with a yard between the shops and the Carnary, to lay stone in, from Michaelmas 1309; rent free but on condition of keeping them in repair. When the New Work should be finished Weldon was to remain in charge of the whole cathedral at the same fees.[1]

The New Work was that of the Lady Chapel, for which preparations were made in 1307 and which was structurally complete by the end of 1312, since Adam le Marbrer took on a contract to pave the four eastern bays on 25 January 1312/13.[2]

[1] CYS, VII, 91–3; [2] SHB, 419–20

WELDON, Thomas de (*fl.* 1272–1278) Mason (*Weldon, Northants.*)

Master in charge of works at *Rockingham Castle*, Northants., from 1272 until about 1276, taking 1s. 4d. a week; the working masons received 1s. 2d. in summer and 1s. in winter. In 1278 Weldon made a round window for the king's great chamber at Rockingham.

(*L.F.S.*)   *PRO*, E.101–480–15; HKW, II, 817

327

WELLS, John (*fl.* 1406–1407) Mason

Master mason in charge of the building of the tower of *Erith ('Earde') Church*, Kent, in 1406. On 9 December of that year John Luffwyk made his will, proved on 8 August 1407; in this he bequeathed 'a certain sum' and £10 for the work to be continued.

(*A.O.*) PCC, 14 Marche; DHC, *West Kent*, vi, 16

'WELLS, Master of' (*fl. c.* 1175–*c.* 1215)

The plan and design of *Wells Cathedral* form a unity to a degree unusual among English churches. The eastern arm has been largely rebuilt, and the west front is an addition in a distinct style, but all between these limits follows in essentials a single design, subject only to minor variations in execution. The dating of the design and of the building has been the subject of much controversy, but it is at least certain on documentary grounds that the plan cannot be earlier than 1174, but must have existed in or before 1186;[1] and that the church, exclusive of the west front, was virtually complete by *c.* 1230.[2] The construction of the five western bays of the nave was certainly separated by a definite break from that of the rest of the church, as is proved by the evidence of masons' marks as well as of details of construction.[3] This break may not have been of long duration, but the building of the western bays can be assigned approximately to the years 1215–30, under Master ADAM LOCK.

No evidence as to the identity of the original designer has so far come to light, but the master was certainly a man trained in the regional traditions of western England, and whose style had reached its full development uninfluenced by the new introduction of French style at Canterbury by WILLIAM OF SENS in 1175. The absolute independence of the Wells master from the influence of the French 'classic' style is extraordinary, and the more so when it is realised that his style, decidedly earlier than any work in France, had completely dropped the characteristics of Romanesque influence. This sudden freedom from the Romanesque tradition is even more remarkable in view of the many Gothic details which Wells has in common with buildings of the Romanesque Transition School of western England and South Wales, such as Worcester (nave bays), Lichfield (choir), St. David's and Glastonbury Abbey.

The contrast between the work at Wells and at Glastonbury is marked, and led Bilson to insist upon a later date for Wells than the documents will warrant. The east end of the great church at Glastonbury was certainly not begun before 1185; yet the Wells charters show that the work of the new church there was already in being by 1186 at the very latest. Any attempt to employ a sequence-dating must therefore be ruled out, and it becomes clear that Glastonbury was the product of a conservative master, trained in the same transitional school of the west, yet devoid of the creative genius of him of Wells.

The crucial documents at Wells, though they give positive evidence of the provision of a fabric fund by 1186 and possibly several years earlier, by no means preclude a start as early as 1175. The scheme was unquestionably initiated by Bishop Reginald, who was consecrated late in 1174, and died in 1191. It is in the highest degree unlikely that a prelate sufficiently energetic to determine upon a complete rebuilding of the church, would allow 10 or 12 years to slip by before taking any definite steps to embody his intentions in stone.

We are thus led to assume a date of *c.* 1175–80 for the production of the plan and general design, almost certainly by a young man in the first flush of his creative powers. The progressive modifications introduced during the building of the transepts and east nave over a period of some 40 years are not sufficient to indicate the advent of a fresh personality, but are such as would arise from second thoughts and more mature consideration by the original architect. There can be no serious doubt that the whole of the church as far as the north porch inclusive, was carried out by a single hand, but the variations in detail and constructional technique introduced in the five western bays are just sufficient to cause hesitation in assigning these also to the first master.

Against this it has to be remembered that a definite break took place, involving the dismissal of the building staff and the engagement of a new body of masons when work was resumed. It is difficult to resist the conclusion that this break coincided with the later years of the Interdict, 1209–13. It cannot be excluded as at least a possibility that the master survived to complete the nave, and in this case, he can only have been Adam

Lock, who would thus have died aged about 80. But should this not have been the case, the extremely conservative adherence to the old design (in spite of the deviations mentioned) suggests that Lock was a reverent pupil of the Master of Wells. The identity of the Master of Wells with THOMAS the Mason III should be borne in mind as a possibility. *J.H.H.* in CWE

[1] J. Armitage Robinson in AJ, LXXXV, 2–3; [2] J. Bilson in AJ, LXXXV, 63, 67–8; [3] SAP, XCIV, 123 ff.; XCV, 180

WELLS, Simon de [? S. le Peyntour, Pictor, Welles] (*fl. c.* 1240–1257) Carver (*Wells, Som.*)

Master; on 24 May 1257 Henry III ordered the Sheriff of Somerset to let Master Simon de Welles have 2 marks (£1 6s. 8d.) to come to Westminster and to dwell there and make a tomb over the body of Katherine the King's daughter in *Westminster Abbey*; and to carry Master Simon's tools to Westminster. Four days later order was given to the treasurer for 80 marks (£53 6s. 8d.) to be paid by instalments to Master Simon during his work on an image of gilt bronze to be placed on the same tomb. Finally, on 11 July further order was given to pay without delay to Master Simon 'who should have made a bronze image over the tomb' 5½ marks (£3 13s. 4d.) for his expenses in coming to London and returning homewards. In the event, an image of silver-gilt, laid on a wooden core, was made by William of Gloucester, the King's Goldsmith, for a total cost of £35 11s. 0d.

It would seem that Master Simon was a carver who either found himself unable to produce a bronze image, or whose design was not accepted. In any case he was probably engaged on the sculptures of the west front of *Wells Cathedral*.

The sculptor was identical with Master Simon le Peyntour (*Pictor*) who witnessed a number of documents of the Dean and Chapter of Wells during the latter part of the reign of Henry III,[1] and whose son Ralph was already one of the cathedral vicars by 1251.[2] 'Pictor' is here presumably used in the sense 'maker or designer of images'. (cf. Martin le Payntour, to whom RICHARD OF GAINSBOROUGH bequeathed two chisels and a 'hakhamer'.)

SGW 113, 145, 261; *PRO*, Issue Roll, 41 Hen. III, m. 4, 5 (Mrs. L. E. Tanner); cf. CLR 1251–60, 376, 385 [1] HMC, *Wells*, I, 315; II, 561, 562, 569, 572; SRS, XLVI (1946), 18; [2] HMC, *Wells.*, I, 132

WELLYS, Richard (*fl.* 1472–   ) Carpenter

Carpenter of *Calais*, was on 3 February 1472 appointed master carpenter of the King's works there and in the marches, with a house and the usual fees of office, in reversion after JOHN PACCHE. The appointment, however, did not take effect.

CPR 1467–76, 313; HKW, II, 1054n.

WELOT, Henry [Wylot] (*fl.* 1386–   ) Mason

Mason of London, sworn one of the Masters of the Mistery of Masons on 13 August 1386.

(*A.O.*)   CLB, 'H', 273–4

WELOT, John [Wilet, Wilot, Wylot] (*fl.* 1356–1388) Mason

Perhaps identical with the John Wilet who worked between July 1349 and October 1351 at the *Tower of London* taking 5½d. or 6d. a day.[1] Was one of the six layers and setters named in the London Regulations for the Trade of Masons in 1356; in 1362–63 he did work at *Windsor Castle*, taking 6d. a day and also receiving £71 10s. 0d. and £13 6s. 8d. for making vaults at task. In 1364 he was paid £295 6s. 8d. jointly with JOHN MARTYN for building a wall at task, in 1365–66 £102 13s. 4d. jointly with Martyn and HUGH KYMPTON for building a wall at task, and in 1367–68, £53 6s. 8d. for building part of a tower at task. In 1386–88, John Wylot, mason, was building walls for the New College manor of *Adderbury*, Oxon., taking 4d. a day.[2]

KJC; **KJI**; HKW, II, 877–80 [1] *PRO*, E.101–471–2, 6; [2] *NCO*, Adderbury Accs., 10–11, 11–12 Ric. II

WELOT, William [Wylot] (*fl.* 1382–1383) Mason

Employed by New College at *Adderbury*, Oxon., in 1382–83 to repair the church vestry.

NCO, Kingham Accs., 'A', 6–7 Ric. II

Welsche, Richard—see WELCH

WENDLINGBURGH, Robert de (*fl.* 1361–   ) Mason (? *Wendlebury, Oxon.*)

Warden (*apparelator*) of the masons at *Windsor Castle* from 12 April to 1 November 1361.

HWC, I, 182, 218

WENDULBURGH, John [Wendelburgh] (*fl.* ? 1380–1413) Mason (? *Wendlebury, Oxon.*)

At Coventry in 1380 two masons, John

Lincoln and (? John) Wendelburgh were assaulted by Thomas Whateley and three others, all masons; Lincoln was killed and Wendelburgh injured. On 31 August 1413 John Wendelburgh, mason, gave a bond in £40 to the Prior of *Coventry Cathedral*, implying that he was to carry out building work there.

DS. XVI, 44; XVII, 65 (*G.M.D.B.*)

WERMINGTON, William de (†*c.* 1350) Mason

Master mason at *Croyland Abbey*, Lincs. His grave-slab, which shows him holding compass and square, is preserved in the abbey church. His name indicates that he came from Warmington, near Oundle, in the great quarrying district. His memorial is inscribed in French in Lombardic capitals of *c.* 1350 (see Appendix I). He cannot have been identical with WILLIAM DE CROYLAND.

(APD; BAA); VCH, *Lincs.*, II, 114; BAH; FNQ, II, 141

Wesey, William—see VESEY

Wespnade—see WYSPENADE

WEST, William, I (–†1390) Marbler

Commemorated on a brass at Sudborough, Northants. Possibly identical with William West, father of WILLIAM WEST II,[1] who may have been the William West who was sworn a master of the Masons' Mistery of London in 1416.[2] In 1422–23, a certain William West, probably a marbler, paid a rent of £7 13*s.* 4*d.* for extensive premises in St. Paul's Churchyard leased from the Dean and Chapter.[3]

[1] DCB, 205; [2] CLB, 'I', 172; [3] PRO, Eccl.2–137–171463 (2); see R. Emmerson in AAJ, CXXXI (1978), 66–7

WEST, William, II (*fl.* 1426–†1453) Marbler

Marbler of London; concerned in many property transactions in the city from 1426 to 1444;[1] died in 1453 after making his will on 20 April bequeathing a tenement to the master of the Hospital of St. Thomas of Acon, and referring to his deceased parents William and Lucy.[2] Some of his property descended to his daughter Joan, who married Thomas Cullyng (dead by 1455) and secondly John Oterton (living 1467).[3] Possibly son of WILLIAM WEST I.

[1] *LHR*, 155 (49), 158 (5, 7), 169 (57), 170 (46), 171 (33), 173 (4, 15); [2] SWL, II, 562; W. J. Williams in AQC, XLI, 136, 155; [3] *LHR*, 183 (34), 197 (26)

WESTCOTE, John (*fl.* 1386–1397) Mason

Mason of London and Maidstone; on 13 August 1386 he was sworn one of the Masters of the Masons' Mistery of London,[1] and on 25 June 1389 was the first of three masons with William Jancook and THOMAS CRUMP, who undertook to build a wharf at the *Tower of London* under the direction of HENRY YEVELEY.[2] On 6 March 1396/7 Westcote was one of the five Maidstone men licensed to impress masons for the repair of the walls and gates of *Rochester*.[3] A sum of £88 seems still to have been due to them in 1400.[4]

[1] CLB, 'H', 273; [2] SHB, 469–70; (*PRO*, E.101–502–10); [3] CPR 1396–9, 137; [4] *Ibid.* 1399–1401, 379

WESTERLEY, Robert [Westley] (*fl.* 1421–1461) Mason (*Westerleigh, Glos.*)

Was commissioned to take 30 masons for service abroad in May 1421, and soon after was working on the round tower of *Rouen Castle*, Normandy. Second mason at *Westminster Abbey* when work on the nave was resumed in March 1423/4, and was paid 3*s.* 4*d.* a week, the same rate as the rest. He also received expenses for travelling to the quarry with 'faussemoldes' and staying there for four days. The roll for 1424–25 is lost but Westerley worked for the whole of 1425–26 and for 48 weeks of 1426–27 and received in each year a special reward of 6*s.* 8*d.* as well as clothing worth 11*s.* In 1427–28 he received this clothing allowance for the last time, though he does not seem to have worked for the Abbey during the year.[1] On 28 February 1429/30 he was commissioned to take stonecutters for the making of cannon-balls,[2] so that he must then have been a mason of some standing in the royal service. Between 1436 and 1439 Westerley was warden of the masons at the palace of *Sheen*, taking 8*d.* a day. After the death of THOMAS MAPILTON he received a grant for life on 6 January 1438/9 of the office of King's Master Mason, at the usual fee of 12*d.* a day, together with his necessary costs and expenses when riding or otherwise.[3] His main work continued to be at Sheen, but in 1440–41 he also designed a new tower with a winding stair for the royal *Mews* at Charing Cross and from 1442 onwards was master mason of the works at *Tutbury Castle*, Staffs., when the south tower at the east end of the hall range was begun. The north tower, in a similar style, was built in 1457–58 while Westerley was still King's Mason and so responsible for works in the Duchy of Lancaster. He also had charge of the continuing works, under royal patronage, of the Bridgettine nunnery at *Syon*, being paid 1*s.* a day for 'working in the trasour' and 'drawing divers patrons'.

Soon after his appointment Henry VI founded the new college of *Eton*, and Westerley had charge of the masons' work there from early in 1441, being undoubtedly the designer of the original scheme for the college. In June he travelled to Oxford and Burford in search of masons, his activities threatening to interfere with the works of All Souls College, Oxford. On 25 April 1442 he had a reward of £10 for purveying freemasons in divers places of England.[4]

Westerley may have been the mason of the lord King who visited *Winchester College* (presumably from Eton) on 13 July 1443 'ad *supervidendum edificacionem Collegij*' and was given 3s. 4d. by the college authorities.[5]

On 1 December 1446 Westerley had a new grant of his office, but was deprived of it by the Act of Resumption of 6 November 1449. After a lapse of two years he was once more given a patent on 11 November 1451,[6] and retained the office until 27 July 1461, when he was superseded by THOMAS JURDAN, who was paid the fees of the office from that day.[7] There can be little doubt that the change was due to the dynastic revolution which had taken place in the spring, for a number of other royal officers of the works were replaced about the same time.

It seems not unlikely that Westerley was the author of the design for a bell-tower for *King's College, Cambridge*, preserved among the Cottonian manuscripts.[8] This agrees in proportions and character with the description given in the so-called will of Henry VI of c. 1448: 'In the myddel of the west pane of the cloistre a strong toure square, conteynyng .xxiiij. fete within the walles, and in height .Cxx. fete vnto the corbel table, and .iiij. smale tourettis ouer that, fined with pynacles, and a dore into the said cloistre ward, and outward noon',[9] and is clearly distinct from the tower proposed at the same period for Eton, which was to be 20 feet square internally and 140 high inclusive of pinnacles, but was not to be provided with turrets.[10] Mr. Gerald Cobb has shown that the unusual detail of the panelling on the turrets, and the general design, were followed by the tower of *St. Mary Aldermary Church, London*, begun in 1510.[11] Since the Cambridge tower was never built, this can only imply that its design on paper had become known to the architect of the London tower, and it follows that the drawing, or some version of it, had been

produced by 1510 at the latest. But it is completely unlike in style to the work of the leading London or King's College architects of that period: ROBERT and WILLIAM VERTUE, JOHN WASTELL, HENRY REDMAN, or JOHN LEBONS. Nor does it resemble in any way the original work of REGINALD ELY at King's College Chapel itself. On the other hand, the closest parallels for the detail suggest a date in the middle of the 15th century, and as there can be no question that the drawing was produced for showing to the King, it is likely that the chief mason at Westminster would be responsible. If Westerley was indeed the author, the design must be dated to within a few years after 1448.

APD; WKM; KJE; HKW, I, 267n., 462–3, 551; II, 848, 1001
[1] *WAM*, 23497–23500; [2] *CPR* 1429–36, 44; [3] *Ibid*. 1436–41, 228; [4] *MEC*, 12; *WCC*, I, 384n.; [5] *WCM*, Compotus 1442–43; [6] *CPR* 1446–52, 22, 500; [7] *PRO*, E.364–100 (B); [8] *BM*, Cotton MS. Aug. I, i, 3; reproduced HGE, Fig. 115; HTD, 100; [9] *WCC*, I, 369; [10] *Ibid*., 355; [11] COC, 73n.

WESTON, John (*fl.* 1433–*c*. 1450) Carpenter
Of Huntingdonshire; in 1433–34 he and Thomas Smart, carpenter, had contracted with John Turvey, prior of St. Neots, to make a roof for the Lady Chapel in *St. Neots Priory* within two years. They entered into a bond in £20 but, by suit of the present prior, Weston had been condemned for the £20 and £5 12s. 0d. besides, and was lying in the Fleet Prison.
PRO, C1–15–15 (*N.L.R.*)

WESTON, Walter (*fl.* 1396–1399) Mason
Subwarden of the masons during works at *Portchester Castle* from 1396 to 1399, under WALTER WALTON. Weston was paid 6d. per day, the same rate as the ordinary masons.
PRO, E.101–479–23, 24

WESTRAM, John (*fl.* 1350–1352) Mason
(*Westerham, Kent*)
Warden (*apparilator*) of the works of masonry at *Windsor Castle* from 26 April 1350, taking 3s. 6d. a week; he was still in charge in 1352.
HWC, I, 132, 134, 140, 144–5, 160, 162, 164; *PRO*, E.101–492–27, 28 (*G.P.J.*)

Westyll—see WASTELL

Wetham—see WYTHAM

WETHERALL, William (*fl. c.* 1540–) Carpenter
Built a house in St. Helen's, Bishopsgate, London, for Balthazar Guercy, surgeon. It consisted of a great hall and great chambers for £24; of which £3, and another £6 for

extras, remained unpaid.

PRO, ECP, 1083, 28 (*L.F.S.*); cf. *PRO*, Ct. of Requests, Hen. VIII, 4–283; 5–28 (*N.L.R.*)

WETYNG, William (*fl.* 1505–1508) Mason (*Weeting, Norf.*)

In or about 1505 whilst employed as a freemason on the King's works at *Westminster* was sent with a commission to impress 'warkfolkis'; at *Peterborough*, where he took up certain work-folk, he and his wife were arrested and imprisoned by the abbot, Robert Kirton, for unpaid rents in the abbot's lordship of Dowsthorp claimed from his wife as executrix of her former husband who had been the abbot's bailiff; as a result of his petition to the chancellor one of the clerks of chancery was sent with a commission, dated 5 February 1506, to obtain the abbot's reply.[1] The work-folk whom Wetyng took up were probably masons employed on the eastern chapels of the Abbey, where he himself had evidently worked before going to Westminster, presumably for employment on *Henry VII's Chapel*. In August 1508 he was one of the masons on the pay-roll at *King's College, Cambridge*, at the rate of 3*s.* 4*d.* a week.[2]

A.O.
[1] *PRO, ECP*, 370/1; [2] *KCM*, Building Acc. 1508–09

Weysey, William—see VESEY

WHALLESGRAVE, Thomas de (*fl.* 1364) Mason (*Falsgrave, Yorks. N. R.*)

Son of Matilda de Whallesgrave, mason (*cementarius*); on 12 July 1364 made a conditional grant of a yearly rent of 40*s.* from his capital messuage and two bovates of land in 'Whallesgrave' (Falsgrave) and Scarborough to the Bailiffs and Commonalty of *Scarborough*. This was a bond for completion of his contract to build a drawbridge of steps (*gradus versibilis*) for the town, perhaps at Aubrough bar.

WVB, 22; collated by Mr. M. Y. Ashcroft with original, *NYR*, DC/SCB

Whatley—see WHETELY

WHELAR, Richard [Wheler] (*fl.* 1441–†1458) Carpenter

Was appointed warden of the King's carpentry works for life on 10 October 1441;[1] he was the master in local charge at *Sheen Palace*, being paid 10*d.* a day, until his death in 1458.

[1] CPR 1441–6, 27; [2] *PRO*, E.101–473–18; 503–15; E. 28–88 (*H.M.C.*)

WHELPDALE, Thomas (*fl.* 1487–   ) Mason

Was paid the sum of 10*s.* 8*d.* for repairs to *Wigtoft Church*, Lincolnshire, in 1487.

APD; NIM

WHELPDALE, William (*fl.* ? 1462–1485) Mason

On 16 February 1461/2 one William Whelpdale was appointed to the office of purveyor of workmen and materials for the works at Westminster and the Tower of London for life, at the accustomed fees.[1] He may perhaps have been identical with a freemason of the same name who was paid 5*s.* in 1485 for making a cross in *Wigtoft Church*, Lincolnshire.

APD; NIM
[1] CPR 1461–67, 113

WHETELY, John, senior [Whytele] (*fl.* 1433–1441) Carpenter

Working at *Windsor Castle* for 14 days in 1433–34 when he was paid 6*d.* a day for repairs to the great stable and other work.[1] In 1439–40 he spent 83 days there, paid at the same rate, working on the new bridge in the lower bailey, repairs to the great stable, bakehouse, etc. He was accompanied by JOHN WHETELY, junior, during the whole of this time.[2] In the next year he worked for 114 days on the bridge in the middle bailey and the roof over the stair to the 'Dongon'.[3]

(*A.O.*)
[1] *PRO*, S.C.6–1302–7; [2] *Ibid.*, S.C.6–1302–8; E.101–546–3; [3] *Ibid.*, E.101–496–9

WHETELY, John, junior (*fl.* 1439–†1478) Carpenter

As John Whetele, junior, worked with JOHN WHETELY, senior, at *Windsor Castle* in 1439–40, and again in the following year, taking 6*d.* a day.[1] He was probably the John Wheteley for whom livery was bought at *Eton College* on 15 December 1448, costing 3*s.* a yard.[2] Presumably related to ROBERT WHETELY; was warden of the carpenters of the *London Bridge House* in 1468, when he certified measurements at certain Bridge properties in the parish of St. Olave, Southwark, with William Basse, carpenter.[3] Citizen and carpenter of London, he made his will on 7 November 1477, and it was proved on 17 April 1478.[4] He wished to be buried in the churchyard of St. Andrew Castle Baynard, London, and appointed Joan his wife executrix, and William Wheteley of London, carpenter, overseer; Richard Wheteley was a witness.

[1] *PRO*, S.C.6–1302–8; E.101–546–3; 496–9 (*A.O.*);

[2] *ECA*, Keys' Compotus *(G.P.J.)*; [3] *LBH*, H.85; I.34; [4] *CCL*, 223 Wilde

WHETELY, Paul [Wheteley] *(fl.* 1445–1446) Carpenter

Working at *Eton College* in 1445–46 when livery was bought for him at 2*s*. 6*d*. a yard (compared with 3*s*. a yard obtained for ROBERT WHETELY).

(G.P.J.)   *ECA*, John Vady's Acc.

WHETELY, Robert *(fl.* 1433–? 1470) Carpenter

In 1433–34 Robert Wheteley worked at *Windsor Castle* on repairing the great stable, with 'John Whytele' (WHETELY) for 14 days, each of the two men taking 6*d*. a day.[1] In 1440–41 he worked there for 22 days at 6*d*. a day, when a new bridge was made in the middle ward and a roof was erected over the stair of the 'Dongon'.[2] Was appointed warden of the carpenters on the works of *Eton College* in 1442, with fees of £10 a year and a livery,[3] and on 30 November 1443 undertook a contract for over £250 worth of carpentry work for the hall and chambers of the college; the final payment of £19 4*s*. 0*d*. for this work was made in 1446, and the hall and north and east sides of the college were in use by 1449.[4]

Whetely was possibly identical with 'the Carpenter of the King's College of St. Mary of Eton' who visited *Winchester College* on 2 April 1445 and was paid in all 10*s*. for a design *(portratura)* of the college's new inn at *Andover*, drawn on a parchment skin, as well as 1*s*. 8*d*. given to his servant *(famulus)*.[5]

In consideration of his good services on the building of Eton College he was granted the reversion of the office of chief carpenter of the works at *Westminster* and the *Tower* on 21 April 1445, to be operative upon the death of JOHN GOLDYNG.[6] This reversion never came into operation, however, as on Goldyng's surrender of the position it was granted on 9 July 1451 to SIMON CLENCHWARTON.

A new design and estimate for the chapel of Eton were prepared in February 1447/8, and a roof of wood is mentioned; later in the year Whetely became master carpenter for the work of the chapel. In 1448–49 he was in receipt of his salary of £10 a year[7] and his livery cost 3*s*. 4*d*. a yard.[8] The roof of the chapel was probably designed by Whetely, for it is clear that Goldyng must have been getting too old for his post. The roof has a clear span of 39 feet, 3 feet more than that of Eltham great hall, the next important roof built by the royal carpenters.

'Wheteley carpentarius de Eton' with his servant, visited King's College, Cambridge, on 17 and 18 May 1459, and was entertained by the Provost.[9] In 1470 Robert Wheteley was master carpenter of *London Bridge*.[10] It is possible that he may have been the Robert Whiteleg', carpenter of *Oxford*, who undertook to build a house in Catte Street there, according to a contract included as a specimen in a formulary of *c*. 1420 or later.[11]

(APD)

[1] *PRO*, S.C.6–1302–7 *(A.O.)*; [2] *PRO*, E.101–496–9 *(A.O.)*; [3] KJE; [4] WCC, I, 390; [5] *WCM*, Compotus 1444–45; [6] CPR 1441–6, 335; [7] *ECA*, Roger Keys' Compotus *(G.P.J.)*; [8] WCC, I, 399; [9] *KCM*, College Accs., vol. ii, *(A.O.)*; [10] LTR, xx, 4–5; [11] SHB, 415–16

Whighte, John—see WHITE

WHINFIELD, James [Whynfeld, Whynfell, Wynfeld] *(fl.* 1464–1485) Carpenter

Free of York in 1464. Master carpenter of *York Minster*; succeeded JOHN FORSTER between 1471 and 1475, and was still in office in 1485, when he and other carpenters were making altars for the use of the King's Chaplains at the time of Richard III's visit to York.

BHY, I, 254, 257–8, 261–2

Whipsnade, John—see WYSPENADE

WHITBY, Ralph de *(fl.* 1322–   ) Mason

Was master mason of *Beverley Minster* in 1322, during the building of the nave; he probably succeeded OLIVER OF STAINEFIELD.

MBM

White—see also WHYTE

WHITE, John [Whighte] *(fl.* 1530–1535) Mason

Freemason of Winchester; was paid £6 in 1534–35 for carving in freestone six hood-mould stops for three doors of the great hall at *Hampton Court*. White had been paid for other jobs of carving there at different dates from 1530 onwards.[1]

SHB, 113; LHC, I, 353
[1] *PRO*, E.36–241, pp. 127, 647

WHITE, William [Whyte] *(fl.* 1511–1512) Carpenter

Made the benches for the 'body of the Chirche' of *Great St. Mary's, Cambridge*, in 1511–12, when he was paid various sums for the work, as the churchwardens' accounts show. These benches have all been destroyed.

He was also paid 3s. 4d. for repairs to the roof and 3s. 4d. 'for Reward'.

(A.O.)   CWM, 38–41

WHYGHTE, John (fl. 1473) Carpenter

Carpenter of Sible Hedingham, Essex. On 17 October 1473 contracted to build a new stable and shippon (chepyn) at Water Hall near Wixoe, Suffolk, for Thomas Peyton the elder. The external dimensions were to be 51 feet by 19 feet 'of the reule', and Whyghte was to be paid £5, of which 40s. in hand and the balance when the work was set up. He was possibly identical with JOHN WHYTE, carpenter.

D. Dymond in VA, IX (1978), 10–11

Whynfeld, James—see WHINFIELD

Whyte—see also WHITE

WHYTE, John (fl. 1477–   ) Carpenter

Senior sworn master of the carpenters' craft of London in 1476/7 when on 26 February a report was made on the Abbot of Winchcombe's house in Fleet Street.[1] He was possibly identical with a timbermonger of the same name who with others had acquired premises in the parish of St. Bride, Fleet Street, in 1437;[2] or with JOHN WHYGHTE.

[1] RLW, II, 565; [2] LHR, 166 (16, 30)

WHYTTEN, John (fl. 1404–   ) Mason

Mason; on 14 September 1404 contracted to build all the stonework of a house on the north side of the church of St. Martin, Exeter, for £6 6s. 8d. The house was to have two gables at each end, two chimneys in the upper rooms, and two latrines, two doors and four windows.

SHB, 477–8; FFE

WIGBERT [Wigberhtus] (fl. c. 1050? –   ) Mason & Carver

An inscription: 'Wigberhtus artifex atque cementarius hunc fabricavit' states that this artist and mason carved the font at Little Billing, Northants. It is in Saxon style and probably dates from the 11th century.

VCH, Northants., II, 187; IV, 76

Wightham, Wihtum—see WYTHAM

Wilde, William de—see DEWILDE

Wilet—see WELOT

WILFRED, Hugh [Hugo Anglicus] (fl. c. 1315–1322) Mason

Master mason working in Avignon, where he built the Chapel of the Angels on the north side of the cathedral of Notre-Dame-des-Doms, c. 1315–22.

LPP, II, 138; SAK, I, 290

WILLAM, John (fl. 1415–   ) Carpenter

Of Basingstoke, Hants.; with WILLIAM AU-STYN, carpenter of the same place, contracted on 14 September 1415 to make the flat roof of the church of Hartley Wintney Priory, Hants., together with a bell-cote. The Prioress agreed to pay them £22, a pig, a wether, a gown worth 10s. or 10s. in cash, and to find William and six men food for a week when they came to set up the roof.

SHB, 492; HMC, 15R (x), 174

WILLIAM (fl. 1333–1335) Carver

Described as Brother William, one of the brethren of the house of St. Robert of Knaresborough, cementarius, was paid 5d. a day for carving stones for the bulwark of the royal lodge of Haywra in 1333–35.

(L.F.S.)   PRO, E.101–544–18

William the Carpenter—see FITZROGER

WILLIAM the Carpenter OI (fl. 1189) Carpenter

In 1189 held of the Abbot of Glastonbury a 'ferling' of land for a rent of 2s. and a gift, and was to serve in the office of carpentry when works were in progress.

LHS, 33

WILLIAM the Carpenter I (fl. 1278–1286) Carpenter

Carpenter to the treasurer of Christ Church Priory, Canterbury, in 1278, when he was paid for work in connection with new houses in Burgate, and had a robe worth 11s. 3d. He continued to receive robes of office until 1285–86, the prices varying from 9s. 7½d. to 12s.

LP, MS. 242, ff. 47v., 48, 55v., 67v., 72

WILLIAM the Carpenter II (fl. 1342–1344) Carpenter

Resident carpenter at Farnham Castle, Surrey, where with two men he rebuilt the bridge in front of the hall in 27 days in 1342. Two years later he made a 'fumerale' or smoke-louvre in the roof of the hall.

RMF, 133–4

W[ILLIAM] the Carpenter III (fl. 1345–   ) Carpenter

Master carpenter at York Minster in January 1344/5, when he was said to be an old man, unable to work at high levels. It was ordered that a young carpenter should be appointed, the old man being employed to survey defects.[1] The young man was presumably PHILIP OF LINCOLN, appointed master carpenter in 1346.

W. may have been identical with the 'Willelmus le carpenter de Copgrave' who took up the freedom of York in 1309–10.[2] In that case he would probably have succeeded RICHARD BRIGGES in office, about 1327.

[1] SHB, 55; [2] YCF

WILLIAM the Engineer [*Ingeniator*] (*fl.* 1195–1196) Mason

Was master mason at *Durham Cathedral* in 1195–96, having presumably succeeded RICHARD WOLVESTON. He may also have worked at *Norham Castle*.

(APD; TCC); DBB, App., v, xi; PR, 8 Ric. I, 255, 260

William the Englishman—see ENGLISHMAN

William the Geometer—see GEOMETER

William FitzThomas the Mason—see FITZ-THOMAS

WILLIAM the Mason [*Cementarius*] (*fl. c.* 1195–   ) Mason

Master mason, probably of *Oseney Abbey*, to which he made a grant of a tenement *c.* 1195. The grant bears seals of Master William and of his wife Agnes, daughter of Reginald.

(*E.M.J.*); OHS, xc (1929), 276

WILLIAMS, Rawlyn (*fl.* 1473) Mason

On 16 February 1472/3, with RALPH SPORRIER, mason, STEPHEN CANON and THOMAS SKIDMORE, carpenters, acted as a viewer of the City of Bristol.

Sothebys Catalogue 13/4/1981, Lot 15 (*G.M.D.B.*)

WILMER, John (*fl.* 1425–1442) Carpenter

A carpenter employed in Normandy during the English occupation, in 1425 at *Harfleur* and in 1429 at *Rouen*. From 1435 to 1442 he held office as Master of the works of carpentry in the bailliage of Rouen, and was an expert consulted in 1441 as to the repair of the *Church of St. Ouen*.

HKW, I, 463

Wilot—see WELOT

WILSON, Alexander (*fl.* 1486–†1510) Mason

Took up the freedom of *York* as a mason in 1486, and was appointed Common Mason of the city on 16 August 1506 in succession to CHRISTOPHER HORNER. He had a fee of 8*s.*; was confirmed in office on 9 January 1509, but died in September 1510.

YCF; RCHM, *York*, II, 174; *YML*, D & C Wills, 2.94

WILTON, Gilbert [Wiltone] (*fl.* 1274–1300) Carpenter

Master Gilbert de Wilton was the first of the working carpenters on the works of the *Tower of London* from 1274, when he was paid 6*d.* a day, his position being subordinate to that of JOHN OSEKYKN.[1]

In 1277–78 the sum of £1 for timber bought for the works was paid to 'Gilbert de Wilton of "Nutteley"', who was probably the same man.[2] In 1281/2 'Gilbert de Wyltone' was a witness to a deed dated at London.[3] In 1300 Isabella and Benedicta, daughters of Alice, the wife of Gilbert de Wiltone, carpenter, disposed of property in the parish of St. Giles without Cripplegate.[4]

[1] *PRO*, E.101–467–6 (4); [2] *Ibid.*, C.47–3–47; [3] *LBH*, Deed, F. 1; [4] *LHR*, 30(50)

'Wilton', Nicholas—see WALTON

WILTON, Richard (*fl.* 1351–1366) Carpenter

Was warden (*apparilator*) of the carpenters at *St. Stephen's Chapel* in 1351–54 under WILLIAM HERLAND. Wilton took 3*s.* 6*d.* a week,[1] and an account of works at Westminster Palace which runs from 4 June 1358 to 30 September 1359 shows that he was still in receipt of the same pay as warden (*apparator*) of the carpenters.[2] In 1366 he was at work at the *Tower of London*, where he was paid £3 6*s.* 8*d.* for making new gates at the entrance of the Tower, and a partition in the lions' house, at task.[3]

[1] BBW, 165; [2] *PRO*, E.101–472–5; cf. CPR 1354–8, 95; [3] *PRO*, E.101–472–17

WILTSHIRE John [Wylteschyre] (*fl.* 1425–1456) Carpenter

Carpenter employed by *New College, Oxford*, for various works over a long period. In 1425–26, with John Tredewell, he was making the great gate for the college manor of *Kingham*, Oxon.; from 1427 to 1439 he spent some part of every year on repairs of the college properties in Oxford. In 1427–29 with JOHN JYLKES he built a new chamber at *Patys Inn* (The Bull) for £14, and in 1430 undertook a task of £8 in the tenement called Hans, where he carried out smaller works for several years. In 1429–30 he also worked on *Merton College* property. In 1433–4 he made a granary door for the New College manor of *Swal-*

cliffe; in 1439–40 worked on the roof of *Shutford Chapel*, and then and in the following year on the stable and bakehouse of Swalcliffe at 6*d* a day. From 1442 to 1445 he was again working in Oxford at *Vine Hall, Studleys Inn*, and elsewhere; in 1444–45 he rode to Stratford on Avon to buy timber for the south chamber of *Swalcliffe Rectory*, and in 1445–46 worked for 34 days in making a stair to the warden's chamber at Kingham. He built a chamber at the west end of the great chamber at Swalcliffe in 1448–49, and was engaged on the choir (*chor' infra cancellam*) of *Swalcliffe Church* in 1450–51. From 1453 to 1455 he was building a new stable at Kingham, and in 1455–56 spent 11 days making a gate next the pinfold at Swalcliffe, taking only 5*d*. a day.

GOC; *NCO*, Accs., Kingham, Oxford City, Swalcliffe

WILTSHIRE, William [Wyltshire] (*fl.* 1412–   ) **Mason**

Was one of the sworn masons of London in 1412 (with WALTER WALTON) when a plot of ground was surveyed for the extension of St. John's Church in Walbrook.

CLB, 'I', 102

WIMUND (*fl.* 1090–1120) **? Engineer**

Was the holder, under the Archbishop of Canterbury, of Leaveland in Kent, in the hundred of Faversham, at a date between December 1093 and October 1096. The holding was of one knight's fee, and Wimund had apparently inherited it from Richard the constable, the Domesday holder of 1086. It was established by the late Sir Charles Clay that the inheritance of Leaveland descended to Nathanael de Levelande son of Geoffrey; that this Geoffrey was GEOFFREY the Engineer who in 1129–30 was keeper of the Old Palace of Westminster; and that this office of keeper was claimed by the Leaveland family 'from the conquest of England', i.e. in 1066.

It appears that until 1157 the hereditary keepers of the 'Leaveland' family had technical qualifications which enabled them to have actual charge of the maintenance of the royal houses at Westminster, and if this was true of Wimund it is likely that he was the designer of the great hall of King William Rufus, built in 1097–99.

C. T. Clay in EHR, LIX (1944), 1–21; cf. HAC, 148

WINCHCOMBE, Richard [Winchecumbe, Wynchecombe] (*fl.* 1398–1440) **Mason**

In the winter of 1398–99 a mason named Richard Wynchecombe worked for 52 days at *Portchester Castle*, Hants., taking 6*d*. a day; it is possible that he was one of the masons impressed for the King's works from Winchester College in July 1398.[1]

Winchcombe was working at the New College manor of *Swalcliffe*, Oxon., in 1404–05 and 1405–06; he was paid 2*s*. for 'forming' stones and it seems likely that he designed the great *Tithe Barn* built there in 1403–06.[2] He was the chief mason employed at the building of the chancel of *Adderbury Church*, Oxon., between 1408 and 1418, for New College, Oxford. He was paid 3*s*. 4*d*. a week besides payments in respect of his apprentice from 1412 to 1417, ranging from 1*s*. 6*d*. up to 2*s*. 9*d*. a week. Winchcombe was absent from the work in the year 1410–11, but was otherwise in charge for the whole or a considerable part of each year. In 1413–14 he visited Taynton to obtain stone, his travelling expenses being charged in the accounts.[3] Between 1410 and 1418 Winchcombe received livery from *New College*, and in 1412–13 was paid 3*s*. 3*d*. for one week's work upon the pinnacles of the college itself.[4] In 1408–09 Winchcombe was master mason to Richard Beauchamp, Earl of Warwick. He was working on a shop cellar in the town of *Warwick* (under the town *Court House*), for 12 weeks and 5 days at a basic rate of 3*s*. 4*d*. a week with an extra 4*d*. per week in respect of his being master (*eo quod stetit magister cementar' ibidem*) until Sunday after All Saints (4 November 1408), and then for 6 weeks at 3*s*. a week plus the reward of 4*d*. a week.[5]

Winchcombe must have had a private practice in Oxfordshire and his style has been found in the Milcombe Chapel at *Bloxham*, certain windows in *Broughton Church*, work at the church of *Deddington* and the reredos at *Enstone* (*c*. 1420), and the Wilcote Chapel at *Northleigh*, which was probably begun in 1439. He probably also designed a doorway at *Balliol College*, originally the entrance to the screens passage of the Master's Lodge (1426–31). Winchcombe very likely designed the transept at *Thame*, built from 1442 by JOHN BECKELEY, perhaps after Winchcombe's death. Similarities of style in *Northleach Church*, Glos., may well be due to close relationship of the 'Henrie Winchcombe' who scratched his name against a mason's mark on a nave column there (Mr. David Verey).

On 4 August 1430, the University of Oxford granted to Master Richard Winchcombe, mason (*lathomus*), while he continued to direct the works at the *Divinity School* (which had been started in 1424), a fee of £2 a year, a gown worth 13*s.* 4*d.*, and 4*s.* a week when engaged on the work there, in addition to lodging for himself and his workmen, and hay for his horse.[6] Winchcombe was succeeded on 16 January 1439/40 by THOMAS ELKIN, and it is possible that this was owing to his refusal or inability to economise on detail, which he had been ordered to do by the university authorities, who were evidently alarmed at the cost of the work.[7] He may, however, have died in 1440. Owing to the troubled period of the Wars of the Roses, work on the Divinity School was stopped for many years, and the vault was not put up until 1480–83, under the direction of WILLIAM ORCHARD. Enstone Church was appropriated to *Winchcombe Abbey*, of which it is highly probable Richard was the master mason.

A certain Master Richard Wynchecombe was paid 1*s.* 8*d.* by the Cellarer of *Worcester Cathedral Priory* in 1395–96 for repairing the latrine by the piggery (*infra Porcar'*), and in 1420 and 1421 Richard Wynchecombe was one of the masons at work on the priory bakehouse, taking 1*s.* 8*d.* a week, with meals at the Prior's expense.[8] An earlier *Richard of WINCHCOMBE* was Master Mason at *Calais* in 1356–62.[9]

KJI

[1] *PRO*, E.101–479–24; *WCM*, Compotus 1397–98; [2] *NCO*, Swalcliffe Acc. roll B; [3] HAR; [4] GOM, 69; [5] *BL*, Egerton roll 8772 (*G.M.D.B.*); [6] SHB, 589; [7] OEA, I, 46, 58, 191; [8] *WCO*, C.77, 83, 84; [9] HKW, I, 427n.; II, 1054

WINCHCOMBE, William de (*fl.* 1278–1282) Mason

Was a working mason at Vale Royal Abbey early in 1278, but from 28 April became undermaster of the works of *Builth Castle* under HENRY DE LEOMINSTER, and later on his own, when his pay was 3*s.* per week.

HKW, I, 295–6

WINCHELSEA, William of [Wynchelse] (*fl.* 1343–1346) Carpenter (*Winchelsea, Sussex*)

Was carpenter and *apparilator* at *Westminster Palace* in 1343–44. In 1346 he was associated with WILLIAM DE RAMSEY III in pressing craftsmen for service in France.

PRO, E.101–469–6; 167–8

Winchester, Thomas of—see WINTON

WINCHESTER, William (*fl.* 1366–   ) Mason

Was warden of the masons (*cementarius et*

apparitor) under HENRY YEVELEY in 1365–66, on the works of *Westminster Palace*, where he took wages of 6*d.* a day.

(APD; LKC); BBW, 196

WINTON, Thomas of (*fl.* 1312–1313)

Master, presumably from Winchester, brought to *Exeter* in 1313 when he spent four weeks from 25 June to 21 July in choosing and felling wood for the Bishop's Throne, which he may have designed. It was made by ROBERT DE GALMETON. Master Thomas was paid 3*s.* a week, and was given 5*s.* on his departure '*versus patriam suam*'. He was evidently identical with THOMAS OF WITNEY.

BPE, 12, 16, 53; *CEF*

WINTRINGHAM, William [Wyntryngham] (*fl.* 1361–†*c.* 1392) Carpenter

Carpenter; from 1 November 1361 to 1365 supervised the erection of the great hall roof of *Windsor Castle*, being paid at the rate of 4*s.* a week. The designer was probably WILLIAM HERLAND, the King's Chief Carpenter, but it was Wintringham who was appointed on 30 July 1362 to impress carpenters and sawyers for the works; one Robert Wintringham was associated with him. In 1367–68 Wintringham made a wooden water gate towards the Thames at *Rotherhithe Manor*.[1]

On 12 March 1372/3 he was granted £20 a year and a vesture by John of Gaunt, Duke of Lancaster, for his good service, which implies that he had already worked for the Duke for some time. The next day a revised grant was issued to include in its terms the office of carpenter to the Duke. On 21 June 1373 an order was made for £10 arrears of his fee to be paid to Wintringham,[2] who on 1 December of the same year contracted to build shops in *Southwark*, by the gatehouse of the Prior of Lewes, Wintringham himself being styled 'of Southwark'.[3] They were to be finished by Christmas 1374, Wintringham receiving £120.

John of Gaunt was evidently engaged on building schemes of considerable size, for on 11 October 1374 he ordered that all the timber within the rape of Hastings, Sussex, should be delivered to William Wintringham 'master and surveyor of all our works in England',[4] and in 1375 he was engaged on work at Gaunt's Palace of the *Savoy*, with HENRY YEVELEY the mason.[5] Meanwhile Wintringham had also been working on the Abbot's house at *Westminster Abbey* where in

1375–76 he was paid £7, besides receiving allowances of food. The timber roof of the Abbot's Hall formed the chief part of the work.[6] This roof was probably to the design of either William or HUGH HERLAND.

Early in 1380 he agreed to build a new chapel and houses within the Duke's *Castle* of *Hertford* for £440, and the formal contract was executed on 1 May.[7] The buildings were to be of timber, and orders were given on 1 July to cut oaks for the work, while instructions were given to the Duke's receiver in Hertfordshire in the following February to provide oak rafters and to cut 12 oaks for the furtherance of the works. On 27 April 1381 a further order was given to cut, by the surveyance of William Wintringham, 6 oaks in the wood of St. Albans Abbey called 'Northaghwode', 6 oaks in the Bishop of Ely's wood at Hatfield, and 12 oaks in the Duke's park at Hertford; the oaks at St. Albans and Hatfield had been given by the Abbot and Bishop to the Duke.

The receiver for Sussex was ordered on 12 May 1381 to pay Wintringham 100 marks yearly for the works at Hertford Castle, and the work must have been approaching completion in December 1382, when 12 fothers of lead were being laid on the roofs by the Duke's plumber, Piers Clete of Lambourne.[8]

In 1386 Wintringham was one of several men who acquired certain houses in the parish of St. Dunstan in the East, London;[9] and in 1388 he was supplying timber for the works of *London Bridge* and also supervised the making of the new drawbridge, for which he was paid £2.[10] Later in the same year he was paid £2 for his labour and supervision of the building of a certain new house to be built by the great door of *St. Paul's Cathedral*, where the old shop of Roger Elys stood.[11] In 1390 he was selling planks and laths to the works of London Bridge.[12]

As John of Gaunt's chief carpenter, Wintringham probably designed the timberwork for the new buildings at *Kenilworth Castle*, though the work was still going on for several years after Wintringham's death in 1391–92. The new great hall at Kenilworth was roofed with a single span of 45 feet, the widest that had been attempted by means of trussing, though to be eclipsed within a few years by the 69 feet of Westminster Hall.

Wintringham, with John Maudeleyn and John Louth, seems to have purchased a house and shop in Westminster in April 1390,[13] but he was dead by 10 February 1391/2, when Robert Wintringham, his cousin and heir, quitclaimed to Robert Lyndesey and others lands in the parish of St. Olave, Southwark, which had been William's property;[14] on 19 February Thomas Bridlyngton, citizen and tailor of London, granted by charter to John Maudeleyn and others all the tenements in Southwark 'late of William de Wyntryngham carpenter and by him new built'.[15] Wintringham was M.P. as burgess for Southwark in the Parliament of October 1377.

Unfortunately, most of Wintringham's known works have been destroyed; the form of the hall roof in Windsor Castle is known from an engraving by Hollar, showing a state banquet,[16] and an Elizabethan plan showing the timber buildings of Hertford Castle has been preserved.[17]

HMA

[1] HWC, I, 185, 219; HKW, II, 881, 991, 993; [2] JGR 1372–6, 590, 854, 1853; [3] SHB, 446–8; (*BM*, Cotton MS, Vesp. F. xv, *f.* 183); cf. SYC, XLIII; [4] JGR 1372–6, 1543; [5] *PRO*, D.L.28-3-1; [6] RAW, 19–20; [7] SHB, 459–60; [8] JGR 1379–83, 148, 276, 278, 921, 339, 448, 466, 519, 521, 738, 738a; [9] *LHR*, 115 (21); [10] LBH, Accs., 7 m.8 (xvii), m.10 (xxxvi), m.12 (Li); P. E. Jones in AAJ, 3 S, XVI (1953), 59; [11] *LBH*, Accs., 8 m.6 (vii); [12] *LBH*, Accs., 9 m. 10 (xli), 10 m.7 (vi); [13] CCR 1389–92, 173; [14] *Ibid.*, 541; [15] *Ibid.*, 552; [16] HWH, Pl. LXIV; [17] CGF, 142

WISBECH, William of [Wysbeche] (*fl.* 1336–1341) Mason (*Wisbech, Cambs.*)

Leading mason at *Ely Cathedral* from 1336 to 1341 under JOHN ATTE GRENE. Wisbech received a yearly robe worth 10*s.* or 11*s.*

CSR, I, 57; II, 84, 97, 110

WISSWALL, Thomas (*fl.* 1542–1591) Mason

Was city mason at *Chester*; in 1542 he did two days' work at 6*d.* a day, on moving the Cross at *St. Mary-on-the-Hill Church*, and worked for a week on the north porch. He did further small works there in the following year, in 1545, and from 1547 to 1549.[1] Wisswall was appointed Master Mason of Chester and Flint on 26 July 1544 and held the office until 1577.[2] He did not surrender his patent as mason of the City of Chester bound to maintain the city walls for 30*s.* a year until 2 January 1591.[3]

[1] ECM, 220–1; [2] HKW, III, 418; [3] EETS, O.S. 108, 146; cf. W. H. Rylands in HSLC, L, 148

Witham—see WYTHAM

Wither, John—see WYTHER

WITNEY, Thomas of [W(h)itteneye, Wyt-

(t)eney(e), Wyttheneye, T. le Maceoun] (*fl.* 1292–1342) Mason (? *Witney, Oxon.*)

Was presumably the Thomas de Witteneye or Whitteneye who worked as a mason (*cementarius*) at 5½*d.* a day and later at 2*s.* 9*d.* a week at the first building of *St. Stephen's Chapel, Westminster*, between October 1292 and September 1293, and again from July to September 1294.[1] The wages earned show that he was already a fully trained, though still junior, craftsman. It is therefore likely that he was born about 1270, and in the town of Witney, Oxfordshire, one of the major manors of the Bishop of Winchester. This fact, and the building of the noble tower and spire of Witney Church shortly before Thomas's time, may have had great influence upon his career. It is also not unlikely that he may have trained at Oxford, where Merton College Chapel was built in 1289–94.

In or before 1311 Thomas de Wyteneye, mason, with his wife Margery, was living in Winchester, and they had by then sold a property in Calpe (St. Thomas's) Street.[2] By this time Witney was certainly prosperous, as he had acquired six acres of valuable meadow at Michelmersh, some 8 miles to the southwest of Winchester, which he granted in November 1313 to the cathedral priory.[3] This was probably part of a transaction to secure a corrody from the priory, a well known form of endowment assurance. It is safe to assume that Witney was already master mason in charge of the cathedral works which included alterations to the eastern arm and the provision of the new choir stalls made by WILLIAM LYNGWODE in 1308–10. He entered into an agreement with the Prior of St. Swithun's, Richard of Enford (1309–27) to undertake the work of the presbytery at the joint cost of the bishop and the priory. This is known only from a surviving mediaeval index to documents now missing from the cathedral chartulary, and he appears as 'Master T. of W., mason'.[4] Later evidence leaves no doubt as to his identity.

By this time Witney was achieving a wider fame, and his association with the building of Exeter Cathedral began. There the great architect ROGER the Mason II had died in July 1310, and his successor Master WILLIAM LUVE cannot have been of the same calibre. Late in April 1311 Master WILLIAM DE SCHOVERWILLE was brought in from Salisbury as a consultant to view the works. Then, when the question arose of choosing suitable timber to fell for the Bishop's Throne, the Exeter chapter brought Master Thomas from Winchester on 25 June 1313 to spend four weeks with the carpenters, looking out timber from the woods of Norton, in Newton St. Cyres, and Chudleigh.[5] From the stylistic equivalence of the design of the Throne to the later work of Witney in Exeter Cathedral, it cannot be doubted that at this stage he must have produced detailed drawings from which the carpenters and carvers could work.

The Exeter accounts for three years are missing, but by Michaelmas 1316 Master Thomas was already in charge, and from April 1317 until June 1324 he was provided with a rent-free house near the Cathedral, which implies that he must have spent much of his time in Exeter.[6] He was not precluded from taking up other work, however, and from 1321 to 1325 was also supervising works in the royal *Castle* there.[7] The cathedral works included not only the completion of the crossing and the building of the nave, but several contained works of monumental art of the highest importance: the reredos and sedilia of 1316–26 and the pulpitum of 1317–25, all in an advanced style to which the wooden Bishop's Throne also belongs.[8]

Witney was paid a regular quarterly fee at the rate of £6 13*s.* 4*d.* a year, besides the annual rent of £1 12*s.* 0*d.* paid for his house. The fee was still being paid in full at Michaelmas 1342, but Witney had presumably died before the opening of the next surviving account in January 1347, when he had been succeeded by WILLIAM JOY. After the middle of 1324, when he ceased to enjoy the rent-free house, it may well be that Witney was often absent from Exeter. On the other hand, he is not likely to have been at Winchester, since in 1328–29 the Bishop of Exeter, John Grandisson, wrote to the Prior there on Witney's behalf to obtain payment of the daily corrody and yearly pension due to him and in arrears for some time past. In the letter Grandisson refers to Witney as 'a dearly loved member of our household and a valuable and willing servant to us and to our church of Exeter (*dilectus familiaris noster ac nobis et Ecclesie nostre Exoniensis serviens utilis et benevolus*)'. Furthermore, within the next year Grandisson wrote to the Abbot and convent of Sherborne commending to them a young man 'J. de Sparkeforde', son of Master Thomas de Wytteneye 'whose industry is of special value for the repair and in part new building, by his skill, of the fabric of our church of Exeter (*cujus industria ad Fabricam ecclesie nostre Exoniensis ejus artificio reparande et in parte de novo construende specialiter est electa*)'.[9] The son's name suggests that he was born either at Sparkford (St. Cross) by Winchester, or at Sparkford, Somerset, the former being more likely in that the date of birth would probably be *c.* 1305–10.

Stylistic resemblances between the clustered piers and general treatment of the Winchester presbytery and Witney's work at Exeter have long been remarked, and receive conclusive confirmation from the documents already quoted. The available records are so far less satisfactory in respect of several other important works which must be attributed to Witney primarily on the evidence of their style. The works in question are at Wells, Somerset; Malmesbury, Wiltshire; and Oxford. At *Wells Cathedral* there is a marked change of style between the chapter-house, completed by the end of 1306, and the Lady Chapel, certainly finished before 1326 and probably by 1319. It is the Lady Chapel, with associated works in the retrochoir, and also the central tower, that show marked similarity to Witney's known work at Exeter. The very unusual bases and mouldings of the retrochoir piers are closely akin to those of the clustered shafts of the Exeter pulpitum. The tracery of cusped 'spherical triangles' of the Wells Lady Chapel is directly paralleled by that of the Exeter Bishop's Throne and by windows in Witney's work in the Exeter north transept (1317–21) and nave. It is this unusual tracery which also indicates his responsibility for the new parts of the nave of *Malmesbury Abbey*, notably the clerestory windows. For Malmesbury no documentary evidence is known, but at Wells two records tend to confirm the presence of Thomas Witney.

In 1323 one Thomas le Masun was a witness to a document in company with members of the Wells chapter; common form in such cases strongly indicates that this was the consultant architect of the time. Secondly, the lay subsidy of 1327 shows that Thomas Mascon was a well-to-do resident of Wells (see THOMAS the Mason V). Some additional confirmation is given by the fact that Witney was succeeded at Exeter by William Joy, who had been in a subordinate position at Wells for some time before his appointment as master in 1329. If he had been undermaster, during Witney's periods of absence from Wells at Exeter, and then succeeded him as master when Witney was growing old, it would be natural that he should later be called to take over at Exeter. The building of the central tower of Wells in its original form is closely documented to the years 1315–21, and its marked resemblance to the tower at Witney Church seems highly evidential.

At Oxford the crossing of the chapel of *Merton College* was built in 1330–32 under Master Thomas the Mason (*Lathomus*), whose identity with Witney is once more suggested by the close likeness between the clustered shafts of the piers and their bases and caps to the comparable details of the nave piers at Exeter (see THOMAS the Mason VI). Retrospectively it is possible to suggest a further association between Merton College, Wells, and Exeter: in the Merton sacristy built in 1309–11 are three-light windows with cusped reticulated tracery of advanced design for their known date. These closely resemble traceries inserted in the south choir aisle at Wells and in the windows of the eastern transeptal chapels, where they are associated with a different but related pattern used by Witney at the west end of the Exeter nave on the south side.

Although by no means all of the works here attributed to Thomas Witney are fully documented, his certain work alone marks him out as one of the greatest creative personalities in English architecture. In the Exeter pulpitum, designed by 1317, he used what may be the first of English four-centred arches. In the vaulting of the Exeter nave, sharply contrasting with the earlier vault of the choir, Witney introduced the method of 'hand-drawn' adjustment to the true geometrical curves of the ribs, in order to present a suave appearance at the springing without the diagonals lurching off awkwardly. This was perhaps more than anything else a revolutionary change indicating the onset of later Gothic. If we accept as his the reticulated windows designed for the Merton sacristy by 1309, Witney was again a distinguished forerunner; and it is indeed hard to think of any other master likely to have introduced such an innovation then. Witney is also exceptional in that his creative designs were not limited to masonry: the wooden Bishop's Throne for Exeter, though made by ROBERT DE GALMETON in 1317, had evidently been designed by Witney four years earlier when he was brought from Winchester to choose specially suitable timber to be seasoned for the job. This overall responsibility for design, including that of carpentry, raises the possibility that it was he who, in or shortly before 1335, designed the hammerbeam trusses of the Winchester Pilgrims' Hall, the first known use of this structural principle on a major scale. It is very likely significant that it was in this year 1334–35 that the receiver of the Winchester Prior's treasury issued clothing to Thomas *cementarius*.

The career of Thomas of Witney is of importance not only for his triumphant genius, exemplified in details such as arches, mouldings and tracery and also in the magnificent spatial effects which he contrived in the Lady Chapel at Wells and in the nave of Exeter with its modified vault profiles. In spite of his early period of employment in Westminster Palace, and his much later supervision for the Crown of works in the Castle at Exeter, Witney worked mainly for private patrons, one of the first instances in England of a large free-lance practice, paralleled only by that of IVO DE RAGHTON and, in early life, that of NICHOLAS DE DERNEFORD, both of them his contemporaries; and by his junior RICHARD OF FARLEIGH. (See Appendix I.)

HME, 133–6; *J.H.H.* in CWE, 76–86, 100; AEC, ii, pp. xx-xxi
[1] *PRO*, E.101–468–6, rot. 25–69, 106–118; [2] KSW, 618–19; [3] CCR 1313–17, 37; [4] GCW, 242; [5] AEC, i, 71; [6] AEC, i, 72–154 *passim*; [7] CCR 1318–23, 662, 667; 1323–7, 66; CMA, no. 2229(a); cf. HKW, II, 649; [8] P. Morris in ANJ, XXIII, XXIV; [9] HRG, I, 218, 225

Adam WITTENEY was a mason-setter on the *Westminster Abbey* cloister from 1349 to 1352 at 2s. 1d. a week,[1] and in 1355 worked at *Westminster Palace* at 5d. and later 5½d. a day.[2]

[1] *WAM*, 23454; [2] *PRO*, E.101–471–11

Witteneye—see WITNEY

WOD, John del (*fl.* 1341) Carpenter
Of Ripon, Yorks.; on 11 September 1341 contracted with Sir Thomas Ughtred to build of good oak a 'mote' with a drawbridge (*pount tretise*) and a defensible chamber 30 feet long with a garderobe. This was to be in the close of land belonging to Sir Thomas near 'Yeveres', i.e. *Yearsley* in Coxwold parish, adjacent to Brandsby where the contract was dated. Del Wod was also to build a barn (*graunge*) the whole length of the 'mote' with posts standing 16 feet above the stone bases, and balks of 20 feet long, with two aisles; with a hall next the (said) chamber having posts and balks of the same sizes. All other timbers were to be according to the pattern (*solonc le scanteloune*) or 'scantling' agreed between the parties. The work was to be completed by 2 February following, del Wod receiving 8 marks of silver and a silk (or serge ?) gown, 40s. in advance and 40s. on 11 November, with £1 6s. 8d. and the gown on completion. An endorsement states that the pattern for the scantling of timber remained with Henry le Stedman and (? followed the sizes of) the roof timbers (*purlens*) of Sir Thomas Ughtred's house in York.

CWA, NS XXI (1921), 200–1; SHB (2nd ed. 1967), 595

WODE, Henry atte (*fl.* 1368–1369) Carpenter
Senior carpenter employed at *Rochester Castle*, in 1368–69 at 6d. a day; he was also paid £26 13s. 4d. for making a new house in the inner gateway at task.
(*A.O.*)   AC, II, 124–5

WODE, John (*fl.* 1436–1440) Mason
Mason of Colchester; contracted to rebuild the western tower of *Bury St. Edmunds Abbey Church* on 25 August 1436, perhaps to the design of THOMAS MAPILTON, who had been called in to advise on this subject in 1429. In Wode's contract it was provided that 'the seyd John Wode schall haue hys bord in the Couentys Halle for hym and hys man, for himself as a gentleman and for his servaunt as for a yoman'. He was to have £10 a year for seven years for himself and his man, and robes of gentleman's livery for himself and of yeoman's livery for his servant. By a second agreement, dated 1 September 1438, Wode undertook to find the wages, food and drink of all the masons employed on the tower at the rate of 3s. per man in winter and 3s. 4d. in summer.[1] On 15 October 1439 he was creditor of one Walter Ranton of Marks Tey, Essex, to the extent of £4 6s. 0d. when he was described as 'late of Colchester alias late of St. Osith, mason'; he may have done work at *St. Osyth Priory* or *Church*.[2] In 1439–40 John Wode and William his mate were paid 13s.

4*d*. in fees for three journeys to *Ely* to survey the defects of the Cathedral Chapter House, and received 6*s*. 8*d*. a week between them for 16 weeks' work on its repair. Richard, their servant, was paid 2*s*. 6*d*. weekly for the same period.[3]

(APD)

[1] SHB, 591–2; A, XXIII, 330; *BM*, Add. MS. 14848, *ff*. 308, 308v.; [2] CPR 1436–41, 324; [3] CUL, Add. 2956, *ff*. 188ff.

WODE, Laurence atte (*fl*. 1382–1397) Mason

Of Maidstone, Kent; on 25 November 1382 was partner with THOMAS CRUMP in a contract for work at *Cowling Castle*, Kent, for which they received £8 in final settlement. Crump seems to have taken atte Wode into partnership to help him out of his difficulties.[1] On 4 August 1387 he was one of nine men of Maidstone and district who gave recognizances for a sum of £360 due to John, Lord Cobham; Henry Yeveley, John Clifford and others.[2] Along with Robert Rowe of Aylesford and three others of Maidstone, atte Wode was on 6 March 1397 licensed to press masons for the repairs of the walls and gates of *Rochester*.[3]

(A.O.)

[1] AC, II, 99; [2] CCR 1385–89, 430; [3] CPR 1396–99, 137

Wode, William atte—see ATWOOD

WODEHAY, Robert (*fl*. 1414–1415) Carpenter

Carpenter of Andover, Hants.; in October 1414 he was given 6*d*. by the Bursars of Winchester College, and was stated to have made the belfry at *Andover*. In May 1415 he visited the college to speak with the warden about the rebuilding of the college's mill at *Shaw*, Berks., and was given 1*s*. 8*d*.

WCM, Compotus 1414–15

WODEHIRST, Robert de [Wadherst, –hyrst, Wodhurst] (*fl*. 1351–†1401) Mason (? *Woodhurst, Hunts.*)

Working as a mason at *Westminster Palace* from 3 October 1351 until 26 May 1352, taking 2*s*. a week under a special agreement, the standard rate being 2*s*. 9*d*.[1] It may be supposed that Wodehirst was a junior craftsman at the time. In 1354–55 he again appears, being paid for 145 days at 5½*d*. and then for 32 days at 6*d*.[2] From 5 June 1357 he was employed as a carver (*talliator*) at *St. Stephen's Chapel*, being paid 8*d*. a day until 24 July; from that date until 5 September, and

again from 24 April to 4 June 1358 he was paid at the rate of 6½*d*. a day.[3] During part of the year ending at Michaelmas 1358 at 3*s*. a week, and for 4 weeks thereafter at 3*s*. 4*d*., he was also working at *Westminster Abbey*, carving vault bosses for the south cloister.[4]

By this time he was receiving the highest specialist's rate of pay, and he probably obtained work of great responsibility elsewhere. It is likely that within the next few years he was in charge of the rebuilding of the presbytery clerestory of *Norwich Cathedral* (*c*. 1361–69) where the tracery designs closely resemble those of the Westminster cloisters. No accounts for this work have survived, but by 1385–86 Robert 'Wadherst' appears as master of the work of the Norwich Cathedral cloister, being paid 6*s*. 8*d*. for 2 weeks' work as well as £1 6*s*. 8*d*. yearly fee for supervision, and a robe worth 13*s*. 4*d*. Wodehirst paid back 10*s*. as a donation to the funds.[5] The traceries of the two western arches of the north walk were inserted at this time.

From 1387 to 1393 Wodehirst was master of the work of the reredos of the high altar (not the Lady Chapel Altar, as usually stated) of *Ely Cathedral*. There he was paid a yearly fee of £4, with his board when at Ely, and a robe; a fir pole 24 feet in length with which he might measure the work was bought for him at the price of 4*d*.[6] In 1392–93 a special gift of 6*s*. 8*d*. was made to Master Robert at the start of the 'new work'.[7] This work is nowhere described, but it seems likely that it may have been the lantern added to the great west tower. In view of the likeness between the windows of this lantern and the east window of the destroyed chapel of Queen's College, Oxford (1373–80), it seems possible that Wodehirst may have been identical with ROBERT the Mason VIII. In 1394 Norwich Cathedral Priory was a patron of the rebuilding of *St. Gregory's Church, Norwich*, which appears to be in Wodehirst's style.

Wodehirst's home was at Norwich, and on 8 July 1399 he appears there as one of the feoffees of the manor of Earlham.[8] He had acquired lands and houses in the city and in Pokethorpe next Norwich, and these he left to his wife Katherine, his son Robert, and daughter Maud, by a will proved on 23 November 1401.[9]

[1] *PRO*, E.101–471–6; [2] *Ibid.*, E.101–471–11; [3] *Ibid.*, E.101–472–4; [4] *WAM*, 23455; [5] *NCM*, roll 1058; [6] *CUL*, Add. 2956, *ff*. 158ff.; Novum Opus rolls 10–13, 16–17, Ric. II; [7] *CUL*, Add. 6388, p. 89; Treasurer's roll 16 Ric.

II; AJ, CXXXVII, 360 (*A.B.W.*); [8] CPR 1396–9, 588; [9] *NMR*, City Court Roll, No. 16, m. 10d.

Wodeman—see also WODMAN

WODEMAN, Richard [Woodeman] (*fl.* 1438–1444) Carpenter

First named of three carpenters, with JOHN TUTTEWYF and PIERS COLYN, all of Woodchurch, Kent, who on 20 December 1438 contracted to make the timberwork for the *Guildhall of Canterbury*. The work was to be finished by 1 August 1439 and the carpenters were to be paid £43 6s. 8d. The Guildhall was wantonly taken down by the corporation of Canterbury, 1950.[1] In 1443 Richard Woodeman made the doors of the new tower of *Lydd Church*, Kent, being paid £5 6s. 8d., as well as £1 13s. 4d. for wood. In the next year he made the new floor for the belfry at a cost of £2 6s. 8d. inclusive of a breakfast and drink for him and his men.[2]

[1] SHB, 510–12; (*CRM*, Bundle LVI A [7]) (*D.G.*); [2] FRL, 86, 89, 97

WODEROFE, James [Woderoffe, -rooff, Woderoue, Woderowe, Wodrove, Wooderofe] (*fl.* 1415–1451) Mason

James Woderoue and his brother JOHN WODEROUE, both masons, were admitted to the freedom of Norwich in 1415–16,[1] and were working together at *Norwich Cathedral* for 10 weeks, at 2s. 4d. each with food, in the same year. In 1420–21 and again in 1421–22 and 1427–28 robes were purchased for the two brothers. Between 1420 and 1422 they were paid £16 for vaulting three bays of the cloister at task, and had a 'reward' of 13s. 4d.[2] In 1424–25 James Wodrove and Henry Sperhawke with other masons were paid £2 18s. 8d. for making arches beneath the relic chamber (above the north ambulatory) and for paving,[3] and in 1427–28 James Woderofe is named as freemason, master of the work of the great cloister, when with JOHN HORNE 'le gravour' and WILLIAM REPPYS 'gravour', he was engaged on the completion of the keys of the cloister vaulting.[4]

In 1440 £1 1s. 8d. was paid to James Woderoue 'freemason' for jambs of freestone for the great gates of the preaching yard, near the north corner of the cathedral's west front.[5] In 1440–41 he was working for 57 days on the new chancel of *Wighton Church*, Norfolk, of which he was presumably the designer. The roof was not made until 1449–50 by WILLIAM BISHOP, and glazing of windows and the

provision of a tiled floor continued in 1455–57 and were not completed until 1470. The chancel survives.[6] In 1443–44 Woderofe made offerings to the fabric funds on behalf of the soul of his brother John, and he continued to have charge of the cathedral works until 1450–51.[6] Woderofe and JOHN JAKES were paid £2 2s. 0d. in 1444–45 for the making of the lavatory in the cloister.[8] In 1446–47 Woderofe was given a robe as livery. On 26 April 1449 James Woderooff of Norwich, mason, with John Jakes, had £4 for their expenses in travelling from Norwich to *Eton College*, and on 4 July Woderoof was allowed additional expenses 'by precept of the King' for coming from Norwich to Eton with his gear, and in the accounts for the year 1449–50 a sum of £7 was allowed for a reward given to James Wooderoffe, mason.[9] James Woderofe had died before 1459, when his widow Alice was buried in the church of St. George Colegate, Norwich, beside her husband.[10] In 1459–60 Nicholas Shaxton, who had been apprentice to Woderofe, took up the freedom of Norwich as a freemason.[11]

Woderofe was almost certainly the designer of the Erpingham Gate (1416–25) at Norwich, and of the remodelled west front of the cathedral (*c.* 1426–50) but he was clearly a recognised specialist of some kind to have been summoned to Eton, where the works were under the architectural control of ROBERT WESTERLEY, the King's Master Mason. The influence of James Woderofe's personal style is widespread in Norfolk and he was probably the designer of the west tower of *Wymondham Abbey*, begun in 1445.[12]

.A.B.W. in AJ, CXXXVII, 315–6; R. Fawcett in ANJ, LXII, 45–54
[1] EFN; [2] D. J. Stewart in AJ, XXXII, 174; *NCM* rolls 1070, 1073, 1074, 1075, 1077; [3] *NCM*, roll 267; [4] AJ, XXXII, 172; *NCM*, roll 1077; [5] *NCM*, roll 287; [6] *NRO*, DCN, Cellarer no. 163 etc. (*S.A.C.* and *P.C.*); [7] *NCM*, rolls 1083, 1088; [8] *Ibid.*, 1083 (*P.C.*); [9] KJE, 105 (38); [10] BHN, IV, 472; [11] EFN; [12] S. Heywood in AJ, CXXXVII, 350

WODEROFE, John (*fl.* 1414–†1443) Mason

With his brother JAMES WODEROFE was admitted to the freedom of Norwich in 1415–16,[1] and from that year onwards they worked together on the cloisters of *Norwich Cathedral*, at first at 2s. 4d. a week each with food, later at 4s. a week at their own board. They also received annual robes from the Sacrist or Communar, and occasional 'recreations'.[2] In 1443–44 James Woderofe made an offering to the funds on behalf of his brother's soul.[3] This seems to indicate that the enrolment of the will of John 'Woderove' on 21 November 1458 in the City Court was a long delayed matter of form.[4] The will enfeoffed Richard Boteler and James Woderove, citizen and freemason of Norwich, of lands in 'Brakendell, Trous, and Carhowe' acquired by John Woderofe and Margaret his wife, for the benefit of Margaret, and after her death for pious uses. Some properties in Trowse had been bought by 'John Woderove of Trous, fremason' and JOHN MARWE, freemason, in 1428–29.[5]

[1] EFN; [2] NCM, rolls 1070, 1073–5, 1077; [3] Ibid., roll 1083; [4] NMR, City Court Roll, No. 19A, m.1; [5] Ibid., Calendar of Deeds, roll 18, m.16, 16d.

Wodman—see also WODEMAN

WODMAN, John (fl. 1395–†c. 1413) Mason

Mason of Hexham; in 1395 owned land in Hawkswell, and on 20 January 1402/3 disposed of lands and tenements in Hexham. In 1404–05 he built the outer bridge of Norham Castle by contract for £26 13s. 4d., of which he was paid £25 in that year by the Receiver of the Bishopric of Durham.[1] He was dead before October 1413, when his son, John 'Horsley', disposed of 2½ burgages and 10 acres of land in Hexham which he had inherited from his father, to Sir Walter Coke, chaplain, and Horsley's brother, Patom Wodman.[2]

(A.O.)

[1] RND, 286; [2] HMC, 11R, VII, 71–2

WOLF, William (fl. 1338–1339) Carpenter

Leading carpenter employed on the repairs of Carmarthen Castle in 1338–39, when he was paid 2s. a week for work on the bakehouse, kitchen, chapel, and the King's great stable.

WWH, III, 58

WOLFEY, John ['Wolsey'] (fl. 1383–†1410) Carpenter

Carpenter of London; on 29 September 1383 contracted to build five houses in Adellane (Addle Street), London.[1] He was a viewer of the London Assize of Nuisance, c. 1405.[2] The will of John Wolfey, carpenter, made on 12 September 1410, was proved in the London Court of Husting on 3 November. It provided for his burial in the church of St. Giles without Cripplegate near his late wife Cristina, and for bequests to his wife Agnes and son John. He owned a brewery called 'le hert on the hoop' and held the lease of

another called 'le Cok on the Hoop', both in Fore Street, with houses and shops, and a close of land called 'Tymberhawe'.[3]

[1] SHB (2nd ed. 1967), 597–8; [2] M. Tatchell in GUM, II (1960–68), 129–31 (N.L.R.); [3] SWL, II, 385

WOLFHOW, Thomas [Wolf', Wolfo] (fl. 1418–1425) Carpenter

Of Petersfield, Hants.; on 6 July 1418 contracted to rebuild the Angel (afterwards Le George) Inn at Alresford, Hants., for the warden (Robert Thurbern) and fellows of Winchester College. The contract provides a detailed specification of the work, which was to be completed by 24 June 1419 at a cost of £50. In fact it was not finished until 1424, when the servant of the college bakehouse was sent to bring Wolfhow to Alresford to meet the Warden for an interview, to settle the price of extras carried out beyond the contract. The work was supervised by ROBERT HULLE, mason. Finally Wolfhow was given a present of £1 6s. 8d. in 1425.

SHB, 493–5; (WCM 1811); WCM, Alresford Farmer's Acc. 3 Hen. VI; Compotus 1418–19

WOLLASSON, Thomas (fl. 1381–1382) Carpenter

Carpenter of Rothwell, Yorks. On 28 July 1382 the receiver of Pontefract was ordered by John of Gaunt, Duke of Lancaster to pay to Thomas Wollasson, the Duke's master carpenter in those parts, fees of 2s. 6d. a week for all the time he had been in the Duke's service, beginning from the preceding Michaelmas.

JGR 1379–83, 716 (p. 235)

Woller, John—see WOLWARD

WOLMAN, John [Wulman] (fl. 1438–1440) Mason

From 1438 to 1440 was master mason at Saffron Walden Church, Essex, being paid at the rate of 3s. 8d. a week. His employment had probably begun earlier, for in 1439 he was paid 6s. 8d. for an old debt in the time of two churchwardens who do not appear in the accounts. The work seems to have comprised the building of the north aisle with its great west window, for the making of which deal boards and parchment were purchased to make 'moulds' for the mason. In 1440 Wolman received 46s. 8d. for buying hard stone in Lincolnshire. In 1439 he contributed a shilling towards the work, as did his successor, JOHN GERARD, who became master mason in 1441.

A.O.   CWW, ff. 5–16

Wolrich, John—see WORLICH

WOLSEY, Michael (*fl.* 1543–1544) Mason

Mason employed by *Chichester Cathedral* for routine repairs in 1543–44, when he was paid 1*s.* 3*d.* for mending a tomb in the Lady Chapel (probably the shrine of St. Richard) broken open by the Commissioners from the Privy Council; and 4*s.* 8*d.* for 9 days' work on pointing and repairs on the north side of the church.

M.E.C. Walcott in GM (1864), pt. i, 233–6

WOLSEY, William [Wulcy] (*fl.* 1479–1487) Carver

Was resident in Bury St. Edmunds in 1479, when he witnessed the will of Giles Cosyn, carver.[1] In 1484 or 1485 a 'gravor' of the same name was admitted a freeman of Norwich.[2] In 1487 an action over a debt of 8 marks was brought against William Wolsey, *late* of Bury St. Edmunds, carver, by John Clopton esquire.[3] This suggests that Wolsey may have been employed by John Clopton on work at his house, *Kentwell Hall, Long Melford*, or in *Melford Church*.

A.O.
[1] *BW*, ia, 297; [2] *EFN*; [3] *PRO*, De Banco Plea Roll, 902, m.41, Mich. 3 Hen. VII

WOLSTON, John (*fl.* 1427–1428) Mason

Freemason of Exeter; was warden of the masons of *Exeter Cathedral* in 1427–28, when he was sent with JOHN HARRY to Beer to purchase stone for the works of the cathedral. He also supervised the erection of houses in *Teignmouth*.

(APD); *FFE*; (*EDC*, No. 2976; Vicars Choral Documents No. 22230)

WOLVESTON, Richard de [*Ingeniator*] (*fl.* 1170–†*c.* 1182) Engineer

Was the chief architect working for Bishop Pudsey (Puiset) of Durham until about 1182. About 1170 he was building the western part of the keep of *Norham Castle*, and shortly afterwards the Galilee Porch at *Durham Cathedral*. He probably also designed the arcaded Constable's Hall in *Durham Castle*, and the old great hall, whose magnificent doorway is still preserved.

Wolveston also built the keep of *Bowes Castle*, Yorks., for Henry II, between 1170 and 1174 when between £400 and £500 was spent.[1] He took his name from lands which he held in Wolviston, county Durham, and which he afterwards gave to the cathedral priory in exchange for a carucate at Pittington. He also held demesne lands at Newton, near Durham, which in 1183, after his death were held by the Abbot of Peterborough.[2] He was probably succeeded as the Bishop's architect by WILLIAM the Engineer and CHRISTIAN the Mason.

Richard's work is the very finest of its period, and well deserves the remarkable contemporary encomiums upon him; he was not only said to be a skilful craftsman and experienced architect (*vir artificiosus fuisset opere et prudens architectus in omni structura artis forissecae*) but was also described as a most noteworthy man in skill and name to all the inhabitants of the district (*cunctis regionis hujus incolis arte et nomine notissimus*); he was said to have become a citizen of Durham.[3] These remarks occur as evidence of his credibility in connection with a miracle attributed to a small fragment of the cloth in which St. Cuthbert's body had been wrapped: Wolveston had been given the fragment by one of the monks who was his friend, and placed by him in a wallet among some 'painted letters which he possessed of very great beauty' (*infra carrecterum picturas, quas pulcherrimas habuit*: possibly illuminated initials which would have served as patterns for enrichment). He had left his wallet in the inn at Berwick-upon-Tweed, when returning to Durham from a visit to Norham. Flung into the fire, it was preserved from the flames. Wolveston is here described as '*simplex laicus*', a simple layman; important evidence of the standing of one of the foremost designers of the 12th century.

(APD; TCB)
[1] VCH, *Durham*, I, 304, 327; VCH, *Yorks. N.R.*, I, 44; [2] DBB, 2; FPD, 140–1n., 198n.; [3] RDL, 94–8, 111–12

WOLVEY, Thomas (*fl.* 1397–†1428) Mason

Mason of St. Albans; he was engaged in building the new work of the church of *Henley-on-Thames*, Oxon., in 1397, when WALTER WALTON of London, mason, and JOHN SWALLOW of Gloucestershire, mason, became sureties for his completion of the work.[1] During the following year he worked at *Westminster Hall*, being responsible for the upper 20 feet of two towers at the north end of the hall, together with their battlements, and the great window in the north gable; for this he was paid £160.[2] The designer of the work was HENRY YEVELEY. The *Clock Tower of St. Albans*, built in 1403–12, and closely resembling

Yeveley's Westminster Palace Clock Tower, was probably designed by Wolvey.[3] A tenement which had belonged to him was rented from St. Mary's Priory, Sopwell, in 1446.[4]

Dr. Eileen Roberts has identified Wolvey's work at Henley as the south chancel chapel, and on the basis of its mouldings has built up a corpus of other works in Hertfordshire which appear to be by Wolvey or to have been strongly influenced by his style. It is likely that he held office as Master Mason to *St. Albans Abbey* for some thirty years before his death, and that his responsibility included the making of the Perpendicular great west window in the front of the abbey church, now destroyed, much of *St. Peter's Church*, St. Albans, and works at other churches, some directly associated with the Abbey, as *Newnham St. Vincent* in the north of Hertfordshire, where work was done for the Abbot soon after 1420. Other work which may be Wolvey's includes the north chancel chapel at *King's Langley* and, far from the county, the surviving four-centred archway related to the 'St. Albans chamber' at *Gloucester Hall*, Oxford, now part of Worcester College, where building was done for Abbot John of Whethamstede, apparently between 1420 and 1426.

Wolvey died in 1428, his will being proved on 7 July; by it he appointed his son John Wolvey to be his executor, and described himself as 'Thomas Woluey de Childewyke' of the parish of St. Michael, St. Albans.[4] He was buried in St. Michael's Church, and his tombstone recorded that he had been one of King Richard II's masons: 'Hic jacet Thomas Wolvey Latomus in arte necnon armiger illustrissimi principis Ric. secundi quondam Regis Anglie qui obiit anno d'ni MCCCCXXX [*sic*] in vigilia S'ci Thome Martyris. Cujus anime propicietur deus. Amen.'[5]

(APD; BAA) **RTW**
[1] CCR 1396–9, 239; [2] *PRO*, E.101–473–11; [3] SAH, NS, I, 298–319; [4] W. Brigg in HGA, II (1897), 231; [5] *PPR*, Archdeaconry of St. Albans, 14 Stoneham; [6] GSM, II, pt. iii, 95

John WOLVEY, son of Thomas and probably a mason, was also buried in St. Michael's Church; he made his will on 27 April 1461, describing himself as of 'Chyldewyk' (Childwick) in St. Michael's parish, and leaving bequests to his daughter Sibyl and son Richard, who was to be his executor. The will was proved on 14 June 1462.

PPR, Archdeaconry of St. Albans, 104 Stoneham

Richard WOLVEY, son of John and grandson of Thomas, was also a mason, and was buried in St. Michael's as he directed 'by the grave of Thomas Wolvey my grandfather'. His will, made on 6 September 1491, describes him as 'of the town of St. Albans', and he left his tenement in 'Fisshpolestret' to Agnes his wife for her life and then to Joan Ive, daughter of John Ive, and her heirs, with remainder to the Master and Brethren of the Guild of the Chapel of All Saints in the churchyard of St. Peter's. Agnes his wife and John Peresson were to be his executors; the will was proved on 3 January 1493/4.[1] On his tomb was the inscription: 'Hic jacet Richardus Wolvey Lathomus filius Johannis Wolvey cum uxoribus suis Agnete & Agnete & cum octo filiis & decem filiabus suis; qui Richardus obiit ann. MCCCCXC [*sic*] quorum animabus. . . .'[2] His widow Agnes made her will on 2 September 1503, and it was proved on 16 September: she wished to be buried in St. Peter's churchyard next the tomb of her first husband John Browne. She left bequests including one to Joan, the wife of Robert Clement, daughter of John Eve, and property at Amersham, Bucks., to be sold and the proceeds spent in good uses 'for the health of my soul and the souls of the aforesaid John Broun and Richard Wolvey late my husbands'.[3]

Agnes's first husband, John Browne, made his will on 26 May 1484, and it was proved on 18 June; Agnes his wife was to be executrix and residuary legatee.[4]

(*A.O.*) (APD)
[1] *PPR*, Archdeaconry of St. Albans 71b Walingford; [2] GSM, II, pt. iii, 95; [3] *PPR*, 113b Walingford; [4] *Ibid.*, 45 Walingford; see also WFM, 582

WOLWARD, John [Woller, Wulward] (*fl.* 1390–1398) Carpenter

Probably master carpenter at *Canterbury Cathedral* during the building of the nave. On 7 February 1389/90 he received a grant of 3 years' exemption from jury service, and on 31 May 1393 a similar grant for a further five years, on account of this work.[1] In 1398 he received livery as an esquire of the Prior of Canterbury, being named immediately after THOMAS HOO.[2] The timber vault of the chapter house may be from Wolward's designs.

(A.O.)
¹ CPR 1388–92, 196; 1391–6, 271; ² Bodl. Tanner MS. 165

Wood, William at—see ATWOOD

Woodeman, Richard—see WODEMAN

Wooderoffe, James—see WODEROFE

Woodman—see WODEMAN; WODMAN; WUDEMAN

WOODWARD, William (fl. 1486–1488) Carpenter

Was master carpenter at *Calais*, succeeding JOHN PACCHE, from 1486 until 1488, when he was succeeded by WILLIAM TEMPLE.

HKW, III, 419

Woolrich, John—see WORLICH

WORCESTER, Ednoth of (fl. 968–974) Monk

A monk of Worcester, who is said to have built the church of *Ramsey Abbey*, Hunts., between 968 and 974.

APD; BAA

WORLICH, John [Wolrich, Wolryche, Wulrich, Wurlyche] (fl. 1443–1476) Mason

Was master mason at *King's College Chapel, Cambridge*, for a short period before the appointment of SIMON CLERK in 1477. He was perhaps identical with the John Worlech, mason, who worked at *All Souls College, Oxford*, for one week in March 1440/1 at 2s. 1d., and again for the second week of August 1442, taking 3s.¹ A fragment of a King's College building account covering four weeks from 6 July to 3 August and referable to the year 1443 contained the name of John Wolrich among the ordinary masons receiving wages for work on the college buildings,² when REGINALD ELY was the master mason. He probably continued to work under Ely on the chapel, when that was begun, until building stopped in 1461. In one of the day-books of the Provost, Robert Wodelark, there is a payment of 6s. 8d. to 'Worliche' under 18 August 1460,³ and on 4 February 1461 he was one of the guests whom the Provost entertained.⁴ For the next fifteen years work on the chapel was almost completely suspended; what little was done seems to have been confined to the side chapels of the choir. 'Worlich', however, appears among the guests in hall on 20 October 1471.

In 1464 a chapel was begun at *King's Hall*, Cambridge, on the site of the present chapel of Trinity College. The fabric seems to have been nearly finished, though wanting its roof, by 1469; work was then discontinued and not resumed until 1480. In the account for 1468–69 there is a payment of 8s. 4d. to 'John Wolryche mason and supervisor of the masons',⁵ from which it would appear that he was then master mason. It is possible, however, that the chapel was designed by Reginald Ely, who had been employed by the college between 1448 and 1452. It seems to have been a brick or brick-faced building. The possibility that John Worlich designed the entrance range of the *Schools* (begun *c.* 1470) or superintended its erection is discussed in the article on Reginald Ely.

If Worlich had worked under Ely from 1443 or earlier he would have been very familiar with his master's designs and intentions, so that when various donations made it possible to resume work at King's College Chapel on a limited scale in 1476, his appointment as master mason is not difficult to explain. The kitchen accounts of the college show that he was a guest on several occasions between January and July of that year,⁴ but it is in a document relating to a dispute between Michaelhouse and Gonville Hall over an 'eaves-drop' into the garden of Fysshwyke or Physwick Hostel that his position is definitely stated. John Wulrich, 'master mason of the King's College Royal of our Lady and Saint Nicholas', was one of the four arbitrators chosen by the Heads of the two colleges; the other three were JOHN BELL, 'Mason Warden in the same works', and two Cambridge carpenters.⁶ This document was brought to the notice of Horace Walpole by William Cole with the result that through the inclusion of his name in Walpole's *Anecdotes of Painting*, John Wulrich has acquired a prominence among English mediaeval architects that he hardly deserves. He had ceased to be master mason by the summer of 1477, when Simon Clerk superseded him, though whether on account of his death, departure, or dismissal the accounts do not reveal. The college Mundum Book for 1476–77 records an expenditure of £77 on the fabric of the new church and a sum of £6 17s. 2d. was paid 'at divers times' to 'John Wolriche and his son masons, working on the said new church'.⁷ Ironwork was being made for the east window and for the first window on the north side, but it is doubtful if their tracery had been inserted before the disappearance of Worlich from the scene. There is good reason for attributing to Simon Clerk the design of the east window, and even if Worlich during his brief term of office was responsible for the tracery of one side window (afterwards followed with only slight modifications for them all), he may merely have used the pattern already given by Reginald Ely. His contribution to the chapel as a designer is therefore negligible.

It is likely that John Worlich had connections with Bury St. Edmunds, and he may thus have begun the relationship with that town and its masons which was established by Simon Clerk and continued by JOHN WASTELL and his two wardens of the masons, one of whom was ROBERT WORLICH. A *John WORLICH alias BRON*, carver, is shown by deeds and other documents to have been living in Bury between 1420 and 1452; he was either the father or grandfather of John Worlich, citizen and salter of London, who died in 1459,[8] and of his brother, also John, citizen and goldsmith of London, who died between 1500 and 1506.[9] A *John WORLICH*, who was probably a mason, was living in Hatter Street, Bury, between 1492 and 1498. On 22 November 1497 he with JOHN BROND and another mason witnessed the will of Elizabeth Galion of Bury,[10] and when he made his own will on 10 June 1498 his executors were his wife Elianore and two masons, John Wastell and John Bayly.[11] His identity with the King's College mason is unlikely because his mother, Anneys Worlyche, of Stanstead, Suffolk, a village near Long Melford, was living in 1492,[12] but he may have been the son mentioned in the entry in the King's College Mundum Book of 1476–77. The will of Anneys Worlyche shows that her husband was dead by 1492 and that she had another son, Robert, who may have been identical with the ROBERT WORLICH below.

A.O.
[1] GOM, 96; [2] CKC, 11; [3] KCM, College Accs., vol. ii; [4] *Ibid.*, Kitchen Accs., s.a.; [5] TCM, KHA, xiv, 46; WCC, II, 450; [6] Bodl., Cambs. Charters, 34; WCC, I, 629; WAP, I, 171; [7] KCM, Mundum Book 1476–77; [8] PPR, CCL, 284 Sharp; [9] PCC, 3 Adeane; [10] BW, vi, 61; [11] *Ibid.*, 13v., 99; [12] *Ibid.*, v, 15

WORLICH, Robert [Worlyche] (*fl.* 1492?–1524) Mason

Of Bury St. Edmunds; probably brother of John Worlich of Bury who made his will 10 June 1498,[1] and perhaps son of JOHN WORLICH,

who was master mason of King's College Chapel in 1476. From 1508 to 1515 he was one of the wardens of the masons at *King's College Chapel* under JOHN WASTELL. Both Wastell and the other warden, HENRY SEMARK, also lived at Bury. Semark and Worlich were paid at the rate of 3s. 8d. a week.[2] They frequently received 'rewards' of 10s. each, and as these payments seem to have been made quarterly, they earned 2 pounds a year more than the masons employed as 'setters'.[3] On 24 August 1508 they and two other Bury masons witnessed the will of their fellow townsman, John Bush, one of the ordinary masons working on the chapel, who died in that or the following year.[4] The will, which was made at Cambridge, was proved 24 September 1509 before the Sacrist of Bury, where Bush had property. Robert Worlich was not named one of the executors, but he figures in that capacity in a deed dated at Bury 16 January 1519 in which he and three others as executors of John Bush, mason, demised to the widow, Katherine Bush and two others a messuage, garden and land in Guildhall Street, Bury.[5] In this deed he is described as 'Robert Worlyche of Bury St. Edmunds, mason'. For the subsidy of 1523–24 Robert Worliche was assessed under South Ward in Bury and he paid a shilling tax on goods valued at £2.[6] In the will of John Fyrmyn of Bury, tanner, dated 28 June 1523, mention is made of his 'tenement called the Crowne and the tenauntries therto annexed. . . in Chirchegovyll Strete [now Crown Street] in Bury. . . down to the hold halle that was Wysemans that I purchasid of Rob't Worlyche'.[7]

A.O.
[1] BW, vi, 13v., 99; [2] KCM, Building Acc. 1508–09; [3] KCM, Building Accs. 1509–1515; [4] BW, vi, 204; [5] Bodl., Cambs. Charters, 143; [6] SGB, x, 349; [7] BW, viii, 108

WORSALL, William de [Wirkesale, Wrsal] (*fl.* 1327–1345) Mason (*Worsall, Yorks., N.R.*)

Mason; probably the William de Wirkesale assessed on 15s. in 1327 in the parishes of St. Helen with SS. Andrew and Maurice in York, among several neighbours named as masons.[1] He took up the freedom of York in 1338.[2] In 1345 he was undermaster of the works at *York Minster*, being called to give evidence as to defects on 11 January 1344/5.[3]

J.H.H. in ACY, 157–8
[1] YRS, LXXIV, Miscellanea ii (1929), 167; [2] YCF; [3] SHB, 55; RFY, 163

WORSELEY, John (*fl.* 1476) Mason

Undertook on 2 March 1475/6 to take down the tower of *Wolverhampton Church*, Staffs., to the base of the windows, and build an octagon 40 feet high, surmounted by an octagonal spire to reach 120 feet, within 4 years. The work was to be according to a 'pateron' left with the churchwardens, who were to pay £110. This design was not carried out, the existing square tower having been substituted not much later.

SHB (2nd ed. 1967), 600

WREK, Thomas [Wreck, Wrenk] (*fl.* 1354–1393) Mason

Mason of London; worked as a *cementarius* at *Westminster Palace* for 133 days in 1354–55.[1] In 1374 he was partner of HENRY YEVELEY in the making of the alabaster monument of the Duchess of Lancaster in *St. Paul's Cathedral*.[2] He was one of the masons on the common council of London in 1376,[3] and in 1379 and 1381 received payments for work done for John, Lord Cobham, perhaps on the latter's house in Tower Street, London; this work was probably done under Yeveley's supervision.[4] Wrek was no doubt identical with the Thomas 'Wrenk' who in 1393 was paid £10 for images of Richard II and Anne of Bohemia with the arms of the King and Queen and of St. Edward to be placed on the tower of *London Bridge*.[5]

Bartholomew WREK was a mason working at *Rochester Castle* at 6*d.* a day in 1368–69.[6]
(*A.O.*)

[1] *PRO*, E.101–471–11; [2] JGR 1372–6, II, Nos. 1394, 1659; [3] AQC, XLI, 130–57; [4] AC, II, 96–7; AQC, XLV, 48, 49 51; [5] WTB, 65; [6] AC, II, 123

WRIGHT, Gruff(yd) le (*fl.* 1408–   ) Carpenter

Repaired the bridge of *Northwich*, Cheshire in 1408, by the advice of WILLIAM DE NEWHALL.
JAB, IV, 8

Wright, John—see FOULFORD

WRIGHT, John [Wryghte] (*fl.* 1484–   ) Carpenter

Of Richmond, Yorks.; on 28 July 1484 contracted to build two parlours, pantry, buttery, larder, four chambers, and kitchen for John Wandesford at his manor house at *Kirklington*, Yorks., for £6 13*s.* 4*d.* The whole was to be comprised in 'one new place of square' 17½ yards long and 10 yards broad.

SHB, 543; WRS, II, 146

WRIGHT, John I [Wryght] (*fl.* 1478–1480) Mason

In an account for *East Dereham Church*, Norfolk, of 1478–80 John Wryght, mason, was paid 6*d.* a day for 28½ days for work on the west window and on repairs to the belfry and 'le Tresory'.

Churchwardens' accounts, P 182D (*P.C.*)

WRIGHT, John II [Wryght] (*fl.* 1508–†1549) Mason

John Wright was one of the setters working on *King's College Chapel, Cambridge*, in the summer of 1508 at the higher rate of 3*s.* 8*d.* a week.[1] In 1532–33 he worked at *Whitehall Palace*,[2] and he was probably identical with the John Wright, freemason of South Mimms, Middlesex, who between 1532 and 1534 supplied stone carvings for the great hall at *Hampton Court*. He provided a lion and a dragon for the gables, at 16*s.* each, 16 beasts to stand upon the crest at the gable ends, at 5*s.* 4*d.* each, 13 beasts and badges in the corbel-table at 4*d.* each, and the 16 corbels to carry the main trusses of the roof, each costing 22*s.* 6*d.*[2] In 1546 he succeeded WILLIAM BAKER as master mason of *Calais*, and died in 1549, when he was succeeded by NICHOLAS THOMPSON.[4]

(*A.O.*)
[1] *KCM*, Building Acc. 1508–09; [2] *WAM* 12257; [3] LHC, I, 346–7, 353–4; SHB, 217; [4] LPH, XXI, i, 302(3); HKW, III, 419

WRIGHT, Lawrence (*fl.* 1354–1380) Carpenter

Was presumably master carpenter at *Ripon Minster* from 1354 to 1380; the only extant fabric rolls for the period are those for 1354–55 and 1379–80. In 1354 he worked on raising the feretory of St. Wilfrid with 'Estriche' boards; in July he repaired the belfry, being paid 3*s.* for a week's work. He was paid the same fee for another week spent on repairs in various parts of the church and in cutting 'thakbordes' for covering the house of the plumbery, a job which he was again doing in the following January when he received the reduced winter rate of 2*s.* 6*d.* a week.

In April 1355 he mended the bell-clappers and did other minor works, and in June erected a scaffold in the choir, with other carpenters, for whom drink was procured at a cost of 8*d.*

During the year to Michaelmas 1380, Lawrence worked for about 5 weeks, generally at 2*s.* 6*d.* a week, on odd jobs, including work in connection with the recasting of a great bell. His position as an official of the Minster is confirmed by his receiving a yearly fee; the amount is lost, but was probably 6s. 8d.

SMR, III

Wright, Thomas—see TURRET

WRIGHT, Thomas (*fl.* 1498–1499)
Carpenter

In 1498–99 made 14 new pews for *St. Margaret's Church, Westminster*; he was paid 20s. for 3 in the Trinity Chapel and £3 2s. 4d. for 11 others priced at 5s. 8d. each.

(*A.O.*)   WMW, 164

WRIGHT, William I [William of Ripon] (*fl.* 1379–1409)
Carpenter

Carpenter of Ripon, Yorks.; in 1379–80 he paid rent of 10s. for a house in Stanbriggate, Ripon, leased to him by the Minster authorities. In the same year the house was re-thatched at their expense, the costs being entered in the fabric rolls. Wright was a timber merchant as well as a carpenter, and in 1391–92 was paid 12d. for timber required for work in the towers of the Minster. In this same year 'William of Ripon' made the wooden high vault of the nave of *Thornton Abbey*, Lincs., and this must have been the same man.[1] Though there are no remains of this timber vault, a very fine pair of late 14th-century gates still hangs in the great gatehouse at Thornton, built at about this time; these gates, with blind reticulated tracery in their heads, may well be the work of William Wright.

At *Ripon* in 1396–97 he was paid 2s. for hanging two bells, and purchases of timber for the bell-frames were made. A sum of 18s. 7d. was also paid to William Wright for making a door in the south part of the choir, with 'bords' of the said William, and 2d. was charged for drink supplied for him while doing the work.

He contracted in 1399–1400 to make a new roodloft in the great church of Ripon for £3 6s. 8d., and another agreement was made with John Spalde for sawing all the timbers for the roodloft for 10s. These contracts are not preserved, but the accounts record the payment of the sums agreed 'by convention'. The Minster paid the cost of timber for the loft, including 4s. worth bought from William Wright himself.

Unfortunately few of the Ripon fabric rolls have survived, but that for 1408–09 shows that in 1409 Wright was doing a great deal of work for the church. He was paid 18d. for timber bought for a locker in the 'purpytyl' or choir-screen, and a further 18d. for a door there for the great organs. He worked on the great bells for three days, being paid 6d. a day, and worked on the choir for the whole week 12–17 June. For the whole of the next week he and one servant were engaged on the cross and nave of the church, taking 3s. each for the week, and Wright was also paid 2s. for timber required for this work.

He was also paid for working the whole week 10–15 July on mending defects in his messuage, which was Minster property, and received 3s. 8d. for timber and panels (*tabulis*) which he supplied for the work. In the following week he worked with another man for 5 days upon the cross (transept) of the church on the north side, and also supplied timber for the same worth 2s. 4d.

Wright was one of an important group of Ripon carpenters and carvers who played a great part in the development of northern English woodwork. (See BROWNFLEET, WILLIAM; WRIGHT, LAWRENCE and THOMAS.)

SMR, III; YAJ, XXIX, 157 ff.
[1] Bodl., Tanner MS. 166

WRIGHT, William II (*fl.* 1381–1383)
Carpenter

Of Lancaster; in 1381 went to *Carlisle Castle* to carry out the timberwork of the gatehouse built by JOHN LEWYN. The work was finished by 1383.

HKW, II, 599

WRIGHT, William le (*fl.* 1353–   )
Carpenter

Built the timber bridge of *Northwich*, Cheshire, in 1353–54, being paid 7 marks (£4 13s. 4d.) for his labour. It is possible that he was identical with WILLIAM DE NEWHALL, though if so he would have been over 80 at the time of his death in 1411; on the other hand, Newhall was 'old and feeble' in 1398.

JAB, IV, 8

Wright, William—see BOYDELL

WRIGHT, William (*fl.* 1480–1484) Mason

Worked at *King's College Chapel, Cambridge*, under SIMON CLERK. The kitchen accounts of the college from 1480 to 1484 show that he was often a guest in hall, usually in the company of Simon Clerk.[1] In a rough account book kept by Thomas Clyff, the clerk of the works, there is an entry dated 5 July 1482: 'for the wage of William Wright freemason 12s.'[2] William Wright was one of the six named in the royal commission of 28 August 1484 for impressing masons and other craftsmen and obtaining materials for the works at King's College.[3] It may be inferred that he was warden of the masons during the second phase of construction.

A.O.

[1] KCM, Kitchen Accs.; [2] Ibid., College Accs., vol. iv; [3] CPR 1476–85, 472

WRYGTH, William (fl. 1496–1497) Carpenter

In 1496–97 William Wrygth provided timberwork for the chancel roof of St. George Colegate, Norwich, and also worked on the stalls there, being paid sums of 8s. 4d. and 1s. 8d.

NRO, DCN, Infirmarer no. 991 (P.C.)

WRYTLE, John de [Writele, Wrytele] (fl. 1293–†1305/6) Carpenter

Probably a native of Writtle in Essex; as 'John de Writele', living in Broad Street Ward, he was taxed 3s. in 1293/4,[1] and was a sworn carpenter of the City of London in 1300. He died in 1305/6 leaving houses in Finch Lane in the parish of St. Benet Fink to his wife Alice for life, with remainder to his sons RALPH and John. His will was proclaimed in the Court of Husting on 24 February 1305/6.[2] His widow Alice in accordance with the terms of this will, in the same year granted a rent to the church of St. Benet Fink in frankalmoign.[3]

(LKC)

[1] WLE; [2] SWL, I, 177; [3] LHR, 34(36)

WRYTLE, Ralph or Ranulph [Writele, Wrytele] (fl. 1303–1317) Carpenter

Son of JOHN DE WRYTLE;[1] is mentioned in various documents from 1303 to 1317, when he disposed of property in the parish of St. Benet Fink, London.[2]

[1] LHR, 45 (129); [2] Ibid., 31 (60), 46 (23); LBH, Deeds C.68, 70; D.93

W[U]DEMAN, Ralph (fl. c. 1175–1200) Carpenter

Carpenter; witness to a grant to Bullington Priory, Lincs., in the late 12th century, with ELIAS the Mason I.

(H.M.C.)   SGC, 94

WULFRIC (fl. 1172–1174) Engineer

Was in charge of work at Carlisle Castle in 1172–73, and in 1174 carried out repairs after the siege by William the Lion, King of Scots. He was possibly identical with URRICUS.

PR

Wulman, John—see WOLMAN

Wulrich, John—see WORLICH

Wulward, John—see WOLWARD

WY, Henry (fl. c. 1324–1326) Mason

Master mason of St. Albans Abbey c. 1324–26 at the rebuilding of five bays of the south nave arcade there, after their collapse in 1323. A head, probably his portrait, is carved in one of the spandrils. (See Appendix I.)

RGA, II, 125; RCHM, Herts.

WYDMERE, John [Wodemer, Wyd(d)emer] (fl. 1389–†c. 1417) Joiner

Joiner of London; from 1389 was acquiring property, mainly in the parish of St. James Garlickhithe, London;[1] his wife Juliana is mentioned in 1389 and 1406,[2] but by 1415 Wydmere had remarried to Joan, widow of Robert Forster, saddler.[3] On 9 October 1391 Wydmere contracted a debt of £5 to Gilbert Maghfeld, merchant;[4] on 14 January 1393/4 he was granted the office of the King's Joiner in the Tower of London in succession to PETER 'DE LOCO'.[5] In 1413 he was sent to Langley to provide the bier on which Richard II's body was brought to Westminster for reburial;[6] early in 1414 he made a chest to stand in the Receipt of the Exchequer to contain truces and other records,[7] while in 1415 he supplied 1,000 lances for Henry V's expedition to France.[8] In 1408 he had enfeoffed his brother Thomas Wydmere of all his lands and tenements in London and suburbs;[9] he was dead by 3 March 1416/17, when ROBERT CONY was appointed to his vacant office.[10] In 1421 his son Thomas Wydmere, clerk, disposed of the family properties.[11] His fees were 12d. a day and he received a yearly robe.[12] Wydmere's son, John WYDDEMER, junior, citizen and joiner of London, made his will on 7 October 1407; it was proved on 11 October.[13] The testator wished to be buried in 'Pardun church hawe' next to his deceased wife Alice, but was a parishioner of St. Michael Queenhithe. His father John Wydmere and uncle Thomas Wyddemere, son Richard, brothers Lawrence and William, servants William, Christopher, Henry, and Agnes, and apprentice Lucas are all mentioned.

[1] LHR, 118 (24), 123 (66), 124 (68, 82), 125 (82–3), 126

(148), 130 (100), 134 (47, 49, 60); [2] *Ibid.*, 118 (24), 134 (49); [3] *Ibid.*, 143 (18); [4] SET, 171; [5] CPR 1391–6, 363; [6] DIE, 326; [7] *Ibid.*, 332; [8] CCR 1413–19, 232; [9] *LHR*, 136 (49), 141 (97); [10] CPR 1416–22, 66; [11] *LHR*, 149 (28); [12] *PRO*, E.101–405–22, *f.* 40d.; [13] *PPR*, Archd. Ct. of London, I, 188

WYKFORD, Nicholas (*fl.* 1467–   ) Carpenter

Nicholas Wykford, wright, contracted on 8 November 1467 to rebuild a watermill (the North Mill) for Sir Humphrey Bohun at *Midhurst*, Sussex; he was to be paid £11 13s. 4d.

SHB, 536–7; (*PRO*, Ancient Deed, D.2747)

WYLLEMER, Thomas [Wyllener'] (*fl.* 1441–   ) Carpenter

Presumably from his name an English master, called in to a conference of experts on 23 January 1440/1 to advise on the condition of the crossing-piers of the church of *St. Ouen, Rouen.* He was master of the works of carpentry within the bailiwick of Rouen.

(APD); **BAF**

Wylot—see WELOT

Wyltshire, William—see WILTSHIRE

WYMARKE, Robert (–†1524) Carpenter

Carpenter and alderman of Lincoln; he held the office of carpenter to *Lincoln Cathedral* until his death, which took place between 3 February and 13 August 1524. By his will he left 'one gowne' to THOMAS BRIGGS who later succeeded to his office at the cathedral.

(*A.O.*)   LRS, XII, 49, 56

Wymbervill, William—see HUMBERVILLE

Wynchelse, William—see WINCHELSEA

WYND', John (*fl.* 1335–1337) Carpenter

Master carpenter at *Haywra*, Yorks. W.R., in 1335–37, when he was paid 2s. 6d. a week for directing work on a peel by the moat. HKW, II, 672

Wynfeld, James—see WHINFIELD

WYNFORD, William de [Wyndeforth, Wyneforde, Wynfort] (*fl.* 1360–†1405) Mason

Perhaps of Winford, Somerset, 6 miles south-west of Bristol; during his career he was connected with Somerset and the West Country on several occasions. He may well have been a member of the manorial family which in 1365 came into the manor of Brympton D'Evercy, Somerset, by marriage

to the heiress of De Glamorgan. This possibility is rendered more likely in that John Wynford of Brympton (died 1431) married Alice, sister of William Lambrooke, Treasurer of Wells Cathedral 1386–1439; Alice in her widowhood in 1432 was a founder of the Holy Cross Chantry in the north transept of Yeovil Church (see below). In 1360 he was working at *Windsor Castle* as warden (*apparellator*) of masons' work under JOHN DE SPONLEE, and from 12 April 1361 was joint disposer (*ordinator*) of the work with Sponlee, taking the same wage of 1s. a day. Wynford, however, was not constantly in attendance at Windsor in 1361 and 1362, being absent for 159 days between April 1361 and 31 October 1362, while Sponlee was paid for every day. From 1360 Wynford is referred to as 'Master' and it is clear that he was already at the top of his craft. William of Wykeham was at this time clerk of the works at Windsor Castle, a position which he held from the autumn of 1356 to 1 November 1361.

On 26 November 1362 Wynford was given a commission for one year to impress masons, and during the following year was paid for 41 weeks spent at Windsor. Sponlee may have been considered less capable than Wynford, and he was evidently growing old; Wynford was spending more time at the castle each year, until in the year to 29 March 1366 he was paid for every day. At this time the Great Gate and the royal lodgings in the upper ward were the principal works in progress, and there are significant resemblances between the plan of the royal lodgings and the plans adopted at Winchester College and New College, Oxford, some years later.[1]

Meanwhile, Wynford had been granted the position of master mason at *Wells Cathedral* on 1 February 1364/5, with a fee of £2 a year and a house in Byestewall Street, Wells, at a nominal rent, with 6d. a day when he should be working there.[2] One of Wynford's masons at New College, Oxford, Thomas Maidstone, was at Wells in 1388–89, for a janitor was sent from Oxford to fetch him back.[3] The fabric roll for 1390–91 shows that Wynford was paid 1s. 6d. in the week ending 28 May 1391 for a visit of three days, and it seems probable that the entry in the account of the Communar of Wells Cathedral for 1392–93 of a payment of £1 to 'William Mason' as his yearly gift for life, refers to Wynford. He may also have been the William Mason of Wells, a

352

legatee of William Hervy of Bristol, who made his will on 10 January 1393/4.[4] William of Wykeham had become provost of Wells at the end of 1363, and it is evident that Wykeham's architectural reputation is due to his employment of Wynford on the building works with which he was connected.

After Sponlee had received a corrody at Reading Abbey in 1364, Wynford was probably the active head of the Windsor operations, and though the detailed accounts have not been preserved after 1368, there is no reason to doubt that he continued to have charge of the works there. He was regarded as a member of the King's household, and with HENRY YEVELEY ranked as an 'esquire of minor degree' on 1 September 1369, when they were issued lengths of black cloth as mourning for Queen Philippa's funeral.[5] In 1370 he was commissioned to impress fifty stone-hewers from the West Country for work at Orewell (*Orwell Haven*, Suffolk), and in the following year to take masons for service abroad. Wynford did not receive payment of his fees and expenses for this last commission until 20 May 1376, when he received £6 13s. 4d. out of £33 6s. 8d. owing to him.[6]

On 2 December 1372 Edward III confirmed to him a pension of £10 a year for life out of the issues of certain lands of Sir John Brocas, knight, in Bray, Clewer, and Windsor;[7] at this time most of the important work at the castle was completed, and only comparatively small sums were spent there during the last years of the old King's reign. Wynford was probably released from the necessity of spending the greater part of his time upon the royal works, and was able to extend his private practice: in 1375–76 he was engaged on the new work of *Abingdon Abbey*.[8] In 1377–78 he was again working for the Crown on the repairs of *Corfe Castle*, Dorset, making five new rooms inside 'le Gloriet' and other works;[9] and in 1378 was commissioned with Henry Yeveley to impress masons for service at Southampton. Wynford was paid for over a year's full-time work at *Southampton* taking 12d. a day, in 1378–79. In 1384–85 he was concerned with HENRY YEVELEY and HUGH HERLAND, on the works of *Carisbrooke Castle*, Isle of Wight.[10]

William of Wykeham, who had been in disgrace during the last year of Edward III, took immediate advantage of the new reign to obtain a licence in mortmain for the foundation of his *New College* at *Oxford*, though the first stone of the present buildings was not laid until 5 March 1379/80, and the college could not occupy them until 14 April 1386. There can on stylistic grounds be no doubt that Wynford was the designer, as he certainly was of Wykeham's second foundation, *Winchester College*, whose first stone was laid on 26 March 1387. Wynford's continued association with Wykeham at this period is proved by his presence at Farnham Castle in 1381; on 16 April Wynford and Henry Yeveley were witnesses to a homage rendered to William of Wykeham in person 'in his chapel within the Castle of Farnham'.[11] In 1388–89 Wynford, with Hugh Herland the carpenter, was paying repeated visits to New College, evidently on business; on 25 March 1389 they dined there at the high table, along with Henry Yeveley. Again on 16 February 1390/1 Wynford and Herland dined at New College, and on 15 September 1391 Wynford was there with a burgess of Southampton, probably his travelling companion from Winchester.[12]

Wynford had surrendered his grant of £10 a year on 29 September 1383, owing to a suit brought against him by Sir Bernard Brocas, who claimed the lands, comprising a messuage, two tofts, 200 acres of land, 8 acres of meadow, and 7s. 7d. of rent, as his by right of inheritance. Brocas was awarded the lands, but the King recompensed Wynford with a grant of £10 a year from the fee-farm of Guildford, Surrey.[13] This grant was made on 14 November 1383,[14] and was to have effect from Michaelmas, when Wynford surrendered his old patent, but it seems that the men of Guildford were slow to obey the King's orders, made on 1 February 1383/4 and repeated on 20 July 1389, when the King had to command that the arrears should be paid over to Wynford.[15]

On 3 March 1389/90 Henry Yeveley, William Wynford, and HUGH HERLAND the carpenter were commissioned to see to the repairs of the walls, turrets, gates, bridges, and houses of *Winchester Castle*, over a period of 7 years, 40 marks (£26 13s. 4d.) a year from the fee-farm of the borough of Winchester being assigned to the work. Payments made in the castle accounts for 1394–95 to Master William the mason for repairs to the great hall, presumably refer to Wynford.[16] Wynford was in any case working in Winchester on the new college, begun early in 1387 and entered by the scholars on 28 March 1394. He probably carried out a number of other works on Wykeham's episcopal manor houses, as he certainly did at *Highclere* in 1394, when he was paid 1s. 9d. for 2 days spent in supervising Wykeham's new works there.[17]

An exemplification of the letters patent of 1383, accidentally lost, was issued to Wynford on 20 October 1391,[18] and the account of the constable of Winchester Castle for the year from Michaelmas 1390 refers to the repairs done 'according to the ordering and advice of Henry Yeveley and William Wyndford the master masons and Hugh Herland the master carpenter of the aforesaid works'.[19]

Winchester College was approaching completion in the summer of 1393, when a surviving account of Wykeham's household expenditure shows that the stained glass for the chapel windows was brought to the college, and also that Wynford, with Herland the carpenter and Simon de Membury the clerk of the works, dined with Wykeham frequently when the Bishop was at Marwell or Wolvesey Palace, Winchester. Wynford dined with the Bishop on thirteen occasions between 24 July and 14 September, and during this period the King and Queen twice visited Wykeham, on 25 July and on 16–17 September. The living quarters of the college were completed by March 1394, but much still remained to be done, and the contract for building the Outer Gate was not let until 1 November, while work was still in progress on the Exchequer Tower at the west end of the hall when, early in 1400, the college spent 2s. 2d. on gloves for Wynford and his masons at the start of the season's work. Wynford and Roger Farham, mason (*latomus*) dined with the household at Winchester College on Thursday 28 December 1396.[20]

Portraits of Wynford, Membury, the Carpenter (doubtless Hugh Herland), and Thomas the glass-painter are included in the glazing of the east window of the college chapel. Wynford appears as quite an old man with thinning hair and a long aquiline nose, with drooping moustaches and forked beard. He is dressed in a deep red robe, while a scroll carries his name: 'Willms Wynfort lathomus'. A carved head, probably another portrait of Wynford, forms the northern label-stop of the east window of the Muniment Room.[21]

On 29 September 1394 the great work at *Winchester Cathedral* began, where the nave was transformed from Norman to Perpendicular without rebuilding. The commission for the repair of Winchester Castle was extended for a further seven years on 28 February 1396/7,[22] and Wynford probably spent most of his time in Winchester during the remainder of his life. On 1 April 1399 the Prior and Convent of Winchester Cathedral Priory granted Wynford a corrody in consideration of his good service past and to come; he was to be free for life to dine and sup in the Prior's Hall at the Prior's own table, with his servant at the servants' table; if he preferred to keep his room, he was to have specified allowances from the Prior's kitchen; he was to retain 'the chamber in which he now dwells in the hospice of the Master of the Work', and to take yearly a robe furred with lamb as one of the Prior's esquires, with a robe for his servant as taken by the Prior's servants.[23] From 1400 to 1402 Wynford was in receipt of payments from *Queen's College, Oxford*, in connection with the building of their hall.[24] He was given licence to have a private oratory in December 1402,[25] and was still acting as disposer of the work at the cathedral when Wykeham made his will on 14 July 1403. The will provided that the work should continue under Wynford's direction; he died in 1405 at Winchester, probably on 26 July.[26] On 7 March 1411/12 ROBERT HULLE was already master mason of Winchester Cathedral.

Nothing is known of Wynford's family, but there can be little doubt that he had a son educated in Wykeham's foundations. John Wynforde of the diocese of Salisbury (perhaps indicating his birth at Windsor) was admitted scholar of New College, Oxford, in October 1389, having presumably been one of the boys maintained by Wykeham at Winchester under a schoolmaster before the building of the college. John was a Fellow of New College from 1391–97, when he graduated B.A. and was ordained acolyte, sub-deacon, deacon and priest during 1396–98. After graduation he became a monk of Oseney Abbey.[27]

Wardour Castle built by John, Lord Lovel from about 1392, when he obtained a licence to crenellate, appears to be in Wynford's style, and it is certain that his work would be known to Lord Lovel, for the latter was one of Wykeham's guests in 1393. The parish church of *Yeovil*, Somerset, built *c.* 1380–1400, shows close resemblance to Wynford's style, and was begun at the expense of Robert de Samborne, rector 1362–82 and Canon of Wells, where he must have met Wynford.[28] Wynford may also have had a hand in the design of *Arundel Church* and *College*, begun *c.* 1380, where some windows are of the pattern employed by him in the cloisters of New College and Winchester College.

More detailed consideration of Wynford's work at Wells, and possibly elsewhere in Somerset, has been left to the end, since it depends less on documentary than on stylistic evidence. That Wynford was the consultant architect to Wells Cathedral itself for forty years, from 1365 until his death, is not in doubt; nor is the independently established date of building of the south-west tower of the cathedral within this period and, more precisely, in the ten years 1385–95. In the building there is abundant evidence of further works at the same period: the transformation internally of the west window of the nave; the masonry work in the north transept which supports the clock was inserted; and, though less certainly, the two-light traceries may have been placed in the windows. This last work may have been completed or even carried out altogether after Wynford's death, but the pattern was used by Wynford for his Winchester College hall windows designed *c.* 1387. It has, moreover, been pointed out by Mr. L. S. Colchester that the Library of not later than 1425 blocks one of the inserted traceries, which must therefore date at the latest within twenty years of Wynford's death.

Outside the church, the gateway inserted beneath the hall of the Vicars Choral by underpinning, and the houses in the Close give every impression of being to designs by Wynford. The early layout of the area is obscure, but it is tempting to suggest that the unique plan of a 'street quadrangle' is due to Wynford, who is altogether more likely in this context than any earlier master of the time of Bishop Ralph of Shrewsbury. It seems probable also that at least a sketch design for the great west tower of *St. Cuthbert's* parish church in Wells was made by Wynford at the time, *c.* 1385–1400, that a major gift towards the work was made by the Palton family.

The effect of Wynford's presence at the centre of the diocese went far beyond Wells itself, and had an influence on later church design which was to go on for centuries. This remarkable impact on English architecture consisted of his sudden introduction of the spireless, square-topped tower. His south-west tower for the cathedral is so designed and built as to preclude any possibility that it was to carry a spire, even one of timber and lead. Yet it is axiomatic that, before this time, all Gothic towers were intended to bear spires of some kind. Henry Yeveley's Westminster Palace bell-tower of 1365 had, as can be seen in Van Wyngaerde's view, a tall spire, and so did the tower at Winchester College, designed by Wynford himself *c.* 1387 and in construction in 1395–96, both of these being of timber and lead. In Wynford's later belfry for New College, however, not built until 1396–1405, there is no sign of provision for a spire of any kind. The chronological sequence is striking: the change in intention coincides with the completion of the Wells tower, with a square top determined at the latest by 1390–94. Clearly a departure was being made from the earlier designs, going back to the middle of the thirteenth century, which existed for completion of the massive towers with their deep buttresses. The only adequate reason for the change would seem to be an aesthetic reaction on the part of Wynford: he felt that square-topped western towers would accord better with the horizontality of the great front, twice as wide as it was high.

The remarkable thing is that it was not only in works actually by Wynford or closely related to his sphere of influence that the new idea spread. Within a very few years the new fashion had become general, and first in Somerset. Detailed consideration of the major church towers in the county has shown that, close to 1400, a different type of design set in, marked notably by paired buttresses set back from the angles, in contradistinction to the diagonal buttresses of most earlier towers in the South-West, which remained normal long afterwards in Gloucestershire and Wiltshire, when Somerset, Dorset, Devon and Cornwall had almost entirely gone over to the paired-buttress design. The new style in buttressing can be dated well after the appearance of Wynford at Wells, but nevertheless before his decision that the cathedral towers should not bear spires. For three parochial towers of distinction, all within 15 miles of Wells, had paired buttresses yet were intended to carry stone spires: Shepton Mallet, where some feet of the spire were built; Cheddar, and Banwell, with squinches to carry spires not actually built. There is some evidence that the lower part of the Cheddar tower was being built in *c.* 1400–13; Shepton is stylistically earlier but probably not before 1385. In the case of Shepton, only five miles from Wells and with a plan reflecting that of the earlier western towers of the cathedral, it is likely that the design was by Wynford himself. It has to be concluded that it was Wynford, as cathedral architect, who was responsible both for the south-western adoption of paired buttresses and also for the spread throughout England in later years of the square-topped tower of the parish church.

Practically the whole of Wynford's known career is connected with the south-west of England, Windsor being no doubt his headquarters in Edward III's time, as Winchester was later. He does not seem to have had any official duties or private work in London, where Henry Yeveley was the most important mason-architect of the day, and it is quite probable that the two masons agreed to keep to their respective territories as far as possible. The styles of the two men, though not unlike, are quite distinct. Comparison should be made between the nave of Winchester, Winchester College, and the western towers of Wells Cathedral, by Wynford, and the naves of Westminster Abbey and Canterbury Cathedral and the recasing of Westminster Hall, with its two northern towers, by Yeveley, and for fine detail, Wynford's tomb and chantry for Wykeham, in Winchester Cathedral, with Yeveley's tombs of Edward III, Richard II, and Archbishop Langham, at Westminster. One of Wynford's favourite details seems to have been a cresting or background of narrow vertical niches or openings, with cusped heads, as in the triforium of Winchester Cathedral, the parapets of the towers and internal parapet of the west window-sill at Wells, and the surfaces behind the canopy-work of Wykeham's tomb and chantry.

Wynford was one of the earliest architects to produce a definite type of domestic plan, and it is extremely fortunate that both his colleges have survived intact, as well as complete records of his royal lodgings at Windsor, sadly though they have been transformed in comparatively modern times. As the leader

or founder of a 'school' of masonry, Wynford is of very great importance, and his was probably the greatest single influence which made the church towers of Somerset the finest in the country. (See Appendix I.)

(APD; BAA; EB (William of Wykeham); KJI; KJY; HMA) HWA; BWO, 156–64; CWC, 77–88, 115–16; HWP, 36–8; **HPS**, 130–6; **HCT**, 166–71; J.H.H. in **CWE**, 89–93
[1] HWC, I, 182, 185, 198; CPR 1361–4, 271; [2] HMC, *Wells*, I, 267; [3] GOM, 115; [4] HMC, II, 24; *WLC* (*L.S.C.*); CWF, 8; WBW, 36 (*E.W.*); [5] LRC, IV, 174; [6] CPR; DTB, 3; *PRO*, E.402–460; [7] CPR 1370–4, 224; [8] AAA, 28; [9] VCH, *Dorset*, II, 334; *PRO*, E.101–461–9 (*L.F.S.*); cf. HKW, II, 623n.; [10] CPR 1377–81, 199; *PRO*, E.364–13 (*L.A.B.*); HKW, I, 213; II, 595; [11] BCL, 42; [12] *NCO*, Bursars' roll 1388–89; Hall Books; [13] CCR 1381–5, 333, 361; [14] CPR 1381–5, 372; [15] CCR 1381–5, 350; 1389–92, 2; [16] CPR 1388–92, 237; Foreign Roll, 13 Ric. II. A (*L.F.S.*); HKW, II, 864; [17] *PRO*, Eccl. 2–159403 (*J.H.B.*); [18] CPR 1388–92, 491; [19] *PRO*, E.101–491–21; [20] *WCM* no. 1 (Wykeham's Household Account 1393) (*H.C.*); LAG, 77; *WCM* 22814 (Hall Book 1396–97); [21] CPW, pl. XXVIb; CWE, pl. 34; [22] CPR 1396–9, 116; [23] HWW, 6; [24] GOM, 66; [25] WRH, II, 543; [26] LWW, App. xvii; *PRO*, E.28–22; [27] *NCO*, Register and Hall Books; WRH, I, 339, 344, 346; Sarum, Reg. Metford, f. 155 (*A.B.E.*); [28] J. Goodchild in SAP, LXXXIX, 87–8

Wyntreton, William—see ROGER BARTON

Wyntryngham, William—see WINTRINGHAM

WYNWICK, John [Wynnewyk] (*fl.* 1435–1455) Mason (? *Winwick, Northants.*)

On 17 December 1435 a commission was issued to John Wynnewyk to take masons, carpenters, and others for the King's works in the *Tower of London*; on 24 January 1436/7 he was paid £1 7*s.* 6*d.* for works done on the door of a house at the end of *Westminster Hall* beneath the Duke of Gloucester's Council Chamber, and to be used for the keeping of the King's Records, and on 18 August 1439 he was appointed warden of the King's works of masonry, with such fees as THOMAS MAPILTON had had, and a gown at Christmas. As his appointment was clearly subordinate to that of ROBERT WESTERLEY, the reference to Mapilton undoubtedly refers back to the period, 1416–18, when Mapilton had been warden, during the mastership of STEPHEN LOTE.[1]

In 1437–38 Wynwick was warden of the masons (*gardianus cementar'*) at the works of the Tower at *Portsmouth*, taking 10*d.* a day.[2]

When the works of *Eton College* began, Wynwick received commissions to impress masons for the works there, in October 1441 and April 1442. At this time the accounts show that for his work at Westminster, the

Tower, and elsewhere he was being paid 10*d.* a day as 'warden of the masons and disposer of the office of masons working on the King's works'.³ With ROBERT CONY, the King's Joiner at the Tower, he was a feoffee of tenements in Mark Lane conveyed to them by the rector and parishioners of St. Olave, Hart Street in 1443.⁴ On 7 October 1447 he had a new grant of office as warden or keeper of the mason's work.⁵ He gave a receipt for his wages of 10*d.* a day as warden of the King's masons from December 1453 to December 1455.⁶

WKM
¹ CPR 1429–36, 526; 1436–41, 297; DIE, 431; *PRO,* E.101–503–9 (*L.F.S.*); HKW, I, 215; ² SHB, 53; *PRO,* E.101–479–7 (*L.F.S.*); ³ CPR 1441–6, 70; *PRO,* E.101–473–18; ⁴ *LHR,* 172(56); ⁵ CPR 1446–52, 111; *PRO,* E. 101–652 (*H.M.C.*)

WYOT, Guy [Withot] (*fl.* 1365–1373) Carpenter

Was carrying out taskwork on doors and other woodwork at *Queenborough Castle* in 1365;¹ and was master carpenter at *Leeds Castle,* Kent, during the works of 1369–73. He was paid £30 for making 3 floors and 3 roofs within the castle, of the King's timber. He also made the timberwork of a new mill within the Castle for £13 6*s.* 8*d.*²
¹ HKW, II, 701, 796n., 797; ² *PRO,* E.101–466–19 (*L.F.S.*)

WYRWODE, Edmund de (*fl.* 1316–1318) Mason

Undermaster of the masons at *Beaumaris Castle* in 1316–18 under NICHOLAS DE DERNEFORD.
(*L.F.S.*)   *PRO,* E.101–486–28

WYSE, William (*fl.* 1397–1415) Carpenter

In 1397 made the woodwork of the belltower of *New College, Oxford;*¹ in 1398 was paid £5 on account of making the roofs of the chancels of *Heston* and *Isleworth,* Middx., while in June 1399 the warden of Winchester College visited Harmondsworth, Isleworth and Heston in connection with Wyse's works there.² In 1399/1400 he went to Winchester from Harmondsworth, Middlesex, bearing a letter to the warden regarding the works of the chancel of *Hampton Church,* a college possession; Wyse was probably in charge of the repairs.³ He was also given commons at New College in the same year. On 15 April 1403 he was appointed master carpenter at *Windsor Castle,* taking 6*d.* a day, and a livery, as THOMAS FRAUNCEYS had done.⁴ Wyse con-

tinued to work at Windsor at least until 1414–15.⁵
GOC
¹ OHS, XVIII, 310–14; ² *WCM,* Custus Operum roll 1397–8; Compotus 1398–99; ³ *WCM,* Compotus 1399–1400; ⁴ CPR 1401–5, 218; ⁵ *PRO,* SC.6–755–6 (*H.M.C.*)

WYSHONGRE, Nicholas [Wyshangre] (*fl.* 1372–1375) Mason (*Wishanger, Glos.*)

Mason (*cementarius*) of Gloucester; on 25 November 1372 contracted to complete the tower of *Arlingham Church,* Glos., in three years; 12 feet were to be built each year. Wyshongre was to be paid 17*s.* and 1 bushel of wheat for each foot of height completed. The work is of simple design with diagonal corner buttresses and the small windows have curvilinear reticulated tracery. On 19 July 1375 the Priory of *Lanthony* by Gloucester made a grant of livery to their mason Nicholas Wyshangre, on condition that he was to work for life at the priory or on the priory's manors. Wishanger is in Miserden parish, in the region of important oolite quarries. Nicholas may have been the son of

John de WYSHANGRE, a mason taking 1*s.* 6*d.* per week for work at *Gloucester Castle* in 1323–24.¹

SHB 445–6; (Berkeley Castle Muniments No. 547); JCB, 174, No. 547; *PRO,* C 115/L1/6688, *f.*89 (*N.M.H.*) ¹ *PRO,* SC 6–854–7

WYSPENADE, John [Wespnade] (*fl.* 1400–1424) Mason (*Whipsnade, Beds.*)

In 1400–01 John Wyspenade, mason, took up the freedom of the City of Norwich.¹ In 1423–24 he was paid £4 for the stone windows of the new chancel of *St. Saviour's Church;* the walls were built by JOHN SPYNK.² It is possible that he was identical with, or closely related to the mason of the same name who worked on a new fireplace at *King's Langley Manor,* Herts., in 1369–70.³
¹ EFN; ² *NRO,* DCN, Almoner no. 531 (*P.C.*); ³ HKW, II, 975

WYTHAM, Reginald [Wihtum] (*fl.* 1325–1335) Mason

Perhaps a son of RICHARD WYTHAM; was working at *Westminster Palace* and the *Tower of London* in 1325, and in 1335 was named after WILLIAM RAMSEY among the masons who were members of the commission to inquire into the state of the Tower of London.¹
LKC; BHT, App. to pt. I, 273

William de WIGHTHAM, another mason who was probably of the same family, worked under Richard of Wytham

at *St. Stephen's Chapel* in 1307.
LKC

WYTHAM, Richard of [Wetham, Witham, Wightham] (*fl.* 1290–1310) Mason

Probably of Wytham, Berks., close to Oxford; in 1290 he was working as a cutting mason at *Westminster Palace* under RICHARD CRUNDALE.[1] During 1298 he quarrelled with SIMON PABENHAM, another London mason, and the two were brought before the Mayor and Aldermen at the Guildhall; they were reconciled on the condition that whichever of them should first renew the quarrel must pay £5 to the funds of London Bridge.[2]

In 1300 Wytham was sworn as a viewer of masons' work in the City of London and in the following year took oath before the Mayor not to make encroachments and the like while fulfilling his duties.[3]

Master Richard 'de Wightham' appears from August 1307 in charge of works at the Palace of Westminster, taking 7*s.* per week as the mason assigned by the treasurer to superintend and direct each of the works of building and to be master in the same office. He worked on St. Stephen's Chapel and the White Chamber in the Palace.[4] On 11 May 1310, as mason in charge of London Bridge, he paid half a mark for admission to the freedom of the City of London.[5]

(WKM; LKC)
[1] *PRO*, E.101–468–1, 2; [2] RML, 38; [3] CLB, 'C', 86; [4] BBW, 109; *BM*, Add. MS. 30263; [5] CLB, 'D', 53

WYTHER, John [Wither] (*fl.* 1267–1274) Carpenter

In 1267 built the great hall of *Silkstead Manor* at Compton, Hants., for St. Swithin's Priory, Winchester. The total cost, including masons' work on the walls, was £23 9*s.* 3*d.* in addition to £6 spent on food for the men, including 15*s.* 6*d.* for meat and bread, 8 quarters of wheat, 48 carcases of bacon, 21 cheeses, and 6 casks of cider.[1] In 1274 John Wither was the master carpenter in charge of works at *Westminster Palace*, and the *Royal Mews*, being paid 5*s.* 3*d.* a week, or at the rate of 9*d.* a day, inclusive of Sundays and feasts.[2]
[1] DCW; [2] *PRO*, E.101–467–7 (2)

XAINTES, Isambert de (*fl.* 1200–1209) ? Architect

A French scholar who gained a reputation for the design of bridges, including those at *Saintes* (Xaintes) and *La Rochelle*. On 18 April 1202 he was invited to England by King John

to complete *London Bridge*, begun by PETER OF COLECHURCH. The work was finished in 1209.
(APD; BAA); **BAF**

Yarmouth, Thomas of—see BARSHAM

YBOURNE, Thomas (*fl.* 1368–1373) Carpenter

Warden (*apparillator*) of the carpenters working on *Leeds Castle*, Kent, in 1368–73, being paid 6*d.* a day. He also did taskwork there, making gates, portcullises and a drawbridge.
HKW, II, 700n., 701

YEMAN, John [Zeman] (*fl.* 1455–   ) Carpenter

On 7 January 1454/5 was appointed, with WILLIAM STORY, mason, to report on the state of the fabric of *Salisbury Cathedral*.
(*L.F.S.*) Salisbury Cath., Act Book 'Burgh'

YERDEHURST, William [Yerdest] (*fl.* 1416–†*c.* 1426) Carpenter

Was probably appointed King's Chief Carpenter *c.* 1416 on the death of WILLIAM TOUTMOND, and was in office by 7 August 1417.[1] He had served with Henry V in France at some time before 19 May 1421;[2] but died before JOHN GOLDYNG'S appointment to the same office on 25 July 1426.
[1] *BM*, Add. 17721, *f.* 39; [2] *PRO*, E.28–34 (*H.M.C.*); CPR 1416–22, 386

YERNEMUTH, John (*fl.* 1398–1399) Mason (*Yarmouth, Norf.*)

In 1398–99 was paid £5 17*s.* 4*d.* by the Chamberlains of (*King's*) Lynn for 9 weeks' work done by him and his associates on a house at the South Gates of Lynn.
LCR, Ea. 40

YEVELEY, Henry [Evelee, Ivele(ghe), 'Revell', Yeevelee, Yeflee, Yevele, Yevelee, Yiffele, Yiffle, Yivele, Yvele(y), Yviele, Zevele(e), -y, Zeweley, Zhevele, Zifflee, Zifle, Zyeveley, Zyvele] (*fl.* 1353–†1400) Mason (*Yeaveley, Derb.*)

Son of Roger and Marion, and brother of ROBERT YEVELEY; his father was probably the Roger de Yeveleye assessed at 18*d.* to the subsidy of 1327, when he was living at Uttoxeter, Staffs., seven miles from Yeaveley, Derbyshire.[1] Roger may have been of the family of John 'le Mazon de Iueleg' who was a Derbyshire freemason in 1278.[2] Soon after 1327 a rental of Uttoxeter shows Roger 'de Zyvelegh' holding 1½ burgages by rent of 18*d.* yearly, 2 acres of land once of Hugh, son of

Cristiana, held by charter at a rent of 8*d.*, and 3 rods of land which had been of Matilda de Staneford, rented at 1½*d*;[3] Roger was evidently a prosperous freeholder, and may well have been a master mason, though there is no direct evidence of this. The facts that both Henry and Robert Yeveley were masons, and that Henry was later much engaged in the making of monuments from Tutbury alabaster do, however, suggest a family background of the mason's craft in this district, which was a part of the Honor of Tutbury, a section of the Duchy of Lancaster.

Henry Yeveley must have been born about 1320–30, and have learned his craft between 1335 and 1350, in all probability on the works going on at one or more of the important buildings of the region. Work was in progress at the time at Lichfield Cathedral (presbytery from 1337, under WILLIAM RAMSEY III, the King's Chief Mason); Uttoxeter Church (tower and spire, *c.* 1325–50); Ashbourne Church (south nave aisle and spire, *c.* 1330–50); Tutbury Priory Church (south aisle, *c.* 1340–60); Croxden Abbey (Abbot's lodging, etc. 1334–36), and Stafford Castle (by JOHN BURCESTRE, from 1348). The Black Death of 1348–49 seems to have been less severe in the Midlands than in the southern counties; in any case a large number of craftsmen bearing northern names reached London soon after the pestilence, and among them were a number of masons of north Midland origin (cf. JOHN PALTERTON with his colleagues John and Thomas Duffield, JOHN MAPILTON, SIMON ROUCESTRE). Henry Yeveley was admitted to the freedom of the City of London, apparently by redemption, on 3 December 1353,[4] and within two years he was among the leaders of his craft in the capital. On 1 February 1355/ 6, he was chosen by the good folks of the trade as one of the six stone-hewers who were members of a commission to inform the Mayor and Aldermen of London concerning the Acts and Articles of the craft.[5]

About 1357 he probably received an appointment as mason to the Black Prince, for whom he had contracted by 15 March 1357/8 to build certain walls, chimneys, and staircases at *Kennington Manor*. This work was to a total value of £221 4*s.* 7*d.*, of which the last instalment was paid on 15 September 1359.[6] On 25 October the Prince ordered his receiver-general to pay £60 to 'Henry de Yevele, the prince's mason'. Yeveley's

practice extended to *St. Albans Abbey*, where the walls were built under licence to crenellate dated 11 June 1357; his deputies on the site were WILLIAM STUBBARD, John Bukkedene and JOHN CLIFFORD (see also below, p. 361).[7]

Yeveley did not confine himself to mason's work, for he engaged also in the export trade, and was presumably in favour at Court for he obtained in 1359 a special licence to discharge victuals at Calais,[8] and soon afterwards he was in the King's service; on 25 June 1360 he was appointed disposer of the King's works of masonry in the *Palace of Westminster* and the *Tower of London* during pleasure, at 12*d.* a day, and on 13 August he was authorised to impress masons for the works.[9] It was at this time that preparations were being made for the building of *Queenborough Castle*, and it seems certain that its design would be within the scope of Yeveley's office, which was by no means confined to works actually executed in London and Westminster. The works at Queenborough lasted from 1361 to 1367, and by 20 August 1360 Yeveley was being described in the accounts for the royal works as the King's deviser of masonry, which implies that he was recognised as an architect (*Devisour de la maceonerie de noz oeveraignes.*).[10] He seems to have received his official post over the head of JOHN BOX, who left London to become the resident master at Queenborough.

At this period Yeveley was already engaging in the purchase and sale of extensive properties in London,[11] and he continued to work for the Black Prince, who ordered allowance of £60 to be made to him in November 1362.[12]

In 1365 when the clock-tower of Westminster Palace was being built, Yeveley was paid for the whole year for ordaining the works, and also for supplying 7,000 Flanders tiles for paving the courtyards of the Palace, and for plaster of Paris;[13] and he was responsible for wages and materials for works at *Eltham, Gravesend*, and *Baynard's Castle*.[14] In the same year he is first mentioned as a warden of London Bridge, an administrative post which he seems to have held continuously until 1396; this brought in a fee of £10 a year.[15] In 1366 he was still master mason of the works at Westminster Palace and elsewhere, drawing his 12*d.* a day, and he continued to have charge of operations at Baynard's Castle,

359

arranged for paving at *Shene* and supplied plaster and brick (*bakston*) for Gravesend.[16] In the next year he was supplying Beer and Caen stone for the works at *Rochester Castle*, and bricks (*valthill* i.e. wall-tile) for paving at Eltham.[17]

Works at Rochester Castle continued in 1368, when Yeveley was paid for supplying 13 tons of Stapleton (Yorkshire) freestone at 8*s*. per ton there,[18] and in the next year on 27 August he had a new grant of office for life, with the usual fees and in addition a winter robe every year.[19] On 1 September when mourning was issued to the royal household for the funeral of Queen Philippa, Yeveley ranked as one of the 'esquires of minor degree'.[20] During the years 1368 and 1369 he had also been active as a London Bridge warden,[21] and with his wife Margaret was acquiring certain city properties and disposing of others.[22]

On 1 March 1369/70 Yeveley was ordered to impress masons for Orewell (*Orwell Haven*, Suffolk),[23] and in the next year for service overseas.[24] He also contracted in 1371 with Sir Walter Manny and the Prior of the *London Charterhouse* to build the first cell and the beginning of the cloister there.[25] Next year Yeveley was paid £73 6*s*. 8*d*. by the Abbot of Westminster for building the bridge between Chelmsford and *Moulsham*, Essex, now destroyed, and was also provided with a robe costing 17*s*. 3*d*.[26] This may indicate that Yeveley had already become consultant mason to Westminster Abbey, but this is uncertain. He was also ordered at this time to impress masons for London and Sandwich, perhaps for service in France.[27]

On 18 July 1373 Yeveley was the first named of the arbitrators before whom the sworn masters of the London carpenters and masons appeared to give evidence in regard to damage to fixtures in a house in the parish of St. Michael 'at Corne', and on 9 November he was himself a claimant in the Court of Husting to a box of deeds brought before the Court for safe custody by John, chaplain to John Rothyng, to whom the deeds had been handed by a carpenter in his employment. There is evidence that at this time Yeveley was a brother of the religious fraternity of Salve Regina in his parish church of St. Magnus.[28]

Yeveley was surety for a ship arrested at Poole on 20 January 1374/5, when it was ordered to be released and taken to the port of London for unloading. The ship, the *Margarete* of Wareham, of 48 tons burthen, was laden with two high tombs of marble for the Earl of Arundel and his deceased wife Eleanor, a great stone for the Bishop of Winchester, and other things of theirs.[29] These tombs were doubtless made in the Isle of Purbeck, and are to be identified with those referred to in the will of Richard, 5th Earl of Arundel, who died on 24 January 1375/6 after making a will in which he desired to be buried beside his wife in the Chapter House of Lewes Priory. It is suggested by Mr. Walter Godfrey that their effigies were removed after the Dissolution to Chichester Cathedral, where they are set on a modern table-tomb which appears to be copied from an original by Yeveley.[30]

Yeveley's official work at the time involved the supply of materials for continuing work at Gravesend and also at *Leeds Castle*, Kent.[31] In addition to working for the King, the Black Prince, Westminster Abbey, and private clients, Yeveley undertook work at the *Savoy* for John of Gaunt, Duke of Lancaster, for which he and WILLIAM OF WINTRINGHAM, carpenter, were paid £30 in 1375, while on 26 January 1374/5 Yeveley and THOMAS WREK, a mason contractor of London, were to receive £108 in part payment of £486 for making the tomb for Gaunt's late Duchess, Blanche, who had died in 1369, and for the Duke himself.[32] Alabaster for this tomb had been ordered on 13 June 1374 to be sent from Tutbury,[33] and work had begun at Michaelmas; it was due to be finished by 1378. It stood in *St. Paul's Cathedral*, but was destroyed by the Great Fire of 1666. Fortunately its design is known from drawings made by Hollar, which show that it was enclosed in an elaborate canopied chantry of great size.

During 1376 Yeveley was granted the wardship of the manor of Langton in Purbeck, Dorset, as from Michaelmas 1375, until Joan, daughter of the late John le Walsh, should come of age,[34] and this may indicate that he had an interest in quarries of Purbeck marble or stone. One of Yeveley's sureties in this connection was ROBERT KENTBURY, the Westminster mason. He was also, with THOMAS BARNET and RICHARD ATTE CHERCHE, concerned in a property transaction in Guildford and its neighbourhood.[35] In the following year he was ordered on 10 July to take masons for works at the Tower of London and the Palace of Westminster,[36] and he probably designed the tomb of the Black Prince in *Canterbury Cathedral*; it may even have been that this was his first association with Canterbury, and that he thus obtained a position there as architect to the new works of the nave which began at this time, though we do not find documentary evidence of his presence at Canterbury until two years later. On the other hand, Yeveley had been paying rent to Christ Church Priory, Canterbury, for property of theirs in the City of London, as early as 1375.[37] During the years 1372–76 his shop was presumably making the great Neville Screen for *Durham Cathedral*, known to have been made in London and which is in a style immediately derived from that of the monument of the Duchess Blanche.[38] The screen, worked in Caen stone, was taken by sea to Newcastle in 1376, and erected by 1380.

Edward III died in June 1377 and Yeveley probably designed his tomb in *Westminster Abbey*, which closely resembles in its details those of Richard II and Cardinal Langham, known to be by Yeveley. It was not actually made until after April 1386, when a cargo of marble for the tomb in a ship at Poole was exempted from impressment. His grant of office as disposer of the works (*dispositor operacionum*) was confirmed by Richard II on 7 March 1377/8.[39] In the same month he was sent to *Southampton* with JOHN DE SPONLEE to advise on the foundations of a tower to be built there, and on 7 May he and WILLIAM WYNFORD were ordered to take masons for Southampton.[40] It was Yeveley who had continuing charge of the work on the tower. On 24 January following he contributed 5 marks to the loan raised in the City of London,[41] and during 1379 he provided a new east window for the chancel of *St. Mary's Church, Battersea*, which belonged to Westminster Abbey.[42] Yeveley was paid £5 for this window, and it is virtually certain that he was by this time master mason to the Abbey, where the fees were £5 a year, with 15s. for dress and furs.

The walls of Canterbury were in need of repair at this time, and the bailiffs of the city had received a writ of aid on 1 October 1378 to assist them in finding masons and labour for the works. Yeveley was no doubt concerned with this work already, though he is not mentioned in public documents in that connection until 1385; it is, however, clear on stylistic grounds that he was the designer of the fine *West Gate* of Canterbury, which was a work of greater importance than would normally be dealt with by the local masons. In the account of the treasurers of Christ Church Priory, Canterbury, for 1379–80, appears a sum of £110 9s. 4d. paid to Master Henry Yeveley, Thomas Elys, and others 'for the debt of John Molasshe cellarer'. Yeveley was commissioned in April 1380 to impress workmen for the fortification of *Carisbrooke Castle* in the Isle of Wight, notably the heightening of the main gatehouse. The work was done under a local warden, RICHARD BRADLE. Yeveley, with WILLIAM WYNFORD and HUGH HERLAND, drew up a contract with ADAM OLIVER in 1384 for carpenter's work there.[43]

It was perhaps about this time that Yeveley visited *St. Albans Abbey* to survey encroachments with the Abbot's steward.[44] He had probably acted as the abbey's architect for the cloister doorway and for the nave screen in the church, as well as for the massive Great Gatehouse.

Defence was also occupying the attention of the City of London at this time, and on 2 October 1380 a commission was set up to prepare a scheme for building a tower on each side of the Thames below the port of London for the protection of shipping.[45] The commission consisted of four men, William Walworth, John Northampton, Nicholas Twyford, goldsmith, and Henry Yeveley. The first three were important civic dignitaries, and in the next year Walworth was knighted for his heroic arrest of Wat Tyler in the King's presence. Walworth, who died in 1385, built a new choir with side chapels to the church of *St. Michael, Crooked Lane*, and founded a college there, and it is extremely probable that Yeveley would be the architect for these works, as St. Michael's was less than 200 yards from Yeveley's own church of St. Magnus by London Bridge.

Meanwhile, Yeveley had acquired an important client in the person of John, Lord Cobham, for whom he had probably designed the quadrangular college at *Cobham*, Kent, about 1370, with the tower, sedilia, and other parts of the church there.[46] Cobham in 1380 obtained licence to crenellate his castle of *Cowling* in Kent. The actual building work was done by three contractors, THOMAS WREK who had worked on the Duchess Blanche's tomb with Yeveley five years before, THOMAS CRUMP, and WILLIAM SHARNHALE. Wrek and Sharnhale built the body of the castle between 1380 and 1384 and Crump the Great Gatehouse, by contract of 26 September 1381.[47] This contract, and a receipt by Sharnhale of 23 July 1382, show that payments were made to them on the basis of measurements made and certified by Henry Yeveley, but there can be little doubt as to his position as designer, for on 24 December 1381 Lord Cobham contracted with NICHOLAS TYPERTON, mason, that the latter should build the south aisle and porch of the church of *St. Dunstan-in-the-East, London*, according to the design (*la devyse*) of Henry Yeveley.[48] This church also was only a few hundred yards from Yeveley's home, and close to the Tower of London, where he must frequently have had official business.

It was at this time that Yeveley's first known contact occurred with William of Wykeham, Bishop of Winchester, who had recently begun to build *New College, Oxford*. Yeveley and William Wynford appear on 16 April 1381 in Wykeham's presence in the chapel of Farnham Castle as witnesses to the homage of a tenant.[49] This cannot have been a chance meeting, and implies that Yeveley must have been called into consultation by Wykeham or by Wynford in connection with some or all of the bishop's architectural projects. While New College recalls the royal apartments built at Windsor Castle while Wykeham was clerk of works there, its regular quadrangle and chamber planning derive also from the layout of Carthusian monasteries and such colleges as that at Cobham. It seems highly significant that Yeveley should have been concerned with just such problems within the preceding years, while his style may be detected in a few details at New College (e.g. the hall windows) which differ from Wynford's usage elsewhere. As will be seen, Yeveley continued to be in close touch with Wykeham and his Oxford foundation.

In the meantime Yeveley had been ordered in the spring of 1381 to press masons for Brittany, to go with the Earl of Buckingham's expedition.[50] In June occurred the Peasants' Revolt, but there is no indication that it affected Yeveley in any way, as he was able to proceed with his work in connection with Cowling Castle almost immediately afterwards.[51] In the winter of 1381–82 he was

installed in shops in St. Paul's Churchyard, London, which he had recently built for himself and for which he paid a rent of £5 to the Chapter. The shops, with a yard and small garden, were next to the Chapter's tracing-house (*trasura*), where Yeveley had charge of work in progress on the Cathedral through the warden STEPHEN LOTE.[52]

On 15 May 1382 Yeveley was again at Cowling Castle, measuring the work done,[53] and gave a certificate on 23 July.[54] Soon afterwards comes evidence that one of his London properties, in Basing Lane, was being leased by John of Gaunt's clerk of the wardrobe as an office and storehouse, at a rent of £3 6s. 8d. a year.[55] No doubt Yeveley's other city tenements were let advantageously, and he must at this time have had a large unearned income as well as what he derived from fees.

A commission was set up on 12 February 1382/3 for the building of *Rochester Bridge*,[56] and Yeveley was a member; he must have visited Rochester when working at Cowling, and also when on his way to Canterbury, apart from actual works at Rochester Castle. On 20 April his wife Margaret was concerned in an indenture then made,[57] and it appears that she was the sister of Isabella, wife of William Palmer, citizen and horse-dealer of London; Margaret died before 1387, when Yeveley had married again.

Yeveley obtained on 2 February 1383/4 a protection against forfeiture for two shops which he held in the parish of St. Martin Outwich, previously in the possession of JOHN TOTENHAM, carpenter.[58] This protection was granted by the King because of the great labours which Yeveley sustained daily in the royal service. On 31 July Yeveley and Thomas Mallyng, mason, appear as Common Councillors for Bridge Ward.[59]

In 1384–85 Yeveley was responsible for the 'ordinance' of works at *Portchester Castle*, Hants., carried out under the immediate supervision of HUGH KYMPTON.[60]

In 1385 an order was made out for the payment of his official fee of 12d. a day, perhaps because he had some difficulty in obtaining it regularly. On 9 December the bailiffs of Canterbury were granted £100 a year for two years from the issues of Kent, which was to be spent on the walls of the city by the survey of Sir John Cobham, two Canterbury men, and Master Henry

Yeveley.[61] Next year he was concerned in the inquiry into the receipts of the Rochester-Strood ferry,[62] and on 3 December was named as overseer of work to be done on the walls of the Cathedral Close at Canterbury by the Prior and Convent of Christ Church.[63] On 5 February 1386 it had been stated that the bailiffs and commonalty of Canterbury were laying out £200 on the walls 'by the oversight and control' of Sir John de Cobham and Henry Yeveley,[64] and it is clear that Yeveley must have been spending a good deal of time in Canterbury, which probably allowed him to act as designer and consultant architect for the new nave of the cathedral.

He was none the less active on official works, and accounts for 1384–87 show that he was supplying large quantities of materials for Shene Palace, and that Katherine 'Lyghtfote', soon to become his second wife, was paid for 2,000 painted tiles for the King's bathroom there.[65] In 1385–86 he was also engaged on works at the College of *St. Martin-le-Grand, London*, where the chancel was being rebuilt at Wykeham's expense.[66] It seems to have been about this period that Yeveley made the munificent gift of a half-mark (6s. 8d.) to every one of the monks of St. Albans.[67] As has been seen above (p. 361) it was in 1386 that marble from Purbeck was being brought to make the tomb of Edward III.

In 1387 Yeveley and JOHN CLIFFORD appear as having entered into an agreement with nine men, most of whom were of Maidstone, whereby the latter were bound to Yeveley and Clifford in £360.[68] Next year Yeveley was paid his fees as master mason of *Westminster Abbey*,[69] though it is likely that he had held this position for some years, at any rate since the new work of the nave began about 1375.

In the year 1387–88 he was paid £66 13s. 4d. for the completion of a contract of £286 13s. 4d. for making a new south doorway and window in St. Paul's Cathedral as well as £6 13s. 4d., a first instalment of his 'new task' of £20.[70] He may perhaps have provided the pulpitum which enclosed the choir on the west. This seems, from Hollar's engravings, to have been in his style, and to have been closely followed by that of Canterbury, designed by Yeveley's partner and successor, Stephen Lote. It seems not unlikely that Yeveley's extensive works at Old St. Paul's may have been due to damage caused by the great earthquake of 1382, which is said to have done serious injury to St. Paul's and Westminster Abbey, as well as to Christ Church, Canterbury.[71]

At this time Yeveley and his second wife Katherine bought a considerable property in Southwark, including two watermills, which in 1388 he had rebuilt by WILLIAM VYNT and two other carpenters.[72] On 25 March 1389, in company with William Wynford and HUGH HERLAND, Yeveley dined at the high table of New College, Oxford.[73]

The method of paying his official fees was altered on 22 October 1389, when he was granted the manors of Tremworth and Vannes, near Wye in Kent, with 25s. a year, the difference between the value of the manors, £17, and the whole of his old fee of £18 5s. 0d., together with a winter robe every year.[74] On 27 September Geoffrey Chaucer, who was then clerk of the works, was instructed to pay over to Yeveley the arrears of his salary.[75] In this year Yeveley supervised work done by contract at the Tower of London, presumably designed by him (see CRUMP, THOMAS).[76]

Further works of a military character next formed a part of Yeveley's duties, for on 3 March 1390 he and William Wynford, with Hugh Herland the carpenter were appointed for a term of seven years to see to the repairs of the walls, turrets, gates, bridges, and houses of *Winchester Castle*,[77] and a surviving account of the constable of the castle for 1390–91 refers to the 'ordinance and counsel' (*ordinacionem et avisamentum*) upon the works, by the three master craftsmen.[78] On 8 May a grant of £200 was made for the repair of the 'dongeon' of *Canterbury Castle* by the advice of the King's Master Mason and Master Carpenter (Yeveley and Herland),[79] and on 29 August Yeveley was granted exemption for life from jury service and from being compelled to hold various offices against his will, in consideration of his being the King's Mason and surveyor of the works within the Palace of Westminster, the Tower of London, and Castle of Canterbury, and of his great age.[80] On 2 August he had been petitioned against before the Mayor and Aldermen of London, by William Kyrton and his wife Elizabeth a city orphan, daughter of John Hadde called 'Lightfoot'; sums of £40 each had been bequeathed to Elizabeth and her brother John by John Hadde, with the proviso that both legacies should go to the survivor of them; John had since died, and the petitioners had not been able to recover the sum of £80 from Henry Yeveley and Katherine, now his wife, the mother of the said Elizabeth, and John Warner and William Jordan, executors of John Hadde. The parties were summoned to appear on the following day, when the petitioners acknowledged that the debt had now been satisfied.[81] It is quite probable that this petition and appearance were simply for the purpose of securing an official enrolment of the transaction. In this year Yeveley bought millstones from Gilbert Maghfeld, a London merchant, for £6, no doubt for his new mills in Southwark.[82]

On 7 December 1390 Yeveley was paid arrears of £6 17s. 1d. and in the following year gave an acknowledgement to Chaucer that he had received payment of all arrears outstanding.[83] In 1391 he was a member of a commission on walls and ditches between Rainham and Aveley in Essex,[84] a district where he had bought property in 1378,[85] and in 1392 he was chosen as one of the twenty-four commissioners of the city who between 19 and 23 June attended the King at Nottingham to plead the city's case in a quarrel with the King, the causes of which seem to have been financial, but are still somewhat obscure.[86] At this time he was also surveying work on the city walls of Canterbury and the building of a new tower next to the West Gate there.[87]

Between 29 April and 3 July 1393 Yeveley was on nine occasions the guest of William of Wykeham, Bishop of Winchester, at the latter's palace in Southwark,[88] and this strongly suggests that Yeveley's professional advice or services were required by Wykeham, possibly in connection with the new design for Winchester Cathedral. Yeveley was still advising upon the repairs of Canterbury Castle.[89]

Towards the end of 1394 Yeveley must have been designing the new *Westminster Hall*, for on 18 March 1394/5 two masons entered into a contract to make the new cornice and corbels according to his design.[90] (See WASHBOURN, RICHARD and SWALLOW, JOHN.) On 1 April Yeveley himself and Stephen Lote contracted to make a tomb for the King and Queen for £250, the work to be completed by Michaelmas 1397; they were to have an extra £20 if the tomb pleased the King.[91] Most of the cost had been paid by July 1397.[92] On 26 November 1394 Yeveley and Lote had been paid an instalment of £20 for work on the tomb of Cardinal Langham, also in Westminster Abbey.[93] Yeveley also constructed a stewpond at *Hertford* for John of Gaunt, for which he was paid £11 16s. 7d. in 1394–95.[94] At the same time Yeveley had entered into an obligation to pay Gilbert Maghfeld £130, no doubt a loan, on behalf of the Bishop of Ely, and the bishop had also borrowed other large sums.[95] It seems possible that Yeveley may have been concerned with works, either at Ely Place, London, or at Ely.

In 1396 Yeveley was still a member of the Salve Regina Fraternity at St. Magnus Church,[96] where he built a tomb for himself, which existed in Stow's time.[97] From 1394 to 1399 the work at Westminster Hall must have occupied a good deal of his time, but on 28 February 1396/7 the commission for repairing Winchester Castle was extended for a further 7 years, with Yeveley, Wynford, and Herland as advisers. Yeveley was doubtless the designer of the new Great Gateway of Westminster Palace begun in 1397 and completed by November 1399. It had polygonal corner turrets and survived until 1706.[98] Yeveley received £90 16s. 0d. in 1396–97 for lead and stone provided by him for the Prior of Christ Church, Canterbury,[99] and, at Christmas 1398, he received livery as one of the Prior's esquires.[100] As has been pointed out by Mr. Arthur Oswald, this fact, taken together with the stylistic evidence, renders it certain that he had acted as consultant architect for the works of the cathedral. It seems extremely probable that the entries among the lists of *intrantes* of the city of Canterbury, paying an annual fine from 1395 to 1400, of one Henry 'Wyffell' or 'Wyuel', refer to Yeveley. The entries are under Burgate, showing the ward in which he had a house. On 29 July 1398 Yeveley was witness to a deed executed at Wennington in Essex, and Stephen Lote was another of the witnesses;[101] it is probable that Yeveley and Lote both lived at Wennington during part of each year. In the summer of 1398 he and HUGH HERLAND were sent to *Great Yarmouth* to report on the harbour.

As Yeveley had been 'a great age' in 1390, he can hardly have been much less than 80 in 1400, as he would have been in middle life when he first served in a prominent capacity in 1356. His last active work in architecture seems to have been the vault of the north porch of Westminster Hall, which in 1399–

1400 was to be made by his 'counsel and discretion' (*avisamentum et discrecionem*).[102] Doubtless on account of his age he was given licence in February 1400 to hear divine service with his wife Katherine in their private chapel in Southwark,[103] and on 25 May he made his will; he died on 21 August[104] and the will was proved in the Commissary Court of London on 12 September. He appointed John Clifford and Stephen Lote, with others, to be his executors, and desired to be buried in the tomb which he had built for himself in St. Mary's Chapel at the church of St. Magnus, London Bridge. He left property consisting of tenements with two quays and a brewery called la Glene in the parish of St. Magnus, where he was a parishioner, with other tenements in Basing Lane and Cordwainer Street in the parish of St. Martin Outwich, and lands at Wennington and Aveley, Essex; all this went to his wife on condition that she maintained two chaplains to celebrate at the altar of St. Mary in St. Magnus Church for the souls of Margaret his late wife, Roger and Marion his parents, and his deceased brothers and sisters, King Edward III, Sir John Beauchamp, and others.[105] Sir John Beauchamp, K.G., who died in 1360, had been standard bearer at Crecy and his tomb in St. Paul's Cathedral was a notable monument in Yeveley's style. Presumably Beauchamp had been one of Yeveley's early friends and patrons. Reference is made in the will to Yeveley's lease of tenements in St. Paul's Churchyard from the Bishop and Dean and Chapter of London, 'with all my marble and latten goods and my tools therein' (*necnon et omnia bona mea marmoria et de latoun ac instrumenta mea ibidem*).

Yeveley's work as an architect certainly included the new Westminster Hall of 1394–99, though its wooden roof was designed by Hugh Herland; and of part of the church of St. Dunstans-in-the-East, destroyed by the Great Fire. He was also in charge of the renewal of work on the nave of Westminster Abbey, where the evidence of the original design of the west front and west porch leaves no doubt that these were his work, though the nave itself followed the general lines of Henry III's church, designed by Master HENRY DE REYNS. Yeveley probably added the porch to the north transept, now lost, which appears in Hollar's views, and he is also the presumed designer of the Abbot's house, built by John Palterton, and of the work of *c.* 1377 on the little chapel of St. 'Erasmus' on the north side of the ambulatory.

His works in fortification seem to have included Queenborough and Cowling Castles in Kent, both erected for coastal defence, and the west gate of Canterbury, besides works on the keep of the castle there. He may also have designed Nunney Castle, Somerset (*c.* 1373), Shirburn Castle, Oxon (1377) and have worked at Arundel Castle, where the great hall and other parts were built *c.* 1380. Also of 1378–80 was the new *Holy Cross Church*, Canterbury, beside the West Gate and altogether in Yeveley's style. On consideration of his known association with Canterbury and Christ Church Priory, and the close resemblances of the nave of Canterbury to his known work, it seems certain that he was its designer, and thus shares with Wynford the credit of designing the two finest Perpendicular interiors now existing. Inasmuch as Wynford's design at Winchester was limited by the decision to utilise the Norman fabric, which conditioned the main lines of his new arcades, Yeveley's nave of Canterbury is the greater as a work of original design, and it was structurally completed under his own supervision, as the vault was being erected in 1400, the year of his death. Of all the English Gothic naves, Canterbury is the most satisfactory in its proportions and bay design, and demonstrates to the full the essential advantage of the Perpendicular style in portraying the sublime and creating the atmosphere of worship and aspiration proper to the body of the church and leading the eye and the mind onwards towards the sanctuary.

Yeveley probably designed many buildings now destroyed and others which exist unrecognised; as architect to Archbishop Courtenay he may have provided designs for the alterations to *Meopham Church*, Kent (1381–96), the gatehouse of *Saltwood Castle*, Kent (*c.* 1383), and the new church and college of *Maidstone*, founded in 1395 but completed for Archbishop Arundel after Yeveley's death, possibly under the supervision of Stephen Lote. Among smaller works, which if not by Yeveley, are close imitations of his style, the tomb of Rahere in the church of *St. Bartholomew the Great, London*, must be mentioned, and his influence is found in *Bodiam Castle*, Sussex, begun in 1385 for purposes of coastal defence, though privately, as was Cowling a few years earlier. During his long association with London Bridge he evidently designed the rebuilt bridge *Chapel of St. Thomas* (*c.* 1384) of which drawings exist, showing it to have been in his style.

Other buildings where Yeveley's style has been recognised are the destroyed church of the Hospital of *St. Katherine-by-the-Tower* (*c.* 1351–); *Arundel Church* and College, Sussex (*c.* 1380–1400); the south porch of *St. Mary's Church, Hitchin* (usually assigned to the late 15th century, but undoubtedly of *c.* 1360–90); and the former west front of *St. Mary Overy, Southwark* (now Southwark Cathedral); with the lower stage of the central tower there. His monumental practice probably included the tombs of Sir William Marney at *Layer Marney,* Essex (*c.* 1360); that of Sir Walter Manny at the London Charterhouse (*c.* 1372); the destroyed monument of Sir Simon Burley in Old St. Paul's (*c.* 1389); and the sedilia of *Selby Abbey,* Yorks (*c.* 1380).

Yeveley has been styled 'the Wren of the fourteenth century', but this hardly does him justice; Sir Christopher Wren was a master of composition and effect, and could at times achieve a delicious lightness and charm, as he showed in St. Stephen's, Walbrook, but admiration for Wren's greatness and bewilderment at the number and variety of his works should not blind us to the alien style in which he worked, quite unsuited to the English climate, materials, and needs. The new St. Paul's Cathedral is Wren's greatest achievement, but regarded as a work of religious architecture it cannot fairly be put on a level with the finest examples of English Romanesque or Gothic.

It is no disparagement of those who went before or came after Yeveley that we should claim him as the greatest English architect; he owed much to the accident of the period in which he was born, and to the good fortune which gave him as patrons two of the greatest of art-loving Kings, Edward III and Richard II, but if it was William Ramsey who introduced the Perpendicular style, it was Yeveley who perfected it and produced the noblest works of its early maturity. (See Appendix I.)

(APD; BAA; DNB; LKC; LWR. 137–152]; **KJI**; KJY; OCC; HHY; HMY; HYR; F. W. Steer in EAS, XXIV; HBP; **HPS**, 97–130; **HSS**, 29–30

[1] WSS, VII, 220; [2] *PRO*, Ass. Roll No. 1238, m. 25d (No. 78) (*C.E.L.*); [3] *PRO*, DL.30–109–1631; [4] HMY, 56n.; *CCL*, 453 Courtney; [5] RML 280–2; [6] BPR, IV, 247–8, 313; [7] *Ibid.*, 327; FSA, 18; [8] *PRO*, C.47–24–11 (*G.P.C.*); [9] CPR 1358–61, 452; [10] *PRO*, E.101–472–8; [11] HYR, 108; *LHR*, 90 (13); [12] BPR, IV, 476; [13] BBW, 189–96; *PRO*, E.101-472-14; [14] *PRO*, E.43–65 (*H.M.C.*); [15] *LBH*, G.79; [16] *PRO*, E.101–464–2; 493–12 (*L.F.S.*); [17] *PRO*, E.101–479–28; 493–29, 30 (*L.F.S.*); [18] AC, II, 112; [19] CPR 1367–70, 301; [20] LRC, III, 174; (*PRO*, E.101–395–2); [21] CPR 1367–70, 94; *LBH*, G.9 (Misc. 2); [22] *LHR*, 96 (209), 97 (4, 142, 170); CAD, I, 207; [23] CPR 1367–70, 378; [24] DTB, 3; [25] DCH, 9–10, 15–16; [26] *WAM*, 19866; [27] *PRO*, Rot. Franc. 46 Edw. III, m.27; [28] CPM 1364–81, 150, 163; [29] CCR 1374–7, 59; [30] SNQ, VI, 56–7; [31] *PRO*, E.101–544–3 (*L.F.S.*); [32] *PRO*, DL.28–3–1, m.3, 4; [33] JGR 1372–6 II, No. 1659; [34] CFR 1369–77, 341, 374; CPR 1374–7, 423; [35] LSF, 145; [36] CPR 1377–81, 7; [37] *CCA*, Bedel's rolls, London, 49 Edw. III etc. (*W.U.*); [38] GDC, 61–2; [39] CPR 1377–81, 146; 1385–9, 127; HKW, II, 842; [40] *Ibid.*, 199; [41] CLB, 'H', 125; [42] *WAM*, 19358; [43] *CCA*, Misc. Accs., vol. ii, f. 323 (*A.B.E.*); HKW, II, 594–5; [44] RGA, III, 186; [45] RML, 444–5; [46] Hussey in *Country Life*, 4 and 11 Feb. 1944; HHY, 30; [47] AQC, XLV, 49, 52; [48] *Ibid.*, XLII, 111; (*BM*, Harl. Ch. 48 E.43); [49] BCL, 42–3; [50] CPR 1377–81, 606; [51] AC, II, 97; [52] *PRO*, E.101–473–1; [53] AQC, XLV, 52; (*BM*, Harl. Ch. 48 E.44); [54] AC, II, 98; [55] HHT, 68; [56] CPR 1381–5, 221; [57] *BM*, Harl. Ch. 58 D.30; *LHR*, 112(41); [58] CPR 1381–5, 382; [59] CLB, 'H', 237–8; [60] *PRO*, E.101–479–22; [61] CPR 1385–9, 103; [62] *Ibid.*, 79; [63] CCR 1385–9, 121, 207; [64] *Ibid.*, 121; [65] *PRO*, E.101–473–2 (*L.F.S.*); [66] *WAM*, 13310; [67] CLH, I, App. vi, 39; [68] CCR 1385–9, 430–1; [69] RNW, 10, 61; *WAM*, 23460; [70] *PRO*, E.101–473–4; [71] College of Arms, MS. Arundel 30, f. 204; [72] *MCO*, Southwark, 135, 138, 139, 8c, 45c (*K.B.M.*); LSF, 154; SHB, 467–9; [73] HMY, 56; *NCO*, Hall Book i; [74] CPR 1388–92, 122–3; [75] AQC, XLIV, 240; (*PRO*, E.101–502–10); LRC, IV, 311; [76] LRC, IV, 311; [77] CPR 1388–92, 237; [78] *PRO*, E.101–491–21; [79] CPR 1388–92, 249, 261; [80] *Ibid.*, 294; [81] CLB, 'H', 354; [82] *PRO*, E.101–509–19; [83] LRC, IV, 290, 311, 312; [84] CPR 1388–92, 522; [85] EAS, XXIV, 48; [86] CLB, 'H', 378; HP, IX, 268–72; [87] *PRO*, E.364–27 (D); [88] *WCM*, Wykeham's Household Acc. 1393 (*H.C.*); [89] CCR 1392–96, 45–6; [90] *PRO*, E.101–473–21; [91] RF; [92] *PRO*, E.101–473–10; [93] *WAM*, 6318; [94] *PRO*, DL.28–32–21 (*K.B.M.*); [95] *PRO*, E.101–509–19; [96] CPM 1381–1412, 239; [97] SSL; [98] CPR 1396–9, 116; HKW, I, 548; [99] *CCA*, Prior's Roll, xvii, 4 (*W.P.B.*); [100] OCC; (*Bodl.*, MS. Tanner 165); [101] CIC; CCR 1405–9, 88; HKW, I, 211; [102] *PRO*, E.101–473–13 (*L.F.S.*); [103] WRH, II, 497; [104] CCR 1399–1402, 154; [105] SWL, II, 346; *CCL*, 453 Courtney '

YEVELEY, Robert (*fl.* 1361–1369) **Mason**

Brother of HENRY YEVELEY;[1] in 1361–62 he undertook certain works at the *Tower of London* by contract, being paid £55 for making a great wall for the house of the constable there, and a vault towards the water-gate, as well as £2 for making a chimney at one of the gates and repairing a wall at task. From 29 May 1362 he was warden of the masons of the Tower, taking 3*s.* 6*d.* a week for ordaining the work of the masons and setters, and was still holding this position on 1 October 1364.[2]

The 'vault towards the water gate' is very probably the vault of the Bloody Tower gateway with lions' faces for bosses.

From 1364 until 1369 or later Robert Yeveley was master mason in charge of works at *Wallingford Castle*, Berks., taking 4*s.* a week.[3]

[1] CCR 1441–7, 480–2; [2] *PRO*, E.101–472–9, 10, 12; [3] *Ibid.*, E.101–490–2; 545–28 (*L.F.S.*)

Ymbar, Lawrence—see EMLER

YONGE, John (*fl.* 1363–1374) Carpenter

Made several timber houses in the royal manor of *Gravesend* in 1363–66, and also built a windmill there in 1373–74. His work was done by contract or by task.

HKW, II, 947–8

YONGE, Maurice [Yong] (*fl.* 1365–1377) Mason

In 1365 and later performed tasks at the *Tower of London*, and with Thomas Hardgrey built the Clock Tower and the Jewel House in *Westminster Palace* to the designs of HENRY YEVELEY.[1] At the same time he and others supplied 8,100 feet of ashlar bought at Maidstone at 3*d.* per foot for the works; he also sold stone for *Havering Manor* in 1374–77.[2] In 1367 Yonge was paid £22 for building walls in the 'Rostynghous' at *Eltham Palace*,[3] and in the same year with JOHN BOX undertook to build the 'Barbican' wall of *Queenborough Castle*, Kent.[4] He made seven fireplaces at the *Manor of Gravesend* in 1374–76,[5] and in 1376 was granted the manor of La Gare in Kent, and out of the rent for the first two years was allowed a sum of £135 owing for the work at Queenborough.[6]

[1] HKW, I, 209, 509, 585; II, 727, 933; [2] R. P. Howgrave-Graham in A, LXXVII (1928), from *PRO*, E.101–472–14; [3] *PRO*, E.101–493–30 (*L.F.S.*); [4] *Ibid.*, E.101–483–25; [5] HKW, II, 948; [6] CFR 1368–77, 352

YVENSON, Thomas (*fl.* 1529) Mason

Freemason of Sewstern ('Sowstorne'), Leics.; on 24 February 1529 undertook to rebuild a vault in the brewhouse at *Croxton Abbey*, Leics., after taking down the vault previously made, for £6 13*s.* 4*d.*

SHB (2nd ed. 1967), 602

Yvele—see YEVELEY

Yvo the Engineer—see IVES

ZANEWORTH, Richard (*fl.* 1379–1381) ? Mason (? *Yanworth, Glos.*)

Possibly a mason; during the building of the new refectory at *Pershore Abbey*, Worcs., in 1379–81, as 'Master Richard Zaneworth' he was paid for 11 visits in 1379–80 and for 8 visits in 1380–81. His yearly fee was £3 6*s.* 8*d.* and he was given allowance for three horses and for his food while at Pershore, a typical example in 1379, for a stay of two nights being 2*d.* for bread, a capon at 3*d.* and 5*d.* worth of ale. The refectory, with the rest of the monastic buildings, is now destroyed.

BAS, LVII, 9–10

Zeman, John—see YEMAN

Zevelee, Henry—see YEVELEY

LAUS DEO

KEY TO CHRISTIAN NAMES

To assist identification of masters described only by their Christian name, the following key includes the whole of the forenames from the text, grouped into periods of fifty years. Thus in a group prefaced by **1200:** will be found all the examples of that Christian name, *the earliest known date* in whose careers falls within the period 1200–49. Names in brackets ( ) are those of men who appear in appendixes subordinate to the life of another man of the same surname. Lists of anonymous masters and of masters known by surname only are included at the end.

ADAM **1200:** Adam M.I, M.IA, Lock; **1250:** Adam M.II, Glasham, Northampton, (Pabenham); **1300:** Adam sculptor, Breton, Carlton, (Rothinge), (Witney) **1350:** Adam J., Helmesfield, Mathie, Newnham, Oliver; **1400:** Powle; **1450:** Lord, Vertue
AELFRIC **1050:** Aelfric M.
AELRIC **1050:** Aelric M.
AILNOTH **1150:** Ailnoth E.
AILRIC **1150:** Ailric carver
ALAN **1250:** Alan C., Fitzgamel; **1300:** Walsingham
ALBERIC **1200:** Alberic M.
ALDUIN **1100:** Malverne
ALEXANDER **1150:** Alexander carver; **1200:** Alexander C., M.I, II, III; **1250:** Abingdon, Alexander M.IV; **1300:** Canterbury; **1350:** Tyneham; **1450:** Wilson
ALWYN **1150:** Alwin M.; **1450:** Newman
ANDREW **1150:** Andrew M.; **1250:** Pritelwell; **1350:** Lengynnour; **1400:** Mason; **1450:** Cowper, (Harward), Swynnow
ANTONIO **1500:** Fagion
ARNOLD **1100:** Arnold M.; **1500:** Hermanzone
ARTHUR **1150:** Arthur M.

BALDWIN **1200:** Araz; **1400:** Dutchman
BARTHOLOMEW **1250:** Massingham; **1350:** Bartholomew C., (Wrek); **1400:** Halley
BEDE **1500:** Oliver
BENEDICT (Benedetto) **1450:** Crosse, Rovezzano
BERTRAM **1200:** Bertram E.
BLITHERE **1050:** Blithere

CHRISTIAN **1150:** Christian M.
CHRISTOPHER **1450:** Hilder, Horner; **1500:** Dickinson, Nedeham, Scune
CLEMENT **1450:** Clement M.
COLMET **1350:** Bateman
CONAN **1100:** Conan M.
CORNELIUS **1500:** Clerk

DAVID **1200:** David C.; **1350:** Aleyn; **1400:** Oswestre; **1450:** Carver, Dam, Orton, Sammesbury
DENIS **1400:** Gabriell; **1450:** Auncell
DURAND **1050:** Durand C.; **1200:** Durand M.
DYRIK **1450:** Vangrove; **1500:** Harrison

EDMUND **1300:** Wyrwode; **1350:** St. Andrew; **1400:** Graveley, Warlowe; **1450:** Arnold; **1500:** Godfrey, More
EDNOTH **950:** Worcester
EDWARD **1000:** Edward M.; **1300:** Edward C.; **1450:** Bolton, Downes; **1500:** Hayght, Leicester, (Semark)
EDWIN **1100:** Edwin C.
ELIAS **1150:** Dereham, Elias E., M.; **1200:** Elias, carver; **1300:** Elias M., Newton
ELLIS **1350:** Harpour

ERNALD **1150:** Ernald M.
EUDO **1250:** Eudo C.

FORTIN **1200:** Fortin E.
FRANCIS **1500:** (Lynsted)

GABRIEL **1500:** Caldham
GEOFFREY **1100:** Geoffrey E.; **1150:** Noiers; **1250:** Geoffrey M.I, Waterden; **1300:** Geoffrey C., Middleton; **1350:** Carlton, Cooper, Doune, Geoffrey C.II, Geoffrey M.; **1400:** Hall, Howell; **1450:** Brook, Kerver
GEORGE **1450:** George M., (Layer), Porter; **1500:** Derwall, Lawson, Simson
GERARD **1200:** Gerard C.
GILBERT **1150:** Gilbert C.; **1200:** Burgo, Corbridge, Eversolt; **1250:** Gilbert C., M., Wilton; **1300:** Acklam, Masoun, **1350:** Gilbert M.
GILES **1450:** Vancastell; **1500:** Fambeler
GODARD **1200:** Godard C.
GODWIN **1050:** Gretsyd; **1150:** Godwin M. (2)
GOLDYNG **1400:** Mapleton
GREGORY **1500:** Bukmer
GRUFFYD **1400:** Wright
GUNDULF **1000:** Gundulf
GUY (Guido) **1350:** Wyot; **1450:** Mazzoni; **1500:** Raff
GWILYM **1400:** Bleddyn

HAMUND **1400:** Jekyll
HANDKEKYN (Hawkin, Hennequin) **1300:** Chesterton; **1350:** Liège
HAROLD **1100:** Harold M.
HENRY **1200:** Henry C.IA, M.IA, Reyns; **1250:** Bray, Henry C., M.I, Hereford, Leominster, Oxford; **1300:** Ellerton, Evesham, Eynsham, Henry M.II, Kingston, (Pabenham), Peyntor, Ryhull, Snelleston, (Tichmarsh), Wy; **1350:** Guelders, Henry C., M.IA, Holme, Lynche, Spencer, Staunford, Welot, Wode, Yeveley; **1400:** Balfront, Denys, (Hancock), Henry M.III, Holm, Luke, Tuddenham; **1450:** Alsebroke, Clerk, (Cobbe), Janyns, Lorymere, Pays, Redman, Sebyste, Semark, Stevens; **1500:** (Bolton), Bullock, (Chalmer), Corant, Harpur, Mumer, Peter, Smyth
HERVEY **1350:** Lyng
HOWEL **1450:** Howel M.
HUBAL **1150:** Hubal M.
HUGH **1050:** Hugh M.I; **1150:** Goldcliff, Hugh carver, M.II; **1200:** Albemunt, Blower, Hugh C.I; **1250:** Hugh M.III, Reyns; **1300:** Boudon, Dymoke, Herland, Huntingdon, Kympton, (Tichemers), Wilfred; **1350:** Frost, Grantham, Hedon, Holbech, Hugh C.II, (Pabenham); **1400:** Prymerose; **1450:** Brasier; **1500:** Bolton
HUGUET **1400:** Huguet M.
HUMPHREY **1100:** Humfrey M.; **1300:** (Hurley); **1450:** Coke

KEY TO CHRISTIAN NAMES

ISAMBERT **1200:** Xaintes
IVES **1150:** Ives E.
IVO **1300:** Raghton

JAMES (Jacob) **1250:** Jacob J., St. George; **1350:** Broyl; **1400:** Palden, Woderofe; **1450:** Dam, Keyley, Remus, Royalton, Whinfield; **1500:** Hales, Nedeham
JOHN (Jean, Giovanni) **1150:** John M.I; **1200:** Canterbury, (Eltham), Flanders, Gloucester, John C.I, M.IA, II, III, Waverley; **1250:** Barnack, Bataile, Blockley, Christchurch, Doget, Gymel, Harting, Hurley, John C.II, III, IV, V, M.IV, V, Langlois, Ledes, Limoges, London, Maghull, Nassington, Ocleye, Osekyn, Pabenham, Puleberg, Wrytle, Wyther; **1300:** Banbury, Boulton, Bourne, Brumleye, Burcestre, Burwell, Bytham, Child, Colwyk, Compton, Corfe, Corscombe, Craneby, Cranswick, Cressing, Englishman, Fifede, Gildene, Glaston, Grene, Gunton, Hacche, Hardyng, Hatherley, Helpeston, Herland, Hungerford, John M.VI, VII, Kent, Kilbourn, Leicester, Maidstone (2), Mason, Massingham, Matheu, Mere, Qwynbergwe, Radwell, Ramsey (3), Rengwyne, Risseburgh, Roke, Stubbard, Teynton, Totenham, Tyryngton, Wakefield, Watton, Weldon, Wod, Wynd', (Wyshongre); **1350:** Abingdon, Alverton, Attleborough, Blounham, Box, Bredon, Broun (2), Byndyll, Clavyll, Clement, Clifford, Clonyer, Clydrowe, Clyve, Cornwall, Dauvyle, Daw, Dinsdale, Dobson, Douve, East, Evesham, Faudy, Frengey, Freton, Goderich, Grantham, Hawardeby, Herleye, Heyward, Hirde, (Hurley), Ickenham, John C.VI, VII, Jylkes, Langton, Lewyn, Long, Lyndesey, Mapilton, Martyn, Massingham, Meppushal, Middleton, Mildenhall, Montfort, More, Mulsham, Newman, Nikel, Offord, Orchard, Page, Palterton, (Patrington), Payn, Pickerell, Podding, Potte, Pratt, Reed, Reynold (2), Rokesacre, Rook, Rothing', Sampson, Sharp, Smyth, Spillesbury, Sponlee, Stafford, Stepul, Stiward, Stone, Stucley, Sutton, Swallow, Tarell, Tichmarsh, Totenham, Waltham, Welot, Wendulburgh, Westcote, Westram, Wodman, Wolfey, Wolward, Wydmere, Yernemuth, Yonge; **1400:** (Antell), Askham, Asser (2), Atkins, Balwe, Bartelot, Barton, Beckeley, Bekham, Bell, Berewik, Bolron, Bolton, Bowde, Branche, Breton, Brown (2), Burton (2), Butler, Campton, Canon, Cantelou, Catelyn, Causton, Chamberlain, Chapman, Clerk, Clife, Coket, Colchester, Cotom, (Couper), Croxton, Denys, Dodyngton, Doraunt Douse, Dover, Downer, [Durrant], Dyncok, East, Essex, Euterpach, Everard, Fayrebowe, Fekenham, Forster, Foulford, Frankelyn, Fuller, Garett, Gerard (2), Goldyng, Goneld, Gowselle, Gryme, Hardy, Hardyng, Harry, Hasill, Hassock, Heley, Herte, Heywod, Hikke, Hill, Hore, Horne, (Hyndeley), Jakes, James, Janyn, (Janyns), Jenyn, John M.VIIA, Kyrton, Langeford, Lewes, Lewisham, Lewys, Lynes, Mafeld, Marwe, Marys, Mason, Massingham (2), Menyver, Morys, Newton, Northampton, Pacche, Pekker, Poleyn, Porter, Poukhill, Rasyn, Reading, Rous, Smyth (2), Spynk, Stacy, (Stanley), Stonard, Tanner, Taverner, Thirsk, Thorn, Todde, Triell, Turnour, Tuttewyf, Tynlegh, Tyrell, Underwood, Wadley, Wassyngle, Wells, Weston, Whetely (2), Whytten, Willam, Wilmer, Wiltshire, Wode, Woderofe, Wolman, Wolston, Worlich, Wyspenade; **1450:** Andrewe, Antell, (Bacon), Barton, Bekke, Bell (2), Bowdon, Brankastre, Bredon, Brian, Brond, Bulford, Bury, Cole, Copdoke, Coryngdon, Couper, Cowper, Crakall, Curteys, Cutting, Derman, Doyle, Drawswerd, Drue, Dymmok, (Elware), Filles, Fisher, Forster, Freman, Galampton, Gelis, Godard, Gower, Graveley, Guynes, Hamme, Hamond, Hampton, Haynes, (Herunden),

Heydon, Hobbs, Howes, Jagryn, Jerveys, John M.VIII, Kale, Kilham, Lee, Leycett, Loose, Lyle, Mason, Morell, Mott, Narburgh, Nicoll, Norton, Nottingham, Pepper, Pollard, Redman, Robson, Roche, Rogers, Rollesby, Roune, Russell, Salter, Sam, Say, Sendele, Sewy, Sherringham, Skynner, Squyer, Stowell, Sturgeon, Swan, Thomas, Tilley, Townshend, Turpyn, Walfray, Walter, Wastell, Whyghte, Whyte, (Wolvey), Worseley, Wright (2), Yeman; **1500:** Allen, Aylmer, Baker, Barbour (2), Bek, Birch, Bird (3), Boore, Bornat, Brereton, Brown, Carter, (Chapman), Coke, Cole, Colonia, Courtley, Daw, Denman, Eastawe, Eleser, Ellis, Forman, Fustyng, Gibbon, Gye, Harresone, Hawkins, Hermer, Herunden (2), Hippis, Howell, (Howes), Hudde, Irlam, Jestelyn, John carver, Kent, Kynge, Lebons, Majano, Manning, Mathu, Mayne, Mileham, Molton, Nun, Orgar, Otes, Padua, Palmer, Pares, Parker, Pasmyche, Penington, Petit, Preston, Revell, Ripley, Robynson, Rogers, Russell, Sakkar, Sallett, Shereff, Skowte, Smyth (2), Sommer, Spark, Syekes, Tempas, Tomson, Warner, White, Wright.
JORDAN **1200:** Jordan C.

LALYS **1100:** Lalys M.
LAMBERT **1150:** Lambert marbler; **1500:** Joyner
LANDRIC **1050:** Landric C.
LAWRENCE **1350:** Longe, (Rokesacre), Wode, Wright; **1450:** Emler, Holbrook, Kerver; **1500:** Bradshaw, Lemyng
LEOFSI **1050:** Duddason
LUKE **1350:** Roger

MARTIN **1300:** Sponbedde; **1450:** Prentice
MATTHEW (Mathy) **1200:** Cambridge; **1250:** Matthew M.I; **1450:** Matthew M.II, More **1500:** Peter
MAURICE **1150:** Maurice E.; **1350:** Yonge
MICHAEL **1200:** Michael M.; **1250:** Canterbury (2), Michael C.I; **1350:** (Herland), Michael C.II; **1500:** Bonversall, Wolsey
MILES **1250:** Carlton

NICHOLAS **1150:** Nicholas C., Walred; **1200:** Aundely, Ely, Nicholas M.I, II; **1250:** Aynho, Chester, Dyminge, Eyton; Nicholas M.III, **1300:** Beare, Campden, Derneford, Eccleston, Ramsey, Turnepe; **1350:** Abingdon, Ailyngton, Obedone, Peyntour, Portland, Typerton, Waleys, Walton, Wyshongre; **1400:** Cowper, Rollesby, Waltham; **1450:** Andrews, Coksegge, Herman, Hill, Tofts, Wykford; **1500:** Andewe, Andrewe, Craven, Ellis, Hermer, Marry, Revell, Thompson

ODO **1200:** Odo (3)
OLIVER **1300:** Stainefield; **1500:** Bolton
OSBERT **1100:** Osbert M.
OSMUND **1150:** Osmund M.

PATRICK **1300:** Patrick M.
PAUL **1400:** Whetely
PETER (Pers, Piers, Pietro) **1150:** Colechurch; **1250:** Koc, Morel, Stone; **1300:** Bagworth, Canterbury, Quadratarius, (Tichmarsh); **1350:** Davyn, Dryng, Loco, Peter M., Steppingley, Webbenham; **1400:** Colyn, (Rollesby); **1450:** Hydes, Lyndon, Torrigiano
PHILIP **1250:** Seroyl; **1300:** Cherche, Lincoln; **1350:** Lessy, Rous; **1400:** Gamston, Mason; **1500:** Philip carver

RADBELL **1050:** Radbell artificer
RALPH **1150:** Ralph M.I, II, Wudeman; **1200:** Bolrun, Burnell, Dartford, Northampton, Ralph M.III; **1250:**

Chichester, Nottingham, Ralph M.IV, Totewyf; **1300:** Marsh, Whitby, Wrytle; **1350:** (Crump); **1400:** Biltham, (Drewry); **1450:** Sporrier; **1500:** Bowman; **1550:** Hilles
RAWLYN **1450:** Williams
RAYNARD (Rayner) **1050:** Rayner C.; **1300:** Fonoyll
REGINALD **1200:** Reginald M.; **1250:** Abingdon; **1300:** Swaffham, Wytham; **1400:** Ely, Knight; **1450:** Langley; **1500:** Bray
RICHARD **1150:** Fitzwiching, Ricardo, Richard carver I, M.I, II, Stow, Wolveston; **1200:** Arches, Eltham, Farnham, Richard C., M.III; **1250:** Abingdon, Acle, Crundale, Kamesham, Lenginour, Machun, Newhall, Norreys, Richard M.IV, Stow, Uppehalle, Waud, Wytham; **1300:** Blaketoft, Brigges, Coterel, Croke, Curteys, Farleigh, Felstede, Gainsborough, Goushill, Legh, Lynne, Machon, Paris, Rothinge, Tayllour, Thwaites, Wallingford; **1350:** Albon, Bisley, Bradle, Bury, Chamberlain, Cherche, Dylkeston, Ercalo, Fayth, Hemmyng, Joy, Kene, Lakenham, Latthebury, Leicester, Mason, Ploughwright, Pode, Richard M.V, Sallynge (2), Shropshire, Swift, Thwayt, Vale, Washbourne, Wilton, Winchcombe (2), Zaneworth; **1400:** Beke, Bird, Bochor, Bright, Buk, Chevynton, (Clerk), Cokker, Cracall, Garald, (Hertanger), Holnerst, Kyng, Meryman, More, Newton, North, Pope, Richard carver II, Russell (2), Smyth, Swift, Tyllok, Whelar, Wodeman, Woodeman; **1450:** Adam, Aleyn, Baker, Bischope, Carpenter, Cheryholme, Combes, Cutting, Dam, Elward, Gylys, Hays, Howes, Myntham, Nymes, Pacche, Philpot, Plantagenet, Richowe, Russell, Rydge, Somere, Thornton, Turner, Wareyn, Welch, Wellys, (Wolvey); **1500:** Ambrose, Burdon, Butler, Daw, Elware, Greyhorse, Gyles, Horssale, Lee (2), Michell, Parker, Plat, Rerey, Rydge, Simpson, Tegge, Tugney, Watchett, Watlington
ROBERT **1050:** Robert M.I; **1100:** (Robert M.), M.IA, Robert carver; **1150:** Blois, Robert M.II, III; **1200:** Albemunt; **1250:** Beverley, Colebrook, Holmcultram, Northampton, Robert M.IV, sculptor, Waleden, Waltham; **1300:** Bagby, Ball, Bedeford, Bokinghale, Dippenhall, Elye, Eye, Fitzgiles, Galmeton, Glasham, Goseden, Gunton, Helpeston, Hendy, Hore, Keten, Lengynour (2), (Lincoln), Mason, Melbourne, Osekyn, Pontefract, Robert M.V, VI, VII, St. Albans, Slegh; **1350:** Bath, Blaston, Brusyngdon, Burwell, Clerk, Corby, Donnom, Dryffeld, Elyngham, Fagan, Frauncys, Frytheby, Gloucester, Goushill, Henwick, Kentbury, Lardyner, Lesyngham, Normanby, Patrington, Pette, Robert M.VIII, Rousby, Scot, Seller, Skillyngton, Snape, Stanlowe, Stretford, Wendlingburgh, Wodehirst, Yeveley; **1400:** (Aldrych), Browne, Bucham, Buk, (Clerk), Cony, Couper, Everard, Fekenham, Gamston, Hertanger, Hulle, Jackson, Janyns, Kerver, Man, Maunsell, Newman, Patrington, Playser, Robert C., (Sharp), Spillesby, Strut, Sutton, Taillour, Wayte, Westerley, Whetely, Wodehay; **1450:** (Antell), Baynes, Beldham, Carow, Crosby, Currant, Davyson, Elis, Fill, Gamelyn, Hunte, Janyns, Kerver, Leget, Mason, Munford, (Russell), Sherborne, Steynforth, Stowell, Sykes, Tonge, Tulley, Vertue, Worlich; **1500:** Ball, Bates, Bellamy, Berty, Bromehall, Clerk, Cobb, Coyny, Day, Grene, Gymboll, Lynsted, Magsden, Mapilsden, Newby, (Pokyll), Rachedale, Robynson, Squyer, Sylvester, Terell, Vertue jun. Watkinson, Wymarke
ROGER **1150:** Enganet, Le Enginnur, Roger artifex, M.I; **1200:** (Blowe), Roger M.IA; **1250:** Crundale, Prittlewell, Roger M.II; **1300:** Blaston, Gunton, Hirton, Roche, Roger M.III, IV; **1350:** Barton, (Crump), Drewry, Frankelyn, Pepper, Stephen; **1400:** Denys, Growdon, Keys; **1450:** (Mapilton), (Peyntour),

Rydge; **1500:** Bell, Coke, Frogbrook, Morwent

SAMPSON **1250:** Sampson M.
SETH **1450:** Derwall
SIMON **1200:** Northampton; **1250:** Canterbury, Pabenham (2), Tresk, Wells; **1300:** Elnington, Humbercroft, Lilye, Simon M.I; **1350:** Hook, (Hurley), (Kentbury), Lawyn, Roucestre, Simon M.II, Snitterfield; **1400:** Clerk, Grove, (Lewes), Tabbard; **1450:** Birlyngham, Clenchwarton
SPROICH **1150:** Sproich C.
STEPHEN **1150:** Stephen C.; **1200:** Estinton, Stephen M.; **1250:** Hors'; **1350:** Barneby, Dunmow, Hoore, Lomherst, Lote, Peyntour, Stephenson; **1400:** (Pette); **1450:** Burton, Canon, Carpenter, Hopkins, Morgan, (Rollesby); **1500:** Haschenperg, Lowe

TEINFRITH **1050:** Teinfrith C.
THEOBALD **1150:** Theobald M.; **1250:** Waus
THOMAS **1200:** Moyses, Norreys, Northwich, Thomas C., M.I, IA, II, III; **1250:** (Crundale), Grantham, Hogun, Houghton, Middleton, Mountsorrel, Thomas M.IV, Tighelere, Waleys, Weldon; **1300:** Bataile, Bolaz, Canterbury, Cook, (Kympton), Ludham, Pacenham, Page, Plumpsted, Rickling, Staunton, Thomas M.V, VI, Winton, Witney; **1350:** Aylmer, Barnet, Bate, Bredone, Cake, Cambridge, Canon, Cleuere, Clopton, Crump, Enemethe, Esshyng, Fant, Gloucester, Hardthong, Hoo, Huy, Mason, (Massingham), (Pette), Thomas M.VII, VIII, IX, Turret, Twyforth, Ufford, Whallesgrave, Wollasson, Wolvey, Wrek, Ybourne; **1400:** Ampilforde, Barsham, Betes, Bird, (Butler), Cobyn, Colyn, Cook, Coventry, Denyar, Dytton, Elkin, Fraunceys, Glasier, Holden, Hore, Hyndeley, (Janyns), Jurdan, (Kentbury), Kerver, Mapilton, Matthewe, Nunton, Pak, Prentys, Rouge, (Smyth), Stanley, Sturgeon, Teynham, Wolfhow, Wyllemer; **1450:** Aldrych, Barowe, Barton (2), Bellamy, Berty, Binks, Briggs, Colyer, Copdoke, Crikylwode, Cutting, Danyell, Dayfote, Dowland, Drawswerd, Emery, Ferrier, Gooch, Grene, Hunter, Hylle, Ide, Jenkyns, Karver, (Leget), Lovell, Marchant, Mason, Mauncy, Nunne, Peyntour, Prowce, Redman (2), (Russell), Simnel, Skidmore, Vile, Wade, Whelpdale, Wright; **1500:** (Barbour), Bele, Bellamy, Briggs, (Brond), Burrey, Chafyn, Chalmer, (Derwall), (Elware), Faunte, Filyon, Hall, Hartshorne, Hermer, Herunden, Jakelyn, Jay, Johnson, Loveday, Lynne, (Michell), Neker, Palmer, Perkyns, Pettyt, Phelypp, Phillips, Pokyll, (Raff), Sellers, Sheres, Simpson, Spendlove, Stafford, Sterlyng, Stockton, Thorngate, Ware, Watlington, Watson, Wisswall, Yvenson
THURUERD **1000:** Thuruerd M.
TIDEMANN **1300:** Tidemann carver
TUROLD **1150:** Turold C.

URRICUS **1150:** Urricus E.

WALDIN **1050:** Waldin E.
WALTER **1000:** Coorland; **1150:** Colchester, Coventry; **1200:** Walter C.I; **1250:** Dixi, Hereford, (Pabenham), Walter C.II, imager, M.I; **1300:** Bole, Canterbury, (Crundale), (Hurley), (Sallynge), Scardebourg, Walter C.II, M.II, III, IV; **1350:** Calne, Capell, Gerard, Gyst, (Sallynge), Walton, Weston; **1400:** Jekyll, Myltone; **1450:** Hill, Nicholl, Prewet, Reve, Symon; **1500:** Martyn, Van Dale
WARIN **1200:** Warin; **1300:** Warin M.
WIGBERT **1050:** Wigbert M.
WILLIAM **1150:** Englishman, Sens, William C.OI, E., M.; **1200:** Bayard, Chancellor, Fitzroger, Kent, Rutier; **1250:** Blound, Dilkyn, Felstede, Fitzthomas,

371

Geometer, Hildolveston, Hoo, Ireland, Marays, Marlow, Mountsorrel, Nottingham, Ramsey, Wauz, William C.I, Winchcombe; **1300:** Abbotsbury, Bokton, Boyden, Bramcote, (Carlton), Eyton, Fulbourne, Gunton, Heose, Herland, Hoton, Hurley, Joy, Kendal, Keylesteds, Luve, Lyngwode, Malton, Mare, Membiri, Montacute, (Pabenham), Preston, Ramsey (2), Repyngdon, Schoverwille, Shockerwick, Underdone, Wakefield, Wermington, William carver, C.II, III, Winchester, Wisbech, Wolf, Worsall, (Wytham); **1350:** Albon, Bodecote, Bodekesham, Brown, Chuddere, Colchester, Crowe, Croyland, Deyster, Edrich, Eland, Farele, Hales, Hancock, Hecham, Helpeston, Hemelhempstead, Hoton, Humberville, Ickenham, Letcombe, Londoneys, Love, Milton, Newhall, Patrington (2), Pruist, Rede, Scot, Selot, Shaldeston, Sharnhale, Stevens, Stubbard, Suthwell, Thornton, Tilney, Ufford, Vynt, Waddeswyk, Warden, Waryn, Welot, Winchester, Wintringham, Wright (3), Wynford, Wyse: **1400:** Addescomp, Aleyn, Arche, Austyn, Berry, Bishop, Boydell, Burdon, Carter, Champneys, Chaumere, (Clavyll), Cobold, Comber, Cottingham, Crofton, Fethurstone, Fisher, Ford, Foundyng, Goldyng, Gravour, Harward, (Hedon), Helle, Hille, (Hobbs), Hockering, Horewode, Hunt, Kerver, Kyppyng, Layer, Lies, Loune, Mody, More, Norffolk, Reppys, Reyner, Roll, Rolles, Rolleston, Serle, Smaldane, Spilbery, (Steynforth), Stonehouse, Thomas,

Toutmond, Vesey, Warlowe, West (2), Wiltshire, Wolsey, Yerdehurst; **1450:** Alcock, Atwood, Bacon, Banston, Bell, Berkeley, Bonevile, Brown, Brownfleet, Bunting, Burgess, Carpenter, (Clavyll), Clyff, Cowper, (Crump), Cutting, East, Elys, Frankelyn, Freemason, Glanforth, Glydon, Graver, Gray, Gyles, Hamond, Hill, Howlett, Hunt, Hyll, Hyndeley, Lee, (Leget), Mason, Mayson, Orchard, Palden, Partryche, Raye, Rede, Rediche, Redman, Reynold, River, Rodes, Smyth, Story, Swayn, (Teynham), Woodward, Wright, Wrygth; **1500:** (Aldrych), Bager, Baker, Bale, Bellamy (2), Benett, Blackshaw, Bolton, Burdon, Buxton, Chapman, Clement, Corvehill, Dewilde, Dowell, Drawswerd, Fels, Grove, Hall, (Hermer), Hort, Hulle, Jackson, Johnson, Kitchin, Moorecock, Netilton, Okey, Oliver, Panton, Pepper, Pondour, Rede (2), Reynold, Robynson, Rotherham, Spencer, Stockton, Taylor, Thacker, Thorne, Vertue, Wetherall, Wetyng, Whelpdale, White

WULFRIC **1150:** Wulfric E.

MASTERS WHOSE CHRISTIAN NAMES ARE UNKNOWN: Alen, Benson, Bouryner, Chambyr, Fawley, Gase, Glosse, Gyles, Hart, Hawes, 'L.', 'N.', Peperton, Pyche, Story

ANONYMOUS MASTERS: Banwell, Bristol, Chester, Chichester, Coventry, Huntingdon, Kirkby Malham, Spalding, Warwick, Wells

KEY TO OCCUPATIONS

THIS key excludes the two main trades of mason and carpenter followed by the majority of those represented in the text, but includes those described as Engineers, Joiners, and Marblers, as well as Clerical Artists, and Sculptors. The last of these categories groups together those described as carvers, gravers, and imagers, as well as such individuals of other trades as are known to have executed sculpture or to have made tombs and monuments.

BRICKLAYERS, BRICKMAKERS: Brikeman, Matthew; Cheryholme, Rich.; Cole, John; Dickinson, Chr.; Dutchman, Baldwin; Johnson, Wm; Lyndon, Pet.; Newby, Robt.; Plantagenet, Rich.; Vesey, Wm.

CARVERS: see SCULPTORS

CLERICAL ARTISTS: *Monastic:* Arnold; Cambridge, Matth.; Colchester, Walt.; Corvehill, Wm.; Eversolt, Gilb.; ? Flanders, John; Gowselle, John; Gundulf; Henry C. I.; Holmcultram, Robt.; John, M. I.; Man, Robt.; Northampton, Ralph; Northwich, Thos.; St. Andrew, Edm.; Stubbard, Wm.; Tulley, Robt.; Walsingham, Alan; Warin; Waverley, John; William, carver; Worcester, Ednoth.

CLERICAL ARTISTS: *Secular:* Colechurch, Pet.; Dereham, Elias; ? Herleye, John; Keyes, Rog.; Langlois, Jean; Ludham, Thos.; Odo, Edw.

ENGINEERS: Ailnoth; Bayard, Wm.; Bertram; Elias; Enganet, Rog.; Fortin; Geoffrey; Gerard; Glasham, Robt.; Grosmont, Ralph; Haschenperg, Step.; Holmcultram, Robt.; Houghton, Thos.; Ives; Jordan; Lee, Sir Rich.; Le Engingnur, Rog.; Lenginour, Rich.; Lengynour, Robt. I, II; Maurice; Radbell; Roger; St. Albans, Robt.; St. George, Jas.; Urricus; Waldin; William; Wimund; Wolveston, Rich.; Wulfric.

GRAVERS: see SCULPTORS

IMAGERS: see SCULPTORS

JOINERS: Adam; Bell, Rog.; Cony, Robt.; Fisher, John; Guynes, John; [Halley, Bart.]; Harrison, Dyrik; Holbrook, Laur.; Jacob; Jagryn, John; Jerveys, John; Joyner, Lambert; Kale, John; Lee, Wm.; Loco, Pet.; Manning, John; Nun, John; Peter, Hen.; Pondour, Wm.; Ripley, John; Sebyste, Hen.; Simnel, Thos.; Stockton, Thos.; Thorngate, Thos.; Ware, Thos.; Wydmere, John.

MARBLERS: Bonevile, Wm.; Canon, Thos.; Chichester, Ralph; Doget, John; Dytton, Walt.; Essex John; (Gibbon, John); Lambert; Lorymere, Hen.; Mapilton, John; Newton, John; Ramsey, John III; Remus, Jas.; Rouge, Thos.; Thacker, Wm.; West, Wm. I, II

SCULPTORS: Abingdon, Alex.; Adam, carver; Adam, Rich.; Alexander, carver; Aleyn, Rich.; Aylmer, John; Bale, Wm.; Banwell, Mr.; Barsham, Thos.; Bateman, Colmet; Bekham, John; Bell, John jun.; Bellamy, Robt.; Bellamy, Thos. II; Bellamy, Wm. I, II; Berkeley, Wm.; Beverley, Robt.; Birch, John; Blackshaw, Wm.; Bowde, John; Bowman, Ralph; Brown, John; Brown, Robt.; Brownfleet, Wm.; Brusyngdon, Robt.; Burwell, John; Burwell, Robt.; Canon, Thos.; Carver, David; Chichester, Ralph; Chuddere, Wm.; Clerk, Robt. II; Clyff, Wm.; Colchester, Walt.; Corant, Hen.; Corvehill, Wm.; Crundale, Rich.; Crundale, Rog.; Dam, David; Dam, Jas.; Dam, Rich.; Davyn, Pet.; Daw, Rich.; Day, Robt.; Drawswerd, John; Drawswerd, Thos.; Drawswerd, Wm.; Dryffeld, Robt.; Durand, M.; Elias, carver; Elis, Robt.; Emler Lawr.; Englishman, John; Essex, John; Fambeler, Giles; Farleigh, Rich.; Fill, Robt., Filles, John; Fisher, John; Flanders, John; Fonoyll, Raynard; Fustyng, John; Glasier, Thos.; Glosse, —; Gooch, Thos.; Gymboll, Robt.; Hales, Jas.; Hamond, John; Harrison, Dyrik; Hermanzone, Arnold; Hill, John; Hill, Nich.; Hill, Walt.; Hippis, John; Hobbs, John; Horne, John; Hubal; Hudde, John; Hugh, carver; Hulle, Wm.;

Hunt, Wm.; Hyndeley, Wm.; Ireland, Wm.; ? Irlam, John; Janyns, Robt.; Johnson, Thos.; Kale, John; Kent, Wm.; Kerver, Geoff.; Kerver, Robt. I; Keyley, Jas.; Kitchin, Wm.; 'L.'; Lakenham, Hen.; Lakenham, Rich.; Langley, Reg.; Leycett, John; Liège, Hawkin; Limoges, John; Lote, Step.; Loveday, Rich.; Lyndesey, John; Majano, Giov.; Malton, Wm.; Mapilton, John; Mapilton, Thos.; Marry, Nich.; Massingham, John III, IV; Mathu, John; Matthew, M.; Mazzoni, Guido; Molton, John; Montacute, Wm.; More, Edm.; Munford, Robt.; Nicholl, Walt.; Nun, John; Okey, Wm.; Oliver, Wm.; Parker, Rich.; Patrington, Robt. I.; Patrington, Wm. I.; Peter, M.; Peter, Hen.; Peter, Matth.; Philip, carver; Phillips, Thos.; Pondour, Wm.; Pratt, John; Prentys, Thos.; Ramsey, John I; Ramsey, Wm. II; (III); Rede, Wm.; Redman, John; Remus, Jas.; Reppys, Wm.; Reynold, Wm. II; Richard, carver, I, II; Robert; Robert, carver; Robert, sculptor; Rogers, John; Roke, John; Rouge, Thos.; Russell, John jun.; Russel, Rich.; Rydge, Rich. I, II; Rydge, Rog.; Sakkar, John; Sampson, John; Say, John; Simon, M.I; Skowte, John; Spendlove, Thos.; Stacy, John; Sterlyng, Thos.; Stockton, Thos.; Stockton, Wm.; Stowell, John; Stowell, Robt.; Stubbard, Wm.; Sutton, John; Sutton, Robt.; Thorngate, Thos.; Tidemann; Tyllok, Rich.; Vancastell, Giles; Van Dale, Walt.; Vangrove, Dirik; Vile, Thos.; Walter, imager; Wastell, John; Watkinson, Robt.; Wells, Sim.; West, Wm. I; White, John; Wigbert; William, carver; Wodehirst, Robt.; Wolsey, Wm.; Wrek, Thos.; Wright, John; Wynford, Wm.; Yeveley, Hen.

TOMB-MAKERS; *see* MARBLERS, SCULPTORS

APPENDIX I

PORTRAITS OF ENGLISH MEDIAEVAL ARCHITECTS

Portraits of mediaeval craftsmen are not uncommon, but can seldom be identified with certainty. The list which follows includes only certain examples, and a few where there is strong presumptive evidence. It is probable that portraits of the reigning sovereign and his queen, of the patron of the work, and of the building staff, were usually included in buildings of importance, and the agreement between different portraits of the same sovereign or patron leaves no doubt that a real likeness was intended. So far as the kings and queens are concerned, it seems that some standard portrait must have existed, which was copied by sculptors, painters, and glaziers responsible for work of the highest class.

Against this it has been customary to allege that portraiture as we know it did not exist in the Middle Ages, and until *c* 1200 it is true that attempts at portraying faces are generally crude and unsuccessful. But by the opening years of the thirteenth century, literary references leave no doubt as to the intention on the part of artists to portray from the life, and towards 1300 an almost photographic realism had been achieved in sculpture. By the reign of Edward I in England, exceedingly fine carved portraits were being made. Westminster Abbey, both in its monuments and on the structure itself, contains many such portraits, and other important series exist in cathedrals and in smaller parish churches, as for instance at Winchelsea, Sussex, where both royal and private personages appear with the most marked individualities. Among a number of prosperous clean-shaven merchants with remarkable head-gear is a bearded face wearing a round cap; this is very probably the master mason who built the church. Fortunately this work can be dated very closely, as the adjoining Alard tomb, clearly by the same hand, has excellent portraits of Edward I (†1307) and his second queen, Margaret of France, whom he married in 1299. The lovely face of the young queen, though small in scale, is one of the finest in mediaeval sculpture. (See the beautiful drawings of these heads by Mr. W. MacLean Homan, in his *Short Account . . . of Winchelsea*, 1936; photographs in J. H. Harvey: *The Plantagenets*, figs. 21–24.)

It is seldom possible to identify craftsmen's heads such as that above mentioned, but where the date of the carving can be fixed approximately, and the succession of master masons is known, there is very strong presumptive evidence. In one case the master mason, carpenter, clerk of works, and glass-painter, are all shown in glass, in the east window of Winchester College Chapel, and all but the carpenter are named, but otherwise we have to rely on monumental slabs and brasses for portraits with a definite ascription.

The following list is short, but has been compiled in the hope of encouraging local research which may lead to further identifications among the many portrait heads which exist. One case deserving special study is the 'mason bracket' in Gloucester Cathedral.

GAINSBOROUGH, Richard of

His tomb-slab, partly defaced, still exists in the cloisters of Lincoln Cathedral. There is a good reconstruction in BAH, p. 120, but the face is now worn away. The inscription reads: 'HIC IACET RICARDVS DE GAYNSBVRGH OLYM CEMENTARIVS ISTIVS ECLESIE QUI OBIIT DVODECIM KALENDARUM IVNII ANNO DOMINI MCCC. . . .' It is certain that several letters have been lost after ·MCCC·, so that the date must have been later than 1300; costume, lettering, and style of canopy preclude a date later than the Black Death.

GLOUCESTER, John of

A fine head high up in the north transept of Westminster Abbey is clearly that of a craftsman; from the part of the building, probably John of Gloucester. (A drawing of it is in LKC, p. 172, and photographs appear in THW, pl. 14; AAJ, 3S, XIII, pl. vii, 1; GMS, fig. 19; HME, pl. 22; SSB, pl. 94)

HERLAND, Hugh

One of the small craftsmen's figures in the glass of the east window of Winchester College Chapel is named 'Carpentarius' and there can be no doubt that the master carpenter in charge of the work was Hugh Herland (*fl.* 1360–1411). The date of the original glazing was 1393, but the present glass is a copy of 1822; the colouring is admittedly inferior, but as regards draughtsmanship, the copy is remarkably exact, wherever it has been possible to compare it with remains of the original glass. (Reproduced in HHH, p. 336; HME, pl. 20.)

JOHN the Mason VII

One of the carved heads on the north-west arch of the Octagon at Ely Cathedral (1322–28) seems to be that of a master craftsman, and this was presumably Master John the Mason.

LOCK, Adam

In the north triforium of the westernmost bay of the nave of Wells Cathedral is a highly individual and fully representational head wearing a mason's cap. This can hardly be anyone else but the master, Adam Lock, placed at the end of his work. (Reproduced in Friends of Wells Cathedral: *Report* 1975, p. 12; CWE, pl. 25)

REDMAN, Henry
The memorial brass of Henry Redman, his wife, and two daughters, is still preserved in the church of St. Lawrence, Brentford, Middlesex, but in a much mutilated condition. Fortunately a drawing of its original state is in the Lysons collection, from which the late Professor Lethaby was able to give a portrait (in LWR, p. 153). Redman died on 10 July 1528.

REYNS, Henry de
In the eastern triforium of Westminster Abbey is the head of a craftsman, with his hand to his head in a meditative posture. This seems to have been a known 'symbol' for the excogitation of design, and is found much later in the head of William Wynford at Winchester College (see below). From its date this should be Henry de Reyns, the original architect. (Reproduced in THW, pl. 17; SSB, pl.91(B); HME, pl. 18)

RICHARD the Mason I
A head in the south-east transept of Lincoln Cathedral is clearly intended for the master, and may be a portrait of Richard the Mason I, who was in charge c. 1195. (Reproduced in GMS, fig. 184; AAJ, 3S, XIII, pl. vii, 3.)

ROGER the Mason II
Among carved heads at the crossing of Exeter Cathedral is one of a lay master, probably Roger the Mason, who died 1310. There has been much discussion about this head, which forms the base of one of the four great corbels, almost certainly carved by William de Montacute in 1312 (AEC, pt. i, 63; pt. ii, p. xxi). Since it forms one of a set with a king and queen, and a pope (? St. Peter, to whom Exeter Cathedral is dedicated), it is certainly not a self-portrait of Montacute, but would normally be the master mason at the time, i.e. William Luve. Coming as it does at the end of the choir, however, it is far more likely to be a memorial to Master Roger, the designer, who had brought the eastern arm almost to completion at his death in July 1310. (Reproduced in BPE, pl. 18(A); GMS, fig. 380; C. J. P. Cave: *Medieval Carvings in Exeter Cathedral*, 1953, pl. 8; HME, pl. 23). (See Thomas Witney, below)

VERTUE, William
The standing figure of a master mason in stained glass, now in the base of the northernmost light of the great west window of St. George's Chapel, Windsor, must certainly represent the architect. The costume is too late in period for Henry Janyns, and there seems little doubt that the figure represents Vertue, in charge at St. George's from 1506 to 1527. (Reproduced in HME, pl. 21, M. F. Bond, *The Romance of St. George's Chapel* (5th ed., 1958), 55 and pl. 4; cf. FSG, 1947, 15; 1962, 92)

WERMINGTON, William de
At Croyland Abbey is the tombstone of Master William de Wermington, mason in the fourteenth century. The inscription reads: 'ICI GIST MESTRE WILLM DE WERMIGTON LE MASON A LALME DE KY DEV (L)Y P(AR) SA GRACE DOUNEZ ABSOLVCION.' (Illustrated in BAH, 119.)

WITNEY, Thomas
It formerly seemed possible that the Exeter head of a master (above, Roger the Mason II) might represent either William Luve or his more prestigious successor Thomas Witney (cf. HME, pl. 23). The full publication of the Fabric Accounts for this period (AEC), however, plainly makes it most unlikely that the corbel was carved later than 1312.

WY, Henry
The five bays on the south side of the nave of St. Albans Abbey (bays 4 to 8 from the tower) were rebuilt after a fall c. 1324–27, and above the four pillars are heads of an abbot, queen, king, and craftsman, the last being presumably Master Henry Wy, the contemporary master mason to the Abbey. (Reproduced in GMS, fig. 378; AAJ, 3S, XIII, pl. vii, 4; HME, pl. 24.)

WYNFORD, William
Appears in the glass of the east window of Winchester College Chapel, next to the carpenter (see Hugh Herland above). The inscription reads: 'WILLMS WYNFORT LATHOMUS'. (Reproduced in LAG, pl. xxv; HHY, fig. 48; HME, pl. 20.) A carved head forming the northern label-stop to the east window of the Muniment Room also seems to be intended for the master mason, and was accompanied on the southern side of the same arch by a portrait of his warden, now defaced. (Reproduced in CPW, pl. xxvi, b; HME, pl. 18; CWE, pl. 34.)

YEVELEY, Henry
The western label-stop of the archway leading from the Parlour to the Abbot's House at Westminster bears the head of a craftsman, now defaced, but probably intended for Yeveley. The carved portrait in wood of a master on a misericord of the stalls from St. Katharine-by-the-Tower may have been intended for him (reproduced in RCHM, London, II, pl. 142, a; HHY, title), and what is probably a posthumous portrait is carved on a boss in the east walk of the cloisters of Canterbury Cathedral. This last gives the impression of having been cut from a death-mask. (Reproduced in HHY, fig. 40.)

APPENDIX II

TABLES OF REMUNERATION

The remuneration of mediaeval master craftsmen varied very greatly, not so much in different periods as in accordance with the status of the individual. I have shown elsewhere* that this depended on a differential standard of education and capacity, and that the ratio between the total pay of the designing master and that of the fully-qualified working craftsmen might often be in the nature of four to one. In using the following tables it should be remembered that the *maximum* yearly earnings of a fully-qualified manual craftsman were about £5 12s 6d. up to 1350; £7 10s. 0d. from 1350 to 1500; and £8 15s. 0d. from 1500 to 1550, and that in the provinces generally rates much lower than these prevailed.

*HGW, 39–52.

APPENDIX II

Chief Masters of the King's Works

C.: Carpenter   D.: per Day   E.:Engineer   KW.: King's Works   M.: Mason   W.: per Week

Date	Person	Office	Fees, yearly			Wages and yearly Perquisites
1174	Maurice, E.	KW (Specialist)	£18	5	0	Robes
1233	Ralph Burnell, C.	KW.				9d. D.
1236	Ralph Burnell, C. and other CC.	KW.	£ 4	11	3	2d. D. when at work
1241	Gerard, C.	—	—			7½d. D.; Gift 13s.4d.; Robe 15s
1257	John Gloucester, M. } Alexander, C. }	KW.				Each 6d. D.; Two Robes each; double pay when travelling
1271	Robert Beverley, M.	KW.	£ 9	2	6	Robe
1275	Robert Beverley, M.	KW.	£18	5	0	Two Robes; 1s. 4d D. when travelling
1278	Walter Hereford	KW.	£36	10	0	Two Robes £2 6s. 8d
1284	Jas. St. George, M.	KW. (Specialist)	£54	15	0	
	Rich. Lenginour, E.	Chester	£18	5	0	
1316	Nich. Derneford, M.	N. Wales	£18	5	0	
1327	Nich. Derneford, M.	N. & S. Wales	£36	10	0	
1331	Thos. Canterbury, M.	Westminster	—			6s. W.; Robe
1336	Wm. Ramsey, M. } Wm. Hurley, C. }	K.W.	£18 each	5	0	Robe; House
1356	John Tichmarsh, M.	{ Chester { Chester Murager	£ 9 £ 6	2 1	6 8	
1360	Hen. Yeveley, M.	KW.	£18	5	0	Robe £1
1372	Wm. Wynford, M.	Windsor Castle	£10	0	0	1s.D.;Robe £1
1375	Hugh Herland, C.	KW.	£24	18	4	} Robe £1; House
1397	Hugh Herland, C.	KW.	£43	3	4	}
1441	John Cantelou, M.	Windsor Castle	£15	4	2	Lodging
1461	Edm. Graveley, C.	KW.	£ 6	1	8	Fees 12d. D.
1481	Hen. Janyns, M.	Windsor, St. George's Chapel	£12	0	0	Robe 10s.; Reward £3 6 8
1484	Thos. Danyell, M. } Edm. Graveley, C. }	KW.	£18 each	5	0	Robe £1 each
1510	Rich. Michell, M.	Berwick	£12	3	4	
1515	Robt. Bates, C.	Tower of London	£12	3	4	
1520	Hen. Redman, M. (joint holder)	KW.	£ 9 (i.e. half of £18 5 0)	2	6	Robe 10s. (i.e. half of £1)
	Hen. Redman, M.	Windsor Castle	£ 9	2	6	Robe
1526	Oliv. Bolton, C.	Chester	£ 9	2	6	
1528	John Baker, M.	Calais	£16	16	4	

Note: Only a few typical examples of the offices of Master Mason and Chief Carpenter of the King's Works are included; the normal fee stood at 12d. D. (for 365 days in the year, i.e. £18 5 0), from Edward I to the sixteenth century.

REMUNERATION: TABLE II

Subordinate Masters of the King's Works

Date	Person	Office	Fees, yearly			Wages and yearly Perquisites
1259	Robt. Beverley, M.	Westminster Abbey	—			3s. W.
1324	Thos. Canterbury, M.	Westminster	—			3s. W.; Robe £1
1354	Geoff. Carlton, M.	Windsor Castle	—			3s. 6d. W.
1364	Hugh Herland, C.	Westminster	£12	3	4	
1366	Hugh Herland, C.	Westminster	£19	0	0	House, etc
c.1420	Wm Lies, C.	Westminster	£15	4	2	
1441	John Wynwik, M.	Westminster	£15	4	2	Gown
1442	Robt. Whetely, C.	Eton College	£10	0	0	(Contracts); Livery
1528	Wm. Baker, M.	Calais	£11	3	10	
1531	Wm. Reynold, M.	Hampton Court	£10	8	0	
1536	Wm. Reynold, M.	Hampton Court	£13	0	0	
1539	Stephen von Haschenperg	(Specialist)	£73	0	0	

APPENDIX II

Date	Person	Office	Fees, yearly	Wages and yearly Perquisites
1278	Walt. Hereford, M.	Winchcombe Abbey	—	Food; Robe; Candles and firewood, with allowance for two servants, two horses.
1334	Wm. Hurley, C.	Ely Cathedral	£ 8 0 0	
c.1330	Wm. Joy, M.	Wells Cathedral	£ 2 0 0	3s. W.
c.1342	Wm. Joy, M.	Exeter Cathedral	£ 2 0 0	
1352	Rich. Farleigh, M.	Exeter Cathedral	£ 1 0 0	3s. W.
1364	Wm. Wynford, M.	Wells Cathedral	£ 2 0 0	3s. W.; House
c.1370	John Lewyn, M.	Durham Cathedral	£13 6 8	(Contracts); Robe 13s.. 4d.
1373	Wm. Wintringham, C.	Duchy of Lancaster	£20 0 0	Vesture
1376	Robt. Lesyngham, M.	Exeter Cathedral	£ 5 0 0	1s. D.; House
1385	Robt. Wodehirst, M.	Norwich Cathedral	£ 1 6 8	3s. 4d. W.; Robe 13s. 4d
1387	Robt. Wodehirst, M.	Ely Cathedral	£ 4 0 0	Robe; Lodging
1388	Hen. Yeveley, M.	Westminster Abbey	£ 5 0 0	Dress 15s
1399	Wm. Wynford, M.	Winchester Cathedral	—	Lodging; Food; Furred Robe; Food for servant
1400	Wm. Colchester, M.	Westminster Abbey	£ 5 0 0	Robe 15s.
1412	Robt. Hulle, M.	Winchester Cathedral	—	3s. 4d.. W.; House 6s. 8d.; Food; Furred Robe; Food for servant
1413	Wm. Colchester, M.	Westminster Abbey	£10 0 0	Robe 15s
1430	Rich. Winchcombe, M.	Oxford University	£ 2 0 0	4s. ' Gown 13s. 4d.; Lodging; Hay for horse
1490	Adam Lord, M.	Bishop of Ely	£ 2 0 0	8d. D.
1510	Chr. Scune, M.	Louth Church	£ 1 0 0	8d. D.; Reward 10s
1520	Wm. Brownfleet, C.	Ripon Minster	6 8	6d. D.
1524	Thos. Briggs, C.	Lincoln Cathedral	13 4	? House
1525	Hen. Redman, M.	Wolsey's Works	£18 5 0	
1532	Thos. Berty, M.	Winchester Cathedral	13 4	
1535	Wm. Kitchin, M.	Lincoln Cathedral	£ 1 0 0	?

REMUNERATION: TABLE IV

Resident Masters of Works

Date	Person	Office	Fees, yearly	Wages and yearly Perquisites
1275	Rich. Abingdon, M.	Oxford, St. Mary the Virgin Church	—	House worth 12s
1299	Roger, M. II	Exeter Cathedral	£6 0 0	House
1310	Wm. Luve, M.	Exeter Cathedral	£6 13 4	House £1 12s.
1316	Thos. Witney, M.	Exeter Cathedral	£6 13 4	House £1 12s
1342	Walt. le Bole, M.	Westminster Abbey	—	(Task-work); Food; Dress; Boots; Gloves
1346	Phil. Lincoln, C.	York Minster	£1 0 0	'Commodities'; office of Close janitor 10s.
1351	Wm. Hoton, jun., M.	York Minster	£10 0 0	House
1352	John Palterton, M.	Westminster Abbey	£2 0 0	2s.W.; Food 1s. W.; Robe 13s. 4d
1359	John Evesham, M.	Hereford Cathedral	£7 16 0	One white loaf D.; House
1369	Robt. Patrington I, M.	York Minster	£10 0 0	House
1370	John Spillesbury, M.	Highclere Manor	£1 0 0	6d. D.
1372	Hen. Staunford, C.	Duchy of Lancaster, Lincs. & Hunts.	£10 0 0	
1386	John Clifford, M.	London Bridge	£1 0 0	3s. 9d. W.; House
1387	John Meppushal, M.	Ely Cathedral	—	4s. W.; Food
1393	Rich. Latthebury, M.	Barton Oratory	10 0	Gown; Food; Feed for horse
1399	John Clement, C.	Duchy of Lancaster, Kenilworth, Leicester, & Tutbury	£6 13 4	
1416	Thos. Hyndeley, M.	Durham Cathedral	£5 6 8	3s. 4d. W.; Robe 13s. 4d.
1417	Rich. Beke, M.	London Bridge	£1 0 0	3s. 9d. W.; ? House
1427	Robt. Playser, M.	Hedon Church	£1 0 0	? 2s. W.; House; Vesture 7s.
1435	Rich. Beke, M.	Canterbury Cathedral	—	4s. W.; House £1; Fuel 8s.; Livery 10s.; Two pairs hose
1438	Robt. Janyns, M.	All Souls College, Oxford	13 4	3s. W.
1446	Wm. Foundyng, M.	Exeter Cathedral	£1 6 8	3s. W.
1466	Robt. Spillesby, M.	York Minster	£1 6 8	3s. 4d. W.
1471	Thos. Peyntour, M.	Ely Cathedral	£7 6 8	Livery; fortnight's holiday
1473	John Kilham, M.	Peterborough Abbey	£2 0 0	Gown
1480	Wm. Smyth, M.	Wells Cathedral	£1 6 8	House
1487	Thos. Wade, M.	London Bridge	£6 13 4	
1488	John Bell, M.	Durham Cathedral	£6 13 4	House; Garment; Reward 10s
1490	Wm. Atwood, M.	Wells Cathedral & Chapter Manors	£1 6 8	House
1512	Thos. Stafford, C.	Arbury Priory	£1 6 8	Meat and drink; 3 yards cloth; barber and laundry W.; Pasture/Hay for horse or cow
1525	John Lebons, M.	Oxford, Wolsey's Works	£10 0 0	£18 5 0
	John Courtley, C.	Quarr Abbey	£1 6 8	House; Robe; 2 white loaves, 2 other loaves, 3 galls. ale; flesh and fish meals as a monk D.; Fuel; Allowances for wife

REMUNERATION: TABLE V

Occasional Consultations

Date	Person	Place	Fee	Journey Money, etc.
1337	Wm. Ramsey, M. of London	Lichfield Cathedral presbytery	£1 0 0 per visit	6s. 8d. trav. exps. for him and servants
1387	Hugh Herland, C. (? from Winchester)	Highclere Manor	6d. D. for four D.	10d. for 6 lb. oats for his horse
1409	Step. Lote, M. of London	Rochester Bridge	6 8	For the hire of his counsel
1422	Thos. Mapilton, M. of London	Rochester Bridge	£4 0 0	For his advice
1429	Thos. Mapilton, M. of London	Bury St. Edmunds Abbey; W. Tower	£1 6 8	6s. 8d. to another mason with him; 3s 4d. to their servants
	'coming from London to survey the great bell-tower and giving his counsel upon repairing the same'			
1439	John Wode, M.	Ely Cathedral	13 4	3s. 4d. W.
1445	? Robt. Whetely, C.	Winchester College	10 0	Design (portratura) on parchment of new inn at Andover
1446	? Rich. Beke, M. (the mason of 'Crystchirche', Canterbury)	Sandwich, St. Mary's Church	5d.	'coming to have ynsyzt yn the Cane stone for the stepill'
1449	Jas. Woderofe, M. of Norwich	Eton College	£7 0 0	£4 for expenses,
			coming from Norwich to Eton with John Jakes, and other payments for 'coming with his gear'.	
1468	Wm. Hunt, carver	Winchester College	3 4	Design and drawing of new roodloft
1470	(See Clem. Mason) the Gloucester M.	Ludlow Church Tower	£1 6 8	For advice and exps.
	The M. of Coventry	Ludlow Church Tower	12 8	For advice and exps.
1509	Humphrey Coke, C. of London	Eton College	6 8	For drawing platt of the cloister
1509	Wm. Vertue, M. & Hen. Redman, M. of Westminster	Cambridge, King's College	£1 17 4	For their advice
1515	Chr. Scune, M. of Ripon	Louth Ch. Steeple	6 8	For 'shewing his councel'
1516	Wm. Vertue, M. & Hen. Redman, M.	Eton College	13 4 each	For devising the 'platte' of the W. side of the College
1517	Wm. Vertue, M.	Oxford, Corpus Christi College	1 8 D.	For his services as architect and consultant
1520	Hen. Redman, M. of Westminster	Chelmsford, Moulsham Bridge	1 0	'For his labor to se the bridge, and to have his counsell, and his brekfast.'
1521	. . . Cheney, M. of Hampton Court	Reading, St. Lawrence's Church	£1 11 8	For making font; 3s. 4d. riding costs;
			and 4s. 4d. 'for a hosecloth to the Surveyor' of Wolsey's Works, for allowing Cheney leave to come	
1560	John Russell, C. of London	Cambridge, Trinity College	£2 13 4	'For his paynes in commynge from London to devise the Chappell worke'

INDEXES

The topographical index is intended to make it possible to see at a glance the architects of specific works, and in the case of large buildings, such as cathedrals, where work went on through several periods, to show so far as is known the dates of the parts for which each architect is responsible. In the case of the ancient English cathedrals, and a few other buildings, dates and details are added where the name of the architect is at present unknown in order to make the information as complete as possible. The dates given are based on documentary evidence, and may be considered exact unless prefaced by 'c'. Where it has not been possible to identify the particular parts of a building the words 'works' or 'repairs' are used.

The English or Welsh county is added after all place-names except where the place is or has been the county town of a county bearing exactly the same name; e.g. Bedford; Buckingham; but Southampton, Hants. The usual abbreviations for the counties are used where such exist, and the remainder should be readily intelligible, e.g. Chs. for Cheshire, Dur. for Durham, N'land for Northumberland, Warw. for Warwickshire.

In all cases where the mention is not directly connected with architectural work, the architect's name is placed within brackets. The name is in **bold type** where a particular craftsman may be regarded with certainty as the designer, or one of the designers, of the work indicated. The capital letters, C, E, or M, after a name, indicate 'the Carpenter', 'Engineer', or 'Mason' respectively.

Where the reference is to a craftsman who occurs only as an appendix to a main article on another man of the same surname, the subject of the main article is given, with an asterisk*, thus under 'Cambridge, Colleges, Trinity, College Chapel 1555–64', the reference '*Dickinson, Chr.' will be found to refer to the notice of Henry Dyckenson which appears at the end of the article on *Christopher Dickinson*.

The County Key refers to the topographical index, where full information will be found; places only mentioned incidentally are enclosed within brackets.

The chronological table comprises information from the topographical index, displayed in historical sequence, so that the names of architects practising at a given period may readily be discovered. Only craftsmen known or supposed to have been the designers of the particular work are included here, suppositious cases being enclosed within brackets.

While it would be impracticable to form a subject index of every detail in so large a mass of material, the attempt has been made to classify the various types of building represented in the topographical index.

Finally, an attempt has been made to include the incidental references to persons and occupations in an index of stray names and matters, which serves also as a general index.

TOPOGRAPHICAL INDEX

Abbotsbury, Dors. (Abbotsbury, Wm.)

Aberconway, see Conway

Aberystwyth, Card.
  Castle: Derneford, Nich.; Lewes, John; Maghull, John; Ocleye, John; Rous, John; Underwood, John
  Building 1277–82; Hereford, Hen.; (Lenginour, Rich.); Mountsorrel, Thos.; **St. George, Jas.**

Abingdon, Berks. (Abingdon, Alex., etc.)
  Abbey: Branche, John; Chevynton, Rich.; (East, Wm.); (Ellis, John); (Howell, John); (Nedeham, Jas.); Stevens, Wm.; (Watlington, Rich.); Welch, Rich.; **Wynford, Wm.**
  Church roof c.1375: Bodecote, Wm.
  Cross (Phillips, Thos.)

Acaster Selby, Yorks. W.R. (Landric)

Acre, Palestine
  Church at: (Englishman, Wm.)

Acre, Castle, Norf. (Kerver, Wm.)

Adderbury, Oxon. Jylkes, John; Welot, John; Welot, Wm.
  Church. Chancel 1408–18; Branche, John; **Winchcombe, Rich.**

Addiscombe, Surr. (Addescomp, Wm.)

Adisham, Kent
  Church: Curteys, John

Afflington, Dors. (Durand, C.)

Aguilar de Campóo, Spain. (Ricardo)

Aire, France (Hermanzone, Arnold)

Aldenham, Herts.
  Church. Works 1538–39: Russell, John j.

Alderney
  Fortifications 1549–51: Bager, Wm.

Aldington, Kent.
  Church. Tower W. door: Wastell, John

Aldworth, Berks.
  Church. Effigy c. 1300: (Abingdon, Alex.)

Allington, Hants. (Crikylwode, Thos.); (Poleyn, John)

Alnwick, N'land.
  Abbey: (Matthew, M.II)
  Walls and Bondgate Tower 1443–50: Matthew M. II

Alresford, Hants.
  Angel Inn (le George) 1418–24: Hulle, Robt.; Ickenham, Wm.; Wolfhow, Thos.

Altarnun, Corn.
  Church. Benches c. 1540: Day, Robt.
  Chancel roof 1534–36: Daw, Rich.

Amersham, Bucks. (More, Edm.)

Amesbury, Wilts. (Hereford, Walt.)

Ampleforth, Yorks. N.R. (Ampilforde, Thos.)
  Church. Bell-tower: Mason, Robt.

Ampthill, Beds.
 Manor. (Sylvester, Robt.)
 Works 1543: **Bradshaw, Lawr.**
Amsterdam, Holland (Hermanzone, Arnold)
Andelys, Les, France (Aundely, Nich.)
Andover, Hants. Kyppyng, Wm.; (Lewys, John); Wodehay, Robt.
 Angel Inn 1445–52; Harding, John II; Holnerst, Rich.; Massingham, John IV; (Whetely, Robt.)
 Church. Belfry 1414: Wodehay, Robt.
Andreskirk, Leics. (St. Andrew, Edm.)
Antwerp, Belgium (Lee, Sir Rich.)
Arbury, Warw.
 Priory: Stafford, Thos.
Ardres, France (Rogers, John II)
Arkholme, Lancs.
 Church. 'Kirkby Malham, Mr. of'
Arklow, Ireland Lenginour, Robt. II
Arlingham, Glos.
 Church. Tower 1372–: **Wyshongre, Nich.**
Arras, France (Araz, Baldwin)
Arreton, I. of W. (Courtley, John)
Arundel, Sx. (Yeveley, Hen.)
 Church 1380–: (Herland, Hugh); (Wynford, Wm.), (Yeveley, Hen.)
 Tomb of Thomas, Earl of Arundel †1416: (Prentys, Thos.)
Ashbourne, Derb. (Yeveley, Hen.)
Ashburton, Dev.
 Church: (Growdon, Rog.)
 Seats 1513–16: **Mayne, John**
 Roodloft &c. 1521–26; (Mayne, John)
 Church House 1487–: **Gray, Wm.**
Ashfield, Suff. (Bell, Rog.)
Ashford, Kent
 Church. Tower c. 1460–90: (Stanley, Thos.)
Ashover, Derb. (Harpur, Hen.)
Ashton, Steeple, Wilts.
 Church c. 1480–1501: Lovell, Thos.
Ashwellthorpe, Norf.
 Church. Roofs 1398–1400: Faudy, John
Askham, Yorks. W.R. (Askham, John)
Aspley, Warw. (Grove, Simon)
Aston Abbots, Bucks. (Wastell, John)
Atherington, Dev.
 Church. Rood-screen c.1530: Pares, John
Attleborough, Warw. (Attleborough, John); (Phillips, Thos.)
Aveley, Ess. (Clifford, John); (Yeveley, Hen.)
Avignon, France. Englishman, John; Wilfred, Hugh
Aylesbury, Bucks. (Wastell, John)
Aylesford, Kent. (Wode, Laur.)
Aynho, N'hants. (Eynho, Nich.)
Ayr, Scotland (Holmcultram, Robt.); (Houghton, Thos.)
Aysgarth, Yorks. N.R.
 Church. Bench-ends c. 1506: (Brownfleet, Wm.)

Bacton, Suff. (Rollesby, John)
Badingham, Norf. (Everard, Robt.)
Bagby, Yorks. N.R. (Bagby, Robt.)
Bagworth, Leics, (Bagworth, Peter)
Bainton, Yorks. E.R.
 Church: (Malton, Wm.)
Bamburgh, N'land. John, C. I.; Osbert, M.
 Castle. Barn 1221: John C.I.
 Works 1244: **Gerard, C.**
 Works 1368–72: **Lewyn, John**

Bangor, Carn.
 Menai Straits Bridge 1282: Lenginour, Rich.; Oxford, Hen.
Banstead, Surr.
 Manor: Letcombe, Wm.; Selot, Wm.
Banwell, Som.
 Church. Tower: (Wynford, Wm.)
 Roodloft 1519–22: 'Banwell, Mr. of'
Bardfield, Ess. (Sturgeon, John); (Swayn, Wm.)
Barking, Ess.
 Abbey. Demolition 1541: (Nedeham, Jas.)
Barkstone, Leics.
 Church. Bench-ends c. 1510: (Brownfleet, Wm.)
Barkway, Herts. Lee, John; (Rikelyng, Thos.)
Barlings Abbey, Lincs. (Tresk, Sim.)
Barnack, N'hants (Semark, Hen.); (Thomas, M. IV)
Barnard Castle, Dur.
 Bridge: (Ampilforde, Thos.)
Barnet, Herts. (Dobson, John)
Barnwell, Cambs. (Dixi, Walt.); (Hall, Geoff.); (Swayn, Wm.)
Barrington, Cambs. (Brown, John II)
Barrington, Glos. (Johnson, Wm.)
Barrow, Suff. (Aleyn, Rich.)
Barsham, Suff. (Barsham, Thos.)
Barton, Cambs. (Ely, Reg.)
Barton, I. of W. (Crikylwode, Thos.); Latthebury, Rich.
Barton Blount, Derb.
 Church. Tomb of 4th Lord Mountjoy c.1530: Parker, Rich.; Smyth, John, M.II
Basingstoke, Hants. (Austyn, Wm.); (William, John)
 Holy Ghost Chapel. (Berty, Thos.)
 Tombs 1536: Hermanzone, Arnold
Batalha, Portugal. Huguet; Stephenson, Step.
Bath, Som. (Hampton, John); Thomas, M. III
 Abbey. Works c. 1324–: **Farleigh, Richard;** (Joy, Wm.)
 New Church 1501–39: Leicester, Edw.; Lynne, Thos.; Molton, John; **Vertue, Robt.; Vertue, Wm.**
 Prior Bird's Chantry. 1515– **Vertue, Wm.**
 St. John's Hospital: Symon, Walt.
Battersea, Surr. (Enganet, Rog.)
 Church. E. window 1379: **Yeveley, Hen.**
Battle, Sx.
 Abbey: Denys, Hen.
 Almonry, Parlour 1443–44: Arche, Wm.
Bawburgh, Norf.
 Church: (Ramsey, John I)
Bearsted, Kent (Alen, M.); (Berty, Robt.); (Berty, Thos.); Pepper, Wm.
Beauchief, Derb.
 Abbey: (Henry, M. I); (John, M. VIII)
Beaulieu, Hants.
 Abbey: **Durand, M.**
Beaumaris, Angl.
 Castle. Irlam, John
 Building 1295–98: Houghton, Thos., **St. George, Jas.**
 Outer curtain &c. 1316–31: Derneford, Nich., Wyrwode, Edm.
Beccles, Suff.
 Church. Tower 1515–47: (Elware, Rich.)
Beckenham, Kent (Ailnoth)
Beckham, Norf. (Bekham, John)
Beckley, Oxon. (Beckeley, John)
 Manor: Milton, Wm.
Bedfont, East, Middx. (*Sallynge, Rich. I)
Bedford (Thomas, C.)
Bedford, Lancs. (Bedeford, Robt.)

Beer, Dev. (Abbotsbury, Wm.); (Foundyng, Wm.); (Harry, John); (Wolston, John)
Beeston, Chs.
Castle: Dymoke, Hugh; Glasham, Robt.; *Hereford, Walt.; Legh, Rich.; Lenginour, Rich.; Warin, M.
Beetham, W'land
Church. 'Kirkby Malham, Mr. of'
Belfast, Ireland (Lee, Sir Rich.)
Bellingham, N'land
Bridge c. 1190: Sproich
Belvoir, Leics. (Bredon, John II)
Bentley, Hants. (Goseden, Robt.); (Hore, Robt.)
Berden, Ess.
Church: Geoffrey, M.I
Bere Regis, Dors.
Church: Daw, John, carver
Bergholt, East, Suff.
Church. N. aisle c.1442: Peperton, R.
Berkhampstead, Herts. (Risseburgh, John)
Castle. Works 1172: **Ives, E.**
Works 1375: Swift, Rich. I
Bermondsey, Surr. (Clifford, John); (Lote, Step.)
Abbey. S. aisle c.1391–92: Londoneys, Wm.
Bernay, France (Colchester, Wm.)
Berrington (near Chipping Campden), Glos. (Elkyn, Thos.); (Johnson, Wm.)
Berwick-upon-Tweed. Coke, Hum.; Fekenham, John; Forman, John; Frytheby, Robt.; Lawson, Geo.; Lee, Sir Rich.; Lewyn, John; Michell, Rich.; (*Pokyll, Thos.); Porter, Geo.; Rogers, John II; Rousby, Robt.; (Ryhull, Hen.); (St. Albans, Robt.); Syekes, John; (Wolveston, Rich.)
Castle: (Houghton, Thos.); St. Albans, Robt.
Bridge 1347–52: Patrick, M.
Bescaby, Lincs. (Walter, M. II)
Betchworth, Surr. (Esshyng, Thos.)
Bettws-y-Coed, Carn.
Pont-y-Pair Bridge 1468–: **Howel, M.**
Beverley, Yorks. E.R. (Rolleston, Wm.)
House of St. Andrew's Prebend. Repairs 1311: Cranswick, John
Minster: (Beverley, Robt.); Burton, John II; (Cranswick, John); (Patrington, Robt. j.)
Choir and Transepts c. 1200–60: (?Beverley, Robt.)
Nave c. 1308–49: Malton, Wm.; Mare, Wm.; **Stainefield, Oliv.**; Whitby, Ralph
Reredos c. 1324–34: (Raghton, Ivo); Stainefield, Oliv.
W. Front and Towers c. 1390–1420: (Rolleston, Wm.)
E. window and inserted windows c. 1416–20
Choir-stalls c. 1520: (Brownfleet, Wm.)
Tombs &c.
Lady Eleanor Percy c. 1340–45: (Malton, Wm.)
Chapel of 4th Earl of N'land c. 1490
North Bar 1409–: Rolleston, Wm.
St. Mary's Church: (Humbercroft, Sim.)
W. Front c. 1390–1411
Chancel 1411–45
Choir-stalls c. 1445
Transept clerestories c. 1450–54
Nave and Tower 1520–24: (Hal, W.)
Roof of N. Chapel c. 1520: Hal, W.
Font 1530
Bicester, Oxon. (Burcestre, John)
Priory. Stalls: Dryffeld, Robt.; Walter, M. III
Bideford, Dev. (Carpenter, Wm.); (Sam, John)
Biggin, Herts. Lee, John
Biggleswade, Beds. (Fustyng, John)
Billing, Little, N'hants.

Church. Font c. 1050?: Wigbert
Billingley, Yorks. W.R. (Eynsham, Hen.)
Bindon, Dors.
Abbey: (Henry, C. I)
Birchanger, Ess. Sturgeon, John; (Sturgeon, Thos.)
Birlingham, Worcs. (Birlyngham, Sim.)
Bisham, Berks.
Priory. Tomb 1421–22: Brown, Robt.
Bishop Auckland, Dur.
Bishop's Palace
Chamber 1490: Robson, John
Chapel. Benches c. 1520: (Brownfleet, Wm.)
Bishop's Hull, Som.
Church. Chancel 1522–40: Bird, John; Denman, John
Bishops Stortford – see Stortford
Bishopstrow, Wilts. (Fayrebowe, John)
Bisley, Surr. (Bisley, Rich.)
Blacktoft, Yorks. E.R. (Blaketoft, Rich.)
Blaston, Leics. (Blaston, Robt.)
Blechingly, Surr. (Burdon, Wm. I)
Bletchingdon, Oxon. (Gloucester, John)
Blithfield, Staffs.
House c.1398: Stanlowe, Robt.
Blockley, Worcs. (Blockley, John)
Blofield, Norf. (Lyngwode, Wm.)
Blois, France. Blois, Robt.
Blo Norton, Norf. (Walton, Walt.)
Bloxham, Oxon.
Church. Milcombe Chapel c. 1430: (Winchcombe, Rich.)
Blunham, Beds. (Blounham, John)
Blythburgh, Suff. (Alcock, Wm.); (Powle, Adam); (Rede, Wm., carver)
Bodiam, Sx.
Castle 1385–: (Yeveley, Hen.)
Bodmin, Corn. (Freemason, Wm.)
Church 1469–72: **Richowe, Rich.**; **Sam, John**; **Carpenter, Wm.**
Seats, Pulpit, and Screen 1491–95: **More, Mathy**
Greyfriars Tomb and Chapel 1442: Ford, Wm.
Boldron, Yorks. N.R. (Bolron, John)
Bolingbroke, Lincs.
Castle: Staunford, Hen.
Bolney, Sx.
Church. Tower 1536–38: Frogbrook, Rog.; Gyles, Rich., M.; **Pokyll, Thos.**
Bolton, Castle, Yorks. N.R.
Castle 1378–: **Lewyn, John**
Bolton upon Dearne, Yorks. W.R. (Eynsham, Hen.)
Bonby, Lincs.
Church. Chancel 1359: Goushill, Robt.; Thornton, Wm.
Bordeaux, France. Gerard
Border, Scottish
Fortifications: Coke, Hum.; Porter, Geo.
(See also Berwick, Carlisle, Norham, Roxburgh, Wark)
Boston, Lincs. (Ely, Reg.); (Gloucester, John); (Lemyng, Lawr.); (Mason, Thos.); (Pays, Hen.); (Scune, Chr.); Tempas, John
Church
Tower c. 1425–70
Lantern c. 1510–20: (Tempas, John)
Bottesford, Leics.
Church. Tomb 1543: Parker, Rich.
Bottisham, Cambs. (Bodekesham, Wm.)
Boughton Monchelsea, Kent (Chafyn, Thos.); (*Crump Thos.); (*Herunden, John I); (Herunden, John

II); (Herunden, Thos.); (Orgar, John); (*Wastell, John)

Boulogne, France (Lee, Sir Rich.); (Nedeham, Jas.)

Bourges, France. Hudde, John

Bourne, Lincs. (Bourne, John)

Bowerham, Lancs. (Bolrun, Ralph)

Bowes, Yorks. N.R.
  Castle 1170–74: **Wolveston, Rich.**

Boxley, Kent. (Chafyn, Thos.); (Londoneys, Wm.)
  Abbey. Cloister 1373–: Lomherst, Step.

Bradfield, Suff.
  Barn 1459–60: **Auncell, Den**.

Bradley, North, Wilts.
  Church. N. Chapel c.1446: (Gabriell, Den.)

Bradwell-juxta-Coggeshall, Ess.
  Church. Window 1389: **Aylmer, Thos.**

Bramber, Sx.
  Bridge. Repairs 1304: Robt. M.V.
  Repairs 1477–78: **Cowper, John**
  Castle: Aundely, Nich.

Bramcote, Notts. (Bramcote, Wm.)

Bramley, Hants.
  Church. Celure 1525: Watson, Thos.

Brancaster, Norf. (Brankastre, John)

Brancepeth, Dur.
  Castle c. 1398: (Lewyn, John); (Middleton, John)

Brandeston, Suff. (Aldrych, Thos.)

Brandsby, Yorks. N.R. (Wod, John)

Brandon, Suff. (Reyner, Wm.); (Wryth, Rich.)

Bratoft, Lincs. (Jackson, Wm.)

Bray, Berks. (Wynford, Wm.)

Bredon, Worcs. (Bredon, John &c.)
  Quarry: (Montfort, John)

Breedon-on-the-Hill, Leics. (St. Andrew, Edm.)

Brent Bridge, Middx. Caldham, Gabr.; *Pokyll, Thos.

Brentford, Middx. (Lote, Step.); Redman, Hen.); (Redman, Thos. II); (Stowell, Robt.)

Brereton, Chs. (Brereton, John)

Bridekirk, Cumb.
  Church: Font c. 1150: Richard Carver I

Bridgewater, Som.
  Church: (Merryman, Rich.); Thomas, Wm.
  Spire 1366: **Waleys, Nich.**
  St. Anne's Chapel 1415–16: Mason, Phil.

Bridlington, Yorks. E.R.
  Priory. Choir-stalls 1518: **Brownfleet, Wm.**

Bridport, Dors. (Gloucester, John)

Brindisi, Italy (Robert, Sculptor)

Brington, Great, N'hants.
  Church. Tomb c. 1522: (Vertue, Wm.)

Bristol, Glos. (Andrews, Nich.); Canon, Step.; (Carver, Dav.); Colyer, Thos.; Crosse, Ben.; (Dymmok, John); (Glosse, —); (Hampton, John); (Herte, John); (Hopkins, Step.); (Joy, Wm.); (Phillips, Thos.); (Skidmore, Thos.); (Somere, Rich.); (Sporrier, Ralph); (Waleys, Nich.); (Walter, John); (Williams, Rawlyn); (Wynford, Wm.)
  Castle: (Mountsorrel, Wm.)
  Bridge 1280–82: Mountsorrel, Thos.
  Great Gate 1305–07: Mountsorrel, Thos.
  Hall, repairs 1321–23: Edward, C.
  Cathedral (Abbey): Derneford, Nich.; Geometer, Wm.; (Ramsey, Wm. III); (Waleys, Nich.)
  Chapter House c. 1154–64
  Elder Lady Chapel c. 1220–30: L., carver; (Lock, Adam)
  Choir c. 1311–32: (Joy, Wm.)
  Tower c. 1466–71

Churches. All Saints
  Library over N. Aisle 1460–64: **Kerver, Geoff.; Roche, John**
  St. Ewen: Hill, John; *Leget, Robt.
  Seats 1476: **Carpenter, Step**.
  St. James. Roodloft 1499: Rydge, Rich. I; Rydge, Rog.
  Screens, etc. 1505–08: Rydge, Rog.
  St. Mary Redcliffe: Norton, John
  St. Michael: (Waleys, Nich.)
  St. Philip: (Mountsorrel, Thos.)
  St. Stephen: Crosse, Ben.; Hart, [?Wm.]; (Rydge, Rich. I)
  House 1472: Morgan, Step.

Britford, Wilts. Dereham, El.

Brittany, France (Herland, Hugh); (Swift, Rich.); (Yeveley, Hen.)

Broad Chalk, Wilts.
  Barn 1477: Brook, Geoff.

Broomfleet, Yorks. E.R. (Brownfleet, Wm.)

Broughton, Oxon.
  Church: (Winchcombe, Rich.)

Broxbourne, Herts.
  Church. E. end of S. Aisle 1476–: **Stowell, Robt.**

Brympton D'Evercy, Som. (Wynford, Wm.)

Bubwith, Yorks. E.R. (Couper, Robt.)

Buckden, Hunts.
  Bishop's Palace: (Cowper, John)

Buckland Monachorum, Dev. (Growdon, Rog.)

Bucklebury, Berks. (Godard, John)

Bucknall, Lincs. (Bokinghale, Robt.)

Budworth, Great, Chs.
  Church. Tower: (Hunter, Thos.)

Builth, Brec.
  Castle: Leominster, Hen.; Winchcombe, Wm.

Bulford, Wilts. (Bulford, John)

Bullington, Lincs.

Bullington, Lincs.
  Priory: Elias, M. I; Wudeman, Ralph

Bumpstead, Steeple, Ess.
  Church. Aisle roof c. 1530: (Loveday, Thos.)

Bungay, Suff. (Ely, Reg.); (Mason, John II)

Burford, Oxon. (Bowdon, John); (Chevynton, Rich.): (East, Wm.); (Janyns, Hen.); (Janyns, Robt. s.); (Westerley, Robt.)
  Church: (Janyns, Robt., j.)

Burghfield, Berks.
  Bridge, Repairs 1278–: **Waus, Theo.**

Burgos, Spain (Ricardo)
  Las Huelgas Convent c. 1180–1223: **Ricardo**

Burlingham, Norf. (Birlyngham, Sim.)

Burnley, Lancs.
  Church. Aisles 1533: **Craven, Nich.; Sellers, Thos.**

Burscough Priory – see Ormskirk

Burston, near Diss, Norf. (Loose, John)

Burton-on-Trent, Staffs. (Harpur, Hen.); (Moorecock, Wm.); (Parker, Rich.) Turold, C.
  Abbey: (Derneford, Nich.)

Burwell, Cambs. (Burwell, John &c.); (Hawes, M.); (Hermer, Nich.)
  Church c. 1454–70: (Ely, Reg.)

Bury, near Ramsey, Hunts. (Redman, Hen.)

Bury St. Edmunds, Suff. (Auncell, Den.); (Bellamy, Wm. I); (Bronde, John); (Bunting, Wm.); (Burdon, Wm. II); Clerk, Sim.; (Derman, John); Forster, John M.; (Goneld, John); (Grene, John) (Hermer, John); Ide, Thos.; (John M. IA); (Koc, Pet.); Layer, Wm.; (Lee, Sir Rich.); Nunne, Thos.; (Rede, Wm., M.); (Semark, Hen.); (Spark, John); Wastell, John; (Wolsey, Wm.); (Worlich, John);

(Worlich, Robt.)
Abbey: Aleyn, Rich.; Bodekesham, Wm.; (Bronde, John); Clerk, Sim.; Cobold, Wm.; Derman, John; Edrich, Wm.; Forster, John M.; Hecham, Wm.; (Hermer, John); Hugh the Carver; (Ide, Thos.); (John M. IA); Kent, John, II; Layer, Wm.; Mapilton, Thos.; Simon M. II; (Walton, Walt.); (Wastell, John); Wode, John
Cross 1467: Ide, Thos.
Houses: Coksegge, Nich.
St. James's Church (Cathedral) 1503–21: (Semark, Hen.); Wastell, John
St. John-at-Hill Chapel. Roof 1439: Heywod, John
St. Mary's Church. Nave 1424–44: Layer, Wm.
St. Saviour's Hospital: (Cobold, Wm.); Simon M. II
Byfleet, Surr.
Manor. Kitchen, etc. 1310– : Kent, John I
Works 1346–51: Wallingford, Rich.
Byland, Yorks. N.R.
Abbey: (Scune, Chris.)
Works c. 1175–1200: Godwin, M. II
Bytham, Castle, Lincs. (Bytham, John)
Church. Repairs 1368–69: Normanby, Robt.
Bywell St. Peter, N'land. Gerard; (Lewyn, John)

Cadishead, Lancs. (Edwin, C.)
Caen, France. (Frankelyn, John)
Caerlaverock, Scotland.
Castle: Glasham, Adam
Caerphilly Castle, Glam.
Castle: (St. George, Jas.)
Hall c. 1326: **Bataile, Thos.**; Hurley, Wm.
Caister, Norf.
Castle 1432–46: Gravour, Wm
Caister, East, Norf.
Church. Roof c.1330: Gunton, John; Gunton, Robt.
Calais, France (Chafyn, Thos.); (Haschenperg, Step.); (Lee, Sir Rich.); (Reynold, Wm. II); (Tyrell, John); Vertue, Wm.; (Yeveley, Hen.)
Castle. Chapel: Pynkhill, John
Fortifications: Acklam, Gilb.; Baker, John; Baker, Wm.; Bates, Robt.; Bird, John II; Box, John; Bukmer, Greg.; (Caldham, Gabr.); Clopton, Thos.; Combes, Rich.; Crofton, Wm.; Dunmow, Step.; Ferrier, Thos.; Frankelyn, Wm.; Fuller, John; Goderich, John; Guelders, Hen.; Hardthong, Thos.; Hemmyng, Rich.; Hockering, Wm.; Jay, Thos.; Lee, Sir Rich.; Mapilsden, Robt.; Mathewe, Thos.; Mody, Wm.; Nedeham, Jas.; Olyver, Bede; Pacche, John; Pettyt, Thos.; Pickerell, John; Pynkhill, John; Rogers, John II; Snitterfield, Sim.; Stucley, John; Thompson, Nich.; Tilney, Wm.; Warlowe, Wm.; Wellys, Rich.; *Winchcombe, Rich.; Woodward, Wm.; Wright, John II
Newenham Bridge: Fuller, John
Caldecote, Cambs.
Church. Tower 1481: (Swynnow, Andr.)
Callington, Corn. (Growdon, Rog.)
Calshot, Hants.
Castle 1539–: **Berty, Thos.**; Boore, John
Camber, Sx.
Castle 1539: Andewe, Nich.; Andrewe Nich.; Haschenperg, Step.; **Molton, John**; Pokyll, Thos.
Cambridge. (Birlyngham, Sim.); (Bury, John); (Cambridge, Matth. &c.); (Cobbe, Robt.); (Hermer, John); (Kale, John); (Loose, John); (Mildenhale, John); (Newman, Alwyn); (Newnham, Adam); (Pekker, John); Plough-

wright, Rich.; (Prentice, Mart.); (*Rede, Wm., M); (Salter, John); (Say, John); (Semark, Hen.)
Castle: Aundely, Nich.; Cooper, Geoff.; (Ely, Reg.); Geoffrey, C. II; *Sharp, John
Building 1286–99: John, C.V; Thomas, M. II
Churches:
Holy Trinity: Ball, Robt. II; Bury, John; Buxton, Wm.; Kale, John; Stockton, Wm.
St. Benet. Nave roof 1452: **Tofts, Nich.**
St. Edward. Work c. 1446: Ely, Reg.
St. John Baptist 1480: Bell, John III; *Burdon, Wm. II; Ely, Reg.; Mott, John; Prentice, Martin; Sturgeon, John
St. Mary the Great: Buxton, Wm.; (Cobb, Robt.); (Robynson, Robt.); Rotherham, Wm.
Nave and Tower (lower stage) 1491–1505; Bell, John III; Clerk, Sim.; Wastell, John
Nave roof 1506
W. ends of Aisles c. 1512–14; **Burdon, Wm. II**; Swayn, Wm.
Benches in Nave 1511–12: **White, Wm.**
Church door 1513–14: **Kale, John**
Seats 1518: **Kale, John**
Roodloft 1520–22: **Bell, Rog.**; **Nun, John**
Tower, belfry stage 1593–1608
St. Mary the Less c. 1352
St. Michael c. 1340
Colleges:
Christ's
God's House 1446–
College 1505–c. 1511: Swayn Wm.
Chapel. Stalls 1510: Bowman, Ralph; **Harrison, Dyrik**
Corpus Christi
Old Court c. 1352–77: (Blaston, Robt.); (Newnham, Adam)
Wall, Bakehouse etc.. 1457–60; Loose, John; Nottingham, John
Emmanuel
Friary of Dominicans. Work c. 1456–81: Clerk, Sim.; Loose, John
Gonville and Caius
Gonville Hall
Chapel c. 1393
Hall, W. and S. Ranges c. 1441
E. Range, 1490
Jesus
St. Radegund's Priory: (Hall, Geoff.)
College 1496–
Chapel. Stalls c. 1490
King's: Brook, Geoff.; (Hall, Geoff.); (Harward, Wm.); Mott, John; Newman, Alwyn; Westerley, Robt.
Chapel 1443–61: Antell, John; Brown, John II; **Ely, Reg.**; Sturgeon, Thos.; (Whetely, Robt.) 1476–85: Bell, John III; *Burdon, Wm. II; **Clerk, Sim.**; (*Cobb, Robt.); *Peyntour, Thos.; **Prentice, Mart.**; Sturgeon, John; Worlich, John; Wright, Wm.
Vaults &c. 1508–15: Bowman, Ralph; Buxton, Wm.; Chapman, Wm.; Cobb, Robt.; Lee, John; (Lee, Rich.); Oliver, Wm.; Otes, John; Redman, Hen.; Robynson, Robt.; Rotherham, Wm.; Russell, John s.; Russell, Rich., C.; Semark, Hen.; (Smyth, Hen.); Stockton, Thos.; Vertue, Wm.; **Wastell, John**; Watlington, Thos.; Wetyng, Wm.; Worlich, Robt.; Wright, John II
Screen and Stalls 1532–36: Buxton, Wm.; Kale,

John; Philip carver

Provost's Lodge 1482–85

             1504–08; Bury, John; Kale, John

King's Hall, see Trinity College

Magdalene

  Chapel c. 1428

  Buckingham College: (Gye, John)

  Hall &c. 1519–

Merton Hall, see 'School of Pythagoras' after Schools

Pembroke: Ely, Reg.

  First Court 1347–c. 1375

Peterhouse

  Hall c. 1286–90

  N. Range 1424–

  W. Range and Library 1431–: Ely, Reg.; **Wassyngle, John**

  Kitchen, Buttery &c. 1450–: Ely, Reg.; **Harward, Wm.**; (Loose, John)

  Stone Parlour 1460–: Bacon, John

Queens'

  First Court 1448–: **Ely, Reg.**; **Sturgeon, Thos.**

  Second Court c. 1460–65

  Hall panelling 1531–32: Fambeler, Giles; Harrison, Dyrik; Joyner, Lamb.

  President's Gallery 1536–37: Cobb, Robt.; Joyner, Lamb.

St. John's: (Cobbe, Robt.); Lee, Rich.; Robynson, John; Robynson, Wm.; (Wastell, John)

  First Court and gate 1511–20: Swayn, Wm.

  Stalls, Roodloft, and gates 1516: **Loveday, Thos.**

  Hall panelling 1538: **Joyner, Lamb.**

Sidney Sussex

  Friary of Franciscans

  Refectory (now Chapel) &c.

Trinity

  Michael House 1324–

  King's Hall: Newman, Alwyn

  1337–: (Baker, Rich.); Bury, John; (George, M.); Gerard, John, M.; Peter, Hen.

  Old Court 1375–1425: Henry, M. III; Mathie, Adam

  Kitchen and Solar 1386–87: **Hoore, Step.; Payn, John**

  Hall 1387–90: Maidston, John, C.; Sharp, John

  Bakehouse and Library 1411–22; **Dodington, John**; Reyner, Wm.; Strut, Robt.

  King Edward's Gate 1427–37: Brown, John II; Coket, John; Douse, John

  Works 1449–52: Ely, Reg.

  Chapel 1464–70: Bell, John III; Clerk, Sim.; Say, John; **Worlich, John**

  Great Gate &c. 1490–95: Salter, John; Swayn, Wm.; **Wastell, John**. 1518–23: Buxton, Wm.; Burdon, Wm. II

  Upper stories 1528–35: **Loveday, Thos.; Shereff, John**

  College Chapel 1555–64: *Dickinson, Chr.; Russell, John j.

Trinity Hall

  Old Court 1352–75: **Bury, Rich.**; Mildenhale, John

Great Bridge: Gye, John

Guildhall: Mott, John

Schools (Old University Library): Hunt, Wm. II; Loose, John; Nottingham, John

  South room &c. 1466–71: Bacon, Wm.; Ely, Reg.; Glanforthe, Wm.; Harward, Wm.; (Worlich, John)

'School of Pythagoras' (Merton Hall): (Harward, Wm.); Sturgeon, Thos.

New work 1374: Mathie, Adam; Meppushal, John

Campden, Chipping, Glos. (Campden, Nich.)

  Church. Tower and Nave c. 1455: Gower, John

  (See also Berrington)

Canewdon, Ess. (Urricus E.)

Canterbury, Kent. (Alexander, C.); (Bellamy, Wm.); Canterbury, Mich.; (Denys, John); Frengey, John; (Lynsted, Robt.); Massingham, John III; (Pepper, Wm.); (Stanley, Thos.); (Vertue, Robt.); (Wastell, John)

  Abbey of St. Augustine: (Canterbury, Mich.); (Nedeham, Jas.); (Ramsey, Wm. III); *Reynold, Wm.; Teynham, Thos.; (Vertue, Robt.)

New Church 1070–91: Blithere

  Great Gatehouse c. 1308: (Canterbury, Thos.)

Archbishop's Palace: (Wastell, John)

Castle. Repairs 1390–: Herland, Hugh; Yeveley, Hen.

Cathedral (Christ Church): Bouryner, J.; Box, John; Clyff, Wm.; Elye, Robt.; Gildene, John; Goneld, John; (Herland, John); John, M. III; Knight, Reg.; *Leget, Robt.; (Londoneys, Wm.); Luke, Hen.; Morys, John; *Pette, Robt.; Ralph, M. III; (Redman, Thos. I); (Robert, M. IV); Roger, Luke; Rouge, Thos.; Smyth, John I; Smyth, Rich.; Teynham, Thos.; Underdone, Wm.; William, C.I

  Lanfranc's Church 1070–77

  Choir, Crypt and E. Transepts 1096–1107

  Choir rebuilt 1175–78: **Sens, Wm.**

  Trinity Chapel and Corona 1179–84: **Englishman, Wm.**

  Choir Screens c. 1304–20: (Canterbury, Thos.)

  St. Anselm's Chapel. Window 1336: (Canterbury, Thos.)

  Black Prince's Chantry c. 1363–: (Box, John); (Yeveley, Hen.)

  Nave and S. Transept 1379–1405: Hoo, Thos.; Lote, Step.; Wolward, John; **Yeveley, Hen.**

  Cloisters 1397–1414: Hoo, Thos.; Lote, Step.; **Yeveley, Hen.**

  Chapter House remodelled c. 1400–12: Lote, Step.; Wolward, John

  Pulpitum c. 1410–40: **Lote, Step.**; (Massingham, John III)

  St. Michael's Chapel 1410–39: (Lote, Step.); (Mapilton, Thos.)

  SW. Tower 1423–34: *Clerk, John; **Mapilton, Thos.**; Smaldane, Wm.; Stanley, Thos.

  Tabernacle work round base 1449–68: Beke, Rich.; Glasier, Thos.

  N. Transept and Lady Chapel c. 1448–55: Beke, Rich.

  Lady Chapel vault c. 1468

  Central Tower 1493–c. 1505: **Wastell, John**

  Christ Church Gate c. 1515–20

  Shrine of Thomas Becket 1220: Colchester, Walt.; Dereham, El.

  Tombs: Bonevile, Wm.

  Archbishop Peckham c. 1292: Canterbury, Mich.

  Archbishop Mepham c. 1333: (Canterbury, Thos.)

  Archbishop Stratford c. 1377: (Box, John)

  The Black Prince c. 1377: (Yeveley, Hen.)

  Henry IV c. 1414: (Lote, Step.); (Prentys, Thos.); (Toutmond, Wm.)

  Cardinal Bourchier c.1480–86: (Janyns, Hen.)

  Cardinal Morton 1486–1500: Wastell, John

  Archbishop Warham c.1503–15: (Wastell, John)

  Churches:

  St. Andrew. Pews and Pulpit 1505: Brown, John, C.; Godfrey, Edm.

Chest 1485: Curteys, John
Holy Cross 1378–80: (Yeveley, Hen.)
Guildhall 1438: Colyn, Piers; Tuttewyf, John; Wodeman, Rich.
Houses in Burgate 1278–79: Robert, M. IV; William, C. I
'The Sun' 1437–38: Goneld, John; Massingham, John III; Smyth, Rich.
Houses 1497: Brown, John, C.
Manor: Caldham, Gabr.; *Reynold, Wm. II
Priory of St. Laurence: (Canterbury, Mich.)
Walls and Westgate 1378–90: Londoneys, Wm.; **Yeveley, Hen.**
Capel, Surr.
Church. Bell-turret and spire: (Walfray, John)
Cardiff, Glam.
St. John's Church. Tower: Hart, [?Wm.]
Cardigan
Castle: Burnell, Ralph; Derneford, Nich.; Lewes, John; Rous, John; Underwood, John
Careby, Lincs. (Kympton, Hugh)
Carisbrooke, I. of W.
Castle: Breton, Adam; Marsh, Ralph; Tayllour, Rich.
Gatehouse heightened 1380–: Bradle, Rich.; Herland, Hugh; Oliver, Adam; Wynford, Wm.; **Yeveley, Hen.**
Carles, Yorks. (Stephen, C.)
Carlingford, Ireland. Aundely, Nich.; (Gerard); (Houghton, Thos.)
Carlisle, Cumb. (Tichemers, Hugh)
Castle: Gerard; Holmcultram, Robt.; Houghton, Thos.; John, M. VI; Preston, Wm.
Works 1172–74: **Wulfric**
Works 1378–83: **Lewyn, John**; Wright, Wm. C. II
Works 1541–43: **Haschenperg, Step.**
Cathedral
Nave and S. Transept c. 1092–1123
Choir Aisles and Arcading c. 1245–92
Choir rebuilt, including piers, and E. bay to springing of window 1293–1322
East front, design of, 1318–22: (Raghton, Ivo)
Upper walls of Choir c. 1363–95
E. window tracery c. 1363–82
Glazing 1382–84
N. Transept and Tower c. 1400–19
Choir-stalls c. 1400–10
Fratry and Monastic buildings c. 1485–1500
Gatehouse 1527
Carlow, Ireland
Castle: More, John
Carlton, Suff.
Church. Screen c.1501: Loveday, Rich.
Carmarthen. (Hereford, Hen.)
Castle: Adam, M. II; Blaston, Rog.; Burnell, Ralph; Derneford, Nich.; (Glasham, Adam); Hirde, John; Hogun, Thos.; Lewes, John; Rous, John; Underwood, John; Wolf, Wm.
Carnarvon (Eccleston, Nich.); (Hereford, Hen.)
Castle: Derneford, Nich.; Huntingdon, Hugh; Irlam, John; (Lenginour, Rich.); St. George, Jas.
Eagle to Chamberlain Towers 1283–92: Ellerton, Hen.; **Hereford, Walt.**
Hall works 1295: London, John
N. Curtain, Towers and King's Gate 1296–1323: Chesterton, Handekyn; Ellerton, Hen.; Eynsham, Hen.; Glasham, Adam; Helpeston, Robt.; Helpeston, Wm.; Mere, John
Walls 1283–: Lenginour, Rich.; St. George, Jas.

Carrickfergus, Ireland. (Urricus, E.)
Carrow, Norf. (Woderofe, John)
Casterton, Little, Rutl. (Boydell, Wm.)
Catterick, Yorks. N.R.
Bridge 1421–: Ampilforde, Thos.; Garrett, John; Maunsell, Robt.
Church
Chancel, Nave and Aisles 1412–: **Cracall, Rich.**; (Newton, Rich.)
Porch 1491
Cave, South, Yorks. E.R. (Barton, John II)
Cavendish, Suff.
Church. S. aisle 1471: (Ely, Reg.)
Cawood, Yorks. W.R. (Forman, John); Palden, Jas.
Manor. Chapel: Patrington, Robt. I
Chalk, see Broad Chalk
Charing, Kent (Wastell, John)
Charing, Middx. Wareyn, Rich.
Mews for Hawks: Beverley, Robt.; Hunt, Wm. I; Kentbury, Robt.; Nottingham, Wm.; Westerley, Robt. (Incidental works at the Mews were under the control of the King's Chief Craftsmen at Westminster Palace)
(See also Eleanor Crosses)
Chart, Great, Kent. (Bouryner, J.)
Chartham, Kent
Fulling Mill 1437: Bochor, Rich.
Château-Gaillard, France (Aundely, Nich.)
Cheddar, Som.
Church: 'Bristol', C.
Tower c.1400–: (Wynford, Wm.)
Chellaston, Derb. (Prentys, Thos.); (Sutton, Robt.)
Chelmsford, Ess.
Moulsham Bridge 1372: **Yeveley, Hen.**
Repairs 1520: Redman, Hen.
(See also Moulsham)
Chenies, Bucks. (More, Edm.)
Chepstow, Mon.
Castle. Works 1278–94: Ralph, M. IV
Cherryholme, Yorks. W.R. (Cheryholme, Rich.)
Chertsey, Surr. (Chapman, Wm.)
Abbey. Demolition 1538: (Howell, John); (Nedeham, Jas.)
Cheshunt, Herts. (Fitzroger, Wm.)
Chester, Chs. (Gerard); (Grantham, Thos.); (Hereford, Hen.); (Leominster, Hen.); (Newhall, Rich.); (Paris, Rich.); (Wisswall, Thos.)
Bridge: Glasham, Robt.
Rebuilt 1347–: **Snelleston, Hen.**
Castle: Bolton, Oliv.; Derwall, Geo.; Drewry, Rog.; Eccleston, Nich.; Frankelyn, Wm.; Helpeston, Robt.; Huntingdon, Hugh; Legh, Rich.; Lenginour, Rich.; Paris, Rich.; Rediche, Wm.; Wakefield, Wm.
Chapel and Apartments 1284: Marlow, Wm.
Outer Gatehouse 1292–93: Marlow, Wm.
(See also Palatinate, below)
Cathedral (St. Werburgh's Abbey)
Norman Church 1093–1140
Choir, Chapter House and Vestibule, Refectory 1194–1250
Choir completed, Lady Chapel c. 1283–1315: **Lenginour, Rich.**
Nave begun c. 1323–
Choir-stalls c. 1390: (Newhall, Wm.)
Nave, N. Arcade 1485–92
Nave completed, Central Tower, S. Transept completed, SW. Porch and SW. Tower begun 1493–1537

III); (Wendulburgh, John)
Cathedral Priory: Reginald, M.; (Wendulburgh, John)
Cross 1542–: Petit, John; Phillips, Thos.
St. Michael's Church. Tower 1373–95: (Skillyngton, Robt.)
Cowdray, Sx.
 Hall c. 1540: (Nedeham, Jas.)
Cowes, I. of W.
 Forts 1539–: **Berty, Thos.**; Molton, John
Cowick, Yorks. W.R.
 Manor: John, C. II
Cowley, Oxon.
 St. Bartholomew's Hospital: Brown, Wm., M; Carow, Robt.
Cowling, Kent
 Castle 1380–85: Crump, Thos.; Sharnhale, Wm.; **Yeveley, Hen.**; Wode, Laur.
Cranswick, Yorks. E.R. (Cranswick, John)
Crecy, France. Campaign: Albon, Rich.
Cressing, Ess. (Cressing, John)
Crewkerne, Som.
 Church. Nave c. 1475—90: (Smyth, Wm.)
Criccieth, Carn.
 Castle: Derneford, Nich.
 Building 1292–: (Lenginour, Rich.); (St. George, Jas.)
Croscombe, Som.
 Church. St. George's Chapel and Vestries 1506–12: **Carter, John**
Croxden Abbey, Derb. (Yeveley, Hen.)
Croxton Abbey, Leics. Walter, M. II; Yvenson, Thos.
Croydon, Surr. (Carter, Wm.); Carver, Wm.; (Fant, Thos.); (Massingham, John)
Croyland, Lincs.
 Abbey: Elnington, Sim.; Keten, Robt.; Wermington, Wm.
 Norman Church 1113–: **Arnold**
 Rebuilding, Tower &c. c. 1392–1427: **Croyland, Wm.**
Crundale, Kent (Crundale, Rich. &c.)
Cubley, Great, Derb.
 Church. Tomb c. 1505: Harpur, Hen.; Moorecock, Wm.
Cudham, Kent (Fant, Thos.)

Damerham, South, Hants. (Thomas, M. IA)
Damme, Belgium (Dam, Jas.)
Darley, Derb. (Stepul, John)
 Hall 1321–: Keylesteds, Wm.
Darnford, Staffs. (Derneford, Nich.)
Darnhall, Chs. Waverley, John
Dartford, Kent. Allen, John; (Caldham, Gabr.); (*Chapman, Wm.); (Dartford, Ralph); Lynsted, Robt.; (Nedeham, Jas.); (*Reynold, Wm. II)
 Church: (Gundulf)
 Manor: Bradshaw, Lawr.
Dartington, near Totnes, Dev.
 Hall 1389–99: (Herland, Hugh)
Daventry, N'hants (Man, Robt.)
Dawlish, Dev.
 Church: Foundyng, Wm.
Deal, Kent
 Castle c. 1540: Clement, Wm.; Dickinson, Chr.; Haschenperg, Step.; Molton, John
Dean, Oxon. Gylys, Richard, C.
Deddington, Oxon.
 Church. Works c. 1430: (Winchcombe, Rich.)
Dedham, Ess.
 Church. Tower c. 1490–: (Wastell, John)
Deerhurst, Glos. (Walton, Walt.)

Deganwy, Carn. Gerard
Denbigh
 Castle and Walls. First work c. 1283–89: (Lenginour, Rich.); (St. George, Jas.)
 Second work, Great Gate &c. c. 1300–22: (Hereford, Walt.); (Stainefield, Oliv.)
Denston, Suff. (Clerk, Sim.)
Dent, Yorks. W.R.
 Church: 'Kirkby Malham, Mr. of'
Depden, Suff. (Payn, John)
Deptford, Kent (Clifford, John); (Danyell, Thos.); (Lote, Step.)
Derby. (Parker, Rich.); (Smyth, John)
 Bridge at 'Wattestonwell': Stepul, John
 Church, All Saints (Cathedral)
 Tower 1510–32: Otes, John
Derby, West, Lancs.
 Castle: Edwin, C.
Dereham, East, Norf. (Hermer, Nich.)
 Church. Steeple work 1463–64: Gyles, Wm.
 S. Aisle work, etc. 1466–67: Narburgh, John
 N. Aisle roof 1467–68: Bishop, Wm.
 Font 1468: Pyche, W.
 Font-cover 1478–80: Munford, Robt.
 W. window, Belfry 1478–80: Wright, John I
 Steeple work 1492–93: Herman, Nich.
Dereham, West, Norf. (Dereham, Elias); (Hermer, John)
Devizes, Wilts.
 Castle. Works 1217: Albemunt, Hugh
Dewchurch, Little, Heref.
 Church. Belfry 1359– : Podding, John
Dieppe, France (Lee, Sir Rich.)
Diserth, Flints. Gerard
Diss, Norf. (Hore, John)
Ditton, Long, Surr. (Dytton, Walt.)
Ditton Valence, see Ditton, Wood
Ditton, Wood, Cambs. (Heywod, John)
Doncaster, Yorks. (Mody, Wm.)
Dover, Kent
 Castle: Adam, M. IA; Alexander, C.; Aynho, Nich.; Chancellor, Wm.; Cressing, John; Freton, John; Gerard; Harting, John; Houghton, Thos.; (Jordan, C.); Lengynnour, And.; Peyntour, Nich.; Peyntour, Step.; Vale, John.
 Windmill 1294: Aynho, Nich.; Harting, John
 Works 1345–48: Peyntor, Hen.
Downton, Wilts. Bulford, John
 Church. Chancel roof 1424–29: Kyppyng, Wm.
 Manor: Banston, Wm.
Drayton, West, Berks. Jylkes, John
Drinkstone, Suff. (Nun, John)
Dublin, Ireland. Corfe, John; Lengynour, Robt. II; Matheu, John; More, John; (Simnel, Thos.)
 Bridge 1386: More, John
 Castle: Bolaz, Thos.; Carlton, Adam; More, John; Walter, C. I
Dudley, Worcs.
 Castle: (Phillips, Thos.)
 St. Edmund's Church: (Phillips, Thos.)
Dumfries, Scotland. Glasham, Adam
Dunbar, Scotland. (Hurley, Wm.)
Dunfermline, Scotland. Bedeford, Robt.; (Houghton, Thos.)
 Abbey: Aelric, M.
Dunmow, Little, Ess.
 Priory. Tower 1528–34: Benson,——
Dunsfold, Surr. (Herland, John)

Dunstable, Beds. Bradshaw, Lawr.; (Farele, Wm.); (Sylvester, Robt.)
(See also Eleanor Crosses)
Dunstanburgh, N'land
Castle. Great Gatehouse and curtains 1313–16: **Elias, M.**
Mantlet, Gatehouse &c. 1380–: Holme, Hen.; **Lewyn, John**
Dunster, Som. Meryman, Rich.
Priory Church. Tower 1442: Marys, John; **Pope, Rich.**
Dunwich, Suff. (Russell, Rich., M)
Durham (Dryng, Pet.); (*Forman, John)
Castle. Old Hall, Constable's Hall &c. c. 1170–80: (Wolverson, Rich.)
Hall roof 1350: **Alverton, John**
Keep rebuilt c. 1360–75: (Lewyn, John)
Cathedral: Chalmer, Thos.; Chaumere, Wm.; Christian, M.; *Forman, John; Harpour, Ellis; More, Rich.; N. . ., R. . .; Scune, Chr.; William, E.
Choir 1093–1104
Nave 1099–1128
Chapter House 1133–40
Galilee c. 1170–75: Lambert; **Wolveston, Rich.**
Chapel of Nine Altars 1242–80: (Dereham, El.); **Farnham, Rich.**; Moyses, Thos.
W. window c. 1341: Roger, M. IV
Kitchen 1366–74: Dryng, Pet.; **Lewyn, John**
Reredos (Neville Screen) 1372–80: (Lewyn, John); (Yeveley, Hen.)
Dormitory 1398–1404: Dinsdale, John; Dryng, Pet.; (Middleton, John)
Cloisters 1390–1418: Hyndeley, Thos.; **Lewyn, John**; Mapilton, Thos.; Rasyn, John; Wadley, John.
Infirmary 1418–29: **Bell, John s.**
Prior's Lodging 1428–32: **Bell, John s.**
Central Tower repaired 1430–37: **Bell, John s.**
Inserted windows and tracery 1438–41: **Bell, John s.**
Central Tower, lower stage 1465–75: Barton, Thos.
Upper stage 1483–88: **Bell, John j.**
Tombs:
Bishop Hatfield c. 1382: Lewyn, John
Bishop Skirlaw 1402–03: Dryng, Pet.; Hyndeley, Thos.
Hospital of St. Mary Magdalene
Chapel 1449: Mason, And.; Taillour, Robt.
Dymock, Glos. (Dymmok, John &c.)

Ealing, Middx. (Redman, Thos. II); (Stowell, Robt.)
Earlham, Norf. (Wodehirst, Robt.)
Earls Colne, Ess.
Priory. Tomb, 13th Earl of Oxford, c.1488–89: Lorymere, Hen.
Easby, Yorks. N.R.
Abbey. Screen c. 1510 (Brownfleet, Wm.)
Eastington, Dors. (Estinton, Step.)
Eastry, Kent. Gildene, John
Eastwell, Kent. **Plantagenet, Richard**
Eccles, Lancs. see Cadishead
Ecclesall, Yorks. W.R. (Henry, M. I)
Eccleston, Chs. (Eccleston, Nich.);(Lenginour, Rich.)
Edinburgh, Scotland (Kilbourn, John); (Lee, Sir Rich.)
Castle. Works c. 1304: Hereford, Walt.; Houghton, Thos.; (St. George, Jas.)
Edmonton, Middx. (Aylmer, John); (Burton, Step.)
Eleanor Crosses (those extant in modern times **in bold type**):
Lincoln; Grantham, Lincs.; Stamford, Lincs.; **Geddington,** N'hants.; **Northampton** (Hardingstone);

Stony Stratford, Bucks.; Woburn, Beds.; Dunstable, Beds.; St. Albans, Herts.; **Waltham,** Herts.; Cheapside, London; Charing, Westminster
Building 1291–94; Abingdon, Alex; **Bataile, John**; **Canterbury, Mich.**; Chichester, Ralph; **Crundale, Rich.**; Crundale, Rog.; Doget, John; **Dyminge, Nich.**; Ireland, Wm.; **Pabenham, Sim. II**; **Stow, Rich. II**
Eling, Hants. (Crikylwode, Thos.)
Ellingham, Norf. (Elyngham, Robt.)
Ellingham, N'land
Church. Chancel 1487–: Mayson, Wm.
Elmham, North, Norf.
Church. Chancel roof c.1382–85: Michael, C. II
Elmley, Worcs.
Castle: Montfort, John
Elsenham, Ess. (Sturgeon, Thos.)
Eltham, Kent (Eltham, Rich.)
Palace: Albon, Rich.; Brown, Wm., M.; Canterbury, Mich.; Capell, Walt.; Cook, Thos. I; (Crosby, Robt.); Davyn, Pet.; Dobson, John; Herland, Wm.; Hoo, Wm.; Hurley, Wm.; (Janyns, Robt.,); (Mauncy, Thos.); (Nedeham, Jas.); Pode, Rich.; (Tichemers, Hugh); Yeveley, Hen.; Vertue, Adam; Yonge, Maur.
Wall 1315–: (Abingdon, Alex.); **Canterbury, Mich.**; Hoo, Wm.
Hall 1475–80: **Graveley, Edm.**; **Jurdan, Thos.**
'Queen's Cross' c.1363–66: Pode, Rich.
Elton, Hunts. (Ailyngton, Nich.)
Elvaston, Derb. (Mapilton, John)
Ely, Cambs. (Burdon, Wm. II); (Ely, Nich. &c.); (Grene, John); (Lee, Rich.); (Lee, Sir Rich.)
Cathedral: (Alexander, C.); Bellamy, Thos. I; Burwell, Robt.; Doraunt, John; Enemethe, Thos.; 'Huntingdon M.'; (John, M.IV); (Koc, Pet.); Lord, Adam; (Nicholas, M.I); Pepper, Rog.; Peyntour, Thos.; (Sampson, M.); Stubbard, John; Thomas, M. VIII; Twyforth, Thos.; Ufford, Thos.; (Walsingham, Alan); Wode, John; Wodehirst, Robt.; (Yeveley, Hen.)
Norman Church 1083–1106
W. Front c. 1174–97
Presbytery 1239–50
Galilee c.1250
Lady Chapel 1321–49: (Ramsey, Wm. III)
Octagon 1322–46; **John, M. VII**; Quadratarius, Pet.
Lantern 1328–42; Burwell, John; **Hurley, Wm.**; Middleton, Geoff.; Page, Thos.; Roke, John; Wisbech, Wm.
Choir 1322–36: Grene, John; John, M. VII; (Ramsey, Wm. II)
Prior Crauden's Chapel c. 1325–35: John, M. VII
Choir-stalls 1336–48: (Hurley, Wm.)
Great Gatehouse (Porta) 1396–1400: Meppushal, John
Octagon of W. Tower? 1392–: **Wodehirst, Robt.**
Tower arch 1476 Peyntour, Thos.
Bishop Alcock's Chapel 1486–1500: **Lord, Adam**
Tomb. Bishop Redman c.1505: (Wastell, John)
Cloisters, E. walk 1509–10: **Palmer, Thos.**
Bishop West's Chapel 1523–36: **Lee, Rich.**; More, Edm.
Emlyn, Carm.
Castle: Machon, Rich.
Emneth, Norf. (Enemethe, Thos.)
Enfield, Middx. (Lynne, Rich.); (Ramsey, Wm. III); (Warner, John)

Enstone, Oxon.
  Church: (Hereford, Walt.)
  Reredos *c.* 1420: (Winchcombe, Rich.)
Ercall, Salop. (Ercalo, Rich.)
Erith, Kent.
  Church. Tower 1406– : Wells, John
Esher, Surr. (Coke, Hum.); (Herland, Hugh)
  Bishop's Palace. Waynflete's Tower *c.* 1480: (Alsbroke, Hen.); (Cowper, John)
Essex, Forest of (Beverley, Robt.)
Etchingham, Sx.
  Church: Esshyng, Thos.
Eton, Bucks.
  College: (Berkeley, Wm.); (Hardyng, John II); (Holnerst, Rich.)
    Building 1441–60: (Beckeley, John); Bryd, Thos.; Burton, Step.; Clerk, John; Clerk, Sim.; Cowper, John; Glasier, Thos.; Goldyng, John; (Gower, John); *Gryme, John; Hampton, John; Hylle, Thos.; (Jakes, John); Janyns, Hen.; Janyns, Robt. s.; Jurdan, Thos.; (Keyes, Rog.); *Leget, Robt.; Norton, John; (Palden, Jas.); *Pette, Robt.; Philpot, Rich.; Reading, John; Smyth, John I; Spillesby, Robt.; Teynham, Thos.; Vesey, Wm.; **Westerley, Robt.**; Whetely, John j.; Whetely, Paul; **Whetely, Robt.**; Woderofe, Jas.; Wynwick, John
  Hall, N. and E. Ranges 1441–49
  Chapel 1448–60
  W. window *c.* 1469: (Clerk, Sim.)
  Roodloft and Stalls 1475–: Nicholl, Walt.
  Antechapel 1476–83: **Orchard, Wm.**
  Lupton's Chantry Chapel *c.* 1512–15: (Vertue, Wm.)
  W. Range, Lupton's Tower &c. 1509–23: **Coke, Hum.**; Jestelyn, John; **Redman, Hen.; Vertue, Wm.**
Evesham, Worcs. (Evesham, John)
  Abbey: Northwich, Thos.
    Chapter House, Dormitory, Refectory, Abbot's House *c.* 1300–19: **Evesham, Hen.**
  Bell Tower *c.* 1530–39: (Vertue, Robt., j.)
  Churches.
    All Saints. Lichfield Chapel: (Vertue, Robt., j.)
    St. Lawrence. Lichfield Chapel: (Vertue, Robt., j.)
Ewhurst, Surr. Lee, Rich.; Lee, Sir Rich.
Ewloe, Flints. (Newhall, Wm.)
Exeter, Dev. (Alexander, M.I); (Carter, John); Coryngdon, John; Glydon, Wm.; (Harry, John); (Jekyll, Hamund); (Pope, Rich.); (Wolston, John)
  Castle: Witney, Thos.
  Cathedral: Beare, Nich.; Corscombe, John; Croke, Rich.; Eleser, John; Farleigh, Rich.; Foundyng, Wm.; Galampton, John; Galmeton, Robt.; Glaston, John; (Gloucester, Thos.); Gyst, Walt.; Harry, John; Jekyll, Hamund; Jekyll, Walt.; (John, M. II); Membiri, Wm.; Michael, C. I; Newton, Elias; (Robert, M. VII)
    Norman Church 1112–36
    Chapter House *c.* 1224–44
    Lady Chapel and Retrochoir *c.* 1275–
    Presbytery, Lady Chapel vaults &c. 1288–1308: Montacute, Wm.; **Roger, M. II**; Walter, C. II
    Crossing and E. bay of Nave 1308–17: Luve, Wm.
    Reredos, Sedilia and Pulpitum 1316–26: **Witney, Thos.**
    Bishop's Throne 1313–17: Galmeton, Robt.; **Witney, Thos.**
    Nave 1328–42: **Witney, Thos.**; Roche, Rog.

Screen of W. Front 1346–75: (Farleigh, Rich.); Joy, Wm.; Pratt, John
Cloisters 1376–82: Cornwall, John; **Lesyngham, Robt.**; Swallow, John
E. window 1390–92: **Lesyngham, Robt.**
Screens of E. Chapels *c.* 1395–1419
Chapter House, upper part 1413–39: **Tynlegh, John**; Wolston, John
Screens of Chapels of St. Paul and St. John Baptist 1433–34: Gabriell, Denis
Oldham and Speke Chantries 1504–19
Exe Bridge 1350: Roche, Rog.
Guildhall 1484; Coryngdon, John
Houses: Glydon, Wm.; Whytten, John
St. Nicholas Priory: (Alexander, M.I)
Eye, Suff. (Ide, Thos.)
  Church. Tower *c.* 1470–85
Eynsham, Oxon. (Eynsham, Hen.)
  Abbey: Christchurch, John

Fairford, Glos. (Ely, Reg.)
Falkirk, Scotland (St. George, Jas.)
Falsgrave, Yorks, N.R. (Whallesgrave, Thos.)
Faringdon, Hants. Harry, John
Farleigh, East, Kent (Herunden, Thos.); (Palmer, John)
Farley, Surr. (Fant, Thos.)
Farnham, Surr. (Dippenhall, Robt.); (Herland, Hugh); (Richard, M. III); (Tighelere, Thos.)
  Castle: Beldham, Robt.; Burgess Wm.; Goseden, Robt.; Hore, Robt.; Kene, Rich.; (Maurice); Potte, John; Thomas, John; Tighelere, Thos.; (Urricus, E.); William, C.II; (Wynford, Wm.); (Yeveley, Hen.)
  'Fox's Tower' 1470–*c.*1475: Cole, John, bricklayer
  Mills: Tighelere, Thos.
Faversham, Kent (Champneys, Wm.)
  Church. Work 1535: Alen, M.
Feckenham, Worcs.
  Manor: Gloucester, John
Felmersham, Beds.
  Granary 1459: Baker, Rich.; George, M.
Felstead, Ess. (Felstede, Rich.)
  Barn 1450–51: Sturgeon, Thos.
Filby, Norf. (Radbell, Artificer)
Fillingham, Lincs. (Alexander, M. III)
Finchale, Dur.
  Priory
    Church remodelled &c. 1364—: Dryng, Pet.; **Lewyn, John**
Finchampstead, Berks. (East, John)
Finedon, N'hants.
  Church: (Wastell, John)
Finmere, Oxon. Aundely, Nich.
Fittleworth, Sx. (Lee, John)
Flamborough, Yorks. E.R.
  Church: (Brownfleet, Wm.)
Flanders (Harrison, Dyrik)
Flint
  Castle: (Dymoke, Hugh); Eccleston, Nich.; Grantham, Thos.; Helpeston, John; Legh, Rich.; Oxford, Hen.; Paris, Rich.; Ryhull, Hen.
  Building 1277–80: **Lenginour, Rich.; St. George, Jas.**
Flintshire, see Chester, Palatinate
Florence, Italy (Torrigiano, Pietro)
  Duomo: (S. Maria del Fiore)
  Dome 1420: (Mapilton, Thos.)
Folkestone, Kent (Baker, Wm.); (Hunte, Robt.)
Fornham All Saints, Suff. (Layer, Wm.)

Foscote, Bucks. (Le Enginnur, Rog.)
Fotheringhay, N'hants.
  Church
    Chancel 1415–: (Lote, Step.)
    Nave and Tower 1434–: Horewode, Wm.; (Wastell, John)
    Tower fan-vault 1529: (Semark, Hen.)
    Tomb of Duke of York c. 1416–: Lote, Step.; Mapilton, Thos.
Fountains, Yorks. W.R.
  Abbey: (Orchard, Wm.)
  Tower c. 1500–: (Scune, Chr.)
Framlingham, Suff. (Ralph, M.IV)
  Castle. Demolition 1175: Ailnoth
Framsden, Suff. (Aldrych, Thos.)
Fransham, Great, Norf. (Neker, Thos.)
Fremantle, Hants. Gerard
Fremington, Dev. (Terell, Robt.)
Frétun, France.
  Peel 1351–52: Acklam, Gilb.; Dunmow, Step.
Frithelstock, Dev. (Lee, Sir Rich.)
Frodsham, Chs. (Doget, John)
  Manor. Repairs 1358: Eccleston, Nich.
Froxfield, Hants. (Hardyng, John II)
Fulbourn, Cambs. (Fulbourne, Wm.)
Fulham, Middx.
  Church. Tower 1441–: Garald, Rich.
Fyfield, Ess. (Fifede, John)

Gainsborough, Lincs. (Gainsborough, Rich.); (Mody, Wm.)
Galmpton, Dev. (Galampton, John); (Galmeton, Robt.)
Garboldisham, Norf. (Walton, Walt.)
Gaywood, Norf. Morell, John
Gazeley, Suff. (Nun, John)
Geddington, N'hants. Thomas, C., see also Eleanor Crosses
Germany (Dutchman, Baldwin); (Haschenperg, Step.); (Tidemann)
Gestingthorpe, Ess. (Loveday, Thos.)
  Church. Roof c. 1525: Loveday, Thos.
Gilling, Yorks, N.R. (Scune, Chris.)
Gillingham, Dors.
  Manor. Works 1253–55: Mountsorrel, Wm.
Glasson, Cumb. (Glasham, Adam &c.)
Glastonbury, Som. (Thomas, M.IA)
  Abbey: (Glaston, John); Northampton, Adam; Thomas, M. IA; ('Wells, Mr. of'); (William, C.OI)
  Works 1308–24: Lengynour, Robt. I
  St. John's Church: Canon, Step; Carver, Dav.
  Porch c.1428: Gryme, John
  Roodloft 1439–40: Hulle, Robt.
  Work c.1465: Smyth, Wm.
Gloucester (Elkin, Thos.); (Hobbs, John); (Mason, Clem.); (Gloucester, John); (Gloucester, Thos.); (Kamesham, Rich.); (Skynner, John); (Swallow, John); (Wyshongre, Nich.)
  Bridge c. 1170: Walred, Nich.
  Castle: Aundely, Nich.; Campden, Nich.; Gloucester, John; Hatherley, John; *Hobbs, John; Teynton, John; Wyshongre, Nich.
  Towers &c. 1390: Clavyll, John
  Cathedral (Abbey of St. Peter)
    Crypt 1089–1100
    Nave c. 1120–60
    Vault c. 1242–45
    S. Aisle 1318–29: (Sponbedde, Mart.)
  S. Transept remodelled 1331–36; (Ramsey, Wm. III)
  Choir remodelled c. 1337–: (Ramsey, Wm. III); (Sponlee, John)
    E. window c. 1350
    Stalls c. 1337–
  N. Transept remodelled 1368–74
  Cloisters c. 1360–1412: Lesyngham, Robt.
  W. Front and S. Porch c. 1421–37
  Tower 1450–60: Gower, John
  Lady Chapel 1457–83: (Hobbs, John)
  Tomb of Edward II c. 1329–34
Churches.
  Lanthony Priory: (Sponbedde, Mart.); (Wyshongre, Nich.)
  St. Bartholomew's Priory: (Walter, M.IV)
  Hospital. First building c.1170: Walred, Nich.
  House 1483: Sammesbury, David
Godstone, Surr. (Berty, Thos.)
Godstow, Oxon.
  Abbey: Fustyng, John
Gold, Field of Cloth of, near Guisnes, France
  Works 1520: **Coke, Hum.**; Stockton, Thos.; **Vertue, Wm.**
Goldcliff, Mon. (Goldcliff, Hugh)
Goodrich, Heref.
  Castle. Barbican c. 1280–85: (Beverley, Robt.)
Goudhurst, Kent. (Thorngate, Thos.)
Goxhill, Lincs. (Goushill, Robt.); (Gowselle, John)
Grafton, N'hants.
  Manor: (Nedeham, Jas.)
Grafton, Worcs.
  Manor. Barn 1428–29: Swift, Rich. II
Grantchester, Cambs. Prentice, Martin; Sturgeon, Thos.; (Wastell, John)
Grantham, Lincs. (Grantham, Hugh &c.); (Robinson, Wm.)
  Church. Tower: (Alexander, M.III)
  (See also Eleanor Crosses)
Graveley, Cambs. (Graveley, Edm.); (Nedeham, Jas.)
Gravesend, Kent. Yeveley, Hen.
  Houses 1363–66: Yonge, John
  Manor. Fireplaces 1374–76: Yonge, Maur.
  Windmill 1373–74: Yonge, John
Greenwich, Kent. (Clifford, John); (Danyell, Thos.); (Vertue, Robt.)
  Palace of Placentia: Coke, John; Martyn, Walt.; Redman, Hen.; Story, C.; Smyth, Hen.; (Stockton, Thos.)
  Works 1499–: Binks, Thos.; (Caldham, Gabr.); Lee, John; Majano, Giovanni; Smith, Hen.; **Vertue, Robt.**
  King's Privy Chamber, roof 1537: Rydge, Rich. II
Grimsby, Lincs.
  Church: Prymerose, Hugh
Grosmont, Mon.
  Castle: Grosmont, Ralph
Guildford, Surr. (Barnet, Thos.); (Cherche, Rich.); (Wynford, Wm.); (Yeveley, Hen.)
  Castle Gateway &c. 1256–: **Alexander, C.**; **Gloucester, John**; Pritelwell, And.
  Market-house 1540: Butler, Rich.
  Palace. Hall repairs 1254–56: Gloucester, John
Guisnes, France
  Fortifications 1539: Bird, John II; (Caldham, Gabr.); Lee, Sir Rich.; **Rogers, John II**
  Castle. Malthouse 1533: Mumer, Harry
  Works. 1540–41: Baker, Wm.
  (See also Gold, Field of Cloth of)

Henley, Oxon. (More, Edm.)
Church. Works 1397–: (Swallow, John); (Walton, Walt.); **Wolvey, Thos.**
Henley, Surr.
Manor. Chapel 1325: Cressing, John
Hensington, Oxon.
Manor: Gloucester, John
Hereford (Denyar, Thos.); Menyver, John; More, Wm.
Castle. Works 1177–79: Grosmont, Ralph
Cathedral: (Reyns, Hugh)
Choir 1079–1110
Nave and Transepts c. 1100–45
Vestibule of Lady Chapel c. 1190
E. Transept c. 1190–99
Lady Chapel c. 1217–25
Presbytery Clerestory and Vault c. 1235–40
N. Transept 1250–68: (Reyns, Hugh)
Inner N. Porch c. 1280–90
Nave outer walls c. 1290–94:**Hugh, M.**
Central Tower c. 1315
Chapter House &c. c. 1364–70: Cambridge, Thos.; Evesham, John
S. Transept Vault c. 1400
Cloister (part) 1412–18: **Denyar, Thos.**
Bishop Stanbury's Chantry Chapel c. 1470
Bishop Audley's Chantry Chapel c. 1500
Vicars' Cloisters c. 1490–1500
Bishop's Cloister c. 1520
N. Porch c. 1520–30
Church of St. Ouen: (More, Wm.)
Wye Bridge c. 1120: Malverne, Alduin
Herstmonceux, Sx.
Castle 1441–: (Vesey, Wm.)
Hertford (Nedeham, Jas.)
Castle: Bisley, Rich.; Bodekesham, Wm.; Canon, John
Houses and Chapel 1380–83: **Wintringham, Wm.**
Gatehouse c.1463–64: Langley, Reg.
Hessett, Suff. (Clerk, Sim.)
Heston, Middx.
Church. Chancel roof 1398: Wyse, Wm.
Hexham, N'land (Wodman, John)
Heyford, Oxon. Jylkes, John
Higham Ferrers, N'hants.
College and Bedehouse 1423–: (Mapilton, Thos.)
Highclere, Hants.
Manor: Emery, Thos.
Works 1370–95: **Herland, Hugh**; Ickenham, Wm.; Spillesbury, John; **Wynford, Wm.**
Hillington, Norf. (Breton, John)
Hindolveston, Norf. (Hildolveston, Wm.)
Hinton, Cambs. (Wassyngle, John)
Hitchin, Herts. (Nedeham, Jas.); (Sturgeon, John); Yeveley, Hen.
Hockham, Norf.
Church and Rectory. Repairs 1521–33: Bele, Thos.
Holbeach, Lincs. (Holbech, Hugh)
Holme Cultram, Cumb. (Holmcultram, Robt.)
Holt, Denbighs.
Castle. Works 1463: 'Chester, Mr. of Abbot of'
Holy Island, N'land. Lawson, Geo.
Holyrood, Scotland
Palace. Tomb of David II 1372: Patrington, Wm. I
Holywell, Lincs. (Kympton, Hugh)
Holywell, Oxon., see Oxford
Honington, Lincs. (Hugh, M. II)
Hope, Flints.
Castle: Lenginour, Rich.; Nottingham, Ralph; Oxford, Hen.

Hornham, Ess., see Thaxted
Horley, Surr. (Hurley, Wm.)
Hornby, Yorks. N.R.
Church. S. Aisle 1410–: (Cracall, Rich.); **Newton, Rich.**
Horsepath, Oxon. Fisher, John
Houghton Conquest, Beds.
Church. Tower 1392–: Farele, Wm.; Lessy, Phil.
Houghton-le-Spring, Dur.
Church: Dereham, El.
Hounslow, Middx.
Priory: Clerk, John
Huddleston, Yorks. W.R.
Quarry: (Palden, Jas.)
Huggate, Yorks. E.R. (Malton, Wm.)
Hull, Yorks. E.R. (Brownfleet, Wm.)
Church of Holy Trinity
Building 1296–1425: (Hereford, Walt.)
Tower c. 1520–30
Fortifications 1542: Reynold, Wm.II; Rogers, John II
Hunsdon, Herts.
House: (Nedeham, Jas.)
Huntingdon (Bell, John III); (Ely, Reg.); (Fitzwiching, Rich.); (Ives, E.); (Prentice, Martyn); (Sturgeon, Thos.)
Bridge c. 1370–75: Albon, Wm.; Hawardeby, John
Hart Inn 1448–51: Ely, Reg.; Hall, Geoff.; *Harward, Wm.; Sturgeon, Thos.
Hurley, Berks. (Hurley, Wm.)
Priory: Aelfric, M.
Hurst, Hants.
Castle 1541–44: **Berty, Thos.**
Hythe, Kent (Bonversall, Mich.)
Church: (Lote, Step.)
Steeple 1480: Hamme, John

Ickenham, Middx. (Ickenham, Wm.)
Ilford, Ess. (Nedeham, Jas.)
Ilkeston, Derbs. (Dylkeston, Rich.)
Ingoldmells, Lincs. (?as 'Weston Admeals')
Church: (Jackson, Wm.)
Ippollitts, Herts. (Nedeham, Jas.)
Ipsley, Worcs. (Swift, Rich.II)
Ipstone, Bucks.
Church. Chancel roof 1391–92: Bath, Robt.
Ipswich, Suff. (Cutting, Thos.); (Hill, Wm.)
Sessions House 1399: Tarell, John
Wolsey's College 1528–29
Gatehouse &c.: Barbour, John; **Lee, Rich.**; Okey, Wm.
Isleham, Cambs.
Church. Nave rebuilding c.1495: (Wastell, John)
Isleworth, Middx. Redman, Thos. II
Church. Chancel roof 1398: Wyse, Wm.
Manor: Selot, Wm.; Warden, Wm.; Waryn, Wm.
Ixworth, Suff. (Vile, Thos.)

Jersey
Bulwarks 1550: (Berty, Thos.)
Jerusalem, Palestine (Langlois, Jean)
Jervaulx, Yorks. N.R.
Abbey: (Brownfleet, Wm.)

Keal, East, Lincs. (Jackson, Wm.)
Kellet, Over, Lancs.
Church: 'Kirkby Malham, Mr. of'
Kelsale, Suff. (Loveday, Rich.)
Kelso, Scotland (Lee, Sir Rich.)

Kempsford, Glos.
Church. Tower *c.* 1470: (Orchard, Wm.)
Kempton, Middx.
Manor: Beverley, Robt.
Hall 1235: Aundely, Nich.
Kendal, W'land. (Kendal, Wm.)
Kenilworth, Warw.
Castle: (Clement, John); Felstede, Rich.; Thwaites, Rich.
John of Gaunt's work 1372–95: Hales, Wm.; Herleye, John; **Skillyngton, Robt.**; Spencer, Hen.; Wintringham, Wm.
Kennington, Surr.
Manor: Ailyngton, Nich.; (Bole, Walt.); Heyward, John; Leicester, John; Leicester, Rich.; **Shropshire, Rich.**; Tyryngton, John; **Yeveley, Hen**.
Kentford, Suff. Aleyn, Rich.
Kersey, Suff. (Wastell, John)
Kessingland, Suff.
Church. Tower *c.* 1436–50: Russell, Rich., M
Ketton, Rutl. (Keten, Robt.)
Keynsham, Som. (Farleigh, Rich.); (Kamesham, Rich.)
Kidwelly, Carm.
Castle: Aleyn, David; Bleddyn, Gw.; Nikel, John
Kilburn, Middx. (Molton, John); (Russell, John j.)
Kildrummy, Scotland
Castle: (Houghton, Thos.); (St. George, Jas.)
Kilkenny, Ireland
St. Canice's Cathedral: (Huguet)
Kimble, Bucks. (Clerk, Sim.)
Kingham, Oxon. Wiltshire, John
Kingsclere, Hants. (More, Edm.)
Kingscliffe, N'hants. (Ely, Reg.)
King's Langley, see Langley, King's
Kingston-upon-Thames, Surr. (Corant, Hen,); (Dewilde, Wm.); (Herland, Hugh); (Herland, John); (Houghton, Thos.); (Hunt, Wm. I); (Kyppyng, Wm.); (More, Edm.); (Stockton, Thos.); (Toutmond, Wm.); (Vertue, Wm.); (Waryn, Wm.)
Bridge, Repairs 1400: Herland, Hugh
Kinver, Staffs. (Carpenter, Rich.)
Kirby-le-Soken, Ess. (Vynt, Wm.)
Kirby Muxloe, Leics.
Castle 1480–84: **Cowper, John**; Doyle, John; Lyle, John; Steynforth, Robt.
Kirkby Malham, Yorks. W.R.
Church: 'Kirkby Malham, Mr. of'
Kirklington, Yorks. N.R.
Manor House 1484–: **Wright, John**
Kirkstall, Yorks. W.R.
Abbey: (Brownfleet, Wm.)
Kirtling, Cambs. (Swayn, Wm.)
Manor: Grove, Sim.
Knaresborough, Yorks. W.R.
Castle: Aundely, Nich.; Boudon, Hugh; Kingston, Hen.; Tichemers, Hugh; William, carver
Masons' lodge, etc. 1307: Bokton, Wm.
Knepp, Sx.
Castle: Aundely, Nich.
Knightsbridge, Middx. (Alexander C.)
Knole, Kent
Manor: Nedeham, Jas.

Lakenham, Norf. (Lakenham, Rich.)
Laleston, Glam. ('Lalys')
Lambeth, Surr. (Clifford, John)
Archbishop's Palace:
Guardroom roof *c.* 1390: (Herland, Hugh)

Lollard's Tower 1434–: Carter, Wm.; Clerk, Sim.; *Hancock, Wm.; Hylle, Thos.; Loune, Wm.; (Mapilton, Thos.); (Norton, John); Thirsk, John
Chapel vestibule work 1434: Russell, Rich., carver
Morton's Tower 1490: (Wastell, John)
Lancaster. (Wright, Wm. II C.)
Castle: Bolrun, Ralph
Lanchester, Dur. (Lewyn, John)
Lanercost, Cumb. Scardebourg, Walt.
Langham, Norf. Morell, John
Langley (near Leafield), Oxon.
Manor: East, Wm.; Lee, John
Langley, King's, Herts. Beverley, Robt.; Lessy, Phil.; Pruist, Wm.; Rede, Wm. le; Wydmere, John; (Wyspenade, John)
Church: (Wolvey, Thos.)
Priory: Pruist, Wm.
Cloister work 1374: Rede, Wm. le
Langleybury, Herts. (Lee, Sir Rich.)
Langton-in-Purbeck, Dors. (Yeveley, Hen.)
Lapworth, Warw.
Manor House. Gatehouse 1313–: Heose, Wm.
La Rochelle, France, see Rochelle, La
Laughton, Yorks. W.R. (Palden, Jas.)
Launceston, Corn. (Daw, Rich.)
Lavenham, Suff.
Church *c.* 1486–1525: (Clerk, Sim.); Rogers, John II; (Wastell, John)
Lawhitton, Corn.
Church: (Daw, John, carver)
Layer, Ess. (Layer, Wm.)
Layer Marney, Ess. (Dyminge, Nich.); Yeveley, Hen.
Leafield, Oxon. See Langley, Oxon.
Leake, Yorks. N.R.
Church. Bench-ends 1519: (Brownfleet, Wm.)
Leaveland, Kent (Wimund)
Leeds, Kent (Ledes, John)
Battle Hall *c.* 1330: (Bataile, Thos.)
Castle: (Bataile, Thos.); (Crump, Thos.); Doune, Geoff.; Gerard, Walt.; Herland, Hugh; Longe, Laur.; Matthew, M.I; *Rokesacre, John; Wyot, Guy; Ybourne, Thos.; Yeveley, Hen.
Priory: Benett, Wm.; (Berty, Robt.)
Leeming, Yorks. N.R. (Lemyng, Laur.)
Leicester. Bagworth Pet.; (Clement, John); (Grantham, John); Keyley, Jas.; (Leicester, Edw. &c.)
Church of St. Martin. Seats 1489: Nicoll, John
College of St. Mary in the Newark: Skillyngton, Robt.
St. Mary's Hospital 1351–54: Stretford, Robt.
Leigh, Glos. (Walton, Walt.)
Leiston, Suff.
Abbey *c.* 1218: Nicholas, M. I
Leith, Scotland. (Lee, Sir Rich.)
Leixlip, Ireland. Lengynour, Robt. II
Lenton, Notts. (Hydes, Pers)
Lérida, Spain.
Cathedral: Fonoyll, Reynard
Letchworth, Herts. (Nedeham, Jas.)
Leverton, Lincs.
Church. Steeple 1498: Mason, Thos.
Lew, North, Dev. (Pares, John)
Lewes, Sx. Kent, Wm.; (Lee, Sir Rich.); (Yeveley, Hen.)
Priory: Alwin, M.; Elias, carver; Roger, M.IA
Lewisham, Kent (Graveley, Edm.); (Lewisham, John)
Lezant, Corn. (Daw, Rich.)
Lichfield, Staffs. (Kerver, Thos.)
Cathedral: Douve, John; Gilbert, M. II
Choir Arcades 1195–1208: ('Wells, Mr. of')

Transepts *c.* 1220–40: Thomas, M. I
Chapter House *c.* 1239–49
Nave and Central Tower *c.* 1265–85: Eyton, Nich.; Fitzthomas, Wm.; Waleys, Thos.
W. Front and lower stage of Towers 1285–93
W. Front and towers completed *c.* 1294–1327: (Abingdon, Alex.)
Lady Chapel *c.* 1320–36: **Eyton, Wm.**
Presbytery and Choir Clerestory 1337–50: **Ramsey, Wm. III**
Choir. Works 1382–85: Driffield, Wm.
St. Mary's Chapel. Roodloft *c.*1490: (Rydge, Rich.I)
Lilleshall, Salop. (Watkinson, Robt.)
Limoges, France (Limoges, John)
Lincoln (Adam, Rich.); (Drawswerd, John); (Hippis, John); (Hugh, M. II); (Lincoln, Phil.); (Nassington, John); (Porter, John); (Richard, M. I); (Spencer, Wm.); (Tresk, Sim.); (Wymarke, Robt.)
Castle: Waldin
Cathedral: (Alexander, C.); Bokinghale, Robt.; Briggs, Thos. II; Burgo, Gilb.; Ernald, M.; Fels, Wm.; Gainsborough, Rich.; Michael; Newby, Robt.; (Pabenham, Sim., I); (Patrington, Robt. j.); (Porter, John); (Stow, Rich. II) Wymarke, Robt.
Norman Church 1074–92
W. Front altered *c.* 1140–50
Choir and E. Transepts 1192–1210: (Blois, Robt.); Noiers, Geoff.; Richard, M. I
Great Transept *c.* 1215–30
Chapter House *c.* 1220–35: **Alexander, M. III**
Nave, completion of W. Front, Galilee, lower two storeys of central tower *c.* 1237–55: **Alexander, M. III**
Angel Choir 1256–80: (Simon, M.I); **Tresk, Sim.**
Cloisters 1295–1305
Central Tower, upper stage 1307–11: **Stow, Rich. II**
S. Transept Gable and 'Bishop's Eye' *c.* 1335–40: (Raghton, Ivo)
Screen *c.* 1340–50
Stalls *c.* 1370
W. window and W. Towers, upper stage *c.* 1370–80: (Geoffrey, M., II); (Wastell, John)
Central Tower Vault *c.* 1380
Bishop Fleming's Chantry Chapel *c.* 1431
Bishop Russell's Chantry *c.* 1493
Bishop Longland's Chantry *c.* 1548: **Kitchin, Wm.**
Tomb of Queen Eleanor 1291–94: Abingdon, Alex.; Crundale, Rog.; **Dyminge, Nich.**
Church. St. Andrew-in-the-Bail: (Nassington, John)
Guildhall 1520: Spencer, Wm.
(See also Eleanor Crosses)
Lingwood, Norf. (Lyngwode, Wm.)
Linlithgow, Scotland
Peel 1301–: Boulton, John; Glasham, Adam; Houghton, Thos.; **St. George, Jas.**
Lire, France (Flanders, John)
Liskeard, Corn. (Daw, John, carver)
Liverpool, Lancs.
Castle. Tower 1431–43: Cowper, Nich.
Tower of Sir John Stanley 1406– : John, M.VIIA
Llandaff, Glam.
Cathedral. NW. Tower 1486–95: (Hart, [?Wm.])
London (Abingdon, Nich.); (Adam, joiner); (Adam, M. I); Alexander, C.; (Ambrose, Rich.); Attleborough, John; Barnet, Thos.; Bataile, John; Bird, Rich.; Bole, Walt.; Bradshaw, Lawr.; (Brasier, Hugh); Bray, Reg.; Bredone, Thos.; Bright, Rich.; Brown, John II; Brown, Robt.; Burton, Step.;

(Cake, Thos.); Caldham, Gabr.; Canterbury, Alex.; Canterbury, Mich.; Canterbury, Sim.; (Catelyn, John); (Chafyn, Thos.); Cherche, Phil.; Cherche, Rich.; (*Clavyll, John); (Clerk, John); Coke, Hum.; Coke, Rog.; (Coventry, Thos.); Crosby, Robt.; Croxton, John; Crundale, Rich.; (Denys, Rog.); (Dewilde, Wm.); (Dippenhall, Robt.); Dobson, John; (Dytton, Walt.); Essex, John; Fant, Thos.; Felstede, Rich.; (Fill, Robt.); (Forster, John, M.); Frankelyn, Rog.; Gerard, John; Graveley, Edm.; (Hancock, Wm.); Hardy, John; Harrison, Dyrik; Hawkins, John; (Haynes, John); (Henwick, Robt.); (Hereford, Walt.); (Herland, Hugh); (Herland, John); (Hertanger, Robt.); (Hoo, Wm.); Hook, Sim.; (Horewode, Wm.); (Hunt, Wm.); Hurley, Wm.; Hylle, Thos.; (John, C.I); (Johnson, Thos.); (Johnson, Wm.); (Joy, Rich.); (Kynge, John); (Lakenham, Rich.); (Langley, Reg.); Lardyner, Robt.; (Lebons, John); (Lee, Wm.); (Lorymere, Hen.); (Lyndesey, John); (Maidstone, John, M.); Mapilton, John; (Massingham, John III); Mauncy, Thos.; (Mody, Wm.); Myltone, Walt.; (Nedeham, Chr.); Northampton, Robt.; Orgar, John; Osekyn, Robt.;Pabenham, Sim., II; (Page, John); (Prentice, Martin); (Prowce, Thos.); (Ramsey, John II); (Ramsey, John III); (Ramsey, Nich.); (Ramsey, Wm. I); (Raye, Wm.); (Rede, Wm., M.); (Remus, Jas.); (Robert, M. III); (Robson, John); Rothinge, Rich.; (Rouge, Thos.); (Russell, John s.); (Rydge, Rich. II); Sallynge, Rich. I; Sallynge, Rich. II; (Shereff, John); Shropshire, Rich.; (Simson, Geo.); (Spark, John); (Stacy, John); (Sturgeon, Thos.); Swaffham, Reg.; (Tichemers, Hugh); Totenham, John I; Totenham, John II; Tyryngton, John; Walton, Walt.; Webbenham, Pet.; (Welot, Hen.); Welot, John; West, Wm. I; West, Wm. II; (Westcote, John); Whetely, John j.; Whyte, John; Wiltshire, Wm.; (Worlich, John); (Wrek, Thos.); Wrytle, John; Wrytle, Ralph; Wydmere, John; Wytham, Rich.; Yeveley, Hen.
Baynard's Castle: Yeveley, Hen.
Rebuilt 1501–: Mauncy, Thos.
Bishop's Palace: Dobson, John
Blackfriars, see Churches
Brewers' Hall: Pekker, John
Bridewell Palace: Molton, John; (Nedeham, Jas.)
Bridges. London Bridge: Beke, Rich.; Brown, John I; Catelyn, John; Clifford, John; Coke, Hum.; Colechurch, Pet.; Conan, M.; Danyell, Thos.; Emler, Lawr.; (Goldyng, John); Hertanger, Robt.; Johnson, Wm.; Jurdan, Thos.; Knight, Reg.; Lewisham, John; Maidstone, John, M.; Mason, Robt. le; Mauncey, Thos.; Orgar, John; Pabenham, Sim. II; Peter, Matt.; Reve, Walt.; (Stockton, Thos.); Wade, Thos.; Whetely, John; Whetely, Robt.; (Wintringham, Wm.); Wrek, Thos.; Wytham, Rich.; Xaintes, Isambert; Yeveley, Hen.
Chapel of St. Thomas *c.* 1384: (Yeveley, Hen.)
London Bridge House, Storehouses: Warner, John
Holborn Bridge 1262: Beverley, Robt.
Carpenters' Hall. Parlour *c.*1500: Simpson, Rich.
Cathedral of St. Paul: Bowman, Ralph; Dobson, John; Goldyng, Wm.; (John, C. I); (Page, John); (Patrington, Robt. II); (Rickling, Thos.); Rothinge, Rich.; (Waltham, Nich.); (Wintringham, Wm.)
Norman Choir *c.* 1090–
Nave *c.* 1110–30: Andrew, M.; Ralph, M. I

Tower *c.* 1200–21
New work, Choir &c. 1251–1312: (Canterbury, Mich.); (Rothinge, Rich.); Weldon, John
Transepts 1256–
Lady Chapel and E. Front *c.* 1307–12; Canterbury, Mich.; (Rothinge, Rich.); **Weldon, John**
Chapter House and Cloister 1332–: **Ramsey, Wm. III**
S. Front *c.* 1382–87: Lote, Step.; **Yeveley, Hen.**
Pulpitum? 1388–: (Yeveley, Hen.)
Tomb of John of Gaunt and Duchess Blanche 1374–78: Wrek, Thos.; **Yeveley, Hen.**
Bell-tower, inspection 1436–37: Rolles, Wm.
Charterhouse
Building 1371–: **Yeveley, Hen.**
Water supply 1442: **Boston, John**
Works 1510–: Dewilde, Wm.
Cheapside, see Eleanor Crosses
Churches:
All Hallows, Staining: Gymboll, Robt.; Sakkar, John
Austin Friars: (Burton, Step.)
Blackfriars: (Warlowe, Edm.)
Works 1259–61: (Gloucester, John)
Works 1278–: (Beverley, Robt.); Canterbury, Mich.; Hoo, Wm.
Greyfriars 1306–27: Eye, Robt.; **Hereford, Walt.**
Tomb of Queen Isabella 1358–59: (Ramsey, Wm.III)
Holy Trinity Priory, Aldgate: (Tidemann)
St. Anthony's Hospital 1501–02: Vertue, Robt.
St. Bartholomew the Great, Priory: (Goldyng, John); (Martyn, Walt.)
Rahere's Tomb *c.* 1400: (Yeveley, Hen.)
Hospital: (Lakenham, Rich.)
St. Dunstan-in-the-East
S. Aisle and Porch 1381–: Typerton, Nich.; **Yeveley, Hen.**
St. Giles without Cripplegate: (Wolfey, John)
St. John's Priory, Clerkenwell: (Hawkins, John)
St. John Walbrook: (Lardyner, Robt.); (Mapilton, Thos.)
Repairs 1412: (Myltone, Walt.); Walton, Walt.; (Wiltshire, Wm.)
St. Katharine's Hospital: (Yeveley, Hen.)
St. Martin-le-Grand 1255–60: (Gloucester, John)
Works *c.* 1385: (Cherche, Rich.); **Yeveley, Hen.**
Works 1446: (Croxton, John)
St. Mary Aldermary. Tower 1510–: (Westerley, Robt.)
St. Mary-at-Hill: (Burton, Step.); Redman, John; Vertue, Robt.; (Wade, Thos.); Warner, John
Roodloft &c. 1427–: Serle, Wm.
St. Mary Eastminster (Abbey), Tower Hill: Reed, John; Reynold, John, C.; Tyryngton, John
Loveyne Tomb 1376: Lakenham, Hen.
St. Michael Crooked Lane: (Yeveley, Hen.)
St. Mildred Poultry: (Fisher, John); Tidemann
St. Nicholas Cole Abbey: (Cherche, Rich.)
St. Olave Hart Street: Coventry, Thos.
St. Olave Jewry: (Burton, Step.)
St. Paul, see Cathedral
St. Stephen Walbrook
Building 1429–38: **Mapilton, Thos.**
St. Thomas of Acon, Hospital: (Nicholl, Walt.); (*Sallynge, Rich. I); (West, Wm. II)
Repairs to church 1383: Hook, Sim.; **Walton, Walt.**
Temple Church –1185: John, M. I; Remus, Jas.
(See also Bridge Chapel, Charterhouse, Ely Place Chapel, Guildhall Chapel, Mercers' Company Chapel, Savoy Chapel, Tower: St. Peter-ad-Vincula)

Drapers' Hall: Nedeham, Jas.
Ely Place: (Yeveley, Hen.)
Chapel of St. Etheldreda *c.* 1290–98: Canterbury, Mich.
Exeter House, St. Lawrence Pulteney
Garden galleries 1530: **Nedeham, Jas.**
Fleet Gaol: (Walfray, John); (Weston, John)
Works 1173–85: Ailnoth
Guildhall
Chapel 1332–37: **Canterbury, Thos.**; Hurley, Wm.
Hall 1411–46; Bird, Rich.; **Croxton, John**;
Hospices. Earl of Huntingdon, of: Lynche, Hen.
Earl of Warwick, of: Grove, Sim.
Hospitals, see Churches
Houses: Addescomp, Wm.; Bird, John, I; Canterbury, Sim.; Causton, John; Cherche, Phil.; Dobson, John; Felstede, Rich.; Frankelyn, Rog.; Gerard, John, C.; Loveday, Thos.; Rerey, Rich.; Revell, Nich.; Rothinge, Rich.; Waltham, Nich.; Webbenham, Piers; Wetherall, Wm.; Wintringham, Wm.; Wolfey, John
Mercers' Company: Thorne, Wm.; Thornton, Rich.
Hall. Louvre 1521–22: **Nedeham, Jas.**
Chapel. Retable 1524: Van Dale, Walt.
Merchant Taylors' Company.
Hall, kitchen 1425–26: Goldyng, John; Mapleton, Goldyng
Old Ford: Birlyngham, Sim.
Pewterers' Company's Hall 1496–98: Birlyngham, Sim.
Rolls Chapel. Tomb of Dr. John Young 1516: **Torrigiano, Pietro**
Rutland House, Temple Bar
Building 1397–: Lawyn, Sim.; **Lote, Step.**
Savoy Palace
Works 1376–94: Lote, Step.; **Wintringham, Wm.**; **Yeveley, Hen.**
Rebuilt as Hospital (with Chapel) 1505–17: Aylmer, John; Bromehall, Robt.; **Coke, Hum.**; Gymboll, Robt.; Sallett, John; **Smyth, Hen.**
Somerset Place: Hilles, Ralph; Revell, Nich.
Temple, see Churches
Tower: Albon, Rich.; Ambrose, Rich.; *Aundely, Nich.; Aylmer, John; Barnet, Thos.; Bataile, Thos.; Bates, Robt.; Blounham, John; Box, John; (Canterbury, Sim.); Canterbury, Thos.; Canterbury Walt.; Colchester, Wm.; Colebrook, Robt.; Conan, M.; Cony, Robt.; Cook, Thos. I; Crump, Thos.; Crundale, Rich.; Dippenhall, Robt.; Dobson, John; Enganet, Rog.; (Flanders, John); Gloucester, Thos.; Hall, Thos.; (Halley, Bart.); Hemmyng, Rich.; Herland, Hugh; Herland, Wm.; Houghton, Thos.; Hungerford, John; Hurley, Wm.; Jerveys, John; Kynge, John; Lee, Wm.; Leicester, John; Lote, Step.; Manning, John; Mapilton, Thos.; Nicholas, M. II; Odo, C.; *Raff, Guy; Ramsey, Wm. III; Reynold, John, M.; Ripley, John; Risseburgh, John; Sheres, Thos.; Stockton, Thos., Stowell, Robt.; Thomas, C.; (*Tichmarsh, John); Tyryngton, John; Vertue, Robt.; (Ware, Thos.); (Welot, John); Westcote, John; Wilton, Rich.; Wydmere, John; Wynwick, John; Wytham, Reg.; Yonge, Maur.
White Tower 1081–: Gundulf
Works 1167–86: **Ailnoth**
Works 1190–1203: **Elias, E.**
Wakefield Tower &c. 1225–29
Traitors' Gate &c. 1239–41: (Reyns, Hen.)
Quay, Towers &c. 1247–69: Beverley, Robt.;

Monk Bretton, Yorks. W.R. (Eynsham, Hen.)
Monkton Farleigh, Wilts. (Farleigh, Rich.)
Montacute, Som. (Montacute, Wm.)
Montblanch, Spain. Fonoyll, Raynard
More, Herts. (Moor Park)
 Mahor: (Caldham, Gabr.); (Nedeham, Jas.)
  Chamber roof 1536: Rydge, Rich.II
Morella, Spain. Church: Fonoyll, Raynard.
Morende Castle (Yardley Gobion), N'hants. East, John
   I; Langton, John
Moretonhampstead, Dev. (More, Mathy)
Morton, Notts. (Osmund, M.)
Moston in Englefield, Flints. (St. George, Jas.)
Mote, The – see Maidstone
Moulsham by Chelmsford, Ess.
 Manor. Hall 1381–82: Mulsham, John
Mount Grace, Yorks. N.R.
 Priory: (Porter, John)

Nantes, France (Colyn, Thos.)
Naunton, Glos. (Hereford, Walt.)
Neath, Glam. 'Lalys'
Needham, High (near Longnor), Derb. (Nedeham, Jas.)
Nettleton, Lincs. (Netilton, Wm.)
Newark, Notts.
 Bridge, Rebuilt 1485: **Downes, Edw.**
 Church. Robert, carver
  Tower: (Alexander, M.III)
  Nave roofs c.1460: (Leycett, John)
  Reredos c.1498: **Drawswerd, Thos**.
Newbiggin-by-the-Sea, N'land. (Porter, Geo.)
Newbrough-in-Tyndale, N'land. (Houghton, Thos.)
Newbury, Berks. (Bulford, John)
Newcastle-upon-Tyne, N'land. (Lewyn, John)
 Castle: Gerard
  Keep 1171–77: **Maurice**
Newenham, Dev. Abbey: (Puleberg', John)
Newhall, Chs. (Newhall, Rich. &c.)
Newhouse, Lincs. (Michael); (Roger, M. I)
Newington-next-Hythe, Kent (Lote, Step.)
Newmarket, Suff. (Clerk, Sim.); (Ufford, Thos.)
Newnham St. Vincent, Herts.
 Church. Work c.1420– : (Wolvey, Thos.)
Newport, Ess. (Page, Thos.); (Sturgeon, Thos.)
Newport, I. of W. (Comber, Wm.)
 Mill of St. Cross: Triell, John
Newstead, Notts.
 Priory: (St. Andrew, Edm.)
Newton, Dur. (Lewyn, John); (Wolveston, Rich.)
Newton-le-Wold, Lincs. (Farnham, Rich.)
Newton St. Cyres, Dev. (Witney, Thos.)
Nonsuch, Surr.
 Palace 1539–: (*Aldrych, Thos.); Clement, Wm.;
  Faunte, Thos.; (*Michell, Rich.); (Molton, John);
  (Nedeham, Jas.)
Norham, N'land.
 Castle: Eland, Wm.; Lee, Sir Rich.; (William, E.);
  Wodman, John
  Keep, W. side 1170: **Wolveston, Rich.**
  W. Gate 1408: Spilbery, Wm.
  New tower 1422: Fekenham, Robt.
  Works 1510–11: *Chalmer, Thos.
Normanby, Lincs.
 Barn 1340: Bourne, John
Northallerton, Yorks. N.R. (Alverton, John)
 Church. Chancel buttress 1480: Hilder, Chr.
 Peel tower 1314: Glasham, Adam
Northampton (Gloucester, John), (Northampton, John & c.)

Castle: (Bray, Hen.)
Priory: (Deyster, Wm.)
(See also Eleanor Crosses)
Northington, Hants. (Northampton, Sim.)
Northleach, Glos. Church: (Winchcombe, Rich.)
Northleigh, Oxon.
 Church. Wilcote Chapel 1439–: (Winchcombe, Rich.)
Northlew, see Lew, North
Northwich, Chs. (Witton)
 Bridge: Newhall, Wm.; Wright, Gruff.; **Wright, Wm.
  le**
 Church. Tower c. 1498: Hunter, Thos.
 Mill: Drewry, Ralph; Eccleston, Nich.; Newhall, Wm.;
  Scot, Wm.
Norton, Derb. (Harpur, Hen.)
Norton, Dev. (Witney, Thos.)
Norton Subcourse (Norton next Haddiscoe), Norf.
 Church. Roofs 1319–20: Gunton, John; Gunton, Rog.;
  Gunton, Wm.
Norwich, Norf. (Antell, John); (Biltham, Ralph);
  (Bishop, Wm.); (Buk, Rich.); Clerk, Robt. I;
  (Couper, And.); Cowper, Wm.; Curteys, Rich.;
  (Dam, Rich.); (Doraunt, John); (Durrant, John);
  (Dyncok, John); (*Elware, Rich.); Elyngham,
  Robt.; Everard, John; Everard, Robt.; (Grene,
  John); (Grene, Robt.); (*Hermer, Nich.); (Horne,
  John); (Howes, John); (Howlett, Wm.);
  (Hyndeley, Wm.); (Marchant, Thos.); Marry,
  Nich.; (Marwe, John); (Mileham, John); (Morell,
  John); (Munford, Robt.); (Ramsey, John I);
  (Ramsey, Wm. II); (Reppys, Wm.); (Say, John);
  (Snape, Robt.); (Spendlove, Thos.); (Tuddenham,
  Hen.); (Vile, Thos.); (Wodehirst, Robt.);
  (Woderofe, Jas.); (Woderofe, John); (Wolsey,
  Wm.)
Castle: (Radbell, Artificer)
Cathedral: Ball, Robt. I; Brankastre, John; Doraunt,
  John; Gase, —; Grene, John; Grene, Robt.;
  (Heydon, John); Hildolveston, Wm.; Howlett,
  Wm.; John, C. II; John, C. IV; John, M. IV;
  (John, M. VII); Machun, Rich.; Massingham,
  Bart.; Michael, C.II; (Nicholas, M.III); Plump-
  sted, Thos.; Ramsey, Wm. II; Tabbard, Sim.;
  Thacker, Wm.; Waterden, Geoff.
Choir and Transepts 1096–1120
Nave and Tower c. 1121–45
Chapter House 1289–1303: Alexander, M. IV; Koc,
  Pet.
Cloister, E. walk 1297–1318: **Ramsey, John I**;
  Upphalle, Rich.
 S. walk 1324–30: Ramsey, John I; **Ramsey, Wm. II**
 W. walk 1344–47: Lilye, Sim.
 N. walk 1385–1415: Lyng, Hervey; **Wodehirst,
  Robt.**
 W. and N. Vaults 1416–30: Horne, John; Reppys,
  Wm.; **Woderofe, Jas.**; Woderofe, John
Lavatory 1444–45: Jakes, John: Woderofe, Jas.
St. Ethelbert Gate c. 1318–30: (Ramsey, Wm. II)
Windows of N. nave aisle 1299–1325: (Adam, carver);
  Ramsey, John I
Carnary Chapel 1310–25: **Ramsey, John I**
Choir images 1314–15: Adam, carver
Cathedral clock images 1323–24: Adam, carver
Presbytery Clerestory c. 1362–69: (Wodehirst, Robt.)
Erpingham Gate 1416–25: Woderofe, Jas.
W. Front and inserted windows c. 1426–50: Woderofe,
  Jas.
Spire and nave vault c. 1464–72: **Everard, Robt.**

Presbytery vault, flying buttresses, tower battlements &c. *c.* 1472–99: Antell, John; (Everard, Robt.)

Hostry, new building 1484–85: Antell, John; Couper, And.; Everard, Robt.

Catton screen, Bishop Nykke's Chantry, and Transept vaults *c.* 1501–36

Churches:

St. George Colegate. Chancel roof, stalls *c.*1496–97: Wrygth, Wm.

St. Gregory. Rebuilding *c.*1394: (Wodehirst, Robt.) Repairs 1453–54: Everard, Robt.

St. Peter Parmentergate. Chancel *c.*1511–12: *Hermer, Nich. and Thos.; Howes, Rich.

St. Saviour. Works 1423–25: Biltham, Ralph; Spynk, John; Wyspenade, John

Conisford Quay 1432–: Marwe, John

Cow Tower 1398–99: Snape, Robt.

Great Hospital: Everard, John; Marwe, John; Tabbard, Sim.

Cloister work 1447–57: Bucham, Robt.

Guildhall 1407–: (*Clerk, John); Clerk, Robt. I; **Marwe, John**

Peacock Inn: (Doraunt, John); Tuddenham, Hen.

Nostell, Yorks. W.R.

Priory. Choir *c.* 1315–25: Pontefract, Robt.

Notley Abbey, Bucks. (Rydge, Rich. II)

Notre Dame de l'Epine, France. 'Patrice'

Nottingham (Elias, E.); Hill, Nich.; (Nottingham, John &c.); (Peter, M.); (Steppingley, Pet.); (Turnour, Wm.); (Urricus, E.); (Yeveley, Hen.)

Bridge. Repairs 1486: Rodes, Wm.

Castle: Child, John.; Dylkeston, Rich.; Gerard; Helmesfield, Adam; Repyngdon, Wm.; Thomas, C.; Turnour, Wm.

Works 1204–14: Aundely, Nich.; **Bayard, Wm.**

Houses 1323: Bramcote, Wm.

Houses 1479: Hydes, Pers

Nuneaton, Warw.

Priory. Choir-stalls 1459: **Karver, Thos.**

Nunney Castle, Som. (Yeveley, Hen.)

Nunton, N'hants. (Nunton, Thos.)

Oakham, Rutl.

Church. Tower vault 1424–: **Nunton, Thos.**

Oatlands, Surr.

Palace. Rebuilt 1537–: Clement, Wm.; Dickinson, Chr.

Occold, Suff. (Hawes, M.)

Offham, Sx. (Rengwyne, John)

Old Sarum, Wilts.

Castle: David, C.; Gloucester, John

Oldham, Lancs.

Church. Rebuilt 1476–79: Hamond, Wm.

Olmütz, Moravia (Haschenperg, Step.)

Ongar, High, Ess. (Keyes, Rog.)

Orby, Lincs.

Church: (Jackson, Wm.)

Orford, Suff.

Castle 1165–73: Ailnoth

Ormesby, Norf. Barn 1434: Berry, Wm.

Ormskirk, Lancs.

Burscough Priory:

Church. Tomb *c.* 1506: Hales, Jas.

Orwell Haven, Suff. Wynford, Wm.; Yeveley, Hen.

Oseney, Oxon.

Abbey: Abingdon, Reg.; (Simnel, Thos.); Walter, M. I; William, M.; (Wynford, Wm.)

Oswestry, Salop. (Oswestre, David)

Otford, Kent. Manor: Russell, John, j.

Otham, Kent (Crump, Thos.)

Ottery St. Mary, Dev.

Collegiate Church. 1337–45: Joy, Wm.

Over Silton, Yorks. N.R.

Church. Bench-end *c.* 1519: (Brownfleet, Wm.)

Oxford (*Aldrych, Thos.); (Bath, Robt.); (Berty, Thos.); (Brown, Wm., M.); Carow, Robt.; (Clerk, Corn.); (Colonia, John); (Ferrier, Thos.); (*Frankelyn, Rog.) (Orchard, Wm.); (Oxford, Hen.); (Phelipp, Thos.); Sampson, John; Simnel, Thos.; (Westerley, Robt.)

Castle: Arches, Rich.; Elias, E.; Gloucester, John; (Humphrey, M.)

Cathedral, see Colleges, Christ Church

Churches:

Holywell: (Herte, John)

St. Mary the Virgin: Carow, Robt.; East, Wm.

Tower *c.* 1270–80: **Abingdon, Rich.**

Choir 1459–65: Chambyr, —

Nave 1487–1503

Pulpit and Congregation House *c.* 1506: **Fustyng, John**

St. Peter in the East: Janyns, Robt. s.

Colleges:

All Souls: Fethurstone, Wm.; (Horewode, Wm.); *Janyns, Robt. s.; (Orchard, Wm.); (Westerley, Robt.)

S. Quad, Chapel &c. 1438–44: **Branche, John; Chevynton, Rich.**; Janyns, Robt. s.; (Keyes, Rog.); (Mapilton, Thos.); Massingham, John III; Massingham, John IV; Tyllok, Rich.; Worlich, John

Cloister *c.* 1491–95: Bell, Wm.

Balliol: (Orchard, Wm.); Winchcombe, Rich.

Library 1431–60

S. Front, Gatehouse 1494–97: Bell, Wm.

Chapel Windows 1522–28: **East, Wm.**; Johnson, Wm.; **Lebons, John**

Brasenose: (Coke, Hum.); (East, Wm.); (Vertue, Wm.)

Front Quad, Gate Tower, Hall *c.* 1509–21

Chapel. Roof from St. Mary's College *c.* 1515: (Coke, Hum.)

Canterbury College. Buildings *c.* 1384–96: Brown, Wm.

Christ Church

Cathedral (St. Frideswide's Priory)

Norman Church *c.* 1158–80

Chapter House, Lady Chapel, Tower (upper stage), and Spire *c.* 1220–50

Latin Chapel *c.* 1350–55

Choir Vault *c.* 1480–1500: (Orchard, Wm.)

College. Tom Quad, Hall and Tower 1525–29: Carow, Robt.; **Coke, Hum.**; (Ellis, John); Johnson, Wm.; **Lebons, John**; Molton, John; Okey, Wm.; **Redman, Hen.**; Watlington, Thos.

Corpus Christi: (*Berty, Thos.)

Main Buildings, Hall and Chapel 1512–18: Carow, Robt.; Clerk, Corn.; **Coke, Hum.**; East, Wm.; Morwent, Rog.; **Vertue, Wm.**

Library desks 1517: Clerk, Corn.

Durham, see Trinity

Lincoln: Hays, Rich.; Jenkyns, Thos.

Hall, Library and N. Quadrangle *c.* 1436–38

Oratory 1478–79: Simnel, Thos.

Magdalen: Brian, John; Cheney, John; Clerk, Corn.; Clerk, Robt. II; Colonia, John; (Cowper, John); East, Wm.; Fisher, John; Hays, Rich.; Jenkyns,

Thos.; Reynold, Wm. I; Rydge, Rich. I; Skowte, John
Enclosing Walls 1467–73
Main Buildings and Chapel 1474–80: **Bowden, John; Orchard, Wm.**
President's Lodgings, Muniment Tower, S. Cloister 1485–90: **Orchard, Wm.**
Great Tower 1490–1509: Carow, Robt.; Fustyng, John; **Orchard, Wm.**; Reynold, Wm.
Stalls 1521: Colonia, John
Merton: (Branche, John); (Fant, Thos.); Janyns, Hen.; Johnson, Wm.; Roger, M. III; Wiltshire, John
Chapel: Brian, John
Choir 1289–94: (Witney, Thos.)
Sacristy 1309–11: (Witney, Thos.)
Crossing 1330–32: Thomas, M. VI; (Witney, Thos.)
S. Transept 1367–68
N. Transept –1424
Tower 1448–52: Atkins, John; Grove, Wm.; *Hertanger, Robt.; **Janyns, Robt. s.**
Roodloft 1486: Fisher, John
Warden's Lodging 1299–1300
Library and Mob Quad 1371–79: Bath, Robt.; **Humberville, Wm.**
Gate Tower 1416–18
Library roof altered 1503: Fisher, John
New College: Branche, John; Brian, John; Carow, Robt.; (Clerk, Robt. II); Hays, Rich.; (Jylkes, John); Martyn, John; (Myntham, Rich.); (Richard, M. V); Sampson, John; (Welot, John); (Welot, Wm.); (Wiltshire, John); (Winchcombe, Rich.)
Main Buildings, Hall and Chapel 1380–86: Brown, Wm., M.; **Herland, Hugh**; Ickenham, Wm.; **Wynford, Wm.**; (Yeveley, Hen.)
Fittings 1398–1406: Adam, joiner
Cloisters and Bell-tower c. 1390–1403: Brown, Wm. M.; Wyse, Wm.
Barn 1402–03: Martyn, John
Oriel: Brown, Wm., M.; Carow, Robt.; (Gylys, Rich.); Hays, Rich.; Roll, Wm.
Stalls 1410–13: Roll, Wm.
St. Mary's College Roof of c. 1515 (see Brasenose): (Coke, Hum.)
Queen's College: Bath, Robt.; Carow, Robt.; Clerk, Robt. II; Fethurstone, Wm.; Johnson, Wm.
Chapel 1373–80: Robert M. VIII; (Wodehirst, Robt.)
Hall 1398–1402: Brown, Wm., M.; **Wynford, Wm.**
St. Bernard's, see St. John's
St. John's
St. Bernard's College 1437– : (Mapilton, Thos.)
Gateway, Tower, and W. Front c.1483– : (Bell, Wm.)
Hall &c. 1502–05: **Orchard, Wm.**
St. Mary's, see Oriel
Trinity
Durham College
Chapel 1406–08
University
Great Gates 1475–76: *Branche, John
Worcester
Gloucester Hall
'St. Albans Chamber': (Wolvey, Thos.)
'Mansiones' c. 1420–1520
Houses: Beckeley, John; Carow, Robt.; Jylkes, John; Wiltshire, John

Divinity Schools: Godard, John
Building 1424–55: (Atkins, John); (Beckeley, John); **Elkin, Thos.**; Fethurstone, Wm.; (Janyns, Robt. s.); Massingham, John III; **Winchcombe, Rich.**
Seating 1466: Godard, John
Vault 1480–83: **Orchard, Wm.**
Holywell Manor 1516–: Gyles, Rich., M.; Phelipp, Thos.

Packwood, Warw. (Grove, Sim.)
Painswick, Glos. (Sponbedde, Mart.)
Palterton, Derb. (Palterton, John)
Paris, France. James, John; (Ramsey, Nich.)
Passenham, N'hants. (Pacenham, Thos.)
Patrick Brompton, Yorks. N.R. (Cracall, Rich.); (Newton, Rich.)
Patrington, Yorks. E.R.
Church: (Patrington, Robt. s.)
Pavenham, Beds. (Pabenham, Sim. I and II)
Pedralbes, Spain.
Monastery: Fonoyll, Raynard
Pembroke (Hirde, John)
Pendennis Castle, Corn.
Building 1542–46: (Haschenperg, Step.); (Molton, John)
Penllyn, Carn. (Howel, M.)
Pennington, Lancs.
Church. Tympanum: Hubal
Penshurst, Kent
Place. Hall &c. 1341–48: (Hurley, Wm.); (Ramsey, Wm. III)
Pershore, Worcs.
Abbey: (Farleigh, Rich.); Newman, Robt.; Zaneworth, Rich.
Tower c. 1330: (Farleigh, Rich.)
S. Transept. Vault c. 1440: (Newman, Robt.)
Perth, Scotland (Hereford, Walt.)
Peterborough, N'hants. (Thomas, M. IV)
Cathedral (Abbey): Kilham, John; (Man, Robt.); Tugney, Rich.
Choir and Transepts 1117–55
Nave 1155–75
W. Transept c. 1177–93
W. Front c. 1193–1230
Galilee Porch c. 1375
New Building c. 1496–1508: Semark, Hen.; **Wastell, John**; Wetyng, Wm.
Petersfield, Hants. (Wolfhow, Thos.)
Petworth, Sx. (Nedeham, Jas.)
Pevensey, Sx. Elias, E.
Pinchbeck, Lincs. (Eynsham, Hen.)
Pinley, Warw. (Clerk, John)
Pirford, Surr. (Beverley, Robt.)
Pistoia, Italy (Rovezzano, Benedetto)
Pittington, Dur. Chaumere, Wm.; (Christian, M.); More, Rich.; (Wolveston, Rich.)
Pleshey, Ess.
Castle: Canon, John
Pluckley, Kent (Bochor, Rich.)
Plumstead, Kent (Wauz, Wm.)
Plumstead, Norf. Brankastre, John; (Plumpsted, Thos.)
Plumstead, Great, Norf.
Chapel of St. Eustachius 1462–63: Brankastre, John
Plymouth, Dev.
Guildhall, Work 1495–96: Andrewe, John
St. Andrew's Church.
Aisles 1481–88: Andrewe, John; Daw, John, M.

Plympton, Dev. (More, Mathy)
Poblet, Spain. Monastery: Fonoyll, Raynard
Poitiers, France. Coorland, Walt.
Pokethorpe, Norf. (Wodehirst, Robt.)
Pontefract, Yorks. W.R. (John, C. II); (Pontefract, Robt.); (Wollasson, Thos.)
  Castle: Filyon, Thos.; Forman, John; Gamston, Phil.; Gamston, Robt.; Sykes, Robt.; Tomson, John
  Great Tower 1323– : Eynsham, Hen.
Ponteland, N'land. (Eland, Wm.)
Pont-y-Pair, see Bettws-y-Coed
Poole, Dors. (Yeveley, Hen.)
Portchester, Hants.
  Castle: Alexander, C.; Elias, E.; Gloucester, John; Herland, Hugh; Kympton, Hugh
  Works 1324–26: Banbury, John
  Works 1396–99: Abingdon, John; Cleuere, Thos.; Denyar, Thos.; Walton, Walt.; Weston, Walt.; Winchcombe, Rich.; **Yeveley, Hen.**
Portland, Dors. (Portland, Nich.)
Portsmouth, Hants. (Bager, Wm.); (Lee, Sir Rich.); (Lote, Step.); Mapilton, Thos.; (Sommer, John); (Thomas, C.); Wynwick, John
  Church of St. Thomas: Dereham, El.; (Lote, Step.)
Prescot, Lancs.
  Church: Pasmyche, John; Rachedale, Robt.
Prittlewell, Ess. (Prittlewell, Rog.)
Purbeck, Isle of, Dors. (Clavyll, John); (Gloucester, John); (Yeveley, Hen.)
Puriton, Som.
  Church. Work 1489: Drue, John
Pyrford – see Pirford

Quarr, I. of W.
  Abbey: Courtley, John
Queenborough, Kent (Herland, Hugh)
  Castle 1361–67: Box, John; Broyl, Jas.; Crump, Thos.; (Gibbon, John); Peyntour, Step.; Rokesacre, John; Thwayt, Rich.; Wyot, Guy; Yonge, Maur.; Yeveley, Hen.

Raby Castle, Dur.
  Kitchen &c. 1378–: (Lewyn, John)
Rainham, Ess. (Yeveley, Hen.)
Rainham, Kent (Champneys, Wm.)
  Church: Allen, John
Ramsey, Hunts. (Ramsey, John &c.)
  Abbey: (Redman, Hen.); *Robert, M. I; Simpson, Thos.; Worcester, Ednoth
Rattlesden, Suff.
  Church. S. porch c.1485–1500: Wastell, John
Raughton, Cumb. (Raghton, Ivo)
Ravenstone, Leics. (Bagworth, Pet.)
Rayleigh, Ess.
  Manor. Repairs 1186: Ailnoth
Rayne, Ess. (Dyminge, Nich.)
Raynham, Norf. (Bekham, John);
Reach, Cambs. (Tofts, Nich.)
Reading, Berks. (Reading, John); Sewy, John
  Abbey: (Sponlee, John)
  Works c. 1333: Farleigh, Rich.
  Churches:
    St. Lawrence
      Nave Arcade and Font 1521–: Cheney, John
Reculver, Kent (Ramsey, Wm. III)
  Ford Manor: (Wastell, John)
Redbridge, Hants.
  Bridge. Repairs 1381: Newman, John

Redenhall, Norf.
  Church. Chancel ceiling 1516: Rede, Wm., carver
Redgrave, Suff. Hall 1545– : **Gibbon, John, M.**
Reigate, Surr. (Leget, Robt.); (Vertue, Robt.)
Repps, Norf. (Reppys, Wm.)
  Church. E. window 1454–55: Everard, Robt.
Repton, Derb. (Repyngdon, Wm.)
Restormel, Corn.
  Hermitage Chapel: Freemason, Wm.
Rheims, France (Reyns, Hen.)
Rhuddlan, Flints.
  Bridge: Legh, Rich.; **Lenginour, Rich.**
  Castle: Melbourne, Robt.
    Works 1277–82: Dymoke, Hugh; **Lenginour, Rich.**; Oxford, Hen.; **St. George, Jas.**
Richmond, Surr.
  Church. Tabernacles 1502–03: Fill, Robt.
  Friary 1501: **Redman, Hen.**; Smyth, Hen.
  Palace c. 1500: Binks, Thos.; (Janyns, Robt.); Smyth, Hen.; Squyer, John
  (See also Sheen)
Richmond, Yorks. N.R. (Wright, John)
Rickling, Ess. (Rickling, Rich.)
Rickmansworth, Herts. (Burton, Step.)
Ripon, Yorks. W.R. (Brownfleet, Wm.); (Turret, Thos.); (Wright, Law.); (Wright, Thos.); (Wright, Wm., C.I); (Wod, John)
  House 1392: Turret, Thos.
  Minster: Penington, John; Turret, Thos.; Wright, Law.; Wright, Thos.
  Norman Church (1154–81): Arthur, M.
  W. Front and Towers c. 1230–40
  E. end rebuilt c. 1288–97
  Roodloft 1399–: **Wright, Wm., C.I**
  Central Tower c. 1460–
  Stalls 1489–94: (Brownfleet, Wm.)
  Nave rebuilt 1502–22: (Cole, John, M.); **Scune, Chr.**; Squyer, Robt.
  St. Wilfrid's Loft 1518: Brownfleet, Wm.
Ripton, King's, Hunts. Hors, Step.
Risborough, Monks, Bucks. (Clerk, Sim.); (Risseburgh, John)
Rocester, Staffs. (Roucestre, Sim.)
Rochdale, Lancs. (Rachedale, Robt.)
Roche, Yorks. W.R. (Thwayt, Rich.)
Rochelle, La, France
  Bridge: **Xaintes, Isambert**
Rochester, Kent (Holbrook, Laur.)
  Bridge 1383–92: **Yeveley, Hen.**
    Repairs: Champneys, Wm.; Goneld, John; Helle, Wm.; Lote, Step.; Mapilton, Thos.
  Bridge Chapel: Hassock, John
  Castle: Alexander, C.; Chamberlain, Rich.; Elias, E.; (Gundulf); (Thomas, C.)
    Works 1368–: Crump, Thos.; Gerard, Walt.; Herland, Hugh; Herland, Wm.; Hook, Sim.; *Pette, Robt.; Sharnhale, Wm.; Wode, Hen.; *Wrek, Thos.; **Yeveley, Hen.**
  Cathedral: Limoges, John; (Nedeham, Jas.)
  Norman Church c. 1077–1108: Gundulf
  Nave c. 1115–30
  W. Front c. 1150–60
  Choir c. 1200–27: (Richard, M. II)
  N. Transept c. 1240–55
  S. Transept. c. 1280–
  Chapter House doorway c. 1352
  Conventual Buildings. Works 1385–6, 1396–7: Doune, Geoff.

W. window *c.* 1470
Nave clerestory *c.* 1490
Lady Chapel *c.* 1500–12: Birch, John
City Walls and Gates 1396–1400: Doune, Geoff.;
Westcote, John; Wode, Laur.
Crown Inn: Holbrook, Laur.
Works 1423–25: Champneys, Wm.; Cony, Robt.;
Holm, Hen.; **Tanner, John**
King's College: Ellis, John; Nedeham, Jas.; (*Reynold,
Wm. II)
Rochford, Ess.
Manor. Chapel 1430–33: Brikeman, Matt.; Norfolk,
Wm.
Rockingham, N'hants.
Castle: Acle, Rich.; Corby, Robt.; Dilkyn, Wm.;
Weldon, Thos.
Roding, Ess. (Rothinge, Rich.)
Rollesby, Norf. (Rollesby, John &c.)
Romford, Ess.
Church: (Taverner, John)
Romsey, Hants. (Berewik, John); (Holnerst, Rich.)
Abbey. Choir *c.* 1120–50: Robert
Ropsley, Lincs.
Church 1380: Bate, Thos.
Ross-on-Wye, Heref. (Podding, John)
Rotherham, Yorks. W.R. (Rotherham, Wm.)
Rotherhithe, Surr.
Manor. Works 1349–70: Albon, Rich.; Cook, Thos. I;
Hemelhempstead, Wm.; Herland, Wm.; Heyward,
John; *Pabenham, John; Stephen, Rog.; Win-
tringham, Wm.
Bridge 1361: Herland, Wm.
Rothwell, Yorks. W.R. (Wollasson, Thos.)
Rouen, France (Prentys, Thos.); Wilmer, John;
Wyllemer, Thos.
Bridge for siege 1418–19: Janyn, John
Castle: Westerley, Robt.
Cathedral: Durand, M.
Church of St. Ouen: Wilmer, John
Rougham, Suff. (Layer, Wm.); (Nunne, Thos.)
Rowington, Warw. (Heose, Wm.); (Phillips, Thos.)
Roxburgh, Scotland
Castle. Works 1335–37: Goushill, Rich.; St. Albans,
Robt.
Works 1378–87: Lewyn, John
Repairs 1419: Fekenham, John
Roxwell, Ess.
Chapel. Chancel altered 1398–1427: **Clonyer, John**;
Richard, M. V
Mill 1399–1400: Clonyer, John
Rudston, Yorks. E.R. (Pabenham, Sim.I)
Rufford, Notts.
Abbey: (Osmund, M.)
Rushden, N'hants. Church: (Wastell, John)
Russia: Czar's works: Chafyn. Thos
Ruthin, Flints. (Helpeston John)
Castle: Grantham, Thos.
Rye, Sx. (Londoneys, Wm.); (Smyth, John 01)

Saffron Walden, Ess.
Abbey: (Prentice, Martin); (Sturgeon, John)
Church: Clerk, Sim.; Cobb, Robt.; Coket, John; Dam,
Rich.; Gerard, John, M.; **Glanforthe, Wm.**;
Hamond, John; Pollard, John; (Semark, Hen.);
Sturgeon, John; Sturgeon, Thos.; Thorn, John;
Wastell, John; Wolman, John
Saham Toney, Norf. (Offord, John)
Saint Albans, Herts. (Bataile, John); (Flanders, John);

(Lee, John); (Lee, Sir Rich.); (St. Albans, Robt.);
(Sylvester, Robt.); (Wolvey, Thos.)
Cathedral (Abbey): (Colchester, Walt.); (Eversolt,
Gilb.); Stubbard, Wm.
Norman Church and Tower 1077–1115; **Robert, M. I**
W. Front *c.* 1195–1214: Eversolt, Gilb.; **Goldcliff,
Hugh**
W. Nave &c. *c.* 1214–35: Cambridge, Matth.
Sanctuary 1235–90
Lady Chapel 1308–26: Boyden, Wm.
Choir-stalls 1314–: **Geoffrey, C.**
Nave, S. Aisle (part) 1324–27: **Wy. Hen.**
Roodscreen *c.* 1360–90: (Yeveley, Hen.)
Gatehouse &c. 1357–90: Clifford, John; Stubbard,
Wm.; Yeveley, Hen.
N. Nave windows 1420–40
W. Nave window *c.*1420–47: (Wolvey, Thos.)
Altar Screen 1476–84
Abbot Ramryge's Chantry *c.* 1500: (Lee, John)
Clock Tower *c.* 1404–11: (Wolvey, Thos.)
Churches.
St. Michael. Wolvey tomb: (Wolvey, Thos.)
St. Peter: (Wolvey, Thos.)
St. Andrews, Scotland
Castle. Works 1304: Bedeford, Robt.
Saint Asaph, Flints.
Cathedral
Tower 1391–: **Fagan, Robt.**
Choir-stalls *c.* 1475–90: (Frankelyn, Wm.)
Saint Benet Holme, Norf.
Abbey *c.* 1020–46: Edward; (Howes, Rich.); Thruerd
Saint Bertin, France. Abbey, see Saint Omer
Saint Cross, Hants.
Hospital: (Hulle, Robt.)
Saint Davids, Pemb.
Cathedral: John, C. VII; ('Wells, Mr. of')
College of St. Mary. Building *c.* 1381–: Fawley,—
Saint Erth, Corn.
Church. Screen: ('Banwell, Mr. of')
Saintes, France. Xaintes, Isambert
Saint-Georges–d'Espéranche, France. St. George, Jas.;
(Waus, Theob.)
Saint Ives, Hunts. (Bytham, John)
Saint Kew, Corn. (Daw, John)
Saint Margaret-by-Rochester, Kent (Hassock, John)
Saint Mawes, Corn.
Castle 1540–43: (Haschenperg, Step.); (Molton, John)
Saint Neots, Hunts. Priory: Weston, John
Saint Omer, France.
Cathedral (former Abbey of St. Bertin).
S. portal 1396: Bateman, Colmet
Saint Osyth, Ess. (Wode, John)
Priory
Gatehouse &c. *c.* 1495–1533
Abbot's Tower oriel 1527
Saint-Quentin, France (Lee, Sir Rich.)
Saint Radigunds, Kent (Englishman, Wm.)
Salcombe, Dev. (Harry, John)
Saling, Ess. (Sallynge, Rich. &c.)
Salisbury, Wilts. (Elys, Wm.); (Hulle, Robt.); (Humber-
ville, Wm.); (Keyes, Rog.)
Cathedral: (Alexander, C.); Dereham, El.; Godard, C.;
Hugh, C. I; Robert, M. VII; Schoverwille, Wm.;
Stevyns, Hen.; Story, Wm.; Yeman, John
Lady Chapel 1220–25: **Ely, Nich.**
Presbytery 1225–37: **Ely, Nich.**
Nave and Great Transept *c.* 1237–58: Ely, Nich.
W. Front *c.* 1258–66

Cloisters and Chapter House *c.* 1263–84: Richard, M. IV

Central Tower and Spire *c.*1320–: **Farleigh, Rich.; Robt., M.VII**

Inverted Arches in E. Transepts *c.* 1388–95: Portland, Nich.

Arches in Great Transepts *c.* 1415–23: Wayte, Robt.

Tomb of Bishop Bridport *c.* 1262–: Richard, M. IV

Inn building 1444: Fayrebowe, John

Leadenhall *c.* 1240: Dereham, El.

St. Anne's Gate and Chapel *c.* 1350–54: (Farleigh, Rich.)

Sallay, Yorks. W.R.

Abbey: Seller, Robt.; (Warin)

Salle, Norf. (Faudy, John)

Saltwood, Kent

Castle. Gatehouse *c.* 1385: (Yeveley, Hen.)

Sandgate, Kent

Castle 1539–40: (Baker, Wm.); **Haschenperg, Step.;** Lynsted, Robt.; (Molton, John); Palmer, John

Sandon, Herts.

Church. Chancel 1348–: Rikelyng, Thos.

Sandown, Kent

Castle *c.* 1540: Dickinson, Chr.; **Haschenperg, Step.;** (Lee, Sir Rich.); (Molton, John)

Sandwich, Kent (Gibbon, John); (Herland, Hugh); (Hurley, Wm.); (Thomas, C.); (Yeveley, Hen.)

Castle 1539: Clement, Wm.

St. Mary's Church. Steeple 1446: (Beke, Rich.); Robert, C.

Walls *c.*1468: Hunte, Robt.

Santes Creus, Spain. Fonoyll, Raynard

Saragossa, Spain. (Janyns, Robt., j.)

Savoy, The, see London

Saxham, Great, Suff. (Aleyn, Rich.); (Hermer, John)

Saxham, Little, Suff.

Hall 1505–11: **Bronde, John**; Burden, Rich.; **Burdon, Wm. II; Loveday, Thos.**; Oliver, Wm.

Scarborough, Yorks. N.R. (Scardebourg, Walt.); Whallesgrave, Thos.

Castle: Brumleye, John; Glasham, Robt.

Constable Tower 1425–29: **Hyndeley, Thos.;** *Michell, Rich.

Scratby, Norf.

Church: Howlett, Wm.

Scrooby, Notts. (Forman, John)

Seasalter, Kent (Blithere)

Seighford, Staffs. (Mason, John III)

Selby, Yorks. W.R. (*Forman, John)

Abbey: Chesterfield, Wm.

E. window *c.*1330– :(Raghton, Ivo)

Sedilia *c.* 1380: (Yeveley, Hen.)

Cloister work 1398–99: Rothing, John; Suthwell, Wm.

N. Aisle work *c.*1432: Couper, Robt.

Sele, Sx.

Priory: (Robert, M. V)

Sens, France (Sens, Wm.)

Sewstern, Leics. (Yvenson, Thos.)

Shalstone, Bucks. (Shaldeston, Wm.)

Shaw, Berks. Wodehay, Robt.

Sheen, Surr. (Birlyngham, Sim.); (Hunt, Wm. I)

Palace, Surr. Brown, Robt.; Lote, Step.; (Mapilton, Thos.); Partryche, Wm.; Prewet, Walt.; Selot, Wm.; Stiward, John; (Vesey, Wm.); Walton, Walt.; Westerley, Robt.; Whelar, Rich.; Yeveley, Hen.

'Byfleet', timber-frame 1413–14: Warlowe, Edm.

(See also Richmond, Surr.)

Sheerness, Kent. Fort: Nedeham, Jas.

Sheldon, Warw.

Church. Steeple 1461– : Dowland, Thos.

Shepperton, Middx. (Teinfrith)

Shepton Mallet, Som.

Church. Tower *c.*1385– : (Wynford, Wm.)

Sherborne, Dors. (Humberville, Wm.)

Abbey–: (Witney, Thos.)

Choir *c.* 1430–45: (Pope, Rich.)

Nave *c.* 1475–93: (Smyth, Wm.)

Castle: Estinton, Step.

St. John's Hospital 1440–42: **Hulle, Robt.**; Jenyn, John; (Pope, Rich.)

Sherburn, South, Dur. (Christian, M.)

Sheriff Hutton, Yorks. N.R.

Castle 1382–: (Lewyn, John)

Sheringham, Norf. (Sherringham, John)

Sherston, Wilts.

Church House 1511: Horsale, Rich.

Shirburn, Oxon. Castle 1377: Yeveley, Hen.

Shockerwick, Som. (Shockerwick, Wm.)

Shorwell, I. of W. (Schoverwille, Wm.)

Shotwick, Chs. Helpeston, Robt.

Shrewsbury, Salop. Fitzgamel, Alan; Gymel, John; John, C. III; Lowe, Step.; River, Wm.

Free School 1551–52; Lowe, Step.

Mill 1452–53: River, Wm.

Stone Bridge 1546–48: Lowe, Step.

Shutford, Oxon.

Chapel. Roof 1439–40: Wiltshire, John

Silkstead, Hants.

Manor. Hall 1267: Wyther, John

Silverstone, N'hants. (Le Enginnur, Rog.)

Skenfrith, Mon. Castle: Grosmont, Ralph

Sloley, Norf. (Ely, Reg.)

Snainton, Yorks. N.R. (Stephen, C.)

Snelson, Chs. (Snelleston, Hen.)

Snitterfield, Warw. (Snitterfield, Sim.)

Soham, Cambs. (Ufford, Thos.); (Wastell, John)

Solarzal, Spain (Ricardo)

Somerton Castle, Lincs. Slegh, Robt.

Sonning, Berks. (Coke, Hum.)

Sopwell, Herts. (Lee, John); Lee, Sir Rich.

St. Mary's Priory: (Wolvey, Thos.)

Southampton, Hants. (Berty, Thos.); Brown, Robt.; Chamberlain, John; (Crikylwode, Thos.); (Gerard); Hardyng, John II; Norton, John; (Royalton, Jas.); Sponlee, John; Stonard, John; Wynford, Wm.; Yeveley, Hen.

Castle. Works 1385–88: Colchester, Wm.; Kympton, Hugh

Gates and Towers 1379–: Swift, Rich. I; **Wynford, Wm.**

Houses: Crikylwode, Thos.

Walls 1428–29: Bartelot, John

Southchurch, Ess.

Chapel 1293–: Prittlewell, Rog.

Southleigh, Oxon.

Church *c.* 1470: (Orchard, Wm.)

Southsea, Hants. Castle: Berty, Thos.

Southwark, Surr. Aylmer, John; (Beke, Rich.); (Canterbury, John); (Clifford, John); (Colebrook, Robt.); (Gibbon, John, M.); (Gloucester, John); Henry, C. IA; (Nicholl, Walt.); (Stockton, Thos.); (Stow, Rich. I); (Tighelere, Thos.); Thomas, John; Vynt, Wm.; (Wintringham, Wm.); (Yeveley, Hen.)

Bridge House: Magsden, Robt.

Cathedral (Priory of St. Mary Overy): (Dereham, El.)

Choir and Retrochoir *c.* 1213–35: Richard, M. III; (Stephen, M.)
N. Transept 1273–
S. Transept (later)
Remodelling *c.* 1385–1410: Yeveley, Hen.
S. Transept restored *c.* 1430–45
Altar Screen *c.* 1520
Central Tower *c.*1520: Berty, Thos.
Mill 1248: Henry C. IA
Mills 1388: Vynt, Wm.
Prior's Houses. Building 1373–: **Wintringham, Wm.**
St. Olave's Church: (Clifford, John)
St. Thomas's Hospital: (Adam, M.I); (Nicholl, Walt.)
Southwell, Notts.
Cathedral
  Norman Church *c.* 1110–50
  Choir *c.* 1234–50
  Chapter House *c.* 1293–1300
  Pulpitum *c.* 1320–35: (Raghton, Ivo)
  W. window *c.* 1450
  Palace. Works *c.* 1525: Forman, John
Spalding, Lincs.
  Priory: Eynsham, Hen.; 'Spalding Master'; (Tresk, Sim.)
Sparkford (by Winchester), Hants. (Witney, Thos.)
Sparkford, Som. (Witney, Thos.)
Sparsholt, Berks. Brown, Wm., M.
  Church. Chancel repairs 1374–75: Brown, Wm., M.
Speen, Berks. (Molton, John)
Spelsbury, Oxon. (Spillesbury, John)
Spilsby, Lincs. (Spillesby, Robt.)
Spoonbed, Glos. (Sponbedde, Mart.)
Spoonley, near Winchcombe, Glos. (Sponlee, John)
Stafford
  Castle 1348: Burcestre, John
Staindrop, Dur. (Colyn, Thos.)
Stainfield, Lincs. (Stainefield, Oliv.)
Stambourne, Ess.
  Church. Roofs *c.* 1530: (Loveday, Thos.)
Stamford, Lincs. (Alexander M. III)
  St. Mary's Church: Richard, carver II
  Nunnery. Works 1445: Boydell, Wm.
  (See also Eleanor Crosses)
Stanhope, Dur. (Lambert)
Stanstead, Ess. (Prentice, Martin)
Stanstead, Suff. (Worlich, John)
Stanton Harcourt, Oxon.
  Church. Harcourt Aisle *c.* 1470: (Orchard, Wm.)
  Manor. Pope's Tower *c.* 1470: (Orchard, Wm.)
Stanwell, Mddx.
  Church. ?Chancel *c.* 1312: Abingdon, Alex.
Stapleton, Yorks. W.R. (Thwayt, Rich.)
Steeple Ashton, see Ashton
Stirling, Scotland. Gelis, John; (Glasham, Adam); (Hereford, Walt.); (Houghton, Thos.); (St. George, Jas.)
  Castle. Repairs 1336–37: Kilbourn, John
Stixwould, Lincs. (Hugh, M. II)
Stockton, Dur.
  Manor: Bolton, John; Tanner, John
Stogursey, Som. Glosse,–; (Marys, John); (Pope, Rich.)
Stoke Holy Cross, Norf.
  Church. Chancel work 1489–90: Elward, Rich.; Sendele, John
Stoke Mandeville, Bucks.
  Church. Chancel 1339: Risseburgh, John
Stoke-by-Nayland, Suff. (Turner, Rich.)
  Tendring Hall 1481–83: Bunting, Wm.; Burton, Step.;

Copdoke, Thos.; Cutting, John; Danyell, Thos.; Gamelyn, Robt.
'Stokhalling', see Stoke Mandeville
Stony Stratford, Bucks. (Clerk, Sim.)
  (See also Eleanor Crosses)
Storeton, Chs., Manor 1372: Barton, Rog.
Stortford, Bishop's, Herts.
  Church. Repairs 1482–1504: Dunmow, M. of; Mason, Wm.
Stow, Cambs.
  House 1198: Stow, Rich. I
Stowell, Som. (Stowell, John); (Stowell, Robt.)
Stratford on Avon, Warws. (Clerk, Hen.); (Cook, Thos. II)
  Church
  Chancel *c.* 1465–90: (Dowland, Thos.)
  Nave *c.* 1495: (Dowland, Thos.)
  Clopton Chapel *c.* 1410–15: **Kyrton, John**
  Guildhall: Grove, Sim.
  Holy Cross Guild Chapel *c.* 1495–1500: **Dowland, Thomas**
  Grammar School 1427–28: **Hasill, John**
  House: Grove, Sim.
Stratton, Corn.
  Church. Roodloft and Screens 1531–39: **Daw, John, carver**; **Pares, John**
Strood, Kent (Champneys, Wm.); (Yeveley, Hen.)
Sudborough, N'hants. (West, Wm. I)
Sudbury, Suff. *Goldyng, John; (Gooch, Thos.); (Ide, Thos.); (Loveday, Thos.); Rollesby, John
  Watermill 1450–51: Goldyng, John
Sudeley, Glos. (Janyns, Robt. s.); (Sponlee, John)
Sunbury, Middx. – see Kempton
Sunninghill, Berks. Hartshorne, Thos.
Surfleet, Lincs. (Elias, E.)
  Church. Chancel 1418–: **Denys, Rog.**
Sutton, Middx.
  The King's House: Toutmond, Wm.
Sutton, Surr. (Urricus E.)
Sutton Valence, Kent (Gerard, Walt.); (Lomherst, Step.)
Swaffham, Norf.
  Church. Tower 1507– : *Antell, John; Cobb, Robt.; **Gyles, M.**
Swalcliffe, Oxon.
  Church. Choir (stalls?) 1450–51: Wiltshire, John
  Rectory: Jylkes, John; Wiltshire, John; Winchcombe, Rich.
  Tithe Barn 1403–06: (Winchcombe, Rich.)
Swarkeston, Derb. (Mapilton, John)
Swineshead, Lincs. (Mason, Thos.)
Syon Convent, Middx. (Redman, Hen.)
  Building 1444: Hardy, John; (Palden, Jas.); Westerley, Robt.
  Altar table *c.*1493–1500: Brown, John, carver; Fill, Robt.

Tabley, Chs.
  Old Hall *c.* 1385: (Newhall, Wm.)
Tadcaster, Yorks. W.R. (Barton, John, II)
Tanworth-in-Arden, Warw. (Grove, Sim.)
Tarporley, Chs.
  Church. Chancel 1289: Newhall, Rich.
Tarragona, Spain. Cathedral: Fonoyll, Raynard
Tarrant Keynston, Dors.
  Tomb of Queen Joan of Scotland 1238: Dereham, El.
Tasburgh, Norf. (Grene, John)
Tattershall, Lincs.

Almshouse 1486: Alsbroke, Hen.

Castle. Building 1433–55: Dutchman, Baldwin

Church 1440–

  Tower 1482: Alsbroke, Hen.; **Cowper, John**

College 1458–86: Alsbroke, Hen.; Lyndon, Pet.

Taunton, Som. (Bird, John, M.)

Tavistock, Dev. (Growdon, Rog.)

Taynton, Oxon. (Atkins, John);(Humberville, Wm.); (Janyns, Hen.); (Janyns, Robt. s.); (Jestelyn, John); (Stevens, Wm.); (Teynton, John); (Winchcombe, Rich.)

Teignmouth, Dev. Wolston, John

Tempsford, Beds.

  Church. Chapel, Reredos, &c. 1512–: Pondour, Wm.

Tendring Hall, see Stoke-by-Nayland

Tenterden, Kent

  Church. Tower *c.* 1460–65: (Mapilton, Thos.); (Stanley, Thos.)

Terrington, Norf. (Bryd, Thos.); (Tyryngton, John)

Tetbury, Glos. (Horsale, Rich.)

Tewkesbury, Glos. (Walton, Walt.)

Teynham, Kent (Teynham, Thos.)

Thame, Oxon. (Rydge, Rich. II)

  Church. N. Transept 1442: **Beckeley, John**; **East, John**; (Winchcombe, Rich.)

Thatcham, Berks. (More, Edm.)

Thaxted, Ess. (Sturgeon, John)

  Church: (Bronde, John); (Ely, Reg.)

  Horham Hall: (Bronde, John); (Loveday, Thos.)

Thelsford, Warw.

  Friary: (Ely, Reg.)

Thetford, Norf. (*Aldrych, Thos.); (Bele, Thos.); (*Wastell, John)

  Cluniac Priory

    E. window 1507: **Aldrych, Thos.**

    Door of Church 1530: **Neker, Thos.**

    Tomb of 2nd Duke of Norfolk 1524: (Wastell, John)

    Holy Trinity Church: (*Wastell, John)

Thirsk, Yorks. N.R. (Thirsk, John); (Tresk, Sim.)

Thorington, Suff.

  Church: Alcock, Wm.

Thornbury, Glos.

  Castle 1511–22: (Janyns, Robt. j.); (Rogers, John, II); Tegge, Rich.; (Vertue, Wm.)

Thornham, Little, Suff.

  Church. Tower *c.* 1485–86: Cutting, Rich.; Tilley, John

Thornton, Lincs. (Thornton, Wm.)

  Abbey. Nave Vault 1391: **Wright, Wm., C.I**

Thorpe Abbotts, Norf. (Tilley, John)

Thorpe Waterville, N'hants. (Lee, Wm.)

Thundersley, Ess. Cressing, John

Thurlton, Norf.

  Church. Chancel work 1441: Durrant, John; **Marwe, John**

Tickenhill, Worcs.

  Manor: Bek, John; Greyhorse, Rich.

    Works 1473–75: Kerver, Laur.; Rogers, John I

Tiköb, Denmark. Alexander, carver

Tilbury, Ess. Fort: Nedeham, Jas.

Tilney All Saints, Norf.

  Church: Burrey, Thos.

    Nave roof 1463: (Arnold, Edm.)

    Landing-place 1434: Bryd, Thos.

Tingewick, Bucks.

  Watermill 1477–80: Myntham, Rich.

Tintinhull, Som.

  Church. Roodloft 1452: **Dayfote, Thos.**

Titchfield, Hants.

Place House 1538–: **Berty, Thos.**; Lee, Sir Rich.

Titchmarsh, N'hants. (Tichmarsh, John &c.)

Tittenhanger, Herts. (Redman, Hen.)

Tivetshall, Norf. (Durrant, John)

  Windmill 1434: Hore, John

Toddington, Beds. (Butler, John)

Toledo, Spain. Cathedral: (Helpeston, Wm.)

Tonbridge, Kent. (Hurley, Wm.)

Torksey, Lincs.

  Priory: Gowselle, John

Totnes, Dev.

  Church. Tower 1449: **Growdon, Rog.**.

Tottenham, Middx. (*Mapilton, Thos.)

Totternhoe, Beds. (Canterbury, Thos.); (Lessy, Phil.)

Trebizond, Turkey (Robert, Sculptor)

Treflan, Carn. Lenginour, Rich.

Tremworth, near Wye, Kent

  Manor: (Yeveley, Hen.)

Triplow, Cambs. (Nun, John)

Trowse, Norf. (Jakes, John): (Marwe, John); Nicholas, M.III; (Woderofe, John)

Troyes, France. Langlois, Jean

Trumpington, Cambs. (Ploughwright, Rich.)

Tuddenham St. Mary, Suff. (Bellamy, Wm.I)

Tunstall, Suff. (Powle, Adam); (Russell, Rich., M.)

Tutbury, Staffs. (Clement, John); (Hirton, Rog.); (Yeveley, Hen.)

  Castle: Townsend, John

    Works 1400: Skillyngton, Robt.

    S. Tower 1442– : Westerley, Robt.

    N. Tower 1457–58: (Westerley, Robt.)

Twickenham, Middx. (Selot, Wm.)

Twyford Bridge, Kent (Herunden, John I)

Tyneham, Dors. (Tyneham, Alex.)

Tynemouth, N'land Lee, Sir Rich.

Upchurch, Kent (Herland, Hugh)

Upnor, Kent. Lee, Sir Rich.

Uttoxeter, Staffs. (Yeveley, Hen.)

Uxbridge, Middx. (Ickenham, Wm.)

Vale Royal, Chs.

  Abbey. Building 1278–85: Bataile, John; Chichester, Ralph; Doget, John; **Hereford, Walt.**; Nottingham, Ralph; *Pabenham, John; Pabenham, Sim., II; Winchcombe, Wm.

    E. Chapels 1359–68: **Helpeston, Wm.**

Vyne, The, Hants. Berty, Thos.

Wadswick, Wilts. (Waddeswyk, Wm.)

Wainfleet, Lincs.

  School 1484: **Alsbroke, Hen.**; (Cowper, John)

Wakefield, Yorks. W.R. (Wakefield, John)

  Chevet Hall 1516–29: Hayght, Ed.; Preston, John

Walberswick, Suff.

  Church: Alcock, Wm.; (*Antell, John); Buk, Rich.; Pays, Hen.

    Tower 1426–50: **Powle, Adam; Russell, Rich., M.**

    Roodloft Stairs 1499: **Cutting, Thos.**

Walden Abbey, see Saffron Walden

Wales, Castles in. Derneford, Nich.; Helpeston, Robt.; Helpeston, Wm.; Lewes, John; Mere, John; Rous, John; Underwood, John

(See also Chester: Palatinate, and under Wales in County Index)

Wallingford, Berks.

  Castle: Humberville, Wm.; Shaldeston, Wm.; Stevens, Wm.; Wallingford, Rich.; Yeveley, Robt.

Walmer, Kent
  Castle *c.* 1540: Clement, Wm.; Dickinson, Chr.; **Haschenperg, Step.**; Molton, John
Walsingham, Norf. (Walsingham, Alan); (Wastell, John)
Walsingham, Little, Norf. Church: Mathu, John
Waltham, Hants. Royalton, Jas.
Waltham Cross, Herts., see Eleanor Crosses
Waltham Holy Cross, Ess. (Harreson, John)
Walton, Suff.
  Castle. Demolition 1176: Ailnoth
Warblington, Hants.
  Castle 1517–18: Gyles, Rich., M.; Perkyns, Thos.
Wardour Castle, Wilts.
  Building 1392–: (Wynford, Wm.)
Ware, Herts. (Hylle, Thos.)
Wareham, Dors. (Vesey, Wm.)
Warfield, Berks. (Watlington, Thos.)
Wargrave, Berks. (Henry, C. IA); (Northampton, Sim.)
Wark, N'land.
  Castle: Rogers, John II
  Works 1543: Pettyt, Thos.
Warkworth, N'land.
  Castle: (Lewyn, John)
Warmington, N'hants. (Wermington, Wm.)
Warton, Lancs.
  Church: 'Kirkby Malham, Mr. of'
Warwick (Brasier, Hugh); (Cook, Thos. II); (Montfort, John)
  Castle. Great Gatehouse *c.* 1392: 'Warwick, Mr. of Earl of'
  Guy's Tower. Work 1392–93: Montfort, John
  Stable *c.*1418–19: Grove, Sim.
  Church of St. Mary
  Chancel *c.* 1381–96: Sutton, John; (Skillyngton, Robt.)
  Beauchamp Chapel 1441–52: (Essex, John); (Kerver, Thos.); Massingham, John III
  Woodwork 1450: **Bird, Rich.**; Haynes, John
  Houses: Grove, Sim.; Winchcombe, Rich.
Washbourne, Glos. (Washbourne, Rich.)
Washingley, Hunts. (Wassyngle, John)
Water Hall (near Wixoe), Suff. Whyghte, John
Waterbeach, Cambs. (Euterpach, John)
Waterden, Norf. (Waterden, Geoff.)
Waterstock, Oxon.
  Church. Danvers Aisle *c.* 1500: (Orchard, Wm.)
Watford, Herts. (Horewode, Wm.); (*Mapilton, Thos.)
Waverley, Surr.
  Abbey. New Church 1204–31: (Waverley, John)
Weeting, Norf. (Wetyng, Wm.)
Weighton, Yorks. E.R. (Brownfleet, Wm.)
Weldon, N'hants. (Semark, Hen.); (Weldon, Thos.)
Wellingborough, N'hants. (Petit, John)
Wells, Som. Atwood, Wm.; Branche, John; Clement, John; *Clerk, John; (*Gryme, John); (Hill, John); (Stowell, John)
  Cathedral: Dereham, El.; Norreys, Rich.; Stowell, John; 'Wells, Mr. of'
  Nave and Transepts and W. bays of Choir *c.* 1175–1230: Lock, Adam; (Nicholas, C.)
  W. Front *c.* 1230–60: **Norreys, Thos.**; Wells, Sim.
  Crypt of Chapter House *c.* 1245–80
  Chapter House *c.* 1293–1306
  Central Tower *c.* 1315–22: Thomas, M. V
  Lady Chapel and Retrochoir *c.* 1310–19: (Witney, Thos.)
  E. window *c.* 1335: **Joy, Wm.**
  Inverted Arches at Crossing *c.* 1338–40: **Joy, Wm.**

Retrochoir and Choir remodelled, Pulpitum *c.* 1329–45: **Joy, Wm.**
SW. Tower and Parapet inside W. window *c.* 1385–95: Stone, John; **Wynford, Wm.**
Bubwith's Chapel 1424: Gabriell, Den.
NW. Tower *c.* 1425–35
Cloisters *c.* 1420–1508: Atwood, Wm.; Stowell, John; Turpyn, John
Crossing vault, Sugar's Chapel *c.* 1475–90: **Smyth, Wm.**
Cloister Lady Chapel 1477–88: **Smyth, Wm.**
St. Cuthbert's Church
  Tower *c.* 1385–1430 (Wynford, Wm.)
  S. Transept Reredos 1470: **Stowell, John**
Close
  Great West (Brown's) Gate *c.* 1445–50
  Penniless Porch Gate *c.* 1445–50
Palace
  House *c.* 1225–40
  Chapel *c.* 1275–80
  Great Hall *c.* 1285–90
  Gatehouse and walls 1340–
  Palace Eye Gate *c.* 1450
  Additions to house *c.* 1525–40
  Deanery. Work *c.* 1473–83: Smyth, Wm.
  Vicars' Close: (Wynford, Wm.)
  Porch, Hall, and Kitchen *c.* 1348–60
  Chapel and remodelling *c.* 1445–70
  Chain Gate 1459
Welwick, Yorks. E.R.
  Church. Priest's tomb: (Malton, Wm.)
Wendlebury, Oxon. (Wendlingburgh, Robt.); (Wendulburgh, John)
Wenlock, Much, Salop.
  Abbey: Corvehill, Wm.
Wennington, Ess. (Clifford, John); (Lote, Step.); (Yeveley, Hen.)
Wensley, Yorks. N.R.
  Church. Screen from Easby Abbey *c.* 1510: (Brownfleet, Wm.)
Westbury-on-Trym, Glos.
  College 1447–74: (Roche, John)
Westenhanger, Kent. (*Janyns, Robt., s.)
Westerham, Kent (Simson, Geo.); (Westram, John)
Westerleigh, Glos. (Westerley, Robt.)
Westley, Suff. (Layer, Wm.)
Westminster, Middx. Blockley, John; Bullock, Hen.; (Burdon, Wm. I); (*Clavyll, John); (Eltham, Rich.); (Eudo, C.); (Gilbert, C. I); John, C. I; (Kentbury, Robt.); (Redman, Hen.); (Redman, John); (Redman, Thos.); (Richard, C.); (Russell, John s.); (Russell, John j.); (Russell, Rich., C.); (Smyth, Hen.); (Stowell, Robt.); (Walter, Imager); (Walton, Nich.); (Wareyn, Rich.); (Whelpdale, Wm.); (Wintringham, Wm.); (Wydmere, John)
  Abbey: (Alexander, C.); (*Barbour, John); Canterbury, Thos.; Canterbury, Walt.; (Cheney, John); (Essex, John); Flanders, John; (Johnson, Thos.); (Leicester, Rich.); Patrington, Wm. II; (Reyns, Hugh); Stafford, John; Waltham, John
  Edward the Confessor's Church, Pyx Chapel –*c.* 1050–65: Duddason, Leofsi; Gretsyd, Godw.; Teinfrith
  St. Katherine's Chapel *c.* 1160: (Ailnoth)
  Refectory. Repairs 1175: Ailnoth
  Lady Chapel 1220–40: Dartford, Ralph
  New work: Presbytery, Chevet, Transept, Chapter House, four N. bays of Cloister E. walk 1245–60:

Alberic, M.; **Alexander, C.**; Gloucester, John; Jacob; Odo, C.; **Reyns, Hen.**
Belfry 1248–: **Alexander, C.**
Second work, E. bays of Nave and four bays of Cloister N. walk 1260–69: **Beverley, Robt.**
Refectory &c. c. 1305: Robert, M. VI
Cloister E. walk, four S. bays 1345–49: **Bole, Walt.**
S. and W. walks 1349–65: East, John I; Henry, C. II; **Palterton, John**; Roucestre, Sim.; Wodehirst, Robt.
Abbot's Hall and House (Deanery), Infirmary rebuilt, Refectory remodelled 1362–76: (Herland, Hugh); Palterton, John; Wintringham, Wm.; (Yeveley, Hen.)
Nave, continued 1377–1539: Brown, John I; Burdon, Wm. I; Colchester, Wm.; East, Wm.; Ellis, John; Ellis, Nich.; Faunte, Thos.; Freeman, John; (Hardy, John); *Hoo, Thos.; Kentbury, Robt.; Lee, John; Long, John; Molton, John; Pacche, John; Pacche, Rich.; Reading, John; Rede, Wm., M; Redman, Hen.; Redman, John; Redman, Thos. I; Redman, Thos. II; Russell, John s.; Russell, John; Russell, Rich. s.: Smyth, John; Stowell, Robt.; Taylor, Wm.; Thirsk, John; (Turnour, Wm.); Vertue, Adam; Vertue, Robt.; Waddeswyk, Wm.; Washbourne, Rich.; Westerley, Robt.; **Yeveley, Hen.**
Henry V's Chantry c. 1422–50: Massingham, John III; **Thirsk, John**
Altar Screen –1441: **Thirsk, John**
Henry VII's Chapel 1503–19: (Drawswerd, Thos.); Emler, Lawr.; (Essex, John); (Hales, Jas.); (Hudde, John); **Janyns, Robt. j.; Lebons, John**; (Leget, Robt.); Mazzoni, Guido; **Vertue, Robt.; Vertue, Wm.**; Wetyng, Wm.
Lady Altar 1526: Rovezzano, Benedetto
Tombs: (Emler, Lawr.)
Katherine 1257: Wells, Sim.
John of Windsor 1272: **Beverley, Robt.**
Henry III c. 1291: (Beverley, Robt.)
Queen Eleanor 1291–93: **Crundale, Rich.; Houghton, Thos.**
Edmund Crouchback c. 1297–: (Canterbury, Mich.)
Aveline of Lancaster c. 1297–: (Canterbury, Mich.)
Aymer de Valence c. 1324–26: (Canterbury, Walt.)
John of Eltham c. 1337–: (Canterbury, Thos.)
Queen Philippa 1367: (Herland, Hugh); Liège, Hawkin
Edward III c. 1378: (Herland, Hugh); (Yeveley, Hen.)
Cardinal Langham c. 1391–95: Lote, Step.; **Yeveley, Hen.**
Richard II 1394–97: (Herland, Hugh); Lote, Step.; **Yeveley, Hen.**.
Henry V c. 1422: Thirsk, John
Abbot Islip's Chantry c. 1530: (Molton, John); (Taylor, Wm.)
Lady Margaret Beaufort 1510–29: Bray, Reg.; Torrigiano, Pietro
Henry VII 1512–18: **Torrigiano, Pietro**
Henry VII's Almshouses 1504: **Coke, Hum**.
Charing Cross, see Eleanor Crosses
Charing Mews, see Charing, Middx.
Churches:
St. Margaret's: Blackshaw, Wm.; (Bullock, Hen.); (Herunden, Thos.); (Reading, John); (Redman, Thos. I.); (Russell, John s.); (Russell, Rich., C.); Sebyste, Hen.; (Smyth, Hen.); Thirsk, John;

Wright, Thos.
S. Aisle c. 1488–91: Stowell, Robt.
N. Aisle and Lady Chapel 1497–1503: Stowell, Robt.
Nave finished 1504: Stowell, Robt.
Tower 1515–22: **Redman, Hen.**
Chancel 1518–23: **Redman, Hen.; Russell, Rich., C.**
St. Martin-in-the-Fields: (Coke, Hum.); (Ripley, John); (Russell, John j.)
Palaces:
Old Palace (Houses of Parliament): Blound, Wm.; Canterbury, John; Canterbury, Pet.; *Carlton, Geoff.; Clenchwarton, Sim.; Colchester, Wm.; Crundale, Rich.; Crundale, Rog.; Dobson, John; East, John I; Enganet, Rog.; Fant, Thos.; Flanders, John; Geoffrey, E.; Gibbon, John, M.; Hoo, Thos.; Houghton, Thos.; Jacob; Ledes, John; (Lewyn, John); Lote, Step.; Mapilton, Thos.; Nottingham, Wm.; Osekyn, Robt.; Radwell, John; Ramsey, John III; Roke, John; (Swift, Rich. I); *Tichmarsh, John; (Wimund); Wynwik, John; Wyther, John
Great Hall &c. 1097–99 (Wimund)
Works 1157–87: **Ailnoth**
Works 1198–: **Elias, E.**
Queen's Chamber, Chapel &c. 1233–39: Albemunt, Hugh; **Alexander, C.**; Burnell, Ralph; Rutier, Wm.; **Waverley, John**
Painted Chamber 1242–44
Works 1259–73: Alexander, C.; **Beverley, Robt.**; Gloucester, John; Hurley, John; Odo, C.; (Stone, Pet.); Wauz, Wm.
Works 1307–: Wytham, Rich.
Works 1325–49: Abbotsbury, Wm.; Bataile, Thos.; Box, John; Dippenhall, Robt; Fulbourne, Wm.; Hurley, Wm.; Lynne, Rich.; Palterton, John; Ramsey, John II; Ramsey, John III; Ramsey, Nich.; Winchelsea, Wm.; Wytham, Reg.
Works 1350–66: **Box, John**; Herland, Hugh; Hook, Sim.; Hurley, Sim.; Massingham, John II; Reynold, John; Roucestre, Sim.; Winchester, Wm.; *Witney, Thos; Wodehirst, Robt.; Wrek, Thos.; **Yeveley, Hen.**; Yonge, Maur.
Hall (Great Hall) remodelled and re-roofed 1394–1400: Brusyngdon, Robt.; Canon, Thos.; Chuddere, Wm.; Crump, Thos.; Davyn, Pet.; **Herland, Hugh**; Kentbury, Robt.; Swallow, John; Walton, Walt.; Washbourn, Rich.; Wilton, Nich.; Wolvey, Thos.; **Yeveley, Hen.**
Great Gateway 1397–99: (Yeveley, Hen.)
Works 1497–1502: Hudde, John; Martyn, Walt.; Mauncy, Thos.; Wetyng, Wm.
St. Stephen's Chapel
Crypt begun 1292–98: Aynho, Nich.; Blound, Wm.; **Canterbury, Mich.**; Canterbury, Mich., j.; Colebrook, Robt.; Flanders, John; Hoo, Wm.; Pabenham, John; Ramsey, Wm. I; Waltham, Robt.; Witney, Thos.
Crypt completed 1319–27: Canterbury, Mich., j.; Canterbury, Walt.; (*Pabenham, John); Roke, John; St. Albans, Robt.; Tyrington, John; Underdone, Wm.
Upper Chapel 1327–46: Abingdon, Nich.; Ailyngton, Nich.; Canterbury, Mich., j.; **Canterbury, Thos.**; Farleigh, Rich.; Herland, John; Herland, Wm.; Hungerford, John; Hurley, Wm.; Lynne, Rich.; Ramsey, John III; Ramsey, Wm. III
Finishings, Stalls &c. 1351–65: Burwell, Robt.;

Church. Tower 1505–25: **Hart**, [?Wm.]
Writtle, Ess. Clonyer, John; (Wrytle, John)
Wroxham, Norf. (Ely, Reg.)
Wyberton, Lincs.
  Church. Rebuilt 1419–: Denys, Rog.
Wycombe, High, Bucks.
  Church
  Chancel. Repairs 1473–: Sherborne, Robt.
  Rebuilding 1508–: **Chapman, Wm.**
Wye, Kent (Yeveley, Hen.)
Wymondham, Norf.
  Abbey Church. W. Tower 1445– : (Woderofe, Jas.)
  Image of St. George 1519–: **Bale, Wm.**; **Sterlyng, Thos.**; (Stockton, Wm.)
Wymondley, Great, Herts. (Nedeham, Jas.)
Wymondley, Little, Herts. (Nedeham, Jas.)
  Priory: (Nedeham, Jas.)
Wynyard, Dur. Hall: Todde, John
Wytham, Berks. (Wytham, Rich.)

Xaintes, see Saintes

Yalding, Kent (Herunden, John I)
  Church: Thorngate, Thos.
Yanworth, Glos. (Zaneworth, Rich.)
Yardley Gobion, N'hants., see Morende
Yarmouth, Great, Norf. (*Barbour, John); (Barsham, Thos.); (Gunton, John); (Gunton, Robt.); (Gunton, Rog.); (Gunton, Wm.); (Lee, Sir Rich.); (Lilye, Sim.); (Yernemuth, John)
  Church: (Newman, Robt., note)
  Harbour 1398–: Herland, Hugh; Yeveley, Hen.
Yatton, Som.
  Church: Bekke, John; Hyll, Wm.; Jagryn, John; Stonehouse, Wm.
  Roodloft 1446–54: **Crosse, John**
  Seats 1447: **Balwe, John**; **Hikke, John**
  Cross 1524–25: Hort, Wm.
Yearsley, Yorks. N.R.
  Hall, barn, etc. 1341–42: Wod, John
Yeaveley, Derb. (Yeveley, Hen.); (Yeveley, Robt.)
Yedingham, Yorks. E.R. (Stephen, C.)
Yeovil, Som. Tyneham, Alex.
  Church c. 1380–1400: (Wynford, Wm.)
York Bagby, Robt.; Barton, Thos.; Baynes, Robt.; (Bell, John); Bischope, Rich.; Blaketoft, Rich.; Bolron, John; Brigges, Rich.; Briggs, Thos. I; (Brownfleet, Wm.); *Carlton, Geoff.; Cotom, John; Cottingham, Wm.; Couper, John; Couper, Robt.; (*Cracall, Rich.); Craneby, John; Dam, Jas.; Davyson, Robt.; (Drawswerd, Thos.); (Fambeler, Giles); (Felstede, Rich.); Fitzgiles, Robt.; Forster, John, C.; Foulford, John; Hardyng, John I; Hirton, Rog.; Jackson, Robt.; *Lincoln, Philip; (Newton, John); (Patrington, Robt. j.); Porter, John; Simon, M. I; Tonge, Robt.; (Waddeswyk, Wm.); (William, C.III); Wilson, Alex.; Wod, John; (Worsall, Wm.)
  Archbishop's Palace: Blaketoft, Rich.; Kingston, Hen.; Watton, John
  Austin Friary: (Bischope, Rich.); (Couper, John)
  Bluecoat School, see St. Anthony's Hall
  Castle: Hardyng, John I; Landric; Wakefield, John
  Repairs 1244: **Northampton, Sim.**; **Reyns, Hen.**
  Bridge 1411: Bolron, John
  Cathedral, see Minster
  Churches:
  All Saints, North Street: (Grantham, Hugh)
  Roof of Choir and Choir Aisles c. 1450: (Foulford, John)

St. Andrew's: Grantham, Hugh
St. John the Baptist, Hundgate
  Building c. 1435: Bolron, John; Cotom, John
St. Martin, Coney Street: (Couper, Robt.); (Fitzgiles, Robt.)
St. Mary's Abbey.
  Church 1270–94: Pabenham, Sim. I; (Tresk, Sim.)
  Abbot's House c.1483: Cheryholme, Rich.
St. Maurice, Monk Bar: (*Hedon, Hugh)
St. Michael-le-Belfry
  Rebuilt 1525–36: **Forman, John**; **Syekes, John**
Dominican Friary: (*Hyndeley, Wm.)
Gaol. Repairs 1377: Barneby, Step.; Dounom, Robt.
Guildhall. Building 1448–60: Barton, John I; **Couper, Robt.**; Foulford, John
Houses: (Wod, John)
  1335: Fitzgiles, Robt.
  1366–68: Craneby, John
  1449: Couper, Robt.
Merchant Adventurers' Hall 1359– : Bagby, Robt.; Colwyck, John; Craneby, John
Minster: Bell, John j.; Bell, John III; Bowde, John; Brigges, Rich.; Briggs, Thos. I; Burton, John I; Couper, John; Dowell, Wm.; Drawswerd, Thos.; Drawswerd, Wm.; Forman, John; Forster, John, C.; Hirton, Rog.; Horner, Chr.; Hyndeley, Wm.; Kitchin, Wm.; Ludham, Thos.; (Malton, Wm.); Porter, John; Whinfield, Jas.
  Norman Church c. 1080
  Choir and Crypt rebuilt 1154–81
  N. Transept c. 1225–34
  S. Transept c. 1230–41: Corbridge, Gilb.
  Chapter House c. 1260–90: (Pabenham, Sim. I)
  Nave and W. Front 1291–1345: Boudon, Hugh; Hoton, Wm.j.; Pacenham, Thos.; **Raghton, Ivo**; **Simon, M. I**; William, C. III; Worsall, Wm.
  W. window c. 1330–39: (Pacenham, Thos.); **Raghton, Ivo**
  Nave, wooden vault c. 1354–70: **Lincoln, Philip**
  Zouche Chapel 1350– : Hoton, Wm., s.
  Lady Chapel and Presbytery c. 1361–73: **Hoton, Wm. j.**; Patrington, Robt. s.
  Choir c. 1380–1405: Donnom, Robt.; Hedon, Hugh
  E. window c. 1400–05: Hedon, Hugh
  Central Tower c. 1408–23: Askham, John; **Colchester, Wm.**; Hedon, Hugh; Long, John; Waddeswyk, Wm.
  SW. Tower 1432–56: Barton, John I; Bowde, John; Cottingham, Wm.; Pak, Thos.; (Waddeswyk, Wm.)
  NW. Tower 1470–74: Bell, John; Forster, John; Spillesby, Robt.; (Waddeswyk, Wm.)
  Central Tower. Roof 1470: Dam, David; Dam, Jas.; Whinfield, Jas.
  Battlements on S. side 1475: Hyndeley, Wm.
  Tomb of Archbishop Gray 1255–60
  Shrine of St. William: (Raghton, Ivo); (Spillesby, Robt.)
St. Anthony's Hall (Bluecoat school) c. 1450: (Couper, Robt.)
St. Leonard's Hospital: Newton, John
Walls: Davyson, Robt.
  1345: Staunton, Thos.
Walmgate Bar. Repairs 1453: Couper, Robt.
York Place – see Westminster, New Palace
Yverdon, France. St. George, Jas.

Zaragoza – see Saragossa

COUNTY INDEX

This Index is in the following order:
  English Counties, alphabetically
  Welsh Counties, alphabetically
  Foreign Countries

No notice has been taken of the changes in local government boundaries made in 1965 and 1974: all English and Welsh counties are to be understood in their historical sense.

On account of the nature of the material and the period dealt with, I have neglected the modern County of London, and places now within its boundaries will be found in Middlesex, Kent, and Surrey. Otherwise, usual lexical divisions are adhered to, e.g. Bristol is included with Gloucestershire, and Lund is given to Sweden, not Denmark. The Isle of Wight appears as a separate sub-section under Hampshire.

Scotland has been considered as a foreign country purely because it is not included in the scope of the book, and the familiar old spelling Carnarvon has been adopted rather than the official Caernarvon, because experience has shown that the older spelling is almost universal in works on history and architecture. I hope that Scottish and Welsh readers (if any) will forgive these liberties.

ENGLISH COUNTIES

(Soham)
Stow
(Triplow)
(Trumpington)
(Waterbeach)
Whittlesford
(Wisbech)

CHESHIRE (Chs.), see:
Beeston
(Brereton)
Budworth, Great
Chester
Darnhall
(Eccleston)
Frodsham
Halton
Macclesfield
(Malpas)
Mobberley
(Newhall)
Northwich
Shotwick
(Snelson)
Storeton
Tabley
Tarporley
Vale Royal
(Wirral)

CORNWALL (Corn.), see:
Altarnun
Bodmin
(Callington)
(Launceston)
Lawhitton
(Lezant)
(Liskeard)
Pendennis Castle
Restormel
(St. Erth)
St. Kew
St. Mawes
Stratton

CUMBERLAND (Cumb.), see:
Border, Scottish
Bridekirk
Carlisle
Cockermouth
(Glasson)
(Holme Cultram)
Lanercost
Raughton

DERBYSHIRE (Derb.), see:
Ashbourne
(Ashover)
Barton Blount
Beauchief
(Chellaston)
(Chesterfield)
Croxden Abbey
Cubley, Great
Darley
Derby
(Elvaston)
(Ilkeston)

(Mappleton)
Melbourne
(Needham, High)
(Norton)
(Palterton)
(Repton)
(Swarkeston)
Wingfield, South
(Yeaveley)

DEVONSHIRE (Dev.), see:
Ashburton
Atherington
(Beer)
(Bideford)
(Buckland Monachorum)
Chudleigh
Chulmleigh
Clyst Gabriel
Corscombe
Dartington
Exeter
(Fremington)
(Frithelstock)
(Galmpton)
Heanton Punchardon
(Lew, North)
(Membury)
(Moretonhampstead)
Newenham
(Newton St. Cyres)
(Norton)
Ottery St. Mary
Plymouth
(Plympton)
Salcombe
(Tavistock)
Teignmouth
Totnes

DORSET (Dors.), see:
(Abbotsbury)
Afflington
Bere Regis
Bindon
(Bridport)
Corfe
(Eastington)
Gillingham
(Langton-in-Purbeck)
(Lyme)
Milton
(Poole)
(Portland)
(Purbeck, Isle of)
Sherborne
Tarrant Keynston
(Tyneham)
(Wareham)

DURHAM (Dur.), see:
Barnard Castle
Bishop Auckland
Brancepeth
Durham
Finchale
Houghton-le-Spring
(Lanchester)

ESSEX

Lumley
(Newton)
Pittington
Raby Castle
(Sherburn, South)
(Staindrop)
(Stanhope)
Stockton
(Wolviston)
Wynyard

ESSEX (Ess.), see:
(Aveley)
(Bardfield)
Barking
Berden
(Birchanger)
Bradwell-juxta-Coggeshall
Bumpstead, Steeple
(Canewdon)
Chelmsford
Chesterford, Great
(Chingford)
Coggeshall, Little
Colchester
Cressing
Dedham
Dunmow, Little
Earls Colne
(Elsenham)
(Essex, Forest of)
Felstead
(Fyfield)
Gestingthorpe
Hacton
Hadleigh
Hallingbury, Little
Halstead
Hatfield Broad Oak
Havering-atte-Bower
Hedingham, Castle
(Hedingham, Sible)
Horham
(Ilford)
(Kirby-le-Soken)
(Layer)
Layer Marney
(Maldon)
(Marks Tey)
Moulsham
(Newport)
(Ongar, High)
Pleshey
(Prittlewell)
(Rainham)
Rayleigh
(Rayne)
(Rickling)
Rochford
(Roding)
(Romford)
Roxwell
Saffron Walden
(St. Osyth)
(Saling)
Southchurch
Stambourne
(Stanstead)

Thaxted
Thundersley
Tilbury
Waltham Holy Cross
(Wennington)
Wethersfield
(Woodford)
Wimbish
(Writtle)

GLOUCESTERSHIRE (Glos.), see:
Arlingham
(Barrington)
(Berrington)
Bristol
Campden, Chipping
(Cirencester)
(Dymock)
(Fairford)
Gloucester
(Harford)
(Hatherley)
Hayles
Kempsford
Leigh
(Naunton)
(Northleach)
(Painswick)
(Spoonbed)
(Spoonley)
(Sudeley)
(Tetbury)
(Tewkesbury)
Thornbury
(Washbourne)
Westbury-on-Trym
(Westerleigh)
Winchcombe
(Wishanger)
(Yanworth)

HAMPSHIRE (Hants.), see:
(Allington)
Alresford
Andover
(Basingstoke)
Beaulieu
(Bentley)
Bramley
Calshot
(Chilcomb)
Christchurch
(Compton)
(Damerham, South)
(Eling)
Faringdon
Fremantle
(Froxfield)
Hamble
Hambledon
Hartley Wintney
Hasilworth
Highclere
Hurst
(Kingsclere)
(Marwell)
(Michelmersh)
(Northington)
(Petersfield)

Portchester
Portsmouth
Redbridge
(Romsey)
(St. Cross)
Silkstead
Southampton
Southsea
(Sparkford)
Titchfield
Vyne, The
Waltham
Warblington
Wight, Isle of:
  (Arreton)
  Barton
  Carisbrooke
  Cowes
  Newport
  Quarr
  (Shorwell)
Winchester

HEREFORDSHIRE (Heref.), see:
Dewchurch, Little
Goodrich
Hereford
Lyonshall
(Marston)
(Ross-on-Wye)

HERTFORDSHIRE (Herts.), see:
Aldenham
(Barkway)
Barnet
Berkhampstead
Biggin
Bishops Stortford
Broxbourne
(Cheshunt)
Hatfield, Bishop's
(Hemel Hempstead)
Hertford
Hitchin
Hunsdon
(Ippollitts)
Langley, King's
(Langleybury)
Letchworth
More
Newnham St. Vincent
(Rickmansworth)
St. Albans
Sandon
(Sopwell)
Stortford, Bishop's
(Tittenhanger)
Waltham Cross
(Ware)
(Watford)
(Wormley)
(Wymondley, Great)
(Wymondley, Little)

HUNTINGDONSHIRE (Hunts.), see:
Buckden
(Bury)
(Elton)

Huntingdon
Ramsey
Ripton, King's
(St. Ives)
St. Neots
(Washingley)
(Woodhurst)

KENT, see:
Adisham
(Aldington)
Ashford
(Aylesford)
Bearsted
(Beckenham)
(Boughton Monchelsea)
Boxley
Canterbury
(Charing)
Chart, Great
Chartham
Chilham
(Chislehurst)
Cobham
Cowling
(Crundale)
Cudham
Dartford
Deal
(Deptford)
Dover
Eastry
Eastwell
Eltham
Erith
(Farleigh, East)
Faversham
(Folkestone)
(Goudhurst)
Gravesend
Greenwich
Hackington
(Hartanger)
(Hartlip)
Hythe
(Knole)
(Leaveland)
Leeds
(Lewisham)
(Loose)
(Luddesdown)
Lydd
(Lynsted)
Maidstone
(Malling, East)
Malling, West
(Meopham)
Newington-next-Hythe
Otford
(Otham)
(Penshurst)
Pluckley
(Plumstead)
Queenborough
Rainham
(Reculver)
Rochester
(St. Margaret-by-Rochester)

417

LANCASHIRE

(St. Radigunds)
Saltwood
Sandgate
Sandown
Sandwich
(Seasalter)
Sheerness
Strood
(Sutton Valence)
Tenterden
(Teynham)
Tonbridge
Tremworth
Twyford Bridge
(Upchurch)
Upnor
Walmer
(Westhenhanger)
(Westerham)
(Woodchurch)
(Woolwich)
(Wye)
Yalding

LANCASHIRE (Lancs.), see:
Arkholme
(Bedford)
(Bowerham)
Burnley
Burscough
(Cadishead)
(Clitheroe)
(Cockersand Abbey)
Derby, West
(Eccles)
Hale
Kellet, Over
Lancaster
Liverpool
(Maghull)
Manchester
Oldham
Ormskirk
Pennington
Prescot
(Rochdale)
Warton

LEICESTERSHIRE (Leics.), see:
(Andreskirk)
(Bagworth)
Barkstone
Belvoir
(Blaston)
Bottesford
(Breedon-on-the-Hill)
Croxton Abbey
Kirby Muxloe
Leicester
(Ravenstone)
(Sewstern)

LINCOLNSHIRE (Lincs.), see:
Barlings
Bescaby
Bolingbroke
Bonby
Boston

(Bourne)
(Bratoft)
(Bucknall)
Bullington
Bytham, Castle
(Careby)
(Corby)
Croyland
(Fillingham)
(Gainsborough)
(Goxhill)
Grantham
Grimsby
(Harbrough)
Harrington
(Hawerby)
(Holbeach)
(Holywell)
(Honington)
Ingoldmells
(Keal, East)
Leverton
Lincoln
Louth
(Nettleton)
Newhouse
(Newton-le-Wold)
Normanby
(Orby)
(Pinchbeck)
Ropsley
Somerton Castle
Spalding
(Spilsby)
(Stainfield)
Stamford
(Stixwould)
Surfleet
Swineshead
Tattershall
Thornton
Torksey
Wainfleet
Wigtoft
Wyberton

MIDDLESEX (Middx.), see:
(Bedfont, East)
Brent Bridge
(Brentford)
Charing
(Ealing)
(Edmonton)
(Enfield)
Fulham
Hackney
Hampton
Harmondsworth
Harrow
Heston
Hounslow
(Ickenham)
Isleworth
(Kilburn)
Kempton
(Knightsbridge)
London
(Mimms, South)

(Shepperton)
Stanwell
Sutton
Syon Convent
(Tottenham)
(Twickenham)
(Uxbridge)
Westminster

NORFOLK (Norf.), see:
(Acre, Castle)
Ashwellthorpe
(Badingham)
Bawburgh
(Beckham)
(Blofield)
(Blo Norton)
(Brancaster)
(Burlingham)
(Burston)
Caister
Caister, East
(Carrow)
(Clenchwarton)
Cley
(Coltishall)
Costessey
Dereham, East
(Dereham, West)
(Diss)
(Earlham)
(Ellingham)
Elmham, North
(Emneth)
(Filby)
(Fransham, Great)
(Garboldisham)
Gaywood
Hardley
(Harleston)
Hempstead-by-Holt
Hillington
(Hindolveston)
Hockham
Langham
(Lakenham)
(Lingwood)
(Lopham, North)
Lynn, King's
Martham
(Massingham)
(Mileham)
Norton Subcourse
Norwich
Ormesby
(Plumstead)
Plumstead, Great
(Pokethorpe)
(Raynham)
Redenhall
(Repps)
(Rollesby)
St. Benet Holme
(Salle)
Scratby
(Sheringham)
(Sloley)
Stoke Holy Cross

Swaffham
(Tasburgh)
(Terrington)
Thetford
(Thorpe Abbotts)
Thurlton
Tilney All Saints
Tivetshall
Trowse
(Walsingham)
Walsingham, Little
(Waterden)
(Weeting)
Wicklewood
Wighton
Worstead
(Wroxham)
Wymondham
Yarmouth, Great

NORTHAMPTONSHIRE (N'hants.), see:
(Aynho)
(Barnack)
Billing, Little
Brington, Great
(Corby)
(Finedon)
Fotheringhay
Geddington
Grafton
Hardingstone
Harlestone
(Helpston)
Higham Ferrers
(King's Cliffe)
Lowick
(Luffield)
Morende
Northampton
(Nunton)
(Passenham)
Peterborough
Rockingham
(Rushden)
(Silverstone)
Sudborough
(Thorpe Waterville)
(Titchmarsh)
(Warmington)
(Weldon)
(Wellingborough)
Yardley Gobion

NORTHUMBERLAND (N'land), see:
Alnwick
Bamburgh
Bellingham
Berwick-upon-Tweed
Border, Scottish
Bywell St. Peter
(Corbridge)
Dunstanburgh
Ellingham
(Hawkswell)
(Hexham)
Holy Island
(Newbiggin-by-the-Sea)
(Newbrough)

419

Newcastle-upon-Tyne
Norham
(Ponteland)
Tynemouth
Wark
Warkworth

NOTTINGHAMSHIRE (Notts.), see:
(Bramcote)
Clipston
Colwick
(Lenton)
(Morton)
Newark
(Newstead)
Nottingham
(Rufford)
Scrooby
Southwell
Wollaton
(Worksop)

OXFORDSHIRE (Oxon.), see:
Adderbury
Beckley
Bicester
(Bletchingdon)
Bloxham
Broughton
(Burford)
Cowley
Deddington
Enstone
Eynsham
Finmere
Godstow
(Headington)
Hensington
Henley
Heyford
Horsepath
Kingham
Langley
Leafield
Milton, Great
Northleigh
Oseney
Oxford
Shirburn
Shutford
Southleigh
(Spelsbury)
Stanton Harcourt
Swalcliffe
(Taynton)
Thame
Waterstock
(Wendlebury)
(Weston Manor)
(Witney)
Wolvercote
Woodstock

RUTLAND (Rutl.), see:
Casterton, Little
Oakham

SHROPSHIRE (Salop), see:

(Ercall)
(Lilleshall)
Ludlow
(Oswestry)
Shrewsbury
Wenlock, Much

SOMERSET (Som.), see:
Banwell
Bath
Bishop's Hull
Bridgwater
(Brympton D'Evercy)
Cheddar
Crewkerne
Croscombe
Dunster
Glastonbury
(Keynsham)
(Montacute)
Nunney
Puriton
Shepton Mallet
(Shockerwick)
(Sparkford)
(Stogursey)
(Stowell)
Taunton
Tintinhull
Wells
(Winford)
(Witham)
Wookey
Yatton
Yeovil

STAFFORDSHIRE (Staffs.), see:
Blithfield
Burton-on-Trent
Darnford
(Kinver)
Lichfield
Repton
(Rocester)
(Seighford)
Stafford
(Tutbury)
(Uttoxeter)
Wolverhampton

SUFFOLK (Suff.), see:
(Ashfield)
(Bacton)
(Barrow)
(Barsham)
Beccles
Bergholt, East
(Blythburgh)
Bradfield
(Brandeston)
(Brandon)
(Bungay)
Bury St. Edmunds
Carlton
Cavendish
(Cherington)
Clare
(Cockfield)

(Copdock)
Denston
(Depden)
(Drinkstone)
(Dunwich)
Eye
(Fornham All Saints)
(Framsden)
Framlingham
(Gazeley)
(Halesworth)
(Hargrave)
(Hartest)
Harwich
(Haverhill)
Helmingham
Hengrave
(Hessett)
Ipswich
(Ixworth)
Kelsale
(Kersey)
Kentford
Kessingland
Lavenham
Leiston
(Long Melford)
(Lowestoft)
Mettingham
(Middleton)
(Mildenhall)
(Newmarket)
(Occold)
Orford
Orwell Haven
Rattlesden
Redgrave
(Rougham)
(Saxham, Great)
Saxham, Little
Stoke-by-Nayland
(Sudbury)
Thorington
Thornham, Little
(Tuddenham St. Mary)
(Tunstall)
Walberswick
? Walton
(Westley)
(Wickhambrook)
Wingfield
Wixoe
(Woolpit)
(Worlington)

SURREY (Surr.), see:
Addiscombe
Banstead
Battersea
(Bermondsey)
(Betchworth)
(Bisley)
(Blechingly)
Byfleet
Capel
Chertsey
(Croydon)
Ditton, Long

(Dunsfold)
Esher
Ewhurst
Farley
Farnham
(Godstone)
Guildford
Henley
(Horley)
Kennington
Kingston-upon-Thames
Lambeth
(Merstham)
Merton
(Mitcham)
Nonsuch
Oatlands
(Pirford)
(Reigate)
Richmond
Rotherhithe
Shene Palace
Southwark
(Sutton)
Waverley
Woking

SUSSEX (Sx.), see:
Arundel
Battle
Bodiam
Bolney
Bramber
Camber
Chichester
Cowdray
Etchingham
(Fittleworth)
Hamsey
(Harting)
(Hastings)
Herstmonceux
Knepp
Lewes
Midhurst
Offham
(Petworth)
Pevensey
(Rye)
Sele
Winchelsea

WARWICKSHIRE (Warw.), see:
Arbury
(Aspley)
(Attleborough)
Claverdon
Coventry
Kenilworth
Lapworth
Nuneaton
(Packwood)
(Pinley)
(Rowington)
Sheldon
(Snitterfield)
Stratford on Avon
(Tanworth-in-Arden)

WESTMORLAND

(Thelsford)
Warwick

WESTMORLAND (W'land), see:
Beetham
(Kendal)

WILTSHIRE (Wilts.), see:
Amesbury
Ashton, Steeple
Bradley, North
Britford
Broad Chalk
(Bulford)
Clarendon
Devizes
Downton
(Haslebury)
Ludgershall
Malmesbury
Marlborough
Mere
Monkton Farleigh
Old Sarum
Salisbury
Sherston
(Wadswick)
Wardour Castle

WORCESTERSHIRE (Worcs.), see:
(Birlingham)
(Blockley)
(Bredon)
(Dudley)
Elmley
Evesham
Feckenham
Grafton
Halesowen
Hanley
Hartlebury
(Ipsley)
(Malvern, Great)
Pershore
Tickenhill
Worcester

YORKSHIRE, EAST RIDING (Yorks., E.R.), see:
(Bainton)
Beverley
(Blacktoft)
Bridlington
(Broomfleet)
(Bubwith)
(Cave, South)
(Cottingham)
(Cranswick)
Flamborough
Hedon
(Huggate)
Hull
Patrington
(Rudston)
(Weighton)
(Welwick)
Wold Newton
Wressle
Yedingham

YORKSHIRE, NORTH RIDING (Yorks., N.R.). see:
(Ampleforth)
Aysgarth
(Bagby)
(Boldron)
Bolton, Castle
Bowes
(Brandsby)
Byland
Catterick
Easby
(Falsgrave)
(Gilling)
Hornby
Jervaulx
Kirklington
Leake
(Leeming)
Mount Grace
Northallerton
Over Silton
(Patrick Brompton)
(Richmond)
Scarborough
Sheriff Hutton
(Snainton)
(Thirsk)
Wensley
Whitby
(Worsall)
Yearsley

YORKSHIRE, WEST RIDING (Yorks., W.R.), see:
(Acaster Selby)
(Askham)
(Billingley)
(Bolton upon Dearne)
(Carles)
Cawood
(Cherryholme)
Cowick
Dent
(Ecclesall)
Fountains
Haywra
(Huddleston)
Kirkby Malham
Kirkstall
Knaresborough
(Laughton)
(Monk Bretton)
Nostell
Pontefract
Ripon
(Roche)
(Rotherham)
Rothwell
Sallay
Selby
(Stapleton)
Tadcaster
Wakefield
(Worsborough)
York

CHANNEL ISLANDS, see:
Alderney
Jersey

WELSH COUNTIES

ANGLESEY (Angl.), see:
Beaumaris

BRECKNOCKSHIRE (Brec.), see:
Builth

CARDIGANSHIRE (Card.), see:
Aberystwyth
Cardigan

CARMARTHENSHIRE (Carm.), see:
Carmarthen
Emlyn
Kidwelly

CARNARVONSHIRE (Carn.), see:
Bangor
Bettws-y-Coed
Carnarvon
Conway
Criccieth
Gyffin
Maenan
? Penllyn
Treflan

DENBIGHSHIRE (Denb.), see:
Denbigh
Holt
Wrexham

FLINTSHIRE (Flints.) see:
Diserth

Ewloe
Flint
Hope
(Moston-in-Englefield)
Rhuddlan
Ruthin
St. Asaph

GLAMORGAN (Glam.), see:
Caerphilly Castle
Cardiff
Laleston
Margam
Neath

MERIONETHSHIRE (Mer.), see:
Harlech

MONMOUTHSHIRE (Mon.), see:
Chepstow
(Goldcliff)
Grosmont
Skenfrith
White Castle

MONTGOMERYSHIRE (Montg.), see:

PEMBROKESHIRE (Pemb.), see:
(Pembroke)
St. Davids

RADNORSHIRE (Rad.), see:

FOREIGN COUNTRIES

BELGIUM:
(Antwerp)
Flanders

CZECHOSLOVAKIA:
Olmütz

DENMARK:
Tiköb

FRANCE:
(Aire)
(Andelys, Les)
Ardres
(Arras)
Avignon
(Blois)
Bordeaux
(Boulogne)
Bourges
(Brittany)
Caen
Calais
(Chateau-Gaillard)
(Clermont-Ferrand)
(Crecy)
(Dieppe)
Frétun

Gold, Field of Cloth of
Guisnes
Harfleur
(Havre, Le)
(Limoges)
(Lire)
Mans, Le
(Nantes)
Notre-Dame-de-l'Épine
Paris
Poitiers
(Rheims)
Rochelle, La
Rouen
(St. Georges-d'Espéranche)
Saintes
St. Omer
St. Quentin
Sens
Troyes
Yverdon

GERMANY:
(Cleves)
(Cologne)
Germany
Hamburg

423

HOLLAND

HOLLAND:
(Amsterdam)

IRELAND:
Arklow
(Belfast)
Carlingford
Carlow
(Carrickfergus)
Dublin
Kilkenny
Leixlip

ITALY:
(Brindisi)
Florence
(Pistoia)

PALESTINE:
Acre
(Jerusalem)

PORTUGAL:
Batalha

RUSSIA
Russia

SCOTLAND:
(Ayr)
Caerlaverock
Coldingham
Dumfries
(Dunbar)
Dunfermline

Edinburgh
Falkirk
Holyrood
(Kelso)
Kildrummy
(Leith)
Linlithgow
Perth
Roxburgh
Stirling

SPAIN:
Aguilar de Campóo
Burgos
Lérida
Montblanch
Morella
Pedralbes
Poblet
Santes Creus
Saragossa
Solarzal
Tarragona
Toledo

SWEDEN:
Lund

SWITZERLAND
Chillon

TURKEY:
(Constantinople)
(Trebizond)

CHRONOLOGICAL TABLE

The dates given are those of the **commencement** of works, and in some instances are only **approximate**. A certain number of small and insignificant buildings have been omitted, but the list includes everything of artistic importance from the topographical index. The letters C, E, M, indicate, as elsewhere, Carpenter, Engineer, or Mason. This table is intended as a ready guide to the masters concerned; dates should not be taken from it without reference to the Topographical index and the text.

Date	*Building*	*Architect*
1020	St. Benet Holme Abbey	Edward, M.; Thuruerd, M.
1050	Westminster Abbey, Confessor's Church	Duddason, Leofsi; Gretsyd, Godwin, M.; Teinfrith, C.
	Little Billing Church, Font	Wigbert, M.
1060		
1070	Canterbury, St. Augustine's Abbey, new Church	Blithere, M.
	Malling Castle	(Gundulf)
1077	St. Albans Abbey, Norman Church	Robert, M. I
	Rochester Cathedral, Norman Church	(Gundulf)
1079	Winchester Cathedral, Norman Church	Hugh, M. I
1081	London, Tower, White Tower	(Gundulf)
1090		
1097	Westminster Palace, Great Hall etc.	(Wimund, E.)
1100		
1110	London, St. Paul's Cathedral, Nave	Andrew, M.; Ralph, M. I
1113	Croyland Abbey, Norman Church etc.	Arnold, M.
1120	Hereford, Wye Bridge	Malverne, Alduin
	Romsey Abbey, Choir	Robert
1140		
1150	Bridekirk Church, Font	Richard carver I
1154	Ripon Minster	Arthur, M.
1157	Westminster Palace, works	Ailnoth, E.
1160	Westminster Abbey, St. Katherine's Chapel	(Ailnoth, E.)
1162	Westminster Palace, Solar	Ailnoth, E.
1165	Westminster Palace, works	Ailnoth, E.
1167	London, Tower, works	Ailnoth, E.
	Windsor Castle, works	Ailnoth, E.; Godwin, M.
1169	Westminster Palace, works	Ailnoth, E.
1170	Bowes Castle	Wolveston, Rich., E.
	Chilham Castle	Ralph, M.
	Durham Castle, Old Hall; Constable's Hall	(Wolveston, Rich., E.)
	Durham Cathedral, Galilee	Wolveston, Rich., E.
	Gloucester, St. Bartholomew's Hospital, first building and Bridge	Walred, Nich, C.
	Norham Castle, W. side of Keep	Wolveston, Rich., E.
1171	Windsor Castle, works	Ailnoth, E.
	Newcastle upon Tyne, Castle Keep	Maurice, E.
1172	Berkhampstead Castle, works	Ives, E.
	Carlisle Castle, works	Wulfric, E.
1173	London, Fleet Gaol	Ailnoth, E.
1174	London, Tower, works	Ailnoth, E.
1175	Canterbury Cathedral, Choir rebuilt	Sens, Wm., M.
	Wells Cathedral	Lock, Adam, M.; 'Wells, Mr.', M.
	Westminster Abbey, Refectory repairs	Ailnoth, E.
	Winchester Castle, Chapel	(Ralph, M.)
1176		
1177	Hereford Castle, works	Grosmont, Ralph, M.
	Woodstock Palace, works	Ailnoth, E.
1178		

1179	Canterbury Cathedral, Trinity Chapel and Corona	Englishman, Wm., M.
	Dover Castle, Keep	Maurice, E.; Ralph, M.
1180	London, Temple Church	John, M. I
1181		
1182		
1183		
1184		
1185	White Castle, works	Grosmont, Ralph, M.
1186	Rayleigh Manor, repairs	Ailnoth, E.
1187	Chichester Cathedral, Retrochoir new work	Coventry, Walt., M.
1188		
1189		
1190	Bellingham Bridge	(Sproich)
	London, Tower, works	Elias, E.
1191		
1192	Lincoln Cathedral, Choir and E. Transept	Noiers, Geoff., M.; Richard, M. I
1193		
1194		
1195	St. Albans Abbey, W. Front	Goldcliff, Hugh, M.
1196		
1197		
1198	Stow, House	Stow, Rich., I
	Westminster Palace, works	Elias, E.
1199		
1200	Rochester Cathedral, Choir	(Richard, M. II)
1201	Beaulieu Abbey, Chevet Chapels	Durandus, M.
1202	Winchester Cathedral, Retrochoir	Richard, M. III; (Stephen, M.)
1203		
1204	Colchester Castle, works	Fortin, M.
	Nottingham Castle, works	Bayard, Wm., E.
	Waverley Abbey, Church	(Waverley, John, M.)
1205		
1206		
1207		
1208	Southwark Cathedral, Choir, etc.	(Richard, M. III); (Stephen, M.)
1209		
1210		
1211		
1212		
1213		
1214	St. Albans Abbey, W. Nave etc.	(Cambridge, Matth.)
1215		
1216		
1217	Devizes Castle, works	Albemunt, Hugh, C.
1218	Leiston Abbey	Nicholas, M. I
1219		
1220	Bristol Cathedral, Elder Lady Chapel	L., carver; (Lock, Adam, M.)
	Canterbury Cathedral, Shrine of Thomas Becket	Dereham, El.
	Lichfield Cathedral, Transepts	Thomas, M. I
	Lincoln Cathedral, Chapter House	Alexander, M.III
	Salisbury Cathedral, Lady Chapel	Ely, Nich., M.
	Westminster Abbey, Lady Chapel	Dartford, Ralph, M.
1221		
1222	Winchester Castle, Hall	Stephen, M.
	Windsor Castle, King's Hall etc.	Jordan, C.; Thomas, C.
1223		
1224	Worcester Cathedral, Choir and Retrochoir	Alexander M. II
1225	Lincoln Cathedral, Nave etc.	Alexander, M. III
	Salisbury Cathedral, Presbytery	Ely, Nich., M.
1226		
1227		
1228		
1229		
1230	Wells Cathedral, W. Front	Norreys, Thos., M.; Wells, Sim.
	York Minster, S. Transept	Corbridge, Gilb., C.
1231		
1232		

1233	Westminster Palace, Queen's Chamber etc.	Alexander, C.; Waverley, John, M.
1234	Havering-atte-Bower Palace, works	(Northampton, Sim., C.)
1235	Kempton Manor, Hall	Aundely, Nich., C.
1236	Windsor Castle, King's Lodgings	Northampton, Sim., C,
1237	Britford, Anchoress's House	(Dereham, El.)
	Lincoln Cathedral, Nave etc.	Alexander, M. III
	Marlborough Castle, works	Blowe, Hugh, M.
	Salisbury Cathedral, Nave and Great Transept	Ely, Nich., M.
1238	Tarrant Keynston, Queen Joan's Tomb	(Dereham, El.)
1239	London, Tower, Traitors' Gate etc.	(Reyns, Hen., M.)
	Windsor Castle, King's Chapel	Northampton, Sim., C.; Reyns, Hen., M.
1240	Salisbury, Leadenhall	(Dereham, El.)
1241		
1242	Durham Cathedral, Chapel of Nine Altars	(Dereham, El.); Farnham, Rich., M.
1243		
1244	Bamburgh Castle, works	Gerard, C.
	York Castle, repairs	Northampton, Sim., C.; Reyns, Hen., M.
1245	Westminster Abbey, Presbytery etc.	Alexander, C.; Reyns, Hen., M.
	Windsor Castle, Barbican etc.	(Northampton, Sim., C.); Thomas, M. II
1246	Clarendon Palace, Houses	David, C.
	Hayles Abbey, first work	Reyns, Hen., M.; Waverley, John, M.
1247	London, Tower, Quay, Inner Curtain etc.	Reyns, Hen., M.
1248	Westminster Abbey, Belfry	Alexander, C.
1249		
1250	Clarendon Palace, Houses	David, C.
	Woodstock Palace, works	Gloucester, John, M.
1251	London, St. Paul's Cathedral, Choir etc.	(Canterbury, Mich., M.)
1252		
1253	Corfe Castle, Bridge	Gerard, C., E.
	Gillingham Manor, works	Mountsorrel, Wm., M.
1254	Guildford Palace, Hall repairs	Gloucester, John, M.
1255	London, St. Martin-le-Grand	(Gloucester, John, M.)
	Windsor Castle, Queen's Lodgings	Alexander, C.; Beverley, Robt., M.; Gloucester, John, M.
1256	Guildford Castle, Gateway	Alexander, C.; Gloucester, John, M.
	Lincoln Cathedral, Angel Choir	Tresk, Sim., M.
1257		
1258		
1259	Westminster Palace, works	Beverley, Robt., M.
1260	Westminster Abbey, E. Nave etc.	Beverley, Robt., M.
	York Minster, Chapter House	(Pabenham, Sim., M.I)
1261		
1262	London, Holborn Bridge	Beverley, Robt., M.
	Salisbury Cathedral, Bishop Bridport's Tomb	Richard, M. IV
1263	Salisbury Cathedral, Cloisters and Chapter House	Richard, M. IV
1264		
1265	Lichfield Cathedral, Nave	Fitzthomas, Wm., M.; Waleys, Thos., M.
1266		
1267	Silkstead Manor, Hall	Wyther, John, C.
1268		
1269		
1270	Hayles Abbey, E. Chapels	(Beverley, Robt., M.)
	Oxford, St. Mary the Virgin Church, Tower	Abingdon, Rich., M.
	York, St. Mary's Abbey, Church	Pabenham, Sim., M.I; (Tresk, Sim., M.)
1271		
1272	Rockingham Castle, works	Carlton, Miles, C.
	Westminster Abbey, Tomb of John of Windsor	Beverley, Robt., M.
1273		
1274	London, Tower, Byward and Middle Towers etc.	Beverley, Robt., M.

1275		
1276		
1277	Aberystwyth Castle	St. George, Jas., M.
	Flint Castle	Lenginour, Rich., E.; St. George, Jas., M.
	Rhuddlan Castle	Lenginour, Rich., E.; St. George, Jas., M.
1278	Burghfield Bridge	Waus, Theo., C.
	Chepstow Castle, works	Ralph, M.IV
	London, Blackfriars Church etc.	(Beverley, Robt., M.); Canterbury, Mich., M.
	Vale Royal Abbey	Hereford, Walt., M.
	Winchcombe Abbey, Cemetery Lady Chapel	Hereford, Walt., M.
1279		
1280	Bristol Castle, Bridge	Mountsorrel, Thos., M.
	Goodrich Castle, Barbican etc.	(Beverley, Robt., M.)
1281		
1282	Bangor, Menai Straits Bridge	Lenginour, Rich., E; Oxford, Hen., C.
1283	Carnarvon Town Walls and Castle, S. Walls	Hereford, Walt., M.; Lenginour, Rich., E.; St. George, Jas., M.
	Chester Abbey, Choir and Lady Chapel	(Lenginour, Rich., E.)
	Conway Castle and Town Walls	Lenginour, Rich., E.; St. George, Jas., M.
	Denbigh Castle and Town Walls	(Lenginour, Rich., E.); (St. George, Jas., M.)
1284	Chester Castle, Chapel and Apartments	Marlow, Wm., M.
	Harlech Castle	St. George, Jas., M.
1285		
1286	Cambridge Castle	John, C. V.; (Thomas, M. II)
1287		
1288	Exeter Cathedral, Presbytery, Choir etc.	Roger, M. II
1289	Harlestone, de Bray Manor House	(Bray, Hen.)
	Norwich Cathedral, Chapter House	Alexander, M. IV
	Tarporley Church, Chancel	Newhall, Rich., C.
1290	Hereford Cathedral, Nave outer walls	Hugh, M.
	London, Ely Place Chapel	Canterbury, Mich., M.
1291	Eleanor Crosses	Bataile, John; Canterbury, Mich., Dyminge, Nich., M.; Stow, Rich., M. II
	Lincoln Cathedral, Queen Eleanor's Tomb	M.; Crundale, Rich., M.; Dyminge, Nich., M.; Pabenham, Sim. M. II; Stow, Rich., M. II
	Westminster Abbey, Queen Eleanor's Tomb	Crundale, Rich., M.; Houghton, Thos., C.
	York Minster, Nave	Boudon, Hugh, M.; Simon, M. I
1292	Canterbury Cathedral, Archbishop Peckham's Tomb	Canterbury, Mich., M.
	Chester Castle, Outer Gatehouse	Marlow, Wm., M.
	Criccieth Castle	(Lenginour, Rich., E.); (St. George, Jas., M.)
	Westminster Palace, St. Stephen's Crypt	Canterbury, Mich., M.
1293	Southchurch, Chapel	Prittlewell, Rog., M.
1294	Dover Castle, Windmill	Aynho, Nich., M.; Harting, John, C.
1295	Beaumaris Castle	St. George, Jas., M.
	Carnarvon Castle, SE. Walls, Towers, Hall.	Hereford, Walt., M.; London, John, C.
1296	Gyffin, Watermill	Chester, Nich., C.; London, John, C.
	Hull Church	(Hereford, Walt., M.)
1297	Norwich Cathedral, Cloister, E. walk	Ramsey, John, M. I
	Westminster Abbey, Lancaster Tombs	(Canterbury, Mich., M.)
1298	Bristol Cathedral, Choir	Geometer, Wm.
	Westminster, York Place, works	Swaffham, Reg., C.
1299	Norwich Cathedral, N. Nave Windows	Ramsey, John, M. I
1300	Denbigh Castle, Great Gate etc.	(Hereford, Walt., M.)
	Evesham Abbey, Chapter House etc.	Evesham, Hen., M.
	Winchelsea, St. Thomas's Church	(Hereford, Walt., M.)
1301	Linlithgow Peel	St. George, Jas., M.
1302		

1303		
1304	Canterbury Cathedral, Choir Screens	(Canterbury, Thos., M.)
	Edinburgh Castle, works	Hereford, Walt., M.
1305	Bristol Castle, Great Gate	Mountsorrel, Thos., M.
	Westminster Abbey, Refectory	Robert, M. VI
1306	London, Greyfriars, Church etc.	Hereford, Walt., M.
1307	Chester, City Walls; Gate	Glasham, Robt., E.
	Knaresborough Castle, Masons' Lodge etc.	Bokton, Wm., C.
	Lincoln, Cathedral, Central Tower upper stage	Stow, Rich., M. II
	London, St. Paul's Cathedral, Lady Chapel	(Canterbury, Mich., M.); Weldon, John, M.
	Westminster Palace, works	Wytham, Rich., M.
1308	Beverley Minster, Nave	Stainefield, Oliv., M.; (Raghton, Ivo, M.);
	Canterbury, St. Augustine's Abbey, Great Gatehouse	(Canterbury, Thos., M.)
	Exeter Cathedral, Crossing, E. Nave, Screen etc.	Luve, Wm., M.
	St. Albans Abbey, Lady Chapel	Boyden, Wm.
	Winchester Cathedral, Stalls	Lyngwode, Wm., C.
1309	Oxford, Merton College, Sacristy	(Witney, Thos., M.)
1310	Byfleet Manor, Kitchen etc.	Kent, John, C.I
	Norwich Cathedral, Carnary Chapel	Ramsey, John, M. I
	Wells Cathedral, Lady Chapel	(Witney, Thos., M.)
1311		
1312	Stanwell Church, Chancel	Abingdon, Alex.
1313	Dunstanburgh Castle, Great Gatehouse etc.	Elias, M.
	Exeter Cathedral, Reredos etc.	Witney, Thos., M.
	Lapworth Manor, Gatehouse	Heose, Wm., M.
1314	Northallerton, Peel Tower	Glasham, Adam, C.
	Norwich Cathedral, Choir images	Adam, carver
	St. Albans Abbey, Choir-Stalls	Geoffrey, C.
1315	Carnarvon Castle, N. Walls and Towers, King's Gate	Ellerton, Hen., M.
	Eltham Palace, Wall	Canterbury, Mich., M.
	Nostell Priory, Choir	Pontefract, Robt.
	Wells Cathedral, Central Tower	Thomas, M. V
	Winchester Cathedral, Presbytery	Witney, Thos., M.
1316	Beaumaris Castle, outer curtain etc.	Derneford, Nich., M.
1317	Hatfield Regis Priory, Choir-Stalls etc.	Page, Thos., C.
	Worcester Cathedral, Nave, N. Arcade	Shockerwick, Wm., M.
1318	Carlisle Cathedral, East Front	(Raghton, Ivo, M.)
	Gloucester Cathedral, South Nave Aisle	(Sponbedde, Mart., M.)
	Norwich Cathedral, St. Ethelbert Gate	Ramsey, Wm., M. II
1319	Norton Subcourse Church, roofs	Gunton, John, Rog., and Wm., C.
	Westminster Palace, St. Stephen's Crypt completed	Canterbury, Walt., M.
1320	Harlestone Church	(Bray, Hen.)
	Lichfield Cathedral, Lady Chapel	Eyton, Wm., M.
	Lincoln Cathedral, S. Transept Gable and 'Bishop's Eye'	(Raghton, Ivo, M.)
	Salisbury Cathedral, Central Tower and Spire	Farleigh, Rich., M.; Robt., M. VII
	Southwell Minster, Pulpitum	(Raghton, Ivo, M.)
1321	Bristol Castle, Hall repairs	Edward, C.
	Darley Hall	Keylesteds, Wm., M.
	Ely Cathedral, Lady Chapel	(Ramsey, Wm., M. III)
	Hamsey Hall	Rengwyne, John, M.
1322	Chester Town Walls, Water Tower	Helpeston, John, M.
	Ely Cathedral, Octagon and Choir	John, M. VII; (Ramsey, Wm. M. II)
1323	Harlech Castle, Bridge	Helpeston, Robt., M.
	Nottingham Castle, Houses	Bramcote, Wm., M.
	Pontefract Castle, Great Tower	Eynsham, Hen., M.
1324	Beverley Minster, Reredos	(Raghton, Ivo, M.); Stainefield, Oliv., M.
	Norwich Cathedral, Cloister, S. walk	Ramsey, Wm., M. II
	Portchester Castle, works	Banbury, John, M.
	St. Albans Abbey, Nave S. Aisle	Wy, Hen., M.
	Westminster Abbey, Aymer de Valence's Tomb	(Canterbury, Walt., M.)
1325	Ely Cathedral, Prior Crauden's Chapel	John, M. VII
	Hadleigh Castle, Houses	Cressing, John, C.

1325	Henley Manor, Chapel	Cressing, John, C.
1326	Caerphilly Castle, Hall	Bataile, Thos., M.; Hurley, Wm.,C.
1327	Westminster Palace, St. Stephen's Chapel	Canterbury, Thos., M.; Herland, John, C.
1328	Ely Cathedral, Lantern	Hurley, Wm., C.
	Exeter Cathedral, Nave	Witney, Thos., M.
1329	Wells Cathedral, Retrochoir etc.	Joy, Wm., M.
1330	Caister, East, Church; roof	Gunton, John and Robt., C.
	Malmesbury Abbey, Nave remodelled	(Witney, Thos., M.)
	Oxford, Merton College, Chapel crossing	Thomas, M. VI
	Pershore Abbey, Tower	(Farleigh, Rich., M.)
	Selby Abbey, E. window	(Raghton, Ivo, M.)
	York Minster, W. Window	Pacenham, Thos., M.; Raghton, Ivo, M.
1331	Gloucester Cathedral, S. Transept remodelled	(Ramsey, Wm., M. III)
1332	London, St. Paul's Cathedral, Chapter House and Cloister	Ramsey, Wm., M. III
	London, Guildhall Chapel	Canterbury, Thos., M.; Hurley, Wm., C.
1333	Haywra, Chapel	Kendal, Wm. C.
	Reading Abbey, works	Farleigh, Rich., M.
1334	Bath Abbey, works	Farleigh, Rich., M.
1335	Haywra, Peel	Wynd', John, C.
	Roxburgh Castle, works	St. Albans, Robt., C., E.
	Wells Cathedral, E. Window	Joy, Wm., M.
	Winchester Cathedral, Pilgrims' Hall, roof	(Witney, Thos., M.)
	York, Houses	Fitzgiles, Robt., C.
1336	Canterbury Cathedral, St. Anselm's Chapel Window	(Canterbury, Thos., M.)
	Ely Cathedral, Choir-Stalls	(Hurley, Wm., C.)
	Stirling Castle, repairs	Kilbourn, John, M.
1337	Gloucester Cathedral, Choir remodelled	(Ramsey, Wm., M. III)
	Lichfield Cathedral, Presbytery	Ramsey, Wm., M. III
	Ottery St. Mary, Collegiate Church	(Joy, Wm., M.)
	Westminster Abbey, John of Eltham's Tomb	(Canterbury, Thos., M.)
1338		
1339	Stoke Mandeville Church, Chancel	Risseburgh, John, M.
1340	Beverley Minster, Eleanor Percy Tomb	(Malton, Wm., M.)
	Normanby, Barn	Bourne, John, C.
1341	Durham Cathedral, W. Window	Roger, M. IV
	Penshurst Place	(Hurley, Wm., C.); (Ramsey, Wm., M. III)
	Yearsley Hall, Barn	Wod, John, C.
1342		
1343		
1344	Norwich Cathedral, Cloisters, W. walk	Lilye, Sim., M.
	Windsor Castle, Round Table	Hurley, Wm., C.; Ramsey, Wm., M. III
1345	Dover Castle, works	Peyntor, Hen., M.
	Westminster Abbey, Cloister, E. walk, S. end	Bole, Walt., M.
	York, Walls	Staunton, Thos., M.
1346	Byfleet Manor, works	Wallingford, Rich., C.
1347	Berwick-on-Tweed Castle, Bridge	Patrick, M.
	Chester Bridge	Snelleston, Hen., M.
	Conway Castle, Windows etc., in Inner Ward	Snelleston, Hen., M.
1348	Sandon Church, Chancel	Rikelyng, Thos., M.
	Stafford Castle	Burcestre, John, M.
1349	Rotherhithe Manor, works	Herland, Wm., C.; Wintringham, Wm. C.
1350	Canterbury Cathedral, Archbishop Stratford's Tomb	(Box, John, M.)
	Durham Castle, Hall roof	Alverton, John, C.
	Exeter, Exe Bridge	Roche, Rog., M.
	Salisbury, St. Anne's Gate and Chapel	(Farleigh, Rich., M.)
	Windsor Castle, Chapter House etc.	Hurley, Wm., C.; Sponlee, John, M. Hoton, Wm., s., M.
	York Minster, Zouche Chapel	Acklam, Gilb., M.; Dumnow, Step., C.
1351	Frétun, Peel	Stretford, Robt., M.
	Leicester, St. Mary's Hospital	Hurley, Wm., C.; St. Andrew, Edm., C.
	Westminster Palace, St. Stephen's Chapel Stalls	

1351	Windsor Castle, Chapel roof	Waryn, Wm., C.
1352	Cambridge, Corpus Christi College, Old Court	Blaston, Robt., C.; Newnham, Adam, C.
	Cambridge, Trinity Hall, Old Court	Bury, Rich., C.
	Westminster Abbey, Cloister, S. and W. walks	Palterton, John, M.
	Windsor Castle, Canon's Lodgings etc.	Sponlee, John, M.
1353	Hampton, Barns	Waryn, Wm., C.
	Westminster Palace, works	Box, John, M.
	Windsor Castle, Cloisters	Sponlee, John, M.
1354	York Minster, Nave wooden vault	Lincoln, Phil., C.
1355		
1356		
1357	Windsor Castle, Gates etc.	Sponlee, John, M.; Wynford, Wm., M.
1358	Hadleigh Castle, works	Herland, Wm., C.; Sallynge, Rich., M. II
	London, Greyfriars, Tomb of Queen Isabella	(Ramsey, Wm., M.III)
	Windsor Castle, Royal Lodgings etc.	Sponlee, John, M.; Wynford, Wm., M.
1359	Bonby Church, Chancel	Goushill, Robt., C.; Thornton, Wm., M.
	Dewchurch, Little, Church; Belfry	Podding, John, M.
	Hereford Cathedral, Chapter House	(Cambridge, Thos., M.); (Evesham, John, M.)
	Vale Royal Abbey, E. Chapels	Helpeston, Wm., M.
	York, Merchant Adventurers' Hall	Bagby, Robt., C.
1360	Durham Castle, Keep rebuilt	(Lewyn, John, M.)
	St. Albans Abbey, Roodscreen etc.	(Yeveley, Hen., M.)
	Winchester Cathedral, W. Front	Thomas, M. VII
	Worcester Cathedral, Nave, S. Arcade etc.	Clyve, John, M.
1361	London, Tower, Bloody Tower etc.	Yeveley, Hen., M.
	Queenborough Castle	Box, John, M.; Yeveley, Hen., M.
	Rotherhithe Manor, Bridge	Herland, Wm., C.
	York Minster, Lady Chapel and Presbytery	Hoton, Wm. j., M.
1362	Norwich Cathedral, Presbytery Clerestory	(Wodehirst, Robt., M.)
	Westminster Abbey, Abbot's House etc.	(Herland, Hugh, C.); Palterton, John, M.; (Yeveley, Hen., M.)
	Windsor Castle, Inner Gate, Hall roof etc.	Herland, Wm., C.; Wintringham, Wm., C.; Wynford, Wm., M.
1363	Eltham, 'Queen's Cross'	Pode, Rich., C.
	Gravesend, Houses	Yonge, John, C.
	Rotherhithe Manor, works	Herland, Wm., C.
1364	Coldingham Priory, works	Lewyn, John, M.
	Finchale Priory, Church remodelled	Lewyn, John, M.
1365		
1366	Bridgwater Church, Spire	Waleys, Nich., M.
	Durham Cathedral, Kitchen	Lewyn, John, M.
	York, Houses	Craneby, John, C.
1367	Westminster Abbey, Queen Philippa's Tomb, Tester	(Herland, Hugh, C.); (Herland, Wm., C.)
1368	Bamburgh Castle, works	Lewyn, John, M.
	Castle Bytham Church, repairs	Normanby, Robt., M.
	Rochester Castle, works	Herland, Wm., C.; Yeveley, Hen., M.
1369		
1370	Cobham Church, College, and Schoolhouse	Pette, Robt., M.; Yeveley, Hen., M.
	Highclere Manor, works	Herland, Hugh, C.; Wynford, Wm., M.
	Huntingdon Bridge	Albon, Wm., M.; Hawardeby, John, M.
	Lincoln Cathedral, W. Towers	Geoffrey, M. II?
1371	London Charterhouse, first work	Yeveley, Hen., M.
	Oxford, Merton College, Library and Mob Quadrangle	Bath, Robt., C.; Humberville, Wm., M.
1372	Arlingham Church, Tower	Wyshongre, Nich., M.
	Chelmsford, Moulsham Bridge	Yeveley, Hen., M.

1372	Kenilworth Castle, works	Spencer, Hen., M.
1373	Boxley Abbey, Cloister	(Lomherst, Step., M.)
	Coventry, St. Michael's Church, Tower	(Skillyngton, Robt., M.)
	Gravesend, Windmill	Yonge, John, C.
	Oxford, Queen's College, Chapel	Robert, M. VIII
	Southwark, Prior's Houses	Wintringham, Wm., C.
1374	Cambridge, Trinity Hall, N. and W. Ranges	Mildenhale, John, C.
	Cambridge, School of Pythagoras, repairs	Mathie, Adam, M.; Meppushal, John, M.
	Gravesend Manor, fireplaces	Yonge, Maur., M.
	Langley, Kings, Priory; Cloister	Rede, Wm. le, M.
	London, St. Paul's Cathedral, Tomb of John of Gaunt	Yeveley, Hen., M.
1375	Abingdon Abbey, Church roof	Bodecote, Wm., C.
	Cambridge, King's Hall, Old Court	Mathie, Ad., M.
	Durham Cathedral, Neville Screen	(Yeveley, Hen., M.)
	Worcester Cathedral, W. Front etc.	Clyve, John, M.; Hugh, C.
1376	Exeter Cathedral, new Cloisters	Lesyngham, Robt., M.
	London, Savoy Palace, works	Wintringham, Wm., C.; Yeveley, Hen., M.
	London, St. Mary Eastminster, Loveyne Tomb	Lakenham, Hen.
1377	Abingdon Abbey, Gatehouse etc.	Wynford, Wm., M.
	Canterbury Cathedral, Black Prince's Tomb	(Yeveley, Hen., M.)
	Corfe Castle, works	Wynford, Wm., M.
	Shirburn Castle	Yeveley, Hen., M.
	Westminster Abbey, Nave continued	Yeveley, Hen., M.
	York Gaol, repairs	Barneby, Step., C.; Dounom, Robt., C.
1378	Bolton Castle	Lewyn, John, M.
	Canterbury, Holy Cross Church	(Yeveley, Hen., M.)
	Canterbury, Walls and Westgate	Londoneys, Wm., M.; Yeveley, Hen., M.
	Carlisle Castle, works	Lewyn, John, M.
	Raby Castle, Kitchen etc.	(Lewyn, John, M.)
	Roxburgh Castle, works	Lewyn, John, M.
	Westminster Abbey, Edward III's Tomb	(Herland, Hugh, C.); (Yeveley, Hen., M.)
1379	Battersea Church, E. Window	Yeveley, Hen., M.
	Canterbury Cathedral, Nave and S. Transept	Yeveley, Hen., M.
	Southampton, Gates and Towers	Wynford, Wm., M.
1380	Arundel Church and College	(Herland, Hugh, C.); (Wynford, Wm., M.); (Yeveley, Hen., M.)
	Carisbrooke Castle, Gatehouse heightened	Herland, Hugh, C.; Wynford, Wm., M.; Yeveley, Hen., M.
	Cowling Castle	Yeveley, Hen., M.
	Dunstanburgh Castle, Mantlet etc.	Lewyn, John, M.
	Durham Cathedral, Neville Screen	(Lewyn, John, M.)
	Hertford Castle, Houses and Chapel	Wintringham, Wm., C.
	Oxford, New College	Herland, Hugh, C.; Wynford, Wm., M.
	Ropsley Church	Bate, Thos., M.
	Selby Abbey, Sedilia	(Yeveley, Hen., M.)
	Yeovil Church	(Wynford, Wm., M.)
	York Minster, Choir	(Hedon, Hugh, M.)
1381	London, St. Dunstan's in the E., S. Aisle etc.	Yeveley, Hen., M.
	Meopham Church, works	(Yeveley, Hen., M.)
	Moulsham by Chelmsford, Manor; Hall	Mulsham, John, C.
	Redbridge Bridge, repairs	Newman, John, M.
	St. Davids Cathedral, St. Mary's College	Fawley,——., M.
	Warwick, St. Mary's Church, Chancel	Sutton, John; (Skillyngton, Robt., M.)
1382	Durham Cathedral, Bishop Hatfield's Tomb	(Lewyn, John, M.)
	Elmham, North, Church; Chancel roof	Michael, C.II.
	Lichfield Cathedral, Choir, works	Driffield, Wm., M.
	Sheriff Hutton Castle	(Lewyn, John, M.)
1383	Cockermouth Castle, works	Barton, Rog., M.
	London Bridge, Chapel	Yeveley, Hen., M.
	London, St. Thomas of Acon Hospital, repairs	Walton, Walt., M.
1383	Rochester Bridge	Yeveley, Hen., M.

1384	London, St. Paul's Cathedral, S. Front	Yeveley, Hen., M.
	Oxford, Canterbury College	Brown, Wm., M.
1385	Bodiam Castle	(Yeveley, Hen., M.)
	London, St. Martin-le-Grand, works	Yeveley, Hen., M.
	Norwich Cathedral, Cloisters, N. walk	Wodehirst, Robt., M.
	Rochester Cathedral, Conventual Buildings, works	Doune, Geoff., M.
	Saltwood Castle, Gatehouse etc.	(Yeveley, Hen., M.)
	Shepton Mallet Church, Tower	(Wynford, Wm., M.)
	Southampton Castle, works	Colchester, Wm., M.; Kympton, Hugh, M.
	Southwark Cathedral, works	Yeveley, Hen., M.
	Tabley Old Hall	(Newhall, Wm., C.)
	Wells Cathedral, SW. Tower	Wynford, Wm., M.
	Worcester Cathedral, N. Porch, Chapter House, Cloisters N. walk	Clyve, John, M.
1386	Cambridge, King's Hall, Kitchen etc.	Hoore, Step., C.; Payn, John, C.
1387	Cambridge, King's Hall, Hall	Maidston, John, C.; Sharp, John, M.
	Winchester College	Herland, Hugh, C.; Wynford, Wm., M.
1388	Salisbury Cathedral, inverted arches in E. Transept	Portland, Nich., M.
1389	Bradwell-juxta-Coggeshall Church, Window	Aylmer, Thos., M.
	Kenilworth Castle, Lancaster Buildings	Skillyngton, Robt., M.; (Wintringham, Wm., C.)
1390	Beverley Minster, W. Front	(Rolleston, Wm., M.)
	Canterbury Castle, repairs	Herland, Hugh, C.; Yeveley, Hen., M.
	Dartington Hall, Hall roof	(Herland, Hugh, C.)
	Durham Cathedral, Cloisters	Lewyn, John, M.
	Exeter Cathedral, E. Window	Lesyngham, Robt., M.
	Gloucester Castle, Towers etc.	Clavyll, John, M.
	Lambeth Palace, Guardroom roof	(Herland, Hugh, C.)
	Lyonshall Castle, Hall	Broun, John, M.
	Oxford, New College, Cloisters and Tower	Brown, Wm., M.; Wyse, Wm., C.
1391	Bermondsey Abbey, S. Aisle	Londoneys, Wm., M.
	Chichester Cathedral, Spire	(Mason, John, M. I)
	Ipstone Church, Chancel roof	Bath, Robt., C.
	St. Asaph Cathedral, Tower	Fagan, Robt., M.
	Thornton Abbey, Nave vault	Wright, Wm., C.I
	Westminster Abbey, Cardinal Langham's Tomb	Lote, Step., M.; Yeveley, Hen., M.
	Winchester Castle, repairs	Herland, Hugh, C.; Wynford, Wm., M.; Yeveley, Hen., M.
1392	Costessey Church, repairs	Elyngham, Robt., M.; Huy, Thos., C.
	Croyland Abbey, Tower, recasing etc.	Croyland, Wm., M.
	Ely Cathedral, Octagon of W. Tower	Wodehirst, Robt., M.
	Houghton Conquest Church, Tower	Farele, Wm., M.; Lessy, Phil., M.
	London, Savoy Palace, works	Lote, Step., M.
	Lumley Castle	(Lewyn, John, M.)
	Wardour Castle	(Wynford, Wm., M.)
	Warwick Castle, Great Gatehouse; Guy's Tower	Montfort, John, M.; 'Warwick, Mr.', M.
1393	Worcester, Edgar Tower, upper story	'Warwick, Mr.', M.
1394	Norwich, St. Gregory's Church, rebuilding	(Wodehirst, Robt., M.)
	Westminster Abbey, Richard II's Tomb	(Herland, Hugh, C.); Lote, Step. M.; Yeveley, Hen., M.
	Westminster Palace, Hall remodelled	Herland, Hugh, C.; Yeveley, Hen., M.
	Winchester Cathedral, Nave	Wynford, Wm., M.
1395	Maidstone, Church and College, Gatehouse etc.	(Yeveley, Hen., M.)
1396	Ely Cathedral, Great Gatehouse	Meppushal, John, M.
	Portchester Castle, repairs	Walton, Walt., M.; Yeveley, Hen., M.
	Rochester Cathedral, Conventual Buildings, works	Doune, Geoff., M.
	Rochester, Walls and Gate	(Westcote, John, M.)
	St. Omer Cathedral, S. Portal	Bateman, Colmet
	Winchester, St. John's Hospital, rebuilding	Portland, Nich., M.
1397	Canterbury Cathedral, Cloisters	(Lote, Step., M.); Yeveley, Hen., M.

1397	Henley Church, rebuilt	Wolvey, Thos., M.
	London, Rutland House	Lote, Step., M.
	Westminster Palace, Great Gateway	(Yeveley, Hen., M.)
1398	Ashwellthorpe Church, roofs	Faudy, John, C.
	Blithfield, House	Stanlowe, Robt., C.
	Brancepeth Castle	(Lewyn, John, M.)
	Durham Cathedral, Dormitory	Dryng, Pet., M.; (Middleton, John, M.)
	Great Yarmouth, Harbour	Herland, Hugh, C.
	Heston Church, Chancel roof	Wyse, Wm., C.
	Isleworth Church, Chancel roof	Wyse, Wm., C.
	Norwich, Cow Tower etc.	Snape, Robt., M.
	Oxford, Queen's College, Hall	Brown, Wm., M.; Wynford, Wm., M.
	Roxwell Chapel, Chancel	Clonyer, John, C.; Richard, M. V
	Selby Abbey, Cloisters, works	Rothing, John, C.,; Suthwell, Wm., M.
1399	Ipswich, Sessions House	Tarell, John, C.
	Ripon Minster, Roodloft	Wright, Wm., C.I
1400	Canterbury Cathedral, Chapter House remodelled	(Lote, Step., M.); (Wolward, John, C.)
	Cheddar Church, Tower	(Wynford, Wm., M.)
	Chichester Cathedral, Pulpitum, Cloisters, Campanile	Walton, Walt., M.
	Hampton Church, Chancel	Wyse, Wm., C.
	Kingston upon Thames, Bridge repairs	Herland, Hugh, C.
	Tutbury Castle, works	Skillyngton, Robt., M.
	Winchester Cathedral, Wykeham's Tomb etc.	Wynford, Wm., M.
	York Minster, E. Window	Hedon, Hugh, M.
1401		
1402	Durham Cathedral, Bishop Skirlaw's Tomb	Dryng, Pet., M.; Hyndeley, Thos., M.
1403	Chichester, Vicars' Close	Mason, John, M. I
	St. Albans, Clock Tower	(Wolvey, Thos., M.)
1404	Worcester Cathedral, Cloisters, N. and S. walks	(Aleyn, Wm., M.)
1405		
1406	Erith Church, Tower	Wells, John, M.
	Liverpool Castle, Tower of Sir John Stanley	John, M.VIIA.
	Oxford, Durham (now Trinity) College Chapel	Appelby, Wm., M.
1407	Norwich Guildhall	Marwe, John, M.
	York Minster, Central Tower	Colchester, Wm., M.
1408	Adderbury Church, Chancel	Winchcombe, Rich., M.
	Norham Castle, W. Gate	Spilbery, Wm., M.
1409	Beverley, North Bar	Rolleston, Wm., M.
1410	Canterbury Cathedral, Pulpitum	Lote, Step., M.
	Hornby Church, S. Aisle	Newton, Rich., M.
	Mettingham College, Chapel	Mason, John, II
	Stratford on Avon Church, Clopton Chapel	Kyrton, John, M.
1411	Cambridge, King's Hall, Bakehouse and Library	Dodington,——., M.; Reyner, Wm., C.
	London Guildhall	Croxton, John, M.
	York Castle, Bridge	Bolron, John, C.
1412	Catterick Church, Chancel, Nave, and Aisles	Cracall, Rich., M.
	Hereford Cathedral, Cloister	Denyar, Thos., M.
	London, St. John's Walbrook, repairs	Walton, Walt., M.
1413	Exeter Cathedral, Chapter House	Tynlegh, John, M.
	Halstead Church, Chancel roof	Taverner, John, C.
	Mettingham College, Stalls	Buk, Rich., C.
	Sheen Palace, 'Byfleet' building	Warlowe, Edm., C.
1414	Canterbury Cathedral, Henry IV's Tomb	(Lote, Step., M.); (Toutmond, Wm., C.)
1415	Bridgwater Church, St. Anne's Chapel	Mason, Phil., M.
	Fotheringhay Church, Chancel	(Lote, Step., M.)
	Hartley Wintney Priory, Church roof	Austyn, Wm., C.; Willam, John, C.
	Salisbury Cathedral, arches in Transept	Wayte, Robt., M.
1416	Arundel, Tomb of Earl of Arundel	(Prentys, Thos.)
	Fotheringhay, Tomb of Duke of York	Lote, Step., M.

1416	King's Lynn, S. Gate	Hertanger, Robt., M.
	Norwich Cathedral, Cloisters, W. and N. Vaults, Erpingham Gate	Woderofe, Jas., M.
1417		
1418	Durham Cathedral, Infirmary	Bell, John s., M.
	Surfleet Church, Chancel	Denys, Rog., M.
	Warwick Castle, Stable	Grove, Sim., C.
1419	Lowick Church, Tomb	Prentys, Thos.; Sutton, Robt.
	Roxburgh Castle, repairs	Fekenham, John, M.
	Wyberton Church, rebuilt	Denys, Rog., M.
1420	Enstone Church, Reredos	(Winchcombe, Rich., M.)
	Newnham St. Vincent Church, works	(Wolvey, Thos., M.)
	St. Albans Cathedral, W. Nave window	(Wolvey, Thos., M.)
1421	Bisham Priory, Tomb	Brown, Robt.
	Catterick Bridge	Ampilforde, Thos., M.; Garrett, John, M.; Maunsell, Robt., M.
	King's Lynn, Guildhall	Rollesby, Nich., C.; Turnour, John, M.
1422	Norham Castle, New Tower	Fekenham, Robt., M.
	Westminster Abbey, Henry V's Chantry	Thirsk, John, M.
1423	Canterbury Cathedral, SW. Tower	Mapilton, Thos., M.
	Higham Ferrers, College and Bedehouse	Mapilton, Thos., M.
	Norwich, St. Saviour's Church	Biltham, Ralph, C.; Wyspenade, John, M.
	Rochester, Crown Inn	Tanner, John, C.
1424	Bury St. Edmunds, St. Mary's Church, Nave	Layer, Wm., M.
	Downton Church, Chancel roof	Kyppyng, Wm., C.
	Oakham Church, Tower vault	Nunton, Thos., M.
	Wells Cathedral, Bubwith's Chapel	Gabriell, Den., M.
1425	Exeter Cathedral, Chapter House, upper part	Wolston, John, M.
	London, Merchant Taylor's Hall, Kitchen	Goldyng, John, C.; Mapleton, Goldyng, C.
	Scarborough Castle, Constable Tower	Hyndeley, Thos., M.
1426	Norwich Cathedral, W. Front etc.	Woderofe, Jas., M.
	Walberswick Church, Tower	Powle, Adam, M.; Russell, Rich., I., M.
1427	Cambridge, King's Hall, King Edward's Gate	Coket, John., M.; Douse, John, C.
	Harmondsworth, Barn	Kyppyng, Wm., C.
	Hedon, St. Augustine's Church, Tower	Playser, Robt., M.
	London, St. Mary-at-Hill, Roodloft etc.	Serle, Wm., C.
	Stratford on Avon, Grammar School	Hasill, John, C.
1428	Durham Cathedral, Prior's Lodging	Bell, John s., M.
	Glastonbury, St. John's Church, Porch	Gryme, John, M.
	Grafton Manor, Barn	Swift, Rich. C.II
	Hale Church, Leyot Tomb	John, M.VIIA.
	Southampton, Walls	Bartelot, John, M.
1429	London, St. Stephen's Walbrook	Mapilton, Thos., M.
1430	Bloxham Church, Milcombe Chapel	(Winchcombe, Rich., M.)
	Deddington Church, works	(Winchcombe, Rich., M.)
	Durham Cathedral, Central Tower repairs	Bell, John s., M.
	Louth Church	(Porter, John, M.)
	Oxford, Divinity Schools	Winchcombe, Rich., M.
	Rochford Manor, Chapel	Brikeman, Matt.; Norffolk, Wm., C.
	Sherborne Abbey, Choir	(Pope, Rich., M.)
	Wingfield Church, alterations	Hawes, M.
1431	Cambridge, Peterhouse, W. Range and Library	(Ely, Reg., M.); Wassyngle, John, M.
	Liverpool Castle, Tower	Cowper, Nich., M.
1432	Caister Castle	Gravour, Wm.
	Norwich, Conisford Quay	Marwe, John, M.
	Selby Abbey, North Aisle works	Couper, Robt., M.
	York Minster, SW. Tower	Pak, Thos., M.; (Waddeswyk, Wm., M.)
1433	Chester, St. Mary-on-the-Hill, S. Chancel Chapel	Asser, John j., M.
	Exeter Cathedral, Chapel Screens	Gabriell, Denis
	Tattershall Castle	(Dutchman, Baldwin)
1434	Fotheringhay Church, Nave and Tower	Horewode, Wm., M.; Russell, Rich.,

1434	Lambeth Palace, Lollards Tower, etc.	(Mapilton, Thos., M.); Thirsk, John, M.
	Ormesby, Barn	Berry, Wm., C.
	Tivetshall Windmill	Hore, John, C.
1435	Clipston Palace, repairs	Butler, John, M.
	Woodstock Palace, repairs	Lewes, John, M.
	Worcester Cathedral, Cloisters, W. walk	Chapman, John, M.
	York, St. John Hundgate	Bolron, John, C.; Cotom, John, M.
1436	Bury St. Edmunds Abbey, W. Tower	(Mapilton, Thos., M.); (Wode, John, M.)
	Kessingland Church, Tower	Russell, Rich., M.
1437	Canterbury, 'The Sun'	Goneld, John, C.
	Oxford, St. Bernard's College.	(Mapilton, Thos., M.)
1438	Canterbury Guildhall	Wodeman, Rich., C.
	Durham Cathedral, inserted Windows	Bell, John s., M.
	Oxford, All Souls College	Branche, John, C.; Chevynton, Rich., M.
1439	Bury St. Edmunds, St. John-at-Hill, Chapel roof	Heywod, John, C.
	Glastonbury, St. John's Church, Roodloft	Hulle, Robt., M.
	Northleigh Church, Wilcote Chapel	(Winchcombe, Rich., M.)
	Oxford, Divinity Schools, second work	Elkin, Thos., M.
	Shutford Chapel, roof	Wiltshire, John, C.
	Windsor Castle, Great Stair to Donjon	Cantelou, John, M.
1440	Sherborne, St. John's Hospital	Hulle, Robt., M.; Jenyn, John, C.
	Wighton Church, Chancel	Bishop, Wm., C.; Woderofe, Jas., M.
	Wingfield, South, Manor	Cobyn, Thos., M.; Cokker, Rich., C.; North, Rich., M.
1441	Eton College, Hall, N. and E. Ranges	Westerley, Robt., M.; Whetely, Robt., C.
	Fulham Church, Tower	Garald, Rich., M.
	Herstmonceux Castle	(Vesey, Wm.)
	Thurlton Church, Chancel works	Durrant, John, C.; Marwe, John, M.
	Warwick, St. Mary's, Beauchamp Chapel	(Essex, John); (Kerver, Thos.); Massingham, John, III
	Winchester, Wolvesey Palace, Great Hall roof	Lewys, John, M.
1442	Bergholt, East, Church; N. Aisle	Peperton, R., M.
	Bodmin, Greyfriars, Chapell	Ford, Wm.
	Dunster Priory, Church Tower	Pope, Rich., M.
	London, Charterhouse, Water supply	Boston, John, M.
	Lydd Church, Tower	Stanley, Thos., M.
	Thame Church, N. Transept	Beckley, John, M.; East, John, C.; (Winchcombe, Rich., M.)
	Tutbury Castle, S. Tower	Westerley, Robt., M.
1443	Alnwick, Walls and Bondgate Tower	(Matthew, M.)
	Battle Abbey, Parlour in Almonry	Arche, Wm., C.
	Cambridge, King's College Chapel	Ely, Reg., M.; Sturgeon, Thos., C.
	South Wingfield, Manor	Kyng, Rich., M.
1444	Norwich Cathedral, Cloister, Lavatory	Jakes, John, M.; Woderofe, Jas., M.
	Syon Convent, works	Hardy, John, M.
1445	Stamford Nunnery, Dormitory roof	Boydell, Wm., C.
	Wymondham Abbey, W. Tower	(Woderofe, Jas., M.)
1446	Bradley, North, Church; N. Chapel	Gabriell, Den., M.
	London, St. Martin-le-Grand, works	(Croxton, John, M.)
	Sandwich, St. Mary's Church, Steeple	(Beke, Robt., M.); Robert, C.
	Yatton Church, Roodloft	Crosse, John, C.
1447	Norwich Great Hospital, Cloister	Bucham, Robt., M.
	Westbury-on-Trym College	(Roche, John, M.)
	Yatton Church, Seats	Balwe, John, C.; Hikke, John, C.
1448	Cambridge, Queens' College, First Court	Ely, Reg., M.; Sturgeon, Thos., C.
	Canterbury Cathedral, N. Transept and Lady Chapel	Beke, Rich., M.
	Eton College Chapel	Westerley, Robt., M.; Whetely, Robt., C.
	Huntingdon, Hart Inn	Ely, Reg., M.; Sturgeon, Thos., C.
	Oxford, Merton College, Chapel, Tower	Janyns, Robt. s., M.
	York Guildhall	Couper, Robt., M.; (Foulford, John, C.)
1449	Durham, St. Mary Magdalene's Hospital Chapel	Mason, And., M.; Taillour, Robt., M.
	York, House	Couper, Robt., M.

436

1450	Cambridge, Peterhouse, Kitchen etc.	Ely, Reg., M.; Harward, Wm., C.; (Loose, John, M.)
	Gloucester Cathedral, Tower	(Gower, John, M.)
	Halton Castle, Gatehouse	Heley, John, M.
	Swalcliffe Church, Choir	Wiltshire, John, C.
	Warwick, St. Mary's, Beauchamp Chapel, woodwork	Bird, Rich., C.
	York, All Saints North Street, Choir roofs	(Foulford, John, C.)
	York, St. Anthony's Hall	(Couper, Robt., M.)
1451		
1452	Cambridge, St. Benet's Church, Nave roof	Tofts, Nich., C.
	Cambridge, King's Hall, works	Ely, Reg., M.
	Tintinhull Church, Roodloft	Dayfote, Thos., C.
	Totnes Church, Tower	Growdon, Rog., M.
1453	Ludlow Church, Tower	Hobbs, John, M.; Mason, Clement, M.
	Norwich, St. Gregory's Church, repairs	Everard, Robt., M.
	York, Walmgate Bar, repairs	Couper, Robt., M.
1454	Burwell Church	(Ely, Reg., M.)
	Lydd Church, roof	Swan, John, C.
	Repps Church, E. window	Everard, Robt., M.
1455	Chipping Campden Church, Tower and Nave	Gower, John
1456	Cambridge, Dominican Friary, works	Clerk, Sim., M.; Loose, John, M.
	Hardley Church, Chancel works	Everard, Robt., M.
	Martham Church, Chancel	Everard, Robt., M.
1457	Cambridge, Corpus Christi College, Bakehouse etc.	Loose, John, M.; Nottingham, John, M.
	Gloucester Cathedral, Lady Chapel	(Hobbs, John, M.)
	Tutbury Castle, N. Tower	(Westerley, Robt., M.)
1458	Tattershall College	Alsbroke, Hen., C.; Lyndon, Pet., M.
1459	Bradfield, Barn	Auncell, Den., C.
	Nuneaton Priory, Stalls	Karver, Thos., C.
	Oxford, St. Mary the Virgin, Choir	Chambyr,——, M.
1460	Bristol, All Saints Library	Kerver, Geoff., C.; Roche, John, M.
	Cambridge, Peterhouse, Stone Parlour	(Bacon, John, C.)
	Newark Church, Nave and Aisle roofs	(Leycett, John, C.)
	Tenterden Church, Tower	(Stanley, Thos., M.)
1461	Sheldon Church, Steeple	Dowland, Thos., M.
1462	Plumstead, Great, Chapel of St. Eustachius	Brankastre, John, M.
1463	Dereham, East, Church; Steeple work	Gyles, Wm., M.
	Hertford Castle, Gatehouse	Langley, Reg., M.
	Holt Castle, works	'Chester, Master of the Abbot of', M.
	Tilney All Saints Church, Nave roof	(Arnold, Edm., C.)
1464	Cambridge, King's Hall, Chapel	Wolrich, John, M.
	Clyst Gabriel Church, Porch	Coryngdon, John, M.
	Norwich Cathedral, Spire and Nave vault	Everard, Robt., M.
1465	Durham Cathedral, Central Tower, lower stage	Barton, Thos., M.
	Glastonbury, St. John's Church, works	Smyth, Wm., M.
	Stratford on Avon Church, Chancel	(Dowland, Thos., M.)
1466	Cambridge, Schools, S. Room etc.	Bacon, Wm., C.; Ely, Reg., M.; Glanforthe, John, M.; Harward, Wm., C.
	Dereham, East, Church; Aisles work	Narburgh, John, M.; Bishop, Wm., C
1467	Midhurst Watermill	Wykford, Nich., C.
1468	Dereham, East, Church; Font	Pyche, Wm., M.
	Hartlebury Castle, Parlour	Carpenter, Rich. C.
	Pont-y-pair Bridge	Howel, M.
	Sandwich, Walls	Hunte, Robt., M.
1469	Bodmin Church	Richowe, Rich., M.; Sam, John, C.
	Eton College Chapel, W. Window	(Clerk, Sim., M.)
1470	Farnham Castle, 'Fox's Tower'	Cole, John
	Kempsford Church, Tower	(Orchard, Wm., M.)
	Southleigh Church	(Orchard, Wm., M.)
	Stanton Harcourt, Harcourt Aisle etc.	(Orchard, Wm., M.)
	Wells, St. Cuthbert's Church, S. Transept, Reredos	Stowell, John, M.

1470	York Minster, NW. Tower	(Spillesby, Robt., M.); (Waddeswyk, Wm., M)
1471	Cavendish Church, S. Aisle	(Ely, Reg., M.)
	Hempstead-by-Holt Church, Chancel	Heydon, John, M.
1472	Bristol, House	Morgan, Step., C.
	Norwich Cathedral, Presbytery vault etc.	Everard, Robt., M.
1473	High Wycombe Church, Chancel repairs	(Sherborne, Robt., M.)
	Tickenhill Manor, works	Kerver, Laur., C.; Rogers, John, M.I
	Wells Deanery	Smyth, Wm., M.
1474	Oxford, Magdalen College	Bowden, John, C.; Orchard, Wm., M.
	Great Milton Manor	Sewy, John, M.; Welch, Rich., C.
	Windsor Castle, St. George's Chapel	Janyns, Hen., M.; Leget, Robt., M.
1475	Crewkerne Church, Nave	(Smyth, Wm., M.)
	Eltham Palace Hall	Graveley, Edm., C.; Jurdan, Thos., M.
	Eton College, Chapel Roodloft	Nicholl, Walt., C.
	Havering-atte-Bower, Queen's Work	Brasier, Hugh, M.
	St. Asaph Cathedral, Stalls	(Frankelyn, Wm., C.)
	Sherborne Abbey, Nave	Smyth, Wm., M.
	Wells Cathedral, Crossing vault etc.	Smyth, Wm., M.
	Worcester, Blackfriars, Powick Chantry	Hobbs, John, M.
	York Minster, battlements on S. side	Hyndeley, Wm., M.
1476	Bristol, St. Ewen's Church, Seats	Carpenter, Step., C.
	Broxbourne Church, E. end of S. Aisle	Stowell, Robt., M.
	Cambridge, King's College Chapel, second work	Clerk, Sim., M.; Prentice, Mart., C.
	Eton College, Ante-Chapel	Orchard, Wm., M.
	Oldham Church, rebuilding	Hamond, Wm., M.
1477	Bramber Bridge	Cowper, John, M.
	Broad Chalk, Barn	Brook, Geoff., C.
	Tingewick, Watermill	Myntham, Rich., C.
	Wells Cathedral, Cloister Lady Chapel	Smyth, Wm., M.
	Windsor Castle, St. George's Chapel, Edward IV Tomb	(Janyns, Hen., M.)
1478	Clare Church, Roodloft	Gooch, Thos.
	Dereham, East, Church; works	Munford, Robt.; Wright, John, M.I
1479	Nottingham, Houses	Hydes, Pers, C.
1480	Cambridge, St. John Baptist Church	Burdon, Wm. II, M.
	Canterbury Cathedral, Bourchier Tomb	(Janyns, Hen., M.)
	Esher Palace, Waynflete's Tower	(Alsbroke, Hen., C.); (Cowper, John, M.)
	Hythe Church, Steeple	Hamme, John, C.
	Kirby Muxloe Castle	Cowper, John, M.
	Northallerton Church, Chancel buttress	Hilder, Chr., M.
	Oxford Cathedral, Choir vault	(Orchard, Wm., M.)
	Oxford, Divinity Schools, vault	Orchard, Wm., M.
	Steeple Ashton Church	Lovell, Thos., M.
1481	Caldecote Church, Tower	(Swynnow, Andr., M.)
	Coton Church, Tower	Swynnow, Andr., M.
	Milton Abbey, Crossing vault	(Smyth, Wm., M.)
	Plymouth, St. Andrew's Church, Aisles	Andrewe, John, M.; Daw, John, M.
	Stoke-by-Nayland, Tendring Hall	Bunting, Wm., C.; Cutting, John, M.
1482	Bishop's Stortford Church, repairs	Mason, Wm., M.
	Tattershall Church, Tower	Alsbroke, Hen., C.; Cowper, John, M.
	Windsor, St. George's Chapel, Stalls	Squyer, John, C.
	Wolvercote Church, Chancel	Bell, Wm., M.
1483	Durham Cathedral, Central Tower, upper stage	Bell, John j., M.
	King's Lynn, Red Mount Chapel	Curraunt, Robt.
	Oxford, St. Bernard's College, Gateway etc.	(Bell, Wm., M.)
	York, St. Mary's Abbey, Abbot's House	Cheryholme, Rich.
1484	Kirklington Manor House	Wright, John, C.
	Norwich Cathedral, Hostry, new building	Antell, John, M.; Couper, And., C.; Everard, Robt., M.
	Wainfleet School	Alsbroke, Hen., C.; (Cowper, John, M.)

Year	Work	Name
1484	Worstead Church, Chancel	Antell, John, M.; Couper, Andr., C.
1485	Newark Bridge, rebuilt	Downes, Edw., C.
	Oxford, Magdalen College, President's Lodgings	Orchard, Wm., M.
	Little Thornham Church, Tower	Cutting, Rich., M.; Tilley, John, M.
	Rattlesden Church, S. Porch	Wastell, John, M.
1486	Canterbury Cathedral, Morton Tomb	Wastell, John, M.
	Ely Cathedral, Bishop Alcock's Chapel	Lord, Adam, M.
	Lavenham Church	(Clerk, Sim., M.); (Wastell. John, M.)
	Nottingham Bridge, repairs	Rodes, Wm., C.
	Oxford, Merton College, Roodloft	Fisher, John
	Tattershall College	Alsbroke, Hen., C.
1487	Ashburton, Church House	Gray, Wm., M.
	Ellingham Church, Chancel	Mayson, Wm., M.
	Helmingham Church, Tower	Aldrych, Thos., M.
	Wigtoft Church, repairs	Whelpdale, Thos., M.
1488	Earls Colne Priory, Tomb of 13th Earl of Oxford	Lorymere, Hen.
	Westminster, St. Margaret's, S. Aisle	Stowell, Robt., M.
1489	Leicester, St. Martin's Church, Seats	Nicoll, John, C.
	Puriton Church, works	Drue, John
	Ripon Minster, Stalls	(Brownfleet, Wm., C.)
	Stoke Holy Cross Church, Chancel works	Elward, Rich., M.; Sendele, John, C.
1490	Bishop Auckland, Bishop's Palace, Chamber	Robson, John, C.
	Cambridge, King's Hall, Great Gate, lower story	(Wastell, John, M.)
	Dedham Church, Tower	(Wastell, John, M.)
	Lambeth Palace, Morton's Tower	(Wastell, John, M.)
	Lichfield, St. Mary's Chapel, Roodloft	(Rydge, Rich., I)
	Oxford, Magdalen College, Great Tower	Orchard, Wm., M.
1491	Bodmin Church, Seats, Pulpit, Screen	More, Mathy, C.
	Cambridge, St. Mary the Great, Nave and Tower	Bell, John, III, M.; Clerk, Sim., M.; Wastell, John, M.
	Chesterford House	Bury, John, M.; Newman, Alwyn, C.
	Oxford, All Souls College, Cloister	Bell, Wm., M.
1492	Dereham, East, Church; Steeple work	Herman, Nich., M.
1493	Canterbury Cathedral Tower etc.	Wastell, John, M.
	Syon Convent, Altar Table	Brown, John, carver; Fill, Robt.
1494	Oxford, Balliol College, Gatehouse	Bell, Wm., M.
1495	Isleham Church, Nave	(Wastell, John, M.)
	Plymouth, Guildhall	Andrewe, John, M.
	Stratford on Avon, Guild Chapel, and Church, Nave	Dowland, Thos., M.
	Woodstock Palace, rebuilt	Brian, John, C.; East, Wm., M.
1496	London, Pewterers' Hall	Birlyngham, Sim., C.
	Norwich, Church of St. George Colegate, Chancel works	Wrygth, Wm., C.
	Peterborough Abbey, new building	Wastell, John, M.
1497	Westminster, St. Margaret's Church, N. Aisle etc.	Stowell, Robt., M.
	Westminster Palace, works	Martyn, Walt., M.; Mauncy, Thos., C.
1498	Leverton Church, Steeple	Mason, Thos., M.
	Newark Church, Reredos	Drawswerd, Thos.
	Northwich Church, Tower	Hunter, Thos., M.
	Windsor Castle, Henry VII's Tower	Janyns, Robt. j., M.; Nymes, Rich., M.
1499	Bristol, St. James's Church, Roodloft	Rydge, Rich., I
	Greenwich Palace	Vertue, Robt., M.
	Walberswick Church, Roodloft Stairs	Cutting, Thos., M.
	Windsor Castle, doors, roofs	Guynes, John.
1500	Bishops Stortford Church, battlements	Dunmow, of, M.
	Bury St. Edmunds, St. James Church, W. Front	(Wastell, John, M.)
	Chulmleigh Church, Roodloft	John the carver
	Fountains Abbey, Tower	(Scune, Chr., M.)
	London Carpenters' Hall, Parlour	Simpson, Rich., M.
	London, Tower, Great Hall, repairs etc.	Vertue, Robt., M.
	Richmond Palace, rebuilt	Mauncy, Thos., C.; Smyth, Hen., M.
	Rochester Cathedral, Lady Chapel	Birch, John

439

1500	Waterstock Church, Danvers Aisle	(Orchard, Wm., M.)
1501	Bath Abbey, New Church	Vertue, Robt., M.; Vertue, Wm., M.
	Carlton Church, Screen	Loveday, Rich.
	London, Baynards Castle, rebuilt	Mauncy, Thos., C.
	Louth Church, Steeple	Cole, John, M.; Scune, Chr., M.
	Richmond Friary	Redman, Hen., M.
1502	Oxford, St. Bernard's College, Hall etc.	Orchard, Wm., M.
	Richmond Church, Tabernacles	Fill, Robt.
	Ripon Minster, Nave rebuilt	Scune, Chr., M.
1503	Bury St. Edmunds, St. James's Church	Wastell, John, M.
	Canterbury Cathedral, Warham Tomb	(Wastell, John, M.)
	Greenwich Palace, works	Vertue, Robt., M.
	Westminster Abbey, Henry VII's Chapel	Vertue, Robt., M.; Vertue, Wm., M.
1504	Westminster Abbey, Henry VII's Almshouses	Coke, Hum., C.
	Westminster, St. Margaret's Church, Nave	Stowell, Robt., M.
1505	Bristol, St. James' Church, Screens	Rydge, Rog.
	Cambridge, Christ's College	Swayn, Wm., M.
	Canterbury Cathedral, Central Tower vault	Wastell, John, M.
	Canterbury, St. Andrew's Church, Pews and Pulpit	Brown, John, C.; Godfrey, Edm., C.
	Ely Cathedral, Redman Tomb	(Wastell, John, M.)
	Great Cubley Church, Tomb	Harpur, Hen.; Moorecock, Wm.
	London, Savoy Hospital	Coke, Hum., C.; Smyth, Hen., M.
	Lynn, King's, Red Mount Chapel; fan vault	Wastell, John, M.
	Manchester College, Church, Stalls	(Brownfleet, Wm., C.)
	Little Saxham Hall	Bronde, John, M.; Burdon, Wm., M. II; Loveday, Thos., C.
	Wrexham Church, Tower	Hart,——, M.
1506	Aysgarth Church, Bench-ends	(Brownfleet, Wm., C.)
	Croscombe Church, St. George's Chapel and Vestries	Carter, John, M.
	Ormskirk Church, Tomb	Hales, Jas.
	Oxford, St. Mary the Virgin, Congregation House	Fustyng, John, C.
	Windsor Castle, St. George's Chapel, Choir vault	Vertue, Wm., M.
1507	Swaffham Church, Tower	Gyles,——, M.
	Thetford Cluniac Priory, Church E. Window	Aldrych, Thos., M.
1508	Cambridge, King's College Chapel, Vaults etc.	Wastell, John, M.
	Chesterfield Church, Tomb	Harpur, Hen.
	High Wycombe Church, works	Chapman, Wm., M.
1509	Ely Cathedral, Cloisters, E. walk	Palmer, Thos., M.
	Eton College, W. Range, Lupton's Tower etc.	Coke, Hum., C.; Redman, Hen., M.; Vertue, Wm., M.
	Windsor Castle, works	Redman, Hen., M.
1510	Barkstone Church, Bench-ends	(Brownfleet, Wm., C.)
	Boston Church, Lantern	(Tempas, John, M.)
	Cambridge, Christ's College, Stalls	Bowman, Ralph; Harrison, Dyrik, C.
	Derby Church (Cathedral), Tower	Otes, John, M.
	Easby Abbey, Screen	(Brownfleet, Wm., C.)
	Norham Castle, works	*Chalmer, Thos., M.
	Wensley Church, Screen	(Brownfleet, Wm., C.)
1511	Cambridge, St. Mary the Great, Nave Benches	White, Wm., C.
	Cambridge, St. John's College, First Court and Gate	(Swayn, Wm., M.)
	Norwich, Church of St. Peter Parmentergate, Chancel	Howes, Rich., M.
	Sherston, Church House	Horsale, Rich., M.
	Thornbury Castle	(Janyns, Robt. j., M.); Tegge, Rich., C.; (Vertue, Wm., M.)
	Windsor Castle, St. George's Lady Chapel vault	Vertue, Wm., M.
1512	Cambridge, St. Mary the Great, W. ends of Aisles	Burdon, Wm., M. II; Swayn, Wm., M.
	Eton College, Lupton's Chantry	(Vertue, Wm., M.)
	Oxford, Corpus Christi College	Coke, Hum., C.; Vertue, Wm., M.
	Tempsford Church, Chapel, Reredos etc.	Pondour, Wm., C.
	Westminster Abbey, Henry VII's Tomb	Torrigiano, Pietro
1513	Ashburton Church, seats	Mayne, John, C.
	Cambridge, St. Mary the Great, Door	Kale, John, C.

1513	London, Tower, Chapel of St. Peter ad Vincula	Vertue, Wm., M.
1514		
1515	Beccles Church, Tower	(Elware, Rich., M.)
	Hampton Court Palace, Base Court, Clock Court, Chapel	Redman, Hen., M.
	Oxford, Brasenose College, Chapel roof	(Coke, Hum., C.)
	Westminster, St. Margaret's Church, Tower	Redman, Hen., M.
	Westminster, York Place, rebuilt	Redman, Hen., M.; Russell, Rich., C.
	Wollaton Church, Willoughby Tomb	Hippis, John.
1516	Cambridge, St. John's College, Stalls, Roodloft, Gates	Loveday, Thos., C.
	Oxford, Holywell Manor	Gyles, Rich., M.; Phelipp, Thos., M.
	Redenhall Church, Chancel ceiling	Rede, Wm., carver.
	Wakefield, Chevet Hall	Preston, John, M.
1517	Oxford, Corpus Christi College, Library desks	Clerk, Corn., C.
	Warblington Castle	Gyles, Rich., M.; Perkyns, Thos., C.
1518	Bridlington Priory, Stalls	Brownfleet, Wm., C.
	Cambridge, St. Mary the Great, Seats	Kale, John, C.
	Ripon Minster, St. Wilfrid's Loft	Brownfleet, Wm., C.
	Westminster, St. Margaret's Church, Chancel	Redman, Hen., M.
	Whaddon Church, Chancel roof	Clerk, Robt., C.II
1519	Banwell Church, Roodloft	'Banwell Mr.'
	Hackington Church, Roodloft	Bonversall, Mich., C.
	Leake Church, Bench-ends	(Brownfleet, Wm., C.)
	Lydd Church, Roodloft	Bellamy, Wm., C.
	Over Silton Church, Bench-end	(Brownfleet, Wm., C.)
	Wymondham Abbey, Image of St. George	Bale, Wm., C.; Sterlyng, Thos., C.
1520	Beverley Minster, Stalls	(Brownfleet, Wm., C.)
	Beverley, St. Mary's Church, N. Chapel roof etc.	Hal, W., C.
*	Bishop Auckland Palace, Benches	(Brownfleet, Wm., C.)
	Cambridge, St. Mary the Great, Roodloft	Bell, Rog., C.; Nun, John, C.
	King's Lynn, S. Gate	Hermer, Nich., M.
	Lincoln Guildhall	Spencer, Wm., M.
	Southwark Cathedral, Crossing Tower	Berty, Thos., M.
	Winchester Cathedral, Presbytery transformed	Berty, Thos., M.
1521	Ashburton Church, Roodloft etc.	(Mayne, John, C.)
	Hockham Church, repairs	(Bele, Thos., M.)
	London, Mercers' Company, Hall louvre	Nedeham, Jas., C.
	Reading, St. Lawrence's Church, Nave Arcade and Font	Cheney, John, M.
1522	Beverley, St. Mary's Church, Nave roof	(Hal, W., C.)
	Oxford, Balliol College, Chapel Windows	East, Wm., M.
1523	Ely Cathedral, Bishop West's Chapel	Lee, Rich.; More, Edm.
1524	London, Mercers' Company, Chapel, Retable	Van Dale, Walt.
	Thetford Cluniac Priory, Tomb of Second Duke of Norfolk	(Wastell, John, M.)
	Yatton Church, Cross	Hort, Wm., M.
1525	Bramley Church, Celure	Watson, Thos., C.
	Gestingthorpe Church, roof	Loveday, Thos., C.
	Hengrave Hall	Eastawe, John, M.; Neker, Thos., C.
	Oxford, Christ Church	Coke, Hum., C.; Lebons, John, M.; Molton, John, M.; Redman, Hen., M.
	Southwell Palace, works	Forman, John, M.
	York, Church of St. Michael le Belfry, rebuilt	Forman, John, M.
1526	Westminster Abbey, Lady Altar	Rovezzano, Benedetto
	Westminster Palace, St. Stephen's Cloister	Redman, Hen., M.; Vertue, Wm. M.
1527		
1528	Cambridge, King's Hall, Great Gate, upper part	Loveday, Thos., C.; Shereff, John, M.
	Ipswich, Wolsey's College	Lee, Rich., M.
	Oxford, Balliol College, Chapel Windows	Lebons, John, M.
	Windsor Castle, St. George's Chapel, Crossing vault	Redman, Hen., M.; Vertue, Wm., M.
1529	Christchurch Priory, Chantries	(Berty, Thos., M.)
	Fotheringhay Church, Tower vault	(Semark, Hen., M.)

1530	Altarnun Church, Benches	Day, Robt.
	Atherington Church, Rood-screen	Pares, John
	Barton Blount Church, Mountjoy Tomb	Parker, Rich.; Smyth, John, M.II
	Steeple Bumpstead Church, Aisle roof	(Loveday, Thos., C.)
	Castle Hedingham Church, roof	(Loveday, Thos., C.)
	London, Exeter House, Garden Galleries	Nedeham, Jas., C.
	Stambourne Church, roofs	(Loveday, Thos., C.)
	Thetford Cluniac Priory, Church door	Neker, Thos., C.
	Westminster Abbey, Abbot Islip's Chantry	(Molton, John, M.); Taylor, Wm. M.
1531	Cambridge, Queens' College, panelling	Fambeler, Giles; Harrison, Dyrik, C.; Joyner, Lamb., C.
	Hampton Court Palace, Hall etc.	Molton, John, M.; Nedeham, Jas., C.
	Stratton Church, Roodloft and Screens	Daw, John, C.; Pares, John, C.
	Westminster, New Palace, works	Molton, John, M.; Nedeham, Jas., C.
1532	Cambridge, King's College Chapel, Screen and Stalls	Buxton, Wm., C.; Philip, carver
	Ely Cathedral, Bishop West's Chapel	Lee, Rich., M.
	London, Tower, Traitor's Gate, repairs	Nedeham, Jas., C.
	Westminster, St. James's Palace	Molton, John, M.
1533	Burnley Church, Aisles	Craven, Nich., M.; Sellers, Thos., M.
	Guisnes Castle, Malthouse	Mumer, Harry, C.
	Mobberley Church, Tower	Plat, Rich., M.
1534	Altarnun Church, Chancel roof	Daw, Rich.
	Wimbish Church, N. Aisle roof	(Loveday, Thos., C.)
1535	Lydd Church, Chancel Seats	Bellamy, Wm., C.
1536	Basingstoke Holy Ghost Chapel, Tombs	Hermanzone, Arnold
	Bolney Church, Tower	Frogbrook, Rog., C.; Pokyll, Thos., M.
1537	Cambridge, Queens' College, President's Gallery	Cobb, Robt., M.; Joyner, Lamb., C.
	More Manor, Chamber roof	Rydge, Rich., II
1538	Cambridge, St. John's College, Hall panelling	Joyner, Lamb., C.
	Greenwich Palace, King's Privy Chamber, roof	Rydge, Rich., II
	Oatlands Palace, rebuilding	Clement, Wm., C.; Dickinson, Chr., M.
	Titchfield, Place House	Berty, Thos., M.
1539	Calshot Castle	Berty, Thos., M.; Boore, John, C.
	Cowes Castle	Berty, Thos., M.; Molton, John, M.
	Camber Castle	Molton, John, M.
	Guisnes, Fortifications	Lee, Sir Rich., E.; Roger, John, M.II
	Nonsuch Palace	Clement, Wm., C.; Molton, John, M. M.
	Sandgate Castle	Haschenperg, Step., E.; Molton, John, M.
1540	Cowdray, Buck Hall, roof	(Nedeham, Jas., C.)
	Deal Castle	Haschenperg, Step., E.; Molton, John, M.
	Guildford, Market-house	Butler, Rich., C.
	Guisnes Castle, works	Baker, Wm., M.
	Heanton Punchardon Church, Guild Chapel	Terell, Robt., M.
	St. Mawes Castle	(Haschenperg, Step., E.); Molton, John, M.
	Sandown Castle	Haschenperg, Step., E.; Molton, John, M.
	Walmer Castle	Haschenperg, Step., E.; Molton, John, M.
	Wormley, House	Harresone, John, C.
1541	Carlisle Castle, works	Haschenperg, Step., E.
	Hurst Castle	Berty, Thos., M.
1542	Coventry Cross	Phillips, Thos., M.
	Hull, fortifications	Rogers, John, M.II
	Pendennis Castle	(Haschenperg, Step., E.); Molton, John, M.
1543	Ampthill Manor, works	Bradshaw, Lawr., C.
	Bottesford Church, Tomb	Parker, Rich.

1543	Helmingham Church, Steeple, battlements	Barbour, John, M.
	Wark Castle, works	Pettyt, Thos., M.
1544		
1545		
1546	Shrewsbury, Stone Bridge	Lowe, Step., M.
1547	Lincoln Cathedral, Bishop Longland's Chantry	Kitchin, Wm., M.
1548		
1549	Alderney, Fortifications	Bager, Wm., C.
1550		
1551	Shrewsbury, Free School	Lowe, Step., M.
	Windsor Castle, Conduit	Ellis, Nich., M.
1552		
1553		
1554		
1555	Cambridge, Trinity College, Chapel	*Dickinson, Chr.; Russell, John, C.
1556		
1557	Windsor Castle, Poor Knights' Lodgings	Bullock, Hen., M.; Russell, John j., C.
1558	Windsor Castle, Fountain	Bullock, Hen., M.; Russell, John j., C.

SUBJECT INDEX OF BUILDINGS

This classification gives all the main types of buildings and furniture, but no attempt has been made to include such details as buttresses, doors, windows, etc. Reference should also be made to the General Index.

ABBEYS and PRIORIES, see:

Abingdon
Alnwick
Arbury
Barking
Barton
Bath
Battle
Beauchief
Beaulieu
Bermondsey
Bicester
Bindon
Boxley
Bridlington
Bristol
Bullington
Burton-on-Trent
Bury St. Edmunds
Byland
Cambridge, Jesus College
Canterbury Cathedral
Canterbury, St. Augustine
Canterbury, St. Laurence
Carlisle Cathedral
Chertsey
Chester Cathedral
Christchurch
Cockersand
Coggeshall, Little
Coldingham
Conway
Coventry
Croyland
Croxden
Croxton
Dunfermline
Dunmow, Little
Dunster
Durham Cathedral
Earls Colne
Easby
Ely Cathedral
Evesham
Exeter, St. Nicholas
Eynsham
Finchale
Fountains
Glastonbury
Gloucester Cathedral
Gloucester, Lanthony
Gloucester, St. Bartholomew
Godstow
Halesowen
Hartley Wintney

Hatfield Broad Oak
Hayles
Hounslow
Hurley
Jervaulx
Kirkstall
Langley, King's
Leeds
Leiston
Lewes
London, Charterhouse
London, St. Bartholomew the Great
London, St. John's Clerkenwell
London, St. Mary Eastminster
London, Temple
Malling, West
Malmesbury
Malvern, Great
Margam
Merton
Milton
Monk Bretton
Mount Grace
Neath
Newenham
Newhouse
Newstead
Northampton
Norwich Cathedral
Nostell
Notley
Nuneaton
Oseney
Oxford Cathedral
Pedralbes
Pershore
Peterborough Cathedral
Poblet
Poitiers, St. Hilaire
Quarr
Ramsey
Reading
Repton
Rochester Cathedral
Romsey
Rouen, St. Ouen
Rufford
Saffron Walden
St. Albans Cathedral
St. Asaph
St. Benet Holme
St. Bertin
St. Neots
St. Osyth
Sallay

SUBJECT INDEX OF BUILDINGS

SUBJECT INDEX OF BUILDINGS

Otford
Oxford, Holywell Manor
Penshurst
Pittington
Rayleigh
Redgrave
Richmond
Rochford
Rotherhithe
Saxham, Little
Shene Palace
Shotwick
Silkstead
Southwell Palace
Stanton Harcourt
Stoke-by-Nayland, Tendring Hall
Storeton
Sutton (Middx.)
Swalcliffe Rectory
Tabley
Thaxted, Horham Hall
Thornbury Castle
Tickenhill
Titchfield, Place House
Tittenhanger
Tremworth Manor
Vyne, The
Wakefield, Chevet Hall
Waltham
Wells, Deanery
Wells, Palace
Westminster Abbey, Abbot's House
Westminster, Palaces
Weston Manor
Wethersfield
Winchester, Wolvesey Palace
Windsor, Old
Wingfield, South
Witney
Woking
Woodstock Palace
Wookey
Writtle
Wynyard
Yearsley
York, Archbishop's Palace
York, St. Mary's, Abbot's House

MILLS, See:
   Chartham
   Dover Castle
   Farnham
   Grantchester
   Gravesend
   Gyffin
   Leeds Castle
   Lynn, King's
   Midhurst
   Newport (I. of W.)
   Northwich
   Roxwell
   Shaw
   Shrewsbury
   Southwark
   Sudbury
   Tingewick
   Tivetshall

Palaces, see MANOR HOUSES and MANSIONS

Priories, see ABBEYS and PRIORIES

PULPITS, see:
   Bodmin
   Canterbury, St. Andrew's
   Chester, St. Mary
   Oxford, St. Mary the Virgin

QUAYS, WHARVES, and HARBOURS, see:

   London, Tower
   Norwich, Conisford Quay
   Orwell Haven
   Rotherhithe Manor
   Tilney All Saints
   Yarmouth, Great, Harbour

REREDOSES, see:
   Beverley Minster
   Durham Cathedral
   Enstone
   London, Mercers' Chapel
   Newark
   St. Albans Cathedral
   Southwark Cathedral
   Tempsford
   Wells, St. Cuthbert
   Westminster Abbey
   Winchester Cathedral
   Windsor Castle

ROODLOFTS and SCREENS, see:
   Ashburton
   Atherington
   Banwell
   Bodmin
   Bridgwater
   Bristol, St. James
   Cambridge, King's College
   Cambridge, St. John's College
   Cambridge, St. John Baptist
   Cambridge, St. Mary the Great
   Canterbury Cathedral
   Carlton
   Chichester Cathedral
   Chulmleigh
   Clare
   Easby Abbey
   Eton College
   Exeter Cathedral
   Glastonbury, St. John
   Hackington
   Kentford
   Lichfield, St. Mary's Chapel
   Lincoln Cathedral
   London, St. Mary-at-Hill
   Lydd
   Norwich Cathedral
   Oxford, Merton College
   Ripon Minster
   St. Albans Cathedral
   St. Erth
   Southwark Cathedral
   Southwell Cathedral
   Stratton
   Tintinhull
   Walberswick
   Wensley

SUBJECT INDEX OF BUILDINGS

Winchester College
Yatton

ROOFS, TIMBER, see:
Abingdon Abbey
Adderbury
Altarnun
Arundel
Ashwellthorpe
Beverley, St. Mary's
Bodmin
Bumpstead, Steeple
Bury St. Edmunds, St. John at Hill
Bury St. Edmunds, St. Mary
Caister, East
Cambridge, Colleges, King's
Cambridge, St. Benet
Cambridge, St. Mary the Great
Cambridge, Schools
Cowdray
Dartington
Dereham, East
Downton Church
Durham Castle
Elmham, North
Eltham Palace, Hall
Ely Cathedral, Octagon
Eton College
Felmersham
Gestingthorpe
Greenwich Palace
Halstead
Hampton Church
Hampton Court
Hardley
Harmondsworth
Hartley Wintney
Hedingham Castle
Heston
Ipstone
Isleworth
Kenilworth Castle
Lambeth Palace
Leeds Castle
London, Guildhall
Lydd
More, Manor
Norton Subcourse
Norwich Cathedral, Hostry
Norwich, St. George Colegate
Oxford, Colleges, All Souls
Oxford, Colleges, Brasenose
Oxford, Colleges, Christ Church
Oxford, Colleges, Corpus Christi
Oxford, Colleges, Magdalen
Oxford, Colleges, New College
Oxford, Colleges, Oriel
Penshurst Place
Pittington Manor
Redenhall
Richmond Palace
Roxwell Chapel
St. Neots, Priory
Southwark Cathedral
Stambourne
Stamford Nunnery
Stoke Holy Cross
Tabley Old Hall

Thame Church
Thornton Abbey
Thurlton
Tilney All Saints
Westminster Abbey
Westminster, Palaces
Whaddon Church
Wighton
Wimbish Church
Winchester Cathedral, Pilgrims' Hall
Winchester Castle
Winchester College
Winchester, Wolvesey Palace
Windsor Castle, Hall
Wingfield, South
Woodstock Palace
Worstead Church
Worcester Cathedral, Guesten Hall
York, All Saints, North Street
York Guildhall
York, Merchant Adventurers' Hall
York, Minster, Central Tower
York Minster, Nave
York, St. Anthony's Hall

Schools, see COLLEGES

SEATING, see:
(see also STALLS, CHOIR)
Altarnun
Ashburton
Aysgarth
Barkstone
Bere Regis
Bishop Auckland
Bodmin
Bristol, All Saints
Bristol, St. Ewen
Cambridge, St. Mary the Great
Canterbury, St. Andrew
Cheddar
Hambledon
Leake
Leicester, St. Martin
Lydd
Over Silton
Oxford, All Souls College
Oxford, Corpus Christi College
Oxford, Divinity Schools
Warwick, St. Mary's, Beauchamp Chapel
Westminster, St. Margaret's Church
Yatton

Spires, see TOWERS and SPIRES

STALLS, CHOIR, see:
(see also SEATING)
Beverley Minster
Beverley St. Mary
Bicester Priory
Bridlington Priory
Cambridge, Christ's College
Cambridge, Jesus College
Cambridge, King's College
Cambridge, St. John's College
Carlisle Cathedral
Chester Cathedral
Ely Cathedral

454

GENERAL INDEX

This index is complementary to the Topographical and Subject Indexes, and excludes references in the text pages 1–367 to the subjects of articles. It includes all stray names and subjects, and supplements the Topographical Index in respect of parishes, places and streets in the larger towns.

Abbeys—*see* Subject Index, pp. 456–7

Aberford, Henry de, Prior of Nostell, 234

Abingdon, Berks.
Holy Cross, Fraternity of, 90
St. Nicholas, 52

Abingdon, Alexander of, 1, 148
Richard of, M., xlvii
(Abyndon), William, 194

Accommodation provided for craftsmen, xlvii, 1, 10, 18, 19, 34, 36, 61, 72, 76, 79, 81, 104, 113, 119, 137, 140, 150, 152, 159, 161, 163, 167, 181, 185, 186, 191, 192, 193, 197, 200, 209, 216, 226, 233, 242, 246, 254, 257, 274, 277, 282, 286, 304, 339, 341, 342

Accounts, xlv, 36, 37, 38, 41, 44, 58–60, 96, 197, 268–9, 272, 280, 293, 294, 295, 312, 313, 316, 332, 336, 356–7
Building, 23, 24, 35, 37, 38, 69, 71, 94, 95, 173, 174, 205, 218, 243, 251, 260, 262, 268, 271, 273, 276, 284, 285, 292, 321, 347, 350
Bursars', xlv, 57–8, 276, 289
Churchwardens', liv, 16, 51, 56, 59, 63, 198–9, 233, 246, 261, 263, 287, 288, 320, 344
Household, xlvi
Kitchen, xlv, 18, 19, 35, 42, 43, 58, 95, 174, 232, 235, 236, 288, 289, 307, 319, 321, 347, 350
Livery, 195
Proctors', 19, 39, 97, 98, 131, 291, 319–20

Adam, Edmond, M., 287
John, spicer, 143
Adams, Katherine, 132
Aelfwin, 125
Agmondesham, John, 308
Ailnoth, E., xliii, 2–3
Maud, wife of, 3
Alabaster, 36, 68, 114, 130, 146, 228, 231, 237, 244, 290, 349, 360
Albon, Margery, 4
Alcock, John, Bishop of Ely, 187
Alexander, C., xliii, 5
Argentine, his wife, 5
Almshouses—*see* Subject Index: Hospitals, p. 464
Alphonso VIII, King of Castile, 253
son of Edward I, 67
Altars 2, 5, 23, 27, 31, 34, 36, 37, 38, 44, 57, 60, 87, 103, 108, 159, 201, 215, 286, 342

see also Subject Index: Reredoses, p. 465
alura, 242
Ambiguity of historical evidence, xiv, xv
Anchoress, 81
Andrew, Geoffrey, 298
Michael, 248
Andrews, F.B., xvi
Anger, Robert, 248
Anne of Bohemia, Queen of England, 139, 187, 349
annexa, 233
Anonymity, vii, 1 (=50)
antyke (antique, Renaissance), 264
apparator, apparitor—see *apparilator* (below)
apparilator, apparator, apparillor (warden, foreman), 4, 28, 46, 47, 48, 69, 76, 120, 134, 142, 154, 169, 186, 189, 199, 224, 241, 250, 268, 305, 329, 331, 335, 337, 352, 358
Apprentices, xlviii, 11, 15, 18, 27, 43, 64, 73, 75, 78, 84, 89, 92, 98, 101, 102, 111, 118, 123, 127, 144, 148, 149, 151, 157, 159, 170, 172, 178, 181, 188, 193, 194, 197, 201, 208, 214, 223, 232, 261, 277, 282, 295, 306, 311, 316, 351
Archeseia, Gervase de, M., 152
Walter de, M., 152
architector, xlviii, li, 100, 106
Architects and Superintendents of Building—see *apparilator*, *architector*, *artifex*, *carpentator*, Clerical Architects, *constructor*, *devisor*, *dictator*, *dispositor operacionum*, *edificatores*, Engineers, *faber lapidarius*, *gardianus*, *iconomus*, *imaginator*, *inceptor operis*, *ingeniator*, Keeper of the Fabric, *latomus*, Laymen as Designers, *magister cementar', magister cementariorum*, *magister cementariorum regis*, *magister cementarius*, *magister fabrice*, *magister lathomorum*, *magister lathomus*, *magister operis*, Master craftsmen, *mestre des masouns*, *ordinator*, *rector fabricae*
Architectural Publication Society, xl, lii
Archive evidence, xlv
Arkill, 53
armiger, 208
see also Esquire
Arthur Tudor, Prince, 30

artifex, 81, 82, 223, 256, 272, 275
Artour, John, C., 310
Arundel, Earls of, 174
Eleanor, Countess of, 360
Richard, 5th Earl of, 360
Thomas, Archbishop of Canterbury, 365
Thomas, Earl of, 237
Ase, Richard, C., 281
Ashfield, Suff. 19
Ashton, Hugh, 63
Richard, Abbot of Peterborough, 320
Ashurst, John, woodmonger, 29
Margery, 29
William, clerk, 29
Askham, William de, 283
Asplond, Mr., 320
Aspour, Roger, 183
assises, 4
Atkinson, Thomas Dinham, viii, liv
Atkyns, John, 221
Attribution, ix, xli, lix
Auerbach, Miss E., 226
Aundely, Huldeburg de, 10
Austen, William, bronzefounder, 101, 200
Aveley, Ess., 61
Aveline, Countess of Lancaster, 45
avisamentum (advice), 56
Awbry, William, 27
Awne, John de, 71
Aylmer, Henry, 11
Joan, 12
Josu, 11
William, 11

Bach family, xlix
Bacheler, Gilbert, 60
Joan, 47
Walter, 47
Baddyng, John, 186
Baggs, A.P., xxiv
Bagot, Sir John, 282
Baillie, H.M.G., xxiv
Baker, Richard, 285
bakston (brick), 360
Baldock, Ralph, Bishop of London, 299, 327
Ballflower, 30, 255
Baly, John—*see* Bayly
Bank, Robert, M., 279
Banyard, Henry, 172
Barber, John le, 217
Nicholas le, 217
see also Barbour
Barber Surgeons—*see* Trades

459

GENERAL INDEX

St. Mary Magdalene, 234
St. Michael-on-the-Mount, 203
St. Peter Eastgate, 6, 234, 302
Sheriff of, 120
Lincoln, Earl of, 266, 282
see also Lacy
Lincoln, John, M., 329–30
Lindsey—see Lyndesey
linseed oil, 238
Lisle, Lord, 175
Literary evidence, xliv
Livermere, Great, Suff., 60
Livery of clothing to craftsmen, xlvi,
xlvii, 4, 5, 7, 8, 12, 16, 17, 18, 20,
23, 26, 28, 29, 31, 34, 37, 39, 40,
45, 47, 48, 51, 52, 55, 62, 63, 66,
69, 72, 73, 75, 79, 80, 87, 90, 93,
103, 104, 107, 109, 112, 115,
117, 118, 119, 121, 122, 124,
138, 148, 152, 154, 156, 158,
159, 162, 166, 167, 168, 169,
171, 181, 184, 186, 187, 190,
191, 195, 199, 203, 204, 208,
215, 216, 217, 219, 226, 227,
229, 230, 233, 238, 240, 241,
242, 246, 247, 251, 254, 255,
262, 272, 275, 277, 280, 281,
284, 295, 296, 297, 298, 301,
304, 306, 313, 316, 326, 330,
333, 336, 337, 338, 341, 342,
343, 346, 351, 354, 357, 360,
363, 364
accounts—*see* Accounts
Local style, li (=51), 86
Lock, Adam, 185, 375
Agnes, 185
Thomas, 185
Lodges, Masons', l (=50), 28, 45, 85,
156, 159, 188, 203, 262, 263,
276, 282, 288, 295
London,
Aldermanbury, 128
Aldersgate, 107, 242, 243
Aldersgate Ward, 47, 243
Aldgate Street, 35, 121
All Hallows, Barking, 4, 14
All Hallows, the Great, 26
All Hallows, the Less, 244
All Hallows, Lombard Street, 212
All Hallows, London Wall, 101
Austin Friars 41
Basing Lane, 362, 365
Bassishaw (Basinghaw), 2, 50, 64
Baynards Castle Ward, 143, 198
Billingsgate Ward, 46
Bishop of, 199, 221, 327, 365
Bishopsgate Street, 26, 301
Blackfriars, 23, 24, 45, 119, 153
Bridge House, 17, 26, 61, 65, 193,
315
Bridge Ward, 259, 362
Bridge Wardens, 61
Broad Street ward, 68, 259, 299
Budge Row, 268
Cannon Street, 12
Chamberlain of, 44, 225
Charterhouse, Prior of, 30, 83, 360
Common Council of, 10, 43, 135
Companies—*see* Guilds
Cordwainer Street, 365
Cornhill, 1, 41
Cripplegate Ward, 217, 313

Crutched Friars, 72
Dowgate Ward, 143
Drapers' Hall, 211
Farringdon Ward, 154
Finch Lane, 351
Fleet prison, 3, 194, 312, 331
Fleet street, 41, 64, 156, 194, 245,
334
Fraternities—*see* Guilds
Friday Street, 116
Golding Lane, 241
Gracechurch Street, 129, 212
Greyfriars, 24, 104, 137, 244
Grub Street, 285
Guilds and Fraternities:
Barber-Surgeons, 200
Brewers, 230
Carpenters, 32, 64, 65, 72, 75,
123, 201, 210, 212, 250, 260,
261, 273, 274
Goldsmiths, 192
Haberdashers, 26
Joiners, 177
Leathersellers, 26
Masons, 11, 33, 43, 54, 61, 76,
93, 120, 129, 148, 163, 246,
275, 314
Mercers, 210, 299, 305
Merchant Tailors, 196
Our Lady of the Assumption of
the Skinners, 196, 296
Pewterers, 26
St. Dunstan, 89, 194
St. John the Baptist of the
Tailors, 194
St. Magnus: Salve Regina, 360,
364
Salve Regina—*see* St. Magnus
(*above*)
Vintners, 26
Gutter Lane, 101
Hart street, 72
Holborn Bridge, 105
Kings Cross Station, 141
Knightrider Street, 313
Lime Street, 1
Lime Street Ward, 259
Lincoln's Inn, Master of, 26
Mark Lane, 188
Mayor of, 11, 17, 155, 177, 201,
225, 244, 358, 359, 363
Mincing Lane, 209
Newgate Street, 15
Old Fish Street, 77
Papey Hospital, 26
Pardonchurchhaw, 80, 351
Paternoster Row, 52, 107
Queenhithe Ward, 142
Rood Lane, 250
St. Alban, 26, 315
St. Andrew Castle Baynard, 29,
191, 314, 332
St. Andrew Hubbard, 241
St. Andrew Undershaft (Cornhill),
1, 54, 259
St. Bartholomew by the Exchange,
223
St. Bartholomew the Great, 121,
197, 365
St. Bartholomew the Less, 11, 68,
217
St. Benet Fink, 61, 199, 223, 301,

351
St. Benet, Paul's Wharf, 143, 198
St. Botolph without Aldersgate,
241, 244, 259
St. Botolph without Aldgate, 26
St. Bride, 334
St. Clement, 12
St. Clement's Lane, 12
St. Dunstan-in-the-East, xlvi, 304,
362
St. Dunstan-in-the-West, 50, 89,
193
St. Faith, 129, 170, 188
St. Giles Cripplegate, 241, 285,
335, 344
St. James Garlickhithe, ?26, 351
St. John Walbrook, 171, 196, 209,
268, 314, 336
St. Katherine Coleman, 33, 254
St. Lawrence Poultney, 210, 244
St. Magnus, 47, 61, 360, 364, 365
St. Margaret Pattens, 26, 46, 189,
241, 250
St. Martin-le-Grand, Dean of, 52,
119
St. Martin Outwich, 254, 301, 362,
365
St. Martin Vintry, 259
St. Mary Aldermanbury, 154
St. Mary Aldermary, 331
St. Mary Bothaw, 143
St. Mary-le-Bow, 26, 45, 124
St. Mary-at-Hill, 41, 129, 241, 249,
272, 306, 311, 315
St. Mary Magdalen, 77
St. Mary Matfelon, 301
St. Mary without Bishopsgate
Hospital, 46
St. Mary Woolchurch, 14
St. Matthew Friday Street, 14
St. Michael Cornhill, 41, 171
St. Michael Hoggen Lane, 313
St. Michael Paternoster, 143
St. Michael-le-Querne, 52, 241,
360
St. Mildred Poultry, 108, 299
St. Nicholas Cole Abbey, 52
St. Olave Hart Street, 72, 357
St. Olave Jewry, 41, 220
St. Paul's Cathedral, xxxix
St. Paul's Cathedral, Dean and
Chapter of, 112, 161, 188, 239,
242, 254, 327, 330, 362, 365
St. Paul's Cathedral, Old Work of,
143, 327
St. Paul's Churchyard, 101, 188,
226, 249, 330, 362, 365
St. Peter Broad Street, 198, 281
St. Peter Cornhill, 301
St. Peter-the-less, Paul's Wharf,
143
St. Peter Westcheap, 275
St. Sepulchre, 80, 114, 225
St. Stephen, Coleman Street, 156,
310
St. Stephen Walbrook, 195, 266
St. Thomas of Acre, 60, 129, 148,
216, 268, 314, 330
St. Thomas Apostle, 14
Sheriffs of, 84, 237
Sworn craftsmen of—*see* Viewers
Temple Bar, 36

312201

*E*nglish Mediaeval Architects, a Biographical Dictionary down to 1550 is the indispensable reference work on the careers of architectural craftsmen working in England in the Middle Ages. The original edition, written in association with the late Arthur Oswald, has long since been unavailable. This completely revised edition, first published in 1984, adds the lives of about 400 new craftsmen to the 1300 or so contained in the original edition, including some masters of considerable stature, such as Ivo de Raghton, the pre-eminent mason in York in the early 14th century, and John Montfort, the master mason to Richard Beauchamp, Earl of Warwick. A number of the existing lives have also been completely rewritten, a notable example being that of Thomas of Witney, one of the major masters of the Decorated period, whose career encompassing Westminster, Winchester and the South-West is now fully expounded; and many other entries for notable craftsmen, such as John Wastell, William Wynford and Henry Yeveley, have been updated and extended. The new information derives not only from the researches of Dr. Harvey and Arthur Oswald since the appearance of the original edition, but also from a great deal of fresh material sent to Dr. Harvey by leading authorities in the field. In addition, there are new introductory sections, including an appreciation of the late Arthur Oswald by his nephew, Philip Oswald, and the indexes and tables have been completely revised by L. S. Colchester and Dr. R. K. Morris. As users of the original edition will be aware, the very extensive tables and indexes are an invaluable aspect of the book as a source for reference, arranged topographically and chronologically, by county and by building type, as well as including a comprehensive general index.

Dr. Harvey is one of the outstanding mediaeval architectural historians of this century. His published writings on architectural and topographical matters stretch back to 1936, and include a number of books which are indispensable works for the study of Gothic architecture – *Henry Yevele, The Gothic World, The Cathedrals of England & Wales* and *The Perpendicular Style* – but amongst which this book, *English Mediaeval Architects*, is generally acknowledged to be his greatest contribution. This is its first appearance in paperback.

ISBN 0-86299-452-7

9 780862 994525

£17.00

ALAN SUTTON PUBLISHING
BRUNSWICK ROAD · GLOUCESTER